District Gazetteers of India Series 123

GAZETTEER
OF THE
BOMBAY PRESIDENCY

District Gazetteers of India Series 123

GAZETTEER
OF THE
BOMBAY PRESIDENCY.

27 VOLUMES (IN 35 BINDINGS)
VOLUME XXI.

BELGAUM.

EDITED BY
JAMES M. CAMPBELL

GYAN

Published by

Gyan Publishing House
5, Ansari Road
Daryaganj, New Delhi-110002
Phone: 011-47034999, 9811692060
E-mail: books@gyanbooks.com

Distribution Network
gyanbooks.com
India, USA, Canada, UK, Australia, France

ISBN: 978-81-212-8560-5 (Set) 27 Volumes (In 35 Bindings)
978-81-212-8508-7 (PB)
First Published, 1884

2nd Impression 2024

Printed at: Gyan Press, Delhi.

GAZETTEER OF THE BOMBAY PRESIDENCY (VOL. XXI)
Editor: JAMES M. CAMPBELL

LIST OF VOLUMES

S. NO.	ISBN NO.	VOLUME	TITLE	AUTHOR	PRICE	PAGES
			ASSAM DISTRICT GAZETTEERS			
1	9788121285926	1st	Cachar	B. C. Allen	600	300
2	9788121285919	2nd	Sylhet	B. C. Allen	750	378
3	9788121285902	3rd	Goalpara	B. C. Allen	400	203
4	9788121285896	4th	Kamrup	B. C. Allen	675	344
5	9788121285889	5th	Darrang	B. C. Allen	725	364
6	9788121285872	6th	Nowgong	B. C. Allen	560	280
7	9788121285865	7th	Sibsagar	B. C. Allen	675	343
8	9788121285858	8th	Lakhimpur	B. C. Allen	690	347
9	9788121285841	9th	Naga Hills and Manipur	B. C. Allen	580	294
10	9788121285834	10th	The Khasi And Jaintia Hills, The Garo Hills And The Lushai Hills	B. C. Allen	675	363
11	9788121285827	11th	The Sadiya and Balipara Frontier Tract	B. C. Allen	375	190
			BENGAL DISTRICT GAZETTEERS			
12	9788121218672	1st	Angul	L. S. S. O'Malley	340	168
13	9788121259637	2nd	Bakarganj	J. C. JACK	970	194
14	9788121218696	3rd	Balasore	L. S. S. O'Malley	450	228
15	9788121259590	4th	Bankura	L. S. S. O'Malley	1000	199
16	9788121218375	5th	Bhagalpur	J. Byrne	390	194
17	9788121218290	6th	Birbhum	L. S. S. O'Malley	300	150
18	9788121259651	7th	Eastern Bengal and Assam - Bogra	J. N. Gupta	940	188
19	9788121218351	8th	Burdwan	J. C. K. Peterson	450	227
20	9788121259538	9th	Calcutta District Gazetteer - Statistics, 1901 - 02		340	68
21	9788121218313	10th	Champaran	L. S. S. O'Malley	410	205
22	9788121259613	11th	Eastern Bengal District Gazetters - Chittagong	L. S. S. O'Malley	1080	216
23	9788121259552	12th	Chota Nagpur Tributary		130	26
24	9788121259415	13th	The Cooch Behar Gazette: Statistics		1460	292
25	9788121218412	14th	Cuttack	L. S. S. O'Malley	490	248
26	9788121261357	15th	Eastern Bengal District Gazetteers Dacca	B. C. Allen	400	207
27	9788121218436	16th	Darbhanga	L. S. S. O'Malley	360	180
28	9789362089335	17th	Darjeeling	L. S. S. O'Malley	500	248
29	9788121259453	18th	Eastern Bengal District Gazetteers - Dinajpur	F. W. Strong	890	178
30	9788121259392	19th	Faridpur	L. S. S. O'Malley	700	140
31	9788121218474	20th	Gaya	L. S. S. O'Malley	540	270
32	9788121214032	21st	Bihar and Orissa District Gazetteer: Hazaribagh	E. Lister	715	234
33	9788121218337	22nd	Hooghly	L. S. S. O'Malley	680	340
34	9788121218191	23rd	Bengal District Gazetteer Howrah	L. S. S. O'Malley	390	199
35	9788121259293	24th	Eastern Bengal and Assam - Jalpaiguri	John F. Gruning	890	178
36	9788121259279	25th	Jessore	L. S. S. O'Malley	960	192
37	9788121259231	26th	Khulna	L. S. S. O'Malley	1100	220
38	9788121259217	27th	Malda	G. E. Lambourn	670	134
39	9788121267854	28th	Manbhum	H. Coupland	600	313
40	9788121218498	29th	Midnapore	L. S. S. O'Malley	500	252
41	9788121218597	30th	Monghyr	L. S. S. O'Malley	560	280
42	9788121259156	31st	Murshidabad	L. S. S. O'Malley	1250	250
43	9788121259576	32nd	Bengal District Gazetteers - Muzaffarpur	L. S. S. O'Malley	940	188
44	9788121259132	33rd	Mymensingh	F. A. Sachse	960	192
45	9788121259118	34th	Nadia	J. H. E. Garrett	1070	214
46	9788121259095	35th	Eastern Bengal and Assam - Noakhali	J. E. Webster	580	115
47	9788121218450	36th	Feudatory States of Orissa	L. E. B. Cobdenramsay	790	395
48	9788121259071	37th	Pabna	L. S. S. O'Malley	710	142
49	9788121218511	38th	Palamau	L. S. S. O'Malley	380	190
50	9788121218634	39th	Patna	L. S. S. O'Malley	500	250
51	9788121218535	40th	Puri	L. S. S. O'Malley	650	328
52	9788121218757	41st	Purnea	L. S. S. O'Malley	440	220
53	9788121258937	42nd	Rajshahi	L. S. S. O'Malley	1080	216
54	9788121256681	43rd	Bihar and Orissa District Gazetteers: Ranchi	M. G. Hallett	1350	278
55	9788121258913	44th	Eastern Bengal and assam - Rangpur	J. A. Vas	890	178
56	9788121218559	45th	Sambalpur	L. S. S. O'Malley	480	242
57	9788121214056	46th	Santal Parganas	L. S. S. O'Malley	940	308
58	9788121218610	47th	Saran	L. S. S. O'Malley	380	190
59	9788121218658	48th	Shahabad	L. S. S. O'Malley	380	190
60	9788121256704	49th	The Gazetteer of Sikhim	H. H. Risley	960	481
61	9788121218573	50th	Singhbhum, Saraikela And Kharsawan	L. S. S. O'Malley	560	280
62	9788121259439	51st	Eastern Bengal District Gazetteers - Tippera	J. E. Webster	730	146
63	9788121259033	52nd	24 Parganas	L. S. S. O'Malley	1420	284

S. NO.	ISBN NO.	VOLUME	TITLE	AUTHOR	PRICE	PAGES
			CENTRAL PROVINCES DISTRICT GAZETTEERS			
64	9789362081728	1st, Vol. A	Akola (Descriptive)	A. E. Nelson, C. Brown	870	436
65	9789362085481	2nd, Vol. A	Amraoti (Descriptive)	S. V. Fitzgerald, A. E. Nelson	1050	524
66	9789362089267	3rd,Vol. A	Balaghat (Descriptive)	R. V. RUSSELL	430	216
67	9789362083494	4th, Vol. A	Betul (Descriptive)	R. V. RUSSELL	610	306
68	9789362085146	5th, Vol. A	Bhandara (Descriptive)	R. V. RUSSELL	580	292
69	9789362088390	6th, Vol. A	Bilaspur (Descriptive)	R. V. RUSSELL	870	434
70	9789362086044	7th, Vol. A	Buldana (Descriptive)	A. E. Nelson	1090	543
71	9789362089014	8th, Vol. B	Chanda (Descriptive)	R. V. RUSSELL	470	234
72	9789362086938	9th	Chhattisgarch Feudatory State	E. A. De Brett	880	440
73	9789362082961	10th	Chhindwara (Descriptive)	R. V. RUSSELL	550	274
74	9789362089342	11th, Vol. A & B	Damoh (Descriptive and Statistical Tables 1891-1901)	R. V. RUSSELL	830	414
75	9789362081230	12th, Vol. A	Durg (Descriptive)	A. E. Nelson	460	232
76	9789362086037	13th, Vol. A	Hoshangabad (Descriptive)	R. V. RUSSELL	860	430
77	9789362086792	14th, Vol. A	Jubbulpore (Descriptive)	A. E. Nelson	950	474
78	9789362089663	15th, Vol. A & B	Mandla (Descriptive and Statistical Tables 1891-1901)	R. V. RUSSELL	370	186
79	9789362086419	16th, Vol. A	Nagpur (Descriptive)	R. V. RUSSELL	790	394
80	9789362080646	17th, Vol. A	Narsinghpur (Descriptive)	R. V. RUSSELL	510	257
81	9789362084835	18th, Vol. A	Nimar (Descriptive)	R. V. RUSSELL	600	299
82	9789362087737	19th, Vol. A	Raipur (Descriptive)	A. E. Nelson	790	396
83	9789362080264	20th, Vol. A	Saugor (Descriptive)	R. V. RUSSELL	570	285
84	9789362081117	21st, Vol. A	Seoni (Descriptive)	R. V. RUSSELL	460	232
85	9789362084965	22nd, Vol. A	Wardha (Descriptive)	R. V. RUSSELL	600	302
86	9789362083401	23rd, Vol. A	Yeotmal (Descriptive)	R. V. RUSSELL	550	277
87	9789362080325	24th, Vol. I, Pt. I	Gwalior (Text and Tables)	R. V. RUSSELL	980	489
88	9789362087133	24th, Vol. I, Pt. II	Gwalior (Maps)	R. V. RUSSELL	400	198
89	9789362086341	24th, Vol. I, Pt. III	Gwalior (Village List)	R. V. RUSSELL	810	406
90	9789362085467	24th, Vol. I, Pt. IV	Gwalior (Photos)	R. V. RUSSELL	1400	698
91	9789362087393	25th, Vol. II	Indore (Text and Tables)	C. E. Luard	1050	524
92	9789362084422	26th, Vol. III	Bhopal (Text and Tables)	C. E. Luard	540	272
93	9789362086815	27th, Vol. IV	Rewah (Text and Tables)	C. E. Luard	500	250
94	9789362087584	28th, Vol. V, Pt. A	Western States - Malwa (Text)	C. E. Luard	1520	762
95	9789362087300	29th, Vol. VI, Pt. A	Eastern States - Bundelkhand (Text)	C. E. Luard	930	463
96	9789362082169	30th, Vol. VI, Pt. B	Eastern States - Bundelkhand (Tables)	C. E. Luard	830	417
			GAZETTEER OF THE BOMBAY PRESIDENCY:			
97	9788121283441	1st, Part I	History of Gujarat	Ed.: James M. Campbell	3220	644
98	9788121285582	1st, Part II	History of the Konkan Dakhan and Southern Maratha Country	Ed.: James M. Campbell	4200	840
99	9788121285568	2nd	Gujarat, Surat and Broach	Ed.: James M. Campbell	2990	598
100	9788121285544	3rd	Kaira and Panch Mahals	Ed.: James M. Campbell	1690	339
101	9788121285520	4th	Ahmedabad	Ed.: James M. Campbell	1860	372
102	9788121285506	5th	Cutch, Palanpur, and Mahi Kantha	Ed.: James M. Campbell	2390	478
103	9788121285483	6th	Rewa Kantha, Narukot, Cambay, and Surat States	Ed.: James M. Campbell	1450	290
104	9788121285469	7th	Baroda	Ed.: James M. Campbell	3260	652
105	9788121285445	8th	Kathiawar	Ed.: James M. Campbell	3790	758
106	9788121285421	9th, Part I	Gujarat Population - Hindus	Ed.: James M. Campbell	3170	636
107	9788121285407	9th, Part II	Gujarat Population - Musalmans and Parsis	Ed.: James M. Campbell	1520	304
108	9788121285384	10th	Ratnagiri and Savantvadi	Ed.: James M. Campbell	2500	501
109	9788121285360	11th	Kolaba and Janjira	Ed.: James M. Campbell	2550	513
110	9788121285346	12th	Khandesh	Ed.: James M. Campbell	3190	638
111	9788121285322	13th Part I	Thana	Ed.: James M. Campbell	2050	413
112	9788121285308	13th Part II	Thana	Ed.: James M. Campbell	1770	357
113	9788121285285	14th	Thana - Places of Interest	Ed.: James M. Campbell	3290	659
114	9788121285261	15th Part I	Kanara	Ed.: James M. Campbell	2340	348
115	9788121285247	15th Part II	Kanara	Ed.: James M. Campbell	1740	348
116	9788121285223	16th	Nasik	Ed.: James M. Campbell	3490	698
117	9788121285209	17th	Ahmadnagar	Ed.: James M. Campbell	3860	772
118	9788121285186	18th Part I	Poona	Ed.: James M. Campbell	2930	586
119	9788121285162	18th Part II	Poona	Ed.: James M. Campbell	2680	537
120	9788121285148	18th Part III	Poona	Ed.: James M. Campbell	2500	503
121	9788121285124	19th	Satara	Ed.: James M. Campbell	3450	692
122	9788121285100	20th	Sholapur	Ed.: James M. Campbell	2730	547
123	9788121285087	21st	Gazetteer of the Bomaby Presidency: Belgaum	Ed.: James M. Campbell	2570	514
124	9788121285063	22nd	Dharwar	Ed.: James M. Campbell	4200	841
125	9788121285049	23rd	Gazetteer of the Bombay Presidency:Bijapur	Ed.: James M. Campbell	3550	712
126	9788121285025	24th	Kolhapur	Ed.: James M. Campbell	2250	450

S. NO.	ISBN NO.	VOLUME	TITLE	AUTHOR	PRICE	PAGES
127	9788121285001	25th	Botany	Ed.: James M. Campbell	2040	408
128	9788121284981	26th, Part I	Materials Towards a Statistical Account of the Town and Island of Bombay - History	Ed.: James M. Campbell	2500	504
129	9788121284967	26th, Part II	Materials Towards a Statistical Account of the Town and Island of Bombay - Trade and Fortifications	Ed.: James M. Campbell	2690	538
130	9788121284943	26th, Part III	Materials Towards a Statistical Account of the Town And Island of Bombay - Administration	Ed.: James M. Campbell	2450	702
131	9788121284929	27th	General Index	Ed.:R. E. Enthoven	2190	428
			MADRAS DISTRICT GAZETTEERS			
132	9788121258814	1st	Anantapur	W. Francis	1140	227
133	9788121258555	2nd	Malabar	C. A Innes & F. B Evans	3010	602
134	9788121258791	3rd	Bellary	W. Francis	1890	377
135	9788121258777	4th	Statistical Appendix For Chingleput		280	56
136	9788121258753	5th	Coimbatore	K. N. Krishnaswami Ayyar	3420	628
137	9788121232814	6th	Madras District Gazetteers District Gazetteer Cuddapah	C. F. Brackenbury	1120	285
138	9788121258715	7th	Statistical Appendix For Ganjam		370	73
139	9788121256766	8th, Vol. 1st	Godavari District Gazetteer	F. R. Hemingway	650	320
140	9788121256803	8th, Vol. 2nd	Godavari District Gazetteer	F. R. Hemingway	160	83
141	9788121258678	9th	Statistical Appendix For Kistna		640	127
142	9788121258654	10th	Statistical Appendix For Kurnool		270	54
143	9788121258616	11th	Madura	W. Francis	1900	379
144	9788121258579	12th	Statistical Appendix For Madura		740	148
145	9788121258630	13th	The Nilgiris	W. Francis	2190	437
146	9788121234276	14th	Madras District Gazetteers Gazetteer Of The Nellore District Brought Upto 1938		1150	386
147	9788121258517	15th	North Arcot		590	118
148	9788121258494	16th, Vol. 1, Part I	Salem	F. J. Richards	1710	343
149	9788121258593	16th, Vol. 1, Part II	Salem	F. J. Richards	1800	360
150	9788121258456	17th	South Arcot	W. Francis	2400	480
151	9788121258470	18th	Statistical Appendix For South Canara		400	80
152	9788121258432	19th, Vol. 1st & 2nd	Tanjore: Main Volume and Statistical Appendix		2070	401
153	9788121258395	20th	Tinnevelly	H. R. Pate	2740	547
154	9788121258418	21st	Statistical Appendix For Tinnevelly		320	64
155	9788121258371	22nd, 1st & 2nd	Trichinopoly: Main Volume and Statistical Appendix	F. R. Hemingway	2440	487
156	9788121241953	23rd	Vizagapatam District Gazetteer	W. Francis	760	385
			PUNJAB DISTRICT GAZETTEERS			
157	9788121255943	1st	Ambala District 1883-84		620	124
158	9788121255967	2nd	Amritsar		1180	236
159	9788121255981	3rd	Delhi		1300	260
160	9788121256001	4th	Ferozepore		950	188
161	9788121256025	5th	Faridkot		350	70
162	9788121256049	6th	Gujranwala 1893-94		1270	254
163	9788121256063	7th	Gujrat	C. E. Luard	1140	228
164	9788121256087	8th	Gurdaspur 1891-92		1260	252
165	9788121256100	9th	Gurgaon 1883-4		1020	203
166	9788121256124	10th	Hazara	H. D. Watson	2290	458
167	9788121256148	11th	Hissar district and Lohar State		1840	367
168	9788121256162	12th	Hoshiarpur		1420	283
169	9788121256186	13th	Jhang		1070	213
170	9788121256209	14th	Jhelam		1010	202
171	9788121256223	15th	Jalandhar District 1883-84		540	108
172	9788121256247	16th, Vol. XIV-A	Jullundur District, with maps and Kapurthala		1990	398
173	9788121256261	17th, Pt. I	Kangra (Proper)		1450	290
174	9788121256285	17th, Pt. II	Kangra (Kulu, Lahual, Spiti)		1800	357
175	9788121256308	18th	Karnal		1930	386
176	9788121256322	19th	Kohat		1540	307
177	9788121256346	20th	The Lahore District 1883-84		1220	244
178	9788121256384	21st	Ludhiana and Maler Kotla		1680	335
179	9788121256407	22nd	Lyallpur		735	147
180	9788121256421	23rd	Mianwali		1170	234
181	9788121256445	24th	Montgomery	P. J. Fagan	1590	318
182	9788121258364	25th	Multan (1901-02)	E. D. Maclagan	2400	480
183	9788121258708	26th	The Rohtak District 1883-84		980	196
184	9788121258746	27th, Vol. III A	Dujana State 1904		500	16
185	9788121256483	28th	Shahpur District		1780	356
186	9788121256506	29th	Simla District		800	159

S. NO.	ISBN NO.	VOLUME	TITLE	AUTHOR	PRICE	PAGES
187	9788121256520	30th	The Chamba State		2040	408
188	9788121256544	31st	The Chenab Colony 1904		1550	310
189	9788121256568	32nd	Kalsia State		270	53
190	9788121256582	33rd	Suket and Mandi		770	154
191	9788121256605	34th	Phulkian States, Patiala Jind And Nabha 1904		2070	414
192	9788121256643	35th	Simla Hill States		2220	443
193	9788121256667	36th	Sirmur		920	183
			RAJPUTANA DISTRICT GAZETTEERS			
194	9789362088994	1st, Vol. I-A & B	Ajmer-merwara (Text and Statistics Tables)	C. C. Watson	1230	246
195	9789362080882	2nd. Vol. II-A & B	Mewar Residency (Text and Statistics Tables)	K.D. Erskine	1700	339
196	9789362088444	3rd, Vol. III-A & B	The Western Rajputana States Residency And The Bikaner Agency	K.D. Erskine	3590	718
			UNITED PROVINCES OF AGRA AND OUDH DISTRICT GAZETTEERS			
197	9789362087560	Vol. I	Agra	H. R. Nevill	2260	452
198	9789362082466	Vol. II	Aligarh	H. R. Nevill	1300	260
199	9789362089779	Vol. III	Allahabad	H. R. Nevill	2050	409
200	9789362081346	Vol. IV	Almora	H. G. Walton	1670	333
201	9789362085658	Vol. V	Azamgarh	D. L. Drake Brockman	1750	349
202	9789362080547	Vol. VI	Bahraich	H. R. Nevill	1410	281
203	9789362085214	Vol. VII	Ballia	H. R. Nevill	1750	350
204	9789362084668	Vol. VIII	Banda	D. L. Drake Brockman	1750	349
205	9789362086518	Vol. IX	Bara Banki	H. R. Nevill	1720	344
206	9789362084101	Vol. X	Bareilly	H. R. Nevill	1640	327
207	9789362086631	Vol. XI	Basti	H. R. Nevill	1610	321
208	9789362083814	Vol. XII	Benares	H. R. Nevill	2290	458
209	9789362086105	Vol. XIII	Bijnor	H. R. Nevill	1820	363
210	9789362081674	Vol. XIV	Budaun	H. R. Nevill	1890	378
211	9789362086891	Vol. XV	Bulandshahr	H. R. Nevill	2100	419
212	9789362081520	Vol. XVI	Cawnpore	H. R. Nevill	2210	442
213	9789362088031	Vol. XVII	Dehra Dun	H. G. Walton	1710	342
214	9789362088710	Vol. XVIII	Etah	E. R. Neave	1600	320
215	9789362082992	Vol. XIX	Etawah	D. L. Drake Brockman	1390	277
216	9789362082220	Vol. XX	Farrukhabad	E. R. Neave	1620	324
217	9789362083869	Vol. XXI	Fatehpur	H. R. Nevill	1890	377
218	9789362085962	Vol. XXII	Fyzabad	H. R. Nevill	1700	339
219	9789362087997	Vol. XXIII	Garhwal	H. G. Walton	1270	254
220	9789362089892	Vol. XXIV	Ghazipur	H. R. Nevill	1600	320
221	9789362085436	Vol. XXV	Gonda	H. R. Nevill	1650	330
222	9789362080271	Vol. XXVI	Gorakhpur	H. R. Nevill	1890	378
223	9789362086129	Vol. XXVII	Hamirpur	D. L. Drake Brockman	1390	277
224	9789362087638	Vol. XXVIII	Hardoi	H. R. Nevill	1680	336
225	9789362081636	Vol. XXIX	Jalaun	D. L. Drake Brockman	1180	236
226	9789362084309	Vol. XXX	Jaunpur	H. R. Nevill	1750	350
227	9789362084187	Vol. XXXI	Jhansi	D. L. Drake Brockman	1960	391
228	9789362089168	Vol. XXXII	Kheri	H. R. Nevill	1650	330
229	9789362086778	Vol. XXXIII	Lucknow	H. R. Nevill	1760	352
230	9789362088635	Vol. XXXIV	Mainpuri	H. R. Nevill	1740	348
231	9789362080424	Vol. XXXV	Meerut	H. R. Nevill	2170	434
232	9789362081087	Vol. XXXVI	Mirzapur	D. L. Drake Brockman	2430	486
233	9789362085443	Vol. XXXVII	Moradabad	H. R. Nevill	1900	380
234	9789362082763	Vol. XXXVIII	Muttra	D. L. Drake Brockman	2140	428
235	9789362089915	Vol. XXXIX	Muzaffarnagar	H. R. Nevill	2260	451
236	9789362086143	Vol. XL	Naini Tal	H. R. Nevill	1890	377
237	9789362086761	Vol. XLI	Partabgarh	H. R. Nevill	1560	312
238	9789362081124	Vol. XLII	Pilibhit	H. R. Nevill	1570	314
239	9789362084453	Vol. XLIII	Rai Bareli	H. R. Nevill	1610	322
240	9789362088284	Vol. XLIV	Rampur	H. R. Nevill	1170	234
241	9789362083654	Vol. XLV	Saharanpur	H. R. Nevill	2190	438
242	9789362083142	Vol. XLVI	Shahjahanpur	H. R. Nevill	1510	302
243	9789362083623	Vol. XLVII	Sitapur	H. R. Nevill	1590	317
244	9789362089939	Vol. XLVIII	Sultanpur	H. R. Nevill	1330	266
245	9789362080851	Vol. XLIX	Unnao	H. R. Nevill	1530	305

GAZETTEER

OF THE

BOMBAY PRESIDENCY.

VOLUME XXI.

BELGAUM.

Under Government Orders.

Bombay:
PRINTED AT THE
GOVERNMENT CENTRAL PRESS.
1884.

THE names of contributors are given in the body of the book. Special acknowledgments are due to Messrs J. L. L. MacGregor, District Forest Officer, G. McCorkell, C. S., W. H. Horsley, C. S., J. F. Fleet, C.S., R. B. Joyner, C.E., and Surgeon-Major C. T. Peters, and to Ráo Sáheb Kalyán Sitárám Chitrey.

Much valuable help has also been received from Messrs. A. A. C. Jervoise, C.S., and T. D. Mackenzie, C.S., the present and former Collectors of Belgaum.

JAMES M. CAMPBELL.

August, 1884.

CONTENTS.

BELGAUM.

BELGAUM.

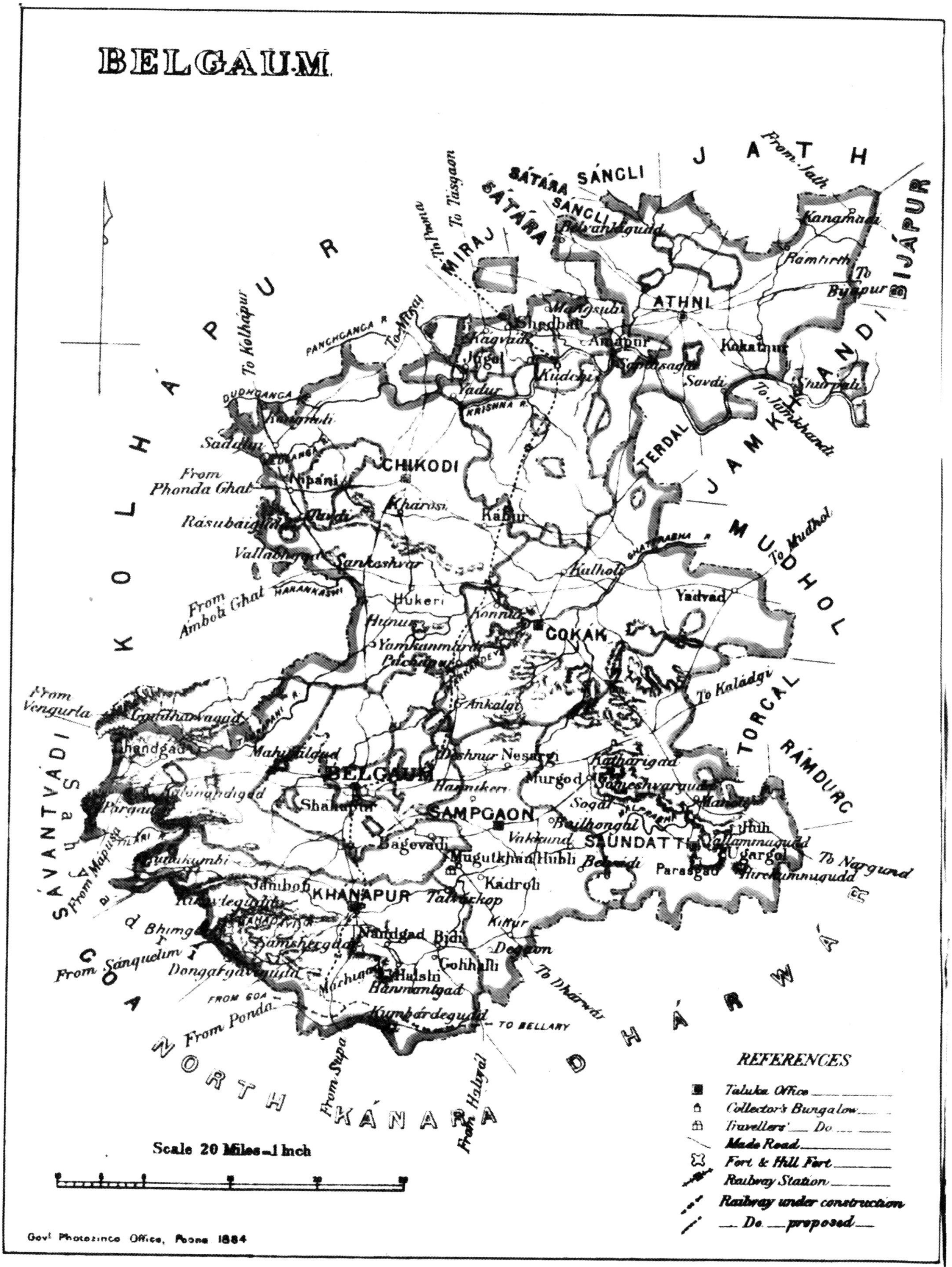

BELGAUM
KOLHÁPUR
JATH
SÁNGLI
SÁTÁRA
MIRAJ
BIJÁPUR
JAMKHANDI
MUDHOL
TORGAL
RÁMDURG
DHÁRWÁR
NORTH KÁNARA
GOA
SÁVANTVÁDI
ATHNI
CHIKODI
GOKAK
SAMPGAON
KHANAPUR
SAUNDATTI
TERDAL
Kanamadi
Ramtirth
To Bijapur
From Jath
To Tásgaon
To Poona
To Miraj
To Kolhapur
PANCHGANGA R.
DUDHGANGA R.
KRISHNA R.
GHATPRABHA R.
Shedbal
Kagvad
Jugal
Yadur
Kudchi
Mangsuli
Kokatnur
Savdi
To Jamkhandi
From Phonda Ghat
Nipani
Rásubaigad
Vallabhgad
Sankeshvar
From Amboli Ghat
HARANKASHI
Hukeri
Konnur
To Mudhol
Yadvad
To Kaládgi
From Vengurla
Gandharvagad
Mahipalgad
Hannikeri
Murgod
Sogal
Bailhongal
Katharigad
Bagevadi
Mugutkhan Hubli
Kadroli
Kittur
Parasgad
Ugargol
To Nargund
Jamboti
From Mapusa
From Sánquelim
Nandgad
Bidi
Degaon
To Dhárwár
Golihalli
Halshi
Hanmantgad
FROM GOA
From Ponda
TO BELLARY
From Supa
From Haliyal
REFERENCES
Taluka Office
Collector's Bungalow
Travellers' Do.
Made Road
Fort & Hill Fort
Railway Station
Railway under construction
Do. proposed
Scale 20 Miles = 1 Inch
Govt Photozinco Office, Poona 1884

BELGAUM.

CHAPTER I.

DESCRIPTION.

Chapter I.
Description.

Belgaum, lying between 15° 23′ and 16° 58′ north latitude and 74° 5′ and 75° 28′ east longitude, has an area of about 4600 square miles, a population of about 864,000 or 185·57 to the square mile, and a realizable revenue of £124,100 (Rs. 12,41,000).[1]

Boundaries.

The district is separated from the west coast by a belt of land twenty-five to seventy-five miles broad. It is bounded on the north by the Miraj and Jath states; on the north-east by Bijápur; on the east by the states of Jamkhandi and Mudhol; on the south-east by the state of Rámdurg and the Navalgund sub-division of Dhárwár; on the south by the Dhárwár sub-division of Dhárwár and the Supa sub-division of North Kánara; on the south-west by Goa; on the west by Sávantvádi and Kolhápur; and on the north-west by Kolhápur and Miraj. The lands of the district are greatly interlaced with those of the neighbouring native states. Within the limits of the district are large tracts of native territory, and many Belgaum villages are surrounded by native states. Of the tracts of native territory that lie within the limits of the district the chief are, in the north of Athni, two patches of Jath and Jamkhandi containing five villages; between Chikodi and Athni, Ráybág, a Kolhápur sub-division with thirty-seven villages; in the west of Chikodi, Lát, a portion of Kolhápur with eleven villages; and in the Belgaum sub-division two tracts of Sángli and Kurundvád. Of the Belgaum villages which are surrounded by the lands of native states, there are some patches in Ráybág, within the limit of the district, and others in Jamkhandi, Miraj, and Kolhápur outside of the district.

Sub-Divisions.

For administrative purposes the area included in Belgaum is distributed over seven sub-divisions Athni in the north, Gokák in the east and centre, Parasgad Sampgaon and Khanápur in the south, and Belgaum and Chikodi in the west. These sub-divisions have on an average an area of 665 square miles, 162 villages, and about 123,400 people:

---

[1] The population and revenue details are for 1881-82.

[2] As these native states are unsurveyed no area details are available. The number of villages has been roughly calculated from the district maps.

Chapter I.
Description.
Sub-Divisions.

Belgaum Administrative Details, 1882.

Sub-Division.	Area.	Villages. Government. Villages. Inhabited.	Uninhabited.	Government. Hamlets. Inhabited.	Uninhabited.	Alienated. Villages. Inhabited.	Uninhabited.	Alienated. Hamlets. Inhabited.	Total. Government.	Total. Alienated.	Total. Total.	Population, 1881.	To the square mile.	Land Revenue, 1881-82.
														£
Athni ...	786	64	1	16	4	17	...	11	65	17	82	105,961	134	15,862
Chikodi ...	840	157	1	50	40	56	1	16	158	57	215	245,614	292	26,144
Gokák ...	670	80	5	33	11	34	1	8	85	35	120	98,029	138	13,144
Parasgad ...	640	103	7	16	12	23	...	1	110	23	133	91,826	143	18,744
Sampgaon ...	424	120	19	10	6	1	...	4	139	1	140	119,843	282	23,918
Belgaum ...	663	120	2	55	28	80	1	53	122	81	203	128,477	193	15,041
Khánápur ...	633	190	25	83	5	24	1	15	215	25	240	79,264	125	11,308
Total ...	4656	834	60	263	106	235	4	108	894	239	1133	864,014	185	124,156

Aspect.

Belgaum,[1] running parallel to the Sahyádri hills, with a very irregular outline, measures about a hundred miles from north to south and fifty to eighty miles from east to west. Kolhápur on the north-west and North Kánara on the south-west separate it in a great degree from the Sahyádri hills. But between these two districts a strip about twenty miles broad passes west to the crest of the Sahyádris. This western tract, and in a less degree the rest of the western fringe of the district, are rugged with forest or bush covered hills, and have a comparatively damp and cool climate. A line drawn through Nipáni, Sankeshvar, Páchápur, Ankalgi, Marihalli and Yellurgad includes the fringe of the district which in character and climate belongs to the hill rather than to the plain country. Within these limits the rainfall is heavierand the vegetation more abundant, and the houses have pent roofs and wide eaves to carry the water clear of the mud walls. The rest of the district, sloping gently to the east, is broken by many ranges of low rolling hills, and by bold single peaks and granite rocks. It is divided from west to east into three belts of varied plain and upland by the courses of three rivers, the Krishna in the north, the Ghatprabha in the centre, and the Malprabha in the south. Most of the plain is of rich black soil, but towards the east it is stony and red and in the north there are in places long stretches of bare rock. In the north-east and centre the country is monotonous and uninteresting, low rolling downs and shallow valleys. In the richer parts are large stretches of black soil, and the higher grounds are almost bare of trees. In spite of numerous well grown trees in the valleys the country is deplorably bare. In the centre where later flows of trap form low flat-headed hills that crown the water-sheds of the larger streams, the country grows less monotonous, and little further west are high bold hills, the remains of still later flows of trap. The west and south are fairly wooded, the plains with mangoes, tamarinds, and jacks; the hills with brushwood, scrub timber, and prickly-pear. The west is watered by the south-west monsoon. Further inland

[1] Chiefly from materials supplied by Messrs. G. McCorkell, C. S., W. H. Horsley, C. S., and J. L. Laird, District Forest Officer.

Chapter I.
Description.
Aspect.
Western Belt.

the south-west rains are light and uncertain. In the north and east want of rain often causes serious loss, and the east and south depend for their supply chiefly on the north-east monsoon.

For descriptive purposes the district may be divided into four parts: the western fringe and the tract of land that runs west to the Sahyádris, and the three belts of the eastern plain that, running east and west, are drained by the Malprabha in the south, by the Ghatprabha in the centre, and by the Krishna in the north. Of the tract that stretches west to the crest of the Sahyádris, the extreme west is a succession of valleys running between spurs that stretch east at right angles to the main range of the Sahyádris. In the hilly west and in other parts of the western fringe the rugged hills, the running streams, and the abundance of trees and brushwood make the country interesting and beautiful. The upper slopes and scarps which are of trap are much like the slopes and scarps near the Bor and Tal passes in Thána. But the scenery changes in the lower slopes where the older quartzites of the Kaládgi series are reached.[1] The tops and upper slopes of the hills are almost bare; the lower slopes and valleys are fairly wooded. The villages are far apart and small with five to fifty huts and a dozen to 200 people chiefly Maráthás, with some Telves and a sprinkling of Lingáyats. Besides the villages there are some Dhangar hamlets of grass-thatched huts, the floors slightly raised and cowdunged, the walls two or three feet high of wattled *kárvi* or Strobilanthus sticks, coated with a wash of mud and cowdung. On the higher ground *rági* Eleusine corocana and *sáva* Panicum miliare are grown sometimes by ploughing and sometimes by coppice-burning. Every village has a little watered rice land on which every year two crops of red rice are grown. Of garden produce there are only plantains and limes. In the hot weather there is no water except low down in the valleys of the chief streamlets. In February when the trees are bare and the grass is bleached or burnt, a few *ráis* or sacred groves alone relieve the general bleakness and barrenness. The fresh leaves of May brighten the hills, but the blackened ground is not hidden till at the beginning of June the rains cover it with grass. Further east the valleys are flatter, broader, and more suited for tillage. Large swelling hills rise on all sides, but they are neither so high nor so steep as in the extreme west. Near Belgaum the smaller hills are rounded, and the larger more distant masses, which are capped by iron-clay, have true table-tops. The land is well watered by deep cut streamlets, which draining into larger streams find their way north to the Ghatprabha. There is a plentiful rainfall from the south-west monsoon, and from the abundance of its evergreen brushwood the country at all times looks fresh and cool. The general features of the western fringe of the rest of the district resemble this tract rather than the open plain to the centre and east. The people grow rice instead of millet, wear coarse woollens instead of cotton, and, instead of in walled flat-roofed villages, live in villages of tiled houses surrounded by deep prickly-pear and *bábhul* fences.

---

[1] Memoir Geological Survey of India, XII. Part I. 172.

Chapter I.
Description.
Aspect.
Southern Belt.

Of the three belts into which the Malprabha in the south, the Ghatprabha in the centre, and the Krishna in the north divide the centre and east of the district, the valley of the Malprabha in the west is covered with hills and forests, some of the hills, especially to the north of Khánápur, being high, rugged, and of striking outline. On either side, as it draws near the Malprabha, the land is more open, and there is much level and arable ground, broken by gentle downs, and sometimes by sudden masses of granite. The banks of the river are fringed with trees and bushes, the south-west rainfall is abundant, and the chief crops are early rice, Indian millet, and sugarcane. There is not much garden tillage. There are many rich well-peopled villages of tiled houses surrounded by huge prickly-pear and *bábhul* tree hedges. Further east, in the extreme south the country is broken by ranges of low hills that run north and south and towards the east become gradually lower and less wooded. Here the early crops yield in importance to the cold weather crops and the north-east monsoon is perhaps the more important. Close to the Malprabha the country along both banks merges into a black or cotton soil plain with few trees, and, except during the south-west rains, with little vegetation or beauty, the barren sandy soil of the quartzites bearing but a scanty growth of forest trees. Only here and there the dullness of the view is broken by ridges of sandstone with sharp broken outlines. The prettiest spots in the country are where the rivers cut through the low ranges of hills. On the Malprabha Rámdurg, Torgal, Basargi, and a few miles to the south the bold rock of Parasgad repay a visit. The deep gorge known as Navil Tirth or the Peacock's Pool has much beauty; the bold wall-like quartz cliffs of Sogal, about ten miles west of Manoli, are adorned with lovely waterfalls and well-grown trees, and, if clothed with timber, the curious Kathárigad valley, about six miles north-west of Sogal, would be higly picturesque. In this part of the country the early and late crops are of about equal importance, but rice is not grown. The chief crops are Indian millet, cajan pea, wheat, gram, cotton, tobacco, and *kusumba* Carthamus tinctorius. There is not much garden land. The villages, which lie close together and at regular intervals, are generally walled and moderately large and rich with many *ráis* or groves of mango, jack, and tamarind.

Beyond the ridges which cross the black soil plain north-east and south-west, especially on the left bank of the Malprabha, is a low rolling plateau of sandstone hills very stony and barren. North of this, between Torgal and Karikol, is a rocky wilderness of poor sandy soil deep cut by streams and covered with scrubby brushwood.

Central Belt.

To the north the drainage area of the Malprabha is separated from the Ghatprabha valley by the Belgaum hills on the west and farther east by a succession of low rather bare sandstone ranges. North of this the Ghatprabha valley, beginning in the west among rugged forest-clad hills, changes eastwards near Dadi and Páchápur into a waving plain, broken by lines of low hills whose sides have a scanty covering of stunted teak. Further east the river passes

Chapter I. Description. Aspect. *Central Belt.*

through a flat black-soil plain, which, towards the north, is suddenly broken by a tableland 300 to 400 feet above the neighbouring valley. Near Gokák, about the centre of the district, on both banks of the Ghatprabha, whose eastern course is tame and uninteresting, the plain is broken by ranges of low rather bare sandstone hills, through one of which the river forces its way in the famous Gokák falls. Close to the falls is the Márkándeya gorge also a spot of great beauty. East of Gokák on both sides of the river stretches a wide plain of rich black soil mixed in places with large patches of poor red. The rivers are fringed with *bábhul,* and along their banks are many garden plots and well-shaded villages. Away from the rivers the country except in the rains is bare and desolate.[1] The fields are treeless, the garden plots few, and the village sites miles apart and poorly shaded. Most of the villages are walled and fortified, and a few are fenced. The main harvest is early, chiefly early grown Indian millet; but especially in the east there is always a large area of late crop. The late crops are millet, Indian millet, cajan pea, gram, barley, and *kulthi.* A peculiarity of the Gokák trap hills, which are flat-topped and terraced, is that the sides are covered with trees and only the tops are tilled. Towards the west in Chikodi the soil is poor, but the south-west rain is more certain than in Gokák where much of the rain is from the north-east.

Northern Belt.

The water-parting between the Ghatprabha and the Krishna is marked in the west by some plateaus of poor soil 300 to 400 feet higher than the plain; further east it is marked by low rolling bare hills. For two or three miles on either side of the Krishna an open well-tilled black soil plain, dotted with many rich villages of flat-roofed houses and garden plots, stretches eastwards, gradually broadening as the western ranges break into single peaks. The banks of the Krishna are thickly clothed with *bábhul* trees. In this tract tillage is almost confined to the valleys of the different streams which run into the Krishna. There is little irrigation and in the west is an immense area of unarable stony ground. In the west the chief rain is from the south-west; further east the fall is less certain and depends more on the north-east monsoon.

North of the Krishna is a belt of deep rich soil with many small villages of thatched houses. Beyond this rich belt the country gradually rises in waving downs. The north-west is, except near villages, badly off for trees. The soil is poor and irrigation is confined to the valleys. In the west, where the soil is rich and the south-west rainfall fairly certain, there is much irrigation, and the barrenness of the plain is relieved by green patches of garden surrounding wells or fringing streams. The villages, which are fairly

[1] In 1791, when during the third Maisur war (1790-92), Captain Little's detachment passed through the district on its way to and from Seringapatam, between Páchápur about twelve miles south of Gokák and Nesargi about fifteen miles south-east of Páchápur, the country was covered by a thick forest called Manoli Bári, the road through which was rugged and stony. The forest lost itself in the south-west of Murgod. In some parts where the rivers took too great a sweep the forest was the boundary between the Marátha and Maisur territories. Moor's Narrative, 15.

Chapter I.
Description.
Aspect.

numerous, are fenced by hedges and are well shaded by trees. Further east a range of low flat-topped hills coming from the north-west disappears near the Krishna. East of these hills the country stretches flatter and poorer, a waving treeless flat, with long stretches of sheet rock. The upper valley of the Don is very fertile and grows unwatered wheat; in other places there is little tillage except in low-lying plots at the sides of brooks and in occasional patches of black soil. Here and there the dull bare plain is broken by steep solitary peaks and granite rocks. Every five or six miles, marked by a few *nim* and tamarind trees and brightened by garden patches, are the sites of villages of flat mud-roofed houses surrounded by more or less ruinous walls. The south-west rain is uncertain and scanty and the people trust mainly to the north-east supply. Most of the crops belong to the late harvest, white *jvári*, millet, cajan pea, linseed, and wheat.

Hills.

Except some parts of Athni in the north and of Sampgaon in the south, the district is thickly covered with ranges of hills, some of them topped with strongly built forts, some of them covered with wild brushwood and prickly-pear, and some with their sides carefully tilled almost to the tops.

North Ghatprabha Spur.

Two great spurs cross Belgaum from west to east, and form the water-partings that divide the drainage area of the Ghatprabha from that of the Krishna on the north and of the Malprabha on the south. The water-parting between the Ghatprabha and the Krishna, which may be called the North Ghatprabha Spur, rises in the Sávantvádi state close above the famous hill-fort of Manohargad about forty miles north-west of Belgaum. After running north-east for more than thirty miles it turns nearly east till it reaches Chikodi. Among the sandstone hills, which in this part of the district go to form the North Ghatprabha Spur, the chief are the table-topped and ironclay-capped hills of Vallabhagad or Hargápur (560 feet high) about fifteen miles south-west, and Hunur or Pavitra or Páijargudd (270) about seventeen miles south, of Chikodi; the flat-topped hills of Mallayan or Ádigudd (630) about twelve miles west, and of Julapengudd (730) and Nágarhál (850) about five miles north, of Chikodi; of Nágarpachmi (390), Jogigudd (875), and Nirvánepan (710) within a mile of Chikodi; and of Shendur or Rásubái (670) with a pointed top, about five miles west of Nipáni. Of these Pavitragudd is alone difficult to climb. All are covered during the rainy months with grass and have no other vegetation; all are infested with jackals and wolves. Except Nágarpachmi, Jogigudd, and Nirvánepan all have their tops or sides tilled with wheat, millet, and rice, by Maráthás, Lingáyats, Jains, Mhárs, and Musalmáns. From Chikodi the main spur passes east right across Belgaum and beyond the Belgaum boundary till it is cut by the valley of the Ghatprabha close to its meeting with the Krishna. It reappears in Kaládgi as a low ridge east of the Ghatprabha and continues eastward for about twelve miles along the southern bank of the Krishna.

North Malprabha Spur.

The second great spur may be called the North Malprabha Spur. Starting from the north side of the Tolkat pass, about twenty-four

Hills.

North Malprabha Spur.

miles west of Belgaum, it rises into the high ridge known as the Kásar Sudda. Of the hills which form the North Malprabha Spur the two most noticeable are Párgad about thirty-six miles, and Kálánandigad about twenty miles west of Belgaum. The peaked hill of Párgad is so steep that it has to be climbed by rock-cut steps. The sides are wooded except where patches have been cleared for wood-ash tillage. It has a ruined fort and several reservoirs. The highest point of the range is the perfectly table-topped hill-fort of Kálánandigad on the Rám pass road between 800 and 900 feet above the plain. Its base is more rugged and its upper slopes are steeper than those of the neighbouring hills. The ascent from the north side is by about one and a half miles of steep footpath. Unlike the neighbouring hills Párgad seems to consist throughout of a very heavy red clayey iron-stone and the capping is sharply scarped all round the edge. The other hills forming the spur are generally neither very high nor very steep. They yield little but grass and a scanty sprinkling of brushwood, and their slopes fall gently almost into the plain leaving near the base large spaces fit for tillage. Though towards the west of Chándgad about twenty-two miles north-west of Belgaum the timber-covered hills are high and abrupt, the main spur sinks to the north of Chándgad, but again rises in the high ridge of Gandharvagad two or three miles further. The Gandharvagad hill with a ruined fort has rather bare sides. The ascent is about a quarter of a mile, steep on one side and easy on the other. At Rájgoli, a little to the east of Gandharvagad, the main spur is crossed by the narrow valley of the Támraparni. In the next ten miles it is broken by the channels of the Islámpur, Márkándeya, Belgaum, Kelvi, Iranhatti, and Nandi, all flowing north-east to join the Ghatprabha. In this part of the district, especially to the north of Belgaum, are long sandstone ridges with grass and brushwood covered sides, and nearly level tops, none of them more than 300 feet high and none of them too steep to be used as grazing grounds. Beyond Nandi, for fifty miles in an unbroken line, the main spur continues to separate the Ghatprabha from the Malprabha. It ends in the Ámingad hills, about ten miles west of Hungund in Kaládgi and 130 miles east of the Sahyádris.

Minor Spurs.

Besides these main ranges three important but minor spurs, the Mahipálgad ridge about ten miles north-west of Belgaum, the Bailur ridge about fourteen miles south-west of Belgaum, and the Jámboti ridge about six miles south of Bailur, stretch east from the Sahyádris. The hills forming the Mahipálgad and Bailur ridges are lofty, their bases large, and their outlines bold and striking. The Mahipálgad hill-fort is perfectly table-topped and is capped with iron-clay. It is the highest point of the range and its sides fairly clothed with wood. The ascent is about 3000 feet long by an easy path. Bailur, which is a table-topped mass, is capped with iron-clay, the capping being sharply scarped all round the edge. It is one of the Trigonometrical Survey Stations, and is the highest point in the district, being 3491 feet above the sea level. After a length of about five miles, the Bailur ridge disappears in

Chapter I.
Description.
Hills.
Minor Spurs.

the valley of a streamlet which runs into the Malprabha. Beyond the valley it again rises in the high and very noticeable hill of Yellurgad. This, which has the ruins of a fine old fort, is one of the Trigonometrical Survey Stations, 3365 feet above the sea level and 797 above the sill of the chief gate of the Belgaum fort. Beyond Yellurgad, the ridge stretches fourteen miles north-east by east when it touches the southward extension of the great North Malprabha Spur. Here the most noticeable hill is the bold and high Kardigudi, a Trigonometrical Station about twelve miles east of Belgaum. After touching the North Malprabha Spur the ridge runs for three or four miles further and sinks into the somewhat raised plain which forms the water-shed between the Ghatprabha and the Malprabha. The Jámboti ridge which is about six miles south of the Bailur hills, has the special interest of being the most southerly mountain mass within the Deccan trap area. The hills which form this ridge are high, more or less wooded to their summits, and press closely on each other. The chief is Kirvalegudd or Goraknáth eight miles west of Khánápur. It is about 2100 feet high and is flat-topped. It has a sloping ascent and the sides are covered with brushwood giving shelter to tigers and spotted deer.

Detached Hills.

Among the isolated hills, unconnected with the Sahyádri spurs, some lie to the north of the Krishna, some to the north of the Ghatprabha, and some both north and south of the Malprabha. Of the hills to the north of the Krishna, the most noticeable are those round the town of Athni and those in the north-west of the Athni sub-division. The hills round Athni town are rolling flat-topped sandstone ranges, 200 to 300 feet above the plain, bare of vegetation except prickly-pear. Those on the north-west of the sub-division belong to a spur that runs south-east from Sátára. Within Athni limits the bare flat-topped hills rise from the plain in clear cut terraces, whose outlines, unbroken by trees or bushes, stand out with marked clearness when caught by the rays of the sun. Of this range the chief hill within Belgaum limits is Junápnála or Belvankigudd, a rugged fortified peak, about fifteen miles north-west of Athni. It rises about 1000 feet above the plain and is covered with short thorny scrub and grass. On its flat top Lingáyat and Marátha husbandmen raise crops of wheat and gram. Of the hills to the north of the Ghatprabha there are the sandstone ranges in Gokák, 200 to 300 feet high, which run north and south and are covered with prickly-pear. About two miles north of Gokák the bold rugged slopes and table-topped mass of Bágedgudd or Bastigudd reaches a height of 2667 feet, and stands 700 to 800 feet above the plain. It is a great mass of trap in which the lines of eight leading flows may be clearly traced. About seven miles east of Gokák is the Manikeri ridge of reddish drab quartzite beds capped with trap. Manikeri, the highest point, is a Trigonometrical Station about 2458 feet above the sea. The top commands a wide view in which the objects of most interest are the Gokák falls and the Gokák scarp. At Hulkund, four miles south-east of Manikeri, the ridge is crossed by a river bed, but it rises again to the east and forms two conspicuous rocky hills. Of the hills to the

Chapter I.

Description.

Hills.

Detached Hills.

north of the Malprabha, the Kathárigad hill, about twelve miles north-west of Saundatti, is 2844 feet above the sea and about 1200 feet above the plain. It is covered with prickly-pear and brushwood sheltering wild hogs and panthers. It has a remarkable flat dome with steep deep-fissured sides. The hill is formed of granite gneiss capped by a mass of quartzite. To the geologist the view from the top is of great interest. South of the Malprabha river and four miles north of the Kel pass, in the extreme west, stands the flat-topped hill-fort of Bhimgad, rugged, steep, and surrounded by a double line of broken hills, rising 1800 feet from the plain. From the north side of the great Mahádáyi ravine looking over the scarp formed by the edge of the trap area, the fort, with the neighbouring limestone peak and several huge masses which have slipped into the valley, forms a view of rock and forest of rare wildness and beauty. The way up is by rock-cut steps, through bush-coverèd slopes which shelter bears, tigers, wolves, and bison. Neither the top nor the sides are tilled. At the foot of the hill is a village inhabited chiefly by Maráthás. About ten miles south-east of Bhimgad is the flat-topped hill of Dongargávgudd. It is about 2400 feet above the plain and is covered with scattered trees sheltering tigers, leopards, and wolves. There is no tillage and there are no hamlets. About twelve miles north-east of Dongargávgudd the flat-topped Samshergudd rises about 1800 feet from the plain. Its gentle slopes are covered with rocks and a few trees which shelter hyænas, wild dogs, and hares. About three miles south of Shamshergudd the flat-topped hill of Máchigad or Bijganigudd rises about 1500 feet above the plain. It is covered with trees and its top and sides are tilled. About eight miles south of Máchigad the flat-topped sloping hill of Kumbhárdegudd rises about 1800 feet from the plain. It is covered with trees which shelter tigers, leopards, and wolves. Sampgaon has three hills, Deshnur about ten miles north, Ganimardi about ten miles south, and Hitalmardi about eighteen miles south-west of Sampgaon. The flat-topped Deshnur hill, about 1320 feet above the plain, is covered with grass and brushwood. Bedars, Lingáyats, and Maráthás till its top with gram, millet, and *rági.* The other two hills, which are also flat-topped, have their sides covered with grass and brushwood. The top of Hitalmardi is tilled and millet and rice are grown on it. The Parasgad hills are flat-topped and are covered with brushwood and prickly-pear sheltering panthers and wild hog. Of these hills Yellamma about 425 feet above the plain is three miles, and Huli about 300 feet above the plain is six miles, north-east of Saundatti; Hirekummi, a Trigonometrical Survey Station, 2572 feet above the sea and 500 to 600 feet above the plain, is about eight miles south-east of Saundatti; Someshvargudd about 350 feet above the plain is about thirteen miles north-west of Saundatti; and the Parasgad hill is about a mile south of Saundatti. The Parasgad hill is about 600 feet above the plain and 2572 feet above the sea and has steep rocky sides difficult to climb.

Rivers.

The district drains eastward along the three lines of the Krishna in the north, the Ghatprabha in the centre, and the Malprabha in the south. None of these rivers is navigable, and between February

Chapter I. Description. Rivers.

and May the volume of the Krishna is much reduced, and the Ghatprabha and Malprabha shrink into small streams. All three have worn deep courses through the surface black soil and laterite, and most of their banks are covered with *bábhul* trees.

The Krishna.

The source of the KRISHNA is near the hill-station of Mahábaleshvar in Sátára, at a height of 4000 feet above the sea. After a south-easterly course of about 175 miles, through Sátára and parts of Sángli Miraj and Kolhápur, it enters Belgaum at the village of Ganeshpur about twenty miles north of Chikodi, and, after flowing about six miles to the south-west, receives from the west the waters of the Panchganga. Below this meeting the united streams turn nearly at right angles to the south-east, cross a narrow strip of Kolhápur, and enter Chikodi, forming for about five miles the boundary between Chikodi and Athni, until at the village of Sháhápur, the river turns nearly west for three miles when it again changes to the south-east. At this point it receives from the west the waters of the Dudhganga, which, with its tributary the Vedganga, drain the north and west of Chikodi. Below the meeting the river runs five miles to the south-east when it again turns north-east for about eight miles. Next it passes through Ráybág of Kolhápur, where, near Chinchi, it is joined by a streamlet called Halhaula in Kanarese, but by Musalmáns called Dudh Nalla or Milk-river from its white water.[1] After a few miles it suddenly turns north and enters Athni, where it winds to the south-east and then to the north-east, receiving the Agrani from the north about eight miles south-west of Athni. Beyond this it flows south-east, and forming the south boundary of Athni, turns north-east till it enters Kaládgi near a village called Janvád. Close to the Krishna are many plots of garden land and the banks are covered with trees. The river sides are steep and scarped from twenty to fifty feet high, generally of black soil or laterite. In the rocky bed are many *bábhul* shaded islands.[2] The monsoon freshes fill the river bed from bank to bank, and, as a rule, from June to December the volume of water is very large. During the dry months the stream greatly dwindles, and between March and June there is but a scanty flow.[3] There are eight ferries at Ainápur, Hálihál, Satti, Mahisvádgi, Savadi, Shirhati, Chikk Padsalgi, and Hire Padsalgi. The ferry boats are round wicker baskets covered with leather, twelve to fifteen feet in diameter, and able to carry thirty to forty passengers.

The Ghatprabha.

From its source in Sundargad to the north of the Rám pass till it joins the Krishna at Kudli Sangam about thirty miles north-east of Kaládgi the GHATPRABHA has a total length of 100 miles.

---

[1] Moor's Narrative, 268.

[2] On one of these islands about a mile east of Kudchi, Lieutenant Moor of Captain Little's detachment found (1791) a beautiful mango grove overshadowing two Musalman tombs. One was of a Musalman saint named Shaikh Muhammud Suraj-ul-Din and the other of a princess of Balkh. Both had travelled so far to make converts to the true faith. They settled on the island and remained for many years doing acts of charity and benevolence. Narrative, 269.

[3] In the middle of May 1791 Lieutenant Moor found the Krishna near Ainápur about 500 yards from bank to bank. There was much water, the deepest part on the north bank being five feet. Narrative, 269, 300.

Chapter I.
Description.
Rivers.
The Ghatprabha.

After flowing about thirty miles north-east through Kolhápur the GHATPRABHA enters the district north of the village of Shedihál at the junction of the Belgaum and Chikodi sub-divisions. From Shedihál, near which it receives the Támraparni from the south, the Ghatprabha flows about twenty miles north-east across the Chikodi sub-division, where it is joined from the west by the Harankáshi. It then enters Gokák between the villages of Sultánpur on the west and Shivápur on the east. From this it takes a sharp turn to the north, running along the boundary of the sub-division. It again turns suddenly to the south-east and flows in an almost straight course to Gokák. Three miles to the west of Gokák rushing through a rugged and picturesque gorge between two ranges of sandstone hills and dashing over a cliff about 175 feet high, the river forms the falls of Gokák, whose thundering roar is heard for about five miles round. Except in the rains, little water is seen in the rocky bed of the river above the fall. It runs in narrow channels deep cut into the rock, till, as it reaches the brink of the cliff, it spreads across the bed of the river. For some distance above the fall the force of the current has worn many large holes which are a favourite bathing-place for Bráhmans and others who come to visit the local deity Mahálingeshvar. The grandeur of the falls varies greatly at different seasons, but from June to December they are almost always worth a visit. A little above the fall the river is about 250 yards across but narrows to eighty as it reaches the brink of the chasm. This narrowing greatly increases the depth and the speed of the mass of water, which, at the rate of ten feet a second, hurries ten feet deep down the shelving tables of rock. The denseness of the body of water, and its dull muddy colour make the fall seem slow and sullen.[1] But the feeling of massive weight is relieved by light and airy clouds of white and amber spray, which, rising from the depth of the gorge in curling wreaths, veil the foot of the fall, except when a fitful gust sweeping up the glen scatters the spray. Above the crest of the gorge the spray vanishes as it rises ; but it again gathers, and at a little distance falls in gentle showers. Spray-bows, of varying brightness, clearness, and size, lend their tints to the ever rising vapour.[2]

About two miles below the falls, and half a mile above the town of Gokák, the Ghatprabha receives the Márkándeya, after a course of about forty miles from the hills to the west of Belgaum. From Gokák the Ghatprabha again runs north-east and passes out of Belgaum into the Mudhol state. Except among hills the banks are low and gently sloping, and, in places, owing to the hardness of the rock, the bed is very shallow. Like the Krishna it is unfit for navigation. In 1835 the water rose so high as to cover three of the flight of steps which leads to the largest of the temples on the right

---

[1] A tumbler of water deposited about one-fiftieth of a fine reddish clay. Captain Newbold in Geological Papers on Western India, 354.

[2] Spray-bows like rainbows are formed only on the surface of the cloud facing the sun. The brightness of their tints depends on the size and closeness of the particles of vapour. They are brightest where the particles are of middle size and closeness and grow dull as the particles are smaller and denser. The largest spray-bows are to be seen in the evening. They form an arch right across the river, and, as the sun sets, rise, withdraw, and vanish. Memoir Geological Survey, XII. Part I. 89.

Chapter I.
Description.
Rivers.

bank of the river at Gokák. The chief ferries are at Hádkal, Ghodgiri, Modga Dodali, Hansibal, Gokák, Tigdi, and Dhavleshvar. Like those on the Krishna the boats are round coracles, wicker-work covered with leather.

The Malprabha or Malapahári.

Unlike the Krishna and the Ghatprabha, which rise beyond the limit of the district, the MALPRABHA has its source among the eastern Sahyádri spurs about eight miles west of Jámboti in Khánápur.

Of the origin of the river this story is told: In the village of Kankumbi, on the eastern brow of the Sahyádris, lived a man who was happy in being the husband of a beautiful and virtuous woman. In spite of his wife's goodness jealousy seized his soul, and he gave his wife neither rest nor peace. At length, driven to despair, she sacrificed to the gods and putting up a prayer to Basava, the patron of Lingáyats, threw herself into a mountain tarn. No sooner did the pool receive this sacrifice than its waters began to rise, and, flowing over their banks, formed a river which was called Malprabha or Malapahári, the Cleanser from Sin.

From its source in Khánápur the Malprabha runs east for about thirteen miles, when it turns south-east for about eight miles, and then north-east past the towns of Khánápur and Lokodi. In this part of its course, though it is shallow in the fair season, it continues to flow throughout the year. Through Sampgaon, across which it next flows in an almost easterly direction, it is a sluggish stream, running in a deep bed between high steep banks.[1] Crossing Parasgad in a north-easterly direction it passes into the Torgal state near the village of Basargi. About four miles north of Saundatti the Malprabha rushes violently through a gorge in the Manoli hills. Before the river wore this gorge through the hills the plain to the west was probably an inland lake, whose surplus waters fell, as at Gokák, over the north face of the cliff. By degrees the fall wore the rock and gradually cut a passage backwards till the lake was reached and its waters drained. On either bank of the gorge is a rock naturally formed into a rough figure. These rocks are the subject of the following story: In former days the river, instead of passing through the hills, crept humbly and slowly round their base. One day a peacock, who sat flaunting his gorgeous tail on the top of the rocks, reproached the river for its humility in creeping round the base of the hill and keeping to the level ground. Enraged at the peacock's taunts the river suddenly changed its course and rushed to the spot on which the peacock was sunning himself. Before the bird had time to take to flight he was changed to stone, and the water bursting the barrier of rocks broke the image of the peacock one-half of it on either bank. From this, it is said, the place took the name of Navil Tirth or the Peacock's Pool.[2] The gorge which

[1] At Sangoli, about five miles south-east of Sampgaon, Lieutenant Moor, of Captain Little's detachment, found (May 1791-92) the Malprabha about two hundred yards across with two feet of water and a good bottom. Narrative, 45, 259.

[2] According to another legend, a peacock, hard pressed by its pursuers, was unable to fly over the chain of hills which rises to the north of the great black plain. In its terror it cried piteously and the deity of the Malprabha, taking pity on the bird, clove a passage through the rocks by which it escaped. Finding the new passage convenient, the goddess adopted it as a channel for her stream, and has

Chapter I.
Description.
Rivers.
The Malprabha.

is about 300 feet deep includes an upper or south-western half not more than fifty yards wide, and a lower half which is broader and with lower banks. The upper or south-western half is so narrow that, even in moderate floods, not an inch of margin is left between the water and the vertical walls on either side. During great floods the water rises thirty to forty feet in the gorge, and rushes with mighty force, forming pot-holes of great size and depth, which at every new-moon in the fair season, when the water is low, are largely resorted to by Hindu devotees. In its lower or northern half, the gorge widens considerably, and the sides decrease in height, till the quartzite beds die out in a level flat which stretches for some distance to the north-east.

At every village along the bank of the river, right down in the bed of the stream, is a small square temple containing a *ling*, and in front of the small low door is almost always an image of Basav in the form of the sacred bull. The banks vary much in character; in some parts they rise sharply from the water's edge, in others they have a gentle slope, and in a few places the river runs almost on a level with the country round. Near Manoli the Malprabha receives from the left the Benákatti, a stream which rising in the trap hills near Sategiri, has a southerly course of about twenty miles. Besides the Benákatti, though both from the north and the south many small streams fall into the Malprabha, it has no important feeders. At Sogal, ten miles west of the Manoli gorge, a stream which after a southerly course of about five miles falls into the Malprabha near Kungari, runs southward through a depression in the quartzite boundary ridge, and forms a very picturesque waterfall in a semicircle cut into the hard quartzite conglomerate. The fall is over a sheer rock fifty to sixty feet high. Above the principal fall are two minor falls, which, with an old temple and a group of trees, form a very pretty scene. The chief ferries on the Malprabha are at Jámboti, Khánápur, Mugutkhán-Hubli, Turmuri, Sangoli, Virápur, Yakundi, and Manoli.

Besides these three main rivers, where, in the south-west, the district stretches to the crest of the Sahyádris, the Mahádáyi, a feeder of the Goa river, and the Tilári, a small river near the Rám pass, drain westward through clefts in the crest of the Sahyádris.

Water.

Except the east of the plain country, which is generally badly off for water, the water-supply is plentiful. In Gokák, the plain from four to six miles wide, between the Ghatprabha and the chain of hills on which Mamdápur stands, is formed of rich black soil everywhere of good depth. The land is capable of yielding the richest crops if only there was water. But the rainfall is so uncertain that only once in three years is there a fair harvest. The east of Parasgad is subject to droughts followed in the hot months by a failure of drinking water. In other parts artificial ponds and reservoirs hold drinking water during most of the year.

Geology.

Geologically[1] the district forms three great belts. In the south

---

used it ever since. The river at this spot is supposed to have great cleansing power. Memoir Geological Survey, XII. Part I. 99.

[1] The geological sketch of the district has been compiled from Mr. R. B. Foote's Memoir on the Geological Features of the Southern Marátha Country and Adjacent Districts. Geological Survey of India, XII. Part I. of 1877.

Chapter I.
Description.
Geology.

is a narrow strip of gneissic rock; in the centre are quartzite and limestone partly overlaid by two great bands of trap; and in the north and west are trap and iron-clay. The earliest traceable event in the history of the Belgaum rocks is the making of the stratified schist. This process was probably continued at intervals through long periods. The schist beds were then forced up, broken, and their character changed by a volcanic eruption, of which certain old highly crystalline trap dykes are a record. After remaining as land through long ages the gneissic rocks sank, were worn by the sea, and as they sank still lower, sandstones and limestones were formed from their ruins and laid over them. Another volcanic eruption forced the sandstones and limestones above sea level, changed their character, and twisted and broke them. For long they continued as land, weathering into hills and valleys, the rivers widening in places into small lakes where cross ridges checked their flow. Next, from the north-west, lava flows rolled over this rugged country, filling valleys and leaving swelling downs and shallow hollows. Of these flows only a few reached the east of the district, but towards the west at least eight great flows came at intervals and lay one over the other. Since the flow of lava ceased the general lie of the country has not changed. The surface has been greatly worn, but the wearing forces have apparently entirely been air-forces, sun, rain, and wind. Though over large areas it has now disappeared the iron-clay capping of Bágedgudd near Gokák shows that the latest lava flow spread at least as far east as the centre of the district. The rivers have long forced their way east through the hardest hills. But rocks formed under fresh water and gravel and shingle beds on river banks, sixty to eighty feet above present flood levels, show that at some period after the latest outflow of lava the country was in places covered with lakes. Since their outflow air and water have changed the latest lava beds into an iron-clay rock that caps most of the higher hills, and in the plains the traps have weathered into red soil, and traps sandstones and gneiss mixed with vegetable matter have weathered into black soil. The rocks are almost entirely without organic remains. Almost the only signs of plant or of animal life are in recent alluvia, where, besides shells, the bones of a wild ox and of an extinct species of rhinoceros have been found.

Beginning from the surface the succession of the geological formations is:

Post Tertiary or Recent:
- 7. Sub-aërial Formations and Soils.
- 6. Alluvia.

Later Tertiary:
- 5. Bone-bearing Deposits.

Upper Secondary:
- 4. Deccan Trap and Associated Formations
  (b) Iron-clay (laterite) Formations. (a) Intertrappean Lake Beds.
- 3. Infra-trappean Formations, Lameta Beds.
- 2. Kaládgi Series of Sandstones and Quartzites (Sub-metamorphic).

Azoic:
- 1. Gneissic (Metamorphic) Series with Associated Intrusive Rocks.

For descriptive purposes the different formations come most conveniently in their true geological or ascending order.

Chapter I.
Description.
Geology.
Gneissic Rocks.

Within Belgaum limits the Gneissic Rocks form a belt that stretches across the south of the district varying in breadth from two to six miles. Besides in this belt gneissic rocks appear as inliers in some cases among sandstones and quartzites, in other cases among trap.[1] It has not been settled whether all the gneissic rocks belong to the same geological age. Full inquiry will probably show that they admit of subdivision and classification. The series includes a very considerable variety of rocks, schistose or granitoid, separated into great sharply-defined bands, which, in many cases, may be traced across the country from the southern boundary of the younger traps, across Dhárwár to the Tungbhadra and away into Bellári and North Maisur.

West of the Dhárwár-Belgaum road the gneiss is greatly obscured by lateritic or lithomargic surface deposits. Beyond these, near Khánápur, about fifteen miles south of Belgaum, is a broad belt of granitoid gneiss, the bedding of which is doubtful. Further west is a great development of very schistose chiefly micaceous gneiss with some very thick beds of crystalline limestone, the strike of which is difficult to indicate as the beds roll at low angles. These beds show much the same position in the several sections at Bhimgad and in the Tilári ravine. The rocks met with in the gneissic series are divided into two great groups, the granitoid, which are highly crystalline and massive, and the schistose, which are less crystalline and often highly foliated and distinctly bedded. The schistose areas differ from the granitoid areas by the much greater smoothness of their surface. Even when they form hills the hills are in most cases gently rounded, the scenery is commonplace and tame, and there is a want of vegetation. A band of granitoid gneiss crossing the Malprabha, and numerous dykes having a north-east to south-west course, appear in the Kathárigad valley, about sixteen miles west of Torgal. Another granitoid band forms some noticeable hills at Ganibáil, twelve miles south of Belgaum, and passes south through Khánápur to the Nandgad hills. Besides, at Saundatti, a very broad band of schistose rocks appears in the upper valley of the Malprabha at Báil Hongal, about ten miles west of the Kathárigad granitoid band, and stretches south-west within a few miles of Khánápur, where it joins the most westerly band of granitoid gneiss.

The commonest type of granitoid gneiss is a more or less porphyritic rock consisting of quartz, felspar, and hornblende in varying proportions. The felspar very frequently predominates. As a rule the granitoid varieties are not distinctly bedded. The transition from the highly crystalline massive form to distinctly bedded and even schistose rocks is often seen near the boundaries of granitoid areas. The granitoid gneiss in those cases shows a broadly banded structure, the bands being parallel to the true

---

[1] There are twelve chief inliers: the Kathárigad inlier thirty miles east of Belgaum; the Halki and Budnur inlier north of the Belgaum-Kaládgi road; west of these are the Vannur and Páchápur inliers; to the north of these are three other inliers at Kelvi, Mamdápur, and Gokák; further south are two inliers in the Belgaum valley; and west of Belgaum close to Patna two small inliers show through the Deccan trap.

Chapter I.
Description.
Geology.
Gneissic Rocks.

foliation of the less altered rocks, and being in fact the true layers of original deposition.

The two chief varieties of schist are micaceous and hæmatite. The micaceous schists, though uncommon in the east, are seen in vast thickness in the ravines of the Mahádáyi and Tilári and in the scarps south of the Párvár and Rám passes. Of hæmatite schists numerous beds are found in the upper valley of the Malprabha in the Báil Hongal schistose band where they form conspicuous ridges among the softer schistose rocks. Their silicious laminæ are generally very fine-grained, and are often as semi-vitreous in texture as true quartzites. Their colour varies from nearly white to bright red or even dull brown. The true foliation or bedding of the rock is almost always perfectly preserved. They are poor in iron, and rarely show much of the red staining, though they are frequently jaspideous in texture. The country is covered with their debris to a remarkable extent. Minute and small quantities of gold are found associated with hæmatite beds in some of the streamlets about Báil Hongal and Belovádi.

Associated with the schistose members of the gneissic series are beds of crystalline limestone. On one of the most conspicuous masses of this limestone stands Bhimgad fort, about twenty-five miles south-west of Belgaum. From the north side of the great Mahádáyi ravine, looking over the scarp formed by the edge of the trap area, Bhimgad, with neighbouring limestone peaks and several huge masses which have slipped into the valley, forms a wild and most beautiful scene. The dolomite beds extend southward from Bhimgad across the Kel or Talevádi pass and up the northern slope of Darshindongar the highest hill in this part of the Sahyádris. Here, as at Bhimgad, the limestone is a light gray sacharoid magnesian with numerous quartz laminæ.[1] Near the east gate of Bhimgad a large quantity of dark blackish brown powder is found on the surface of the dolomite from which it has evidently weathered. The face of the limestone which is here greatly hid by vegetation is darker than in the main mass of the mountain. There are three other chief instances of crystalline limestones. A gray crystalline limestone underlying the hæmatite-schist bed which forms the crest of the ridge south of Báil Hongal in the upper valley of the Malprabha; a small outcrop of very silicious gray limestone which forms two small inliers four miles east of Nesargi on the Belgaum-Kaládgi road; and to the east of Gudganhatti, six miles north-east of Nesargi, a very considerable bed of gray limestone associated with argillaceous and micaceous schists.

Of trap, granite, and quartz the three chief foreign dykes or reefs that cross the South-Marátha gneiss, the only reefs of any size within Belgaum limits, are trap dykes. A numerous set of dykes, with a north-east to south-west course, cross the gneiss inlier in the Kathárigad hills. The largest of this group is a very broad dyke which, rising from the black soil three miles north-west of Behvur,

---

[1] An analysis of the dolomite showed water and organic matter 4·0; carbonate of lime 56·4; carbonate of magnesia 34·8; oxide of iron with a little alumina and manganese 3·6; insoluble 2·2.

Chapter I.
Description.
Geology.
Gneissic Rocks.

runs for about eight miles, till it joins another very large dyke. Beyond this dyke it does not reappear, or is again immediately lost under the alluvium of the Krishna at Mudukop. An intrusion of dioritic trap, surrounded by a vast unbroken spread of cotton soil, occurs at Asmatti, about twelve miles east of Parasgad, and forms a long low rocky hill. To the north and south the ridge dies away rapidly under the cotton soil, but groups of large masses stand out at intervals showing that it stretches north-west and south-east for about three miles with a width of two-thirds to three-quarters of a mile.

Kaládgi Series.

A great series of quartzite, sandstone, and limestone rocks, in many respects closely resembling the Kadapah series,[1] forms a well marked basin, lying mainly between the banks of the Krishna and the Malprabha rivers. In geological sequence these rocks are next in age to the gneissic series on which they directly and unconformably rest. Their broken ridges of varied outline relieve the dullness of the central and eastern plain, but their barren sandy soil is unfavourable to vegetation. Within Belgaum limits the rocks that belong to the Kaládgi series are of two leading varieties, quartzites and limestones. The quartzites are found in a line that runs from Daddi in the west to Rámdurg in the east, about two-thirds from the north of the district. The limestones, which are of later formation than the quartzites, occur in an inner basin in the eastern centre of the district, a space about fifteen miles from north to south and about thirty miles from east to west. Beyond these limits, quartzite and limestone rocks appear in many parts of the district both as outliers resting on older rocks, and as inliers, exposed by denudation within the area of younger rocks. The chief of the inliers are to the west, the Mángaon inlier in the upper valley of the Harankáshi, the Shengaon and Assangaon inliers in the valleys of the Vedganga and Dudhganga in Kolhápur, and a group of large and small inliers on the south bank of the Ghatprabha near Yádvád about nine miles south-west of Mudhol. Of the outliers one of some importance caps the Parasgad hill and two small ones occur a little to the north-east.

The series, as a whole, where disturbed, is decidedly metamorphic. The disturbed parts lie within the Kaládgi basin, the undisturbed parts are, with few exceptions, the western outliers. As no trace of any organism has been detected the series may for the present be regarded as lifeless or azoic.

The whole series may be subdivided as follows in descending order :

	Feet.
B.—*Upper Kaládgi Series.*	
6. Shales Limestones and Hæmatite Schists ...	2000
5. Quartzites with local Conglomerates and Breccias ...	1200-1800
A.—*Lower Kaládgi Series.*	
4. Limestones Clays and Shales	5000-6000
3. Sandstones and Shales	3000-5000
2. Silicious Limestones and Hornstone or cherty Breccias	3000-5000
1. Quartzites Conglomerates and Sandstones	3000-5000

[1] This series takes its name from Kadapah a British district in the Madras Presidency between 13° 12′ and 16° 19′ north latitude and 77° 52′ and 79° 48′ east longitude.

Chapter I.
Description.
Geology.
Kaládgi Series.

The total thickness of the series is not clearly known. Near Kaládgi the depth is not less than 10,000 to 15,000 feet, and in the west, among the Sahyádris, where all the rocks apparently belong to the lower series, the thickness is not less than 1000 feet.

Rocks belonging to the upper series are found only over small areas in the east of the district. The chief places are to the west of Lokápur and to the west and east of Yádvád. Of the upper series of rocks the limestones of the higher portion are found only in the east. This limestone tract is on the eastern boundary about fifteen miles from north to south, from about five miles south of Mudhol to about ten miles north of Rámdurg. It stretches in a broken belt about thirty miles north-west into the trap country, narrowing till it ends near Beshati on the right bank of the Ghatprabha about twenty miles below Gokák. The remaining rocks of this series belong to the quartzites and shales, the lowest section of the Lower Kaládgi Series. These form au irregular winding belt, which, beginning about five miles on either side of Rámdurg in the east, stretches first north-west to Gokák, and then south-west to Daddi in a band ten to twenty miles broad.

The base of the Kaládgi series rests on the gneissic rocks whose surface was so uneven that in places the basement beds of the quartzites and sandstones may be seen lapping round prominences rising from the surface of the older rocks. The silicious rocks of the lowest Kaládgi sections are entirely of materials taken from worn gneiss. The two sections of the Lower Kaládgi series may be further divided as follows:

II. 4. Limestones Clays and Shales.
3. Sandstones and Shales.
I. 2. Silicious Limestones and Hornstone Breccias.
1. Quartzites Conglomerates and Sandstones.

Lower Kaládgi Series.

The three lowest subdivisions are so closely connected that they may be best taken together in the same section. The basement beds of the Lower Kaládgi Series consist of conglomerates, grits, sandstones, and quartzites of great aggregate thickness. There are occasional beds of shale or shaley flags, and in one place several beds of hæmatite schists. All the outliers belong to this section of the series. In the rocks of the series there is great local diversity of texture and colour. At the same time the relative characters of the more important subdivisions are to a great extent constant, and the gradual decrease in coarseness of texture from below upwards holds good almost everywhere. Resting upon the basement beds, in the east and south of the basin, are found beds of intensely silicious limestone, which in many places pass or seem to pass into very characteristic hornstone or cherty breccias. Resting upon these come in most parts of the basin the clays, shales, and limestones that are grouped together in sub-section 4. In the south and west of the basin an important group of sandstones and shales appears between the breccia beds and the base of sub-section 4. But the imperfect character of the local sections and the presence of a broad band of Deccan trap combine to make the relations of the beds obscure and doubtful. As a rule the rocks of this section lie somewhat upturned,

Chapter I.
Description.
Geology.
Lower Kaládgi Series.

the outer boundary scarps forming a true basement edge. Within the basin, they are usually waving, but in some places are horizontal, and in others are much disturbed and crumpled. In the western outliers the conglomerates and sandstones are almost undisturbed and show a minimum of metamorphic action.

The colour of the conglomerates and lower grits varies much more than the colour of the higher beds. Among the conglomerates the chief shades are purplish-gray and dark purple, pinkish-gray from the decomposed granite-gneiss, whitish-gray where there are many quartz pebbles, and much light reddish-brown. The shaley beds are usually drab or pale ashy-gray. Near the jaspery hæmatite schists of the gneiss the conglomerates are in many places almost entirely composed of rolled or angular fragments of the jaspery hæmatite of all colours peculiar to those beds.

The cherty breccia beds, which are peculiar features of the Kaládgi basin, by weathering into disconnected masses, obscure the relations between the underlying and the overlying rocks. The position and the relations to the great bands of very silicious limestone, which occur to the north and north-west of Manoli, seem to show that the breccias are altered silicious limestone. The change from limestone to breccia was probably caused by highly acidulated water soaking in and carrying away so much chalky matter that the cherty skeleton was broken by the weight of the overlying rocks. Subsequent infiltration of flinty chalky and iron-clay matter formed the crushed chert into a breccia with variable cement. The greater part of this change probably took place during the period of volcanic energy which produced the Deccan trap.

The following details of sections show the character of the Kaládgi quartzite hills in different parts of the district:

Lower Kaládgi Quartzites.

At Gokák, the great series of pebbly and gritty quartzites are remarkably uniform in colour and texture. Drab to reddish brown are the leading colours. The best section is in the gorge of the river just below the fall. Here the exposed thickness of quartzites and conglomerates cannot be much less than 400 feet, of which more than 300 are exposed in the cliff on the north side of the falls.[1] The curved lines showing the outcrops of the quartzite beds are very conspicuous on the face of the cliff. For some distance above the fall the water [2] runs at a great pace, and in consequence has worn in the very hard quartzite many fine specimens of pot-holes some beds of which both here and in many neighbouring sections are typical waxy quartzites showing beautifully preserved rippling.

[1] The cliffs flanking the right side of the river below were found by Captain Newbold rent by nearly vertical fissures from summit to base. Two of the largest, with a direction of east-south-east, were crossed nearly at right angles by minor cracks, which thus insulated portions of the rock. The bases of these tottering pinnacles were often undermined by the action of the water and the mass tumbled headlong into the stream. Geological Papers on Western India, 355.

[2] At Konur, about two miles and a half above the Gokák falls, a tumblerful of the turbid water deposited one-fiftieth of its bulk of a fine reddish clay, not calcareous. The pebbles brought down were chiefly quartz, granite, and hypogene schist, with a few calcedonies; the sand contained grains of magnetic iron. Geological Papers on Western India, 355.

Chapter I.
Description.
Geology.
Lower Kaládgi Quartzites.

A large fissure[1] in the cliff which forms the south side of the gorg is really composed of joint fissures much enlarged by the partis sliding forward of the rocky masses.

In spite of the hardness of the rock, the gorge is cut fully a mill back from the general scarp of the Gokák hills. This scarp muse have had something of its present shape before the outpouring of the Deccan trap. And there can be little doubt that these quartzite rocks were more worn away before than they have been since the outpouring of the trap flows.

Two small but very marked outliers of the basement conglómerate beds cap isolated and almost conical schistose hills, one on either side of the Ghatprabha where it issues from the gorge below the falls. These conglomerate beds form sharply scarped table tops to two hills of hornblendic and micaceous schist. The larger hill, which rises more than 600 feet above Gokák, overlooks a great part of the quartzite plateau which stretches away far to the south-west.

Very beautiful quartzite cliffs, whose bright red contrasts splendidly with the encircling green brushwood, occur in the valley of the Márkándeya, two miles south-west of Gokák, and especially in a great ravine that opens into the valley from the Karabgatti plateau on the south. Round many parts of the Gokák scarp the edges of the conglomerate beds form wall-like cliffs, and occasionally from the more rapid weathering of the schistose beds in the underlying gneiss, fallen quartzite and conglomerate masses strew the sides and bases of the hills.

The Gokák scarp disappears northward under the Deccan trap at Arbhavi, four miles north of Gokák. To the south it forms two bold headlands jutting east. Further south it is lost, and the beds forming it dip southward, and then roll generally at low angles over a large area covered with small wooded hills on the banks of the Kelvi and its tributaries. It stretches south through Lakhmápur and Deshnur to Marihal, about ten miles east of Belgaum, east to Mamdápur and Nandi, and west to the Márkándeya river on the Páchápur-Ankalgi valley. Throughout this region the sandstones less frequently assume the character of quartzites, having been exposed to a decidedly smaller degree of metamorphism. The coarser beds, as conglomerates and grits, show little change, but

---

[1] The head of the fissure is elliptical in form, with mural sides of sandstone, which, in its lower portions, is interstratified with layers of shale of a purplish-brown and yellowish-brown colour, with minute spangles of mica disseminated and between the laminæ containing incrustations of common alum. The head appears to have been cut back about 100 yards by the wearing of the water. Large rocks with angular unworn surfaces evidently dislodged from the rocks on the spot are seen in the bed and on the sides of the river below the deep receptacle of the fallen waters and on its margin. At the bottom of the deep fissures in the sandstone cliffs there were heaps of fallen fragments of rocks intermingled with bones and dung of bats, rats, wild pigeons, sheep, and goats. The upper portions of the fissures, with their sides marked with shallow polished grooves, were also choked with rubbish and rocks. Captain Newbold made two holes through the floor of the chief fissure. After penetrating the surface layer of loose stones a fine red earth was found imbedding angular fragments of sandstone and a few rounded pebbles of sandstone and quartz. Geological Papers on Western India, 355, 356.

Chapter I.
Description.
Geology.
Lower Kaládgi Quartzites.

some of the fine grained beds, even where they lie horizontally or very nearly horizontally, are true quartzites. Where the beds have been disturbed the amount of metamorphism is in direct proportion to the amount of disturbance.

The same characteristics are found in the rocks that stretch west across the Márkándeya river to the Kákti and Kankumbi scarps near Belgaum and along the upper valley of the Ghatprabha past Konur, Ghodgiri, Majti, Vatmuri, Sutgatti, and Daddi to the extreme west of the Kaládgi basin at Vatangi. The two gneiss inliers of Iranhatti and Yellápur seem to be high points of the old gneissic surface, round which the true basement beds of the quartzite series are not exposed.

The lower Kaládgi quartzites and sandstones at Vatangi in the extreme west are covered on three sides by Deccan trap flows. Beyond the ridge of trap, which covers the quartzites west and north of Vatangi, the quartzites reappear in the valley of the Harankáshi, occupying a considerable area near the village of Mángaon. The rocks that form this inlier present no peculiar features. They are quartzites and grits which mostly dip northward or north-west at low angles. They are best exposed in the row of hills which runs south-east from Salgaon on the bank of the Harankáshi and joins the trap ridge. The quartzites and grits are mostly pale coloured and fine-grained, and form a series of beds several hundred feet thick. Of the same character of rock are the beds that form smaller inliers in the valley of the Vedganga, eight miles north-west of Mángaon. These lie in the centre of the valley between Yengol and Shengaon and are four in number, the southmost, close to the village of Yengol, forming a small outstanding hill 200 to 300 feet high. Here all the beds dip north-west 5° to 10°. The other inliers are simply exposures on the flanks of the great ridges.

Passing to the south-west limit of the quartzite series, at Kákti, about five miles north of Belgaum, the rock forms a scarp whose base is hidden by a thick talus, or slope of fragments, abutting on a broad alluvial flat, which has gathered in the valley of the Márkándeya above the gorge by which that river flows through the cougeries of hills and small quartzite plateaus that lie between Kákti and the Ankalgi valley. This scarp is merely the north-west continuation of the scarp that forms the boundary of the quartzite plateau to the north of the Belgaum valley, and along the entire base of which the underlying metamorphic rocks are to be seen. From the relative position of the trap flows that form the base of the great flat-topped One Tree Hill to the north-east of Belgaum, it is clear that the Kákti scarp was formed before the outpouring of those particular trap flows, and not improbably before the very earliest trap flows. It is not unlikely that this scarp extends far to the north-west under the overlying trap. The form of the ground at Rájgoli on the Támraparni, and at Yengol in the valley of the Vedganga, suggests the idea that the scarps there seen are really the great boundary scarp of the westward extension of the Kaládgi basin, although the base of the scarp is not sufficiently uncovered to show the underlying metamorphics.

Chapter I.
Description.
Geology.
Lower Kaládgi Quartzites.

Both above Kákti and along the south scarp above Kankumbi a succession of conglomerate and grit beds, with some compact quartzites intercalated between them, are seen to dip north or north-east at low angles. Farther north other gritty and pebbly beds are met overlying the beds which form the scarp. These scarp beds pass across the slightly inclined plateau to the gorge of the Márkándeya near Nandi, north of which come other quartzites which stretch to the valley of the Ghatprabha near Sutgatti and Vantmuri about half-way between Daddi and Páchápur. The very gritty and conglomerate character of the beds in the Kákti plateau changes gradually eastward, so that near Hoskatti and Hanbarkatti quartzite beds predominate. How very greatly this part of the Kaládgi basin was worn before the trap was poured out is shown by the quartzite beds that cap the Budnur hill, a gneissic inlier among the trap. A fine section of the quartzites, which there form the basement of the Kaládgi Series, occurs in the valley north of Siddápur, where the Budnur stream enters the Kaládgi basin by a picturesque gorge. The beds dip 12° north-east. At the next gorge eastward from Siddápur the edge of the basin is more than usually uptilted and the quartzite beds have a dip of 30° to 35° north-east.

At Murgod, in the west of Parasgad, a set of quartzite beds forms the actual base of the series, and is overlaid by a set of conglomerates with sandstone forming the surface of great part of the plateau east of the village. The surface of this plateau has been greatly broken by weathering, but has reformed into a breccia pavement made of an iron cement apparently of sub-aërial origin. The pebbles included in the conglomerates are mostly of an older quartzite, probably of gneissic age. The beds which form the plateau east of the village rise eastward to the apex of the flat dome of Kathárigad. The arch of the dome is seamed by deep fissures, which, cutting through the mass of quartzites, show the underlying granite gneiss. East of Kathárigad the quartzites sink rapidly into the valley of the Benákatti, a tributary of the Malprabha. To the south of Kathárigad, the rocks at the Sogal waterfalls are hard quartzite conglomerate, pale, reddish-brown, or purplish, and numerous bright red jasper pebbles form the hæmatitic beds of the Malprabha valley. The southern boundary of the Kathárigad erosion valley is formed by a considerable fault which runs west 29° north, and has caused an upthrow of the beds on its southern side. The fault stretches along the south of the ravine north-west of Karlhatti.

The rocks that form the beautiful gorge of the Peacock's Pool, or Navil Tirth, nine miles east-south-east of Sogal, are hard quartzites extremely polished within water reach. The polished surface is in most places covered with a thin film of dark grayish-black, a striking contrast to the delicate pale-red and pink of the other quartzite rocks. In the gorge, bed after bed may be traced upward or downward without a sign of doubling. The dip varies from 10° to 15° and averages about 12°. The leading colours are pale light red and pink and drab, with a few beds of light bluish-gray. Near the base some of the quartzite beds are of bright red salmon colour, or even of a pale peach blossom. Many minor beds among the quartzites are very pebbly,

Chapter I.

Description.

Geology.

Lower Kaládgi Quartzites.

in fact are perfect conglomerates. Among the included pebbles and fragments are many of red and gray jasper from the hæmatite beds in the gneiss. Pebbles of quartz and other quartzites, also of hornblendic schist and of pistacite, are common among the inclusions. The quartzite beds often contain isolated pebbles, which, especially when of red jasper, contrast strongly with the generally uniform texture of the matrix. Taking the length of the section at one and a quarter miles directly across the ridge the total thickness of quartzite and conglomerates cannot be estimated at less than 1200 to 1300 feet, the average dip of 12° being perfectly steady throughout the greatest part of the section. Most of the faces of the cliffs exposed in the Peacock's Gorge correspond with some of the principal lines of jointing by which the whole quartzite series is permeated.

To the north the quartzites dip under a thick series of clay schists which stretch across the flat immediately north of the gorge to a low quartzite ridge, formed by a reappearance of the upper basement series in a sharply flexed anticlinal which abuts on the left bank of the river close to Manoli. Beyond Manoli the quartzite again disappears under schists. To the west this anticlinal sinks very low, and then rises and joins the south-east extension of the Kathárigad plateau south of Madlur. The large village of Manoli stands on the clay schists and is chiefly built of a flaggy variety exposed during the dry season in the bed of the Malprabha immediately opposite the village east of the Peacock's Pool. The Kaládgi basin is bounded by a line of bluff quartzite hills, showing here and there precipitous scarps, whose bases are everywhere hidden by fragments of rock. The underlying gneiss is seldom seen. The chief outlier of the quartzite beds to the south is the Parasgad hill, about eight miles south of Manoli. The quartzites of this hill along their northern boundary are faulted against the gneiss and form a great inclined plain with an average dip of 7° north. In many parts the surface shows vast sheets of bare rock. In a cave about 200 feet below the edge of the scarp is a very interesting spring, whose water must drain through joints in the rock from the brow of the hill.

Lower Kaládgi Limestone.

The clay schists that overlie the basement quartzites at Manoli stretch from some distance north-west of Yargatti, south-east to the Malprabha at Manoli, and across the Malprabha into the spurs of the hills that run north-east parallel with the river, and pass into quartzite or sandstones among the hills south-west of Rámdurg. To the north of the clay schists comes in sometimes a 'dirty' hornstone breccia, sometimes a set of highly silicious (cherty) limestones, whose extension is in great measure masked by the great accumulations of cherty debris derived from the weathering of the cherty beds, together with great spreads of cotton soil and also of sand formed by the decay of the silicious beds on the higher grounds. These silicious limestones appear to be distinct from the great limestone formation that occupies the Ghatprabha valley near Kaládgi. They stretch from Ujenkop south-east to Jakkabal on the Malprabha north-east of Manoli, and are connected with a patch of similar character that occurs at Goraganur further down the river. To the west of Yargatti, on the Belgaum-Kaládgi road about

Chapter I.
Description.
Geology.
Lower Kaládgi Limestone.

ten miles north of Manoli, the limestone beds roll in low reefs forming a rocky wilderness six to eight miles square. Over this area to the west of Yargatti the 'dirty' breccia is not seen. To the north-east of Yargatti are some beds of pink and pinkish gray limestone of less silicious character. In the hilly ground to the south-west and north of Torgal a thick series of sandstones with a few conglomerate and quartzite beds overlies the silicious limestones and dirty breccia, and forms a low rolling plateau very stony and barren. To the north, between Torgal and Karikol, the land is mostly a rocky wilderness of sandy soil, deep cut by streams and covered with scrubby brushwood. Further north the sandstones are represented by the drab shaley series and the overlying quartzites. The only remaining section of the quartzite basement series is a narrow strip to the north of the long spur of Deccan trap that forms the watershed between the Malprabha and the Ghatprabha. The most westerly part of this strip forms a high rocky ridge culminating in the Manikeri hill about twenty miles east of Gokák. Its red and drab quartzite beds have a north-east dip of 30° to 40°. At Hulkund the ridge is crossed by a stream, but rises again to the east and forms two conspicuous rocky hills, the southmost of which dies down in an anticlinal ellipse. To the west the anticlinal character of the ridge is obscured by the trap which surrounds the hill to a great height. Rather more than half a mile east of the elliptical end of the anticlinal other sandstone and quartzite beds are exposed. These probably belong to a rather higher horizon in the series.

The lower Kaládgi limestones and associated shales are found chiefly on the north-east part of the Kaládgi basin. A considerable extent of them occurs between Lokápur north-west to the Ghatprabha. These rocks lie partly within Belgaum limits to the east south and west of Yádvád, and partly in the Mudhol and Jamkhandi villages in the east of Belgaum. These limestones occupy a basin within the Kaládgi basin, and with boundaries in many parts fairly parallel to those of the great basin. The western boundary is formed almost entirely of the overlying traps, and there are a small number of limestone inliers beyond the north-west corner of the limestone basin. The limestone basin includes within its area a number of minor basins and outliers of rocks, quartzites, limestones, and shales that lie conformably on it and form the upper division of the Kaládgi series. From their low position, and from the great amount of contortion to which they have been subjected, it is difficult to fix the precise relations of this section of the Kaládgi Series.

At and round Yádvád is one of the largest shows of limestone in the whole region. The prevalent beds, mostly seen in the bed and banks of the Yádvád stream, are gray in various shades, but other colours as white-banded gray and white, greenish gray with pink, and white bands and grayish green are also found. The great plain south of Yádvád is covered by an almost unbroken sheet of typical cotton soil or regur through which rocks show only in a few widely scattered places. A little to the north-east of Monami banded green and white limestone, with some white and pink bands, occurs in

Chapter I. Description. Geology. *Lower Kaládgi Limestone.*

small sections. The broken outliers from them in a limestone basin west of Yádvád stretch about twelve miles north-west to Beshati near the Ghatprabha. Large shows occur between Hal Yergudri and Uradi, six to eight miles north-west of Yádvád; between Bisankot and Beshati from ten to twelve miles north-west; at Kulgur about ten miles west; and between Has Yergudri and Temápur, between four and six miles west. In the long valley that stretches south from Temápur the limestones are red, pink, and banded with gray, green, and brown. The beds are mostly much crumpled and the true dip is often doubtful. At Alimati, about eight miles north-west of Yádvád, are handsome brecciated beds of drab limestone cemented by a purple matrix. At Manápur, about one and a half miles south of Alimati, beds of dull red earthy limestones are associated with red chert, lumps of which are scattered on the surface.

The limestone on the two outliers south of the limestone basin near Sidanhal, eight miles north-west of Torgal, shows flaggy purple beds, sometimes rather earthy. They roll a good deal at low angles, and to the south are underlaid by beds of cream-coloured and whitish limestone which occur in the Tolagati stream a little to the south of Sidanhal. Returning to the main limestone basin by the Belgaum-Kaládgi road, gray and whitish limestones, some of them very cherty, are crossed on the north-east of the Panchgaon travellers' bungalow about eight miles north-east of Sidanhal. To the north-west of these is a large show of earthy sub-crystalline beds of red and pink which dip under the Lokápur synclinal. Further east, at Varatsgal in Mudhol, about two miles south of Lokápur, are numerous beds of gray limestone. To the east and west of Lokápur gray and bluish-banded limestones are largely exposed, and make the largest show in the whole limestone basin. The Belgaum limestones are almost entirely free from quartz reefs and veins. A few veins are found to the south-east and north-west of Hoskati, about a mile to the west of Lokápur.

Upper Kaládgi Series.

Rocks of the Upper Kaládgi Series, quartzites below and limestones and shales above, are found in bands resting conformably on the lower series, and occupying a number of small basins which form elliptical synclinal valleys. They lie on the whole east and west. The series nowhere passes beyond the limestone basin, and the area it occupies is extremely small. The chief are to the west of Lokápur, to the north-east of Yádvád, and some smaller outcrops on the Deccan trap area, near Alimati, about eight miles to the north-west of Yádvád. The quartzites of this upper series are very uniform, pale, and frequently conglomeratic, with local patches of brecciation. It is worthy of note that all the ridges of this series are cut by streams on their way to the Ghatprabha through weak spots caused by excessive jointing. A section in the gorge through which the Lokápur stream enters the basin from the south shows in descending order

3. Breccia of Quartzite.
2. Calcareous Shales with Limestones.
1. Quartzites with Pebbly Beds.

Fragments hiding Calcareous Shales.

The calcareous series that rests on the upper quartzites consists

Chapter I.
Description.
Geology.
Upper Kaládgi Series.

almost entirely of calcareous shales purplish or gray and overlaid by purple and gray argillaceous shales; limestones show only occasionally and generally in thin bands. In some parts the purple shales are highly ferruginous, being richly charged with earthy red hæmatite. As a rule the surface of this series is thick covered by cotton soil or by thick, red, ferruginous, gravelly soil formed by the decay of the hæmatitic shales. Limestones of this series occur at Murgar in Mudhol about four miles east of Yádvád, at Jembigi about four miles further east, at Yenkatpur a little to the north of Lokápur and at Varatsgal about two miles to the south of Lokápur.

Intrusive Rocks.

The only Intrusive Rocks in the Kaládgi basin are trap dykes, which are sparingly distributed and occur only in the upper part of the series. There are three trap dykes near Lokápur, all of compact green diorite weathering in concentric ellipsoidal masses unlike any of the older diorites seen in the gneissic area. Their course is north-west by west to south-east by east, and they show only in the centre of the valleys among the shales. In the absence of organic remains and from its isolated position it is impossible to correlate the Kaládgi series closely with other series rich in quartzites. Still, the character of its rocks is much like the character of the rocks of the Kadapa Series and of the Gwalior or Bijávar Series of Central India.

Infra-Trappean Rocks.

Underlying the great Deccan trap, and resting sometimes on the gneissic and sometimes on the Kaládgi series, are certain deposits of sedimentary origin of small thickness and extent. They are interesting, as some of them may represent the pre-trappean deposits of Central India which are known as Lameta beds from the Lameta pass near Jabalpur. Unlike the hard rocks of the Kaládgi Series these deposits are in a soft unconsolidated or half-consolidated state. They are formed of the ruins of various older rocks with a considerable mixture of the red earthy clay called bole in isolated lumps, or in strings, or generally spread through the mass. The most common form of these deposits is gritty marly clay or clayey grit, as at Malanhatti three miles north-east of Gokák, and at Kulgur twelve miles north-east of Malanhatti. Coarse shingle, mainly gneiss and quartz pebbles, seen largely at Nágarhál east of Yellurgad near Belgaum, is the remains of former pre-trappean deposits. The most extensive exposure of these infra-trappean beds is near Sigihalli, about ten miles south-east of Belgaum. The sandstones here are seen in very thin courses in soft sandy marl resting on hornblendic schistose gneiss. These infra-trappean beds are eight to ten feet thick. As far as is known they contain no fossils. The presence of bole in so many of the pre-trappean deposits appears to be due to the heating action of the trap flows poured on to beds of fine clay. The quantity of the bole is always largest close to the trap, where it occasionally occurs pure and much broken by minute cracks. The pure bole is rarely many inches thick. In some cases it is very markedly affected by a system of prismatic jointing on a small scale; but the mass is so friable that it is impossible to collect any of the very pretty little prisms; they crumble even with the most delicate handling. From the circumstances under which they occur, from

Chapter I. Description. Geology. *Deccan Trap.*

their limited extent, and from their strong resemblance to the fresh water deposits among the lower trap flows the infra-trappean beds may be set down as of limestone origin.

The north half of the district and two great spurs, one that runs from near Gokák south-east to near Rámdurg and the other that runs from Belgaum about twenty-five miles north-east, that is about three-fourths of the district, are trap. The depth of trap grows gradually greater from the east to the west. In the east where only a few flows have spread are low rolling downs with shallow valleys between; further west later flows rise in flat-topped ridges between the water-sheds of the larger rivers; and still further west the latest flows are piled into high and massive hills.

The chief varieties of trap are basalt, amygdaloid trap, vesicular trap, and clayey trap. These, with some few intertrappean sedimentary beds and numerous highly iron-charged clayey beds make up the mass of the trap flows. By far the commonest rock is basalt. This includes, besides compact and vesicular basalt, the highly weathered earthy trap so common throughout the Deccan. In form basalt is either massively shapeless, rudely tabular, or rudely columnar, the two last forms being the most common. The lower flows are mostly basaltic, the middle flows alternately basaltic and amygdaloid, and the upper chiefly basaltic, capped by beds of laterite and clay. The lower trap flows were poured over an exceedingly rough surface. The upper flows often overlap the lower and rest on the higher parts of the older rocks. In the west, when studied from some commanding point, the flows are seen to dip at a low angle to the north-east. About twenty-five or thirty miles from the Sahyádris the dip becomes more easterly, and so gradual as to be hardly perceptible. The absence of centres of eruption and the rarity of beds of volcanic ash seem to show that the volcanic centres through which the trap was poured were north of the Belgaum district. That the trap flows were poured out in the air and not under water is now generally accepted as proved. Of the age of the trap nothing has yet been determined. The intertrappean beds occur near the local base of the traps. These beds are of small extent, and are found only along or near to the south-east edge of the trap area.

The grandest sections of trap are to be seen in the great western scarp of the Sahyádri hills. Their great thickness, some of them forming cliffs several hundred feet high, makes the flows very difficult to study. But they can be well examined in the cuttings on the roads over the Phonda and Ámboli passes. To the east the best sections are the bare hills round Chikodi, Bágedgudd north of Gokák, and Yellurgad south of Belgaum.

The series of trap flows seen in the bare hills round Chikodi consists of six basaltic flows. The three lowest are separated from each other by thin beds of amygdaloid trap and red bole. The highest flow is separated from the rest by thin boliferous beds, part of which may be volcanic ashes. The two middle flows, though distinct, show no intercalated matter. The whole makes up a thickness of 600 to 700 feet, of which the three lower basaltic flows occupy fully two-thirds.

Chapter I.
Description.
Geology.
Deccan Trap.

The bare slopes of Bágedgudd, about two miles north of Gokák, give a very good section. This is the most easterly point at which the uppermost trap flows occur. From the south eight chief flows may be seen over the water-shed ridge that divides the valleys of the Ghatprabha and the Krishna. They are best seen from a distance, as close at hand the ruggedness of the slopes masks the terrace structure. Beginning from the highest the succession is (1) iron clay (laterite); (2) amygdaloid; (3) basalt; (4) basalt; (5) amygdaloid, red and brown; (6) basalt; (7) amygdaloid, purplish and soft; and (8) basalt. The lower beds stretch far on all sides, and may be traced for many miles in the spurs that branch from the great central mass. Its lower flows connect Bágedgudd with the Chikodi hills about twenty-five miles to the north-west, with the Manoli hills about the same distance to the south-east, and with the lower basaltic plateau that stretches along the north frontier of Mudhol about the same distance to the north-east. To the north of Gokák the lower Bágedgudd flows form several rocky ridges which stretch into the Krishna valley. The hills near Athni and Gateh may be said to be extensions of the Bágedgudd series. The dolerite and basalt flows that form the group of hills at Gosbal and Kauljalgi about fifteen miles east of Gokák represent the three lower members of the Bágedgudd sections.

The iron-clay bed which caps Bágedgudd is the youngest known, the most constant, and the most safely determinable member of the local Deccan trap series. As it caps all the highest ridges and peaks in Kolhápur and Belgaum it may be called the summit bed. Of all the mountains those which it caps are the most perfectly table-topped, and in most cases the capping is sharply scarped all round the edge. As these scarped plateaus crown all the highest hills and were easily made very strong, many of them were chosen by native chiefs as sites for their strongholds. Such are Gandharvgad about twenty and Mahipálgad about twelve miles north-west of Belgaum, Kálánandigad about sixteen miles west of Belgaum, and Yellurgad about eight miles south of Belgaum. Further north the same rock forms the hill-forts of Samángad and Bhudargad, about twenty-five and forty miles north of Belgaum in South Kolhápur, and of Vallabhgad and Páijargudd in Chikodi. Underlying the great iron-clay bed is a bed of clayey trap often purple and much softer than the overlying bed. The more rapid weathering of this clayey trap bed is the reason why the scarp so constantly and sharply defines the iron-clay summit bed. This clayey trap generally passes into ordinary purple or reddish brown amygdaloid, below which are basaltic and other amygdaloid flows. The clayey trap is largely developed on Kálánandigad about sixteen miles west of Belgaum, and on Bailur fourteen miles south-west of Belgaum, the highest hill in the district 3491 feet above the sea. Further north the clayey trap is well seen on Vallabhgad and Páijargudd in Chikodi.

A somewhat striking feature of one of the basaltic flows, which, at many parts of the southern boundary, forms the basement bed is the weathering into great rude blocks, some of which might almost be reckoned small tors. These blocks frequently rest directly on the underlying gneiss. At Bastvád about eight miles south-west of

Belgaum, at Nágarhál about two miles east of Yellurgad, and to the north-west of Murgod in Parasgad, a few big blocks remain isolated on the gneiss at small distances from the boundary of the basalt flow. At Bavihal two miles north of Sampgaon, an unusual variety of trap occurs below the blocky basalt flow which generally forms the base in that quarter. This exceptional variety differs from any other Deccan trap in being much more crystalline in texture and resembling far more a highly hornblendic diorite of gneissic age. The upper part of the intermediate bed consists of pure bright-red bole, two to three inches thick, which shows very distinct prismatic columnar cleavage.

Typical basalt which occurs in innumerable places, is largely quarried on the slopes of One Tree Hill north of Belgaum. It is a fine close-grained brownish black stone with a few small vesicular cavities. A variety which is porphyritic from enclosing rather large crystals of green glassy-looking olivine, was observed on the high hill which forms the north-eastern extremity of the Yellurgad ridge.

Volcanic ash-beds are not numerous. They are found in the flanks of Vallabhgad about fourteen miles south-west of Chikodi, and in the north Ghatprabha range between Chikodi and Valur in south Kolhápur. The beds may at first sight be easily taken to be amygdaloid flows, but examination shows that they are chiefly of fragments, lapilli, or volcanic ashes and dusty particles of vesicular trap cemented by the deposition of calcite and zeolitic matter in strings and films between the fragments as well as in the vesicular cavities. The lapilli are mostly reddish or purplish, and much red bole is spread through the mass, which, by contrast with the whitish calcite and zeolite, makes the whole reddish or pinkish gray.

Columnar cleavage of basalt is occasionally seen in the west, but is generally rude and unworthy of note. The best case is probably the cutting at the top of the Phonda pass. In the Konkan, west of the Rám pass, Mr. Wilkinson noted fallen masses of perfectly columnar trap.

The mineral substances enclosed in the trap flows are not very numerous. Zeolites, chiefly scolecite and stilbite are very abundant in small or large vesicular cavities in many trap flows. An uncommon crystalline form of heulantide was found in a purple amygdaloid at Dandápur, nine and a half miles north of Gokák. The crystals occurred lining irregular clefts in the rocks.

Small agates are found in large numbers on the weathered surfaces on the ridge north of Chinchni three miles west of Chikodi, at Kurgaon eight miles south east of Chikodi, and near Hamámságar twenty-miles south-east of Gokák.

Some curious fungoid concretions of chalcedony and rock crystal are found in a soft clayey amygdaloid flow south-east of Dehmangi, about four miles south-east of the Belgaum fort. Similar concretions also occur on Kálánandigad sixteen miles west of Belgaum. Calcspar occurs frequently both in basaltic and in amygdaloid traps. Magnetic iron is spread in considerable quantities through the mass of the basaltic and doleritic trap. Arragonite occasionally occurs in doleritic

Chapter I. Description. Geology. *Deccan Trap.*

trap flows. Red bole frequently occurs in amygdaloid beds and in some volcanic ash-beds as in the slopes of Vallabhgad in Chikodi. Olivine is not very often seen. The best specimens occur in the first high basaltic hill south-west of Nesargi on the Belgaum-Kaládgi road.

Inter-trappean Beds.

Between the flows of lava that make up the Deccan trap, sedimentary rocks, chiefly sandy deposits, conglomerates, grits, and clay beds sometimes occur. In a few of these fossils have been found, whose organic contents show them to be of fresh water origin. The similarity of their mineral character leaves little doubt that all these rocks were formed in fresh water lakes. Though their mineral character differs, the fossils, Physa prinsepii, Lymnea, and Unio deccanensis, prove that the traps of the Southern Marátha Country and of Central India belong to the same period.

The Southern Marátha intertrappean beds lie near the base of the trap series. In one important case a fresh water marl was found resting on the gneiss rocks, and thus underlying what locally appears to be the lowest trap-flow. This may have been caused either by the flow overlapping some older flow or by its representing the deposits in a fresh water lake older than the first outpouring of the Deccan traps. In two intertrappean beds within Belgaum limits, at Mamdápur, six and a half miles north-east of Gokák, and at Uparhati, a mile north of Mamdápur, organic remains have been found.

The intertrappean beds near Mamdápur in Gokák seem to have been formed on the shore of a lake. They have a considerable show of bright red sandy marl, the red being due to the somewhat abundant presence of bole. Under the red sandy marl with lime nodules and many gneiss and quartzite pebbles is a bed of pale-drab sandstone with lumps of quartzite and Unio shells. This sandstone rests on red marl, and the red marl on a greenish-yellow marly-looking bed of decomposed vesicular trap that passes into dark greenish-black vesicular trap, with many small and a few large agate amygdaloids. The whole thickness of marls and sandstones ranges from fifteen to twenty feet.

A little more than a mile from the Mamdápur section, separated from it by an exposure of gneissic rock, rises a low flat-topped ridge, on the west side of which, close to the village of Uparhatti, the intertrappean rocks again show. The exposed beds are quartzite and gneiss shingle of uncertain age; weathered basaltic trap; red sandy marl with three or four sandstone partings containing *Unio*[1] shells and decomposing whitish amygdaloid trap.[2]

Patches of shingle, chiefly of quartzite, appear from their position to be the relics of some intertrappean formation that has been worn

[1] The *Unio* beds are about twenty feet thick, and were formerly continuous with those of Mamdápur. The fossil *Unios* in both sections are well preserved, even the beautiful lining or nacre being kept in some instances.

[2] This section represents the beds north of the village in order to introduce the quartzite and gneiss shingle. The *Unios* were found a few dozen yards south of the village.

Chapter I. Description. Geology. *Deccan Trap.*

away or masked by surface fragments. Of the latter class are the patches of quartzite gravel at Kolik and Chiguli, on the south side of the Tilári ravine, eighteen miles south-west of Belgaum. A similar gravel patch occurs at Volmani, a mile east of Jámboti, about fifteen miles south-west of Belgaum, and at much the same level relative to the trap-flows. Near the western end of the great trap spur north-west of Párgad, about four miles west of the Rám pass, there is another gravel patch in which quartz pebbles predominate. To the class of gravels that represent worn intertrappean beds most likely belongs a large spread of quartzite shingle that lies on the surface of the trap on rather high ground three or four miles north of Yádvád. The curious bed of quartzite shingle that caps the Uparhati hill near Mamdápur may also belong to this class of relics.

The position of some of the lateritoid or iron-clay rocks intercalated between trap-flows in the high western ridges suggests that they may be of intertrappean sedimentary origin. This is the case with some iron-clay beds on the south side of the Jámboti ridge seen on the path leading from Chikhli to Ámti. Other iron-clay deposits occur here and there over the trap area, which, though very likely the results of sub-aërial atmospheric action might, from their position, be regarded as intertrappean relics similar to the quartzite gravels.

The only instances of intertrappean limestone are two small exposures of flaggy light-brown oolitic limestones that occupy depressions in the surface of the trap and are obscured by the surrounding cotton soil. One of these is in the hollow at the foot of a hill south-west of Nesargi on the Belgaum-Kaládgi high road. The other is at Ghone, a village six miles east of Nesargi. Neither bed seems to have any signs of organic remains.

Iron-Clay.

The traps in many parts of the district are overlaid by an iron-clay rock. This rock is of two kinds somewhat hard to distinguish, and both of them formed of decomposed trap. The first are much changed from their original state by weathering; the second are collections of ruins of rocks of the first class. The rocks of this second class are probably partly made of altered sedimentary rocks, but they are chiefly altered lava flows. It is convenient to call the altered lava flows iron-clay rocks, and the altered sedimentary rocks laterite, the name originally given to the fringe of ferruginous deposits that surrounds the southern part of the Indian peninsula, and almost certainly appears in the South Konkan or Ratnágiri laterite. When the Southern Marátha iron-clay was formed the country had probably acquired nearly its present features. The weathering of trappean rocks into iron-clay rocks is well seen in the cutting on the Phonda and Ámboli pass roads. The basaltic rocks graduate into a moderately hard brown earthy mass, which encloses many nuclei of the original rock. The infiltration of surface water charged with iron has solidified the decomposed mass. The summit bed, which has already been noticed as capping many of the highest hills, seems to have been formed of a trap rock entirely without silicious segregations.

The underlying trap into which the summit bed is seen to graduate at the principal sections, as Vallabhgad and others, is a very clay-like rock without any enclosed minerals. In colour and fineness of

Chapter I. Description. Geology. *Iron-Clay.*

texture it resembles many of the purple, brown, reddish amygdaloid beds that occur so largely elsewhere, but differ in the total absence of vesicular cavities whether empty or full. Besides the highest ridges and peaks in the Belgaum section of the Sahyádris, which have their summits capped with iron-clay, there are many others on which an iron-clay capping forms a very marked feature. Some of the most important of these cappings form outliers[1] on the older rocks where the latter are of great elevation and stand above the general mass of the trap flows, but are overlapped by the ferruginous beds. Owing to the superior hardness of the highly ferruginous summit bed, and the more rapid weathering of the underlying beds, the surface of the underlying beds is generally covered by ruins or by great fallen masses of the upper beds. In other sections a quasi-stalactitic ferruginous rain-wash often affects the appearance of the surface of inaccessible cliffs. And the presence of numerous delicate gray, orange, pale-pink, and flesh-coloured lichens in many cases so greatly changes the colour of the scarp faces that they can be made out only on close inspection.

Within Belgaum limits the three best sections of the Deccan trap iron-clay are at Kálánandigad sixteen miles west of Belgaum, and at Vallabhgad and Páijargudd in Chikodi. The iron-clay rocks of Kálánandigad are best seen on the path up to the north gate of the fort. The hundred feet at the top of the hill consist of mottled purplish and white or purplish clayey rock, which, without any sudden change, passes into a compact lateritoid mass.[2] The hill-sides become scarped as soon as the level of the summit bed is reached.

At Vallabhgad the clayey under-rock shows a good deal of quasi-vesicular structure in the arrangement of colours. Numerous thin films of white are seen like other vesicles enclosing darker portions of the general mass. The ruling colours are purple and reddish-brown, much flecked with white vesicle sections. The iron-clay summit bed, instead of showing horizontal or approximately horizontal vesicular cavities in the mass, is permeated by vertical tubuli running nearly through it. The upper beds of these tubuli, which vary in

---

[1] The chief outliers of the summit bed, counting from the southern extremity of the trap area northward, are : (1) The Jámboti ridge ; (2) Bailur with a peak 3491 feet high ; (3) the Kárle and Báknur hills south-west of Belgaum ; (4) Kálánandigad and Mátungi and the high spur connecting them with (5) the Mahipálgad ridge ; (6) the Gandharvgad ridge ; (7) the Vágbud and Kásarsudda plateau west and south-west of Chándgad ; (8) the high ridge between the Ghatprabha and Harankáshi south of Ámboli, and also from a little north of the Belgaum and Vengurla road north-east to the Khánápur Trigonometrical Station hill near Ajra ; (9) the high ridge dividing the valleys of the Ved and Dudhganga rivers, including the well marked plateau north of Pyáh ; (10) the Vallabhgad outlier ; (11) the two Bágedgudd outliers, on the eastern of which is a Trigonometrical Station ; (12) the group of outliers west and south-west of Gokák, two of which overlap the Kaládgi quartzites ; (13) the Páijargudd group of four small outliers, with a fifth forming the summit of Huligarkit hill three miles to the east ; (14) the Arlehatti outlier four miles west of Páchápur resting directly on the quartzites ; and (15) the Yellurgad outlier eight miles south of Belgaum, the last of the summit bed outliers. Several other outlying patches of similar iron-charged clayey rocks occur in the more eastern parts of the trap area, but they are too distant to be safely correlated with the summit bed.

[2] Captain Newbold supposed that the beautiful lilac colour of the lithomargic earth underlying the iron-clay of the Bidar plateaus was due to the presence of manganese. This supposition is probably correct. Memoir Geological Survey of India, XII. 206.

Chapter I.
Description.
Geology.
Iron-Clay.

diameter from a quarter to three-quarters of an inch, but which are generally less than half an inch across, are empty for a little distance, giving the surface a pitted appearance. But the tubes are generally filled with lithomargic clay and have their walls lined with a glaze very like the glaze which occurs in the vermicular cavities of ordinary laterites. The height of the tubuli which are less distinct in the lower parts of the bed, and whose formation is due to the action of percolating water depends upon the thickness of the bed, and the glazed sides show much stalactitoid waviness of surface.

The section seen in Páijargudd hill shows a thick-bedded mass of iron-clay with little or no tubulation, resting on a clayey trap of generally gray or purplish colour, finely streaked and mottled with reddish-brown, orange, or dull yellow. The vesicular markings noticed at Vallabhgad are also seen here, but are less common.

Pisolotic Iron-Clay.

A very peculiar pisolitic form of the iron-clay, varying in colour from pale brownish pink to bright or deep red or purple, is observed in several places, chiefly on Yellurgad, on Bailur, and on the Kásarsudda ridge south-west of Chándgad. Where this pisolitic iron-clay occurs the rock has a decidedly jaspideous texture and look, its colour varying from pale brownish pink to bright or deep red or purple according to the percentage of peroxide of iron.

A very extensive show of lateritoid iron-clays occurs at and to the east and west of the Rám pass. The rock there forms a nearly level ridge with a ragged scarped edge and a slope of great fallen masses. This ridge stretches north-east into the higher spur west of Hire, while, to the west, it joins the Isápur plateau north of Párgad, along the north side of which it forms a very distinct and generally vertical scarp thirty to sixty feet high. The Rám pass bed rests in some places direct on a basaltic flow without the intervention of the thick clayey trap. It is probably distinct from the summit bed, as it is considerably lower and does not lie in a level plane.

At apparently the same level are several ragged-edged plateaus south and west of the high Kásarsudda ridge about the head waters of the Ghatprabha. To the same set belong the beds on the high ground south-west of Patna and at Kodali on the north side of the Tilári ravine.

Sedimentary Iron-Clay.

South of the Tilári ravine at Kolik, Chigoli, Kankumbi, Huland, and stretching west towards Chorle and to the extreme western points of the Sudda fort spur, overlooking Goa, are continuous sheets of the iron-clay belonging to a bed or beds occurring very much at the same level. Southward, past the top of the Párvár pass, these sheets join those at the foot of the Jámboti ridge and pass south-east, forming, near Ambgaon and Chapoli, a well-defined plateau which caps the extreme southern promontory of the great Deccan trap area overlooking the Mahádáyi ravine. From the edge of this ravine the iron-clay beds seem to be represented on its southern side by a similar set which form a plateau round Gausi. To the north of the Rám pass, this set, which for convenience may be called the water-shed series, is represented in the plateau near the source of the Ghatprabha and in the valley of the Harankáshi.

The bed of iron-clay which forms a well defined plateau on the

Chapter I.
Description.
Geology.
Sedimentary. Iron-Clay.

high spur south of Chapoli is of sedimentary origin. The sides which are well scarped show a vertical thickness of fifteen to twenty feet of the tubulated variety of iron-clay, the tubulation being very strongly and clearly developed.

From the number of quartz pebbles imbedded in the clayey mass it may be inferred that this iron-clay represents wholly or in part an altered intertrappean pebbly clay of the kind found in various typical intertrappean beds.

Along the south side of the Jámboti ridge, on the path leading from Chikhli to Ámti, are several alternations of iron-clay and basalt at different levels, the iron-clay apparently forming distinct terraces corresponding to altered trap-flows or intertrappean beds.

Three sets of small iron-clay plateaus, occupying rather lower levels than those of the water-shed series, occur in the valleys of the Márkándeya, Támraparni, and Ghatprabha. Those of the first and last sets form small groups of barren flat-topped hills, those on the Márkándeya near Unchgaon on the Belgaum-Vengurla road, and those on the Támraparni to the south of Arkur. Besides these there are similar minor and less marked plateaus in the upper parts of the valleys of these rivers.

The iron-clay at Belgaum occupies a deep bay or hollow on the east side of the basaltic rise on which the new European barracks have been built. The basaltic high ground here forms an angle, the apex of which lies north-west of the town, and, in that angle, the iron-clay is most largely exposed in two sections, one in the well in the soldiers' garden, the other in a deep well-like pit. In the soldiers' well the iron-clay had not been pierced at a depth of thirty-five to forty feet, and in the pit the thickness exposed exceeded (in 1872) a depth of fifty feet vertical and yet the underlying trap rock was not reached. In the well section the rock is not so clearly shown from the smaller size of the opening, but in the quarry the unweathered surface of the walls shows the rock to great advantage. The rock is very different in character from the summit bed or water-shed series. Instead of being vertically tubulated or nearly horizontally disposed, this iron-clay consists of an aggregate of nodular fragments in a quasi-conglomeratic mass, the quasi-pebbles being arranged in rudely horizontal lines. Beyond these lines there are no traces of bedding, but the downward decrease of the percentage of iron in the rock is very clearly shown. No traces of any enclosed mineral of pre-trappean origin are to be found. The whole formation appears to be a sub-aërial accumulation of pluvial detritus of older iron-clay beds. The iron-clay exposed in ballast pits close to the reservoir north of the pit and close to the post office and *Idgáh* is truly vesicular and far more ferruginous. No sections showing the relations between the vesicular iron-clay of the pit and the nodular rock are exposed in the hollow east of the cantonment or in the church hill. Both varieties are much covered by thick red sandy soil which is so largely developed over both iron-clay and trap and gneiss, and in places is so much charged with nodular pieces of iron-clay that it is often impossible to draw any line showing the true boundary of the trap and the older iron-clay and gneiss.

Sedimentary. Iron-Clay.

Beds of iron-clay strongly resembling the typical iron-clay beds are found as outliers of the trap area. In most cases they were probably once continuous with iron-clay beds belonging to the Deccan trap series.

The iron-clay plateau, the boundary between the Belgaum and Kánara districts, extends from Gausi southward up the slope of the eastern spur of the Darshnidongar in North Kánara. The iron-clay[1] resting upon and passing down into the weathered surface of the underlying gneiss is continued along the ridge to the very summit of the mountain where it is cut short by a sudden scarp. This scarp trends from the summit to the east on both sides of the ridge, the northern scarp joining the west scarp of the main mass of the Gausi plateau, and the southern scarp running east by south of Mendil and ending in a bluff to the east of Degaon. The passage of the base of the iron-clay into the lower gneiss is clearly seen in various sections in the scarped edges of the iron-clay plateau, in the beds of the streamlet near Gausi, and in the stream that flows west from Talevádi. In these beds the descent from the pure iron-clay into decomposing gneiss is clear, the quartzose laminæ remaining after the softer parts have been replaced by the clayey mass. In the small stream that rises south-west of Mendil south of Talevádi, the upward passage of a micaceous schistose gneiss into iron-clay is very clear. The iron clay is frequently a breccia in structure owing to the presence of numerous small angular fragments of white vein quartz which are very frequently seen in similar iron-clays far away from the gneiss rocks and wholly of trappean origin.

A small and well-marked iron-clay plateau, twenty to thirty feet thick, forms an outlier on the top of the Bidarbhávi hill five miles south-east of Yellurgad. It shows much vertically tubular structure, and the amount of iron contained decreases speedily with the depth. The rock is also very distinctly bedded. Below the base of the scarp no rock is satisfactorily seen in place; but the sides of the hill are covered with broken iron-clay or masses doubtfully in place. Nor is the gneiss exposed for some distance from the base of the hill, the nearest visible portion of Deccan trap being the south spur of Yellurgad. From its external resemblance, as compared with Yellurgad, it probably represents an altered inter-trappean or infra-trappean deposit.

Tertiary Deposits.

Of later tertiary and alluvial deposits there are three; fresh-water sedimentary rocks, fossil-bearing river rocks, and old and new river alluvia. Of these the most noticeable are the fossil-bearing river rocks under a covering of black clay. They are of dark brownish-black stiff clay with partings and thin beds of gritty or sandy clay. The fossil-bearing beds are shown in the banks of a stream that flows into the Ghatprabha at Chikdauli, three miles north-east of Gokák. At the point where the bones were found[2] the section is, (4) regur or

---

[1] Though, as seen from the north, from various points along the Jámboti ridges or from the lower iron-clay terraces of Ambgaon and Chapoli, the Gausi plateau strongly resembles a normal iron-clay capped trap area, no positive trace of the Deccan trap was found by Mr. Foote.

[2] Of the fossils the most interesting is an extinct species of rhinoceros. A number

Chapter I.
Description.
Geology.

cotton-soil passing into (3) black clay which contained the head of a rhinoceros, (2) clayey grit, two beds with clayey parting and numerous specimens of *Unio* and *Corbicula* in the gritty bands, and (1) reddish-brown black clay with bovine remains.[1] The bones are in a friable state, somewhat distorted by pressure, and much comminuted or broken by the action of numerous shrinkage cracks in the clay. Some of the bones are much encrusted by chalky deposits.

Alluvial Basins.

The alluvia of the several rivers agree very closely in character. They consist almost entirely of alluvial regur or black soil, with some beds of sand and gravel, frequently cemented by limestone nodules into coarse conglomerate. On the smaller rivers the alluvium in some cases is confined to a well-marked flat surrounded by higher grounds. Four cases of this kind are noted on the Ghatprabha and its tributaries, and in each of the four the alluvial flat or basin lies above a narrow gorge through which the river forces its way. Two of these alluvial areas occur, and both occupy shallow valleys above the eastern edge of the trap hill region. The one occurs along the course of the Márkándeya, some two miles north of Belgaum, and the other along a stream that rises in the Yellurgad hill and joins with those that drain the Belgaum downs. Both end abruptly eastward by the streams entering narrow gorges in the quartzite hills, and in both cases the alluvium is a black clay or a quasi regur.

A third basin to the south of Páchápur is at the meeting of the Márkándeya and the Belgaum river. The black regur-like alluvium in the upper part of the flat contains much nodular limestone. The lower part is wholly covered by thick regur, but in the upper parts between Ankalgi and Hudali there is a great development of pale-reddish and yellowish sandy loam with much limestone in filtration, strongly resembling the tertiary deposit known as loess, which forms steep cliff-like banks twenty-five to thirty feet high.

The fourth alluvial basin begins immediately below Gokák and stretches nearly eleven miles north-east to Tegdi. The lower part of the basin is hidden by a thick covering of cotton-soil through which only one section penetrates. The bone-bearing beds under the regur, which are exposed only in the Chikdauli stream are dark coloured clays with gritty clayey sands, and contain mammalian bones and fresh water shells. The space between is completely masked by cotton soil. It is probable that the Gokák basin joins the alluvial deposit which fills the valley of the Kelvi, a tributary of the Ghatprabha from the south. These alluvial deposits are gravels and coarse loam, the latter resembling the loam of the Belgaum stream at Hudli. These gravels rest on the various older formations that form the bottom and sides of the old valley, namely the gneiss, quartzites, Deccan trap, and inter-trappean beds. The gravel is in

---

of bones were found loose in the bed of the stream, and others were obtained in 1871 by digging in the fields. Many of these are bovine and a few belong to a smaller specimen of Rhinoceros deccanensis, the nasal bones of which were not found. The specimen was just adult, and from the absence or very small size of the incisors the animal had probably a large horn.

[1] The bovine animal was in the shape of its molars nearly allied to the bison Gavæus gaurus which still inhabits the thickly-wooded slopes of the Sahyádris.

Chapter I.
Description.
Geology.
Alluvial Basins.

great part sub-angular and contains pebbles of all the older rocks that occur in the neighbourhood. The gravels or loam have no organic remains.

The river alluvia consist very largely of regur or cotton soil partly washed up by the river action and partly washed down by rain action from higher grounds. In many cases this reguroid alluvium is undistinguishable from the true regur, as it in great measure assumes the same character if broken by innumerable sun cracks, by which in time the laminated structure due to its sedimentary origin is wholly lost.

Gravel beds of two classes are found, one of them river deposits the other lake deposits. Almost all the larger Karnátak rivers have on their banks deposits of gravel and shingle sixty to eighty feet above ordinary flood level. These shingle beds, there can be little doubt, are relics of the time when the spurs of hills through which the river channels are now cut were barriers that dammed back the river waters into lakes. Of these high level gravel beds the only case noted within Belgaum limits is on the Malprabha, nine miles west of Saundatti. Gravel beds, probably of lake or river origin, are found along the foot of the Kathárigad hills near the village of Tolur, about eight miles north-west of Manoli. In the Tolur bed, though not in such quantity as in some beds near Bádámi, rather water-worn chipped stone tools have been found lying on the surface.

Sub-Aërial Formations.

The reproductive action of open-air influences have produced five formations. Of the iron-clay, which is the chief of these open-air formations details have already been given. The others are (1) conglomerates formed mechanically by the deposition of clay and iron cements; (2) deposits cemented by the chemical precipitation of calcareous matter; (3) pluvial or rain rain caused aggregations; and (4) blown sand.

Cases of the cementing of the remains of the lower Kaládgi quartzites by the deposition of iron-clay are noticed at Somápur a little south-east of Kathárigad, and three miles further west on the plateau east of Murgod. At these places numerous large quartzite pebbles weathered out of sandstone conglomerate have been recemented in very nearly their original position. The new rock looks much like an artificial pavement. A very similar, but even more striking effect, is produced by the cementing of rounded quartzite fragments in the valley south-west of Tumurgudi about eleven miles north-east of Belgaum. This pavement stretches for several hundred yards.

A case of cementation of angular fragments of gritty quartzite into a breccia by the introduction of a red sandy cement is observed in the saddle between the north-east side of One Tree Hill at Belgaum and the south-east corner of the quartzite plateau to the north-east. This breccia might, from its position, be easily mistaken for part of the lower Kaládgi quartzites, the coarse pebbly basement beds of which are exposed close by and seem to rest on highly upturned micaceous schistose beds in a section a little to the north-east of Kanburgi. Instances of the formation of small patches of sub-aërial conglomerates and breccias by the lateritoid decomposition of ferruginous rocks are very common.

Chapter I.
Description.
Geology.
Pluvial Formations.

Pluvial aggregations are common chiefly on the slopes of tray hills and at the sides of some of the larger valleys. Much of the quasi-lateritic soil and rock met in such positions is of purely pluvia origin, but as a rule this class of deposits is so mixed with the local results of weathering that no line of separation can be traced Considerable areas in the neighbourhood of Belgaum are covered with formations thick enough to mask the true sub-rocks.

Large tracts of the quartzite region along the northern slope of the hills north-east of Mamdápur in Gokák are covered with almost pure sand.

Ruined Rock.

Accumulations of ruined rock are met everywhere, and are often very widespread, especially at the foot of the quartzite slopes and scarps where they make the ground very rough and impassable. To the north-east of the Nesargi travellers' bungalow, on the Belgaum-Kaládgi road, they are so thick as to a very great extent to obscure the geological boundary lines.

Soils.

From a geological view point the soils may be divided into two main classes the red and the black. The red soils are primary soils, that is they are the direct result of the decomposition of iron-bearing rocks. The black soils are secondary soils, that is they are the result of primary decomposition changed by accession of organic matter. The black soil is not solely the result of the weathering of trap rocks. Black soil occurs quite as largely and as typically on the gneiss and other azoic rocks as it does on the trap.

Climate.

The pleasantest climate in the district is in a tract parallel with the crest of the Sahyádris, between the western forests and the treeless east. Within this belt lie Belgaum, Kitur, Páchápur, Sankeshvar, and Nipáni.[1]

The dry east winds which blow from October to March and the heavy south-west rains which last from June to October make the climate of Belgaum trying to new-comers. At the same time to the robust and to those who are accustomed to the climate, the two thousand feet above the sea, the moderate heat, and the early and fresh sea-breeze, make Belgaum pleasant and healthy.

The healthy influence is especially noticed in European children who thrive wonderfully and have a bloom on their cheeks during the colder months. Still a long residence enervates. Europeans who have grown up in Belgaum as a rule are pale, delicate, and weak. Newcomers again suffer in consequence of the sudden change from the extreme dryness of the air in the fair season to the great dampness of the rains. Unless with very active exercise the skin does not act, the liver grows sluggish and congested, and languor and drowsiness pass into sleeplessness, loss of appetite, and listlessness. The strong with the help of active exercise after a time throw off these feelings and enjoy vigorous health; but so long as they remain in Belgaum the weakly are doomed to suffer more or less. The climate of Belgaum is unsuitable to those who are liable to

---

[1] Kies' Southern Marátha, 24.

suffer from sluggishness of the liver, asthma, heart-disease, rheumatism, Bright's disease of the kidneys, or consumption; on the other hand those who have suffered from malarious fevers as a rule improve by a residence in Belgaum.

Chapter I.
Description.
Climate.
Seasons.

The Belgaum year may be arranged into three seasons, the cold and dry season from the middle of October till the middle of February; the hot and dry season from the middle of February till the beginning of June; and the wet season from the beginning of June till the middle of October. About the middle of October the cold weather perceptibly sets in, the evening air begins to be chilly, heavy fogs gather soon after sunset, and towards the morning and for some time after sunrise the country is shrouded in thick mist. Towards the end of December or early in January the night temperature is at its minimum. In 1879 December showed a mean temperature of 67°. During the whole period the weather is fine with strong dry easterly winds which make the cold of the coldest month less felt than the damp chill of July and August. The cold season lasts till the middle of February, when both the day and the night temperature begin to rise. The common cold-weather diseases are bronchitis, dysentery, dyspepsia, and malarious fever, which last, though prevalent all the year round, is at its highest from November to January. The hot season sets in about the middle of February and the temperature rises rapidly until it reaches 100° in May. The prevailing wind is from the west. In April and May the great heat causes occasional heavy showers attended with easterly winds, thunder, lightning, and sometimes with hail.[1] Even in May the nights are cool, almost chilly. Dew forms from sunset to sunrise and is sometimes as heavy as gentle rain. Even in the hottest days *pankhás* or damped grass screens

---

1 The following accounts of thunderstorms which passed over Belgaum in 1847 (7th April) and 1849 (24th April and 2nd June) are taken from the Transactions of the Bombay Geographical Society, IX. 191-194. During the week ending the 9th of April 1847 the weather was warm, the thermometer at 2 P.M. ranging from 88° to 92°. The afternoons were ushered in by strong squalls from the south-west and north-east, with occasional clouds of dust and whirlwinds. These were usually followed by heavy clouds, and by thunder and lightning at night. About four in the evening of the 7th April the wind rose almost to a storm, accompanied by rattling peals of thunder followed by a fall of hail and rain which lasted for an hour. The thermometer which before the storm had stood at 90°, had at its close fallen to 70°. Upwards of half an inch of rain fell. A native man and woman were struck dead by lightning near the Collector's office. During the whole of April 1849 the weather was very trying. Every evening large dense clouds hung over the town and threatened a thunderstorm. But on every occasion they were blown off by a current of high wind and dust, followed by thunder and most vivid lightning. Up to the 24th there were three or four smart showers of rain and one slight hail shower. On the evening of the 2nd of June (1849) an extremely severe storm of wind and rain passed over Belgaum. Slight rain began at four, but the storm did not burst till five. The rain lasted from five till half-past eight during twenty minutes of which there was an awful hailstorm. Such large hailstones had never been seen at Belgaum. They were neither spherical nor oval, but irregular-shaped as if a number of small stones had united in their descent from the clouds. The thunder was deafening and the lightning very vivid and frequent. The hurricane ruined the plantain groves and smaller fruit trees. Five inches of rain were registered in the Highlanders' Hospital and in the fort a little more than two inches. Scarcely a house escaped without being stripped of some of its tiles. Several lives were lost in the neighbourhood of Sháhápur about a mile to the south of Belgaum.

Chapter I. Description. Climate. *Rain.*

are never required. The occasional showers of April and May become more frequent and heavy as the south-west rains draw near. So gradual is the approach of the south-west monsoon that in some seasons it is hard to tell which storm is the burst of the true monsoon. The break of the south-west monsoon, which supplies the district with most of its rain, is generally looked for about the 5th of June. The south-west rains last till the middle of October. They are not followed by a period of complete dryness. At Belgaum showers fall during almost every month in the year. In June July and August the air is so moist that stoves or *sigris* are required to dry houses and clothes.[1]

Near the Sahyádris the south-west monsoon is very constant and heavy. Further east it is fitful, coming in showers separated by breaks of fair weather. To the east of a line drawn from Nipáni, through Sankeshvar, Páchápur, Ankalgi, Marihalli, the Yellurgad ridge, and the Malprabha crossing on the Belgaum-Dhárwár road, the decrease of rain is sudden, and is accompanied by a marked change in the look of the country and in the style of the houses. To the west of this line the houses have tiled pent roofs with wide eaves to carry the water clear of the mud walls. To the east of the line the greater number of houses have flat-terraced roofs of beaten mud able to stand only a moderate rainfall.[2] The eastern plain, besides fitful showers from the south-west monsoon, receives a scanty supply from the north-east or Madras monsoon. The north-east monsoon is looked for by the middle of October. But in some seasons it does not burst till the end of October or even till the middle of November. As a rule the north-east monsoon has little effect west of Kaládgi. Its supply of rain is much less and lasts much shorter than the rainfall of the south-west monsoon. Only in exceptional seasons as in 1874 do the north-east rains pass west to the Sahyádris.[3] The general rule regarding the south-west monsoon is that it is heaviest in the west along the crest of the Sahyádris and grows lighter and less certain as it leaves the western hills and passes over the eastern plain. At the same time the distribution of the supply is greatly affected by the lines of the rivers, by hills, and by other local features. In Sampgaon, which is thirty to fifty miles east of the Sahyádris, the fall both from the south-west and north-east rains is ample and certain. If the south-west rains fail, the want is almost sure to be made good by the north-east rains. The eastern villages sometimes suffer from a scanty fall in the south-west monsoon; but a total failure of crops from drought is said to be unknown. In Parasgad, forty to seventy miles from the Sahyádris, the fall of rain varies greatly in different parts; it is plentiful and certain in the west and grows gradually more uncertain as the plain stretches east, where, along the borders of Navalgund and Nargund in Dhárwár, the seasons are uncertain and the crops are liable to fail. In east Parasgad too the supply of drinking water is very scanty, and in some villages, during the hot weather, water has to be carried several miles.

---

[1] Climate and season details are compiled from materials supplied by Surgeon-Major C. T. Peters, M.B.

[2] Mr. Foote in Mem. Geo. Surv. XII. 14.

[3] Mr. Foote in Mem. Geo. Surv. 15, 16.

Chapter I.
Description.
Climate.
Rain.

The hills which enclose Gokák on the south and west, and which are about sixty miles from the Sahyádris, seem to intercept the monsoon showers and make the plain to the east of them very subject to drought. In the plain to the east it is a common saying that a good monsoon comes only once in twelve years.

Rain[1] returns registered for the twenty-three years ending 1882 at the seven sub-divisional stations give for the whole district an average fall of nearly thirty inches. Arranged in order of rainfall, 1863 and 1865 are lowest with twenty inches; 1860 and 1876 are next with twenty-one inches; 1864 and 1873 third with twenty-two inches; 1871 fourth with twenty-three inches; 1861 and 1872 fifth with twenty-five inches; 1867 sixth with twenty-six inches; 1862 and 1866 seventh with twenty-seven inches; 1869 and 1880 eighth with twenty-eight inches; 1868 ninth with twenty-nine inches; 1881 tenth with thirty-two inches; 1870 eleventh with thirty-three inches; 1875 twelfth with thirty-five inches; 1879 and 1882 thirteenth with thirty-seven inches; 1877 fourteenth with thirty-nine inches; and 1874 and 1878 are highest with forty-one inches. Considering how near the district is to the Sahyádris the average fall of thirty inches is low. In Khánápur, whose sub-divisional station is twenty miles from the Sahyádris and in which are situated nearly all the forest reserves, the yearly rainfall varied from twenty-three inches in 1861 to seventy-seven inches in 1878, and averaged fifty-one inches; and in Belgaum, which is twenty-five miles from the Sahyádris, the fall varied from thirty-three inches in 1880 to seventy-one in 1882, and averaged forty-seven inches; at Chikodi, about fifty miles from the Sahyádris, the fall varied from eight inches in 1869 to thirty-seven inches in 1877, and averaged twenty-one inches; at Gokák, about sixty miles from the Sahyádris, it varied from seven inches in 1876 to thirty-three inches in 1877, and averaged seventeen inches; at Athni, about ninety miles from the Sahyádris, it varied from seven inches in 1876 to thirty-four inches in 1878, and averaged nineteen inches; at Saundatti, about sixty miles from the Sahyádris, it varied from ten inches in 1863 and 1865 to forty-one inches in 1874, and averaged twenty inches; and at Sampgaon, about forty miles from the Sahyádris, it varied from nine inches in 1863 to thirty-eight inches in 1874, and averaged twenty-three inches. The following statement gives the details:

Belgaum District Rainfall, 1860-1882.

Station.	1860.	1861.	1862.	1863.	1864.	1865.	1866.	1867.	1868.	1869.	1870.	1871.
Belgaum	38	58	51	53	39	46	46	39	50	49	55	36
Sampgaon	15	22	25	9	16	14	20	19	24	28	27	17
Khánápur	30	23	44	30	27	34	47	36	57	59	66	50
Chikodi	14	23	26	16	18	17	23	26	21	8	23	17
Saundatti	13	14	15	10	23	10	19	26	18	23	25	15
Gokák	10	14	16	12	12	11	18	17	18	22	21	13
Athni	27	20	17	12	13	19	15	18	16	16	18	13
Average ...	21	25	27	20	22	20	27	26	29	28	33	23

1 The rain figures must be received with caution as in several cases the returns do not agree.

Chapter I.
Description.
Climate.
Rain.

Belgaum District Rainfall, 1860 - 1882—continued.

Station.	1872.	1873.	1874.	1875.	1876.	1877.	1878.	1879.	1880.	1881.	1882.	Average.
Belgaum	45	40	57	64	36	46	54	54	88	41	71	47
Sampgaon	15	15	88	34	18	30	37	36	27	26	30	23
Khánápur	51	49	74	67	51	64	77	70	46	70	65	51
Chikodi	16	11	25	23	16	37	34	32	21	22	27	21
Saundatti	15	13	41	20	16	37	28	26	24	26	21	20
Gokák	15	10	26	18	7	33	25	22	21	18	27	17
Athni	20	16	31	23	7	31	34	21	23	24	20	19
Average ...	25	22	41	35	21	39	41	37	28	32	37	29

The following statement gives for the twenty-seven years ending 1882 the rainfall at the town of Belgaum for each month in the year. Of the twelve months in the year, February is the driest month with a fall varying from 0·53 of an inch in 1873 to 0·04 of an inch in 1865, and averaging 0·02 of an inch; January comes next with a fall varying from 0·94 of an inch in 1870 to 0·04 of an inch in 1860, and averaging 0·03 of an inch; December is third with a fall varying from 2·88 of an inch in 1863 to 0·02 of an inch in 1865, and averaging 0·33 of an inch; March fourth, with a fall varying from 2·44 of an inch in 1876 to 0·02 of an inch in 1866, and averaging 0·48 of an inch; November fifth, with a fall varying from 5·37 inches in 1878 to 0·04 of an inch in 1877, and averaging 1·13 inches; April sixth, with a fall varying from 4·85 inches in 1865 to 0·03 of an inch in 1866, and averaging 1·85 inches; May seventh, with a fall varying from 10·68 inches in 1856 to 0·67 of an inch in 1861, and averaging 2·77 inches; September eighth, with a fall varying from 9·26 inches in 1874 to 0·09 of an inch in 1860, and averaging 3·29; October ninth, with a fall varying from 7·97 inches in 1880 to 0·18 of an inch in 1864, and averaging 4·47 inches; August tenth, with a fall varying from 22·43 inches in 1861 to 2·25 inches in 1876, and averaging 8·68 inches; June eleventh, with a fall varying from 17·61 inches in 1862 to 0·54 of an inch in 1881, and averaging 9·85 inches; and July is the wettest month, with a fall varying from 29·37 inches in 1882 to 2·78 inches in 1877, and averaging 14·57 inches. The goodness or badness of a year depends less on the fall for the whole year than on its distribution during the rainy months. In 1871, though the fall was only thirty-six inches, it was not a famine year, because the rain was evenly distributed, eight inches in June and July, seven inches in August, one inch in September, and five inches in October. So also the 1880 fall of thirty-three inches was fairly distributed, five inches falling in June, eight in July, three in August, two in September, and seven in October. On the other hand, the year 1876 with a fall of thirty-six was a famine year, because the rain was badly distributed. Six inches fell in June, twenty-one in July, two in August, one in September, and 0·97 of an inch in October. In 1877 of a fall of forty-six inches, sixteen fell in June, three in July, eight in August, seven in September, and seven in October. Owing to the failure of rain in July the year would have been one of great scarcity, but for a timely fall in September and October. The year of heaviest rainfall was 1882 with seventy-one inches. Next to 1882 were 1875, with sixty-four inches, and 1861 with fifty-eight inches. The limit of the yearly normal rainfall may be said to be between forty and fifty inches :

Chapter I.

Description.

Climate.

Rain.

BELGAUM CITY RAINFALL, 1856-1882.

Month.	1856.		1857.		1858.		1859.		1860.		1861.		1862.	
	In.	C.	In.	C.	In.	C.	In.	C.	In.	C.	In.	C.	In.	C.
Jan. ...	0	00	0	00	0	00	0	00	0	04	0	00	0	00
Feb. ...	0	00	0	00	0	00	0	00	0	00	0	00	0	00
March..	0	00	0	40	0	72	0	36	0	09	0	66	0	37
April ...	1	56	2	45	1	05	2	87	3	87	0	49	0	37
May ...	10	68	7	71	6	08	2	87	0	93	0	67	1	11
June ...	11	66	13	08	3	49	4	98	6	74	4	25	17	61
July ...	12	10	6	58	13	08	22	61	10	23	25	36	8	79
Aug. ...	6	33	17	52	4	06	6	11	11	66	22	48	10	41
Sept. ...	2	88	1	17	2	87	5	24	0	09	2	38	5	18
Oct. ...	2	57	7	10	6	76	3	40	5	17	1	48	6	20
Nov. ...	0	08	3	14	1	31	1	74	0	00	0	07	0	19
Dec. ...	0	16	0	00	0	00	0	00	0	00	0	00	0	77
Total...	48	00	59	11	38	72	50	18	38	28	57	83	50	95

Month.	1863.		1864.		1865.		1866.		1867.		1868.		1869.	
	In.	C.	In.	C.	In.	C.	In.	C.	In.	C.	In.	C.	In.	C.
Jan. ...	0	00	0	00	0	00	0	00	0	00	0	00	0	00
Feb. ...	0	00	0	00	0	04	0	00	0	00	0	00	0	00
March..	1	59	0	03	0	38	0	02	0	74	0	66	0	00
April ...	2	63	1	45	4	85	0	08	0	86	2	32	0	69
May ...	0	00	2	16	2	96	0	53	1	94	5	22	0	64
June ...	18	60	8	18	8	91	11	39	7	95	15	04	13	97
July ...	9	37	19	31	14	68	17	71	11	39	10	06	14	33
Aug. ...	11	04	6	64	13	88	9	17	7	75	13	08	7	69
Sept. ...	1	47	1	17	0	27	1	11	1	83	1	26	3	14
Oct. ...	3	44	0	18	4	21	6	40	6	07	2	49	4	70
Nov. ...	1	69	0	12	0	31	0	00	0	00	0	00	1	79
Dec. ...	2	88	0	00	0	02	0	06	0	00	0	00	1	79
Total...	52	70	39	24	45	51	46	42	38	53	50	18	48	74

Month.	1870.		1871.		1872.		1873.		1874.		1875.		1876.	
	In.	C.	In.	C.	In.	C.	In.	C.	In.	C.	In.	C.	In.	C.
Jan. ...	0	94	0	88	0	00	0	00	0	00	0	00	0	00
Feb. ...	0	00	0	00	0	00	0	53	0	00	0	00	0	00
March..	0	26	0	43	0	12	0	22	0	00	0	80	2	44
April ...	2	47	1	33	2	22	2	05	0	60	3	64	1	19
May ...	2	96	1	84	1	05	5	43	5	04	1	37	0	00
June ...	9	43	8	33	11	30	4	16	12	64	15	40	6	01
July ...	18	60	8	22	15	13	14	42	15	31	25	01	21	11
Aug. ...	8	61	6	54	3	62	4	78	6	26	8	29	2	25
Sept. ...	6	14	1	65	5	69	4	80	9	26	3	30	1	94
Oct. ...	5	22	5	24	3	48	3	49	6	76	4	74	0	97
Nov. ...	0	66	1	85	0	04	0	58	0	77	1	11	0	00
Dec. ...	0	00	0	00	2	74	0	00	0	00	0	02	0	00
Total...	55	29	36	24	45	39	40	46	56	64	63	68	35	91

Month.	1877.		1878.		1879.		1880.		1881.		1882.		Average.	
	In.	C.	In.	C.	In.	C.	In.	C.	In.	C.	In.	C.	In.	C.
Jan. ...	0	00	0	00	0	00	0	00	0	00	0	00	0	3
Feb. ...	0	00	0	00	0	05	0	00	0	00	0	00	0	2
March..	0	00	0	00	0	00	1	59	0	00	1	13	0	48
April ...	3	66	2	63	0	64	1	58	1	01	2	07	1	85
May ...	1	23	1	20	5	85	1	13	1	63	3	23	2	77
June ...	16	43	5	60	13	40	5	30	0	54	16	74	9	85
July ...	2	78	12	09	8	66	8	72	18	40	29	37	14	57
Aug. ...	7	69	14	34	17	13	3	63	10	00	6	61	8	68
Sept. ...	6	03	6	10	1	40	2	54	8	27	8	81	3	29
Oct. ...	7	42	6	64	3	81	7	97	1	96	2	82	4	47
Nov. ...	0	04	5	37	4	40	0	59	4	36	0	34	1	13
Dec. ...	0	60	0	00	0	07	0	00	0	00	0	08	0	88
Total...	46	48	53	97	54	91	33	05	41	17	71	15	47	47

Information[1] compiled by Mr. Chambers shows that in Belgaum city, during the sixteen years ending 1872, the average number of rain days varied from 0·1 in February to 25·2 in July. The details are :

BELGAUM CITY RAIN DAYS, 1856-1872.

Month.	Days.	Month.	Days.	Month.	Days.	Month.	Days.
January ...	0·2	April ...	4·7	July ...	25·2	October ...	10·8
February ...	0·1	May ...	6·3	August ...	24·3	November..	2·2
March ...	1·5	June ...	20·3	September.	14·2	December..	1·1

The greatest fall recorded in any one day in each month varied from 6·07 inches in August to 0·05 in February. The details are:

BELGAUM CITY GREATEST RAIN DAYS, 1856-1872.

Month.	Inches.	Month.	Inches.	Month.	Inches.	Month.	Inches.
January ...	1·06	April ...	2·28	July ...	5·83	October ...	2·87
February ...	0·05	May ...	4·63	August ...	6·07	November..	2·19
March ...	0·83	June ...	5·51	September.	2·20	December..	2·60

[1] The climate details from pages 43-51 are from Chambers' Meteorology of the Bombay Presidency, 131-167.

Chapter I.
Description.
Climate.
Warmth.

The two daily observations taken at the Belgaum Observatory at 9-30 A.M. and 3-30 P.M. show for the nineteen years ending 1874 a mean temperature of 77·7. The greatest excess of temperature was 1·0° in 1869 and the greatest decrease was 1·6° in 1857. The details are:

Belgaum City Mean Temperature, 1856-1874.

Year.	Mean.	Over Mean.	Year.	Mean.	Over Mean.	Year.	Mean.	Over Mean.
1856 ...	76·8	−0·9	1863 ...	...	...	1870 ...	77·3	−0·4
1857 ...	76·1	−1·6	1864 ...	77·7	0·0	1871 ...	77·6	−0·1
1858 ...	76·8	−0·9	1865 ...	78·0	+0·3	1872 ...	78·2	+0·5
1859 ...	78·6	+0·9	1866 ...	78·2	+0·5	1873 ...	77·7	0·0
1860 ...	77·9	+0·2	1867 ...	77·3	−0·4	1874 ...	77·0	−0·7
1861 ...	77·9	+0·2	1868 ...	78·4	+0·7			
1862 ...	78·0	+0·3	1869 ...	78·7	+1·0			

At the Belgaum Observatory, which is (1878) in the enclosure of the European General Hospital, besides rainfall, thermometer and barometer readings have been recorded since 1851. The observations are under the charge of the senior medical officer. The record comprises two sets of observations made every day at 9-30 A.M. and at 3-30 P.M., and a complete set of twenty-four hourly observations for one day in every month. The instruments and phenomena noted at each observation include the barometer, dry and wet bulb thermometers, the direction of the wind, the cloudiness, and the rainfall. Once a day the maximum and minimum thermometer reading in the shade, the maximum thermometer reading exposed to the sun's rays during the day time, and the minimum thermometer reading laid upon grass exposed to the sky at night are recorded. The observations are registered on printed forms, which when filled are forwarded by the head of the medical department to the Superintendent of the Colába Observatory in Bombay where the calculations are checked and the results compiled. Once a year the registers and compilation are sent by the Superintendent to Government to be forwarded to Her Majesty's Secretary of State for India. In the Belgaum Observatory the self-registering thermometers are placed in a wooden revolving stand, at a distance of 18½ feet from the nearest building, and four feet from the ground: they are fully exposed to the air, and protected from the sun's rays, but it is impossible to prevent rain from getting at them during the revolving storms which occur at the beginning of the south-west monsoon. The thermometer readings are supposed to be too high, as the stand is not suited to a tropical sun. The barometer, and dry and wet bulb thermometers are in a shed in the north-east veranda of the hospital guard-house. The shed which measures thirteen feet by eight by six is built of wooden bars two inches apart; it has a flagged floor, and a post in the middle stretching from floor to roof: this post supports the barometer on one side and the dry and wet bulb thermometers on the other side, the thermometers being four feet seven inches from the floor and two feet seven inches and three feet one inch from the wall.

An examination of the temperature returns in the city of Belgaum for the nineteen years ending 1874 shows that during five months in the year February, March, April, May and June the temperature was

Chapter I.
Description.
Climate.
Warmth.

above, and that during the seven remaining months the temperature was below the mean. Adopting the return corrected for the daily inequality, August was the coldest month with an average of 3·3° below the mean, December came next with 3·2°, January third with 2·9°, July fourth with 2·4°, September fifth with 2·2°, November sixth with 1·5°, and October seventh with 0·3°. Of the five hot months February and June are the coolest with 0·4° in excess of the mean, March comes next with 3·8°, May next with 4·7°, and April is the hottest, being 6·4° above the mean. The details are:

Belgaum City Monthly Temperature, 1856-1874.

Month.	At 9-30 A.M. and 3-30 P.M.	Corrected.	Month.	At 9-30 A.M. and 3-30 P.M.	Corrected.
January ...	−2·1	−2·9	July ...	−4·8	−2·4
February ...	+2·1	+0·4	August ...	−5·0	−3·3
March ...	+6·1	+3·8	September.	−3·3	−2·2
April ...	+8·2	+6·4	October ...	−1·0	−0·3
May ...	+5·8	+4·7	November..	−1·6	−1·5
June ...	−1·5	+0·4	December..	−2·9	−3·2

The corrections are found from the daily inequalities at the several hours in each month. They are the means of these inequalities for the hours 9 A.M. and 10 A.M. and 3 P.M. and 4 P.M., and are applied subtractively.

The following table shows for the city of Belgaum, for each month, for the monsoon quarter June to August, and for the whole year, the excess of the mean temperature at the several hours of the day above the mean temperature of the twenty-four hours; also the number of complete days' observations, which are generally not more than one in each month, of the year from which the means are derived:

Belgaum Temperature in Local Civil Hours, 1856-1874.

Month.	6	7	8	9	10	11	12	13
January	−8·2	−7·3	−4·6	−1·2	+2·0	+4·4	+6·3	+7·0
February	−9·3	−7·9	−4·0	0·0	+3·2	+5·8	+7·6	+9·2
March	−8·8	−6·6	−3·1	+0·7	+4·0	+6·7	+8·6	+10·1
April	−7·8	−5·6	−2·8	+0·5	+4·8	+7·2	+9·3	+10·8
May	−6·0	−4·3	−2·1	+0·4	+2·8	+5·4	+7·8	+9·2
June	−2·4	−1·3	−0·8	+0·9	+2·1	+2·9	+3·5	+4·2
July	−1·6	−1·1	−0·0	+0·8	+1·6	+2·2	+2·3	+3·8
August	−2·7	−2·0	−0·7	+0·8	+2·1	+3·0	+3·9	+4·3
September	−3·5	−2·5	−1·0	+0·6	+2·5	+4·1	+5·3	+5·7
October	−4·4	−3·5	−1·9	−0·2	+1·9	+3·7	+4·7	+5·5
November	−6·7	−5·8	−3·4	−0·2	+2·2	+4·1	+5·5	+6·4
December	−7·2	−6·4	−4·0	−0·6	+2·2	+4·1	+5·8	+6·9
June to August ...	−2·3	−1·5	−0·3	+0·8	+1·9	+2·7	+3·2	+3·8
Year	−5·7	−4·5	−2·8	+0·2	+2·6	+4·5	+5·9	+6·9

Month.	14	15	16	17	18	19	20	21
January	+9·0	+9·6	+9·1	+7·8	+5·1	+3·3	+0·6	−1·0
February	+10·4	+10·2	+9·6	+8·1	+5·9	+2·3	+0·4	−1·7
March	+11·1	+10·9	+9·8	+7·7	+4·0	+0·8	−1·6	−2·9
April	+11·4	+10·4	+8·1	+5·0	+2·3	+0·3	−1·5	−2·6
May	+10·0	+9·3	+7·8	+5·1	+1·9	−0·2	−1·5	−2·5
June	+3·8	+3·0	+2·8	+1·6	+0·4	−0·5	−0·9	−1·2
July	+3·0	+2·4	+1·8	+1·3	+0·3	−0·2	−0·6	−0·9
August	+4·2	+3·7	+3·0	+1·9	+0·6	−0·4	−1·1	−1·4
September	+5·4	+5·0	+4·0	+2·3	+0·7	−0·2	−1·0	−1·6
October	+5·9	+6·0	+5·6	+4·3	+2·1	+0·8	−0·3	−1·1
November	+7·4	+7·4	+6·7	+5·7	+3·6	+2·0	+0·6	−0·9
December	+7·9	+8·1	+7·7	+6·4	+4·2	+2·2	+0·8	−0·7
June to August ...	+3·7	+3·0	+2·4	+1·6	+0·4	−0·4	−0·9	−1·2
Year	+7·6	+7·2	+6·3	+4·8	+2·6	+0·9	−0·5	−1·5

Chapter I.
Description.
Climate.
Warmth.

BELGAUM TEMPERATURE IN LOCAL CIVIL HOURS, 1856-1874—continued.

MONTH.	22	23	0	1	2	3	4	5	Complete Days.
January ...	−2·1	−3·7	−4·1	−5·4	−6·1	−6·7	−6·9	−7·6	16
February ...	−2·6	−3·9	−5·3	−6·1	−6·8	−7·4	−8·2	−8·3	17
March ...	−4·0	−5·0	−5·7	−6·5	−7·0	−7·9	−8·3	−8·6	17
April ...	−3·6	−4·2	−5·2	−6·0	−6·7	−7·5	−8·1	−8·0	17
May ...	−3·4	−4·4	−4·9	−5·2	−5·7	−6·0	−6·5	−6·8	17
June ...	−1·6	−1·9	−2·2	−2·2	−2·5	−2·8	−2·8	−2·7	17
July ...	−1·2	−1·4	−1·5	−1·5	−1·7	−1·8	−1·9	−1·9	17
August ...	−1·8	−2·0	−2·3	−2·4	−2·7	−2·8	−2·9	−3·1	16
September ...	−2·1	−2·5	−2·7	−3·2	−3·2	−3·5	−3·6	−3·9	16
October ...	−1·6	−2·4	−2·8	−3·5	−3·9	−4·4	−5·0	−5·1	16
November ...	−1·9	−2·6	−3·6	−4·5	−5·0	−5·4	−5·8	−6·3	18
December ...	−1·7	−2·5	−3·3	−4·2	−5·0	−5·7	−6·5	−7·0	18
June to Aug.	−1·5	−1·8	−2·0	−2·0	−2·3	−2·5	−2·5	−2·6	
Year	−2·3	−3·0	−3·6	−4·2	−4·7	−5·1	−5·5	−5·8	

The average daily range of temperature for the year is almost double the range for the wet months from June to August. The range during the cold half-year is generally large, compared with the range of the hot and wet half. The daily range for the year is 13·3° and for the wet months 6·4°.

A comparison of the range of the mean temperatures of the different months for the same series of years shows that the variation is least 11·5° in July, August comes second with 12·4°, June third with 16·3°, September fourth with 16·5°, October fifth with 21·7°, November sixth with 23·9°, December seventh with 25·4°, May eighth with 27·5°, January ninth with 28·3°, February tenth with 30·1°, April eleventh with 32·0°, and March twelfth with 32·8°. The details are :

BELGAUM CITY DAILY RANGE, 1856-1874.

MONTH.	Mean Maximum.	Mean Minimum.	Range.	Annual Variation.	MONTH.	Mean Maximum.	Mean Minimum.	Range.	Annual Variation.
January ...	86·1	57·8	28·3	+5·1	August ...	78·8	65·9	12·4	−10·8
February ...	80·8	59·7	30·1	+6·9	September.	81·4	64·9	16·5	−6·7
March ...	96·0	63·2	32·8	+9·6	October ...	86·2	64·5	21·7	−1·5
April ...	98·4	66·4	32·0	+8·8	November..	85·0	61·1	23·9	+0·7
May ...	94·5	67·0	27·5	+4·3	December..	84·1	58·7	25·4	+2·2
June ...	83·3	67·0	16·3	−6·9					
July ...	78·0	66·5	11·5	−11·7	Year ...	86·8	63·6	23·2	

During the same period the highest recorded monthly mean temperature varied from 92·5 in July to 109·5 in April, and the lowest from 46·7 in December to 62·7 in July. The details are :

BELGAUM CITY HIGHEST AND LOWEST MONTHLY TEMPERATURE, 1856-1874.

MONTH.	Maximum.	Minimum.	Range.	MONTH.	Maximum.	Minimum.	Range.
January ...	95·4	50·0	45·4	July ...	92·5	62·7	29·8
February...	99·7	47·3	52·4	August ...	93·5	61·5	32·0
March ...	103·9	50·2	53·7	September.	93·0	59·4	33·6
April ...	109·5	54·4	55·1	October ...	95·7	53·0	42·7
May ...	108·2	59·0	49·2	November..	94·0	49·0	45·0
June ...	103·1	61·2	41·9	December..	92·6	46·7	45·9

The following statement gives for each of the six years ending 1882 the thermometer readings taken at Belgaum :

Chapter I.
Description.
Climate.
Warmth.

BELGAUM CITY HIGHEST AND LOWEST MONTHLY TEMPERATURE, 1877-1882.

Year.	January. Max.	January. Min.	January. Mean.	February. Max.	February. Min.	February. Mean.	March. Max.	March. Min.	March. Mean.	April. Max.	April. Min.	April. Mean.	May. Max.	May. Min.	May. Mean.	June. Max.	June. Min.	June. Mean.
1877	79	62	73	89	64	71	93	68	80	98	71	89	100	70	90	92	71	78
1878	78	64	72	88	63	73	96	67	82	97	73	83	95	74	83	95	72	79
1879	81	61	70	87	64	73	93	62	78	99	70	84	101	71	80	66	70	74
1880	84	58	68	86	64	75	98	70	79	99	71	72	97	74	79	90	69	76
1881	82	56	73	86	59	71	96	65	85	97	72	84	99	71	84	95	73	80
1882	83	60	71	88	61	73	89	63	77	90	70	84	89	74	85	85	71	76

Year.	July. Max.	July. Min.	July. Mean.	August. Max.	August. Min.	August. Mean.	September. Max.	September. Min.	September. Mean.	October. Max.	October. Min.	October. Mean.	November. Max.	November. Min.	November. Mean.	December. Max.	December. Min.	December. Mean.
1877	84	70	76	81	70	74	82	71	75	81	68	75	84	60	72	84	62	76
1878	85	70	76	85	71	76	86	72	78	85	70	77	88	64	74	82	58	69
1879	87	70	74	78	70	72	80	67	71	81	68	70	80	58	69	81	59	67
1880	71	69	70	78	68	72	76	69	72	85	67	81	82	65	76	81	58	71
1881	80	71	73	81	70	73	80	67	78	88	66	74	84	61	69	82	57	71
1882	83	70	74	79	70	74	77	70	73	84	65	75	84	62	74	88	61	71

The mean is the mean of four daily observations.

Pressure.

The mean barometric pressure for each year of complete observation is shown for the city of Belgaum in the following table. The means are derived from two daily observations one at 9-30 A.M. the other at 3-30 P.M.:

BELGAUM CITY BAROMETRIC PRESSURE, 1856-1874.

Year.	Mean.	Excess.	Year.	Mean.	Excess.	Year.	Mean.	Excess.
1856 ...	27·369	+·046	1863 ...	...	...	1870 ...	27·289	—·034
1857 ...	27·326	+·003	1864 ...	27·345	+·022	1871 ...	27·304	—·019
1858 ...	27·331	+·008	1865 ...	27·338	+·015	1872 ...	27·292	—·031
1859 ...	27·325	+·002	1866 ...	27·335	+·012	1873 ...	27·303	—·020
1860 ...	27·324	+·001	1867 ...	27·337	+·014	1874 ...	27·298	—·025
1861 ...	27·322	—·001	1868 ...	27·331	+·008			
1862 ...	27·302	—·021	1869 ...	27·308	—·015			

The observations during the same series of years (1856-1874) show that, in the six months between October and April, the barometric pressure is over the mean, and in the six months between April and October the pressure is below the mean. The month of least pressure is June with 0·096 below the mean, July is next with 0·095, August third with 0·062, May fourth with 0·049, September fifth with 0·025, and April sixth with 0·016. Of the six months of excessive pressure, October is lowest with 0·011, March second with 0·030, November third with 0·062, February fourth with 0·064, December and January fifth and sixth with 0·089 each. The details are:

BELGAUM CITY MONTHLY BAROMETRIC VARIATION, 1856-1874.

Month.	At 9-30 A.M. and 3-30 P.M.	Corrected.	Month.	At 9-30 A.M. and 3-30 P.M.	Corrected.
January ...	+·094	+·089	July ...	—·096	—·095
February ...	+·067	+·064	August ...	—·062	—·062
March ...	+·030	+·030	September.	—·032	—·025
April ...	—·019	—·016	October ...	+·009	+·011
May ...	—·048	—·049	November..	+·065	+·062
June ...	—·098	—·096	December..	+·089	+·089

Chapter I.

Description.

Climate.

Pressure.

In the following table are shown for Belgaum, for each month and for the whole year, the excesses of the mean barometric pressure at the several hours of the day above the mean barometric pressure for the twenty-four hours :

Belgaum City Hourly Barometric Pressure, 1856-74.

Month.	Local Civil Hours.							
	6	7	8	9	10	11	12	13
January	+·012	+·028	+·050	+·066	+·065	+·046	+·022	—·010
February	+·005	+·025	+·046	+·061	+·058	+·045	+·023	—·005
March	·000	+·022	+·045	+·059	+·059	+·048	+·027	—·001
April	+·012	—·027	+·046	+·056	+·055	+·045	+·028	—·001
May	+·014	+·028	+·043	+·055	+·055	+·035	+·017	—·002
June	—·006	+·006	+·020	+·030	+·026	+·020	+·011	—·000
July	—·008	+·002	+·016	+·024	+·030	+·024	+·016	+·001
August	—·004	+·009	+·026	+·038	+·038	+·030	+·016	+·001
September	—·007	+·012	+·032	+·042	+·087	+·026	+·010	—·015
October	+·004	+·021	+·040	+·050	+·048	+·032	+·009	—·016
November	+·011	+·029	+·019	+·065	+·064	+·042	+·014	—·015
December	+·002	+·020	+·041	+·053	+·056	+·040	+·017	—·013
Year	+·003	+·019	+·038	+·050	+·049	+·036	+·017	—·007
June to August ...	—·006	+·006	+·021	+·031	+·031	+·025	+·014	+·001

Month.	Local Civil Hours.							
	14	15	16	17	18	19	20	21
January	—·033	—·049	—·051	—·044	—·033	—·016	·000	+·010
February	—·031	—·046	—·052	—·045	—·033	—·016	+·001	+·016
March	—·025	—·046	—·055	—·048	—·035	—·017	—·002	+·014
April	—·030	—·049	—·056	—·049	—·032	—·017	—·007	+·009
May	—·024	—·041	—·051	—·047	—·033	—·019	—·008	+·007
June	—·011	—·023	—·029	—·028	—·017	—·005	+·007	+·013
July	—·010	—·019	—·028	—·027	—·020	—·009	+·004	+·014
August	—·015	—·027	—·037	—·031	—·022	—·008	+·006	+·020
September	—·033	—·047	—·049	—·039	—·029	—·013	+·005	+·021
October	—·038	—·049	—·048	—·036	—·020	—·004	+·011	+·020
November	—·039	—·051	—·054	—·044	—·032	—·014	+·005	+·017
December	—·036	—·046	—·049	—·039	—·029	—·014	+·002	+·014
Year	—·027	—·041	—·047	—·040	—·028	—·013	+·002	+·014
June to August ...	—·012	—·023	—·031	—·029	—·020	—·007	+·006	+·016

Month.	Local Civil Hours.								
	22	23	0	1	2	3	4	5	Complete Days.
January ...	+·013	+·008	—·002	—·008	—·017	—·025	—·025	—·014	16
February ...	+·018	+·014	+·003	—·009	—·016	—·023	—·022	—·011	17
March ...	+·020	+·014	+·005	—·008	—·016	—·022	—·023	—·015	17
April ...	+·016	+·015	+·002	—·008	—·017	—·019	—·015	—·004	17
May ...	+·013	+·016	+·009	—·004	—·014	—·020	—·018	—·006	17
June ...	+·020	+·021	+·012	+·001	—·007	—·016	—·021	—·022	17
July ...	+·019	+·017	+·011	—·001	—·009	—·017	—·019	—·013	17
August ...	+·026	+·020	+·006	—·006	—·016	—·025	—·026	—·021	16
September ...	+·029	+·022	+·014	+·005	—·004	—·008	—·011	·000	16
October ...	+·024	+·015	+·006	—·006	—·013	—·021	—·024	—·015	16
November ...	+·023	+·015	+·005	—·004	—·015	—·022	—·024	—·015	13
December ...	+·019	+·011	+·008	—·001	—·010	—·016	—·016	—·005	13
Year	+·020	+·015	+·006	—·004	—·013	—·020	—·021	—·012	
June to August.	+·022	+·019	+·010	—·002	—·011	—·019	—·022	—·019	

The following table shows for each month of the year the greatest and least values of the barometric pressures observed at 9-30 A.M. and at 3-30 P.M. :

Chapter I.
Description.
Climate.

Belgaum City Monthly Range of Barometric Pressure, 1856-1874.

Month.	Maximum.	Minimum.	Range.	Month.	Maximum.	Minimum.	Range.
January ...	27·624	27·192	·432	July ...	27·411	27·078	·333
February...	27·602	27·200	·402	August ...	27·426	27·104	·822
March ...	27·534	27·185	·349	September..	27·470	27·085	·385
April ...	27·538	27·111	·427	October ...	27·518	27·085	·433
May ...	27·466	27·082	·384	November .	27·599	27·196	·403
June ...	27·403	27·043	·360	December ..	27·650	27·202	·448

Vapour.

The values of the pressure of vapour made use of have been calculated by Glaisher's Hygrometrical Tables from the observed temperatures of the dry and wet bulb thermometers. The annual variations give high values of the vapour pressure in the hot and wet months, that is from May to September, and low values in the cold months. The month of maximum pressure is June. The mean daily variation for the year shows a minimum towards the end of the night hours with a fairly regular progress during the intervals. The variation during the wet months has high values during the day and low values during the night. The daily range of the wet months is very small compared with the daily range of the cold months, and the low range continues till late in the year with the late continuance of the rains.

The following table shows for the nineteen years ending 1874 the mean pressure of vapour from observations taken at 9-30 A.M. and at 3-30 P.M.

Belgaum City Pressure of Vapour, 1856-1874.

Year.	Mean.	Excess.	Year.	Mean.	Excess.
	In.	In.		In.	In.
1856 ...	·634	+·044	1866 ...	·571	—·019
1857 ...	·580	—·010	1867 ...	·643	+·053
1858 ...	·615	+·025	1868 ...	·602	+·012
1859 ...	·571	—·019	1869 ...	·586	—·004
1860 ..	·560	—·030	1870 ...	·594	+·004
1861 ...	·551	—·039	1871 ...	·599	+·009
1862 ...	·585	—·005	1872 ...	·619	+·029
1863 ...	...	...	1873 ...	·608	+·018
1864 ...	·547	—·243	1874 ...	·599	+·009
1865 ...	·595	+·005			

Clouds.

The cloudiness of the sky is estimated in lengths of the celestial hemisphere, the unit being one-tenth of the whole sky. Cloudiness is great during the wet months, and small during the cold months. The following table shows the average cloudiness of the sky in each month of the year from observations taken at 9-30 A.M. and 3-30 P.M., during the same series of nineteen years :

Belgaum City Cloudiness, 1856-1874.

Month.	Tenths.	Month.	Tenths.
January	2·7	July	8·6
February	2·3	August	8·4
March	3·1	September	7·6
April	4·1	October	6·0
May	5·2	November	4·0
June	8·2	December	3·0
		May to October	7·3
		November to April	3·2
		Year	5·3

Chapter I.
Description.
Climate.
Winds.

From March to September the prevailing winds are from the west and south, and from October to February from the east and north. The easterly element continues to some extent until April or May, and does not cease until the south-west rains begin. On the other hand, the westerly element is present all the year round, beginning at about two or three in the afternoon and continuing until eight the following morning. Thus during the fair and during the hot months, that is from November till May, while the sun is above the horizon, the wind blows from inland, and towards the interior when the sun is below the horizon. This shows that the prevailing Belgaum winds are essentially different from the coast winds, where in the fair season the land wind blows at night and the sea breeze during the day. The winds of May and October are intermediate between those of the south-west monsoon and those of the dry weather. The observations of the direction of wind taken at Belgaum at 9-30 A.M. and 3-30 P.M. have been grouped together in months. Each group includes the observations of the nineteen years ending 1874 for each month. The following are the results:

Belgaum Winds, 1856-1874.

Direction.	At 9-30 A.M.											
	Jan.	Feb.	Mar.	April.	May.	June.	July.	Aug.	Sept.	Oct.	Nov.	Dec.
N. ...	13	33	50	54	29	4	...	4	7	46	16	11
N.N.E. ...	...	...	2	6	...	1	...	...	...	1	...	...
N.E.N. ...	68	79	106	92	28	6	1	7	7	62	109	66
E.N.E. ...	4	12	8	11	2	...	...	1	1	9	2	2
E. ...	162	103	78	53	11	3	1	2	5	114	232	232
E.S.E. ...	15	15	4	6	...	1	...	1	...	12	24	16
S.E. ...	135	82	42	24	6	5	...	...	1	34	57	111
S.S.E. ...	10	3	4	2	...	...	...	...	...	3	5	7
S. ...	29	25	20	20	12	8	...	2	8	35	12	6
S.S.W. ...	1	...	...	1	...	10	5	1	...	...	...	...
S.W. ...	29	31	50	65	64	156	191	109	78	29	8	10
W.S.W. ...	...	...	1	...	4	19	40	57	23	2	1	...
W. ...	23	52	84	81	265	269	238	316	305	101	8	8
W.N.W. ...	...	2	2	4	12	6	12	8	17	1	...	...
N.W. ...	...	15	28	33	55	11	...	8	27	17	3	3
N.N.W. ...	...	1	1	3	8	...	...	...	2	...	...	...
Calm ...	38	26	47	55	31	9	6	11	34	59	33	24
Sums ...	527	479	527	510	527	508	494	527	510	525	510	496

Direction.	At 3-30 P.M.											
	Jan.	Feb.	Mar.	April.	May.	June.	July.	Aug.	Sept.	Oct.	Nov.	Dec.
N. ...	9	12	16	13	7	...	...	...	3	28	21	7
N.N.E. ...	...	2	1	...	...	...	...	...	...	...	1	..
N.E. ...	60	79	40	37	4	1	1	...	5	68	110	100
E.N.E. ...	4·5	8	2	3	...	...	...	...	1	2	2	...
E. ...	173·5	104	80	32	6	1	...	3	2	113	283	243
E.S.E. ...	11	4	1	2	...	...	...	...	...	6	13	11
S.E. ...	87	50	30	18	4	...	1	...	4	23	23	53
S.S.E. ...	8	4	1	1	...	...	...	1	...	1	2	2
S. ...	26	23	17	16	7	5	1	..	2	43	18	9
S.S.W. ...	2	...	...	...	1	7	8	6	1	...	1	...
S.W. ...	53	76	123	185	114	167	191	106	83	55	7	23
W.S.W. ...	1	1	3	7	15	29	45	44·5	23	8	...	3
W. ...	34	84	167	212	333	268	237	356·5	350	117	14	5
W.N.W. ...	...	1	1	2	10	5	2	1	7	2	...	...
N.W. ...	4	10	25	11	22	4	1	4	8	14	5	2
N.N.W. ...	...	...	...	2	...	...	...	...	...	...	...	...
Calm ...	59	21	30	19	4	4	8	5	20	45	49	38
Sums ...	527	479	527	510	527	491	495	527	510	525	509	496

Chapter I.
Description.
Climate.
Winds.

The coefficients and angles of formula representing the daily variation in the duration of different winds are:

BELGAUM CITY DURATION OF WINDS, 1856-1874.

Hours.	November to January.				February to April.				June to September.				Total.			
	c1	c1 (° ′)	c2	c2 (° ′)	c1	c1 (° ′)	c2	c2 (° ′)	c1	c1 (° ′)	c2	c2 (° ′)	c1	c1 (° ′)	c2	c2 (° ′)
6 ...	1·11	78 35	1·17	164 11	·49	291 22	·68	161 2	1·87	253 53	1·52	149 33	·53	254 39	1·14	157 16
7 ...	1·13	81 52	1·21	168 2	·41	278 20	·73	172 53	1·87	253 13	1·51	148 0	·56	248 0	1·14	162 41
8 ...	1·06	80 48	1·08	162 44	·22	333 26	·89	146 29	1·86	254 41	1·48	150 50	·47	251 34	1·13	154 48
9 ...	1·39	92 53	0·96	182 59	·22	65 46	·72	146 19	1·86	253 25	1·48	150 30	·35	229 34	·97	161 56
10 ...	1·55	98 55	0·80	198 53	·27	70 12	·82	165 7	1·87	255 9	1·53	152 12	·35	226 10	1·00	166 40
11 ...	1·58	95 18	0·87	203 38	·51	79 48	·59	194 45	1·86	256 56	1·50	155 9	·25	216 52	·89	174 14
12 ...	1·68	92 23	1·05	186 2	·57	87 59	·73	175 18	1·86	258 25	1·46	148 10	·25	198 26	·97	168 49
13 ...	1·72	90 20	1·17	186 53	·73	67 19	·35	154 53	1·83	251 52	1·41	145 24	·19	188 58	·90	159 9
14 ...	1·65	97 18	1·08	185 52	·52	76 46	·95	146 39	1·75	252 42	1·33	145 43	·26	204 37	1·07	156 48
15 ...	1·48	98 11	1·01	184 82	·07	146 19	1·20	155 22	1·81	250 58	1·35	145 15	·43	224 4	1·13	165 56
16 ...	1·39	96 12	1·23	186 5	·37	239 18	1·17	153 39	1·85	251 4	1·47	145 14	·51	231 20	1·22	155 19
17 ...	1·27	92 15	1·27	188 36	·47	252 43	1·18	154 18	1·87	255 27	1·54	154 36	·58	246 32	1·26	162 0
18 ...	·85	104 22	1·08	184 14	·75	263 4	1·44	158 25	1·88	255 13	1·54	152 36	·76	248 29	1·31	160 19
19 ...	·60	107 32	1·06	166 21	1·36	264 5	1·58	173 49	1·90	255 58	1·59	153 55	1·00	258 44	1·38	162 18
20 ...	·39	94 24	1·12	164 29	1·39	265 2	1·61	173 85	1·88	253 36	1·53	148 54	1·04	255 2	1·38	160 54
21 ...	·47	106 7	1·10	175 19	1·27	257 43	1·51	164 39	1·88	255 49	1·56	154 6	1·02	252 17	1·36	161 34
22 ...	·42	98 8	1·20	170 23	1·26	263 9	1·38	171 13	1·87	256 42	1·54	156 36	1·02	256 22	1·37	163 25
23 ...	·48	79 9	1·15	155 26	1·17	261 58	1·46	172 9	1·87	254 29	1·52	151 45	·96	255 32	1·34	159 57
0 ...	·46	98 51	1·24	157 10	1·24	259 19	1·18	165 44	1·89	256 51	1·58	156 11	·99	255 58	1·34	160 21
1 ...	·53	70 12	1·20	161 34	1·38	261 42	1·27	172 46	1·89	256 33	1·59	154 43	1·03	258 48	1·35	161 26
2 ...	·57	62 50	1·04	155 39	1·26	272 16	1·31	180 0	1·89	257 8	1·59	156 40	·98	261 13	1·27	161 42
3 ...	·61	64 32	1·07	151 31	1·23	275 37	1·07	179 27	1·89	255 36	1·58	158 16	·95	263 19	1·19	159 54
4 ...	·68	65 42	1·14	150 30	1·06	288 7	1·16	188 24	1·88	254 56	1·57	151 48	·86	223 42	1·22	160 23
5 ...	·72	67 1	·99	151 7	·82	282 41	1·23	175 49	1·88	255 49	1·54	153 46	·80	263 30	1·25	159 49
Means ...	·97	90 0	1·06	172 52	·54	270 0	1·07	167 32	1·87	254 46	1·51	151 34	·65	250 10	1·19	160 48
Complete Days.	42				47				68				188			

CHAPTER II.

PRODUCTION.

Chapter II.

Production.

Minerals.

Diamonds.

In the latter part of the sixteenth century (1585), two English travellers Fitch and Newberry mentioned Belgaum as a great diamond market.[1] The Belgaum diamonds probably came from the Golkondah and other mines in the Nizám's territories. Still, it is worthy of note that part of the sandstone towards the Kolhápur side of the district is the same old diamond sandstone which is found at Kadapah in Madras and at other diamond fields.[2]

Gold.

The geological conditions necessary for the development of gold are present in much of the Belgaum rock. In 1852, an examination showed that gold occurs in much of the coarse-grained gravel or local drift, so abundant on the sides of hills in many parts of the district. Gold was also found in the valley of the Malprabha near Chikop, about twenty-five miles east of Belgaum. The first basin of Chikop gravel yielded two minute grains of fine gold with much worn corners. After the gravel was washed, there remained a black iron sand with yellow grains of gold standing out clearly from the dark ground. The result of this and of other trials was to show that every basin of gravel contained one or two minute grains or scales of gold. Under black soil, on the left bank of the right branch of the stream, which passes by the village of Markumbi two miles west of Chikop, was gravel and marl, and below the marl was conglomerate limestone resting on disturbed and hardened chlorite slate. The gravel in the bed of the stream contained gold. And gold was also found at Belevádi on the south side of the Malprabha, where the stream flows in a hollow between two parallel ridges of metamorphic rock. In the whole gold-yielding area very few quartz veins occur, and none are found with a north and south course.

In this part of the country were professional gold-washers, some of them settled and others wanderers. The settled gold-washers used a trough about four feet long nine inches high and one foot broad. In washing the gravel this trough was propped on sloping stones on the bank of the stream. One man threw in a basketful of gravel and another stirred the gravel with his hand and poured on water.[3] The larger gravel was thrown out and the sand was again washed in a round shallow dish about eighteen inches across and four inches deep. The gold dust was amalgamated with mercury and the mercury sublimed on charcoal.[4] The greatest proportion of gold, though the amount was small, was found in a small stream to the west of Belevádi.

Iron.

Iron,[5] nearly equal to Swedish iron, was formerly made

---

[1] Hakluyt's Voyages, II. 385.
[2] Bom. Gov. Sel. VIII. 6.
[3] Trans. Bom. Geo. Soc. XI. 2-6.
[4] Mem. Geo. Surv. XII. 259.
[5] This and the remaining mineral sections are from materials supplied by Mr. G. V. Gáyatonde, Assistant Engineer.

Chapter II.

Production.

Minerals.

Iron.

near Kánur, Punare, and Pátne in Belgaum; at Kaitnal and Távaj in Gokák; at Kitur in Sampgaon; and near the Rám pass.[1] The ore is generally peroxide of iron with a mixture of clay, quartz, and lime. All the laterite of the district is charged with iron though in too small a proportion to make it worth smelting. In smelting iron the practice was to gather small nodules with iron ore and crush them to powder with iron hammers. The powdered ore was then mixed with charcoal and put into a round upright furnace which was kept at an intense heat by air blown continuously by hand-bellows. No flux was used as the ore contained all that was wanted. As it smelted, the liquid metal flowed into a round hole at the bottom of the furnace. When all the metal had run into the hole the mass of iron was dragged out by a pair of large pincers, placed on an anvil, and beaten by hammers. The metal contained a great deal of foreign matter which was removed by heating it in a common smith's furnace, and, while red hot, by beating it with quick blows of five or six heavy hammers worked by men grouped round the anvil. The hammering was continued till the metal was considered pure. This iron was of first class quality. The chief difficulty in the way of iron-smelting was the large quantity of charcoal it consumed. Brown hæmatite, which forms the matrix in a hornstone-breccia at Basargi, is smelted at Tegihál, both the villages lying on the left bank of the Malprabha, between Manoli and Torgal. The manufacture of iron has now ceased, partly on account of the increased price of fuel and partly because of the fall in the price of iron. Besides iron the only metallic ore which occurs in any quantity is an earthy powdery form of binoxide of manganese which is found among weathered dolomite at Bhimgad.[2]

Stones.

There are stone quarries at Pátne, Halkarni, Chándgad, Dukurvádi, and Dolgarvádi in Belgaum; at Chikodi and Nipáni in Chikodi; and at Kágvád, Ainápur, Shedbál, Kakmari, and Athni in Athni.[3] The stones are green basalt or trap, gneiss, quartzose sandstone, gray sandstone, reddish gray sandstone, and laterite. Green basalt or trap is found in most parts of the district in hills, in boulders, and in river-beds. With some exceptions it is hard and lasting. It has been used in several bridges and large buildings. The fort of Belgaum is partly of this stone brought from a village named Kanbargi, three miles north-east of Belgaum, and partly of sandstone from hills nine or ten miles to the north. The stone has worn well as the fort is now 400 years old and the masonry is still fresh.

Gneiss is found in the Khánápur sub-division. It is used for rough work and for road-metal, but on account of its hardness it is not

---

[1] In 1822, at Nersa, about six miles west of Khánápur, iron was worked by a wandering tribe who came yearly in the fair season from Goa or the Sávantvádi state. Mr. Marshall found common clayey ironstone exposed in abundance about the hills, but it did not yield much metal. The villagers were wholly unacquainted with the nature of the process by which the metal had been extracted. Marshall's Statistical Reports, 98. [2] Memoirs Geological Survey, XII. 250, 263.

[3] The forts of Kálánadigad, Vallabhgad, Páijargudd, and the temple at Chándgad Kankumbi are built of laterite or iron clay, which, except as road-metal, is now little used. Memoirs Geological Survey, XII. 268.

Chapter II. Production.

Minerals.

Stones.

generally used in cut-stone work. Quartzose sandstone is found near Sutgati in the valley of the Ghatprabha at Gokák and at Saundatti. It is gray in colour, very hard, gritty, porous, and lasting, and is used where great strength is required as in the arch stones of bridges. At Gokák and Saundatti it is made into millstones from one to three feet in diameter. Gray and reddish-gray sandstone is found in Parasgad. Thongh very soft and absorbent, it may be used in inferior kinds of work instead of brick. The hones that used to be quarried in a bed of very hard clay schist at Kákti north of Belgaum are not now in demand. Laterite of varying quality is found in the west near the Sahyádri range. Near Belgaum is a claystone enriched with iron in the form of red and yellow ochres, with a perforated and cellular structure. The heavier claystone with more iron is generally harder and more lasting than the claystone with less iron. Near where it occurs this stone has been used for many buildings and a few bridges. The cost of laterite bricks varies from 10*s.* to 12*s.* (Rs.5 - 6) the hundred cubic feet. It is quarried in rectangular blocks. Magnesian limestones or dolomites occur in the gneissic series on the slopes of the Sahyádris east of Goa. The beds exposed in Bhimgad hill are unfit for polishing, as numerous thin folia of granular quartz permeate the rock.

In making and repairing roads three kinds of metal are used, trap, quartzose sandstone, and laterite. The price of trap and quartzose sandstone varies from 10*s.* to 11*s.* (Rs. 5 - 5½), and of laterite from 3*s.* to 6*s.* (Rs.1½ - 3) the hundred cubic feet. For fair weather and cross country roads hard red gravel is used which costs about 2*s.* (Re.1) the hundred cubic feet. Good sand or gravel is found in the beds of most streams and rivers. The rates vary from 3*s.* to 8*s.* (Rs.1½ - 4) the hundred cubic feet. The metallic sand which is used instead of blotting paper is found in several rivers at places where they pass through black soil. The best is the Krishna sand. A very good white clay for earthenware, which burns gray and hard, is found near Khánápur.

Lime.

The lime in general use is made from calcined nodules or *kankar* of limestone which are found on the surface in detached patches throughout the district, and at some places in quarries. The lime nodules contain a mixture of sand and clay, and so do not want much sand or *surki*, to make good hydraulic mortar. Calcined lime costs £3 16*s.* to £4 (Rs.38 - 40) the hundred cubic feet. At Yádvád in Gokák a bed of bluish-gray limestone is quarried for lime. These stones, when calcined, yield lime which is too pure or fat but makes good mortar when freely mixed with sand. This is the best lime for whitewashing. Crystalline limestone is also found in south Khánápur.

Bricks and Tiles.

Good brick-earth is found in several places, the best at Kákti, Yamkanmardi, Sankeshvar, and Nipáni in Chikodi. Burnt bricks measuring 10″ × 4″ × 3″ cost 17*s.* 9*d.* (Rs.8⅞) the thousand; half round tiles 16″ × 6″ cost £1 1*s.* 6*d.* (Rs.10¾) the thousand; and ridge tiles cost 6*s.* (Rs.3) the hundred.

Forests.

In 1863 Dr. Gibson described the forest towards the Sahyádris as all inferior or jungle timber, but much of it of superior quality. In the thirteen previous years the forest had suffered greatly by fires and from other causes. Teak and blackwood forest began about six miles east of the Sahyádris and stretched through Ghotgali and Kakkeri. The teak had formerly stretched to Dhárwár. Deep woody valleys under the hill of Sidh on the North Kánara border, about five miles south of Ghatgalli, had suffered much from the spread of tillage. Of young growing teak there was still a respectable quantity in the west of the forest abutting on Sidh hill. Further east the trees, though numerous, were stunted and would probably never yield more than rafters and small posts. One kind of timber, which was of great account for building and occurred both on Sidh hill and in the neighbouring forests, was the *hasan* or *hone* Pterocarpus marsupium, a beautiful tree of easy growth. The only forest to the north of Belgaum was in Páchápur. It contained *ain* Terminalia glabra, satin wood or *halda* Chloroxylon swietenia, *nirmali* Strychnos potatorum, and other trees too stunted to be of use except for firewood and tent pegs. A *bábhul* preserve was also set apart in Athni.[1]

Besides[2] a few square miles of private forest the present (1883) area of Government forest is 819 square miles. Of these 688 square miles, chiefly in Khánápur, have, under the Forest Act VII. of 1878, been declared reserved, and 131 square miles protected.[3] The forest is very unevenly distributed, the large sub-divisions of Athni and Parasgad having till lately little or no forest, while Khánápur has twice as much forest as tillage.

The Belgaum forests[4] may be roughly divided into moist and dry, the dry lying east of the Poona-Dhárwár road and including the forests of Chikodi, Sampgaon, and Gokák; and the moist lying west of the Poona-Dhárwár road, including the forests of Belgaum and Khánápur. The Poona-Dhárwár road runs nearly north and south, skirting the Sahyádri range and its outliers from Nipáni to Belgaum, and then bending slightly east into the more level country. In the moist forest the rainfall is heavy, varying from fifty inches to an unknown quantity, probably not less than 200 inches. About one-half of the moist area belongs to the Sahyádris, a mass of laterite-covered mountains, cut by deep densely wooded ravines and open to the full force of the south-west monsoon. Except an occasional patch of rice or *rági* the forest is unbroken. Here the population is scanty and the area fit for plough cultivation

[1] Handbook to the Forests of the Bombay Presidency, 74.

[2] The sections on Forests, Animals, and Birds are from materials supplied by Mr. J. L. Laird-Macgregor, District Forest Officer.

[3] The sub-divisional forest details are :

Belgaum Forests, 1883.

Sub-Division.	Square Miles.		Sub-Division.	Square Miles.	
	Reserved.	Protected.		Reserved.	Protected.
Belgaum ...	150	62	Chikodi ...	36	18
Khánápur ...	308	...	Athni ...	2	...
Gokák ...	101	51	Parasgad ...	65	...
Sámpgaon ...	26	...			
				688	131

[4] Mr. W. H. Horsley, C.S.

Chapter II.
Production.
Forests.

is small. In those villages which lie actually along the crest of the Sahyádris these conditions are most marked. The area culturable with the plough is insufficient even for the small population, and from time immemorial they have chiefly lived on the proceeds of what is known as *kumri* or wood-ash tillage. The steep slopes of the Sahyádris are suitable for this form of cultivation. The dense coppice growing on such slopes is cut down, allowed to dry, and then burnt. The ashes are hoed into the soil and *náchni* or *rági* Eleusine coracana is sown. If the patch chosen has had its due period of fallow, a very abundant crop results. During the second season a crop of *sáva* Panicum miliare is grown on the same ground. The field is then relinquished and requires a long period of fallow. If left alone for about twenty years it will be found to be again densely covered with coppice. In fact the practice of *kumri* under proper conditions is eminently favourable to the growth of dense coppice. At the introduction of the revenue survey nearly thirty years ago an attempt was made to put a stop to *kumri* under the impression that it must result in denudation. The consequent distress became so marked that in 1875 further allotments were granted in Khánápur and in 1879 similar arrangements were made in Belgaum. These arrangements were inadequate as they did not allow a sufficiently long period of fallow. It has lately been suggested by the Conservator of Forests, Southern Division, that *kumri* allotments should be granted on condition that the people plant with useful trees an area equal to one-third of the area held for *kumri* cultivation. This suggestion has been approved by Government and arrangements are in progress for carrying it out.

The commonest trees are the *jámbul* Eugenia jambolana, *kumba* Careya arborea, *máti* Terminalia tomentosa, *harda* T. chebula, *hela* T. bellerica, *páiri* Ficus cordifolia, *kel* Ficus infectoria, *umar* F. glomerata, *kindali* Terminalia paniculata, *báva* Cassia fistula, *karanj* Pongamia glabra, *anjan* Memecylon edule, *nána* Lagerstræmia lanceolata, *ávla* Phyllanthus emblica, small bamboo, and *kárvi* Strobilanthus grahamianus. There is a sprinkling of *jámba* Xylia dolabriformis, *sisva* Dalbergia latifolia, *shemba* Acacia concinna, and other acacias, *hasan* Pterocarpus marsupium, *ápta* Bauhinia racemosa, *palas* Butea frondosa, and *pángera* Erythrina indica, but no teak. Of these trees *máti, jámbul, nána, harda, sisva,* and *hasan* are valuable timber trees; *kárvi* and small bamboos are useful only for fencing and roofing; and *kumba* is chiefly used for field tools. *Anjan,* a useful wood, is confined to very moist places on the crest-line of the Sahyádris where it forms unmixed woods of considerable extent. Here and there, dense *ráis* or groves of huge evergreen tree, sometimes covering more than a hundred acres, stand out like dark islands in the grey sea of withered grass and leafless coppice. The commonest trees in these evergreen hill groves are soft woods, *nánás,* jacks, and mangoes with a sprinkling of *mári* palms Phœnix sylvestris, whose sap is drawn for liquor, and of cinnamon trees whose bark is used as a spice. Along the Sahyádris there is comparatively little large timber, though large *mátis, nánás,* and other valuable trees are by no means uncommon in ravines and remote places.

Chapter II.
Production.
Forests.

Of minor produce, the *harda* and *hela* furnish myrobalans, the *shemba* supplies the *ritha* or soapnut which is used in cleaning clothes, and the large stretches of bare or thinly wooded slopes furnish grazing for thousands of cattle, which flock to them every year from the grassless eastern plains. As already remarked this western tract is badly wooded. Probably not more than one-twelfth of the whole forest area is stocked with trees. But the moist climate and heavy rainfall cause a free growth wherever there is soil enough for plants to take root. There is little doubt that, when fully guarded from fire, the forest will gradually spread upwards from the lower slopes and watercourses and clothe much that is now bare and useless.

The eastern parts of the moist forest, though not cut off by any natural line of demarcation from the more western parts, may, for convenience, be considered separately. The country is less hilly and is partially sheltered from the south-west monsoon by the crests of the main range of the Sahyádris. The rainfall varies roughly from forty-five to sixty inches, enough to ensure vigorous vegetation. Besides the trees mentioned in the purely Sahyádri forest the timber includes *dhámin* Grewia asiatica, *honangi* Adina cordifolia, *kalam* Stephegyne parvifolia, *siris* Albizzia spp., teak, and large bamboos. The commonest trees are *kumba, jámba, harda,* the dwarf date-palm Phœnix farinifera, *palas, ávla, jámbul,* bamboo, *kindali, máti, nána,* and in the south a good sprinkling of teak and blackwood. The produce is chiefly superior firewood poles from fifteen to thirty feet long, with here and there large standards of *sávari* Bombax malabaricum, *hela, pángera, karambál,* and other soft woods, and less often of *máti, kindali, jámbul,* and other hard woods. The forest increases in heaviness towards the south where are some fifty square miles of good timber, including much clean straight-stemmed teak, *máti,* and blackwood. These tracts are much better wooded than the main range. Probably one-fourth of the forest area is stocked. Teak occurs only in the south and is commonest on the granite hills south of Nandgad. It is generally mixed with *jámba* and bamboo. But between Távarkatti and Bidi there is much pure teak of vigorous growth.

The forests of the dry tract east of the Poona-Dhárwár road are on the trap and sandstone hills of Chikodi, Gokák, and Sampgaon. They stretch east as far as the town of Gokák, north to Hukeri, south to Deshnur, and west to the moist forest. These dry forests are about the same height (2000 feet above the sea) as the moist forests, but being further inland, the rainfall is much less, probably on an average not more than thirty inches. Cultivation is confined to the valleys and some of the flat-topped trap-hills. The forest-land, about one-eighth of which is stocked with useful wood, is very poor and stony, yielding only firewood scrub with a sprinkling of small poles, fit for hut-building, and of an average height of about ten feet. The produce is chiefly cactus, four or five kinds of fig, *dindal* Anogeissus latifolia, *mashvál* Chloroxylon swietenia, *bandurgi, ávla, gorvi* Ixora parvifolia, *tarvár* Cassia auriculata, *máti* Terminalia tomentosa, *kindali, as* Hardwickia binata, sandal, bamboo, and numberless thorns. Near Nipáni and Degaon there is a little outlying

Chapter II.
Production.
Forests.

forest-land, and near Suldhál and Yamkanmardi teak-scrub also occurs. *Dindal* is perhaps the commonest tree and is useful for firewood but is generally too small for building purposes. *Tarvár* bark is much prized for tanning and *gorvi* bark for making torches. There is also a good deal of small and a little large bamboo. The most widespread shrub is the cactus. Fully half the forest area is covered with cactus. It is rapidly creeping from the cultivated valleys to the tops of the hills, threatening, as has already happened in Mamdápur and other parts of Gokák, to choke all other vegetation. The rapid spread of the cactus appears to be mainly owing to two kinds of thrush, Malacocercus griseus and Argya malcolmi, which live on the fruit and scatter the seeds far and wide. In this part of the Belgaum reserves, the putting down of cactus is the problem of the future. Its eradication is not easy. No ill-treatment short of burning both roots and branches kills it. An attempt is being made to dig it up and burn it, but the result is still doubtful.

The forests of the main Sahyádri range are not at present worked. Most of their valuable firewood and small timber could easily be worked and is sure to improve. Acre for acre, their present value cannot be less than that of the forest tract east of the Poona road, for, though not nearly so regularly stocked, the vigour and quality of the timber make them a far more valuable property. Experiments seem to show that, exclusive of the value of the land, the present net value of the dry forest is not less than £123,634 (Rs. 12,36,340) or £1 4*s.* (Rs. 12) an acre, and that the yearly yield of firewood available without trenching on the capital stock, is about 46,000 cartloads, or 1,150,000 cubic feet, a quantity which more than meets the present firewood demand for the whole district.[1] The eastern part of the Sahyádri forest tract is roughly

[1] This estimate is based on the results of clean cuttings on 439 acres of the Biranholi forest. The details are :

Biranholi Forest Cuttings.

RECEIPTS.

Poles.		Bamboos.		Firewood.				Acre Yield.								Money Yield.	
				Stems.		Branches.		Poles.		Bamboos.		Firewood.					
												Stems.		Branches.			
Number.	Value.	Number.	Value.	Number.	Value.	Number.	Value.	Number.	Value.	Number.	Value.	Number.	Value.	Number.	Value.	Total.	Acre.
5034	Rs. 926	36,850	Rs. 490	Carts. 7046	Rs. 10,569	Carts 909	Rs. 909	11	Rs. 2·1	84	Rs. 1·1	Carts. 16	Rs. 24	Carts. 2	Rs. 2	Rs. 12,894	Rs. 29·2

EXPENDITURE.

Cutting and stacking 5034 poles at Re. 1 the hundred	50
Ditto ditto 36,850 bamboos at 4 *annas* the hundred	92
Ditto ditto 7046 cartloads of (stem) firewood at 4 *annas* each	1762
Establishment: two guards at Rs. 7 each, one clerk at Rs. 12 a month, for twelve months	312
Total £221 12*s*. or Rs.	2216

That is, total receipts of Rs. 12,894 minus Rs. 2216, or Rs. 10,678, and acre receipts of Rs. 29 less Rs. 5 that is Rs. 24. The Biranholi forest is somewhat above the average of the dry forest, but if the average is taken at one-half the above yield, the error is not likely to lie on the side of exaggeration. On the

Chapter II.

Production.

Forests.

estimated as equal to the western Sahyádri forests, or 150,000 acres that is about 234 square miles. It supplies the Khánápur store with timber, of which the following statement gives the details for the two years ending 1880:

Sahyádri Timber Sales, 1878-1880.

Timber.	No.	Cubic Feet.	Realized.	Cost.	Net.	The cubic foot.
			£	£	£	s. d.
Teak Logs	1074	26,350	3625	1102	2523	1 10
Blackwood Logs	106	2875	352	121	231	1 7
Miscellaneous Logs ...	303	8712	773	364	409	1 0
Teak Pieces	413	3312	337	56	281	1 8
Blackwood Pieces ...	27	250	18	4	14	1 1
Miscellaneous Pieces ...	56	625	35	10	25	0 9
Teak Poles (superior) ...	11,689	42,862	2103	508	1595	0 9
Do. (inferior) ...	1363	...	71	28	43	0 7
Blackwood Poles... ...	28	162	4	2	2	0 4
Miscellaneous Poles ...	153	550	20	6	14	0 6
Sandal	9	12½	2	$\frac{1}{16}$	1$\frac{9}{16}$	3 0
Total ...	...	85,710½	7840	2201$\frac{1}{16}$	5138$\frac{9}{16}$	...
Yearly Average ...	...	42,855	3670	1101	2569	...

The immediate supply of large timber is nearly exhausted, but fifty or sixty years hence there ought to be no difficulty in securing a constant yield fully equal to the above, as length is more sought than girth and as there is a good stock of young growth. In 1882-83, 115,908 bamboos worth £1222 (Rs. 12,220) were cut.

Firewood forests are worked partly on the toll-house or *náka* system, partly by departmental cuttings. *Nákás*, or forest toll-houses, for collecting fees levied on loads cut and gathered by the buyers, are posted at Nandgad, Gokák, Suldhál, Biranholi, Chinchani, Piranvádi, and Kanburgi. The foresters in charge of the three wood-stores also issue permits for collecting revenue in this way. In 1882-83 the receipts for wood so collected amounted to £2411 (Rs. 24,110). The fees are 1*s.* (8 *as.*) for each cartload drawn by two bullocks, 6*d.* (4 *as.*) for each beastload, 1⅛*d.* (¾ *anna*) for a man's, ¾*d.* (½ *anna*) for a woman's, and ⅜*d.* (¼ *anna*) for a child's headload.

Departmental cuttings were begun in 1879-80. The practice is to fell all trees within certain limits and to stack the wood in heaps 5′ × 4′ × 10′, equal when air-dried to about one cartload or twenty-five cubic feet solid measure. In the 1879-80 auction sales of 6000 stacks, the average stack rate was 3*s.* (Rs. 1½) and the net proceeds of all departmental cuttings came to £1030 (Rs. 10,300). In 1882-83, 17,813 stacks of firewood were sold for £1068 (Rs. 10,680) net. The system of departmental cuttings has so many advantages that it may

basis of half the Biranholi yield, or Rs. 12 an acre, the net value of the 103,028 acres of dry forest reserves in Sampgaon, Gokák, and Chikodi would amount to Rs. 12,36,336. This represents the estimated value of the crop as it now stands, with only about one-eighth of the ground stocked with useful wood; it will increase as the forest land becomes better stocked. Taking the cartload, or stack, of firewood at 25 cubic feet solid measure and the cartload of branches at twenty-three cubic feet, the average acre yield of stems would amount to 200 cubic feet and the yield of the whole forest area would be 20,605,600 cubic feet of stem wood and 2,369,644 cubic feet of branches. Coppice will renew itself in fifteen years or at twenty years at most. Taking the revolution, as it is called, at twenty years, the area yearly available for cutting would be 103,028 by twenty years, or 5153 acres, yielding 46,377 cartloads or 1,149,119 cubic feet of firewood, that is, at five per cent, or twenty years' purchase, a total value, excluding minor produce, of £139,132 (Rs. 13,91,320).

Chapter II. Production. Forests.

seem strange that the toll system should be continued.[1] The objection to stopping the tolls is that a number of people who live near the larger towns depend for their daily bread on gathering wood. It is hoped that by degrees they will find some other means of subsistence as the toll system is wasteful and incompatible with good forest management.

The chief minor produce is the myrobalan-nut or *harda,* which is sent in large quantities to Bombay. From Bombay the best find their way to Europe and the rest are kept for Indian use. Up to 1876-77 the right to gather myrobalans in each sub-division was every year publicly sold by the mámlatdárs to the highest bidders. In 1877-78 the Conservator of Forests, Colonel Peyton, determined to try departmental collection. The nuts were gathered at twenty-nine stores dotted over the myrobalan tracts, and sold to merchants.[2] The result was satisfactory; £4587 (Rs. 45,870) were netted, or more than half as much again as the previous season, though the returns for that year had been higher than those of any former season. The revenue has never again been so high as it was in 1877-78. Still the average for the three years since 1877-78 has been £3275 (Rs. 32,750) compared with an average of £1850 (Rs. 18,500) for the eight preceding years. In 1882-83 the net receipts amounted to £2718 (Rs. 27,180). The receipts vary greatly because both the market and the crop are uncertain, and the last two seasons have not been favourable. A full myrobalan crop is estimated at 1000 tons in Khánápur and at 375 tons in Belgaum.

Other minor products are honey, *fungi, tarvár* and other bark for tanning, corinda, *hela, ávla, ritha,* and other fruits, and grass. Of these grass alone brings in (1882) an appreciable net revenue of about £100 (Rs. 1000) a year. Up to 1881 grass was sold by the mámlatdárs at yearly auctions. In 1881-82 the management of the grazing was undertaken by the forest officers. The receipts for the first year came to over £1200 (Rs. 12,000). After deducting twenty-five per cent which are credited as land revenue, there remained nearly three times as much as the largest sum ever obtained under the old system. The increase would have been more than threefold if the number of cattle had not been greatly reduced by disease immediately before the new system came into practice. The rates charged for one year are: for every head of horned cattle 3*d.* (2 *as.*), and for each goat or sheep ¾*d.* (½ *anna*).

During the eighteen years ending 1882-83 forest receipts have risen from £3094 (Rs. 30,940) in 1865-66 to £14,215 (Rs. 1,42,150) in 1882-83, and the average has risen from £2667 in the five years

---

[1] The chief advantages are: It admits of organized management and the determination of the sustained yield of the different forest tracts. As the cuttings are confined to a small area, they can be easily watched, easily renewed, and easily guarded from fire and theft. And as the wood is air-dried before it is moved, it is more easily carried. Finally, as no work is carried on in it, the rest of the forest is safer from fire and theft.

[2] In Khánápur there are eleven stores, at Khánápur, Hemádgi, Shitavade, Gunji, Vátre, Shiroli, Ghotgáli, Chápoli, Jámboti, Kankumbi, and Kongle, the whole yielding on an average about 4000 *khandis* of 560 lbs. each; in Belgaum there are sixteen stores, Kátgali, Vághavade, Kinie, Báilur, Hajgoli, Mahálungi, Kitavade, Pátne, Kalasgade, Gulavde, Vághotre, Umgaon, Bhogoli, Chandgad, Sundi, and Chinchani, with a total average yield of about 1500 *khandis* of 560 lbs. each.

ending 1870 to £11,766 in the five years ending 1882. During the same period, from increase of staff and from the introduction of departmental cuttings and myrobalan gatherings, charges have risen from £966 (Rs. 9660) in 1866 to £4361 (Rs. 43,610) in 1882. Profits have risen from an average of £756 in the five years ending 1870 to an average of £6739 in the five years ending 1882. The following statement gives the details :

Belgaum Forest Finances, 1865-66 – 1882-83.

Year.	Receipts.	Charges.	Profit.	Year.	Receipts.	Charges.	Profit.
	£	£	£		£	£	£
1865-66 ...	3094	966	2128	1874-75 ...	7589	4837	2752
1866-67 ...	1079	1194	...	1875-76 ...	8169	4040	4129
1867-68 ...	2529	1164	1365	1876-77 ...	7976	3696	4280
1868-69 ...	4347	939	3408	1877-78 ...	9534	4667	4867
1869-70 ...	2288	408	1880	1878-79 ...	10,778	5739	5039
1870-71 ...	5132	1435	3697	1879-80 ...	11,579	4488	7091
1871-72 ...	6287	2236	4051	1880-81 ...	9537	3602	5935
1872-73 ...	8428	4759	3669	1881-82 ...	12,720	6945	5775
1873-74 ...	9295	2640	6655	1882-83 ...	14,215	4361	9854

These increased profits are due not to larger timber cuttings, for less timber is now cut than was formerly cut. The increase is due to better prices, to a greater demand for bamboos and firewood, and to improved methods of working the myrobalan and firewood forests.

The permanent staff consists of one deputy conservator of forests on £50 (Rs. 500) a month and his personal establishment, one head-clerk on £3 10*s*. (Rs. 35), one vernacular clerk on £2 (Rs. 20), and three messengers on 16*s*. (Rs. 8) each. The rest of the staff is one ranger on £10 (Rs. 100) a month ; five foresters, one on £4 (Rs. 40), two on £3 (Rs. 30) each, and two on £2 (Rs. 20) each ; six sub-foresters, three on £1 4*s*. (Rs. 12) each, and three on £1 (Rs. 10) each ; and twenty-one guards, eight on 16*s*. (Rs. 8) each, and thirteen on 14*s*. (Rs. 7) each, at a yearly cost of £1248 (Rs. 12,480). During the working season which lasts from November to June the permanent staff is strengthened by thirty-six myrobalan and firewood clerks on £1 4*s*. (Rs. 12) a month; one clerk in the deputy conservator's office on £2 (Rs. 20) a month; nineteen sub-foresters, one on £2 (Rs. 20), three on £1 10*s*. (Rs. 15), and fifteen on £1 (Rs. 10) ; and seventy-one forest-guards, fifteen on 16*s*. (Rs. 8), and fifty-six on 14*s*. (Rs. 7), at a total cost of £825 (Rs. 8250). The deputy conservator has general charge of the Belgaum forests. Under him are three executive officers, rangers, and foresters, one in charge of Khánápur, one of Belgaum and Sampgaon, and one of Chikodi and Gokák, who keep sub-divisional accounts and carry out cuttings, plantings, and other executive work. Under them the sub-foresters patrol sub-ranges, see that each guard is on his beat, and that he does his work properly. The guard patrols his beat, catches thieves, puts out fires, and guards the forest from harm, a heavy task as a guard's beat averages twenty square miles of forest mixed with tillage.

Near Pátne in Belgaum a plantation which was begun in 1879 numbered in 1881, 2393 seedlings from one to three years old. The plants are nearly all myrobalans which grow well and yield valuable fruit. In starting this plantation the land was given for tillage for two or three years, free of rent, the husbandmen

Chapter II. Production. Forests.

undertaking to plant the seedlings and guard them from fire for two or three years without charge. The only outlay has been the cost of raising the plants in the nursery. This has hitherto averaged 30*s*. (Rs. 15) an acre, a high rate owing to the difficulty of getting the seeds to sprout. The seed is sown in January, and in June and July, when four to eight inches high, the seedlings are planted twelve feet apart.

Trees.

[1]All forest trees occasionally occur in the open country. Some trees, such as figs, chiefly *pairi* Ficus cordifolia, banian Ficus indica, and *umbar* Ficus glomerata, *báva* Cassia fistula, *ápta* Bauhinia racemosa, *siris* Albizzia spp., *bor* Zizyphus jujuba, *pándre máti* Terminalia arjuna, *karanj* Pongamia glabra, *jámbul* Eugenia jambolana, *nána* Lagerstrœmia lanceolata, and *sávri* Bombax malabaricum are found far from forest tracts. Others, such as *kála máti* Terminalia tomentosa, sandal Santalum album, *mashvál* Chloroxylon swietenia, *ávla* Phyllanthus emblica, *dindal* Anogeissus latifolia, and teak are seldom seen far from forests. Many trees are grown for their fruit, timber, or shade. Cultivated trees are most often found in the east of the district. Many trees such as the guava, lime, mango, and tamarind, which require care in the east, grow wild in the damp western forests. The *karanj*, the willow Salix tetrasperma, the *pándre máti*, and the *jámbul*, grow best in moist places generally on river and pond banks and in rice fields. The well-to-do are fond of planting groves or *ráis*, an acre or two in area, generally mango or jack trees.

Field Trees.

The chief field trees are the *pipal* Ficus religiosa, *umbar* Ficus glomerata, *vad* Ficus indica, *pimpri* Ficus wightiana or Urostigma pseudo-tjiela, and *nándruk* Urostigma retusum or Ficus benjamina. These are generally planted along roadsides and near temples. The following ornamental and flowering trees are also planted along roadsides and in gardens : Albizzia procera and Albizzia lebbek, the large *gulmohr* Poinciana regia, and the small *gulmohr* Poinciana pulcherrima, known locally as *sankeshvari ;* the silk cotton tree, *simul* or *sávari* Bombax or Salmalia malabaricum, whose wood is used for making Gokák figures; the sandalwood tree, *shrigandh* or *chandan* Santalum album; the Belgaum walnut, *jangli akrot* Aleurites triloba ; *saru* Casuarina muricata, and the cypress also called *saru,* Cupressus glauca ; the *ápta* Bauhinia racemosa ; the *kánchan,* Bauhinia variegata of two varieties, the B. purpurescens and the B. candida, yielding beautiful purple and yellow and green flowers ; the Bengal almond, *badám* Terminalia catappa ; the *asoka* Guatteria or Polyalthia longifolia; the *pila chámpha* Michelia champaca ; the *nág chámpha* Messua ferrea; and the *son chámpha* Plumeria acuminata, are grown near houses and roadsides. The *nág chámpha* is very rare.

Fruit Trees.

Among fruit trees are the Mango *ámba* Mangifera indica ; the Jack *phanas* Artocarpus integrifolia ; the Loquat Eriobotrya japonica, which is quite naturalised ; the Custard-apple *sitáphal*

[1] The paragraphs on Trees, Plants, Shrubs, Creepers, Grasses, and Exotics have been contributed by Surgeon-Major C. T. Peters, M.B.

Chapter II.
Production.
Trees.
Fruit Trees.

Anona squamosa; the Bullock's-heart *rámphal* Anona reticulata; the Cashewnut *káju* Anacardium occidentale; the *jámbul* Eugenia jambolana; the Bael *bilva* Ægle marmelos; the Woodapple *kavit* Feronia elephantum; the Pummalo *popnas* Citrus decumana; the Sweet Lime *mitha nimbu* Citrus limetta; the Citron Citrus medica; the Lime *nimbu* Citrus bergamia; the Orange *nárangi* Citrus aurantium; the *kokam* Garcinia purpurea; the *ávla* or *ámla* Phyllanthus emblica; the *bor* Zizyphus jujuba; the *turan* Zizyphus rugosa; the *guti* Zizyphus xylopyra; the *chinch* Tamarindus indicus; the *agasti* Agati grandiflora, the flowers of which, with wheat salt and chillies, are cooked into a kind of cake, and the pods and leaves are eaten as curries; the Horse Radish Tree *shenga* or *shegva*, Moringa pterygosperma, whose leaf, flower, and pod are eaten as curries, whose bark is used as a poultice, and by Europeans instead of the horse-radish; an inferior kind of peach, Amygdalus persica; the Guava *jám* Psidium pyriferum and P. pomiferum; a superior kind of Pomegranate *ánár* Punica granatum is grown in Báil Hongal; the *papav* or *pápya* Carica papaya, is grown largely as a dessert fruit; *karanda* Carissa carandas, grows wild about the hill sides and hedges; *kamrak*, Averrhoa carambola and A. bilimbi, bear acid fruit; the Fig *anjir* Ficus carica, is found but the fruit is not so good as the Poona fig; the Mulberry *tut* or *shetut* Morus indica, is grown but not to any large extent; there are different kinds of Plantains *kele* Musa paradisiaca, the fruit of which is used as a dessert fruit, and some varieties, along with the pith and blossoms of the different kinds of plantains, are cooked as curries; and the Pineapple *ananás* Bromelia ananasa.[1]

Among other useful plants are the Soapnut *ritha* or *aritha* Sapindus emarginatus, and the Markingnut *bibva* or *bhilávan* Semecarpus anacardium; the frankincense tree, *dhupsálái* Boswellia thurifera, found on Shendur hill in Chikodi; the Givotia rottleriformis, also called *ritha*, whose light wood is used for making Gokák figures; and the Wild Nutmeg *jaji kai* Tyrrhosia horsfieldii, whose scentless fruit is a little larger than the true nutmeg. Among palms are the Wild Sago Palm *bherli mád* Caryota urens, whose pith yields a coarse sago and is cooked as gruel and the trunk is used as water conduits; the Betelnut *phophal* or *supári* Areca catechu, which is rarely grown; the Wild Date *shendi* Phœnix sylvestris, which is common in Khánápur and Belgaum and on the banks of streams in the east; the Cocoa Palm *náriel* Cocos nucifera, which is grown only in the east in the gardens of the rich; and the Brab or Palmyra *tád* Borassus flabelliformis, which is not very common.

Roadside Trees.

Many miles of roadside have been planted with trees and bamboos. The trees chiefly used are the banian, *páiri*, *umbar*, *ápta*, *siris*, *bábul*, mango, tamarind, *nim*, and bamboo. These trees are useful either as timber or for fences. The figs are the hardiest class of tree and grow well on rocky soil where nothing else thrives.

Many exotics have been introduced near the Belgaum cantonment. Some of them, as the Casuarina, India-rubber, and Pithe-

[1] In 1791 the neighbourhood of Chikodi was famed for producing grapes of extraordinary size and flavour. Moor's Narrative, 14.

Chapter II.

Production.

Trees.

colobium dulce, are apparently hardy trees. Others, as the logwood, the Australian Eucalypti or blue gums, and the acacias have been less successful. Coffee has been lately introduced and grows well in evergreen clumps on or near the Sahyádris.

Hedge Plants.

The chief hedge plants are the *adhalsa* Adhatoda vasica, the *nirgundi* Vitex negundo, the *lantana* Lantana indica, the Mexican aloe Agave americana, the Aloe *kuar* Aloe perfoliata, and the *mendi* Lawsonia alba. The Prickly Pear Opuntia dillenii, is used as a hedge-plant about gardens, but harbours rats and snakes; hedges of the Milk Bush *sher* Euphorbia tirucalli, are also common. The *bor* Zizyphus jujuba, the *bábhul* Acacia arabica, and the Physic Nut *erunde* Jatropha curcas, are used for field enclosures, while the quick-growing Indian Coral Tree *pángera* Erythrina indica, and *shevri* Sesbania ægyptica, are used to support the Betel vine *pán* Piper or Chavica betel.

Water and Marsh Plants.

Of water plants there are the Lotus, *kamal,* of three kinds, Nymphœa stellata, N. rubia, and N. pubescens, the Ipomia reptans, growing in ponds and used in some places as a pot-herb, and the *sola* Æschynomene aspera, growing in marshes and used for making wedding garlands and coronets. The roots of some of the Polygonums which are found on the banks of rivulets were used as food during the 1876-77 famine.

Shrubs and Weeds.

Among the Shrubs and Weeds that grow in waste lands and on hill sides are the *vágáti* Capparis roxburghii with large white showy flowers, the Nettle *bichuti* Urtica or Fleurya interrupta, the Thorn-apple *datura* Datura alba and D. fastuosa, the *supti* Tephrosia suberosa growing on rocky hills, the *tarvár* Cassia auriculata and C. tora, the *kanguni* Solanum incerta and S. jacquinii, a diffuse plant armed with prickles bearing yellow berries of the size of a plum, the Mexican Thistle *pila dhotra* Argemone mexicana, the Swallow Wort *mádár* or *rui* Calotropis gigantea, the *tumba* Leucas linifolia, the *agáda* Achyranthes aspera, and different kinds of Coleus grow as weeds in waste ground. The *ghols* Portulaca quadrifida and P. oleracea are found in moist shady places, while the Lepidagathis cristata and *káli musli* or *musli khund* Curculigo brevifolia and C. graminifolia, prefer more rocky grounds.

Creepers.

Of Creepers there are several convolvuluses, among them the Argyreia; some of the Cucurbitaceæ, such as the Citrullus colocynthis *indráyun,* which grows in hedges along with the milk bush; *tendla* Coccinia indica which bears a beautiful red oblong fruit; and the *gulvel* Cocculus cordifolius a twining shrub found among hedges.

Grasses.

The chief Grasses are: spear grass *kántha gavat* which is not used as fodder for horses, *chirkyáche gavat* which looks like a variety of *kántha gavat, kánta márvel* or *makunche gavat* Andropogon scandens which grows during the rains and is considered good fodder, *madhádche gavat* or *kátgod mandi,* a kind of Eleusine, is eaten by cattle, *jangli rala* Panicum italicum is eaten by horses and cattle, *kutta phanda* is not good for horses, *sipi* is considered good fodder, *hariyáli* Cynodon dactylon is excellent fodder for horses and sheep but not for cattle, *phanda* is also not good for cattle, *mol munda* bears large seeds which were used as food during the 1877 famine, *lohora* a kind of Andropogon, is not used as fodder, *bimba* is supposed to be a variety of *lohora, gávti náchni* or wild *náchni* is a variety of Eleusine, *kavdyáche phombi* also called *bhojráche gavat* and *kolya* or *jangli rála* is a kind of Panicum, and *kusliche gavat* or *gávti sáva* whose seeds are eaten is probably the Panicum frumentaceum.

Chapter II.
Production.
Grasses.

Besides the above, there are the Lemon grass *cha gavat* Andropogon schœnanthus, which with ginger sugar and milk is used as a drink in fevers and colds, and the scented Andropogon muricatus which is used in making wind screens and fans.

The chief Ferns are: Adiantum lunulatum and A. cappillus-veneris, two varieties of maiden hair, growing in moist shady places, the Silver Fern Cheilanthes farinosa and C. tenuifolia found chiefly in the western hills, two brackens Pteris cretica and P. pellucida found at a height of more than 2000 feet, the Oak Leaf Fern Aspidium cicutarium, Lastrea bergiana, Hemionitis arifolia, Gymnopteris contaminans, and the Royal Fern Osmunda regalis. The Tree Fern is occasionally found and a shrubby Alsophila occurs among the western hills; so also do a few varieties of the Trichomanes and Ophioglossum. The Pleopeltis membranacea is found growing on trees.

Mosses and Lichens.

Of the Club Moss family or Lycopodiaceæ, L. selaginella is seen in shady hill sides and L. clavatum in marshes. Beautiful mosses are found in the hills near Jámboti and the Ámboli pass.

Exotics.

With care many European fruits and vegetables can be grown in Belgaum. The Reverend J. Smith, of the London Missionary Society, has grown English apple and pear trees, but the pear trees do not bear. Peaches and strawberries succeed with care, while the raspberry and Cape gooseberry Physalis peruviana, grow of their own accord after they have been once planted.

A very large number of English flowers have been grown from seeds or from cuttings. Among the most successful are Achimenes, Amaranthus, Aralias, Arbutilons, Arums, Caladiums, China Asters, Balsams, Begonias, Bignonias, Bonganuvillias, Camellias, Cannas, Coryopsis, Coleus, Crotons, Dahlias, Fuschias, Gardenias, Geraniums, Gloxinias, Heliotropes, Hoyas, Iresines, Maurandyas, Mignonette, the Marvel of Peru, Nasturtiums, Passion Flowers, Phloxes, Pinks, Poinsettias, Roses, Sweet Peas, Violets, and Zinnias. Of European vegetables, cabbages are grown all the year round, but thrive best during the cold weather. Cauliflowers are fair but never very large. A continual supply of peas may be kept up but during the dry months they want much care. Nolkohl and turnips are good if carefully grown. French beans, beet, lettuce, carrots, Jerusalem artichokes, asparagus, celery, parsnips, radishes, small onions, tomatoes, cucumber, and water-cresses all thrive.

Domestic Animals.

Cattle are mostly bred by the Dhangars, who live chiefly in the forest tracts of the Khánápur and Belgaum sub-divisions. A large number of cattle are brought for sale from Maisur and other distant places. The principal cattle marts are Nipáni, Báil Hongal, Gokák, Belgaum, Kitur, and Nandgad.

Chapter II.

Production.

Domestic Animals.

Donkeys.

Of MAMMALS, Elephants are used by the Commissariat Department for transport purposes, and by a few rich natives for show.

Donkeys are used chiefly by Vadars for carrying their camp-gear and stones, and their charcoal, of which they are the sole makers. Beldárs or stone-masons and potters also keep asses for carrying their wares and washermen keep asses for carrying their clothes. The price of a good four-year old donkey is about £2 (Rs. 20).

Dogs.

Dogs are chiefly kept by Bedars and Vadars, who use them for hunting, and most villages have generally some ownerless pariah dogs. The dogs kept for sport are of the pariah breed but are better fed and larger than the ordinary village dogs. They have good noses, and sufficient pace and endurance to run down pig, the chief object of the chase, and keep them at bay until the hunters come up. They are unable to run down deer in a fair course. But by surrounding them and letting the dogs in from all sides, *sámbhar*, *chital*, and other deer are sometimes brought to bay and killed.

Horses.

Besides by European residents, among natives, Government officials, merchants, and others of the rich and well-to-do classes keep horses for riding, driving, and carrying loads. They are fed on gram, *kadbi*, grass, *masála*, and *bájri*. Country-bred or *deshi* animals are seldom over fourteen hands and generally under thirteen. They are wiry little animals able to do a great deal of work on very poor food and to stand exposure; but they are ugly, vicious, and obstinate. Their price varies from £2 to £20 (Rs. 20-200).

Mules.

Mules are used almost exclusively by the Commissariat. They have lately been employed in the coaches which run between Belgaum and Dhárwár.

Camels.

Camels are used almost solely by the Commissariat. A few are kept by rich families for carrying loads. They are fed on shrubs, grass, gram, and *kulthi*, and cost £5 to £20 (Rs. 50-200).

Pig.

Pig of a lighter-coloured smaller breed than the wild pig are reared by Native Christians, and by Vadars and other low-caste Hindus. They are dirty feeders and are generally the only village scavengers.

Buffaloes.

Buffaloes do not thrive on the Sahyádris though a few are kept in most villages. The best buffaloes come from Sampgaon and Gokák and the country to the east. She-buffaloes, which are bred by cultivators and milkmen, have their first calf at the age of five and go on bearing till they are about sixteen. They are of four breeds, *gavli* or *hanbari* so called because they are reared by milkmen of the Gavli and Hanbar castes, *nagdi*, *javári* or *deshi* that is local, and *dhangari* so called because they are kept by shepherds or Dhangars. The *gavli* breed, which is weaker and smaller than the *nagdi*, have slender bent horns, and the *nagdi* breed have long straight horns. Except that it is taller and stronger the *dhangari* breed differs little from the country breed. When in full milk a good she-buffalo gives five to ten quarts (5-10 *shers*) of milk a day and keeps in milk for ten months at a time. The price of a milch buffalo, which has just calved, is about £2 10*s*. (Rs. 25) if she gives three quarts (3 *shers*) of milk a day, and £1 (Rs. 10) more for every quart above three. He-buffaloes begin to work when

Domestic Animals.

Buffaloes.

four years old and are used for ploughing, draught, and burden. For heavy work a pair of he-buffaloes are often kept and are most useful on account of their great strength and, when well broken, on account of their steadiness. Though slower than oxen they are much more powerful, being able to pull nearly double the weight on heavy ground. Their great defect is that they cannot stand the sun; they must be worked in the early morning or evening and are so useless when the sun is high that the husbandmen sometimes plough by moonlight. The trade between Sávantvádi, Goa, and Belgaum is carried on almost entirely by pack bullocks and buffaloes, which take down grain, fruit, and tobacco, and bring back salt, cocoanuts, and dried fish. The price of a draught-buffalo varies from £3 to £5 (Rs. 30-50).

Cows.

Cows are found all over the district. Those living on the Sahyádris are smaller than those of the more level country and give little milk. The breed further inland is on the whole better fed and larger; but in all parts of the district small cattle always far outnumber the large. Cows first calve when three to four years old, and go on bearing till they are about fifteen. They feed on grass, millet stalks, cotton seeds, and oil-cakes. A good cow when in full milk gives about four quarts (4 *shers*) of milk and continues in milk about six months. The price of a young full grown cow varies from £1 10*s.* to £4 (Rs. 15-40). There are eight breeds of bullocks: *sorti, mudla, kundalvari, nagdi, dhangari, khillári, hanabari,* and *chilhar*. Of the first four the *sorti* or South Káthiáwár bullocks are the strongest and largest, about 13½ hands at the shoulder. They have thick black horns, large ears, and long thick tails. Though they are slow, no team for ploughing is considered complete without one or more pairs of *sortis*. The *mudla* bullocks are strong, active, and of middle size, and have straight long horns, slender tails, and small ears. The *nagdi* bullocks are short, about ten hands at the shoulder, stout, and active. They are found in numbers both in the plain and hilly country. Though useful and hardy they are not so strong as the *sortis* or *mudlás*. The *kundalvari* bullocks, the weakest of the four breeds, have large ears, long tails, thick hair, and bent horns. The *dhangari* and *khillári* bullocks differ from the *hanabari* and *chilhar* bullocks by having longer faces, and being stouter, taller, and larger. Bullocks are generally reared by the cultivating classes and are put to work when they are three years old. A pair of *mudla* or *nagdi* bullocks ploughs four acres of land in six days, while three or four pairs of *sorti* and *kundalvari* bullocks, working together at one plough, take ten days to plough an equal area of land. A pair of bullocks of the *sorti* breed costs £6 to £20 (Rs. 60-200), of the *mudla* breed £5 to £20 (Rs. 50-200), of the *kundalvari* breed £3 to £10 (Rs. 30-100), and of the *nagdi* breed £2 10*s.* to £8 (Rs. 25-80). On a fair level road, a pair of good well-fed oxen can, as an ordinary day's work, draw a load of half a ton sixteen miles a day. For carriages, or *dhamanis,* fast trotting bullocks of the Maisur breed are often used, which sometimes cost as much as £30 (Rs. 300) a pair. Pack-bullocks owned by peddlers and traders

Chapter II. Production. Domestic Animals. Goats.

carry about 200 pounds (8 *mans*) of grain or cloth packed in gunny bags.

Goats are kept by all classes except Bráhmans, Lingáyats, and Jains. They are of four breeds, local, *kumyadu, kui sheli*, and *dhangari*. The country breed has longer legs than the *kumyadu*, and the *kui sheli* goats are short and white, and yield specially good milk. Goats are chiefly kept in villages near bushlands and are most numerous in Gokák. The price of a full-sized she-goat varies from 6*s*. to 16*s*. (Rs. 3-8) and averages about 8*s*. (Rs. 4) for one in full milk which gives about a quart (1 *sher*) of milk a day. Some goats give as much as two quarts, but most do not give more than three quarters of a pint to a pint and a half.

Sheep.

Dhangars breed three kinds of Sheep, country, *kenguri*, and *yelga*. Country sheep are either white or black, and their wool is somewhat stronger than the *kenguri's* wool. The *kenguri* sheep have red soft wool. The *yelga* sheep is either white or red. Sheep are reared solely in the east, the climate of the west being too damp for them. They are sheared twice a year, in June and in December, and their wool is made into blankets. The price of a full-sized sheep weighing about twenty-five pounds is about 4*s*. (Rs. 2).

Fowls.

Hens, reared chiefly by Maráthás, Musalmáns, and Christians, are of two breeds, large and small. Hens of the smaller breed cost 6*d*. to 1*s*. (4-8 *as*.) and hens of the large breed 4*s*. to 16*s*. (Rs. 2-8). Eggs of the smaller breed cost 3*d*. (2 *as*.) and of the large breed 6*d*. (4 *as*.) a dozen. Ducks, turkeys, and guineafowls are reared by Christians and Musalmáns. A duck costs 2*s*. to 4*s*. (Re. 1 - Rs. 2), and a duck's egg ⅜*d*. (¼ *anna*); a turkey costs 4*s*. to £1 (Rs. 2-10), and a turkey's egg 1½*d*. (1 *anna*); a guineafowl costs 1*s*. to 4*s*. (8 *as*.-Rs. 2), and a guineafowl's egg ⅜*d*. (¼ *anna*).

Especially in the west of the district cattle suffer much from epidemic disease. The worst time is at the opening of the south-west rains in the first fortnight in June, when they are reduced by bad and scanty fodder and are unable to stand the sudden change from heat to damp cold. One of the commonest and most fatal diseases is derangement of the liver. Other common complaints are foot-rot and inflammation of the lungs.

Wild Animals.

Among *WILD ANIMALS*, of QUADRUMANA, the BLACKFACED MONKEY, *kari mangia* or *vánar*, Presbytis entellus, is common all over the country, frequenting groves, river banks, and woodlands. The REDFACED MONKEY, *kempu mangia* or *mákad*, Macacus radiatus, is not nearly so common as the blackfaced variety, but is generally distributed.

Of CHEIROPTERA or Bats, the FLYING FOX, *gádal*, Pteropus edwardsii, is common all over the district wherever there are tamarinds, figs, or other trees with edible fruit. Its fat is used as a cure for rheumatism and its flesh is eaten by Musalmáns and Hindus as a medicine. Cynopterus marginatus is very common. Hipposideros murinus occurs, but is rather rare. Nycticejus heathii is common.

Of CARNIVORA or Flesh-eaters, the COMMON MUSK-SHREW, *chuchundri*, Sorex cœrulescens, frequents most buildings though it is not very numerous. The BLACK BEAR, *asval* or *kardi*, Ursus labiatus, is common on the Sahyádri range and occurs also in the heavy forest on the Kánara border. Bears are much less numerous than they formerly were. Between 1840 and 1880 no less than 223 bears were killed. Of these 137 were killed between 1840 and 1850; fifty-one between 1850 and 1860; thirty-two between 1860 and 1870; and three between 1870 and 1880. The INDIAN BADGER, Mellivora indica, is common in woodland and open country. It is said to dig up and eat dead bodies. The COMMON INDIAN OTTER, *niranái*, Lutra nair, is common on the banks of the larger streams. The TIGER, K. *huli*, M. *vágh*, Felis tigris, is not very common. It is confined to the Sahyádri range and the strip of heavy forest in the extreme south. When the crops are on the ground tigers sometimes wander far from the forest and one was lately shot near Kitur. The people distinguish two kinds *dhánia* and *patáit*, but the only difference seems to be in size. Man-eating tigers, if they do occur, are rare, though man-eating panthers have been reported. Tiger's flesh is sometimes eaten by the depressed castes. In Belgaum during the thirty-seven years ending 1877, 372 tigers were killed. Arranging these thirty-seven years into three terms of nine years and one term of ten years the returns show a marked fall in the number slain, 128, 121, fifty-four, and sixty-nine, or a yearly average of fourteen, thirteen, six, and seven. The following statement shows the details of the five years ending 1882:

Chapter II.
Production.
Wild Animals.

BELGAUM TIGERS, 1878-1882.

YEAR.	Tigers killed.	Rewards		Loss of Life.	
				Persons	Cattle.
		£.	s.		
1878	3	5	8	1	39
1879	2	4	16	0	9
1880	1	2	8	4	10
1881	2	4	16	4	22
1882	5	7	4	1	27

The LARGER PANTHER, K. *yemme kerkál*, Felis pardus, does not often occur east of the Poona-Dhárwár road, but is common all along the Sahyádris, in the Belgaum and Khánápur sub-divisions, and in the heavier forests of Khánápur bordering on Kánara. People have been wounded and killed by panthers, but there is no certain case on record in which a panther has attacked a man with the object of eating him. Felis Panthera, K. *kerkal*, the smaller darker and bolder panther, is found in all forest tracts. To the north of Belgaum and in the hilly parts of the Gokák and Chikodi sub-divisions they frequent the dense thickets of prickly-pear Opuntia dilenii in which they find a secure retreat. There is no way of driving or cutting them out of these thickets. The only plan to circumvent them is either to watch over their kills, or to picket out goats near to some thicket into which they are known to have gone, and then await their approach from a tree or rock. It is useless to sit down behind a bush or in a hole to await their coming. Panthers are much feared at Gokák, for they have hurt and killed many people. In Gokák their flesh is sometimes eaten by Mhárs and

Chapter II.
Production.
Wild Animals.

Mángs. Between 1840 and 1877, 830 panthers were killed. The rewards paid and the number of cattle killed are not mentioned. The details for the five years ending 1882 are :

Belgaum Panthers, 1878-1882.

Year.	Killed.	Rewards.	Loss of Life.	
			Persons.	Cattle.
		£. s.		
1878	12	12 12	9	30
1879	11	10 10	6	71
1880	10	11 8	2	81
1881	16	16 10	18	22
1882	16	15 0	3	52

The Leopard-cat, M. *vágat,* is rare, occurring only on the Sahyádris and in the south Khánápur forests. Though scarcely bigger than a full-grown cat, the people say that it sometimes kills the largest buffaloes. It climbs trees, pounces on the back of its prey, and kills it by tearing its throat. The Common Jungle Cat, K. *arive bekku,* M. *rán mánjar,* Felis chaus, is common all over the district. Some years ago when antelope were common in the Belgaum plains, Hunting Leopards, *chita* or *chircha,* Felis jubata, were kept by the Mudhol chief. The Striped Hyæna, K. *katta kiráb,* M. *taras,* Hyæna striata, is common all over the country. It is commonest in open hilly woodlands. Since 1840 seventy-nine hyænas have been killed. The Civet Cat, K. *punagala bekku,* M. *kasturi mánjar,* Viverrina malaccensis, is common in the woodlands at Khánápur, Belgaum, and Gokák. The Common Tree or Toddy Cat, K. *matta bekku,* M. *hejjat,* Paradoxurus musanga, is common everywhere. The Madras Mongoose, K. *mungali,* M. *mungus,* Herpestes griseus, is common all over the district. Herpestes smittii occurs on the Sahyádris, and probably in the Gokák and Chikodi forests. Herpestes monticolus has been noticed in the Gokák forest land. Herpestes vitticollis, a much larger mongoose than H. griseus or H. smittii, occurs on the Sahyádris. The Indian Wolf, K. *tola,* Canis pallipes, is not uncommon in the open east but is seldom seen in the forest tracts. Since 1840 ten wolves have been killed. The Common Indian Jackal, K. *kapalnari,* M. *kola,* Canis aureus, abounds everywhere. The Jungle Dog, K. *arive nai,* M. *jangali kutra,* Cuon rutilans, is very common in the southern forests but rare in the east. The Indian Fox, K. *chandak nari,* Vulpes bengalensis, is common in the open east, but is seldom seen in well-wooded tracts.

Of Glires or Gnawers, the Common Porcupine, M. *salindar,* Hystrix leucura, is found in all forest tracts, especially on and near the Sahyádris. The Bombay Red Squirrel, M. *shekra,* Sciurus indicus, the S. elphinstonii of Jerdon, is common in the tall Sahyádri and south Khánápur forests, but does not occur further inland. The Common Striped Squirrel, K. *yenchi,* Sciurus palmarum abounds everywhere. The Brown Flying Squirrel, Pteromys petaurista, is rare and is confined to the south Khánápur forests. The Jerboa Rat, Gerbillus indicus, is common, and Gerbillus speciosus somewhat darker and about an inch smaller than G. indicus, is common in the thinly wooded parts of Khánápur. The Mole Rat, Nesokia indica, is found in the eastern sub-divisions. The BANDICOOT, *ghus*, Mus bandicota, is common in houses and granaries. The MIGRATORY RAT, Mus decumanus, is the common house-rat found everywhere. The LONG-TAILED TREE MOUSE, Mus oleraceus, is found in wooded parts of the district, living in trees. The COMMON INDIAN HOUSE MOUSE, Mus urbanus, from two to three inches long, may be seen in most houses, but is not very numerous. Animals of this genus are eaten by Vadars and other low-caste men. Mus terricolor is common in the more open parts of Khánápur. Leggada lepida is common in the thinly wooded parts of Khánápur. The BROWN SPINY MOUSE, Leggada platythrix, is found in Gokák. The FIELD RAT, Golunda meltada, is found in the open parts of the country, and is said to appear without any explainable cause, sometimes in great numbers, and to do much damage to crops as happened in the eastern sub-divisions in 1878, the year after the famine. The BLACKNAPED HARE, K. *mala*, M. *sasa*, Lepus nigricollis, is rare in the Sahyádris and does not frequent tall timber forests. It is common in the open country and in the scrub forests of Chikodi and Gokák.

Of MULTUNGULA, or animals whose hoof is divided into more than two parts, the WILD PIG, K. *handi*, M. *dukar*, Sus indicus, is common in all forest tracts and is eaten by Maráthás and by several of the early or depressed castes. It is a dirty feeder and will even eat carrion and cows which have died of disease, and in this way sometimes becomes infected with cattle-disease and falls a victim to its gluttony.

Of BISULCA or CUD-CHEWERS there are, the SÁMBHAR, K. *kadivi*, M. *sambar*, Rusa aristotelis, which is rare, occurring almost solely on the Sahyádris and in the Khánápur forests. One or two live in the scrub forest near Gokák, but east of Belgaum they are almost extinct. It never leaves the cover of the forests and keeps to the thickest parts. The SPOTTED DEER, K. *sárang*, M. *chital*, Axis maculatus, is common in the south Khánápur forests but rarely further north. In Gokák it has been almost exterminated by the villagers, who beat the forests regularly once a week and kill large quantities of game. It never leaves the forest tract, but unlike the *sámbar* prefers low open bushland to tall timber. The BARKING DEER, K. *kondákuri*, M. *bekar*, Cervulus aureus, is not uncommon in most forests, especially on the Sahyádris and in south Khánápur. It never leaves the forest tract. The MOUSE DEER, M. *pisái*, Memimna indica, is common in the Khánápur forests and is also met with on the Sahyádris. It does not occur east of Belgaum. The FOURHORNED ANTELOPE, K. *kondákuri*, M. *bekar*, Tetraceros quadricornis, has the same Kánarese and Maráthi name as the Barking Deer. Their general appearance is much the same and they frequent the same tracts. T. quadriconis is commonest in the open Sahyádri forests which it never leaves. The BLACK BUCK, K. *chiggari*, M. *haran*, Antelope bezoartica, was common thirty years ago in the fields about Belgaum. Now it is scarcely found west of Gokák, and even in the open east it is not numerous. It avoids woodlands, though it is sometimes found in low scrub on the borders of cultivated land. The INDIAN GAZELLE, K. and M. *madar*,

Chapter II.
Production.
Wild Animals.

Gazella bennettii, is not uncommon in the east. It frequents the low bushland east of Belgaum, but is not found further west.

The BISON, M. *gava*, Gavæus gaurus, is rare occurring only in one or two places on the Sahyádris and in the heavy forest in the extreme south. It is very shy. When in herds it seems never to attack the patches of *rági* and *sáva* which are grown in the centre of its haunts; but solitary bison do sometimes graze on the crops and cause much annoyance to the hillmen, who often find it difficult to drive them away. It is said that many years ago a large bull was shot by Mr., now Sir Frank Souter near One Tree Hill about a mile and a half to the north of Belgaum.

Of EDENTATA or Toothless Animals, the INDIAN ANT-EATER, K. *hanch bekku*, M. *khápar mánjar*, Pholidotus indicus, is fairly common in the forest tracts both east and west of Belgaum.

Bees.

There are no tame bees. The wild bees are of six classes: *Naraj jenu* (K.) or *Murkut* (M.) are small, scarcely the size of the small house-fly; the honey is pale yellow and is used in medicine. *Sunna nonajenu* (K.) or *Pove* (M.) is like the *Murkut* in many respects. Both *murkut* and *pove* make their nests round small twigs in bushes and also in the ground. *Nonajenu* (K.) or *Katyali* (M.) is of the size of an ordinary English bee. It builds its nests in trees and its honey is pale yellow and good. *Kondge* (M.), called variously in Kánarese *Kadujenu, Jagrijenu, Kuddujenu, Hebbajenu,* and *Sabarjenu,* is very large. Its honey is coarse and of a golden brown. It makes large combs stretching along large branches and also in rocks. *Sateru* (K.) or *Sátvani* (M.) is of the ordinary size. The honey is good though rather dark in colour. It makes a peculiar nest of seven layers of cells in trees. There is also a bee called *Atak,* but, except that the honey is thin and pale, nothing further is known about it. Besides from bees, honey is made from the *nána* Lagerstræmia lanceolata, mango, tamarind, *bábhul,* and *nim* Melia azadirachta, and from the blossoms of the *halli, tatta, bettavari,* and other creepers. The market price of honey varies from 3*d*. to 6*d*. (2-4 *as*.) the pound. There is no trade in honey.

Birds.

Among *BIRDS,* of RAPTORES, OTOGYPS CALVUS (Scop.), the Black Vulture, is common everywhere and most numerous in forest tracts, especially on the Sahyádris and in Khánápur. It is a resident. PSEUDOGYPS BENGALENSIS (Gmel.), the Whitebacked Vulture, is a resident and common everywhere. NEOPHRON GINGINIANUS (Lath.), the Common Scavenger Vulture, is a resident and common near all large villages, especially towards the east. FALCO SUBBUTEO (L.), the European Hobby, has been once procured by Captain Butler. It is a cold-weather visitant and occurs only as a straggler. CHIQUERA FALCO (Daud.), the Redheaded Merlin, a cold-weather visitant, is rare, occurring only in the open country. CERCHNEIS TINNUNCULUS (L.), the Kestrel, is a very common cold-weather visitant. CERCHNEIS NAUMAUNII (Fleisch.), the Lesser Kestrel, is very rare occurring if at all only as a straggler in the cold season. CERCHNEIS AMURENSIS (Radde.), the Orangelegged Kestrel, is very rare occurring only as a cold-weather straggler. ASTUR BADIUS (Gm.), the Indian

Chapter II. Production. Birds.

Sparrow Hawk, is very common; it probably leaves before the beginning of the rains. ACCIPITER NISUS (L.), the European Sparrow Hawk, is very rare, occurring only as a cold-weather straggler. ACCIPITER VIRGATUS, the Besra Sparrow Hawk, occurring in the Khánápur forests, is rare and probably leaves during the rains. AQUILA MOGILNIK (S. G. Gm.), the Imperial Eagle, is very rare, found only in the open country east of Belgaum. AQUILA VINDHIANA (Frankl.), the Tawny Eagle, is very common, especially in thinly wooded parts. It probably leaves at the beginning of the rains. HIERAËTUS PENNATUS (Gm.), the Dwarf Eagle, is rare. It is obtained, recorded by Captain Butler, from Belgaum in the cold season. NISAËTUS FASCIATUS (Vieill.), Bonelli's Eagle, is rather rare, but occurs in open forest and in open country near forests. CIRCAËTUS GALLICUS (Gm.) is rare, but is a resident. SPILORNIS MELANOTIS (Jerd.), the Crested Serpent-Eagle, is a resident, very common on the Sahyádris where only it seems to be found. BUTASTUR TEESA (Frankl.), the White-eyed Buzzard, is very common particularly in the Khánápur and Sahyádri forests. It probably leaves at the beginning of the rains. CIRCUS MACRURUS (S. G. Gm.), the Pale Harrier, a cold-weather visitant, is common in the open parts. CIRCUS CINERACEUS (Mont.) is common in open parts. CIRCUS ÆRUGINOSUS (Lin.), the Marsh Harrier, a cold-weather visitant, is very common near ponds and rice-fields in Khánápur but less common further north. HALIASTUR INDUS (Bodd.), the Maroon-backed Kite, a resident, is found near almost all large ponds and reservoirs. MILVUIS GOVINDA (Sykes), the Common Kite, is a resident, very common in the fair weather and less common during the rains. PERNIS PTILORHYNCHUS (Tem.), the Crested Honey Buzzard, is very common in all eastern forest tracts and open country. It probably leaves during the rains. ELANUS CŒRULEUS (Deel.), the Blackwinged Kite, is very common everywhere, particularly in the forests of Khánápur and on the Sahyádris. It probably leaves during tho rains.

STRIX JAVANICA (Gm.), the Indian Screech Owl, a resident, is common in the thinly wooded east, but does not occur on the Sahyádris or in other well-timbered parts. SYRNIUM INDRANEE (Sykes), the Brown Wood Owl, is rare, probably confined to the Sahyádris. SYRNIUM OCELLATUM (Less.), the Mottled Wood Owl, is common in thinly-wooded tracts, especially in Khánápur. ASIO ACCIPITRINUS (Pall.), the Shorteared Owl, is rare, occurring only in the cold season in open grass land. BUBO BENGALENSIS (Frankl.), the Rockhorned Owl, is a resident occurring in open tracts and in certain thinly wooded parts of the Sahyádris. KETUPA CEYLONENSIS (Gm.), the Brown Fish Owl, is common in the south and west forests, and sometimes occurs in open tracts. SCOPS PENNATUS (Hodgs.), the Indian Scops Owl, a resident, is often heard but seldom seen, and is probably confined to the Sahyádris and their immediate neighbourhood. CARINE BRAMA (Tem.), the *pingala*, is very common in open and thinly wooded parts, but does not occur in thick woods or on the Sahyádris.

GLAUCIDIUM MALABARICUM (Bly.), the Malabár Owlet, is a resident,

Chapter II.
Production.
Birds.

common in the Khánápur timber forests, less common on the Sahyádris, and not found outside of the belt of heavy rainfall. NINOX LUGUBRIS (Tick.), rare but probably a resident, occurs in the Khánápur forests.

Of INSESSORES, HIRUNDO RUSTICA (Lin.), the Common Swallow, is a cold-weather visitant found everywhere. HIRUNDO FILIFERA (Steph.), the Wiretailed Swallow, a resident, is common everywhere in open country and thin bushlands. HIRUNDO ERYTHROPYGIA (Sykes), the Redrumped Swallow, is a resident and common everywhere. PTYONOPROGNE CONCOLOR (Sykes), the Dusky Crag Martin, a resident, is common in most parts, especially on the Sahyádris.

CYPSELLUS AFFINIS (J. E. Gr.), the Indian Swift, a resident, is common in most parts, but does not occur everywhere or in the forests. DENDROCHELIDON CORONATA (Tick.), the Crested Swift, is very common in all forest tracts west of Belgaum, but does not occur in the open country.

CAPRIMULGUS INDICUS (Lath.), the Jungle Nightjar, a resident, is common in Khánápur in the open as well as in the forests. CAPRIMULGUS ATRIPENNIS (Jerd.), the Ghát Nightjar, a rather rare bird, occurs on the Sahyádris and in the Khánápur forests. CAPRIMULGUS ASIATICUS (Lath.), the Common Indian Nightjar, a resident, occurs in the eastern bushlands. CAPRIMULGUS MAHRATTENSIS (Sykes), occurs, but is rare. CAPRIMULGUS MONTICOLUS (Frankl.), Franklin's Nightjar, a resident, is common in all forest tracts. HARPACTES FASCIATUS (Forst.), the Malabár Trogon, a resident, is found, but rarely in the heavy south Khánápur forest; it occurs nowhere except in the outlying bit of Belgaum forest at the foot of the Rám pass. MEROPS VIRIDIS (Lin.), the Common Indian Bee-eater, a resident, occurs everywhere except in heavy forest. MEROPS SWINHOII (Hume), the Chestnutheaded Bee-eater, occurs occasionally on and at the foot of the Sahyádri range. NYCTIORNIS ATHERTONI (Jard. and Selb.), the Bluenecked Bee-eater, is rather rare on the Sahyádris and in south Khánápur and does not occur anywhere else. CORACIAS INDICA (L.), the Indian Roller, a cold-weather visitant, is common all over the district.

PELARGOPSIS GURIAL (Pearson), the Brownheaded Kingfisher, a resident, occurs only on the Tillarnádi at the foot of the Rám pass, where it is common. HALCYON SMYRNENSIS (Lin.), the Whitebreasted Kingfisher, a resident, is common everywhere. ALCEDO BENGALENSIS (Gmel.), the Common Kingfisher, a resident, is common everywhere in suitable places. ALCEDO BEAVANI (Wald.), Beavan's Kingfisher, probably a resident, is said to have been shot in the Rám pass. CERYLE RUDIS (Lin.), the Pied Kingfisher, a resident, is common near all the larger streams and ponds.

DICHOCEROS CAVATUS (Shaw), the Great Hornbill, a resident, is common on the Sahyádris and in the lofty forests of Khánápur. Stragglers are sometimes found in the open east. HYDROCISSA CORONATA (Bodd.), a resident, is very common in all forest tracts. TOCKUS GRISEUS (Lath.), the Grey Jungle Hornbill, a resident, is common in the lofty forests of Khánápur and on the Sahyádris.

Palæornis torquatus (Bodd.), the Roseringed Paroquet, a resident, is common everywhere. Palæornis purpureus (P. 4. S. Müll.), the Roseheaded Paroquet, a resident, is common in the cold and hot weather in the Khánápur and Sahyádri forests, and during the rains in the east. Palæornis columboides (Vig.), the Bluewinged Paroquet, a resident, is common on the crest of the Sahyádris, but occurs nowhere else. Loriculus vernalis (Sparrm.), the Indian Loriquet, a resident, is found during the cold and hot weather only on the crest of the Sahyádris. During the rains it is common also in the east. Picus mahrattensis (Lath.), the Yellowfronted Woodpecker, a resident, is very common in all woody parts of the country. Yungipicus nanus (Vig.), the Southern Pigmy Woodpecker, is not uncommon in the heavy Khánápur forests. It has not been found elsewhere, but probably occurs on the Sahyádris. Yungipicus gymnothalmus (Blyth.), is rare, occurring in the heavy south Khánápur forests. Hemicercus cordatus (Jerd.), the Heartspotted Woodpecker, a resident, is common in the Khánápur and Sahyádri forests. Chrysocolaptes delessertii (Malh.), the Southern Large Goldenbacked Woodpecker, a resident, is very common in the Khánápur and Sahyádri forests.

Chrysocolaptes festivus (Bodd.), the Blackbacked Woodpecker, is rare, occurring in the south of Khánápur and probably on the Sahyádris. Thriponax hodgsoni (Jerd.), the Large Black Woodpecker, a resident, is not uncommon in the heavy south Khánápur forest. Gecinus striolatus (Blyth.), the Small Green Woodpecker, is rare, occurring in the Khánápur forests and probably on the Sahyádris. Chrysophlegma chlorigaster (Jerd.), the Southern Yellownaped Woodpecker, a rather rare resident, occurs in the Khánápur forests and on the Sahyádris. Micropternus gularis (Jerd.), the Madras Rufous Woodpecker, a resident, is common on the Sahyádris and in the low Khánápur forests. Brachypternus puncticollis (Malh.), the Lesser Goldenbacked Woodpecker, a resident, is very common on the Sahyádris and in the southern Khánápur forests. Yunx torquilla (L.), the Wry Neck, is a rather rare cold-weather visitant in the open east. It does not occur west of Belgaum. Megalæma inornata (Wald.), the Western Green Barbet, a resident, is common in the Khánápur and Sahyádri forests. Megalæma viridis (Bodd.), the Small Green Barbet, a resident, is common in woodlands and tree-clumps throughout the district. Xantholæma hæmacephala (Müll.), the Crimsonbreasted Barbet, a resident, is common everywhere. Xantholæma malabarica (Blyth.), the Crimsonthroated Barbet, a rare resident, occurs in the Khánápur forests and at the foot of the Rám pass.

Cuculus sonnerati (Lath.), the Banded Bay Cuckoo, is not uncommon on and near the Sahyádris during the rainy season. It does not seem to remain during the rest of the year. Cuculus miscropterus (Gould.), the Indian Cuckoo, occurs on and near the Sahyádris during the rainy season. It is rare, and leaves when the rains are over. Hierococcyx varius (Vahl.), the Common Hawk Cuckoo, a resident, is common everywhere west of Belgaum, except in dense forest. Cacomantis passerinus (Vahl.), the Plaintive Cuckoo, a resident, is common in all forest tracts except in the

Chapter II.
Production.
Birds.

lofty forests of the south. COCCYSTES JACOBINUS (Bodd.), the Pied Crested Cuckoo, a resident, is common in all scrub forests east of Belgaum and in north Khánápur. It occurs also in the open country during the hot and cold seasons.

EUDYNAMYS HONORATA (Lin.), the Koel, a resident, is common in the north and east, but is rare in Khánápur. RHOPODYTES VIRIDIROSTRIS (Jerd.), the Small Greenbilled Cuckoo, a resident, is common in the scrub forests of the east and of Khánápur, but seems not to occur on the Sahyádris. CENTROCOCCYX RUFIPENNIS (Illq.), the Common Crow Pheasant, a resident, is common in open scrub forest and gardens all over the district. It does not frequent tall timber forests. TACCOCUA LESCHENAULTI (Less.), the Southern Sirkeer, is probably a resident, but is rare, occurring only in the scrub forests east of Belgaum. ARACHNOTHERA LONGIROSTRA (Lath.), the Little Spider Hunter, a resident, is not uncommon in the Khánápur forests. It occurs also at the foot of the Rám pass.

ÆTHOPHYGA VIGORSI (Sykes), the Violet-eared Red Honeysucker, a resident, is common on the Sahyádris and in the Khánápur forests. CINNYRIS ZEYLONICA (Lin.), the Amethyst-rumped Honeysucker, is a common resident. CINNYRIS MINIMA (Sykes), the Tiny Honeysucker, a resident, is common on the Sahyádris and in the Khánápur forests, but does not occur in the eastern bushlands. CINNYRIS ASIATICA (Lath.), the Purple Honeysucker, probably a resident, is not uncommon on the Sahyádris and in Khánápur. DICÆUM ERYTHRORHYNCHUS (Lath.), Tickell's Flowerpecker, a resident, is common in Khánápur and Belgaum. DICÆUM CONCOLOR (Jerd.), the Thickbilled Flowerpecker, is a resident of all forests and open forest fringes. DENDROPHILA FRONTALIS (Horsf.), the Velvet-fronted Blue Nuthatch, a resident, is very common in the thick forests of the south and near Belgaum.

UPUPA EPOPS (Lin.), the European Hoopoe, a cold-weather visitant, is common everywhere. UPUPA CEYLONENSIS (Reich.), the Indian Hoopoe, a resident, is found all over the district. It is commonest in thinly-wooded parts during the fair season.

LANIUS LAHTORA (Sykes), the Indian Grey Shrike, a resident, is common in the open country to the north and east, but is not found west of Belgaum. LANIUS ERYTHRONOTUS (Vig.), the Rufousbacked Shrike, a resident, is very common everywhere west of the Poona road except in dense forests. Towards the east it is replaced by Lahtora, the representative species of the open country. LANIUS VITTATUS (Valenc.), the Baybacked Shrike, a resident, is common in the low bushlands east of the Poona road, where it almost entirely replaces L. erythronotus. LANIUS CRISTATUS (L.), the Brown Shrike, a cold-weather visitant, is common throughout the district especially in Khánápur. TEPHRODORNIS SYLVICOLA (Jerd.), the Malabár Wood Shrike, a resident, is common in the big forests of Khánápur, but appears not to occur elsewhere. TEPHRODORNIS PONDICERIANUS (Gm.), the Common Wood Shrike, a resident, is common in all forest tracts. HEMIPUS PICATUS (Sykes), the Little Pied Shrike, probably a resident, is not uncommon in the tall forests of Belgaum and Khánápur; it does not occur further east. VOLVOCIVORA SYKESI (Strickl.), the Blackheaded Cuckoo Shrike, probably a resident, is very common in all woodlands. GRAUCALUS MACII (Less.), the Large Cuckoo Shrike, a resident, is common in the Khánápur forests and, generally, in moderate-sized thick forests. It does not occur east of Belgaum. PERICROCOTUS FLAMMEUS (Forst.), the Orange Minivit, a resident, is common in the Khánápur and Belgaum forests. PERICROCOTUS PERIGRINUS (Lin.), the Small Minivet, a resident, is very common everywhere. PERICROCOTUS ERYTHROPYGIUS (Jerd.), a resident, is occasionally found in the Ghatprabha forests near Sutgatti, but nowhere else. BUCHANGA ATRA (Herm.), the Common Drongo Shrike, a resident, is common everywhere except in the Khánápur forests where it is replaced by BUCHANGA LONGICAUDATA (Hay.), the Longtailed Drongo, a resident, common in the Khánápur forests and on the Sahyádris and passing to the eastern districts during the rains and cold weather. BUCHANGA CŒRULESCENS (Lin.), the Whitebellied Drongo, a resident, is common on the Sahyádris and in the Khánápur forests, but does not occur further east. CHAPTIA ŒNEA (Vieill.), the Bronzewinged Drongo, a resident, is rather common in the tall forests of Khánápur and extends to the Sahyádris within Belgaum limits. DISSEMURUS PARADISEUS (Lin.), the Malabár Racket-tailed Drongo, a resident, is common in the tall Khánápur forests but does not occur elsewhere. MUSCIPETA PARADISI (Lin.), the Paradise Fly-catcher, a resident, is common in all woodlands, especially in the dense Khánápur forests. HYPOTHYMIS AZUREA (Bodd.), the Black-naped Blue Flycatcher, a resident, is not uncommon in the low thick Khánápur woodlands and occurs also on the Sahyádris. LEUCOCERCA AUREOLA (Vieill.), the Whitebrowed Fantail, a resident, is common in all forest tracts except those on the crest of the Sahyádris. LEUCOCERCA LEUCOGASTER (Cuv.), the Whitespotted Fantail, a resident, is common everywhere. CULICICAPA CEYLONENSIS (Swians.), the Gray-headed Flycatcher, a cold-weather visitant, is found in the scrub forest near Gokák. ALSEONAX LATIROSTRIS (Raffl.), the Southern Brown Flycatcher, a cold-weather visitant, is not uncommon in the scrub forest east of Belgaum. ALSEONAX TERRICOLOR (Hodgs.), found at Belgaum, is rare. STOPOROLA MELANOPS (Vig.), the Verditer Flycatcher, probably a resident, is common in the Khánápur and Belgaum forests. CYORNIS RUBECULOIDES (Vig.), the Bluethroated Redbreast, is a rare cold-weather straggler. Only two specimens have been procured. CYORNIS TICKELLI (Blyth.), Tickell's Blue Redbreast, a resident, is common in all forest tracts. CYORNIS RUFICAUDUS (Sws.) may occur as a straggler. In October 1880 a female bird was found in the scrub forest of Belgaum which seemed to belong to this species. CYORNIS PALLIPES (Jerd.), the Whitebellied Blue Flycatcher, probably a resident, has been found only on the Sahyádri hills and rarely even there. ERYTHROSTERNA PARVA (Bechst.), the Whitetailed Robin Flycatcher, a cold-weather visitant, is common everywhere.

MYIOPHONEUS HORSFIELDI (Vig.), the Malabár Whistling Thrush, a resident, is common in dense thickets and ravines on the Sahyádris where only it is found. PITTA BRACHYURA (Lin.), the Indian Ground Thrush, is found only during the period of migration, on the Sahyádris and at Belgaum in May and June. CYANOCINCLUS CYANUS (Lin.), the Blue Rock Thrush, a cold-weather visitant, is common in all the more

Chapter II. Production. Birds.

open parts of the country including the Sahyádris. PETROPHILA CINCLORHYNCHA (Vig.), the Blueheaded Chat Thrush, a resident, is very common in the Khánápur and Belgaum forests. GEOCICHLA CYANOTIS (Jerd. and Selb.), the Whitewinged Ground Thrush, a resident, is common on the Sahyádris and in the Khánápur forests. GEOCICHLA UNICOLOR (Tick.), the Dusky Ground Thrush, is rare. One specimen was procured by Captain Butler at Belgaum in April. MERULA NIGROPILEA (Lafr.), the Blackcapped Blackbird, a resident, is common on the Sahyádris, but is not found east of Belgaum. PYCTORIS SINENSIS (Gm.), the Yelloweyed Babbler, a resident, is common throughout the district. ALCIPPE POIOCEPHALA (Jerd.), the Nilgiri Quaker Thrush, a resident, is common in the Khánápur and Belgaum forests. ALCIPPE ATRICEPS (Jerd.), the Blackheaded Wren Warbler, is common in the west of Khánápur, but is not found elsewhere. DUMETIA ALBOGULARIS (Bly.), the Whitethroated Wren Babbler, a resident, is common in all forest tracts. PELLORNEUM RUFICEPS (Swains.), the Spotted Wren Warbler, a resident, is found only in the Khánápur forests where it is common. POMATORHINUS HORSFIELDI (Sykes), the Southern Scimitar Babbler, a resident, is common on the Sahyádris and rarer in the southern Khánápur forests.

MALACOCERCUS GRISEUS (Lath.), the Whiteheaded Babbler, a resident is common in the bushlands of Gokák and Chikodi, but disappears, towards the east. MALACOCERCUS SOMERVILLII (Sykes), the Rufous-tailed Babbler, a resident, is common in the Khánápur forests and on the Sahyádris. ARGYA MALCOLMI (Sykes), the Large Grey Babbler, a resident, is common in the forests north of the Ghatprabha river and in the open country towards the east; it does not occur further south. LAYARDIA SUBRUFA (Jerd.), the Rufous Babbler, a resident, is found nowhere except in the forests about Hemadgi and Mendil in south-west Khánápur, and even there it is rare. CHATARRHÆA CAUDATA (Dum.), the Striated Bush Babbler, is rare, occurring only in the open country about Belgaum. SCHŒNICOLA PLATYURUS (Jerd.), the Broadtailed Reed Warbler, is rare, occurring about Belgaum in the rains and hot weather, and breeding there.

HYPSIPETES GANEESA (Sykes), the Black Ghát Bulbul, a resident, is very common on the Sahyádris but is found nowhere else. CRINIGER ICTERICUS (Strickl.), the Yellowbrowed Bulbul, a resident, is common in the Khánápur forests and on the Sahyádris. IXOS LUTEOLUS (Less.), the Whitebrowed Bulbul, a resident, is common in the low thick forests on the borders of the Sahyádris. RUBIGULA GULARIS (Gould.), the Rubythroated Bulbul, a resident, is common at the foot of the Rám pass, but has not been observed elsewhere. BRACHYPODIUS POLIOCEPHALUS (Jerd.), the Grayheaded Bulbul, a resident, is not uncommon in the south-west corner of the Khánápur sub-division, but is found nowhere else. OTOCOMPSA FUSCICAUDATA (Gould.), the Southern Redwhiskered Bulbul, a resident, is common in all forests west of Suldhal, particularly in Khánápur and on the Sahyádris. MOLPASTES HÆMORRHOUS (Gm.), the Common Madras Bulbul, a resident, is very common all over the district. PHYLLORNIS JERDONI (Blyth.), the Common Green Bulbul, a resident, is common in Khánápur except in the tall timber forests. It is also common along the Sahyádris. PHYLLORNIS MALABARICUS (Gm.), the Malabár Green Bulbul, is a resident, frequenting the same parts of the district as the last. IORA TIPHIA (Lin.), the Blackheaded Green Bulbul, a resident, is common throughout the district. IRENA PUELLA (Lath.), the Fairy Blue Bird, a resident, is not uncommon at the foot of the Rám pass; it is also found in the extreme south of Khánápur in tall timber forest but, as a rule, does not occur above the Sahyádris. ORIOLUS KUNDOO (Sykes), the Indian Oriole, probably a resident, is common in the open country and in low bushland but is seldom seen in the Sahyádris. ORIOLUS MELANOCEPHALUS (Lin.), the Blackheaded Oriole, a resident, is common in the Khánápur forests and on the Sahyádris. COPSYCHUS SAULARIS (Lin.), a resident, is common in all forests and passes to the open country. CERCOTRICHAS MACRURA (Gm.), the Shama, a resident, frequents thick forests; it is common on the Sahyádris, but is seldom found east of Belgaum.

THAMNOBIA FULICATA (Lin.), the Indian Black Robin, a resident, is common all over the district. PRATINCOLA CAPRATUS (Lin.), the White-winged Bushchat, is common everywhere. PRATINCOLA INDICUS (Bly.), the Indian Bushchat, a cold-weather visitant, is common in open and thinly wooded tracts. RUTICILLA RUFIVENTRIS (Vieill.), the Indian Redstart, a cold-weather visitant, is common throughout the district, except in thick forest. LARVIVORA SUPERCILIARIS (Jerd.), the Blue Woodchat, a rather common resident, is confined to the Sahyádris. CYANECULA SUECICA (Lin.), the Redspotted Bluethroat, a cold-weather visitant, is common all over the district except on the Sahyádris and in thick forest. ACROCEPHALUS STENTORIUS (Hemp. and Ehr.), the Large Reed Warbler, a cold-weather visitant, occurs occasionally in the more open country but is not found in the forest tracts. ACROCEPHALUS DUMETORUM (Bly.), the Lesser Reed Warbler, a cold-weather visitant, is common in the more open country. ACROCEPHALUS AGRICOLUS (Jerd.), the Paddyfield Warbler, a cold-weather visitant, has been found by Captain Butler at Belgaum. LOCUSTELLA HENDERSONI (Cass.), Henderson's Locustelle, probably only a visitant, is not uncommon about Belgaum during the rains, frequenting rice-fields and high grass. ORTHOTOMUS SUTORIUS (Penn.), the Indian Tailor Bird, a resident, is common in the open country, generally near wells, ponds, or streams; it does not occur in forests. PRINIA SOCIALIS (Sykes), the Ashy Wren Warbler, a resident, is common in the open country, but is seldom found in thick forest. PRINIA ADAMSI (Jerd.), one specimen has been obtained which appears to belong to this 'lost' species. PRINIA GRACILIS (Frankl.), Franklin's Wren Warbler, a resident, appears to be not uncommon in the opener forest land near the Sahyádris. PRINIA HODGSONI (Bly.), the Malabár Wren Warbler, a resident, is not uncommon in the opener forests near the Sahyádris. CISTICOLA CURSITANS (Frankl.), the Rufous Grass Warbler, is common in grass-lands in the open country. DRYMŒCA INORNATA (Sykes), the Earthbrown Wren Warbler, a resident, is common in the open country. HYPOLAIS RAMA (Sykes), the Tree Warbler, is a cold-weather visitant. HYPOLAIS CALIGATA (Sicht. Sykes), the Allied Tree Warbler, a cold-weather visitant, is found in the eastern scrub forest. PHYLLOSCOPUS TRISTIS (Blyth.), the Brown Warbler, is found at Belgaum. PHYLLOSCOPUS MAGNIROSTRIS (Blyth.), the Largebilled Tree Warbler,

Chapter II. Production. Birds.

recorded from Belgaum by Captain Butler, appears to be rare. PHYLLOSCOPUS NITIDUS (Blyth.), the Bright-green Tree Warbler, recorded from Belgaum, by Captain Butler, appears to be rare. PHYLLOSCOPUS INDICUS (Jerd.), the Olivaceous Tree Warbler, a cold-weather visitant, is found in the east. REGULOIDES OCCIPITALIS (Jerd.), the Large-crowned Tree Warbler, a cold-weather visitant, seems to be rare. REGULOIDES HUMII (Brooks), Hume's Crowned Tree Warbler, found by Captain Butler at Belgaum, appears to be rare. SYLVIA JERDONI (Blyth.), the Blackcapped Warbler, a cold-weather visitant, is not uncommon in the east. SYLVIA AFFINIS (Blyth.), the Allied Grey Warbler, a rare cold-weather visitant, has been found by Captain Butler at Belgaum. MOTACILLA MADERASPATENSIS (Gm.), the Large Pied Wagtail, is common throughout the district. MOTACILLA PERSONATA (Gould.), the Blackfaced Wagtail, is recorded from Belgaum by Captain Butler. MOTACILLA DUKHUNENSIS (Sykes), the Whitefaced Wagtail, a cold-weather visitant, is common everywhere. CALOBATES MELANOPE (Pall.), the Gray and Yellow Wagtail, is a common cold-weather visitant. BUDYTES CINEREOCAPILLA (Savi.), the Slatyheaded Wagtail, a cold-weather visitant, is common everywhere.

BUDYTES MELANOCEPHALA (Licht.), the Blackcapped Field Wagtail, a cold-weather visitant, has been found by Captain Butler at Belgaum, where it seems to be common. BUDYTES FLAVA (L.), the Grayheaded Yellow Wagtail, has been recorded from Belgaum by Captain Butler. LIMONIDROMUS INDICUS (Gm.), the Wood Wagtail, probably a resident, is common in the tall forests in Khánápur but seldom occurs east of Belgaum. ANTHUS TRIVIALIS (Lin.), the European Tree Pipit, a cold-weather visitant, is common in the open country. ANTHUS MACULATUS (Hodgs.), is common in open wooded tracts. CORYDALLA RUFULA (Vieill.), the Indian Titlark, a resident, is common. ZOSTEROPS PALPEBROSA (Tem.), the White-eyed Tit, a resident, is common in all forest tracts west of Suldhal. PARUS NIPALENSIS (Hodgs.), the Indian Gray Tit, a resident, is common in the Belgaum and Khánápur forests. MACHLOLOPHUS APLONOTUS, (Blyth.), the Southern Yellow Tit, a resident, is common in the Belgaum and Khánápur forests.

CORVUS MACRORHYNCHUS (Wagl.), the Carrion Crow, a resident, is common everywhere. CORVUS SPLENDENS (Vieill.), the Common Graynecked Crow, a resident, is common everywhere, except on the crest of the Sahyádris and in the heavy Khánápur forest. DENDROCITTA RUFA (Scop.), the Common Magpie, a resident, is common in all forests.

ACRIDOTHERES TRISTIS (Lin.), the Common Myna, a resident, is common in the open country. ACRIDOTHERES FUSCUS (Wagl.), the Dusky Myna, a resident, is common in the better-wooded parts of the country. STURNIA PAGODARUM (Gm.), the Blackheaded Myna, a resident, is common in Belgaum and Khánápur, and also occurs in the opener country. STURNIA MALABARICA (Gm.), the Grayheaded Tree Myna, a resident, is fairly common in Khánápur and Belgaum. STURNIA BLYTHI (Jerd.), the Whitebreasted Tree Myna, a resident, is fairly common in the Khánápur forests in the cold and hot weather,

Chapter II.
Production.
Birds.

and in the open country during the rains. PASTOR ROSEUS (Lin.), the Rosecoloured Starling, a cold-weather visitant, is common everywhere except in thick forests. PLOCEUS PHILIPPINUS (Lin.), the common Weaver Bird, a resident, is common everywhere except in forests. PLOCEUS MANYAR (Horsf.), the Striated Weaver Bird, a resident, is fairly common in the open country.

AMADINA MALACCA (Lin.), the Blackheaded Munia, a resident, is common in the open country. AMADINA PUNCTULATA (Lin.), the Spotted Munia, is fairly common in the forests east of Belgaum, and less common in Khánápur. AMADINA PECTORALIS (Jerd.), the Rufousbellied Munia, is very rare, found only at Hemádge in the south-west corner of Khánápur. AMADINA STRIATA (Lin.), the Whitebacked Munia, common in the Khánápur and Belgaum forests, is not confined to the Sahyádris. AMADINA MALABARICA (Lin.), the Plain Brown Munia, is common in the open country and in the Khánápur forests. ESTRELDA AMANDAVA (Lin.), the Red Waxbill, a resident, is common in the tracts east of Belgaum, being specially fond of sugarcane fields. PASSER DOMESTICUS (Linn.), the Common Sparrow, a resident, is common everywhere in towns and large villages. GYMNORIS FLAVICOLLIS (Frankl.), the Yellowthroated Sparrow, a resident, is common in all forests passing into the more open country. EMBERIZA BUCHANANI (Blyth.), the Graynecked Bunting, found by Captain Butler at Belgaum, seems to be rare. EUSPIZA MELANOCEPHALA (Scop.), the Blackheaded Bunting, a cold-weather visitant, is common on tilled lands. EUSPIZA LUTEOLA (Sparrm.), the Redheaded Bunting, a cold-weather visitant, is not uncommon in the open country. CARPODACUS ERYTHRINUS (Pall.), the Common Rosefinch, a resident, is common in the open woodlands of Khánápur and Belgaum and in the forest tract in the east.

MIRAFRA AFFINIS (Jerd.), the Madras Bushlark, a resident, is common in the eastern scrub forests, but is found nowhere else. MIRAFRA ERYTHROPTERA (Jerd.), the Redwinged Bushlark, a resident, is common in the eastern scrub forests. AMMOMANES PHŒNICURA, (Frankl.), the Rufoustailed Finchlark, a resident, is common in the open country east of Belgaum. PYRRHULAUDA GRISEA (Scop.), the Blackbellied Finchlark, a resident, is common in the open country west of Belgaum. CALANDRELLA BRACHYDACTYLA (Leisl.), the Social Lark, a cold-weather visitant, is common in fields in the open country. SPIZALAUDA DEVA (Sykes), the Small Crown-crested Lark, a resident, is common in the open country, but does not occur on the Sahyádris. SPIZALAUDA MALABARICA (Scop.), the Large Crown-crested Lark, a resident, is very common in Belgaum and Khánápur. ALAUDA GULGULA (Frankl.), the Skylark, a resident, is not found on the Sahyádris but is not uncommon in the open east.

Of GEMITORES, CROCOPUS CHLORIGASTER (Blyth.), the Southern Green Pigeon, is common in the cold and hot weather; it seems to leave the district during the rains. OSMOTRERON MALABARICA (Jerd.), the Grayfronted Green Pigeon, probably a resident, is not uncommon in the south Khánápur forests, where only it seems to be found. PALUMBUS ELPHINSTONII (Sykes), the Nilgiri Wood Pigeon, is not uncommon on the crest of the Sahyádris to which it is

Chapter II. Production. Birds.

confined. COLUMBA INTERMEDIA (Strickl.), the Indian Bluerock, a resident, is common in the open country and on the crest of the Sahyádris. TURTUR PULCHRATUS (Hodgs.), the Indian Turtle Dove, a cold-weather visitant, is common in the low forests of Khánápur and Belgaum. TURTUR MEENA (Sykes), the Rufous Turtle Dove, a cold-weather visitant, is common in the low forests of Khánápur and Belgaum. TURTUR SENEGALENSIS (Linn.), the Little Brown Dove, a resident, is very common everywhere except in tall forests. TURTUR SURATENSIS (Gm.) the Spotted Dove, a resident, is common in all forest tracts. TURTUR RISORIUS (Linn.), the Common Ring Dove, a resident, is very common east of Belgaum both in woodlands and in the open country. TURTUR TRANQUEBARICUS (Herm.), the Vinous Ring Dove, is very rare; only one specimen in the open country at Linganmáth has been recorded. CHALCOPHAPS INDICA (Lin.) is rather rare. It has been found in the Khánápur and south Belgaum forests and is probably a resident.

Of RASORES, PTEROCLES FASCIATUS (Scop.) (A),[1] the Painted Sandgrouse, a resident, is very common in and is confined to the scrub forests of East Belgaum. PTEROCLES EXUSTUS (Temm.) (A), the Common Sandgrouse, a resident, is very common in the open east, as a rule frequenting open grass lands. PAVO CRISTATUS (Lin.) (A), the Peacock, a resident, is very common in the scrub forests of Gokák and Chikodi, but is comparatively rare in the Sahyádris and in the Khánápur forests. GALLUS SONERATI (Tem.) (A), the Gray Junglefowl, a resident, is common in Khánápur and on the Sahyádris, and is less common in the eastern scrub forest. GALLOPERDIX SPADICEUS, (Gm.) (A), the Red Spurfowl, a resident, is found in the same parts of the district as Gallus sonnerati, and is equally numerous. GALLOPERDIX LUNULATUS (Valenc.) (A), the Painted Spurfowl, a resident, is rare, being found only in the forest near Gokák. FRANCOLINUS PICTUS (Jard. and Selby) (A), the Painted Partridge, a resident, is common on most black soil tracts, and is seldom found far from trees. ORTYGORNIS PONDICERIANUS (Gm.) (A), the common Gray Partridge, a resident, is very common in the low scrub forests of Gokák and Chikodi; it is less common in the open country.

PERDICULA ASIATICA (Lath.) (A), the Jungle Bush Quail, a resident, is common on the Sahyádris and in the eastern scrub forests. PERDICULA ARGOONDAH (Sykes) (A), the Rock Bush Quail, a resident, is common in the open east and in bush lands. MICROPERDIX ERYTHRORHYNCHUS (Sykes) (A), the Painted Bush Quail, a resident, is common but very local, being found only in fields studded with bushes or trees. COTURNIX COMMUNIS (Bonn.) (A), the Large Gray Quail, a cold-weather visitant, is common in the open country east of the Sahyádris. COTURNIX COROMANDELICA (Gm.) (A), the Blackbreasted Quail, a resident, is common in all grass-lands and fields. TURNIX TAIGOOR (Sykes) (A), the Blackbreasted Bustard Quail, a resident, is fairly common in the fields of the scrub forest tracts east of Belgaum. TURNIX JOUDERA (Hodgs.) (A), the large Button Quail, is very rare; only one specimen has been obtained. TURNIX DUSSUMIERI

[1] Birds marked (A) are game birds.

(Temm.) (A), the Small Button Quail, a resident, is common but very local in grass-lands near Belgaum.

Of GRALLATORES, EUPODOTIS EDWARDSII (J. E. Gr.) (A), the Indian Bustard, probably a resident, occurs in the east in Parasgad. SYPHEOTIDES AURITA (Lath.) (A), the Lesser Florikin, is common in the hot weather in fields and grass-lands in the open country. Most leave during the rains and cold weather, but a few remain all the year. CURSORIUS COROMANDELICUS (Gm.), the Courier Plover, is common in the eastern scrub tracts and in the open country east of Belgaum. CHARADRIUS FULVUS (Gm.,) the Eastern Golden Plover, probably a cold-weather visitant, is common on all grass-lands all over the district, except on the Sahyádris. ÆGIALITIS DUBIA (Scop.), the Common Ring Plover, is common on open grassy expanses generally near ponds, in the plain country. CHETTUSIA GREGARIA (Pall.), the Blacksided Lapwing, has been recorded by Captain Butler. LOBIVANELLUS INDICUS (Bodd.), the Redwattled Lapwing, a resident, is very common near water from the crest of the Sahyádris inland. LOBIPLUVIA MALABARICA (Bodd.), the Yellow-wattled Lapwing, a resident, is common everywhere; on the Sahyádris it is commoner than L. indicus. It chooses drier ground. ŒDICNEMUS SCOLOPAX (S. G. Gm.), the Stone Plover, a resident, does not occur in tall forests, but is otherwise fairly common in the Khánápur and Sahyádri woodlands. SCOLOPAX RUSTICOLA (L.) (A), the Woodcock, is rare, appearing only as a straggler in the season of migration in the forests west of Belgaum. GALLINAGO STHENURA (Kühl.), (A), the Pintailed Snipe, a cold-weather visitant, comes in September and stays till May. It is very common in the cold weather. When in January the open country begins to dry, it retires to the patches of summer rice in the forest tracts where it stays at least till the hot weather rains set in. GALLINAGO CŒLESTIS (Fren.) (A), the Common Snipe, a cold-weather visitant, chooses the same ground as G. sthenura but is not nearly so common. GALLINAGO GALLINULA (Lin.) (A), the Jack Snipe, a cold-weather visitant, occurs everywhere, but is not nearly so common as the common or pintailed variety. RHYNCHÆA BENGALENSIS (Lin.) (A), the Painted Snipe, is probably a resident. It is very local as it seems to require much thicker cover than the other snipe and is never found in bare rice-fields. Twenty-five couple of snipe is considered a good bag for one gun in a day.

NUMENIUS LINEATUS (Cuv.) (A), the Curlew, a very rare cold-weather visitant, is recorded by Captain Butler from near Belgaum. MACHETES PUGNAX (Lin.), the Ruff, is recorded by Captain Butler from Belgaum in the cold season. RHYACOPHILA GLAREOLA (Lin.), the Spotted Sandpiper, is common about ponds and rice-fields in the cold season. TOTANUS OCHROPUS (L.), the Green Sandpiper, is a very common cold-weather visitant. TRINGOIDES HYPOLEUCUS (Lin.), the Common Sandpiper, is common in the cold season. TOTANUS GLOTTIS (Lin.), the Green Shank, is common in the cold weather. TOTANUS FUSCUS (L.), the Spotted Red Shank, is rare but occurs at Belgaum. HIMANTOPUS CANDIDUS (Bonn.), the Stilt, is common near most ponds in the cold weather but is somewhat locally distributed. PARRA INDICA (Lath.), the Bronzewinged Jacana, a resident, is common in Khánápur.

Chapter II.
Production.
Birds.

HYDROPHASIANUS CHIRURGUS (Scop.), the Pheasant-tailed Jacana, probably leaves in the cold weather. It is rarely found in the rains in Khánápur and Belgaum. PORPHYRIO POLIOCEPHALUS (Lath.) (A), the Purple Coot, probably a resident, is very locally distributed but is common in the reedy ponds in Khánápur. FULICA ATRA (Lin.) (A), the Bald Coot, a resident, is very common, found on almost every reedy pond in the cold weather. GALLINULA CHLOROPUS (Lin.), the Common Water Hen, a resident common on weed and lily-covered ponds in Khánápur. ERYTHRA PHŒNICURA (Penn.), the Whitebreasted Water Hen, a resident, is common in ponds in Khánápur and along river banks. PORZANA AKOOL (Sykes), the Brown Rail, one specimen said to have been caught on its nest was found in October at Belgaum. PORZANA BAILLONI (Vieill.), Baillon's Crake, a cold-weather visitant, is common all over the district. HYPOTÆNIDIA STRIATA (Lin.), the Bluebreasted Rail, occurs in the rains. Captain Butler obtained specimens at Belgaum. XENORHYNCHUS ASIATICUS (Lath.), the Black-necked Stork, a rare bird is recorded by Captain Butler from Hubli. DISSURA EPISCOPA (Bodd.), the Whitenecked Stork, a resident, is common in the Khánápur forests and Sahyádris as well as in the more open country.

ARDEA CINEREA (Lin.), the Common Blue Heron, is very common in the cold weather in the open country near ponds. ARDEA PURPUREA (Lin.), the Purple Heron, is rare; one specimen is recorded from Sampgaon. HERODIAS TORRA (B. Ham.), the Large Egret, is common everywhere in the cold weather. HERODIAS INTERMEDIA (Han.), the Little White Heron, is common in the cold weather throughout the district. HERODIAS GARZETTA (Lin.), the Little Egret, is common in the cold weather. DEMIEGRETTA GULARIS (Bosc.), the Ashy Egret, probably a resident, is found on river-banks in the better wooded parts of Belgaum, Khánápur, and Gokák; it is not common.

BUBULCUS COROMANDUS (Bodd.), the Cattle Egret, a resident, is common in all forest tracts. ARDEOLA GRAYI (Sykes), the Pond Heron, a resident, is common everywhere. BUTORIDES JAVANICA (Horsf.), the Little Green Bittern, a resident, is common on woody river banks. ARDETTA CINNAMOMEA (Gm.) the Chestnut Bittern, a resident, is rather rare; it is recorded from Belgaum and Khánápur. GOISAKIUS MELANOLOPHUS (Raffl.), the Malayan Tiger Bittern, is very rare; one specimen is recorded from the foot of the Rám pass. NYCTICORAX GRISEUS (Lin.), the Night Heron, a resident, is locally distributed, but is not rare. TANTALUS LEUCOCEPHALUS (Forst.), the Pelican Ibis, is found on the Ghatprabha, and probably occurs on all the larger streams in the cold weather. INOCOTIS PAPILLOSUS (Temm.) (A), the Wartyheaded Ibis, a cold-weather visitant, is not uncommon in the more open parts in rice fields and along river-banks.

Of NATATORES, SARCIDIORNIS MELANONOTUS (Penn.) (A), the Nukhta, probably a visitant, is very rare, occurring occasionally near Belgaum. NETTOPUS COROMANDELIANUS (Gm.) (A), the Cotton Teal, is fairly common in the cold season in Khánápur and Sampgaon, and is probably generally distributed. DENDROCYGNA JAVANICA (Horsf.) (A), the Whistling Teal, probably occurs only in the rainy season when it is not uncommon. SPATULA CLYPEATA (Lin.) (A), the Shoveller, is

Birds.

a common cold-weather visitant. ANAS BOSCHAS (L.) (A), the Wild Duck, is recorded by Captain Butler from Hubli; it is rare. ANAS PŒCILORHYNCHA (Forst.) (A), the Spotbilled Duck, probably a resident, is not uncommon. CHAULELASMUS STREPERUS (Lin.) (A), the Gadwall, is a very common cold-weather visitant. DAFILA ACUTA (Lin.) (A), the Pintailed Duck, occurs in the cold weather, but is not rare. QUERQUEDULA CRECCA (Lin.) (A), the Common Teal, is a common cold-weather visitant. QUERQUEDULA CIRCIA (Lin.), the Bluewinged Teal, is common in the cold-weather. FULIGULA FERINA (Lin.) (A), the Redheaded Pochard, a rare cold-weather visitant, is recorded from Hubli by Captain Butler FULIGULA NYROCA(Güld.)(A), the White-eyed Pochard, a rare cold-weather visitant, is recorded by Captain Butler from Belgaum. FULIGULA CRISTATA (Lin.) (A), the Tufted Duck, a cold-weather visitant, is recorded by Captain Butler from Belgaum. PODICEPS MINOR (Gm.), the Little Grebe, is a common resident. HYDROCHELIDON HYBRIDA (Pall.), the Small Marsh Tern, a rare cold weather visitant, is found at Belgaum. STERNA MELANOGASTRA (Tem.), the Blackbellied Tern, is a rare cold-weather visitant. PELECANUS PHILIPPENSIS (Gm.), the Grey Pelican, is recorded by Captain Butler as shot at Belgaum. PHALACROCORAX PYGMÆUS (Pall.), the Little Cormorant, is very common. PLOTUS MELANOGASTER (Penn.), the Indian Snakebird, is a common resident.

Snakes.

Snakes are common everywhere, especially on stony ground. The Cobra Naga tripudians, and *Phursa* Echis carinata, are perhaps the commonest of poisonous snakes. Pythons are occasionally seen, and little green snakes, scarcely to be known from the blades of grass in which they lie, are numerous.

Crocodiles.

Crocodiles are common in all the larger streams. They seldom attack men, but frequently kill goats, and sometimes cows, and even the largest buffaloes. The flesh of the crocodile is eaten by people of the Goll caste, who hunt and kill it in the water. When they have seen a crocodile enter the water, the Golls make a great noise and splash some distance above and below the spot where he is supposed to be. This so frightens the beast that he tries to hide under the first cover he can find in the bed or bank of the river. After some minutes of noise and splashing divers go in search, and, when the animal is found, secure it with nets, or, if it is small, despatch it without the use of nets. The Golls have dogs specially trained to help in securing the game.

Fish.

Fish[1] in abundance, but for the most part small and of little value, are caught in the Malprabha, Támraparni, Ghatprabha, and Márkándeya, as well as in the smaller streams and ponds. Except during the rainy season floods, which is the breeding or spawning time, fish are caught all the year round. In this way the breeding fish and the fry are to some extent spared, though the fishermen never fail to destroy them when they can get them. The chief fresh-water fish caught in rivers and ponds are the *aval, bali, bam* or *balvi, dhoke, godach, gácháli, ghogre, harági, hánu, kute, kavli, kulogi, kavnya malag, muluga purgi, sannat* and *thunga*.

---

[1] The fish portion is compiled from Day's Fish and Fisheries, Appendix LII. and LX., and from a contribution from Mr. G. McCorkell, C.S.

Chapter II.
Production.
Fish.

The fishery rights of Government and of private persons have never been fixed. The people of the river bank villages net fish for their own use. Besides river-bank villagers there are professional fishers of the Bhoi, Koli, Rajput, and Marátha castes. Except Musalmáns, who fish mostly for home use, these fishers catch in order to sell. In addition to fishing they work as servants, palanquin-bearers, basketmakers, and husbandmen. Breeding and young fish are caught in nets made of cotton thread dyed brown with a mesh of about one-sixth or one-fourth of an inch from knot to knot. In and near Belgaum a net called *jhinginjál,* with even smaller meshes, is used for catching prawns and a small fish called *mori* known to Europeans as whitebait. Nets with minute meshes are used during the rains for small fish, and with larger meshes during the cold and hot seasons. Besides these, there are drag-nets *mahájál,* band-nets *charejál,* and stake-nets *kundál.* Besides being netted, fish are trapped in irrigated fields. They are carried in by the rush of water, and once inside, they are easily caught. In the hot weather, the rivers brooks and ponds are dammed and poisonous drugs are thrown into the water, so that the fish either die, or, becoming stupefied, float on the top and are easily caught. This practice of poisoning fish to a certain extent has been stopped in Gokák, as the cutting of the poisonous twigs and leaves has been forbidden. Rod fishing and long line fishing are occasionally resorted to where the water is too deep to dam. Bottom fishing by dragging small pools with a piece of cotton cloth is carried on by persons from the banks throughout the year. Of the fish thus caught, the largest are eaten, but many small fry are left on the banks to die. No fishing boats are employed in any part of the district. Except during the heavy rains when fishing is stopped, none of the rivers have water enough to float a boat much larger than a cockle shell. The bait used is either the common earthworm or grubs found in manure.

All classes of people except Bráhmans, Lingáyats, Jains, Márwár Vánis, Bhátiás, Vaishyas, Gujarát Vánis, and Panchals eat fish. As the markets are well supplied with salt-fish from Goa and the coast, there is little demand for fresh fish, which are dear and bad. The only exception is near Belgaum, where the European demand exceeds the supply. Local opinion differs as to whether the supply of fish is or is not falling off.

CHAPTER III.

POPULATION.

Chapter III. Population. Census Details. *1872-1881.*

According to the 1881 census[1] the population of the district was 864,014 or 185·57 to the square mile. Of these Hindus numbered 791,277 or 91·58 per cent; Musalmáns 66,262 or 7·66 per cent; Christians 6322 or 0·73 per cent; Jews 89; and Pársis 64. The percentage of males on the total population was 50·28 and of females 49·71. The corresponding returns for 1872 were a total of 944,985 or 205·83 to the square mile, of whom Hindus numbered 865,776 or 91·61 per cent; Musalmáns 72,065 or 7·62 per cent; Christians 6931 or 0·73 per cent; Jews 123 or 0·01 per cent; and Pársis 90. Compared with the 1872 returns the 1881 returns show a decrease of 80,971 or 8·56 per cent. The decrease is due partly to the mortality caused by the 1876-77 famine, and partly to the emigration of the labouring classes to the neighbouring districts which took place at that time.[2]

Birth-place.

Of 864,014 (males 434,485, females 429,529), the total population, 783,187 (males 400,119, females 383,068) or 90·64 per cent were born in the district. Of the 80,827, who were not born in the district, 25,755 were born in Kolhápur; 24,060 in the Southern Marátha states; 8404 in Dhárwár; 4403 in Sátára; 4252 in Kaládgi; 2430 in the Konkan and Konkan states; 1930 in Goa, Daman, and Diu; 1390 in Sholápur; 1389 in Madras; 1150 in Kánara; 889 in the Nizám's Territories; 886 in Gujarát; 840 in Poona; 338 in Maisur; 240 in Bombay; 188 in Ahmadnagar; 171 in Khándesh; 55 in Násik; and 2057 in other parts of India and outside of India.

Language.

Of 864,014, the whole population, 556,397 (males 277,640, females 278,757) or 64·39 per cent spoke Kánarese. Of the remaining 307,617 persons, 225,008 or 26·04 per cent spoke Maráthi; 65,731 or 7·60 per cent spoke Hindustáni; 10,757 or 1·24 per cent spoke Telugu; 1810 or 0·20 per cent spoke Gujaráti; 1670 or 0·19 per cent spoke Tamil; 1270 or 0·14 per cent spoke English; 682 spoke Portuguese-Konkani or Goanese; 614 spoke Hindi; 36 spoke Tulu; 33 spoke Panjábi; 4 spoke German; and 2 spoke Arabic.

Age.

The following tabular statement gives the number of each religious class according to sex at different ages, with, at each stage, the percentage on the total population of the same sex and religion. The columns referring to the total population omit religious distinctions, but show the difference of sex:

---

[1] In 1837 and in 1846 the people of the Belgaum district as it was then constituted were numbered. The territorial changes which have since taken place make those figures useless for purposes of comparison.

[2] Some details of the Emigration during the famine time are given in Chapter IV.

Chapter III.
Population.
Census Details.
Age.

BELGAUM POPULATION BY AGE, 1881.

Age in Years.	Hindus.				Musalma'ns.				Christians.			
	Males.	Percentage on Males.	Females.	Percentage on Females.	Males.	Percentage on Males.	Females.	Percentage on Females.	Males.	Percentage on Males.	Females.	Percentage on Females.
Up to 1 ...	10,490	2·64	10,290	2·61	959	2·87	898	2·71	17	1·98	75	2·81
1 to 4 ...	33,379	8 40	34,178	8·67	2815	8·42	2846	8·65	238	6·36	253	9·50
5 to 9 ...	56,178	14·13	54,996	13·96	4881	14·61	4756	14·47	370	10·10	370	13·90
10 to 14 ...	56,355	14·18	46,981	11·92	4859	14·55	3863	11·75	305	8 33	271	10·18
15 to 19 ...	31,980	8·04	27,798	7·05	2668	7·98	2115	6·43	279	7·62	200	7·51
20 to 24 ...	30,849	7·76	34,525	8·76	2535	7·59	2878	8·75	339	9·25	240	9·01
25 to 29 ...	38,000	9·56	37,867	9·61	3168	9·48	3236	9·84	428	11·69	312	11·72
30 to 34 ...	36,001	9·06	37,529	9·52	2991	8·95	3162	9·62	427	11·66	256	9·62
35 to 39 ...	25,399	6·39	23,154	5·87	2105	6·30	1877	5·71	289	7·89	137	5·14
40 to 49 ...	40,553	10·20	38,677	9·81	3279	9·80	3160	9·61	300	8·19	238	8·94
50 to 54 ...	16,640	4·18	18,852	4·78	1321	3·95	1546	4·70	209	5·70	114	4·28
55 to 59 ...	6530	1·64	7168	1·81	513	1·53	579	1·76	88	2·40	40	1·50
Above 60 ...	14,978	3·76	21,935	5·56	1300	3·89	1957	5·95	323	8·82	155	5·82
Total ...	397,332		393,945		33,394		32,868		3661		2661	

Age in Years.	Pa'rsis.				Jews.				Total.			
Up to 1 ...	1	2·22	...	...	...	...	2	5·55	11,521	2·65	11,260	2·62
1 to 4 ...	4	8·88	2	10·52	3	5·66	1	2·77	36,434	8·38	37,275	8·67
5 to 9 ...	3	6·66	4	21·05	7	13·20	6	16·66	61,439	14·14	60,132	13·99
10 to 14 ...	9	20·00	4	21·05	7	13·20	4	11·11	61,535	14·16	51,123	11·90
15 to 19 ...	2	4·44	1	5·26	3	5·66	8	22·22	34,932	8·04	30,122	7·01
20 to 24 ..	5	11·11	1	5·26	15	28·30	2	5·55	33,743	7·76	37,646	8·76
25 to 29 ...	7	15·55	2	10·52	5	9·43	2	5·55	41,608	9·57	41,419	9·64
30 to 34 ...	4	8·88	..	...	1	1·88	4	11·11	39,424	9·07	40,951	9·53
35 to 39 ...	1	2·22	...	...	1	1·88	4	11·11	27,795	6·39	25,172	5·86
40 to 49 ...	7	15·55	4	21·05	8	15·09	1	2 77	44,147	10·16	42,080	9·79
50 to 54 ...	1	2·22	1	5·26	3	5·66	1	2·77	18,174	4·18	20,514	4·77
55 to 59 ...	...	...	...	...	...	...	...	...	7131	1·64	7787	1·81
Above 60 ...	1	2·22	...	...	...	...	1	2·77	16,602	3·82	24,048	5·59
Total ...	45		19		53		36		434,485		429,529	

Marriage.

The following table shows the proportion of the people of the district who are unmarried, married, and widowed :

BELGAUM MARRIAGE DETAILS, 1881.

	Under Ten.		Ten to Fourteen.		Fifteen to Nineteen.		Twenty to Twenty-nine.		Thirty and Over.		Total.	
	Males.	Females.	Males.	Females.	Males.	Females.	Males.	Females.	Males.	Females.	Males.	Females.
HINDUS.												
Unmarried ...	96,796	80,724	43,899	11,989	15,346	1191	10,251	1751	3657	2681	169,949	98,286
Married ...	3006	17,984	11,334	32,448	15,348	24,477	54,825	62,243	115,956	71,163	200,469	208,315
Widowed ...	245	751	1122	2594	1286	2190	3773	8398	20,488	73,471	26,914	87,344
MUSALMA'NS.												
Unmarried ...	8492	7977	4456	2375	1986	283	1869	181	521	191	17,326	11,007
Married ...	154	502	369	1409	624	1716	3611	5359	9521	6044	14,289	15,030
Widowed ...	9	16	32	79	48	116	223	574	1467	6046	1779	6831
CHRISTIANS.												
Unmarried ...	670	698	289	221	235	56	427	36	594	29	2215	1029
Married ...	4	5	16	47	43	138	324	435	938	433	1325	1058
Widowed ...	...	...	...	3	1	12	16	81	104	478	121	574

Chapter III.
Population.
Census Details.
Marriage.

BELGAUM MARRIAGE DETAILS, 1881—continued.

	Under Ten.		Ten to Fourteen.		Fifteen to Nineteen.		Twenty to Twenty-nine.		Thirty and Over.		Total.	
	Males.	Females.	Males.	Females.	Males.	Females.	Males.	Females.	Males.	Females.	Males.	Females.
JEWS.												
Unmarried ...	10	9	6	4	3	1	5	...	1	...	25	14
Married ...	...	...	1	...	...	7	15	4	12	8	28	19
Widowed ...	...	...	...	...	...	...	...	...	...	3	...	3
PA'RSIS.												
Unmarried ...	8	5	8	3	2	...	3	1	3	...	24	9
Married ...	...	1	1	1	...	1	9	2	9	4	19	9
Widowed ...	...	...	...	...	...	...	...	...	2	1	2	1

Occupation.

According to Occupation the 1881 census returns divide the population into six classes :

I.—In Government Service, Learned Professions, Literature, and Arts, 17,082, or 1·97 per cent.
II.—In Domestic Service, 9207 or 1·06 per cent.
III.—In Trade, 4085 or 0·47 per cent.
IV.—In Agriculture, 275,345, or 31·86 per cent.
V.—In Crafts, 133,653, or 15·47 per cent.
VI.—In Indefinite and Unproductive Occupations, including children, 424,642 or 49·14 per cent.

BRÁHMANS.

Bra'hmans[1] include nine divisions with a strength of 30,400 souls or 3·84 per cent of the Hindu population. The following statement gives the details :

BELGAUM BRÁHMANS, 1881.

CLASS.	Males.	Females.	Total.	CLASS.	Males.	Females.	Total.
Deshasth ...	13,888	12,806	26,694	Shenvi ...	999	959	1958
Golak ...	75	71	146	Telang ...	53	33	86
Gujaráti ...	50	6	56	Tirgul ...	45	41	86
Karháda ...	260	220	480				
Konkanasth..	448	425	873				
Márwári ...	15	10	25	Total ...	15,833	14,571	30,404

Deshasths.

DESHASTHS, with a strength of 26,694, originally from the Deccan, are found all over the district. They are darker than Chitpávan or Konkanasth Bráhmans. They speak Maráthi but the home tongue of many is Kánarese. They are strict vegetarians. Most of them are *grahasthas* or laymen taking no alms and earning their living as writers, merchants, traders, moneylenders, and landowners. Among the religious Bráhmans or *bhikshuks* are *vaidiks* or reciters of the *Veds*, *shástris* or expounders of the law, *joshis* or astrologers, *vaidyas* or physicians, *puránike* or readers of sacred books, and *haridáses* or singers and story-tellers. The chief subdivisions of Deshasths found in the district are Rigvedis, Ápastambs, Yajurvedis, Kánnavs, and Mádhyandins. Rigvedis, who are a large

[1] From materials supplied by Ráo Sáheb Kalyán Sitárám Chitre, Mámlatdár of Belgaum.

Chapter III. Population. Bráhmans.

subdivision intermarry with Ápastambs, and both consider it an act of merit to marry their daughters with their sisters' sons. In rare cases the maternal uncle marries his niece. White and black Yajurvedis do not intermarry. Kánnavs were formerly considered inferior, and though of late years they have risen in social rank, some religious Rigvedis scruple to eat food cooked by Kánnavs. Mádhyandins, who are found in large numbers in Parasgad, Sampgaon, and Athni, hold a low position among Deshasths. Unlike Rigvedis they do not marry their daughters with their sisters' sons. Though some live on charity, and a few work as cooks and water-bearers, Deshasths, as a class, are well-to-do.

Golaks. GOLAKS or GOVARDHANS are returned as numbering 146 and as found in Athni, Gokák, and Belgaum. They are divided into Kund Golaks who are said to be descended from a Bráhman woman by a Bráhman man who was not her husband, and Rand Golaks who are said to be descended from a Bráhman widow. They are medium-coloured, neither very dark nor very fair. They speak either Maráthi or Kánarese and are moneychangers, shopkeepers, astrologers, and husbandmen. They send their boys to school and are in easy circumstances.

Gujarátis. GUJARÁT BRÁHMANS, of three subdivisions Nágar, Shrimáli, and Pokarna, with a strength of 56, are found in Chikodi and Belgaum where some Gujarát Vánis and Bhátiás are settled. They act as priests to Gujarát Vánis and Bhátiás. They are goodlooking and fair, but weak. Their home speech is Gujaráti and they speak Maráthi in public. They have no houses of their own, and generally live in the houses of their patrons the Gujarát Vánis and Bhátiás. They are strict vegetarians. Their dress differs from that of local Bráhmans only by their wearing a small turban instead of a headscarf or *rumál*. They hold aloof from other Bráhmans, and do not eat with them.

Karhádás. KARHÁDÁS from Karhád near the meeting of the Krishna and Koyna about fifteen miles south of Sátára, are returned as numbering 480 and as found over the whole district. As a class they are darker, less well-featured, and sturdier than the Konkanasths. Their home tongue is Maráthi. They are priests, traders, writers, landholders, cooks, and water-carriers. They are staunch goddess worshippers, their chief family goddess being Lakshmi. Cases of intermarriage among Karhádás, Deshasths, and Konkanasths are not unknown. Karhádás are frugal, businesslike, and intelligent. On the whole they are well-to-do.

Konkanasths. KONKANASTHS or CHITPÁVANS with a strength of 873, are scattered over the district. They have come from the Konkan and are family priests, Government servants, moneylenders, cooks, and beggars. The men are generally fair and tall, and the women well-formed and graceful. They speak Kánarese, but their home tongue is Maráthi. They are frugal, intelligent, hardworking, and enterprising. Many of them are well-to-do, and a few are rich.

Márwáris. MÁRWÁR BRÁHMANS are found in very small numbers in large towns. They have not permanently settled in the district. Except a few who serve as cooks to Márwár Vánis, they are well-to-do as merchants and dealers in cloth and metal vessels. Some of them have their wives and children with them.

Shenvis. SHENVIS, with a strength of 1958, are found chiefly in the Belgaum and Khánápur sub-divisions. A few are found in the

Sampgaon sub-division, and there are a considerable number in the town of Sháhápur, which is about a mile to the south of Belgaum and belongs to the chief of Sángli. Goa was their original Konkan settlement, where, according to the Sahyádri Khand, they are said to have come at Parashurám's request from Tribotra or Tirhut in Northern India. This legend is thought to be confirmed by the fact that, especially in Goa and the surrounding parts, Shenvis like Bengális freely rub their heads with oil and also like them are fond of rice gruel called *pej* and fish. The honorific Báb, as in Purushottam-báb, is perhaps a corruption of Bábu in Bengáli.[1] Shenvis have some peculiar names taken from their gods, such as Mangesh, Shántárám, Shántábái, and others. Their broad pronunciation of the vowel sounds is also said to be like the Bengáli pronunciation.[2] Their family gods,[3] for whom they have much reverence, are still in Goa from which some are said to have fled to escape conversion by the Portuguese. They hold themselves bound to visit Goa at least every four or five years to pay their devotion to the family god. Others are probably older settlers in Belgaum as some of the Deshpándes, Inámdárs, and Khásnis of Khánápur, Chandgad, and other places hold deeds or *sanads* from the Bijápur Government (1489-1686). The fact that Shenvis are the hereditary *kulkarnis* in the greater part of the Khánápur and Belgaum sub-divisions and in part of Dhárwár seems to show that some were settled in the district before the beginning of Bijápur rule. The Shenvis belong to ten stocks or *gotrás*: Atri, Bháradváj, Gautam, Jámdagnya, Kaundinya, Káshyap, Kaushik, Vasishta, Vatsa and Vishvámitra. They are Sárasvat Bráhmans of the Panch Gaud order, and their priests or *upádhyás* belong either to their own class or to the class of Karháda Bráhmans. They have a few original surnames as Achmáne, Bhándáre, Bichu, Brahme, Kánvinde, Karnik, Kekare, Mánge, Rege, Telang, and Velang. A few are taken from their past and present occupation, as Dalvi or commander, Desái or village headman, Deshpánde or district accountant, Fadnis or accountant and seal-keeper, Haváldár or subordinate revenue officer, Khot or revenue farmer, Kulkarni or village accountant, Khásnis or deputy, Mantri or counsellor, Nádgonda or head of a district, Nádkarni or district accountant, Náik or headman, Sabnis or chief clerk, and Saráph or moneychanger. Most surnames are taken from the names of places as Punekar, Shahápurkar, Jámbotkar, and others. In religion Shenvis are either Smárts or Vaishnavs, each sect being under the jurisdiction of a separate *sanyási* head priest called *svámi*.[4] The Smárt *svámi* has a monastery at Khánápur where he occasionally lives, and which enjoys a grant of the two villages of Mansápur and Lákudvádi. The two sects dine

[1] Ráo Bahádur Shankar Pándurang Pandit, Oriental Translator to Government.

[2] Professor R. G. Bhándárkar, M.A., Hon.M.R.A.S. The tombs or *samádhis* of two of the first settlers, named Shivasharma and Devasharma the ancestors or *mulpurush* of the Vatsa and Kaundinya stocks or *gotrás* are still shown and worshipped at Kona near the village of Mangeshi.

[3] Their chief house gods and goddesses are Mahálakshmi, Mangesh also called Mángirish and supposed to mean the god of Mungir in Bengal, Mhálasa, Nágesh, Rámnáth, Shántádurga, and Saptakotishvar.

[4] The Smárt *svámi* generally lives at Sonavda in Kánara and the Vaishnav *svámi* in Goa. They have rich monasteries at Kárwár, Bombay, Násik, and Benares.

Chapter III.
Population.
BRÁHMANS.
Shenvis.

together and intermarry and do not hate each other as in Bombay. Of the several minor divisions of Shenvis, only a few Kudáldeshkars and Kárwár Sárasvats are found in the district. Shenvis are fair. The women are well-made and graceful, and, like the women of Goa, are fond of decking their hair with flowers. Both men and women speak Maráthi and occasionally Kánarese. At home they speak the Konkani language which they brought from Goa, though the accent has been changed to a Kánarese accent, and a good many Kánarese words have been added. Their houses, especially in Nandgad and in the Sángli chief's town of Sháhápur, are strong and well-built. Most Shenvis eat fish and keep to rice as their daily food. As a class they are well-to-do, some of them in Nandgad and Sháhápur being bankers and moneychangers; the rest are Government servants chiefly village clerks and district hereditary officers. A few are pleaders, traders, contractors, shopkeepers, and landholders, some of whom till with their own hands. They are fond of show and somewhat extravagant, but in intellect and energy hold their own with any class in the district. They have no peculiar customs.[1] Caste disputes are settled at meetings of the members of the caste, the caste decisions being referred for confirmation to the head priests or *svámis*. They are eager to educate their children, and seem likely to keep the place they hold as one of the most intelligent and prosperous classes of West India Hindus.

Telangs.
Tirguls.

TELANGS, with a strength of 86, are scattered over the district. They are wandering beggars, and are not settled in the district. They come from the Madras Presidency in the fair season. TIRGULS, with a strength of 86, are scattered over the district. They are said to have come from the Madras Presidency. They have settled in the district and are cultivators. In dress, habits, and manners they resemble Kunbis. They are dark, well-built, and hardworking. Deshasths and other local Bráhmans drink water brought by a Tirgul, but do not eat food cooked by one.

Bráhmans are found all over the district. They are family priests, merchants, traders, moneylenders, Government servants, pleaders, cooks and water-bearers, and landholders. The landholders own both Government and alienated lands. Some of them till with their own hands. The priestly class beg, conduct the worship of house gods, make leafplates, teach children Sanskrit prayers and other texts, and help in performing religious rites. The *bhikshuks* or religious Bráhmans are idle and lazy. Except some elderly widows who serve as cooks in rich Bráhman houses, women have nothing to do except housework.

The houses of the rich are large, two or three storeys high, with tiled roofs and walls of stone. Those of the poor are small with tiled roofs and mud walls. The outer face of the house wall is covered with clay and mortar and painted with upright stripes alternately white and red. The inside face is decorated with pictures of gods,

---

[1] In some families at the yearly Ganpati worship in August-September a picture of the god drawn on paper is laid beside his image. This custom is believed to have taken its rise in the time when the Portuguese forbade the open worship of Hindu gods.

giants, and other Puránic personages. Every Bráhman house has generally a back and sometimes a front yard, a cook-room which opens on the backyard, a middle hall where household furniture and provisions are stored and where the children sleep at night, and two or three bedrooms for the married people and a large hall. Outside the front door is a veranda raised one to two feet above the ground where the members of the family sit talking of an evening. In front of the door in the front or backyard or garden is a highly ornamented pedestal on which is a pot with a sweet basil plant to which the house people bow when they go out. There is a shed close by for cows, she-buffaloes, and horses. The yard is daily swept, cowdunged, and decorated with lines of powdered quartz. In the backyard are plantains and a variety of flowering shrubs and a number of basil plants, whose leaves and the flowers of the shrubs are used in the worship of the house gods. Their household furniture includes metal pots and pans, wooden boxes stools and cots, bedding and pillows. In addition to these, a few houses have chairs tables and cupboards.

The daily food of Bráhmans includes rice, Indian millet bread, pulse curry, butter, curds, and milk. Except Shenvis they are strict vegetarians and some do not eat onions, garlic, or carrots which they consider impure. Some do not drink the milk of a cow until the tenth day after she has calved. When one of them intends to give a caste feast he goes round to the houses of the different guests accompanied by his wife, a relation or two, a servant, and the family priest. They take with them two cups, one filled with grains of rice, the other with red-powder. When they reach a house the men stand on the veranda and call out the name of the owner of the house, and the women of the party walk into the part of the house where the women live. When the head of the house appears, the priest in the name of the host asks him to a feast, naming the place, the day, and the hour at which he should attend, and lays a few grains of rice on the palm of his right hand. The head of the house takes the grains of rice if he can come; if he has another engagement he makes an excuse. Inside of the house the women of the party mark the brow of the chief woman of the family with red-powder and give their invitations. On the feast day when the dinner is ready a near relation of the host goes to the houses of his guests and tells them that the feast is ready and that the host waits to receive them. When the guests arrive the host receives the men and the hostess receives the women, and they are led into different rooms. Each of the guests brings a waterpot and cup. The women are in full dress and decked with ornaments; the men have no turban and are bare to the waist which is girt by a silk waistcloth which falls to the feet. In the men's room the guests are seated in two rows about four feet apart facing each other. In front of each guest a leafplate is laid. In the women's room the hostess marks with red-powder the brow of each guest as she enters, and they are seated in two rows facing each other like the men. When the guests are seated a band of people of the house, relations and friends, both men and women, serve the dishes, putting a little of each dish into the leafplate in front of each guest.

When the dishes are served, the host goes to the god's room

Chapter III.
Population.
BRÁHMANS.

and the family priest offers the god food or *naivedya*. He then sets on a plate a cupful of holy water or *tirth*, some sandal-paste, some grains of rice, some flowers and basil leaves, and going in front of each male guest, pours a spoonful of the holy water on his right palm and this the guest sips. He then rubs the guest's brow with sandal-paste and fixing a few grains of rice in the paste, lays a *tulsi* or sweet basil leaf or a flower in his hand. When all have sipped the holy water the family priest sprinkles a little water and a little sandal-paste on the ground in front of him and calls in a loud voice the name of the host's family god and all the men guests join in the shout, *Jay, Jay Rám*, Victory, Victory to Rám. The priest bows and asks the guests to begin. While the guests are eating, the host goes up and down among the men guests and the hostess among the women guests, pressing them to eat and chiding them for their want of appetite. When dinner is over the guests are handed betelnut and leaves, scented oils and powders are rubbed on their arms, and garlands of flowers or nosegays are placed in their hands. Money is given to such of the guests as belong to priestly families, and in return they throw grains of rice over the host's head, who bows before them and receives a blessing. Their holiday dishes are *bundis*, balls of gram flour mixed with sugar and boiled in butter; *besans*, solid balls of gram mixed with sugar and boiled in butter; and *dales*, wheat balls boiled in butter and mixed with sugar, raisins, bits of almonds, and sugarcandy; *khir* or boiled milk mixed with sugar and pieces of almonds; *shrikhand*, curds mixed with sugar, nutmeg, saffron, and bits of almonds; *keshar-bhát*, rice cooked with sugar, saffron, and almonds; *vánge-bhát*, rice cooked with butter and split brinjals; *jilbi*, small cake of wheat flour fried in boiling butter and syrup. A sweet cake called *chavda* is peculiar to the Shenvis.

Bráhmans take two meals a day. They do not dine without bathing and put on a silk robe which has not been touched since it was washed and dried. A Bráhman who has been girt with the sacred thread, before he begins to eat, offers some of the food to his gods, and sprinkles a ring of water round his plate. He places from three to five pinches of cooked rice mixed with butter on the right side of his leafplate, pours water on the rice, and pours a spoonful on the palm of his right hand, sips it, and eats six pinches of rice, and then begins to eat. At the evening meal some Vaishnavs do not place the pinches of rice on the ground and do not sip water or eat the pinches of rice. All they do is to touch their eyes with water. After their meal is over, all Bráhmans sip a spoonful of water and wash their hands and feet. During dinner if two men touch, and this often happens, they are polluted, and have to apply water to the eyelids before again beginning to eat. A few old orthodox Bráhmans do not eat again till the evening or even till next day. If they choose they may avoid the fast by eating dishes called *phaláhár* which have been cooked in butter. In like manner, if a server touches one who is dining, the server has to throw away the dish and may not go into the cook-room again till he has washed his hands and feet. Except a wife, who can eat from her husband's plate, no one can eat out of a plate which has been used until it is washed and cleaned. A used leaf-plate is cast away.

At home a Bráhman wears a waistcloth. On going out he winds a scarf or *rumál* round his head, and puts on a coat, a waistcoat, and a sleeveless jacket. Both in and out of doors the women wear a robe and a bodice. The robe is passed round the waist and the lower end drawn back between the feet and tucked into the waist-band behind, the robe falling on each side of the end that is drawn back so as to hide the limbs nearly to the ankle. The upper end of the robe is drawn from the waist over the right shoulder and is then passed across the bosom and tucked into the waistband on the left side. The bodice has a back and short sleeves stopping above the elbow. It is fastened in a knot in the middle of the bosom. Children under six are allowed to play about the house without clothes. Out of doors boys and girls wear caps and coats reaching to the knee. After six years of age a girl begins to wear a robe. A boy when he is nine or ten, that is after he has been girt with the sacred thread, wears a waistband in the house and a waistcloth when he goes out. Before a Bráhman puts on a new waistcloth he rubs turmeric and red-powder on the corners at both ends, and folding it lays it before the house gods and prays them to give him a better garment next time. Finally before it is worn the new garment is sometimes laid across the back of a horse.

Yellow robes with red silk borders and lace fringes called *pátals* are a favourite dress for women during their first pregnancy. Red or crimson silk waistcloths with lace borders are worn both by men and women on holidays. The rich have introduced petticoats. Compared with the women the men wear few ornaments. The men wear the earring called *bhikbáli*, finger rings, the armlet called *pochi*, and the neck ornaments called *gop* and *kanthi*. The boys wear pearl earrings, finger rings, the bracelets called *válás* and *todás*, gold or silver waistchains, the gold necklaces called *gops* and *kanthis*, and silver anklets. The women wear on their heads *nágs* or cobras, *ketaks*, *chandrakors* or moons, and flowers or *phuls* round the back hair. Sometimes the hair is plaited and allowed to hang down the back with a number of flowers braided with the hair. In the ears they wear *bugdis*, *bális*, and *karnaphuls*. Their nose-rings are of three kinds, a ring of twenty pearls called *nath*, a ring of four or five pearls called *gádi*, and a ring with one large pearl called *mugati*. The neck is the chief object of decoration. The first ornament is the lucky-thread or *mangalsutra* which is tied to the bride's neck by the husband at the time of the marriage. Other necklaces called *tikis* are of many kinds, *geji-tikis gudin-tikis* and *vajra-tikis*; circles of gold coins, *putalis*, *jomálisars*, or *chandrahárs*, are also worn. Armlets called *vánkis* and *bájubands* are worn above the elbow, and wristlets called *pátlis* and *todás*. A thick broad gold or silver belt called *patta* clasps the waist and keeps the robe tight. Anklets of silver called *sarpolis* and *paijans* adorn the feet, and silver rings embellish the toes. Young children wear pearl earrings called *mukhs* or *mudis* and *chalatumbs* or *bhokhars*. The neck is adorned with a circlet called *hasli* and *gáthli* of gold coins or *putalis* in the

Chapter III. Population. BRÁHMANS.

middle of which are two tiger claws worked in gold. *Nágmurgis* of gold and silver are worn above the elbows and gold *bindlis* and *gunds* round the wrists. In addition to these ornaments male infants wear a gold or silver belt round the loins and anklets called *halgadag* and *kalgadag*. The infant's cap or *jhulpi* is adorned with three gold flowers, and on the lap is fastened an *arbeli* or *padak*, studded with precious stones. Most of a Bráhman's savings are invested in ornaments.

A Bráhman rises early, washes his hands and face, and repeats verses. He goes to the backyard, plucks some flowers and basil leaves for the gods, and attends to his business till ten or eleven. When he comes home he bathes, repeats prayers, worships his house gods, and dines. After dinner he takes a short nap, attends to his business, visits some neighbouring temple, and returns home in the evening. When supper is ready he washes his hands and feet, prays, eats, and goes to bed between nine and ten. A woman rises early, sweeps the house, draws water, arranges the vessels in the cook-room, removes the bedding, and lights a fire. She combs her hair, marks her brow with red-powder, puts on her nose and ear-rings, and bathes. She puts things in order in the god's room, arranges the vessels of worship, rubs sandalwood to powder, and cooks. When dinner is ready she serves it to the people of the house, and after they have dined bows to the house gods and dines. She removes what is left, cowdungs the hearth and the dining place, and washes the cooking and dining vessels, plates, and cups. She then washes the waistcloths robes and bodices, and perhaps the children's clothes, and prepares cotton wicks and leafplates. After a short nap, she sets to work again, cleaning rice, cutting vegetables, cooking and serving supper, supping, cowdunging the place where supper was eaten, and cleaning vessels, and then goes to bed.

The customs of the Belgaum Bráhmans differ little from those of the Dhárwár Bráhmans which are given in the Dhárwár Statistical Account. In religion, Bráhmans are either Vaishnavs or Smárts. Vaishnav men mark their brow, shoulders, and chest with lines and marks of the conch-shell and discus in yellow sandalwood or *gopi-chandan* earth. They daily mark their bodies with special metal seals bearing Vishnu's shell and discus. Smárt men mark the brow with a single or double level line of sandal and Vishnav men with a single upright line of *gopi-chandan*. They also mark the shoulders and chest with level lines. The wives of Vaishnavs mark the brow with an upright and the wives of Smárts with a level line of red-powder or *kunku*. They rub their cheeks and arms with turmeric at the time of bathing to give the skin a yellowish tinge. Both married and unmarried women are careful to rub the brow with red-powder. Widows are not allowed to use either turmeric or red-powder. Their heads are shaved, and, if they are Vaishnavs, the brow is marked with an up-and-down line of charcoal or *gopi-chandan* earth. Their priests are Bráhmans whom they treat with great respect. They observe all the Hindu fasts and feasts and make pilgrimages to Benares, Rámeshvar, Venkatraman, and Giri or the mountain of Venkatraman in the Madras Presidency. The head of the Vaishnav Bráhmans is Madhváchárya and of the Smárts is the Shankarácharya. These two pontiffs settle all religious disputes. They send their boys to school and are well off.

WRITERS.

Writers include three castes with a strength of 426 or 0·05 per cent of the Hindu population. Of these 98 (males 52, females 46) were Káyasth Prabhus; 284 (males 162, females 122) Mudliárs or Valalans; and 44 (males 20, females 24) Náidus.

Káyasth Prabhus.

Ka'yasth Prabhus are returned as numbering ninety-eight and as found chiefly in Belgaum and Chikodi. Three families who are settled in Párgad in Khánápur are said to have been brought by Shiváji from the Kolába district. One of these three families has the title of Subhedár, and enjoys certain cash allowances. The other Káyasth Prabhus, who are in Government service, are all from the Kolába district. They have no subdivisions. The local Káyasths are darker and stronger than those of Kolába or Ratnágiri. The men wear the headscarf, or *rumál*, instead of the turban; in other respects their dress does not differ from that of their castemen in the Konkan. They speak Maráthi and have no separate dialect. They eat fish, mutton, and game, but not domestic fowls. They are clean, neat, and hard-working, hospitable and fond of show and pleasure. Most of them are landowners, and a few who have come from Kolába are in Government service. Their household deities are Khandoba and Bhaváni. Deshasth Bráhmans are their family priests. Caste disputes are settled according to the opinion of the majority of the castemen. The Svámi of Sankeshvar is their religious teacher or *guru*. They burn their dead, forbid widow marriage, and shave their widows' heads. They send their boys to school and are a prosperous class.

Mudliárs.

Mudlia'rs or **Valalans** are returned as numbering 284 and as found chiefly in the town and sub-division of Belgaum. They are somewhat dusky in colour varying from light brown to nearly black. They are smaller and weaker than Lingáyats. The hair is always black and the eyes black, bright, and intelligent. Their home tongue is Tamil. They are clean, neat, hardworking, sober, thrifty, even-tempered, hospitable, and orderly. A Mudliár is most kind to his relations. If he is prosperous, relations flock to him from all sides and take up their abode with him. Most Mudliárs are land-owners. But they will not touch the plough if they can help it, and, as a rule, do all field-work with the help of hired labour. Some are merchants, shopkeepers, Government servants, messengers, and domestic servants. The Commissariat Department is full of Mudliárs. Except a few of the rich who own large and comfortable buildings, their houses are simple and small. They eat rice, vegetables, fish, mutton, and fowls, and drink liquor. The men wear a waistcloth, a shouldercloth, and a coloured *rumál* or headcloth. The women wear a shortsleeved bodice and a coloured robe fourteen to eighteen feet long, covering the body from the feet to the neck. They wear precious stones and pearls in the ears, pearls in the nose, gold necklaces and bracelets, and silver anklets and toe-rings. Even the poorest must wear an ornament in the ear. Widows dress in white. When a child is born, the family priest is sent for and prepares the horoscope.

Chapter III.
Population.
WRITERS.
Mudliárs.

On the twelfth or thirteenth day the priest is called, and the child is named. The parents sit on the ground, and the mother takes the child in her arms. The name is repeated thrice; an offering is made to the family god; the family priest receives a present and castefellows are given a feast. Girls are generally married between eight and nine, but sometimes not until they have come of age. When a man is on the point of death, his relations press forward, put a basil leaf and a few drops of water into his mouth, and shout the name of God. This is said to be done in the hope that the dying person may go to heaven. When life is gone the eldest son washes the head and anoints it with oil. The body is wrapped in a new cloth, stretched on a litter, and rice and betelnut are laid in the mouth. The women weep and the eldest son walks in front of the bier holding by a string a pot with fire. Between the chief mourner and the bier come musicians. Only men join the funeral party. If the dead was a person of position, cloths are spread on the ground over which the procession passes, the pieces being at once picked up and laid again in front. At the burning ground the body is laid on the funeral pile with the feet to the south, so that the head may point to the north. The mourners thrice throw a few grains of rice over the corpse's mouth. The chief mourner walks thrice round the pile with a lighted torch in his hand and an earthen waterpot on his shoulder. He thrusts the lighted torch into the north end of the pile, and lets the waterpot fall so that it breaks and the water is spilt. The chief mourner bathes in a running stream or river, and goes straight home without looking back. If he looks back it is believed that his father's sin will come on his head. Hired corpse-burners do what more is required for the burning of the body. On the next day the chief mourner, with relations and friends, goes to the burning ground, gathers the bones and ashes, washes them, pours milk over them, and places them in a small earthen pot. This pot is either carried to the nearest stream, or sent to some sacred river and buried in its sandy bed. Mourning lasts for sixteen days. During this time only one meal a day is eaten. On the seventeenth the caste is feasted, and every twelve months a memorial feast is held, when Bráhmans are fed and presented with clothes. The Mudliárs are a religious people and have images of their gods in their houses. They treat their priesst who are Bráhmans with respect. The Mudliárs formerly had a strong caste organization, and settled social disputes at meetings of the men of the caste. Of late this system of caste settlement has fallen into disfavour, and most disputes are settled in the law courts. They are in easy circumstances, not scrimped for food or for clothes. They save at ordinary times, but their marriage and other special expenses swallow their savings. They send their boys to school and take to new pursuits. On the whole they are a rising people.

Náidus.

Na'idus, numbering forty-four, are found only in Belgaum. They came into the district from Madras about forty years ago in search of work. They have no subdivisions. They are strong and well-made, and in colour and features do not differ from Mudliárs. Their home speech is Ándhra or Telugu. Most of them live in houses of the

Chapter III.
Population.
WRITERS.
Náidus.

better sort, with walls of brick and tiled roofs. Their staple food is rice and Indian millet, but they eat fish, mutton, fowls, and game, and drink liquor. They dress like Mudliárs. They are hardworking, even-tempered, hospitable, and orderly. They are writers, traders, and shopkeepers, and as English clerks write a good hand. They eat and meet socially on an equal footing with the Mudliárs, but they do not marry with them. They worship all the ordinary Bráhmanic gods, and their family god is Venkatraman. They respect Bráhmans and employ them as priests, calling them to conduct their chief ceremonies. They observe all Hindu holidays and fasts. Their customs are the same as those of the Mudliárs. They are bound together as a body. Caste disputes are settled by a headman called Desái Shetti, who is chosen from among the Náidus in consultation with the headman of the Mudliár caste. The office is not hereditary, a man is chosen because of his reputation for sense and wisdom. They send their children to school and are a rising class.

TRADERS.

Traders include eight castes with a strength of 48,837 or 6·17 per cent of the Hindu population. The following table gives the details :

BELGAUM TRADERS.

Caste.	Males.	Females.	Total.	Caste.	Males.	Females.	Total.
Bándekars ...	633	654	1287	Komtis ...	91	67	158
Bhátiás ...	43	27	70	Márvádis ...	36	14	50
Gujar Vánis ...	58	44	102	Nárvekars ...	1089	1013	2102
Jains ...	22,719	22,272	44,991				
Kalváris ...	36	41	77	Total ...	24,705	24,132	48,837

Bándekars.

Bándekars, that is people of Bándivde a village in Goa, are returned as numbering 1287 and as found in most large towns except Parasgad, Gokák, and Athni. They say they fled from Goa to escape conversion by the Portuguese, and some families still have relations in Goa. All speak Maráthi with many Konkan peculiarities like those of the Shenvis. They are divided into Bándekars, Pánavres, Sangameshvaris, and Pátáne Vánis, who do not eat together or intermarry. Their surnames are Bhogte, Vanajari, Pilankar, Nevaji, Mahájan, Patgáskar, Bandivdekar, and Karmalkar. Sameness of surname does not prevent marriage. The names in common use among men are, Venkteshshet, Rámshet, Vithushet, Pándushet, and Mahádevshet; and among women, Rukmini, Káshi, Vithábái, and Sundari. They rank with Shudras but hold themselves superior to Maráthás with whom they do not eat, though a Marátha eats food cooked by them. They have no family stocks or *gotras*. They look like Nárvekars, being of middle size, dark, strong, and muscular. Most live in untidy ill-cared for houses with walls of mud and tiled roofs. They have a couple of servants and keep dogs, goats, cows, buffaloes, and bullocks. Their every-day food is rice, pulse, millet, vegetables, milk, curds, and butter. They eat fish and crabs, and the flesh of goats, sheep, fowls, and wild hog. They give feasts at marriages and on the anniversary of their fathers' deaths. They do not offer the animals to a god before they eat them, nor do they eat animal food on holidays. They are said to have taken to flesh-eating

Chapter III.
Population.
TRADERS.
Bándekars.

and to liquor-drinking since their arrival in Belgaum. All smoke tobacco and some smoke hemp. It is the cost and not any religious scruple that prevents them regularly eating animal food. They are hardworking, honest, sober, thrifty, even-tempered, hospitable, and orderly. They are grain-sellers and grain-parchers, selling rice, millet, wheat, pulse, sugar, oil, and parched grain. They buy from Gujars and other wholesale dealers. Their boys begin as apprentices and at twelve years of age know their work thoroughly. Their occupation is steady, neither improving nor falling. Wedding and other special expenses have thrown some of them in debt. They borrow at about twelve per cent a year. They do not differ in religion or customs from the Nárvekars. Their house gods are Nágesh, Ravalnáth, and Lakhsmi, whose temples are in Goa. Their priests are Deshasth Bráhmans to whom they show much respect ; their religious head is the Shankaráchárya of Sánkeshvar. They either bury or burn the dead. They form an organized social body settling disputes according to the opinion of the majority. They send their boys to school till they are about twelve. They do not take to new pursuits but are steady and fairly prosperous.

Bhátiás.

Bha'tia's, with a strength of seventy, are found only in Belgaum and Chikodi. They have come from Cutch through Bombay within the last thirty years. They speak Cutchi and look like Gujarát Vánis. They are strong, sturdy, inclined to stoutness, and some of them fair with handsome regular features. Most live in large well-built houses with walls of stone and tiled roofs ; and have chairs, tables, boxes, metal pots and silver cups and drinking vessels. They have generally a horse, two or three cows, a couple of buffaloes and bullocks, and servants. Their staple food is wheat, rice, pulse, vegetables, and butter. They are strict vegetarians. They take no intoxicating drinks, but smoke and chew tobacco. The men and women are neat and clean in their dress and have a special liking for gay colours. Except that they wear a Gujaráti coat and Hindustáni shoes, the men dress like Deshasth Bráhmans. They formerly wore the double-peaked Bhátia turban but they now use a silver-bordered headscarf. The women wear a shortsleeved bodice, a petticoat, and a robe. They are clean, neat, hardworking, and sober, but hot-tempered. They mostly deal in cotton, grain, cocoanuts, betelnuts, dates, cocoa-kernels, sugar, butter, oil, and iron. Their chief dealings are with Hubli, Vengurla, and Bombay. They are bold and skilful traders, and are prosperous and well-to-do. They worship the usual Bráhmanic gods and their chief god is Krishna. They respect Bráhmans and call Deshasth Bráhmans to conduct their ceremonies, except that for their marriages they bring a Pokarna Bráhman from Bombay. They make pilgrimages to Benares, Mathura, Dwárka, Ayodhya, Gaya, Prayág, Pandharpur, Gokarn, and Rámeshvar. They are Vaishnavs of the Vallabháchárya sect. They burn their dead. They do not allow widows to marry, but do not force them to shave their heads. Bhátiás have a strong caste association and settle social disputes at meetings of the castemen. They send their boys to school. They are ready to take advantage of any new opening or industry, and seem likely to hold the place they have gained as the leading traders in the district.

Chapter III.
Population.
TRADERS.
Gujarát Vánis.

Gujara't Va'nis, generally called Gujar Vánis, with a strength of 102, are scattered over the district and are settled in large numbers in Chikodi. Most of them have been in the district for three generations. They are of middle size, fair, strong, and healthy. Their home tongue is Gujaráti mixed with Hindustáni, and besides their home tongue most of them speak both Hindustáni and Maráthi. They are active, hardworking, sober, thrifty, and hospitable. They are less exacting and more popular than Márwár Vánis. They live as shopkeepers, grocers, moneylenders, pearl-merchants, grain and cloth dealers, and sellers of butter, oil, and other miscellaneous articles. Many Gujarát shopkeepers are permanently settled in Belgaum villages. A few who have become landowners do not till with their own hands, but employ field labourers whose work they supervise. Except helping in village shops, the women and children add nothing to the men's earnings. Most of them live in good two-storied houses with walls of stone and tiled roofs. Their houses are clean and well kept and the walls are painted with bright fantastic colours. They are strict vegetarians. They have servants and clerks and keep cows and buffaloes. The clerks usually belong to their own caste. When castemen are not available they employ Bráhmans or qualified men of any of the other higher local castes. A clerk's salary varies from £10 to £12 (Rs. 100-120) a year, which is paid either in a lump sum or in instalments every three or four months. A clerk keeps the accounts and writes the *khatávni* or daybook. They sometimes act as their masters' agents buying and selling goods for him. A clerk generally enters a trader's service about eighteen and has finished his training by twenty-four. The men wear the small tightly-wound Gujarát Váni turban or a headscarf, a long coat, a waistcloth, and a shoulder-cloth. Except the turban there is no difference between the dress of the Gujarát and the local trader. The women draw the upper end of the robe over the left instead of over the right shoulder, and not tuck the skirt back between the feet. They are either Shraváks that is Jains, or Meshris that is Vaishnavs of the Vallabhácharya sect. The Gujarát Jains do not dine or have any social intercourse with the Belgaum Jains. Both classes are strongly opposed to the destruction of life. They keep marriage relations with Gujarát and spend large sums in marrying their children. Marriages are generally celebrated in Belgaum, but when they cannot get a suitable local match they go to Gujarát. Most of their savings are spent on their children's marriages. Though they do not allow widow marriage, they do not always enforce the rule that a widow's head should be shaved. The married dead are burnt and the unmarried dead are buried. When a death occurs in a family the female relations and caste women beat their breasts. They have their own Gujarát Bráhman priests who generally live in their houses. Gujarát Vánis keep most Hindu fasts and feasts, and during the *Diváli* holidays in November worship the goddess Lakshmi in their shops. They have a caste council and settle social disputes according to the decision of the majority of castemen generally. They send their boys to school and are a well-to-do people.

Jains.

Jains are returned as numbering 44,991 and as found all over

Chapter III. Population. TRADERS. *Jains.*

the district, chiefly in large villages. They are divided into Shetváls, Chaturtharus, Bogárs, and Panchams, who eat together but do not intermarry. Both men and women look like Lingáyats. The men wear a tuft of hair on the crown of the head and shave the moustache but not the beard or whiskers. They rub sandal-ashes on their brow and wear the sacred thread. The women mark their brow with red-powder and wear the lucky marriage-string or *mangalsutra*. They speak Kánarese. They are clean, neat, hardworking, hospitable, and timid. They are merchants, traders, husbandmen, and labourers, and a few are in Government service. Most Jains live in houses of the better class two storeys high and with walls of brick. They rear cows, buffaloes, oxen, and horses, and have metal vessels in their houses. They seldom use European articles of furniture. Their daily food is Indian millet, bread, rice, vegetables, milk, and curds. They do not touch assafœtida. They eat only in the daytime before sunset. The men wear silk or woollen waistcloths while cooking, dining, and worshipping the house gods. The men dress in a waistcloth, a coat, and a headscarf, and a second waistcloth hangs from their shoulders. The women wear a bodice and a robe without passing the skirt back between the feet. On the fifth day after the birth of a child the goddess Satvái is worshipped, and on the thirteenth the child is named and the caste people are feasted. During the first year of a boy's life his head is shaved except a tuft of hair on the crown. In his seventh year the *munj* or thread-ceremony is performed when the boy is girt with the sacred thread. A girl should be married after she is four and before she comes of age. Betrothal is confirmed by the boy's parents presenting the girl with an ornament, and after this the marriage ceremony can be performed at any time before the girl comes of age. Before the wedding a ceremony called *bhástagi* is observed and sugar and packets of betelnut and leaves are offered to relations and friends. The bride and bridegroom are rubbed with turmeric on the day before the marriage, and in the evening a ceremony called boundary-worship or *simantpuja* is performed when the boy is visited by the girl's parents, worshipped, and presented with clothes and ornaments. Before the time appointed for joining hands the house gods are worshipped and the boy and girl at their homes are rubbed with turmeric and bathed four times in hot water. Then the boy is seated on a horse and with music and a party of relations and friends goes to the girl's house. Here the priests repeat verses and the guests throw rice mixed with red-powder on the heads of the boy and girl, and the couple throw garlands of flowers round each other's necks. The festivities last for a week among the rich, sumptuous dinners being given daily to relations, friends, and castefellows, and, surrounded by a number of women, the boy and girl daub one another with sandal and red-powder and play games of luck with betelnuts. The expenses vary from £100 (Rs. 1000) among the rich to £2 (Rs. 20) among the poor, with whom marriage lasts only a day or two days at most. They burn their dead. On the third day they gather the ashes and bones and throw them into a river or the nearest stream. On the tenth day rice balls are offered to crows. On the twelfth and thirteenth days relations and castefellows are feasted. The higher classes, such as merchants and traders, do not allow widow marriage, but husbandmen and labourers practise it freely. The Jain widow is stripped of her bangles but her head is not shaven. During her monthly sickness a woman is held impure for four days and is purified by bathing in water.[1] The Shetváls and Chaturtharus are greatly devoted to the worship of Vithoba of Pandharpur and Tuljápur. The Panchams are the followers of Lakmeshvar Svámi who lives at Kolhápur. The Teacher or *guru* of the Shetváls is Dimudra Kártik who lives at Hombad near Honávar, and the Teacher of the Bogárs is Balutkárgun who lives at Málkhed in the Nizám's dominions. The Chaturtharus' Teachers have their head-quarters at Kurundvád thirty-five miles west of Athni. The Jains have their own priests and do not employ Bráhmans. They fast on the eighth and fourteenth day of every fortnight, and keep the regular Hindu holidays. They do not admit men of other castes into their community. If any one of them eats or intermarries with any one who is not a Jain he is excommunicated. Each of the four local communities, Shetváls, Chaturtharus, Bogárs, and Panchams, has its own Teacher or *svámi* who has power to fine or excommunicate. Those who are put out of caste may rejoin it by the payment of a fine. A few Jains send their boys to school. As a class they are well-to-do.

Kalvaris.

Kalvaris, with a strength of seventy-seven, are found in the town of Belgaum. They came into the district about forty years ago from Cawnpur in Upper India. They live in houses of the better sort with walls of mud and tiled roofs. Their staple food is rice, wheat, pulse, butter, and vegetables. They eat fish and the flesh of sheep, goats, pigeons, and partridges. They eat animal food on holidays and at any other time when they are able to pay for it. They drink country and foreign liquor and smoke tobacco. The men dress like Kunbis, the only peculiarity being that they pass both ends of the waistcloth between their legs. Formerly they wore a headscarf or *pheta*, a cap, or a turban folded after the Márwári fashion; they have now adopted the Marátha style. The women wear a short bodice and petticoat over which they roll a robe or *sádi* drawing one end across the right shoulder. The women mark their brows with red-powder or *kunku*, and wear glass bangles but not the lucky necklace or *mangal-sutra*. They are clean, neat, and hardworking, but hot-tempered. They are moneylenders and messengers. They worship the ordinary Bráhmanic and local gods, and pay special respect to Mahádev. They have no images in their houses. Their priests are Sarvariya Bráhmans to whom they show much respect. They keep the usual Hindu holidays. They have no spiritual head or guide, but have faith in lucky and unlucky days regarding which they consult their priests. They name their children on the day of birth. When a girl becomes ten or twelve years old, her father seeks a husband for her of not more than sixteen years of age. When he finds a suitable lad he goes to the lad's father and they talk over the matter in company with near relations and friends. After they have settled the sum to be given to the boy, which varies from £10 to £50 (Rs. 100-500), the girl's father

1 Fuller details of Jain customs and religion are given in the Dhárwár Statistical Account.

Chapter III. Population. TRADERS. *Kalvaris.*

hands packets of betelnut and leaves and retires. Next the girl's parents send 2*s.* (Re. 1), ¾*d.* (½ *anna*), a piece of turmeric root, and some betelnut and leaves to the boy's parents, and the marriage is considered settled. On a lucky day both the boy and girl are rubbed with turmeric at their homes and at the lucky moment a cloth is held between them and the priest repeats marriage verses, and rice is thrown on their heads. Packets of betelnut and leaves are handed round and the priest retires. Two or three days after a feast is held, but the parents of the bride never eat at the bridegroom's house. When a Kalvari dies the chief mourner has his moustache shaved on the ninth day if the dead is a female, and on the tenth day if the dead is a male. On the thirteenth a feast is given to the castemen. They are bound together as a body, and settle social disputes according to the opinion of the majority of the men. They send their children to school, taking away their girls at ten and their boys at fifteen. They are a well-to-do class.

Komtis.

Komtis, with a strength of 158, are found in small numbers over the whole district. They are said to have come to Belgaum from Madras. They call themselves Vaishyas. As a class they are dark, strong, and regular featured. Their home tongue is Telugu. They are hardworking, even-tempered, thrifty, and hospitable. They deal in grain, spices, clothes and jewels, act as moneychangers, make necklaces of sweet basil beads, make snuff, till, and work as writers and clerks. In poor families the elder women help in the shop, stitch leafplates, and parch pulse. Few Komtis wear the sacred thread and some like the Lingáyats hang a *ling* round their necks. They allow polygamy, and forbid widow marriage, but seldom force the widow to shave her head. Their headman, who is called *sheti,* is required to be present at all their ceremonies. He settles their social disputes in accordance with the opinion of the majority of the men. Komtis send their boys to school, and are a rising class.

Márvádis.

Ma'rva'dis, or MÁRWÁR VÁNIS, are a small community numbering about fifty scattered over the district. They say they have come from Márwár for trade purposes within the last fifty years. They are of two main divisions, Shrávaks or Jains and Meshris or Vaishnavs, who neither eat together nor intermarry. The men wear a lock of hair curling over each temple and a top-knot. They formerly wore beards, but of late they have taken to shaving the face except the moustache. They speak a little Kánarese and Maráthi, but their home tongue is Márwári. They are hardworking, miserly, and sober. They are notorious usurers and unscrupulous in their dealings. Husbandmen who fall into their power are generally treated without consideration or pity. They deal in cloth, grain, and spices, but the chief source of their profits is moneylending. They live in houses generally one storey high, with walls of brick and stones and tiled roofs. They have cattle and servants generally Kunbis or Musalmáns, whom they pay 6*s.* to 12*s.* (Rs. 3-6) a month. They have also a clerk or two, a man of their own caste, who is paid £7 10*s.* to £20 (Rs. 75-200) a year. They are strict vegetarians and drink no liquor. The men dress in small tightly-wound red and yellow or pink turban, a tight-fitting fulltailed coat, and a waistcloth.

Chapter III. Population. TRADERS. *Márvádis.*

The women wear an open-backed bodice, a petticoat and a robe or *odni*, whose upper end is drawn from the band of the petticoat and falls like a veil over the left side of the head and face. They wear a gold armlet above the elbow and gold and bone bracelets. To marry their boys many go to their native country and give the girl's parents £10 to £100 (Rs.100-1000). A week to three weeks before a marriage the bridegroom's and bride's parents form separate processions called *bindoris*, and move through the streets. They burn their dead. They do not allow widow marriage, but do not shave their widows' heads. The Shrávaks are said to worship Vishnu and Báláji, as well as their own saints or Tirthankars. They have their own Márwár Bráhmans, who officiate as priests in their houses and perform their religious ceremonies. They fast on the second, sixth, eighth, and tenth day of the first fortnight of *Bhádrapad* or September, and keep the leading Hindu holidays. Their social disputes are settled at meetings of the castemen. They teach their boys themselves, and are well-to-do, carrying away large fortunes when they return to their native country.

Nárvekars.

Na'rvekars, or inhabitants of Nárve in Goa, are returned as numbering 2102, and as found in Khánápur, Belgaum, Sampgaon, Chikodi, and Parasgad. They are said to have come into the district about two hundred years ago for purposes of trade. They call themselves Vaishyas, and have no subdivisions. They are fair and their women are well-made. They speak Konkan-Maráthi, and live in substantial buildings with tiled roofs. The well-to-do, among the men, and all the women dress like Bráhmans and the poorer men like Maráthás. Their staple food is rice, pulse, and Indian millet-bread, but they eat fish and flesh and drink liquor. They eat twice a day at noon and between eight and nine at night. They are clean, hardworking, sober, and hospitable. They are moneylenders and grocers, dealing in clarified butter and cloth. Some of them parch rice, and make and sell sweetmeats, while others are husbandmen. Their women and their children of sixteen and over help them in their work, and they generally have small sums of money at their credit. They do not work as labourers. They name their children when they are twelve days old, clip their boys' hair for the first time when they are between two and five, and invest them with the sacred thread at the time of marriage. They marry their girls before they come of age, and their boys generally before they are twenty. They do not allow widow marriage. They are Shaivs and worship Mahádev, Ganpati, Bhagvati, Kanakádevi, Yellamma, Rámling, Venkatpati, Mhálsa, and Tukái. The ordinary Marátha Bráhmans are their priests. They keep all Hindu fasts and feasts, and make pilgrimages to Benares, Gokarn, Mahábaleshvar, and Yellamma in Belgaum. In common with other Hindus, they believe in sorcery, witchcraft, and soothsaying. Petty disputes are settled by the men of the caste. More serious matters, as when a widow becomes pregnant, when a girl comes of age before she is married, and when a member of the caste eats with a person of another caste, are referred to the Svámi of Sankeshvar when he visits the district in his yearly tour. The Nárvekars send their boys to school, and are a rising class.

Chapter III.

Population.

HUSBANDMEN.

Husbandmen include thirteen classes, with a strength of 208,074 or 26·29 per cent of the Hindu population. The following statement gives the details:

BELGAUM HUSBANDMEN.

CLASS.	Males.	Females	Total.	CLASS.	Males.	Females	Total.
Chhatris ...	7126	7163	14,289	Maráthás ...	60,358	58,944	119,302
Guravs ...	698	704	1402	Mithgávdás ...	4	...	4
Hanbars ...	7086	7083	14,169	Radis ...	3163	3147	1310
Kámátis ...	11	8	19	Rajputs ...	1343	1354	2697
Kulmarus ...	36	39	75	Tiláris ...	2819	2753	5572
Kunbis ...	21,546	21,105	42,651				
Lamáns ...	562	414	976				
Lonáris ...	299	309	608	Total ...	105,051	103,023	208,074

Chhatris.

Chhatris, or **Khetris,** are returned as numbering 14,289 and as found all over the district. They seem to be long settled in the district and are said to have no tradition of any former home. They have no subdivisions. Families having the same surname do not intermarry. They are dark and tall and speak Kánarese. Most of them live in thatched huts and dress like cultivating Maráthás. Their staple food is Indian millet bread, rice, pulse, and vegetables; but they eat fish and the flesh of goats, sheep, domestic fowls, and game. The monthly food expenses of a family of six is about 16*s.* (Rs. 8). They are clean but hot-tempered, and work as husbandmen, village servants, and labourers. Their customs do not differ from those of Kunbis with whom they eat. Their family gods are Venkoba and Máruti, and their priests are Deshasth Bráhmans. They keep the usual Hindu holidays and fast either on Saturday or on Sunday. Their social disputes are settled by meetings of the castemen. They do not send their boys to school nor take to new pursuits, but are a steady class.

Guravs.

Guravs are returned as numbering 1402 and as found chiefly in Athni, Chikodi, and Gokák. They are strong and well-made with regular features. The men wear the top-knot, but neither the beard nor whiskers. The home speech of most of the Guravs is Kánarese, but those in Khánápur, Belgaum, and Chikodi speak Maráthi. They are honest, sober, even-tempered, and hospitable. Some serve at the shrines of the village gods and live on the villagers' offerings of food and grain. At harvest time the villagers give them a small share of the grain. A few hold rent-free lands in return for performing the service in certain temples. They are husbandmen and musicians, beating drums and playing fiddles. They accompany dancing-girls when they go to perform on festive occasions, and also teach them to sing and dance. A majority of them live by selling leafplates, which they supply without charge to public servants on tour and to villagers who give them a share of the crop. Their women and children help them in their work. Some keep cows and she-buffaloes, and sell milk and butter. Their houses are small and ill-furnished, with nothing but a few earthen pots and one or two blankets and waistcloths. They neither eat flesh nor drink liquor. Their staple food consists of Indian millet, rice, vegetables, and pulse. Indoors the men wear a waistcloth, and out of doors they draw a second cloth over the shoulders, and either wear a turban or roll a handkerchief round the head. Their women wear the robe and bodice, but do not pass the end of the robe between the feet. The average monthly expenses of a family of six vary from 14*s.* to £1 (Rs. 7-10). They worship the goddess Páchvi or Satvái on the fifth day after the birth of a child and name the child on the thirteenth. Their marriage customs are the same as those of Gondhlis. Bráhmans officiate at their marriages. They allow widow marriage. They burn their dead and throw the ashes into a running stream on the third day. They offer a ball of rice to the crows on the tenth, and perform the *shráddha* ceremony on the eleventh or twelfth when they feast the caste. They are a religious people. Their chief gods are Shiv, Vishnu, Ravalnáth, and Máruti. Their priests are the ordinary Marátha Bráhmans. They do not become ascetics. They have no *gurus* or religious teacher, and they never go on pilgrimage. They say they do not believe in sorcery or witchcraft, but they have faith in soothsaying. The local soothsayers are generally learned Deccan Bráhmans, well versed in astronomy, who are consulted in cases of sickness. They keep the usual Hindu holidays. They have no headman and settle their disputes at meetings of the castemen. They do not send their boys to school and are a falling people. The demand for their leafplates has of late greatly fallen as most people now make their own plates.

Hanbars.

Hanbars are returned as numbering 14,169 and as found all over the district. They are numerous in the hilly tracts of Belgaum, Khánápur, and Chikodi. Of late they have been obliged to live in or near villages in consequence of the spread of reserved forests. They are divided into Hosa or New Hanbars and Hale or Old Hanbars who eat together and intermarry. They are dark, tall, and strong, with regular features, thin lips, high nose, and lank hair. The men wear the top-knot often in a matted state, and the moustache. Their home tongue is Maráthi. They generally live in houses with thatched roofs and walls of wooden planking. Those living in villages dress like Kunbis and those in the hilly tracts in a loincloth, a waistcloth, and a small piece of cloth rolled round the head. Their staple food is rice, *jvári*, and *rági* or *sáva* bread, but they eat fish and flesh and drink liquor. They smoke *gánja* and both chew and smoke tobacco. They are dirty and hot-tempered, but thrifty and honest. Some keep cows and she-buffaloes, the cows worth £1 to £2 (Rs. 10-20) and the buffaloes £2 to £3 (Rs. 20-30). They sell milk and butter. Those who live in villages and in the eastern parts of the district are either husbandmen or day-labourers. The labourers are paid by the day either in cash at the rate of 3*d.* (2 *as.*) for a man, 2¼*d.* (1½ *as.*) for a woman, and 1½*d.* (1 *an.*) for a child over thirteen; when paid in grain it is generally Indian millet at the daily rate of 4-6 pounds (2-3 *shers*). The Hanbars are peasant-holders, under-holders, and field-labourers. They grow both watered and dry crops. They are skilful husbandmen being helped by their women and their children of over twelve or thirteen. Their household gods are Máruti and Yellamma. Their family priests are Deshasth Bráhmans who officiate at their marriages, and are consulted for lucky days and names for their children. They

Chapter III.
Population.
HUSBANDMEN.

say they do not believe in witchcraft or sorcery, but have faith in soothsaying. When a soothsayer is consulted a packet of betelnut and leaves and a copper coin or two are laid before him, and he opens his book and after pondering over it gives an answer. The Hanbars fast on Friday, and keep the usual Hindu holidays. They have no headman and settle social disputes at meetings of the castemen. They do not send their boys to school and as a class are poor and unprosperous.

Kámáthis.

Ka'ma'this,[1] with a strength of nineteen, are found only in Belgaum. They say that they came from the Madras Karnátak about sixty years ago in search of food. They have no subdivisions. They look like Maráthás and speak Telugu at home and Maráthi out of doors. They live in small houses with walls of mud and tiled roofs. Their houses are neither neat nor clean and they rear no useful or pet animals. They are great eaters but not good cooks. Their everyday food is rice, Indian millet, pulse, and vegetables. Whenever they can afford to get them, they eat fish and the flesh of goats, sheep, hogs, and domestic and game birds. Their only caste feasts are at the time of weddings. They are excessively fond of liquor, drinking both country and foreign spirits. All smoke tobacco and some smoke hemp. The men wear a top-knot, moustache, and whiskers; and the women tie their hair in a knot at the back of the head and neither decorate it with flowers nor use false hair. Neither men nor women are neat or clean in their dress. The men wear a waistcloth, a headscarf or *rumál*, a shouldercloth, and a short coat; and the women a shortsleeved bodice and a robe or *lugade* whose end they do not draw back between the feet. Their family gods are Venkoba and Máruti. They respect Bráhmans and call them to conduct their chief ceremonies at the time of birth, marriage, puberty, and death. Their Bráhman priests are either Karhádás or Deshasths. They keep the regular Hindu holidays, and fast on the elevenths of *Ashádh* in July. They do not make pilgrimages. They believe in soothsaying, omens, and lucky and unlucky days. Their customs do not differ from those of Kunbis. They allow widow marriage and bury their dead. They are bound together as a body and their social disputes are settled at mass meetings of the caste. They do not send their boys to school and are a poor class.

Kulmarus.

Kulmarus, or IRON-WORKERS, from *kulume* the Kánarese for a forge, with a strength of seventy-five, are found in Khánápur and Sampgaon. They have no subdivisions and speak Maráthi. They look like Kunbis, the men wearing the top-knot and the moustache. They live in small houses with walls of mud and thatched roofs. They rear cows, bullocks, and buffaloes. Their staple food is Indian millet or *náchni*. They eat fish and flesh, drink liquor, and smoke tobacco. The men wear a headscarf or *rumál*, a shouldercloth, and

[1] The word Kámáthi is supposed to come from *kám* work and to mean a labourer. But there are many classes of Kámáthis of all positions and occupations from Bráhmans to Mhárs. The name seems to come from Komometh a tract in the Nizám's dominions.

a loincloth or *langoti*. The women wear a bodice and a robe whose end they do not pass back between the feet. They are dirty and untidy, but hardworking and orderly. They have given up their old craft of iron-smelting and work as husbandmen, some being under-holders and others field-labourers. Their women help in the fields. They rank below Kunbis who do not eat from them. They respect Bráhmans and call them to conduct their birth and marriage ceremonies. They worship the ordinary Bráhmanic and local gods and their household deity is Yellamma. They keep the regular Hindu holidays but do not fast or go on pilgrimage. They believe in soothsaying and witchcraft and their customs do not differ from those of Kunbis. They bury the dead and allow widow marriage. They are bound together as a body and settle social disputes at caste meetings. They do not send their boys to school and are a poor class.

Kunbis.

Kunbis[1] are returned as numbering 42,650 and as found in the Athni, Belgaum, Chikodi, and Khánápur sub-divisions. They are divided into Konkanis also known as Detale or Kále Kunbis and Maráthás also called Kunbis proper or Kulvádis. The Kulvádis eat from the Káles, but the Káles do not eat from the Kulvádis.. They do not intermarry. The Detale or Kále Kunbis are found only in Khánápur into which they seem to have come from North Kánara, where their caste is numerous. They speak Konkani, the common speech in the neighbouring sub-division of Supa in North Kánara and in Goa.

The names in common use for men of the Detale Kunbi caste are, Bábi, Govind, Gangápa, Ithu, Jánu, Náru, Phondu, Punna, Rám, Shába, Topána and Yenku; and for women, Bhágirthi, Chimna, Duvárki, Gangái, Jánki, Mánkái, Rámái, Remani, Sámni, Umi, and Yesu. They contract marriages only with certain families which have been fixed by their forefathers. Their house gods are silver or copper plates called *tákis* with embossed humanlike figures. The names of the deities are Birámani, Pánchmáya, and Sáteri.

The Maráthi or Kulvádi Kunbis seem to have come from the Maráthi-speaking districts of the Deccan. Their home speech is Maráthi and their family gods are, Kedárling also called Jotiba whose chief shrine is in the Kolhápur state; Tulja Bhaváni whose head shrine is in Tuljápur in the Nizám's territory; Somnáth in South Káthiáwár; Yellamma in Ugargolla in the Parasgad sub-division of Belgaum; and Khandoba in Jejuri in the Purandhar sub-division of Poona. They have two hundred and ninety-two surnames.[2] Of

---

[1] The word *kunbi* is pronounced as *kulbi* in the Belgaum and Khánápur sub-divisions and as *kunbi* in the Athni and Chikodi sub-divisions. It is nowhere pronounced *kurumbi*.

[2] These surnames are, Áble, M., Abhag, M., Abhire, U., Ábhore, M., Abrut, M., Advele, M., Age, M., Ahir, M., Akhade, S., Anag, B., Anag, M., Andhak, M., Aushadhárarao, M., Ávcháre, M., Ávade, S., Ávati, S., Áváre, M., Bábar, B., Bádale, M., Badáre, S., Barage, S., Bhádolkar, S., Bhadurge, B., Bhále, M., Bhanvase, M., Bhand, M., Bhápkar, M., Bhayásur, M., Bhejan, S., Bhis, S., Bhodave, B., Bhoite, B., Bhoják, M., Bhore, M., Bhosale, B., Bhudke, M., Bhujag, U., Biraje, B., Bodake, S., Bodhe, M., Budhe, B., Chándel, B., Chavhán, M., Ched, M., Cheke, U., Chikane, B., Chitravade, B., Chodháre, U., Chor, B., Chorade, B.,

Chapter III.
Population.
HUSBANDMEN.
Kunbis.

the whole, number one hundred and two trace their origin to the moon; seventy-eight trace their origin to the sun; and eighty-one to the god Brahma. The twenty-nine remaining surnames are said to belong to miscellaneous tribes. Marriage between persons of the same surname is forbidden. They are generally stoutly made, sallow, and over the middle height. The face is oval, the eyes small, the nose high, the lips thin, the cheekbones low, the cheeks gaunt, the head hair lank, and the face hair thick. They are not liable to any special disease and are generally longlived. The Maráthi spoken by the Kulvádis is rougher and less clear than Bráhman Maráthi. Among the peculiarities of their dialect may be noticed, *máj*, to me; *tuj*, to you; *jevos*, to eat; *lai*, much; *khate* or *khalete*, where; *váich* or *ullas*, a little; *gont* (Kánarese), to know; *háya*, is; *nháya*, is not; and *mula* (Kánarese), a corner. Detale Kunbis speak the Konkani which prevails in Goa and in the north of Kánara. In towns and large villages most Maráthi Kunbis live in houses with mud walls and tiled roofs. Most village Kunbis live in thatched huts. Their dwellings are untidy and ill-cared for. The only household goods are field tools, one or two brass or copper pots, and a number of earthen vessels used in cooking

---

Chukaliya, B., Dágade, S., Dágal, B., Daire, S., Dalavi, U., Darekar, M., Dásháde, B., Davekar, B., Dhámpále, M., Dhamadhere, S., Dhamále, B., Dhanik, B., Dhápál, B., Dharmaráj, B., Dhavle, M., Dhek, B., Dhisale, B., Dhitak, S., Dhobare, M., Dhoke, U., Dhole, S., Dhomse, U., Dhone, U., Dorik, B., Dubal, B., Dubule, S., Dudhare, M., Duduskar, M., Dumáge, M., Dunage, M., Durátma, B., Dure, M., Gadagopál, M., Gadavarg, M., Gádave, S., Gágule, S., Gáikavád, S., Garud, B., Gávde, M., Gavde, M., Gavhár, M., Gharáte, S., Ghátage, S., Ghorade, S., Ghorapade, B., Ghule, S., Gole, B., Goli, B., Gore, S., Gujádhe, B., Gudhe, S., Gujakar, B., Gujar, M., Gujávade, B., Guje, S., Gurusále, S., Haran, M., Honmáne, M., Idalakar, B., Igavale, B., Ignale, B., Isidage, S., Itápe, U., Jachak, S., Jádhav, M., Jagdále, M., Jagmal, B., Jagnivás, M., Jamdáde, B., Jágdale, B., Jávale, U., Jitakar, S., Kadam, S., Kájale, S., Kákde, S., Kalam, S., Kalamb, S., Kalebhar, M., Kále, B., Kálge, M., Kálmukh, S., Kalaskar, B., Kalyánkar, M., Kankále, S., Kánpháte, B., Kánte, B., Kapále, B., Kápse, B., Karáde, B., Karálkar, M., Kárle, S., Karmukh, S., Kasále, M., Káshte, B., Kátaváde, M., Kaustube, S., Kantuke, M., Kavade, B., Kavále, M., Kavre, U., Kesarkar, S., Khádekar, S., Khadágale, M., Khaláte, U., Khánadáre, B., Khándekar, M., Khárát, S., Khilláre, M., Khirságar, U., Khogane, U., Khule, S., Kirdatt, M., Kodag, M., Kodhe, M., Kadu, U., Kokare, M., Kokáte, S., Kolhár, M., Kollále, S., Kuráde, U., Lad, M., Lád, M., Ládak, U., Ládge, M., Lahule, M., Lavte, U., Lokhande, S., Londe, B., Machále, B., Mádhav, M., Madge, B., Madikar, S., Madukar, S., Magar, B., Mahale, B., Mahate, B., Mákhmakhle, M., Male, M., Máne, B., Máskar, S., Maske, S., Mede, M., Mhade, S., Mhadik, S., Mohite, M., Morbhe, M., More, M., Marik, M., Nád, S., Nágidave, U., Náglilek, U., Nagne, U., Nagváde, U., Nalga, S., Nalvade, B., Navle, B., Nikalank, S., Nikam, S., Nimbálkar, M., Páchpore, M., Páchpute, M., Páde, U., Panchánan, M., Pansamble, B., Parihár, S., Pavár, M., Phadtare, B., Phanindre, U., Phátak, S., Pisále, B., Pol, B., Polat, S., Pratihár, S., Ráchode, S., Ragte, S., Rajhanse, B., Randive, M., Rankhámbe, B., Ranpise, B., Ránrákshas, B., Ranvágure, S., Rananavar, B., Rasál, S., Rastkunde, M., Rautrao, B., Rumále, M., Sáble, M., Sáde, M., Saildar, S., Sákle, M., Sakpál, M., Sále, B., Sálokhe, B., Sánge, U., Sáráte, B., Sarkate, B., Satpal, M., Sátpute, M., Sávle, S., Setge, S., Shedger, S., Shelár, S., Sinágare, M., Sinde, U. Sirke, M., Sirsát, B., Sisode, B., Sitole, S., Sokávant, B., Sonvane, B., Sukhe, S., Surkar, U., Surpale, U., Sursen, M., Sámvant, B., Suryavanshi, S., Táde, M., Tágmoge, B., Tákare, M., Talkar, U., Támbe, M., Tanvade, M., Taváre, S., Thorát, S., Thote, S., Tibole, S., Todmale, M., Tode, M., Tungáre, B., Tupe, S., Upáse, U., Vádágare, B., Vágchávare, M., Váge, M., Vagmode, M., Vákde, M., Vánve, U., Waráde, S., Vayále, B., Virdatt, M., Voge, M., Yádhav, M., Yáharu, B.*

* M = Moon, S = Sun, U = Uncertain, B = Brahma.

and for storing grain and oil, one handmill *ukhal-musal*, a grinding slab or *páta-varvanta*, and a few bamboo baskets. They generally have one or more pairs of bullocks and buffaloes and one or two cows or she-buffaloes. Most of them rear hens and keep a dog. They rarely own goats, and never have sheep. Among Detale Kunbis, the grown members of a family generally live in one house. As one of these undivided Kunbi families includes fifty to a hundred and fifty members, their oblong thatched houses are very large and are divided into separate lodgings by wattled walls of *kárvi* or Strobilanthus stems. The furniture in a Konkani Kunbi's house is much the same as in a Maráthi Kunbi's, and like the Maráthi Kunbis they keep dogs and cattle; but they do not rear domestic fowls as they neither eat nor sell them. They have separate houses for their cattle. Both classes are temperate in eating and drinking, their every-day food being *náchni* bread and *náchni* gruel or *ámbil*. The well-to-do take a little rice every day, and the poor take rice on holidays. Their holiday dishes are round cakes of rice, wheat, and pulse called *vadas;* fried cakes of wheat, gram, and coarse sugar called *telchiás;* sweet cakes of rice balls or *undes;* plantain-shaped wheat or rice cakes filled with coarse sugar, boiled gram or parched rice flour or *rájgira* (Amaranthus tristis) seed boiled in steam; rice vermicelli or *shevaya;* rice cakes called *ghávan;* broad round cakes of wheat filled with boiled gram and coarse sugar called *polyás;* and milk boiled with rice and coarse sugar called *khir*. The Maráthi Kunbi eats fish, crabs, sheep and goats, the wild hog, the deer, and the hare. They do not eat beef. They eat eggs, and cocks and hens, but not ducks, geese, peacocks, guineafowls, or turkeys. Of wild birds they eat the partridge, snipe, quail, wild duck, and pigeon. When the Kunbis, whether Maráthás or Konkanis, go to hunt, they visit the temple of the village god and pray for success. If they kill they lay the game before the village god, offer him a piece, and take the rest home. The flesh offered to the god becomes the property of the temple-ministrant or *pujári*. The Konkani Kunbi eats all the animal food which is eaten by the Maráthi Kunbi except sheep, goats, cocks and hens, and eggs. He gives no reason for this except that they are forbidden by caste rules. Neither Konkani nor Maráthi Kunbis eat animal food daily. They take it only on special occasions and on certain holidays. This is because they cannot afford meat oftener; it is not from any religious or other scruple. Neither Maráthi nor Konkani Kunbis drink palm-juice. The Konkanis take no liquor but Maráthi Kunbis drink country and European spirits. Both classes smoke tobacco. Except in the west of the district, Kunbis take only two meals a day, one between eleven and twelve in the morning, the other between seven and eight at night. In the west the Kunbis take three meals a day. At eight breakfast, consisting of two cakes of *náchni*, a cup of gruel or *ámbil*, some chillies, garlic, and salt, and sometimes a cooked vegetable; dinner about twelve of bread, gruel, butter, milk, and vegetables; and supper at seven of bread, rice and curry.

Kunbis of both classes are generally poorly clad and show little

Chapter III.
Population.
HUSBANDMEN.
Kunbis.

regard for cleanliness or neatness. The men of both classes shave the head once a month except the top-knot or *shendi* and the face except the moustache and occasionally the whiskers. The men wear round the head a scarf or *rumál* six to eight feet square of coarse local handwoven cloth costing 1*s.* to 1*s.* 6*d.* (8 - 12 *as.*). The upper part of the body from the shoulders to the loins is covered by a piece of rough country cloth three to three and a half feet broad and seven to eight feet long and varying in price from 9*d.* to 1*s.* 1½*d.* (6 - 9 *as.*). When at work in the fields this cloth is tied so as to form a jacket. The waistcloth is spread over the head and back and the upper ends drawn through the armpits; then the right-hand end is passed over the left shoulder and the left-hand end over the right shoulder and both ends are tied together at the nape of the neck. The loincloth or *langoti* is a rough country cloth two or three feet square costing 1½*d.* to 3¾*d.* (1 - 2½ *as.*). To gird the loins they also wear the *kácha*, a long narrow country cloth three or four inches broad and five or six yards long, varying in price from 3*d.* to 4½*d.* (2 - 3 *as.*). They wear sandals or *vaháns*, which are generally made by Chambhárs and cost 6*d.* to 1*s.* (4 - 8 *as.*). Besides these the *kámbli* or blanket is worn over the head and used both as a cloak to keep off the sun, cold, and rain and as bedding. These blankets are generally three to four feet broad and eight to eleven feet long. They are made in the district of black wool by Kurburs or Dhangars and range in price from 2*s.* to 3*s.* (Rs. 1 - 1½). During the cold and rainy seasons Kunbis generally wear a jacket made from worn-out blankets. Some Maráthi Kunbis wear short breeches or *cholnás* reaching to the knee and a waistcoat or *bandi* or a sleeveless jacket or *kabcha* of country cloth. The breeches cost 4½*d.* to 7½*d.* (3 - 5 *as.*) and the waistcoat 7½*d.* to 10½*d.* (5 - 7 *as.*). On holidays they wear a new headscarf, generally black, a silk-bordered shouldercloth or *dhotar*, and a coat or *angarkha* of white cotton or of cheap black or red woollen. Men of both classes wear gold earrings or *bhikbáli* worth 4*s.* to 6*s.* (Rs. 2 - 3) in the upper part of the right ear; a silver armlet or *kade* worth £1 4*s.* to £2 10*s.* (Rs. 12 - 25) round the left wrist; and a silver girdle or *kadadora* worth £1 10*s.* to £2 (Rs. 15 - 20) round the waist. Besides these ornaments the Konkani Kunbis always wear gold earrings or *gots* worth 4*s.* to 10*s.* (Rs. 2 - 5) in the lobes of both ears. The women of both classes braid their hair, doing it up once a week or once a fortnight, generally on Mondays. On holidays they deck their hair with flowers and the Konkani women with a fragrant herb called *tirap.* Maráthi Kunbi women wear the robe or *sádi*, and the bodice or *choli.* Unlike a Bráhman woman who passes the skirt of the robe between the feet and tucks it in at the back, the Maráthi Kunbi woman does not pass the ends between her feet but gathers the folds on her left hip. The upper part of the robe is drawn over the head. Konkani Kunbi women wear no bodice. They gather the folds of the robe exactly in the middle just as Bráhman women do, and tuck it in at the waist behind. The upper part of the robe is drawn up from the waist under the armpits and the ends tied in a knot between the shoulders, leaving the arms, shoulders, neck, and head bare. The robes are three feet broad and fifteen to twenty-two feet long. They are made in handlooms at Murgod, Gokák, Sankeshvar, Bail Hongal, Kittur, Deshnur, and other places in the district. The commonest colour in use is black or red or a mixture of black and red. The robes vary in price from 3*s.* to 6*s.* (Rs. 1½ - 3). The bodice costs from 6*d.* to 1*s.* (4 - 8 *as.*). On holidays the women wear a silk-bordered robe ranging in price from 10*s.* to £2 10*s.* (Rs. 5 - 25) and a silk-bordered bodice valued at 1*s.* 6*d.* to 3*s.* (12 *as.*- Rs. 1½).

The ornaments worn by a Maráthi Kunbi woman are toe-rings or *jodvis* of queen's metal worth 6*d.* to 1*s.* (4 - 8 *as.*); in the nose a *nath* worth 10*s.* to 14*s.* (Rs. 5 - 7) or a *moti* worth 8*s.* to 16*s.* (Rs. 4 - 8); in the ears, *gáths* worth 6*s.* to 8*s.* (Rs. 3 - 4) and *bugdis* worth £1 to £2 10*s.* (Rs. 10 - 25); round the neck the lucky-thread or *mangalsutra* worth 2*s.* to 3*s.* (Rs. 1 - 1½) and a *tiki* worth 10*s.* (Rs. 5). On the upper arm or elbow a pair of silver bracelets *tolbandis* valued at £2 to £3 (Rs. 20 - 30), on the wrists two pairs of silver bracelets or *kákans* valued at 8*s.* to 12*s.* (Rs. 4 - 6) and glass bangles. Girls wear anklets, generally of queen's metal, and seldom of silver. A married girl, on reaching womanhood, generally gives up wearing anklets. Girls also wear a waistbelt or *patta.* Except the lucky-necklace or *mangalsutra,* anklets, and toe-rings or *jodvis,* widows wear all the ornaments worn by married women. But they do not mark the brow with red-powder or *kunku.* Konkani Kunbi women wear gold earrings or *tanviddás,* worth 6*s.* to 12*s.* (Rs. 3 - 6); a number of strings of small red and white glass beads round the neck, worth 3*d.* (2 *as.*); a lucky necklace, armlets or *tolbandis,* brass bracelets or *pátlis* worth 1½*d.* to 3*d.* (1 - 2 *as.*), and toe-rings. Though neither clean nor neat, Kunbis are honest and simple people, hardworking, and generally sober, thrifty, orderly, and hospitable. The women are hardworking, simple, virtuous, and obedient. Most of them are landholders and the rest are field-labourers. Most grow rice, *rági, sáva,* and millet, but some are skilled husbandmen, raising sugarcane and other garden crops. Their women and children work with them in the field. Field-workers are paid in grain during the reaping season and at other times in cash. When there is nothing doing in the fields they work as day-labourers. They also grow fruit and vegetables in their back yards and sell them in the nearest markets. Some gather and sell firewood. They also make butter and sell it in the nearest market. In towns they sell milk and curds. In spite of their hard work, as a class Kunbis are in debt. The debt is caused both by ordinary and by special expenses. They borrow at twelve to twenty-five per cent a year. Though they are still indebted their standard of comfort is considerably higher than it formerly was. Every one wishes to have a pair of bullocks, copper pots, a better house, a cart, ornaments, and good and clean clothes. In these small luxuries their balance of saving is spent and nothing is left to meet special expenses. Formerly few husbandmen had carts, copper pots, or valuable clothes and ornaments. They kept all their savings by them in cash, ready to meet special expenses.

During the rainy season the men of the family go early to the fields. The rest of the household tend the cattle or fetch firewood

Chapter III.
Population.
HUSBANDMEN.
Kunbis.

or grass. They return home about ten, take their morning meal, and after eleven again go to work, returning between five and six. Women generally rise at four, grind corn, and prepare bread-gruel and vegetables. After sunrise they go to some well, pond, or stream to fetch water, and on their return sweep the house. After the morning meal they start about ten to work in the fields with their husbands. From seed time in June to harvest in November-December both men and women are busy in the fields and when the crops are ripening many of them watch by night as well as by day. During the hot season Kunbis go to their fields in the early morning. About eight breakfast is brought by one of the children or women who stay and work with the men. They go home at noon, dine, and returning at two, work till sunset. Sometimes, if they have much to do, they remain all day in the field. Boys from eight upwards tend cattle, and from ten to fifteen are taught the lighter parts of husbandry. A boy of fifteen or sixteen is fit for most branches of field work. Kunbis are busy all the year round, but with those who have no garden crops work is light in January, February, and part of March. Monday is a day of rest for the bullocks, and and with some full-moon days are holidays, and are kept as days of new-moon days rest. The property of a Kunbi family fairly off and living in a style of reasonable comfort may be estimated at about £22 (Rs. 220). Of this £2 10*s.* to £5 (Rs. 25-50) represent the value of the house; £11 10*s.* to £14 (Rs. 115-140) the value of the furniture and household goods;[1] and £3 to £4 (Rs. 30-40) the value of the clothes. The yearly charges of a family of five persons, a husband wife two children and an aged relation or dependent, living in fair comfort, are estimated at £15 to £20 (Rs. 150-200). Of this amount food and drink charges are estimated at £7 to £9 (Rs. 70-90); dress charges at £1 10*s.* to £2 10*s.* (Rs. 15-25); the wages of a servant are estimated at £4 to £6 (Rs. 40-60); and the keep of the cattle at £2 10*s.* to £3 (Rs. 25-30) a year. The estimated charges for special expenses are, for a birth 5*s.* to 10*s.* (Rs. 2½-5); for a marriage of a son £10 to £15 (Rs. 100-150); for the marriage of a daughter £2 to £3 (Rs. 20-30); for a daughter's coming of age 10*s.* to 15*s.* (Rs. 5-7½); and for her first pregnancy 10*s.* to 15*s.* (Rs. 5-7½); and for a death 10*s.* to 15*s.* (Rs. 5-7½). Both branches of Kunbis are religious. The family gods of the Maráthi Kunbis are Kedárling otherwise called Jotiba, Tulja Bhaváni, Somnáth, and Yellamma; those of the Konkani Kunbis are Birámani, Sáteri, and Panchamáya. Their family priests, who are Deshasth or Karháda Bráhmans, are treated with great respect. They are called to conduct marriage and death ceremonies and in some families perform the *tulsi* marriage on the twelfth day of the first fortnight of *Kártik* or October-November and to the garland-hanging or *mál-lávane* ceremony performed in honour of dead

[1] The details are: Beds, drinking and cooking vessels £2 (Rs. 20); two bullocks £4 to £5 (Rs. 40-50); two other cattle £2 10*s.* to £3 (Rs. 25-30); one cart £3 to £3 10*s.* (Rs. 30-35); two axes 2*s.* to 4*s.* (Rs. 1-2); two picks 4*s.* to 5*s.* (Rs. 2-2½); two spades 2*s.* to 3*s.* (Rs. 1-1½); one crowbar 1*s.* 6*d.* to 2*s.* (12 *as.* - Re. 1); and other goods £1 10*s.* to £2 (Rs. 15-20).

ancestors during the second fortnight of *Bhádrapad* or August-September. Most Kunbis are disciples of a *guru* or religious teacher, a Gosávi who initiates them and performs the garland or spirit-laying ceremony. They consider Mahádev the chief god but do not belong to any sect.

They keep seventeen yearly holidays. The first festival is *Sansár-pádva* or New Year's Day. This comes on the first of the bright fortnight of *Chaitra* or March-April. On this day they set up a bamboo pole or *gudi* capped with a small brass pot and with a new piece of cloth hanging to it as a flag. They break cocoanuts before the family and village gods and refrain from animal food. Their dinner consists of cakes, rice, split pulse, and vegetables. The second holiday is the full-moon of *Chaitra* or March-April. Cakes or sweet milk is the special dish for the day. The third holiday is *Áshádhi Ekádashi*, the eleventh of the first fortnight of *Áshádh* or June-July. On this day Kunbis live on roots and fruits. Newly married sons-in-law spend a week at the bride's house. Their fourth holiday is *Undyáchi-pornima* or the *Unda* full-moon in *Áshádh* or June-July. On this day they worship their bullocks with sandal-powder and flowers, and break cocoanuts before them. The fifth holiday is the first Monday of *Shrávan* or July-August and a certain holiness attaches to all the Mondays of the month. On the first and last Mondays all the members of each Kunbi family abstain from food till four in the afternoon, when they take a meal of sweet milk and rice *shevayás*. The sixth festival is *Nág-panchami* or the Cobra's Day. It comes on the fifth of the first fortnight of *Shrávan*, generally about the end of July. On this day Kunbis worship a clay cobra or *nág*. During the day they eat *tambit* made of the flour of rice or panic-seed *rále*, and mixed with milk or water and coarse sugar, and *láhya* or roasted *jvári* rice or other grain, and in the evening have a good meal of sugared milk. The seventh festival is the *Povatyáchi-pornima* or thread-hank full-moon. On this day, which falls on the full-moon of *Shrávan* or June-July, Kunbis make a number of hanks of cotton thread of five skeins each and about three feet in circumference. They dip the hank in turmeric paste and throw one round the neck of each of the men and women of the family, and round every lampstand, cart, and other farm implements. The dish for the day is sweet milk. The eighth festival is *Ganesh-chaturthi* or Ganpati's Fourth. This comes on the fourth of the first fortnight of *Bhádrapad*, generally in August. On this day the Kunbis worship a painted clay figure of the god Ganesh and offer it sweet milk and rice or wheat balls shaped like a fig and filled with cocoa-kernel and coarse sugar or with boiled gram and coarse sugar. On the next day the rat or *undir*, Ganesh's carrier, is worshipped, cooked mutton and country liquor are offered to it, and then consumed by the people of the house. The next day is sacred to the goddess Gauri. At an early hour fixed by the Bráhman priest a band of girls from several houses go to some public well, pond, or river. Each fills with water a small brass or earthen pot spotted below the neck with lime. Each lays a bunch of different kinds of flowers in her pot and worships it with sandal-powder and sugar.

Chapter III.
Population.
HUSBANDMEN.
Kunbis.

They then lift the pots on their heads and return home singing. On reaching home they set the pots on the right side of the god Ganpati. Next day, the ceremony called *vanshe* is performed. Newly married girls fast till evening and then worship Gauri with an offering of sweetened milk *khir* or *pátolya* that is cooked rice flour rolled into a ball, placed between two turmeric leaves, rolled, and cooked in steam. After the worship is over the girl has to visit five or ten houses. At each house she presents Ganpati and Gauri with some rice balls, a piece of cocoa-kernel, some betelnut and leaves, and some parched rice. After making her offering she bows before the deities and the elders of the house and in return has her lap filled with rice by a married woman belonging to the family. After visiting all the houses she returns home and takes a meal. Next day any newly married son-in-law who may have been asked to the house is sent back to his father's house with his wife. Both are presented with new clothes and the girl's father and sisters together with a band of five to fifty friends and relations accompany the son-in-law to his father's house. The girl's father takes with him fifty to two hundred sweet wheat cakes or *nevaris*, or pulse cakes *vadás*, which are distributed among the caste people in the village by the son-in-law and his wife. After remaining a day or two in the son-in-law's house the party return leaving the girl. During their stay the son-in-law's father has to give two dinners, one of sweetmeats costing 2*s.* to 10*s.* (Rs.1-5), and the other of mutton costing 10*s.* to £1 (Rs. 5-10).

The ninth festival is the *Mahál* or *Shráddha* which is held in honour of dead ancestors during the second fortnight of *Bhádrapad* in August-September. Unlike Bráhmans, who perform the *shráddh* on the day in the fortnight which corresponds to the day on which the deceased died, Kunbis perform it either on the first, second, or third day of the fortnight. From one to ten couples of the host's caste, whether or no they belong to the same family stock, are asked to fast and afterwards to break their fast at the host's house. The couples come, and after the host has worshipped the household gods the women's laps are filled with rice, betelnut and leaves, and they are feasted along with their husbands. The chief dishes are pulse cakes or *vadás* and sweet milk or *khir*. Relations and friends are also asked to dine. The tenth festival is the *Navarátra* or nine nights and the *Dasara* or tenth in honour of Durga Devi. These holidays last from the first to the tenth of the first fortnight of *Áshvin* or September-October. The first nine days are not held so holy by Kunbis as by Bráhmans. The head of each family fasts till the evening. He then worships his family gods and hangs a garland from the ceiling over an earthen or metal pot representing the goddess Durga. In the pot are water, five copper coins, a betelnut, and a piece of turmeric. The pot is covered with a bunch of mango leaves and a cocoanut. The head of the house worships it in the same way as he worships his household gods. On the eighth day dishes of sugared milk and cakes are prepared and are eaten after being offered to the gods and to the goddess Durga. On the next day all tools and implements made of iron are laid in a row and worshipped. This is called the *Khande-puja*. A sheep or goat or a cock or hen is killed and the flesh cooked and eaten. Cakes or *ghávans* are also eaten and liquor is sometimes drunk. On the tenth or *Dasara* Day Kunbis feast on sweetmeats and offer cocoanuts to the village gods. In large villages and towns Kunbis, Bráhmans, and other high-caste Hindus go outside the village to worship the *ápta* Bauhinia racemosa and *shami* Prosopis spicegera, offering their leaves to their friends and acquaintances. They return home in the evening. The eleventh festival is on the full-moon of *Áshvin* or September-October which is known as the Pándavs' full-moon. The Kunbis spend the day from noon till evening in their fields. They take with them to their fields one to five dishes such as cakes and sugared milk. On reaching their fields they gather six stones and smear them with lime and spot them with red. Five of them they place in a row along an untilled strip of ground and worship them in the name of the Pándavs. The sixth stone, which is set at the foot of a stalk of corn opposite the five stones, represents Kunti the mother of the Pándavs. They break a cocoanut before the Pándavs, offer them the dishes they have brought, and take their meal. On their way home they pluck an ear of corn and lay it on the shrine of the family god. The twelfth festival is *Diváli* or the feast of lights. This feast lasts for three days, the last two days of *Áshvin* and the first day of *Kártik* or October-November. The day before the feast the Kunbis buy a large earthen waterpot, smear it with lime, set it on the hearth, and fill it with water. Several other large waterpots are also filled with water. Next morning, before sunrise, all the members of the family are anointed with cocoanut oil and bathed in hot water. About nine in the morning married woman waves a lamp round the face of all the men of the family who stand in a row. Each man puts some money or at least a betelnut in the lamp-plate. This lamp-waving is again repeated on the first day of *Kártik*. A newly married son-in-law is always invited to his wife's house for *Diváli*. He has to put 2*s*. (Re. 1) in the lamp-plate at the first waving and a bodice-cloth or *khan* at the second. On the first of *Kártik* he receives in return a waistcloth or a headscarf. Several dishes are eaten in honour of *Diváli;* the commonest are *sánnás* and *undás*. The thirteenth festival is *Kártiki Ekádashi* that is the eleventh day of the first fortnight of *Kártik* or November. The observances are the same as on the third festival, the *Áshádhi Ekádashi*. The fourteenth festival is the *Tulsi-lagna* or marriage of the *tulsi* or holy basil plant. On the evening of the twelfth day of the first fortnight of *Kártik* (November) the basil plant is worshipped in honour of the marriage of Tulsi with Vishnu. Parched rice or *churmurás* and pieces of cocoa-kernel are distributed. With the marriage of Tulsi the Hindu marriage season opens and from this day Kunbis begin to eat new tamarind, new *avalás* Phyllantheus emblica, and new sugarcane.

The fifteenth festival is the *Makar Sankránt* on the twelfth of January or *Pausha,* the day on which the sun passes into the sign of Capricorn and begins to move to the north. There are no observances. But the Kunbis keep the day as a holiday, eating sweetmeats and occasionally animal food. The sixteenth festival is the *Shivarátra* or Shiv's night. This falls on the fourteenth

Chapter III.
Population.
HUSBANDMEN.
Kunbis.

day of the second fortnight of *Mágh* or January-February. The elders of the family fast, and if there is a Shiv's temple in the village they pay it a visit. The seventeenth and last festival is *Shimga* or *Holi*. The main day of the feast is on the full-moon of *Phálgun* or February-March. But small boys begin to keep holiday from the second day of the bright fortnight. As soon as they see the moon they begin to shout the names of the organs of generation. They also cry aloud and beat their mouths. In the Bombay Karnátak this feast is believed to be held in honour of Kám the god of love, who they say was burnt by Shiv. Festivities go on till the end of the bright fortnight. During the night boys and youths sit at the village cross or *chaváta* late at night singing obscene songs and gathering firewood and cowdung cakes.[1] They try to steal the cakes and firewood from their neighbours' yards, though stealing is not always easy as people are on the look-out and sleep in their yards. In the afternoon of the full-moon day after feasting on cakes the Kunbis go into the bushlands and cut a long pole, which is called the *holi*. Next morning the stump of last year's pole is dug out and the new pole is fixed in its place. A stone is worshipped at the bottom of the pole, and the head of each Kunbi family breaks a cocoanut before it. The wood and cowdung cakes, together with what remains of the last year's pole, are piled in a heap and set on fire. Then the people march through the village in bands throwing dust and filth at each other and return to their homes at midday. The pole is cut in the evening of the next full-moon day, leaving about three feet out of the ground.

Marátha Kunbis make pilgrimages to Yellamma's hill in the Parasgad sub-division of Belgaum and sometimes to Jotiba's hill in Kolhápur. They have a spiritual head or *guru*, who belongs to one of the ten sects of Gosávis, generally a Giri, a Puri, or a Bhárati. Of the Konkan Kunbis some have a spiritual teacher or *guru*, others have not. Those who have a spiritual teacher are called *guru-márgis* or teacher-followers. If a young Kunbi, whether a man or a woman, wishes to become the disciple of a *guru*, he goes to the *guru* either when the *mál* or garland ceremony is performed in honour of the dead, or he goes to the teacher's monastery on the eighth day of the *Navarátra*. The disciple presents the teacher with 3*d.* to 1*s.* (2-8 *as.*) in cash and a bottle of country liquor. The teacher tells the disciple to respect his teacher, to speak the truth, not to steal, not to dine if a neighbour has died and is not buried, and not to go on eating after the lights have gone out. Kunbis ask their teachers to dine with them and make them presents or *dakshina*. If a *guru* has no children a successor is adopted. Kunbis of both classes believe in witchcraft, sorcery, and soothsaying. The sorcerers and witches are said to belong to the Hatkar and other classes of weavers. Of late years cases of witchcraft and sorcery are said to be rarer than formerly, and faith in them is said to be passing away. The soothsayers are Bráhmans,

---

[1] The *chaváta* is the place where four roads meet, the chief haunt of spirits.

Ghádis, or Guravs, and the Kunbis have great faith in their powers of foretelling. When a person is sick or in difficulty, the village Bráhman or a Gurav is consulted. The Bráhman brings out his almanac and his bag of shells. He places the almanac and the shell-bag before him on a low wooden stool and the visitor lays three to seven pice (¾ - 1¾ *anna*) on the stool and bows. The visitor then explains his troubles and the Bráhman, bowing before the almanac and the bag, pours out the shells, which are twenty-seven in number, and divides them into three heaps. Each of these three heaps he divides by three, and answers in accordance with the numbers that are left over. Thus, if the remainder is 1, 1, and 1, the Bráhman says that the sick person will be well in fifteen days. If the remainders be 2, 0, and 1, he says that the sick person will not recover. Again certain Sanskrit verses tell that certain remainders represent certain stars or planets. If a sick or anxious Kunbi goes to consult a Gurav, the Gurav takes him to the village temple, where flowers, leaves, or grain are dipped in water and fixed on the body of the image. The Gurav burns incense before the god, and prays him, if a certain result which he names is to happen, to let a certain leaf or flower which he points fall. In some places, as in Chandgad and Bailur in Belgaum, some Guravs become possessed. When a Gurav into whose body the god enters grows old or diseased, he goes with his grown up sons or brothers and prays the god to cease coming into his body and asks the god henceforth to enter the body of some one else among those present. Then one of the number becomes possessed, and from that time he becomes the medium between the god and his worshippers. The days on which Guravs generally become possessed are New Year's Day in *Chaitra* or April, *Dasara* in October, *Diváli* in November, *Pádava* in *Kártik* or November, and the full-moon of *Mágh* or February. They also get possessed when the village is attacked by an outbreak of cholera or of small pox. At such times the *desái, deshpánde, pátil, kulkarni,* and other village office-holders meet in the village temple, while the village Mhár stands in front of the god, outside of the temple, and red rice-grains and flowers are handed round. The Gurav who is to be possessed stands in front of the god with a cane close beside by him. Another of the Guravs burns frankincense and lays the village sorrow or *gárháne* before the god. While he is speaking the Mhár now and then utters a longdrawn *Svámi* or Lord; and the others who are present repeat *Har Har,* that is Máhádev, and at the same time throw grains of rice and flowers on the Gurav who is to be possessed. As soon as the matter has been explained to the god the Gurav begins to shiver, moves to and fro, and takes the cane in his hand twisting it and lashing himself with it. Then he is asked a number of questions, and the villagers take such steps as he suggests for driving away the disease.

On the fifth day after the birth of a child a waterpot is filled with cold water and set on a low wooden stool in the lying-in room. A cocoanut is placed in the mouth of the pot and the pot is worshipped in the name of the goddess Satti or Satvái, that is Mother Sixth. A goat is offered, and the midwife, who is a Kunbi, a

Chapter III. Population. HUSBANDMEN. *Kunbis.*

Musalmán, or a Goa Christian, is asked to dinner. Some Kunbis perform this ceremony on the night of the sixth instead of the fifth. They put the knife with which the navel-cord is cut under the mother's bed for ten days. Neither people of the house nor the midwife sit up all night on the *Satti* day, they place no writing materials for the goddess to write the fortune of the child, and call no Bráhman. On the eleventh day the mother is bathed and purified. On the twelfth day a dinner of sweet dishes is prepared and friends and relations are called. In the evening the child is laid in the cradle and given a name, the first letter of which is fixed by the village astrologer, who consults his almanac after being told the day and hour at which the child was born. Thus, if the astrologer says the name must begin with *A*, the head of the family suggests Ápána, Ákápa, Ánápa, Ápa, Ápu, or Átma, and the rest choose whichever of these names is most pleasant or most suitable. The hair both of boys and girls is cut on any day between the beginning of the seventh and the end of the twelfth month. The cut hair is thrown into a river without any ceremony being performed over it. The barber is given one day's food and from 1½*d.* to 6*d.* (1-4 *as.*) in cash. Among well-to-do Kunbis, when a boy is from twelve to fifteen years old, his father looks for a suitable girl of seven or eight. Among poor Kunbis boys are not married till they are twenty or twenty-five, and girls not before twelve or fourteen or even older, as there is no rule that a girl should be married before she comes of age. No ceremony is held when an unmarried girl comes of age. It is kept secret and the monthly sickness is not considered to bring ceremonial uncleanliness. If the boy's father approves of the girl he settles the amount to be paid to her father in the presence of some respectable members of the caste. This present, which is sometimes partly in cash and partly in grain but is generally in cash, varies from £2 to £3 (Rs. 20-30) and is called *dyája*. The surname and badge or *devak* of each of the families must be ascertained as no marriage can take place between families who have the same badge.

Soon after this on a day chosen as lucky by the Bráhman priest the boy's father and mother, with a few neighbours, go to the girl's house with betelnut and leaves, turmeric and red-powder, sugar, a robe and bodice, and a silver girdle or anklets. At the girl's house, a party of men and women have assembled in whose presence the girl is dressed in the robe, bodice, and ornaments. The turmeric and red-powder are given to all the married women present, and sugar and betelnut are handed to all. This ceremony is called *vida-ghálane* or the distribution of betel-leaves. It confirms the marriage contract and the ceremony may take place on any subsequent day. The fathers of the boy and girl go together to a Bráhman priest and ask him to name the marriage day. A week before the day preparations are begun. The boy's father pays the father of the girl the fixed *dyája* or dowry. Two or three days before the wedding day, in the presence of the Bráhman priest, the boy is anointed with oil and covered with turmeric, and Ganpati worshipped by the boy's father. On the right side of the outer door of the house a mango pole is set up and rubbed with turmeric and red-powder, frankincense is burned before it, and two betel-leaves and one betelnut are laid on the ground in front of it. This is called *devakácha khámb* or the guardian-pillar. An earthen jar or *kara* is brought from the potter's, for which he receives a day's food or *sidha* and five copper pice (1¼ *anna*). Then the priest prepares ten strings or *kankans* with a piece of turmeric and a mango leaf fastened to each. Five married women rub the bridegroom with oil and turmeric and bathe him. When the bridegroom has been bathed, five or six men and one or two married women with five of the ten strings and such of the oil and turmeric as remain over, go with music to the bride's house. The bride is seated on a low stool, and in the presence of five married women has her lap filled with a cocoanut, rice, dates, plantains, lemons, betelnuts, a comb, and a box of red-powder. Then the bride is rubbed with oil and turmeric and bathed. Of the five strings which have been brought from the bridegroom's house, one is tied to a pestle in the bride's house; a second to the guardian-pillar which has been set at the door of the marriage-booth; and a third is wound round a small earthen pot, *kalash* or *kara*, which, with a hole in its side, has been spotted with lime, and its mouth closed by a cocoanut. The two remaining strings are kept for the wedding. The bridegroom's party, after a dinner of cakes and sugared milk, called the turmeric-dinner or *kaladiche-jevan*, return to the bridegroom's house. Next day a booth is set up in front of the bridegroom's house and a dinner of sweetmeats called the *deva-jevan* or god's dinner is given. When the dinner is over, some friends and relations dress the bridegroom in a waistcloth, an over-waistcloth, a long coat, and a headscarf. A marriage-crown or *báshing* made of pith is fastened to his forehead and a dagger is placed in his right hand. Of the five strings which were received from the priest, one is tied to the earthen jar, one to the mango post, a third to the dagger, and the two others are taken to the bride's house. Then the bridegroom, with his father and mother and a party of male and female friends and relations, leaves the village at an hour fixed so that they may reach the bride's house shortly before the wedding hour. Without waiting at the border of the bride's village, they at once go and sit in a temple or other public place and send word to the bride's father. When everything in the bride's house is ready, a few married women go to where the bridegroom is sitting and take the robe and ornaments brought for the bride and return to her house. When the bride is dressed in her new robes a few men and women go with music to escort the bridegroom and his party to the bride's house. The bridegroom is seated on a low wooden stool under the booth. A curtain is held before him by two Bráhman priests and the bride is brought from within the house and made to stand beyond the curtain facing the east. Then the bridegroom rises and stands facing the west. The priests from both the bride's and bridegroom's houses then begin to repeat the lucky verses and grains of red rice are given to all the guests. When the verses are over the priests shout out, Take care, *Sávadhán*; the curtain is dropped; and the guests throw the red rice grains over the heads of both the bride and bridegroom. The bride then throws a garland of flowers round the bridegroom's neck

Chapter III.
Population.
HUSBANDMEN.
Kunbis.

and the bridegroom throws a garland round the bride's neck. Of the two sacred strings brought by the bridegroom's father one is tied to the right wrist of the bridegroom and the other to the right wrist of the bride. Of the two strings that were formerly left in the bride's house one is tied to her father's right wrist and the other to her mother's. After this, if it is customary with the bridegroom's family, a sacrificial fire or *hom* is kindled and worshipped. Then the skirts of the bridegroom's and bride's robe are tied together and they bow before the bride's family gods, the bridegroom offering a new cloth or a rupee in cash which becomes the property of the family priest. After this, betelnut and leaves are distributed to the village gods and to the hereditary village officers and others who attend the wedding. Then the bride and bridegroom are seated side by side and the village officers touch their brows with red rice, place betelnut and leaves in their hands, and wave a copper coin (¼ *anna*) round their faces to take away the evil eye. The coin is afterwards given to the village Mhár. Then friends and relations touch the brows of the young couple with red rice, place betelnut in their hands, wave a copper coin round their faces, and present them with rings or with two or four *anna* pieces. The bridegroom's father gives the Bráhman priest 2*s*. to 10*s*. (Rs. 1-5), and the bride's family treats the company to a dinner of sweetmeats. After the dinner is over the whole company escort the pair to the house of the bridegroom's father, a ceremony which is known as the house-filling or *ghar-bharani*. When this procession reaches the bridegroom's house a measure of rice filled to the brim is laid on the threshold. Before she enters the house a lamp with five lighted wicks is put in the hands of the bride. The bridegroom's sister stops the way and does not let him pass until he promises to give his daughter in marriage to her son. In passing through the door the bride oversets the measure of rice with her right foot. The spilt rice is gathered into the measure, and if the measure is as full as before, the bride is considered lucky. After bowing before the family gods,[1] the bride and bridegroom are seated together and a new name is given to the bride. When this over the people are presented with betelnut and leaves, and rice thrown over the heads of the newly married pair. The father of the bride gives one or two grand dinners and sweetmeat parties. Afterwards, generally on the fifth day, the strings are loosened from the wrists of the bride and bridegroom and the last of the wedding ceremonies is over. Among Marátha Kunbis child marriage, widow marriage, and polygamy are allowed. Among Konkani Kunbis widow marriage is not allowed. There are no traces of polyandry.

When a married Kunbi girl comes of age no special ceremony is observed. She is seated by herself for three days and after that is presented with a new robe and bodice and a small dinner is given to the castewomen. When she becomes pregnant for the first

---

[1] In bowing before the family gods the worshipper generally raises his joined hands to the brow and bends four times till the brow is between the heels. The old and strictly religious sometimes throw themselves full length on the ground before the gods; the younger and less religious content themselves with raising the joined hands to the brow.

time, in the fifth or seventh month, her lap is filled by an elderly married woman of the house with rice grains, a cocoanut, lemons, plantains, dates, a piece of kernel, betelnut, and betel-leaves, and she is presented with a new robe and bodice both of them green, and a small dinner is given to friends and relatives.

Kunbis bury the dead. They prepare no place to lay out the dying person, and leave him to breathe his last in any part of the house where he may happen to be. Two or three persons go to the burying ground and dig a grave. When the bier is ready the dead body is washed with hot water, laid on the bier, covered with a white sheet, tied with a string, and carried by the four nearest relations on their shoulders. The bearers do not repeat any words as they go to the grave. A married woman is dressed in a white robe by married women. Her brow is marked with red-powder, and her lap is filled with a cocoanut and bodice, and she is laid on the bier. The women accompany the body wailing and beating their breasts. There is no fire and no music. The bearers stop on the way to change shoulders, but do not pick up a stone of life or *jiv-khada* or make a small heap of pebbles. On reaching the burying ground three or four copper coins are laid near the grave and the body is lowered and buried. The Mhár takes the coins. No other ceremony takes place at the grave and nothing is done at the house except that a light is kept burning for ten days. They do not place food or water near the tomb or at the house for the spirit of the dead. They make no presents to Bráhmans or other beggars in the name of the deceased, neither do they give away the deceased's clothes. They do not inquire to see into what animal the spirit has gone. Neither the *guru*, nor a Bráhman, nor the potter, takes any part in the burial ceremony. On the eleventh day the family priest goes to the mourner's house with water. The sons of the deceased or the chief male mourners have their heads shaved, except the top-knot, and their faces including the moustache, and a sacrifice is performed. The priest then gives all the mourners water to drink and sprinkles it through the house. The priest is either given a cow or four to ten shillings in cash. Soon after being purified by the priest, on the thirteenth day after the death, or, if they are too poor, at any later date, most Kunbis pacify the spirit of the dead by hanging a garland, a ceremony which is known as the *mál lávne* or garland-hanging. All followers of a *guru* or religious teacher must hang the garland. Those who have not become followers of a religious teacher may hang the garland and then be initiated by the teacher. Two or three days before the Kunbi visits his teacher and tells him he is going to hang a garland. The teacher asks him to bring ten or fifteen cocoanuts, the same number of plantains and dates, half a pound of betelnut, fifty betel-leaves, half a pound of cocoa-kernel, half an ounce of camphor, a few fragrant frankincense sticks, a goat, a bottle of country liquor, and a waist-cloth and headscarf if the dead was a man, and a robe and bodice if the dead was a woman. On the appointed day, after supper, at about eight, the teacher and those who have received or intend to receive advice at the ceremony meet in a room. A space six feet

Chapter III. Population. HUSBANDMEN. *Kunbis.*

long by ten feet broad is smeared with cowdung, a grass mat or *dáli* is spread on the space, and on the mat a folded blanket is laid filling a space about two feet square. A new kerchief is spread on the blanket, and on the kerchief some rice grains are strewn and on the rice a copper waterpot full of cold water is set. This pot is spotted with sandal and red-powder, and in the pot from two to five copper coins (½ - 1¼ *as.*) and some betel leaves are put and a cocoanut is laid on the top. Three or four sticks of any kind, about four feet six inches long, are set up and their ends tied, and from the knot a wreath of flowers is hung over the pot. The teacher or Gosávi sets all the fruits and the bottle of liquor before the pot, and worships it in the name of the dead, and all present hold some grains of rice in their hands. The teacher then sits at the left corner, with his face to the east, and the goat is made to stand in front of the pot. The teacher worships the goat with sandal powder and flowers, and whispers in his ears that he is to be offered to the soul of the dead. On this the people throw rice grains on the pot, place cocoanuts before it, prostrate themselves before it and the teacher, and sing songs. Afterwards the goat is killed and the teacher begins to give advice to his new followers. A dinner of mutton is prepared and liquor is served, and the feasting goes on till near daybreak. There is no music and no merriment, and even if the death happened on an unlucky day no Kumbhár or potter is brought to tell what is wanted before the dead will be at rest.

The Kunbis have a fairly strong caste organization. In some places ordinary social disputes are settled by a committee of the caste. Such serious questions as when a widow becomes pregnant or a man eats with a caste with whom he is forbidden to eat, are referred to the *svámi* or religious head of Sankeshvar. In other places the headmen settle social disputes. The Kunbi headmen, among whom one of the chief is the Desái of Jamboti, are hereditary. Disobedience to a caste decision is punished by loss of caste. Of late there has been no change in the caste authority. The teacher or *guru* has no voice in settling social disputes. Kunbis do not send their children to school, nor do they take to new pursuits. They are rather a falling class.

Lamáns.

Lama'ns, returned as numbering 976, are found over the whole district, especially in Parasgad, Chikodi, Bidi, and Gokák. They say they are Rajputs and that they came from Gujarát about two hundred years ago, and that their relations still hold land in Gujarát. They are different from Vanjáris. They are divided into Chohâns, Jhálods, Ráthods, and Parmárs, and except these clan names have no surnames. They eat together. They observe the Rajput rule against intermarriage of families of the same clan name. The four clans intermarry, except that Ráthods do not marry with Jhálods, nor Parmárs with Chohâns. The Lamáns are fair, tall, and strong, generally with high features. Their head hair is dark and the men wear the top-knot, moustache, and whiskers. Their home tongue is Gujaráti. They are clean, hard-working, honest, even-tempered, sober, and hospitable. The women are hardworking and well-behaved. They till the land, but without much skill or labour. They sell firewood, which they cut in the bush-lands, and sell at ¾*d.* to 4½*d.* (½ - 3 *as.*) a headload. They own pack-bullocks which they use for carrying grain and sell salt which they bring from the Konkan. While the main body of the caravan with the women and children and loaded cattle move slowly, a band of the able-bodied sometimes leave them, travel quickly to a distant village, commit a robbery, and rejoin the caravan with the booty. They also join the Korvis in stealing cattle, and are accused of kidnapping women and children and of issuing false coin. Some of them, who are professional robbers, disguise themselves as carriers and waylay travellers, rob, and sometimes strangle them. They live outside of villages in clusters of square huts three or four feet high with mud walls and thatched roofs. They leave their cattle in the open air both by night and day. They eat fish and the flesh of fowls and goats, drink liquor, and smoke tobacco. Their staple food is Indian millet and vegetables. The men wear a turban, a short coat, and a pair of breeches or a waistband, and sometimes shoes; and the women, a petticoat and an openbacked bodice. They cover their arms from the wrists to the elbows with circles of ivory or horn costing 6*d.* to 1*s.* (4 - 8 *as.*), and their ears with tin rings costing 1½*d.* to 3*d.* (1 - 2 *as.*) hung with silk knobs. They braid their hair and allow it to hang down their backs with two or more silk knobs at the end. A feast is held on the birth of a child and the child is named by its near relations. On the fifth day the goddess Páchvi is worshipped and a feast is given to near relations. At marriages the boy's father gives the girl's father £4 (Rs. 40) in cash and three bullocks. If he is unable to pay this amount the bridegroom has to serve his father-in-law for two or three years. Their priests are Deshasth Bráhmans, who unite the hands of the boy and girl and enjoin them to be true to each other. For this service the priest is paid 2*s.* 6*d.* (Rs. 1¼) and sometimes more. They allow widow marriage and polygamy, but not polyandry. A younger brother marries his elder brother's widow, but an elder brother is not allowed to marry a younger brother's widow. They bury their dead and give caste dinners on the third, twelfth, and thirteenth days after death. At these death-dinners no animal food is eaten. They mourn thirteen days. Their family goddesses are Tulja Bhaváni, Durga Bhaváni and the god Báláji, of whom almost every family has images. No animal food is ever eaten in feasts in honour of Báláji. Their headman or *náik* settles social disputes. Owing to the opening of cart roads across the Sahyádris the pack-bullock traffic has of late years suffered severely. They are now a poverty-stricken class. They do not send their boys to school.

Lonáris.

Lona'ris, or SALT-MEN, with a strength of 608, are found in Belgaum, Chikodi, Athni, and Gokák. They are divided into Mith Lonáris or salt-sellers and Chune Lonáris or cement-makers, who eat together but do not intermarry. Their home speech is Kánarese, but they look like Kunbis, the men wearing the topknot, moustache, and whiskers. They live in small houses with walls of mud and tiled roofs. They rear cows, buffaloes, bullocks, asses, and dogs. Their staple food is Indian millet and vegetables, but they eat the

Chapter III. Population. HUSBANDMEN. *Londris.*

flesh of goats, sheep, fowls, partridges, and pigs. They drink to excess and smoke both tobacco and hemp-flower. They feast their castemen at the time of marriage. They are careless and untidy in their dress. The men wear a waistcloth, a headscarf or *rumál*, a shirt, and a shouldercloth; and the women a shortsleeved bodice and a robe whose skirt is not passed back between the feet. The women mark their brows with red-powder or *kunku* and wear glass bangles and the lucky necklace *mangalsutra*. Except the married woman's bangles and necklace neither men nor women wear ornaments. They are hardworking, hospitable, and well-behaved. The Mith Lonáris or salt-sellers make nitre or *sor-mith* and work as husbandmen. The Chune Lonáris or cement-makers make and sell charcoal, carry stones on asses, and sell firewood. Their women help the men in their work. They respect Bráhmans and call Karhádás or Deshasths to conduct their births, marriages, and deaths. They worship the ordinary Bráhmanic gods and have images of Khandoba and Yellamma in their houses. They keep the regular Hindu holidays, the chief of which are *Shimga* in March, *Yugádi* in April, *Dasara* in October, and *Diváli* in November. They have no religious head or *guru*, and believe in soothsaying and in lucky and unlucky days. Their customs scarcely differ from Kunbi customs. They allow widow marriage and bury the dead. They are bound together as a body and settle social disputes at meetings of the men of the caste. They are a poor class.

Maráthás.

Mara'tha's are returned as numbering 119,300 and as found all over the district. They have come into the district from Sátára and other parts of the Deccan. Several of the higher Marátha families claim, and probably with right, a strain of Rajput or North Indian blood. Among these may be noticed the Pavárs who claim connection with the Rajput Pavárs or Parmárs, the Ghádges, Shirkes, Jádhavs, and Bhosles. The handsome appearance and martial bearing of many of the higher families support their claim. They wear the sacred thread and are careful to perform the regular Hindu observances. At the same time no line can be drawn between them and the cultivating Marátha Kunbis in whom the strain of northern blood is probably much weaker. One subdivision of Maráthás is the Akarmáshes or eleven parts, that is one part short, also called Shindes, a term applied to the illegitimate offspring of the mistresses of Bráhmans or Maráthás. Their caste is that of the mother, and various privileges are withheld them. Cultivating Maráthás are called Kunbis or Kulvádis. The Maráthás have no objection to dine with them, but they do not as a rule intermarry. There is no objection to the son of a Marátha marrying a Kunbi's daughter, and occasionally the daughters of poor Maráthás are given in marriage to a rich Kunbi. Shindes try to get Marátha girls as wives for their sons, and when they are well-to-do succeed. The son then calls himself a Marátha, and if he is a rich man he passes as a Marátha without difficulty. A Marátha of good family so far admits the Kunbi's claims to equality that he considers him higher than the Shindes. The Maráthás are hardworking, strong hardy, and hospitable, but hot-tempered. As soldiers they are brave and loyal. The men wear the top-knot, the moustache, and whiskers. Their home speech is Maráthi, but they know Kánarese and Hindustáni and a few of them English. They are landholders, husbandmen, pleaders, traders, labourers, soldiers, writers, messengers, and servants. The houses of the well-to-do are large and roomy, while those of the poor are little better than huts. The house of a well-to-do Marátha has four or five rooms, one for cooking, another for storing grain, and the rest for bed-rooms. They have front verandas, which serve as reception and sitting rooms, and the wings as cattle sheds. The Marátha's staple food is millet bread, rice, and a liquid preparation of split pulse or *dál.* They use milk in large quantity and occasionally eat fish and flesh, and drink liquor.

Some of the men dress like Bráhmans and the gentry or *jahághirdárs* and families of rank or *sardárs* wear trousers, a tight-fitting coat, and a three-cornered turban worn tilted up over the right ear of twisted cloth about a foot broad and a hundred feet long with ends of gold. Poor Maráthás wear a *rumál* or headscarf, a blanket to cover the shoulders, and a waistcloth wrapped round the middle. A rich Marátha woman dresses like a Bráhman woman in a long robe with the end drawn back between the feet and a bodice with short sleeves and a back. They generally wear a number of ornaments. The poor dress like the rich, but in coarse fabrics and with ornaments of silver, brass, or zinc. On the fifth day after the birth of a child, five little girls are feasted in honour of the goddess Satvái. On the thirteenth day they lay the child in a cradle and name it. On the day before a marriage the boy and girl are rubbed with turmeric at their own houses. A feast is held and the *gondhal* ceremony is performed. In the third and the seventh month of her first pregnancy a woman is presented with a bodice and robe. Lines with red-powder or *kunku* are drawn on her feet, turmeric is rubbed on her body, and a feast is given to relations and friends. In the evening the woman is richly dressed and ornamented, and with her husband is seated in the midst of a crowd of relations and friends. Two married women rub with red-powder the brows of the husband and wife and wave lighted lamps before their faces, while the women guests sing songs. The wife repeats her husband's name in a verse, adorns him with flowers, and rubs his body with scented powder and oil, daubs his brow with sandal, offers him a packet of betelnut and leaves, and again repeating his name in a couplet bows before him. The husband then adorns his wife with flowers, rubs her brow with red-powder, and repeats her name in a couplet. A couple of married women then wave lights in front of the faces of the husband and wife and the guests retire, but not till each of the women repeats her husband's name in a couplet. They bury infants, and all except the very poor burn persons of mature age. The chief mourner shaves his head except the top-knot and his face except the eyebrows, and tying a piece of gold with the hair burns it on the funeral pyre. They mourn ten days, and on the twelfth and thirteenth perform ceremonies in honour of the dead, when the castefellows are feasted and uncooked rice or *shidha* is

Chapter III.
Population.
HUSBANDMEN.
Maráthás.

given to Bráhmans. The higher Maráthás do not allow their widows to marry, but the poor do. The Maráthás are religious and believe in the usual Hindu gods and in their sacred writings. Their chief gods are Vishnu and Shiv. Most of them have no house deities, but a few keep images of Khandoba and Amba Bhaváni. They show great respect to Bráhmans, and employ them as their priests. They keep all Hindu fasts and feasts, and some of them wear the sacred thread or *jánva.* They fast on *Rámnavami* in April, the Mondays of *Shrávan* in August, and on the *Ekádashis* of *Áshádh* and *Kártik,* July and November. On the new-moon of *Bhádrapad* or September, during the *Pola* festival, bullocks are decorated with flower garlands and wreaths and painted red, especially the horns, and paraded round the town or village with great show and merriment. The right to have the leading bullock in the procession is keenly prized and is generally enjoyed by the headman of the village. When the procession returns to the village cross or *chávdi,* the village priest applies red-powder to their brows and is presented with money. In the evening every family gives as rich a feast as they can afford. They have a caste community and settle social disputes in accordance with the opinion of the majority of the castemen. They send their boys to school and take to new pursuits. Except husbandmen and labourers, who have to borrow to meet special expenses, they are in easy circumstances.

Mith-gávdás.

Mith-ga'vda's, or SALT-MEN, with a strength of twenty-four, are found in Chikodi only. They seem to be of Marátha origin. They came into the district from Vengurla and Shirvada, but when and why is not known. They have no subdivisions. Their surnames are Cholán, Jádhav, and Shinde; families bearing the same surnames cannot intermarry. They look like Kunbis and speak Maráthi in their homes. They live in small houses with walls of mud and tiled roofs. They rear cows, buffaloes, and bullocks. They are temperate in eating and drinking, and their every-day food is *jvári* or *náchni* and rice. They are not good cooks and eat fish, crabs, and the flesh of sheep, goats, and fowls. They drink both country and foreign liquor and smoke tobacco. They give feasts to their castemen during marriages and on the anniversaries of deceased ancestors. The men wear a waistcloth, a headscarf or *rumál,* a shirt, and a shouldercloth. The women wear a shortsleeved bodice and a robe whose skirt they draw back between the feet. The men's ornaments are, the earrings called *bhikbáli* and the bracelet *kada*; the women wear the earrings called *bugdis, bális,* and *káps,* the nose-ring called *nath,* the necklaces called *mangalsutras, saris,* and *putlis,* the armlets called *vákis* or *cholbandis,* and the bracelets called *pátlis, vales,* and *kanganis.* Neither men nor women are neat or clean in their dress and they have no special liking for gay colours. They are hardworking and sober, but hot-tempered. Some of them are landholders and some peasant-holders, but none of them are skilful husbandmen. Their women help them in their work, and also by selling milk, butter, and curds. They are poor, many of them in debt. They have little or no credit and have to pay twenty-four per cent of interest. They worship the ordinary Bráhmanic gods and show special reverence to Mahádev. Their house god is Ravalnáth. They respect and call Karhádas to conduct their birth, marriage, puberty, and death ceremonies. They keep the regular Hindu holidays. They fast on the *Áshádhi Ekádashi* in July and on the *Kártiki Ekádashi* in November, and undertake no pilgrimages. They believe in sorcery and in lucky and unlucky days, and consult ordinary Bráhmans at the time of birth, marriage, puberty, and death. Their customs do not differ from those of Maráthás. They allow widow marriage and bury their dead. They are bound together as a body and their social disputes are settled at meetings of the men of the caste. They do not send their boys to school or take to new pursuits. They are a poor class and in debt.

Radis.

Radis, with a strength of 6290, are found over the whole district except Khánápur and Belgaum, and are most numerous in Gokák. They are divided into Matmat Radis and Pakpak Radis, who eat together but donot intermarry. They are strong and dark, the men wearing the topknot and moustache. They are hardworking, honest, thrifty, and miserly. They are husbandmen, graindealers, and moneylenders, and enter Government service as messengers. They rear cows, buffaloes, horses, and other domestic animals. Their houses are like those of ordinary Hindus, one or two storeys high. They do not eat fish or flesh or drink liquor. Their staple food is rice, Indian millet bread, and vegetables. Their holiday fare is sweetmeats and other rich dishes. The only peculiarity in their way of eating is that the Pakpaks set a low wooden stool under the plate from which they eat. They do not differ in their customs from Kunbis, and allow widow marriage. They bury the unmarried and burn the married dead. In religion the Matmats are Vaishnavs and rub their brows with sandal and red-powder. The Pakpaks are Shaivs, rub their brows with ashes, and wear the *ling.* The Matmats' priests are ordinary Bráhmans and the Pakpaks' are Jangams or Lingáyat priests. Both divisions observe the ordinary Hindu holidays. They call their headmen *katimaniyavars* and leave all disputes to their decision. A few send their boys to school. They are a well-to-do class.

Rajputs.

Rajputs are returned as numbering 2697. They are scattered all over the district but are chiefly found in large villages especially in Parasgad and Chikodi. They state that they have been long settled in the district and their forefathers kept Marátha and other lowcaste women. The offspring of these mixed marriages, who are scattered all over the district, call themselves Rajputs and keep some of the customs of their fathers. A few have kept relations with Rajputana. Among them are representatives of several tribes, Ahirs, Báhiriyás, Báris, Gardiyás, Korachmalás or Koris, Kohárs, Lads, Loniyas, Muráis, and Pasis. Families belonging to these different tribes neither eat together nor intermarry. Some of the families of purer descent belong to the Chandrágan, Garga, Káshap, Raghuvanshi, and Bisen *gotras* or family stocks. Families belonging to the same *gotra* cannot intermarry. Besides the division into tribes who neither eat together nor intermarry, and into family stocks or *gotras,* the Rajputs are distinguished by surnames, the traces of old tribal or clan distinctions which so far correspond to family

Chapter III.
Population.
HUSBANDMEN.
Rajputs.

stocks or *gotras* that families must marry into families with other surnames. The chief of these surnames are Povár, Chandel, Rána, Bhidáriya, Maidpuri, Chohán, Dháránagari, Kashvai, Solanki, Háda, and Ráthod. They are larger and more strongly made than other Belgaum Hindus, but with a coarser skin and less intelligence than Bráhmans. Some men shave the head except the top-knot; others let the whole head hair grow. All wear the moustache. Some wear whiskers and no beard, and others wear both beard and whiskers; and some grow a tuft of hair over each ear. Women wear the hair tied in a knot on the back of the head but do not deck it with flowers. Their home tongue is Hindustáni; most of them live in clean and neat houses two storeys high with walls of brick or mud and tiled roofs. They eat Indian millet or *jvári* bread, rice, pulse, and vegetables. Their pet dishes are sugared milk or *básundi* and wheat cakes or *puris*. They give caste feasts during marriages and holidays. They eat fish, crabs, fowls, and the flesh of sheep, goats, and game on holidays and whenever they can afford it. Most Rajputs drink no liquor. A few take a little on holidays and other great days and others daily, but not to excess. Their dress does not differ from the Kunbi dress. Both men and women are neat and clean in their dress. Some of the women wear large gold noserings or *naths* about a foot round. To ease the nostril of its weight the ring is chained to the hair over the left ear. Other women wear a nosering only a little larger than that used by Kunbi women. Married women wear the nosering,[1] earrings,[2] the lucky necklace *mangalsutra*, and other neck ornaments. They wear gold, silver, and glass wristlets, silver anklets or *painjans*, and a silver ring on each toe. Widows are not allowed to wear the lucky neck-thread or *mangalsutra* or glass bangles. The men hang a gold coin or *mohor* round their neck and wear a necklace of the *rudráksha* beads sacred to Shiv. They wear a gold armlet or *pochi*, and gold wristlets or *kadis*. They are fond of gay colours. Except that it is costlier, their holiday dress does not differ from their everyday dress. They are clean, neat, sober, thrifty, and hardworking, but not very agreeable or hospitable. They are landholders, overholders, peasant-holders, and under-holders. Some are only field-labourers. Some, but not all, are skilful husbandmen growing garden and other rich crops. The women and grown up children of the poorer families help the men in the fields; but well-to-do women do not appear in public or work in the fields or on the roads. Very few of them are traders or craftsmen. Some of them make and sell sweetmeats and others are cattle-keepers and milk-sellers. A few are in Government service as watchmen, constables, revenue messengers, clerks, and soldiers. A few are moneylenders. Among them a boy begins to earn his living at about fifteen. Most of them are in good condition. Some are in debt due to marriage and other special expenses. They have credit and can borrow at about eight

---

[1] There are two ways of wearing the nosering. Some wear it in one of the nostrils, others bore the centre cartilage of the nose and the ring hangs on the upper lip.

[2] They bore about ten holes in each ear in which they wear gold rings set with pearls.

Chapter III.
Population.
HUSBANDMEN.
Rajputs.

or nine per cent a year. They are Shaivs by religion, worshipping all Hindu gods but chiefly Mahádev. They have copper, brass, silver, and gold images of Mahádev, Vishnu, Ganpati, Máruti, and Devi in their houses. They show much respect to their priests who are the ordinary village Bráhmans. They require the help of a Bráhman at naming, threadgirding, marriage, and death. They keep the regular Hindu holidays, and make pilgrimages to Gokarn, Rámeshvar, Benares, Dwárka, Mathura, Allahabad, and Triveni. Their spiritual guide is Shankaráchárya of Sankeshvar. They believe in sorcery, witchcraft, and soothsaying, and consult wizards and astrologers when sickness or misfortune overtakes them. Rajputs claim to keep all the sixteen ceremonies or *sanskárs* but some perform only *páchvi* or the ceremony on the fifth day after birth, naming, marriage, puberty, and death. They wear the thread only at marriage time. Child marriage and polygamy are allowed, but widow marriage is forbidden and polyandry is unknown. They are bound together as a body and their social disputes are settled by the majority of the adult male members. Some send their children to school, but girls are removed as soon as they are married or reach the age of twelve. They are ready to take to new pursuits and on the whole are a steady and prosperous class.

Tilária.

Tila'ris, or ÁDI BANAJGERS, with a strength of 5570, are found only in Belgaum and Chikodi. They have no subdivisions. Their commonest surnames are Ningmudri and Sankpál. The names in common use among men are Bassapa and Mallápa, and among women Lingava and Yellava. Their home speech is Kánarese. They look like Lingáyats. The men wear the top-knot and moustache, and the women tie their hair in a knot behind the head but do not deck it with flowers or mix it with false hair. They live in small houses with walls of mud and tiled roofs, and keep cows, bullocks, and buffaloes. Their staple food is Indian millet, pulse, and vegetables. They are not good cooks and almost their only feasts are on marriage occasions. They eat neither fish nor flesh and drink no liquor. The men wear a waistcloth, a headscarf or *rumál*, a shirt, and a shouldercloth; and the women, a shortsleeved bodice and the robe without passing the end back between the feet. The men's ornaments are the earrings called *bális*, the armlets called *kadás*, and the waistchain called *kadadora*; the women's ornaments are the earrings called *bugdis* and *bális*, the nosering called *moti*, the necklaces called *saris*, *tikás*, and *mangalsutras*, and the bracelets called *pátlis*, *chdbundis*, *kanganis*, and glass bangles. Both men and women wear a *ling* in an oblong silver box hung round the neck or tied round the right arm near the shoulder, or, among the poor, tied in the turban. The sect-mark which is worn both by men and women is a level streak of white ashes. They are neat, clean, hardworking, honest, and sober, but not orderly. They are husbandmen and milk-sellers and their women and children help them in weeding and sowing. Their family priest is a Jangam and they do not respect Bráhmans or call them to their ceremonies. They keep the regular Hindu holidays and fast on *Shivarátra* in February. They have the greatest respect for Shiv and their house god is Malaya. They do not go on pilgrimage

Chapter III. Population. HUSBANDMEN. *Tilaris.*

and have no teacher or *guru.* They believe in lucky and unlucky days, numbers, sights, and events, for which they consult the Jangams. Of the sixteen sacraments or *sanskárs* they keep five, birth, marriage, puberty, pregnancy, and death. They name the child on the thirteenth day and feast Jangams and castefellows. Before marriage they rub the boy and the girl with turmeric and oil and the Jangams conduct the marriage ceremony by throwing rice grains over the couple's head and repeating verses. After being handed betelnuts and leaves the guests retire. On the following day they feast Jangams and castemen and the marriage is over. They allow widow marriage and bury the dead. Before the body is taken out of the house a dinner of buns and boiled milk is given and alms are distributed among the Jangams. The body is seated on a wooden frame covered with flower garlands, and with music is carried to the burial ground. The only sign of mourning is that for three days the relations of the dead are considered impure. They are bound together as a body and their social disputes are settled at mass meetings of the adult male members of the caste. They do not send their boys to school and take to no new pursuits. They are a steady class.

CRAFTSMEN.

Craftsmen include sixteen classes with a strength of 60,050 or 7·58 per cent of the Hindu population. The details are:

BELGAUM CRAFTSMEN.

Class.	Males.	Females.	Total.	Class.	Males.	Females.	Total.
Badgis ...	2097	1990	4087	Otáris ...	32	45	77
Ghánigerus ...	2810	2908	5718	Pánchâls ...	5092	4828	9920
Ghisádis ...	37	40	77	Patvegárs ...	270	293	563
Hatkárs and Jádars ...	1804	1743	3547	Sális ...	6540	6227	12,767
				Shimpis ...	1908	1861	3769
Jingars ...	274	260	534	Sonárs ...	2079	1952	4031
Kásárs ...	109	103	212	Uppars ...	4278	4275	8553
Kumbhárs ...	2022	1979	4001				
Lohárs ...	1166	1028	2194	Total ...	30,518	29,532	60,050

Badgis.

Badgis, or CARPENTERS, are returned as numbering 4087 and as found in large villages all over the district. They say that they are the descendants of one of the five sons of Vishvakarma, the world-builder. They are divided into Pancháls or Karnátaks, Maráthás, and Konkanis. The last two eat food cooked by Pancháls, but Pancháls do not eat food cooked either by Maráthás or by Konkanis. None of the classes marry with the others. The Maráthás and Konkanis are believed to have come from Ratnágiri, Sávantvádi, and Goa, and the Pancháls from the Karnátak. They are of middle height, fair, regular-featured, and rather slightly made. The men shave the head and face except the topknot and moustache. The Pancháls' mother-tongue is Kánarese, and the Maráthás and Konkanis speak Maráthi. They live in houses with walls of mud and tiled roofs. The men wear a headscarf or *rumál,* a waistcloth, a shouldercloth, and a coat or waistcoat. Their women dress like Kunbi women, and do not draw back the end of the robe. They are hardworking, hospitable, and intelligent, but extravagant and not honest. They earn their living as carpenters, blacksmiths, and cultivators. Except a few in Belgaum and one in Kittur in Sampgaon, they are not trained to handle European tools. The following are the names and prices of their chief tools: the adze or *báchi*, costing 3*s*. to 4*s*. (Rs. 1½ - 2); the chisel or *uli*, costing 9*d*. to 1*s*. (6-8 *as*.); the saw or *karangas*, costing 1*s*. to 14*s*. (8 *as*.-Rs. 7); the plane or *uchgorada*, costing 2*s*. to 3*s*. (Rs. 1 - 1½); the borer or *hidsál*, costing 1*s*. (8 *as*.); and the file, costing 4½*d*. to 3*s*. (3 *as*. - Rs. 1½). They make tables, chairs, boxes, and cupboards, and earn 4½*d*. to 1*s*. (3-8 *as*.) a day. Youths do not begin to work regularly till they are between sixteen and eighteen. They buy wood from timber merchants who bring it from Sávantvádi and Kánara. They buy iron from local Márwár Vánis. Very few of them have capital and they do not keep ready-made articles in store. There is nothing particular either in their houses or dress. The staple food of the Badgis is millet and rice, but except the Panchâls, they eat flesh and drink liquor. They work from morning to lamplight. A Badgi never dines until he has bathed, said his prayers, and worshipped his house gods. Their women mind the house and do not help the men in their work. Panchâls perform the thread ceremony of their boys before they are ten years old, the ceremony costing £1 10*s*. to £3 (Rs. 15 - 30). Girls are married before they come of age and the marriage expenses vary from £3 to £20 (Rs. 30 - 200). Widow marriage is allowed, but women who marry again are not held in much respect. If the husband agrees the wife is allowed a divorce and is at liberty to form a second marriage. The Badgis including the Panchâls either burn or bury the dead; those who can afford it burn. They keep all Hindu fasts and feasts. The men rub their brows with sandal-powder, and the women, excepting widows, with vermilion. Their chief gods and goddesses are Kálamba, Lakshmi, Khandoba, and Jotiba. Their family gods are Ravalnáth, Malhár, and Yellamma. The Panchâls have their own caste priests, who eat and intermarry with them. The Maráthis and Konkanis employ the ordinary Deccan and Konkan Bráhmans. The Panchâl Badgis worship the goddess Lakshmi.[1] Her image, which is always of wood, is kept in a carpenter's house. The goddess has few special shrines. The local Bráhmanic story of the origin of the worship of Lakshmi is that she was the daughter of a Bráhman who married a Mhár. The Mhár was a sweeper and every morning swept the Bráhman's house, and, while sweeping, overheard the Bráhman teach his children the Veds and learnt them by heart. He then moved to a neighbouring village and there lived as a Bráhman. After some time he went to the house of the Bráhman he used to serve, and having repeated the Veds, demanded his daughter in marriage. They were married, had children, and for some years lived in her father's house. They then left the Bráhmans and went to live with the husband's parents. On finding out to what caste he belonged, she caused her husband and children to be murdered. The Bráhmans would not receive her back and she went to the house of a Badgi who welcomed and worshipped her. Since then the carpenters continue to worship

---

[1] In almost all villages which have towers the guardian of the tower is Lakshmi and the ministrant of Lakshmi's shrine is the Badgi or village carpenter.

Chapter III. Population. CRAFTSMEN. *Badgis.*

the image of Lakshmi. At a yearly fair in honour of the goddess a buffalo and several sheep are offered. This is part of the early Kánarese village goddess worship, and the Bráhmans seem to have invented the Mhár-Bráhman husband story to reconcile these blood offerings to the worship of Lakshmi and to explain their taking part in the rite. The buffalo which is sacrificed is the Mhár and the sheep the Mhár-Bráhman children. The day on which the yearly fair is held is fixed by the Badgis. A week before the day of the fair the image of Lakshmi is set in a consecrated place and daily worshipped. On the morning of the chief day the image is set in a large car and dragged through the main street of the village. When it is brought back a he-buffalo and a sheep are made to stand in front of the goddess and the village headman or *pátil* touches their necks with a drawn sword, and the village Mhár cuts off their heads. So much excitement and expense attend these yearly fairs that *kuri kon bidon,* the killing of the sheep and buffalo, is a proverbial phrase for any great effort. When the buffaloe's head is cut off the village Mhár raises it on his own head, and followed by a crowd walks round the village, the people strewing rice dipped in buffaloe's blood to pacify evil spirits and keep them friendly. Under former rulers it was the custom for the head-carrying Mhár to be followed by a band of men of his caste with drawn swords. If he fell with the head, it was considered most ill-omened and he was cut to pieces by the swordsmen. Besides presents of clothes the carrier of the head is paid 8*s.* (Rs. 4) in cash. On the fifth day after the birth of a child Badgis worship the goddess Satvái and name the child on the twelfth. Boys have their hair cut at six months old, and girls are married before they come of age. They allow widow marriage and polygamy, but polyandry is unknown. The Panchals have a headman or *guru* of their own caste, who settles ordinary disputes. Serious breaches of caste rules are referred to the Shankaráchárya. The Maráthás and Konkanis have no headmen and settle disputes at a meeting of the men of the caste. They are a well-to-do class. Some have good employment as Public Works carpenters and foremen; others earn about 1*s.* (8 *as.*) a day. Few send their boys to school or take to new pursuits.

Ghánigerus.

Gha'nigerus, or MILLWORKERS (*ghána* a mill and *geru* a workman), that is Oilmen, are returned as numbering 5718 and as found over the whole district. They say that the founder of their class was a certain Ghánád Kanyapaya, a pious but poor Lingáyat who is said to have been a devoted worshipper of Revansiddheshvar, an incarnation of Shiv. His chief worship consisted in lighting a lamp called *dipárádhan* in Shiv's temple every evening and in this duty he never failed. He pressed only so much oil as sufficed to light the lamp and maintain himself and his family. To try his faith Shiv took from him his mill and everything in his house, and left him destitute. Kanyapaya, finding himself bereft of everything, went to the temple and standing in front of the god set his long hair on fire and lighted the temple. Shiv was so pleased with his devotion that he carried Kanyapaya to heaven. The Ghánigerus are divided into Sajan, or pure; Kare, or black; Bile, or white;

Chapter III.
Population.
CRAFTSMEN.
Ghánigerus.

Vantiyat, or men with one bullock; Pasti, of unknown meaning; Puncham, belonging to the five crafts; Kemp, or red; and Vaishnav, or followers of Vishnu. Most of these names are Kánarese. All except the Vaishnavs eat together, but none of the classes intermarry. The men are dark and strong and the women are fair. Both men and women wear a *ling* and rub their brows with ashes. Some of the Vantiyat or one-bullock-men wear both the *ling* and the sacred thread or *jánva*. Their home tongue is Kánarese. They are dirty, but sober, thrifty, even-tempered, and hospitable. Almost all are oil-pressers and the rest husbandmen. They trade and extract oil from linseed, groundnuts, and sesamum. Two or three kinds of seeds are generally mixed in equal quantities. Their mill consists of a solid stone cylinder with a mortar-like hollow in which the seed is ground by a heavy block of wood called *diki* which turns round in the hollow and to which bullocks or buffaloes are yoked. They buy the raw seed from husbandmen either directly or through brokers and sell the oil to wholesale or retail dealers. Their women help and their boys after the age of twelve. Their work is constant, but they do not make more than 1*s.* (8 *as.*) a day. About half of them have capital; the rest are labourers, most of whom are in debt. Besides pressing oil the women make cowdung cakes which are useful for fuel and for burning the dead. The Ghánigerus of Belgaum, besides pressing oil, keep bullock carts and let them for hire, and this greatly adds to their income. In Belgaum their houses are generally larger than those of other Hindus, being two storeys high and with tiled roofs. Inside, near the front door, their mill stands on ground two or three feet lower than the rest of the house. Except the Vaishnavs all eat fish and flesh and drink liquor. They dress like Lingáyats. They name children on the twelfth day after birth, and their other ceremonies such as hair-cutting, marriage, pregnancy, and death closely resemble those of the Lingáyats. The followers of Shiv bury, and the rest burn their dead. The clothes of the dead are brought home, worshipped on the seventh day, and given to Jangams or Lingáyat priests. They do not observe mourning. Except the Sajans and Pastis they allow widow marriage. They give a feast to the *jangams* and castemen, visit Lingáyat temples, and pay money to the Jangams. They are either followers of Shiv or Vishnu. They consider it a sin to close the eyes of their bullocks while they are yoked to the mill. They have also a belief that it is sinful to work with a pair of bullocks and hence the class of Vantiyats or one-bullock-men (*vanti* one and *yattu* ox) has arisen. The Ghánigerus have a headman who settles disputes with the help of the men of the caste. Breaches of caste rules are punishable by excommunication, but a feast or *diksha* to castefellows restores the offender to his place. Few send their boys to school. The Ghánigerus are in easy circumstances, but are soon likely to suffer from the competition of kerosine oil.

Ghisádis.

Ghisa'dis, or WANDERING BLACKSMITHS, are returned as numbering seventy-seven, and as found over the whole district. They are also called Bailne Kombárs or outside-ironsmiths, because they work in open places outside of the village. They are said to have come from Gujarát about a hundred or a hundred and twenty-five years ago.

Chapter III. Population. CRAFTSMEN. *Ghisádis.*

They have no subdivisions, and among their surnames are Chohán, Povár, Solanke, and Suryavanshi. They are healthy and well-made, and the colour of their skin is sallow. Their home tongue is Gujaráti. Being a wandering tribe they have no built houses, but remain wherever they are overtaken by the rains outside the village under rag-roofed booths or *páls* which they carry from place to place on the backs of donkeys. The men wear a cloth round the waist and another round the body, and a turban; and the women dress like Kunbis. They eat fish and flesh and drink liquor. They are hard-working, quarrelsome, intemperate, and extravagant. Though they do not take part in gang robberies they are at times connected with them supplying the robbers with spearheads and other weapons. On such occasions they are staunch in refusing to tell who were their employers. They make iron spoons, sickles, reaping hooks, and other field tools. Their women and children help by blowing the bellows. Their chief gods are Kálamma, Khandoba, and Ambábái; and their priests are Deshasth, Konknasth, and Karháda Bráhmans. On the fifth day after the birth of a child they worship the goddess Páchvi, offer her a sheep, and feast their castefellows. On the ninth day they lay the child in the cradle, name it, and distribute cooked gram and wheat to female relations and friends. They marry their children at any age. A day before the marriage the parents of the boy and girl worship the goddess Bhaváni and perform the *gondhal* dance. They practise polygamy and allow widow marriage. They bury the unmarried and burn the married dead. On the eleventh day after a death the chief mourner has his moustache, whiskers, and beard shaved. Their tribe has no recognized head, each gang choosing the most intelligent and enterprising to settle its disputes. They do not send their boys to school or make any effort to improve their position. They save a little to meet marriage and other special expenses, but much of what they save goes in drink. Their condition is middling.

Hatkars.

Hatkars, or HANDLOOM WEAVERS, are returned as numbering 3547 and as found over the whole district except in Khánápur and Belgaum. At one time all were Lingáyats. Several hundred years ago a certain Devángad Ayya persuaded some of them to wear the sacred thread instead of the *ling* and to rub their brow with sandal instead of cowdung ashes. The obstinacy with which they have stuck to their new religion, from *hat* obstinacy, is generally believed to be the origin of the name Hatkar. But this seems improbable as Hatkar-Dhangar is the name of many classes of shepherds to whom the epithet obstinate seems to be in no way applicable. Some of them in time lost faith in Devángad Ayya and went back to Lingáyatism. There are now two divisions, the Kulácháris or followers of Devángad Ayya, who wear the sacred thread; and the Shivácháris who are Lingáyats and wear the *ling*. The Kulácháris observe the rules of the Bráhman religion, bathing daily, wearing freshly washed or silk waistcloths at worship and dinner; offering food to the gods before they eat it, laying out pieces of food at dinner time to please spirits, making a circle of water round the dining plate, and rubbing the brow with sandal and red-powder. The Shivácháris assert that Shiv is the supreme being, and observe the Lingáyat rites. The two divisions neither eat together nor intermarry. They are generally fair, like goldsmiths or coppersmiths. Their home tongue is Kánarese. Most of their houses are one-storeyed with mud or brick walls and tiled roofs. They keep them neat and clean and have no servants. Some own a cow or a she-buffalo. The men wear a headscarf, a coat, and waistcloth. Flesh and liquor are forbidden, and only a few of the men smoke. They are hardworking and honest, but hot-tempered. They consider begging a great disgrace and work hard for their bread. They are clean and neat and hospitable to their caste-fellows. Their chief calling is weaving. The clothes they weave are robes, *sádis* and *lugdis,* worth 4*s.* to £2 10*s.* (Rs. 2 - 25); cotton waistcloth *dhotars,* worth 2*s.* to £1 4*s.* (Rs. 1 - 12); and silk waistcloths *mugtás,* worth 8*s.* to £3 (Rs. 4 - 30). Some of them are moneylenders. Boys begin to learn weaving at twelve and are skilful workers by twenty. They sell their goods, sometimes wholesale to big cloth merchants, sometimes retail to consumers. Their daily earnings average 7½*d.* to 9*d.* (5-6 *as.*). They sometimes work to order, but they seldom sink to a position of dependence on men of capital. Their craft is hereditary. Some have capital and others buy their materials on credit. Among the Kulácháris or Bráhmanic Hatkars on the fifth day after a male child is born a party of elderly married women meet and gird the child's waist with a cotton string called *kadadora.* Each of the women is presented with a little turmeric, which they rub on their own cheeks, at the same time marking their brows with red-powder. In the evening sweet cakes and sugared milk are handed round. Among the Shivácháris on the fifth day after birth the child's father, or in his absence the head of the family, hangs a *ling* round the child's neck, and keeps it in some safe place till the child is able to bear its weight. A party of children not fewer than five are fed in honour of the ceremony. Both divisions name the child either on the twelfth or on the thirteenth day after birth. Before a marriage the boy's father has to pay the girl's father £2 10*s.* to £5 (Rs.25-50) if she is under eight; £5 to £7 (Rs. 50-70) if she is between eight and ten; but sometimes as much as £10 (Rs.100) when she is over ten and nearly able to work at the loom. A father may agree to accept less than the full amount, or he may return part of it as dowry. The fathers of widows of mature age and who are able to weave are sometimes paid more for a widowed than for an unmarried daughter. Two or three days before the marriage day a formal betrothal, or *bástáyikárya,* takes place in the presence of the Shetis, Mahájans, Deshmukhs, and other leading men of the town, and the boy's father presents the girl with a necklace and robe. They allow widow marriage and mark the event by a caste dinner. They practise polygamy. The Kulácháris burn their dead. The chief mourner shaves his moustache and mourns eleven days. They remove the ashes on the third day and throw them into a river or running brook. They feed their priests and relations both on the twelfth and on the thirteenth days. The priests who perform their funeral ceremonies are Devángadáyás or followers of the priest who

Chapter III. Population. CRAFTSMEN. *Hatkars.*

induced the Kulácháris to give up being Lingáyats. They say that the seat of their head is at Hampi in Bellári and that he has representatives in several important towns. The Shivácháris or Lingáyat Hatkars bury their dead and do not mourn. The Kulácháris respect their priests and the Shivácháris worship theirs. Among the Kulácháris the men wear the sacred thread and mark their brows with sandal, while the women rub theirs with red-powder; the Shivácháris, both men and women, wear the *ling* and mark their brows with cowdung ashes. Neither of them employ Bráhman priests at their marriages, except that they ask a Bráhman to fix the lucky moment. Their headmen are their teachers or *gurus*, who live in monasteries. The condition of Hatkars is generally good, but those who depend solely on their looms are liable to suffer in times of drought. During the 1876 and 1877 famine their sufferings were very severe. There was no demand for clothes and grain was ruinously dear. They have not yet regained their former state of comparative comfort. They send their boys to school, but only till they learn to read and write a little and cast accounts. They are a steady and well-to-do class.

Jádars.

Já'dars are found over the whole district, especially in Gokák where they are numerous. They are divided into Pátsális, Samedvárs, Kurinvárs, and Helkárs, who do not intermarry or eat together except in their monasteries or *maths*, and when their *svámis* are present. The Nilkatbalkis, who are a subdivision of the Kurinvárs, have the peculiar custom of the *ling* and *bhasm* or sacred ash tied to and rubbed on the calf of the right leg. The Kurinvárs do not eat with the Nilkatbalkis and never give them their daughters in marriage, but they sometimes take their girls in marriage after they have performed some purifying ceremonies. The men wear the moustache but not the top-knot, and apply cowdung ashes to their brows. Their home tongue is Kánarese. They are clean, hardworking, honest, sober, thrifty, even-tempered, and hospitable. The women help the men in their work. They are weavers, weaving excellent robes and waistcloths both of cotton and silk; they also trade in cloth. Some of them rear cows, buffaloes, and horses. Their houses are generally roomy and well suited for their looms. Their dress, like that of other Lingáyats, is simple and plain. Their jewelry is the same as that of high caste Hindus. Their staple food is Indian millet bread, rice, pulse, and vegetables. Those who are not Shaiváits eat flesh and drink liquor, but never allow their food to be seen by any one of another caste. They worship the goddess Satvái on the fifth day after the birth of a child, and their children are named on the thirteenth day by a Lingáyat priest, who ties the *ling* round the child's neck. There is no rule that a girl should be married before she comes of age. A poor person has to pay the girl's father a sum not exceeding £4 (Rs. 40). The rich make presents of clothes and ornaments. They allow their widows to marry, paying them double what is paid during the first marriage. The children by the first husband are left to his relations. They practise polygamy freely saying that they require women to help them in their work. The Shaiváits bury their dead; the others burn. When a Jádar dies a Jangam places his foot on the dead man's head. The foot is then washed and worshipped, and the water is dropped into the corpse's mouth. The body is carried to the burying ground on a wooden frame, accompanied by friends, relations, and music. After the burial is over the clothes are brought back and worshipped, a practice which is said to be prevalent in this district only. Their headman called Katimaniyavaru or Shetti, with the help of the adult male members of the caste, settles social disputes. Owing to the competition of European and Bombay cloth the handloom-weavers are not so well off as they used to be. Still they are not scrimped for food or clothing and are able to save. Most of those who wear the *ling* worship Shiv; the others worship Vishnu, but like the Shaiváits they respect Bánáshankari whose shrine is at Bánáshankar in Bádámi where is a large temple and two fine ponds. A fair is held every year attended by thousands of pilgrims. In times of sickness her worshippers take a vow that if the sick recovers he will pass across the pond near the temple. On the big day the child or grown person for whom the vow has been made is seated in a cradle-shaped platform of fresh plantain stems, joined together with spikes, bound by plantain thread or ropes and let into the water. The child is attended by two fishermen or Ámbigs, one of whom swims holding a rope tied to the cradle in his teeth and another follows in case of accident. Thus the child is drawn across the whole breadth of the pond. This practice is common among all classes who worship the goddess. The priests of the Jádars are Jangams. They have no images in their houses and keep the ordinary Hindu holidays. They send their boys to school till they learn to read and write and cast accounts. They are well off.

Jingars.

Jingars are returned as numbering 534 and as found all over the district, but chiefly in large villages. They have no subdivisions. Some of their chief surnames are Ámblekar, Chaván, Gaoli, Honkalasgár, Kámblekar, Kutasvár, and Karjgár. They are fair and good-looking, and speak both Kánarese and Maráthi. They live in houses with tiled roofs and walls of brick, one or two storeys high, which they keep clean and tidy. They have servants in their houses and keep cows and she-buffaloes. Both the men and women are clean and neat in their dress, the men wearing a coat, waistcoat, waist and shouldercloth, a turban folded in Deccan Bráhman fashion, and shoes; and their women wear a bodice and a robe one end of which they tuck between the feet. Their staple food includes Indian millet, rice, curds, and milk, but they eat fish or flesh and drink liquor. The Jingars are clean, hardworking, intelligent, and clever workers, and fair in their dealings. Their hereditary calling was to make saddles, cloth scabbards, and harness. They now work as carpenters, blacksmiths, coppersmiths, book binders, picture-painters, and makers of clay and wood toys. The Jingars of Gokák and Deshmur in the Sampgaon sub-division are famous for their wood toys, imitating fruit, and the figures of men and animals. Their boys help them after the age of twelve and are skilful workers at eighteen. Their daily wages vary from 9*d.* to 2*s.* (6 *as.* - Re. 1). They buy the raw material in the local markets and sell a cradle at 6*s.* to 12*s.* (Rs. 3 - 6) and a saddle at 4*s.* to 10*s.* (Rs. 2 - 5). The earthen images of Ganpati, so much

Chapter III. Population. CRAFTSMEN. *Jingars.*

worshipped in the month of *Bhádrapad* or September, are made by these people. The Jingars are small capitalists and generally work to order. Their chief goddess is Shakti. They keep all the Hindu fasts and feasts and their priests are the ordinary Deshasth Bráhmans. They gird their boys with the sacred thread, and forbid widow marriage. Their marriage ceremonies last for three days. On the first day a feast is held in honour of the house deities. On the second the boy and girl are set facing each other, a cloth is held between them, verses are repeated by the priests, and grains of rice are thrown over the heads of the boy and girl by the guests. The lighting of the sacred fire or *hom* ends the day's proceedings. On the third day the girl's father gives a feast to castefellows and the marriage ceremony is over. The Jingars have a caste council and settle their social disputes at meetings of the castemen. They send their boys to school, take to no new pursuits, and are a falling people.

Kásárs.

Ka'sars are returned as numbering 212 and as found scattered all over the district. They are Jains and are the same as the Bogár or coppersmith subdivision of the Panchams. Kásárs greatly resemble Maráthás. The men wear the top-knot and moustache, but no beard; and the women tie the hair in a knot behind the head. They neither use false hair nor deck it with flowers. Their home speech is Kánarese. Their dwellings are generally small. None of them live in houses of two or more storeys high. They do not eat fish or flesh, drink liquor, or dine with any castes who are not Jains. The men wear a waistcloth, a headscarf, a long fine coat, and sometimes a shirt or a blanket. They wear native shoes or sandals called *chapals*. Their holiday dress is the same as their every-day dress, but finer and carefully kept. The women wear a robe twenty-one to twenty-three feet long, with one end thrown over the head and the other allowed to fall in front like a petticoat. They also wear a bodice. They are hardworking, honest, sober, thrifty, even-tempered, and hospitable. They make their living by selling bangles and by cultivating. The women help their husbands in the field but do not sell bangles. They have fallen to the rank of unskilled labourers and their position in the local caste list is not higher than that of Maráthás and other cultivators. Their working hours are from morning to sunset, and they are busiest during festive and marriage seasons. They do not worship the ordinary Bráhman gods and do not respect Bráhmans. Except themselves no one is allowed to enter their temple. Their priests, who are Jains, are called *upádhyás* and officiate at their houses. Their religious teacher or *guru* wears ochre-coloured clothes and has neither a top-knot, moustache, nor beard. He has power to punish breaches of religious and social rules by fine. Their customs do not differ from those of other Jains. On the fifth day after a birth the goddess Páchvi is worshipped, and on the twelfth day the child is given a name which is chosen by the village astrologer. The boy is girt with the sacred thread when he is about eight years old and a girl is married before she comes of age. They burn their dead and mourn for twelve days. They practise polygamy and of late have begun to allow widow marriage. Social disputes are settled according to the opinion of the majority of the caste and with the consent of their *guru*. They do not send their boys to school nor do they take to new pursuits. Their condition is middling. They do not save, and to meet special expenses have to borrow at twelve to twenty-four per cent.

Kumbhárs.

Kumbha'rs, or POTTERS, are returned as numbering 4000 and as found all over the district, chiefly in large villages. They are divided into Goremaráthe, Pardeshi, and Karnátak or Pancham Kumbhárs. The Karnátak Kumbhárs think themselves higher than the other Kumbhárs, and do not eat with them. The different subdivisions do not intermarry. Kumbhárs are of middle size. The men of all classes wear the top-knot, moustache, and whiskers, but no beard. They speak Kánarese, and are hardworking, sober, thrifty, even-tempered, and hospitable. They are reckoned among the twelve *balutdárs* or members of the village community, and make bricks, tiles, and vessels of different sizes and shapes. Some cultivate but they are not considered good husbandmen. Their vessels are made on the wheel and show considerable skill, but have no special excellence or popularity. The Goremaráthis are a wandering tribe who live away from villages in small tents or cloth huts. Unlike the Goremaráthis neither the Pardeshi nor the Karnátak Kumbhárs eat flesh or drink liquor. All three divisions dress like Kunbis. The poorer men wear the loincloth and cover their bodies with a blanket. The women wear a robe wrapping it round the loins and covering the breast with the upper end. The men spend their whole time in making, drying, and burning pots. The women, besides doing housework, collect horsedung to mix with the earth. The Kumbhárs hold a ceremony on the fifth day after a child is born and name it on the thirteenth day. They marry their girls before they come of age, the boy's father paying the girl's father about £4 (Rs. 40). They allow widow marriage. They either bury or burn their dead. The Karnátak or Lingáyat dead are carried to the grave in a cart. Before removing the body a Lingáyat priest puts his foot on the dead man's head. Water is poured over the foot and some of the water is dropped into the corpse's mouth. The clothes of the dead are brought back to the chief mourner's house and worshipped on the fifth day and the caste is feasted in honour of the dead. They do not offer cakes to the soul of the dead or hold feasts in his memory. During their monthly sickness the women sit apart for three days. Kumbhárs worship Shiv, Lakshmi, Máruti, Ravalnáth, Jotiba, and Yellamma. They keep Hindu holidays and make pilgrimages to Virbhadra in Yedur on the banks of the Krishna, and to Uḷvi in Yellápur in Kánara. They ask Bráhmans to perform their religious ceremonies. Their *guru* is a Lingáyat and he settles their caste disputes. They do not send their boys to school and are a steady class.

Lohárs.

Loha'rs, or BLACKSMITHS, are returned as numbering 2194 and as found over the whole district. The tradition of their origin is that Brahma created Manu, and Manu became the father of Prajápati. Prajápati had eight wives one of whom gave birth to the five-faced and ten-handed Vishvakarma, the heavenly architect. Vishvakarma had five sons, Daivadnya who became a goldsmith, Manu who became a blacksmith, Maya who became a coppersmith, Tvashta who became a

Chapter III.
Population.
CRAFTSMEN.
Lohárs.

carpenter, and Shilpi who became a mason. They hold Vishvakarma in great reverence as their father, and worship him as a god. They perform the six Bráhman *karmas*, studying and teaching the Veds, sacrificing and causing others to sacrifice, and giving and receiving alms. The word Lohár from *loh* iron means iron-workers. They have no subdivisions. The men wear the top-knot, moustache, and whiskers, but not the beard. The men wear the sacred thread and rub their brows with sandal. The women wear a robe and a bodice and apply red-powder to their brows. Their home tongue is Kánarese. They are hardworking, extravagant, and quarrelsome. They make vessels, ploughshares, field tools, nails, locks, key-latches, and similar articles of iron. They generally work to order, only those who have some capital keeping ready-made articles. A man's daily wage is about 6*d.* (4 *as.*). Their work is constant and their craft hereditary. From fourteen or fifteen boys begin to help by blowing the bellows. Some Lohárs are skilful workers in brass, silver, and gold. Some make excellent images of Hindu gods, and others are employed as foremen in the Public Works Department. A few work as husbandmen, but they are not skilful. Children begin to herd cattle about seven and their women take their bread to the fields. They live in good dwellings one or two storeys high, and rear cows, buffaloes, and sheep. They do not eat animal food but drink liquor. Their staple food is Indian millet bread, rice, and vegetables, and on special occasions they make wheat cakes, mixed with sugar and with large quantities of butter or milk. Those who cannot afford to buy butter or milk eat cakes soaked in water and molasses. Most of them dress like middle class Hindus, but the rich dress like Bráhmans. The men work from morning to noon, when they bathe, go to Kálamma's temple, and dine. After resting an hour or two they again set to work and work till after lamplight. The women do not help in their work. However old they may be before they marry, men do not put on the sacred thread till a couple of days before the marriage day. The day before the sacred thread is put on the family gods are worshipped and the caste feasted. Their marriages last for three days. A booth is set up and a yellow piece of cloth, in which are a betelnut and a piece of turmeric root, is tied to one of the posts. On the first day a feast is held in honour of the marriage gods. On the second day the bridegroom, dressed in new and handsome clothes, is taken to the bride's. Here the boy and girl are seated facing each other on low wooden stools, a cloth being held between them. The priest repeats marriage verses and at the end throws rice grains over their heads and the bride throws a flower garland over the neck of the bridegroom, and they are husband and wife. That evening the bridegroom dines at the bride's, and during the night leaves with his wife. Next day he gives a caste feast. They allow widow marriage and polygamy, the bridegroom paying the bride's father a sum of not more than £2 10*s.* (Rs. 25). They burn the dead and mourn ten days. On the eleventh the mourners bathe and feast the caste. They worship Shiv, Yellamma, Khandoba, and Kálamma. They do not consult Bráhmans but have priests of their own caste. They observe the principal Hindu holidays. Their headman is of their own caste whom they style teacher or *guru*. He is unmarried and is chosen by the caste. They send their boys to school. Their work is steady and well paid, but their craft has in some degree declined owing to the competition of European tools and vessels. As a class they are well-to-do.

Otáris.

Ota'ris, or SMELTERS, with a strength of seventy-seven, are found all over the district. Except that they seem to have come from the Deccan nothing is known of their origin or history. They have no subdivisions. Their surnames are, Áhir, Ándil, Dále, and Gotbágar. Families bearing the same surname do not intermarry. They look like Maráthás, having no peculiarity of face, figure, or bearing; and their home speech is Maráthi. They live in small but neat and clean houses with mud walls and tiled roofs. They keep cows and buffaloes. They are temperate in eating, and their every-day food is rice, Indian millet bread, pulse, and vegetables. They eat fish and the flesh of goats, sheep, and fowls without offering them to any deity; it is the cost alone which prevents them using animal food regularly. They drink country and foreign liquor and smoke tobacco and sometimes hemp-flowers or *gánja*. The men wear a headscarf or *rumál*, a waistcloth, shouldercloth, and shirt. The women wear a bodice and a robe without passing the skirt back between the feet. They tie their hair in a knot behind the head, and neither deck it with flowers nor use false hair. The men and women are neat and clean in their dress and have a special liking for gay colours. They are quarrelsome and drunken, but hardworking. They make molten images of Hindu gods, platters, and *jodvis* or toe-rings. Their women help in making moulds. Their work is steady. In social position they are below the Maráthás who do not eat with them. They worship all Bráhmanic gods, and hold Máruti in special honour. Their house images are generally Mhasoba, Kálamma, and Yellamma. Their priests are Deshasth or Karháda Bráhmans to whom they show great respect and whom they call to preside at their births, marriages, puberty ceremonies, and deaths. They keep the usual Hindu holidays. They do not go on pilgrimages. Their teacher or *guru* is Shankaráchárya of Sankeshvar. They believe in soothsaying, omens, and lucky and unlucky days. Their customs do not differ from those of Maráthás. They bury their dead. They are bound together as a body, and settle social disputes at meetings of the castemen. Few send their boys to school. On the whole they are a steady class.

Pánchâls.

Pa'ncha'ls are returned as numbering 9920 and as found in almost all large villages and towns. The tradition of the origin of the Pánchâls is that in the beginning the goddess Kálamma created Vishvakarma or Virátpurush who had five faces or *panchánan* and was the ancestor of the Pánchâls. From his five mouths were produced five seers or *rishis* named Sán, Sanátan, Abhuvan, Prashthan, and Suparn. These five seers had five sons. Sán's son was Manu, Sanátan's Maya, Abhuvan's Tvashta, Prashthan Shilpi, and Suparn's Daivadnya. These five persons took to the five different crafts of working in iron, copper, wood, stone, and gold. Their descendants followed their fathers' callings and hence the five divisions of Pánchâls. They appear to be old residents and there is no record

Chapter III. Population. CRAFTSMEN. *Pánchâls.*

of when and whence they came into the district. They are divided into Sonárs or goldsmiths, Kásárs or coppersmiths, Sutárs or carpenters, Lohárs or blacksmiths, and Pátharvats or Shilpis stone-masons. None of these classes eat together or intermarry. They have no tribe or clan names, but some have local names taken from a former residence. The names in common use among men are, Kálappa, Krishnáppa, Rudráppa and Rámchandráppa; and among women, Kálamma, Lakshmava, Sitava, and Yammava. They are dark, short, lively, roundfaced, and stout. They are notable for a formal style of walking and talking. Most of them live in houses with mud walls and tiled or thatched roofs. Their household goods consist of copper brass or clay pots and pans and wooden boxes. They generally own a cow or a she-buffalo. They are temperate in eating and do not cook their food in earthen vessels. Their every-day food consists of Indian millet, split pulse, vegetables, and chillies, and rice in the western districts. Their special holiday dishes are wheaten cakes stuffed with coarse sugar and *tur* pulse, sugared milk mixed with spices, and *páyas* a sort of liquid preparation. They feast their friends and relations on marriage and other ceremonial occasions. They do not eat animal food or drink liquor. Their articles of dress and their way of wearing them do not differ from those of Bráhmans. They generally wear local handwoven cloth. The members of the different subdivisions generally follow their hereditary calling. Pánchâls eat and associate with no Hindus except of their own caste. They generally work from morning to evening resting an hour or two at midday. They do not work on *amávásya* or the no-moon day that is the last day of every lunar month. Kálamma is their goddess, and they also worship Ishvar-Párvati and Gauri. They show no respect to Bráhmans and never call them to conduct their chief ceremonies. They have their own Pánchál priests. Pánchâls keep the usual Hindu holidays. They do not go on pilgrimages. They are bound together as a body. Social disputes are settled by the *guru* and his decisions are enforced on pain of loss of caste. They send their boys to school and keep them there till they are ten or twelve years old. They are a well-to-do and successful people.

Patvegárs.

Patvega'rs take their name from making the silk bands or *patás* which women formerly wore to keep the robe tight. They are returned as numbering 563. A few are found in Belgaum, but most live in Gokák. They are said to have come from Gujarát to Bijápur and to have moved from Bijápur to Belgaum about a hundred years ago. Their surnames are, Chaudri, Dalvekar, Kalekar, Nákvád, Pavár, Sirolkar, Sátpute, and Rangrej. They have no subdivisions and all eat together and intermarry. They are generally fair with regular features. The men wear the top-knot and moustache. Their home tongue is Gujaráti with several Musalmán and Maráthi words.[1] To every proper name they add *sa*

[1] What work did you do this morning, *Áj sakál ti káya kám karyo*; He went to Bombay, *Tyo Mumbain gayo*; News of his arrival has been received, *Tyo pohochi khabar lagad diyo*; He is my brother, *Tyo hamára bhái chhe*.

Chapter III. Population. CRAFTSMEN. *Patvegárs.*

corresponding to the Maráthi *pant* or *ráv.* Thus Nágu becomes Nagusa and Tuku Tukusa. They claim to be Kshatriyas. They have lost all memory of a former settlement in Gujarát. Their family priests are Deshasth Bráhmans. They are hardworking, sober, thrifty, and honest. They prepare colours, dye robes red green black and purple, and weave. They sell the robes wholesale to big cloth merchants and sometimes retail. Few of them have capital. They buy their materials on credit and repay the amount borrowed after they have sold their goods. They also, but less often, work to order. A boy begins to help at twelve and is a trained worker at twenty. Their women do not weave, but help, in other parts of the work. Their craft is hereditary. Their houses are large, and do not differ from those of Jádars, Hatkars, and other weavers. They eat fish and flesh and drink liquor. The men smoke tobacco about four times a day and at night before going to bed. The women as a rule do not smoke. They gird their boys with the sacred thread before they are ten years old; the ceremony is not accompanied by prayers, but lasts for two days. Some days before the ceremony a caste feast is given. The boy is invested with the help of the Bráhman family priest, who lights a sacrificial fire or *hom,* and retires with his fee which is generally 7½*d.* (5 *as.*). The guests are handed packets of betelnut and leaves, and near relations are feasted. The priest is given two handfuls of wheat, rice, gram pulse, molasses, butter, and salt. Before a marriage a *gondhal* dance must be performed. Their marriages last three days. On the first day a feast is given in honour of the marriage gods and in the evening the relations and friends of the boy and girl meet in the village temple, and the girl's parents worship the boy. The girl's mother pours water over the boy's feet and the girl's father gently rubs the feet and dries them with the hem of his waistcloth. Packets of betelnut and leaves are handed and the guests retire. Next day the marriage is performed at a lucky moment either in the morning or evening when the cattle come home. The boy and girl stand face to face, a cloth is held between them, and when the repetition of the marriage verses is at an end grains of rice are thrown over their heads. On the third day the ceremonies end by a feast which the girl's father gives to the boy's party. They allow widow marriage and polygamy. They burn the dead and mourn ten days. They worship Khandoba, Mahálakshmi, and Yellamma. They have no headman and settle disputes according to the opinion of the majority of the castemen. A Bhát or genealogist comes from Gujarát with a record of the Patvegár families. He reads the records to the Patvegárs, and they give him a present of £1 (Rs. 10) or less. He has no fixed abode and wanders from village to village visiting the Patvegárs. Patvegárs are mostly well-to-do. They occasionally trade in cotton. They send their boys to school, but take them away as soon as they are able to read and write a little and cast accounts. On the whole they are a prosperous people.

Sális.

Sa'lis, or WEAVERS, returned as numbering 12,767, are found in Gokák, Parasgad, and Athni. They are also called Aryádru apparently meaning Maráthás or northerners. They are divided into Bijápurkarsális, Padamasális, Sagunsális, Suksális, and Suntásális.

Chapter III.
Population.
Craftsmen.
Sális.

Except the last all eat together but do not intermarry. Their surnames are Ambrole, Bade, Bhándáre, Kandekar, Kámbale, Khirságar, Gángatade, Lád, and Vupre. The Suntásális are reverts from Islam and are so called because they still keep up the practice of circumcision or *sunta*. The customs of Suntásális are partly Musalmán and partly Hindu. The Sális look like Kunbis. The men wear the top-knot and moustache, and the women tie the hair in a knot behind the head, but do not deck it with flowers nor use false hair. The women of the Sális are fair, and rub their brow with sandal ashes. Their home tongue is corrupt Maráthi. They are clean, neat, hardworking, sober, thrifty, hospitable, and dislike begging. Their women are equally hardworking and help their husbands in preparing thread for weaving. They weave undyed white cloth and also trade in thread and cloth. They weave robes or *lugdis*, waistcloths, and headscarves or *phadkis*. They buy the thread from Márwár and Gujarát Vánis and sell the cloth to dealers or to wearers. Their daily profits represent 4½*d.* to 6*d.* (3-4 *as.*) a head. Their boys begin to help them after ten or twelve, and by the end of three or four years are trained workers. They are generally well-to-do and purchase the materials on credit. They also work to order. Their calling is hereditary. They do not till land but rear cows and buffaloes. Their houses are of mud with tiled roofs, and have long verandas suited to prepare the thread for the loom. They eat fish and flesh and drink liquor, several of them eating from the same plate at the same time. Their staple food is millet bread, rice, and vegetables. The men wear a headscarf or *rumál*, a waistcloth, a coat, and a shouldercloth. The women dress in a robe and bodice. They wear the lucky necklace or *mangalsutra*, glass bangles, and generally all the ornaments worn by Bráhman women. On the fifth day after birth, the goddess Satvái is worshipped by one of the elderly women of the house; women guests are presented with turmeric and red-powder or *kunku*, and few neighbouring children are feasted. On the twelfth day the child is laid in a cradle and named, and the laps of married women are filled with a handful of rice and betelnut. They marry their girls before they come of age. The boy's father has to give the girl's father at least £3 (Rs. 30). Their priests are Deshasth Bráhmans. They perform the *gondhal* dance in honour of Tulja Bhaváni, and feast their castefellows with flesh and liquor. The Sális' family deities are Kedárling and Ambábái or Tulja Bhaváni of Tuljápur, and Bráhmans conduct their marriages. Besides these they worship the Bráhmanic gods, Ganpati, Máruti, Vishnu, and Mahádev, but have no images in their houses. They keep the usual Hindu holidays. They make pilgrimages to Kedárling in Kolhápur. They allow widow marriage, the ceremony being performed by the people of the caste without the help of Bráhmans. They practise polygamy. A widow with child is put out of caste until she gives birth to the child and parts with it. Sometimes when the father is known and willing to take charge of the child, it is made over to him, or it is given to a person of another caste who is willing to take charge of it. Sometimes the mother herself keeps the child and is put out of caste. As a

Chapter III. Population. CRAFTSMEN. Salis.

rule she disposes of the child and is allowed back into caste. Formerly a widow's child if it was a girl, was given away or sold for prostitution, but this practice is growing uncommon. In any case before she is allowed to rejoin the caste, the mother is required to feast the caste, and to drink water in which a Bráhman's toe has been washed. Formerly the widow's head was altogether shaved. Now, as a rule, they only shave five lines or *pánch pát.* Sális burn their dead and mourn ten days. Their religious teacher or *svámi* lives at Bangalor and is called Shesh Naik. He occasionally visits his people and keeps a register of their families and reads it to them. He instructs his people and offers them a few drops of the sacred water or *tirth* in which his feet have been washed. They have a caste organization and decide social disputes at meetings of the castemen. They suffer from the competition of European and Bombay cloth. They do not send their boys, and are a falling people.

Shimpis.

Shimpis, or TAILORS, are returned as numbering 3769 and as found over the whole district. They are divided into Námdevs or the followers of the saint of that name; Yaktátes or diners from separate dishes; Gopál Kalis or diners from the same dish, who are also called Rangáris or dyers; and Akramásis or bastards. Besides the Shimpis proper some Maráthás are called Shimpis because they make their living by sewing. The different subdivisions neither eat together nor intermarry. The men wear the top-knot and moustache, and a few wear whiskers. Their home tongue is Maráthi. They are quiet, hardworking, thrifty, and skilful workers. Most of them make their living by sewing, but a few are cloth-dealers and husbandmen. They sew caps, coats, waist-coats, frocks, ornamental umbrellas or *abdágirs,* and *kunchis* or children's cloaks. Their boys generally begin to work at fifteen or sixteen if they go to school, and at eleven or twelve if they do not. Their employment is fairly constant, but they suffer from the competition of tailors who do not belong to their caste. Their daily wages vary from 3*d.* to 1*s.* (2-8 *as.*). In Belgaum they are largely employed by Europeans and are paid £1 (Rs. 10) a month. The women help the men in sewing bodices and quilts called *godadis.* They live in houses with mud walls and tiled or thatched roofs, and own cows, she-buffaloes, and ewes. They have little furniture and cook and eat in earthen pots. The men wear a waistcloth rolled loosely round the waist, a headscarf or *rumál,* and a shouldercloth. The women dress in a robe and bodice. They are temperate in eating and drinking. Their every-day food is Indian millet or *jvári,* split pulse, and sometimes rice. The Indian millet bread is usually eaten with vegetables and a relish or seasoning of chopped chillies, salt, onions, tamarind, and split pulse. They eat mutton and poultry, but neither beef nor pork, and drink both country and foreign liquor. They work from morning till night, resting for a short time in the afternoon, and their women help them from noon till evening. On the fifth day after the birth of a child, a goat is sacrificed to the goddess Satvái and the child is named on the twelfth day. The child's hair is cut either before the end of the

Chapter III. Population. CRAFTSMEN. *Shimpis.*

first or during the third year after birth. They do not wear the sacred thread. No age is fixed for a boy's marriage. But girls are generally married before they come of age. Among Gopál Kalis, after the marrige ceremony is over, the bridegroom goes to the bride's, steals one of the house gods, and goes home. The bride putting on man's clothes goes to the bridegroom's house, beats him on the back with a light rattan, and persuades him to go with her to her house. They burn their dead. The priests of the Shimpis are Deshasth Bráhmans, and their disputes are settled by the men of the caste. A few send their boys to school. One or two Shimpis at Belgaum use sewing machines.

Sonárs.

Sona'rs are returned as numbering 4030 and as found chiefly in large villages. They are divided into Pánchál or Kánarese Sonárs, and Konkani or Maráthi Sonárs. They are fair and good-looking and their home tongue is Kánarese. They generally live in houses with mud walls and tiled or thatched roofs, and they dress like Bráhmans and wear the sacred thread. They eat fish and the flesh of sheep, goats, and fowls, and drink liquor. They are clever, hardworking and well-behaved. Besides making and repairing gold and silver ornaments, they work in precious stones, and the poor among them make copper and brass ornaments and sell them to low-class people. Some are husbandmen and a few are moneylenders and in Government service. As goldsmiths they earn 6*d.* to 2*s.* (4 *as.*-Re. 1) a day. Their women do not help in their work, boys begin to learn about ten, making copper rings, armlets called *táits,* and other articles that require little skill. At twenty they are trained workers. They work to order and are constantly employed. Sonárs believe in sorcery and witchcraft. The Konkani or Marátha Sonárs have no priests of their own caste and do not call themselves Bráhmans. The Pánchál or Karnátak Sonárs have their own priests and think themselves equal if not superior to the ordinary Marátha Bráhmans, whose manners and customs they imitate wearing silk waistcloths or *madis* at meals. They have raised one of their castemen to the post of *jagadguru* or world-teacher and do not call Bráhman priests to their houses. Their chief god is Nágesh. In common with other Sonárs they worship all Hindu gods and goddesses and keep their fasts and feasts. They worship the goddess Páchvi on the fifth day after the birth of a child and name the child on the twelfth. They clip the boy's hair when he is a year old, and gird him with the sacred thread when he is nine or ten. They marry their girls before they come of age, and their boys at or before twenty. They burn their dead, do not allow widow marriage, and practise polygamy. They hold caste councils and settle social disputes in accordance with the opinion of the majority. They send their children to school. There is an assistant school mistress of the Sonár caste in the Belgaum female school. They are a well-to-do people.

Uppárs.

Uppa'rs, or SALTMAKERS, are returned as numbering 8550 and as found chiefly in towns and large villages. They are called Uppárs from their former trade of making salt for which the Kánarese name is *uppa.* Since salt-making has been stopped they have taken to stone-cutting. They are black, small, and strong. They speak Kánarese and live in houses with mud walls and tiled or earth roofs. Their staple food is rice, Indian millet, and pulse, but they eat fish and flesh and drink liquor. Their women wear a robe and bodice, and do not pass the skirt of the robe back between the feet. They do not deck their hair with flowers or use false hair. They are clean and hard-working, but rather quarrelsome and extravagant. Their chief calling is stone-cutting, but they also cultivate and trade in grass and firewood. They formerly made images of Hindu gods and saints, and sold them at great profit. They work to order, and earn a daily wage of about 9*d.* (6 *as.*) The women do not help the men in their work, but boys begin to learn about fifteen or sixteen. Their craft is hereditary and their work is constant, especially in the fair weather. Women help by working in the fields. Their family gods are Venkatraman and Yellamma; and their priests are Deshasth Bráhmans, whom they respect and ask to officiate at their marriage, puberty, and death ceremonies. They keep the usual Hindu holidays. They go on pilgrimage to the shrine of Venkoba near Tirupati in Madras, to Vithoba of Pandharpur in Sholápur, and to Yellamma near Parasgad in Belgaum. Their spiritual teacher or *guru* lives in the town of Anegundi. It is not known why the Uppárs made him their spiritual guide. He sends his disciples every third or fourth year to this part of the country, and gathers 1*s.* to 6*s.* (8 *as.*-Rs. 3) from the head of each family. Serious breaches of social and religious rules, as when a widow gives birth to an illegitimate child, are referred to this guide. They name a child before it is a month old and feast relations and friends. Among them the betrothal ceremony generally takes place a few days before marriage, when an agreement is passed, the boy's father gives the girl's father £4 (Rs. 40), and the guests withdraw with presents of sugar and packets of betelnut and leaves. On a day before the marriage a feast is held in honour of the family gods, and the next day the boy and girl are married. Feasts and presents of clothes and ornaments are exchanged between the boy's and girl's parents and the marriage is over. They bury the dead, allow widow marriage, and practise polygamy. Their social disputes are settled by a family who are forbidden widow marriage on pain of losing their post as arbitrators. They send their boys to school and are a rising class.

LINGÁYATS.

Linga'yats,[1] with a strength of about 236,950 or thirty per cent of the Hindu population, are found over the whole district. They take their name from wearing a *ling* the emblem of the god Shiv. The principal divisions are the Ádibanjigs or grocers; Agas or washermen; Árebanjigs or traders; Hogárs or flower-sellers; Jangams or priests; Málgárs or fruiterers and vegetable sellers; Kudvakligs or husbandmen; Kumbhárs or potters; Nágliks or cotton-thread dyers; Panchamsális, Shilvants, and Padsáligs or coarse white cloth weavers; Semsáligs and Nilkants or weavers; Raderus or husbandmen of the Raddi caste; and Saibarus or flower-sellers. The members of all these classes look like local Hindus. The home speech of all is Kánarese. As a class they are even-

[1] Fuller details of Lingáyat customs are given in the Kaládgi Statistical Account.

Chapter III.
Population.
LINGÁYATS.

tempered, orderly, and kindly; and those whose calling does not prevent it are clean. Among them are writers, merchants, traders, husbandmen, oil-pressers, tailors, dyers, goldsmiths, weavers, potters, flower-sellers, musicians, barbers, washermen, labourers, and beggars. None of them are shoemakers. Their houses are generally divided into two parts. The right-hand side is used by the house people; it is about two feet higher than the left-hand part, which is used for keeping cattle. Many of their houses are built so that almost no air can come in except by the front and back doors. They are vegetarians and do not allow strangers to look at their food or water or to touch their wells. Their dress differs little from that of other Hindus. The men wear a headscarf or *rumál*, a coat and a waistcoat, a waistcloth, and a shouldercloth. The women wear a shortsleeved bodice with a back and the robe without passing the skirt-corner back between the feet. Both men and women wear round their neck a silver box containing a *ling*. On the day the child is born the priest fastens a *ling* round its neck. After a short time the *ling* is tied to the cradle in which the child is laid and is kept there until the child grows strong enough to wear it. The practice of tying the *ling* on the fifth day instead of on the first day has recently become common. On the thirteenth the child is named and relations and friends are feasted. When a Lingáyat thinks of marrying his boy he sends a priest or a friend to the girl's house, and if her parents approve of the match, they feast the messenger. This concludes the betrothal. The marriage ceremony is performed by a Jangam, and the boy and the girl are married in the house. They allow widow marriage. When a Lingáyat is on the point of death he is bathed in warm water, and a few drops of water in which a priest's feet have been washed are put into his mouth. A feast is given to Jangams, relations, and friends, and a little of the food is laid in the dying man's mouth. Alms are handed to priests and the poor, a necessary part of the gift being a ball of ashes. The Jangam touches the dying person's head with his right foot. The dead body is again bathed, and the nostrils, ears, mouth, and other openings are stuffed with cotton. To enable relations and friends to attend the funeral the corpse is allowed to remain in the house for a couple of days. It is seated on a high wooden stool and supported on both sides with split bamboos. The priest five times places his right foot on the corpse's right thigh and is worshipped and presented with money. The body is then seated in a bamboo frame and carried to the burial ground by men and women, relations and friends, and music. They bury their dead, except people who have died of leprosy or women who die within thirteen days of child-birth. These they burn because they say that their bones will be disturbed by snake-charmers in search of charms. On the tenth day a grand feast is held. They observe most Bráhmanical fasts and feasts. Their chief god is Shiv, but Virbhadra, Mallikárjun, and Basavanna are regarded as gods and worshipped. Their priests are Jangams whom they treat with great respect. The well-to-do keep Jangams in their houses. The poor content themselves with worshipping the priests whenever there is a marriage or death ceremony in their houses or on big days. Social disputes are settled by their priests with the help of the headman or *sheti* and a council of the leading men of the community. The Lingáyats send their boys to school and have made good progress in education. Some of them are in Government service holding high positions. Most classes of Lingáyats are on the whole prosperous.

PERSONAL SERVANTS.

Personal Servants include three castes with a strength of 8249 or 1·04 per cent of the Hindu population. Of these 117 (males 55, females 62) were Madrásis; 5079 (males 2713, females 2366) Nhávis, and 3053 (males 1561, females 1492) Parits.

Madrásis.

Madra'sis, with a strength of 117, are found only in Belgaum town. Madrási is a general term applied to some Christian and low-class Hindu families who came from Madras about sixty years ago and took service with European officers in Belgaum. They are dark, with small eyes, a dreamy expression, and generally regular features. Their home tongue is Tamil, but they speak Hindustáni in public. They live in houses with walls of mud and tiled roofs. Their staple food is Indian millet, pulse, and vegetables. Except on holidays they eat fish, crabs, mutton, beef, and domestic fowls. They drink both country and foreign liquor, some of them to excess. They are not neat or clean in their dress and some of the men wear a loincloth and others pantaloons, a cap or headscarf, a jacket, a long coat, and boots. Their women wear the robe without passing the skirt-corner back between the feet, and a bodice which covers the back and breast. They are hardworking, but neither sober nor hospitable. Most of them are in the service of Europeans. They earn 10*s.* to £2 (Rs. 5-20) a month, and begin to earn their living when they are about fifteen. They are well paid, but some are in debt and they have no credit. Most of them waste their money in drink. Some of them send their boys to school.

Nhávis.

Nha'vis, or BARBERS, with a strength of 5080, are found in all large towns and villages. They are divided into Marátha and Lingáyat Nhávis who neither eat together nor intermarry. The Lingáyat barbers do not differ from other Lingáyats in appearance, food, dress, or customs. The Marátha barbers consider themselves superior to the Lingáyat barbers. They say that they came from Kolhápur and Sátára about fifty years ago. They look like cultivating Maráthás and say that they belong to that stock, though, on account of their calling, Maráthás do not eat or marry with them. They speak Maráthi and live in small houses with thatched roofs. Both men and women dress like Maráthás. Their staple food is Indian millet bread, rice, pulse, and vegetables. They occasionally eat fish and flesh, and drink liquor. They are an orderly, sober, thrifty, and hardworking people. They start to shave early in the morning and do not return till late in the afternoon. They never rest except in April during the *Shimga* holidays. Their women do not help them in their calling, or act as midwives or as women-doctors. In towns barbers are paid in cash and in villages in grain. The Lingáyat Nhávis shave the heads of all classes. The Marátha Nhávis do not shave Berads, Buruds, Jingars, or other degraded Hindus. Some besides acting as barbers own land, but they are not good husbandmen. Their family gods are Jotiba, Kedárling,

Chapter III. Population. PERSONAL SERVANTS. *Nhávis.*

and Tulja Bhaváni, and their priests, to whom they show much respect, are Deshasth, Karháda, or Konkanasth Bráhmans. They keep all Hindu holidays. They believe in witchcraft, sorcery, soothsaying, omens, and lucky and unlucky days. Whenever any of them sickens or if any misfortune overtakes them, local gods, Bráhmans, and Pingle and other Joshis are consulted. Their customs do not differ from the customs of cultivating Kunbis. They bury their dead, and allow widow marriage and polygamy. They are bound together as a body and their social disputes are settled by a caste council. They do not send their boys to school, and are in easy circumstances.

Parits.

Parits, or WASHERMEN, with a strength of 3050, are found over the whole district. They are most numerous in Parasgad. They have four divisions, Maráthás, Karnátaks, Rajputs, and Telangis. The Maráthás and Karnátaks are said to have been long settled in the district, and the Rajputs and Telangis to be comparatively new-comers, the Rajputs from Hindustán and the Telangis from Madras. They neither eat together nor intermarry. They do not vary much in appearance, most of them being of middle size, strong, and dark, with high nose and thick lips. The men wear the top-knot, moustache, and whiskers. The Maráthás and Karnátaks speak Kánarese and some speak Maráthi; the Rajputs speak Hindustáni, and the Telangis Telugu. They are hardworking and hospitable, but thriftless and given to drink. They wash clothes and are helped by their women and children. In washing and cleaning clothes they use rice-starch, lemon-juice, soap, indigo, and sugar. They live in towns in one-storeyed houses with walls of mud and tiled roofs. They own bullocks and asses and use them in carrying clothes. All but the Rajputs drink liquor and eat flesh, except beef or pork. Their staple food is Indian millet bread. The only thing peculiar about their dress is that they generally wear their employer's clothes. The Maráthás and Karnátaks worship the goddess Páchvi on the fifth day after a birth, and name the child either on the twelfth or thirteenth, when a dinner is given to friends and relations. They marry their girls when they come of age. Some burn and others bury the dead. They mourn ten days, but perform no rites except giving a caste feast on the third or fifth day. The Telangi washermen perform their marriage and funeral ceremonies without the help of a Bráhman or other priest. Rajput washermen name their children on the twelfth day after birth, gird the boys with the sacred thread at ten or twelve, and call Marátha Bráhmans to their marriages. They conduct their funeral ceremonies without the help of a Bráhman. All allow widow marriage. They worship Shiv, Vishnu, Lakshmi, and Yellamma, and their priests are Deshasth Bráhmans. Each subdivision has a caste council and settle their disputes at meetings of the men of the caste. Their condition is middling. They do not send their boys to school.

SHEPHERDS.

Shepherds include two castes with a strength of 60,274 or 7·61 per cent of the Hindu population. Of these 59,727 (males 29,598 females 30,129) were Dhangars, and 547 (males 289, females 258) Gavlis.

Chapter III.
Population.
SHEPHERDS.
Dhangars.

Dhangars, that is COWHERDS, called Kurubars that is Shepherds in Kánarese, are returned as numbering 59,730 and as found over the whole district, especially in Belgaum and Khánápur. They are old residents and have no traditions of a former home. Their commonest surnames are Amogasiddaru, Bannenavaru, Bhádanavaru, Hálináveru, Hulenavaru, Kharatanavaru, and Sarvaru. They are divided into Jaude Kurubar, Hande Kurubar, Hatikankan, Unnikankan, and Vader, who eat together but do not intermarry. They are dark and strong, dirty and untidy. The hair is uncared for, the beard and moustache long, the eyebrows shaggy, and the expression sullen and morose. Their home tongue is Kánarese. They are ignorant and slothful, but innocent, honest, thrifty, grateful, and hospitable. They tend and sell sheep and goats and a few of them till. The women help in spinning wool and in selling sheep's milk and butter. They sometimes take their flocks long distances to graze and for sale, and for the sake of the manure are occasionally highly paid for penning them in fields. Some of them weave blankets nine feet by four. A blanket, of which they keep five to twenty in store, takes eight days to weave and fetches 3*s.* to 8*s.* (Rs. 1½-4). Besides minding the house a Dhangar woman spins about a quarter of a pound of wool a day. They live in houses with walls of stone and clay, and roofs of branches covered with earth. Inside they have a cooking room, a god-room, and a central dining hall, and a separate place for cattle. The houses of the poor, which are of mud and the roof thatched with straw, are divided into two or three rooms. A plot in front of the house is generally set apart for weaving. Their staple food is Indian millet bread and vegetables, and their special dishes are mutton, fowls, hare, and fish. They are fond of liquor. Among the men the well-to-do wear a pair of short breeches and a headkerchief or *rumál,* and the poorer a waistband and blanket. The women wear a bodice and robe. They have few ornaments, but those who can afford them wear ear and nose rings, gold and silver bracelets, and silver anklets. They name their children on the thirteenth day and worship the well or water-spirit within twenty days after delivery. They shave a boy's head when he is three years old. They marry their boys generally about twelve, and their girls between ten and the time they come of age. A few days before a marriage a ceremony, called *aitán,* corresponding to the thread or *munj* ceremony is performed. A Lingáyat priest or Jangam is called, or in his absence they go to a Lingáyat monastery or *math,* pile five waterpots or *kalash* on a layer of rice, and cover them with betel leaves and cocoanuts, and, after worshipping the pots, tie a *ling* round the neck of the boy. Contrary to the strict Lingáyat rules they are careful to marry their girls before they come of age, saying among other things that an unmarried grown up girl cannot ride an ox or she will pollute Basava. Two of the subdivisions, the Hatikankans and the Vaders, seek the aid of Bráhmans at their marriages. On the marriage day the girl, accompanied by her male and female relations, goes to the boy's house, where they are made to stand under an open umbrella and have grains of rice thrown over them. Then the couple, accompanied by relations and friends, go with music to the temple of one of their gods, burn camphor before the image

Chapter III.
Population.
SHEPHERDS.
Dhangars.

and return after offering a cocoanut. A feast to the guests completes the marriage. When a girl comes of age she is seated in a bamboo frame, and, on a lucky day after five days have passed, a feast is given to relations and friends. They burn the dead and mourn fifteen days. Among the well-to-do, if the deceased, whether a man or a woman, was over twenty years old an embossed silver plate is set among the household gods and worshipped once a year. The poor set up a betelnut instead of a mask and some families have a number of masks or betelnuts. These are kept in a four-legged wooden frame called *chauki* placed on a raised seat or *gadigi* leaning against a wall in one of the rooms in the house facing the east. They allow widow marriage. They are Shaivs by religion but do not wear the *ling*. Their family gods are Alákmirsid, Birappa, Kárisid, Mailárling, Máyana, and Rámsid. Besides the ordinary Bráhmans whom they call to marriages and who repeat marriage verses, throw grains of rice over the boy and girl, and tie the thread or *kankan*, they have a family priest belonging to the Vader subdivision called Shivalingayya whom they ask to dinner on marriage and other special occasions and present with a money offering. The duty of this priest is to purify any one who breaks religious or social rules by giving him *tirth* that is water which has been used in washing the gods. They go on pilgrimage to the temples of Birappa and Alákmursid in villages near Kolhápur. They have Lingáyat or Dhangar *gurus* or teachers each of whom within a certain area has power to settle caste disputes and if necessary punish offenders by putting them out of caste. They do not send their boys to school. About fifty years ago they are said to have been in easy circumstances, but they have not yet recovered their losses in the 1876 and 1877 famine. The spread of tillage and the taking of waste lands for forest have also reduced the area of free grazing and made the rearing of sheep more difficult and more costly. They do not take to new pursuits.

Gavlis.

Gavlis, or MILKMEN, with a strength of 550, are found throughout the district especially in large towns. They are said to have come into the district about a hundred years ago from Sángli, Miraj, and parts of Sátára. They say they originally belonged to Upper India and left their homes as camp-followers. They are divided into Maráthi Gavlis who speak Maráthi, and Rajput Gavlis who speak Hindustáni. In no point of face, figure, or bearing does a Maráthi Gavli differ from a Maráthi Kunbi. They are thrifty, even-tempered, hospitable, and hardworking. They live in tiled or thatched houses of one storey, very ill-kept and untidy, shared by them with their cattle whose number varies from five to thirty. The men wear short trousers or *cholna* reaching to the knee, a headscarf or *rumál*, and a waistcoat. The women wear the robe in Maráthi fashion passing the skirt-corner back between the feet and throwing the upper end over the shoulder; they also wear the bodice. They do not deck their hair with flowers, nor do they use false hair. Men and sometimes women wear sandals. Their staple food is rice, Indian millet bread, powdered chillies, and a liquid preparation of *tur* pulse. They do not eat fish or flesh nor do they drink to excess. They smoke tobacco. Most of them are cow and buffalo keepers, selling milk,

SHEPHERDS. *Gavlis.*

curds, whey, and butter. The women help the men in milking the cows, in selling the milk, and in cleaning the stables. After about eight their boys help in watching the cattle. A milkman rises at half-past five or six, milks his cattle, and takes the milk and curds and butter to sell. He returns about one, bathes, and dines between two and three. He then goes out to bring fodder for his cattle. He returns home, and in the evening ties up the cattle, takes his evening meal, and sits talking with his neighbours or house people, sees that the cattle are all right for the night, and goes to bed. A milkwoman gets up as early as the man, washes the pots, sweeps the house, serves breakfast, sweeps the stable, makes dinner ready, grinds corn, and attends to the house. In the evening she cooks supper. They allow widow marriage and polygamy. Their family gods are Khandoba and Shidoba. They have no family priest, but they respect Bráhmans and call them to their marriages and funerals. They seldom go on pilgrimage. Their teacher or *guru* is a Lingáyat *svámi*. Whenever he visits their village the head of each family pays him 1*s.* to 10*s.* (8 *as.*-Rs. 5). Except this the *guru* has no authority over the people and does nothing for them. Most of them are in debt, borrowing to meet special expenses at eighteen to twenty per cent a year. They are bound together as a body and their social disputes are settled by a meeting of the men of the caste. They do not send their boys to school, and are a steady class.

FISHERMEN.

Fishermen include three castes with a strength of 17,440 or 2·20 per cent of the Hindu population. Of these 1267 (males 625, females 642) were Bhois; 12 (males 7, females 5) Gábits; and 16,161 (males 8035, females 8126) Kolis.

Bhois.

Bhois, PALANQUIN-BEARERS OR FISHERMEN, with a strength of 1267, are found in villages on the banks of the Krishna, Malprabha, Márkande, and Harankáshi. The Bhois are divided into Marátha or Koli Bhois, Kar Bhois, Masande Bhois, and Paratgi Bhois. They eat together but do not intermarry. Besides these there are some Mhár and some Musalmán Bhois who act as palanquin-bearers. The Mhár Bhois are chiefly employed by Europeans. The Bhois are black and strong with regular features and of middle size. Those who live in the north and south of the district speak Maráthi; the rest speak Kánarese. The houses of the well-to-do are substantial, with tiled roofs; and those of the poor are thatched huts. They seldom rear poultry. The men wear a small cheap turban, a waist-cloth, and short trousers; the women wear a robe and bodice. Some men shave the head, while others keep the top-knot. The men wear the moustache but not the beard. The women tie their hair by a cotton string and do not deck it with flowers or use false hair. They are not clean in their dress and have a liking for gay colours. Except glass bangles neither men nor women have any ornaments. Their staple food is Indian millet bread, fish, and vegetables, but on high days they eat flesh and drink liquor. They are dirty, active, hardworking, thrifty, and even-tempered. A few are given to drink, but they are not extravagant. The Marátha or Koli Bhois are palanquin or litter bearers; the Masande Bhois are fishermen; and the Paratgi Bhois are cement-makers. Very few cultivate. They

Chapter III. Population. FISHERMEN. *Bhóis.*

are religious and worship Shiv, Vishnu, Khandoba, Jotiba, and Amba Bhaváni. At their marriages they employ Bráhmans, and at their funerals Gosávis. Except at marriage and death they have no ceremonies. Girls marry before they come of age, the boy's father having to pay £2 10*s.* (Rs. 25) to the girl's father. They allow widow marriage. They bury their dead and mourn ten days. Rites on behalf of the dead are performed between the eleventh and the thirteenth. Either on the tenth or eleventh a Gosávi priest or *gosávi-guru* cowdungs a spot of ground in a room in the deceased's house and marks off a square with lines of flour, and in the middle of the square a pot full of cold water is placed and worshipped. The Gosávi mutters a few verses and hangs from a rafter a cotton wick twisted with leather about four feet long, and offers a goat. The wick is lighted and if it burns the soul of the deceased is supposed to have gone to heaven. If the wick goes out the soul is supposed to have gone to hell. A feast of flesh and liquor ends the ceremony. These funeral occasions are considered the proper time for the initiation or *upadesh* ceremony. Only those who are or who are about to become the followers of a religious teacher or *guru* are allowed into the room where the goat is offered. Disciples of the Gosávi are called *gurumárgis.* A man who wishes to have a religious teacher asks the Gosávi, and if the Gosávi agrees the disciple promises from that day forward to break all family ties, renounce worldly pleasures, obey the *guru* in all matters, and follow him wherever he goes. When the novice has promised, the Gosávi lays his hand on his head saying, 'Rise, from this day you are my disciple.' These disciples keep Monday as a day of rest and abstain from fishing. Formerly fishers used to throw the contents of the first net back into the water as an offering to the spirit of the water but this practice is not now observed. They have a caste organization and hold caste meetings. They do not send their boys to school, nor take to new pursuits. Since the opening of roads palanquins have almost ceased to be used and many have suffered in consequence of the change.

Gábits.

Gábits, or FISHERS, with a strength of twelve, are found only in Sampgaon. They have come from Ratnágiri and Vengurla, but when they came is not known. They have no subdivisions. They speak Maráthi and look like Kolis. The well-to-do live in houses with walls of mud and tiled roofs; the huts of the poor are thatched. Their staple food is rice, Indian millet, and vegetables; but they eat fish and flesh and drink liquor. All smoke tobacco and a few *gánja.* The men wear a loincloth or *langoti* and a blanket; and the women a robe without drawing back the end. Most of them catch and sell fish; the rest are husbandmen. The women help the men in their calling. Their work is uncertain and poorly paid. The men pass their time in fishing, and the women in selling the fish. They respect Bráhmans and call them to conduct births, marriages, deaths, and other chief ceremonies. They worship the ordinary Bráhman gods, but their chief object of worship is Vetál. They keep the regular Hindu holidays but not the fasts. They do not make pilgrimages and have no religious teacher or *guru.* They believe in spirits and ghosts, and in lucky and unlucky omens, numbers, sights, and events. They allow widow marriage and bury the dead. They are bound together as a body, and settle social disputes at mass meetings of their caste. They do not send their boys to school, and are a steady class.

Kolis.

Kolis, with a strength of 16,160, are found all over the district. They claim descent from the sage Válmiki, the famous author of the Rámáyan. The Kolis are also called Kabbers or Kabbulgers that is fishermen, Ambigers that is boatmen, Chunáris or lime-burners, and Jalgars or Zárekaris that is dust-searchers. Except in occupation there is no difference in the subdivisions who eat together and all call themselves Kolis. The names in common use among men are, Bharmáppa, Chanáppa, Kalláppa, and Takkáppa; and among women, Bharmava, Gangava, Lukshmava, Shivava, and Yellamma. The Kolis are divided into several *kuls* or clans of which the chief are Adakis, Baggas, Bilechhatragis, Ghantis, Honnamutta-bile-chhatragis, and Koris. The different clans intermarry, but marriage is forbidden between members of the same clan. Kolis do not differ in appearance from Kunbis. Their home tongue is Kánarese and they live in houses with mud walls and tiled or thatched roofs. Their staple food is Indian millet and rice. They eat fish, mutton, domestic fowls, and game, but neither tame pork or beef. They consider the wild pig a delicacy. They eat animal food only on holidays or on special occasions, but it is its cost alone that prevents them making regular use of animal food. On special occasions they take intoxicating drinks, both country and foreign. In dress they do not differ from Kunbis. Their chief calling is husbandry, some being over-holders and others under-holders. They are weavers, labourers, lime-burners, boatmen, and dust-sifters, and a few are in Government service as village watchmen and messengers. The women help the men in field-work, in weaving, and in burning lime. Their work is generally steady, but most of them are poor and some have to borrow to meet their special expenses. They are generally clean, hardworking, and well-behaved. They do not eat at the hands of barbers, oilmen, washermen, carpenters, Jingars or saddle-makers, and Buruds or bamboo-workers. They are religious. Their family gods are Bhaváni, Kedárling or Jotiba, Khandoba, and Yellamma. They respect Bráhmans and employ them as their priests, calling them to conduct their marriage and death ceremonies. They keep all the chief Hindu holidays. They go on pilgrimage to Yellamma's hill in Parasgad and to Tuljápur. They have no special religious teacher. They believe in sorcery and soothsaying. Many of them are exorcists, who drive evil spirits out of the bodies of those who are possessed by them. They are also believed to have power to kill by means of evil spirits and incantations called *bhut-mantra*. One class of Kolis called Budbudkars foretell events from the chirping of birds whose language, which is called *hállaki* in Kánarese, they know. After midnight they go outside the town to a group of trees and begin to sound the *budbudki* a noisy shrill-toned pipe. This awakens the birds which move from tree to tree, and as they move make sounds from which the divines know what

Chapter III.
Population.
Fishermen.
Kolis.

is going to happen in the town during the next few days. In the morning they come into the town, and while begging from door to door sing the events which they have heard from the birds. On the fifth day after a birth the goddess Satvái is worshipped, and on the twelfth day the child is named. A boy can be married at any time, a girl should be married between eleven and fifteen when she comes of age. The parents of the bridegroom have to pay £1 to £1 4*s*. (Rs. 10 - 12) to the parents of the bride before the marriage takes place. Before the marriage the *gondhal* ceremony is performed, the Gondhlis being paid 2*s*. to 8*s*. (Rs. 1 - 4) besides food. A goat is generally sacrificed at this ceremony. In other respects a Koli marriage is the same as a Kunbi marriage. When a girl comes of age during four days she is not allowed to touch other members of the family, but on the fifth day her husband gives her a new robe and a bodice. Well-to-do Kolis burn and the poor bury their dead. On the twelfth day after a death, a Bráhman is required to visit the house to purify it by sprinkling it with water. Child marriage, widow marriage, and polygamy are allowed, and polyandry is unknown. They are bound together as a body and settle their social disputes at a meeting of the men of the caste. Caste decisions are enforced by excommunication. They do not send their boys to school, and are on the whole a steady class.

Musicians.

Musicians include three castes with a strength of 182 or 0·01 per cent of the Hindu population. Of these 105 (males 53, females 52) were Devlis; 21 (males 11, females 16) Ghadsis; and 50 Kalávants.

Devlis.

Devlis, or Temple Servants, with a strength of 105, are found in Belgaum, Khánápur, and Gokak. They have neither subdivisions nor surnames, proved relationship being the only bar to marriage. Among Devlis the men as a rule are tall and good-looking, and the women fair, graceful, and refined with the manners of dancing-girls. Their home speech is Maráthi. Most are husbandmen and the rest are labourers. They eat fish and flesh, and drink liquor. Their staple food is rice, millet, pulse, and vegetables. They live in houses with walls of brick or mud and tiled roofs. The men wear the top-knot, moustache, and whiskers; and the women tie their hair in a knot at the back of the head and deck it with flowers. The men and women are neat and clean in their dress and have a special liking for gay colours. They dress like Maráthás and wear both local handwoven and European clothes. The women pass the skirt-corner of the robe back between the feet. They are not allowed to sing or dance in public and in social position rank below professional singers and dancers who do not eat with them. Both men and women are servants in temples, the women being dedicated to the service in their childhood. It is usual among the class of temple servants who are called Guravs to dedicate some of their female children to the worship of the village gods, such as Ravalnáth, Satái, and Mahuli. Those who can afford it burn their dead; the rest bury. Their customs differ in no point from those of Maráthás. They keep dogs as pet. The women sweep the temple of the god to whom they are married and also act as courtezans. Of their children one daughter is wed to the god and the rest marry the sons and daughters of Devlis. They worship the ordinary local and Bráhmanical gods. They believe in omens, witchcraft, lucky and unlucky days, number, sights, and events. They consult Karháda or Deshasth Bráhmans when they are in difficulty or at times of birth, marriage, and puberty. They settle disputes by calling caste meetings. They do not send their boys to school and are in middling circumstances.

Ghadsis.

Ghadsis, with a strength of twenty-seven, are found only in Chikodi. They came into the district about forty years ago from Sángli, Miraj, and Kolhápur. They have no subdivisions, and their surnames are Bhosle, Gáikwád, Ghorpade, Sálunke, and Yádav. Families bearing the same surname do not intermarry. They are dark, stout, well-made, and strong, and look and speak like Maráthás. They live in thatched huts and have a very scanty store of household goods. A few of the well-to-do own a cow or a buffalo. Their every-day food is Indian millet, pulse, and vegetables. They eat fish and the flesh of goats, sheep, domestic fowls, and wild game. They never give feasts except on the occasions of marriage. They have no objection to animal food, but their poverty prevents them using it regularly. They drink liquor and smoke tobacco; and some of them smoke hemp-flowers or *gánja*. The men wear a headscarf or *rumál*, a short waistcloth, and a shouldercloth; and the women a bodice and robe passing the skirt-corner back between the feet and drawing the upper end over the right shoulder. They are neither clean nor sober, but are hardworking and even-tempered. They are held to be the most skilful of local musicians. They worship the ordinary Bráhmanic gods, but their chief object of worship is Máruti. They keep house images of Mhasoba and Kedárling or Jotiba. They respect Bráhmans and call them to conduct their marriage, puberty, and death ceremonies. They believe in lucky and unlucky days, numbers, sights, and events, and consult Deshasth Bráhmans. They name their children on the twelfth day after birth, when they distribute sugar. Their marriage ceremonies last for a couple of days. The boy and the girl are rubbed with turmeric at their homes and at the time of marriage a cloth is held between them. The Bráhman repeats verses and throws rice over their heads. The guests are presented with packets of betelnut and leaves, and retire. Next day the marriage ceremony ends with a feast. They bury the dead and feast the caste people on the thirteenth, giving uncooked food or *shidha* to their Bráhman priest and to many other Bráhman beggars. They are bound together as a body and their social disputes are settled at meetings of the men of the caste. They do not send their boys to school or take to new pursuits. They are a steady class and fairly well-to-do.

Kalávants.

Kala'vants, with a strength of about fifty, are found in Belgaum, Yankammardi, Saundatti, and Athni. They belong to five classes, Maráthás, Kánarese or Lingáyats, Konkanis, Telangs, and Musalmáns. The Marátha and Lingáyat dancing-girls are said to be descended from the earliest settlers in the district. The Lingáyats do not eat from the hands of any of the other divisions; Maráthás and Konkanis eat together, but not from Lingáyats;

Chapter III. Population. MUSICIANS. *Kalávants.*

Telangs, who originally belonged to Madras, eat from all except Musalmáns, and the Musalmáns eat from all except Telangs. None of the divisions intermarry. As a class they are fair and good-looking. Except a few of the Musalmán families who speak Kánarese the different divisions speak at home the language of their own country. Their houses are large and airy, but in appearance and plan do not differ from those of other Hindus. The women dress in rich well-fitting clothes and wear shoes and mark their brows with red-powder or *kunku*. Lingáyat girls at home mark their brows with ashes and wear the *ling*, but when they attend weddings or other joyful occasions in families who are not Lingáyats, they mark their brows with red-powder. On such occasions Musalmán girls also mark their brows with red-powder. All, except Lingáyats, eat fish and the flesh of goats, sheep, and fowls; and the Musalmáns beef and drink liquor. They sing, dance, and act as courtezans. Marátha and Lingáyat Kalávants do not receive visits from Musalmán men on pain of loss of caste. Telangs receive Musalmáns and Konkanis receive Christians but not Musalmáns. They generally begin to learn to sing and dance when about seven or eight years old and their training lasts for about ten years. They practise singing and dancing every morning and evening. Their charges vary according to the season and the demand for their services. The ordinary charge for a troop or *táfa* of five, two dancers and three players, for a thread-ceremony varies from 10*s.* to £1 10*s.* (Rs. 5-15); for a marriage from £3 to £20 (Rs. 30-200); for public feasts from 10*s.* to £2 10*s.* (Rs. 5-25); and for house-warming from 10*s.* to £1 10*s.* (Rs. 5-15). The monthly earnings of a Kalávant vary from £1 10*s.* to £5 (Rs. 15-50) and most earn £2 to £2 10*s.* (Rs. 20-25) a month. Only a few Telang and Konkani dancers earn as much as £5 (Rs. 50) a month. Their expenses vary with their incomes, but if they choose they can save £3 (Rs. 30) out of every £5 (Rs. 50) they earn. They adopt girls whose parents are unable to support them. The daughters of dancing-girls, as a rule, take to their mother's profession. They were formerly allowed to buy girls but this is now forbidden and in consequence of the restriction their numbers are said to be decreasing while the number of prostitutes or *kasbins* is said to be on the increase. They get a Bráhman to give their child a name on the twelfth day after birth. Among Marátha, Lingáyat, and Musalmán dancing-girls between the time when a girl is seven years old and the time she comes of age she is presented with a set of ankle-bells called *cháls*. Unless this ceremony, which is called *tila*, is performed she is not a regular dancing-girl and is not allowed to sing or dance in public. After the bell ceremony comes the marriage which is performed either before or after a girl comes of age, but always before she is pregnant. The ceremony is performed with the same details as a marriage in the class to which they belong, all the honours which are generally shown to a bridegroom being in their marriage shown to a dagger or *katár*. Instead of the bell-wearing and dagger-marriage Telang and Konkan dancing-girls, before they come of age undergo a form of marriage called *shes*, in which a girl dressed as a man and with a dagger in her hand

Chapter III.
Population.
Musicians.
Kalávants.

acts as bridegroom. The sons of dancing-girls are called either *saffardáiks* a respectful or *sájindás* a somewhat contemptuous Hindustáni term for a musician. The occupation of these men is playing the fiddle and drum or singing. They generally begin to learn when they are about twelve or thirteen and are kept under training six or seven years. Some dancing-girls' sons with the help of their mothers, sisters, or paramours' funds have become wealthy moneylenders and cloth-dealers. Others own land, or teach music and dancing, charging 10*s.* to £3 (Rs. 5-30) a month. The Telangi musicians are dirty, hot-tempered, and drunken; the Musalmán, Konkan, and Marátha musicians drink moderately; and the Kánarese musicians abstain. Except the Telangs, musicians as a class are good-tempered, hospitable, and well-behaved, but thriftless. Their manner is notably formal and respectful. They marry the daughters of prostitutes or orphan or destitute girls. Even when they are married they live in some corner of their sister's or their mother's house. Their widows do not become dancing-girls nor do they remarry. Some of them become mistresses living with their protectors and cease to belong to the dancing-girl caste. Besides the Saffardáiks there is a class of Bráhman music-masters who are generally Konkanasths and are known as Pandits, Gavais, and Vastádjis. They live in Bráhman quarters and their occupation in no way affects their position as Bráhmans. Konkani Kalávants when they pass temples or the houses of Government officials, out of respect untie the part of the robe called *kásta* which they tuck into the waistband behind. They also used to go and sing at the house of the headman and Government officers, but except in some of the neighbouring Native States this practice is falling into disuse. Dancing-girls consider oilmen, barbers, Jingars or saddle-makers, and washermen low, and never perform at their houses. The troop or *táfa* includes one or two or sometimes three dancing-girls, two fiddlers, and one drummer. The dancing-girl stands in front, and on either side of her stands a fiddler and behind her the drummer. Konkani, Maráthi, and Telangi dancing-girls have priests, generally Deshasth, Konkanasth, and Karháda Bráhmans. Lingáyat dancing-girls employ Jangams or *ayyás* and Musalmán dancing-girls employ the *káji*. Konkani, Maráthi, and Telangi dancing-girls burn the dead. No priest goes with the body and no religious ceremony is performed on the day of death. On the third day relations and friends throw the ashes in water. From the ninth to the twelfth day with the help of a priest balls called *pinds* are offered to the deceased. On the thirteenth day the caste is given a dinner. They mourn ten days. Lingáyats and Musalmáns bury the dead. Among the Lingáyats the *ayya* or priest attends the funeral and before the body is buried touches it with his foot and is paid 2*s.* 6*d.* (Rs. 1¼). On the third and seventh days the caste is feasted. Lingáyats observe no mourning. The Musalmáns ask the *káji* to attend the funeral and he repeats verses from the Kurán after the body is buried. They feast the caste on the ninth and eleventh days. Dancing-girls are religious. Except the Musalmáns they worship all Hindu gods, and even Musalmán girls sometimes worship Hindu gods and follow Hindu customs.

Chapter III.
Population.

They have no headman. Each section has its own board or council, but they have no fixed rules for its guidance. When a dispute arises one of the parties calls the elderly dancing-girls, who meet in one of their houses and settle the matter. They do not send their children to school but a few read and write Maráthi and are well-to-do, holding lands for services rendered to temples and to the tombs of Musalmán saints.

LABOURERS.

Labourers and **Miscellaneous Workers** include seventeen castes with a strength of 49,934 or 6·31 per cent of the Hindu population. The details are:

BELGAUM LABOURERS AND MISCELLANEOUS WORKERS.

Caste.	Males.	Females	Total.	Caste.	Males.	Females	Total.
Beldárs ...	842	850	1692	Korvis ...	1775	1935	3710
Bhandáris ...	694	600	1294	Korchars ...	129	164	293
Bisdarus ...	18,649	18,628	37,277	Medárs or Buruds	544	548	1092
Deshávals ...	270	230	500	Rámoshis ...	92	75	167
Dombárs ...	478	528	1006	Rávals ...	126	132	258
Golls or Gopáls ...	173	151	324	Shikáris ...	14	15	29
Ilgers ...	568	640	1208	Vadars ...	90	107	197
Kaikádis ...	63	52	115				
Kaláls ...	25	23	48				
Kolátis ...	352	372	724	Total ...	24,884	25,050	49,934

Beldárs.

Belda'rs, or QUARRYMEN, with a strength of 1692, are found all over the district. They are of Gujarát origin, and came into the district from Sátára in search of employment about sixty years ago. They look like Kunbis. They can speak Maráthi, but their home tongue is Gujaráti. Most of them live in thatched huts and a few in houses with mud walls and tiled roofs. They keep bullocks, buffaloes, cows, and dogs. Their staple food is Indian millet, rice, pulse, and vegetables. They never hold caste feasts except on the occasion of a marriage. They eat fish, and when they can afford it the flesh of goats, sheep, poultry, partridges, and wild game. The cost alone prevents them from using animal food regularly. They smoke tobacco and drink country and foreign liquor but not to excess. They dress like Kunbis, wear the same ornaments, and the women mark their brows with red-powder. They are not clean, neat, or honest, but they are hardworking and orderly. They are quarrymen, sometimes employing servants. Boys help their fathers from the age of sixteen. The craft is hereditary, constant, and well paid. The men work from early morning to evening, and the women look after the house. Some burn and some bury their dead. They worship all Hindu gods and pay special respect to Vithoba. Their priests are Deshasth and Karháda Bráhmans, whose help they seek at births, marriages, comings of age, and deaths. They keep the usual Hindu holidays. They believe in omens and in lucky and unlucky days regarding which they consult Bráhmans. Their customs differ in no point from those of Kunbis. They are bound together as a body and settle social disputes by the opinion of the majority of the castemen. They do not send their boys to school. They are free from debt, and are a steady class.

Bhandáris.

Bhanda'ris, or PALM-TAPPERS, with a strength of 1294, are found all over the district except in Sampgaon and Athni. They came into the district about sixty years ago from Rantágiri in search of work.

Their home speech is Maráthi. They live in good and neatly kept houses with walls of mud and tiled roofs. They drink to excess. Their staple food is Indian millet, pulse, and vegetables. They feast the caste on marriages and after deaths. Whenever they can afford it, they eat fish, crabs, mutton, poultry, hares, wild game, pigeons, and partridges. They drink country and foreign liquor and palm-spirit. They smoke tobacco and some of them hemp-flower or *gánja*. The men wear the moustache and sometimes the whiskers, but never the beard. Their heads are shaved, except the top-knot, once a week. The women wear their hair rolled in a ball on the back of the head, decking it with flowers, and mixing it with false hair. A few of them are clean and neat in their dress, but most are dirty. The only peculiarity in the dress of women who have come from the Konkan is that they draw the skirt of their robes back between their feet. They are hardworking, even-tempered, and orderly. Some of them are husbandmen and others messengers and constables. A lad generally begins to earn his living about fifteen. Their women help in weeding and sowing and in selling milk and butter. They worship the usual Hindu gods, Shiv being the chief object of their adoration. Their priests are Deshasth and Karháda Bráhmans to whom they show great respect. They keep Hindu fasts and feasts, and go on pilgrimage to Pandharpur, Gokarn, and, if well-to-do, to Benares. They believe in sorcery, witchcraft, soothsaying, omens, and lucky and unlucky days, and consult Bráhmans at the time of birth or marriage or whenever they are in difficulty. Their customs do not differ from those of Kunbis. They either bury or burn the dead. They are bound together as a body, and settle social disputes at meetings of the men of the caste. Some of them send their children to school. They take their girls away about twelve and their boys about fifteen. They attempt no new pursuits and are on the whole a steady people.

Biadarus.

Biadarus, or **Berads**, are returned as numbering 37,280 and as scattered all over the district. They form a distinct tribe corresponding to the Gujarát Kolis, the Khándesh Bhils, and the Poona Rámoshis. Páchhápur about twenty miles north of Belgaum is said to have formerly been a capital of the Berads and many villages near Páchhápur are occupied chiefly by Berads; they are also found near Satagati on the Belgaum-Poona road in the hills bordering the Ghatprabha. In former times they were much feared by travellers whom they waylaid in hilly parts by rolling stones on them from high ground near the roadside. Gangs of Berads still occasionally waylay and rob the travellers. The common names for men are Balya, Bhima Hanmya, Lingya, and Shettya; and for women Gangi, Lagmi, and Yelli. Their surnames are Basgalvar, Gadaldavar, Gorla, Gujaldavar, Metkar, Metkuppi, Motmalnavar, Mumudlavar, Nágalnavar, and Phodenavar. Persons bearing the same surname do not intermarry. As a class Berads are strong, robust, and able to bear fatigue and hardship. Most of them are dark, but some are fair, clean, and tidy. Their home tongue is Kánarese; some of them live inside the villages in houses with flat roofs and stone walls and rear cattle. Others, in hilly tracts, live in grass huts and do not rear animals. Their staple food

Chapter III.
Population.
LABOURERS.
Biadarus.

is millet bread or rice and pulse. They eat mutton, beef, pork, domestic fowls, and wild game. They drink to excess. They have no objection to eating with Musalmáns. The higher classes of Hindus look down on them and never associate with them. The men wear a pair of light short trousers reaching a little below the knee, a shirt and a headscarf or *rumál*. The women wear a backed bodice with short sleeves, and a robe whose skirt they do not pass between the feet. Berads, as a class, are simple in their manners, civil and goodhumoured in their bearing, talkative, and brave; they are lazy, cunning, and cruel. They are clever thieves, skilful in eluding search and hiding stolen property, and are much feared by travellers. They steal cattle with such cleverness and send the stolen animals such long distances, that the greatest energy and caution often fail to find any trace of them. The owner has to go and ask the Berad's help, and if he promises a reward the animal is found and restored. Near Satagati if an animal is missing it is almost sure to have fallen into the hands of the Berads. They are said to cut its throat, hang its head down to the branch of a tree, kindle a fire underneath it, and with their wives and children feast on its flesh. Though notorious thieves, the Berads are honest guardians of public property. They are village watchmen, husbandmen, and labourers. Under the Peshwa the village of Chikaddine about twelve miles north of Belgaum was the centre of a small Berad state. At the time of the British conquest of the country in 1817 they had a strong organization under a *náik* or chief. In the early years of British rule they caused some trouble, but were reduced to order in 1820. They were still very unwilling to settle to regular work and preferred to sublet their land even at a small rent rather than be at the trouble of farming it. In 1829 there was a great Bedar outbreak under a famous leader named Rajappa Sangoli. So successful was he that for a time the fort of Belgaum was believed to be in danger. Of late years they have become skilful both as field and as day labourers, hunters, and snarers. They have no family priests. They believe in sorcery, witchcraft, and soothsaying. They worship all local deities, especially Yellamma and Máruti, and consult Bráhmans. Their chief ceremonial occasions are birth-naming, hair-cutting, coming of age, marriage, and death. On none of these occasions is a Bráhman called to officiate. On the fifth day after the birth of a child they worship the goddess Páchvi and feast three or four relations. On the twelfth or nineteenth day the elders choose a name generally either of a deceased relation, or of one of the gods, lay the child in a cradle, repeat its name three times, the women sing songs, and a few relations are feasted. When a male or a female child is a year old the maternal uncle cuts five hairs with a pair of scissors and asks the barber to cut the rest. A girl is married before she comes of age; the bridegroom, in company with relations, goes to the bride's at the time fixed by the village Bráhman; the bride is led by her maternal uncle to where the marriage party are met; the couple are seated on a mattress face to face, and a cloth is held between them; the elders throw grains of rice over their heads, and they are husband and wife. The next day the married pair go to the village temple accompanied by

Chapter III.
Population.
LABOURERS.
Biadarus.

relations and music. They stand outside of the building, give a cocoanut, betel-leaves, and a ¼ *anna* (⅜*d.*) to the temple ministrant, bow to the god, return to the bride's house, distribute sugar to the guests and give a feast to near relations. Polygamy and widow marriage are allowed and practised. When a girl comes of age she keeps aloof for three days. On the fourth day she bathes, when if the husband is well-to-do, he gives her a new robe and bodice, and a married woman fills her lap with rice, betelnut, and a cocoanut. A few burn, but most bury their dead. The dying person is laid in the centre of the house with the head towards the north. When life is gone the body is bathed, shrouded in a new cloth, and carried to the burning ground. A Mhár always goes with the body and is paid 1½*d.* (1 *anna*). On the twelfth day the chief mourner brings water from the village Brahman, sprinkles it in the house, and, if the deceased was married, a silver plate impressed with the deceased's figure is bought from a goldsmith for 6*d.* or 1*s.* (*annas* 4 or 8). On the thirteenth day the relations of the deceased worship the silver plate which is kept in the house and worshipped once in a year. They are bound together as a body. Their social disputes are settled at meetings of the caste under an hereditary headman called *nádigye.* They do not send their boys to school.

Deshávals.

Desha'vals, with a strength of 500, are found in Belgaum, Parasgad, and Athni. They came into the district from Bangalor about sixty years ago. They live in small houses with walls of mud and tiled roof; and keep cows, goats, dogs, and poultry. Their home speech is Telugu. Their staple food is wheat or Indian millet bread, rice, pulse, and vegetables. They eat fish, mutton, and poultry, but there is a caste rule against eating animal food daily. They are great drunkards, using both country and foreign liquor. They smoke tobacco and some of them hemp-flower or *gánja*, eat opium, and *májum* an inebriating preparation of *bháng* mixed with sugar and spices and formed into cakes. The men wear the top-knot and moustache; and the women tie the hair in a bunch on the right side of the head without using either flowers or false hair. The men wear the loincloth, headscarf or *rumál*, waistcloth, coat, shirt, and shouldercloth; and the women the shortsleeved bodice and a robe the skirt-corner of which they pass between the feet and draw the other end over the left shoulder. They are neither neat nor clean in their dress, and use both country-made and European cloth. They bake and sell loaves, biscuits, and ginger-bread, the women and children helping in their calling. They worship the ordinary Bráhmanic gods and have the greatest respect for Mahádev. Their household god is Venkoba and they are the priests of Náidus and Mudliárs. Their priests are Deshasth Bráhmans, whom they call to conduct their chief ceremonies such as birth, marriage, puberty, and death. They have no teacher or *guru*, and make no pilgrimages. They believe in soothsaying, omens, and lucky and unlucky days. They bury their dead, and their customs do not differ from those of the Náidus. They are bound together as a body, and settle social disputes according to the opinion of the majority of the caste people. They send their boys to school and teach them Telugu and Maráthi. Their craft is poorly paid, and is declining.

Chapter III.
Population.
LABOURERS.
Dombárs.

Domba'rs, with a strength of 1006, are found throughout the district. Tumblers, rope-dancers, and gymnasts are called Dombárs. They are divided into Vále or Váliar that is Holia also called Mhár Dombárs, Gopálgani Dombárs who perform feats on *gopálganis* or long bamboo poles, and Musalmán Dombárs. These three classes have no subdivisions and no surnames. They do not intermarry or eat together. The Vále Dombárs speak Kánarese, the Gopálganis Maráthi, and the Musalmáns Hindustáni. The men are generally hardworking and good-tempered, though not sober. The Gopálganis are clean, neat, and well-behaved, and the Vále women are thieves. The Gopálganis, besides performing rope-dancing and other athletic feats, amuse the people by buffoonery. Two bamboos ten or twelve feet long are set up some sixteen feet apart and a strong rope is tied to their tops. On this they dance and while dancing keep making ludicrous remarks like buffoons in theatres. They are excellent stilt-walkers and also perform feats of strength on the ground. The Gopálgani women are expert prostitutes persuading people to visit them and to pay them well. For this purpose good-looking girls are set apart and called *sonchedis* or golden daughters. The Váles make combs and other articles of horn and hide which the women hawk from house to house, losing no chance of pilfering anything they can lay their hands on. Like the Gopálganis the Musalmán Dombárs earn their living by performing athletic feats and by begging. When they beg they are accompanied by their women who dance and sing, and both women and children take part in performing athletic feats. Sometimes they go begging from door to door, one beating a drum or *daf,* and the other playing the one-stringed fiddle called *tuntune.* The women also make bamboo sieves and barter them for old clothes. Dombárs wander from place to place stopping outside the villages in small huts of straw matting supported by bamboo sticks which they carry with them wherever they go. They halt during the rains wherever they happen to be when the rain begins. They rear no domestic animals except some asses which carry their mat huts and their gear. They eat the flesh of cows, buffaloes, goats, sheep, deer, and hogs; but not of horses, *nilgáis,* lizards, serpents, porcupines, asses, or monkeys. The men wear short tight trousers and wrap a long cloth round the loins. They occasionally wear a waistcloth, a short coat, and a turban. The golden girls of the Gopálganis who are set apart as courtezans have a silk-bordered robe and bodice, deck their hair with flowers, and wear gold and silver ornaments on the head, ear, nose, neck, arms, and feet like those worn by dancing-girls. The dress of the rest of the women is poor and coarse. In the morning the men teach their children athletic exercises and to sing songs, and then perform from two till sunset. The women, after setting apart some food for the evening, go about begging and pilfering. They marry their girls at any age, the husband having to pay a sum of money to the girl's parents. Some of the men have more wives than one and live on their wives' earnings as courtezans. They bury their dead. Hindu Dombárs worship Yelloba and Yellamma, and Musalmán Dombárs reverence Pirs. They have no class organization. Each family roams by

Chapter III. Population. LABOURERS.

itself careful to avoid others lest they should spoil each other's prospects. The Gopálganis are well-to-do, but the Váles are extremely poor. They do not send their boys to school or take to new pursuits. On the whole they are a falling people.

Golls.

Golls or **Gopa'ls,** with a strength of 324, are found only in Sampgaon and in Athni. They are a wandering people from Madras whose home speech is Telugu. They are dark and middle-sized with long faces, thick lips, gaunt cheeks, and long necks. The men wear the top-knot, moustache, and whiskers, and a few the beard. They live in thatched huts and keep dogs. Their staple food is Indian millet bread, pulse, and vegetables. Their only caste feasts are in honour of marriages. They eat fish and the flesh of sheep, goats, the hare, domestic fowls and wild game. They drink palm-spirits. Most smoke tobacco and some hemp-flower or *gánja.* They dress and wear ornaments like Kunbis. They prepare medicines from metals and from forest plants. Some of them are clever at drawing out guineaworms with a needle and at cupping. Their women and children weave mats and sell them in the local markets. Some of them are beggars. They respect Bráhmans and call them to their marriages. They worship the ordinary Bráhman gods and have the greatest respect for Máruti, whose image, along with those of Venkoba, Narsoba, and Yellamma, they keep in their houses. They have no spiritual teacher or *guru,* and believe in lucky and unlucky days. On the birth of a child they worship the goddess Páchvi or the spirit of the fifth, and name their children on the ninth. Their boys are shaved for the first time in presence of the village Máruti. Their marriage customs do not differ from those of the Kunbis. They bury their dead and mourn for five weeks, when they call a Jangam or Lingáyat priest who makes them pure by ringing a bell and blowing a conch-shell. For this he is given uncooked food or *shidha.* They have a caste organization and settle their social disputes at meetings of the castemen. Some of them earn enough to maintain themselves and their families decently and a few lay by a little. They do not send their boys to school and are a steady class.

Ilgers.

Ilgers or **Shindiga'rs,** with a strength of 1208, are found in all large villages of the district except in Khánápur. They are chiefly found in the villages and towns near which fan-leaf or *tád* palms and wild date-palms grow. They say they came into the district about a hundred years ago from Bellári in Madras in search of work. Their home tongue is Kánarese, but in Chikodi, Athni, and Belgaum they speak Maráthi out of doors. They look like Lingáyats, and are dark, strong, and muscular. Most of them live in houses of the better class, with walls of brick or mud, and tiled roofs. Their staple food is wheat and Indian millet bread, rice, pulse, milk, butter, curds, and vegetables. They eat fish and the flesh of goats, sheep, deer, hare, and domestic fowls. They do not sacrifice the animal before eating it. They do not drink country or foreign liquor, not even fresh palm-juice, neither do they smoke tobacco or any other drug. They dress like Lingáyats and wear the same ornaments. They are not clean, but they are hardworking, sober, thrifty, even-tempered,

Chapter III. Population. LABOURERS. *Ilgers.*

hospitable, and well-behaved. They are drawers and sellers of palm-juice. Boys begin to earn a living when they are about fourteen. Some of them are moneylenders and one contracts to supply bread to the Belgaum troops. Some are over-holders, some under-holders, and some field-labourers, but none are skilful husbandmen. The women help the men in sowing and weeding. Their religion and customs do not differ from those of the Maráthás. Their priests, who are Karháda Bráhmans, officiate at their houses at birth, marriage, coming of age, and death ceremonies. They worship the usual Bráhmanic gods, and have the greatest respect for Vithoba. They bury their dead. They have a caste organization. They do not send their boys to school. Since they came into the district they have improved the palm-juice trade, and made money. They are well paid and prosperous.

Kaikádis.

Kaika'dis, with a strength of 115, are found in Chikodi, Gokák, and Athni. The men wear the top-knot and moustache, and the women tie their hair in a knot without using false hair or flowers. They live either in houses with mud walls and tiled roofs or in thatched huts. They rear bullocks, buffaloes, donkeys, and dogs, and their every-day food is Indian millet bread and vegetables. No one but Mhárs eat from their hands. They eat fish, the flesh of sheep, goats, pigs, hare, deer, partridges, and fowls. They are fond of drinking both country and foreign liquor, and smoke tobacco and hemp-flower or *gánja.* Their habits are dirty and untidy. The men roll a piece of cloth round the loins and another round the head, and draw a third over the shoulders. Their women wear a robe without passing the end between the feet; they seldom wear a bodice. They make baskets of the wild date leaves and some are husbandmen under-holders or field-labourers. All have a bad name as robbers and housebreakers. They worship all Hindu gods, honour Yellamma as their house goddess, and reverence Muhammadan saints. They consult village Bráhmans as to their children's names, but do not call them to their marriages. The boy and girl are rubbed with turmeric at their houses, a caste feast is given with plenty of liquor, and the parents of the girl tie the hem of the girl's robe to the boy's waistcloth, and the boy and girl are husband and wife. The marriage agreement has the unusual condition that the son-in-law must live with his wife's family and help to support them until his wife has given birth to three children. If he separates from his wife by mutual consent, he has to make an allowance to his wife's parents. Kaikádis have no headman and settle disputes by a committee of four or five members of the caste. They do not send their boys to school or take to new pursuits. They are a poor class.

Kaláls.

Kala'ls, or LIQUOR-SELLERS, with a strength of forty-eight, are found in large villages and towns throughout the district. They are generally fair and goodlooking. The men wear the topknot, moustache, and whiskers, but no beard. The women braid their hair behind, but do not deck it with flowers or wear false hair. They speak Kánarese. Most of them live in houses with tiled roofs. The men dress like Lingáyats in a headscarf *rumál,* waistcloth, coat, and shouldercloth; and the women in the robe and bodice. The men wear the sacred

LABOURERS.
Kaláls.

thread. They eat fish and the flesh of sheep, goats, the hare, and domestic fowls, provided they are slaughtered by a Musalmán priest or *mulla*. If there is no available priest a Kalál slaughters the animal himself, washing his hands and mouth and repeating some words from the *Kurán*. Their hereditary calling is to make and sell liquor, but since 1881, when a central or *sadar* distillery was established at Belgaum, their calling has been confined to the sale of liquor prepared at the distillery. They also work as labourers and cultivate, though as cultivators they do not show much skill. Their women work in the fields and as day-labourers. They worship Shiv, Vishnu, and Máruti, and show much respect to their priests who are Deshasth, Konkanasth, and Karháda Bráhmans. Their marriage and death ceremonies are the same as those of Kunbis. Their marriages last three days. On the first day castemen are feasted and the bride and bridegroom are rubbed with turmeric. The next day the bridegroom goes to the bride's house and is seated on a blanket. A cloth is held between them and the priest repeats verses and at the end throws grains of rice over their heads, and they are husband and wife. Packets of betelnut and leaves are handed round, and the guests retire. On the second evening the boy walks with the girl to his house accompanied by music and friends and relations. At his house the goddess Lakshmi is worshipped. On the third day a castefeast is given. On the first day after a death 2*s*. to 4*s*. (Rs.1-2) are spent in preparing the pile, in buying flowers which are thrown over the body, and in buying clothes for the corpse. On the third day sons, brothers, and other near male relations go to the burning ground, sprinkle milk over and round the ashes, take the ashes to some river, and throw them into the water. On their return such alms as they can afford are given to the poor. On the twelfth or thirteenth day a dinner is given to near relations and friends. A Bráhman priest attends only on the twelfth day and gets cash or *dakshina* and uncooked food or *shidha*. They practise child marriage and polygamy; widow marriage is forbidden and polyandry is unknown. Their caste rules allow them to spin wool in a spindle but not to spin cotton. If they touch quilt patch-work they have to bathe. They have no priest of their own, but they generally call Bráhman priests to their marriages. They do not go on pilgrimage. Under the new excise system they have become little more than the servants of the contractor. They borrow to meet special expenses. They have no headman and settle social disputes by the opinion of a majority of the castemen. They send their boys to school but only till they can read and write a little. Their condition is at present somewhat depressed.

Kolátis.

Kola'tis, with a strength of 724, are found only in Chikodi. They are divided into pure and impure Kolátis who do not eat together or intermarry. They speak a mixture of Maráthi and Hindustáni, and are intelligent, slight, and active, of fair complexion, with dark eyes, and short-cut black hair. The men wear the top-knot, the moustache, the beard, and whiskers; and the women tie the hair in a knot behind the head. They generally live outside of villages and

Chapter III.
Population.
LABOURERS.
Kolátis.

move from place to place, carrying long low mat huts, nicknamed *kádi-maháls* or straw-halls. They live together in small groups of four or five families. They keep donkeys which they use in travelling from place to place. Their staple food is Indian millet bread and vegetables. They eat fish, crabs, mutton, domestic fowls, pigs, deer, hare, and partridges. They drink both country and foreign liquor and palm-juice. All smoke tobacco and some hemp-flower or *gánja*. Their dress is untidy and dirty. The men wear a small twisted turban, a rough shouldercloth, and short tight trousers; the women wear a shortsleeved bodice and a robe whose skirt corner is passed back between the feet. They are tumblers and rope-dancers, and live by begging. Their social position is as low as that of Mhárs. They worship the ordinary Hindu gods but Hanumán is their chief object of worship; their family deities are Khandoba and Mari. They believe in ghosts and spirits. When she comes of age every Koláti girl is called on to choose between marriage and prostitution. If she prefers marriage she is jealously watched and is usually well-behaved. If she choose prostitution and tumbling, her parents have to call a caste council and get their leave and give a feast. She is then at liberty to follow the calling. The children of unmarried Koláti women are admitted to the full privileges of the caste. They are an intelligent class anxious to rise from their position.

Korvis.

Korvis, with a strength of 3710, are found over the whole district except in Khánápur. They are divided into Sanádis, Konchis, Advis or Kal Kaikádis, and Modi Korvis. The Sanádis are considered the highest subdivision of Korvis and neither eat nor marry with the others. They are strong and dark, the women being a little fairer than the men. The men wear the top-knot, the moustache, and whiskers. Their home tongue is Telugu mixed with Tamil, in which three-fourths of the words are Kánarese. They are dirty, cruel, idle, given to thieving and drinking; and their women are prostitutes. They are musicians and makers of baskets, cornbins, slings, and grass ropes. They do not cultivate. The Modis or sorcerers play on a pipe called *pungi* and make baskets; and the Konchis catch and sell peacocks and partridges. The Advis enter villages during the day under pretence of selling brooms and baskets. They find a good house to rob, and at night return and carry off clothes, vessels, ornaments, or cattle. The Advi women are also thieves. They frequent villages on the pretence of begging and rob by day in regular gangs headed by a female leader called *jamádárin*. Each gang is provided with a bunch of keys and pick-locks. When they see a locked house in an unfrequented lane, one of them stands in front of the door, as if begging alms. The *jamádárin* picks the locks and the rest are posted round watching. When the leader comes out with the booty she locks the door, and they all walk away. Should any one happen to pass while the leader is in the house, the woman at the door produces a silver coin and asks the man if the coin is good. She then begins to dispute with him, and laying hold of him calls to her comrades that the man has abused her or taking liberties with her. One woman after another runs up and they jostle the man away from the door. When a number of people have gathered the leader escapes with the booty. Again, an old woman will go from house to house pretending to be a fortune-teller. If she finds a house with no one in it but a single woman she flatters and astonishes the housewife by telling the chief events in the housewife's life, how many children she has, and how many more are coming. When the woman of the house is satisfied that the Advi woman has superhuman powers she allows the witch to cover her face with her robe and shuts her eyes while the Advi woman breathes on them and blows in her ears and sits muttering charms. Meanwhile one or two of her friends who have been lurking close by, walk into the house and carry away whatever they can lay their hands on. When they have left the house the woman's face is uncovered, and the Advi woman takes her presents and leaves her dupe to find out that her house has been robbed. Such of the Korvis as have given up a wandering life live either in or outside of villages in small houses either with thatched or tiled roofs. They rear pigs and fowls. While travelling they carry straw mats which with the help of a few sticks they make into huts. They keep dogs and asses to watch and carry their goods. Except cows, horses, rats, and dead animals, they eat most kinds of flesh and drink liquor. Their staple food is Indian millet. On fast days they prepare cakes or *polis* and rice like other Hindus. They dress like low-caste Hindus, generally in dirty clothes. Their women wear a bodice and a robe. The Modis or sorcerers wear a long coat, a pair of breeches, and a turban with some feathers fastened to it. Well-to-do women wear a nosering or *mukra* of gold, and silver rings or *tolbundis* above the elbows. Except a coil of black beads round the neck and glass bangles, a poor woman wears no ornaments. On the fifth day after a birth the goddess Páchvi is worshipped, and the child is named on the twelfth, the name being given by an astrologer. All children have their heads shaved before they are a year old. They have no rule that a girl should be married before she comes of age. The betrothal is settled by the payment of 8*s.* (Rs. 4) to the girl's father in presence of relations and friends. Shortly before the marriage day a second sum called *mahár* of not less than £3 (Rs. 30) is given to the girl's father. Three days before the marriage the boy and girl are rubbed with turmeric at their homes and instead of red-powder or *kunku* a mixture of turmeric and cement is rubbed on their brows. A cocoanut wrapped in a piece of cloth is tied to the boy's right and a three-cornered piece of cloth called *pál* is set up as a canopy in front of the boy's house. On the wedding-day the boy goes with his relations and friends to the girl's house and sits by the girl surrounded by women. Neither widows nor widowers are allowed to enter the house. The boy's and girl's hands are joined, and two married women, one a relation of the boy, the other of the girl, ask the elder women present whether they agree to the marriage. When they state that they are willing, the musicians play the marriage song and the ceremony is completed. Then the boy and girl sit facing each other and they feed one another with sweetened rice, and the rest of the rice is given to guests whose

Chapter III. Population. LABOURERS. *Korvis.*

first wives or husbands are alive. The boy takes the girl to his house and feasts the caste with meat and liquor. A widow who has daughters may not marry until all the girls are married; a widow who has sons can never marry. Korvis, as a rule, bury the dead, but they burn a woman who dies within ten days after child-birth. Their death ceremonies are like those of low-caste Hindus. The only peculiarity is that two near relations or friends are chosen to be corpse-bearers and after the funeral remain in the house for three days. On the third day the ashes of the dead are gathered and thrown into a river or pond. After bathing the two bearers and a party of caste people are feasted and are then free to go where they please. The gods of the Korvis are Máruti, Yellamma, Huligeva, Mailar, Basápa, and Márgav or Lakshmi. They believe and worship all other Hindu gods and goddesses. Their priests are ordinary Bráhmans. They fast on Saturdays and observe *Pádva* in April and *Nág-panchmi* in August as holidays. They go on pilgrimage to Huligeva in the Nizám's dominions, to the shrine of Yellamma at Saundatti, and to a Musalmán saint's tomb at Yamanur. Her monthly sickness is not thought to make a woman unclean. Though the Korvis hold a very low social position high-caste Hindus do not consider that their touch defiles. The Sanádis have a headman of the Támil caste whom they term *sheti* or *mahánandi*. The other subdivisions settle social disputes at meetings of the men of the caste. Among the Korvis if a woman is found guilty of adultery or of any other serious crime she is put out of caste and not allowed back until she passes through the following ordeal: Three stakes of Indian millet are set on the ground their tops touching. The woman is made to stand under them and they are set on fire. Then her tongue is branded with a piece of heated gold. After all these rites have been performed she is clean and fit to come back into caste. The Korvis do not send their boys to school. They are a very poor class, many of them living entirely on alms.

Korchars.

Korchars, with a strength of 293, are found in Belgaum and Gokák. They are black, strong, and well-made, and look like Korvis. Their expression is lively, the nose high, the cheeks round, and the hair lank. The men wear a top-knot, moustache, and whiskers; and the women tie their hair in a knot on the right side. Their home tongue is Tamil; out of doors they speak Hindustáni. They live in small dirty and untidy houses with walls of mud and tiled roofs. Their staple food is Indian millet bread, pulse, and vegetables. They eat fish and the flesh of goats, sheep, fowls, and game. They are given to drink, using both country and foreign spirits and palm-juice. All smoke tobacco and some smoke hemp-flowers or *gánja*. The men wear a headscarf, a short coat and waistcoat, and a waist and shouldercloth; the women wear a shortsleeved bodice and a robe whose skirt-corner is not passed back between the feet. Some are day-labourers, while others are hunters or *shikáris*. They eat from Maráthás and Maráthás eat from them. They are hardworking, but not honest, sober, or thrifty. The men go hunting or work as labourers, and the women earn something by tattooing. They worship the usual Bráhmanic gods and have the greatest respect for Máruti. Their family goddess is Durgamma and their family priests are Bráhmans whom they call to conduct their marriage, age-coming, and death ceremonies. They observe the regular Hindu holidays. They have no religious teacher or *guru*. They believe in soothsaying, omens, and lucky and unlucky days, and consult Deshasth Smárt Bráhmans at the time of birth and marriages and when in difficulty. They name the child on the twelfth day after birth and give a dinner, most of the guests being women. Their marriage ceremonies last two days. On the first day they rub the bride and bridegroom with turmeric and oil, and on the second day a Bráhman conducts the marriage ceremony. A cloth is held between the boy and girl, verses are repeated, and the ceremony is completed by throwing rice over their heads. On the third day a feast is held at both the boy's and the girl's. They bury their dead, and give a feast on the thirteenth day to relations and castemen including the four bier-bearers. They allow widow marriage. They are bound together as a body and settle their social disputes according to the opinion of the majority of the castemen. They neither send their children to school, nor take to new pursuits. They are very poor.

Medárs.

Medárs or **Buruds**, WORKERS IN BAMBOO, with a strength of 1092, are found over the whole district, chiefly in large villages and towns. They claim descent from one Kyataya, a Lingáyat, to which sect they say they formerly belonged and lost their position from eating and drinking in Shudras' houses during a famine. The Medárs do not now wear the *ling*. They have no subdivisions. The men are dark, strongly made, and regular-featured; the women are a little fairer than the men. The men wear the top-knot and moustache, and sometimes the beard and whiskers. The women coil their hair in a knot and tie it with a woollen string or *mandidhar*. Their home tongue is Kánarese. They are hardworking and hospitable but extravagant and drunken. They make bamboo baskets and blinds. They seldom cultivate; many of them trade in bamboo. As a labourer a Medár man earns about 6*d*. (4 *as.*) a day. Their women are equally hardworking, and besides minding the house plait baskets and matting. A man wears a turban or headscarf, a waistcoat, short pantaloons or *chadis*, and sometimes a shouldercloth and shoes or *chapals*. The women wear a robe and a bodice. They eat fish and flesh and drink liquor. Their every-day meal consists of Indian millet bread and vegetables, a few eating rice. They worship the goddess Páchvi on the fifth day after child-birth and name it on the thirteenth. They shave the child's hair for the first time before it is two years old and throw the hair into the river. Medárs allow widow marriage, the children of the first husband being left to his relations. A woman who marries a second husband is considered impure and is not allowed to take part in religious ceremonies. The Medárs bury and do not burn their dead. The Chalvádi, who carries a bell in front of the Lingáyats' funerals, heads their burial parties. Before the dead is carried to the burying ground a Lingáyat *ayya* sets his

Chapter III. Population. LABOURERS. Medárs.

right foot on the head of the corpse. The priest's foot is worshipped by the relations of the dead, washed, and the water poured into the corpse's mouth to wash away its sins. Except this the Medárs observe no Lingáyat customs. They mourn the dead for ten days and perform the funeral ceremonies or *shráddh* from the eleventh to the thirteenth day. They worship Shiv, Basavana, Yellamma, and other Hindu gods. They keep in their houses and worship silver or brass images of their ancestors. They call Bráhmans to their houses to perform all religious ceremonies except funerals which are conducted by Lingáyat priests. Like Konkan and Deccan bamboo-workers the Medárs are not held unclean. They have a caste organization. Their headmen who are called *gauda* and *chavga* belong to their own caste and with the help of the caste people, settle social disputes. The two headmen are paid certain fees on marriage and other joyful occasions and no marriage contract is settled without their consent. Medárs are not scrimped for food or clothing, earning enough to keep themselves and their families, but not saving enough to meet marriage and other special expenses. Many have to borrow and are in debt. They do not send their boys to school or take to new pursuits, and are not a rising class.

Rámoshis.

Ra'moshis, with a strength of 167, are found in Belgaum, Sampgaon, Chikodi, Athni, and Gokák. According to their own story they are of the same caste as the Berads with whom they eat but do not marry. They have no subdivisions. Their surnames are Ándil and Banni, and families bearing the same surname cannot intermarry. They look like Kunbis. The men, who wear the top-knot, moustache, and whiskers, are dark, strong, and regular featured. Their home speech is Kánarese. A comparatively well-to-do Rámoshi has a house with three rooms, the back room for cattle, the middle room for the women and for dining and sleeping, and the front room for men and visitors. Except six or seven brass and several earthen vessels, they have few household goods. They keep cows, bullocks, buffaloes, and dogs. Their staple food is Indian millet, rice, pulse, and vegetables. They eat fish and the flesh of goats, sheep, fowls, and buffaloes. Their use of animal food is not limited to sacrificial or other great occasions; if they could afford it they would eat meat regularly. They drink both country and foreign liquor and eat opium; almost all smoke tobacco and some smoke hemp-flower. The men dress like Kunbis in a headscarf, shouldercloth, and waistcloth, but their clothes are dirty and untidy. The women wear a shortsleeved bodice and the robe without passing the end back between the feet. They are quarrelsome and given to drink. They make their living as watchmen, husbandmen, and labourers, and some of them are robbers. They grow *náchni* and *vari* with the help of their women. Field-workers are paid either in grain or in cash, at the rate of 3*d.* (2 *as.*) a day. Their work is steady, but most of them borrow to meet special expenses, and as they have generally to pay as much as twenty-four per cent interest many of them are involved in debt. They do not respect Bráhmans nor call them to conduct their ceremonies. Their family goddess is Yedeva and they have the greatest respect for Máruti. They worship their deceased ancestors as well as the cobra or *nág,* holding it sacred and never

Chapter III. Population. LABOURERS. Rámoshis.

destroying it. They keep no images in their houses. Their priests are Lingáyat Jangams who perform their birth, marriage, and death ceremonies. They make no pilgrimages and except their Jangams have no religious head or *guru*. When a child is born they give a Jangam ⅜*d.* (¼ *anna*) and ask him to name the child. The Jangam asks the name of the child's ancestors and after consulting his almanac tells them by what name to call the child. They have no betrothal or puberty ceremonies. The marriage age for girls varies from five to ten, and for boys from ten to twenty. When his first wife is barren, a man may take a second or even a third wife. But if he has children by his first wife he seldom marries again during her lifetime. They allow and practise widow marriage. There is a rule that if a man suspects his wife of unfaithfulness, with the consent of the caste he may divorce her. They bury their dead. Nothing is spent on the burial of the unmarried, but in memory of the married dead, whether men or women, a caste feast is given on the thirteenth day after death. They are bound together as a body and settle caste disputes at meetings of the adult male members. They do not send their boys to school.

Rávals.

Ra'vals, with a strength of 258, are found all over the district. They are divided into Rávulnáths and Padamroti Rávals who neither eat together nor intermarry. Both divisions look like Maráthás and speak Maráthi at home. They live in small houses with walls of mud and tiled roofs. They keep cows, bullocks, goats, and fowls, and are temperate in eating and drinking. Their staple food is rice, Indian millet, pulse, and vegetables, but they do not object to eat fish or flesh or to drink liquor. They smoke tobacco and hemp-flowers. The men wear a headscarf or *rumál,* a coat, a shirt, a waistcloth, and a shouldercloth; and the women a shortsleeved bodice and a robe or *lugade* whose end is not drawn back between the feet. They are hardworking, sober, and thrifty, but dirty. They are messengers, weavers, landholders, field-workers, and beggars. They weave coarse robes or *sádis* which they sell to shopkeepers, their women helping them in their work. They are not skilful husbandmen. Their women help them in weeding and sowing, and their children in looking after the cattle. They sell milk, butter, and curds. They worship the ordinary Bráhman gods, and have the greatest respect for Mahádev. Their priests are Deshasth Bráhmans whom they call to conduct their birth, marriage, puberty, and death ceremonies. They do not make pilgrimages, and have no religious guide or *guru*. They believe in soothsaying and lucky and unlucky days and consult the ordinary Bráhmans at the time of birth and marriage or whenever they are in difficulty. Their customs do not differ from those of Kunbis. They bury their dead and allow widow marriage. They are bound together as a body and their social disputes are settled at meetings of the adult males of the caste. A few send their boys to school. As a class they are fairly prosperous.

Shikáris.

Shika'ris or HUNTERS, also called Párdhis or Snarers, with a strenth of thirty, are a wandering tribe who seem to be the same as the Gujarát Vághris. Their home tongue is Gujaráti. They are

Chapter III.
Population.
LABOURERS.
Shikáris.

divided into Mir or noble Shikáris, Haranpárdhis or deer-hunters, and Korchers or basket-makers. These divisions neither eat together nor intermarry. They have no surnames. They are dark, dirty, and thin. The men allow the hair to grow like a woman's hair and wear the moustache and beard. They are bird-catchers, hardworking, sober, and such skilful whistle-players that the birds gather round them. They also catch them with nets. The birds they generally catch are peafowl, partridges, rock-quail, and parrots. The quail are taught to fight and the parrots to speak. The Haranpárdhis catch deer by throwing large nets over them or disabling them with sticks. They sell the young deer and the skins of the old ones. Some carry matchlocks, swords, and spears, and hunt large game. They are also gang-robbers. When in towns and villages selling game they try to find a suitable place for a robbery. They commit burglaries, rob fields, and steal when the chance offers. The Korchers, besides hunting and robbing, work as basket-makers. They eat deer, fowls, goats, sheep, hares, hogs, peacocks, partridges, and quails, and almost all feathered game, but not cows, buffaloes, horses, asses, rats, cats, monkeys, *nilgáis*, porcupines, lizards, or serpents. They drink liquor and smoke tobacco and hemp-flower. They wear a loincloth, a headscarf, and a bodycloth. The women wear the robe and bodice, glass bangles, and brass earrings. They live in bamboo huts seven feet by four and five feet high with walls and slanting roofs of straw matting which they roll up and carry off in a few minutes. In the fair season they generally live near hills in clusters of about a dozen huts. When overtaken by rain they take shelter in the nearest village. On the fifth day after the birth of a child the goddess Satvái is worshipped and a feast is given to the caste to satisfy the goddess. A Deshasth Bráhman gives the child a name. If the child is a boy the mother should keep the house for three and if it is a girl for two months. In practice the confinement seldom lasts for more than a month. At the end of the three months in the case of a boy or of the two months in the case of a girl a feast is given to the caste. Until this feast is given the mother is considered impure and is not allowed to join in any ceremony such as a marriage. On the day the child is named a feast is held. The child is laid in its mother's lap, songs are sung, and the child is named by a Deshasth Bráhman and sugar is handed to the guests. They marry their girls at any age. The boy's father has to give the girl's father £4 (Rs. 40) in cash. If his father cannot pay the amount the bridegroom has to serve in his father-in-law's house for a stated period. Their marriages are performed by Deshasth Bráhmans and the festivities last for two or three days according to the parents' means. On the first day the boy and girl are rubbed with turmeric and a dinner is given in honour of the family gods. On the second day the pair are seated on a blanket, the priest repeats verses and at the end throws grains of rice over their heads and they are husband and wife. They are taken to bow before the village god and a feast is given by both the fathers. They bury the dead and mourn twelve days and end with a caste feast. They allow widow marriage. Their chief objects of worship are Lakshmi, Durgava, and Dyámava. They respect

Bráhmans. They do not go on pilgrimage and have no spiritual head. They have a caste organization and decide social disputes at meetings of the castemen. They do not send their boys to school or take to new pursuits. They are a poverty-stricken class, with an uncertain and poorly paid calling. They are generally dressed in rags and are sometimes scrimped for food.

Vadars.

Vadars, or DIGGERS, are a wandering tribe, returned as numbering 197 and as found over the whole district. They are divided into Bhoj-Vadars who hold aloof from the rest, Kal-Vadars, Man-Vadars, and Bhandi-Vadars who eat together and intermarry. They are dark with regular features, high noses, thin lips, and long necks, and are strongly made. They speak a mixture of Telugu and Kánarese. The men are hardworking but thriftless and given to drink, and their wives are hardworking and well-behaved. Bhoj-Vadars prepare and sell charcoal and cement. Kal-Vadars are stone-cutters; Man-Vadars are diggers, and Bhandi-Vadars are cartmen. They also prepare corn handmills. They rear asses, sell pickaxes and shovels, and build mud walls. Formerly all were plunderers, robbing both by day and night. Bhoj-Vadars live in small thatched houses, and the other divisions live in bamboo and mat huts about three and half feet high, three broad, and six or seven feet long. They keep buffaloes, asses, and fowls, and, except beef, eat all animal food including serpents and rats. They drink liquor and their staple food is Indian millet and vegetables. They dress like low-caste Hindus, the men in a turban, a pair of breeches reaching the knee, and a blanket or waistcloth; the women wear a robe without a bodice. On the fifth day after the birth of a child Vadars feast married women and name the child on the night of the eleventh. They do not consult astrologers for lucky days or for a name. They marry their children on Monday afternoon at any time either before or after they are of age, though it is considered wrong to put off a girl's marriage until she comes of age. A feast to the caste seals the marriage contract. When the boy and the girl are to be wedded the boy is seated on a blanket on open ground in front of the girl's house, and two pieces of turmeric root along with betel leaves are wrapped in a cloth and tied to the right wrist of both the boy and the girl. The girl wears a glass bangle on her left wrist, and the boy ties a black bead necklace round her neck with a piece of white thread. Friends and relations throw rice on the couple's heads, and they are husband and wife. On the next day they are thrice rubbed with turmeric and the marriage ceremony is over. The whole costs 10*s.* to £2 (Rs. 5-20). Except very old persons the Vadars bury the dead. The death ceremony generally costs 4*s.* to 10*s.* (Rs. 2-5). They worship Venkatraman, Yellamma, and Máruti, but do not employ Bráhmans to officiate at their houses. The headmen of the Bhojs, who are termed *shetis* and *mahánadis* are of the Tamil caste. The social disputes of the other subdivisions are decided by elderly persons at a meeting of the castemen. The Vadars do not send their boys to school, but are fairly off, not scrimped for food or clothing and free from debt.

Chapter III.
Population.
BEGGARS.

Beggars include fourteen classes with a strength of 2500 or 0·31 per cent of the Hindu population. The following statement gives the details:

BELGAUM BEGGARS.

Class.	Males.	Females	Total.	Class.	Males.	Females	Total.
Bágdis ...	6	6	12	Kánphátes ...	36	33	69
Bháts ...	43	27	70	Kelikelars ...	47	61	108
Dandig Dásarus	3	5	8	Oshtams ..	41	52	93
Dásarus ...	274	300	574	Pichátis ...	48	57	105
Davris ...	53	52	105	Pinales ...	21	22	43
Gondhlis ...	163	207	370	Vásudevs ...	4	6	10
Gosávis ...	464	440	904				
Joshis ...	25	4	29	Total ...	1228	1272	2500

Bágdis.

Ba'gdis, with a strength of twelve, are found in Belgaum only. They are wandering beggars who occasionally come into the district from Kolhápur. They have no subdivisions, and families bearing the same surname cannot intermarry. Their home speech is Maráthi. The men wear the top-knot and moustache, and the women tie their hair in a knot behind the head. They are black, lively, and well-featured and look like Kolis. They live in thatched huts, and their staple food is Indian millet, fish, and vegetables. They eat fish and the flesh of sheep, goats, and domestic fowls. They drink country liquor and smoke tobacco. The men wear a loincloth, a shouldercloth, and a headscarf. The women have no bodice, and wear the robe without passing the end back between the feet. They mark their brows with red-powder, and wear the lucky-necklace or *mangalsutra* and glass bangles. They are neither neat nor clean in their dress and get their clothes by begging. They are dirty and lazy, but sober and even-tempered. They are beggars and fishers holding a low social position. They worship the usual local and Bráhman gods, and regard Mhasoba as their family deity. They have no priests, but respect Bráhmans and call them to conduct their birth, marriage, and death ceremonies. They keep the regular Hindu holidays, but do not fast or go on pilgrimages. They believe in ghosts and spirits. On the fifth day after the birth of a child, they perform the *páchvi,* and on the twelfth day name the child and give a feast to the castemen. The marriage ceremony lasts for two days. On the first day the boy and girl are rubbed with turmeric and oil. On the second day a Bráhman repeats verses or *mantras,* holding a cloth between the boy and girl, and throws rice over their heads. The ceremony ends with a feast. They practise polygamy and allow widow marriage. They bury their dead, and give a feast to their castemen on the thirteenth day. They are bound together as a body and their headman or *mehtar* settles their social disputes by fining offenders one or two shillings (8 *as.*-Re. 1). They are a poor people.

Bháts.

Bha'ts are returned as numbering seventy and as found over the whole district. They were probably settled in the country before the introduction of Muhammadan rule. They are divided into Marátha or Bráhman Bháts and Thákur or Joshi Bháts. The Bráhman Bháts always repeat the name *Brahma* before beginning to sing; the Joshi Bháts foretell the future. They neither eat together nor intermarry. They look and speak like Kunbis. They are wandering beggars having no houses and living in temples or inns. They sometimes have horses, cows, dogs, and fowls. Their staple food is rice, Indian millet bread, pulse, and vegetables. They do not give caste dinners, but during marriages they give each guest about a quarter of a pound of uncooked rice or wheat, pulse, and coarse sugar. They eat fish, crabs, mutton, fowls, wild game, pigeons, and partridges. They are great drinkers, being specially fond of palm-juice. They get their clothes by begging. They smoke tobacco and hemp-flowers or *gánja*. The men go begging and singing from six in the morning to one. In the evening they go fishing, staying away till the early morning. They are not a religious people. They worship the ordinary village gods, but their favourite deity is Máruti. In their houses are images of Sidoba and Máyaráni. Their priests are Bráhmans, whose help they seek only at marriages. They do not fast but keep the usual Hindu holidays. Bháts believe in sorcery, witchcraft, soothsaying, and lucky and unlucky days. They consult Bráhmans whenever they are in difficulty. A few days after child-birth they go into the bushlands and offer a goat to the goddess Mukiáyi. Their only customs are at marriages and they are the same as Kunbi customs. They have no caste council and leave social and religious disputes to be settled by their teacher or *guru*. The Bháts do not send their boys to school. They are a steady people.

Dandig Dásaru.

Dandig Da'sarus, with a strength of eight, are found only in Chikodi. They came into the district from Madras. They have no subdivisions and families bearing the same surname do not intermarry. Their home speech is Telugu and they look like Dásarus. They live in small houses with walls of mud and tiled roofs. They do not rear any useful or pet animals. Their houses are neat and clean. Their every-day food is rice, Indian millet bread, and vegetables. They give feasts on marriage occasions, eat fish, and the flesh of sheep, goats, and domestic fowls. They drink liquor and smoke tobacco. They dress like the Dásarus. The only difference between the Dásarus and the Dandig Dásarus is that the former are Shaivs and the latter Vaishnavs.

Dásarus.

Da'sarus, apparently the servants or *dás* of the god Máruti, are wandering beggars, returned as numbering 574. They are found throughout the district, but chiefly in Gokák and Athni. They appear to belong both to the Telugu and the Karnátak stock, but there is nothing to show when and from where they came into the district. Their head-quarters are at Bijápur where they live during the rains. They are divided into Telangi Dásarus, Karnátak Dásarus, Valu Dásarus, and Holár or Mhár Dásarus. None of these classes either eat together or intermarry. The men are of middle size and dark, with a quick lively look; and the women are strong and muscular. The Telang Dásarus speak Telugu and the Karnátak and other Dásarus speak Kánarese. The Dásarus are quiet, hospitable, and sober, but idle and thriftless. They are wandering beggars, singers, and musicians, the Karnátak Dásarus in addition performing plays and allowing their wives to act as courtezans. Before starting to beg they pray to Máruti and Vishnu

Chapter III.

Population.

BEGGARS.

Dásarus.

for a bagful of grain. The Telang Dásarus, who are also called Vakalgerus, carry a lamp at the end of a long pole and rest a gong and a conch-shell on their right shoulder. They beg on Saturdays only. Among the Hindus of the district when one of a family is sick, it is common to vow that if he recover a number of Dásarus will be feasted. This is done because they are believed to be favourites of Máruti, one of the chief local gods. Excepting a few in Belgaum and other towns, who live in small houses, Dásarus have no dwellings. They eat Indian millet bread, rice, vegetables, fish, and flesh, and drink liquor. The men dress like Kunbis and the women like dancing-girls braiding the hair and tying it in a knot behind the head as if resting on the neck. They are clean and neat in their dress, wear rich robes with broad silk borders, sometimes with gold ends, drawing one end over the head and bringing the lower end back between the feet. They wear a tight bodice of fine cotton or silk cloth and mark their eyebrows with red-powder or *kunku*. They wear a profusion of gold and silver ornaments and like dancing-girls are fond of show and pleasure. Karnátak and Valu Dásarus invest their sons with the sacred thread between the age of nine and twelve. All allow widow marriage. When a Telang Dásaru dies a conch-shell and discus are tied to his arm, and again untied when he is buried. They are kept in some safe place and brought out for worship on the fifth day by the chief mourner. If they are lost the person responsible for them is put out of caste. The Dásarus worship Vishnu, Bálájí, and Máruti. The Telang and Karnátak Dásarus employ Deshasth Bráhmans to perform their thread-girding, marriage, and other ceremonies. The Valu Dásarus perform them themselves and act as priests to the Holárs. Except the Karnátak Dásarus who have a headman, they settle social disputes in accordance with the opinion of the majority of the castemen. The Telang and Valu Dásarus send their boys to school for a short time. Those Dásarus who know how to sing and dance and whose women act as courtezans are in easy circumstances. The rest are poor, living from hand to mouth.

Davris.

Davris, or DRUMMERS, are returned as numbering 105 and as found throughout the district, especially in large towns. They have no subdivisions. They look like Maráthás and those at Belgaum, Chándgad, and Khánápur speak Maráthi; the Davris of other parts of the district speak Kánarese. They generally live in thatched huts. The men wear a small close-fitting turban, breeches or a waistcloth, and a few of them a coat. Women wear a robe and bodice. Their staple food is millet, pulse, and sometimes rice. They eat fish and flesh, and drink liquor. They are idle and dirty and beg by beating the drum called *daur*. The women retail wooden combs, needles, and beads. They generally buy from the carpenters on credit and pay them when the combs are sold. On the fifth day after a birth the goddess Satvái is worshipped, and on the thirteenth the child is laid in a cradle and named, friends and relations being presented with cooked gram and millet. When the child is twelve years old the lobes of its ears are bored, and the teacher or *guru* with his own hands puts into the holes a pair of light silver rings worth about 3*d.* (2 *as.*). Before a marriage the bodies of the boy and girl are rubbed with turmeric, the god Kedárling and the goddess Amba Bhaváni are worshipped, and verses are repeated and rice is thrown over the heads of the couple by the Bráhman priest who is generally a Deshasth. They bury their dead. On the third day after a death the mourner lays cooked rice mixed with milk on the grave, and when it has been touched by a crow, returns home. If no crow comes he makes an earthen crow and touches the rice with its beak. On the twelfth day the funeral ceremonies end with a dinner to caste-fellows. Though not a religious people the Davris keep a small metal image of Kedárling in their house and worship it every Sunday morning. They sacrifice no animal to Kedárling, but sometimes vow to make a pilgrimage to Kolhápur or to feast his begging devotees. Their emblems are small metal bells and a basket-shaped pot. Vows are made in order to get children or to be cured from sickness. The Davris do not act as sorcerers. They are bound together as a body and their social disputes are settled by mass meetings of the caste. They do not send their boys to school, and still suffer from the decline in alms-giving which followed the famine distress.

Gondhlis.

Gondhlis are returned as numbering 370 and as found only in a few villages and towns throughout the district. They seem to have entered the district from the Bombay Deccan. They have no subdivisions. They look like Maráthás, being dark and strong, with high noses and thin lips. Their home tongue is Maráthi. Most of them live in houses with thatched roofs. They eat fish and flesh, and drink liquor. They dress like Maráthás, but the men beg and dance the *gondhal* in peculiar long coats which reach to the feet. They wear shell-necklaces and caps stuck over with shells. The *gondhal* dance is performed among Marátha Bráhmans in honour of the goddess Bhaváni on the occasion of a thread-ceremony, a marriage, or in the seventh month of a woman's first pregnancy. Among other Hindus the dance is performed only at the time of marriage, either before or after the ceremony. The dance always takes place at night. In the evening, in the women's hall, the dancers spread on a high wooden stool a piece of new black bodice-cloth, about two feet three inches long and a foot and a half broad. On this cloth thirty-six pinches of rice grains are laid and sprinkled with turmeric and red-powder. On the rice is set a copper water-pot or *támbya* filled with mixed milk and water, and the mouth is covered with betel leaves and a cocoanut. On the high wooden stool in front of the pot are laid five betelnuts and an equal number of plantains, dates, and lemons, and, with the help of the chief Gondhli, the male head of the family worships the pot as the goddess Tulja Bhaváni. The five dancers then light five torches, and set them in the hands of five men of the family, and the torch-bearers march five times round the goddess repeating the word Amba Bhaváni. The head Gondhli now approaches and takes his stand in front of the high wooden stool, three of his company stand behind him with musical instruments, and the fifth generally stands to the right of the headman with the lighted torch in his hand. On both sides of the head dancer men and women look on, seated on

Chapter III.
Population.
BEGGARS.
Gondhlis.

carpets and mats. Then the head Gondhli begins to dance, to sing in praise of the goddess, at times stopping to explain the meaning of the songs. This lasts the whole night and is not over till day-break. At the end of the dance a lighted lamp is waved round the goddess. The dancers are paid about 2*s.* (Re. 1) and retire. The only ceremonies which the Gondhlis are said to perform are the putting on of the shell-necklace and marriage. The shell-necklace is put round the novice's neck at a meeting of the castemen, who after the ceremony is over retire with a handful of sugar and packets of betelnut and leaves. Their marriage ceremony lasts for three days. On the first day they feast the caste in honour of the family gods. On the second day the boy and girl are seated face to face on two low wooden stools. Marriage verses are repeated by Bráhman priests, and grains of rice are thrown over their heads. The guests are offered packets of betelnut and leaves and retire. The marriage ceremony ends with a feast on the third day. They generally marry their children before they come of age. They practise polygamy, but polyandry is unknown and widow marriage is forbidden. Besides begging, a few work as husbandmen. Their priests are Deshasth Bráhmans. Their family goddesses are Amba Bhaváni and Tulja Bhaváni in honour of whom they fast on Tuesdays and Fridays. They are bound together as a body and settle social disputes according to the opinion of the majority of the castemen. A few send their boys to school. They are a poor people, hardly earning enough to live on.

Gosávis.

Gosa'vis are returned as numbering 904 and as found all over the district except in Parasgad and Gokák. They are divided into Náth Gosávis, Davri Gosávis, and Bálsantoshis. The Náth Gosávis are considered higher than the others and neither eat nor marry with them. The Davris and Bálsantoshis eat together and intermarry. They have no family stocks or *gotras.* They speak Maráthi in their homes, and, except that they wear rings in their ears, they look like Kunbis. The commonest names among men are Ambarnáth, Appánáth, Kirnáth, and Rámnáth; and among women, Báli, Santi, and Tuki. They are middle-sized, strong, muscular, and long-lived. They are dark with clever faces, small eyes, regular features, high nose, thin lips, and high cheek bones. They live in houses with mud walls and tiled roofs, generally untidy and with very little furniture. Most families have a couple of bullocks or cows as well as sheep, goats, and fowls. Their every-day food is Indian millet, rice, pulse, and vegetables. But when they can afford it they eat fish, crabs, and the flesh of goats, sheep, hare, wild hog, game birds, and domestic fowls. On holidays and whenever else they can afford it, they drink both country and European liquor, but not to excess. They smoke tobacco and hemp-flowers or *gánja* and do not eat opium. Before beginning to eat they offer food to their family god Jotiba, who is also called Bahiri and Kedárling. Caste feasts are given in honour of marriages and deaths. When they start begging the men wear ochre-coloured clothes, a wallet hanging from the left arm, and a pale-coloured gourd in the right hand. With this exception neither men nor women differ in dress from Kunbis.

They are thrifty, even-tempered, hardworking, and orderly. They live chiefly by begging. The Náths, besides begging, cultivate, and a few lend money. All the Bálsantoshis live by begging, while among the Davris there are husbandmen and traders as well as beggars. The traders sell thread and needles, glass beads, combs, stoneware, metalware, looking-glasses, buttons, and boxes. The women help in the fields, beg, and sell small wares on market days, squatting by the road and spreading their goods before them on pieces of blanket. They also work as day-labourers. Children of twelve years and upwards help their parents. The Davris buy their wares from Márwár Váni shopkeepers in large towns and cities, and hawk them from village to village. Their work is constant and their calling hereditary. Very few are well-to-do; some are fairly off and some are in debt. Many borrow to meet marriage and other special expenses for which they have to pay about six per cent a month. They are a religious people. Their family god is Jotiba who is called Kedárling or Bhairavnáth. His chief temple is in Battisral near Pandharpur. They worship the god Jotiba daily with flowers, rice, and sandal-powder. They offer him sugar every day and mutton on *Dasara* Day in October. His image is a brass, silver, or gold mask with four arms. They respect Bráhmans and call them to all their ceremonies except to the ear-boring, to which they call their teacher or *guru*. They worship the ordinary Bráhman gods but have the greatest respect for Shiv. They keep the regular Hindu holidays. They do not make pilgrimages. They have a spiritual teacher or *guru* who belongs to the Dorivike sect of Gosávis. He bores the ears of their male children and they pay him 2*s.* 6*d.* (Rs. 1¼). He is succeeded by one of his disciples and makes no attempt to gain new followers. They believe in sorcery, witchcraft, and soothsaying. The soothsayers are Bráhmans, Joshis, and Pinglis. Their chief ceremonies are the worship of the goddess Satti on the fifth day after a child-birth, when rice and fish are presented and a feast is given to the caste people. On the twelfth day the child is named. When the boy is twelve years old his ear is slit and he puts on the begging garb and is eligible for marriage. The ceremony is performed by their teacher. He plants a trident in the ground and after worshipping it and offering it a cocoanut, plantains, sugar, betel leaves and nuts, and dates, pierces with a needle the lobes of the young disciple's ear and puts silver or gold rings into the holes. A wallet with a pot in it is tied to his left arm and the teacher enjoins him henceforth to live solely by begging. He starts on his new calling, gathering plantains and dates from the guests. The ceremony ends with a dinner to castemen. On betrothal, the father of the boy invites the girl's father and their friends to a dinner. Sugar and betelnuts are handed, and the girl's father is presented with £3 (Rs. 30) which is called *dej*. On a lucky day the female relations carry turmeric to the girl's house and rub her with it. Then the women of the girl's family bring turmeric and rub it on the boy's body, who with a party of his relations goes to the girl's house where the marriage is solemnised, and a feast is held. When a girl reaches womanhood the *phalshobhan* or lap-filling ceremony takes place.

Chapter III.
Population.
BEGGARS.
Gosávis.

When a person dies his body is washed with warm water, covered with a new white cloth, and carried to be buried. On the third day after death the bearers are feasted, and on the eleventh the mourning ceases and the mourners are purified by drinking the five products of the cow. On the twelfth day a goat or two are sacrificed, and the day ends with a feast. On the morning of the thirteenth day the ceremonies end by presenting a pipe of tobacco to friends, relations, and castefellows. There has not been any recent change in their customs. Child marriage, widow marriage, and polygamy are allowed. Social disputes are settled by the votes of the majority of the men of the caste, though of late the power of the majority is said to have declined. They do not send their boys to school neither do they take to new pursuits. They are a poor class.

Joshis.

Joshis are returned as numbering thirty and as found chiefly in Khánápur and Belgaum. They are divided into Maráthás and Kidbides. They eat together and intermarry. In appearance they resemble well-to-do Kunbis, being neither very fair nor very dark. They are not strongly made but have regular features. Their home tongue is Maráthi. Their dress consists of a long coat, a waistcloth, and a turban. They eat flesh of all kinds except beef, but are not allowed to drink liquor. They are persistent beggars but refuse all regular work. They object to be classed as beggars and say that as astrologers they have a claim on the public alms. They are neat, sober, and even-tempered, and hospitable to their castefellows whom they never send away empty-handed. They wander in gangs of ten to twenty with their wives and children and return to their head-quarters after tours varying from six to nine months. They call themselves Joshis or astrologers because they foretell events. They beg from door to door in the mornings from six or seven to twelve. Each has a small drum called *bud-budki* which he beats in front of a house and offers to tell what has happened to the family and what is in store for it. In answer to questions he tells how the head of the house had once a narrow escape, and that another misfortune hangs over his head and will fall on him unless he walks a certain number of times round the god Máruti, or keeps a lamp in the temple lighted for a certain number of days, or pours oil over the god. In return for this advice the people of the house give him money or clothes. Joshis generally carry a set of small square pictures of a *tulsi* pot, Mahádev and Párvati, Máruti and Rámchandra, as good omens; and of an eclipse, a tiger, or a snake, as bad omens. Their priests are Bháts. They do not employ Bráhmans at any of their ceremonies. Their family gods are Kedáreshvar and Sidoba; and their chief holidays are *Shivarátra* in February, *Nágpanchami* in August, *Dasara* in October, and *Diváli* in November. They seldom go on pilgrimage. They believe in divination and soothsaying. They are said not to practise witchcraft and to have no faith in the evil eye. They believe Tuesday and Friday are lucky days and the rest unlucky. Marriage is their only ceremony. The members of the caste meet and the Bháts throw rice on the boy's and girl's heads and the ceremony ends with a dinner. They allow widow marriage.

BEGGARS. *Joshis.*

Their funeral ceremonies are performed by themselves without the help of priests. They bury the dead except lepers whom they burn. They have a headman who is chosen by the votes of the castemen from the leading elders of the community. He settles their social disputes with the help of the castemen. He also directs their begging excursions, and, in case any of them neglects his orders, he fines them 4*s.* to 6*s.* (Rs. 2-3). A few send their boys to school but only for a short time to learn to read Maráthi. They are a falling people.

Kánphátes.

Ka'npha'tes or SLIT-EARED JOGIS are returned as numbering seventy and as found in Chikodi. They have no subdivisions, speak Maráthi, and look like Kunbis. Some of them marry and others remain single. They live in temples or inns and rear buffaloes and dogs. They eat fish and the flesh of sheep, goats, and domestic fowls. They drink liquor and smoke tobacco and hemp-flower, and eat opium. Their staple food is rice, Indian millet bread, and vegetables. They wear a brick-coloured dress including a loin-cloth, a cap, a blanket, and a waistcloth. From their left arm hangs a wallet, and when they go begging they carry a trident or *trishul* in the right hand and a pale-coloured gourd in the left. The ornaments worn by men are a silver chain called *gop,* silver armlets called *kadis,* and the wooden or ivory earrings, which are the distinguishing mark of the sect. The women wear a short-sleeved bodice and a robe or *lugade,* whose skirt-corner they do not pass back between the feet. Ornaments include a gold nosering, a necklace of glass and metal beads with a small central gold brooch or *galsari,* and three sorts of earrings called *bugdis, bális,* and *kúps.* A woman whose husband is alive marks her brow with red-powder or *kunku* and wears glass bangles and the lucky necklace or *mangalsutra.* They are neat, clean, and well-behaved, but lazy. Both men and women beg from door to door. Some of them are husbandmen, either over-holders or under-holders, but none of them are skilful cultivators. Their women help them in sowing and weeding. Their house god is Gorakhnáth, and they respect Bráhmans and call them to their marriage and death ceremonies. They worship the ordinary Bráhmanic gods and keep the regular Hindu holidays. They make pilgrimages to Benares, Prayág or Allahabad, Rámeshvar, and Gokarn in Kánara. They believe in witchcraft and in lucky and unlucky days. Their customs do not differ from those of Gosávis. They are bound together as a body and settle their social disputes at meetings of the castemen. They are a steady class.

Killiketars.

Killiketars or KATABUS are a class of cattle-keepers and picture-showmen. They are returned as numbering 108 and as found in Sampgaon, Chikodi, Parasgad, Gokák, and Athni. They are much like Maráthás and seem to have come from the north, either from Kolhápur or Sátára. They have no subdivisions. The men wear a top-knot about three inches long, whiskers, and moustache. The women comb their hair once a fortnight and tie it in a knot on the back of the head. They do not deck it with flowers nor do they use false hair. Their home tongue is Maráthi. They generally live outside

Chapter III.
Population.
BEGGARS.
Killiketars.

of the village in huts. Every family owns a dog, two to four buffaloes, two or three cows, and four or five goats. Their daily food is Indian millet. They eat fish and the flesh of sheep, goats, hares, and domestic fowls. The women do not drink, and the men are temperate in their use of liquor, drinking only on special occasions, at marriages, on holidays, and when they entertain guests. The men smoke tobacco. They dress like Maráthás. They are clean, neat, honest, thrifty, and quiet. Their chief occupation is showing pictures of the Pándavs and Kauravs, and other heroes. The pictures are drawn on deer skins and cost 3*d.* to 6*d.* (2 - 4 *as.*). They always show them at night. One of the men sits behind a curtain with a lighted torch and shows from one to two hundred pictures. Another man sits outside and explains. The women beat a drum. The show lasts five to seven hours beginning about nine or ten at night. The villagers club together and pay them about 4*s.* (Rs. 2), half in cash and half in grain and oil. At harvest time they go from village to village collecting grain which the husbandmen give them in charity. Their women are expert tattooers and are paid in grain and old clothes. They tattoo women of all castes. The figures are traced with ink before they are pricked into the skin. The figures which they generally tattoo are a line with a crescent above it and a small circle below, called *chandram* or moon, and generally tattooed on the brows of Bráhman women; The head ornament or *muttin botta*, a line with an ornament of eight pearls a central pearl and seven round it above the line and a small circle below the line, tattooed on the forehead of women of all castes except Bráhmans; A pair of plain or ornamental brackets called in Kánarese *kannu suge* or outer eye-corners, and worn by all women except Bráhmans at the outer corners of the eyes; A slender oval mark called the wheat grain or *godlkál* worn by Rajput women on the left side of the nose; A circle about the size of a pea called *nasal* worn by Dombári women between the eyes and by women of other castes on the cheek or chin; *Sitecha padar* or Sita's fringe, a line like four teeth of a saw, worn on the arm. Besides these emblems figures of the *tulsi* plant or sacred basil, and of the incense tree *sura-honne* or Boswellia thurifera are worn on the forearm. Lotuses, snakes, and scorpions are tattooed on the back of the hand and small spots are worn even on the backs of the fingers. Shri Rám, Shri Rám Jay Rám, Jay Jay Ram, and other names of household or favourite gods are tattooed on the forearms of Bráhman women.

They are a religious people, and daily worship their box of pictures. Their family deities are Yellamma, Máyava, and Bhaire. They have no priests, but they keep all the chief Hindu holidays. They keep no fasts, make no pilgrimages, and do not believe in witchcraft or soothsaying. They worship the goddess Satvái on the fifth day after the birth of a child and name the child on the eleventh. They marry their girls at the age of four or five and their boys between ten and twelve. The boy's father has to go in search of a wife for his son. When a suitable match is found the marriage is settled, and the boy, his parents, friends, and relatives go

Chapter III. Population. BEGGARS. *Killiketars.*

to the girl's village. When they have reached the village boundary a cocoanut is broken, and about five in the evening the boy and his party are taken into the village and feasted. Next morning the boy and girl are rubbed with turmeric and oil and they are made to stand face to face, the girl looking east and the boy west. A curtain is held between them for a few moments and then dropped. The boy ties a string of black and green beads round the girl's neck. The girl ties a piece of turmeric root with a cotton thread round the boy's right wrist and the boy in return ties another wristlet of turmeric root round her wrist. A few grains of red rice are handed to the guests who throw them on the heads of both the boy and girl shouting *Shám Dhám*, a corruption of the Bráhman *sávadhán* or Take care. On the second or third day, the boy and his party walk with the girl to the boy's village, and the marriage is over. When a girl comes of age she is considered impure and is not allowed to touch any one. This rule is observed only on the occasion of the first monthly sickness. They allow widow marriage and polygamy. They bury their dead. They do not send their boys to school. Though a poor class they are almost never in debt.

Oshtams.

Oshtams, with a strength of ninety, are scattered over the district except in Belgaum and Athni. They have come into the district from Madras. Their home speech is Telugu. They have no subdivisions. They look like Kunbis, speak Maráthi out of doors, and live in small but neat and clean houses with mud walls and tiled roofs. Their every-day food is Indian millet and vegetables. They eat fish, and the flesh of sheep, goats, and poultry. They drink both country and foreign liquor and smoke tobacco. They get their clothes by begging. They respect Bráhmans and call them to their birth, marriage, and death ceremonies. They worship the ordinary Bráhman gods and hold Máruti in special respect. In their houses are images of Máruti and Venkoba. They keep the usual Hindu holidays. They have no teacher or *guru*. They believe in sorcery and witchcraft. Their customs do not differ from those of Mudliars. They allow widow marriage and bury their dead. They are bound together as a body and settle social disputes according to the opinion of the majority of the men. They do not send their boys to school and as a class are badly off.

Pichátis.

Picha'tis, with a strength of 105, are found in Chikodi and Athni. They have no subdivisions and families bearing the same surname cannot intermarry. They look like Kunbis and speak Maráthi. They live in thatched huts and keep no animals. Their staple food is Indian millet or *náchni* bread and vegetables. They eat fish and the flesh of sheep, goats, and domestic fowls, whenever they can afford it. They drink country liquor and smoke tobacco. The men wear the waistcloth, shouldercloth, and turban; and the women a robe whose lower end they do not pass back between the feet. They get their clothes by begging. Both men and women beg, and in addition the women sew quilts. They worship the ordinary local and Bráhmanic gods, and their chief house goddesses are Ambabái and Satvái. Their priests are the ordinary Marátha Bráhmans, whom they respect and call to their births, marriages,

Chapter III.
Population.
BEGGARS.

and deaths. They observe the regular Hindu holidays. They believe in lucky and unlucky days, numbers, sights, and events. On the fifth day after the birth of a child, they worship the goddess Páchvi and name the child on the twelfth. The marriage lasts one day, when the boy and girl are rubbed at their houses with oil and turmeric and the marriage ceremony is performed in the presence of caste people. If they are able, the parents give a feast. They bury the dead. Widow marriage is allowed. They settle social disputes according to the opinion of the majority of the castemen. They are very poor.

Pingles.

Pingles, who foretell events by the help of the *pingla* or little spotted owl, are returned as numbering forty and as found in Belgaum, Khánápur, and Parasgad. They say they came into the district from Kolhápur about sixty years ago. They rank below Maráthás. They have no subdivisions, and their surnames are Garud, Máne, and Shingán. Families bearing the same surname cannot intermarry. Their home speech is Maráthi and they look like Kunbis. They live in thatched huts, and their staple food is Indian millet, rice, and vegetables; but they do not object to eat fish or the flesh of goats, sheep, or fowls, or to drink liquor. All smoke tobacco and some smoke hemp-flowers or *gánja*. The men wear a waistcloth, a head-cloth, a long coat, and a waistcoat, and a silk-bordered shoulder-cloth. The women wear a shortsleeved bodice and a robe or *lugade* whose lower end is not passed back between the feet. They get their clothes by begging. They are wandering fortune-tellers, and go begging from door to door. Their women do nothing but house-work. They worship the ordinary Bráhmanic gods and their family goddess is Margái to whom they sacrifice a goat once a year or whenever they can afford it. They respect Bráhmans and call them to conduct their marriage and death ceremonies. They keep the regular Hindu holidays. They do not fast and have no religious teacher or *guru*. They believe in spirits, ghosts, soothsaying, lucky and unlucky numbers, sights, and events. Their customs are generally the same as those of Kunbis. They burn the dead, and allow widow marriage and polygamy. They are bound together as a body and settle their social disputes according to the opinion of the majority of the castemen. They send their boys to school for a short time, and take to no new pursuits. They are a poor class.

Vásudevs.

Va'sudevs are found in small numbers over the whole district. They seem to have come from the Deccan. They have no sub-divisions. Their surnames are Dhurve, Gavli, Reke, and Sálunke. They are of middle height and dark, with high nose and thin lips. The men wear the top-knot, moustache, and whiskers, but no beard. Their home tongue is Maráthi. They are sober, thrifty, even-tempered, and idle. They are professional beggars and go from one village to another all the year round carrying two metal cups or *tâls*, two wooden pincers or *chiplyás*, brass bells, jingling rings, and a wooden whistle. Except a few who have settled as husbandmen, they wander from place to place, halting in temples and rest-houses and carrying with them no tents, mats, or other shelter. Their staple food is Indian millet bread, rice,

Chapter III. Population. BEGGARS. *Vásudevs.*

and vegetables, but they eat fish and the flesh of goats, sheep and fowls, and drink liquor. They dress like Maráthás, but when they go begging they wear a long hat adorned with peacock's feathers and a brass top, and a long full-skirted coat. Their women wear the bodice and robe passing the end between the feet and rub their brows with red-powder or *kunku*. On the fifth day after the birth of a child they worship the goddess Satvái and feast married women after presenting them with turmeric and red-powder or *halad-kunku.* They begin their marriage ceremonies by invoking the aid of the goddess Bhaváni and end them with a *gondhal* dance. They allow widow marriage and burn their dead. They are Vaishnavs, worshipping Vishnu, Vithoba, and Mahákáli; their house gods are Bhairoba, Jotiba, Khandoba, and the goddess Bhaváni. They employ Deshasth Bráhmans at their marriages and when a youth is invested with his begging robes. On the initiation day the Bráhman priest dresses the boy in the long hat and coat repeating verses and marking his brow with sandal. By this he becomes a Vásudev fit to wear the hat and to beg. The Bráhman is given five copper coins ($1\frac{1}{4}$ *annas*) and a packet of betelnut and leaves. A feast to the castefellows ends the day. They have no headman. They refer disputes to an intelligent member of the caste who decides in the presence of the castemen. They do not send their boys to school and are a poor people.

DEPRESSED CLASSES.

Depressed Classes include seven castes with a strength of 68,000 or 8·59 per cent of the Hindu population. The details are:

BELGAUM DEPRESSED CLASSES.

Class.	Males.	Females	Total.	Class.	Males.	Females	Total.
Bhangis ...	64	45	109	Láds ...	507	517	1024
Chalvádis ...	49	58	107	Mángs ..	8059	8790	16,849
Chámbhárs ...	3291	3163	6454				
Dhors ...	879	838	1717				
Hollars ...	20,132	21,608	41,740	Total ...	32,981	35,019	68,000

Bhangis.

Bhangis, or **Halálkhors,** with a strength of 109, are found in all municipal towns. Some of them appear to belong to Gujarát, others to Upper India especially the neighbourhood of Delhi and Cawnpur. Thirty or thirty-five years ago a few came into the district from the native states of Sángli and Miraj. The rest have come within the last five years since more regular conservancy measures have been taken in the larger towns. They have no divisions. The men are tall and either swarthy or fair; the women are generally plump and well-featured. Their home tongue is Hindustáni. They live in huts with thatched or tiled roofs. They are greedy eaters; they eat fish and the flesh of goats and sheep and domestic fowls, and drink liquor. Their staple food is millet, rice, and pulse. A man wears a waistcloth or trousers, a coat, a head-scarf or *rumál,* and either English or Maráthi shoes or sandals; the women wear a robe and bodice and sometimes a petticoat. The robe is wound round the waist, the skirt-corner being passed between the feet and tucked behind. They coil their hair behind the head and sometimes deck it with flowers. When at work their clothes are filthy and ragged, but several among them have a stock of rich

Chapter III. Population. DEPRESSED CLASSES. *Bhangis.*

clothes. They are hardworking, but quarrelsome, dirty, and thriftless. They are town-sweepers and removers of nightsoil. Their women and children from the age of thirteen or fourteen help in their calling. On the fifth day after a birth they worship Páchvi or the Fifth, and on the twelfth name the child distributing cooked grain and millet to female relations and friends. On the marriage day the boy and girl are rubbed with turmeric, the goddess Amba Bhaváni is worshipped, and the *gondhal* ceremony performed. They bury their dead. On the third day after a death the chief mourner lays a ball of rice mixed with curds on the grave and does not leave until it has been touched by a crow. If the crows will not touch the rice and the mourner is rich he presents a cow to his priest, if he is poor he presents his priests 1*s.* to 4*s.* (8 *as.* - Rs. 2). On the tenth day they feast relations and friends including the four bier-bearers. They allow widow marriage. They worship Yellamma and Brahmadev. They do not worship the minor village deities or their ancestors. The Bráhmans who cast horoscopes and fix lucky names and dates for the Bhangis are not outcaste or of any special order. Any Bráhman may act as a Bhangis' priest. They do not observe Hindu fasts, but keep all the usual festivals. Bhangis are bound together as a body. They settle social disputes at mass meetings of the adult male members of the caste. They do not send their boys to school and are poor.

Chalvádis.

Chalva'dis, with a strength of 107, are found in all towns with a considerable Lingáyat population. The Chalvádis have no subdivisions and no surnames. The names of men and women are the same as those of other Lingáyats. They are dark and like Mhárs, only that they are less strongly made. Their home speech is Kánarese which does not differ from the local Kánarese. Their staple food is millet which is eaten either with *tur* or *masur* pulse. They do not eat fish or flesh, drink no liquor, and use no drug except tobacco. Like other Lingáyats the men wear the waistcloth, a white turban, and sometimes a jacket; and the women a robe and a bodice. The women sometimes wear silver wristlets or *talbandis,* silver or pewter toerings or *jodvis,* and silver bracelets and glass bangles. Both men and women wear a silver box or *chanka* which contains the *ling,* and rub their foreheads with ashes. The Chalvádis' chief office is to carry the ladle and bell in front of Lingáyat processions. They live by begging, and on money distributed by Lingáyats on festive or funeral occasions. A Chalvádi generally has in his house images of Mahádev in the form of a *ling* and of Basaveshvar in the form of a stone or silver bull or *nandi.* They bathe and worship the *ling* before their morning meal. They also venerate such village deities as Yellamma, Kariamma, and Mariamma. Their priests are Jangams whom they worship, drinking the water in which the priest's feet have been washed. Their customs are like those of the Lingáyats. They neither eat nor associate with Mhárs. Social disputes are settled at meetings of the leading Lingáyats. Any one who fails to obey the public decision loses his office. They do not send their boys to school, but any one holding the office of Chalvádi is required to read the sacred books and must

Chapter III.

Population.

DEPRESSED CLASSES.

Chámbhárs.

therefore know how to read and write Kánarese. Beyond this their children have no schooling. They are a poor class.

Cha'mbha'rs, or LEATHER WORKERS, with a strength of 6454, are found throughout the district. They are divided into Lingáyat, Maráthi, and Konkani Chámbhárs. Maráthi and Konkani Chámbhárs eat together and take food from the Lingáyats, but the Lingáyats do not eat with them. As regards marriage all three subdivisions are separate. They have no surnames or family names. They are fair, regular-featured, and strong. The men generally shave the head except the top-knot. Some of the children have beautiful faces, refined and intelligent. They speak both Kánarese and Maráthi. They are hardworking, even-tempered, and hospitable, but thriftless, dirty, and given to drink. They work in leather, cut and dye skins, and make bridles, whips, and harness, sandals, shoes, ropes, and water-bags. They sell their wares either at their houses or in the local markets, and earn about 6*d.* (4 *as.*) a day. The women help by fringing the shoes with silk. Their boys begin to work at twelve to fourteen and generally earn about 3*d.* (2 *as.*) a day. They buy their leather from Dhors and their silk from weavers. Except a few of the poorest they have capital enough to buy their materials without borrowing. As tent-pitchers, a work which gives them a good deal of employment in Belgaum, they earn 9*d.* (6 *as.*) a day. They both keep ready-made leather articles in stock and work to order. They are said not to mend Jingars' shoes as they hold themselves equal to if not higher than them. The Lingáyats stop work in the afternoon, as they are not allowed to touch leather in the evening. Some are cotton-weavers not leather-workers. Their houses are poor with tiled or thatched roofs and wattle and daub walls. They are generally untidy, the ground in front being littered with pieces of skins. They eat Indian millet bread and *náchni* gruel except the Lingáyats who neither eat animal food nor drink liquor. They eat fish and flesh but not carrion or pork, and drink liquor. The men wear a loincloth and occasionally a waistcloth and a turban or headscarf. They seldom wear coats or waistcoats but cover their bodies with a waistcloth. The women dress in the usual Kunbi bodice and robe reaching to the knee. The men work from early morning till noon, when they dine and take a nap and again work till five after which they go about the streets hawking shoes. The women mind the house and help the men in making shoes. They name their children on the thirteenth day after birth, and cut the child's hair for the first time in the third year. Some of them worship the holy basil and wear the sacred thread. They bury the dead. The Maráthi or Konkan Chámbhárs on the third day after a funeral make a ball of cooked rice mixed with curds and lay it on the grave and do not leave till it has been touched by a crow. Relations as well as the corpse-bearers mourn ten days. They worship the ordinary Hindu gods and keep the usual fasts and feasts. Some Lingáyats worship the sweet basil before they take their meals. They have a community and settle disputes at meetings of the men of the caste. They do not send their boys to school. They earn enough to maintain themselves, and if they were less unthrifty and drunken, they would be well-to-do.

Chapter III.
Population.
Depressed Classes.
Dhors.

Dhors, or Tanners, with a strength of 1717, are found in small groups of one or two families in all the larger villages in the district. They are divided into Marátha, Hindustáni, and Karnátak Dhors who neither eat together nor intermarry. All are dark and strong. The Marátha Dhors speak Maráthi, the Hindustáni Dhors Hindustáni, and the Karnátak Dhors Kánarese. Except a few belonging to the rich, their houses are small, dirty, and untidy. They dress in a loin and waistcloth and a turban often in rags; and their women like Chámbhár women wear a robe falling like a petticoat with the upper end passed over their shoulder, and a bodice. They tie their hair in a knot behind and neither deck it with flowers nor mix it with false hair. Their dress is of country cloth fairly clean, and most of them have a spare holiday suit. The women wear glass or if they are well-to-do silver bangles. Their staple food is Indian millet, split pulse or pulse-curry, and chilly powder mixed with salt. Only occasionally can they afford rice. They eat fish and flesh of all kinds except beef, and drink liquor but not to excess. They sacrifice goats on *Dasara* Day in October. Their pet dish is goat's flesh or *ghos*. Animals who die a natural death are not considered fit for food though they are occasionally eaten in secret. Besides tanning they make water-bags, buckets, drums or *dhols,* bridles or *lagáms,* horse's mouth-bags or *tobres,* boxes or *petárás,* and other articles. Some work as day-labourers. Women never help the men in their work, but boys begin to be of use after twelve. They employ Bráhmans at their marriages, reciting verses and throwing grains of rice over the heads of the boy and the girl. They bury their dead. A Lingáyat priest or *ayya* attends and the body is carried to the grave. A pit is dug and the body is sprinkled with ashes by the priest and laid in the pit and earth is thrown in. The priest offers a Kánarese prayer asking the Almighty to take the dead to heaven, and claps his hands together which is supposed to inform the dead that the gates of heaven are open to him. The mourners strew flowers over the grave, bathe, and return. A funeral costs 2*s.* to 4*s.* (Rs. 1-2). On the ninth or tenth day after a death castemen are feasted at a cost of 8*s.* to 10*s.* (Rs. 4 - 5). When the funeral service is properly performed the Dhors think that the dead is highly pleased and acts as their guardian and intercessor. They worship Mahádev, Khandoba, and Tulja Bhaváni, and consult oracles. They are religious, and hold their priests in great esteem. They have no headman and settle disputes by the arbitration of some of the older members of the community. They do not send their boys to school. Except a few who are well-to-do the Dhors live from hand to mouth. The demand for leather articles is of late said to have been very slack, and the Dhors to have suffered in consequence.

Holids.

Holia's, or **Mha'rs,** with a strength of 41,740, are found throughout the district. They are divided into Karnátaks, Telangs, and Maráthás. The first two eat together and intermarry but not with the third. They are generally tall, strong, and dark. They hold a low position among Hindus, their touch being thought to defile. The men shave the head except a long tuft on the crown and wear

Chapter III.
Population.
Depressed Classes.
Holiás.

whiskers and moustache. The Karnátaks speak Kánarese, the Maráthás Maráthi, and the Telangs Telugu. They are dirty in their habits, fairly temperate and thrifty, but revengeful. They are notable for their want of reverence for Bráhmans and Bráhmanic gods, for the looseness of their morals, and for their worship of evil spirits. They are village servants, watchmen, boundary markers, treasure-carriers, escorts, removers of dead animals, drummers, and bugle and horn blowers. In large villages they guard the village door, keep a muster of all persons entering or leaving, and after the door is locked take the keys to the headman. They also guard the stackyard during harvest time, attend to travellers in the name of the village, letting them know where they can buy food, and supplying them with grass and firewood. They also attend Government officials and carry messages. In spite of the lowness of their caste they have considerable power in the village, their decision being generally accepted in boundary disputes. Besides working as village servants they are husbandmen, labourers, and weavers of coarse cloth. They take service in the Bombay army and are employed as constables. Their houses are small, either tiled or thatched, and with wattle and daub walls. Their staple food is Indian millet bread eaten with a preparation of chillies and salt. On holidays, marriages, and other ceremonies they eat rice, fish, and flesh. They also eat the flesh of dead cattle and drink liquor of which they are excessively fond. The men wear a loincloth, a waistcloth or short trousers, a waistcoat, and roll a scarf round the head; the women wear a robe and bodice. The Holiás worship Satvái on the fifth day after the birth of a child and name their children on the same day. They marry their girls before they come of age. A Chalvádi is called to the marriage to sound his ladle and bell, and in return receives rice, a cocoanut, and a few copper coins. They allow widow marriage, the children by the first husband being left to his relatives. They practise polygamy. They bury their dead and mourn ten days. On the third day after death they go with a ball of rice mixed with curds to the burying ground, and burning incense on the spot where the deceased was buried place the ball on it and do not go home until the ball has been touched by a crow. They perform anniversary ceremonies on the fifth of *Bhádrapad* or August-September. Their chief goddesses are Lakshmi, Márvir, and Yellamma. The fair and sacrifice described in the Carpenters' account as a rule is not held unless the Mhárs first sacrifice a buffalo to Lakshmi. Bráhmans do not officiate at their houses, but are consulted as to the lucky moment for marriage and other ceremonies. They fast only once in the year on the full-moon of *Paush* that is December-January. The Holiás make pilgrimages to the shrine of Yellamma at Saundatti in Belgaum where a fair is held on the fifteenth lunar day of *Márgashirsha* or November-December. They have a teacher or *guru* of their own caste who lives in Kolhápur. He supports himself by begging among his own people. His office is hereditary and when he visits a village the Holiás of the place defray his expenses so long as he stays with them. As a parting fee he is paid 2*s.* 6*d.* (Rs. 1¼). The Holiás do not send their boys to school, neither do they take to new pursuits.

Chapter III.
Population.
DEPRESSED CLASSES.
Láds.

La'ds, with a strength of 1024, are found all over the district. They claim to be Kshatriyas of the solar race and wear the sacred thread. They are divided into Brahmakshatri Láds, Sáv Láds, Hálvekari Láds, and Káyit Láds, who do not eat together nor intermarry. Láds are dark and strong, the men wearing the top-knot and moustache and looking like Maráthás. The women are small, fair, and good-looking. Their home tongue is Maráthi. They are a hardworking, sober, thrifty, and hospitable people, but hot-tempered. They follow various callings. They are betel-leaf sellers, grain merchants, makers and sellers of *attar* of roses and pastils, husbandmen, and at Belgaum and Athni mutton-sellers. The goat or sheep is slaughtered by a Musalmán *mulla*, who makes it stand facing the south, repeats some texts from the Korán, and cuts its throat. He is paid ¾*d*. (½ *anna*) for each goat or sheep. They claim mutton-selling as one of their hereditary callings. They own good strong and plain houses. They drink liquor both country and foreign, and eat fish and the flesh of sheep and goats, hares, and fowls. Their staple food is rice, Indian millet bread, pulse, and vegetables. They dress like Maráthás, but their customs differ in some respects. They gird their boys with the sacred thread before they are ten years old without performing any ceremony. They have no rule that a girl should be married before she is of age. The boy's father has to pay the girl's father not more than £5 (Rs 50). Brahmakshatri and Sáv Láds do not allow widow marriage; the others do. Polygamy is allowed, and such of them as cannot afford to burn their dead, bury them. They mourn ten days and on the third day place cooked rice and milk on some open spot, and after it is touched by a crow they return home satisfied that the soul of the deceased is at peace. On the eleventh day after a death they worship a silver plate with an embossed mask of the deceased and feast relations and friends including the four corpse-bearers. Their chief god is the sun, but they worship Venkoba, Khandoba, and the goddess Tulja Bhaváni. After a marriage they perform the *gondhal* dance in honour of Khandoba, and in honour of Bhaváni they kill a goat and sacrifice it to her after burning its hair. They also observe the *Gopál* feast, when on certain days of the week they go begging in gangs, and cook and eat together the grain they collect. Their priests are the ordinary Marátha Bráhmans, whom they respect. They have no headman and settle social disputes at caste meetings. Some send their boys to school till they can read and write a little and cast accounts. Though not a rising people they earn enough for their ordinary expenses.

Mángs.

Ma'ngs or **Ma'digers,** with a strength of 16,849, are found throughout the district. They are divided into Mádigerus, Mochi Mádigerus, and Máng Rauts, who do not eat together or intermarry. They are dark, strong, and regular featured, and their head hair is black and thick. The men shave the head except the top-knot, and wear the moustache and whiskers, but not the beard. The home tongue of the Karnátak Mángs is Kánarese and of the Telangs Telugu. They are hardworking, cunning, passionate, and revengeful. They rank as the lowest of Hindus and will take food from all except Bhangis. They are leather-rope and shoemakers, musicians, executioners, and cattle-gelders. Some of them are village watchmen, husbandmen, and labourers. The Rauts are leech-sellers whose special calling has made them a separate class. They live in tiled or thatched huts and eat pork but not beef. They also eat the flesh of dead animals and drink liquor. They are great eaters and their staple food is Indian millet *náchni* or *sávi*, split pulse, and chillies. They occasionally eat rice. They name their children either on the ninth or the eleventh day after birth. The parents arrange for the marriage of their children, the boy's father having to pay the girl's father £2 4*s.* to £3 (Rs. 22-30). Their marriage ceremony is simple and lasts for only one day. The ceremony is performed by a woman of the caste who knows the formula. This woman is not called by any particular name nor is any woman specially appointed for the purpose. Any goodnatured experienced elderly woman is chosen at the time from among the guests. They have no special marriage songs but sing those which are used on other merry occasions. Soon after the guests are met the woman who is to conduct the ceremony is chosen; she makes the pair sit on a blanket face to face when a cloth is held between them and a song is sung.[1] When the song is over grains of rice are thrown on the heads of the boy and girl; the marriage coronet or *báshing* is tied to their brows and they are husband and wife. A feast to the caste people ends the ceremony. The husband sometimes makes the wife a present of not more than £1 (Rs. 10). They allow widow marriage, the children of the first husband being given to his relations. Second marriages are simple. A caste meeting is called and before the assembled people the widow agrees to marry the man, and the man expresses his willingness to marry the widow. They either bury or burn the dead, and mourn eleven days. They feast their castemen on the third day, the entertainment costing about 4*s.* (Rs. 2). The expenses on the day of the death are not more than 1*s.* (8 *as.*). They are religious, and worship goddesses more than gods. The names of their chief goddesses are Lakshmi, Tulja Bhaváni, and Yellamma. They are said not to believe in or practise divination, soothsaying, or witchcraft. They have no special holidays, lucky or unlucky numbers, sights, and events, but consult the ordinary Bráhmans. They have no headman, and settle disputes at meetings of the caste. Adultery is punished with loss of caste, but the offender is re-admitted if he repents and begs for pardon. They do not send their boys to school, neither do they take to new pursuits. None of them have entered the Government service as soldiers.

---

[1] One of the commonest wedding songs runs as follows: Rub turmeric, women, on my king's daughter; rub the well-omened turmeric on my sister, the wife of one who rules justly. Clothe, women, the daughter of Shri the goddess of wealth and the wife of a king, in a princess' garment. Dress, women, auspiciously the wife who is like Subhadra, the wife of the five Pándavs. Bind, women, the strings of flowers on the head of the beautiful daughter. Bind, women, auspiciously the strings of flowers on the head of the wife of the leader of an army. Put, women, the bodice on my Indra's daughter and wife of a king; put, women, the bodice auspiciously on the wife and my sister. Rub, women, the red-powder on my Indra's daughter; rub, women, auspiciously red-powder on the wife of a king, my sister.

Chapter III. Population. MUSALMÁNS.

They earn enough to maintain themselves, but their savings are swallowed in heavy marriage expenses. They are a poor people.

[1]According to the 1881 census, Belgaum Musalmáns numbered 66,200 or 7·66 per cent of the whole population. The Musalmán section of the Belgaum population includes thirty-eight classes, of whom ten intermarry and are separate in little more than in name, and twenty-eight form distinct communities marrying only among themselves. The classes who intermarry belong to two groups, four general divisions, Syeds, Shaikhs, Moghals, and Pathans, and six local divisions, of whom two Attárs or perfumers and Manyárs or dealers in hardware are traders, three Kaláigars or tinsmiths Kharadis or wood-turners and Nálbands or farriers are craftsmen, and one Baidaras are servants.

Of the twenty-seven separate communities who marry among themselves, six are of outside and twenty-one are of local origin. The six of outside origin are Bohorás and Mehmans from Gujarát and Cutch; Labbeys from the Malabár Coast; and Mukeris, Gáo-kasábs, and Kákars from Maisur, the first four classes being traders, the fifth craftsmen, and the last servants and labourers. Of the twenty-one classes of local origin one is a special community of Gair-Mahadis; two are traders Baghbáns or fruiterers and Támbolis or betel-leaf sellers; two are dealers in animals, Kanjars or poultry and egg sellers and Pendháris or pony-hirers; eight are craftsmen, Bojgars or millet beer brewers, Gaundis or bricklayers, Jhárakars or dust-sifters, Ládkasábs also known as Sultánis or mutton-butchers, Momins or weavers, Patvágars or silk tassel twisters, Pinjáras or cotton carders, and Sikalgars or armourers; four are servants, Bhatyáras or cooks, Dhobis or washermen, Halálkhors or scavengers, and Pakhális or watermen; and four are musicians performers or players, Darveshis or tiger-showmen, Gárodis or jugglers, Kasbans or dancing-girls, and Taschis or kettle-drummers. Of the four general divisions, Syeds, Shaikhs, Moghals, and Patháns, the Moghals are a very small body. The other three divisions include large numbers and are found in all parts of the district. They are probably the descendants of local Hindus who on embracing Islám took the title Shaikh or Pathán in honour of the religious or the military leader under whom they were converted. At the same time almost all claim, and probably most of them claim with right, to have some strain of foreign or of Upper Indian blood. The earliest foreign element was the traders, especially the horse-dealers, the religious leaders, and above all the mercenaries and military adventurers who, before the beginning of Musalmán power about the close of the thirteenth century, found their way to the courts of the early Hindu kings of the Deccan and the Karnátak. The first large arrival of foreign Musalmáns was probably the Turki and North Indian troops who accompanied the armies of Alla-ud-din Khilji in their conquests in the Deccan during the first twenty years of the fourteenth century. A second Central Asian and North Indian element, no doubt resulted from the conquests of Mubárik Khilji in 1318 and of Muhammad Tughlik in

[1] From materials supplied by Mr. Syed Dáud, clerk, Registration Department.

1328. In 1347 the establishment of the independent Bahmani dynasty severed the connection between the Deccan and the north. The result was to introduce through the Konkan and Kánara ports a strain of Persian, Arab, and East African blood. The number of these foreigners who reached the Karnátak was small, until in the latter part of the sixteenth century the Karnátak was conquered by Bijápur. Except a few who can trace their descent from some early religious leaders the memory of these early Musalmán settlers has disappeared. Almost all the classes who admit their descent from local Hindus trace their conversion to one of three great spreaders of Islám, the Emperor Aurangzeb who ruled the South Deccan from 1687 to 1707, Haidar Ali who ruled Maisur from 1763 to 1782, and Haidar's son Tipu who ruled Maisur from 1782 to 1800.[1]

Except the Memans who speak Cutchi and the Bohorás who speak Gujaráti at home, almost all Musalmáns, both villagers and townspeople, speak Hindustáni with a mixture of Maráthi and Kánarese words.

Food.

The village Musalmáns as a rule are tall, sturdy, and dark, but the large eyes, fair skin, and high features of many of the townspeople point to a strain of northern or of western blood. Musalmáns of all classes take at least two meals a day. They breakfast about ten in the morning on wheat or millet-bread and pulse and vegetables, and if rich on mutton; they sup about eight in the evening on millet and pulse, and in some of the richer families on wheat and rice and mutton or vegetables. Some of the richer classes, and almost all husbandmen, have three meals, the richer breakfasting on tea, wheat-bread, milk, and eggs; and the husbandmen taking a cold breakfast about seven, a midday meal in the fields, and a supper on reaching home in the evening. The field-working Musalmáns are very fond of chillies and onions which in many cases take the place of a relish or curry. In a husbandman's family of four persons four to six pounds of chillies are used every month. The rich give costly public dinners at which the chief dishes are *biryani* and *jarda*. *Biryani* is a dish of mutton, clarified butter, rice, cardamoms, cloves, black pepper, cinnamon, and fresh ginger or saffron; *jarda* is a sweet dish of rice, clarified butter, sugar, almonds, saffron, and other spices. A dinner at which both of these dishes are given costs about £3 10*s*. (Rs. 35) for a hundred guests. Among the middling classes and the poor the chief dish at public dinner is a *puláo* of boiled rice and clarified butter eaten with *dálcha* or pulse and mutton curry; a *puláo* dinner costs £1 10*s*. to £2 10*s*. (Rs. 15-25) for every hundred guests. Many rich families eat mutton daily, and most have mutton either once a week, or at

---

[1] Of twenty classes who admit a Hindu origin, fourteen, Attars or perfumers, Bhágváns or gardeners, Bhatyáras or cooks, Bojgars or brewers, Gaundis or masons, Jhárakaris or dust-washers, Kaláigars or tinsmiths, Kharadis or wood-turners, Manyárs or hardware dealers, Nálbands or farriers, Patvágars or tassel-makers, Pinjárás or cotton teasers, Sikligars or armourers, and Támbolis or betel-sellers trace their conversion to Aurangzeb (1687-1707); three, Baidaras or Bedars, Dhobis or washermen, and Halálkhors or scavengers, trace their conversion to Haidar Ali (1763-1782); and three, Kanjars or poulterers, Sultánis or butchers, and Pakhális or watermen to Tipu (1782-1800).

Chapter III.
Population.
MUSALMÁNS.
Food.

special dinners, or on the Ramzán and Bakar Id or Bull festival. Except Bohorás, Mehmans, and members of the four main divisions, almost all Belgaum Musalmáns prefer mutton to beef, and many of the local communities, especially the mutton-butchers and the fruiterers, will on no account touch beef. Buffalo beef is considered unwholesome and is avoided by all. Fowls and eggs are generally used by the rich and by the poor when they entertain friends and relations, and when they sacrifice to any Hindu god or Musalmán saint. Fish, both dry and fresh, is eaten by all without objection. The staple food of all classes is grain and pulse. Among the rich and well-to-do, perhaps about twenty per cent of the whole, the grains in ordinary use are wheat, Indian millet, rice, and pulse; the remaining eighty per cent use Indian millet, millet, and pulse. The monthly cost of food in a rich Musalmán family of five varies from £3 to £6 (Rs. 30-60); in a middle-class family from £1 10*s*. to £2 (Rs. 15-20); and in a poor family from 10*s*. to £1 (Rs. 5-10). Water is the only beverage drunk by all classes of Musalmáns. Milk is taken with tea or coffee by the rich or with bread in the morning. In spite of the religious rules against its use, country liquor is largely drunk, and in some villages even sold by Musalmáns. On account of their cost imported wines and spirits are little used. Of intoxicating drugs, *bháng* or *gánja* that is hemp leaves, *charas* also made from hemp leaves, and *madat* small balls made of bábul leaf ashes soaked in opium water, are largely used by servants and beggars. Of other stimulants and narcotics tobacco is smoked by almost all either in the form of cigarettes rolled in plantain leaves, or in pipes, and in the form of snuff by some old men of the trading classes. Opium is occasionally used by servants and beggars.

Dress.

Except the men of the four leading divisions of Musalmáns who wear the Musalmán turban, coat, shirt, waistcoat, and trousers, the men of almost all classes dress in the Hindu style. The men wear indoors a headscarf or a skull cap, a shirt or a waistcoat, and a waistcloth. Out of doors, if rich on all occasions, and if middle-class or poor on festive occasions or holidays, they put on a Hindu-shaped turban either twisted or loosely wound, a coat, and a pair of shoes. The whole of the every-day dress is made of cotton, but for festive or ceremonial occasions almost all have a silk turban, a silk-bordered waistcloth, and a silk handkerchief. They generally have their turbans dyed on the Ramzán or Bakar Id festivals. Except the Pirzádas or religious teachers and the Syeds, who prefer green or white, the usual colour of the turban is red, yellow, or orange. A rich man's wardrobe is worth £10 to £20 (Rs. 100-200) and his yearly clothes charges vary from £2 to £3 (Rs. 20-30); a middle-class man's wardrobe is worth £3 to £5 (Rs. 30-50) with a yearly cost of £1 to £2 (Rs. 10-20), and a poor man's wardrobe is worth £1 to £2 (Rs. 10-20) with a yearly cost of 10*s*. to 15*s*. (Rs. 5-7½).

Women of almost all classes wear the Hindu robe or *sádi* generally eight yards long by a yard and a quarter broad, and a bodice or *choli* covering the back and fastened in a knot under the bosom with short tight-fitting sleeves covering the upper arm only. When

Dress.

the women of the four main divisions go out of doors they cover themselves with a white sheet, and the Bohora women shroud themselves in a large black chintz or silk cloak which falls from the crown of the head to the feet leaving a gauze opening for the eyes. Other Musalmán women, as a rule, appear in public in the dress which they wear indoors. Except on festive or ceremonial occasions almost all women dress in cotton. The festive or ceremonial dress consists of one or two sets of silk or embroidered robes called *pitámbars* and bodices. These rich garments are given by the husband at marriage and generally last during the whole of the woman's life. A rich woman's ceremonial dress is worth £10 to £20 (Rs. 100-200), and a middle class or poor woman's £3 to £8 (Rs. 30-80). The yearly cost of dress varies for a rich woman from £2 to £3 (Rs. 20-30), and for a middle class or poor woman from £1 to £2 (Rs. 10-20). Except courtezans who always wear shoes and women of the better class families who wear embroidered broadcloth slippers for a year or two after marriage, Musalmán women never wear shoes.

Ornaments.

The men of some of the lower classes, butchers, water-carriers, and sweepers, when they can afford it, are fond of wearing a large gold ring in the right ear, and a silver chain called *toda* 1¼ to 2½ lbs. (50 to 100 *tolás*) in weight on the right ankle. The men of the other classes seldom wear any ornament except finger rings. All who can afford it are fond of ornamenting their boys with a large thick gold or silver neck-ring called *hansli*, a pair of silver or gold wristlets called *kadás*, and a pair of silver ankle chains or *todás*. Almost all Musalmán women begin married life with a good store of ornaments. Their parents must give them at least one nosering, a set of eight to ten gold or silver earrings, and silver finger rings; and their husbands must invest in ornaments for the bride as much as the amount of the dowry which is generally £12 14*s.* (Rs. 127). Among the poorer classes a woman seldom keeps her full stock of wedding jewels. Most of them disappear by degrees in meeting special expenses and in tiding the family over times of dear food or scanty employment.

Houses.

Townsmen of the four main divisions are fond of luxury and good living. Their houses are generally one-storied with tiled roofs. Many of them have a front or back yard enclosed by a stone wall five to seven feet high. A few of the better class of houses have walls of cut-stone and cement, and a framework of good timber. But the walls of most are of rough stone and clay smeared with a wash of cowdung; the timber framework is scanty and cheap. Few houses have much furniture. Almost none have tables or chairs or other articles of European pattern. They have a few mats and carpets, a few low stools, a cot or two, some quilts or blankets, and cooking and drinking vessels. Some of the rich and well-to-do have Persian or English carpets and China mats in the sitting or public room called *baithak* or *dálan*, and large cushions or bolsters laid against the walls to lean on. The houses of the rich and well-to-do generally contain five or six rooms, built round a square or central yard which occasionally has a well of drinking water. Of the five rooms the front room is set apart as a public room, and

Chapter III.
Population.
Musalmáns.
Houses.

the last as a cook-room; the rest are kept either as sleeping rooms or as store rooms. A rich man's house built of cut-stone and cement with a good timber frame costs £50 to £300 (Rs. 500-3000) to build and 10*s.* to 16*s.* (Rs. 5-8) a month to hire; a lower, middle, or poor man's house costs £10 to £30 (Rs. 100-300) to build and 1*s.* to 4*s.* (8 *annas*-Rs. 2) a month to hire. Village houses are built in much the same style as the poorer class of town houses. They have generally three or four rooms. The front room, which is always the biggest, is set apart as a cattle-shed; the middle room or rooms are used for sleeping and for storing grain; and the back room for cooking. The houses have little furniture, a cot or two with blankets, and a few brass and clay vessels.

Some landholders or *jágirdárs* and rich traders keep one or two house servants and grooms, and pay them 8*s.* to 16*s.* (Rs. 4-8) a month. With this exception the only servants which Musalmáns employ are barbers, washermen, and water-carriers. These men work for several families. Each family pays the washerman £1 to £2 (Rs. 10-20) a year, the water-carrier 10*s.* to £1 (Rs. 5-10), and the barber 8*s.* to 12*s.* (Rs. 4-6).

Calling.

Village Musalmáns are almost all land or estate holders. Town Musalmáns follow all callings, trading in piecegoods and grain, and taking timber contracts, and supplying provisions to the Commissariat Department. Two callings forbidden to the faithful are commonly followed by well-to-do townsmen, moneylending and liquor-selling. Even the descendants of some of the highest religious families freely and openly exercise these callings. The bulk of the men of the four main divisions are servants and messengers.

Character.

Except trading Bohorás and Mehmans, and some classes of craftsmen, the bulk of the townsmen, though clean and orderly, are somewhat idle and fond of drink and good living; the villagers, especially the husbandmen, are hardworking and thrifty, but untidy and occasionally somewhat turbulent.

Condition.

Except traders and a few craftsmen, husbandmen, and servants who are well-to-do, most town Musalmáns are badly off. Some live comfortably on their earnings though forced to borrow to meet special expenses, while others are pinched living from hand to mouth. All but the very richest suffered severely in the 1876-77 famine not only from the very high prices of grain but because of the failure of the demand for their labour or for the articles which they produce. Many were forced to part with the bulk of their property, and others incurred debts which they have not been able to pay.

Customs

The only specially Musalmán ceremony which all classes practise is circumcising their sons. Of other specially Musalmán rites the main body of Belgaum Musalmáns observe the sacrifice or *akika* ceremony either on the seventh, twelfth, or fourteenth day after the birth of a child, and the initiation or *bismilla* that is in God's Name when the child is four years four months and four days old. The mass of craftsmen, husbandmen, and labourers avoid the sacrifice and the initiation ceremonies partly from ignorance partly from poverty. Women of all classes are careful to keep *chhati* or

Chapter III. Population. Musalmáns. Customs.

the sixth day after the birth of a child, and to observe the shaving or *mundan* of the child's head on the fortieth day after its birth or when it is a year or two old. On the shaving ceremony they spend large sums on dinners. A few craftsmen and labourers in a woman's first pregnancy hold a *satvása* ceremony in the seventh month, spending a little on dinners to friends and relations. All classes rub the bride and bridegroom with turmeric and henna; and the first four Fridays after a marriage, called *jumagis*, are kept as festive days and a little is spent on dinners to friends and relations. The new-moon day of the first Muharram after marriage is unlucky for a married couple. They are separated for a month, the bride going to her father's house where the husband is not allowed to see her for some days. On the third day after a death a *ziarat* or third day mourning is held. About seven in the morning the mourners with some friends and relations go to the mosque and all read the Kurán. When the reading is over two trays are handed round, one with parched rice mixed with fruit, the other with flowers and a cup of scent. The parched rice and fruit are taken by those present. Of the flowers each picks one, dips it into the scent cup, and puts it back on the tray. The flowers are afterwards taken to the grave. On the tenth day a grand dinner is given at a cost of £3 to £8 (Rs. 30-80), and after every tenth day for six months the Kurán is read and prayers are offered to God beseeching him to show pity to the soul of the dead, and alms are given.

Religion.

Except members of the four main divisions and some servants and traders, who teach their children to read the Kurán, few Musalmáns teach their children any religious books. Almost all are careful to have their boys circumcised and to get their marriages and funerals performed by the *kázi*, that is the judge or marriage registrar, or his deputy. Though few attend the mosque service daily, almost all are careful to be present at the special services on the Ramzán and Bakar Id festivals. They are also careful to give alms and to pay the *kázi* his dues. Their religious officers are the *kázi* or judge, the *mulla* or priest, and the *mujávar* or beadle. The *kázi*, who under Musalmán rule was both a criminal and civil judge, has now no function except to register marriages. The office of *kázi* is in most cases hereditary, the family holding some estate granted by the Moghals. As marriage registrar the *kázi* is paid 5*s.* (Rs. 2½) for registering a marriage, and 2*s.* 6*d.* (Rs. 1¼) for registering a remarriage. He is much respected and his services are considered of high value. Next in importance to the *kázi* comes the *mulla* or priest who is commonly *náib* or deputy *kázi*. He is generally a man chosen from some poor family because of his knowledge of the Kurán and of Urdu, and is deputed by the district *kázi* to register marriages in a certain village. Each village has one *mulla* or priest who receives one-fourth part of the *kázi's* fee, that is 6*d.* to 2*s.* 3*d.* (4-10 *as.*) for a marriage and 3*d.* to 7½*d.* (2-5 *as.*) for a remarriage. Besides these fees, the priest makes small sums by cutting the throats of goats, sheep, and fowls with the proper Musalmán purifying ceremonies.[1] He cuts the throats of animals not only for

[1] This ceremony is called *halál karna* or making lawful.

Chapter III. Population. MUSALMÁNS. Religion.

Musalmáns but for Hindu landholders as well, as they never eat the flesh of an animal which has not been killed by a *mulla*. In some villages, in reward for this service, the hereditary *mulla* holds land granted by the villagers for his services. This he generally himself tills. The ministrants or *mujávars* are chiefly employed as the guardians of the shrines of Musalmán saints. The office, as a rule, is not hereditary and holders occasionally give up the post if they find better employment. They live either by begging or on the offerings made to the shrine of which they have charge. They pray to the saint on behalf of all who offer cocoanuts, sweetmeats, or flowers, or who sacrifice sheep or fowls at the saint's shrine. Besides the offerings which he receives for the saint the *mujávar* is presented with 1*d.* to 1½*d.* (⅔-1 *anna*) as *chiraghi* or lamp-money which he keeps for himself. Ministrants, whose shrines do not yield enough to support them, go from village to village begging in the name of their saint, and sometimes journey to Poona or to Bombay staying several months and returning for the yearly *urus* or fair. The spiritual guides or *pirzádás,* that is saint-sons, are held in high respect. The chief saintly families in Belgaum are the Bashebans who are descended from Pir Syed Umar Idrus and Pir Syed Muhammed bin Syed Ali Khatál. The representatives of these holy men live chiefly on the rents of their estates and by moneylending. They have no specially religious character, and do not attempt to gain converts to Islám.

Community.

Most Musalmáns belong to the sect of Sunnis that is they accept the succession of the four Imáms, Abubakar-Sidik, Umar, Usman, and Ali. They form a body bound together by strong religious ties. They worship in the same mosque, keep the same holidays, perform the same religious and social ceremonies, and respect and employ the same *kázis*. Musalmáns who are not members of the main community of Sunnis either belong to the minor Musalmán sects or to the bodies of local converts who have either never given up or who have again taken to Hindu practices. The minor Musalmán sects are represented in Belgaum by the Bohorás, people of Gujarát origin who belong to the Ismaili branch of Shiás. They are known as Daudi Bohorás from the name of the pontiff or Mula Sáheb whose claims in a disputed succession they supported.[1] Another sect of some consequence, the Ghair Máhdis or anti-Máhdis, hold that the Máhdi or looked for Imám or leader has come.

---

[1] Shiás that is holy, generally called *ráfjis* or heretics, are the second of the main Musalmán sects. They reject three of the four Sunni Imáms, Abubakar-Sidik, Umar, and Usmán, and in their stead honour twelve Imáms of whom the first is Ali the son-in-law of the Prophet. Shiás are divided into two classes, Mustálians and Ismailians. The division arose on the death of the sixth Imám, Jáfer Sadik who died in 1300 (H. 698). This pontiff had quarrelled with his eldest son and passed him over in favour of his younger son Ismáili. Those who supported the elder brother are known as Mustálians and those who supported the younger brother as Ismáilians. The chief representatives of the Mustálians are the Khojás the followers of H.H. Agáh Ali Sháh Khán, and the chief representatives of the Ismáilians are the Dáudi Bohorás. The chief points of difference between Sunnis and Shiás are that the Sunnis hold that Abubakar, Umar, and Usman were the lawful successors of the prophet; and the Shiás believe that Ali was the lawful heir to the Khaliphát and was kept out of his rights by the three others. The Shiás leave out certain passages from the Kurán which they say were written by Usman; and add a chapter in praise of Ali under the belief that it was kept back by Usman.

Chapter III.

Population.

Musalmáns.

Community.

Among the separate communities the mutton-butchers or Kasáis, the betel-sellers or Támbolis, and the fruiterers or Bágbans, have such strong Hindu leanings that they do not associate with other Musalmáns. They almost never come to mosque, eschew beef, keep Hindu holidays, and openly worship and offer vows to Hindu gods. Almost all of these special communities who marry among themselves only, have a union or committee called *jamát* which settles their disputes at meetings of the men of the community each under a head called *patel* or *chaudhari*. The headman is chosen from among the oldest and richest members of the community. If the majority of the men of the class agree the headman has power to fine any one who breaks the caste rules. Almost all of these distinct communities obey the *kázi*, and sometimes refer social disputes to him for disposal.

Prospects.

The want of education, thrift, and forethought greatly interferes with the prospects of the Musalmáns. Except the pushing well-to-do trading Memans and Bohorás, who teach their boys Maráthi and Urdu, not more than thirty per cent of the Musalmáns send their boys to school. Few learn English or enter Government service as clerks.

Movements.

Few Musalmáns leave the district in search of employment or for other causes. On the contrary a considerable number of Musalmáns, especially military pensioners, are drawn to settle at Belgaum by the cheapness of provisions, the pleasantness of the climate, and because of the openings for employment which the presence of so large a body of troops causes. The ten classes that form the main body of Musalmáns, who intermarry and are separate in little more than in name, include, besides the four general divisions of Syeds Shaikhs Moghals and Patháns, six small communities of whom two are shopkeepers, Attárs or perfume-sellers and Manyárs or bangle-sellers; three are craftsmen, Kaláigars or tinsmiths Kharádis or wood-turners and Nálbands or farriers; and one, the Bedras, are servants.

Syeds or Pirzádás.

Syeds or **Pirza'da's,** also known as **Mashaiks,** number about a thousand, and claim descent chiefly from two Belgaum saints, Syed Muhammad bin Syed Ali Katáli known as Katálwali or Saint Katál, and Syed Umar Idrus Basheban. Both of these men came from Arabia as missionaries during the rule of the Adilsháhi kings of Bijápur (1489-1686). They hold estates which were granted to them by the Bijápur kings and the Moghal emperors. Though mixture of blood has greatly changed their appearance, these Syeds trace their origin to Ali and Fatima the son-in-law and daughter of the Prophet. The men take the word Syed that is holy, or Mir that is head, before, and Sháh that is king, after their names; and the women add Bibi to theirs. Their home speech is Hindustáni. The men are tall or of middle height, well-built, strong, and fair. They shave the head, wear the beard full, and dress in a white or green turban or a headscarf, a long coat, a shirt, a waistcoat, and loose trousers. The women, who are either tall or middle-sized and refined, with arched eyebrows, long straight nose, full limbs, and fair skin, wear the Hindu robe and bodice. They do not appear

Chapter III. Population. MUSALMÁNS. *Syeds or Pirzádás.*

in public, and perform no work except minding the house. Both men and women are neat and tidy in their habits. The rich are landlords or *jágirdárs*, traders, and commissariat contractors; the poor are soldiers, constables, messengers, and servants. Though hardworking, they are apt to fall into a luxurious and intemperate way of living. Most of them are well-to-do and not scrimped for food. As a rule they marry among themselves but they occasionally give their daughters to Shaikhs of high family. Their customs do not differ from those of other Musalmáns. They follow the regular *kázi* and employ him in their marriage and funeral ceremonies. In religion they are Sunnis of the Hanafi school. Most of them are religious, but the bulk of the young men are careless about saying their prayers. They take much interest in teaching their children Arabic, Persian, and Maráthi, and of late some have begun to send their boys to English schools.

Shaikhs.

Shaikhs, that is ELDERS, are found in large numbers throughout the district. They are of two main branches, the Sidikis who trace their descent to Abábakr Sidik the father-in-law, and the Farukis who trace their descent to Umeral-Faruk the son-in-law of the Prophet Muhammad. Besides those who may have some strain of foreign blood many local converts have received the title of Shaikh from the masters who induced them to embrace Islám. Their appearance and dress do not differ from those of the Syeds and like them their home speech is Hindustáni. The men take the word Shaikh or elder before, and the women the word Bibi or lady after their names. Their women, like Syed women, do not appear in public or do any work except managing the house. Both men and women are neat and clean. They are hardworking, thrifty, and hospitable. The rich are traders and landlords or *jágirdárs*, and the poor are soldiers, constables, servants, and messengers. A few are rich and well-to-do, but most are poor and in debt. They marry either among themselves or with any of the ordinary classes of Musalmáns, from whom they do not differ in manners or customs. They obey the *kázi* and have no special headman. In religion they are Sunnis of the Hanafi school. As a class they are religious, most of them, except the young, being careful to say their prayers. They teach their children Urdu and Maráthi, and of late some have begun to send their boys to English schools.

Moghals.

Moghals, the representatives of the Moghal invaders of the Deccan in the seventeenth and eighteenth centuries, are found in small numbers. The men add Mirza to their names and the women Bibi; they speak Hindustáni and do not differ in appearance or dress from Syeds or Shaikhs. Both the men and women are neat and clean and the women neither appear in public nor add to the family income. They are hardworking, but many of them are fond of drink and few are well-to-do or able to save. They are either constables, messengers, servants, or husbandmen. Except with Syeds, who do not as a rule give their daughters to Moghals, they marry with all the main classes of Musalmáns. They are Sunnis of the Hanafi school, but few are religious or careful to say their prayers. They obey the *kázi* and their manners and customs do not differ from those of other regular Musalmáns. They teach their children Urdu and Maráthi. None have learnt English or risen to high position.

Patháns.

Patha'ns, or WARRIORS, said to come from *paithna* to penetrate, are found in large numbers throughout the district. They represent the Afghans who came to the Deccan in the service of the Bijápur kings and Moghal emperors. Some of them are local converts who took the title of Pathán because they joined Islám under the patronage of some Afghan general or missionary. They speak Hindustáni among themselves and Maráthi with others. They are tall or of middle height, well-made, strong, and dark or olive skinned. The men shave the head, wear the beard full, and dress in a Marátha turban, a short shirt, a tight-fitting jacket, and a pair of tight trousers or a waistcloth. The women, who are either tall or of middle size, with regular features and wheat-coloured skins, wear the Hindu robe and bodice. They neither appear in public nor add to the family income. Both men and women are neat and tidy in their habits. They are soldiers, constables, messengers, servants, and husbandmen. Though hardworking, many of them are fond of smoking hemp and drinking fermented millet beer or *boja*, and palm-spirit. As a class they are badly off, many of them being in debt. They marry among themselves or with any of the main Musalmán divisions. Except the villagers who abstain from the use of beef and offer vows to Hindu gods, their manners do not differ much from those of the ordinary Musalmáns. They are Sunnis of the Hanafi school, but few of them are religious or careful to say their prayers. They teach their boys Urdu and Maráthi, and of late some have begun to send their children to Government schools to learn English. None have risen to any high position.

Attárs.

Atta'rs or PERFUMERS, local converts from the Hindu class of the same name, are found in small numbers in some of the larger towns. According to their own account, they were converted to Islám by the Emperor Aurangzeb (1687-1707). Their home tongue is Hindustáni, but with Hindus they speak Maráthi and Kánarese fluently. The men who are middle-sized, well-made, and dark or olive skinned, shave the head, wear the beard full, and dress in a Marátha turban or headscarf, a tight-fitting jacket, and tight trousers or a waistcloth. Their women, who are of middle size, delicate, with good features and of a wheat colour, dress in the Hindu robe and bodice, appear in public, but except when they grow elderly do not help the men in selling perfumes. Both men and women are neat and clean in their habits. They are *attárs* or perfume-sellers and find a fairly constant demand for their wares. They sell several sorts of perfumes and tooth-powders, chiefly extracts of rose, jessamine, and other flowers, at prices varying from 2*s.* to £1 (Rs. 1-10) the *tola* of ⅖ths of an ounce; frankincense or *agarbatti* at one to two shillings (8 *as.*-Re. 1) the pound; aloewood or *argaja* at one to two shillings the *tola*; dentrifice or *missi* at 1*s.* (8 *ans.*) the pound; red-powder or *kunku* at one shilling (8 *as.*) the pound; red thread or *náda* for women's hair-nets at 1*s.* (8 *as.*) the pound; and the thread garlands or *sahellis* which are worn during the Muharram festival at 1½*d.* to

Chapter III. Population. MUSALMÁNS. *Attárs.*

3*d.* (1-2 *as.*) the pair. Of these articles, the tooth-powder or *missi*, and the red-powder or *kunku*, are the only articles sold in any large quantity. The flower extracts or *attar*, the frankincense or *agarbatti*, and the other perfumes are sold only occasionally to the rich. The thread garlands are sold only during the latter five of the ten days of the Muharram festival, and are bought by both Hindus and Musalmáns. Their yearly income does not exceed £50 (Rs. 500). Most have shops; but some of the poor hawk their wares from street to street or from village to village. They are hardworking, thrifty, and sober, and some of them are fairly well-to-do and able to save. They do not form a separate community nor have they any special organization. They marry either among themselves or with any of the regular classes of Musalmáns, and have nothing peculiar in their manners or customs. They are Sunnis of the Hanafi school, most of them fairly religious or careful to say their prayers. They do not send their children to school. Of late some have begun to teach their boys Maráthi and Urdu, but none have risen to any high position.

Manyárs.

Manya'rs, Dealers in hardware and glass bangles, are local converts, probably of mixed Hindu origin. They are found in small numbers in Belgaum and other large towns. They are said to have been converted by the Emperor Aurangzeb between 1687 and 1707. Their home speech is Hindustáni and out of doors Maráthi or Kánarese. They are tall or of middle size, well-made, and of a brownish colour. The men shave the head, wear the beard full, and dress in Hindu fashion in a shirt, a waistcoat, and a waistcloth. The women, who are like the men in face, wear the Hindu robe and bodice, appear in public, and help the men in their work. Both men and women are neat and clean in their habits. Chinese and European competition has forced the Manyárs to give up making glass bangles and take to trading in hardware and miscellaneous articles. Of bangles they sell two kinds of Chinese glass bangles which they buy from wholesale Hindu dealers in Bombay, a dearer bangle at 1*s.* 6*d.* (12 *as.*) the dozen and a cheaper bangle at 6*d.* to 9*d.* (4-6 *as.*) the dozen, and common or country glass bangles at 4*d.* (2½ *as.*) the dozen. They make and sell lac bracelets at 9*d.* to 1*s.* (6-8 *as.*) the dozen. Of hardware they sell iron vessels, buying them cheap from Ghisádi tinkers or wandering blacksmiths and selling them at a good profit to Pinjáras or cotton-teasers and Momins or weavers. They buy cotton ropes by weight and sell them by the yard. Of European articles they sell match-boxes, mirrors, brass ornaments, and lanterns, which they buy from wholesale Bohora or Hindu merchants. Some of them stay in their shops, and others go to villages which have weekly markets. When the men are away the women sit in the shops and sell. They are hardworking, thrifty, and sober, and, though their profits are small, they are fairly off and able to save for emergencies. They marry either among themselves or with any of the regular Musalmáns. They have two different craft names: Bangarharas who sell bangles, and Manyárs who deal in bangles and hardware. These are not separate communities as they intermarry and eat together. They have no special organization and no headman except the *kázi* who settles their social disputes. Their manners and customs do not differ from those of ordinary Musalmáns. They

MUSALMÁNS. *Kaldigars.*

are Sunnis of the Hanafi school but are not religious or careful to say their prayers. They do not send their boys to school or take to new pursuits.

Kala'igars, or TINSMITHS, probably local converts of mixed Hindu origin, are found in small numbers in Belgaum and in some other large towns. They are said to have been converted by Aurangzeb (1687-1707) and call themselves Shaikhs. Their home tongue is Hindustáni, but with Hindus they speak correct Maráthi or Kánarese. They are middle-sized, thin, and either dark or olive-coloured. The men shave the head, wear the beard full, and dress in a large Marátha-like white or red turban, a shirt, a tight-fitting jacket, and a pair of tight trousers or a waistcloth. The women, who are like the men in face, weart he ordinary Marátha robe and bodice. They do not appear in public, and add nothing to the family income. Both men and women are neat and clean in their habits. They are tinsmiths by craft and are hardworking, but some of them are excessively fond of intoxicating drinks on which they spend most of their earnings. They are neither rich nor scrimped for food, but have to borrow to meet special expenses. They coat copper and brass vessels with tin and work for all classes, being paid 1*s.* 6*d.* to 2*s.* (12 *as.*-Re. 1) for tinning a dozen vessels. Their employment is said of late to have declined as many of the poorer Musalmáns and Hindus are said to have taken to cooking their every-day food in clay vessels to save the cost of tinning brass and copper. Many are said to have gone to Haidarabad, Poona, or Bombay. They marry either among themselves or with any of the regular classes of Musalmáns. They form a well-organizod body and hold meetings to settle social disputes under a headman or *chaudhari* chosen from the oldest and most respected members. If the majority agree, the headman has power to fine any one who breaks the class rules. In other ways their manners or customs do not differ from those of the regular Musalmáns. They obey the *kázi* and employ him at their marriage and funeral ceremonies. They are Sunnis of the Hanafi school, but few of them are religious or careful to say their prayers. They send their boys to school and teach them Maráthi. None have risen to any high position.

Kharádis.

Khara'dis, or WOOD-TURNERS, local converts probably of the Sutár caste, are found in small numbers in Belgaum and in other large towns. They are said to have been converted by Aurangzeb. Among themselves they speak Hindustáni, and Maráthi or Kánarese with others. The men are tall or of middle size, well-made, and dark. They shave the head, wear the beard either short or full, and dress in a large red Marátha turban, a tight-fitting jacket, and a waistcloth. The women, who are like the men in face, wear the Hindu robe and bodice. They appear in public and help the men in their work. Both men and women are dirty and untidy in their habits. They are wood-turners by craft, and turn bed-legs, cradles, and children's toys, and colour them with red, yellow, orange, green, and blue lac. They are hardworking and thrifty, and most of them are sober. They earn one to two shillings (8 *as.* - Re. 1) a day, but their work is so uncertain that many have given up their craft

Chapter III. Population. MUSALMÁNS. *Kharádis.*

and become servants and messengers or gone to Bombay or Haidarabad in search of work. They are not well-to-do, and live from hand to mouth. They marry either among themselves or with any of the regular classes of Musalmáns. Though they form a separate body, they have no special organization and no headman except the *kázi* who settles their social disputes. Their customs do not differ from those of ordinary Musalmáns. They are Sunnis of the Hanafi school, but are not religious or careful to say their prayers. They do not give their boys any schooling. On the whole they are said to be a falling class.

Nálbands.

Na'lbands, or FARRIERS, probably local converts of mixed Hindu origin, are found in small numbers in Belgaum. They are said to have been converted by Aurangzeb, and call themselves Shaikhs. They speak Hindustáni among themselves and Maráthi or Kánarese with others. The men are tall or of middle height, strong, and dark or olive-skinned. They shave the head, wear the beard either short or full, and dress in a Marátha turban, a shirt, a jacket, and a pair of tight trousers or a waistcloth. The women, who are of middle size, well-featured, and wheat-coloured, wear the Hindu robe and bodice, and neither appear in public nor add to the family income. Both men and women are neat and clean in their habits. They make their living as farriers, shoeing horses and bullocks. They are hardworking, but excessively fond of drink and of smoking hemp or *gánja*. Except a few, who are fairly off, most are in debt. They are paid 1*s.* to 2*s.* 6*d.* (8 *as.*-Rs. 1¼) for shoeing a horse and 3*d.* to 6*d.* (2-4 *as.*) for shoeing a bullock. They go from house to house in search of work, and some of the poorer sit by the roadside or near places where laden bullock-carts stop. Their work is uncertain and they do not earn more than 14*s.* to £1 6*s.* (Rs. 7-13) a month. They marry either among themselves or with any of the general classes of Musalmáns. They are separate only in name. They have no class organization, and their manners and customs do not differ from those of the regular Musalmáus. They obey the *kázi* and through him settle social disputes. They are Sunnis of the Hanafi school but are not religious or careful to say their prayers. They teach their children Maráthi, but none teach them English. Besides as Nálbands some earn their living as messengers and servants.

Bedars.

Bedars, or FEARLESS, Hindu converts from the local tribe of Baidarus, are found in small numbers in Belgaum. They are said to have been converted by Haidar Ali of Maisur (1763-1781), who considered them among his most trusty soldiers. They are said to have come from Maisur to Belgaum about seventy years ago. They call themselves Kháns. Their home speech is Hindustáni, but with others they talk Maráthi and Kánarese. The men are tall and robust, with large eyes, long straight noses, broad chests, with dark or olive skins. Some shave the head; others let the hair grow. They wear long and full beards, and dress in a turban, a coat, a shirt, and tight trousers. Their women, who are either tall or of middle height, well-made, with regular features and fair skin, dress in the Hindu robe and bodice. They appear in public but do not add to the family income. Both men and women are neat and clean in

Chapter III. Population. MUSALMÁNS. *Bedars.*

their habits. They are servants and messengers. They are hardworking but excessively fond of liquor. They are neither well-to-do nor scrimped for food, and on marriages and other special occasions have to borrow. They do not form a separate community. They marry with the main body of Musalmáns and do not differ from them in manners and customs. They have no special organization and no headman except the regular *kázi* who settles their social disputes. They are Sunnis of the Hanafi school, and are generally religious and sometimes strict in saying their prayers. Some of them teach their boys Maráthi, but none teach them English. None have risen to any high position.

Of the twenty-eight separate communities, the six of outside origin are the Bohorás, Gáokasábs, Labbeys, Memans, and Mukeris.

Bohorás.

Bohora's,[1] the only Shiás in the district, are found in small numbers in Belgaum. Originally partly Hindu converts and partly descendants of Arab and Persian immigrants, they are said to have come from Surat and Bombay to Belgaum about forty years ago. They are Ismaili Shiás in religion and are known as Daudis from Daud, the name of a pontiff or Mulla Sáheb whose claim they supported in a case of disputed succession. Their home speech is Gujaráti, and with others they speak Hindustáni or Maráthi. They are active and well-made with an olive skin and regular clear-cut features. The men shave the head, wear the beard long, and dress with considerable care and neatness in a white tightly wound turban, a long shirt hanging to the knee, a waistcoat, a long overcoat, and a pair of loose trousers of white cloth or striped chintz. The women are fair and delicate, with regular features. They are very clean, neat, and modest and are particularly fond of dyeing the soles of their feet and the palms of their hands red with henna. They appear in public muffled in a long cloak from head to foot. Except by house work they add nothing to the family income. Their dress is a petticoat of three or four yards of silk or chintz, a headscarf, and a backless bodice with short and tight-fitting sleeves. The large cloak or *burkha* which they wear out of doors is made of striped black silk or chintz. They deal chiefly in Bombay piecegoods and in hardware. They are said to be honourable traders and to have a good name for fair dealing. They are hardworking, thrifty, and sober, very economical, and well-to-do. They eat and drink with other Musalmáns but marry only among themselves. They have a well-organized community with a *mulla* at their head, the deputy of the pontiff or chief *mulla* of Surat, who performs their marriage, circumcision, and death ceremonies, and collects the dues which they are bound to pay to the chief *mulla*. They lay in the hands of the dead a paper written by the chief *mulla* praying the Almighty to have pity on the dead man's soul[2]. Printed copies of this prayer are

---

[1] The word Bohora is probably from the Gujaráti *vohorvu* to trade.

[2] The words of this prayer are, I seek shelter with the Great God and with his excellent nature against Satan, who has been overwhelmed with stones. Oh God, this slave of your's who has died and upon whom you have decreed death is weak and poor and needs your mercy. Pardon his sins, be gracious to him, and raise his soul with the souls of the Prophets and the truthful, the martyrs, and the holy, for

Chapter III. Population. MUSALMÁNS. *Bohorás.*

sent from Surat to the deputy *mulla* who is paid a fee varying from £2 to £30 (Rs. 20-300). The manners and customs of Bohorás do not greatly differ from those of ordinary Musalmáns. They do not pray in the ordinary mosques but have a separate meeting-room or *jamát-khána* where they meet to pray and settle social disputes. Though they do not obey or respect the regular *kázi*, they are allowed to bury their dead in the regular burial ground. They send their boys to Government schools to learn Maráthi and teach them Gujaráti at home. None teach their boys English and they follow no calling but trade. They are pushing and prosperous.

Gáokasábs.

Gá'okasá'bs, or BEEF-BUTCHERS, immigrants from Maisur, are found in small numbers in the Belgaum cantonment. They are said to have come with General Wellesley's army in 1803. They are believed to be descendants of Abyssinian slaves. They are either tall or of middle height, well-made, strong, and dark. Their home speech is Hindustáni. The men shave the head, wear the beard full, and dress in a headscarf, a shirt, a waistcoat, and a pair of tight trousers. The women, who have the same cast of face as the men, dress in a Hindu robe and bodice, appear unveiled in public, and help the men in selling the smaller parts of beef. Both men and women are dirty and untidy in their habits. They generally kill cows and have fixed shops, selling the beef to Christians and Musalmáns, and to Mhárs, Bhangis, and other low-class Hindus. They are hardworking, but much given to intoxicating drinks, and are said to be hot-tempered and quarrelsome. A few of them are rich, but the bulk are in debt. They form a separate community, and marry only among themselves. They have a well-managed union with a headman or *chaudhari*, who, with the consent of the majority of the men, has power to fine any one who breaks caste rules. Their manners and customs do not differ from those of ordinary Musalmáns and like them they obey and respect the regular *kázi*. In religion they are Sunnis of the Hanafi school, but they are not religious or careful to say their prayers. Being themselves illiterate, they do not send their boys to school. They take to no new pursuits.

---

to be with them is good. This is thy bounty. Oh God, have mercy on his body that stays in the earth and show him thy kindness that he may be freed from pain and that the place of his refuge may be good. By your favourite angels, by the serene angels, by your messengers, the Prophets, the best of the created, and by the chosen Prophet the choice Amin, Muhammad the best of those who have walked on earth and whom heaven has overshadowed, and by his successor Ali, the son of Abi Tálib, the father of the noble Imáms and the bearer of heavy burdens from off the shoulder of your Prophet, and by our Lady Fatima-tuz Záhera, and by the Imáms her offspring Hasan and Hussain, descendants of your Prophet and by Ali son of Hussain and by Muhammad son of Ali, and Jáfer son of Muhammad, and Ismail son of Jáfer, and Muhammad son of Ismail, and Abdulah-al-Mastur, and Ahmad-al-Mastur, and Hussain-al-Mastur, and our Lord Mahadi, and our Lord Káim, and our Lord Mansur, and our Lord Moiz, and our Lord Aziz, and our Lord Hakim, and our Lord Zahir, and our Lord Mustansir, and our Lord Mustali, and our Lord Amir, and our Lord the Imám-ul-Tyab Abul Kasim Aminal-Mominain, and by their deputies and their representatives and by the apostles and by the Kaimal Akharilzamán, and his representatives and by the religious Imáms of his time, may the blessings of God be upon them, and by the apostle *dái* (a) for the time being our Syed and Lord, and our Syed (a) the deputy of his Lordship, and our Syed (a) the neighbour of his Lordship, and (a) the ministers of law who are learned and just, God is the best representative and the best defender. There is no power nor virtue but in God.

(a) The name of the present holder is entered.

Chapter III.

Population.

Musalmáns.

Kákars.

Ka'kars, originally of the Kakarzahi tribe of Afgháns, are found in considerable numbers in the Belgaum cantonment. According to their story, about the middle of the eighteenth century they came to India as mercenaries of Ahmad Sháh Abdáli, and in 1758 on the defeat of the Abdáli governor of Sirhind by Raghunáth Rao, the Kákars wandered in bands through Málwa, the North-West Provinces, and Gujarát, leading the life of outlaws. At last, hearing of the rise of Haidar Ali's power in Maisur, they joined him and remained in his service in the mounted battery till the fall of Tipu in 1799. Some of them state that their forefathers came into Belgaum with Haidar Ali, and others that they came with General Wellesley about 1803. Among themselves they speak a peculiar dialect, a mixture of rough Hindustáni, Brij, Málvi, and Maráthi. With others they speak Deccan Hindustáni. The men are tall, strong, and well-made, and dark or olive skinned. The men either shave the head or let the hair grow, wear the beard full and long, and dress in a headscarf or a white Marátha turban, a shirt, a tight-fitting jacket, and a pair of tight trousers or a waistcloth. Like the men, the women are tall, thin, regular-featured, and dark, and wear the Hindu robe and bodice. They appear in public and by their earnings add to the family income. Both men and women, though hardworking, are dirty and untidy, and being very fond of drink are not well-to-do. The men are servants, messengers, and pony-keepers, and the women sell poultry and head-loads of fuel. The men make 12*s.* to £1 (Rs. 6 - 10), and the women 8*s.* to 10*s.* (Rs. 4 - 5) a month. They form a separate body marrying only among themselves. They are a well-organized community with a headman styled *jamádár* chosen from among their oldest and richest members. The present *jamádár* at Belgaum is learned in Persian, Maráthi, and Urdu, and is highly respected not only by the Kákars of Belgaum, but also by those of Dhárwár, Hubli, and Kaládgi. With the consent of the majority of the castemen the *jamádár* has power to fine any one who breaks caste rules. Their manners and customs differ little from those of ordinary Musalmáns, and they respect and obey the regular *kázi*, employing him in their marriage and funeral ceremonies. They are Sunnis of the Hanafi school and some of them are religious and careful to attend prayers at the mosque. They have begun to teach their children Maráthi and Urdu. None of them teach their children English nor has any of them risen to a high position.

Labbeys.

Labbeys, who are traders in skins and leather, are temporary immigrants from the Madras Presidency. They are the descendants of the Arabs and Persians who in the seventh century fled from the tyranny of Hajjaj-ibn-Yusuf, the governor of Irák, and of the Arab and Persian merchants in whose hands the foreign trade of West India remained until the establishment of the Portuguese ascendancy in the beginning of the sixteenth century. Their home speech is Arvi or Malabári and with others Hindustáni. Their thin oval faces, small and dark eyes, high cheek-bones, and pale skins prove a strain of foreign blood. The men are tall or of middle height, well-made, and strong. They shave the head, wear the beard full, and dress in a white skull-cap around which on going out a kerkchief of striped cotton is wound, a long shirt falling to the knees, and a red or black

Chapter III. Population. MUSALMÁNS. *Labbeys.*

striped waistcloth not drawn back between the feet like the Maráthi waistcloth. They are neat and clean in their habits. As they stay in Belgaum for only a few months they do not bring their women with them. They are hardworking, thrifty, mild, honest, and sober, and for the most part are well-to-do, and have good credit as traders. They are of great help to the local butchers to whom they advance £10 to £100 (Rs. 100 - 1000) to keep them from passing into the hands of rival hide-merchants. They buy skins from the butchers at 8*s*. to 12*s*. (Rs. 4 - 6) a dozen and send them in salt to Madras or Bombay where they have tanneries. In religion they are Sunnis of the Sháfai or Arab school. They are said to be strictly religious, and careful to say their prayers and to keep the rules of their faith. They are on the whole a rising class.

Mehmans.

Mehmans, properly MOMINS or BELIEVERS and chiefly converts of the Cutch Vánia and Lohána castes, are believed to have come from Cutch and Káthiáwár about sixty years ago. Among themselves they speak Cutchi and Hindustáni with others. They number about forty houses and nearly a hundred souls, all of whom are settled in Belgaum. The men are tall, well-made, and strong, and of a brownish colour. They shave the head, wear the beard full, and dress in an embroidered or silk headscarf, a long coat, a shirt, a waistcoat, and a pair of loose trousers. The women are either tall or of middle height, rather inclined to stoutness, with large and black or grey eyes, straight nose, and fair skin. They wear a long shirt or *aba* falling to the knee, a headscarf or *odna,* and a pair of loose trousers rather tight at the ankles. Except the old women who sometimes sit in the shops, they do not appear in public or add to the family income. Both men and women are neat and clean in their habits. Some of the richer Mehmans contract to supply the commissariat with fuel and provisions, others deal in piece-goods, and others in hardware and miscellaneous European articles such as matches, candles, glass buttons, mirrors, threads, pins, and furniture. They are hardworking, thrifty, sober, and well-to-do. They are able to save and to spend on special occasions. They marry among themselves or take wives from Bombay Mehmans. They form a separate community but have no special class organization and no headman to settle their social disputes, except the regular *kázi* who presides over the meetings of the adult male members, and, with the consent of the majority, fines any one who breaks caste rules. Their manners and customs do not differ from those of ordinary Musalmáns. They are Sunnis of the Hanafi school, and are religious or careful to say their prayers. They send their boys to school to learn Maráthi and Urdu, but none learn English. None of them have taken to any calling except trade. On the whole they are a rising class.

Mukeris.

Mukeris, that is DENIERS, local converts probably of the Lamán or Banjári castes, are found in small numbers in Belgaum. They are said to have come from Maisur as settlers with General Wellesley's army in 1803. They speak Hindustáni among themselves and Maráthi with others. The men are tall or of middle size, and dark or olive skinned. They either wear the hair or shave the head,

Chapter III.
Population.
MUSALMÁNS.
Mukeris.

have full beards, and dress in a Hindu-like turban or a headscarf, a shirt, a waistcoat, and a pair of tight trousers or a waistcloth. The women, who are like the men in face, wear the Hindu robe and bodice, appear in public, but add nothing to the family income, and have no very high character for modesty. Both men and women are neat and clean in their habits. Mukeris are grain-sellers and grocers. They are hardworking, thrifty, and sober, but have no character for honesty. Most of them are well-to-do and able to save. They form a separate community, marrying among themselves only. They settle social disputes at meetings of the men of the class under a headman or *chaudhari* chosen from among the richest and most respected families, who, in accordance with the wish of the majority of the members, has power to fine any one who breaks caste rules. They are Sunnis of the Hanafi school, but are seldom religious or careful to say their prayers. They obey and respect the *kázi* and employ him to conduct their marriages and funerals. They teach their children Maráthi and Urdu, but none learn English and none have risen to any high position.

Ghair Máhdis.

Ghair Máhdis, or ANTI-MÁHDIS, believe that the looked for Máhdi, the last of the Imáms, has come. Their Máhdi was a certain Muhammad Máhdi who was born in A.D. 1443 (H. 847) in Jaunpur, a village near Benares, and who at the age of forty began to act as a saint or *vali*. He drew around him a large body of followers at Jaunpur, and afterwards at Mecca. He returned to India in 1497 and in 1499 at Pátan in Gujarát openly laid claim to be the looked for Máhdi. His public career was marked by the working of miracles; he raised the dead, gave sight to the blind, and speech to the dumb. He travelled much, accompanied by two companions Syed Khondmir and Syed Muhammad. In Farrah, a city of Khorásan, in the year 1504 (H. 910) Muhammad Máhdi died of fever, maintaining to the last that he was the promised Máhdi. His grandson Muhammad, after being persecuted in the North-West Provinces and at Ujjain, was well received by Burhán Nizám Shah of Ahmadnagar (1590), who not only allowed him to remain in his dominions and to spread his faith, but gave his daughter in marriage to the Máhdi's son. With the help of Burhán's patronage the Ghair Máhdis met with considerable success and gained a large body of converts. They continued a powerful community till towards the end of the seventeenth century they were repressed by Aurangzeb. Though they are now free to profess their opinions, the Ghair Máhdis still practise concealment or *takiyah*, and always endeavour to pass as orthodox Muslims. There are very few in Belgaum. Their head-quarters are at Ahmadnagar and Haidarabad where they form a large circle or *diaras* and live apart from other Musalmáns. They speak Hindustáni, but have nothing special in their appearance or dress. They are clean, neat, and hardworking, and as a class are fairly off. Some of them are servants and messengers, and others are husbandmen. They marry among themselves only, but do not form a separate community and have no special organization. They do not respect and obey the *kázi* except that they employ him to register their marriages. They keep the sacrifice, circumcision, and initiation ceremonies and their marriage and death rites do not differ from those practised by ordinary Musalmáns. In religion they profess to be Sunnis, and hold that their saint was the last Imám and expected Máhdi. As he is come they neither repent for their sins nor pray for the souls of the dead. They teach their children Urdu and Maráthi but no English. None have risen to any high position.

Bágbans.

Bá'gbans, or GARDENERS, local converts of the Kunbi caste, are found over almost the whole district. They are said to have been converted by Aurangzeb about 1687. Among themselves they speak Hindustáni, and Maráthi with others. The men are tall or of middle size and dark. They shave the head and either shave or wear the beard. They dress in white turbans, a tight-fitting jacket, and a waistcloth. The women are either tall or middle-sized, thin, well-featured, and brown. They dress in the Hindu robe and bodice, appear in public, and help the men in selling vegetables and fruit. Both men and women are dirty and untidy in their dress. They are hardworking, orderly and sober, and are fairly off making their living by selling fruit and vegetables. The fruit they sell is partly of local growth and partly brought from other districts. Of local fruit the chief varieties are plantains, guavas, oranges, watermelons, pomegranates, and sugarcane. Of outside fruit they sell grapes, sometimes brought from Poona, Goa mangoes, and Poona pummeloes and pomegranates. Of vegetables they sell Poona and Mahábaleshvar potatoes, cabbages, carrots, and turnips. Some have fixed shops and others attend weekly markets and fairs. When the men are away the women sit in the shop and sell. They marry among themselves only and form a separate community with a well-organized union, settling their social disputes at meetings under a *chaudhari* or headman who is chosen from the richest and oldest members of the community. With the consent of the majority of the men the headman has power to fine any one who breaks caste rules. They have a strong Hindu feeling against the use of beef. They differ from the regular Musalmáns in observing Hindu festivals, offering vows to Hindu gods, and in failing to perform the *akika* or sacrifice and the *bismilla* or initiation ceremonies. Their one Musalmán rite is that they circumcise their sons. In religion they are Sunnis of the Hanafi school, but they are not religious or careful to say their prayers. They respect and obey the *kázi*, and employ him to conduct their marriage and death ceremonies. They are illiterate themselves, and do not send their boys to school. None have risen to any high position.

Támbolis.

Tá'mbolis, or BETEL-SELLERS, local converts of the Kunbi caste of that name, are found in considerable numbers throughout the district. They are said to have been converted by Aurangzeb. Among themselves they speak Hindustáni and with others they speak Maráthi. The men are tall or of middle size and of olive colour. They shave the head, wear the beard full, and dress in a Hindu-like turban, a tight-fitting jacket, and a waistcloth or a pair of tight trousers. The women are generally tall, thin, and fair, with regular features. They wear the Hindu robe and bodice, appear in public, and help the men in selling betel. Both men and women are clean and neat in their habits. They buy betel leaf from the

Támbolis.

village Kunbis or bring it from other districts, and sell it at 1½d. (1 *anna*) the hundred leaves. They also buy Konkan and Mangalor betelnuts from Hindu merchants who get them through their Bombay agents. They retail tobacco and snuff, buying the stock from wholesale dealers. They are hardworking, thrifty, and sober, and fairly off, earning £10 to £20 (Rs. 100 - 200) a year. They have fixed shops, and some of them keep bullocks to bring loads of betel leaf from outlying villages. In the absence of the men, the women look after the shop. They marry among themselves only and form a separate community with a well-managed union settling social disputes by mass meetings under a *chaudhari* or headman chosen from the richest and most respected families. With the consent of the majority, the headman has power to fine any one who breaks caste rules. Their manners and customs do not differ from those of ordinary Musalmáns. They are Sunnis of the Hanafi school, but they are not religious or careful to say their prayers. They obey and respect the *kázi*, and teach their children a little Maráthi but no English. Their calling is prosperous and gainful and they never take to other pursuits.

Kanjars.

Kanjars, or FOWLERS, local converts from the Hindu tribe of the same name, are found in small numbers in Belgaum. They are said to have been converted by Tipu Sultán (1783 - 1799). Among themselves they speak a dialect of their own, which is a mixture of rough Hindustáni and Maráthi. With others they speak Maráthi. The men are tall or of middle height, thin, and dark. They shave the head, wear the beard full, and dress in a Hindu turban, a waistcoat, and a waistcloth. The women are generally short, thin, dark, and ill-featured. They wear the Hindu robe and bodice, appear in public, and add to the family income by selling poultry, eggs, and headloads of fuel, and by making hemp ropes. Both men and women are poorly clad and dirty in their habits. Kanjars are hardworking but neither honest, sober, nor well-to-do. All live from hand to mouth, some in fair comfort, others much scrimped for food. The men are servants and labourers earning 10*s.* to 14*s.* (Rs. 5 - 7) a month, and the women make 3*d.* to 6*d.* (2 - 4 *as.*) a day. Most of their earnings are spent on liquor. They form a separate community marrying among themselves only. They have a well-organized body with a headman or *mukâdam*, under whom social disputes are settled according to the opinion of the majority of the castemen. Breaches of caste rules are punished by fine. They differ from ordinary Musalmáns in worshipping and offering vows to Hindu gods. They circumcise their sons but do not keep the sacrifice or the initiation ceremonies, and, except employing him to register their marriages, they do not respect or obey the regular *kázi*. In religion they are Musalmáns in little more than name, many of them passing their whole lives without entering a mosque. They do not send their children to school, and none of them has risen to any high position.

Pendháris.

Pendha'ris, found in small numbers in Belgaum, are converts of mixed Hindu origin, partly local and partly North Indian. In the early part of the century, till in 1817, 1818, and 1819 they were suppressed by the British, the Pendháris were the scourge of the greater part of

Chapter III.
Population.
MUSALMÁNS.
Pendháris.

India. Their home tongue is a mixture of rough Hindustáni, Málvi, and Maráthi; with others they speak Maráthi and Hindustáni. The men are tall or of middle size, well-made, and of a dark or olive colour. They shave the head, wear the beard full, and dress in a Hindu-like turban or a headscarf, a tight-fitting jacket, and a pair of tight trousers or a waistcloth. The women, who are like the men, are tall or of middle size, dark, and generally rough-featured, and dress in the Hindu robe and bodice. They appear in public and add to the family income chiefly by selling fuel. Both men and women are poorly clad and dirty in their habits. The men keep ponies for hire or work as labourers or servants, and the women sell grass, fuel, and eggs. They are hardworking, but neither sober, honest, nor well-to-do. They marry among themselves only, and form a separate community with a headman styled *jamádár*, and have a good organization for punishing social offences. Till lately they were half-Hindus, openly worshipping Hindu gods, eschewing beef, and, except that they circumcised their boys, keeping none of the specially Musálman ceremonies. Of late they seem of their own accord to have taken a dislike to the worship of Hindu gods, and now rank among ordinary Musalmáns with whom they eat and drink. Their women still keep most Hindu customs, and most of the men abstain from the use of beef. They respect and obey the regular *kázi* and employ him to conduct their marriage and funeral ceremonies. In religion they are Sunnis of the Hanafi school, and a few of them are religious and careful to say their prayers. Of late some have begun to teach their children Maráthi and Urdu. On the whole they are a falling class.

Bojgars.

Bojgars, or MILLET-BEER BREWERS, apparently local converts of mixed Hindu origin, are found in small numbers in Belgaum and in some other large towns. They are said to have been converted by Aurangzeb. They speak Hindustáni among themselves and Maráthi with others. The men are middle-sized and lean, with small eyes, outstanding cheekbones, and dark skins. Some men shave the head and others wear the hair; all grow the beard which is generally long and full. They dress in a white Marátha-like twisted turban, a waistcoat, and a waistcloth. The women, who are like the men in face, wear the Hindu robe and bodice, appear in public, and add nothing to the family income. Both men and women are poorly clad and dirty in their habits. They make beer by boiling Indian millet with a herb called *gulbel*, hemp-seed or *bháng*, and *kuchhla* Strychnos nuxvomica. They sell the beer which is largely drunk by servants and labourers at 1*d.* (⅔ *anna*) a bottle and earn 2*s.* to 4*s.* (Rs. 1-2) a day. Being thriftless, lazy, and fond of drink, they spend almost their whole income on liquor and sweetmeats. Though they form a separate community and marry only among themselves they have no special headman and no special social organization. They obey the regular *kázi* and employ him in settling social disputes, and differ little in customs from the regular Musalmáns. They are Sunnis of the Hanafi school, but are neither religious nor careful to say their prayers. Being themselves illiterate they do not give their boys any schooling. On the whole they are a falling class.

Chapter III.
Population.
MUSALMÁNS.
Gaundis.

Gaundis, or BRICKLAYERS, local converts of the Hindu class of the same name, are found in small numbers in Belgaum and other large towns. They are said to have been converted by Aurangzeb. Their home tongue is Hindustáni, but with others they speak Maráthi. The men are tall or of middle size, well-made, strong, and dark. They shave the head, wear the beard full, and dress in a large loosely wound Hindu-like turban, waistcoat, and waistcloth. The women, who are either tall or of middle height, are thin, well-featured, and olive-skinned. They wear the Hindu robe and bodice, and appear in public, but add nothing to the family income. Both men and women are neat and clean in their habits. They are hardworking and thrifty, but, partly because they get no help from their wives, and partly from what they lost during and after the 1877 famine, they are not well-to-do. They are bricklayers by craft, and earn 1*s.* to 2*s.* (8 *as.*-Re. 1) a day. But work is not constant, and a large number have moved to Kolhápur, where many public buildings have lately been made. Though they marry among themselves only and form a separate community, they have no special social organization and no headman to settle their disputes, except the *kázi* who among them holds the position of judge as well as of marriage-registrar. They differ from ordinary Musalmáns in eschewing beef, offering vows to Hindu gods, and keeping Hindu festivals. They circumcise their boys, but do not keep either the initiation or the sacrifice ceremonies. In religion they are Sunnis of the Hanafi school, bnt they are seldom religious or careful to say their prayers. They do not send their boys to school, or take to new pursuits.

Jhárakers.

Jharakers, or DUST-WASHERS, converted by Aurangzeb from the Hindu caste of Dhuldhoyas, are found in small numbers in some of the larger towns. Among themselves they speak Hindustáni, and with others Maráthi. The men are of middle size, thin, and dark. They shave the head, wear the beard short or full, and dress in a Hindu-like turban or a headscarf, a shirt, a waistcoat, and a pair of tight trousers or a waistcloth. The women, who like the men are short and thin, are well-featured and olive-skinned. They wear the Hindu robe and bodice, and appear in public, but add nothing to the family income. Both men and women are neat and clean in their habits. Dust-washers buy and sift the sweepings of goldsmith's workshops, paying 2*s.* to 4*s.* (Rs. 1-2) a month. They find small particles of gold and silver, and if lucky sometimes make about £1 (Rs. 10) a month. Though hardworking, thrifty, and sober, they are not well-to-do, but live from hand to mouth, and have to borrow to meet their special charges. They form a separate community, marrying among themselves only, but have no special social organization nor any headman except the *kázi* who settles their social disputes and registers their marriages. They differ from ordinary Musalmáns in eschewing beef, offering vows to Hindu gods, and keeping Hindu festivals. They circumcise their boys, but keep neither the initiation nor the sacrifice ceremony. In religion they are Sunnis of the Hanafi school, but are not religious or careful to say their prayers.

Chapter III.
Population.
MUSALMÁNS.
Kasábs.

Some of them teach their boys Maráthi, but none English. None of them has risen to any high position.

Kasa'bs, or BUTCHERS, also called **Sulta'nis** because they were converted by Tipu Sultán, are local converts from the Lád Khátik caste of Hindus. They are found in considerable numbers all over the district. Among themselves they speak Hindustáni, and with others Maráthi. The men are tall or of middle size, and dark or olive-skinned. They shave the head, either shave or wear the beard, and dress in a Hindu-like turban, a tight-fitting jacket, and a waistcloth, and if they can afford it put a large gold earring in the right ear. The women, who are either tall or of middle height, delicate, with good features, and brown, wear the Hindu robe and bodice, appear in public, and help the men in selling mutton. Both men and women are clean in their habits. Mutton butchers buy sheep and goats from Dhangars or shepherds, according to their wants, kill them, and sell to Christians, Muhammadans, Pársis, and some Hindus. They buy sheep at 4*s.* to 8*s.* (Rs. 2-4) each and from each sheep get thirty to forty pounds of mutton which they sell at 3*d.* to 4½*d.* (2-3 *as.*) a pound. They have fixed shops and earn £30 to £40 (Rs. 300-400) a year. They are hard-working, thrifty, and sober, generally well-to-do, and able to save. They form a separate community and marry among themselves only. They are a well organized body under a headman or *pátil* chosen from the richest families, and under penalty of a fine, force members to respect the wishes of the majority. They have a very strong Hindu feeling, neither eating nor drinking with other Musalmáns, and shunning beef butchers, whose touch they hold impure. Except that they circumcise their sons, and employ the *kázi* to register their marriages, they are Musalmáns in little more than in name, worshipping the Hindu gods Khandoba, Mhasoba, and Yellamma, and keeping Hindu festivals. They do not send their children to school nor take to other pursuits.

Momins.

Momins, properly BELIEVERS, are local converts of the Koshti or Sáli castes of Hindu cotton handloom weavers. They are found in considerable numbers in Belgaum and other towns and large villages. They are said to have been converted by Syed Makdum Gaisudaráz also called Banda Nawaz of Gulbarga in 1418 (H. 820). Among themselves they speak Hindustáni, and with others Maráthi. The men are tall or of middle size, and dark or olive-skinned. They shave the head, wear the beard full or short, and dress in a white Marátha turban, a shirt, a waistcoat, and a waistcloth or a pair of tight trousers. The women, who like the men are either tall or middle sized, are thin, well-featured, and wheat-coloured. They wear the Hindu robe and bodice, appear in public, and add to the family earnings by weaving. A Momin woman earns by her weaving as much as a man, and for this reason some weavers have two or even three wives. Both men and women are rather dirty and untidy. They are hardworking and thrifty, but they are not sober and as a class few are rich or well-to-do. The bulk live from hand to mouth, and have to borrow to meet special charges. They suffered severely in the 1877 famine and are always depressed by the

Chapter III.
Population.
MUSALMÁNS.
Momins.

competition of English and Bombay mill-made cloth. The rich and well-to-do employ the poor either from their own funds or from advances made by shopkeepers and exporters. The poorer weavers work about twelve hours a day and in return do not earn more than 6*d.* (4 *as.*). As they are so ill-paid they do not take holidays except on special and unavoidable occasions. The chief products of their looms are bordered robes or *sádis* eight yards long and a yard and aquarter broad. These, if of cotton, sell at 3*s.* to 10*s.* (Rs. 1½-5) each; if half-silk half-cotton or if silk-bordered they fetch £1 to £2 (Rs. 10-20); turbans of coarse cotton are worth 2*s.* to 6*s.* (Rs. 1-3), and of fine cotton and with silver or gold embroidered borders £1 to £3 (Rs. 10-30); bodice-cloths three quarters of a yard square called *khans*, if of cotton, are worth 6*d.* to 1*s.* (4-8 *as.*), and if half-silk half-cotton with silk borders are worth 2*s.* to 4*s.* (Rs. 1-2); waistcloths or *dhotars* two and a half yards long and a yard and a quarter broad, are worth 1*s.* to 2*s.* (8 *as.*-Re. 1), and if of fine cotton and with silk borders 4*s.* to 10*s.* (Rs. 2-5). They also make striped cotton chintz or *susi* which fetches 6*d.* to 1*s.* (4-8 *as.*) a yard. They, for the most part, use English and Bombay mill yarn which they buy from Hindu wholesale dealers who draw their supplies from Bombay by Vengurla. The middle class weavers, who work for themselves with small capital, take their goods daily to the shopkeepers, or hawk them about the villages, and attend weekly markets; the poor, who cannot afford to buy yarn and a loom and other appliances, live by working at the houses of the rich. They form a separate community, marry among themselves only, and have a well organized union with a headman of their own chosen from the richest and most respected families, who, with the consent of a majority of the men, has power to fine any one breaking caste rules. Their customs do not differ from those of ordinary Musalmáns and they respect and obey the regular *kázi* employing him to register their marriages. In religion they are Sunnis of the Hanafi school, and most of the old men are said to be religious and careful to say their prayers. Few of them give their boys any schooling and none of them take to other pursuits.

Patvágars.

Patva'gars, or SILK-TASSEL-MAKERS, local converts of the Hindu class of the same name, are found in small numbers in Belgaum and other large towns. They are said to have embraced Islám during the reign of Aurangzeb. Among themselves they speak Hindustáni and with others Maráthi. The men are tall and muscular, and dark or olive coloured. They shave the head, wear the beard full or short, and dress in a Hindu-like turban, a tight-fitting jacket, and a waistcloth. The women are either tall or of middle size, and fair with good features. They dress in the Hindu robe and bodice, and appear in public, but add nothing to the family income. Both men and women are neat and clean in their habits. They are hardworking, thrifty, and sober, earning 6*d.* to 1*s.* (4-8 *as.*) a day as day-weavers, and fairly off, but not rich. They work in silk buying from Hindu silk-merchants and preparing the waistband or *kardotas* of silk threads with silk tassels worn round the waist by Hindus and Musalmáns which they sell at 1*d.* to 1½*d.* (⅔-1 *anna*);

Chapter III.
Population.
MUSALMÁNS.
Patvágars.

they deck golden beads and pearl necklaces and other ornaments with silk, getting 1½*d.* to 3*d.* (1-2 *as.*) for each ornament; and they sell horse-tail fly-flappers and false hair for women worth 6*d.* to 1*s.* (4-8 *as.*) each. Some have fixed shops; others go from village to village and attend weekly markets in search of work. Their work is not constant, but most of them earn about 6*d.* (4 *as.*) a day. They marry among themselves only and form a well-organized community, who, under a headman, meet and settle social disputes. The headman or *chaudhari*, who is chosen from the oldest and richest families, if the majority agree, has power to fine any one who breaks caste rules. Their manners and customs do not differ from those of ordinary Musalmáns. They respect and obey the regular *kázi* and employ him to conduct their marriage and funeral ceremonies. Some of them teach their children Maráthi, but none of them teach them English, nor has any of them risen to any high position.

Pinjárás.

Pinja'ra's, or COTTON-CLEANERS, local converts of the Hindu class of the same name, are found in small numbers in Belgaum and in other large towns. They are said to have been converted by Aurangzeb. Their home tongue is Hindustáni but with others they speak Maráthi. The men are of middle size, thin, and dark. They shave the head, wear the beard full, and dress in a coarse white Hindu-like turban and a waistcloth. Some of them on going out wear a tight-fitting jacket. The women who have the same cast of face as the men, wear the Hindu robe and bodice, appear in public, and help the men in cotton-cleaning. Both men and women are dirty and poorly clad. They clean old or new cotton for filling beds and pillows. They walk about the streets twanging the string of their cotton-teaser and travel from village to village in search of work. They also buy cotton from village shopkeepers, clean it, and make it into small rolls called *hanjis*, which they sell to weavers at 5*d.* (3½ *as.*) the pound. In cleaning cotton for beds and pillows they charge about 5*d.* (3½ *as.*) the *man* of forty pounds. Their work though constant is poorly paid. They are hardworking, thrifty, and sober, but seldom well-to-do, living from hand to mouth and borrowing to meet special charges. They marry among themselves only and form a separate community with a headman or *chaudhari*, who settles social disputes, and, with the consent of the majority of the castemen, has power to fine any one who breaks the caste rules. Except that they circumcise their sons and employ the *kázi* to register their marriages, they keep no Musalmán customs. In religion they are Sunnis of the Hanafi school; but they are neither religious nor careful to say their prayers. They give their children no schooling and take to no new pursuits. On the whole they are a falling class.

Sikalgars.

Sikalgars, or ARMOURERS, local converts perhaps from the Hindu caste of Ghisádis, are found in small numbers in Belgaum and other large towns. They are said to have been converted by Aurangzeb. Among themselves they speak Hindustáni and with others Maráthi. The men are tall or of middle height, thin, and dark. They either let the hair grow or shave half of the head, wear the beard full, and dress in dirty untidy Hindu turbans, waist-coats, and waistcloths. The women, who are like the men in face and little less dirty or untidy, wear the Hindu robe and bodice. They appear in public and help the men in their work. They grind and sharpen knives and swords, and are hardworking, but neither sober nor well-to-do. They grind the knives on a stone wheel which their women or children turn with the help of a leather strap. They work for blacksmiths and other people and are paid ½*d.* to 1½*d.* (¼-1 *anna*) for sharpening a knife or a razor; their monthly earnings are not more than 16*s.* (Rs. 8). They marry among themselves only and form a separate community, settling social disputes at meetings of the castemen. They have a headman called *mukádam*, chosen from the oldest and most respected members, who has power to fine any one who breaks their caste rules. They are Musalmáns in little more than in name, almost never going to the mosque, keeping Hindu gods in their houses, eschewing beef, and except circumcision observing no special Musalmán rites. They employ the *kázi* to register their marriages but do not pay him much respect. They do not send their boys to school nor take to new pursuits.

Bhatyáras.

Bhatya'ras, or COOKS, probably local converts of mixed Hindu origin, are found in small numbers in Belgaum. They are said to have been converted by Aurangzeb. Among themselves they speak Hindustáni, and with others Maráthi. They are of middle size, thin, and dark or olive-skinned. The men shave the head, wear the beard full, and dress in a dirty untidy Hindu turban, a waistcoat, and a waistcloth. The women, who are like the men in face, wear the Hindu robe and bodice, and are neither tidy nor clean. They appear in public and help the men in their work. They have shops at which cooked meat, pulse, vegetables, and bread are offered day and night. They are also employed by Musalmáns to cook marriage and other great dinners, and are paid 2*s.* to 4*s.* (Rs. 1-2) a day. Their work as public cooks or lodging-house keepers is not constant. They seldom have lodgers, except travellers and poor labouring or depressed Hindus like Mhárs and Bhangis. A few of them serve as private cooks and messengers. Though hardworking they are much given to drink, and are seldom well-to-do. They form a separate community, marrying among themselves only. They have no special social organization and no headman, except the *kázi* who settles their social disputes and registers their marriages. Their manners and customs do not differ from those of ordinary Musalmáns. They are Sunnis of the Hanafi school, but are neither religious nor careful to say their prayers. They do not send their boys to school, and on the whole are a falling class.

Dhobis.

Dhobis, or WASHERMEN, local converts from the Hindu caste of the same name, are found in small numbers all over the district. They are said to have been converted by Haidar Ali of Maisur (1761-1782). Among themselves they speak Hindustáni and Maráthi with others. The men are of middle size, thin, and dark. They shave the head and face, or wear the beard short, and dress in a Hindu turban, a tight-fitting jacket, and a waistcloth. The women, who have the same cast of face as the men, wear the Hindu robe and bodice, appear in public, and by their earnings add to the family income. Both men and women are neat and clean, and as a

Chapter III.
Population.
MUSALMÁNS.
Dhobis.

rule well dressed as they generally wear their employers' clothes. They are employed by Europeans and natives. They are paid 12*s.* to £1 10*s.* (Rs. 6-15) a month by Europeans, and 2*s.* to 8*s.* (Rs. 1-4) a month by natives, as a washerman generally works for only one family of Europeans and for several families of natives. They also wash at the rate of 8*s.* (Rs. 4) for a hundred garments if ironed, and 4*s.* (Rs. 2) if unironed. From their native employers, besides their wages, they receive presents in money or in grain on festive and other ceremonial occasions. Though hardworking they never save and spend all they can spare on liquor. They have generally to borrow to meet their special charges and have a specially good name for the care with which they pay their debts, even at excessive rates of interest. They marry among themselves only, and form a separate community with a well-organized council under a chosen headman or *chaudhari*, who, with the consent of the majority of the castemen, has power to fine any one who breaks caste rules or to put out of caste any one who refuses to pay the fine. A person put out of caste is allowed back on paying a double fine. All fines are kept by the headman, and, when they amount to a large enough sum, are spent on liquor and dinner parties. They differ from ordinary Musalmáns in eschewing beef, worshipping Hindu gods, and keeping Hindu festivals. Except that they circumcise their boys, they do not keep any special Musalmán customs. In religion they are Sunnis of the Hanafi school; but they follow Islám in little more than in name, never attending the mosque and seldom fasting during the month of Ramzán. They do not send their boys to school, and none have risen to any high position.

Halálkhors.

Halálkhors, that is those who earn their bread lawfully, also called Shaikhdas or little Shaikhs, and commonly known as Bhangis, are found in small numbers in the town of Belgaum. They are converts from the Hindu caste of Bhangis and are said to have been converted by Haidar Ali of Maisur. Among themselves they speak Hindustáni and with others Maráthi. They are of middle size, thin, and dark, the men either shaving the head or letting the hair grow, wearing the beard full, and dressing in a Hindu-like turban, a waistcoat, and a pair of tight trousers or a waistcloth. They are fond of wearing a large gold ring in the right ear. Their women, who are like the men in face, wear the Hindu robe and bodice, appear in public, and add to the family income. Both men and women are dirty and untidy. The men are either employed in the Belgaum and other municipalities as scavengers and by European and some native families; and the women are generally employed by Europeans as sweepers. The men earn 10*s.* to 12*s.* (Rs. 5-6), and the women 6*s.* to 8*s.* (Rs. 3-4) a month. Though hardworking, both men and women are very fond of liquor and spend almost the whole of their earnings in drink. They are poorly clad and badly off. They marry among themselves only, and form a separate and well-organized community, settling social disputes at caste meetings under a headman called *mehtar* or *patel*, who, with the consent of the majority, has power to fine any one who breaks caste rules. The amount levied in fines is spent by the caste on liquor. They are Musalmáns in name only, and are not allowed to enter the mosques nor to have any connection with other Musalmáns. They know little of their religion and believe in Hindu gods, many of them worshipping the goddess Marimáta. Except that they circumcise their boys, they keep no Musalmán ceremonies; and do not respect the *kázi*. They do not send their children to school or take to new pursuits.

Pakhális.

Pakhalis, or WATER-MEN, local converts of the Hindu class of the same name, are found in small numbers in Belgaum. They are said to have been converted by Tipu Sultán. Among themselves they speak Hindustáni and Maráthi with others. The men are of middle height, thin, and dark. They shave the head, wear the beard short or full, and dress in a Hindu-like turban, a tight-fitting jacket, and a waistcloth. If their means allow they are fond of wearing a large gold earring in the right ear and a silver wristlet on each wrist. The women, who like the men are of middle size, are delicate, with good features and wheat-coloured skins. They wear the Hindu robe and bodice, and appear in public, but except the old do not add to the family income by helping the men in their work. Both men and women are neat and clean in their habits. They carry water in leather bags on bullock back or on their own backs and supply both Christians and Musalmáns. A bag or *pakhál* holds about thirty gallons of water. They are paid 12*s.* to £1 (Rs. 6-10) a month by a European family, and 4*s.* to 8*s.* (Rs. 2-4) by a Pársi, and 1*s.* to 2*s.* (8 *as.*-Re. 1) by a Musalmán as they generally work for a single European family or for several native families. In selling water retail they charge about 6*d.* (4 *as.*) a bag. They are hard-working, but excessively fond of liquor on which they spend most of their earnings. They are fairly off and some of them are able to save. They marry among themselves only, and form a separate well-organized community who settle social disputes under a head or *patel* chosen from the oldest and most respected members, who, if the majority agree, has power to fine any one breaking caste rules. They eschew beef, believe in Hindu gods, and observe Hindu festivals. In religion they are Sunnis of the Hanafi school, but they are neither religious nor careful to say their prayers. They obey and respect the *kázi* and employ him in their marriage and funeral ceremonies. They do not send their children to school nor take to any other pursuits.

Darveshis.

Darveshis, literally religious beggars, seem to be local converts perhaps of the Shikári caste. They are a class of wandering bear and tiger showmen. They are said to have been converted by the saint Syed Makhdum Gaisudaráz, commonly known as Khwaja Banda Nawaz of Gulbarga, whom they regard with much veneration. Among themselves they speak Hindustáni, and with others Maráthi. They are tall or of middle size, sturdy, and dark. The men let the hair grow, have long and full beards, and wear a heavy necklace of glass beads. They dress in dirty and untidy white Hindu turbans, a shirt, a waistcoat, and a pair of tight trousers or a waistcloth. The women, who like the men are tall or middle-sized, are thin, with good features and wheat-coloured. They dress in the Hindu

Chapter III. Population. MUSALMÁNS. *Darveshis.*

robe and bodice and appear in public, but add nothing to the family income. They are not neat or clean in their habits. Darveshis rear bear and tiger cubs, and carry them from place to place asking alms. Both Hindu and Muhammadan women give them corn or money and receive some tiger's or bear's hair which they keep in a gold or silver locket, and hang round children's necks to ward off evil spirits and ghosts. They are a lazy class much given to intoxicating drinks and drugs, and are poorly clad and badly off. They marry either among themselves or with any other religious beggars, and form a separate community and settle social disputes at meetings of the men under a headman or *sargiro* who has the power of fining any one who breaks their caste rules. They are Sunnis of the Hanafi school, but are neither religious nor careful to say their prayers. Their only connection with the *kázi* is that they employ him as marriage registrar. Their manners or customs differ from those of ordinary Musalmáns. They are illiterate, and do not send their boys to school. Within the last twenty years their number has greatly decreased. Almost all of them have taken to new pursuits; some earning their living as husbandmen and others as servants and messengers.

Gárodis.

Ga'rodis, apparently called after a snake-charm of that name, or **Mada'ris,** apparently called after the holy and healing *madar* or *rui* Calotropis gigantea, a wandering tribe of jugglers, who move in bands of four or five families. They are local converts from the Hindu class of the same name. Their head-quarters are at Miraj near Kolhápur. They are said to have been converted about the middle of the sixteenth century by Mir Shamsuddin commonly known as Mira Shamna whose shrine at Miraj they hold in high respect, and are careful to visit at the yearly fair held in April or May. Their home speech is a coarse Hindustáni with a large mixture of Maráthi words. The men are middle-sized, sturdy, and dark or olive. They either shave the head or wear the hair and the beard full, and dress in a dirty and untidy carelessly wound twisted turban, a short tight-fitting jacket, and a pair of short tight trousers covering the legs as far as the knees, and fasten round the neck a large necklace of glass beads. The women, who like the men are middle-sized, are thin, well-featured, and dark or olive. They dress in a Hindu robe and bodice and appear in public, but add nothing to the family income. They are dirty and untidy. The men are jugglers, tumblers, and snake-charmers. They are hardworking, but are much given to intoxicating drinks and drugs and are poorly clad and scrimped for food. They marry among themselves, and form a separate and well-organized community, settling social disputes at meetings of the adult male members under a headman or *patel,* who has power to fine any one who breaks their caste rules. Except circumcising their boys they keep no Musalmán customs, and are Muhammadans in little more than in name. Few of them ever enter a mosque. They do not respect or obey the *kázi* except in employing him as a marriage registrar. They are illiterate, and do not send their boys to school, or take to any other pursuits. On the whole they are a falling class.

Chapter III.
Population.
MUSALMÁNS.
Kasbans.

Kasbans, or professional dancing-girls and courtezans, are local converts of mixed Hindu origin. They do not claim to belong to any of the general divisions of Musalmáns, and being a mixed class they have no special peculiarity of feature or form. Fair girls with shapely figures and good features, are adopted by some elderly dancing-girl and trained to dance and sing. Dark girls with coarse features and clumsy figures are taught no accomplishments and form a lower class of courtezans. All are careful to be neat and clean. They generally wear the Hindu robe and bodice, and a tight-fitting jacket, and at least a pair of gold earrings, a silver girdle or *pati* which they wear over the robe, and loose bell anklets known as *kadús* to whose chimes they walk with a mincing step. The most noticeable point of difference in the dress of a Musalmán courtezan and of a private woman is that the courtezan wears shoes. They have two separate communities, one known as Ramjánis or Kalávants who are also called Náikans or mistresses; the other called Takáis or Kamáus that is prostitutes. The Kalávants are high class courtezans who generally live under the protection of a rich man who pays them £2 to £5 (Rs. 20-50) a month, and allows them to add to this by dancing and singing. The Takáis or prostitutes live solely by prostitution. They are considered low and the dancing-girls neither eat, drink, nor associate with them. The Ramjánis or dancing-girls are generally well-to-do, but they are very luxurious and fond of pleasure and intrigue, and they are proverbially crafty and faithless. The strumpets are poor, often hardly able to make a living. When a dancing-girl begins to age she looks out for some good-looking girl who has misbehaved or been left destitute, or she buys the daughter of some poor family and adopts the girl. They generally treat their adopted children with care and kindliness and take pains to make them good dancers and singers. The girl calls her adoptive mother *bái* or madam. When the girl comes of age she is generally patronised by some rich man who pays £5 to £10 (Rs. 50-100). The girl's teeth are dyed black as a bride's teeth are blackened, a ceremony which is called *missi* or tooth-powder. To the £5 to £10 (Rs. 50-100) which the girl's patron gives, her adoptive mother adds £2 to £4 (Rs. 20-40) and from the joint amount gives a dinner party to the members of the community who spend a few nights in dancing and feasting. From that day the girl is admitted a member of the class, and recognized as a professional dancing-girl. The daughters of dancing-girls are brought up to their mother's profession; the sons are left to choose a calling. They marry and keep their wives in the same seclusion as private women. Dancing girls do not follow any Musalmán customs and do not respect the *kázi*. They form an organized community under a head-woman called *náikin* or *bái*, that is lady, who settles disputes and is treated with much respect. They do not send their boys to school. On the whole they are a falling people partly because the class of rich Musalmáns who were their chief patrons is dying out, partly it is said, as the husband can no longer safely punish an erring wife, because women are less chaste than they used to be.

Táschis.

Ta'schis, or KETTLE-DRUMMERS, local converts of mixed Hindu origin, are found in small numbers in Belgaum and other large

Chapter III. Population. MUSALMÁNS. *Táschis.*

towns. Among themselves they speak Hindustáni and Maráthi with others. They are tall or of middle size, well-made, and dark or olive-skinned. The men shave the head, wear the beard full or short, and dress in a dirty and untidy Hindu turban, a waistcoat, and a pair of tight trousers or a waistcloth. The women, who are like the men in face, wear the Hindu robe and bodice, appear unveiled in public, and add nothing to the family income. They are neither clean nor neat in their habits. Kettle-drummers are engaged both by Hindus and Musalmáns to play during their marriages and other rejoicings. A band of four men is paid about 2*s.* (Re. 1) a day, which is divided equally among the players. Their work is not constant. In the rainy season they have to employ their time either in tilling the ground or in acting as messengers or servants. They are much given to intoxicating drinks and drugs, and are seldom well-to-do or able to save. They form a separate community marrying only among themselves, but they have no special organization and no headman, except the regular *kázi* who settles their social disputes and registers their marriages. Their manners and customs do not differ from those of ordinary Musalmáns. In religion they are Sunnis of the Hanafi school, but they are neither religious nor careful to say their prayers. They do not send their children to school.

CHRISTIANS.

Christians, with a strength of 6322 or 0·73 per cent of the population, include two main divisions, Europeans and Natives. The Europeans numbering 1178 (1013 males and 165 females) include, besides the district officers, the officers of the two Native regiments and the officers and men of the European regiment and of the Artillery which together generally forms a force 1500 to 2000 strong. Of 5063 Native Christians about 500 are Protestants and about 4500 are Roman Catholics.

Native[1] Protestant Christians, numbering about 500, are found in the town of Belgaum and in other towns and large villages. They do not live apart. Some are immigrants from Madras and others are local converts. The Madras Christians came as domestic servants to officers of the Madras army when Belgaum was garrisoned from Madras. Many of them take service with officers and follow their masters when they go to other parts of India. Of the local converts some were Bráhmans, some Lingáyats, some Maráthás, some Hindus of other classes, and a few were Musalmáns. The home tongue of the Madrásis is Tamil; that of the local Christians is either Kánarese, Hindustáni, or Maráthi. Except that the Madrásis are dark and the local converts wheat-coloured, they differ little in appearance being short, round-featured, and inclined to stoutness. They live in one-storeyed houses with mud or stone walls with either tiled or thatched roofs and open verandas. Their furniture includes low wooden stools, palm-leaf mats, wooden benches and boxes, brass lamps, and metal pots. The well-to-do keep servants. The staple food of the Madras or Tamil Christians is boiled rice or wheat bread, beef, coffee, and dry fish. Most local converts eat millet bread

---

[1] Partly from materials supplied by the Reverend J. G. Hawker.

Chapter III.
Population.
CHRISTIANS.

and boiled rice with *chatni*[1] or pulse curry or spiced pulse soup. On holidays they prepare sweetmeats and one or two dishes of flesh with unleavened bread. The Madras Christians are fond of animal food and spirituous drinks, but most local converts use flesh and spirits sparingly and some touch neither flesh nor spirits. They are good cooks and moderate eaters their chief dainties being hot and sour condiments and oil. The Madras men wear a white headscarf, a waistcloth, a long white coat, and country shoes; the local converts wear a short coat or a shouldercloth instead of the long coat, and generally a white cotton headscarf with country shoes. The husbandmen often wear a country blanket on their shoulders, especially during the rainy season and in the cold weather. The women of both classes wear the shortsleeved bodice with the robe hanging like the petticoat. They cover the head with the upper end of the robe and wear gold and silver head, nose, neck, and wrist ornaments. On the whole the well-to-do incline to imitate European dress. Except a few who are clerks in public offices and one who is a land proprietor or *inámdár*, as a class the Protestant Christians are badly off. Some are catechists or religious preachers, some are pastors or ministers in the service of the London Missionary Society; and some are Government servants, dyers, weavers, husbandmen, carpenters, fishers, and servants. The women mind the house. As among Hindus the wives of Government servants and carpenters add nothing to the family income, while the wives of dyers, weavers, husbandmen, fishers, and servants either help their husbands in their calling or work as labourers. They mix with Musalmáns and Native Roman Catholics with whom they eat but do not marry. Hindus look down on them and they find it difficult to get Hindu barbers and washermen to work for them. Those who are servants attend on their masters from sunrise to sunset, their women either working as maids or *ayas* or preparing rice for home use and for sale. They also make and sell rice pancakes called *pánpoli* (M.) or *doshi* (K.) The daily life of the rest does not differ from that of the Hindus who follow the same calling. Except servants most rest on Sundays and on New Year's Day in January, Good Friday in March-April, and Christmas Day in December. A family of five generally spends 10*s.* to £1 (Rs. 5-10) a month. A birth costs 2*s.* to 10*s.* (Rs. 1-5), a marriage £2 to £10 (Rs. 20-100), and a death 4*s.* to £1 10*s.* (Rs. 2-15). Some of them belong to the London Missionary Society and some to the English Episcopal Church. The later converts all belong to the London Mission Society which is the only missionary body in the district. It began work in 1820. The first missionary was the Reverend J. Taylor, who was sent from Bellári at the request of Major-General Pritzler for the benefit of the troops under his command. At first the progress of the mission was slow, the only converts being a small number of Madras servants. After a time, when the missionaries were able to preach Kánarese and Maráthi their labours were more successful. In 1858 or after thirty-eight years' work there were over 400 local converts. But of these, partly apparently because the

[1] *Chatni* is a mixture of long pepper, salt and tamarind ground together and mixed with sesamum oil.

Chapter III.
Population.
CHRISTIANS.

teachers or catechists were Tamils, only forty-five were Kánarese. Since 1858 more attention has been paid to the conversion of Kánarese. Their ceremonies at births, marriages, and deaths do not differ from those of the churches to which they belong. All attend divine service on Sundays, New Year's Day, Good Friday, and Christmas Day which they keep as complete holidays. They are said to have no faith in soothsaying, ghosts, or sorcery. Some of them keep to the old practice of wearing gay clothes and cooking certain dishes on certain Hindu holidays.

They are said not to observe any particular ceremonies on the occasions of a birth or of a girl's coming of age. On the wedding day the bride and bridegroom accompanied by friends go separately from their houses to church and are there married by the minister. When the marriage service is over the couple come in procession to the bride's father's where a dinner is served. There is no settled dowry, but parents often present their daughters and daughters-in-law with ornaments, clothes, and furniture. Women are confined in the house like Europeans and they do not think that either birth or death causes impurity to the members of the family. They employ midwives who are paid 2*s.* to 4*s.* (Rs. 1-2). On a convenient day after birth the child is baptised by the minister in the church. When life is gone the body is laid in a coffin or carried covered with a shroud to the graveyard where it is buried after the minister has read the funeral service over it. The only expense at a funeral is the gravedigger's fee and the cost of the shroud or coffin. Those who are Government or mission servants are anxious to give their boys a good education and to teach their girls reading, writing, and needle-work. The London Missionary Society supports five schools in the district of Belgaum, three of them boys' schools and two girls' schools. One of the boys' schools is an Anglo-Vernacular school teaching up to the matriculation standard. The total number under tuition at the end of 1882 in the five schools was 720 boys and 135 girls. Cases of misdemeanour are enquired into and punished by the minister.

Madras Catholic Christians, numbering about 500, are found in the town of Belgaum. Like the Madras Protestant Christians and Hindus they came from Madras either in 1817, when the district passed to the British or afterwards up to about 1830 while Belgaum was garrisoned by Madras troops. They do not differ from Protestant or Hindu Madrásis in appearance, character, calling, house, or food. They are Roman Catholics subject to the jurisdiction of the Jesuit Bishop of Bombay and their religious ceremonies are performed according to the Roman ritual. Their holidays and fast days are the same as those observed by Bombay Catholics. They pay particular devotion to patron saints, the chief of whom is the Blessed Virgin. As most of them are house servants they cannot rest on Sundays and holidays. Their women are confined with the help of midwives and their children are baptised on the eighth day by the chaplain at the church where Madras or other Catholics answer for them at the font. There is no fixed age for marriage. Girls are generally married between fifteen and twenty and boys between eighteen and twenty-five. Beginning from the first Sunday or holiday

CHRISTIANS.

after betrothal the bans or proclamation of marriage are published by the priest in the church. On the wedding day the bridegroom and bride with friends and relations, go to the church in separate parties and are there married by the priest. Cases of misdemeanour are enquired into and punished by meetings of married castemen called the council or *panch*. The *panch* has a caste-headman appointed by the priest. Those who refuse to obey the decisions of the council are put out of caste, but on submission are again admitted. They teach their boys to read and write Tamil, but do not take to new pursuits.

Konkani or **Goa Catholics,** numbering about 4000, are found throughout the district, chiefly at Khánápur, Turkanvádi, Patnya, and Bidi. They are immigrants from Goa and are under the jurisdiction of the Archbishop of Goa. They do not differ in any important points from the Christians of Ratnágiri and Kánara.[1]

JEWS OR BENI-ISRAELS.

Jews or **Beni-Israels,** numbering about ninety, are found in the town of Belgaum. They are natives of the island of Bombay and of the neighbouring districts of Thána and Kolába. They have come to Belgaum with Native regiments in which they are employed as sepoys, officers, and medical attendants. In appearance, character, religion, customs, and other particulars they do not differ from the Konkan Beni-Israels. They are a vigorous pushing class, sending their boys to English schools and showing much readiness to take advantage of opportunities to improve their position.

PÁRSIS.

Pa'rsis, numbering sixty-four, are found only in the town of Belgaum. They came from Bombay and Surat about fifty years ago for purposes of trade. They do not consider Belgaum their home, and keep family and marriage relations with the Pársis of Bombay and Surat. Their home speech is Gujaráti. Out of doors they speak Maráthi and English and a few Kánarese. As shopkeepers, merchants, and contractors the Belgaum Pársis are well-to-do and prosperous. They have priests of their own. As there is no Tower of Silence in Belgaum they bury their dead, and as there is no fire-temple they go to Poona or to Bombay to have their marriages performed.

Villages.

According to the 1881 census there was one village or town to every 4·32 square miles of land, each village containing an average of 175 houses and 810 people. Fourteen towns had more than 5000 and three of the fourteen more than 10,000 people. Excluding these fourteen towns, which together held 122,074 or 14·12 per cent of the population, the 741,940 inhabitants of Belgaum were distributed over 1055 villages, giving an average of one village for every 4·40 square miles and of 700 people to each village. Of the 1055 villages 103 had less than 100 people, 159 had between 100 and 200, 325 between 200 and 500, 256 between 500 and 1000, 135 between 1000 and 2000, 49 between 2000 and 3000, and 28 between 3000 and 5000. From a distance a Belgaum village is generally pleasing. Most villages are well shaded and many are surrounded by so high and thick a fence of *bábhuls* and prickly-pear,

---

[1] Details are given in Bombay Gazetteer, X. 134-136 and XV. 380-394.

Chapter III. Population. Villages.

that a stranger might easily pass them as a plot of bush and brushwood. The entrance generally leads through a ruined gate into a central street lined by houses of considerable size, showing signs of comfort, occasionally of wealth. The houses in the side rows, which run at right angles to the main street, are smaller and show fewer signs of comfort; and beyond these, generally outside of the village fence, is a fringe of huts of the lowest classes and the tents and booths of wanderers. Except the huts of Mhárs, which are often of bamboo and millet stalks, the walls of the houses are generally of sun-dried brick. In the rainier west most of the roofs are peaked and covered with overlapping semicircular tiles; in the drier east the roof is generally a flat mud terrace with a parapet. Almost every village has its temple or shrine and its holy tree. A few of the larger towns have walls and a tower, but most villages find their deep circle of thorn a complete shelter from robbers and wild animals.

Houses.

According to the 1881 census, of 188,694 houses 154,806 or eighty per cent were occupied and 33,888 or eighteen per cent were empty. These figures give an average of forty-one houses to the square mile and of five inmates to each occupied house. [1] Except in the larger towns and occasionally in villages the houses are one-storeyed. The better class of house is built on a plinth, generally of dressed stone, rising three or four feet above the street. From the street a flight of two or three steps let into the plinth lead to the house-door. Of the veranda or *katti* on the top of the plinth on either side of the central steps one-half is generally open and the other half closed by bamboo matting. The veranda is covered by the eaves whose outer edge rests on a row of wooden pillars. Except as a waiting place for servants and beggars, and sometimes in playing games, the veranda is little used. The back of the veranda is the front wall of the house. This is pierced about the centre by a doorway about five feet high by three feet broad closed by a solid wooden door not unfrequently relieved by bosses of iron or other metal. On each side of the door a window about two feet square is generally guarded by heavy upright bars of wood let into the masonry. Some houses are built round a courtyard; others have no central open space. In houses with a central yard each of the four inner faces of the house has a room fronted by a low veranda. In houses without a central yard the rooms open into one another, and a central passage sometimes runs between the rooms from the front door to the back yard. In central yard houses the room between the street and the yard is used as a receiving room, by business men as an office, and by traders as their shop. When not in public use the women of the family sit in this room, and into it a dying member of the household is carried some days before his death. The central courtyard is known as *ángala* when open to the air, and as *padsále* when roofed. There is sometimes no room between the front veranda and the *padsále* or roofed court. Among the rooms, which surround the central court, are the *devar máne* or god-room, the cooking room, the sleeping room, and the

---

[1] Contributed by Mr. G. McCorkell, C. S.

Chapter III.
Population.
Houses.

eating or dining room. In some parts of the district the cook-room is also used as a bath-room. In other parts the bathing room is separate at the back of the house and is known as the *bachchala.* Among Lingáyats ornaments and other valuables are kept in a box in the god-room; Bráhmans and others keep them in a separate room answering to the strong-room of an English mansion, and in some instances they are kept in boxes in the sleeping rooms. Some houses have walls and every house has a well-like cistern to store rain water. The dwelling of any well-to-do family must have these rooms and conveniences. A rich man's house has more rooms. But even in the houses of the rich the rooms are low and dark. There are almost never side windows. The light comes from the front and back doors or where there is a central yard from the front door and the courtyard. The floors are of beaten earth covered with a wash of cowdung which is renewed every Monday, every new or full-moon day, and on most holidays. The dwellings of the poor have walls of mud and straw. The doors are of plaited or woven slips of bamboo. As a rule they have only one or two rooms with a front veranda formed by the overhanging eaves. The poorest live in huts whose walls, except a few bamboos to bear the roof, are of woven millet stalks or palm leaves, sometimes but not always daubed with mud. There is little difference between town and village houses. The wealthier a man the better his house. He will have more rooms, but the arrangement will not be changed. The cost of building a first class house varies from £500 to £2000 (Rs. 5000-20,000); the ordinary labouring villager or townsman is content with a house costing £10 to £20 (Rs. 100-200); and a few shillings represent the cost of the poorest huts.

Furniture.

A wealthy man's house contains the following furniture: One to three *palangs* or cots varying in price from £1 10*s.* to £5 (Rs. 15-50), two or three cupboards each valued at 10*s.* to £2 (Rs. 5-20), a few chairs each worth 8*s.* to 10*s.* (Rs. 4-5), a few boxes each worth 10*s.* to £2 10*s.* (Rs. 5-25), carpets or *jájams* each worth 6*s.* to £3 (Rs. 3-30), bedding for each member of the family worth 10*s.* to £2 10*s.* (Rs. 5-25), and brass and copper water pots and cooking and dining vessels and dishes worth £20 to £30 (Rs. 200-300). A wealthy man will have ten to forty silver vessels used for dining and drinking and for show. As these silver vessels are chiefly for show and as a form of investment the number of them depends on the wealth and taste of the house-owner. It may be said that few families who are locally classed as rich, have less than £20 (Rs. 200) or more than £200 (Rs. 2000) invested in silver vessels; apart from these silver vessels a wealthy man's furniture varies in value from £50 to £100 (Rs. 500-1000); the furniture of a man in easy circumstances from £10 to £15 (Rs. 100-150); the furniture of a family in middling circumstances from £2 to £5 (Rs. 20-50); and a labourer's house gear, bed, matting, a brass pot or *lota*, and some earthen cooking vessels, is not worth more than £1 (Rs. 10).

Dress.

Among men, except by a very few Bráhmans and by the highest class of Government servants, the broad flat-rimmed Bráhman turban is not used. In its place is worn a white cotton headscarf

Chapter III.
Population.
Dress.

or *rumál* eight to ten feet square generally plain but sometimes with a gold border. Numbers of these headscarves are brought from Madras. Those who wear the turban wear it only in public. In private the head is either bare or is covered by a plain headscarf or by an ornamented skull-cap. The rich and the well-to-do wear local hand-woven waistcloths of varying fineness with silk-embroidered borders. Middle class men use English and Bombay machine-made cloth, and poor men wear coarse local hand-woven cloth. A poor husbandman wears a minimum of clothing, a loincloth or *langoti* and a blanket or *kámbil.* The loincloth is of coarse cotton cloth about two feet long by one foot broad. The blanket is of locally woven coarse wool and costs 4*s.* to 6*s.* (Rs. 2-3). By day it supplies the place of clothes and by night it serves as bedding. Instead of the loincloth a pair of coarse drawers reaching half-way down the thighs are occasionally worn. Hindu women generally wear the robe called *shiri* (K.) or *lugade* (M.) and the bodice called *kuppas* (K.) or *choli* (M.) The bodice or *kuppas* covers the back between the shoulders and is fastened in front. The sleeves are short and reach about half-way down the upper arm. Among the rich the meeting of the sleeve with the rest of the bodice is hid by a narrow armlet of gold called *váki* in Maráthi and *vanki* in Kánarese. The robe or *shiri,* which is either of cotton or of silk, is of two sizes: the full robe of twenty-seven feet by 3¾ which is worn by women and the smaller robe of eighteen feet by three which is worn by girls. In putting it on the robe is wound round the waist so as to leave two parts of unequal length, the longer part to serve as a skirt and cover the limbs and the shorter part to serve as a cloak or mantle and cover the shoulder and breast and in some cases one side of the head. The women of most Kánarese castes catch the lower part together in front in a number of plaits and allow it to fall like a petticoat to within two or three inches of the ankle. Bráhman and Marátha women, instead of letting it fall like a petticoat, draw one corner of the skirt back between the feet and fasten the end into the waistband behind. This divided skirt among the higher classes is loose and generally falls below the knee. Among the poorer classes it is tightly girt and drawn up so as to leave the greater part of the leg bare. The upper end of the robe is by girls of the higher classes and by the women of all other classes worn over the right shoulder and tucked into the waistband in front close to the left hip. The women of the higher classes use the upper end as a veil drawing it over the right side of the head instead of over the shoulder, and holding the end in the right hand below the level of the bosom. The clothes worn by a rich woman vary in price from £1 to £1 4*s.* (Rs. 10-12); those worn by a middle class woman are not worth more than 10*s.* or 12*s.* (Rs. 5 or 6); and those worn by a poor woman are not worth more than 3*s.* or 4*s.* (Rs. 1½-2).

Communities.

The office of village headman called *pátil* (M.) or *gauda* (K.) is hereditary. He has generally the revenue and police charge of the village, the duties in some cases being divided between a police headman who is responsible in all matters connected with crime, and a revenue headman who collects the Government dues. The headmen

Chapter III.
Population.
Communities.

of some villages are paid entirely in cash. As a rule their sole or their chief source of profit is an allotment of rent-free land. Most of the headmen are Lingáyats. Few of them are able to write. The clerk or accountant called *kulkarni* (M.) or *shánbhog* (K.), keeps the village accounts, writes up the landholders' receipt-books, and prepares returns and the findings of village juries. With few exceptions the post of village clerk is hereditary. It is paid partly in land partly in cash. Almost all village clerks are Bráhmans of the Deshasth, Konkanasth, Shenvi, or Golak divisions. Their charge is generally confined to a single village, but in some cases they have a group of two or three villages. Most of the village watchmen and beadles belong to the depressed caste who are called Mhárs (M.) or Holiás (K.) and a few belong to the less depressed Bedar and Rámoshi tribes. There are generally three or four families of Mhárs in each village, who are supported partly by the grant of rent-free land and partly by grain payments from the villagers. The villagers of late have shown a tendency to dispute the Mhárs' rights to their old dues alleging that the Mhárs neglect their duties, while the Mhárs contend that they never neglect their duties when the villagers pay them their dues. The Mhárs' duties are heavy and important. For Government they act as village police, messengers, and revenue carriers; for the villagers they act as watchmen, boundary settlers and scavengers. Of other village office-bearers the priest and astrologer called *grám-joshi* (M.) or *joisaru* (K.) is generally a Bráhman, who performs the birth, marriage, and death ceremonies of the Bráhmanic Hindus of the village. Besides the astrologer every village has a ministrant who is called a *pujári* when he is a Bráhman, and a *gurav* when he is a Shudra. Lingáyats have a *jangam*, and Musalmáns a *mulla*. All the village office-bearers are paid by rent-free lands or by voluntary offerings made by the people whom they serve.

Of village craftsmen there are in large villages the carpenter called *sutár* (M.) or *badagi* (K.) Besides in building houses and making and mending field tools, the carpenter is in most villages the ministrant called *pujári* (M.) or *archak* (K.) in Lakshmi's shrine, who is the favourite Kánarese village guardian. The carpenter is paid partly by land held at low rates but chiefly by an allowance of grain from each landholder. When employed to perform other than field work he is paid in cash. Blacksmiths called *lohárs* (M.) or *kammár* (K.) make and mend the iron parts of field tools and carts and carpenter's tools, also locks, hinges, nails, and other articles required for ordinary house purposes. He is paid in cash when employed on other than a field work. They have seldom lands granted at low rents and are chiefly paid by allowances of grain from villagers. Potters called *kumbhárs* (M.) or *kumbárs* (K.) are found in most good-sized villages. They make earthen pots, tiles, and bricks, act as torch-bearers, and perform certain rites when a village is attacked by an epidemic. They are to some extent paid by grain allowances but chiefly by cash payments for the vessels, tiles, or bricks supplied. Besides these office-bearers some goldsmiths or *sonárs* (M.) used to act as *potdárs* whose duties were to test the coins received in payment of Government dues. The barber called

Chapter III.
Population.
Communities.

nhávi (M.) or *navilgia* or *kelaser* (K.) is found in almost all villages. He almost always belongs to the Kánarese barber caste and is generally a Lingáyat. Besides shaving the men, the barber acts as torch-bearer, musician, and social messenger. He is entirely paid by the villagers partly in cash and partly in grain. The washerman called *parit* (M.) or *agasa* or *madival* (K.) is found only in the larger villages. He belongs to a separate caste and is generally a Lingáyat by religion. He washes the clothes of all well-to-do villagers. He holds no rent-free or low-rent land and lives chiefly on allowances of grain given by the villagers. The shoemaker *chambhár* (M.) or *sambgár* (K.) is found in almost all villages. He supplies landholders with all leather work for field purposes and sandals, *vhána* (M.) or *chupals* (K.). He is always paid in grain. A family of *Mángs* (M.) or *Mádigerus* (K.) is found in every group of four or five villages. They remove dead cattle and supply leather ropes. They are paid in grain. The bulk of the people in most villages are Lingáyats and Jains. There is probably no village whose entire population belongs to one caste.

Movements.

The movements of the people into and out of Belgaum limits are confined to the neighbouring British districts of Dhárwár, Kaládgi, Kánara, Sátára, Sholápur, and Ratnágiri, and to Kolhápur and other Southern Marátha native states. Of traders Lingáyats and Marwár Vánis leave their Belgaum homes after the *Dasara* holiday in October and go to Poona, Bombay, and Bellári in Madras to fetch cloth for the *Diváli* festival in November. Very few high-caste Hindus leave the district in search of employment. The people of the Sahyádri villages, who are chiefly Maráthás, originally practised coppice-burning or *kumri*. About 1850, at the introduction of the survey, coppice-burning was stopped as it was believed to have stripped the hills of their trees. Though they remained in their old villages the people during the rains were forced to go to Goa and Sávantvádi where coppice-burning was allowed. As the restriction pressed hard on the people since 1875 arrangements have been made to allot land for coppice-burning, and since then the people have been freed from the necessity of leaving their homes. Of the labouring classes, Marathás, Kunbis, Berads, Buruds, Vadars, and Musalmáns every year between January and March go to Dhárwár, Hubli, Kaládgi, Kolhápur, and Vengurla, and return to their homes for field work early in June.[1] The local cotton-carrying trade is in the hands of Bombay traders and Vengurla Shenvis who engage cartmen to take cotton to Vengurla for shipment to Bombay. These cartmen remain at Vengurla for a couple of days, where, as in other parts of the Konkan, they are put to much inconvenience as they can neither get *jvári* for themselves nor good fodder for their cattle. Of those who come to the district in search of work, the most noticeable are the Ratnágiri Maráthás and Kunbis who are largely found as house servants among the rich families of Belgaum.

[1] The 1881 census shows that 29,145 people born in Belgaum were in that year found in different parts of the Bombay Presidency. The details are, Dhárwár 13,557, Kánara 6700, Kaládgi 4469, Sátára 1735, Poona 1155, Sholápur 630, Ratnágiri 480, Ahmadnagar 205, Khándesh 87, Násik 86, and Kolába 41.

CHAPTER IV.

AGRICULTURE.

Chapter IV.
Agriculture.

According to the 1881 census returns agriculture supported about 612,000 people or seventy per cent of the population:

Belgaum Agricultural Population, 1881.

Age.	Males.	Females.	Total.
Under Fifteen ...	121,133	113,240	234,373
Over Fifteen ...	186,776	191,158	377,934
Total ...	307,909	304,398	612,307

Husbandmen.

The bulk of the regular husbandmen are Lingáyats and Maráthás; next in strength to Lingáyats and Maráthás come Jains, Musalmáns, Dhangars, Mhárs, Berads, and Bráhmans. Husbandmen of the better class live in tiled houses, own £30 to £100 (Rs. 300-1000) worth of ornaments and metal vessels, and have grain enough in store to meet all demands for food and for seed. Sometimes they have a surplus which is lent on interest. The poorer class of husbandmen live in mud-roofed houses or in grass huts, own £5 to £10 (Rs. 50-100) worth of goods, and have a store of grain barely enough to keep them for half a year. During the remaining months they have either to work as labourers or to run into debt. All are well-behaved, orderly, and religious, and, except the poorer classes who are a little given to drinking, sober. Bráhmans, Lingáyats, and Jains are clean in their persons and in their houses; most of the other classes are more or less dirty and untidy. On the whole they are thrifty. Though hardworking, especially in Belgaum and Khánápur, their character as husbandmen is not high. As a rule they are landholders or *khátedárs* who till their own land; the rest are under-holders or labourers. As much land has passed into the hands of moneylenders there is a considerable body of under-holders. But these are not all dependent on the moneylender as well-to-do landholders or *khátedárs* not unfrequently, in addition to their own holdings which as a rule they inherit, become the tenants of a moneylender, and till part of his land either as sharers in the produce or on payment of a money-rent. During the off season, that is from about February to May, the ordinary husbandman uses his oxen and carts for carrying grain and other produce to the two great grain markets of Nipáni and Belgaum. He also makes considerable profit by carrying cotton to Vengurla in Ratnágiri whence there is always a large return traffic in salt for local use and in the stores required by the residents in the large civil and military station of

Chapter IV.
Agriculture.
Husbandmen.

Belgaum. Besides by carrying, the better class of husbandmen add to their income by moneylending, by the sale of dairy produce, and by cotton-spinning, cotton-ginning, and blanket-weaving. Poor husbandmen eke out their gains by fishing, hunting, and fowl-rearing. These additions to their incomes vary from £1 to £50 (Rs. 10 - 500). About twenty-five per cent of the husbandmen are free from debt; the remaining seventy-five per cent are indebted. This indebtedness is owing to expensive family ceremonies, law suits, crop failures, and unwillingness to part with their land. The amount of debt varies from £2 to £50 (Rs. 20-500). In almost all cases the indebtedness of husbandmen may be traced to family ceremonies. To meet the expenses which attend family ceremonies savings are spent, then the store of grain goes, next an ox or it may be a pair of oxen are sold, and last the family jewels are pawned. Stripped of his store of seed and food-grain, so soon as his stock of food is exhausted, the husbandman has to go to the moneylender. Once in the hands of the moneylender, charge gathers on charge, until the holding is mortgaged, at first without possession, but generally in the end possession passes to the lender. The moneylender's name appears in the Government books and the landholder sinks to a labourer. The yearly rates of interest vary from twelve to thirty per cent. Though in most parts of the district the people have to a great extent recovered from the 1876-77 famine, in Gokák and some other red and poor soils the effects of the famine are, in places, still apparent in ruined houses, in arable waste, and in impoverished husbandmen. Of late years the chief agricultural change has been the growing desire of the lending classes to get possession of land.

Soil.

Geologically the soils of the district may be divided into two classes, the red and the black. The red soils are primary soils, that is they are the direct result of the decomposition of the iron-bearing rocks. This variety of soil is generally found all along the western border; it also occasionally occurs in the plain country as in the tableland between the Ghatprabha and the Krishna, and in the Belavádi and Ambadgatti village groups or *khariyats* of Sampgaon. This red soil is mostly coarse and poor, and, as in these western parts the rainfall is plentiful, the chief products are the early, called the *kharif* (M. and H.) or *mungári* (K.) crops. In parts of Athni red garden lands are watered from wells. The black soils are secondary soils, that is, they are rock-ruins changed by the addition of organic matter. The black soil is not solely the result of the weathering and enriching of the ruins of trap rocks. Black soil occurs as largely and as typically in tracts where the rock is gneiss as it occurs in tracts where the rock is trap. The black soil covers most of the plain country and is best suited for the growth of cotton, Indian millet, wheat, and gram. In east Gokák it is so rich as not to need fallows. The husbandmen by careful changes secure a yearly crop. In the north-east of the district, bordering on the Don, are loamy plains of noted richness. Only in seasons of extreme drought do the crops in these lands fail, and in average seasons the harvest is almost always fair. The black soil of the Krishna valley is of most uncertain depth, the waving trap lying sometimes several feet, at other times only a few inches below the surface. Near the sandstone hills in Chikodi,

Chapter IV.
Agriculture.
Soil.

Gokák, and Parasgad, owing to the crumbling of the sandstone, the soil is little better than sand. This sandy soil does not want much rain, but it wants constant enriching, and, with the aid of manure, yields fair crops of cereals, pulse, and oilseeds. Locally the black soil is divided into four classes: *káli* or rich deep black, *movat* or red and black mixed of middling richness, *karak* or thin black over stone, and *mali* or alluvial which near the Krishna is of unusual richness. For cotton-growing the *káli* and the *movat* are grouped together as *regur* (Tel.) or pure black. Two other varieties of black soil are recognised, a brown less-matured *regur* and a gray-black largely mixed with lime nodules and with a layer of lime two to ten feet below the surface. The pure black soil is best suited for local cotton and the brown soil is best suited for American cotton of which very little is now grown; the gray-black soil is inferior to the other two. Kánarese husbandmen describe their cotton soil as *yera bhumi* or melted earth. The cotton soil is very dense and is improved by a mixture of sand and pebbles. Its chemical properties show that it contains all the elements of vigorous growth. Much of this land is very deep. Three feet and upwards is common, and depths of twelve or fifteen feet and even of thirty and forty feet are not unusual.[1]

Arable Area.

The revenue survey returns give Belgaum an area of 2,979,840 acres. Of these 1,163,738 or 39·05 per cent are alienated, paying Government only a quit-rent; 1,179,300 acres or 39·57 per cent are arable; 398,720 acres or 13·38 per cent forest; 156,572 or 5·25 per cent unarable waste; and 81,510 acres or 2·73 per cent village sites and roads. Of 1,179,300, the total Government arable area, 1,072,820 acres or 90·97 per cent were in 1881-82 held for tillage. Of this 7860 or 0·73 per cent were garden land; 53,600 or 4·99 per cent rice land; and 1,011,360 or 94·27 per cent dry-crop land.

Holdings.

In 1881-82 the total number of holdings, including alienated lands in Government villages, was 63,201 with an average area of 25·50 acres. Of the whole number of holdings 8904 were of not more than five acres, 11,079 were of five to ten acres, 18,902 of ten to twenty acres, 18,207 of twenty to fifty acres, 4343 of fifty to a hundred acres, 1304 of 100 to 200 acres, 378 of 200 to 500 acres, sixty-four of 500 to 1000 acres, fourteen of 1000 to 2000 acres, and six of above 2000 acres. Of holdings above 500 acres, ten were in Chikodi, seventeen in Parasgad, twenty-three in Athni, twenty-eight in Gokák, and two each in Belgaum, Khánápur, and Sampgaon.

A Plough.

One pair of good oxen can work twelve to sixteen acres of dry-crop land and four to ten acres of garden land. In Chikodi and Athni the general practice in ploughing black soil, which when dry becomes very hard, is to use two to four pairs of bullocks. It

---

[1] An analysis of the best cotton soil showed, in 4500 grains, 3324 grains of very fine soil, 936 grains of impalpable powder, and 240 grains of coarse pebbles like jasper, with pieces like burnt tiles strongly retentive of moisture. The impalpable portion consisted of 18·000 grains of water, 0·450 of organic matter, 0·083 of chloride of sodium, 0·007 of sulphate of lime, 0·027 of phosphate of lime, 0·450 of carbonate of lime, 0·013 of carbonate of magnesia, 15·200 of peroxide of iron, 16·500 of alumina, 0·085 of potash, 48·000 of silica combined and free as sand, and 1·185 of loss. Walton's Belgaum and Kaládgi Cotton, 88.

Chapter IV. Agriculture.

is roughly estimated that twenty to forty acres of the better class of dry-crop land or six to ten acres of garden might enable a cultivator to live like an ordinary retail dealer, and that, except in seasons of failure of rain, forty to sixty acres of dry-crop land or ten acres of rich garden land would enable him to support himself, his wife, and two children and one field-labourer comfortably without being obliged to have recourse to other work or to the moneylender.

Stock.

According to the Collector's yearly returns the 1881-82 field stock included 60,204 ploughs, 22,510 carts, 206,313 bullocks, 127,089 cows, 138,719 buffaloes of which 89,975 were females and 48,744 males, 6218 horses mares and colts, 3598 donkeys, and 283,936 sheep and goats.

Field Tools.

The chief field tools are, two kinds of plough the large or *negali* (K.) and the small or *ranti* (K.), the large hoe-harrow or *kunti* (K.), the seed-drill or *kurgi* (K.), the grubber or *yedi-kunti* (K.), the weeder or *belli-salla* (K.), and the pick-axe or *báigudli* (K.)

The Plough.

Of the two ploughs the heavy or *negali* consists of a massive three-cornered block of very hard wood, rudely shaped by the village carpenter, so that the broad lower part forms the share on which a strong iron bar is fixed as a tongue. The hinder part under an acute angle forms the breast of the plough into which, near its upper end, a handle is let in from behind, while from the front side the plough-bar is fixed below the handle. This plough-bar consists of a somewhat bent or crooked beam, at least twelve feet long. It is laid on the necks of the rear pair of bullocks, which are always the strongest of the team. Instead of bullocks the rear pair are sometimes buffaloes which when well broken are heavier and steadier than bullocks. The team includes four, five, six, sometimes even eight pairs of bullocks, all harnessed with small cords to a long leather rope, which passes round the beam and the hinder part of the plough. An old man usually leads the team, while on the yoke of the third pair of bullocks a boy is seated, who with a strong leather whip belabours and urges the bullocks both before and behind him. This heavy plough is difficult to manage. In spite of every effort the ploughman is unable to keep it in anything like a straight line, while the acute angle between the share and the beam of the plough is constantly choked with earth. Still it is specially useful in bringing neglected black soil under tillage by uprooting the grass and weeds which stifle the crop. A heavy or *negali* plough costs 8*s*. to 16*s*. (Rs. 4-8) and is seldom owned by the poorer landowners. It turns over the soil to a depth of fifteen inches. Three ploughings are necessary, the first along, the second across, the third cornerwise. It takes about seven months to bring about twenty-four acres of black land under tillage. The light or *ranti* plough, costing about 4*s*. (Rs. 2), is used for ploughing the red and especially the sandy soils. It is of the same make as the big plough, but is so much smaller and lighter that the husbandman usually carries it to the field on his shoulder, and can work it with one pair of bullocks. It scratches the field three to six inches deep which in the red soil can be done only either immediately after harvest or when the occasional rains of March and April or the regular thunderstorms of May have again wetted the soil.

Chapter IV.

Agriculture.

Field Tools.

The Hoe-harrow.

The hoe-harrow or *kunti* (K.) is a large rude tool. The chief part is a stout slightly crescent-shaped blade of iron about three feet long and four to five inches broad bladed on one side. This blade or cutting edge is turned forward and the ends are tightly fastened in stout timbers, which are again secured slopingly in a heavy bar of wood that has two narrowing poles passing to the yoke to which it is harnessed by strong leather ropes. This tool is drawn by three or four pairs of bullocks. As it moves the earth is forced between the iron knife and the bar of wood. On the wooden bar the driver and sometimes a second man or boy stand to make it heavier and force the blade deeper into the ground, so that the clods are completely cut and the grass and other weeds are rooted out and brought to the surface. The hoe-harrow is used both before and after ploughing; it costs about 6*s.* (Rs. 3).

The Drill.

The seed is sown by the seed-drill, called *kuri* or *kurgi* (K.) a rude but a most suitable and simple contrivance. At the top it is a wooden cup pierced with a number of diverging holes. Into each hole the upper end of a hollow bamboo is fastened, whose under end is fixed into a wooden bill standing out from a wooden bar and armed with a small iron tongue. As the bullocks move the driver keeps feeding the cup with grain from a bag under his arm; the seed runs down the hollow bamboos, while the outstanding iron spikes at the lower end pass through the soil opening small furrows into which the seed drops. The number and the distance of the bills and the hollow bamboos vary according to the seed and also according to the soil. Through this drill all grains are sown. The seeds of the pulses and oilseeds called *akkadi* or mixed crops, which are sown in separate rows between the grain rows, are dropped through a supplementary thick hollow bamboo with a sharp point called in Kánarese *bukkada, kolu,* and *sudiki.* This thick bamboo is always tied to the drill and held by a ploughboy, who, walking some paces behind the drill, drops the pulse and oilseeds through the thick bamboo. If the pulse or oilseed ought to be unmixed with grain the corresponding hole in the cup is stopped. On account of its bulk and the greater distance between the rows cotton-seed is always sown through the extra big bamboos, two of which are fastened to the bar of the drill with only two furrowing bills and without the cup and its small hollow bamboos. The seed drill costs about 2*s.* (Re. 1).

The Grubber.

The grubber or *yedi-kunti* (K.) is used to clear grass and weeds between the rows of cotton, and to earth up the soil at the roots of the cotton plants. It is a kind of broad spud or share, made of iron, a little shorter than the distance between the cotton rows. The lower edge is sharp, and to each side of the spud a strong light bamboo is fastened to join it with the yoke. Two are worked together and the four bamboos are brought up at their proper place to the bullocks, the one bullock working between one set of rows, and the other between another set of rows, that is there is a row of cotton between them. The two grubbers clear the grass and weeds on either side of this row, and between it and the next, thus weeding two rows at a time. Near the handle of each grubber is a stick forked

Chapter IV.
Agriculture.
Field Tools.

at the lower end and fastened by a rope to the horns of the bullocks. With these the driver can readily put on one side plants that come in the way of the machine, which, without this device, would be damaged. The grubber costs 2*s.* to 3*s.* (Rs. 1-1½).

The Weeder.

The weeder or *belli-salla* (K.) is worth about 8*s.* (Rs. 4). It consists of two shares or spuds, one at each end of an arched crescent-shaped frame, whose arch passes over the row of corn, while the shares loosen the earth between the rows, tear up weeds, and heap the soil close to the roots of the seedlings.

The Hand-hoe.

The hand-hoe or *báigudli* (K.) is a pickaxe with one end pointed and the other end bladed into a sharp adze. It is most effective in cutting and uprooting grass and other weeds after the land has been ploughed.

Carts.

Besides these field tools there are a weeding hook or *khurpi* worth 6*d.* (4 *as.*), a spade or *salki* worth 2*s.* 6*d.* (Rs. 1¼), an axe or *kodli* worth 2*s.* (Re. 1), and a sickle or *kudgolu* worth about 1*s.* (8 *as.*). Sometimes for travelling in a large company within a narrow area, and almost always for bringing thrashed grain and loads of fodder to town, most well-to-do husbandmen have field carts. The field cart, which in Kánarese is called *hallibhandi*, is rudely shaped and heavy, requiring four to eight bullocks to drag it. It is nearly fourteen feet long and not more than four feet broad. The floor is made of two strong side bars of teak scarcely less than nine inches square joined by four cross pieces of about the same size, the spaces being filled either by planking or by small bamboos. The sides are generally temporary additions either of bamboo or of wicker work. The wheel is of solid wood, about four feet across, formed of two or three well-fitted sections, with edges three or four inches thick, and gradually thickening from the edge to the nave. It is generally of tamarind wood and is bound by a strong iron rim from two to two and a half inches thick. The nave is an iron cylinder. The whole machine is strong and well made and may last for nearly a century. It costs £6 to £8 (Rs. 60-80).

Irrigation.

[1] The greater part of the arable land of Belgaum is under dry crops. Except along the banks of rivers and near ponds little land is watered. As so much of the land trusts solely to rain for its moisture the outturn varies greatly from year to year. Still, only in rare cases is the rainfall scanty enough to cause failure of food. In 1881-82 of 16,000 acres under irrigation, 15,870 were garden land and 130 were rice land. The total area of watered land bears a consolidated assessment of £5268 (Rs. 52,680) of which four-fifths are credited to Irrigation and one-fifth to Land. Except on land watered from the Gaddekeri or Swamp lake at Mugutkhán-Hubli in Sampgaon no separate water-rate is charged. In 1881-82, besides wells, there were 1055 water-works, including reservoirs, dips, and water-courses. Of these 377 are in Khánápur, 249 in Sampgaon, 190 in Chikodi, ninety-nine in Belgaum, eighty-three in Gokák, forty-five

---

[1] Except the account of the Gokák canal the irrigation section has been contributed by Mr. A. Clarke-Jervoise, C.S.

in Athni, and twelve in Parasgad. The eastern sub-divisions, Athni, Gokák, and Parasgad, are worst off for water-works. It is these parts of the district which generally suffer most severely from a partial or a total failure of rain. Of the 1055 water-works, 561 are permanent, watering 9215 acres assessed at £3277 (Rs. 32,770), and 494 are temporary, watering 6785 acres assessed at £1991 (Rs. 19,910). Of the water-works, seventy-four water over fifty acres, 205 water between fifty and twenty acres, and 776 water less than twenty acres. Of the whole number of water-works 663 are reservoirs, 146 are watercourses, and 246 are river and stream dips. Of these three classes of water-works the reservoirs are the most important. Most of the larger reservoirs are in such a state that they cannot hold more than one season's supply, and many, however heavy the rainfall, are dry before the end of the next hot season. Of late, especially during the 1876-77 famine, much has been done by Irrigation engineers to improve the reservoirs. Of the improved reservoirs the chief is the Gaddekeri lake at Mugutkhán-Hubli about fifteen miles south-east of Belgaum. The Gaddekeri lake has an area of 126 acres and a maximum depth of five feet. The catchment basin measures 4·62 square miles and the average rainfall is 26·33 inches. Before the 1876 famine it was intended to raise the water surface 2·38 feet, thereby increasing the gross storage from 14¼ to 27½ millions of cubic feet, and to build two waste weirs one at each end of the dam. The dam was begun as a relief work in 1877 and completed in 1878. The estimated cost of the proposed improvements was £1616 (Rs. 16,160); the expenditure on famine relief labour up to the end of 1877-78 amounted to £831 14*s*. (Rs. 8317); and the value of the work done, at normal rates, was £798 6*s*. (Rs. 7983). Since 1877, at a cost of £1130 (Rs. 11,300), the water surface as originally intended has been raised 2·38 feet, thus increasing the storage by thirteen millions of cubic feet. The improved lake will furnish a supply for 450 acres. On lands watered from the Gaddekeri lake a special acre cess of 10*s*. (Rs. 5) is levied for rice lands, and of £1 (Rs. 10) for garden lands. The rates are levied not according to the fitness of the land for rice or for garden crops, but according to the crop for which the water is actually used.

Three water-drawing appliances are in use, *mots* or leather-bags, *páts* or channels, and *dols* or bamboo baskets. The *mot* is a large leather-bag with two holes. One hole which is nearly the entire breadth of the bag, is kept at full stretch by a square or round frame with cross pieces, the other hole is narrow and pipe-like. A stout rope fixed to the bars of the great hole, is passed over a roller supported by side posts above the level of the reservoir, and is fastened to the yoke of the bullocks who draw up the bag. A smaller rope, fastened to the pipe-like hole of the bag, passes over a second roller below the first roller, and is fixed to the greater rope near the yoke. An inclined plane is prepared, down which the bullocks walk and draw up the full bag till at the top it spills into a masonry cistern. Then, while the empty bag falls into the water and fills, the bullocks back to the top of the slope and again walk down the slope dragging up another bagful. From the cistern into which the bag spills channels carry the water all over the land. Leather-bags are also used in drawing water

Chapter IV.
Agriculture.
Irrigation.

from holes dug near rivers and streams. Channels or *páts* are built to carry off water from rivers, streams, and reservoirs. The channels are supplied with water without the aid of bags from streams or other water-courses where water can be dammed to the proper level and turned into the channel. When the water in a stream or reservoir is below the level of the channel or *pát* the water is raised by a basket or *dol*, a three-cornered bamboo basket large enough to hold an ordinary jar of water. At two corners of the basket ropes are tied. The end of each rope is caught by a strong man, for the work is heavy, and they dip the basket into the water, and when it is full, lift it up and toss into the channel as much water as remains in the basket. In some places two to six baskets are worked at the same time.

Wells.

Of 11,818 wells used for watering, 3374 are step-wells and 8444 are dip wells. Of the 11,818 wells, 4214, of which 948 are step-wells and 3266 are dip-wells, are in Chikodi; 3073, of which 136 are step-wells and 2937 are dip-wells, are in Belgaum; 1832, of which 1191 are step-wells and 641 are dip-wells, are in Athni; 1028, of which 533 are step-wells and 495 are dip-wells, are in Gokák; 905, of which 337 are step-wells and 568 are dip-wells, are in Sampgaon; and 766, of which 229 are step-wells and 537 are dip-wells, are in Parasgad. In Khánápur no wells are used for watering. Water is always drawn from wells by the leather-bag or *mot*. Water is found near the surface in a small area close to the Nágzari springs in the Belgaum Cantonment and in the Chikodi villages along the Krishna. In other parts of the district, especially in Parasgad, wells have sometimes to be sunk as much as a hundred and fifty feet. The depth of wells varies from five to sixty feet in Belgaum, from twelve to forty feet in Sampgaon, from ten to fifteen feet in Chikodi, from twenty to 150 feet in Parasgad, from twenty-five to fifty feet in Gokák, and from thirty to fifty feet in Athni. The cost of building a step-well varies from £50 to £400 (Rs. 500-4000), and of building a dip-well from £10 to £200 (Rs.100-2000). At a good well four water-bags can be worked. With a sufficient supply of water one bag can water five acres, the area largely depending on the soil and the crop. In ordinary cases one bag waters from one-fourth of an acre to an acre in a day. The crop is watered by channels carried from the top of the well, where the bag is emptied, to the fields. The channels are made so as to allow the course of the water to be changed every two or three yards so that each row of crops may have an equal supply. The crops irrigated are rice, sugarcane, potatoes, onions, garlic, cabbage, and other vegetables, plantain trees, groundnuts, chillies, sweet potatoes, and turmeric. The husbandmen value irrigation, but few are able to bear the expense of sinking wells and building channels. Within the last five years the returns show a gradual fall in the area of irrigated garden land. In 1878-79 the garden area under irrigation was 17,900 acres, in 1879-80 it fell to 16,222 acres, in 1880-81 to 16,520, and in 1881-82 to 15,870 acres. This decline in the irrigated area is believed to be due to the fact that the lands are mortgaged to moneylenders and that as the mortgager may any day be foreclosed, the holders are unwilling to be at the expense of irrigating them.

Chapter IV.

Agriculture.

Irrigation.

Gokák Canal.

A great water-work called the Gokák canal is at present being made at the expense of Imperial revenues. A project for a large canal with headworks on the Ghatprabha above the Gokák falls was first brought to notice in 1852 by Captain, subsequently Sir George, Wingate. A preliminary survey, made by Colonel, now Lieutenant-General, Walter Scott, R.E., showed remarkable facilities for leading a canal from a point about two miles above the falls to water the tract lying between the Ghatprabha and the Krishna and comprising portions of Gokák in Belgaum and Bágalkot in Bijápur and of the Mudhol and Jamkhandi states. The river has a sheer descent of about 170 feet at the lowest part, and at the spot chosen for the canal-head the total command is about 220 feet. Colonel Scott showed that, by cutting through a ridge of hills on the left of the valley, the canal could at once be brought out with complete command of the country beyond. From 1865 to 1867 the project was surveyed in detail by Lieutenant now Major Smith R. E., under the orders of Colonel now Lieutenant-General Fife R. E. It comprised a total length of 162 miles of main canal at an estimated cost of £485,000 (Rs. 48,50,000). Owing to the difficulties of carrying the canal through the native states the larger project was placed in abeyance, and a fresh scheme was drawn up for a definite project for watering only the lands of Gokák in Belgaum. In 1868 the project was submitted. It comprised fifty miles of main canal commanding an area of 135 square miles. The cost for works only was estimated at £150,000 (Rs. 15,00,000) and the return on expenditure at six and a quarter to six and three quarters per cent. The Government of India did not consider the scheme sufficiently satisfactory to admit of its being sanctioned from loan funds, and suggested further revision of the designs and estimates. This revision was in progress, when, in 1871, under orders from the Government of India, all large irrigation projects in the Bombay Presidency were placed in abeyance. In 1873 the revision of the scheme ordered in 1869 was carried out by Major now Colonel C. B. F. Penny R. E., and plans and estimates were made ready for an immediate beginning of the work. According to Major Penny's plan a masonry weir was to be thrown across the Ghatprabha at a site about two and a half miles above the falls. The great natural height thus obtained would allow the canal to be led from the left bank at right angles to the course of the river. The canal would run north for about nine miles where it would cross the Pamaldini streamlet by an aqueduct of thirteen arches each of thirty feet span. From this point the canal would take an easterly course generally parallel to the river and from six to eight miles from it. The canal would tail at the village of Shivápur forty miles from the head. A branch about twelve miles long would be taken off at the third mile. The scheme included provision for complete regulation and distribution. The canal was designed to carry 430 cubic feet a second at the head and to command a total arable area of 77,319 acres or 121 square miles at an estimated cost of £97,500 (Rs. 9,75,000). During the 1876 famine the Gokák canal project was brought forward as a means of usefully employing the

Chapter IV.
Agriculture.
Irrigation.
Gokak Canal.

people. Between the end of 1876 and December 1877 the earthworks on a length of nine miles of canal, beyond the deep cutting in the first 3½ miles, were partially completed. The highest number of people employed was 11,946, the outlay was £17,788 (Rs. 1,77,880) on wages and charitable relief, and the value of the work done was £7646 (Rs. 76,460). In October 1877 a gang of about 600 convicts was employed on the heavy cuttings through the ridges in the first 3½ miles of the canal. The works during the famine were in the charge of Mr. H. G. Palliser, the Executive Engineer for Irrigation in Belgaum and Dhárwár, acting under the orders of Colonel now Major-General Merriman R. E., then Chief Engineer for Irrigation. In December 1877 the Mudhol Chief desired to have the Gokák canal extended through his territory. Steps were taken to ascertain how far it was possible to modify the designs so as to allow the canal to debouch on to the watershed between the Krishna and the Ghatprabha near the village of Mantar about 110 miles from the head works, from which point branches could be thrown to command the Bágalkot sub-division of Bijápur on both sides of the water-shed. In April 1879, Sir Richard Temple, then Governor of Bombay, visited the country intended to be cut by the canal. As he considered it necessary as far as possible to utilize the work already done by famine and convict labour, fresh plans and estimates were made. The part of the new project sanctioned in March 1882 comprised the weir and headworks on the Ghatprabha four miles above Gokák with two and a half miles of main canal and a branch eleven miles long to the village of Vaddarhatti eight miles north-east of Gokák. This section which is nearly completed (February 1884) commands the country between the Ghatprabha and its tributary the Pamaldini which includes about 25,200 acres of good arable land. The cost is estimated at at £45,800 (Rs. 4,58,000) including all charges.[1] The extent to which the scheme, as sketched out by Sir Richard Temple, may eventually be expanded, comprises a length of about 180 miles of main canal with very extensive storage works to supplement the natural supply of water in the river during the dry season. The total area that would thus be commanded is about 625 square miles, of which about 375 square miles are in British territory and the remainder in the neighbouring native states. The entire cost of such a scheme is estimated at £1,400,000 (Rs. 1,40,00,000) and the return at four and a half per cent. The canal would have a discharging capacity at head of 1200 cubic feet a second and the storage works would impound 10,580 million cubic feet.[2]

Manure.

Pure black soil does not require manure, but the yield from red and sandy soils depends on the amount of manure they receive. Husbandmen value manure highly. Each landholder has his manure-pit into which every morning house sweepings, ashes, and cattle litter are thrown. To this all kinds of rubbish and decayed vegetable

---

1 The works have been designed and carried out by Mr. R. B. Joyner, C. E., Executive Engineer for Irrigation in Belgaum, Dhárwár, and Bijápur.

2 Fuller details are given by Mr. R. B. Joyner under Gokák in Places of Interest.

Chapter IV.
Agriculture.
Manure.

matter and fallen leaves are added. By the time it is ready for carting the rubbish and litter have decayed to powder which is generally spread in the fields from about the middle of March till the end of May between the thunderstorms which are commonly known as the mango showers. The supply from the manure-pit is supplemented by gathering into heaps in the field and burning roots of the former crop, dried weeds, and rubbish. In rare cases, as soon as the first rain falls, a farmer plants some quick-growing crop and ploughs it green into the land as manure for the main crop. Bone manure is not used. The supply of manure would be much greater if the bulk of the cattle dung was not burnt as fuel. The husbandman's belief in liberal manuring is shown by the high price house-sweepings, litter, and other garbage command in all large towns and villages. To manure an acre of land ten to fifteen cartloads are required, each cartload costing 1*s*. to 2*s*. (8 *as*. - Re. 1).

Rotation.

Millet is the least exhausting and cotton is the most exhausting crop. In places where land is scarce, husbandmen frequently raise red millet for many years from the same red soil fields without change; and on rich black soil there is no more profitable course than to grow an unbroken succession of crops of white millet. It is believed that yearly crops of white millet might be raised for a century without wearing out the land. As a rule, cotton and other cold-weather or *hingári* crops are raised in alternation with each other. Cotton, particularly, does not thrive two successive years on the same ground; it must be followed by white millet or by wheat. Among the various rain or *mungári* crops, when other considerations admit of such a course, some variety, though not a systematic circle of changes, is observed.

Wood-ash Tillage.

Formerly large tracts in the more open parts of the forests were cultivated by brushwood-burning or *kumri*. The chief brushwood burners were Maráthás. In the cold season, on a space of ground, commonly on a hill-side, the Maráthás cut down the bushes and the lower branches of the larger trees. They let the brushwood and dead branches dry during the hot season and burnt them before the rains set in. The effects of the fire pass three to six inches below the surface. In some places, without touching the surface with a tool, on the fall of the first south-west rain, the seed is sown in the ashes. In other places before the seed is sown the ground is ploughed or hoed by the hand. *Rági* Eleusine corocana, and in the next year *sáva* Panicum miliare occasionally mixed with pulse, are the grains raised by bush-burning. After the second year's crop the plot is considered exhausted and is left. After ten or twelve years, when the ground is again clothed with bushes and its surface regains something of a turfy texture, the process is repeated. This form of tillage, because of the destruction it caused to the brushwood, was for many years very greatly restricted. The restriction pressed heavily on the hill-people. They found no other employment and yearly made long journeys to Sávantvádi and Goa where wood-ash tillage was allowed. Under these circumstances, subject to certain conditions, arrangements have been made for allotting tracts of bush-land for wood-ash tillage.

Chapter IV.
Agriculture.
Tillage.

Tillage is either dry, *kádáramba* (K.), or wet, *periráramba* (K.). The dry field tillage varies according as the soil is black or red and sandy. For dry tillage a black soil field is first ploughed and cleared of grass and weeds by the heavy or *negali* plough. Three ploughings by this heavy plough, one along, one across, and one cornerwise, are almost always given. These, especially in cotton fields, are necessary to uproot a grass called *karige* Cynodon dactylon which, eight to ten inches below the surface, forms a thick mat and chokes all other growth. If after three ploughings any bushes are still standing they have to be uprooted by the hoe. When the large clods left by the plough, after having been thoroughly burnt by the sun, are slightly softened by the first south-west rains, they are crushed by drawing a block of heavy wood over them and the ground is two or three times loosened by the hoe-harrow or *kunti*. When a black soil field has been once brought under tillage it requires no more ploughing. The only care of the husbandman in after-years is to keep the surface as firm and consistent as possible. All that is wanted before the yearly sowing is to hoe or harrow the field so that all weeds may be cleared from it and the surface loosened. To save himself the trouble of using the heavy plough, whenever he sees new shoots of *karige* or other grass the farmer removes them by digging the weedy spots during the dry season with a hand-hoe. If he is careless and allows the weeds to grow, their turfy roots year after year gain strength and widen the area that is unfit for crops. Red and sandy soils, especially sandy soils which are apt to harden and cake after rain, are kept loose and friable by ploughing the field every year with the light plough or *ranti*. Two, if not three, ploughings are necessary; the first lengthwise, the second across, and the third, if at all, cornerwise. Hardworking landholders generally give the first ploughing immediately after the crop has been cleared and the second ploughing after the first heavy fall in the next south-west rainy season. Afterwards the clods are broken and the surface smoothed and prepared for sowing by a scalping knife which cuts up the old stubble *hanchichuru* (K.), stout stalks of weeds, and whatever else presents itself. If a considerable time has passed since the last scuffing this operation is repeated immediately before sowing. Both in red and in black soils the seed is sown from the drill or *kurgi*. After the seed has been sown it is covered with loose earth and the field is harrowed. Delicate seeds in particular soils are sometimes sown broadcast and then covered by having a bundle of prickly bamboos or other thorny bushes drawn over the field. The same is sometimes done in detached and uneven spots that do not admit of the use of the seed-drill.

Crops.

According to their seed times and harvest times Belgaum crops belong to three classes, early-rain or *tusi* (H.); main-rain called *kharif* (H. and M.) or *mungári* (K.); and late or cold-weather called *rabi* (M. and H.) or *hingári* (K.). Crops sown in the latter half of May and the first half of June and gathered before the end of September are called *tusi* or early-rain crops. To this class belong *náchni* (M.) or *rági* (K.), Eleusine corocana; *udid* (M.) or *uddu* (K.), Phaseolus mungo; *til* (M.) or *yallu* (K.), Sesamum indicum; maize, *makái* (M.)

or *mekke jala* (K.), Zea mays; and *rála* (M.) *káng* (M.) or *navni* (K.), Panicum italicum. The *kharif* or main monsoon crops include crops sown towards the end of June and in the beginning of July, that is when the first heavy fall of rain is supposed to be over, and reaped in December and January. The main monsoon crops are Indian millet, *jvári* (M.) or *jvála* (K.), Sorghum vulgare; spiked millet, *bájri* (M.) or *saji* (K.), Penicillaria spicata; rice, *bhát* (M.) or *bhatta* (K.), Oryza sativa; *math* (M.) or *madki* (K.), Phaseolus aconitifolius; *tur* (M.) or *togri* (K.), Cajanus indicus; *kulthi* (M.) or *hurli* (K.), Dolichos biflorus; *mug* (M.) or *hesru* (K.), Phaseolus radiatus; *pávta* (M.) or *avri* (K.), Dolichos lablab; *javas* (M.) or *agsi* (K.), Linum usitatissimum; *tág* (M.) or *sanbu* (K.), Crotalaria juncea; and *ambádi* (M.) or *pundi* (K.), Hibiscus cannabinus. The *rabi*, that is the late or cold-weather crops, comprise all cold-weather crops that is those which require little or no rain. They are sown in September and October and are reaped in January and February. The chief cold-weather crops are gram, *harbhara* (M.) or *kadli* (K.), Cicer arietinum; wheat, *ghau* (M.) or *godi* (K.), Triticum æstivum; cotton, *kápus* (M.) *hatti* (K.), Gossypium herbaceum; tobacco, *tambáku* (M.) or *háge soppu* (K.), Nicotiana tabacum; castor, *erand* (M.) or *audla* (K.), Ricinus communis; and safflower, *kardai* (M.) or *kusbi* (K.), Carthamus tinctorius.

In 1881-82, of 1,072,820 acres held for tillage, 196,815 acres or 18·34 per cent were fallow or under grass. Of the remaining 876,005 acres 69,921 were twice cropped. Of the 945,926 acres under tillage, grain crops occupied 698,337 acres or 73·82 per cent, 422,945 of them under Indian millet, Sorghum vulgare; 64,774 under rice, Oryza sativa; 63,499 under wheat, Triticum æstivum; 58,381 under spiked millet, Penicillaria spicata; 38,016 under Italian millet, Panicum italicum; 30,016 under *rági* or *náchni*, Eleusine corocana; 9416 under *sáva*, Panicum miliare; 4360 under *harika*, Paspalum scrobiculatum; 1972 under maize, Zea mays; 57 under barley, Hordeum hexastychon; and 4901 under other grains of which details are not given. Pulses occupied 92,767 acres or 9·80 per cent. Of these 29,757 were under cajan pea, Cajanus indicus; 25,534 under gram, Cicer arietinum; 23,975 under *kulthi*, Dolichos biflorus; 3379 under peas, *vatána*, Pisum sativum; 2381 under *mug*, Phaseolus radiatus; 1337 under *masur*, Ervum lens; 564 under *udid*, Phaseolus mungo; and 5840 under other pulses. Oilseeds occupied 36,578 acres or 3·86 per cent, of which 4668 were under gingelly seed, Sesamum indicum; 1507 under linseed, Linum usitatissimum; 1082 under rape, *sarau*, Brassica napus; 108 under mustard, Sinapis racemosa; and 29,213 under other oilseeds. Fibres occupied 92,988 acres or 9·83 per cent, of which 91,407 were under cotton, Gossypium herbaceum; 982 under Bombay hemp, Crotalaria juncea; and 599 under brown hemp, Hibiscus cannabinus. Miscellaneous crops occupied 25,256 acres or 2·67 per cent, of which 4176 were under sugarcane, *us* (M.) or *kabbu* (K.), Saccharum officinarum; 9314 under tobacco, Nicotiana tabacum; 7967 under chillies, Capsicum frutescens; 84 under coffee; and the remaining 3715 under various vegetables and fruits.

The chief details of some of the most important crops are: Indian

Chapter IV.
Agriculture.
CROPS.
Indian Millet.

millet, *jvári* (M.) or *jvála* (K.), Sorghum vulgare, in 1881-82 covered 422,945 acres or 44·71 per cent of the whole tilled area. It is grown all over the district, especially in Athni, Parasgad, Chikodi, Sampgaon, and Gokák. It is the chief main-rain or *mungári* crop and is grown in all red soils, except in the lighter and more sandy lands where spiked millet is often mixed with it. Sometimes it is mixed with one or several pulses together with a few seeds of Bombay hemp. The reason why pulses are sown with Indian millet is that in case the rains fail and the corn crop is scanty, the pulses, which can bear up against drought and ripen with the help of dew alone, may yield some return. Where the millet does well, it smothers the pulse without taking any harm. In growing millet after the first heavy fall of rain generally early in June, the field is three times ploughed under ordinary circumstances with the light plough or *ranti*. The seed is sown by the seed-drill or *kurgi* (K.), one row out of every two or three being sown with pulse. The sowing season is the second half of June and the first half of July when the first heavy fall of rain has softened the soil. Indian millet as a rule is ready for reaping about the middle of November, nearly a fortnight after the end of the south-west rains. Several weeks before the crop ripens, as soon as the corn heads begin to form, guards, some on foot others on stages or in trees, are set to keep off birds and pilferers.[1] When the reaping is over the grain is trodden out by the feet of cattle and winnowed. It is then ready for use. Indian millet is the common food of the people and the straw is used as fodder for horses and cattle. After years of scarcity millet straw becomes so valuable near Belgaum that much of the cotton land is given to millet. One advantage of millet is that it takes very little out of the soil. Where land is scarce, farmers often raise Indian millet on the same red fields year after year. The pulses which are grown with Indian millet take longer to ripen, and remain in the fields till after the beginning of January nearly two months after the millet has been reaped.

Spiked Millet.

Spiked Millet, *bájri* (M.) or *saji* (K.), Penicillaria spicata, in 1881-82 covered 58,381 acres or 6·17 per cent of the tillage area. It is grown chiefly in Athni, Gokák, and Chikodi. The time and the way of growing spiked millet are almost the same as the time and way of growing Indian millet. In sandy plains they are often sown together. The chief difference is that spiked millet ripens about the end of October, that is a fortnight before Indian millet. Spiked millet is eaten chiefly by the labouring classes. The straw makes excellent thatch. It is also eaten by cattle but is not esteemed as fodder.

Rice.

Rice, *bhát* (M.) *bhatta* (K.), Oryza sativa, in 1881-82 covered 64,774 acres or 6·84 per cent of the tillage area. It is chiefly grown in Khánápur, Belgaum, and Sampgaon. There are five modes of rice tillage, three regular modes, and two extra modes which are used only when the regular modes fail. The first and best form of rice tillage is called *rop* (M.) *natihackhona* (K.), or planting, but many

---

1 A head of Indian millet commonly contains 400 to 500 grains; in a remarkably fine head 2000 grains have been counted. Marshall's Belgaum, 10.

Chapter IV.
Agriculture.
Crops.
Rice.

husbandmen shrink from it because of the cost and the heaviness of the labour. In Khánápur and Belgaum during April or early May a small nursery or seed-bed, a plot to which water has easy access, is covered with leaves, wood, straw, and rubbish, and this covering is burnt in late May before the first rainfall. At the same time the fields into which the seedlings are to be planted are being got ready. The field-banks are mended, the water-ways cleared, stiff plants and stalks are cut out, and as much of the ground as possible is covered with grass, weeds, and rubbish, and burnt. When the first rain falls the seed-bed is thrice ploughed and harrowed. When well soaked it is covered with a thick broadcast sowing of rice in husk. The ploughing of the fields into which the seedlings are to be planted is not begun until the bullocks sink in the mud to the knees, a dreadful toil both to man and bullocks. Every field is thrice ploughed, and after the third ploughing, to clear it of roots, is harrowed with a long-toothed harrow. In a good season, that is heavy rain with gleams of sun, after five weeks or early in June the seedlings are fifteen to eighteen inches high and fit for planting. When the seedlings are ready, if possible in a break of bright weather, cowdung-ashes, litter, and leaves decayed to dust in the manure-pit are brought from the village, spread equally over the field, and trodden deep into the mud. When the field is manured the surface is levelled by dragging over it a loaded board called *hendor* (M.) or *karadu hodiyona* (K.). A day or two later, still if possible in fine weather when the field is not deep in water, the seedlings are rooted by the hand out of the seed-bed and brought to the fields in baskets. A rake with short teeth, ten to twelve inches apart, is drawn over the smooth ground to mark the lines in which the seedlings are to be set. The workers, who are generally women, follow with baskets from which they take small handfuls of eight to ten plants, and, at ten to twelve inches apart and as far as possible opposite the middle of the interval of the next row, thrust them about a foot deep. Except so much as is wanted to flood the lower fields the water is kept in the field and when each field has had its share the channel to it is blocked. Two weedings are given, but, as the field has been so carefully cleaned, the weeds are seldom strong. In ordinary years planted rice is ready for cutting in November or December. The second mode of growing rice is the *kivri* or *kurgi*, that is the seed-drill plan. This system is adopted in the hope that enough rain will fall within a week after the seed has been sown to make the soil muddy. It saves much labour, but should the rain hold off for about a fortnight the ground becomes heated and the seed suffers from the dryness and is eaten by birds and lizards. At best the outturn is small. The third method is adopted when the early rain is so heavy that the seed-drill cannot be worked. Furrows are made by the light plough and the seed is sown in the furrow. This furrow-sowing system never yields a good crop. When one of the three regular modes fails, in the hope that the harvest may not be entirely lost, sprouted seed or *málaki* (K.) is sown. A sackcloth or matting bag is filled with grain, dipped in water, and laid in a warm close place. In three or four days the seeds sprout and are thrown

Chapter IV. Agriculture. Crops. Rice.

thick and broadcast on the field. The fifth mode of growing rice is to root out the sprouted rice seedlings where they have come too thickly and plant them into the bare fields. This is the rice-grower's forlorn hope. It is called *surdi* (K.) or the cold crop, perhaps because it does not ripen till the close of the cold weather.

Ripe rice is reaped and thrashed either by striking the ears against a board, or by beating them with a stick. After winnowing the grain is carried home and dried in the sun. The husks of as much as is wanted for immediate use are beaten off in a stone mortar, *ukhal* (M.) or *varalu* (K.), by a wooden pestle, *musal* (M.) or *vanaki* (K.), and the rest is stored in high cylindrical baskets called *kungi*, the openings in which within and without are closed by a coating of cowdung.

In parts of Khánápur near the Sahyádris two crops of rice are grown every year. The first crop is sown with a seed-drill about the end of June, or is sown sprouted in August. It ripens towards the end of October and is called the *Kártik* or October-November crop. The second crop is sown sprouted in November and December, and ripens towards the end of April. It is called the *Vaishákh* that is the March-April or the *sugi* crop. The April crop is reckoned better than the October crop because it is not exposed to the cold weather winds.

Wheat.

Wheat, *gahu* (M.) *godi* (K.), Triticum æstivum, in 1881-82 covered 63,499 acres or 6·71 per cent of the tillage area. It is grown in Belgaum, Sampgaon, Parasgad, Athni, Gokák, and Chikodi. Three varieties of wheat are grown in Belgaum, *támbda* or red, *khapli*, and *holi*. The *támbda* or red is the best variety and is like English wheat. The *khapli* is a bearded wheat like English barley except that the grain is oblong. It is grown as a watered crop in garden lands. The *holi* is an inferior wheat grown in rice lands after the rice has been carried. Wheat is a cold-weather or *rabi* crop. It prospers only in good black soil. In October, soon after the first heavy burst of the north-east or Madras monsoon, the wheat is sown like *jvári* in carefully prepared and manured land and is reaped in January and February. The quantity of seed varies from twelve to thirty-two pounds the acre. In wheat-growing lands the best succession of crops is said to be Indian millet the first year, cotton the second year, wheat the third year, Indian millet the fourth, cotton the fifth, and wheat the sixth, and so on in the same rotation. In some places wheat alternates with sugarcane and gram; occasionally *kusbi* or safflower is raised two to six feet apart between the rows of wheat. The safflower does not ripen till one month after the wheat, that is about the end of March, and in no way interferes with its growth. Instead of safflower, linseed or gram is often grown. Wheat takes three to three and a half months to ripen and grows eighteen inches to two feet high in good soils and one foot high in poor soils. Towards the end of December one good shower is wanted to make the wheat crop safe. Southerly winds are said to be bad for wheat, northerly or easterly winds are preferred. An excessively cold wind causes a blight called *ittangi* (K.), also called *kunkam rog*, which turns the wheat red and reduces the outturn. The average wholesale rupee price of wheat is about 2*s*. the quarter (28 pounds the rupee). Wheat is not the staple food of the people. Only the rich and well-to-do can afford it for everyday use. The poorer classes eat it only on holidays. Wheat is brought from Dhárwár and Bijápur, and is sent to Goa, Vengurla, and other Konkan ports, and thence to Bombay. A small quantity goes to Kolhápur. Wheat from Athni finds its way to Belgaum, Kolhápur, Vengurla, Chiplun, and Rájápur. No wheat is carried to any railway station from any part of the district. The nearest stations are Poona 210 and Bársi 140 miles from Belgaum. The cart-hire to these stations varies from £1 to £2 (Rs.10-20). The hire of a cart which carries 1000 pounds from Belgaum to Vengurla, a distance of about sixty miles is 16*s.* to £1 (Rs.8-10). Belgaum traders buy wheat from the Bijápur growers and send it to Vengurla and to Bombay on their own account.

Sugarcane.

Sugarcane, *us* (M.) *kabbu* (K.), Saccharum officinarum, in 1881-82 covered 4176 acres or 0·44 per cent of the tillage area. It is grown chiefly in Chikodi, Belgaum, Sampgaon, and Khánápur. It is raised in the same lands as rice, and it is usual to have one crop of cane followed by two crops of rice. The first step in growing sugarcane is taken in the first half of January when the land receives three ploughings with the light plough, one lengthwise, one across, and one cornerwise. As much manure as the landholder is able to gather is harrowed into it; about three tons an acre is a fair quantity. All roots bushes and rubbish are harrowed out. In the beginning of February furrows are drawn all over the field by the light plough nine or ten inches deep and nine or ten inches apart. Water is let into the furrows till the bottom is deep in mud. Into the mud sugarcane cuttings, fifteen to eighteen inches long and with three to five joints, are laid flat and firmly pressed into the bottom of the furrow by the foot. The plough is driven between the furrows to cover the cane-cuttings. If the cane is the common white kind no more watering is required, and the field is levelled by drawing over it a cross beam of wood. It is covered with straw to keep the surface from parching in the sun and is enclosed with a hedge. Except two hand weedings, no further expense is incurred. If they are of the black cane, after the cuttings are covered with earth, the furrows are not entirely filled with earth, as, from February until the rains in June, water must be let into the field at least once every fourteen days. The cane ripens at the end of a year. To plant an acre of sugarcane 20,000 cuttings are required. They cost about 1*s.* (8 *as.*) the thousand for the white kind and 2*s.* (Re.1) for the black. In the raw state as the black is sweeter it fetches a higher price than the white, the black cane selling for ¾*d.* (½ *anna*) and the white for ⅛*d.* ($\frac{1}{12}$ *anna*) a piece. Both varieties are used for making molasses or *gur.* Molasses is made in a press of two upright solid wooden cylinders on one of which is cut an endless male screw and on the other an endless female screw. These are set in pivots cut in a strong plank which is fixed at one edge of the bottom of a pit two or three feet deep. The pit is large enough to hold, besides the press, the boiling apparatus and the workmen. The male screw cylinder is about a foot higher than the female and into its head a horizontal bar is let to

Chapter IV.
Agriculture.
Crops.
Sugarcane.

which a bullock is yoked and keeps the machine constantly revolving. The bullock's path is on the level ground outside the mouth of the pit, and the bar as it circles passes clear of the top of the female cylinder. The canes are broken off close to the ground and cut into pieces about a foot long. A man sits above and keeps feeding the cylinders with pieces of cane. The juice is thoroughly squeezed out, and runs into a large earthen vessel at the base of the press. A bamboo spout leads it into a flat copper pan under which a hole is dug for the fire, and the juice is kept gently and constantly boiling. When it has gained a proper consistency it is baled into a cloth which lies loosely over a hole in the earth about a foot across and four or five inches deep. The molasses is thus formed into a flattish cake called *dhep*.

Ragi.

Rági or *náchni*, Eleusine corocana, in 1881-82 covered 30,016 acres or 3·17 per cent of the tillage area. It is grown chiefly in Khánápur, Belgaum, Chikodi, and Sampgaon. *Rági* is one of the early monsoon crops, being sown in April or May and reaped in September. It is grown on all red soils in West Belgaum and Khánápur. *Rági* is sometimes raised on fallow ground to make it fit to yield a crop of *sávi* Panicum miliare in the next year. In some places it is grown on plots that have yielded a *til* crop in the previous year and in the year after will yield *sávi*. The ground is prepared by burning on it wood, leaves, and rubbish. Commonly some pulses and not unfrequently a few seeds of mustard and Indian maize are sown with the *rági* for home use. In parts of the country *rági* seed is mixed with cowdung and a small quantity is dropped with the hand at intervals of about nine inches apart into furrows drawn by the small plough about seven inches apart. After this the seeds are covered and the field smoothed either by the levelling block or *karadu* or by a smaller scalping knife called *balsál*. In every seventh furrow some pulse or other bush grain as *mung, tur, pávta* and *udid* are sown. *Rági* is sown with the first shower of the south-west monsoon, that is immediately after the thunder-storms in April and May. It ripens and is ready for gathering in September before the end of the rains. It is cut by the sickle, tied in small sheaves, and stacked on the spot until the October rains are over, when it is thrashed. *Rági* is a very productive crop and can be raised in places too steep for the plough or harrow. The grain is generally eaten by the poorer classes. It is ground into flour and dressed in various ways. *Rági* straw is reckoned better than rice straw for all kinds of cattle.

Tobacco.

Tobacco, *tambáku* (M.) *hágesoppu* (K.), Nicotiana tabacum, in 1881-82 covered 9314 acres or 0·98 per cent of the tillage area. It is grown chiefly in Athni and Chikodi in gardens or on favourable plots near villages or along rivers and streams. The best tobacco is raised on the deep alluvial lands near the Krishna. The seed is sown in nursery beds, usually in gardens, about the beginning of July. For the first month, if there is no rain, the beds must be watered every other day, and, after the first month, every fifth day. The seedlings are fit for planting towards the end of August. Before this the field, which is generally of the best soil, is manured

Tobacco.

by penning sheep and cattle on it for several nights. Then the light plough is drawn over it, once lengthwise and once across, about two feet apart. Where two furrows cross the seedlings are planted and watered from a pot whenever the weather keeps fair for more than a day or two. After a fortnight a little dung is put to each plant and the field is hoed with a scalping knife. This hoeing has to be repeated several times to keep the soil open and powdered. At the end of about six weeks the top shoots are pinched off, and the pinching is repeated several times after. In December or January when it begins to whiten, the tobacco is fit for cutting. The stems are cut within two or three inches of the ground and are then split lengthwise, and the halves strung in a line and spread to the sun and air for twenty days, being turned every third day. After this the leaves are taken into the house, piled in a heap, covered with straw, and pressed with a large stone, and turned every fourth day. After this pressing and turning has been repeated four or five times the tobacco is fit for sale. Tobacco is generally grown every third year. In Chikodi and Athni, at a cost at £2 5*s.* (Rs. 22½), the acre yield in a good season is 420 pounds, but over a series of several years the average outturn is probably not more than 280 pounds. This at 5*s.* to 6*s.* (Rs. 2½ - 3) for twenty-eight pounds brings to the husbandman from £2 10*s.* to £3 (Rs. 25 - 30) or a net acre profit of 5*s.* to 10*s.* (Rs. 2½ - 5).

Cotton.

Cotton,[1] covering 91,407 acres or 9·66 per cent of the tillage area, is the most valuable and next to Indian millet the largest crop grown.

As cotton-growers the different sub-divisions of Belgaum come in the following order, Parasgad, Athni, Sampgaon, Gokák, Chikodi, Belgaum, and Khánápur.[2] The soil, roads, climate, and position of Sampgaon fit it to hold the first rank among the Belgaum cotton-growing tracts. The reason why it holds the third place is that its nearness to the Belgaum market makes grain pay better than cotton. As regards climate the Belgaum cotton plain has two great advantages. Its 1500 to 2000 feet above the sea keeps it comparatively cool, and the two fairly light monsoons in which it shares prevent the air from growing excessively dry, save the roots from being rotted with damp, and help the under-soil to keep moist far into the hot weather. In the cotton plains of Belgaum the average yearly rainfall for the twenty-three years ending 1882 varied from seventeen to twenty-three inches. Thermometer readings at Belgaum show a greatest heat of 101° in May and a least heat of 57° in December. Mr. Mercer, the American planter, who in 1840 travelled over a considerable part of India, noticed that the climate of the Bombay Karnátak was more like that of Mississipi than any climate he had experienced in India and that this had probably

[1] The account of Belgaum cotton is prepared from a pamphlet written by Mr. W. Walton, late superintendent of cotton gin factories and cotton improvements.

[2] In 1881-82 the areas under cotton in the different sub-divisions were, Parasgad 26,607 acres, Athni 24,258, Sampgaon 15,949, Gokák 13,784, Chikodi 9395, Belgaum 1405, and Khánápur 5 acres.

Chapter IV.
Agriculture.

much to do with the exceptional success of Mississipi seed in Belgaum and Dhárwár.[1]

Crops.
Cotton.
Kinds.

Three kinds of cotton are grown in Belgaum. Gossypium arboreum or *devkápus* (M.) that is God's Cotton, used in making sacred threads; Gossypium indicum or *juvári-hatti* (K.) that is country cotton; and Gossypium barbadense or *viláiti-hatti* (K.) that is foreign cotton. Of these three kinds Gossypium arboreum, a perennial bush growing ten to twelve feet high is much like the Peruvian or Brazilian cotton plant. It is raised in small quantities all over the district, both in the black eastern plains and close to the hilly forest-clad west. The cotton is white silky and of long staple, but too brittle to be used for ordinary purposes. It is never grown as a field plant and its wool never comes to market. Bushes are occasionally grown in gardens beside wells and streams and near temples. From the cotton of this plant Bráhmans make their sacred threads spinning it from a small reel called *bhirki,* temple servants make their lampwicks, and Bráhman and other high caste Hindu women spin it into thread for other purposes. Gossypium indicum or *juvári-hatti,* generally known as Kumta cotton, is largely planted everywhere. Gossypium barbadense, which is planted only sometimes and to a small extent in Parasgad and Sampgaon, is the American cotton which was introduced in 1845 by Government planters. Both Kumta and American cotton are grown as annuals.

Seed.

In former times great care was paid to the seed. Landholders, when their seed showed signs of losing strength, sent for a fresh supply from any part of the district where the crop was specially good. Of late years less care has been shown in the choice of seed, and the seed is also allowed to suffer from the practice of leaving the cotton unpicked after it is ripe. Showers fall and the damp seed tends to sprout and loses vigour. Cotton whose seed is meant for planting should be separately ginned. Separate ginning is necessary because seed for sowing should be as well preserved as possible, while the seed of cotton ginned for wool must be thoroughly dried in the sun before ginning. Seed for sowing must be kept in a dry and even temperature, and through the early rains must be often looked at and aired to check untimely sprouting. The people pay great care to the seed, keeping it in well covered dry earthenware pots, and taking it out and examining it every now and then until sowing time. It is easy to tell if cotton seed is good or is bad. Cut across it with a sharp knife and look at the kernel. If the seed is good the kernel is cream-coloured, moist, and speckled with little dark spots; if the seed is bad the kernel is a dirty yellow or brown and is shrivelled. In sending cotton seeds from one district or one country to another, especially by sea, the greatest care should be taken. The seed should

---

[1] Observations in the American cotton country between 30° and 34° north latitude and 78° and 96° west longitude show for eight towns in the more western tract (96°-90° west), a variation from 64° to 74° in means and from 47° to 87° in extremes, and for six places in the more eastern tract (82°-78° west) a variation from 57° to 72° in means, and from 42° to 83° in extremes.

Chapter IV. Agriculture. Crops. Cotton. *Seed.*

be packed in a cool, dry, airy place, where the temperature is as even as possible. On board ship the parcels should when practicable be in cabins or rooms on deck. Stowing below hatches often does much mischief to cotton seed. Some German authorities go so far as to say that no seed can keep its life if packed in the hold below the ship's water-line. This is not the case, as instances are known in which seed so packed sprouted and gave a middling crop. Still great risk is run and serious harm is almost always caused. With the more delicate kinds of cotton it is best to send the seed with the wool, just as picked from the plant. No seed should ever be placed near a ship's engines or boilers.

Soil.

In India for the growth of cotton, the soil should be loose and open enough to allow the air and sun to pass below the surface and still more to let excessive and untimely rain drain under the roots. These qualities the crumbling gaping soil of the deep black Belgaum plain has in an unusual degree. The black cotton soil, which the Kánarese husbandmen call *yera bhumi* (K.) or melted earth is of three classes, *regar* (Tel.) or pure black, a brown soil much like *regar* but geologically less matured and containing much disintegrated trap, and a gray black soil largely mixed with lime nodules and an underlayer of lime two to ten feet below the surface. The *regar* or pure black is best suited for the local cotton and the brown for the American cotton. The gray black is inferior to the other two, the staple being poorer and scantier. One great merit of the black and brown soils is the wonderful time the under-soil keeps moist. It is this underground dampness that enables the cotton plant to mature as late as March. When the surface is baked and gapes with the heat the cotton bushes are still green because the tap-roots are down in the cool moist undersoil. Cotton is seldom grown on red soil; the outturn is too small to pay at ordinary prices. Mr. D'Oyley, an assistant collector, once experimented with foreign cotton on red soil. He found the plants flourish so long as the rains lasted, but as soon as the dry weather set in they withered. Examination showed that the hardness of the soil had kept the roots from passing any distance below the surface.

Watering.

Much interesting information was collected in 1855 as to the effect of watering cotton in Belgaum. Mr. Goldfinch, of the Civil Service, stated that water was considered unnecessary if not hurtful. Some New Orleans plants failed in watered land, while others throve near at hand in the same soil without water. Mr. Seaton-Karr, of the Civil Service, had never seen cotton watered; he believed that watering would harm the plant. The late Colonel Meadows Taylor, C.S.I., who had paid close attention to the subject, condemned the watering of cotton. He tried several kinds at the same time some with and some without water. In all cases, except only with the Sea Island, watering was a failure. With Sea Island, up to a certain time, watering did good, but continued watering did harm. He thought that in deep black soils watering would always harm cotton, but in stony and shallow soil one or two judicious waterings might do good. In any case water should never be given after the 15th of December. He thought that the staple of watered

Chapter IV. **Agriculture.** CROPS. Cotton. *Watering.*

cotton would always prove weaker than the staple of unwatered cotton. The husbandmen whom Colonel Taylor consulted had never tried irrigation and agreed with him in all essential points. The result of experiments in watering cotton in Belgaum was in red soil an outturn of cotton worth 2*s.* 6*d.* (Rs. $1\frac{1}{4}$) at a cost of £1 0*s.* 8*d.* (Rs. $10\frac{5}{16}$); in black soil an outlay of 11*s.* 10*d.* (Rs. $5\frac{15}{16}$) yielded little more than half the quantity grown without water. Between 1845 and 1851, Mr. Channing, an American planter who was engaged by the East India Company and was sent by Government to Belgaum, made some experiments in red and clayey soils. He thought that in these soils water helped cotton, but it must be applied most carefully, after sunset and before sunrise and without wetting the leaves. He also held that the watered plants were more liable to blight and to injury from insects. In 1854, Mr. L. R. Ashburner, of the Civil Service, noticed that watering made cotton run to wood and seed and lessened the outturn of wool and weakened the staple. This view was supported by the American planters who declared that after the tap-roots had taken hold, soil and climate could hardly be too dry. In Dhárwár watering the cotton plants showed the same result. On one occasion, when want of rain threatened to destroy his crop, Mr. W. Shearer (1867-1875), the superintendent of cotton experiments, endeavoured to save it by watering. The watered plants yielded no more cotton than the unwatered plants, and the staple of the watered plants was exceptionally weak. So far as Mr. Shearer's experience went the only effect of watering either foreign or local cotton was to develop the plant at the expense of the fibre. Apart from the difficulty of keeping the plants in health during the whole of an ordinary hot season the annual cotton plant would seem to yield better cotton than the plant yields when it is allowed to remain in the ground for more than one season. In 1874, Mr. Walton, the superintendent of cotton gin factories in Belgaum, noticed that after a very heavy and late rainfall cotton was deficient in quantity and unusually weak in staple. At the beginning of the next rains the plants were so green that some landholders allowed them to stand till the next season. This attempt to make cotton perennial failed. In every place where it was tried the yield was very small, and the length and strength of the fibre much less than usual, while in the fields grown in the regular way, that is treating the plant as an annual, the crop was unusually large and good.

Change.

Mr. Mercer, an American planter, who was in Dhárwár between 1841 and 1846, came to the conclusion that, though poverty often prevented him from doing what was best, no one understood the benefit of a regular change of crops better than the Indian husbandman. On the other hand Dr. Wight maintained that in his rotation of crops the Indian husbandman was more governed by chance or caprice than by system. Mr. Walton's experience during the fifteen years ending 1880 satisfied him that Mr. Mercer's view was the correct view. The Belgaum husbandman, when well-to-do, is careful to change his crop according to regular rules. He knows that cotton takes much out of the soil, and, unless he is tempted by high prices, does not grow cotton oftener

Chapter IV. Agriculture. Crops. Cotton. *Change.*

than once in three years. Other circumstances besides a tempting price of cotton lead to the rule of rotation being broken. A landholder may make the proper field ready for cotton but the rain may be unsuitable for cotton and another crop may have to be sown. Cotton is one of the late, called *rabi* (M. and H.) or *hingári* (K.), crops. If rain falls well for the early crops the husbandman leaves less land than he ought for the late crops; if the early rain fails more land than he ought to leave is left for the late crops. Again as high cotton prices tempt the husbandman to grow more cotton than he ought to grow, so high grain prices tempt him to grow less cotton than he ought to grow. Still cotton is the husbandman's great money-bringing and rent-paying crop and he is always anxious to grow as much cotton as he can. Enquiries into the composition of cotton seem to show that the cotton or wool absorbs potash, lime, phosphoric acid, magnesia, and sulphuric acid, the proportions being about half of the whole potash, one-quarter lime, one-fifth phosphoric acid, and the greater part of the small remainder magnesia with a very little sulphuric acid. The total quantity absorbed is very small. It was calculated that some twelve pounds of the above ingredients were amalgamated in about two thousand pounds of cotton wool, so that the total quantity was only about one ounce to an acre. An analysis of the seed showed that the seed absorbed half as much again as the wool. Of ninety-six parts forty-five were phosphoric acid, thirty lime, twenty potash, and the small remainder sulphuric acid. No analysis of the plant is available.

Manure.

Manure is not put on the ground in the same year in which the land is sown with cotton. The husbandmen say that fresh manure heats the soil too much for cotton; they therefore put on the manure the year before the cotton is sown. The manure is the pulverised produce of the manure-pit in which dung, cattle litter, house sweepings, fallen leaves, ashes, and rubbish of all sorts have been laid to rot. Three to six cart-loads of manure an acre are generally spread on the fields in the hot season (March-May) between thunder-showers. To this is added the burnt roots of the former crop and occasionally some quick-growing crop is raised and ploughed in.

Tools.

The field tools used in growing cotton have been already described.

Tillage.

Mr. Mercer, the American planter (1841-1846), came to the conclusion that the system of growing cotton in the Kánarese country was not nearly so defective as was supposed. Many of the better class of husbandmen take great care in preparing their cotton land. It is cleared of all the stumps of the previous crop, partly by hand partly with the hoe or *kunti*. It is then ploughed either with the smaller or larger plough. The main object of working the large plough is not so much to turn the soil as to cut out the roots of weeds and wild plants, particularly the entangled and almost incredibly strong webs which the matted roots of *harrihalli* (M.) or *kariki* (K.) grass, Cynodon dactylon, form eight to twelve inches below the surface. Unless the *kariki*, which though hurtful as a weed is the best horse grass in the Karnátak, is cleared the cotton roots have no chance of striking into the subsoil and the

Chapter IV.
Agriculture.
Crops.
Cotton.
Tillage.

plants rapidly wither as the moisture withdraws from the surface to the subsoil. Even repeated workings of the heavy plough are not always sufficient to remove the roots of this grass. After several ploughings the weeds have often to be destroyed by men going round separately and cutting and uprooting them with a bladed pick or *bái-kudali.* After the ground is cleared the hoe is used to break the clods, but these are often so large and stubborn that they have first to be roughly separated by a heavy beam of wood, locally called the *koradu* (K.), dragged by several pairs of bullocks. After the beam the hoe or *kunti* (K.) is used. Even this is sometimes not enough and the clods have to be softened by rain before it is possible to break them. Another effectual way is to break the land by manual labour. Large numbers of labourers turn out with pickaxes or *bái-kudalis* (K.) and dig the land often two feet deep. This is very slow and hard work, but the result repays the severe labour and expense. The soil thus broken and smoothed is ready for seed.

A point which was often urged by the American planters, and which has since been strongly recommended by many outsiders, is early sowing. It is often stated that Belgaum cotton has to pass through many hardships because the seed is not sown soon enough. No rule can be laid down as to the correct time for sowing. In each district the time depends on the rainfall. No cotton seed can be successfully sown until enough rain has fallen to bring the soil into proper condition for starting the seed. This condition of the earth is much better understood by the local husbandman than by any stranger. In 1860, Mr. Mansfield, who had long known the Kánarese country, drew the attention of Government to an advertisement of the Bombay Chamber of Commerce, in which people were advised to sow cotton in May and November. All persons who followed this advice would, Mr. Mansfield observed, inevitably lose both their seed and their labour. In May the Belgaum soil is much like cinders at a temperature of one hundred and fifty degrees; and, if sowing is delayed till November, the cotton has not time to ripen before the fierce sun forces open the half-ripe bolls.

Cotton is sown in August, early or late according to the rainfall, but generally in the latter part of the month. As a rule cotton-sowing begins in the west fully a fortnight before it begins in the east. This is owing to the difference in rainfall. In fact the eastern country has often to wait for what the Kánarese call the *muggi mulli,* or return monsoon, that is rain from the east, before their land is in proper order for cotton and other late or *hingári* sowings. By the latter part of August the land has been thoroughly soaked, and is so far drained that the surface is comparatively dry. Land fairly dry on the surface with much moisture below is in the proper state for sowing cotton. It helps the seed to sprout and it draws the roots deep enough to support and bring the plant to perfection when the hot weather and trying east winds set in. Between the time of smoothing and of sowing the land the surface generally becomes more or less covered with weeds and grass. The husbandman easily removes these weeds with his hoe, and the hoeing also stirs the surface and makes it ready for the seed. The seeds are rubbed in fresh bullock-dung and water, which gives them a hard smooth surface, prevents their sticking together, and enables them to run freely through the sowing drill. The rubbing with cowdung is also said to quicken and help the sprouting. The seed is sown with the aid of the seed-drill or *kurgi* (K.), which has two iron teeth as far apart as the distance between the two rows of cotton. To each of the teeth a hollow bamboo tube called *yellishedi* (K.) is fastened. Bullocks are yoked to the seed-drill, and as the drill moves the iron teeth plough two drills, and in these the cotton seed is dropped through the bamboo tube. Two rows are thus sown about eighteen inches apart. The seed-drill is immediately followed by the hoe which closes the drills. The seed-leaves show in six to twelve days. In about a month, when the plants are three or four inches high, the farmer takes his simple but effective grubber or *yedi-kunti* (K.), and works it between the cotton plants doing two rows at a time. The grubber roots out all young weeds and grass, and, at the same time, turns over the surface soil and prevents it from souring, and also heaps the soil at the roots of the young plants. This heaping of the soil is repeated several times, the oftener the better, until the plants grow too high. The more hardworking and careful husbandmen besides the grubber employ hand labour. For this men women and children are hired on 3*d.* to 6*d.* a day (2-4 *as.*), weeding at a surprising speed with a *kurchigi* or miniature sickle. By the middle of October hard cutting east winds set in which are very trying to the cotton plants. These east winds last fully a month, when the strain is eased by occasional genial westerly breezes, and sometimes by timely showers. Then easterly winds again set in, and with an occasional break blow more or less heavily, until January and sometimes February. Meanwhile the plants have flowered, and these steady east winds rapidly mature them and ripen the bolls, so that the crop is ready for a first picking late in February or early in March. A good crop yields five and sometimes six pickings; a poor crop not more than three or four. All the picking, and in the case of the local cotton all the ginning, is done by women and children, the labour of the men ceasing when the plants reach maturity. The main anxiety with cotton is to plant it so that it will be ripe and get picked when there is no danger of rain. This essential is too often overlooked by those who think that the Belgaum husbandman might sow his cotton earlier, and thus have it sooner ready for export. Experience has taught the people that by sowing in August the chances of success are greater than by sowing at any other time.

The payment of the cotton-pickers causes frequent disputes. When the price of the staple rules high the husbandman wishes to pay the women in cash. When the price of the staple is low he wishes to pay them in kind. The pickers know well how cotton is selling, and as their interests are the opposite of the husbandman's, disputes are common. When the crop is large labour is generally scarce, then the women strike in the most determined way, and generally make the owner of the cotton come to terms.[1] In America when

---

[1] In 1850, according to Mr. Channing, the people were paid 1½*d.* (1 *anna*) for every

Chapter IV.
Agriculture.
Crops.
Cotton.
Tillage.

it grows too freely the cotton plant is topped or pruned. This is done to prevent the plant running to wood and leaf and to make it flower and fruit. Belgaum cotton plants are never pruned. During the fifteen years ending 1880 only in the heavy rains of 1874 did the plants grow to any great size. Even then they were no larger than the usual height in America. European agriculturists, both practical and amateur, have often remarked upon and condemned the crowded way in which the people of Belgaum grow their cotton. In this, to a considerable extent, the people are right. That at times they overcrowd the plants is true. Still in so dry a climate and so dry a soil moderately thick planting is required. What injures the staple most is the practice of picking whether the day is dry or wet, and at the picking time wet days or at least thunderstorms are not uncommon. The women bring in the cotton packed in large bundles on their heads. These loads are weighed or the weight is guessed at and the bundles are thrown on the rest of the heap in the room, shed, or cattle-house, where the husbandman may be storing his seed cotton. This goes on for days, often for weeks, and when the huge heap is finished, it is often allowed to lie for months without being examined or even looked at. The result is that the huge mass steams and heats through the rainy months, and the fibre is hopelessly weakened and impaired. When the raw cotton is brought out of such a store-room it is never fit to gin, either with the saw-gin or the foot-roller. No machine will work it; they clog and choke and will not turn out the cotton wool until it has been thoroughly dried in the sun, and often until it has been flogged with bamboos, a process which, to some extent, damages the fibre.

Disease.

Though naturally very hardy sudden changes of weather sometimes harm cotton. What tries cotton most are untimely sudden and heavy falls of rain, frequent changes of wind, and cloudy weather. Frost also injures the plant, but frost seldom happens in Belgaum. The people often say their cotton plants are smitten with disease when unusual heat and excessive dryness occur before the tap-roots have passed into the cool subsoil. When this happens the branches and leaves droop, then dry and turn brown, and in the end look as if they had been burnt. The people distinguish six blights or diseases from which cotton is apt to suffer. These are *Banti Rog* (K.), the yellow disease, caused especially in badly drained fields by untimely rain and flooding. The stems and branches become a dirty yellow, the leaves grow red, and the bush droops, and if the flooding or excessive damp lasts long enough the plant dies. *Banji Rog* (K.), the barren disease, is caused by hard east winds blowing night and day accompanied by cloudy weather. This disease seems to stop growth. The plant almost ceases to show fresh leaves, and the flowers and bolls no longer develope. The name *Gugari Rog* (K.), that is the half-cooked grain disease, shows that the soil and air have partially boiled or cooked the cotton plants. It is caused by excessive moisture and dull weather with heavy clouds and slight changing winds. The leaves shrivel and dry. *Shidi Hayu* (K.) of

---

twenty-eight pounds of American unginned cotton. With local cotton they were paid in kind, generally about one-sixth of what was brought in.

Disease.

unknown meaning is caused by long continued harsh north-east winds. The leaves droop but the plant seldom dies. *Majghi Rog* (K.), or the white disease, is brought on by excessive dews at night followed by heavy winds during the day. The leaves turn a dull white and both leaves and flowers droop and die. *Kari Jigi Rog* (K.), the black sticky disease, is the worst of all cotton ailments. When it takes hold of a field and the plants are far advanced they hardly ever recover. It is caused by long continued dews and unceasing easterly winds. The leaves become so thickly covered with a dark gumlike substance, that leaves flowers and half-formed bolls die and drop, and, in a short time, a field of strong green healthy bushes turns to charred-looking dirty sticks. Both kinds of cotton are subject to these ailments, but the acclimatised American suffers more than the local cotton. The plants show wonderful life and hardiness in recovering from disease when the cause of disease is removed, and healthy weather again gives the bushes a chance. Genial seasonable weather stops all forms of disease. Young plants generally recover, but the full grown suffer and yield short weak and often dull fibre.[1]

Yield.

According to the season the acre yield of clean cotton ranges from forty to fully one hundred pounds. In America the outturn is higher, the average yield over the whole states varying from one hundred and thirty to one hundred and seventy-five pounds. In considering these results the further difference in the proportion of yield of wool to seed in Indian and American cottons has to be remembered. In Indian cotton the usual outturn is three parts seed to one part fibre; in the American cotton it is two parts seed to one part fibre. In other words the American yields fully thirty-three pounds of fibre to every one hundred pounds of seed cotton, and the Indian twenty-five pounds. According to the 1882-83 Bombay Cotton Report, during the five years ending 1882-83 the average estimated acre yield was of American cotton twenty-two pounds and of local cotton thirty-two pounds.[2]

Cost.

The cost of growing cotton is difficult to determine. Much depends on the condition of the grower, the number of cattle he owns, the area of land he holds, the number of persons in his house,

---

[1] Dr. Forbes, then Cotton Commissioner, has left the following detailed description of a deadly blight from which the cotton suffered in 1867. In December unusually dark and cloudy weather accompanied by untimely and heavy rain, checked the plants and made them droop. Towards the middle of December the first signs of wind blight were seen, and from that time forward the plants passed from bad to worse. The American plants suffered first in their foliage. The leaves grew dark and shrivelled as if blasted and soon after dropped leaving the pods unsheltered. The most advanced pods soon lost their plumpness and opened prematurely, while the younger bolls withered and fell to the ground. The local plant kept its leaves and for a time seemed likely to yield a fair crop. But the bad weather continued, the pods suffered, and their failure was almost as complete as the failure of the American crop.

[2] The details are: In 1878-79 ten pounds of American and twenty-eight pounds of local cotton; in 1879-80 fifteen pounds of American and thirty-four pounds of local cotton; in 1880-81 sixteen pounds of American and thirty-two pounds of local cotton; in 1881-82 thirty-seven pounds of American and twenty-eight pounds of local cotton; and in 1882-83 thirty-one pounds of American and thirty-seven pounds of local cotton. These figures are probably of little value.

Chapter IV.
Agriculture.
Crops.
Cotton.

and many other conditions which more or less affect his actual cash outlay on cotton operations. Roughly the acre cost of growing cotton is *6s. 3d.* (Rs. $3\frac{1}{8}$) and the value of the produce is £1 *4s.* (Rs. 12) leaving a net profit of *17s. 9d.* (Rs. $8\frac{7}{8}$) an acre.[1]

In the care and skill which they give to the growth of cotton the small landholders are in no way inferior to the large proprietors. Since the intoduction of the survey settlement between 1849 and 1857, especially in Athni and Chikodi, the area under cotton has surprisingly increased.

Experiments.
1819.

In 1819, soon after the Karnátak passed to the British when Belgaum was still under Madras, the commercial residents of Bellári recommended that Brazil cotton should be introduced along the Krishna, Malprabha, and Ghatprabha. There is no evidence to show whether these views were approved or acted on. In 1820, Mr. Marshall, then statistical reporter to Government, recommended the growth of Bourbon cotton. Some of it was tried in Belgaum and did well on dry and rather gravelly soils.[2] *1828.* In 1828 the Court of Directors authorized the Bombay Government to pay premiums or to give some other encouragement to native cultivators who would prepare approved parcels of cotton of not less than five *khandis* grown from local seed or from foreign seed supplied from Government farms. Soon after this, selected foreign seed, chiefly American, was sent to Bombay with two Whitney saw-gins and several books on the growth of cotton. In the same year Lord Ellenborough, the chairman of the Indian Board, pressed on the East India Company the importance of improving the cotton supply. *1829.* In 1829, a beginning was made by Dr. Lush as superintendent of botanical experiments for the Bombay Government. The chief aims of these experiments were to procure a better variety of cotton, to introduce a better system of growing cotton, and to improve the ginning or cleaning of the staple. In the Kánarese country Dr. Lush's operations were in great measure confined to Dhárwár. *1832.* In 1832 the produce was decided to be no better than common field cotton, and the experiments in the Kánarese country were pronounced a failure. In 1832, at Báil-Hongal in Sampgaon experiments were made with Sea Island cotton, Black-seeded Barbadoes, and

---

1 The details are: Government land rent Rs. $1\frac{1}{4}$, seed 1 *a.* first hoeing 6 *as.* ploughing 7 *as.* second hoeing 6 *as.* drill sowing and hoeing 7 *as.* grubbing 9 *as.* picking 10 *as.*, total Rs. $3\frac{1}{8}$. In 1846, Mr. Inverarity, the Collector of Belgaum, estimated that an acre of cotton returned a sum of £1 *15s.* (Rs. $17\frac{1}{2}$) of which £1 *6s.* (Rs. 13) had been spent in raising the crop, and *9s.* (Rs. $4\frac{1}{2}$) was a balance of profit. The land on which Mr. Inverarity's calculations were based paid the exceedingly high acre rental of *10s.* (Rs. 5) and in 1846 cotton was worth only half of what it was worth some years later. In spite of the much higher land rates then in force it paid to sell Belgaum cotton in Bombay at *2d.* a pound. In 1850, Mr. Channing calculated the cost of growing cotton, exclusive of assessment, at *3s.* (Rs. $1\frac{1}{2}$) an acre. He also estimated the cost of manuring at *4s.* (Rs. 2) an acre. As the land is manured the year before the cotton is sown only half of it belongs to the cost of cotton-growing. For the five years ending 1856-57 excluding assessment the mean acre cost of cotton-growing was roughly estimated by local officers at *4s.* (Rs. 2) in 1852-53 and 1853-54, and at *3s.* (Rs. $1\frac{1}{2}$) in 1854-55, 1855-56, and 1856-57.

2 Marshall's Belgaum, 61. Mr. Walton thought the *dev-kapás*, Gossypium arboreum, a remnant of the Brazil cotton introduced in 1819. It seems unlikely that so recent a foreigner should gain a place among the holy plants of India.

Chapter IV. Agriculture. Crops. Cotton. *Experiments. 1832.*

Gujarát. Some of the seed did not sprout and all failed. The American saw-gins were condemned as unsuitable, which they certainly are for ginning local cotton. To tempt landholders to improve their cotton Government stated that they were willing to take their rents in cotton instead of in cash and that for specially well cleaned cotton they were ready to pay twenty per cent over the market price. No advantage was taken of these offers. Only a very small quantity of clean well-picked cotton was secured. A special agent was appointed to try and improve the preparation of cotton in Belgaum, Dhárwár, and Bijápur, but his endeavours met with little success. In or shortly after 1832, under Dr. Lush, a Government experimental farm was started at Sigihalli in Khánápur. The site of the farm was badly chosen as Khánápur is the part of the district least suited for cotton. The objects aimed at in establishing the Sigihalli farm were to introduce new and better kinds of cotton, and to improve the growing, cleaning, and packing of the local variety. In 1834 a committee of Pársi cotton merchants in Bombay reported so highly on some of the Sigihalli cotton, that Government sent it to England. In England it was pronounced clean and showy, but much injured in cleaning, containing very objectionable small white knots. Of nine lots sent from Bombay the valuation varied from five pence to nine pence the pound. The experts, who made the valuations, added that the value of the injured cotton could not be given with confidence as spinners might refuse to take it, though it might be bought in moderate quantities at the prices named by candlewick-makers, jewellers, and others. These opinions were repeated on another sample of the same white-seeded perennial kind subsequently sent to England from the Sigihalli farm. Relieved by occasional successes the result of the Sigihalli farm continued disappointing till it was closed in 1836 by Sir Robert Grant, then Governor of Bombay (1835-1838), who held that enough had been done to show that the attempt to improve the Karnátak cotton was a failure.

1835.

In 1835, Lord Ellenborough, President of the Board of Commissioners for the Affairs of India, suggested that Egyptian seed should be tried in Western India. He also suggested that, to ascertain the best means of cleaning cotton, specimens of the machinery used in America, Brazil, India, and Egypt, should be sent to London. To carry out these views Dr. Lush sent a foot-roller and a common ginner or *charka*. At the same time Dr. Lush noticed that he had not found the foot-roller able to clean any foreign cotton; he probably meant any New Orleans. In 1836, when the experiments to improve the cotton were stopped, Government offered for five years to forego the assessment on all Government land under cotton. This concession did not meet with the approval of the Court of Directors, and the remission was cancelled in January 1838. In 1839 further enquiries into the causes of the unsatisfactory state of Western India cotton led Sir J. Rivett-Carnac, then Governor of Bombay (1839-1841), to the conclusion that dirty cotton gave the local dealers and middle men a better return than clean cotton. About this time the Court of Directors determined to try how far Indian cotton could be

Chapter IV. Agriculture. Crops. Cotton. *Experiments. 1840.*

improved by employing American planters in India. Captain Bayles, of the Madras Army, was sent to America. He not unnaturally met with great opposition. The cry was raised that it was an English scheme to ruin the American cotton trade; the American papers urged that it was a public duty to prevent Captain Bayles securing planters; he had to go about armed and was forced to work in secret. At last twelve planters accepted his terms and agreed to come to India to conduct experiments in growing cotton. Three of the twelve arrived in Bombay in 1840. In 1841 Mr. Mercer one of the American planters, with two assistants Mr. Hawley and Mr. Channing, was sent to Dhárwar, where they began an experimental cotton farm at Kushgal, five miles north east of Hubli.

The American planters came to the country with the object of introducing the American system of growing cotton. They naturally at first paid little attention to the local modes of tillage, and viewed their roughness and imperfection with contempt. Experience taught them that American tools and American rules were unsuited to the country, and that the local tools and the local rules were suited to the country. Only after adopting local methods did their operations prove at all successful. In 1841 the American planters noticed adulteration as one of the chief causes of the depression of the Indian cotton trade. They said that both European and native merchants found that dirty and falsely packed cotton yielded a better return than clean.[1]

1845. In 1844-45, 185,388 and in 1845-46 117,188 acres were under cotton. In 1845 experiments were begun in Belgaum with the view of introducing foreign cotton and saw-gins. Mr. J. W. Channing, who since 1841 had been Mr. Mercer's assistant in Dhárwár, was transferred to Belgaum. In March 1845, Mr. Frere the Collector of Belgaum, reported that Mr. Channing had decided to begin work at Neganhál in Sampgaon and wished to have three hundred acres of land. Government considered Mr. Channing's estimate too high and thought the experiment would succeed better farther east. Mr. Channing kept to his opinion that Neganhál was the most suitable place for experiments, and a farm was accordingly started at Neganhál. Mr. Channing proposed to sow his fields with New Orleans, Broach, and Sea Island cotton. Broach seed was ordered, and New Orleans, probably supplied by Mr. Shaw the Collector of Dhárwár, was largely planted. In October the prospects of the American cotton were so promising that the superintendent applied for two gins of twenty-five saws each. The stock of machinery was so small that Government could spare only one machine of fourteen saws. Early
1846. in 1846 some American gins arrived in Bombay for sale, and two of these, one of twenty-two, the other of twenty-five saws, were secured for the Belgaum cotton farm. Mr. Channing proposed to keep one for his own work and sell the other, and this was sanctioned. Early in February 1846 bad weather set in, and the superintendent complained that, though the plants looked healthy

[1] Adulteration was no new feature in the Bombay cotton trade. As early as 1810, before the Karnátak came under the British, the Court of Directors called the attention of the Government of Bombay to the disgraceful state in which cotton arrived from India.

and showed quantities of flowers, the crop would not mature, but fell off just as the bolls were forming. When Government heard of this failure they asked whether it was due to the unfavourable season and not rather to the unsuitable situation of the farm. In reply Mr. Channing reported a great improvement in the crop, and begged that for the present judgment regarding the farm might be suspended. He also brought to notice a demand among dealers for the use of gins, and asked that spare machinery lying at Broach might be sent to him. This was sanctioned, and he recommended that for two shillings (Re. 1) 756 pounds (27 *mans* at 28 lbs. the *man*) of well picked and 672 pounds (24 *mans*) of average seed-cotton should be ginned. Though the result was not completely satisfactory the market price of the New Orleans was twelve per cent above that of the local staple. The results with Broach seed were encouraging and the crop turned out a success.

In 1845-46 the American planters came to the conclusion that the local cotton was nearly as good as any cotton grown in India. It was the dirt-trash mixed with it, in most cases wilfully, that ruined its name in European markets. The Bombay cotton trade showed so serious a decline that in 1844 and again in 1846 a committee was appointed in Bombay to enquire into the reasons and to suggest a remedy.[1] In 1846-47, from the experience of the previous season, Mr. Channing recommended that at Neganhál he should cultivate only as much land as could be managed by his two pairs of bullocks and that he should be authorized to make contracts at four Parasgad and at two Sampgaon villages to have twenty acres in each village cultivated on Government account. These proposals made necessary another ginning establishment at Murgod, about fifteen miles north-west of Saundatti. The superintendent considered these new measures so successful that, towards the end of the year, he asked leave to give up the Negauhál farm, and carry out all his operations on the contract plan. In supporting this proposal the Collector stated that 1300 acres were under Orleans seed and 726¾ under Broach. He believed that these two varieties would be grown to any extent that Government might wish if the produce could find a market. Government sanctioned the superintendent's proposals and granted him two gin-learners. On the whole, as in the previous year, the Broach was a success, but New Orleans after a good promise failed to ripen. Further experience showed that Broach cotton was unpopular with the people because of the difficulty in clearing the stumps of the old plants. In addition to the experiments with New Orleans and Broach the superintendent planted 248 pounds of Narma or Central Indian cotton, eighty-eight pounds of Georgia, fifty-six pounds of Sea Island, and thirty-six pounds of Bourbon. None of these sowings succeeded. The purchases and sales of cotton in 1846-47 showed a considerable balance in favour of Government. New Orleans, which cost Government £7 15*s*. (Rs. 77½) to lay down in Bombay, was sold in Bombay for £12 (Rs. 120); Belgaum-grown Broach cost £6 15*s*. (Rs. 67½) to lay down in Bombay and fetched

[1] Details are given in the Trade Chapter.

Chapter IV.
Agriculture.
CROPS.
Cotton.
Experiments.

£12 10*s.* (Rs. 125); local Belgaum cost Government £7 1*s.* (Rs. 70½) to lay down in Bombay; what it fetched is not stated. In this year Belgaum New Orleans sold at 14*s.* (Rs. 7) a *khandi* above Dhárwár New Orleans. In 1846 Mr Mansfield, the Collector, in describing the results of the American experiments recorded the opinion that the Indian system of tillage was better suited for India than the American system. In his opinion the American system was more costly than India either could afford or required.

1847.

In 1847-48, 2617 acres were under New Orleans and 115,888 under local cotton. The result of the sowings of New Orleans was far from encouraging, the rainfall was scanty, and much of the crop was lost by heavy wind and rain in the picking season. Mr. Channing feared that so few fields had yielded a good crop that in the next year many of the people would keep from sowing New Orleans cotton. The superintendent was unable to buy in Belgaum all the New Orleans cotton required by Government. He bought the balance in Ron, Hungund, and Bágalkot, where the growth of New Orleans had spread. At this time the tillage in some parts seems to have been very slovenly, the average acre return of clean cotton varying from thirty to fifty-five pounds or about one-third to one-half of the yield of well-tilled ground. In 1847, about nine thousand pounds of New Orleans, Broach, and local cotton, the produce of the Neganhál farm, together with four hundred bales of bought local staple cleaned by the saw-gins at Báil-Hongal and Saundatti, were sent to Vengurla. On the way to Bombay the native vessel met such severe weather that eight of the packages had to be thrown overboard and most of the rest was so damaged that it had to be sold at Bombay by public auction.

In the same year (1847) the Belgaum and Dhárwár experiments were united under one superintendent, and it was proposed that Mr. Channing should have the double charge and should be transferred from Belgaum to Kushagal in Dhárwár, with a mechanical assistant under him. Under instructions from the Board of Directors Government ordered Belgaum to provide a yearly supply of seven hundred and fifty bales of local and seven hundred and fifty of New Orleans. The number was afterwards reduced to five hundred bales of each kind and from the want of saw-gins the actual purchases came only to about two hundred bales. The Bombay Government applied to the Court of Directors for five thousand more saws for fitting new gins. In some places the cultivation of New Orleans had taken such a hold of the country, and the farmers understood its cultivation so well, that Mr. Channing estimated that some landholders near Báil-Hongal had raised crops yielding an acre outturn of about one hundred and twenty pounds of clean cotton. The actual area under New Orleans seed in five sub-divisions, two of which are now in Bijápur, was slightly under four thousand two hundred acres.

News of the unusually heavy crops that were gathered near Báil Hongal brought some Bádámi and Hungund landholders to buy the American seed. The President of the Manchester Commercial Association declared that some of the cotton received from Mr.

Channing was superior to American uplands. New Orleans now fetched fifteen per cent more than the local Belgaum. Through the agency of the Government planters, Mr. Turner, a Manchester merchant, bought (1847) a quantity of the Southern Máratha acclimatized New Orleans. The cost of delivering the cotton in Manchester was $3\frac{3}{8}$*d.* ($2\frac{1}{4}$ *as.*) the pound, and Mr. Turner realized 6*d.* to $6\frac{1}{2}$*d.* (4 - $4\frac{1}{4}$ *as.*) a pound. He also had fifty pounds of it tested with ordinary Orleans from America. The result was in favour of the Indian Orleans which when unadulterated beat the American by about two and a half per cent. The result of Mr. Turner's purchases shows what could be done, even in those days, when the staple was carefully grown and honestly ginned and packed. The high value of the Indian New Orleans was again recognized in September 1847. Some five hundred bales of Belgaum and Dhárwár New Orleans sent to England by Government were shown for sale in the Manchester Exchange. The cotton caused a considerable sensation. Before the day was over nearly four hundred of the bales were sold at $6\frac{1}{2}$*d.* ($4\frac{1}{4}$ *as.*) a pound, when the highest price of other Surats was only 5*d.* ($3\frac{1}{4}$ *as.*) The spinners thought the Belgaum unadulterated American equal to middling Boweds and well suited for all counts of yarns under forties.[1] The Manchester newspapers strongly urged the local manufacturers to buy their cotton direct in the Indian districts. So long as Bombay afforded a ready market for dirty dishonest cotton Government efforts to stop the evil were futile. The papers thought that a large and certain supply of honest Indian cotton could be secured only by the co-operation of the Lancashire manufacturer. This appeal seems to have had little practical effect. For many years Government were left, almost unaided, to the work of attempting to suppress fraud and secure pure cotton.

At the same time (1847) the high value of the Belgaum cotton in the English market was being seriously threatened by the prevalence of adulteration and fraud. This adulteration of cotton was in a great measure due to the small number of saw-gins. Only three gins were in use on Government account and of the three one at Saundatti was sold during the season for £22 (Rs. 220). Sixteen more were being made for Government and four for private persons. During the season adulteration was so rife that many officers recommended that a law should be passed making adulteration penal. Government thought that the provision of Regulation III. of 1829 if enforced would do much to suppress the evil. Notices were printed and circulated warning growers and dealers in cotton that Government were determined to put down gross adulteration and false packing. These threats and warnings had little effect. Before a committee of the House of Commons, Mr. Turner, who, as noticed above, had large dealings in Belgaum cotton, stated that his firm were on an average out of pocket £7000 (Rs. 70,000) every year from the clay, sand, twigs, and seed which were mixed with the cotton. So bad a name did this adulteration give Indian cotton that

---

[1] This cotton was called Boweds because before the saw-gin was invented it was cleared by the Indian cotton-bow.

Chapter IV.
Agriculture.
Crops.
Cotton.
Experiments.
1848.

as a rule spinners used it only when they could find nothing else to use.

In 1848-49, partly in Belgaum partly in Bijápur, the area under New Orleans rose to 6750 acres. The yield was good, but the people found it difficult to get buyers. The want of a market for New Orleans was more felt than for the local cotton, as large quantities of the local cotton were spun and woven in the district. In this year two proprietors or *jágirdárs* and two cotton dealers in private villages applied to the Collector for saw-gins. An English cotton broker's report on the staple sent to England in 1847-48 described the Belgaum New Orleans as clean and bright, of good colour and staple, in every respect superior; the Belgaum local cotton was good ordinary Surat with leaf and dirt, of short staple, and similar to average Surat. The 1848-49 shipments of New Orleans are described as of rather high colour, good staple, and very clean; and of the local cotton as of high colour, but of good staple and clean. Both kinds sold at 7½*d.* the pound. Early in 1848, the Honourable Mr. Reid, then Member of Council, stated that Belgaum and Dhárwár cotton was quoted at £11 4*s.* (Rs. 112) a *khandi* while no other Indian cotton fetched more than £8 10*s.* (Rs. 85). He urged that more saw-gins should be sent from England and that a fresh supply of Orleans seed should be brought from America. At this time in Liverpool, ordinary Orleans cotton was worth 6¾*d.* a pound, Belgaum Orleans 6¼*d.*, and the best Surat 5¼*d.* At the same time Belgaum Broach seed sold in Bombay at five per cent above Belgaum Orleans. Next year, in consequence of Mr. Reid's representations, twelve hundred new saws were brought from England and sent to Belgaum.

In the same year (1848) the Board of Directors, in London, reviewed the recent attempts to introduce New Orleans into the Kánarese districts. They thought that the time had come when the growth of New Orleans might be left to make its own way. They wished Government to limit their action to supplying new seed and introducing improved ways of preparing the staple. They also stated that they were sending from Liverpool one hundred bushels of New Orleans and fifty of Georgian seed from the best selections of the forthcoming American crop. The Georgian was recommended for poor soil. In 1848, according to Mr. Channing, the practice in the Belgaum cotton trade was for the dealers to make advances to the landholders on the security of the growing crop. The ordinary interest for an advance on the security of a growing crop was thirty-eight per cent. Not content with this heavy interest, when the dealers received the cotton they exacted a further levy of about fourteen per cent (3-4 lbs. the *man*). The landholders resented these exactions and to be revenged on the dealers wilfully mixed dirt with the cotton. Mr. Inverarity, the Collector, confirmed Mr. Channing's explanation of the origin of much of the dirt in cotton. He doubted if adulteration could be put down except by opening roads and letting in capital to compete with the local dealers. In the same year (1848) the Bombay Chamber of Commerce drew the attention of Government to the grave injury to the cotton

1848.

trade caused by adulteration. They suggested that inspectors should be appointed to examine and stamp the staple before shipment, and that every package should have marks which would make it easy to trace the person who had ginned it and grown it. In America provisions of this kind had nearly put an end to fraud. Adulterated cotton should, they thought, be taken before a magistrate, and half of the penalty given to the informer. If Government approved, the Chamber were ready to submit a draft Cotton Frauds Bill. Of all the cotton that came to Bombay perhaps the worst and the most fraudulently packed came from the Kánarese districts. The Chamber's proposals were referred to some leading firms who did not belong to the Chamber, and, with one exception, the Chamber's statements were confirmed and their proposals approved.[1] Government officers were less agreed than the merchants as to the wisdom of the Chamber's proposals. Mr. Townshend, the Commissioner, thought that the Chamber's proposal could not be carried out in Belgaum and matters were allowed to remain unchanged.

1849.

In 1849-50, 3059 acres were under Orleans and 145,216 under local cotton. The crop was good in the east and poor in the north. The average acre yield of clean cotton was estimated at about thirty-seven pounds for Orleans and thirty-nine pounds for local cotton. There was a good demand for the cotton. Government bought about a quarter of the experimental crop. The indebtedness of the landholders made them indifferent. Mr. Townshend, the Commissioner, noticed that the superintendent gave 1*s.* 4½*d.* (11 *as.*) for twenty-eight pounds of well-picked Orleans and only 1*s.* 1½*d.* (9 *as.*) for twenty-eight pounds of well-picked local cotton. These terms Mr. Townshend thought unduly favourable to the New Orleans. He thought the American cotton might now be left to take its natural place in the market. The superintendent explained that the native dealers were hostile to the New Orleans and that unless Government bought it, it would find no sale. Mr. Inverarity, the Collector, supported the superintendent, noticing that the dealers failed to see that the crop which paid the grower best must in the end pay the dealer best.

In 1850, Mr. Mackay, the special commissioner sent by the Manchester Chamber of Commerce to enquire into the condition of the cotton trade in India, was struck with the injury caused to the cotton trade by adulteration. He found bales whose ropes were so thickly coated with mud that instead of four and a half pounds they weighed fourteen and a half pounds. In the same year (1849) the Bombay Chamber of Commerce wrote to Government complaining of the state in which Belgaum American reached Bombay. It was not cleaned in any way and was so full of seeds and dirt as to be nearly unsaleable.

1850.

In 1850-51, 2332 acres were under New Orleans and 181,728 under local cotton. The season was marred by exceptionally trying

[1] The exception was Messrs. Forbes and Co. who expressed the opinion that the only way to improve the cotton trade was to abolish the land-tax. This proposal Lord Falkland, then Governor of Bombay (1848-1853), described as not worthy of notice.

Chapter IV.
Agriculture.
Crops.
Cotton.
Experiments.
1850.

and severe east winds. In five sub-divisions the experiments failed and in four there was only half a crop. The average acre yield of New Orleans was thirty pounds of clean cotton. Government, who were anxious to encourage private enterprise, refrained from buying. Mr. Davis, the first recorded English agent, was sent by Messrs. Lancaster and Company of Bombay to buy and gin cotton. Mr. Davis was provided with gins by Government but most were faulty and were returned. In his report for this year Mr. Channing noticed that much might be done to prevent seed from declining by shifting it from one part of the district to another. His experience also showed him that large plants did not yield the best staple. Plants of about two feet high gave the best and largest crops. Mr. Walton's experience during the fifteen years ending 1880 confirmed the correctness of Mr. Channing's views on both of these points.

At this time the Manchester Commercial Association repeatedly pressed on the Court of Directors the advisability of inducing the people of Belgaum and Dhárwár to grow their cotton earlier in the year. Mr. Channing strongly supported this recommendation and did his best to help the change. He did not succeed. It has already been noticed that further experience has shown that in the choice of the seed-time the people were right and Mr. Channing and the Manchester Association were wrong.

In 1850, Government approved a suggestion of Mr. Shaw, Collector of Dhárwár, that when cotton was not wilfully ill-treated the penalties of Regulation III. of 1829 should be sparingly inflicted. No information has been traced to show how far this proposal was carried out in Belgaum. In the same year the Bombay Chamber urged Government to take steps to improve the state of the local Belgaum cotton. In the Chamber's opinion it was the worst adulterated and the most fraudulently packed cotton that came to Bombay.

In 1850, Government distributed foreign cotton seed sent by the Court of Directors. It was called sugar-loaf cotton seed and was probably the variety best known as Bourbon kidney seed cotton. Three barrels, containing about three hundred pounds of seed, were sent to Belgaum, and it was planted in about thirty-two acres at Saundatti. About two-thirds of the seed failed to sprout. The plants that did come were at first small and sickly. In November they looked healthy and promised fairly, though inferior to New Orleans cotton. The Collector advised that no more of this kind of seed should be sent. In this year Government insisted on the importance of keeping the Orleans seed unmixed. New Orleans seed was also distributed in Chikodi and Sampgaon.

In 1850, Mr. Townshend, then Revenue Commissioner, expressed the opinion that experimental farms were costly and were of little use. That certain cotton could be grown in an experimental farm at a profit was no proof that it would pay the ordinary landholder to grow it. The Governor, Lord Falkland (1848-1853), approved of Mr. Townshend's views and expressed the opinion that more good might be done by improving the cleaning, growing, picking, and carrying of the local cotton than by introducing foreign varieties.

In 1851-52, 2212 acres were under New Orleans and 158,372 acres under local cotton. During this year Mr. Channing died. He was succeeded by Mr. Blount who had been in charge of cotton experiments in Dhárwár. The season was unfavourable. Mr. Blount estimated that the average acre yield of clean Orleans was not more than six pounds.

In 1851, Mr. Reeves, then Collector, reported that he had sent to Bombay 46,256 pounds of Orleans and 76,040 of local cotton of this and of the previous year's crop. This was only half of what he had been asked to send, but the rest of the crop had been bought by outside merchants. Two more cotton-gins were ordered and Mr. Reeves was asked to send Belgaum New Orleans for trial to Sindh.

Meanwhile Mr. Mackay, the special commissioner of the Manchester Chamber of Commerce, had drawn up a lengthy report in which among other things he made some remarks on the system of tillage in Belgaum. Mr. Mackay's report was sent to the Collector of Belgaum for opinion. With reference to Mr. Mackay's remarks, Mr. Havelock, then (1851) for some time in charge of Belgaum, wrote that he thought that if Mr. Mackay knew more of the country he would change his views about the defects of the Belgaum system of tillage. In his own case increased knowledge of the local system had led to increased respect for it. He knew that some of the American planters frankly admitted that there was much in the native system of farming to admire and that it was well suited to the circumstances of India. Mr. Walton's experience (1865-1880) confirmed this opinion. No experiments had succeeded except those which were based on local methods.

In 1851 adulteration was as bad as ever. The Bombay Chamber again complained that the Southern Marátha cotton had all the worst characteristics of Indian cotton in the days of its greatest shame. Nothing but the strong hand of authority could stop the wholesale mixing of seed. Government asked merchants to help by giving information whenever they received falsely packed and adulterated cotton. This the merchants said they could not do; only Government could stop the export of unmarketable cotton. Government called on the Collector to enforce the provision of Regulation III. of 1829 as strictly as possible. In the same year (1851) Mr. Channing, shortly before his death, urged on the Collector of Belgaum the necessity of securing pure seed. Strict attention to purity of seed was the more necessary because Government were retiring from the cotton trade and were trying to introduce Bombay agencies into Belgaum. As regards the mixing of cotton, Mr. Reeves, the Collector, after examining much of the growing crops, was satisfied that the mixing was not as a rule done in the fields, but at the gins. Mr. Reeves also reminded Government that much of the cotton which reached Bombay so shamelessly adulterated was not grown or ginned in Belgaum though it had passed through the district.

In 1852-53, 1950 acres were under New Orleans and 168,427 acres under local cotton. The New Orleans was almost a complete failure. In 1852 adulteration was as bad as ever. The coast

Chapter IV.
Agriculture.
Crops.
Cotton.
Experiments.
1852.

dealers petitioned Government to pass an enactment to punish cotton frauds. They were helpless. If they refused to take adulterated cotton their rivals took it or the up-country dealers sent it straight to Bombay. In 1853-54, 1386 acres were under New Orleans and 192,284 were under local cotton. The east of the district suffered from drought and over large tracts the cotton crop was an almost total failure. Mr. Inverarity the Collector, and Mr. Courtenay the Revenue Commissioner, agreed in recommending that the experiments should cease. Government approved of their opinion and said that if it was found to pay New Orleans would of its own accord spread north from Dhárwár to Belgaum. In 1853 the experiments were given up. At the same time orders were issued that every encouragement should be given to any undertaking that tended to a free and natural extension of the cultivation of New Orleans. Orders were also issued to give every facility for the repair of saw-gins and the distribution of seed.

In 1853, a decision of the Belgaum Judge, which was confirmed on appeal, made the provision of Regulation III. of 1829 almost a dead letter by allowing the owner of adulterated cotton to plead the credulity, negligence, and error of his servants. In 1854-55, 1911 acres were under New Orleans and 167,317 acres under local cotton. In 1855-56, 1728 acres were under New Orleans and 124,185 were under local cotton.

In the discussions about the evils of mixing and false packing it had often been said that the saving of the cotton trade would be for a European merchant to go or to send a European agent to the cotton country to buy as nearly as possible from the grower. In 1855, one English merchant went to Belgaum. He found he had to travel hundreds of miles with his rupees on his back, and that he had no resting-place but the ground. He had to weigh the cotton himself in little lots and when he bought it he had no place to warehouse it and no means of carrying it to the coast. In 1856-57, 4461 acres were under New Orleans and 183,091 acres under local cotton. In 1856, the Court of Directors noticed that in 1854-55 in Belgaum only 1911 acres were under New Orleans. They considered that the experiments had led to no results of any consequence and that a continuance of them was unlikely to bring any permanent good effect. Except the distribution of improved seed the Court thought that experiments might be left to private enterprise.

For the three years ending 1846-47 the cost of Government cotton experiments in Belgaum, including the superintendent's pay during some of the time, appears to have been about £827 (Rs. 8270); while the receipts in India were only about £26 (Rs. 260). Of the value of the cotton which was sent to England, which in every case formed the bulk of the crop, no details are available. In 1847 the charges are entered at about £385 (Rs. 3850) and the receipts at £21 (Rs. 210) apart from the proceeds of more than 100 *khandis* which were sent to England. In 1848, the operations cost £1581 (Rs. 15,810) and the receipts amounted to £221 (Rs. 2210) in addition to over one hundred *khandis* of cotton shipped to England. In 1849, the cost amounted to £1949 (Rs. 19,490) and the

Chapter IV.
Agriculture.
Crops.
Cotton.
Experiments.
Cost.

recoveries to 8*s.* (Rs. 4) besides about ninety-five *khandis* sent to Great Britain. In 1850, the expenses were £2522 (Rs. 25,220) and the receipts about a hundred and fifty-six *khandis* exported. In 1851, the expenditure was £2306 (Rs.23,060) and the receipts about £213 (Rs. 2130) and about fifty-eight *khandis* shipped to England. In this year an adjustment of cotton transactions was made between the Dhárwár and Belgaum collectorates, by which Belgaum was credited with refunds of about £1162 (Rs. 11,620). A farther shipment of about twenty-five *khandis* was also made on account of the Belgaum experiments. In 1853-54 the staff was reduced to one clerk and the charges fell to £18 (Rs. 180) and the receipts to £1 15*s.* (Rs. 17¾). In this season there is no record of any shipment of cotton. In 1854-55, as experiments had been altogether discontinued, the only expenditure was £1 10*s.* (Rs. 15) paid for lithographing a number of vernacular notices telling husbandmen how to obtain the best seed and cotton-ginning machinery. Experiments were thus carried on for about ten years (1845-1855), and during the greater part of that time were under the control of an experienced planter. The total cost appears to have been £9590 (Rs. 95,900), which, with receipts in India returned at £1646 (Rs. 16,460), leaves a net cost of £7946 (Rs. 79,460). The records show that during these ten years some five hundred and thirty-four *khandis* of cotton were shipped to England to be sold on Government account and more than this was probably sent. Even if only 534 *khandis* were sent the cost would be only £15 (Rs. 150) a *khandi*. In Mr. Walton's opinion the long series of experiments showed that New Orleans cotton was well suited to Belgaum. It suffered from the uncertainty of the climate, but accidents of climate also injured, sometimes destroyed, the outturn of the local crop. The chief difference was that the New Orleans seed tended to deteriorate. Mr. Walton believed that if Government had adopted Mr. Reeves' advice to have the saw-gins repaired by the superintendent at the owner's cost as was done in Dhárwár, Belgaum like Dhárwár might still have a large trade in New Orleans. The New Orleans crop was much more valuable than the local crop. It took less time to ripen, it was in more general demand in Europe, it yielded a greater outturn of uncleaned cotton, and the proportion of wool to seed was much greater in New Orleans than in the local cotton. Mr. Walton estimated that with the same tillage area, if, over Belgaum and Bijápur, New Orleans had taken the place of local cotton, the addition to the crop, partly from greater outturn partly from the higher proportion of wool, would represent 40,000 bales at the average prices of 1878, worth £400,000 (Rs. 40,00,000).

1857.

In 1857-58, 1487 acres were under New Orleans and 230,548 acres were under local cotton. In 1857, the Chamber of Commerce represented to the Government of Bombay that from the systematic mixture of the seed cotton in the gins the name of American Belgaum and Dhárwár cotton had greatly suffered in Bombay. They also complained that the American and the local were mixed in the same field. Government ordered their officers to take such steps as they thought advisable to check the evils of which the Chamber complained. In this year experiments were made with Egyptian staple in three sub-divisions of Belgaum and in two of Bijápur. The results were

Chapter IV.
Agriculture.
Crops.
Cotton.
Experiments.
1857.

unsatisfactory and Mr. Seton-Karr, the Collector, feared that the seed had been damaged in transit. It was sown much more thickly than usual, but not half the seeds sprouted. Mr. Seton-Karr thought it might succeed if watered, but the people were unwilling to undertake further experiments. Nearly fifty acres were planted in thirty-four Bijápur villages. Only in a portion of these did the seed come up, and even there the return was miserable. In five Athni villages there was no outturn. Forty acres were planted in three Parasgad villages, but the average acre yield was only seven pounds of cleaned cotton. Samples sent to the Bombay Chamber of Commerce were found damaged by insects. The uninjured cotton was superior, and if well ginned would fetch a price equal to Egypt-grown Egyptian. In 1858-59, 1558 acres were under American and 244,787 under local cotton. Almost the whole area under New Orleans between 1854 and 1858 was in Bádámi in Bijápur and not in the present Belgaum. In 1858 the Bombay Chamber said that it was useless for European firms to send agents to the cotton districts in the absence of security against frauds and impositions in preparing and packing cotton. In 1859-60, 1977 acres were under New Orleans and 288,668 under local cotton. In the same year Egyptian seed was distributed gratis in twenty-two Bijápur and eighteen Belgaum villages which had some of the best cotton land in the district. Instructions were given regarding the sowing. Of the Bijápur villages in Bádámi the seed came up in two villages and failed in other two; in Hungund it sprouted in six villages and failed in nine; and in Bágalkot it came up in one and failed in two. Of the Belgaum villages the seed sprouted in twenty-four fields and failed in two; in Tásgaon, now in Sátára, it came in five and failed in two; and in Gokák it failed in nine and came in one. Mr. Seton-Karr believed that the seed was good and sound. The results were miserable and the people were averse from any further attempt to grow Egyptian cotton. Mr. Seton-Karr sent Dr. Gibson four pounds of the seed and asked him to try it in the Government gardens at Dápuri and Hewra in Poona. The seed was sown at the end of April, and when they seemed to want it the plants were helped with water. Mr. Walton doubted if the Belgaum people had given the Egyptian seed a fair trial. In 1859 the Bombay Chamber of Commerce explained the fall in the quality of the Belgaum Orleans by supposing that it had been crossed with the local variety. This seems to have been a mistake. Dr. Forbes, the Cotton Commissioner, made enquiries which satisfied him that the decline in the quality of Orleans was not due to crossing with the local cotton.[1]

1859.

In 1859, the Bombay Chamber again appealed to Government for help against adulteration. The merchants had no means of inducing

---

[1] In 1845 Mr. A. Elphinston, the Collector of Ratnágiri, paid much attention to the crossing of cotton. He succeeded in getting some seeds which he called mixed Bourbon. These seeds were distributed by Government, but the result was unsatisfactory. In 1872 experiments were made in Sind and it was hoped that they had succeeded in producing a cross, but this proved a mistake. Mr. Walton's experience led him to agree with Dr. Wight of Madras that, though by a freak of nature a cross might take place, there was no reason to hope that local Indian and American cotton could ever be hybridised.

Chapter IV. Agriculture. Crops. Cotton. *Experiments. 1861.*

the landholder to improve his cotton. They could not refuse to accept mixed or adulterated cotton because the mixing was universal. In 1860-61, the Civil War in America increased the area under New Orleans to 6514 acres and under local cotton to 243,823 acres, and in 1861-62 New Orleans rose to 6620 and local cotton to 278,963 acres. In 1860 it was stated, in Mr. Walton's opinion, correctly, that the chief cause of the badness of the Belgaum cotton was the greed and the fraud of the local cotton-dealer or middleman as he was called. The local dealer was said to be able to secure for himself the benefit of all the improvements effected by Government. It was a common practise in the ginning yards to find a large heap of trashy local cotton and near it a pile of American of about the same bulk. The space in front of the ginning room was covered with a mixture of the two heaps spread in the sun to dry. It was this mixture which was being cleaned in the gins. No cotton details are available for 1862-63 and 1863-64.

Adulteration.

The unusual demand and rapid rise of price caused during these years by the war in America led to a great increase in adulteration, mixing, and false packing. The Commissioner, Mr. Hart, found the local officers unable to prevent these frauds. They urged him to move Government to take measures to check these abuses which they were satisfied must end in making Belgaum cotton unsaleable. It was found that the presence of European agents in the cotton-growing districts caused no diminution in the frauds. The agents represented merchants, not manufacturers; they bought to sell again, and in the turn-over dirty cotton might yield more profit than clean. The penal provisions of Regulation III. of 1829 were practically a dead-letter chiefly owing to the fact that the possession of mixed or dirty cotton was not an offence unless, which was often impossible to prove, the cotton was shown to be offered for sale. About the same time the Bombay Chamber once more drew the attention of Government to the ruin which adulteration was working in the cotton trade. Matters were worst in the Bombay Karnátak where cotton adulterating was a recognised calling. These representations and special inquiries satisfied Government that fraud was so widespread that, unless it was checked, the value of Bombay cotton must seriously suffer. They appointed a Commission who took evidence in Bombay and visited and made enquiries in the cotton-growing districts.[1] In the Kánarese districts the Commission found many of the traders and growers so anxious that adulteration should cease that they were willing to pay fees to support the necessary establishment. An examination of the evidence collected by the Commission led Government to ask them to prepare a draft Act for the suppression of cotton frauds. After much discussion and with various changes the draft became Act IX. of 1863. The value of the Act was greatly lessened by the absence of a definition of what constituted adulteration. This point was to a great extent left to the discretion

[1] The Commissioners were: Mr. G. Inverarity, Commissioner of Customs, president; Messrs. Forbes and Forjett, appointed by Government; and Messrs. Scott, Hannay, and McIlwraith, chosen by the Chamber.

Chapter IV.
Agriculture.
Crops.
Cotton.
Adulteration.

of the magistrate, and, as many magistrates were disinclined to convict, prosecutions often broke down. Still, in Mr. Walton's opinion, the fear of punishment to some extent reduced the amount of adulteration.

In 1864-65 Bijápur was formed into a separate collectorate. In that year within the limits of the present Belgaum were 3731 acres under American and 145,928 acres under local cotton. The American staple was so largely mixed with the local that no pure American was available. In 1865-66, 3730 acres were under American and 163,676 under local cotton. The season was unfavourable and there was a marked deficiency both in the quantity and quality of the crop. In 1865, Mr. Walton attempted to revive the growth of American cotton in some of the best central sub-divisions of Belgaum. The seed was sent to Sampgaon and grew well, but the attempt failed for want of gins. Under the Cotton Frauds Act Kánarese cotton was carefully examined at the Ratnágiri port of Vengurla. This had a marked effect in checking adulteration. In 1866-67, 1865 acres were under American and 130,810 acres under local cotton. Under the influence of the cotton inspectors New Orleans was grown much more purely than formerly. In 1866 Mr. Bulkley, the Inspector-in-Chief of Cotton, brought to the notice of Government that the existing provisions of the Cotton Frauds Act failed to check the mixing of different kinds of cotton and the adding of seed or uncleaned cotton at the ginning establishments which were scattered all over the district. Unless the inspector caught a gin-master in the act of mixing the prosecution failed. The people knew when the inspector was at hand and the mixing stopped till he was gone. In the yards were the heaps of different kinds of cotton ready for mixing and the seed-cotton ready to be thrown in to make weight. The inspector knew with what object the different cottons and the seed were there, but he could not interfere. The cotton must be offered either for pressing or sale, and as there were no local presses and the cotton was not sold till it reached Bombay the mixers and dirt-adders were safe. In 1867-68, 2825 acres were under American and 122,191 under local cotton. The increase in the area of New Orleans was chiefly due to the improved arrangements for keeping the saw-gins in repair. The opening of a new ginning factory at Navalgund in Dhárwár proved a great convenience to the people of Parasgad. Early in the year the bushes were attacked by a blight which, it was calculated, destroyed thirty-five per cent of the crop. The local cotton suffered more than the American.

In 1868-69, 3098 acres were under American and 120,677 under local cotton. The cultivation of American was well maintained. Blight reappeared and did great damage, in some places destroying nearly the whole crop. In Parasgad the adulteration of American by foot-rolling local staple into it was detected. In 1869-70, 7588 acres were under American and 205,672 under local cotton. These are the largest areas on record. In 1869 a draft Bill to amend the 1863 Cotton Frauds Act was introduced into the Bombay Legislative Council by the Honourable A. H. Campbell. After much discussion and several changes the Bill was passed. But it was not sanctioned by the Government of India and the Act of 1863 was continued for nine years more. In 1870-71, 13,166 acres were under American and 163,072 were under local cotton. This rise in the area of American cotton was owing to an improved arrangement for repairing gins. The new arrangements were not continued and the spread of American ceased. The arrangement with the Navalgund ginning factory for repairing gins in Belgaum villages came to an end and the area under American fell to 7295 acres. In 1871-72, 7295 acres were under American and 154,181 under local cotton. The fall in the cotton area was partly due to the discouragement caused by the blight in the previous year, partly to a decline in the quality of the American seed. Many attempts to adulterate cotton were detected. This was a bad year for cotton. The growers tried to make up for the shortness of the crop by increased adulteration which to some extent was checked by several successful prosecutions. The Collector urged the need of a more efficient Frauds Act. The question was not solely a merchant's question. The fortune of the most valuable export in Western India was at stake. In 1872-73, 7570 acres were under American and 161,232 under local cotton. The crop was fair, there was much less adulteration than in the previous year, and the cotton came to market in fair order. In this year the efficiency of the Act was much increased by extending its working to the villages of the estate-holders or *jágirdárs* of the Kánarese districts. Many prosecutions had broken down on the plea that the cotton had been mixed in a private or estate village.

In 1872 an inquiry into the working of the Cotton Frauds Act of 1863 showed that in Belgaum the dealers were in favour of stronger provisions for repressing fraud. The reason why the dealers as a class were so much more in favour of penal provisions in 1872 than they had been in 1863 was that in the years between 1863 and 1872, they had lost much from frauds in cotton. The wealth which had come to the cotton-growers during the American War to a great extent had made them independent of their former patrons, the cotton-dealers. Instead of the uncleaned cotton coming into the hands of a comparatively small body of dealers and being ginned at a few centres and under their control many of the growers had set up gins and ginned and mixed the cotton before selling it to the dealers. Much when it reached Bombay was found dirty and mixed and was thrown on the dealers' hands.

In 1873-74, 7570 acres were under American and 160,622 were under local cotton. A blight seriously damaged the crop. In 1874-75, 2139 acres were under American and 175,589 under local cotton. In Bombay, American sold at $5\frac{5}{8}d.$ and local cotton at $4\frac{1}{2}d.$ the pound. The crop was large and late and there was much adulteration. *Kumta,* that is the local Belgaum cotton, was in much demand in the Bombay mills. In 1874-75 the adulteration was so great that in six cases the fraudulent mixture ranged from thirty-four to forty-seven per cent. The Collector urged Government to import fresh American seed and to take steps to check the destructive state of the saw-gins. In 1874 in consequence of an agitation in

Chapter IV. Agriculture. Crops. Cotton. *Adulteration.*

Bombay to put a stop to special measures for preventing cotton adulteration a Commission was appointed to consider whether a Cotton Frauds Act should be continued, and if it should be continued, what changes should be made in the existing Act.[1] The Commission collected a large amount of evidence. The majority were of opinion that though it was not advisable to annul the Act, it was advisable to place it in abeyance for a time. The report of the Commission was considered by Government and the papers were forwarded to the Secretary of State. The Secretary of State held that the majority of the evidence taken before the Commission was in favour of the continuance of the Act. Certain portions of the Act, he thought, should be modified and other portions made more stringent. He directed the Government of Bombay to prepare a fresh Act, with the object of remedying the defects of the existing measure.

In 1875-76, on account of the success of the previous year, the area under American cotton rose to 5941 acres and under local to 214,983. But the price fell and the season was not successful. Adulteration was more general than it had been for some years.

In the famine year of 1876-77 the area under American cotton fell to fifty-nine and the area under local cotton to 70,281 acres. Except in a few spots in the west what was sown failed to come to maturity, and next year the people were left almost without seed cotton.

In 1877-78, 167 acres were under American and 146,701 acres were under local cotton. Considering the losses and trials of the previous season the farmers showed wonderful energy and command of resources. Still cattle were scarce and the crop suffered much from the failure to keep it clear of weeds. Sir Richard Temple, then Governor of Bombay (1877-1880) visited Belgaum and enquired into the cause of the fall in value of the American cotton. The Cotton Department was ordered to resume the control of the gin-repairing establishments, but Government shortly afterwards decided that, for the present, operations were to be confined to Dhárwár. A supply of five hundred pounds of new American seed was ordered.

In 1878-79, 984 acres were under American and 177,374 under local cotton. The outturn of cotton suffered again from the dearness of food grains and from the want of cattle to clean the fields. These evils were small compared with the plague of rats which swarmed over Dhárwár and part of Belgaum. They attacked all crops, and to none did they do more harm than to cotton. They cut the bolls off the bushes before they were ripe, opened them and devoured the seed, leaving the unmatured fibre strewed over the field. In some places not thirty per cent of the crop was gathered. This plague seriously reduced the already scarce supply of cotton seed. Much of the produce of the five hundred pounds of fresh American seed was destroyed. Not more than three thousand pounds were available for distribution. A second supply of 500 pounds was brought from

---

[1] The Commission were: The Honourable A. Rogers, President; and the Honourable E. W. Ravenscroft, the Honourable Narayen Vásudev, and Messrs. H. P. LeMesurier and E. M. Fogo, members.

America. In 1878, after long discussion, Act VII. of 1878 was passed. The provisions of this Act, though milder than those of the former Act, were more effective and they worked well. In September 1879 the Government of India recommended that all special legislation for the suppression of cotton frauds should cease. The Secretary of State did not agree with the view held by the Government of India. At the same time, on the 4th of March 1880, he sanctioned the proposals of the Government of India and desired the Bombay Government to do away with the special cotton fraud preventive establishment. According to Mr. Walton the opinion of the local European agents and native merchants was opposed to the giving up of Government efforts to check fraud.

In 1879-80, 592 acres were under American and 174,103 under local cotton. People sometimes spoke and wrote as if false packing and mixing would cease if English merchants or their agents came into the district. It was certainly less hopeless for English merchants to come to the district and buy than it had been in 1855; roads had been opened and rest-houses had been built. Still in Mr. Walton's opinion it was impossible for the exporter to buy small quantities from the growers without the help of a local dealer. In 1880 most of the cotton trade was carried on by a number of middlemen or local dealers who either went from village to village or remained in country towns and bought for their employers who were either local export merchants or the representatives of Bombay firms. Many of the local dealers instigated frauds both in cleaning and in packing in which the grower had seldom any objection to join. In spite of their losses in the famine which had reduced many of the smaller holders to their old position of dependence on the local dealer, the cotton growers were to a considerable extent independent of the local cotton-dealer or middleman. The cotton-growers knew the market price and were in a position to demand it. In Mr. Walton's opinion the chief drawback to the change was that the local dealer's profit was so reduced that he was forced to be more tricky than ever, and practised his ingenuity in devising fresh modes of cotton adulteration and false packing. The usual method of mixing local cotton is to store in a small room two heaps of cotton, a good and a bad, an old and a new, a damaged and a sound. Two men go into the room, each with a bundle of thin canes in his hand. They tie cloths over their mouths and noses and shut the door. They spread out the two kinds of cotton together and keep whipping the mixture, every now and then throwing on handfuls of seed-cotton or seed. The whipping is done with such thoroughness and skill that the mixture is surprisingly passable. Mixing with saw-gins is still easier and more perfect. The saw-gin is wilfully kept in disrepair because in that state it lets an immense weight of heavy dust and rubbish pass through powdered among the ginned cotton so as not seriously to take from its appearence. According to Mr. P. Chrystal, a Bombay merchant who is well acquainted with the Belgaum and Dhárwár cotton trade, the Bombay dealers and merchants in American Dhárwár and Kumta cotton think (1883) that the Cotton Frauds Act failed to stop adulteration in the Bombay Karnátak. Since the Act has been stopped he thinks there has been no noticeable increase in

Chapter IV.
Agriculture.
CROPS.
Cotton.

adulteration. The American Dhárwár has declined in staple and lost its silkiness but this he thinks is due not to more mixing but to deterioration in the American seed.

The following table for the thirty-five years ending 1882-83 gives the areas under the two varieties of cotton, American and local:

BELGAUM COTTON AREA, 1846-1882.[1]

Year.	American.	Local.	Total.	Year.	American.	Local.	Total.
	Acres.	Acres.	Acres.		Acres.	Acres.	Acres.
1846-47 ...	2017	110,103	112,120	1866-67 ...	1865	130,810	132,675
1847-48 ...	2617	115,888	118,505	1867-68 ...	2825	122,191	125,016
1848-49 ...	4190	134,514	138,704	1868-69 ...	3098	120,677	123,775
1849-50 ...	3059	145,216	148,275	1869-70 ...	7588	205,672	213,260
1850-51 ...	2332	181,728	184,060	1870-71 ...	13,166	163,072	176,238
1851-52 ...	2212	158,372	160,584	1871-72 ...	7295	154,181	161,476
1852-53 ...	1950	168,427	170,377	1872-73 ...	7487	161,232	168,719
1853-54 ...	1386	192,284	193,670	1873-74 ...	7570	160,622	168,192
1854-55 ...	1911	167,317	169,228	1874-75 ...	2139	175,589	177,728
1855-56 ...	1728	124,185	125,913	1875-76 ...	5941	214,983	220,924
1856-57 ...	4461	183,091	187,552	1876-77 ...	59	70,281	70,340
1857-58 ...	1487	230,548	232,035	1877-78 ...	167	146,701	146,868
1858-59 ...	1558	244,787	246,345	1878-79 ...	984	177,374	178,358
1859-60 ...	1977	288,668	290,645	1879-80 ...	592	174,103	174,695
1860-61 ...	6514	243,823	250,337	1880-81 ...	21	192,106	192,127
1861-62 ...	6620	278,963	285,583	1881-82 ...	344	163,504	163,848
1864-65 ...	3731	145,928	149,659	1882-83 ...	929	230,090	231,019
1865-66 ...	3730	163,676	167,406				

Famines.

1396. On account of its uncertain rainfall Eastern Belgaum is one of the parts of the Bombay Presidency which is most liable to suffer from failure of crops. The earliest recorded failure of rain is the great Durga Devi famine. It began in 1396 and is said to have prevailed over the whole of India south of the Narbada and to have lasted for nearly twelve years. This famine was caused by the total want of seasonable rain. Almost no revenue was recovered and a large proportion of the people died. There is no record that any measures were adopted to relieve the distress.[2] In 1419 no rain fell and there was a grievous famine throughout the Deccan and Karnátak. Multitudes of cattle died from want of water. Ahmad Sháh
1419. Bahmani (1419-1431) increased the pay of his troops and opened public stores of grain for the use of the poor. In 1420, there was again a failure of rain and the country was much disturbed.[3] The
1472. years 1472 and 1473 are described as seasons of exceptional distress. No rain fell and no crops were sown for two years. Many died and many left the country. In the third year when rain at last fell scarcely any one was left to till the land.[4] In consequence of continued drought and great swarms of locusts there was a gradual failure of crops which began from 1787-88 and continued to 1795-96 and caused great distress among all classes.
1790. In 1790 the march of the Maráthás under Parashurám Bháu through Belgaum and Dhárwár to Maisur was accompanied by such

[1] From 1846-47 to 1861-62 the figures include those of the three sub-divisions of Bágalkot, Bádámi, and Hungund in the present district of Bijápur. For 1862-63 and 1863-64 no figures are available. From 1864-65 to 1882-83 the figures are for the present district of Belgaum including alienated lands in Government villages and native state lands mixed with Government lands. In 1881-82 the cotton area in Government villages was 91,400 acres.

[2] Grant Duff's Maráthás, 26.

[3] Briggs' Ferishta, II. 405.

[4] Briggs' Ferishta, II. 494.

Chapter IV. Agriculture. Famines. 1790.

devastation that on its return from Maisur the victorious army almost perished for want of food. In the following year 1791-92 the complete failure of the early rain caused awful misery. Hardly any records have been found regarding this famine. But tradition speaks of it as the severest famine ever known, extending more or less over the whole of the Bombay Presidency except Sind and to Madras and the Nizám's territory. In Belgaum the distress seems to have been heightened by the disturbed state of the country and by vast crowds of immigrants from more afflicted parts. Under these influences grain could hardly be bought. Some high-caste Hindus, unable to get grain, and rejecting animal food, poisoned themselves, while the poorer classes found a scanty living on roots, herbs, dead animals, and even corpses. The famine was so severe that it was calculated that fully half the inhabitants of many villages died; of those who survived many wandered and never returned. In 1791-92, in the town and district of Gokák, from starvation alone twenty-five thousand people are said to have perished.[1] A story remains that a woman in Gokák under the pangs of hunger ate her own children, and in punishment was dragged at the foot of a buffalo till she died. From the numbers of uncared-for dead this famine is still remembered as the *Dongi Bura* or the Skull Famine. The estate-holders or *jágirdárs* are said to have done what they could to relieve the distress, but the Peshwa's government seems to have given no aid.[2] Plentiful rain fell in October 1791 and did much to relieve the distress.[3] In 1791 from the 7th to the 15th of May the rupee price of rice was six pounds (3 *shers*) at Dudhvad, Murgod, Bendvád, Ráybág, and Kudsi, eight pounds (4 *shers*) at Gokák, and ten pounds (5 *shers*) at Athni. The rupee price of gram was six pounds (3 *shers*) at Dudhvad and Murgod, eight pounds (4 *shers*) at Ráybág and Kudsi, and ten pounds (5 *shers*) at Athni. The rupee price of Indian millet was eight pounds (4 *shers*) at Dudhvad, Murgod, Ráybág, Kudsi, Gokák, and Bendvád; and twelve pounds (6 *shers*) at Athni.[4] In 1802-3 Belgaum again suffered severely from famine. This famine was less due to want of rain than to the depredations of Pendhári and other robbers, which, over large tracts, were so constant as to put a stop to tillage. The local distress was heightened by the arrival of crowds of people from the Godávari districts which the ravages of Holkar's army had turned into a desert. In the Gokák sub-division 15,000 people are said to have died of famine. The Peshwa's government seems to have made no attempt to relieve the distress.[5]

1802.

1832-33.

In 1832-33 almost no rain fell and almost no crops were reaped in the east of the district. The distress, though very severe, hardly amounted to famine. Many cattle died and some people are said to have sold their children for food. In 1853 the drought in the

---

[1] Walton's Cotton, 65. [2] Walton's Cotton, 6.
[3] Colonel Etheridge's Report on Past Famines, 103.
[4] Moore's Narrative of Captain Little's Detachment, 232.
[5] Colonel Etheridge's Report on Past Famines, 103.

Chapter IV. Agriculture. Famines. *1876.*

east of the district caused distress which was heightened by crowds of the destitute from Sholápur, where the failure of rain was more complete. Government granted considerable remissions.[1]

In 1876 a scanty and ill-timed rainfall of 21·34 led to failure of crops and distress amounting to famine over nearly half of the district.[2] The early crops failed almost entirely in Athni and Gokák, and over the greater part of Chikodi and Parasgad; in the three remaining sub-divisions they were less than half the average. In addition to the failure of the early rains, September and October passed with only a few showers, and, except on river banks, little or no cold-weather crops were sown. With high grain prices, Indian millet at fourteen instead of forty-three pounds the rupee, and no demand for field labour, large numbers of the poorer classes fell into distress. The need for Government help began about the middle of September, when relief works from local funds were started. Early in November there was scarcity of grain and increasing distress. Soon after large supplies began to pour in and the pressure lightened. In the hot months, with rising prices, distress returned, and the scanty fall of rain in July and August caused much anxiety and suffering. The timely and plentiful rainfall of the next two months saved the growing crops, and the condition of the people gradually improved. At the close of November the demand for Government help ceased.

The following details show, month by month, the phases through which the distress passed and the measures taken to meet it. In September 1876 rain held off and the early crops almost wholly perished in Athni, Gokák, and the east of Chikodi; elsewhere they were withering. Cold-weather crops could not be sown, and the loss caused by the very scanty early rains began to deepen into distress. On the 28th of the month 1·28 inches of rain fell in Belgaum and 1·88 inches in Sampgaon and did great good to the early crops. In Gokák and Athni water was failing, and, especially in Gokák, fodder was so scarce that the Collector asked that the usual order against cutting *asan* Briedelia retusa branches should not be enforced. Cattle were being fed on the withered crops and numbers were dying. About the middle of the month local fund relief works were started. Late in October three inches of rain fell in Parasgad, one inch in Belgaum, and showers in some Gokák and Chikodi villages. In a few places cold-weather crops were sown. The condition of the early crops was generally unfavourable. They had almost entirely failed in Athni and Gokák, nearly three-fourths had gone in Chikodi and Parasgad, and, in the rest of the district they were withering. In the beginning of the month grain was scarce in the Belgaum markets. Later large quantities were imported by sea, but, as most of the imported grain passed through Belgaum to Dhárwár, Kolhápur, and the Patvardhan states, the local supply was only slightly improved. Water and

[1] Walton's Cotton, 58, 65.

[2] The estimate was in area 2660 square miles of a total of 4600, and in population 500,000 out of 940,000.

1876.

fodder were growing scarce, and, in the north, people were moving about in search of work, and were sending their cattle to the Sahyádri hills. The scarcity of food and the want of water caused an increase of crime, and for a time the unsafe state of the roads interfered with the import of grain. Local fund relief works gave employment to large numbers, but more works were wanted. November passed without rain and most of the early harvest perished. Except on river banks few cold-weather crops were sown, and where they had been sown they were withering from want of moisture. In Gokák and Athni there was great distress. People were moving to Dhárwár and Maisur, and cattle were dying in great numbers from want of fodder and water. Grain kept pouring in freely from Vengurla for export to Kaládgi, Bágalkot, and other inland towns. The Belgaum market was plentifully supplied, but in Gokák and Athni, owing to the stoppage of exports from Mudhol and Jamkhandi, traders found it so difficult to get supplies that grain had to be sent to the Parasgad relief works. In the beginning of the month, *jvári* rose as high as twelve pounds the rupee, but quickly fell to sixteen pounds. Public works were started. Of 9573, the average daily number relieved during the month, 8839 were able-bodied expected to do a full day's work and superintended by ordinary public works officers, and 734 were aged or feeble expected to do two-thirds of a day's work and superintended by assistant collectors, mámlatdárs, and special officers.[1] December passed without rain and with no change in crop prospects. Grain continued to be largely imported and *jvári* fell from seventeen pounds at the beginning of the month to twenty pounds near the close. About the middle of the month cholera broke out. During the month the numbers of the destitute rose on public works from 8839 to 11,471, and on civil works from 734 to 7749.

1877.

In January no rain fell. Grain importations continued, and the supply was plentiful, except in Athni, where prices slightly rose. *Jvári*, after rising in the beginning to nineteen pounds, fell about the close of the month to twenty pounds the rupee. Cholera continued prevalent. On the 19th of the month the pay of weakly workers was reduced.[2] The result of this change was a fall in the number of civil agency workers from 10,088 in the beginning of the month to 6966 at its close. At the same time, by enforcing distance and task tests, the numbers on public works fell from 18,133 to 8909. During the month 388 persons were charitably relieved. Late in February eight cents of rain fell. Grain supplies continued sufficient, and *jvári* remained steady at nineteen pounds the rupee. In Athni and Gokák water was very scarce. Cholera continued prevalent and the mortality was high. The numbers on relief fell, on public works from 19,106

---

[1] The original wages were, for a man 3*d.* (2 *as.*) a day, for a woman 2¼*d.* (1½ *as.*), and for a boy or girl 1½*d.* (1 *anna*). About the middle of November a sliding scale was introduced, providing that when prices rose over sixteen pounds the rupee, the money rate should vary with the price of grain, and that a man should always receive the price of one pound of grain in addition to one *anna*.

[2] The new rates were, for a man, the price of one pound of grain and ¾*d.* (½ *anna*) instead of 1½*d.* (1 *anna*); for a woman, the price of one pound and ⅜*d.* (¼ *anna*) instead of ¾*d.* (½ *anna*); and for a boy or girl, the price of half a pound of grain and ⅜*d.* (¼ *anna*).

Chapter IV.
Agriculture.
Famines.
1877.

to 13,235, and on civil works from 7910 to 4507; on charitable relief they rose from 388 to 451. March passed without rain. There was a general, and, in some places, a very great scarcity of water. Grain continued to pour into the district and *jvári* remained steady at eighteen pounds the rupee. The mortality from cholera was very heavy. Against a fall on civil works from 4507 to 4113, the numbers on public works rose from 13,235 to 19,659, and on charitable relief from 451 to 1000. About the middle of April rain began to fall and before the end of the month had averaged 1·20 inches. In Athni grain was scarce; elsewhere, though dear, the supply was sufficient; *jvári* rose from eighteen pounds at the beginning of the month to fifteen pounds about the close. In Athni the scarcity of water was very severe. The cholera mortality was heavy but was decreasing. The numbers on relief rose, on public works from 19,659 to 25,670, on civil works from 4113 to 5615, and on charitable relief from 1000 to 2974. In May good rain fell in Athni, Belgaum, Sampgaon, and Parasgad, and showers in other parts. The sowing of quick-growing crops and rice made considerable progress. In a few places the ordinary early crops were sown, but more rain was required before sowing could be general. Grain supplies continued sufficient, and *jvári* remained steady at fifteen pounds the rupee. Cholera was still prevalent. The numbers on public works rose from 25,670 to 40,389, and on charitable relief from 2974 to 7631. On civil works the numbers fell from 5615 to 2807. In June there was an average fall of 10·89 inches of rain. Rice-sowing was nearly completed, and the sowing of the other early crops was progressing. Over the whole district people were coming back and setting to work on their fields. Grain importations ceased, but the supply was sufficient. *Jvári* rose from fourteen pounds in the beginning of the month to twelve pounds about the close. Cholera continued prevalent but was on the decline. Partly from the good prospects, partly because the distance test was more strictly enforced, the numbers receiving relief fell on public works from 40,389 to 26,818, and on civil works from 2807 to 1638; on charitable relief there was a rise from 7631 to 7972. July passed with very little rain, an average of only 1·61 inches. The break in the monsoon caused much anxiety. Except in Sampgaon the early crops were withering. In Parasgad and Khánápur grain was scarce, and *jvári* rose from eleven pounds in the beginning of the month to 8½ pounds near the close. By the end of the month cholera had almost disappeared. The numbers on relief fell, on public works from 26,818 to 22,294, on civil works from 1638 to 287, and on charitable relief from 7972 to 5486.

In August there was an average fall of 4·80 inches of rain. The fall was chiefly in the west, where the crops considerably improved. In the east there were only a few showers, and in some villages the fields were withering. About the end of the month good rain fell, and such crops as were not past recovery were much benefited. The supply of grain continued sufficient and *jvári* fell from 9½ pounds in the beginning of the month to ten pounds about the close. Cholera, of a mild form, continued prevalent. The numbers on public works rose from 22,294 to 24,995, and on charitable relief from 5486 to 8898. On the 4th of the month all civil agency works were stopped.[1] In September there was an average fall of 15·44 inches. Except in a few places in the east where the rain came too late to save the crops, by the end of the month, over almost all the district, the prospects of the early harvest were good and the sowing of the cold-weather crops was begun. Grain continued abundant and *jvári* fell from 10½ to eighteen pounds the rupee. There was a marked improvement in the state of the people. Cholera altogether disappeared, and against a rise on charitable relief from 8898 to 13,807, the numbers on public works fell from 24,995 to 21,319. In October rain fell so heavily, 8·98 inches, as, in some places, to harm the ripening crops. *Jvári* rose in the beginning of the month to 15½ pounds but before its close had again fallen to 16½ pounds the rupee. The numbers on public works fell from 21,319 to 9662, and on charitable relief from 13,807 to 9234. In November the weather continued favourable. Except in a few places the sowing of the late crops was over and the harvesting of the early crops was vigorously pushed on. The rupee price of *jvári* fell from nineteen to thirty-one pounds. The numbers on public works fell from 4699 in the beginning of the month to 112 on the 24th when all works were closed; on charitable relief they fell from 9234 to 1260. In December there were a few showers at Belgaum and Khánápur. The late sowing was completed, and the harvesting of the early crops was nearly over. By the end of November all relief-houses were closed.

The following statement of prices and numbers relieved shows that, during the first two months of 1877, grain prices ruled at nineteen pounds the rupee or more than twice the ordinary rates, that its price rose steadily till in July and August it averaged something less than ten pounds, and that between August and November it fell to twenty-seven pounds. As early as December 1876 the numbers on relief works reached 19,220. By lowering wages and enforcing task and distance tests the total was in February reduced to 17,742. From this it advanced till, in May, it stood at 43,196, when it again fell. The decrease was slow in July, August, and September, and more rapid in October and November, when the works were closed. The numbers on charitable relief rose steadily from 388 in January to 7972 in June. They then fell to 5486 in August, and, after rising to 13,807 in September, fell in November to 1260, when almost all charitable relief ceased:

---

[1] Though civil works were stopped, payment at civil agency rates was continued at the public works to labourers, who, under Government orders, were not entitled to the full wages.

Chapter IV.
Agriculture.
Famines.
1876-77.

BELGAUM FAMINE, 1876-77.

MONTH.	AVERAGE DAILY NUMBER RELIEVED.				JVA'RI, Pounds the Rupee.	RAIN-FALL.
	On Works.			Free.		
	Civil.	Public.	Total.			
1876.						
November	784	8839	9573	...	14¾	·11
December	7749	11,471	19,220	...	18½	...
1877.						
January	7910	19,106	27,016	388	19	...
February	4507	13,235	17,742	451	19	·8
March	4113	19,659	23,772	1000	18¼	...
April	5615	25,670	31,285	2974	16¼	1·20
May	2807	40,389	43,196	7631	15⅛	2·3
June	1638	26,818	28,456	7972	12½	10·89
July	287	22,294	22,581	5486	9⅝	1·61
August	128	24,995	25,123	8898	9⅜	4·80
September	...	21,319	21,319	13,807	13⅜	15·44
October	...	9662	9662	9234	16	8·98
November	...	1526	1526	1260	27	0·5
December	...	...	...	56	34	0·79
Total ..	35,488	244,983	280,471	59,157	...	47·43
Average ...	3548	18,845	21,575	4929	...	...
Cost in Rs. ...	...	...	9,98,648	1,55,314	...	...
			1,153,962			

Relief Houses.

Twenty relief-houses or camps were opened in the district. Of these the camps at Chikodi, Hukeri, Kubbur, Eksambe, Saundatti, Yergatti, Herekop, Gokák, Athni, Kokatnur, Shedbal, and Telsang were opened in the month of November 1876; those at Nándgaon and Páchhápur in the following December; those at Sampgaon and Deshnur in January 1877; those at Yádvád in March, and at Pamaldini in April 1877; and those at Belgaum and Mudalgi in May 1877. The relief-houses at Páchhápur and Eksambe were closed in January 1877, those at Kabbur and Mudalgi in July, at Deshnur in August, at Belgaum and Nándgaon in October, and the rest in November. At Belgaum a rest-house was for long used as a relief-house. Afterwards in the rainy season a shed was built about a mile from the town. In other places no relief houses were built, usually some rest-house or other large building was turned to account. The total number of men women and children fed at the relief-houses was 2,071,838, giving an average of 103,592 for every relief-house, or a monthly average of 172,653 for the whole. Some of the upper and middle classes, weavers and dyers, thought it a disgrace to go on the relief works or to the relief-houses. To help these people Government placed £150 (Rs. 1500) at the disposal of the Collector. From this sum raw materials were bought and advanced to the people, who, on the receipt of the manufactured articles, were paid their market value minus the amount of advance they had received in the shape of raw materials. In this way many families of weavers and dyers in Gokák, Chikodi, and Athni were relieved.

Relief Staff.

In November 1876 the permanent mámlatdárs of Sampgaon, Parasgad, Gokák, and Athni were relieved of their usual duties and deputed to superintend relief works, to inspect crops, and inquire into the condition of the people. In May 1877, when the number

Relief Staff.

of immigrants passing through Belgaum and the number of the relief works were increasing, it was found necessary to appoint a relief mámlatdár for the Belgaum sub-division also. Mr. T. H. Stewart, C.S., was relieved of his ordinary duties as an assistant collector from December 1876 till the end of the famine, and was deputed for famine duty. Captain G. Coussmaker remained on special famine duty from the 8th of May to the 25th of November 1877. Mr. A. Dalzell, of the survey department, was also appointed temporarily to famine duty from the 23rd of September to the 2nd of December 1877. Captain Coussmaker was detached for duty in Chikodi and Athni and Mr. Dalzell for duty in Gokák. In addition to these officers, from February 1877 to the end of the famine, two sub-overseers on £5 (Rs. 50) a month were appointed to superintend the civil agency relief works. The mahálkari of Chándgad was also appointed on famine duty to help the relief mámlatdár at Gokák as the distress in that sub-division was specially severe. Besides the above staff of officers fifty-two circle inspectors were appointed, ten for Athni, twelve for Gokák, eighteen for Chikodi, and twelve for Parasgad. A group of villages was placed under each of these inspectors. Each village in the inspector's beat was to be visited by him at least twice a week to see that the village officers did their relief duty properly.

Grain.

In October and November 1876 the certainty of a failure of crops induced the holders of grain to hoard their stocks. So closely were the stocks held that in some places grain was most difficult to get. The local stocks were not very large and the holders were chiefly husbandmen and a few local dealers. The people who believed that there were immense stores of grain became discontented and committed many acts of violence and robbery. Very inferior grain was brought to market and sold at very high prices. The better sorts of grain were kept back until the scarcity increased. At this stage of the famine, when no grain was to be had, the Belgaum municipality brought from Vengurla £200 (Rs. 2000) worth of grain which they retailed at cost price to the poorer classes. Municipal sales of grain lasted only about two weeks. Then a few Belgaum, Nipáni, and Gokák merchants began to import grain from Nágpur, Sind, and parts of the Bengal Presidency, either direct or through Bombay agents. Many dealers also bought grain from Bombay merchants. The only Government help offered to grain merchants was by issuing money-orders at par on its being shown that the order was to pay for grain. To the grain-dealers of other districts every facility was offered for importing by stopping the levy of octroi duties on grain. Special police arrangements were made to protect the main roads and on several roads grass was stored. With these encouragements large quantities of grain poured in. Bohorás and cloth-merchants, whose own trade was at a stand, joined in the import. The grain was brought by sea through Vengurla to Belgaum, Gokák, Saundatti, and Khánápur, and through Chiplun and Rájápur to Nipáni, Chikodi, and Athni. It was also brought in smaller quantities from Kárwár by the Kodra and Unshi passes to Belgaum, and was sent from Belgaum to the interior. Every effort was made to help the passage of grain

Chapter IV.
Agriculture.
Famines.
1876-77.

towards Bijápur where the distress was severer and grain dearer than in Belgaum.

Cart-rates.

Before November 1876 the ordinary monthly rate of cart-hire was £2 18*s.* (Rs. 29). During the fourteen months ending December 1877 the monthly cart-rate rose from £2 10*s.* (Rs. 25) in February 1877 to £4 (Rs. 40) in July 1877, and from that fell to £2 16*s.* (Rs. 28) in November and December.[1] About the middle of the famine and before grass stores were opened so many cattle died from overwork and want of food that labourers had to be employed in dragging the grain-carts from Vengurla.

Emigration.

Of the number of people who left the district during the famine no accurate estimate can be formed. It is known that from the west a considerable number of labourers and poor husbandmen went to Kánara, Goa, Kolhápur, and other places in search of work and food, and that from the east numbers went to Haidarabad and Bijápur. Compared with 1872 the 1881 census shows a fall of 80,900 in population. The addition of the normal yearly increase of one per cent during the remaining seven years gives 147,000 as the loss of population caused by death and migration in 1876 and 1877.

Famine Census.

On the 19th of May 1877, when famine pressure was general and severe, a numbering of relief workers showed that of 44,757 labourers, 41,447 on public and 3280 on civil works, 28,447 belonged to the sub-divisions where the works were carried on; 10,218 belonged to different sub-divisions of the same district; 1721 were from other districts; and 4371 from neighbouring states. As regards their occupation, 1309 were manufacturers or craftsmen, 19,731 were holders or sub-holders of land, and 23,717 were labourers.

Cost.

The total cost of the famine is returned at £115,396 (Rs. 11,53,960), of which about £99,865 (Rs. 9,98,650) were spent on public and civil works and £15,531 (Rs. 1,55,310) on charitable relief. Of the whole amount £106,126 (Rs. 10,61,260) were paid from Imperial and £9270 (Rs. 92,700) from local funds.

Effects.

Compared with those of the previous year, the crime returns of 1877 showed an increase of 1209 offences, almost all of which were due to the pressure of want on the lower classes. Of the 1209 offences, 848 were thefts, 293 cattle thefts, nineteen cases of mischief, fourteen criminal breaches of trust, eleven culpable homicides, twelve dacoities, seven house-trespasses, three robberies, and two grievous hurts. The loss of farm stock during the famine to some extent interfered with the carrying of grain and in a marked degree hampered field work. Many landholders who had lost their cattle had to give up their land and a large amount of revenue remained outstanding. The yearly village returns show a fall in the number of cattle from 432,634 in July 1876 to 320,267 in July 1878, a loss of 112,367 head.

---

[1] The details are: November and December 1876 £2 14*s.* (Rs. 27), January 1877 £3 12*s.* (Rs. 36), February £2 10*s.* (Rs. 25), March and April £2 18*s.* (Rs. 29), May £3 4*s.* (Rs. 32), June £3 12*s.* (Rs. 36), July £4 (Rs. 40), August £3 6*s.* (Rs. 33), September and October £3 2*s.* (Rs. 31), November and December £2 16*s.* (Rs. 28).

Chapter IV. Agriculture. Famines. 1877. *Effects.*

This loss was not so serious as the numbers suggest. The majority of the animals which perished were maimed or diseased bullocks or cows which had ceased to give milk. Still the working and rent-paying power of the district was a good deal affected. The tillage area fell from 946,203 acres in 1875-76 to 651,325 in 1876-77, in 1877-78 it rose again to 868,632 acres, and in 1878-79 to 838,020 acres. In 1876-77 the revenue for collection was £126,473 (Rs. 12,64,730) of which £114,178 (Rs. 11,41,780) were collected in the year. In 1877-78 the amount for collection was £126,679 (Rs. 12,66,970), of which £122,978 (Rs. 12,29,780) were collected in the year. Of the balance of £15,996 (Rs. 1,59,960) £13,632 (Rs. 1,36,320) were collected in subsequent years and £2163 (Rs. 21,630) were remitted.

Rat Plague.

In October 1878, rats, of which there are no less than ten local varieties, swarmed in the northern and eastern sub-divisions of Gokák, Athni, and Parasgad, and in a less degree in Chikodi. Of the ten varieties of which some details are given in the Production Chapter the most destructive to crops was the large-eared field-rat, Golunda mettada. In June and July 1879, though not in such swarms as in some of the Deccan districts, rats were again found in great numbers in the north and east of the district. They did much damage by scratching out and eating the seed grain. Some fields had to be thrice sown. In July 1879, Government offered a reward of 2*s.* (Re. 1) for every hundred rats killed, and the district officers were urged to rouse all classes to bestir themselves to help in ridding the country of the plague of rats. The bulk of the husbandmen from their dislike to take life were of little service. Low-caste Hindus and Musalmáns, though willing to help, were too ignorant of the habits of the rats to be of much service. The Vadars proved excellent rat-catchers digging the burrows and killing the rats in large numbers. Between August and October about 135,000 rats were destroyed and £135 (Rs. 1,350) spent in rewards. Before a reward was paid the rats had to be produced at a Government treasury, where the tails were cut off. The reward was paid to the rat-catcher and the tail-less bodies were returned to him to be eaten. Rewards were continued till the 15th of October 1879. Though the employment of rat-catchers to destroy the rats probably saved the crops from considerable loss, the disappearance of the rats was not solely or even chiefly due to the skill of the Vadars. Towards the end of the year large numbers of rats were killed by very heavy rain and afterwards by cold. The bodies of many rats were also covered with a red tick which was believed to have been the cause of death. By the end of December 1879 the rats had disappeared.

CHAPTER V.

CAPITAL.

Chapter V.

Capital.

UNDER the heads of Traders and Capitalists the 1882-83 license tax returns show 1801 persons assessed on yearly incomes of £50 and upwards. Of this number, 865 had £50, 316 from £50 to £75, 195 from £75 to £100, seventy from £100 to £125, 110 from £125 to £150, ninety-nine from £150 to £200, sixty from £200 to £300, thirty from £300 to £400, thirty-four from £400 to £500, thirteen from £500 to £750, and five from £750 to £1000.[1] Of these 1801 capitalists and traders 1295 were moneylenders, 239 were traders, and forty-nine were brokers.

Currency.

[2] Before Belgaum became a military station (about 1818) ordinary business was carried on either by the Sháhápur or by the Shambhu rupee which was coined at Vádi in the South Konkan. The Sháhápur rupee was a sound coin with a certain and uniform proportion of silver and alloy. The Shambhu rupee, which weighed about 173 grains Troy and was worth 1*s.* 8*d.* (13⅓ *as.*), was less certain and uniform in its proportion of silver and alloy and was rated at four or five per cent below the Sháhápur rupee. In 1822 these were the only coins used by villagers. The establishment of the Division Pay Office at Belgaum, and the necessity of supplying from the Ceded Districts in Madras funds to meet the expenses of the civil and military establishments, brought into use numerous other coins.[3] Of these the Company's Madras rupee was worth eleven per cent and the Bágalkot rupee was worth two per cent more than the Sháhápur coin; on the other hand the rupee from Chándor in Násik was two and a half per cent, the Hukeri current in Kolhápur was nine per cent, and the Haidarabad, Udváni, and Govind Bakshi rupees were twelve per cent below the Sháhápur rupee.[4] All of these coins were freely used by the shopkeepers in their daily dealings. Among them, from its intrinsic worth, the Company's rupee bore a high price, and it was sent in large numbers as bullion to the Sháhápur mint. In 1822 the only copper

---

[1] Since 1879 incomes under £50 have been free from the license tax. The 1878 license tax returns showed 13,810 persons with yearly incomes of £10 to £50, 7838 with £10 to £15, 3462 with £15 to £25, 1714 with £25 to £35, and 796 with £35 to £50.

[2] Marshall's Statistical Reports, Bombay 1822, 21, 49-50, 55-56.

[3] In March 1820 the Belgaum troops were paid in no less than twenty-one different sorts of money. Many of these coins were unknown to the petty dealers in the market and they passed into the hands of the moneydealers who made large profits on the transaction. Marshall's Statistical Reports, 49.

[4] In 1822 a bill was not procurable on Haidarabad at a better rate than 100 Sháhápur for 106 Udváni, the difference of six per cent being regarded as the carriage and insurance of the cash to Haidarabad. Marshall's Statistical Reports, 55.

coin in circulation was the *Sháhu Paisa,* apparently coined at Sátára by Sháhu (1708-1750) the grandson of Shiváji. In 1822 it weighed about 154 grains Troy; the impression was generally worn away. At present (1884) the Imperial rupee is the standard coin over the whole district.

Bills.

Except at Sháhápur there is little trade in *hundis* or exchange bills. In the towns of Athni, Belgaum, Gokák, Hongal, Nandgad, Nipáni, Sankeshvar, and Saundatti not more than twenty persons, chiefly Lingáyats Bráhmans and a few Márwár-Vánis Jains and Musalmáns, issue exchange bills. In Athni these bills go to £1000 (Rs. 10,000), in Belgaum to £250 (Rs. 2500), in Gokák to £500 (Rs. 5000), in Hongal and Nandgad to £200 (Rs. 2000), in Nipáni to £300 (Rs. 3000), in Sankeshvar to £200 (Rs. 2000), and in Saundatti to £100 (Rs. 1000). In 1822 the Sháhápur bankers were merely agents for the bankers of New Hubli and Miraj. They did not grant bills on towns beyond a circle of about a hundred miles. If the place on which the bill was required was one of the few that to any large extent dealt direct with Sháhápur the price of the bill was nearly the market rate of the coin of the same place with an additional half or one per cent for agency charges.[1] At present (1883) at Sháhápur exchange bills to the amount of about £80,000 (Rs. 8,00,000) a year are issued on Bombay, Chiplun, Gadag, Madras, Nipáni, Poona, Sátára, and Vengurla. These exchange bills are generally discounted at one-fourth to one and a half per cent. In March, April, and May, when traders lay in stock for the rainy season, the rate of discount rises to three per cent.

Savings.

The classes who save are Government servants, pleaders, moneylenders, and large traders and shopkeepers, chiefly Bráhmans, Lingáyats, and a few Gujarát and Márwár Vánis. The land proprietors or *inámdárs* are improvident. They keep establishments which they are unable to support, and spend sums which they can ill afford on caste dinners and in holding marriages and other ceremonies. The agricultural classes as a rule are badly off, their holdings being generally too small to enable them to save any considerable sums. The few husbandmen who save generally spend their savings in improving their land. Craftsmen, especially town craftsmen, are better off. If they do not save much, they are at least freer from debt than most of the other middle and lower classes. Except those who are in the service of Europeans servants do not save.

Before 1876, when there was no restriction as to the amount any one person might invest in them, moneylenders put large sums in the Savings Banks. Since 1876, when the amount which any one

---

[1] Such a bill was the conveyance of a real mercantile balance and the trade of Hubli and Miraj afforded such bills to a much greater extent both as to the field and the amount than the limited transactions of Sháhápur. The bill transactions even of the Sháhápur bankers were on no very large scale. If they drew largely they were frequently obliged to make real remittances of specie to answer their own bills, in which case the exchange rate was very nearly the actual cost of sending the specie. Marshall's Statistical Reports, 55.

Chapter V. Capital. Investments. *Securities.*

person might lodge was limited to £300 (Rs. 3000), the Government Savings Banks are used mostly by Government servants and pleaders, sometimes by moneylenders and shopkeepers, and rarely by husbandmen. In 1882 the investments in Savings Banks amounted to £9067 (Rs. 90,670). In 1882, £16,260 (Rs. 1,62,600) were invested in Government promissory notes. The whole amount was held by twenty-seven investers, £5850 (Rs. 58,530) being held by three moneylenders, £5500 (Rs. 55,000) by six land-proprietors, £2330 (Rs. 23,300) by eight Government servants, £1650 (Rs. 16,500) by five wives and widows of Government servants, £500 (Rs. 5000) by two shopkeepers, and £430 (Rs. 4300) by three Government pensioners.

Land.

Except by moneylenders little or no capital is invested in land or in house-building. Land is bought neither by Government servants nor by pleaders, but it is often taken in mortgage by moneylenders, and of late years much has passed into their hands. Moneylenders seldom invest money in improving their land. During the last twenty years the price and the rent of land have greatly risen. Garden land fetches £10 to £30 (Rs. 100-300) the acre, rice land £2 to £10 (Rs. 20 - 100), and dry-crop land £1 to £1 10*s*. (Rs. 10 - 15). As a rule moneylenders do not themselves till the land which is mortgaged to them. They rent it generally to the former holder at three or four times the assessment, or they take half of the produce and from their share pay the Government assessment. The tenant or under-holder usually pays his rent in kind.

Houses.

In rural Belgaum investment in house-building is unknown. New houses are almost always built by persons who mean to live in them. In small villages houses are often let rent-free on condition that the tenants keep them in repair. In large villages house-rent varies from 10*s*. to £4 (Rs. 5-40) a year, and in towns from £1 4*s*. to £10 (Rs. 12-100). Even in the city of Belgaum there is little house-building. The houses built for Europeans, if not occupied, are allowed to fall into disrepair, and no new houses have lately been built. The houses held by Europeans pay monthly rents varying from £1 to £8 (Rs. 10-80), and the houses in the native town of Belgaum yield monthly rents of 4*s*. to 16*s*. (Rs. 2-8). The few new houses generally belong to moneylenders. These are better built and better placed than those built thirty years ago, both air and light are more freely admitted. As land, timber, and labour are dearer, the cost of house-building is much greater than it formerly was.

Ornaments.

With all classes ornaments are the favourite form of investment. Those who can afford it, almost always spend part of their savings in buying ornaments whose workmanship varies with the rank and position of the wearer. The lowest classes have silver bangles and bracelets with an occasional gold necklace or *tika* and as a hair ornament a gold plate laid on brass. Many of the richer classes have gold earrings and necklaces, in many cases set with stones, and hair ornaments of solid gold.

Moneylending.

In Belgaum shopkeeping and moneylending go hand in hand. The trader who finds it difficult to develop his business invests his profits in moneylending. Of all investments moneylending is considered the most profitable. Of £3822 (Rs. 38,220), the total amount collected under the license tax in 1882-83, £2942 (Rs. 29,420), or about seventy-five per cent, were collected from 1295 moneylenders who had yearly incomes of £50 (Rs. 500) and upwards. About forty per cent of the moneylenders are found in large towns and sixty per cent in villages. The chief moneylenders, both in towns and in villages, are Lingáyat or Karnátak Vánis, Bráhmans, and a few Jains, Maráthás, and Musalmáns. Of Márwár and Gujarát Vánis and Cutch Bhátiás, who are generally both traders and moneylenders, there are not more than 300. Of these about thirty are found in Belgaum, 200 in Chikodi, and the rest in Parasgad, Gokák, and Athni. The Bhátiás are a very small body. The Gujarát and Márwár Vánis are said to have come to the district about eighty years ago and they have since slowly but steadily increased in number and wealth. Still they are not strong enough to cause any serious interference with the moneylending of the local Lingáyats and Bráhmans. Few Gujarát or Márwár Vánis have permanently settled in the district; most of them go home for their marriages and other religious ceremonies. As creditors the outside Vánis are considered harsher and more unscrupulous than the local lenders. A poor man seldom escapes if he falls into a Márwári's clutches. The Lingáyats and Bráhmans who form the bulk of the moneylending class have comparatively a good name. Besides these professional moneylenders pleaders sometimes lend money to a small extent. Village headmen and Nárvekar husbandmen also often lend money, usually small sums, but sometimes as much as £20 to £50 (Rs. 200 - 500) to the people of their own village. They have a better name than professional moneylenders, being more tolerant of delay in paying and showing more regard to their debtors' circumstances. Besides the moneylenders of Belgaum, in the Sángli town of Sháhápur about a mile south of Belgaum, there are thirty moneylenders, 250 traders, and 320 weavers. Of all the towns within Belgaum limits Sháhápur is the foremost in wealth and has the best trade in cloth, pearls, and jewelry. Many of its moneylenders and traders carry on business both in Sháhápur and in Belgaum, and a large share of the district moneylending is in the hands of the Sháhápur moneylenders. They lend larger sums than other Belgaum moneylenders generally to persons of known credit and at less than the usual rate of interest. Rural traders and moneylenders sometimes borrow from the Sháhápur bankers. They are the only men of capital in the district whose credit is so good that people think it safe to lodge their savings in their hands. On sums lodged with them the Sháhápur moneylenders generally grant yearly interest at one and a half or two per cent. Village moneylenders generally lend at small sums, seldom more than £50 (Rs. 500). Town moneylenders lend larger sums on safer security and at lower interest. The commonest forms of security are a mortgage, pledge, or bill of sale of any property the borrower may own. Land, and sometimes houses, trees, cattle, and standing crops, are taken in mortgage, and ornaments and sometimes stock in trade are pledged. With people

Chapter V.
Capital.
Moneylending.

of good credit a simple bond or a bond with a surety is a sufficient security for a loan. Of moneylenders the people say, 'They save us and they ruin us.' They save the husbandman by advancing him money and grain when his crop has failed, or when his store is exhausted and the new crop is not ripe; they ruin the husbandman by the burden of heavy and compound interest, a burden from which he can seldom set himself free.

Márwár and Gujarát Vánis and Bhátias keep ledgers or *kirdas* and day-books or *khatávnis* in which balances are made up daily, weekly, or fortnightly. Other moneylenders keep only rough books called *botakhátás* and bonds.[1] When a husbandman is embarrassed his different creditors do not combine to share his property. Each works for himself, tries to realise what he can, and never writes off an amount as a bad debt. The only exception is that in some cases creditors, gaining nothing by keeping a debtor in prison, let him out and allow their claim to become time-barred. A debtor has generally current dealings with one creditor. The growing crop is generally pledged to this creditor, who often has it attached and sold in execution of his decree. In no case is the power of the creditor independent of the civil court. The civil court is the last resort of all moneylenders except those who advance only on gold and silver ornaments and are never forced to go to court. The moneylender does not rest satisfied with what payments he can extract from his debtor under fear that the decree will be put into execution. Before putting the decree into execution the creditor waits for some time to induce his debtor to come to terms. As a last resource he throws the debtor in jail or he sells the debtor's property. The immoveable property, which is generally previously mortgaged or otherwise encumbered, when put to sale seldom fetches a good price. The indebtedness of the poorer cultivators almost never leads to agrarian crime.

Interest.

Except among Márwár and Gujarát Vánis who use the *Samvat* year beginning from *Kártik* or November, the *Shak* year beginning from *Chaitra* or March - April is in general use.[2] As interest is charged monthly and not yearly, an extra sum is levied when an additional or intercalary month occurs. The rate of interest depends partly on the credit of the borrower and partly on the amount borrowed. In the case of a borrower of good credit the yearly rate of interest for sums between £50 and £100 (Rs. 500-1000) is eight to twelve per cent and for sums of more than £100 (Rs. 1000) lent to bankers six to nine per cent. One case is mentioned in which one moneylender borrowed from another, at different times, sums amounting to as much as £2200 (Rs. 22,000) at a yearly interest of five and a quarter per cent. For large traders with good credit the rate of interest varies from eight to twelve per cent; for small traders and craftsmen it varies from twelve to twenty-four per cent; and for husbandmen and labourers it varies from eighteen to thirty-seven and a half per cent. The interest

---

1 The *botákháta* is never produced in court and its existence is denied.
2 The *Samvat* era begins with B.C. 56, the *Shak* era with A.D. 78.

charged when property is mortgaged varies from six to twelve per cent when ornaments are pledged, and from nine to twenty-four per cent when land is pledged. During the last thirty years there has been no considerable change in the rate of interest.

Borrowers.

Almost all classes borrow to meet wedding and other special charges. Of all borrowers husbandmen are the worst off; traders and craftsmen have better credit, and labourers have so little credit that they cannot sink deep into debt. Large traders, who sometimes borrow to meet special expenses or to face some mercantile loss, can raise money at eight to twelve per cent on bonds with or without security. To lay in a sufficient stock for the rainy season small traders generally raise loans in April and May at twelve per cent and more by pledging their goods. In the larger towns the craftsmen are fairly free from debt. Weavers often borrow to meet their daily expenses, but blacksmiths, goldsmiths, carpenters, masons, potters, and shoemakers are seldom in want of funds. Their credit is fair. To meet wedding and other special expenses the town craftsman can raise a loan from professional moneylenders at twelve to twenty-four per cent, and the village craftsman, who is sometimes a husbandman as well as a craftsman, at eighteen to twenty-four per cent. During the rains, when their services are in little demand, craftsmen have sometimes to borrow to meet their daily expenses. Of husbandmen about one-fourth are well-to-do and free from debt. The rest except the poorest are able to live comfortably without the help of moneylenders in an ordinary year, but, on account of their small holdings, they are forced to incur debts in times of unusual scarcity and on occasions of marriages and other family events. During the rains the poorer husbandmen have sometimes to seek advances of grain either for food or for seed from the richer landholders or from moneylenders who generally store grain in pits. An advance of grain is generally paid in kind at harvest time with an addition of one-fourth to one-half of the quantity advanced. Husbandmen often raise loans to supply the loss of cattle, to build a new house, to pay wedding and other special expenses and, during years of scarcity and bad crops, to buy food and seed for the next year's crops and to pay the Government assessment. If his land is unburdened a husbandman can easily raise £5 (Rs. 50). But, even among husbandmen whose credit is good, not more than twenty per cent can raise a loan of over £8 (Rs. 80) without mortgaging land, house, or other property. The credit of a large portion of the husbandmen is poor and they have to pay extremely heavy interest. For husbandmen with fair credit the yearly rate of interest varies from eighteen to twenty-four per cent on the security of land or house property, from nine to twelve per cent on the security of ornaments, and from twenty-four to thirty-seven and a half per cent on personal security. For husbandmen with little or no credit the rate of interest is invariably thirty-seven and a half per cent. When the nominal rate of interest is between twenty-four and thirty-seven and a half per cent, if the principal and interest are paid in time, the moneylender sometimes remits part of the interest on closing the account. During the 1876-77 famine, Belgaum, specially Athni Parasgad and Sampgaon, suffered severely. The

Chapter V.

Capital.

famine greatly reduced the husbandman's credit. Want of money, rather than any growth of thrift or forethought, has led most husbandmen to reduce their marriage expenses by one-third. At the same time there seems to be some increase of forethought, as since the famine the practice of storing grain in pits is commoner than it was. During the six years ending 1882 borrowing is said to have become more general among the husbandmen than it was before the famine. The chief causes are the famine of 1876 and 1877, and the scanty and irregular rainfall and consequent bad seasons between 1878 and 1881.

Land Transfers.

A good deal of land changes hands in one of three ways, from the failure of the holder to pay the assessment, under the orders of the civil courts, and by voluntary sale or mortgage. Cases of land being given up by its holder or sold by Government on account of the holder's failure to pay rent are not common. If the land is worth keeping, the holder, if in difficulty, usually prefers to borrow to pay the assessment rather than lose his land. During the three years ending 1882 the sales of land under the orders of the civil court averaged fifty-six. Land which is sold under the orders of the civil courts is generally of poor or middle quality; it is mostly bought by Lingáyat and Bráhman moneylenders. Land is seldom transferred by voluntary sale. Unless it is very poor, landholders do their utmost to keep the land in their own cultivation even if they are forced to part with the ownership to moneylenders. The usual forms of land mortgage are mortgages with or without possession. In the beginning most husbandmen who till their own lands raise loans by mortgaging land without possession. The rate of interest demanded in such cases generally ranges from eighteen to twenty-four per cent. So high a rate of interest leaves little chance of clearing the debt. Part of the interest remains unpaid and the gathered interest gradually increases the principal until principal and interest together equal the value of the land mortgaged. The moneylender then practically takes possession of the land, though he seldom appeals to the civil court to have his possession legally recognized. The fear of losing his land usually induces the husbandman to continue tilling on almost any terms the moneylender may lay down. In this way land which is once mortgaged without possession passes into the hands of the moneylender as completely as if it was mortgaged with possession. When land is mortgaged to a moneylender with possession, though it stands in the name of the husbandman and though he may continue to till it, the land is in the possession of the lender and the husbandman's ownership is nominal. Cases of mortgage with possession are common. One-fourth and sometimes more than one-fourth of the gross produce is paid as the interest of the mortgage, but one-fourth is seldom enough to meet the amount due under interest, so that the husbandman becomes more and more involved and his chance of recovering his land continues to grow smaller.

Labour Mortgage.

Bráhmans Jains and Lingáyats sometimes, and workmen and husbandmen, chiefly shepherds Mhárs and Mángs, often raise money by mortgaging their labour for a term of years. The rate at

Chapter V.
Capital.
Labour Mortgage.

which the pledger's service is valued depends on his need, his credit, and his power of work. Bráhmans, Lingáyats, and others belonging to the higher classes pledge their labour either as writers, accountants, or clerks; workmen and husbandmen pledge their labour generally as house or field workers. Formerly the practice of raising loans by labour-mortgages was common among labourers. Of late, as work has been fairly plentiful and wages regular, the practice of workmen mortgaging their labour has become less common. The labour-mortgage bond is always written on stamped paper. The bond generally provides that the workman who pledges his labour shall be supplied with food and clothing, usually two waist-cloths, a blanket, and a pair of shoes a year. The bond also lays down the condition that, in default of service, the debt or the remaining portion of the debt shall be paid or interest be charged at twelve to thirty-six per cent for the time for which the debt shall remain unpaid. The relations of the labour-mortgager and mortgagee are the same as those of master and servant, the chief difference between a free and a pledged labourer being that the free labourer receives daily wages, while until his debt is paid the pledged labourer enjoys less freedom and receives only food and clothing.[1]

Wages.

About thirty years ago (1853) skilled labourers, carpenters, black-smiths, and masons, were paid 6*d.* (4 *as.*) and bricklayers 4½*d.* (3 *as.*) a day. At present (1883) carpenters, blacksmiths, and masons are paid 9*d.* to 1*s.* (6-8 *as.*) and bricklayers 6*d.* to 9*d.* (4-6 *as.*) a day. These wages are paid in cash, either weekly or daily. The skilled labourers are chiefly Lingáyats, Maráthás, and Musalmáns. Even during the rains, when little is going on, skilled town labourers

---

[1] The following are translations of two Belgaum labour-bonds :

[1]. I, Venkáji Rámchandra, having received from you, Gopálráo Anna Dámle, a loan of rupees 100, sign, of my own free will, the following agreement for service in liquidation of my debt. I will live in your house for the next two years and do whatever service you may require, field labour, dunning debtors, and other miscellaneous work. I will claim no payment in cash for these services, but you should supply me with a blanket, two waistcloths each costing a rupee, and a pair of shoes. In this way shall my debt be paid by my service for a period of two years. In case I fail to complete the term of my service I agree to remain subject to the payment of what portion of my debt remains after deducting an amount proportionate to the time I shall have served, at the rate of rupees four a month. I further agree to pay such sum as shall remain if I do not complete my term of service, in a lump sum, and in case that sum be not paid at once I bind myself to pay interest at the rate of three rupees per cent a month in addition to the principal. My bond is to be returned to me when I pay off the debt by service or in money. This agreement is given of my free will and herein I will not fail.

Date ———. Name ———.

[2]. I have borrowed from you a sum of rupees one hundred for my own necessities. By way of paying that debt I agree to serve you in tending cattle and other field labour. I bind myself hereby to serve in this way for a period of four years from the date of this bond and to do in addition to the above service any similar work that you may impose upon me. At the end of the four years the sum borrowed is to be considered as fully paid and I am to be at liberty to offer my services to any other master. During the four years I will not cease to serve you. If I cease to serve you before the end of the four years, a sum proportionate to the period for which I shall have served, shall be taken from the original amount borrowed, and for the remaining amount from that date interest at the rate of one rupee per cent a month shall be paid. The further conditions are that you shall feed me twice a day and every year provide me with a pair of waistcloths, a pair of shoes, a handkerchief, a blanket, and two shirts. Under these conditions I agree to serve you.

Date ———. Name ———.

Chapter V.
Capital.
Wages.

and those employed by the Public Works Department find constant work of eight to ten hours a day. Their wives, who do not help them in their work, look after their houses and sometimes do a little spinning and weaving. Their condition is fair, though the rise in the price of grain takes considerably from the value of the increase in money wages. At present the services of skilled workmen are in good demand, chiefly by the Public Works Department and by railway contractors. On public works skilled labourers generally receive high daily wages, masons 10½*d.* to 1*s.* 6*d.* (7-12 *as.*), carpenters 9*d.* to 1*s.* 6*d.* (6-12 *as.*), blacksmiths 9*d.* to 1*s.* 3*d.* (6-10 *as.*), painters, tailors, and shoemakers 1*s.* (8 *as.*), and thatchers 9*d.* (6 *as.*). Village craftsmen are not nearly so well off as town craftsmen. During the rains their services are in little demand, even during the busy season the demand is not always enough to occupy their whole time. They generally combine tillage with their special calling. Most village carpenters and blacksmiths, who are usually village servants, supplement their daily wages by receiving at harvest time a grain allowance or *aya* from husbandmen whose field tools they repair. Of unskilled labourers, who are mostly Lingáyats, Maráthás, Musalmáns, Mhárs, and Mángs, town labourers are generally paid in cash and field labourers in grain. The daily wages of town labourers are for men 3*d.* to 5¼*d.* (2-3½ *as.*), for women 1½*d.* to 3*d.* (1-2 *as.*), and for children ¾*d.* to 1½*d.* (½-1 *anna*). Thirty years ago the wages of unskilled labour were about two-thirds of the present rate. Labourers who find work in the city of Belgaum and on public works are generally better off than the rest of their class. As a rule town labourers have little work during the rains. The chief employment of labourers, especially of female labourers, is carrying, digging, and doing the rougher parts of house-building. On market days they earn twice or three times what they earn on other days. At harvest time town labourers occasionally work in the fields, when they are mostly paid in grain. Field labourers who are paid in grain get daily wages of 4 pounds to 10 pounds (2-5 *shers*) of grain for a man, 3 pounds to 4½ pounds (1½-3 *shers*) for a woman, and 1 pound to 2 pounds (½-1 *sher*) for a child. They work six to nine hours a day, and sometimes by doing night work earn half as much again as their regular day's wages. Their busiest time is ploughing and sowing in May and June, and weeding reaping and thrashing between September and December. As a rule field workers are paid daily wages, but reaping is sometimes paid by the piece. When employed in house-building or in digging a well, labourers sometimes bind themselves for a fixed sum or a fixed quantity of grain to attend daily till the work is finished. During the harvest months, that is from September to December, when work is harder and wages are higher than at other times, the labourers often save enough to keep them in fair comfort during the remaining eight months of the year. For the five months between January and May, when there is almost no field work, field labourers work in large towns, picking cotton and getting employment in the carrying trade to the Kánara, Goa, and Ratnágiri coast.

Prices

Yearly price details, some of which are little more than estimates, are available for the fifty-nine years ending 1882. During these fifty-

Chapter V.

Capital.

Prices.

nine years the rupee price of Indian millet or *jvári*, which is the staple grain of the district, varied from seventeen pounds in 1863 to 112 in 1849, and averaged sixty-one pounds. Of the fifty-nine years, in four the price was below 100 pounds the rupee, 112 in 1849, 108 in 1851, 103 in 1832, and 102 in 1850; in four it was between 100 and ninety pounds, ninety-eight in 1834, ninety-seven in 1829, ninety-two in 1844, and ninety-one in 1831; in four it was between ninety and eight pounds, ninety in 1842, eighty-five in 1845, and eighty-one in 1830 and 1852; in eleven it was between eighty and seventy pounds, seventy-nine in 1836 1848 1853 and 1856, seventy-eight in 1835 1843 and 1847, seventy-six in 1841, seventy-five in 1840, seventy-four in 1854, and seventy-one in 1839; in six it was between seventy and sixty pounds, sixty-eight in 1827 and 1837, sixty-six in 1857, sixty-three in 1828, and sixty-two in 1825 and 1855; in nine it was between sixty and fifty pounds, sixty in 1824 and 1858, fifty-nine in 1838, fifty-eight in 1846 and 1859, fifty-six in 1881, fifty-three in 1860, and fifty-two in 1826 and 1882; in seven it was between fifty and forty, forty-seven in 1833, forty-five in 1875, forty-four in 1868 1869 and 1874, and forty-three in 1862 and 1871; in six it was between forty and thirty pounds, forty in 1867, thirty-nine in 1861, thirty-eight in 1880, thirty-six in 1876, thirty-three in 1870, and thirty-two in 1873; and in eight it was between thirty and fifteen pounds, twenty-six in 1872, twenty-five in 1879, twenty-four in 1878, twenty-one in 1865, twenty in 1864 and 1877, eighteen in 1866, and seventeen in 1863. Till 1857, except in 1826 1833 and 1838, the price was below sixty pounds the rupee. Since 1857 the price has never been below sixty pounds.

The fifty-nine years may be divided into nine periods. In the five years ending 1828 the price varied from sixty-eight in 1827 to fifty-two in 1826 and averaged sixty-one pounds. Except in 1833 when the price was forty-seven pounds in the second period of eight years ending 1836, the price varied from 103 in 1832 to seventy-eight in 1835, and averaged eighty-four pounds. In the third period of the five years ending 1841, the price varied from seventy-six in 1841 to fifty-nine in 1838, and averaged seventy pounds. Except in 1846 when the price was fifty-eight pounds, in the fourth period of twelve years ending 1853, the price varied from 112 pounds in 1849 to seventy-eight in 1843 and 1847, and averaged eighty-seven pounds. In the fifth period of the nine years ending 1862 the price varied from seventy-nine in 1856 to thirty-nine in 1861 and averaged fifty-nine pounds. In the sixth period of the four years ending 1866 the price varied from twenty-one pounds in 1865 to seventeen in 1863 and averaged nineteen pounds. Except in 1872 when it was twenty-six pounds, the price during the seventh period of the ten years ending 1876 varied from forty-five in 1875 to thirty-two in 1873 and averaged thirty-nine pounds. In the eighth period of the three years ending 1879, the prices varied from twenty-five in 1879 to twenty pounds in 1877, and averaged twenty-three pounds. In the ninth period of the three years ending 1882 the price varied from fifty-six in 1881 to thirty-eight in 1880 and averaged forty-nine pounds :

Chapter V.
Capital.
Prices.

Belgaum Grain Prices in Pounds the Rupee, 1824-1882.

Produce.	First Period.					Second Period.								Third Period.	
	1824.	1825.	1826.	1827.	1828.	1829.	1830.	1831.	1832.	1833.	1834.	1835.	1836.	1837.	1838.
Indian Millet	60	62	52	68	63	97	81	91	103	47	98	78	79	68	59
Wheat	53	57	46	56	56	87	57	76	77	28	49	52	66	69	61
Rice	43	46	47	50	53	60	67	69	55	33	28	47	47	35	40

Produce.	Third Period—contd.			Fourth Period.											
	1839.	1840.	1841.	1842.	1843.	1844.	1845.	1846.	1847.	1848.	1849.	1850.	1851.	1852.	1853.
Indian Millet	71	75	76	90	78	92	85	58	78	79	112	102	108	81	79
Wheat	45	63	39	78	74	76	71	53	69	69	87	84	105	89	83
Rice	35	49	38	61	67	67	57	42	49	53	72	63	62	61	65

Produce.	Fifth Period.									Sixth Period.				Seventh Period.	
	1854.	1855.	1856.	1857.	1858.	1859.	1860.	1861.	1862.	1863.	1864.	1865.	1866.	1867.	1868.
Indian Millet	74	62	79	66	60	58	53	39	43	17	20	21	18	40	44
Wheat	81	53	78	61	58	55	37	22	41	17	12	15	10	21	39
Rice	65	48	41	39	41	41	34	27	30	17	13	15	15	21	25

Produce.	Seventh Period—contd.								Eighth Period.			Ninth Period.		
	1869.	1870.	1871.	1872.	1873.	1874.	1875.	1876.	1877.	1878.	1879.	1880.	1881.	1882.
Indian Millet	44	33	43	26	32	44	45	36	20	24	25	38	56	53
Wheat	31	11	19	16	20	34	38	29	14	14	12	18	35	40
Rice	18	18	27	..	18	32	31	24	13	16	19	22	23	21

Weights and Measures.

Precious stones and pearls are not sold by weight. Their price is fixed by their size and quality according to rules which are known only to dealers in those articles. Gold and silver are bought and sold by small weights. The table used in weighing gold and silver is eight *gulugunjás* or Abrus seeds one *mása,* and twelve *másas* one *tola.* One *tola* is equal to 180 Troy grains. The *tola* is almost always represented by the Imperial rupee. Silver ornaments are almost always weighed against rupees. Copper, brass, tin, lead, iron, and grain are sold by *shers* and *mans.* The *sher* varies from twenty to eighty *tolás.* The eighty *tolás sher* is the full or Government *sher* and is equal to two English pounds. The *man* contains forty and occasionally forty-one *shers.* Green and dry grass are sold in small bundles called *pendis* or *sivadus,* of which about 200 go to the rupee. Lucern grass, which is in great demand in the Belgaum cantonment, is sold at eighty to ninety pounds the rupee. Rice straw is usually sold by the cart and millet stalks or *karbi* by the cord that is in bundles containing as many stalks as can be bound in a rope six to eight feet long. Cotton, both cleaned and uncleaned, is bought and sold on the basis of fifty-two *shers* to the *man*, and twenty *mans* to the *khandi*. Of liquids, milk and sesamum castor and cocoanut oil are sold by a capacity measure which is equal to twenty rupees in weight. Fragrant and valuable oils are sold according to the table of weights used for gold and silver. Salt is bought wholesale according to the standard measure called *páili* which is equal to four *shers* or 320 *tolás*. It is sold retail by the standard *sher* of eighty *tolás*. The *páili* is made of iron or copper and is cylindrical in form. Bamboos are sold by tale, gravel and sand by the cartload, and cement and lime by ordinary capacity measures.

Of measures of length the *háth* or cubit, that is a foot and a half, is the unit of long measure. It is the length from the top of the middle finger when the hand is open to the point of the elbow joint, and in an adult averages eighteen inches. Two *háths* are equal to one *gaz, vár*, or yard. Nearly all soft goods are sold by the *háth* or cubit. But such articles as *chidis* or women's robes, *rumáls* or headscarves, and *kháns* or bodicecloth, are sold by tale, and waistcloths by the pair; carpets are sold according to their size; masonry is either contracted for as piece-work or at a fixed rate for the hundred cubic feet. Of stones large stones and coping stones are sold by cubic contents; paving stones and stones of a uniform section, only surface dressed, are sold by surface measurement; dressed stones are sold by cubic or surface measurement; and stones with varying sectional areas by tale. Roadmetal is sold by the cart-load. Timber, both green and seasoned, is sold by the cubic contents according to English measurement. The land measures at present in use are the acre and the *guntha* or one-fortieth of an acre. The people do not use the division into fortieths but apply the division into sixteenths speaking of the parts as *annás*. The use of weights of known form is now to a certain extent compulsory. Still in outlying villages rude lumps of lead or iron and stones and pieces of broken stone and earthenware are sometimes used as weights.

CHAPTER VI.

TRADE.

I.—COMMUNICATIONS.

Chapter VI.
Trade.
Roads.
1820.

In 1820 so liable were almost all villages to be cut off for weeks together by swollen streams and flooded rivers that before the rains the people were forced to lay in a four or five months' store of provisions.[1] In 1826 Captain Clunes noticed that five main lines of road centred at Belgaum.[2] Two went north to Poona, one went north-east to Kaládgi and Sholápur, one went south-east to Dhárwár, and one went west to Goa and Vengurla in Ratnágiri. Of the two Belgaum-Poona roads, one, after passing about sixty miles through Kungarli, Yamkanmardi, Hukeri, and Chikodi, left the district at Gokarvádi in Chikodi. It then crossed Kolhápur and Sátára till it reached Poona after a further distance of about 150 miles. The second Belgaum-Poona road was 241 miles long. Of the whole length seventy-eight miles lay within Belgaum, passing through Kalkumbe, Marihal, Konur, Nagarmanoli, Kerur, and Sidápurhatti. It left the district at Kágvád about twenty-four miles west of Athni, and beyond Kágvád passed through Tásgaon and Koregaon in Sátára to Poona. From this second Belgaum-Poona road two lines branched, one to the north-west the other to the north-east. The north-west branch had a length of 128 miles of which about eight lay within Belgaum limits. It started from Sidápurhatti about ten miles north-east of Athni, and reached Karád in Sátára through Miraj. The north-east branch had a length of 191 miles, of which about twenty-six lay within Belgaum limits. It started from Konur about eight miles north-west of Gokák and reached Sholápur through Bijápur. The Belgaum-Sholápur road in the north-east for the first thirteen miles formed part of the Belgaum-Poona road which left the district at Kágvád. From Marihal the road passed east for about twenty-five miles when it left the district near Manikeri. It then for about thirty miles crossed the Mudhol state to Kaládgi. From Kaládgi it went north for about 135 miles through Bijápur to Sholápur. From Guchan-Kurbet on this line, about three miles north of Gokák, a road of about 150 miles, of which about seventeen lay within Belgaum limits, branched north to Sholápur through Jamkhandi and Bijápur. The Belgaum-Dhárwár road of about fifty miles formed part of the Belgaum-Bellári road and the Belgaum-Harihar road. From Belgaum a road ran west for about twenty-five miles, passing through Sinoli, Turakvádi, and Kálánandigad,

[1] Marshall's Statistical Reports, 64.

[2] Clunes' Itinerary, 32-34, 68-73.

Chapter VI.
Trade.
Roads.

and after descending the Rám pass reached Kudási in Sávantvádi. At Kudási it divided in two, one branch about thirty miles long passing north-west to Vengurla, the other of twenty miles passing south-west to Goa. Few if any of these roads were in good order.

1829-1877.

In 1829 the roads joining the district with the coast were described as wretched tracts unworthy of the name of roads.[1] After 1829 for upwards of fifteen years little seems to have been done to improve the roads. Early in 1847 the Collector, Mr. J. D. Inverarity, brought to notice the injury which the cotton trade suffered from want of roads and bridges. In 1848, Mr. Townshend, the Revenue Commissioner, urged the necessity of improving the communications with the coast. The badness of the roads added seventeen to twenty per cent to the cost of carrying Belgaum cotton to Bombay.[2] In the same year, when Government made liberal concessions with the object of improving Belgaum cotton, one of the Members of Council, the late Mr. L. R. Reid, urged the necessity of supplementing the concessions by opening either railways or roads which would be passable at all seasons. In 1849, the Bombay Chamber of Commerce urged that good roads and railways should be made from the cotton districts to the coast and to Bombay, as until communications were improved it was impossible to establish up-country agencies.[3] Lord Falkland, the Governor of Bombay, (1848-1853) in recording the Chamber's recommendations recognized the importance of their advice. He regretted that funds were not available to carry out the improvements which Government had so much at heart. The Court of Directors expressed the hope that at no distant period they would be able to sanction the expenditure needed for improved communications. Shortly after this the Collector again urged on Government the necessity for improving the roads. But want of funds prevented Government doing anything beyond making a road through the Phonda pass to Vijayadurg in Ratnágiri. In 1850 the Dhárwár-Belgaum road was unfit for traffic as it was unbridged and as the Malprabha sometimes rose to a great height. During the rains carts could pass the river only at intervals sometimes of a fortnight. When the river was fordable the carts had to be dragged through the stream by two bullocks when unloaded and by four to six bullocks when loaded. There were generally about a dozen men shoulder-deep in water round each cart helping to turn the wheels and urging the frightened bullocks. The height of the wheels prevented much damage; still in some cases grain was considerably injured by the water.[4] Since 1864 the local funds system has placed increased means for constructing and improving roads in the hands of the Commissioner and Collector. Communications have been greatly improved. During the 1876-77 famine, many new roads were opened and many old roads were improved as relief works.

1883.

At present (1883), of forty-six roads, varying from a few furlongs to seventy-eight miles, one is Imperial, five are provincial, and forty

---

[1] Walton's Cotton, 8. [2] Walton's Cotton, 164. [3] Walton's Cotton, 165. [4] Mackay's Western India, 393.

Chapter VI.
Trade.
Roads.
1883.

are under local funds management. The total length represented by these roads is 792 miles, being twenty-nine of Imperial, 266 of provincial, and 497 of local funds roads. Yearly repairs cost on the Imperial roads about £800 (Rs. 8000), on the provincial roads about £9300 (Rs. 93,000), and on the local funds roads about £2550 (Rs. 25,500). The Imperial roads are the roads in the cantonment of Belgaum. Of the five provincial roads the first of seventy-six miles is part of the Poona-Harihar trunk road. This enters the district at Kangoli about twenty miles north-west of Chikodi, and passing through Nipáni, Sankeshvar, Yamkanmardi, Kákti, Belgaum, Bágevádi, and Kittur, leaves the district about four miles south-east of Kittur. It is metalled and bridged throughout, and has a large cart traffic during the fair months chiefly in grain and tobacco. The cost of making the road is estimated at £120,000 (Rs. 12,00,000). Of the second provincial road from Kaládgi to Vengurla there are two sections, one of seventy-eight miles west of Belgaum to Vengurla by the Ámboli pass of which thirty-one miles are within Belgaum limits and the rest are in Sávantvádi in Ratnágiri, the other section of seventy-three miles stretches east from Belgaum to Kaládgi, forty-two miles of it lying within the district. The western or Ámboli pass section, which is bridged and metalled throughout, was made in 1871 at a cost of about £140,000 (Rs. 14,00,000). During the fair season, when the port of Vengurla is open, a heavy cart traffic passes along this line. The whole line from Belgaum to Vengurla is repaired by the Executive Engineers of Belgaum and Kolhápur. The eastern or south Bijápur section is metalled and drained for the first fifteen miles only. It is a fair road thirty-six miles to Yargatti. Beyond Yargatti parts of it in black soil are almost impassable during the rains. Even in the fair weather the steep banks of many of the streams make it somewhat difficult for carts. In the dry season the cart traffic, especially in cotton, is heavy. The third road of about fifty miles starts from Dhárwár west to Linganmat about twenty miles south-east of Khánápur and runs through the southern part of the Khánápur sub-division to the Tinai pass in Kánara. This road, which is under the Executive Engineer of Dhárwár, is partly bridged and is in fair order for cart traffic all the year round. The fourth road of forty miles runs south to Khánápur and from Khánápur south-west to Bidi till it meets the Dhárwár and Tinai pass road at Linganmat. It has a few drains but no bridges and is passable for carts all the year round. The fifth road is of seventeen miles from Khánápur south to Sitavda on the Dhárwár-Tinai pass road beyond which the line runs to Supa in Kánara. This is passable for carts at all seasons. Of the local funds slightly repaired roads, which are mostly fair-weather tracks, there are four of some importance, the old Poona-Belgaum road, the Kolhápur-Bijápur road, the Sankeshvar-Yádvád road, and the Gokák-Nargund road. The old Poona-Belgaum road enters the district at Kágvád, and passing through Mánjri, Akhli, Chikodi, Vudurhal, and Kamatmur, joins the new or mail road at Gotur. This is the old mail road to Sátára by Tásgaon which was used before the Kolhápur route was opened. It is partly drained, but the larger streams are unbridged and the old metal is disappearing.

Chapter VI.

Trade.

Roads.

1883.

Though now merely a local road it has considerable cart traffic, especially north of the Krishna at Mánjri. During the monsoon, for six or seven miles north of Mánjri, the road is almost impassable owing to its deep black soil and to the widespreading floods of the Krishna. The Kolhápur-Bijápur road, of 106 miles, crosses the Athni sub-division from west to east, and passes through the towns of Berag, Kempvád, Athni, Aigal, and Telsang. In the fair season this road has a good deal of cart traffic, but during the rains many portions of it in black soil are almost impassable. The Sankeshvar-Yádvád road, forty-eight miles long, runs east and west through Chikodi and Gokák, passing Hukeri, Guras, Arbhavi, Vadurhátti, Musgupi, and Kulgod, to Yádvád. It has some cart traffic in the fair weather, but during the rains parts of it in black soil are almost impassable. A line, thirty-six miles long, running south from Athni, passes through Darur, Terdal, Kankanvádi, Kalloli, and Arbhavi on the Sankeshvar-Yádvád road to Gokák. From Gokák it stretches south-east through Yargati on the Belgaum-Kaládgi road and Manoli, and, after crossing the Malprabha, runs through Sindogi and Halikati to Nargund in Dhárwár. Part of this road between Arbhavi and Yargatti is sandy and stony and difficult for carts. Beyond Yargatti, though not bridged, the road is at all seasons passable for carts and gives easy access to the market town of Manoli. Besides these four main lines of local funds roads there are several smaller lines and country tracks. From Athni, besides the roads already noticed, six lines radiate, one north towards Balgeri, one north-east towards Kanmari, one south-east with a branch at Nándgaon leading to Kokatnur, one south joining the Athni-Gokák line at Terdal, one south-west joining the old Belgaum-Poona road at Kágvád, and one north-west to Belanki. Besides the main road three lines centre at Chikodi, one from Kankanvádi on the Athni-Gokák line in the east, one from Kurundvád in the north which after passing south and crossing the Poona-Belgaum road at Yamkanmardi ends at Daddi, and one from Nipáni in the west. A line from Kurundvád passes through Borgaon and joins the Poona-Harihar road at Savdalgi in Chikodi. Other roads run from Yádvád twenty miles to Yargatti on the Belgaum-Kaládgi road in Parasgad; from Arbhavi in Gokák thirty miles to Modga on the Belgaum main line; from Bágevádi on the mail road in Belgaum twenty miles to Murgod in Parasgad; from Hongal through Kittur twenty-five miles to Bidi; from Belgaum twenty-nine miles to the Rám pass; from Hulki on the Belgaum-Kaládgi road eighteen miles to Sindogi and Murgod and Saundatti in Parasgad; a road from Macha on the Belgaum-Khánápur road twenty-six miles running through Jámboti to Kankumbi, where it splits, one branch leading six miles to the Mangeli pass and the other seven miles to the Chorle pass; from Jámboti to Khánápur ten miles; and from Khánápur to the Kel pass twenty-two miles.

Passes.

Across the Sahyádris, within Belgaum limits or on the main lines between Belgaum and the sea, are eight chief passes of which three are crossed by roads fit for carts. Beginning from the north and working south these are the Ámboli or Párpoli Pass on the Belgaum-Vengurla road in the Sávantvádi state forty-three miles west of

Chapter VI.
Trade.
Passes.

Belgaum. It is an excellent pass nine and a half miles long with an easy gradient. It is bridged, drained, and metalled throughout, and in the fair season has a very great cart traffic. The Rám Pass lies about thirty miles west of Belgaum on the old Belgaum-Vengurla road. In 1826 it was the great pass to the upper country from Sávantvádi, Málvan, Vengurla, and Goa. The approach to the pass, both above and below, was a made road, and the ascent was easy and passable for every sort of wheeled carriage. The tract of country below was wild, hilly, and covered with large trees, clumps of bamboos, and thick underwood with partial tillage in the valleys. Since the opening of the Ámboli pass road in 1871, the Rám pass has been abandoned and cannot now (1883) be used by loaded carts. It is little frequented except by traders from Goa and by Vanjári bullocks taking salt from the coast and bringing grain from inland. About twelve miles south of the Rám pass and about twenty-five miles south-west of Belgaum is the Chorle Pass on the road between Sánkhali to Kankumbi. It is a mere foot-track though it can be used with difficulty by bullocks carrying salt. A mile or two to the south-east of Chorle is the Párva Pass, and about eight miles south-east of the Párva pass is the Kel Pass on the road which starts from Khánápur and runs south through Heneghe. Both the Párva and Kel passes are, like the Chorle pass, fit for foot passengers and with difficulty for cattle. About twelve miles south-east of the Kel pass is the Támeri Pass, a mere foot-path. About twelve miles south-east of the Támeri pass is the Tinái Pass. In the actual descent the road is well suited for carts, but immediately below, in the Goa territory, it is almost impassable with axle-deep ruts. The section in British territory is under the care of the Executive Engineer of Dhárwár.

Bridges.

There are six large bridges, three of stone and three of iron. The three stone bridges are on the Poona-Harihar road. One with seven forty-five feet spans is across the Vedganga in the 165th mile from Poona, the second is over the Harankási in the 187th mile, and the third is across the Ghatprabha in the 197th mile. The three iron bridges are on the Belgaum-Ámboli pass road. One, the Senavli bridge, in the seventh mile from Belgaum, has one Warren girder of sixty feet span and two plate girders each of thirty feet span; a second across the Kálánadi in the seventeenth mile has three Warren girders each of sixty feet span; and the third in the thirtieth mile across the Ghatprabha has two Warren girders each of sixty feet.

Tolls.

Of twenty toll-bars eleven are on provincial and nine are on local funds roads. Of the provincial toll-bars four, at Támbulvádi and Kanur on the Belgaum-Vengurla road, at Kudchi on the Belgaum-Kaládgi road, and at Desur on the Belgaum-Linganmut road, are in the Belgaum sub-division; two, at Sidanbhavi and Timápur on the Belgaum-Harihar mail road, are in Sampgaon; one, at Bidi on the Belgaum-Linganmut road, is in Khánápur; three, at Sutgatti, Sankeshvar, and Savdalgi, are on the Poona-Harihar mail road in Chikodi; and one, at Halki on the Belgaum-Kaládgi road is in Parasgad. Of the nine tolls on the local funds roads, two, at Turkevádi and Vaghotre on the Belgaum-Vengurla road across the Rám pass, are in Belgaum; two, at Chorle on the road from Belgaum to the Chorle pass and at Talevádi on the Khánápur-Talevádi road, are in Khánápur; one is at Chikodi on the Sutgatti-Chikodi road; one is at Vatnal on the Gokák-Saundatti road in Parasgad; two are at Tigdi and Gudas, both on the Sankeshvar-Lokápur road in Gokák; and one is at Kágvád on the Chikodi-Kágvád road in Athni. In 1881-82 the provincial toll-bars yielded £5401 (Rs. 54,010) and the local fund toll-bars £789 (Rs. 7890).

Rest Houses.

At Hukeri on the Sankeshvar-Gokák road two mosques are kept in repair for the use of district officers, and with the same object at Saundatti, the head-quarter station of Parasgad, some rooms in the fort are kept in order. Besides these there are ten bungalows for European and forty-two rest-houses or *dharmshálás* for Native travellers. Of the travellers' bungalows, four, one each at Belgaum, Támbulvádi, Pundre (Kanur), and Turkevádi, are in Belgaum; three, one each at Sutgatti, Gotur, and Nipáni, are in Chikodi; two, one each at Mugutkhán-Hubli and Nesargi, are in Sampgaon; and one is at Yargatti in Parasgad. The travellers' bungalow at Belgaum, which was built at a cost of £252 (Rs. 2520) is on the Poona-Harihar mail road; it has three rooms and is kept at a yearly charge of £13 4*s*. (Rs. 132); the bungalow at Támbulvádi, which in 1869 was built from provincial funds at a cost of £726 (Rs. 7260), is on the Belgaum-Vengurla road, has two rooms, and is kept at a yearly charge of £22 16*s*. (Rs. 228); the bungalow at Pundre or Kanur, which in 1868 was built from provincial funds at a cost of £700 (Rs. 7000), is on the Belgaum-Vengurla road, has two rooms, and is kept at a yearly charge of £20 8*s*. (Rs. 204); the two-roomed bungalow at Turkevádi, which was built at a cost of £219 (Rs 2190), is on the Belgaum-Rám pass road and is kept at a yearly charge of £8 8*s*. (Rs. 84). Of the three bungalows in Chikodi all are on the Poona-Harihar mail road and have two rooms. Of these the Sutgatti bungalow was built in 1848 at a cost of £290 (Rs. 2900) and has a yearly establishment at a charge of £18 (Rs. 180); the bungalows at Gutur and Nipáni were built in 1858 at a cost of £275 (Rs. 2750) each, and are kept at a yearly charge of £15 12*s*. (Rs. 156) each. Of the two Sampgaon bungalows the Mugutkhán-Hubli bungalow, which was built in 1839 at a cost of £321 (Rs. 3210), is on the Poona-Harihar mail road, has two rooms, and costs £18 (Rs. 180) a year to keep; and the Nesargi bungalow, which was built at a cost of £300 (Rs. 3000), is on the Belgaum-Kaládgi road, has two rooms, and costs £20 8*s*. (Rs. 204) a year to keep. The Yargatti bungalow in Parasgad is on the Belgaum-Kaládgi road; it has two rooms, was built at a cost of about £209 (Rs. 2090), and costs about £14 8*s*. (Rs. 144) a year to keep. Under the supervision of the Collector these bungalows are in the charge of a servant whose duty is to satisfy the wants of travellers. Only at the Belgaum bungalow is there a messman who has a small supply of oilman's stores, but is not licensed to sell wines and spirits. A daily fee of 2*s*. (Re. 1) is charged to any one using the bungalow.

Of the forty-two rest-houses or *dharmshálás* with room for ten to

Chapter VI. Trade. Rest Houses.

150 native travellers, eight are in Belgaum, six in Sampgaon, five in Khánápur, eleven in Chikodi, seven in Parasgad, one in Gokák, and four in Athni. All are in the charge of servants paid out of local funds. They have been built from local funds since 1865 at a cost of £7 to £543 (Rs. 70-5430). The rest-houses are used free of charge and the Local Funds Committee repairs them when necessary. Except by Lingáyats who stay in monasteries or *maths* and some others who lodge in the porches and out-houses of temples these rest-houses are used by all Native travellers.

Ferries.

No public ferries are worked throughout the year; all the rivers are fordable during the dry season. Of the thirty-eight public ferries which are worked during the rains, eight, at Ainápur, Hálihál, Satti, Mahisvádgi, Savadi, Shirhatti, Chik Padsalgi, and Hire Padsalgi, are on the Krishna; nine, at Hadkal, Ghodgeri, Modga, Hansihal, Gokák, Daddi, Konur, Tigdi, and Dhavaleshvar, are on the Ghatprabha; two, at Bhoj and Bedakihal, are on the Vedganga; two, at Páchhápur and Gokák, are on the Márkándiya; three, at Mángaon, Kovad, and Chinchani, are on the Támraparni; twelve, one at Jámboti, two at Khánápur, and one each at Parasvad, Mugutkhán-Hubli, Hansikatti, Turmuri, Sangoli, Vákund, Korvikop, Virápur, Yakundi, and Manoli, are on the Malprabha; and one at Ghotgevadi is on the Tilári. These ferries are all maintained at the expense of local funds and are yearly farmed the proceeds being credited to local funds. The revenues from the different ferries vary from 2*s.* to £130 (Rs. 1-1300). Of three ferries which yearly yield £50 (Rs. 500) and upwards, one is at Mugutkhán-Hubli, one at Manoli on the Malprabha, and one at Gokák on the Ghatprabha.

Of the thirty-eight public ferries sixteen have large ferry boats, eight have large canoes of which four are double canoes, thirteen are leather-baskets or *tokarás*, and one is an iron pan or *káil*. The boats and the canoes are made either by the executive engineer or by contractors at the cost of the local funds. They are of teak, mango, or *sávri* wood. The leather-baskets or *tokarás* are circular and are built of bamboo sticks covered with leather. They are generally built at the places where they are kept, or at the nearest sub-divisional head-quarters station. It requires no great skill to build a coracle. The large iron pan or *káil* is made by a village blacksmith. The ferry boats vary in size from eight feet long by eight broad and one and a half deep, to thirty-nine feet long by fourteen broad and three deep. They carry a quarter to two tons (15 to 120 *mans*) of goods, fifteen to 200 passengers, and some of them two to eight carts. Their fees are $\frac{3}{8}$*d.* to $\frac{3}{4}$*d.* ($\frac{1}{4}$-$\frac{1}{2}$ *anna*) for a man, 9*d.* to 1*s.* (6-8 *as.*) for a cart, and 1$\frac{1}{2}$*d.* (1 *anna*) for a horse buffalo or ox. The crew varies from four to sixteen on a boat, from one to ten on a canoe, and one to four on a basket. The crews are Bagdis, Bedars, Kabalgers or Thákurs, Kolis, Lingáyats, Maráthás, Mhárs, and Musalmáns. The boats cost £15 to £250 (Rs. 150-2500), the canoes £1 to £15 (Rs. 10-150), the leather boats £1 to £3 (Rs. 10-30), and the iron pans £1 10*s.* to £3 (Rs. 15-30). Besides these public ferries eleven ferries are kept by *inámdárs* or holders of alienated villages. All yield a yearly revenue of less than £50 (Rs. 500) except the

Chapter VI.

Trade.

ferry at Mánjri in Chikodi across the Krishna on the old Belgaum-Poona road, about fifty-five miles north-east of Belgaum. The private ferry boats vary in size from thirteen feet long by six broad and two deep, to twenty-eight feet long by eight broad and three deep. They carry ⅓ to 1⅔ tons (20 to 100 *mans*) of goods and fifty to 150 passengers; five of the eleven private ferries are charitable ferries and charge no tolls. The fees levied on the rest are ¾*d.* (½ *a.*) for a passenger, and 1*s.* (8 *as.*) for a cart. They do not carry animals. In 1881-82 the total public ferry revenue amounted to £473 4*s.* (Rs. 4732).

Railway.

The system of railways which is being introduced into the Southern Marátha and Kánarese districts of Bombay includes the East Deccan or Hutgi-Gadag, the South Deccan or Bellári-Marmagaon by Dhárwár and Hubli, and the West Deccan or Poona-Londa by Miraj and Belgaum. The West Deccan railway strictly ends at Belgaum; the thirty-three miles from Belgaum to Londa are called the Belgaum branch. Of these the lines which will directly affect Belgaum are the Bellári-Marmagaon and the Poona-Londa railways.

The line of the Bellári-Marmagaon railway passes east and west through about twenty-one miles of Khánápur in the extreme south of the district. It begins at 165⅓ miles west of Bellári and about ninety east of Marmagaon at the station of Alnávar, a small village on the road from Belgaum by Khánápur and Bidi to Haliyál in North Kánara. From Alnávar it passes almost west along a low narrow saddle of the Sid Pagoda range eight and three-quarters miles to Nágargali. At Nágargali, 174¼ miles from Bellári and about eighty from Marmagaon, the line crosses the road to Hulsi and Nandgad both places of some little importance, and ascends north-west till it reaches the top of the Sid Pagoda range near Suligali 2325 feet above the sea and only seventy feet below Dhárwár. The line then crosses the Punda river and passes along its left bank till it crosses the river Turva near Londa station about twelve miles west of Nágargali. Close beyond Londa, at 186¼ miles from Bellári and about sixty-eight from Marmagaon, the line passes out of Belgaum limits. The estimated cost of the twenty-one miles within Belgaum limits amounts to £162,393 (Rs.16,23,930) or £7733 (Rs.77,330) a mile.

The Poona-Londa, the beginning of which was sanctioned in December 1883, passes north and south about a hundred miles through Athni, Chikodi, Gokák, Belgaum, and Khánápur, almost the whole length of Belgaum. This line will start from Poona, pass south-east through 46¾ miles of the Poona district and 117 miles of the Sátára district, and enter Belgaum at Shedbal in west Athni 169¼ miles from Poona. From Shedbal it will pass south about seventy-two miles to Belgaum and from Belgaum about thirty-three miles further south to Londa in the extreme south of Khánápur where it will meet the Bellári-Marmagaon line. The cost of the line between Poona and Belgaum is estimated at £8274 (Rs. 82,740) a mile or a total expenditure within Belgaum limits of £827,400 (Rs. 82,74,000). The works will be begun in 1884-85; they are expected to be completed in 1889. After Miraj 159 miles south-east of Poona the line passes eighteen miles east to secure a good crossing over the

Chapter VI.
Trade.
Railways.

Krishna. It enters Belgaum limits near Shedbal station about six miles north-west of the Krishna. From the Krishna it passes south-west sixty-six miles to Belgaum by Kudchi three miles, Nágral eleven miles, Chikodi Road near Kabur eight miles, Gokák Road near Sirdan ten miles, Páchhápur twelve miles, Khángaon twelve miles, and Belgaum ten miles. Except about four miles north-east of Belgaum, where the line turns south-east to avoid some hills and rough ground, the whole sixty-two and a half miles are practically straight. The limiting gradient is one in 100 and seventeen and a half miles of the section are level. There is no curve with a smaller radius than 600 feet. The only large village passed between the Krishna and Belgaum is Páchhápur, about twenty miles north-east of Belgaum with about 1500 people. The chief bridge is across the Krishna about 175 miles from Poona and three miles north-west of Gundigvar. The Krishna bridge has eleven spans of 150 feet girders, that is a total length of about 550 yards. Like the other big bridges on the Southern Marátha railways the Krishna bridge has breadth enough to allow a cartway to run alongside of the line. The piers are of masonry, those in the north founded on rock, those in the south founded on hard *muram*. The bridge is estimated to cost £73,500 (Rs. 7,35,000); of this the iron work in the girder is estimated to cost £23,600 (Rs. 2,36,000) and the erecting of girders £8500 (Rs. 85,000). The other large bridges are, Bekeri Bridge at 185 miles from Poona, with five spans of forty feet arches and an estimated cost of £3331 (Rs. 33,310); the Jágnur at 202 miles with eight spans of forty feet arches and a cost of £4841 (Rs. 48,410); the Ghatprabha at 208 miles with sixteen spans of fifty feet arches and a cost of £13,063 (Rs. 1,30,630); the Márkándiya at 221 miles with seven spans of fifty feet arches and a cost of £7076 (Rs. 70,760); the Bellári No. 1 at 225 miles with five spans of fifty feet arches at a cost of £5572 (Rs. 55,720); the Bellári No. 2 at 231 miles with four spans of forty feet arches at a cost of £2216 (Rs. 22,160). All these bridges have rock foundations for the piers, the piers of the Márkándiya and Bellári bridges resting on sandstone and the others on trap. For the section seven third class stations and one second class station are proposed, that is an average of one station to every nine miles of line. The details are, Shedbal at 169 miles from Poona, Kudchi 179 miles, Nágral 190 miles, Chikodi Road 198 miles, Gokák Road 208 miles, Páchhápur 220 miles, Khángaon 232 miles, and Belgaum 242 miles. The exact position of Belgaum station has not been fixed; it will depend chiefly on military considerations. As this section will form an integral part of the Southern Marátha Railway, the permanent-way, rolling stock, stations, and fencing will be similar to those in use on the rest of the company's line. From Belgaum the line runs south thirty-three miles and joins the South Deccan section near Londa station 186¼ miles west of Bellári. From Belgaum the line runs through cultivated ground about seven miles straight south to Desur. From Desur, where a high ridge is crossed, the line passes through forest falling 286 feet down a rather difficult hill slope seven and a quarter miles to Khánápur on the Malprabha. In this descent the line curves to the east and has a limiting gradient of one in 100. The Malprabha will be crossed near Khánápur by a

Railways.

bridge of eight fifty-foot arches whose piers will probably be founded on granite. From the Malprabha the line runs through thick forest eight miles straight south to Gunji. From Gunji, still through thick forest, the line passes over a *kotal* or saddle near Kirvale and then gradually descends till it joins the South Deccan railway half a mile east of Londa station. Three third class stations are proposed, at Desur 249 miles from Poona and about seven miles south of Belgaum, at Khánápur 258 miles from Poona and about sixteen miles from Belgaum, and at Gunji 266 miles from Poona and about twenty-four miles from Belgaum. Over the whole line there is abundance of granite and no scarcity of water. The only places at which much traffic is likely to be received are Belgaum and Khánápur. To help traffic the Kaládgi-Belgaum and the Bidi-Khánápur roads want improving. The cost of the thirty-three miles from Belgaum to Londa is estimated at £230,000 (Rs. 23,00,000) or £6970 (Rs. 69,700) a mile.

Post Offices.

Belgaum forms part of the Southern Marátha or Bombay Karnátak postal division. Besides the chief receiving and disbursing office at Belgaum it contains two town sub-offices, twenty-seven sub-offices, and twelve village post offices. Of the twenty-seven sub-offices and twelve village offices, seventeen sub and nine village offices are within British limits, and ten sub and three village offices lie in the Bombay Karnátak states. All are supervised by the superintendent of post offices, Bombay Karnátak division, and are paid by the Belgaum disbursing office. The chief disbursing office at Belgaum is in charge of a postmaster who draws a yearly salary of £180 (Rs. 1800) rising to £240 (Rs. 2400) in five years. The two town sub-offices, one in the city of Belgaum the other between Belgaum and Sháhápur, and of the twenty-seven sub-offices the seventeen within British limits, at Athni, Báil-Hongal, Chándgad, Chikodi, Gokák, Gokák Canal, Hukeri, Khánápur, Kittur, Mugutkhán Hubli, Murgod, Nandgad, Nipáni, Sampgaon, Sankeshvar, Saundatti, and Yamkanmardi, and the ten in state limits, at Gad-Hinglaj, Gargoti, Jamkhandi, Katkol, Mahálingpur, Mudhol, Rabkavi, Rámdurg, Ráybág, and Terdal, are in charge of sub-postmasters drawing £9 12*s*. to £36 (Rs. 96-360) a year. Of the twelve village post offices the nine within British limits are at Bágevádi, Garl-Husur, Hera, Manoli, Nesargi, Páchhápur, Vantundri, Yádvád, and Yakkundi, and the three in state limits are at Ajra, Angol, and Torgal. Of these twelve, five are in charge of village postmasters, drawing £9 12*s*. (Rs. 96) a year; five are in charge of village schoolmasters who in addition to their pay as schoolmasters receive yearly allowances varying from £2 8*s*. to £4 16*s*. (Rs. 24-48); and two are in charge of local residents who are yearly paid £2 8*s*. (Rs. 24) in one village and £4 16*s*. (Rs. 48) in the other. At the towns and villages which have either sub or village post offices, letters are delivered by twenty-seven postmen who are yearly paid £7 4*s*. to £12 (Rs. 72-120), and at the villages without post offices by fifty-four village postmen who are yearly paid £9 12*s*. to £12 (Rs. 96-120). Of the fifty-four village postmen nineteen are paid from Imperial and thirty-five from provincial funds. Besides by these postmen, letters are delivered in some places by postal runners who receive yearly from £1 4*s*. to

Chapter VI.
Trade.
Post Offices.

£4 16s. (Rs. 12 - 48) for this additional work. Besides delivering letters the village postmen clear letter-boxes stationed in villages, receive articles tendered for registration, and for the use of the village people carry with them postage labels, blank declaration forms of insured articles, and money-order applications. Except at all the twelve village offices and three sub-offices at Chándgad, Gargoti, and Mugutkhán-Hubli, where money orders only are issued, money orders are issued and savings banked at all the forty-two post offices including the disbursing post office at Belgaum. Mails from and to Bombay are carried by the Peninsula railway from Bombay to Poona. The mails from Poona to Belgaum are carried in pony carts or *tonga dáks* which run between Poona and Hubli through Sátára, Kolhápur, and Belgaum, to Dhárwár. Except the disbursing post office at Belgaum and the two town sub-offices at Belgaum and Belgaum-Sháhápur, which are directly subordinate to the disbursing postmaster of Belgaum, the Belgaum post offices are supervised by the superintendent of post offices, Southern Marátha or Bombay Karnátak division, who has a yearly salary of £240 (Rs. 2400) and whose head-quarters are at Belgaum. The superintendent is assisted in Belgaum by an inspector who draws £96 (Rs. 960) a year and whose head-quarters are at Chikodi.

Telegraph.

There is one Government telegraph office in the city of Belgaum.

II.—TRADE.

Traders.

The leading traders are Bráhmans, Lingáyats, Jains, Gujarát and Márwár Vánis, Maráthás, Komtis, Musalmáns, and Pársis. Their capitals vary from £500 to £20,000 (Rs. 5000 - 2,00,000). Except some agents of Bombay, Konkan, or inland merchants, most Belgaum merchants trade on their own and some on borrowed capital. The chief trade is with Bombay by Vengurla, Chiplun, and Goa. The agency for distributing imports and gathering exports may be roughly brought under five heads, local trade centres, fairs, markets, village shopkeepers, and travelling carriers.

Trade Centres.
Belgaum.

The chief trade centres are, Belgaum, Báil-Hongal in Sampgaon, Nandgad in Khánápur, Nipáni and Sankeshvar in Chikodi, Gokák, and Athni. BELGAUM has about 250 traders, chiefly Bráhmans, Lingáyats, Nárvekars, Maráthás, Gujarát and Márwár Vánis, Pársis, and Musalmáns, with capitals varying from £500 to £20,000 (Rs. 5000-2,00,000). Some have capital of their own and some trade on borrowed funds. Almost all are independent traders. The chief imports are timber, ironware glass and other European articles, metal vessels, salt, and cocoanuts. Timber is bought at the Government stores in Kánara and sold at Belgaum to private persons and contractors. Ironware, glassware, and other European articles are brought from Bombay by Vengurla in the fair season and by Poona during the rains; they are sold to petty dealers and to consumers. Brass and copper vessels are brought from Poona and Sángli for local use; salt and cocoanuts are brought from Goa and Vengurla both for local use and to be sent inland. The chief exports are of grain, rice, wheat, gram, *jvári*, and pulse; and of cloth, *dhotars* or waistcloths and *sádis* or women's robes. Grain is bought by grain merchants at

Belgaum from petty corn dealers and growers and sent to Goa and Vengurla. The waistcloths or *dhotars* and the robes or *sádis* are bought by cloth merchants from local weavers and are either sold to Konkan merchants or sent to Dhárwár and Kaládgi.

Báil-Hongal.

BÁIL-HONGAL in Sampgaon, about twenty-seven miles east of Belgaum, has about thirty traders, chiefly Lingáyats, Jains, and Bráhmans, with capitals varying from £500 to £10,000 (Rs. 5000 - 1,00,000). All are independent traders. The chief imports are silk and cotton yarn, *sádis* or women's robes, *chol-kháns* or bodicecloths, waistcloths and headscarves, and betelnuts molasses and indigo. Silk and cotton yarn are bought in Bombay through agents or *dalâls* and brought in steamers and native craft to Vengurla and from Vengurla to Báil-Hongal in carts. These articles are sold to outside traders as well as to local weavers. *Sádis* or women's robes are brought for local use from Gadag in Dhárwár and *chol-kháns* or bodicecloths from Guledgudd in Bijápur and from Hubli in Dhárwár. Betelnuts and molasses are brought from Yellápur in Kánara both for local use and for transport to Sholápur and Kaládgi. Indigo, waistcloths, and headscarves are brought from Madras for local use. Of exports cotton is the chief. Cotton is bought on market days from husbandmen and petty dealers and also from the surrounding villages by local traders and by the agents of Belgaum and Vengurla merchants. It is then sent to Vengurla.

Nandgad.

NANDGAD in Khánápur, about twenty-two miles south of Belgaum, has about thirty traders, chiefly Shenvi Bráhmans, Lingáyats, and Jains, with capitals varying from £500 to £3000 (Rs. 5000 - 30,000). Of the thirty traders three trade on their own capital and twenty-seven partly on their own and partly on borrowed capital. Most of them are independent traders and a few are agents of coast and inland dealers. The chief imports are cocoanuts, betelnuts, cocoanut oil, salt, and dates. These articles are brought either in carts or on pack-bullocks from Native Christian traders of Goa, and are sold to local traders. None of these imported articles are passed inland or sent to Dhárwár by Nandgad traders. But from the agents of Goa traders at Nandgad most of these articles are bought in exchange for wheat and other grain by the agents of Hubli, Navalgund, and Gadag traders in Dhárwár. At Nandgad there is no direct export trade. Formerly almost all the coast traffic was on pack-bullocks; since the opening of roads across the Sahyádris much of the pack-bullock traffic has given place to carts.

Nipáni.

Of NIPÁNI and SANKESHVAR, the two Chikodi trade centres, Nipáni, about forty-two miles north of Belgaum, has 100, and Sankeshvar, about thirty-two miles north of Belgaum, has fifty traders, chiefly Lingáyats, Jains, Shimpis, Márwár and Gujarát Vánis, and Bráhmans, with capitals varying from £500 to £2500 (Rs. 5000 - 25,000). Except a few agents or *dalâls* the merchants are independent, some trading on their own and some on borrowed capital. The chief imports are betelnuts, cardamums, and pepper from Havig traders at Sirsi in Kánara; salt, cocoanuts, cocoa-kernel, dates, betelnuts, and copper sheets from Bhátiás, Gujarát and Márwár Vánis, and Musalmáns of Rájápur and Vengurla; and cloth, brass

Chapter VI.
Trade.
Trade Centres.

vessels, catechu or *kát*, nutmegs, almonds, and cloves from Bombay and Poona traders. All these articles are sold to local consumers and petty dealers. The chief exports are cotton, molasses, tobacco, chillies, hemp, and country cloth to Vengurla and Rájápur.

Gokák.

Gokák, about thirty miles north-east of Belgaum, has thirty traders, chiefly Lingáyats, Komtis, Bráhmans, Patvegars, Jains, and Musalmáns, with capitals varying from £1000 to £20,000 (Rs. 10,000-2,00,000). Nearly all the traders are independent, some carrying on business on their own and others on borrowed capital. The chief imports for local use are, silk, cotton yarn, and piece-goods from Bombay, *kháns* or bodicecloths from Guledgudd in Bijápur, rice from Haliyál in Kánara, and *gánja* or hemp from Rabkadi in Sángli. Of exports the chief are *sádis* or women's robes which are woven in large quantities at Gokák. Most of the robes are bought at Gokák by Konkan and Rájápur traders who carry them to the coast on pack-bullocks and ponies.

Athni.

Athni, about eighty miles north-east of Belgaum, has thirty traders, chiefly Bhátiás, Jains, Bráhmans, Lingáyats, and Márwár Vánis, with capitals varying from £2500 to £10,000 (Rs. 25,000-1,00,000). Of the thirty traders nine are independent and the rest are agents of Bombay, Chiplun, Miraj, and Jamkhandi merchants. The chief imports are sugar, dates, and gunny-bags from Bombay, and salt from Chiplun. The chief exports are cotton, wheat, and clarified butter. During the fair season the exports and imports from and to Athni find their way to Bombay in steamers and native craft by Chiplun and during the rains by rail from the Bársi Road station about ninety miles north of Athni.

Fairs.

Of nine fairs held in the district one is in Belgaum at Chándgad; one in Sampgaon at Báil-Hongal; two in Chikodi at Sankeshvar and Yedur; three in Athni at Mangsuli, Kokátnur, and Kanmadi; and two in Parasgad at Ugargal. These fairs last one to six days, have an attendance of 2500 to 60,000, and an estimated sale of goods worth £150 to £3500. The fairs are chiefly distributing centres. The articles sold are cloth, metal and earthen vessels, camphor, glass bracelets, wheat, rice, cocoanuts, plantains, and other fruit, and cows bullocks horses ponies and other cattle. Some of the sellers are husbandmen, but most are retail dealers, chiefly Jains, Lingáyats, Bráhmans, Gujarát and Márwár Vanis, and Musalmáns. The buyers are generally local consumers. There is little barter:

Belgaum Fairs, 1882.

Name.	Month.	Days.	Patron.	People.	Sales.
					£
Chándgad ...	Feb. - Mar.	1	Ravalnáth ...	2500	150
Báil-Hongal ...	Nov. - Dec.	1	Basvana ...	4000	150
Sankeshvar ...	Feb. - Mar.	1	Shankarling...	25,000	1000
Yedur ...	Mar. - Apr.	1	Virabhadra ...	10,000	500
Mangsuli ...	Apr. - May.	3	Mártanddev...	3000	3500
Kokátnur ...	Dec. - Jan.	5	Yellama ...	1000	1400
Kanmadi ...	Apr. - May.	6	Darideva ...	3000	1600
Ugargal ...	Dec. - Jan.	1	Yellama ...	60,000	1700
Ditto ...	Apr. - May.	1	Ditto ...	10,000	...

Chapter VI. Trade. Markets.

Besides at the seven trade centres of Belgaum, Báil-Hongal, Nandgad, Nipáni, Sankeshvar, Gokák, and Athni, weekly markets are held at Bágeshvari and Pátna in Belgaum, at Kittur in Sampgaon, at Khánápur in Khánápur, at Saundatti and Murgod in Parasgad, and at not less than fifty other large villages. The estimated attendance at weekly markets in the chief local trade centres varies from 2500 to 10,000, 8000 being the estimate for Belgaum, 6000 for Báil-Hongal, 5000 for Nandgad, 10,000 for Nipáni, 7000 for Sankeshvar, 3000 for Gokák, and 2500 for Athni. The weekly markets are both distributing and gathering centres. The chief articles for distribution are butter, salt, grain, cattle, cloth, molasses, and sugar, iron brass copper and earthen vessels, oil, spices, and tobacco. The sellers, who are generally retail dealers and sometimes producers, are Lingáyats, Jains, Gujárat and Márwár Vanis, Maráthás, and Musalmáns. The buyers are generally consumers who live at or near the market towns. There is little barter. The articles which are gathered at these markets are local produce chiefly cotton, tobacco, oil, salt, rice, horns, hides, fat, butter, and molasses. The sellers are grocers and petty dealers, and the buyers are local traders and agents of Bombay, Vengurla, and Rájápur merchants.

Shopkeepers.

Almost every village, except the smallest, has its shop. The shopkeepers are chiefly Lingáyats, Jains, Gujárat and Márwár Vánis, Nárvekars, Native Christians, and Musalmáns. They sell to villagers and travellers rice, pulse, salt, tobacco, chillies, oil, molasses, clarified butter, spices, and other necessaries. They are chiefly distributors. Barter prevails to some extent. The shopkeepers take cotton, millet, rice, and other grain and give salt, oil, molasses, and spices. They neither lend nor advance money to the villagers. They go to market towns to bring supplies and are not connected with large trading firms.

Carriers.

Carriers are either cartmen or pack-bullockmen. The cartmen are Maráthás, Lingáyats, Native Christians, Jains, and Musalmáns. They carry various kinds of grain, cocoanuts, betelnuts, salt, cloth, tobacco, molasses, cotton, hemp, chillies, sugar, blankets, myrobalans, dates, cocoa-kernel, iron, copper, brass, and other articles. They visit Goa, Vengurla, Rájápur, Poona, Sirsi, Haliyál, Yellápur, Hubli, Gadag, and Tálikoti. A few are traders and the rest carry goods for hire. The trading cartmen buy grain and other local products from merchants and producers, and carry them to places where they can sell them at a profit. Of late the number of cartmen has increased in consequence of the opening of new roads. Pack-bullockmen are chiefly Lamánis, Musalmáns, Native Christians, Lingáyats, and Nárvekars. They generally carry grain, salt, and cocoanuts. They visit Haliyál, Hubli, Tálikoti, Goa, Vengurla, and Rájápur. All are traders. They buy grain from up-country dealers and sell it to coast merchants and buy salt and cocoanuts from coast merchants and sell them to inland dealers. The number of pack-bullockmen has fallen as the bulk of the carrying trade is now done by carts.

Of Imports the chief articles are: Of timber, teak, jack,

Chapter VI.
Trade.
Imports.

and *matti* or Terminalia tomentosa are brought from the Government stores in Kánara and from Bombay, Sávantvádi, and Chiplun, and sold to local contractors and craftsmen. This timber is used in building houses and in making carts, boxes, tables, and chairs. Of house furniture, ironware, chiefly locks, hinges, bars, and nails; copper and brass vessels, dishes, plates, and water pots; and glasses, ornamental chairs and tables, and clocks and watches are brought from Bombay, Poona, Hubli, and Sángli by Márwár Váni, Jain, Pársi, and Musalmán traders. These articles are either sold to the people or to retail dealers. Copper and brass vessels are either sold by retail dealers in their shops, or the retail dealers sometimes go from village to village and sell their vessels for cash or for valuable second-hand clothes. Of food grains, rice is brought from Haliyál in Kánara and from Kolhápur, and millet wheat and gram from Dhárwár and Kaládgi, and from the Jamkhandi, Jath, Mudhol, Rámdurg, and Sángli states. These food grains are generally brought by grain-dealers and sometimes by grocers. Part is sold locally and the rest is sent to the Konkan. Sugar, dates, cocoanuts, cocoa-kernel, sweet oil, kerosine oil, and salt are brought from Goa, Vengurla, Chiplun, Rájápur, and Bombay, and molasses from Yellápur in Kánara. Some of these articles are sent to Dhárwár and Kaládgi. Fruits of different kinds are brought from Goa and Kolhápur by petty dealers and sold locally. European spirits and wines and drugs are brought from Bombay by Pársi, Musalmán, and Native Christian merchants, and sold in the town and cantonment of Belgaum. Of fine tools and appliances anvils, hammers, saws, files, and scissors are brought from Bombay by Márwár Vánis and Musalmáns and sold locally to craftsmen and other consumers. Of dyeing and colouring materials indigo is brought from Madras. Of cloth, European cotton goods, shawls, woollen and silk cloths, machine-spun yarn, raw and coloured silk, and silk waistcloths or *pitámbars* are brought from Bombay and Poona, *rumáls* or headscarves and *dhotars* or waistcloths from Madras, *sádis* or women's robes from Gadag, and *chol-kháns* or bodicecloths from Kaládgi. The importers are cloth traders, most of them Gujarát and Márwár Vánis and Lingáyats. Except silk and yarn, which are chiefly bought by weavers to make *sádis* and *dhotars*, the imported cloth is partly sold to local consumers and petty dealers and partly sent to Goa. Cards chessmen and other toys are brought from Sávantvádi; jewels and gold ornaments are brought by Poona, Kolhápur, and Miraj merchants and sold to the rich; pearls and coral are brought from Bombay by Márwár Váni traders called *motikars* or pearlmen. Pearl merchants generally stay in the large towns and make one or two trips in the district.

Exports.

[1] Cotton is the most important of Belgaum exports. Belgaum has no European cotton agents and no agents of Bombay European houses. A few persons in the larger towns represent native firms, but more business is done between Bombay and the up-country

---

[1] Most of the details about cotton trade and cotton industries are taken from Walton's History of Cotton in Belgaum and Kaládgi (1880).

dealer at the South Konkan ports than in the cotton-growing districts. The system of trade in Belgaum is by no means uniform. Most landholders sell their own cotton and are consequently to this extent cotton-dealers as well as cotton-planters. After the cotton has been picked and ginned the season is generally too far spent to allow any but the very small outturn of American cotton to reach the coast before the latter half of May when traffic ceases. The bulk of the Belgaum cotton crop, at the expense of a considerable loss in value, is generally stored in damp godowns and dirty sheds and kept there till about the end of October. It is then taken out and weighed into bundles or *dokrás* of about 224 pounds which are covered with sacking and sewn with strong twine into packages about three feet long by two and a half broad. The cotton is neither pressed nor half-pressed; it is not even tightened by ropes. Most of these Belgaum bundles or *dokrás* find their way to Vengurla in Ratnágiri. Till 1871 when the new road to Vengurla across the Ámboli pass was opened, much cotton was carried on bullock-back down the Rám pass about thirty miles west of Belgaum. This route is no longer used, and the practise of carrying cotton on pack-bullocks is confined to a few packages from the north and north-east which make their way over the Sahyádris to the small Ratnágiri ports. The present road over the Ámboli pass has an easy gradient and is almost all that can be desired for bullock-cart traffic. This opening of the Ámboli pass road has affected the Kárwár and Kumta trade. Much traffic that formerly went from South Belgaum to Kárwár and Kumta now goes to Vengurla. Large quantities of cotton from the northern sub-divisions of Belgaum go to Chiplun in Ratnágiri about twenty-five miles from the mouth of the Váshishti river. In the customs returns this cotton appears as shipped at Anjanvel, on the south shore of the entrance to the Váshisti. A small quantity occasionally makes its way to the small ports between Vengurla and Anjanvel, but for practical purposes Vengurla and Anjanvel may be considered the ports for Belgaum cotton. The great drawback to Vengurla is that it is only a roadstead which is closed to shipping from June to October, and in heavy westerly winds is at all times dangerous. The cost of carriage from the ginning districts to the coast to a great extent depends on the number of carts available and on the time of year. The cartmen are generally husbandmen, and as soon as the sowing season draws near they rush to their villages often at great distances, to prepare and sow their land. From South Belgaum to Vengurla, a cart carrying some one thousand pounds of cotton is generally paid about £1 8*s*. (Rs. 14); to this at Belgaum has to be added a transit-agent's fee of 6*d*. (4 *as*.) With slight variations £1 8*s*. (Rs. 14) may be taken to represent the average cost of carting one thousand pounds of cotton from the Belgaum cotton fields to the coast, a distance from the farthest point of about 120 miles. This is a heavy charge. Taking 30*s*. a ton of 2240 pounds as the average of the cotton freight by steamers from Bombay to Liverpool during the year 1882, the charge from the Belgaum cotton fields to the coast is nearly twice as heavy as the charge from Bombay to Liverpool. Compared with Hinganghát, Dholera, and

Chapter VI.

Trade.

Exports.

Cotton.

Broach cotton the local Kánarese cotton has the disadvantage of being much later of getting to market. The necessity for choosing a dry time of the year for picking prevents the cotton ripening before February and March. With the help of railways and quicker ginning it may soon be possible to send forward the cotton so that the new crop may reach Bombay before the end of May. Besides the interest on the money locked in the cotton for six or seven months, the early delivery of the crop in Bombay will save the damage from storage in dirty sheds and leaky godowns, a damage which is roughly estimated at about a farthing a pound. The returns for the Vengurla customs division for the five years ending 1882 show an average export of cotton worth £249,976 (Rs. 24,99,760). The bulk of this comes from Belgaum. From Vengurla some of the cotton goes by steamer to Bombay, a passage, including stoppages, of twenty-six to thirty-two hours; the bulk is shipped in the native craft known as *phatemáris* which take three to twelve days to reach Bombay. There are agents of Bombay native firms at Vengurla, but no agents of Bombay European firms. The customs charges are light; a one *anna* stamp and two manifests costing ¼ *anna* each that is a total charge of 2¼*d.* (1½ *anna*). The cotton bundles or *dokrás* are allowed to remain on the landing for forty hours before any port charges are levied. Some of the cotton shipped from Vengurla comes from Dhárwár, but the bulk of it is from Parasgad and Sampgaon in Belgaum, and from Hungund Bágalkot and Bádámi in south Bijápur. All of it comes down the Ámboli pass. The shipments from the other parts of the district come by the routes that merge into the main coast-road not far from Ámboli. The bulk of the Vengurla shipments is of local Kánarese cotton; very little American goes by that route. The cost of freight by steamer and *phatemári* to Bombay ranges from 6*s.* to 14*s.* (Rs. 3-7) a local *khandi* of 756 pounds that is $\frac{18}{30}$ to $\frac{40}{30}$ times the average 1882 steamer freight from Bombay to Liverpool. The bulk of the trade is in the hands of Lingáyats, Gujarát Vánis, and Bhátiás. There are no transactions in Vengurla on European account. The bulk of the staple is brought from up-country for sale at the coast; comparatively little is bought in the cotton-growing districts. The growers or the local dealers consign it to agents at Vengurla who are the middlemen between the local dealer and the Bombay merchant. The Vengurla middleman's charges amount to 2*s.* 7*d.* (Re. 1$\frac{5}{16}$) on every 756 pounds (1 *khandi*) of cotton.[1]

North Belgaum cotton goes to Chiplun and much that is grown in other parts besides Belgaum and Bijápur is carried there. The best cotton that reaches Chiplun comes from Athni and its neigbourhood; in Bombay this Athni cotton is known as *kacha kumta* or poor Kumta. The staple from the rest of north and north-east Belgaum is inferior to the Athni cotton. No American is grown so far north. All the cotton carried by this route goes down

---

[1] The details are: Brokerage 2*s.*, weighing charges for scale ⅜*d.*, weighing charge for labour ¼*d.*, grant to a priest ⅜*d.*, grant to temples 3*d.*, grant to a charity fund 3*d.*, total 2*s.* 7*d.* The Vengurla municipality makes no charge.

the Kumbhárli pass, and nearly the whole of it reaches Bombay in *phatemáris*, as it is difficult and costly to get it into steamers which cannot pass so far up the Váshishti as Chiplun. During the five years ending 1882, the declared yearly value of the cotton shipped at Anjanvel, the Customs House at the Váshishti mouth which clears Chiplun shipments, averaged £147,466 (Rs. 14,74,660). The cost of carriage from Chiplun to Bombay varies from 1*s.* to 2*s.* (Re. ½-1) the *dokra* of about two hundredweights, and the same weight costs another 1½*d.* (1 *anna*) in porterage from the agent's godown to the vessel. The only other charges are 1*s.* (8 *as.*) a cart, for brokerage equal to about 2*s.* (Re. 1) a ton, and a fee of about three pounds of cotton, generally paid in kind, which the Chiplun dealers charge the up-country people for weighing the staple. At Chiplun nothing is levied by the municipality or for temples or charity. No permanent agents either of native or of European Bombay houses are settled at Chiplun; the trade is entirely in the hands of residents of Chiplun, who are the middlemen between the up-country dealers and the Bombay merchants. The voyage from Chiplun to Bombay takes three to twelve days. The system of trade at the small ports or landings between Vengurla and Chiplun is the same as the Chiplun system.[1] The owners of the vessels begin to beach them early in May when the south-west swell sets in. By or soon after the middle of May the Ratnágiri ports are closed till October.

During the last forty years Government have made repeated efforts to improve the Belgaum cotton trade. In 1841 the price of cotton in Bombay fell as low as 3*d.* (2 *as.*) a pound. In 1842 the expense of sending a *khandi* of 756 pouns of cotton from Belgaum to Bombay was estimated at £1 15*s.* (Rs. 17½).[2] In 1844, the Bombay cotton trade was so unsatisfactory that, at the request of the leading firms, a Commission was appointed of ten Government officers and merchants. This Commission made many valuable and business-like proposals. The proposal of most importance to Belgaum was the improvement of the roads between the Belgaum cotton fields and the coast. Regarding the growth of cotton the Commission made no recommendations beyond suggesting the introduction of better sorts of cotton. They strongly urged the need of improved cleaning and packing. The trade was also unfavourably affected by a considerable customs duty of about ⅛*d.* the pound (Rs. 5¼ the *khandi*). This duty had been fixed when the price of cotton was much higher, it was a heavy charge, and the Commission thought that it should be reduced. The Commission went into the question of the pressure of the land-tax and came to the conclusion that in some places the pressure was severe. Government adopted most of

---

[1] Beginning from Vengurla, the names of these small ports, of which there are nine, are Nivti, Áchra, Devgad, Vijayadurg, Jaytápur, Purangad, Ratnágiri, Jaygad, and Borya. The Vengurla shipments include shipments from Nivti and the Anjanvel shipments include shipments from Borya. The average yearly value of the cotton shipped from the remaining seven ports is £3859.

[2] The details were: Bullock hire Rs. 10, bagging and packing Rs. 3½, freight to Bombay Rs. 2¼, Bombay charges Rs. 1¼, total Rs. 17½.

Chapter VI.
Trade.
Exports.
Cotton.

the Commission's leading suggestions. Orders were issued that the road to Kumta should at once be made fit for carts; the customs export duty was abolished; and a temporary reduction in land-tax was made in places where the pressure had been shown to be specially heavy. In 1845, in answer to inquiries made with the object of starting an English cotton company in the Bombay Karnátak, Mr. Mercer, the American planter (1841-1846), expressed the opinion that a company with £50,000 to £60,000 (Rs. 5-6 *lákhs*) might, on the plan he proposed, monopolize the cotton trade and return immense profits. Since Mr. Mercer made his calculation the cotton trade has so increased that in the opinion of Mr. Walton, who was cotton inspector in Belgaum from 1865 to 1880, a dozen companies each with the capital named by Mr. Mercer would fail to carry on all the present business. In September 1846 the Bombay cotton trade was still so bad that Government appointed a second Commission to inquire into the causes of the decline of the trade and to suggest remedies.[1] In March 1847, the Commission reported that they had no suggestions to offer regarding improvements in tillage. They were told by the American planters, who had experience in Belgaum and other districts, that the native methods were well adapted to the country. As regards the trade in Belgaum cotton the Commission recommended the abolition of all duties on raw cotton, an improvement in the port of Vengurla and in roads from Vengurla to the interior, and the opening of the Deccan by railways. They thought that the stagnation and loss in trade were due to the decline in the price of cotton.

In 1847, Mr. Jamsetji, a Pársi merchant, came to Belgaum to buy and export cotton. He wrote to the local authorities, told them he was anxious to buy and ship as much American cotton as he could get, and asked their support and help. He was promised every help compatible with the interests of the district, and was warned to be careful in his purchases, as the Collector was aware that acclimatized American cotton was being mixed and adulterated by the local dealers. In 1847, in a special report on the Belgaum cotton trade, Mr. J. D. Inverarity, the Collector, expressed the opinion that nothing would benefit the trade so much as the making of roads and the bridging of rivers and streams. The cost of carrying cotton from the fields to the coast was about 2*s.* 6*d.* (Rs. 1¼) the hundred pounds. At this time in the Belgaum markets cotton fetched about 1½*d.* to 2*d.* a pound (Rs. 50-60 a *khandi* of 756 lbs.) The competition of the local weavers was keen, and they paid as high as 2¼*d.* the pound (Rs. 70 the *khandi*) for the best cleaned cotton. In 1848, Mr. Townshend, the Revenue Commissioner, showed that the cost of carrying cotton from Belgaum to Bombay added seventeen to twenty per cent to its price. In this year Captain Meadows Taylor urged that good roads should be made through the cotton plains to join into one main highway, on which the staple could be

[1] The Commission were: Messrs. H. B. E. Frere the present Sir Bartle Frere, H. H. Glass, R. Spooner, J. D. Inverarity, J. Bowman, R. W. Crawford, J. Smith, S. D. Murray, Kharsetji Jamsetji, and Kharsetji Káwasji.

Chapter VI.
Trade.
Exports.
Cotton.

carried in carts down the Phonda pass to Vijaydurg in Ratnágiri, which he stated had a port fit for ships large enough to carry the cotton direct to Europe instead of round by Bombay. A fairly large quantity of the staple was then carried through Sankeshvar in Belgaum to Rájápur in Ratnágiri, a famous place of trade during the latter part of the seventeenth century. About the same time the Collector of Belgaum calculated that the average cost of carrying 756 pounds (1 *khandi*) of cotton was £1 (Rs. 10) to Kumta and 18*s*. (Rs. 9) to Vengurla. Besides by the cost of getting it to Bombay the export of cotton to England was burdened by heavy freights between Bombay and England which in 1847 were about £7 the ton. In 1848 the Collector reported that on its way to Bombay, Belgaum cotton was exposed to every form of evil. Moving at the rate of one or two miles an hour in rude carts or on bullock-back, over bad roads, the dew and the dust did their worst. The bullocks were loaded and unloaded twice a day, generally near watering places, and their packs were rolled in the mud. During the march each bullock consoled himself by keeping his nose in his leader's pack, and steadily eating the cotton. The loss in weight, which had not been made good by dust, was too often supplied by water and mud at the journey's end. Half of the night was lost in loading and unloading and the bullocks seldom did more than eight miles a day. All along the way petty chiefs and village headmen demanded tolls and stopped the cotton if the toll was not paid. Even after it was on board ship exactions did not cease. Till 1840 when his state lapsed to the British Ángria the chief of Kolába made all vessels stop off Kolába till his officers came on board, examined the cargo, and levied heavy and vexatious exactions. Mr. Townshend, the Commissioner, confirmed what the Collector said about the perils by land. The want of roads to the sea was the ruin of the inland people.

In 1849, the Bombay Government recommended merchants to establish up-country agencies. The Chamber of Commerce replied, that in the backward state of roads up-country agencies could not succeed. They urged Government to open the cotton districts by roads and railways to the coast and especially to Bombay. If this was done all other improvements would follow without trouble or expense. Lord Falkland then Governor of Bombay (1848-1853), recognized the great value of roads. He regretted that want of funds prevented Government from doing what they wished. Mr. J. P. Willoughby, one of the members of Council, thought that the financial pressure should not be allowed to stand in the way. If trade was not looked to the financial pressure must grow greater. Trade was sick, if not dying. He never remembered such a forest of masts waiting for freight in Bombay harbour. The Board of Directors in acknowledging the papers hoped at no distant period to be able to sanction the expenditure needed to improve communications. One result of the want of roads was a great inequality in local prices. In places with an easy outlet the price of cotton was double or treble its price in a place where export was difficult or impossible. In some places the cost of exporting it made the growth of cotton impossible. About this time (1849-50) Mr. Channing the

Chapter VI.
Trade.
Exports.
Cotton.

superintendent of cotton experiments calculated that taking Bijápur and Belgaum together the average cost of carrying a *khandi* of 756 pounds of cotton to the coast was a little over £1 8*s*. (Rs. 14). The full expense of carriage from Bijápur to Bombay he estimated at an average of £1 11*s*. (Rs. 15⅝), from Belgaum to Bombay he thought £1 2*s*. (Rs. 11) covered the cost. Mr. Channing expected that the opening of the Phonda pass route to Vághotan would do much for the Belgaum and Bijápur cotton trade. In 1849 the revised assessment was introduced in Gokák and Parasgad. The survey officers estimated that in the whole of Belgaum, which at that time included a large area of the best cotton lands of South Bijápur, about one million two hundred thousand acres were suitable for cotton. On a proper system of crop rotation this would give an available yearly area of about three hundred and seventy thousand acres. It was estimated that the land rent or assessment represented about seventeen per cent of the value of the gross produce. This proportion would become less as roads were opened and cultivation improved.

In 1847 the attention of Government had been drawn to the difficulty and danger of shipping cotton from the South Konkan and Kánara ports in April and May. After several years of examination and surveying Government decided that Vijaydurg, about thirty miles south of Ratnágiri, was to be the cotton port of the future, and that the trade was to centre at Vághotan, about ten miles up the river, where was a depth of eighteen feet at low water spring tides. From Vághotan good roads were to be made over the Sahyádri passes to Kolhápur about eighty, and to Belgaum about a hundred miles. When these roads were finished it was hoped that the bulk of the Belgaum and Bijápur produce would be sent to Vághotan, and that the agents would there put it in boats and send it to ships at Vijaydurg. These hopes have not been realized. The trade is too fluctuating to send large ships regularly to Vijaydurg. The advantages of direct shipments would probably be more than counterbalanced by the increased freight and higher insurance that would be demanded by ships that had to go to Vijaydurg instead of to Bombay. Trade never took to the Vághotan and Vijaydurg route and since 1871 when the excellent A'mboli pass road was opened it has centred at Vengurla.

The Government cotton experiments during the three years ending 1848-49 did not do much to increase the cotton trade. The yearly average outturn was only a little over a hundred and seventy bales each of 392 pounds. Even of this Government had bought two-thirds and the merchants less than a third. In 1849, the Manchester Chamber of Commerce urged Parliament to inquire into the unsatisfactory condition of the Indian cotton trade. In 1850, as the House of Commons refused the inquiry, the Manchester Chamber of Commerce, with the help of the Chambers of Liverpool Blackburn and Glasgow, sent an agent to India. Most of the inquiries of their agent, Mr. A. Mackay, were made in the Bombay Presidency. Mr. Mackay, who travelled through the Bombay Karnátak in 1851, reported to the Manchester Chamber of Commerce

Chapter VI.
Trade.
Exports.
Cotton.

that the bad state of roads greatly interrupted the trade of the district; that only paltry sums were spent by Government on road improvement; that the few good roads were useless for trade as they were made for military convenience; and that improved not extended cultivation of cotton was what was wanted.[1] In reply to Mr. Mackay's statements Mr. H. W. Reeves then Revenue Commissioner S. D., and other District Officers including Messrs. W. H. Havelock and M. J. M. Shaw-Stewart pointed out that so far as external commerce was concerned the Karnátak districts were well off for roads; that there were two outlets for the produce of the country, the Vengurla road across the Rám pass for the districts north of the Malphrabha, and the Kumta road for the southern districts; that considering the difficulty of the country much had been done to improve roads; that besides the metalled roads mentioned by Mr. Mackay many fair weather roads were fit for carts; that the necessity of improving roads had engaged the attention of District officers and of Government as early as 1845, and that steps were being taken to improve roads; that the metalled roads made by Government for military purposes were of the greatest use to trade, as the military stations were excellent and convenient markets for local produce; that Mr. Mackay underrated the value of the important road from Belgaum to Vengurla by the Rám pass; that an unbroken and very rich traffic was carried on between Vengurla and Belgaum throughout the fair season; and that the improvement of the cotton trade must come from the merchants of Bombay establishing direct agencies in the cotton districts, and thus dispensing with the host of native middlemen who ate up a large portion of the profit which would otherwise fall to the husbandmen.[2]

In 1850, the Collector of Belgaum complained of the apathy of the Bombay merchants in not making arrangements for up-country buying. The merchants replied that until roads were opened no up-country agency could succeed. In 1850 Messrs. Lancaster and Co., of Bombay, sent a Mr. Davis as their agent to Belgaum. He made large advances to secure American cotton. Mr. Reeves, the Collector, expected that during that season the firm would spend fully £20,000 (Rs. 2,00,000). Mr. Davis was also empowered to buy for other firms. Under these circumstances Mr. Reeves thought that Government should cease to buy. Mr. Davis found it difficult to get seed-cotton as in return for the Government seed the cotton-growers were bound to bring all the seed cotton to the Government gins. He begged that this hindrance might be removed; he stated he was making ginning houses at every five or six miles through the cotton country; and, in return for concessions, he offered to rent all the Government ginning establishments, and to guarantee that he would purchase every pound of the American crop. The Collector supported Mr. Davis' application, and Government approved of Mr. Reeves' proposals. They directed that, except in cases where the landholder was anxious to carry out his engagement with Government, the Collector was to cease buying cotton on Government account.

---

[1] Mackay's Western India, 414. [2] Rev. Vol. 55 of 1855.

Chapter VI.
Trade.
Exports.
Cotton.

In 1852 Mr. Young, the Collector of Customs in Bombay, brought to the notice of Government that the cotton received from Belgaum on Government account was inferior to what the Bombay merchants were buying in the same district. As the spinners and others in England had come to look on the yearly Government consignments as the standard of what India could produce, he thought it his duty to bring the inferior state of the cotton to the attention of Government. He recommended that this consignment of cotton should not be sent to England. Government ordered the superintendent of experiments to Bombay to examine the cotton. The examination of the parcels showed that out of 4553 bales of American cotton 723 contained inferior and dirty staple. On this, early in 1853, Government issued orders that on receipt of the cotton which had already been ordered, no more was to be bought, that the quantity on which advances had already been made was to be carefully examined, and that none but what was good was to be sent to England. In 1854, under orders from the Court of Directors the accounts of all Government shipments were made up by the Accountant General. These shipments included nine consignments. They amounted to 5574 packages, of which 5419 were bales, 152 were half bales, and three were bundles or *dokrás*. Of the nine consignments seven showed a profit of £7950 (Rs. 79,500) and two showed a loss of £1677 (Rs. 16,770), that is on the whole transactions a net profit of £6273 (Rs. 62,730). No details are available to show what portion of the whole amount was Belgaum cotton, but it is worthy of note that there was no Belgaum cotton in the two shipments that showed a loss.

In 1855, an enterprising merchant, Mr. A. C. Brice, settled in Dhárwár and did a large cotton business. A sub-agency was established at Saundatti to buy Belgaum cotton, and he projected more agencies in the same district. Mr. Brice owned upwards of a thousand head of draught cattle and a corresponding stock of cotton carts.

Ten years later during the American war the Belgaum cotton trade greatly increased, though fraud and dirt-mixing prevented the cotton from realizing nearly so high a price as it would have fetched had it been clean. The efforts made to check fraud and to improve the outturn of cotton by spreading the use of American seed and of sawgins have been shown under the heads of Adulteration and Ginning. The immense number of small ginning places made it almost impossible to check the mixing of cotton and the adding of dirt, and the difficulty of keeping saw-gins in order and the damage caused by saw-gins in bad order prevented the efforts to improve the cotton trade from succeeding. Since 1870 partly from the decline in the value of the American cotton, but chiefly from the difficulty of getting it ginned, the growth of American cotton and the use of saw-gins have almost ceased. Since 1876 the Government supervision of the trade and of the gins has been withdrawn.

The whole exports of Belgaum cotton, together with a small quantity from South Bijápur and neighbouring Native State, reach

Bombay through the Ratnágiri ports. The famine of 1876 and 1877 lowered the value of the Ratnágiri exports from £400,750 in 1874-75 to £330,946 in 1877-78 and to £331,738 in 1878-79. For the five years ending 1882-83, the returns of the customs divisions of Anjanvel, Ratnágiri, Vijaydurg, Málvan, and Vengurla give the highest value of cotton at £494,240 in 1879-80, the lowest at £331,738 in 1878-79, and the average at £401,300. The details are:

Chapter VI.
Trade.
Exports.
Cotton.

COTTON EXPORTS, 1878-1882.

Customs Division.	Value of Exports.					
	1878-79.	1879-80.	1880-81.	1881-82.	1882-83.	Total.
	£	£	£	£	£	£
Vengurla ...	210,112	261,532	294,278	228,431	255,527	1,249,880
Anjanvel ...	118,364	228,090	176,814	102,795	111,266	737,329
Ratnágiri ...	5	314	20	14	239	592
Vijaydurg ...	8187	1592	2261	2907	1699	11,646
Málvan ...	70	2712	291	276	3708	7057
Total ...	331,738	494,240	473,664	334,423	372,439	2,006,504

According to rough estimates by Bombay merchants and cotton dealers, of the total supply of American cotton or as it is called sawginned Dhárwár received at Bombay from the Bombay Karnátak about sixty-eight per cent is from Dhárwár and the remaining thirty-two per cent from Belgaum, Bijápur, and the Bombay Karnátak states; and of the Kumta or local cotton supply, about sixty-eight per cent comes from Belgaum and Bijápur and thirty-two per cent comes from Dhárwár. Nearly the whole of the American goes from Bombay to Europe; none is used locally and very little remains in Bombay. The Kumta when pure, though not very white has a strong and fairly long staple. It is particularly well suited for spinning the lower counts of yarn up to twenties and is largely used in the Bombay mills. Very little goes to Europe. According to the Bombay Cotton Report for 1882-83 in the Bombay market sawginned Dhárwár averaged about $5\frac{1}{4}d.$ the pound in 1879-80, $5\frac{1}{16}d.$ in 1880-81, $5d.$ in 1881-82, and $4\frac{7}{8}d.$ in 1882-83; in the Liverpool market it averagod $6\frac{3}{16}d.$ the pound in 1879-80, $5\frac{1}{2}d.$ in 1880-81, $5\frac{9}{16}d.$ in 1881-82, and $5\frac{1}{4}d.$ in 1882-83. In the Bombay market Kumta or local cotton sold for $5\frac{1}{8}d.$ the pound in 1879-80, $4\frac{3}{4}d.$ in 1880-81, $4\frac{7}{8}d.$ in 1881-82, and $4\frac{7}{32}d.$ in 1882-83; in the Liverpool market it sold for $5\frac{3}{4}d.$ the pound in 1879-80, $4\frac{13}{16}d.$ in 1880-81, $4\frac{7}{8}d.$ in 1881-82, and $4\frac{5}{16}d.$ in 1882-83. Inquiry in Bombay shows that in the Bombay market a *khandi* of 784 pounds of sawginned Dhárwár is at present (December 1883) worth £2 (Rs. 20) more than a *khandi* of Kumta. In November 1879 a *khandi* of Broach was worth £1 10*s.* (Rs. 15) more than a *khandi* of sawginned Dhárwár and £3 to £3 4*s.* (Rs. 30-32) more than a *khandi* of Kumta; at present (1883) Broach is worth £2 10*s.* (Rs. 25) more than sawginned Dhárwár and £4 10*s.* to £5 (Rs. 45-50) more than Kumta. In November 1879 a *khandi* of good Dholera was worth 10*s.* (Rs. 5) more than a *khandi* of good sawginned Dhárwár and £1 10*s.* (Rs. 15) more than a *khandi* of Kumta; at present there is no difference between the value of Dholera and of sawginned Dhárwár and a *khandi* of Dholera is worth £2 (Rs. 20) more than a *khandi* of Kumta. In 1879 a pound of American Mid Orleans was

Chapter VI.
Trade.
Exports.

worth $\frac{3}{8}d.$ more than a pound of good sawginned Dhárwár and $1\frac{1}{2}d.$ more than a pound of good-fair Kumta; at present a pound of American Mid Orleans (November 1883) is worth $1\frac{5}{16}d.$ more than good sawginned Dhárwár and $1\frac{15}{16}d.$ more than good-fair Kumta.

Miscellaneous.

Besides cotton the chief Belgaum exports are brassware, grindstones, grain, butter, and cloth. Of brassware the chief articles are brass lampstands or *samais*, small water-sipping ladles and cups or *pali panchapátris*, small round god-boxes or *sampushtas*, waving lamps or *niránjans*, and other articles used in worship. These are made by the Otari casters of Gokák and sold at Gokák to dealers from Kolhápur, Dhárwár, and Hubli. Grindstones are made at Arbhavi in Gokák by masons or Pátharvats, and taken for sale in carts or on pack asses to Poona, Sátára, and Dhárwár. Rice wheat millet and gram, molasses, and tobacco are bought from the Lingáyat, Jain, Marátha, and Musalmán growers by the trading carriers and traders of the market towns, and sent to Kaládgi, Dhárwár, Goa, Vengurla, Rájápur, Sirsi, and sometimes to Bombay. Clarified butter is bought from Marátha Lingáyat and Jain husbandmen either in their own villages or in market towns on market days, and is sent in tin boxes by a few Nárvekar dealers to Bombay by Vengurla. Of cloth, *sádis* or women's robes are best woven at Belgaum, Gokák, and Báil-Hongal, and *dhotars* or waistcloths at Belgaum and Báil-Hongal in Sampgaon. Robes waistcloths and other coarse cotton cloth are generally bought from the weavers by the local traders and either locally sold to Goa, Rájápur, and other Konkan traders or sent for sale to Dhárwár and Kaládgi. Myrobalans or *hirdás* are sent in large quantities from Belgaum. They grow wild in the forests of Khánápur, Belgaum, and Chikodi, and are gathered for the forest officers during the fair season and kept at Government stores where they are sold to contractors. The contractors send the myrobalans to Vengurla where they are sold to agents of Bombay and European merchants.

There has of late been a considerable increase in the import of European cotton yarn and cloth, boots and stockings, and among articles of house furniture clocks, watches, glasses, ornamental chairs, and tables. These articles are used by the well-to-do, especially by those who have received an English education. Kerosine oil and matches are largely imported and are used by all except the poorest.

III.—INDUSTRIES.

Industries.

The chief Belgaum crafts are cotton-ginning, cotton spinning and weaving, calico-printing, dyeing, toy-making, copper and brass work, pottery, and oil-pressing.

Cotton-ginning.

One of the chief industries of the district is the ginning of cotton, that is the separating of the cotton wool from the cotton seed. Though the practice is greatly neglected, the cotton should be dried before it is ginned. If it is not dried the fibre is stained or otherwise harmed. To dry it the cotton is spread in the sun and is frequently turned so that every part of it, especially the seed, may be thoroughly dried. Seed-cotton or *kapás* is not in good order for ginning unless the seed cracks, and does not crush between the teeth of the gin. Cotton cannot be rightly ginned in wet or even in damp weather. A short smart shower unless followed by a steady dry wind will stop cotton-ginning for days.

Each landholder is careful to put on one side part of his best local cotton for home spinning. This is ginned separately and with much more care than what is meant for sale. The quantity set apart for home spinning depends on the number of women in the household and the leisure they have for working the spinning machine or *nalu-rati.* For home-spinning the staple is so well cleaned that not a single seed can be found in a dozen pounds. Three machines are used for ginning cotton, the ginning wheel or *charkha,* the foot-roller or *hattigudda,* and the sawgin. The ginning wheel or *charkha,* though still found in a few remote villages in the north of the district, has for many years been discarded in favour of the foot-roller. The ginning wheel is a very rough machine. It consists of two cylinders, one of wood the other of iron, which revolve on endless screws at the ends of rollers. The cylinders, which are twenty to twenty-four inches long, are fixed touching each other, parallel and horizontal, in a strong wooden frame twelve to sixteen inches high. The iron cylinder which works on the wooden cylinder is about half an inch in diameter. It is thickest in the middle and tapers slightly and gradually towards the ends. The wooden roller is much thicker. It is one and a half to two inches in diameter, and on one end has a rude wheel sixteen to twenty inches in diameter fixed on the centre. A piece of wood stuck in the rim of the wheel serves as the handle for working the roller. On the other side of the ginning wheel, at the end of the iron roller, is a second handle for turning it. When in work, the ginning wheel is fixed on the ground between two persons, each of whom takes a handle and turns it in an opposite direction, and by turns feeds the wheel with seed cotton. The seed is turned out on one side and the wool on the other. Nothing but cotton is cleaned in the wheel. It turns out more work than the foot-roller, but does not work so well. The cost of ginning with the wheel is about half-way between the cost of ginning by the saw gin and by the foot-roller.

The chief local appliance for ginning cotton is the foot-roller called *hattigudda* in Kánarese. The foot roller is a rude primitive machine which does not cost more than 1*s.* (8 *as.*). Its chief parts are the *tevantghi* that is the three-legged stool on which the ginner sits worth 2*d.* (1½ *as.*); the *aru-kul* or flat-stone about one foot by six inches and two inches thick worth 3*d.* (2 *as.*); the *kuda* an iron roller about one foot long and tapering from about three-quarters of an inch in the middle to a point at the ends worth 6*d.* (4 *as.*); and two wooden soles or *pavantgis* for placing under the feet when turning the roller, generally made of flat pieces of split bamboo costing little or nothing. The foot-roller is worked only by women and girls. In cleaning cotton by the foot-roller the seed cotton is laid in the sun, frequently turned, and when well dried is sharply beaten with a thin bamboo called *shedi* that it may be as loose as possible for ginning. When a heap of cotton is ready the ginner sits on her three-legged stool. She sets the stone on the ground before her and on

Chapter VI.
Trade.
Industries.
Cotton-ginning.

the stone lays the iron roller whose ends stand about three inches beyond the side of the stone. On each end of the roller she sets one of the bamboo soles. She leans forward still sitting but partly balancing herself on her feet which she rests on the bamboo soles at the ends of the roller. She takes a handful of seed cotton in her right hand and pressing with her feet on the bamboo soles moves the roller back and forwards on the stone. As the roller moves she drops seed cotton under it and the pressure of the roller on the seed cotton separates the wool from the seed. The seed comes out in front and the cotton wool comes out behind. As the cotton wool comes out the ginner keeps pulling it under her stool with her left hand.

The rates for cleaning with the foot-roller vary in different places. The following are perhaps about the commonest. The owner of the cotton or the owner's man, serves the seed cotton to the women in a body. As each woman brings her cleaned cotton back, it is weighed and she is paid at a rate equal to about 3*s*. 4*d*. (Rs. $1\frac{11}{16}$) the hundredweight of ginned cotton. Another plan is to serve seed cotton to each woman, and pay her by the weight of the seed cotton. In this case the rate represents about 3*s*. 3*d*. (Rs. $1\frac{5}{16}$) the hundredweight of cleaned cotton. On the other hand, if they wish the cotton to be really clean and free from seed or dirt the woman is paid by the amount of seed and dirt she takes out of the cotton at rates which represent a charge of about 4*s*. 4½*d*. (Rs. $2\frac{3}{16}$) a hundredweight. The system of having two ginning rates, a high rate to ensure clean cotton for the local spinners and a low rate to ensure dirty cotton for the Bombay buyers, prevails over the whole district. If honestly worked the foot-roller cleans local cotton better than any other machine. It is the only machine that does no harm to the fibre. At the same time the process is very slow. This slowness is a serious evil as the local cotton cannot be ginned in time to reach Bombay before the rains, and by being packed in leaky godowns and dirty sheds loses much of its value.

Saw-ginning.

The outturn of American Belgaum is now so trifling that few sawgins are used and these few are in bad repair. Most of these sawgins have ten to eighteen saws. The machine is worked by the hand in a room eighteen feet by fifteen. The room is divided into two spaces separated by firm bamboo matting. Of the two spaces the smaller about twelve feet is used as a lint room, and the larger is set apart for the gin. The gin must be firmly placed against the partition of the smaller room. In the partition-matting a hole should be cut of the size of the gin-flue and the flue should be placed in the hole and passed two or three inches beyond it. The small or lint room should not be too air-tight; if it is too air-tight the flue gets choked and hinders the working of the gin. The gin must be perfectly level as well as firm. It must be so firmly secured either by strong pegs or masonry that while at work it remains perfectly still. The smaller strap should then be put on the inner and larger rim of the saw pulley, and over the top of the brush pulley; this will make the brush pulley move inwards, that is in the opposite direction to the saws. The band must be fixed round the wheel of a pulley post at the back of the gin and tightened by a rack fastened to the pulley post. Care must be taken that the fans or brushes keep the flue clear of ginned cotton, and at the same time raise enough draught to drive the ginned cotton twelve or fourteen feet. If the fans are not properly arranged, the ginned cotton will gather close to the mouth of the flue, and stop the gin. The spindle of the driving wheel must be placed eighteen feet from the saw pulley, and the wheel should be placed in a line with the gin so that the strap or band may run freely and smoothly. The band should have holes in its joining ends so that it may be tightened or slackened at will. When the band is arranged the wheel should be firmly fixed, so that it may work with perfect steadiness. Five workers are wanted, four drivers at the wheel and one to feed the gin. The feeder places a quantity of seed-cotton on the top of the machine, and with his back to the driving wheel stands opposite and close to the gin, facing the hopper-box which receives the seed-cotton and in which the saws revolve. Experience is wanted to make a good feeder, so that the roll of the cotton in the hopper-box may revolve equally and steadily. At starting it is well to fill the hopper with a mixture of equal parts of seed and seed-cotton. The feeder should then lift the box on its hinges, high enough to keep the saws clear of the mixture in the hopper. Then the drivers should begin and as soon as the gin is in motion, the box should be put down sharply, evenly, and firmly. The working of the saws forces the contents of the box to go round, and the feeder must keep on supplying cotton neither too slowly nor too fast. The roll or contents of the box should move steadily with the hopper full, but not overcharged. If the roll of cotton in the box does not begin to go round as soon as the saws are in motion the box should be lifted once, or if necessary twice, and be again carefully set down in the way described. This lifting will also be necessary every now and then to clear the box of the cleansed seed that may gather at the bottom of the grates. In fine bright weather, for damp at once injures ginning, an eighteen-saw gin in good work will in an hour gin one hundredweight of seed cotton. In starting and working a gin care must be taken that the saws revolve through the cotton only, and that they do not rub against the grates. To make sure of this the hopper should be allowed to become empty or almost empty, and, with the hand resting on the saw whirl, the saws should be made to revolve slowly. If any of the saws gives the slightest touch to the sides of the grates, the adjustment is wrong. The saws are easily put right by seizing the saw in a pair of plyers or pincers and working it until it is seen to revolve in the exact centre of the space between the grates. If all the saws press on one side, the whole of them and the spindle are wrong, and to put them right the spindle must be properly replaced on the bearings. Unless these adjustments are made the fibre will be damaged. Every time that the saws are examined, the seed board must be carefully replaced, or the seed will either fall too freely and not properly stripped of the wool, or, if the opening is too small, the seed will not fall away at all and the gin will be stopped. The seed board is easily replaced by the travelling nuts that are fitted for the purpose. Every care should be taken that the cotton seed is free

Chapter VI.
Trade.
Industries.
Saw-ginning.

from stones, lumps of earth, or other matter likely to injure the teeth of the saws. The gin should be kept carefully clean and all its bearings well oiled. Of the three modes of ginning the sawgin is much the most rapid. An eighteen saw-gin driven by four men and fed by a fifth will turn out twenty pounds of clean cotton in less than half an hour. Two men working a wheel gin or *charka* turn out about twenty pounds of clean cotton in twelve hours. The foot-roller works still more slowly. Ginning with the foot-roller costs about half as much again as ginning with the saw-gin, and the cost of the wheel gin is about half-way between the cost of the foot-roller and of the saw-gin.

The arrangements for working saw-gins vary greatly. The richer dealers often employ their own staff of men so that it is not easy to calculate what the ginning costs them. When the owner of the seed cotton has neither a gin nor his own men he commonly gives 694 pounds of American seed cotton to five labourers four of whom drive and one feeds the gin. These men are bound to give the owner 482 pounds of ginned seed and the 212 pounds of cotton wool. For this they are paid 4*s.* 6*d.* (Rs. $2\frac{1}{4}$) which is about 2*s.* $4\frac{1}{2}$*d.* (Rs. $1\frac{3}{16}$) the hundredweight of clean staple. The charge for the use of a gin varies from 2*s.* (Re. 1) the 694 pounds of cotton seed in the slack season to 4*s.* or 6*s.* (Rs. 2-3) in the busy season. The nominal outturn of clean cotton is 212 pounds in 674 pounds. This is much above the actual outturn and to bring the weight of clean cotton to what is required the labourers have to add weight. To increase the weight of the clean cotton they let as much dirt as they can pass among the clean cotton and with this object always prefer to use gins which are out of order. A saw-gin in really good order if honestly worked, gives much less than 212 pounds of good clean cotton wool from 694 pounds of the present poor and mixed American. Mr. E. P. Robertson, when Collector of Dhárwár (1868-1875) brought to notice that gin-owners kept their saw-gins unrepaired for years till the teeth of the saws were almost worn away. Saws worn to knives cleaned more cotton and cleaned it more easily than when the saws were fresh. The fact that saws worn to knives cut the cotton into masses of fluff made no difference to the gin owners.

Though the saw-gin is intended only for American cotton, it is often used in the Kánarese districts for ginning the local staple, especially when the local cotton has been dulled or soiled by rain or has been beaten down on the ground. With the foot-roller it is impossible to give damp and dirty local cotton anything like a good appearance so the holder passes it through a saw-gin, which freshens it and makes it look better. The dealer generally does his best to pass this sawginned local cotton as sawginned American, and those who do not know sawginned American are often deceived.

A serious objection to the general use of the saw-gin is the difficulty of keeping the teeth of the saws in order. Many experiments have failed because the teeth of the saws were either badly shaped or were too sharp. The tooth should be a not too blunt hook, in shape much like a rose thorn. As the saws move round in the hopper, the tooth catches the fibre. To do its work properly the tooth must be sharp enough to catch the fibre and blunt enough to hold the fibre without in the least cutting it. If the tooth is too flat or blunt it will catch the cotton and crush it, and often the seed as well, in lumps against the grates of the gin. If the brushes or fans are in proper order, they sweep off the fibre as soon as the tooth has laid hold of it. If the brush does not sweep off the fibre, the fibre is carried round back into the hopper, and the tooth, blocked with the fibre, forces its way through the seed cotton doing much harm. To keep the teeth at the proper sharpness and curve Mr. Walton (1865-1880) found it necessary to make a special file. Every workman who filed the teeth had the model of a perfect tooth with him and was told to file the tooth to the shape of the underpoint of a man's little finger. Many American planters object to bran-new saw-gins. The planters take off the roughness of fresh teeth by working them for a little with cotton seed and sand.

The following is a summary of the efforts which have been made to introduce the use of saw-gins into Belgaum. Saw-gins were brought into India as early as 1828. In 1828 one of two Whitney saw-gins sent by the Court of Directors to the Bombay Government was forwarded to the Bombay Karnátak for trial. So long as the saws were under skilled European control and care they worked well. But all officers agreed that it was unsafe to trust them to cotton-growers or cotton dealers. The mistake was at first made of ginning the local cotton in the saw-gins. In many cases the result was that the cotton was cut to pieces. In fact the saw-gin is suited only to New Orleans cotton, whose fibre clings so tightly to the seed that the ordinary gin cannot separate it. In 1835, Lord Ellenborough, President of the Board of Commissioners for the Affairs of India, suggested that specimens of the machinery used in cleaning cotton in America, Brazil, India, and Egypt, should be sent to London, and that Indian seed cotton should be sent with the gins that experts might determine which was the best machine. A foot-roller and a wheel-gin were sent by Dr. Lush from Belgaum. In 1836 to encourage the cotton trade, the Bombay Government abolished the 5*s.* 6*d.* (Rs. 2¾) tax on wheel gins. This measure did not much affect Belgaum. In 1838 Dr. Lush condemned the American Whitney gins. He said much time had been lost by assuming that because the machine did well in America it must do well in India. He added that a gin was wanted which would do the same for India that the Whitney gin had done for America. On this the Court of Directors offered a prize of £100 (Rs. 1000) to encourage mechanics to invent a gin suitable for Indian cotton. The result was unsatisfactory. Saw-gins were first made in the Karnátak about 1845. Nearly at the same time, with the aid of local craftsmen, Mr. Mercer the American planter succeeded in making a saw-gin in Dhárwár and Mr. Channing in Belgaum. The local saw-gin though somewhat imperfect worked fairly so long as it was under skilled supervision and management. Under every other condition it failed. As the number of local saw-gins increased, it was found impossible to keep wooden framed gins in repair.

Chapter VI.
Trade.
Industries.
Saw-ginning.

They were also found unsuited for permanent use by the husbandmen. No matter how well seasoned the wood and excellent the workmanship, they fell to pieces under the rough treatment of the gin owners and their servants. In the towns and villages the local saw-gin was never successful till every possible part of it was made of the strongest iron. Even iron gins are so roughly used that it takes the most constant efforts to keep them in anything like good order. When he has bought a saw-gin, the local dealer thinks he has done all he should be called on to do, and that his first expense should be his last. He does not understand that saw-gins want keeping up to the mark. So long as it can go round, he is most unwilling to spend even the smallest sum to keep his gin in repair.

In 1844 some cotton dealers objected to the saw-gins because the cotton they turned out was too clean. About the same time the Collector reported that the cotton dealers at Báil-Hongal and Saundatti, had applied that saw-gins might be put up in their towns. The Collector was allowed to grant their request and Mr. Channing set up the gins in some old Government buildings at the cost of about £20 (Rs. 200). In the same year (1845) Government set up two more saw-gins one at Murgod and another of fourteen saws on the Government farm at Nágenhál. Except the gin on the Government farm these saw-gins were let to local dealers. To encourage careful picking the ginning charges were 2*s.* (Re. 1) for 756 pounds (twenty-seven *mans*) of well picked and 672 pounds (twenty-four *mans*) of ordinarily picked seed-cotton. Mr. Channing represented that, if the price of saw-ginning was brought within the means of the local merchants, he believed saw-gins would come into general use throughout Belgaum. He asked to be allowed to make two machines at a cost of £19 16*s.* (Rs. 198) each, which, he added, was about half the price at which such gins could be procured from England or America. Early in 1847 these proposals were sanctioned.

Mr. Channing estimated that he could make and issue twenty good saw-gins at about £16 16*s.* (Rs. 168) and good twenty-five saw-gins at about £17 8*s.* (Rs. 174) and at ten per cent less if more than six were made at one time. These machines could be made and fitted on the spot, except the saws, which must be brought from England. So long as these gins were under direct European management and were mended and adjusted by skilled mechanics, they answered their purpose well. They ceased to work well when they were taken to dealers' ginning houses, and subjected to rough and ignorant usage. A machine fitted for such rough treatment was never made until every part of it was made of strong iron. Even the iron gins went wrong if workmen were not constantly going round with inspectors after them to see not only that the workmen mended the gins properly, but that the gin-owners allowed them to mend them. Later in the same year (1847) the available saw-gins were found to be too few. To increase ginning facilities the Bombay Government applied to the Court of Directors for 5000 saws for new gins. Only four saw-gins were kept on Government account and during the season one of these was sold for £22 (Rs. 220).

Chapter VI.
Trade.
Industries.
Sawginning.

Sixteen more were being made for Government and for private persons. In the same year the cost of cleaning American cotton by the saw-gin was 5*d.* (3⅓ *as.*) for eighty pounds, and the cost of cleaning local cotton by the foot-roller was 6¾*d.* (4½ *as.*) for eighty pounds. In 1848 the demand for saw-gins spread in some of the neighbouring states. Government suggested that prizes should be offered to the local craftsmen for the best saw-gin. Mr. Simpson, the superintendent of cotton experiments, opposed this suggestion. The native craftsmen had much skill in imitating, but, without training, they could not make a machine that required such nicety and exactness as a saw-gin. He thought no one should be allowed to sell saw-gins who had not spent six months in the Government factory.

In the same year in consequence of the representations of the Honourable Mr. Reid twelve hundred new saws were received from England in Belgaum. Even this did not meet the demand. About this time some of the sawginned cotton sent to England was found to be damaged; it was said because the gins were worked at too great a speed. There was some difference of opinion among experts as to the best number of revolutions in the minute. All agreed that hand labour, which implied slow turning with occasionally extremely fast spurts, was bad for the staple. In 1852, to improve the ginning machinery and to settle the disputed point regarding the best rate of speed, Government determined to hold a public trial in Calcutta and offered a prize of £500 (Rs. 5000) to the maker of the best gin. Mr. Channing, who had at first said that the best rate was 180 turns in the minute, afterwards raised his estimate to 200 or 250 turns a minute. The Dhárwár superintendent thought even a higher rate than 250 turns was advisable. Opinions still differ as to the best rate of speed.

Early in 1849, at the suggestion of the Manchester Commercial Association, the Court of Directors sent out 200 cottage saw-gins. Great pains were taken with this handy machine. No less than four models were made; one chiefly of wood, the rest of iron. Each was worked on a different plan and all were made under the advice and suggestions of those who were well acquainted with India and its cotton trade. Dr. Forbes Royle who was present at the trials, thought the gin made of iron with saws and brushes moved by wheels and bands the best. He recommended that it should be introduced into India chiefly on the ground that if each landholder had one of these handy machines in his house, he would be independent of other labour, and his family would gin his cotton crop. He thought there would not be much difficulty in introducing the gin, as it could be no novelty in Belgaum and other districts where the people were already acquainted with sawginning. The iron model was farther improved, and the Court of Directors ordered two hundred to be sent to India. It was calculated that with this small machine one man would be able to gin sixteen pounds of seed-cotton in the hour at an expense of less than 6*s.* (Rs. 3) for five hundred pounds of cleaned cotton, while the hand-power gins at work were found to turn out for each man less than one pound an hour, at an expense of nearly 8*s.* (Rs. 4) for five hundred pounds of clean staple, and the old Indian wheel-gin cleaned

Chapter VI.
Trade.
Industries.
Saw-ginning.

fifty pounds of seed-cotton a day at a cost of 10*s.* (Rs. 5) for every five hundred pounds of clean cotton. It was estimated that the cost of wear and tear, to every bale of cotton cleaned by these three machines, was for the cottage gin a little over 1*s.* 4*d.* (10⅔ *as.*), for the saw-gin about 1*s.* 8*d.* (13⅓ *as.*), and for the Indian wheel gin a little over 6*d.* (4 *as.*). A number of the cottage gins were distributed in Belgaum and Bijápur. They were worked for a time, were never repaired, and in the end were thrown on one side as lumber. In Mr. Walton's opinion these cottage gins did not get a fair trial When worked by skilled Europeans, as by Dr. Wight in Madras, these cottage-gins succeeded well. With eight of them Dr. Wight ginned about 4000 pounds of cotton; if he had had them Dr. Wight could have kept 200 gins at work. Even with a fair trial Mr. Walton doubted if the cottage gins would have answered in Belgaum. They would be roughly used and get out of order and there was no means of putting them right if they once went out of repair.

In 1850 the demand for saw-gins in Belgaum was at its greatest height. Forty were at work in twenty-one towns and villages and orders for thirty-seven were registered. In the same year (1850) the Collector of Belgaum calculated that ginning with the foot-roller cost 12*s.* to 14*s.* (Rs. 6 - 7) and with the saw-gin 7*s.* (Rs. 3½) the *khandi.* About the same time Mr. Channing calculated that with the saw-gins then in work in Belgaum, with an assistant, he could clean about 1,200,000 pounds of raw or seed cotton, and without an assistant about 700,000 pounds of raw cotton a year. To meet the great demand for saw-gins it was arranged that ten Government saw-gins should be sent from Dhárwár and that small machines should be made which could be sold to landholders for 16*s.* (Rs. 8). It was hoped that the people would buy the small machines and keep them in their houses, and that this would remove one of the main objections to the growing of New Orleans cotton. These efforts ended in failure, as these small cheap gins were unsuited to stand the rough and ignorant treatment they received. Up to this time it does not seem to have been noticed that to saw-gin the local cotton in the same way as the American did it incurable harm. The demand for gins which was so brisk in 1850 soon passed away. In 1851 of twenty-six Government gins only five were at work and of fifty-six private gins only twenty-two were at work. This collapse seems to have been partly due to the failure of the American crop and partly to faults in the gins. Mr. Davis, the first European agent in Belgaum, took twenty-five of the Government gins, but returned them as he found they did not work well.

About 1851 the Bombay Government sent to Belgaum some cotton cleaning machines, designed and constructed by a Mr. Mather, for which he had received a prize of £50 (Rs. 500) and the Bengal Agricultural Society's Medal. Captain, afterwards Sir George Wingate, the head of the Southern Marátha Revenue Survey, who had paid particular attention to cotton cleaning machinery, tested the Mather gin and pronounced it a poor adaptation of the native wheel-gin and inordinately dear at £8 (Rs. 80). In this opinion all officers who tried the Mather gin agreed. In 1852 of fifty Government saw-gins only two were at work and of thirty-nine private saw-gins only thirteen were at work. In 1855 Mr. Reeves brought to notice the damage done by saw-gins in bad order. The landholders and local dealers of Dhárwár and Belgaum looked solely to the quantity of cleaned cotton they could turn out in a day. They were reckless as to the way in which the cotton was cleaned; they worked their saw-gins so long as they could be kept going. In 1856 when the orders of the Court of Directors to stop cotton experiments reached Belgaum the Government ginning houses were valued at about £712 (Rs. 7120). The order stopping experiments was modified as regarded saw-gins as it was found that no one but Government could supply them. The damage done by careless ginning, of which Mr. Reeves complained, proved so serious that some new machines of the best quality were ordered. The new machines were carefully distributed in Dhárwár, but in Belgaum and Bijápur little was done. To keep the cotton-ginning machinery in repair apprentices, all of them Indo-European youths were (1857) trained under the superintendents. Some of the apprentices learned well, but none stuck to the work as all found better-paid employment. Government sold the English-made gins at £40 (Rs. 400) for an eighteen and £20 (Rs. 200) for a ten saw-gin complete including the driving gear. The machines were of the best class and were always put up and thoroughly tested before they were made over to purchasers. During the American War (1862-1865) immense numbers of gins were imported and made in the country.

In 1866 and 1867 Mr. Walton, the superintendent of Government cotton ginning, established repairing factories at Navalgund and Ron in Dhárwár. As these factories were near the Belgaum and South Bijápur frontiers they were entrusted with the gins of those two districts. The factories were much used till, in 1870, Mr. Walton left for England, and it was arranged that the Dhárwár factories were not to mend gins beyond Dhárwár limits. Since then the Belgaum and Bijápur saw-gins have fallen more and more out of order, until the people have almost ceased to grow American cotton because they have no machinery to clean it with. So far as is known only about thirty saw-gins are left in the district. Of the thirty, twenty-eight are in seven villages of Parasgad and two are at Báil-Hongal a large village in Sampgaon. Of these thirty gins few are in use, partly because of the want of means for repairing them. The price of gins which during the American war was as high as £120 (Rs. 1200) now ranges from £5 to £8 (Rs. 50-80).

Cotton Pressing.

No Belgaum cotton is either full-pressed or half-pressed. In 1847 Mr. Channing devised a cotton-press at an estimated cost of £8 (Rs. 80) which the Collector said could be made and put up by any local mechanic. Mr. Channing was allowed to set up this press in the town of Saundatti. Many other attempts have been made to introduce the use of presses. All have failed. The failure has been due partly to the difficulty of keeping the machinery in order, but chiefly because the exporters cannot trust the local dealers. The exporter knows that when opportunity offers, the up-country ginner

Chapter VI.
Trade.
Industries.

and dealer will always adulterate and pack falsely. So the cotton he buys must be loosely packed that his hand may be able to reach any part of the bundle. So long as this well-founded distrust continues no press can succeed. A minor objection to pressing was that the cartmen charged as much and often more for carrying pressed than unpressed cotton. It is doubtful whether half presses would be a gain; but there is no doubt that the cotton trade would greatly profit if bales could be full pressed in Belgaum and Dhárwár and sent unopened to Europe.

Cotton Weaving.

The chief cotton weaving towns are, in order of importance, Gokák with a yearly outturn of goods valued at about £15,000 (Rs. 1,50,000), Chikodi Sankeshvar and Báil-Hongal each with a yearly outturn valued at about £12,000 (Rs. 1,20,000), Belgaum with a yearly outturn valued at about £11,500 (Rs. 1,15,000), Mundgod Athni Páchhápur and Deshnur each with a yearly outturn valued at about £10,000 (Rs. 1,00,000), Manoli and Garl Hasnar each with a yearly outturn valued at about £9500 (Rs. 95,000), Saundatti with a yearly outturn valued at about £9000 (Rs. 90,000), Kittur with a yearly outturn valued at about £7500 (Rs. 75,000), Mugutkhán-Hubli Bágevádi Maribal and Sulibhávi each with a yearly outturn valued at about £7000 (Rs. 70,000), Nesargi with a yearly outturn valued at about £6500 (Rs. 65,000), and Sampgaon with a yearly outturn valued at about £4000 (Rs. 40,000). Weaving is also carried on to a fair extent at Tailsang, Kágvád, Shailbal, Ainápur and Kunmadi, in Athni; at Ankalgi, Yádvád, Kavjalgi, Mamdápur, and Kurbat in Gokák; at Nipáni, Hukeri, Bhoja, and Kangoli in Chikodi; at Kovad and Chándgad in Belgaum; at Bidi, Khánápur, Nandgad, Itgi, Parasvad, Kitávad, Bogánar, and Haidur in Khánápur; at Sangoli, Manketti, Nágenhál, Tarmeri, and Hanchkalti in Sampgaon; and at Yekundi, Asundi, Sutigeri, Susanghi, Hasur, and Hanchinhal in Parasgad. The yearly outturn of all the hand looms of the district is estimated to be worth about £200,000 (Rs. 2,00,000).[1]

Spinning is carried on all over the district except in Belgaum and Khánápur, and is practised more or less by the women of every caste except Bráhmans. The women spend most of their spare time in making cotton yarn. In most black plain villages the yarn is made either from cotton grown on the spinner's land, or from the cotton which has been paid to the women and children of the house for picking their neighbours' crop. The yarn is taken to market and is there either sold for ready money, or bartered for salt, grain, curry stuff, and other articles. Petty dealers move about the country and attend the village weekly markets to gather yarn. When they have gathered a large quantity, they take it for sale to one of the leading hand-loom weaving towns.

Process.

For spinning into yarn and weaving into cloth the Belgaum and Bijápur people use nothing but the local cotton. They say that they

[1] These are Mr. Walton's estimates for 1879 (Belgaum Cotton, 142). Since 1879 chiefly from the competition of Bombay steam made cloth the hand-loom weaving has declined. The opening of railways and the establishment of mills at Hubli and probably at other Kánarese trade centres will further depress the local hand-loom industry.

cannot spin sawginned American, they use none of it and the whole crop is exported. As has been noticed they take the greatest pains that the cotton they spin is pure. The cotton is picked with special care and they ensure thoroughness and honesty on the part of the foot-roll ginners by paying them, not as they do when the cotton is to be exported by the weight of the ginned cotton, but by the weight of the seeds and dirt ginned out of the cotton. The local cotton cleaned by the foot-roller makes a strong and good though somewhat coarse and uneven yarn, and the local hand-loom cloth is wonderfully strong and lasting. The local cotton is also largely used in the Bombay mills and the demand would be greater if the growers took anything like the care of the cotton they export which they take of the cotton they spin. The immense number of foot-roller ginning-places, for every holder of cotton works foot-rollers in his own house or yard, makes the checking of mixing an almost hopeless task.

Teasing.

Before cotton is ready for spinning, it has to be teased by the Pinjáris or cotton-teasers most of whom are Muhammadans. These Pinjáris tease the cotton by laying it on the tight gut string of a harp-shaped frame called *bessi* which they set trembling by beating it with a dumb-bell shaped blackwood mallet.[1] In teasing cotton the harp-shaped frame or *bessi* is fastened to the roof of the house with the wooden part up. The sieve or *tutti* is set on the ground below the frame and on the sieve cotton is piled. The teaser sits on the left of the sieve and taking the frame in his left hand and the dumb-bell mallet in his right hand, draws the gut string of the frame among the pile of cotton and deals the string so sharp and heavy a blow that the quivering gut tosses the cotton into the air and opens it letting the dust and dirt pass through the sieve on to the floor. With two or three teasing frames at work the air is so thick with dust and fluff that no one but a teaser can stay in the room. When the teaser thinks he has made the cotton clean and soft enough, he takes the tapering bamboo stick in his right hand and rolling it deftly on his thigh gathers at the stick point a finger-long curl or roll of cotton called *hanji*. A teaser is paid 3*d.* (2 *as.*) for cleaning about six and a half pounds called a *dhada* of these curls or rolls. Sometimes, instead of cleaning other men's cotton, the teaser buys cotton from petty hawkers or from small village shopkeepers who take cotton from pickers in exchange for salt, grain, and curry stuff; teases it; and sells the rolls at 5¼*d.* (3½ *as.*) the pound. These rolls are seldom so well cleaned as the rolls which a teaser turns when he is called to a man's house and paid to tease the cotton.

Reeling.

The next process in working cotton into yarn is reeling. Cotton is

[1] The parts of the teasing appliance are a blackwood frame called *bessi* (K.) worth 10*s.* (Rs. 5); a goat-gut cord called *bihu* (K.) fastened as tight as a harp-string from end to end of the frame, worth 2*s.* (Re. 1); a dumb-bell shaped blackwood mallet called *korathi* (K.) worth 1*s.* (8 *as.*); a bamboo bow with a common string called *billa* (K.), worth ⅜*d.* (¼ *anna*); a bamboo sieve called *tutti* (K.), on which the teased cotton rests letting the dust and dirt pass through, worth 6*d.* (4 *as.*); a tapering eighteen inch long stick called *gania* (K.) round which the teaser winds the teased cotton in curls or *hanjis* worth ⅜*d.* (¼ *anna*), and a bamboo stick called *shedi* to gather the teased cotton. The whole cost of the teaser's tools is 13*s.* 7*d.* (Rs. 6¾).

Chapter VI. Trade. Industries. *Reeling.*

reeled on the spinning wheel or *nulu-rati* (K.) which is worth 1*s*. 3*d*. to 1*s*. 6*d*. (10-12 *as*.) and is much like the old English distaff. On the frame shaft a small wooden upright is set, and on the upright an iron pin called *kadaru*. This pin is fixed upon two short pegs on the outside, and is held together by the shaft thread which passes round the wheel. The wheel is worked by the right hand, the cotton roll or *hanji* from which the yarn is twisted being held in the left hand. As the wheel turns, the pin spins round and rapidly twists the fibre into yarn. As the yarn forms it is reeled on the pin and when the reel has grown to a certain size it is taken off and another is begun. These oblong reels of cotton twist or yarn are called *kudali*. As soon as the spinner has enough of these reels, she again fixes them one by one to the iron pin or *kadaru*, the end of the twist being passed through a bamboo tube called the *kuvinghi*. The yarn is then arranged on a rack-like wooden machine fitted with pegs, called *hassamari* and costing about 1*s*. (8 *as*.). The yarn is worked in and out among the pegs until enough has been wound to make a hank or *putti*. The hank is taken off and a new one begun.

Spinning.

In a Hindu house there is next to no sewing. Almost all clothes are worn as they come from the loom, so that when there is no field work, after their housework is over, the women have a good deal of spare time. As a class the women are very hardworking and spend all their spare time in spinning. Most women spin five hours a day, and others whose housework is light spin still longer. Ripening crops are generally watched by women, many of whom may be seen sitting on some raised part of the field working the thread-wheel and scaring birds and other thieves. A clever woman will spin four ounces of cotton in five hours. The return is small. On a market day the women take the hanks to the nearest town. A hank of coarse yarn weighing about eight ounces and six yards long, sells for about 3⅜*d*. (2¼ *as*.) and a hank of fine yarn five yards long and weighing six ounces fetches 2⅝*d*. (1¾ *as*.). Taking off the price of the cotton rolls this leaves only ⅜*d*. (½ *anna*) for two days' spinning. These starvation rates are the result of the competition of English and Bombay machine-made yarn; formerly the thread wheel yielded a fair return. The spinners sell their hanks of yarn to weavers and to tape and rope makers.

Dyeing.

If he is going to weave coloured cloth the buyer hands his hanks to the dyer. For the best fast colours the dyer charges 4½*d*. to 5¼*d*. (3-3½ *as*.) and for less lasting or brilliant colours 1½*d*. to 3*d*. (1-2 *as*.) for each hank. The coarser yarn is generally dyed with the cheaper dyes and the finer yarn with the dearer dyes. After being coloured, the hanks are dried by spreading them along a pair of stands called *hudithers* (K.) costing about 1*s*. (8 *as*.). Uncoloured yarn is soaked in water for about three days and is then spread on the drying stands. Little yarn is spread to dry at the same time as the yarn should be washed or dyed just before it is arranged on the loom.

Warping.

In dyeing, the yarn is as far as possible arranged so that each fibre may lie separate and in proper order for weaving. To arrange the yarn, a number of flat bamboo sticks, called *khumbhis*, together worth about 1½*d.* (1 *a.*), are laid between the upper and lower fibres. After the sorting or *hassu* is finished the yarn is taken off the stands to be sized. The size used in the Bombay Karnátak is Indian millet starch. It is thoroughly worked into the yarn by hand, and the yarn is again stretched on the stand or *hudither*. After this second stretching, to make it fair and even and take off surplus size, the yarn is most carefully and repeatedly brushed with an instrument called the *kunchghi* worth about 7*s.* (Rs. 3½). For the finer cloths this brushing or combing takes much time and requires great skill. The brushed yarn which is called *vunki* is taken off the stand and arranged on the loom, a process known as *hanaji*. In arranging the yarn on the loom one end of the fibres is fastened to four round sticks or *koles*, which in weaving are at the extreme other end of the web from the weaver and then each fibre is passed between the teeth of the comb or *tutt* which lies across the web in front of the weaver. Two flat sticks called *shullis* (K.) are shoved in to keep the upper and lower fibres of the web from entangling. When the fibre-sorting is finished the web is again fixed on the stand or *hudither*, and then the threads are placed in their final position according to the texture of the cloth which is to be woven. After this final process the yarn which is called *hormatgki* is taken from the stands and fixed to the loom or *mugga*, when it gets its final name of warp or *negi*. The whole process of preparing the warp yarn is carried on in the open air.

The yarn used for the woof or cross threads is differently prepared. Local yarn if undyed is well soaked in water. Dyed yarn is not soaked and neither dyed nor undyed yarn is sized. It is next stretched between two rude stands called the *hari*, rough upright wooden posts with several pegs in them, for the proper arrangement of the yarn. When the yarn is ready the end is taken off and fastened to a conical reel called *hati* worth 1½*d.* to 3*d.* (1-2 *as.*). English or Bombay yarn is not put on the round *hari*, but on a wheel of bamboo sticks called a *rattal* worth about 3*d.* (2 *as.*). This change of process is needed because English yarn is made in such short hanks that no peg-winding is wanted. When the yarn is ready it is reeled on to small bobbins called *kankis* on a wheel called *rutti*, almost the same as the spinning-like wheel or *naluratti*. In reeling English or Bombay yarn the bamboo stick wheel *rattal* is placed close to the spinning-like wheel or *ratti*, and over the iron pin or *padaru* is drawn a hollow reed or millet stalk; the end of the yarn is brought from the bamboo-stick wheel and fastened to the hollow reed; the spinning-like wheel is turned, and as much yarn as is wished is reeled off. In reeling local yarn the peg-post or *hati* is brought close to the spinning-like wheel and the yarn is reeled. The bobbins or *kankis* are laid in a basket close to the weaver who fastens one on an iron pin in the shuttle, uses it and when it is empty fastens a new one. After a piece of cloth is finished, it is unrolled from the *kunti* or weaver's beam at the top of the loom and neatly folded square. It is then considered ready for the local market or for export.

The Kánarese call the loom *magga*; the Musalmáns call the loom

Chapter VI.
Trade.
Industries.
Weaving.

kúm. Looms vary considerably in quality and cost.[1] The price ranges from about 10*s.* to £1 (Rs. 5-10) and even higher. The size of the weaving room for one loom is about eighteen feet by eight, for two looms eighteen by twelve, and for three eighteen feet square; each loom wants six feet extra. In towns where weaving is carried on to a large extent few work-rooms have only one loom. Most have two or three, and some, especially at Belgaum and Guledgud in Bijápur, have four. A new loom is rare. Many looms are for sale at a half or a third of their cost.

Beginning from the weaver's end the parts of a loom are: The pit or *mugga teg,* thirty inches by fifteen and twenty inches deep, in which the weaver sits as he weaves. In front of the pit is the weaver's beam or *kunti,* a solid square bar about four feet long by four inches broad. It has a ridge on one side in which a thin round stick called the beam-stick or *kunta da shull* is fixed. To this beam-stick are fastened the ends of the warp yarn. The beam has socket ends and is so fixed, that, as his work advances, the weaver can turn the beam and roll the web loosening the warp at the other end by a pulley and rope which is fastened to a peg close to his right hand. The beam is kept in its place by two strong pegs the *nali ghut* and the *honkal ghut.* Across the warp hung from the roof by strings and a stick is the frame or batten called the *hulghi* which encloses the comb or reed called *tutt* between whose reeds the warp yarn is passed. Next to the batten is the heddle harness with heddle strings hanging from two thin bamboo tubes fastened to heddle sticks or *biza koles* which are attached to the roof. The heddles are provided with loops or eyes through which the warp yarn is passed. The heddles communicate by strings and sticks with the treadles or *havanpads* in the pit by pressing which alternately with his foot the weaver

---

[1] The names and the cost of the different parts of a loom are: One comb-frame or *hulgi* of tamarind or blackwood, worth 9*s.* to £1 (Rs. 4½-10); one reed comb for common cloth very neatly made, 1*s.* 3*d.* (10 *as.*); one comb for fine cloth made with English thread, 3*s.* 6*d.* (Rs. 1¾); one *hanaghi* which in addition to the comb holds two *biza* to keep the warp separate and regular, 1*s.* 9*d.* (14 *as.*); one *kunti* or weaver's beam with two peg for rolling the cloth as it is made, 3*s.* 6*d.* (Rs. 1¾); one *ard dunghi* or cross bar to lift the warp, 7½*d.* (5 *as.*); one *kai guta* 1½*d.* (1 *anna*); one *amar* or *ambar dunghi,* 4½*d.* (3 *annas*); one *nevghi haggi* or rope to keep the warp stretched, 4½*d.* (3 *as.*); one *chingi koli* or stick to which the warp ends are fastened, 3*d.* (2 *as.*); one *meni guta* peg for fastening the rope, 1½*d.* (1 *anna*); two *tankoles* the sticks that are attached to the *biza* holes, with the two wooden soles, the *havinpads,* 2¼*d.* (1½ *as.*); two *kal pavantgis* complete, 3*d.* (2 *as.*); two *khumbis* for regulating the texture of the cloth, 1⅛*d.* (¾ *anna*); two *shulls,* ¾*d.* (½ *anna*); two *chaker gards* or rude pulleys, 3*d.* (2 *as.*); one pair of *shed kutgis* with needles, 1½*d.* (1 *anna*); two *lattis* or shuttles made of buffalo horn, 1*s.* 3*d.* (10 *as.*); one *nali ghut,* ¾*d.* (½ *anna*); one *honkal ghut,* 1⅛*d.* (¾ *anna*); one pair *nimbada ghut,* for keeping the *kal paratghi* in its place, 3*d.* (2 *as.*); total £1 (Rs. 10). This is about the cost of a good medium loom fit for ordinary work. Some much commoner and not so complete can be bought as cheap as 10*s.* (Rs. 5); others for making fine goods out of the higher counts of machine-made yarn with silk ornament, cost £2 to £2 10*s.* (Rs. 20-25). The more expensive looms have the following extra fittings: One *pata gad* complete, a frame fitted over the loom with sixteen pulleys for cords to pass through, to keep separate all the different silks. This is used in making elaborately patterned borders in expensive cloth. They cost 2*s.* (Re. 1) to 2*s.* 6*d.* (Rs. 1¼) each. A set of five to nine light iron and wooden rods or *sulls* hang by the pattern frame to keep the silk and other rich border threads distinct so that in weaving the woof thread may pass through them. They cost 1*s.* 9*d.* (14 *as.*) to 2*s.* 9*d.* (Rs. 1⅜) the set. The Kánarese call the warp *negi* and the woof *hoke.*

forces the heddles to carry up and down the warp yarns which are passed through their loops or eyes and so leave a passage for the shuttle between the two rows of warp yarn. The treadles are fastened by ropes to two pegs in the bottom of the loom-pit. Beyond the reed and the heddle harness is the cross bar or *ard dundghi* fixed to the ground on two pegs or *pevigutas* and used for raising the warp. Beyond the cross bar three sticks are placed across the warp to keep the yarn from getting out of place. The further end of the warp is fastened to the *chingi koli* (K.), a round wooden bar, and to the bar another shorter piece of wood is wound by a strong twine in the centre of which a rope called the *veigi hagga* (K.) is fastened and secured to a strong peg called the *meniguta* (K.). From the peg the rope is drawn back close to where the weaver sits and is fastened to another peg called the *raiguta* (K.). This rope the weaver loosens whenever he has web enough to wind round the beam. When the loom is ready, the weaver sits on the ground with his legs in the pit and works the heddles one by one by pressing his feet on the treadles. He passes the shuttle with its reel of thread sharply from right to left and back again as he lifts and lowers the fibres of the warp by working the treadles. After each passage of the shuttle, the weaver brings the woof yarn home by drawing the batten or reed frame heavily against the edge of the web. To keep the web from shrinking until there is enough to wind on the beam two bent rattan sticks with a needle in either end are fastened at the sides of the cloth.

Outturn.

The cloths woven in the Belgaum hand-looms are women's robes *sádis* (M.) or *siris* (K.), seven to nine yards long and one and a quarter yards wide. They vary in price from 2*s.* 3*d.* to 10*s.* (Rs. 1⅛ - 5) when made of coarse village yarn, and from 5*s.* to £1 10*s.* (Rs. 2½-15) when made of fine machine-made twist with silk borders and costly colours. Bodices, *holis* (M.) or *kubsas* or *kubassas* (K.), vary from coarse plain cloths to rich showy stuffs. The size for grown women is about three quarters by half a yard. The price varies from 6*d.* to 3*s.* (Rs. ¼ - 1½) a piece. Girls' robes or *kirgis* (K.) worn by girls of five to thirteen are two and a half to five yards by two to two and a half feet. They are sold at 1*s.* 3*d.* to 6*s.* (Rs. ⅝ - 3) a piece. Men's waistcloths are generally woven in pairs. The size of each is three yards by one for grown men and they are smaller in proportion for youths and boys. A pair of coarse waistcloths varies in price from 1*s.* to 3*s.* (Rs. ½ - 1½), and a pair of superior waistcloths with silk edgings cost 2*s.* to £1 4*s.* (Rs. 1 -12). Báil-Hongal is noted for its fine waistcloths. Boys' waistcloths or *bhuchkhanis* (K.) are one and a half to two and a half yards long by three quarters of a yard broad. They are worn by boys of five to fifteen and vary in price from 6*d.* to 2*s.* 9*d.* (Rs. ¼ - 1⅜) a pair. Headscarves or *rumáls* (K.), are three to five yards square. The way of wearing the headscarf varies according to the wearer's caste. Most are made of machine-spun yarn. They vary in price from 9*d.* to 6*s.* (Rs. ⅜ - 3). At Chikodi and Deshnur a larger and costlier headscarf called *mundar* (K.) is made fifteen to fifty yards long and eight to twelve inches broad. These headscarves are worn by Maráthás, Musalmáns, and others, who, though natives

Chapter VI.
Trade.
Industries.
Outturn.

of the country, dress differently from the ordinary Kánarese. At Chikodi their price varies from 3*s.* to £1 10*s.* (Rs. 1½-15) and at Deshnur some sell as high as £3 (Rs. 30). The costlier turbans have the outside end elaborately adorned with silk and gold or silver tinsel. Longcloths called *khádis* (M.) or *hachdás* (K.) when taken off the loom are about eleven yards long by one yard broad. They are used as bedding, as veils for Musalmán women when they walk abroad, and for making into coats for Musalmáns, and at Gokák, Murgod, and Manoli for printing with coloured designs. These longcloths are always made of hand-spun yarn; cloths made of coarse yarn are chosen for printing, as they take the stamp and show the designs much better than finer cloth. Their price varies from 2*s.* 6*d.* to 5*s.* (Rs. 1¼-2½). Coloured handkerchiefs or *vastras* (K.) are woven at Sankeshvar. They are two feet to one and a half yards square and are used among the forest tribes as head coverings, and among the labouring classes as waistbands. Their price varies from 1½*d.* to 9*d.* (1/8-6 *as.*). At Belgaum and at Mugutkhán-Hubli is made a cloth of various patterns known as *susi* (K.) about eight yards long by one yard broad. These cloths are used for making coats trousers and other articles worn by Musalmáns, by Maráthás for bedding, for clothing by Goanese Christians, and a large quantity is bought by Government for various uses in regimental hospitals. *Susi* varies in price from 2*s.* 6*d.* to 4*s.* (Rs. 1¼-2) a piece. At Bágevádi a coarse sheeting called *nadka* (K.) is made. These are two and a half by one yard in size and in price vary from 10½*d.* to 1*s.* 3*d.* (7-10 *as.*).

Of the local goods those woven at Báil-Hongal are of what are known as the Dhárwár and Sholápur patterns and those at Páchhápur as the Sháhápur pattern; at Áthni the favourite patterns are known as the Jamkhandi, Sátára, and Chiplun; at Gokák the favourite patterns for robes are the Kolhápur, and for waistcloths the Sángli, Kolhápur, and Miraj; and at Deshnur the favourite patterns for headscarves and waistcloths are the Jamkhandi and Rámdurg, and for robes and bodices the Sholápur and Konkan.

Carpets.

Carpets or *jemkhanis* (K.) are made chiefly at Belgaum, Báil-Hongal, and Mugutkhán-Hubli. Carpet-making, which from the Hindustáni names for all the parts of the loom seems to have been brought from North India, is almost entirely in the hands of Musalmáns. Unless the carpets are small, a special loom is used which like the ordinary loom is called *mugga*. It consists of two *thaklás* or wooden bars with posts and pegs worth 12*s.* to £7 (Rs. 6-70), two *gulis* worth 3*d.* to 6*d.* (2-4 *as.*), one *pesbhánd* worth 4½*d.* to 9*d.* (3-6 *as.*), one *pansa* worth 1*s.* 3*d.* to 2*s.* 3*d.* (Re. ⅝-1⅛), and one *kamán* worth 3*d.* to 6*d.* (2-4 *as.*), the whole costing 14*s.* to £7 4*s.* (Rs. 7-72) according to the size and quality of the loom and the kind of carpet to be made. The *thaklás* are two long wooden bars about eight inches in diameter either round or eight-sided, which are fixed one about eight feet from the ground the other close above the ground, on two upright wooden posts, thus making the loom an upright frame. This upright frame is set in the workshop or *kárkhána* where a hole is dug three feet square by two and a half feet deep. The threads of the carpet are made from the usual country yarn. They are twisted to the proper size for the kind of carpet required and are fixed from the upper to the lower cross bar. Two *gulis* or sticks, secured with twine in the same way as the *hanagis* of the cloth-loom, are fixed to the carpet thread. In passing the cross thread the workman pulls these two sticks one after the other, and he closes and tightens the texture by working the iron comb called *panja*. The *gulis* or sticks are supplemented by the *kamán*, a semicircular stick secured by string at each end and fixed to the *peshband*, a long bamboo which stands on pegs behind the weaver. Carpets five to fifteen feet long by twenty inches to fifteen feet broad sell at 1*s*. 6*d*. to £1 2*s*. (Rs. ¾ - 11). The small pieces are used by Musalmáns as praying carpets. The patterns are various, most of them being in gaily coloured stripes. Every colour is brought into use from sober gray to brilliant orange.

Ropes.

Cotton is worked into twine and rope varying from the finest cord of two or three strands of yarn to heavy ropes. They are six feet to ten yards long and sell at 1½*d*. to 1*s*. (1-8 *as*.). From this cordage whip-lashes, horse reins, and yoking bands are made. These ropes are made on a primitive machine called *kám*. This includes a *kám* which is either a wooden frame if a rope of three strands is to be made, or a board if a rope of six strands is to be made, and is worth 6*d*. (4 *as*.); *vuttis* or sticks, three being used for a rope of three strands and six for a rope of six strands, worth nothing; a *putti*, a flat wooden board with holes, into which the strands are put and rolled, to give the proper twist to the rope, worth 1½*d*. (1 *anna*); a *bagai* a cone-shaped piece of wood, often a fragment of a Pinjári's hammer, in which six fair leaders are cut, through which the strands of the rope are passed, to keep them in place, is worth 3*d*. (2 *as*.); a mantt, a large piece of wood forked into two stems, to which an iron hook the *bore khudi* is fastened, to fix the end of the rope, and on the wood a large stone is placed heavy enough to give the needed drag on the rope, to prevent it curling into coils while being made, worth 6*d*. (4 *as*.).

Other miscellaneous goods are *páls*, in Kánarese called *guddars*, which are strong cloths or rather light carpets twelve to thirty feet long by eight to twenty-five broad, made by sewing firmly together stripes of strong stuff called *gudar putti*. Making these *guddarputtis* is a separate, and in Amingad, Ganjnihal and Bijápur in Bijápur, and Mugatkhán-Hubli, in Sampgaon a fairly large industry. These cloths are used to cover the big family-cart when the women and children are going to any domestic festival or religious fair; for making booths in markets; for rude tents used when on a long journey, especially by the Vanjáris, to protect their packs; for sorting oilseeds and grains; and for carrying grain from the fields. They are also used as carpets. A finer cloth called *padam* is used in the same way as the *guddar* and also for making bags and curtains. The *padams* are generally about fifteen feet by nine, of various colours, red and white and blue and white being the favourites; they cost 1*s*. to 2*s*. (Re. ½ - 1) a piece.

Chapter VI. Trade. Industries. *Tape.*

Tape or *ladi* is generally three to six feet long by three quarters to one and a half inches broad; it costs ½*d.* to 1*d.* (⅓-⅔ *as.*) a piece. Tape is of many sizes and sorts, both white and coloured, for binding and ornamenting native saddles, for embellishing horses' head gear, for making bridles, for fastening travelling and money bags, for binding bedding, and for making tents. A very broad thick strong tape called *navár* is much used in making tents, for stretching on sleeping cots, for waistbands for labouring people and regimental sepoys, and for messengers' belt or badges. Belts or *puttis* sown together are made into cloths or *páls* and *gudars* or carpets, and into bags for pack-bullocks, travelling bags, and other uses. All these articles are made from the yarn spun by the women on the spinning wheel during their leisure hours. Head harness for horses called *muki* is made of heavy tape about twenty by one and a quarter inches, woven from strong thick thread. They sell at 3*d.* to 6*d.* each (2-4 *as.*). Horse reins or *lagáms* are round ropes about as thick as a man's little finger and five to six and a half feet long; they sell at 6*d.* to 1*s.* (4-8 *as.*). *Guddarputtis* or carpet belts are generally coloured in red and white stripes, of different lengths, and of various breadths though seldom more than nine inches broad. A piece eighteen feet long costs 1*s.* to 2*s.* (Re. ½-1) according to quality. The machine used in weaving floor-cloths and tape is distinct from the loom. It is called a *tána*, is very rude and rough, and can be bought complete for 9*d.* (6 *as.*). It includes three parts, the *tána* frame worth 6*d.* (4 *as.*), the *ghut* or pegs worth 1½*d.* (1 *anna*), and the *hatha* or knife worth 1½*d.* (1 *anna*). The *tána*, a strong square wooden frame, is firmly fixed in the ground. Two cross sticks are fastened to the side posts, the upper stick being flat and the lower round. At the middle of the lower stick are a number of strings called the *biza*, through which the yarn to be woven is passed, and carried over to the top on the flat stick. The full length is then stretched and passed round a strong wooden peg or *guta* and brought back to the side of the *tána*, and there fastened to a second peg. This gives the length to be worked at full stretch. The weaver sits beside the frame with his reel of woof yarn, and passes the reel through the warp backwards and forwards giving the cloth a drive at each pass with the knife or *hatha*. This industry is almost entirely in the hands of the poorer class of Muhammadans. When he intends to make these miscellaneous articles, the weaver goes to the nearest market on market day, and buys hanks or *puttis* of coarse yarn. He takes the hanks home and opens and sorts them carefully into as many threads as the thickness of the intended article requires. These are then twisted into the necessary strands, or thick threads, by a largish spinning reel called a *bhirki*, worth 3*d.* (2 *as.*) This spinning reel is a cone-shaped piece of wood through whose centre a long thin stick is fastened. It is worked by taking the stick in the right hand, and fastening to it the end of the thread to be twisted. Then with the palm of his hand the man gives a quick rolling motion to the thread on his thigh, with the reel hanging down and rapidly revolving. When this length has been sufficiently twisted, he winds it round the reel, and starts with another length, and so on, until he has enough to fix the frame.

Chapter VI. Trade. Industries. *Weavers.*

The Belgaum weavers belong to many castes: Hatkars, Patvigars, Sális or degraded Patvigars, Padamsális, Lingáyats, Maráthás, Khatris or Chutris, and Musalmáns. The weavers are an orderly, quiet, and respectable class. Except some of the more wealthy who make expensive goods and employ workmen most weavers get all the work done by their own households and employ no outside labour. The engagement is always by contract, and a fair workman, on a long day's work, earns about 3¾*d.* (2½ *as.*). A weaver noted as a skilful and rapid worker earns more.

Shopkeepers and exporters make considerable advances to the weavers of the town in which they live, and the weavers are bound to deliver the goods within a certain time. Breaches of contract are rare. The richer townspeople order expensive cloths to be made of a particular size and description. They generally advance money while their orders are being carried out. Weavers of coarse cloth are fairly busy throughout the year. Weavers of the finer cloths are busy only during the eight fair months. Weavers work about eight hours a day, keep all the important holidays, and stop work on every *amávásya* or no-moon day. The average monthly earnings of a man his wife and two children vary from 8*s.* to 16*s.* (Rs. 4-8) if employed in weaving coarse cloth, and from 16*s.* to £1 12*s.* (Rs. 8-16) if employed in weaving the finer cloths.

Trade.

After meeting local wants, the different cotton goods are sent to other parts of the district and to places outside of the district. The cheaper and coarser goods are sold by the weavers, in the villages on market days, and they also go hawking them in the small places that have no regular markets. The higher class of goods are sold to shopkeepers and exporters. Numbers of pack-bullocks travel all over the country, whose owners both buy and sell local cotton goods. The Sampgaon and Kittur goods for the most part are made to meet the wants of the *malládu* or rainy country near the Sahyádris where the bulk of the people are poorer than the people of the black plains. The goods are bought by these people at the weekly fairs or are taken to them by peddlars. The goods from Athni go to Sháhápur and Kágvád and to Bágalkot and Jamkhandi; the Gokák goods go to Belgaum, Sháhápur, Nipáni, and Sankeshvar, and to Kolhápur and Bágalkot; the Chikodi goods go to Sankeshvar, Nipáni, Belgaum, and Sháhápur, to Kolhápur, Miraj, and Sángli, and to Málvan, Rájápur, and Vengurla in Ratnágiri; the Belgaum goods go to Sháhápur and Nandigad, and to Goa, Vengurla, Ratnágiri, Sávantvádi, and Málvan in the Konkan; the Sampgaon goods to Belgaum, Sháhápur, Nandigad, and the hill country, to Mudhol, Bágalkot, Jamkhandi, and Sholápur, and to Vengurla and other coast towns; the Parasgad goods go to Belgaum, Nipáni, Nandigad, and Dhárwár, Nargund, Mudhol, Bádámi, Kaládgi, Jamkhandi, Miraj, Kolhápur, Poona, Sholápur, and in small quantities to the coast; the Khánápur goods occasionally go in small quantities to Belgaum and the coast.

Weaving.

In 1817, when Belgaum and Bijápur came under British rule, almost all the cotton which was a very small crop was used locally. The number engaged in spinning and weaving was small, but with

Chapter VI.
Trade.
Industries.
Weaving.

increased security for life and property the number rapidly increased until the weavers became an important class. The demand for raw cotton and the supply of raw cotton increased together. This went on till 1840, when the local weaving trade was worth lákhs of rupees a year. The first known estimate of the amount of cotton used locally appears in 1852-53, when 3332 *khandis* of 784 pounds each are estimated to have been used in the district, against 4937 exported. The district at that time included the three important cotton-growing sub-divisions of South Bijápur, Bágalkot Bádámi and Hungund. For the five years ending 1853-54 an average is recorded of about 5063 *khandis* exported against 2772 *khandis* kept for home use. In 1854-55 the estimate is 3597 *khandis* kept for home use and 5792 *khandis* sent away; in 1855-56 the estimate is 2979 *khandis* kept for local use and 3865 *khandis* sent away; and in 1856-57 3913 *khandis* kept for local use and 5779 *khandis* sent away. For the five years ending 1856-57 the average is 3547 *khandis* kept for home use and 5416 *khandis* sent out of the country. In 1857 in Sampgaon about two hundred looms were at work in the villages of Deshnur, Báil-Hongal, and there were several looms in Sampgaon, Mugutkhán-Hubli, Mankatti, and other villages, over the whole sub-division supplying work for an estimated total of about five thousand. What they chiefly made were robes turbans and waistcloths of coarse cotton cloth, part to meet the local demand and the rest to send to the Konkan through Belgaum. Most of the weavers worked on their own account, a few employed labour and owned four or five looms. At Belgaum there were four to five hundred weavers who made coarse cloth only. The coarse Belgaum cloth and similar cloth made close by in Sháhápur was all used in the neighbourhood. Most other villages had ten to thirty weavers.

In 1857 in Chikodi the revenue survey officers found that slightly over two thousand persons were maintained by weaving in addition to about another thousand equally divided between the towns of Nipáni and Sankeshvar. Of the two thousand, over five hundred lived in Yamkanmardi, and about two hundred and fifty in Chikodi; the rest were scattered in small numbers among the different villages. No high-class goods were made. Only the usual waistcloths, turbans. women's robes, and coarse cloths; almost the whole was used locally, In the Ankalgi petty divsioin of the old Páchhápur sub-division less than five hundred persons were engaged in cotton weaving; of these three hundred were in Páchhápur, and the rest were scattered over the other thirty-two villages. The Kittur petty division of the Bidi sub-division contained forty-one villages, and had close upon eighteen hundred and fifty persons supported by weaving, nearly half of these being in Kittur itself, a town of over seven thousand five hundred inhabitants; the others were scattered through the rest of the petty division.

Large as it still is hand-loom weaving is a falling industry and grows less year by year. The competition of English that is Manchester goods, locally called *manaji peit mál,* that is goods made at the town of Manaji, has been growing stronger during the last twenty-five years, and during the last twelve years the competition

Chapter VI.
Trade.
Industries.
Weaving.

of Bombay-made yarn and cloth has been still more severe. The branch of the local weaving industry that has been most affected is the weaving of the more costly and better paying goods. Many places that used to do a large trade in piecegoods now weave nothing but the coarser cloths. At one time, the weavers were one of the wealthiest of up-country classes. But for many years the margin of profit left to the weaver has been so small that many came to poverty. The 1876 famine fell with peculiar severity on the weavers as they had no store of grain, and as soon as grain became dear the demand for their cloth ceased. Most of them were unfitted for the heavy labour of the ordinary relief works. Still some of them took to labour and are said to be better off than they were as weavers. Since 1877 the position of the weavers has been improved by a brisker demand for cloth and by the cheapness of yarn and of grain. The hand-loom weavers are likely to suffer from the opening of railways. Railways will tend to raise the local price of grain and will cheapen the price at which English and Bombay cloth can compete with the produce of the local hand-looms. To this will probably be added the still more ruinous competition of local weaving mills. In 1880 Mr. Walton estimated that about twenty per cent of the cotton crop was used locally. All that is used is Kumta that is local cotton.

Printing.

At Murgod, Gokák, and Manoli, cloth is stamped or printed with wooden blocks in various patterns and colours. This was at one time a large and important industry. Even now more calico-printing is done at Murgod than in the whole of the rest of the Bombay Karnátak. At Murgod about fifteen Shimpi families find constant employment as calico-printers. They work about eight hours a day and keep all the leading Bráhmanic and local holidays. Their women and children help in washing the cloth. Their average daily earnings vary from 6*d.* to 9*d.* (4 - 6 *as.*). They sell their prints from place to place or at their houses to cloth dealers. They suffered severely during the 1876 famine, and are depressed by the constant fall in the price of imported prints. In brilliancy, purity, and fastness the dyes used by these Belgaum block printers are better than those in imported English prints. In spite of the hardest treatment in washing, a local print keeps its colour and lustre, till it is worn threadbare. The printing is done by hand with small blocks of *hasan* Briedelia retusa wood worth 6*d.* to 8*s.* (Rs. ¼ - 4) on which designs are skilfully and tastefully carved in relief by men of the Jingar caste. The printers work the blocks with great speed and skill, and their wares are still very popular. The fall in price prevents the present printers from doing such good work as their fathers did. Still they have a surprising knack of choosing patterns and colours which please both at a distance and close at hand. In their competition with the local printers the outside prints have the advantages of cheapness and variety.

Calico Printing.

Only the coarser *khádi* or *hachda* cloths are used in block printing, as coarse cloth shows the prints and colours much better than fine cloth. In calico-printing the cloth is taken to water, if possible running water, and is thoroughly soaked and well shaken.

Chapter VI.
Trade.
Industries.

The washing and drying go on between three and four days until all trace of size has disappeared. The cloth is then soaked for three days and pulled about in a mixture of oil and water. It is again taken and washed in the river, and after a second thorough drying it is steeped in a mixture of myrobalans or *hirdas* and water. After this second drying it is ready for printing.

The articles used in making dyes are *hirdás* or myrobalans, *nil* or indigo, *kusbi* Carthamus tinctorius oil, iron filings, anters gum, *máephals* or gallnuts, and *surang* a brown dye. Indigo is brought from the Madras Presidency and gallnuts and *surang* from Sholápur. The other materials are of local origin. In making ready the dye, iron filings are dropped into water and kept in water for three days. The iron-laden liquid is drawn off little by little, as much water as has been taken away being each time added. When enough iron-water has been stored gum is mixed with it until the compound becomes thick soft and sticky. If the ground-work is to be coloured the cloth is soaked in a dye of the desired shade. After the ground-work is dyed, the stamping begins with the iron-water and gum, mixed with the required colour, or, if no other shade is added, the iron-water and gum print a dark ironstone. After stamping so as thoroughly to fix the prints and colours, the cloth is boiled in *surang* and water. The printed cloth is dried and again taken to a river and gently washed. It is then finished by a dressing of rice starch and dried and the starching and drying are repeated time after time for six days. The charge for the whole process is 2*s.* 6*d.* (Rs. 1¼) for each piece ten yards long by one yard wide. Among the cloths printed are *józams* a light carpet for floors, *pachodis* large cloths for covering the body, chintzes, dark red spotted prints much used for clothes by Muhammadans, *palangpuds* for bed coverlets, waistcloths and turbans, *asmangiris* or ceiling cloths, and *pardás* or curtains used in Musalmán houses, tapes for cushions and mattresses, rose-coloured chintz, tent lining, a variety of red printed cloths for bedding, native saddle-cloths, and book-binding cloths. As a rule, one yard of printed cloth costs 9*d.* to 1*s.* (6 - 8 *as.*) The floor-cloths or *józams* vary in price from 6*s.* to £1 12*s.* (Rs. 3 - 16) according to the length and breadth of the cloth, a *pachodi* costs 4*s.* to 16*s.* (Rs. 2 - 8), and a bed cover 1*s.* 6*d.* to 2*s.* 6*d.* (Rs. ¾ - 1¼). Murgod, the long established head-quarters of calico-printing, still sends a considerable quantity of goods to Sháhápur, Belgaum, Dhárwár, Kaládgi, Kolhápur, Miraj, Sángli, Jamkhandi, and the coast.

Dyeing.

Cotton thread dyeing is a separate industry at Gokák and Manoli in Parasgad. It supports 250 families of Bandhgárs or workers in red, who belong to the Náglik division of the Lingáyat sect, and eleven families of Nilgárs or indigo-workers who, except two families of which one are Chunárs and the other are Musalmáns, are mostly Maráthás and Námdev Shimpis. The Bandhgárs are said to have come about a century ago from Kalyán in the Nizám's country and Adváni or Adoni in Bellári. About 1850 there were three hundred families. Of the origin of the Nilgárs nothing is known. Since 1850 their number has increased from nine to eleven families. A cotton-thread dyer's appliances are simple. They are a mortar and a few pestles for powdering *surang* root and *pápdi* or carbonate of soda, a copper vessel for boiling the yarn, and two or more large wide-mouthed earthen vessels to prepare and store the dyes. As a rule each dyer makes his own dye-stuffs. The chief dyes for colouring red are the roots of the *surang* which come from Sholápur and *pápdi* which is used when a fast colour is not wanted. The black dye is indigo. In preparing the red dye the *surang* root or *papdi* is pounded to fine powder. To 4½ pounds of this powder are added half a pound of alum powder, a pound of oil, and some water. Besides indigo the black dye contains *tarvad* (Cassia auriculata) seed, lime, and milk-bush or plantain ashes. Indigo and *tarvad* seed are powdered and put into a large-mouthed earthen vessel partially buried in sheep or goat dung, and over the indigo and *tarvad* a solution of lime and ashes is poured into the vessel. The mixture is stirred every day and is left for five days in the earthen vessel, when it is considered fit for dyeing. The thread they dye is both of local and of Bombay manufacture. Bombay thread being finer is greatly used by rich Bandhgárs and is woven into fine cloth. The usual steps taken to make the yarn ready for the dye is to boil it in a strong caustic lye in which carbonate of soda plays an important part. Alum is one of the commonest mordants. The lye consists of goat or sheep dung, milk-bush or plantain tree ashes, oil, and water. The yarn to be dyed is steeped in the lye, trampled under foot, and dried in the sun. This process is repeated for eight days. On the ninth day, the yarn is soaked in water, boiled for some time, washed in clean water, and dried in the sun. It is then dipped into the prepared colour, and the dipping is repeated four to eight times according to the desired brilliancy. In some places yarn is boiled; in other places it is simply washed and dipped into the colouring matter, and steeped in the dye-stuff a larger or a smaller number of times according to the required blackness.

The Bandhgárs find much work all the year round, and the Nilgárs are busiest between June and October As a rule both Bandhgárs and Nilgárs work eight or nine hours a day, from seven to eleven or twelve in the forenoon, and, after the midday rest, from two to six. They never work at night. If work is pressing they rise about four and go to a river or reservoir to wash the yarn. They keep most of the leading local and Brahmánic holidays. The Musalmán Nilgár family keep three Musalmán holidays, but stop work on many Hindu holidays because the weavers their employers are mostly Hindus. The women help the men. A Bandhgár earns 6*d.* to 9*d.* (4-6 *as.*) a day. The rich Bandhgárs dye their own yarn and sell it to weavers at 16*s.* to £1 12*s.* (Rs. 8-16) a *chaukdi* of twenty-four hanks, each hank weighing sixteen *tolás*. Bandhgárs who have no capital remain as dyers in the service of their richer castefellows. Bandhgárs' yarn is used locally, and when the local market is overstocked and dull, it is sometimes taken to the surrounding towns. Nilgárs dye weavers' yarn and are paid according to the quality of the colour. Poor Nilgárs work under rich Nilgárs. Of two hundred Bandhgár families fifteen are rich living in substantial houses and owning £200 to £5000 (Rs. 2000-50,000), eighty-five are middle class, and a hundred are poor. Of the eleven families of Nilgárs the two richest

Chapter VI. Trade. Industries.

are said to be worth about £500 (Rs. 5000), three are middle class, and six are poor. The Bandhgárs suffered much during the 1876-77 famine. The competition of outside goods is rapidly ruining their calling, and some of the families who were reduced to distress by the last famine are said to be likely to leave their homes and settle in some other part of the country. The Nilgárs also suffered during the last famine. Neither Bandhgárs nor Nilgárs are bound by any trade rules.

Silk-Dyeing.

About forty families of the Sankar caste in Belgaum and about ten families of Sális at Gokák spin and dye raw silk. The silk-workers at Belgaum are labourers and those at Gokák capitalists. Their business is dull during the rainy season and brisk at other times. The raw silk comes from Bombay. After it is coloured it is generally sold to local weavers at about £1 8*s*. (Rs. 14) a pound. The workers are well off and the industry is rising.

Wooden Toys.

Fancy furniture and wooden toys are made here and there in the district. Gokák and Deshnur in Sampgaon are noted for their wooden toys. Toy-making supports twelve families in Gokák and three in Deshnur. All of them belong to the Jingar caste who claim to be Kshatriyas or corruptly Chhatris. They are said to have been brought into Belgaum about a century and a half ago by one Bhimráv son of Anandappa, the headman of Kágal in Kolhápur. Bhimrav's grandson Bápu Jingar, a skilful painter and wooden toy-maker, was patronised by a chief of Kolhápur about eighty years ago. He lived for ten years in the service of the prince and after his patron died he went to Gokák and lived among his relations, maintaining himself by making wooden toys, palanquins, and the *abdágirs* or ornamental umbrellas which are carried over native chiefs. It was he who taught his relations how to make wooden toys. The Jingars are also employed to paint temples and rich men's houses. They have given up their old craft of leather-working and every member of their small community is forbidden to work in leather on pain of losing caste, though in practice this offence is condoned by a caste feast. The wood generally used for toys is all local woods, silk-cotton *sávar* Bombax malabaricum, *umbar* Ficus glomerata, and teak. Besides wood, the chief materials used are varnish, beeswax, coloured tin plates called *begad* (M.), and gold-leaf. These things are brought from Belgaum or bought of local dealers. The material generally used for colouring red is vermilion, for yellow orpiment, for white whitelead, and for black indigo. A wooden toy-maker has six tools, a saw worth 1*s*. to £1 (Rs. ½-10), an adze worth 4*s*. to 8*s*. (Rs. 2-4), a plane worth 2*s*. to 8*s*. (Rs. 1-4), a file worth 1*s*. to 2*s*. (Re. ½-1), and two chisels one for coarse work worth 1*s*. to 4*s*. (Rs. ½-2), and the other for fine work with a very sharp point worth 3½*d*. to 6*d*. (2¼-4 *as*.).

They make cradles, palanquins, toys, fruit, animals, men, and gods.[1] They are skilful workmen, and their wares are much

[1] The chief articles made and their prices are: A Bráhman his wife and child Rs. 5; a Marátha his wife and child, Rs. 5; a Váni his wife and child Rs. 5; a Váni at work, Rs. 3; a cultivator Rs. 5; a weaver Rs. 3; a blacksmith Rs. 3; a potter Rs. 2½; a goldsmith Rs. 2½; a tailor Rs. 2; a calico-printer Rs. 2; a Nilgár dyer Rs. 2; a Bandhgár dyer Rs. 2¼; a Kurub blanket-weaver

Chapter VI.

Trade.

Industries.

Wooden Toys.

admired especially by Europeans. The figures are life-like and the fruit is surprisingly natural and highly finished. Their wares have a local sale among rich Hindus and Pársi merchants of Belgaum, but most of them go to Bombay to the agents of Bombay work-box makers. From Bombay their wares find their way all over India. At times advances are made and the demand is strong, but, as a rule, it is rather dull. Wooden toy-makers generally work about nine hours a day, from seven to eleven in the morning, and from two to six in the afternoon. When orders are pressing they work extra hours sometimes till nine. During these extra hours they do not carve or paint; they mix dyes and make other preparations. Boys help the men in preparing colours, the women do not help the men. The average yearly income of a toy-making family is said to vary from £10 to £30 (Rs. 100 - 300). They generally make articles to order, and seldom have more than two or three pounds (Rs. 20 - 30) invested in stock. They are unsteady workers and never finish in time. They take few holidays, but are often idle from want of work. During the 1876 famine, except a few families who were supported by the Chief of Jamkhandi, they were reduced to distress. Many had to sell their property and a few had to leave their homes. The low price of grain in some of the years since the famine has helped them and some have recovered from their famine losses. They are

---

Rs. 2½; a Teli oil-presser Rs. 8; a butcher Rs. 3; a comb-maker Rs. 2½; a barber Rs. 4; a washerman and his ass Rs. 3; a Bhisti or water-carrier Rs. 3; a Bhisti with his water-bag by his side, Rs. 2; a Burud or basket-maker Rs. 2; a Vadar with his cart Rs. 5; a banker Rs. 3; a Jingar or harness-maker Rs. 3; a painter Rs. 3; a shoemaker Rs. 4; a woman spinning cotton Rs. 3; a woman ginning cotton Rs. 2; a schoolmistress Rs. 3; a Kásár putting bangles on the hands of a woman Rs. 5; a Patvegar twisting silk Rs. 5; a well for watering Rs. 12; a water-spring for bathing Rs. 7; a well for drinking Rs. 7; a Korvanji with her child Rs. 3; a liquor-seller Rs. 7; a Máng or a carrier of dead cattle Rs. 2; a snuff-maker Rs. 5; a dancing girl Rs. 9; a Jangam or Lingáyat priest Rs. 2; a Chalvádi with bell and ladle Rs. 3; a Bairági or ascetic Rs. 2; Gondhalis or beggars Rs. 2; a Kid-bid-joshi or gipsy Rs. 3; a Dasáyya beggar Rs. 2½; a horn-blower Rs. 2; an old man and an old woman Rs. 5; a Puránik or reciter of hymns Rs. 5; four wrestlers Rs. 8; a snake-charmer Rs. 9; a Sudgad-Shiddi or sexton Rs. 2½; a Lamáni or carrier with his wife Rs. 9; a Mena Rs. 9; a palanquin Rs. 10; a Moglai carriage Rs. 10; a Chopdár or mace-bearer Rs. 2; a Pattevála or peon Rs. 2; a Kázi or Musalmán priest Rs. 2; a Mulla or Musalmán school-master Rs. 2; a Pársi Rs. 2½; an Emperor Rs. 30; five princes Rs. 15; five rich men Rs. 15; a Bráhman bathing Rs. 3; a cow Rs. 2; an elephant Rs. 10; a camel Rs. 3; a panther Rs. 10; a she-buffalo Rs. 2; a she-goat Rs. 2; a he-goat Rs. 2; a ram Rs. 2; a tiger Rs. 3; a bear Rs. 2; a boar Rs. 2; a stag Rs. 2; a deer Rs. 2; a hare Rs. 2; a jackal Rs. 2; a mouse Re. 1; a scorpion 8 *as.*; a *heggana* or rat Re. 1; a lizard 8 *as.*; a *jhural* or beetle 8 *as.*; a dog Rs. 2½; a monkey Rs. 2½; an ape Rs. 2½; a lizard Re. 1; a snake Rs. 3; a large serpent Rs. 3; a parrot Re. 1; a dove Re. 1; a sparrow Re. 1; a starling Re. 1; a crane Rs. 2; a crow Re. 1; a hen Rs. 2½; a cock Rs. 3; a lion Rs. 3; a *Kámdhenu* or cow of paradise Rs. 3; a *tás* a kind of skylark Re. 1; a fish Re. 1; a tortoise Rs. 3; a crab Rs. 2; a bunch of mangoes Rs. 1½; a bunch of plantains Rs. 1½; a jack fruit Rs. 1¼; a watermelon 12 *as.*; a pomegranate 6 *as.*; a fig 6 *as.*; a jujub fruit 6 *as.*; an almond 4 *as.*; a sugarcane 8 *as.*; an apple 6 *as.*; a tamarind pod 8 *as.*; a bunch of grapes Re. 1; a pine-apple Rs. 1½; a pair of maize heads 6 *as.*; a guava 6 *as.*; a cashewnut 6 *as.*; a lemon 6 *as.*; an orange 7 *as.*; a *papanas* pumelo 10 *as.*; a *sitáfal* or custard-apple 6 *as.*; a *bhendi* 2 *as.*; a brinjal 4 *as.*; a gourd 8 *as.*; garlic 4 *as.*; chillies green 1 *a.*; chilli red 1 *a.*; a *padval* or snake-gourd 6 *as.*; a *rátále* or sweet-potato 2 *as.*; a *dodke* 4 *as.*; *tondle* a vegetable 2 *as.*; a cucumber 3 *as.*; a *kavit* or wood-apple 4 *as.*; *máhulung* a fruit 6 *as.*; *popai* a fruit 4 *as.*; *rámfal* or sweet sop 6 *as.*; a white gourd 6 *as.*; a *gájar* 2 *as.*; Cassia fistula pod 2 *as.*; *kárle* or bitter gourd 4 *as.*; a radish 6 *as.*; a carrot or onion 4 *as.*; *shevaga* or horse-radish pod 2 *as.*; an *avala* or emblic myrobalan 8 *as.*; a *karvand* or corinda 8 *as.*

Chapter VI.
Trade.
Industries.

not bound by a guild, every one is free to sell his things at any price he chooses.

Copper.

Copper vessels are made in Belgaum by sixty families of Jain Bogars and by Musalmán labourers. The copper comes from Bombay in sheets chiefly by sea through Vengurla. The copper is beaten into cooking and drinking vessels of different forms. The demand is steady. The Bogars sell their articles direct to consumers at Belgaum and other market towns and fairs. The price varies from 3*d.* to £5 (Rs. ⅛ - 50) according to weight, the rule being 6¾*d.* (4½ *as.*) the *sher* of twenty *tolás*. The workers are well off and the trade is steady.

Pottery.

Earthen pots are made throughout the district by Marátha and Lingáyat Kumbhárs who make earthen pots of various sizes, tiles, and bricks. The pots and tiles are made on a wheel turned on a short pole fixed upright in the ground. Bricks are made in a quadrangular wooden frame. Potters are busy during the hot season and idle during the rains. They work about ten hours a day. They keep all local and Bráhmanic holidays and rest on every no-moon or *amávásya*. The women and children help the men in preparing the earth for the pots. They take their pots for sale to market towns and sell the tiles at home. The price of a pot varies according to size from ⅛*d.* to 1*s.* ($\frac{1}{12}$-8 *as.*). The price of tiles varies from 8*s.* to 16*s.* (Rs. 4 - 8), and of burnt bricks from 4*s.* to £1 4*s.* (Rs. 2 - 12) a thousand. The average yearly earnings of a family range from £5 to £20 (Rs. 50 - 200). As a class potters are poor. The craft is neither rising nor falling.

Oil-Pressing.

Oil is pressed from *til* Sesamum indicum, *kusbi* Carthamus tinctorius, *bhuising* or groundnuts Arachis hypogea, and *ambádi* or hemp Hibiscus cannabinus. The oil-pressers are Lingáyats, Maráthás, Khatris, and Musalmáns. Telis or oilmen are found in almost all towns and large villages. Their chief settlements are Belgaum, Kittur in Sampgaon, and Athni. The oilseed is partly grown in the district, partly brought from Bijápur, Sátára, and Kolhápur. Most families have some capital. The oil-mill includes a *gán* or cylindrical stone block half buried in the ground, and a *kani* or wooden roller to which a heavy weight is hung and which is turned by two bullocks. About thirty-five or forty pounds of *til*, *bhuising*, *kusbi* flour, or *ambádi* are thrown into the hole of the block, and the roller is placed on the block and turned. When the seed is crushed the powder is mixed with water and the roller is again put in motion till all the oil is pressed out. The employment is steady. The mill is generally at work twice a day from six to eleven and from two to seven. Oil-pressers never work on Mondays. The women help them in grinding the oil-seed. The average daily earnings of a family are 4½*d.* to 9*d.* (3 - 6 *as.*). The pressers sell the oil to oil-dealers or direct to consumers at their houses, and sometimes hawk it from door to door and from village to village. The price of oil is about 6*s.* (Rs. 3) for twenty-six pounds (1 *man*). Oil-pressers as a class are well off. Within the last few years their profits have been greatly reduced by the competition of kerosine oil which almost all classes have taken to use as a lighting oil.

CHAPTER VII.

HISTORY.

Chapter VII.
History.
Early History.

BELGAUM has none of the rock temples, and, so far as is known, none of the inscriptions which in so many parts of Western India determine the rulers of the country during the centuries before and after the Christian era. But, chiefly through the labours of Mr. J. F. Fleet of the Bombay Civil Service, for the history of the eight hundred years ending with the close of the thirteenth century, materials in the shape of thirty stone and nine copperplate inscriptions have been discovered, deciphered, and translated.

Early Kadambas, A.D. 500.

As far as present information goes, the oldest place in the present district of Belgaum is Palasige, Halasige, or Halsi ten miles south-east of Khánápur and twenty-three miles south of Belgaum. Seven copperplates found within three miles of Halsi show that about the fifth century after Christ it was the capital of a dynasty of nine Kadamba kings.[1] Almost all these early Kadamba plates begin and end with a Jain salutation, and, except one which records a grant of land to a private person, all record grants of land or of villages in furtherance of the Jain religion. Five of the plates mention Palásika or Halsi and one records the building of a Jain temple at Halsi.

The later Early Hindu history of the district, till the Musalmán conquest in the beginning of the fourteenth century, belongs to four periods: An Early Chalukya and Western Chalukya period lasting to about A.D. 760; a Ráshtrakuta period from about A.D. 760 to A.D. 973; a Ratta period (850-1250) during which the district was directly governed by a dynasty of Ratta chiefs at first as feudatories of the Ráshtrakutas and the Western Chálukyas and then (1170) of their own authority till their final conquest by the Devgiri Yádavs about 1250; and the fourth or Devgiri Yádav period from 1250 till their overthrow by the Muhammadans about 1320.

Though no inscriptions or copperplates of the Early (550-610) or of the Western Chalukyas[2] (610-760) have been found within

[1] The exact date of the early Kadamba dynasty cannot be fixed as the plates contain no reference to any known era. Still, from the fact that the plates are all in the Sanskrit language, and in the Western India Buddhist cave alphabet characters not yet developed into old or Hála Kánarese, and from the allusions which they contain to contemporary events the plates may be approximately assigned to about the fifth century. Fleet's Kánarese Dynasties, 9-10.

[2] The name Chalukya is derived by tradition from *chulka*, *chuluka*, or *chaluka*, a waterpot, from which their ancestor is said to have sprung. This appears to be a late story, as though *chulka* a waterpot may be the origin of the later forms of the name Chálukya in the Deccan and Chaulukya in Gujarát, it cannot be the origin of the early name which is written Chalkya, Chalikya, and Chalukya. They claim to belong to the Soma-vansh or lunar race and mention a succession of fifty-nine kings, rulers of Ayodhya and after them sixteen more who ruled over the region of the south. The names of seven early Chalukya kings have been found who reigned from about 550 to 610. In 610 the Chálukya dominions were divided into an eastern kingdom whose head-quarters were Vengi in the delta of the Krishna and the Godávari, and a western kingdom whose head-quarters are believed to have been at Bádámi in Bijápur. Of this western branch called the Western Chalukyas the names of six kings have been found who ruled from 610 to 760 about which time they were overthrown by the Ráshtrakutas. Details are given in Fleet's Kánarese Dynasties, 17-30.

Chapter VII.
History.

Belgaum limits, the large number of Early and Western Chalukya inscriptions which have been found in Dhárwár and Kaládgi and the mention of their sway over the Kuhundi or Kundi Three Thousand make it almost certain that the Early and Western Chalukyas held the Belgaum district.[1] About 760 when the Ráshtrakutas overthrew Western Chálukya sovereignty, Belgaum, or the Kuhundi Three Thousand, passed with the rest of the Chalukya dominions to their conquerers. Though no inscriptions recording gifts by Ráshtrakuta kings have been found within Belgaum limits, a trace of Ráshtrakuta power and dominion long survived in the Ratta Great Circle Lords or Mahámandaleshvars.[2] This family, for about 350 years, first as feudatories of the Ráshtrakutas (875-973), then as feudatories of the Western Chálukyas (973-1170), and then apparently of their own authority, until their conquest by the Devgiri Yádavs about 1250, held the government of the Kuhundi or Kundi Three Thousand. Their capital was Sugandhvarti the modern Saundatti in Parasgad, forty miles east of Belgaum, and afterwards (1210) Venugrám or Velugrám the modern Belgaum. Their inscriptions have been found at Belgaum in the Belgaum sub-division, at Bhoj and Sankeshvar in Chikodi, at Kalhole and Konnur in Gokák, at Badli Saundatti and Sogal in Parasgad, at Bail-Hongal Hannikeri Nesargi and Sampgaon in Sampgaon, at Mulgund in Dhárwár, at Khánápur and Ráybág in Kolhápur, and at Lokápur on the Belgaum-Kaládgi road about sixty miles north-east of Belgaum.[3] These inscriptions throw much light on the Ratta system of administration. Territorial divisions are mentioned, varying from a group of six to a province of twelve thousand villages, as the Nesargi Six, the Saundatti Twelve, the Hubli Twelve, the Banihatti Eighteen, the Venugrám or Belgaum Seventy, the Belvola Three Hundred, the Konkan Nine Hundred, the Kundi Three Thousand, the Palasige or Halsi Twelve Thousand, and the Banavási Twelve Thousand. Among the different grades of officials mentioned, the *Mahámandaleshvar* or *Mahásámanta* the Great Lord of the Circle, the *Mandaleshvar* or *Sámanta* the Lord of the Circle, and the *Dandnáyak* or Commander of the Forces appear as the local representatives of the reigning monarch; the *Rájguru* or royal spiritual preceptor with his counsellors appears as minister under the three chief officials; a *Náyak* appears in charge of a circle of villages; and, finally, the *Gávundu* or village headman

Rattas, 850-1250.

[1] The Kuhundi or Kundi district of three thousand villages, a division of the Kuntala province, included the greater part of the Belgaum district and the native states to the north of it, and the south-western parts of the Kaládgi district. Dynasties of the Kánarese Districts, 20 note 1.

[2] It is not certain whether the Ráshtrakutas were northerners or a family of Rattas or Reddis the widespread tribe of Kánarese husbandmen who were formerly the strongest fighting class in the Karnátak and Maisur. Mr. Fleet seems to incline to a northern origin and to trace the name to Ráshtrakuta or Ráshtrapati, a title meaning a district head who is subordinate to some overlord. But it seems not improbable that the Ráshtrakutas were Rattas or Reddis, and that the main branch when they rose to supreme power Sanskritised their name, while the side branch of Rattas kept their original name. The names of twenty-two Ráshtrakuta kings have been found the seventh of whom Dantivarma II. overthrew Western Chalukya power about 760. His fifteen successors were powerful sovereigns who ruled till 973 when the last of their race Kakka III. was defeated and slain by the revived Western Chalukyas, better known under the slightly changed name of Western Chálukyas. Details are given in Fleet's Kánarese Dynasties, 31-38.

[3] Journal Bombay Branch Royal Asiatic Society, X. 167-278.

Chapter VII.
History.
Rattas, 850-1250.

appears sometimes with a council of traders in charge of each village. The modern *taraf, kariyát, mahál, táluka,* and *pargana* represent the division of the country into circles of specified numbers of villages, and the present hereditary district and village officers represent the lowest of the old grades of functionaries.[1] In some of their inscriptions the Rattas call themselves Ráshtrakutas; and in one or two passages they profess to belong to the lineage of the Ráshtrakuta Krishna II. (875-911). In the majority of instances they use the name Ratta, and were probably (like the Ráshtrakutas) a local division of the Reddi or Ratta caste. They were of the Jain religion. They held the title of *Lattalur-puravar-ádhisvara* or *Lattanur-puravar-ádhisvara,* Supreme lord of Lattalur or Lattanur, the best of cities. Their banner was a golden Garud or man-vulture, their mark was redlead, and their musical instrument was the *trivali* or three-stringed harp.[2]

---

[1] Journal Bombay Branch Royal Asiatic Society, X. 118 note 2.

[2] The Ratta family tree is :

- Merada.
  - Prithvirâma. *Saka* 797 A.D. 875.
    - Pittuga.
      - Shántivarmá. *Saka* 902 A.D. 980.
        - ⋮
          - Nanna.
            - Kártavirya I. *Saka* 902 A.D. 980.
              - Dávari, or Dáyima.
              - Kannakaira I.
                - Erega.
                  - Sena I.
                    - Kannakaira II. *Saka* 1004 and 1008. A.D. 1082 and 1096.
                    - Kártavirya II. *Saka* 1009 and 1018. A.D. 1087 and 1096.
                      - Sena II.
                        - Kártavirya III. *Saka* 1065 and 1086. A.D. 1143 and 1164.
                          - Lakshmideva I. *Saka* 1130 A.D. 1208.
                            - Kártavirya IV. *Saka* 1121 and 1140. A.D. 1199 and 1218.
                              - Lakshmideva II. *Saka* 1150 A.D. 1228.
                            - Mallikárjuna. *Saka* 1123 and 1130. A.D. 1201 and 1208.
                - Anka. *Saka* 970 A.D. 1048.

Chapter VII.
History.
Rattas, 850-1250.

Merada and his son Prithvirâma were originally teachers of the Jain Kâreya sect of the holy Mailâpatirtha. About A.D. 875-6[1] (*Saka* 797) Prithvirâma was invested with the rank and authority of a *Mahásámanta* or *Mahámandaleshvara* by the Ráshtrakuta king Krishna II. Of Pittuga, the son of Prithvirâma, except that he repulsed a certain Ajavarmá, and that his wife was Nijikabbe or Nijiyabbe no record remains. Pittuga's son, Shántivarmá or Shánta, whose wife was Chandikabbe, is described in an inscription found at Saundatti and dated 980-1 (*Saka* 902, the Vikrama *samvatsara*),[2] as a feudatory of the Western Chálukya king Taila II. (972-997).[3] The inscription records a grant of land to a new temple of Jina built by Shántivarma in Saundatti and notices a gift of two pounds (4 *sers*) of oil from each oil-mill for the lamp of the god at the festival of *Dipávali* in October-November. After Shántivarma a break in the genealogy leaves nothing to show in what relation he stood to his successor. Of Nanna, also called Nannapayyarána, no details are known. Of Nanna's son Kártavirya I. or Katta I., one inscription has been found at Sogal fifteen miles north-west of Saundatti. It is of the same date (A.D. 980-1) as the inscription of his predecessor Shántivarmá, and records that Katta was governing the Kundi country as the feudatory of the Western Chálukya king Taila II. (973-997). Another and later inscription again speaks of Katta as the feudatory of Taila II. (973-997), who is mentioned by his title Áhávamalla I. It also records that Katta fixed the boundaries of the Kuhundi or Kundi country. Of Dávari or Dáyima, Kannakaira I. or Kanna I., and Erega or Eraga, no inscriptions have been found. Of Anka two inscriptions occur at Saundatti. One of them is the first part of a tablet which also bears a later inscription. It is dated A.D. 1048-9 (*Saka* 970, the Sarvadhári *samvatsara*), and records that Anka was a feudatory of the Western Chálukya king Someshvar I. (1042-1068). The other inscription in which Anka is named is a fragment of the same date. Of Sena I. or Kálasena I., and his wife Mailáladevi, no details are known. His eldest son, Kannakaira II. or Kanna II., is mentioned as one of the feudatory *Mahámandaleshvaras* in a Bijápur grant dated A.D. 1082-83, of the Western Chálukya king Vikramáditya VI.[4] Kanna II. is also mentioned as a feudatory of the same king and of his son Jayakarna, in an inscription at Konnur near Gokák dated 1087-8 (*Saka* 1009, the Prabhava *samvatsara*).[5] Kanna seems to have been alive and to have remained in power, with his younger brother Kártavirya II., up to 1096-7 (*Saka* 1018, the Dhátu *samvatsara*), as one of the Saundatti inscriptions mentions him in connection with that date.[6]

---

[1] Journal Bombay Branch Royal Asiatic Society, X. 194; Páli Sanskrit and Old Kánarese Inscriptions, No. 88.

[2] Journal Bombay Branch Royal Asiatic Society, X. 204.

[3] This is the earliest mention that the over-lordship had passed from the Ráshtrakutas to the Western Chálukyas. As Shántivarma's successors down to Sena II. (about A.D. 1128) continued feudatory to the Chálukyas, this part of the country seems like Dhárwár to have passed back from the Ráshtrakutas to the Chálukyas towards the end of the tenth century.

[4] Indian Antiquary, I. 80.

[5] Journal Bombay Branch Royal Asiatic Society, X. 287; Páli Sanskrit and Old Kánarese Inscriptions, No. 93.

[6] Ditto, 194; Pali Sanskrit and Old Kánarese Inscriptions, No. 88.

Of Kártavirya II. or Katta II., who was also called Senana-Singa or the Lion of Sena and his wife Bhagaladevi, four inscriptions remain. These are a dateless fragment at Saundatti, whose preamble shows that Katta held office under the Western Chálukya king Someshvar II. (1068-1075);[1] a second at Saundatti dated 1087-8 (*Saka* 1009, the Prabhava *samvatsara*); a third at Vatnál four miles north of Saundatti dated either in the same or in the following year; and the already mentioned Saundatti inscription of A.D. 1096-7. Of Sena II. or Kálasena II., and his wife Lakshmidevi, no details are known. Of Kártavirya III. or Kattama, and his wife Padmaladevi or Padmávati, four inscriptions have been found, two at Khánápur in Kolhápur dated 1143-4 (*Saka* 1065, the Rudhirodgári *samvatsara*) and 1162-3 (*Saka* 1084, the Chitrabhánu *samvatsara*);[2] one at Bail-Hongal six miles east of Sampgaon dated 1164-5 (*Saka* 1086, the Tárana *samvatsara*);[3] and one at Konnur, the date of which is effaced.[4] In the Khánápur inscription Kattama is described as the feudatory of the Western Chálukya king Jagadekamalla II. (1138-1150), and in the Bail-Hongal inscription, as having been the feudatory of Taila III. (1150-1162) of the same dynasty. In the Konnur inscription Kattama has the title of *Chakravarti* or Emperor. This title and the fact that Kattama's descendants, though they keep the title of *Mahámandaleshvar*, speak of themselves as enjoying sovereignty or *sámrájya*, show that Kattama took advantage of the confusion that prevailed during the last years of the Chálukya dynasty (1153-1164) to establish himself as an independent ruler.

Chapter VII.

History.

Rattas, 850-1250.

Of Lakshmideva I., Lakshmana, or Lakshmidhara, whose wife was Chandaladevi or Chandrikádevi, one inscription remains at Hannikeri about six miles north-west of Sampgaon, dated 1208-9 (*Saka* 1130, the Vibhava *samvatsara*). This inscription has the first mention that the Ratta capital was moved from Sugandhavarti or Saundatti to Venugrám or Belgaum, and that, in addition to the Kundi Three-thousand, they held the Belgaum Seventy, which they seem to have won from the Goa Kádambas (1000-1250). This inscription speaks of Lakshmideva I. as a descendant of the Ráshtrakuta king Krishna II. to whom it gives the title of *Kandhára-puravarádhisvara* that is Supreme lord of Kandhárapura, the best of cities, probably the modern Kandhár in the Nizám's territory about 125 miles north-east of Sholápur and 120 miles north of the Ráshtrakuta capital of Málkhet.[5] Kandhár may have been one of the original Ráshtrakuta cities; but so far no other mention of it has been traced. Of Kártavirya IV. and his brother Mallikárjun, who reigned with him as heir-apparent or *Yuvarája*, seven inscriptions have been found, one at Sankeshvar fifteen miles south-west of Chikodi, dated 1199 (*Saka* 1121, the Siddhárthi *samvatsara*) and

---

[1] Journal Bombay Branch Royal Asiatic Society, X. 213.
[2] Sir Walter Elliot's MS. Collection, II. 547 and 548.
[3] Indian Antiquary, IV. 115.
[4] P. S. and O. C. Inscriptions, No. 94; Burgess' Third Archæological Report, 103.
[5] Ferishta (Brigg's, II. 349) mentions Kandhár as one of the leading cities, where, in 1380, the fifth Bahmani king Muhammad I. (1378-1397) founded orphan schools. The other six places were Bidar, Chaul, Dábhol, Daulatabad, Ilichpur, and Kulbarga.

Chapter VII.
History.
Rattas, 850-1250.

1202 (*Saka* 1124, the Dundubhi *samvatsara*);[1] one at Ráybág fifteen miles north-west of Chikodi, dated *Saka* 1124 for 1123 (A. D. 1201), the Durmati *samvatsara*;[2] two, which were formerly at Belgaum but are now lost, dated *Saka* 1127 for 1126 (A.D. 1204), the Raktákshi *samvatsara*;[3] one at Kalhole seven miles north-east of Gokák, of the same date;[4] one, a copper-plate grant, at Bhoj near Chikodi, dated *Saka* 1131 for 1130 (A.D. 1208), the Vibhava *samvatsara*; and one at Nesargi seven miles north of Sampgaon, dated *Saka* 1141 for 1140 (A.D. 1218), the Bahudhánya *samvatsara*.[5] The dates of his earlier inscriptions show that Kártavirya IV. first shared the government with his father Lakshmideva I. His wives were Echaladevi and Mádevi or Mahádevi. Of Lakshmideva II., who is also called Boppansing or the Lion of Boppa, one inscription has been found at Saundatti; it is dated *Saka* 1151 for 1150 (A.D. 1228), the Sarvadhári *samvatsara*.[6] This is the last notice of the Rattas. Lakshmideva II. seems to have been the last of his race, and to have fallen before the rising power of the Yádavs (1150-1310) of Devgiri in the North Deccan.

Devgiri Yádavs, 1250-1320.

In 1228 the Yádav Singhana II. (1209-1247) appears making grants and setting up inscriptions near Kolhápur, in Bijápur, in the Torgal Six-thousand,[7] in the Belvola country, and in Dhárwár and Maisur. These grants are numerous enough to show that the country on the north, east, and south of the Kundi Three-thousand was subject to him, though, as is shown by the date of the inscription of Lakshmideva II., he had still left the Rattas unharmed. In 1249-50, Singhana's son Krishna is mentioned as holding the Kundi Three-thousand. The overthrow of the Rattas by Singhana's minister and general Vichana, which is recorded in a grant of the seventh Devgiri Yádav king Krishna, dated 1253, found at Behatti fifteen miles east of Dhárwár, must have taken place towards the close of Singhana's reign.[8] An inscription at Bágevádi ten miles south-east of Belgaum, dated 1249, mentions Krishna's minister Mallisetti as governing the Kundi country from Mudugal, the modern Mudgal in the Nizám's country eighty miles east of the Belgaum frontier, and another at Manoli six miles north of Saundatti, dated 1253, mentions Krishna's great minister Chaundráj, son of the Ratta conqueror Vichana, as in charge of the southern parts of his kingdom.[9] From 1253 the

---

1 Elliot MS. Collection, II. 561.
2 Elliot MS. Collection, II. 564; Jour. Bo. Br. R. As. Soc. X. 182.
3 Elliot MS. Collection, II. 571 and 576.
4 Jour. Bom. Br. R. As. Soc. X. 220; P. S. and O. C. Inscriptions, No. 95.
5 Jour. Bom. Br. R. As. Soc. X. 240.
6 Jour. Bom. Br. R. As. Soc. X. 260; P. S. and O. C. Inscriptions, No. 89.
7 One of Singhana II.'s inscriptions, dated 1223 (*S.* 1145) has been found at Manoli six miles north of Saundatti. It mentions Singhana II.'s commander Jagadala Purushottam as governing the Torgal Six-thousand. Jour. B. B. R. A. S. XII. 2, 11.
8 Jour. Bom. Br. R. As. Soc. XII. 42.
9 It is doubtful whether the Goa Kádambas (1000-1250) and their cotemporaries the Kádambas of Banavási and Hángal (1050-1203), who appear from their traditional origin to belong to the same family stock, were of local origin or were northerners. Compare Bombay Gazetteer, XV. Part II. 82-83. The successions of the Goa Kádambas are Guhalla, Shasthadev I. or Chatta, Chattala and Chattya (1007), Jayakeshi I. (1052), Vijayáditya I., Jayakeshi II. (1125), Permádi or Shivchitta (1147-1175), Vijayáditya II. or Vishnuchitta (1147-1171), Jayakeshi III. (1175-1188), Tribhuvanmalla, and Shasthadev II. (1246-1250). Fleet's Kánarese Dynasties, 90.

Chapter VII.
History.
Goa Kádambas, 1000-1200.

Devgiri Yádavs held Belgaum till their final overthrow by Mubárik Khilji about 1320.

Inscriptions found in various parts of the district, at Belur, Degámve, Gudikatti, Golihalli, Halsi, and Kittur, show that during the greater part of the twelfth and the early years of the thirteenth centuries the Kádambas of Goa (1000-1250) held part of the Halsi Twelve-thousand and the small division known as the Venugrám or Belgaum Seventy.[1] The earliest mention of the Goa Kádambas in Belgaum is in an inscription of the fifth Kádamba chief Jayakeshi II. at Narendra five miles north-west of Dhárwár, dated 1125, which mentions him as governing, among other districts, the Palasige or Halsi Twelve-thousand under the Western Chálukya king Vikramáditya VI. (1075-1126). About 1130 Jayakeshi II. was conquered by the third Hoysala king Vishnuvardhan (1117-1137) by whom the Halsi district is recorded to have been held for a time.[2] The sons of Jayakeshi II. were Permádi, who is also called Perma, Paramardi, and Shivachitta, and Vijayáditya II. who is also called Vijayárka II. and Vishnuchitta. Permádi had also the title of *Malavara-mári* that is the Slayer of the Malavas or Sahyádri tribes which corresponds to *Malaparol-ganda* one of the titles of the Hoysala dynasty. Vijayádidya II. had also the title of Vánibhushana or Sarasvatibhushana. The two brothers reigned together from 1147-4 (4248 *Kaliyuga, Saka* 1069, the Prabhava *samvatsara*). It was Permádi's wife Kamaládevi who built at Degámve three miles south-west of Kittur the small richly carved temple of the god Kamala-Náráyana and the goddess Mahálakshmi which contains three inscriptions of this family; this temple was built by Tippoja, the *sutradhári* or mason of the god Bankeshvaradev and the son of the mason Holloja of Huvina-Bágе probably Raybág in Kolhápur, and by Tippoja's son Bajoja.[3] The earliest of their inscriptions, at Golihalli a mile south of Bidi, is dated 1160-6, in the fourteenth year (*Saka* 1082, the Vikrama *samvatsara*); 1163-4 the seventeenth year (*Saka* 1085, the Svabhánu *samvatsara*); and 1172-3, the twenty-sixth year (*Saka* 1094, the Nandana *samvatsara*) of the reign of Permádi.[4] Permádi was then at his capital of Gove or Goa, ruling over the Konkan Nine-hundred, the Palasige or Halsi Twelve-

---

1 Fleet's Kánarese Dynasties, 73.

2 Fleet's Kánarese Dynasties, 66, 92. The Hoysalas, who are best known as the Hoysalas of Dvárasamudra in Maisur, ruled from about 1039 to 1312. Their name is also written Hoysana, Poysala, and Poysana. They belong to the lineage of Yadu and seem to be connected with the Yádavs of Devgiri (1189-1312) as they both have the family titles of Yádav-Náráyan and of Dvárávati-Puravarádhishvar, supreme lords of Dvárávati the best of cities, apparently Dvárasamudra, the modern Halebid in West Maisur. Vinayáditaya (1039) was the first of the family to secure any considerable share of power. The two chief men of the family were Vishnuvardhan from about 1117 to 1138 who was independent except in name, and Ballála II. (1192-1211) who overthrew the Kalachurya successors of the Chálukyas and also defeated the Yádavs of Devgiri. His son Narsimh II. (1233) was defeated by the Yádavs, and his great-grandson Ballála III. by Ala-ud-din's general Malik Káfur in 1310. They sustained a second and final defeat from a general of Muhammad Tughlik's in 1327. Their successions are: Vinayáditya (1047-1076), Ereyanga, Ballála I. (1103), Vishnuvardhana (1117-1137), Narsimh I., Ballála II. (1191-1211), Narsimh II. (1223), Someshvar (1252), Narsimh III. (1254-1286), and Ballála III. (1310). Fleet's Kánarese Dynasties, 64; compare Wilson's Mackenzie Collection, New Edition, 64.

3 Jour. Bo. Br. R. As. Soc. IX. 294

4 Jour. Bo. Br. R. As. Soc. IX. 296.

Chapter VII.
History.
Goa Kádambas, 1000-1200.

thousand and the Venugrám or Belgaum Seventy. The Bailur inscription four miles south-west of Kittur is dated 1167-8, the twenty-first year of his reign (*Kaliyuga* 4268, *Saka* 1089, the Sarvajit *samvatsara*); and also in his twenty-second year (the Sarvadhári *samvatsara*). One of the Halsi inscriptions records in the twenty-third year of his reign, 1169-70 (*Kaliyuga* 4270, *Saka* 1091, the Virodhi *samvatsara*), a grant of the village of Sindvalli in the Kálagiri sub-division of Halsi. One of the Degámve inscriptions in the twenty-eighth year of his reign, A.D. 1174-5 (*Kaliyuga* 4275, *Saka* 1096, the Jaya *samvatsara*), mentions Permádi as reigning at Gopakpuri or Goa, and making a grant of the village of Degámve in the Degámve sub-division of Palásika or Halsi.[1] Another inscription at Golihalli, dated 1175 (*Kaliyuga* 4283 or more correctly 4276, the Manmatha *samvatsara*), records that Permádi and his mother Mailáladevi were reigning at Gove. Of Vijayáditya II. only one inscription has been found. It is at Halsi, dated 1171-2 (*Kaliyuga* 4270 for 4272, the Khara *samvatsara*), and the twenty-fifth year of his reign, and records the grant of the village of Bhalaka in the Kálagiri sub-division of Palasi or Halsi.[2]

Permádi's successor was Vijayáditya II.'s son Jayakeshi III., who also had the title of *Malavara-mári* or Hill-men Slayer. Of his time two inscriptions have been found, a copper-plate grant at Halsi, which is dated 1187-8, in the thirteenth year of his reign, (*Kaliyuga* 4288, *Saka* 1109);[3] and a stone-tablet at Kittur, which is dated 1188-9, in the fifteenth year of his reign (*Kaliyuga* 4289, *Saka* 1110).[4] The copper-plate records that he established the god Ádivaráh in a temple in front of the already existing temple of Narsimh at Palásika or Halsi town, and gave to the idol the village of Kiri-Halasige, or the smaller Halasige, and a variety of other grants. His second inscription at Kittur contains an interesting account of a trial by ordeal. In consequence of a dispute regarding the ownership of a field between Shivshakti, the *Áchárya* or priest of the god Kalleshvardev of Kittur, and Kalyánshakti the *Áchárya* of the *Mulsthándev* or Place God, the two parties met before the commandant or *Dandanáyak* Ishvar, and agreed to put their claims to the test of the *phaladivya* or red-hot ploughshare. On Sunday the dark seventh of *Áshádh* (June-July) the claimants met in the presence of the principal villagers of Degámve, at the temple of the god Mallikárjun. Kalyánshakti declared that the field belonged to the *Mulsthándev* or Place God, while Shivshakti, holding a red-hot ploughshare in his hand, made oath that the field belonged to the god Kalleshvar. Next day, the leading villagers examined Shivshakti's hand and finding it unharmed, decided that the field in dispute belonged to his god Kalleshvar. Jayakeshi's successors lost the Kádamba territories in Belgaum. By 1208 even the small Venugrám or Belgaum Seventy had passed to the Rattas.[5]

Trial by Ordeal, 1188.

---

[1] Jour. Bo. Br. R. As. Soc. IX. 266, 287. [2] Jour. Bo. Br. R. As. Soc. IX. 280.
[3] Jour. Bo. Br. R. As. Soc. IX. 241. [4] Jour. Bo. Br. R. As. Soc. IX. 304.
[5] Fleet's Kánarese Dynasties, 82; see above p. 357.

Chapter VII.

History.

Delhi Emperors, 1294-1350.

Till 1294, with the title of emperor or *chakravarti*, Rámchandra, the ninth Yádav king of Devgiri (1271-1310), was supreme over the Deccan, Konkan, and Karnátak.[1] In 1294 a Musalmán army was for the first time led into Southern India by Allá-ud-din the nephew and afterwards the successor of Jelál-ud-din the first Khilji emperor of Delhi (1288-1295). Advancing by forced marches from Karah-Mánikpur on the Ganges, Allá-ud-din surprised Rámchandra, or Rámdev as Ferishta calls him, at Devgiri, took the city, and forced Rámdev to pay tribute and acknowledge the supremacy of the Khilji emperors of Delhi.[2] Between 1295 and 1306 the Yádavs were not again molested and seem to have continued overlords of the south. In 1306 Allá-ud-din, who, in 1295, had assassinated his uncle and usurped the Delhi throne, under his general Malik Káfur, sent a second expedition against Rámchandra who had become irregular in paying his tribute. Malik Káfur subdued a great part of the Marátha country, besieged Devgiri, and forced Rámchandra to submit.[3] Rámchandra returned with Malik Káfur to Delhi, was treated with honour, and was not only restored to his old government but was presented with fresh territory for all of which he did homage and paid tribute to Allá-ud-din.[4] Rámchandra died in 1310. He was succeeded by his son Shankar who was ill-affected to the Musalmáns. In 1310 Allá-ud-din sent an army under Malik Káfur and Khwája Háji to reduce Dvársamudra the capital of the Hoysala ruler Ballála III. (1290-1310). Leaving part of their forces at Paithan on the Godávari to overawe and hold Shankar of Devgiri in check, Malik Káfur and Khwája Háji marched south, entered and laid waste the Hoysala kingdom, defeated and captured Ballála III. and took and plundered his capital of Dvársamudra. In 1311 Malik Káfur returned to Delhi with rich spoils.[5] In 1312, as Shankar of Devgiri withheld his tribute, Malik Káfur entered the Deccan for the fourth time, seized Shankar and put him to death. He laid waste Maháráshtra and the Karnátak from Cheul in Kolába and Dábhol in Ratnágiri in the west as far east as Mudgal and Ráichur in the Nizám's country. He established his head-quarters at Devgiri, and from Devgiri realized the tribute of the princes of Telingana and the Karnátak and remitted it to Delhi.[6] Malik Káfur shortly afterwards returned to Delhi. During his absence Harpál, the son-in-law of Rámchandra, stirred the Deccan to arms, drove out a number of Musalmán posts, and restored the former Devgiri territories to independence. The troubles at Delhi, the assassination of Allá-ud-din (1316) by Malik Káfur and then shortly afterwards

---

[1] Fleet's Kánarese Dynasties, 74. The title of *chakravarti* or emperor is given to Rámchandra in a manuscript written in 1297 at Suvarngiri in the Konkan, probably Suvarndurg in Ratnágiri.

[2] Briggs' Ferishta, I. 307; Elphinstone's History of India, 332.

[3] Briggs' Ferishta, I. 367.

[4] Briggs' Ferishta, I. 367.

[5] The spoils included 312 elephants, 20,000 horses, 96,000 *mans* of gold, several boxes of jewels and pearls and other precious effects. During this expedition to the Karnátak no metal other than gold was taken. There were no silver coins; no person wore bracelets chains or rings of any metal but gold. All the plate in the houses of the great and in the temples was of beaten gold. Briggs' Ferishta, I. 365.

[6] Briggs' Ferishta, I. 379.

Chapter VII.
History.
Delhi Emperors, 1294-1350.

Malik Káfur's own assassination, prevented the immediate reduction of the Deccan. In 1318 the emperor Mubárik (1317-1321) led an army into the Deccan, captured Harpál, and flayed him alive.[1] In 1327 the emperor Muhammad Tughlik (1325-1351) subdued the Karnátak even to the shore of the sea of Umán that is the Indian Ocean.[2] Among the noblemen who were appointed to govern the conquered country two were stationed within Belgaum limits, one at Hukeri about twenty-five miles and the other at Ráybág about forty-five miles north of Belgaum.[3] The Deccan and the Karnátak soon passed out of the hold of the Delhi emperors.

Vijayanagar.

About this time (1328-1335) a new Hindu kingdom was founded at Vijayanagar or the City of Victory, originally called Vidyánagar or the City of Learning, on the south bank of the Tungbhadra about thirty-six miles north-west of Belári. The founders were two brothers Hakka and Bukka of doubtful origin. By one account they were of the Yádav line; by a second account they were descended from under-lords of the Hoysala Ballálas; by a third account they belonged to the Banvási Kadambás; and by a fourth account they were shepherds or Kurubars and were treasury guardians of Pratápruda king of Varangal who was overthrown by the Musalmáns in 1323.[4] Hakka and Bukka were helped by a sage named Mádhav, the head of the great Smárt monastery of Shringeri in West Maisur, by whom Hakka was crowned as Harihar. By 1342 the power of Vijayanagar had spread to the Kánara coast, and two years later (1344), with the help of the chief of Telingana, Harihar seized the country occupied by the Musalmáns in the Deccan and drove them out, so that, according to Ferishta, within a few months Muhammad Tughlik's Deccan possessions were reduced to Devgiri, whose name in 1338 he had changed to Daulatabad or the City of Wealth.[5] Ferishta's statement that in 1344 the Musalmáns lost all their Deccan possessions except Daulatabad seems exaggerated. In 1347 among the new nobility or *Amir Jádidás,* whom the emperor summoned to Daulatabad and who revolted, were the *amirs* of Ráybág, Hukeri, and Bijápur.[6] Ferishta's statement that in 1347 Musalmán nobles held Ráybág, Hukeri, and Bijápur, together with the fact that till 1472 the Belgaum fort was held by a Hindu chief subordinate to Vijaynagar, shows that about the middle of the fourteenth century, Belgaum north of the Ghatprabha including Athni and Chikodi was in Musalmán hands and was part of the Deccan, and Belgaum south of the Ghatprabha was part of the Hindu kingdom of the Karnátak.

The Bahmanis, 1347-1489.

In 1347 the successful revolt of the new nobles against Muhammad Tughlik resulted in the founding of the Bahmani dynasty (1347-1490) and the separation of the Deccan from Northern India. The founder of the Bahmani dynasty was an Afghán, named Hassan Gangu, whose capital was at Kulbarga nearly midway between Bijápur

---

[1] Briggs' Ferishta, I. 389. [2] Briggs' Ferishta, I. 413.
[3] Stokes' Belgaum, Bom. Gov. Sel. CXV. 11.
[4] Details are given in the Kánara Statistical Account, Bombay Gazetteer, XV. Part II. 96. [5] Briggs' Ferishta, I. 420, 427. [6] Briggs' Ferishta, I. 437.

Chapter VII.
History.
The Bahmanis, 1347-1489.

and Haidarabad. Within a short period the whole country between the Bhima and Adoni or Adváni about forty miles north-east of Belári and between Cheul and Bidar, including the west Nizám's Deccan and Karnátak, the Bombay Deccan and the north Bombay Karnátak, and the central Konkan, was brought under the authority of Allá-ud-din the first Bahmani king (1347-1358).[1] In 1357 Allá-ud-din Bahmani divided his kingdom into four chief governments. His Belgaum possessions were included in the first of these divisions which stretched from Kulburga west to Dábhol in Ratnágiri and south to Ráichur and Mudgal. This was placed under Malik Seif-ud-din Ghuri.[2] Part of the Karnátak, as far west as the Kánara frontier, including south Belgaum, acknowledged as overlords the Vijayanagar kings. Thus, as before, the border line of the Deccan and the Karnátak continued to pass through the present district of Belgaum. The Bahmanis and the Vijayanagar kings kept up an almost constant rivalry. The usual seat of their wars seems to have lain beyond the limits of the Bombay Karnátak, and the record of their wars is probably one-sided as Ferishta dwells on Musalmán victories and passes over Musalmán defeats. In 1368 Bukka, the second Vijayanagar king (1350-1379) suffered a series of defeats at the hands of Muhammad Sháh Bahmani (1358-1375), the first Muhammadan sovereign who, in person, crossed the Tungbhadra and entered Vijayanagar territory. Ferishta describes the Vijayanagar territory of 1375 as comprising the sea-port of Goa, the fortress of Belgaum, and other places not included in the Karnátak proper.[3] The woods and hill forts of the Vijayanagar country, between the Krishna and the Tungbhadra, guarded it against foreign invasion, and the country was filled with a prosperous and loyal people.[4] In 1375 Mujáhid Sháh Bahmani (1375-1378) demanded from Bukka the Vijayanagar king the territory east of the Tungbhadra, the fort of Bankápur in Dhárwár, and other places among which Belgaum was probably included.[5] Bukka refused. In the war which followed he was driven through the forests to Cape Rámas in Goa, but successfully evaded capture.[6] Mujáhid Sháh then besieged Adoni or Adváni but without success. From Adoni, Mujáhid, under the advice of Malik Seif-ud-din Ghuri the governor of his south-west province, turned his arms against the forts from Goa to Belgaum and Bankápur, but here too he met with little success.[7] Taking advantage of the troubles which followed Mujáhid's assassination in 1378, the Vjayanagar king Harihar II. (1379-1401) completely defeated the Musalmáns. From 1378 to 1397 the country seems to have been at rest. This period of rest was followed by the awful ruin of the Durga Devi famine during which, beginning with 1396, twelve years are said to have passed without rain. The country became a desert and the hill forts and strong places fell from the Musalmáns into the hands of petty chiefs and leaders of bandits.[8] In 1398,

---

1 Briggs' Ferishta, II. 291.
2 Briggs' Ferishta, II. 295.
3 Briggs' Ferishta, II. 313; Scott's Deccan, I. 27.
4 Briggs' Ferishta, II. 337-338.
5 Briggs' Ferishta, II. 330; Stokes' Belgaum, 14.
6 Briggs' Ferishta, II. 332.
7 Briggs' Ferishta, II. 389.
8 Grant Duff's Maráthás, 26.

Chapter VII.
History.
The Bahmanis, 1347-1489.

1406, 1417, and 1423 the Bahmani and Vijayanagar kings were at war, but the general limits of the two territories seem not to have been greatly changed. 1423 and 1425 were years of drought and famine.[1] During the first three-quarters of the fifteenth century the issue of the wars was in favour of the Bahmani kings.

Under Dev Ráya (1401-1451), Mallikárjuna (1451-1465), and Virupáksha (1465-1479) the power of Vijayanagar gradually waned. The Musalmáns claim that the wars in 1435 and 1444 reduced the Vijayanagar kings to be tributaries. Some disastrous campaign may have forced Vijayanagar to buy off the Musalmáns, but the little advance of the Musalmán borders shows that the permanent position of the two powers was not greatly changed.[2] In 1470 the capture of Goa by Máhmud Gawán Giláni, the prime minister of Muhammad Sháh Bahmani II. (1463-1518), was a severe blow to Vijayanagar.[3] In 1472 under orders from Virupáksha of Vijayanagar, Vikram Ráy Rája of Belgaum, helped by the Hindu chief of Bankápur in Dhárwár, made an attempt to retake Goa. Muhammad Sháh Bahmani put himself at the head of a large army and marched against Belgaum, which is described as a fortress of great strength, surrounded by a deep wet ditch, and near it a pass whose only approach was fortified by redoubts.[4] According to Ferishta Vikrama Ráy, who commanded the fort, at first asked terms which were refused. He then defended himself with great vigour and prevented Khwája Máhmud Gawán the Bahmani general from filling with wood and earth the wet ditch in which lay the chief strength of the fort. The besiegers then began to form trenches and dig mines, apparently at this time a new feature in Deccan warfare. Three mines were sprung and made practicable breaches in the fort wall. The breaches were at once stormed, and, in spite of a gallant defence and the loss of two thousand of the besiegers, Muhammad Sháh succeeded in gaining the ramparts. The inner citadel had yet to be carried, but Vikram Ráy despairing of success, disguised himself and was admitted to the Bahmani king's presence as a messenger from the Belgaum chief. In the king's presence he threw his turban round his neck and discovered himself, saying that he had come with his family to kiss the foot of the throne. Muhammad admiring his courage received him into his order of nobles. The new territories were added to the estates of Khwája Máhmud Gawán who had distinguished himself during the siege.[5] Dyámavva the guardian of Belgaum fort was taken out by the Musalmáns. In a small temple near the fort she is still worshipped once in twelve years, when, along with goats sheep fowls and cocoanuts, twelve buffaloes are sacrificed to her.[6] In 1472 and 1473 the country was wasted by famine. So many died or

Siege of Belgaum, 1473.

---

[1] Briggs' Ferishta, II. 405. [2] Stokes' Belgaum, 17.
[3] Briggs' Ferishta, II. 485. According to Faria (Kerr, VI. 130) Goa belonged to the Moors of Honávar before it was taken by the Bahmanis; and according to other Portuguese chroniclers quoted by Mr. Fonseca (Goa, 125) Goa was independent of Vijayanagar between 1440 and 1470. [4] Briggs' Ferishta, II. 491.
[5] Briggs' Ferishta, II. 491-493; Scott's Deccan, I. 160-161.
[6] Stokes' Belgaum, 21.

Chapter VII.
History.
The Bahmanis, 1347-1489.

left their homes that in the third year when rain fell scarcely any remained to till the land.[1]

The capture of Belgaum and the conquest of its dependencies brought the whole of the Bombay Karnátak under Musalmán rule and for a time crushed the power of the Vijayanagar king. In 1478 the Bahmani minister Khwája Gawán, a Persian of great learning and power, finding so large a territory unwieldy, divided the Bahmani kingdom into eight *tarafs* or provinces. Each province had its own governor appointed by the king, and each governor had several officers under him also appointed by the king for the management of the different parts of the province. The practice of leaving all the forts in each province in the hands of each provincial governor was stopped. One fortress only was allowed to the governor. The others were kept in the hands of officers and troops appointed by the king and paid from head-quarters. Under this new distribution the country from Junnar, including several dependent districts in the south, Indápur in Poona, Wái and Mán in Sátára, and the forts of Goa and Belgaum, were placed under the governorship of Fakr-ul-Mulk.[2] In 1481 some Bahmani officers, whose power suffered under the new system of control, plotted against Khwája Gawán. He was falsely accused of treason and was put to death by the king's order. Muhammad's power never recovered the loss of Khwája Gawán who alone was able to control the rivalries and disaffection of the ambitious nobles of the Bahmani court.[3] About the same time (1479), under Narsingh, who according to one account was the slave of the last king Virupáksha, according to a second account was a chief of Telingana, and according to a third account was of a Tulav or South Kánara family, a fresh dynasty arose at Vijayanagar whose energy once more made the Hindu Karnátak a fit rival for the Musalmán Deccan. In 1481 the new Vijayanagar king Narsingh attempted to recover Goa. The attack was repelled by Muhammad Sháh who is mentioned as visiting Belgaum and examining the city and fortifications.[4] The ambition of the provincial governors, which Khwája Gawán had succeeded in curbing, after his death did not long remain at rest. In 1489 Ahmad Nizám Khán the governor of the Junnar province and Yusuf Adil Khán the governor of Bijápur, though they continued to pay nominal allegiance to Máhmud Bahmani (1482-1518) assumed independent power. Of these nobles, Yusuf Adil Khán, who,

---

[1] Briggs' Ferishta, II. 494.

[2] Briggs' Ferishta, II. 502-503; Scott's Deccan, I. 168-169; Grant Duff's Maráthás, 29.

[3] According to Ferishta Khwája Gawán, who was connected with the family of the Sháh of Persia, alarmed by the intrigues and jealousies of the court of Persia, left his native land, travelled as a merchant through many countries, and formed the acquaintance of the learned men of each. Partly for trade and partly to visit the learned men of the Deccan, Khwája Gawán landed in 1455 at Dábhol in Ratnágiri, and travelled to Bidar. Allá-ud-Din Bahmani (1435-1457) was charmed by his learning and information and raised him to the rank of a noble. Under Allá-ud-Din's successors he received title after title until he became the first man in the state. He fought several successful campaigns, his greatest exploit being the capture of Goa in 1470. He was a strict Sunni, very learned and liberal, an accomplished writer, and a profound scholar. He left a library of three thousand volumes. Briggs' Ferishta, II. 510-512; Scott's Deccan, I. 172-175.

[4] Briggs' Ferishta, II. 516-517.

Chapter VII.
History.
Bijápur Kings, 1489-1686.

as the founder of the Bijápur dynasty (1489-1686) is one of the most important characters in Belgaum history, was a foreign soldier of fortune, surnamed Savaia from the Persian city of Sáva,[1] and is believed to have been a son of Agha Murád or Amurath Sultán of Turkey.[2] About the time when Ahmad Nizám Khán and Yusuf Adil Khán quietly assumed independence another noble of the Bahmani court Bahádur Giláni, the governor of the Konkan, broke into open rebellion. He seized Belgaum and Goa, established his head-quarters at Sankeshvar about thirty miles north of Belgaum, and afterwards (1489) possessed himself of Miraj and Jamkhandi. An attempt to establish a navy on the Konkan coast stirred the dangerous enmity of Máhmud Begada (1459-1511) the greatest of the Gujarát Ahmadabad Sultáns, who at this time held the Konkan coast as far south as Cheul. Under Begada's remonstrances and threats Máhmud Sháh was forced to take active measures against the rebel Giláni. In 1493, with the help of 5000 horse sent by Yusuf Adil Khán of Bijápur, who probably looked with disfavour on Giláni's attempt to secure the whole Konkan sea-board, Máhmud Sháh took Jamkhandi and gave it in charge to Yusuf Adil Khán's troops. From Jamkhandi Máhmud passed to Sankeshvar whose fortifications were still unfinished and which in three days yielded to the king. From Sankeshvar Máhmud marched against Miraj, twenty-eight miles west of Athni, defeated Giláni's troops, and took the town. Giláni, after one or two more reverses beyond Belgaum limits, was (1493) slain by an arrow, and his estate including Belgaum was conferred on Ein-ul-Mulk Giláni.[3] In 1498, though they continued to acknowledge their nominal supremacy till 1526, that is a century after (1426) the Bahmanis had moved their capital from Kulburga to Bidar, the three strongest of the Bahmani nobles, Yusuf Adil Khán of Bijápur, Ahmad Nizám Khán of Junnar afterward of Ahmadnagar, and Kutb Khán of Golkonda agreed to divide the Deccan. In this division Ein-ul-Mulk Giláni's estate of Belgaum and the neighbouring districts was assigned to Bijápur. Ein-ul-Mulk Giláni did not resist the transfer of his allegiance from Bidar to Bijápur and in token of his approval went with 6000 horse to the capital of his new overlord. About this time Hukeri twenty-five miles north of Belgaum and its neighbourhood was in charge of Fateh Bahádur a captain of one thousand horse.[4] In 1502 Yusuf Adil Shah, jealous of the growing power of Ein-ul-Mulk Giláni, took from him his command in the Bijápur army, and reduced his

[1] Yusuf's title Savaia is the origin of the Portuguese Sabaio, a name by which the Bijápur kings are always known in early Portuguese books.

[2] The received story of Yusuf's life is that he was born about 1443. After his father's death in 1451 to save him from his elder brother who had succeeded to the throne, Yusuf was secretly delivered to Khwája Imád-ud-din, a merchant of Sáva in Persia who took and educated him till he was seventeen. In 1459, led by a dream, he sailed for India, and, in 1461, reached Dábhol in Ratnágiri. Here he was sold or got himself sold to Khwája Máhmud Gawán the Bahmani minister. His engaging manners rapidly raised him from a simple soldier to the command of the royal body-guard. Invested with the title of Adil Khán and adopted by Khwája Gawán he was made governor of Daulatabad and afterwards of Bijápur, where in 1489 he was crowned king. Gibbon's Decline of the Roman Empire, XII. 186; Briggs' Ferishta, III. 4-9.

[3] Briggs' Ferishta, II. 539-543.

[4] Stokes' Belgaum, 23.

Chapter VII.
History.

Bijápur Kings, 1489-1686.

The Portuguese, 1510.

possessions to the districts of Hukeri and Belgaum. Ein-ul-Mulk continued to hold Hukeri during the forty-three years ending 1546, where several tombs and water-courses remain as a trace of his government.[1]

During the first half of the sixteenth century the power of Bijápur was prevented passing south by the alliance between Vijayanagar and the Portuguese. From 1498, when, under Vasco da Gama they reached the Malabár coast, till, towards the close of 1510 they finally ousted Bijápur from Goa, the Portuguese fought not against the Hindus but against the Muhammadans. From the first the Portuguese did their best to gain Vijayanagar as an ally. But Narsingh and after his death in 1508 his successor Krishna Ráy themselves had designs on Goa, and gave the Portuguese little support till, in 1510, the Portuguese proved themselves strong enough unaided to defeat Bijápur.[2] The final success of the Portuguese at Goa was quickly followed by a close alliance between Krishna Ráy and the Portuguese. The power of Vijayanagar was greatly increased by the ammunition and guns, the horses, and the trained artillerymen supplied by the Portugese, and during Krishna Ráy's long reign (1508-1542) Vijayanagar was perhaps the richest state that ever held sway in Southern India.[3] At the same time, apparently shortly before the final conquest of Goa by the Portuguese, Bijápur was weakened by the death of its great ruler Yusuf Adil Sháh.[4] In March 1510, when the news of Dalboquerque's capture of Goa reached Belgaum, the Hindus rose, drove out the Bijápur garrison and resumed their former allegiance to the Vijayanagar kings.[5] Though the Belgaum Hindus were soon reduced and though Belgaum and Hukeri long belonged to Bijápur, Krishna Ráy of Vijayanagar seems to have spread his power as far north as Ráybág. A Kánarese inscription dated 1514-15 (*S.* 1436), at Ugargol three miles south-east of Saundatti, mentions the name of Bommappa of Bági that is Ráybág, as one of Krishna Ráy's military officers or *náiks*.[6] In 1511 Belgaum was taken from Ein-ul-Mulk, and, together with the title of Asad Khán, was granted to Khusru Turk, a Persian of the province of Lár and a Shia by religion, in reward for delivering the young king Ismáil Adil Sháh (1511-1535) from the treachery of his guardian Kamál Khán Dakhani.[7] Asad Khán held Belgaum for thirty-eight years (1511-1549) during which he was the mainstay of Bijápur power. His is the greatest name the local history can boast. He is the hero of the Belgaum

Asad Khán, 1511-1549.

---

[1] Stokes' Belgaum, 23.

[2] Goa was taken by Dalboquerque on the 5th of March 1510. It was recovered by the Bijápur troops on the 23rd of May 1510 and was again taken and finally held by Dalboquerque on the 25th of November. Compare Briggs' Ferishta, III. 30; Commentaries of Dalboquerque, II. 89, 91, 125. Decadas De Barros, II. liv. v. 511, Faria in Kerr's Voyages, VI. 131, 133, 146. Details are given in the Statistical Account of North Kánara, Bombay Gazetteer, XV. Part I. 101-110.

[3] Rice's Mysore, I. 230.

[4] According to the Portuguese historians Yusuf died before the first capture of Goa by Dalboquerque. According to Ferishta (Briggs, III. 30) Yusuf died after the recapture of Goa by the Bijápur troops in May 1510.

[5] Commentaries of Dalboquerque, III. 37.

[6] Jour. Bom. Br. Roy. Asiatic Soc. XII. 343.

[7] Briggs' Ferishta, III. 45.

Chapter VII.
History.
Bijápur Kings, 1489-1686.
Asad Khán, 1511-1549.

Musalmáns, and is now a saint whose power keeps the cholera spirit from ruining his beloved town of Belgaum. In 1519, in a war with the brother kings of Vijayanagar, Krishna Ráya and Achyuta Ráya (1508-1542), Asad Khán saved the Bijápur army from the danger into which the rashness of Ismáil Adil Sháh had brought them and led the troops back in safety to the capital. For this service he was rewarded with the title of Sipáh Sálár or Commander-in-Chief. Several districts were added to his estate and from that time Asad Khán became the king's chief adviser.[1] In 1523 he was Bijápur envoy at Sholápur when the king's sister Mariam was married to Burhán Nizám Sháh of Ahmadnagar (1508-1553).[2] In 1524 near Sholápur Asad Khán gained a brilliant victory over the confederate kings of Ahmadnagar and Berar and the regent of Bidar, the bone of contention being the fort of Sholápur with its five and a half districts which were said to have been ceded by Bijápur to Ahmadnagar as the marriage portion of the Bijápur princess. In this battle Asad Khán took Burhán Sháh's standard, forty elephants, cannon, and baggage. He was presented with eleven of the elephants and the pay of every soldier in his army was raised. To enable him to bear this expense Ismáil gave to Asad Khán's troops the land allotted for the support of the harem and half the customs levied at the forts.[3] In 1528 Asad Khán once more completely defeated the Ahmadnagar king, and took much of his baggage, and twenty elephants. Except one elephant called *Alla Baksha* or The Gift of God, which Ismáil kept for himself, these animals were presented to Asad Khán whom in his letters or *firmáns* Ismail addressed as *Farzan* or son.[4] In 1529 Asad Khán accompanied his master Ismáil against Amir Barid the regent of Bidar, an old, experienced, and crafty prince. The Bijápur troops won the day chiefly through the skill of Asad Khán, whom, when the battle was over, the king embraced in the sight of the whole army. Asad Khán followed this success by surprising the Bidar regent in a fit of debauchery and carrying him prisoner to the Bijápur camp. In 1531 Asad Khán gained a fourth victory over Ahmadnagar and established the superiority of Bijápur throughout the Deccan.[5] In 1534, on his death-bed, Ismáil Adil Khán appointed Asad Khán Protector of the Kingdom and guardian of his eldest son Mallu Adil Sháh. Disorders which threatened to break out on the king's death were firmly suppressed by Asad Khán. Afterwards, disgusted with the conduct of the young king, Asad Khán resigned his post at court and retired to Belgaum. He was accompanied by Yusuf Khán, a Turkish nobleman who had an estate at Kittur about twenty-five miles south-east of Belgaum.[6] The conduct of Mallu Adil Sháh not only disgusted his guardian, it alienated his friends, even his grandmother took part against him. After a reign of six months he was deposed and blinded by Yusuf Khán of Kittur and his brother Ibráhim was placed on the throne. Ibráhim Adil Sháh (1535-1557) abjured

[1] Briggs' Ferishta, III. 51.
[2] Briggs' Ferishta, III. 51.
[3] Briggs' Ferishta, III. 52-55.
[4] Briggs' Ferishta, III. 56.
[5] Briggs' Ferishta, III. 57-62.
[6] Briggs' Ferishta, III. 76.

the Shia tenets of his father and grandfather and ordered Asad Khán to enlist Deccanis in his service and to adopt the Sunni faith. Asad Khán dismissed six hundred foreigners out of a thousand, but refused to change his faith, and, both in his camp and on his estate, publicly practised the Shia rites, an indulgence which the king prudently allowed.[1] Under the new king Ibráhim II. Asad Khán resumed his post of Commander-in-Chief. Through his advice an army marched to Vijayanagar, and, on their return Asad Khán went to attack Adoni or Adváni, concluded a peace, and returned.[2] Asad Khán's enemies tried to persuade Ibráhim that the peace was against Bijápur interests and was due to corruption. Ibráhim refused to believe this charge, and, on Asad Khán's return, presented him with robes and made him Prime Minister as well as Commander-in-Chief. This still more enraged Asad Khán's enemies. Yusuf Khán of Kittur accused him of meditating the surrender of the Belgaum fort to Burhán Nizám of Ahmadnagar, who, like Asad Khán, was a Shia. This time his enemies succeeded. Under Yusuf's advice the king summoned Asad Khán to Bijápur, but Asad Khán pleaded sickness and remained at Belgaum. After fruitless attempts to poison him, lands near Belgaum were given to Yusuf that, when the chance offered, he might seize the minister. Once near Belgaum, while Asad was riding alone some distance ahead of his guard, Yusuf Khán attacked him with a troop of horse. Asad Khán, who was a man of giant strength and a famous swordsman, attacked and put Yusuf Khán to flight, and with the help of his guard made Yusuf's men prisoners.[3] King Ibráhim professed much anger at Yusuf's conduct, confined him, and asked Asad Khán to do with him what he pleased. Asad Khán blamed his own ill-luck and set Yusuf's men free with presents.[4] Taking advantage of this quarrel between Ibráhim and Asad Khán, Burhán Nizám of Ahmadnagar and Amir Barid of Bidar spread abroad reports that Asad Khán had promised to give them Belgaum. In 1542 the Ahmadnagar king attacked the Bijápur territory and moved south towards Belgaum. According to Ferishta Asad Khán was not in treaty with Bijápur's enemies. Still, to save his estates from plunder, he joined Burhán Nizám with six thousand horse and his example was followed by Ein-ul-Mulk of Hukeri. Ibráhim Adil Sháh retired to Kulbarga leaving the country as far as Bijápur at the mercy of the invaders. Asad Khán explained to Imad Sháh, the king of Berar, that he was not really in alliance with Ahmadnagar and asked him to help his master Ibráhim. Imad Sháh agreed and the siege of Bijápur was raised. Asad Khán left his nominal allies and went over to Imad Sháh through whom he was restored to his master's confidence. In proof of his favour towards Asad Khán Ibráhim Sháh imprisoned Yusuf's agents, and conferred Yusuf's estates among them Kittur on Ein-ul-Mulk the governor of Hukeri, who, under the persuasion of Asad Khán, had rejoined the Bijápur service.[5] The enemy was driven from Bijápur and peace was

---

[1] Briggs' Ferishta, III. 80. [2] Briggs' Ferishta, III. 87.
[3] Lead-weighted shoes, too heavy for a man to lift, in which Asad Khán used to exercise himself are still treasured in the Sáfa mosque at Belgaum. Stokes' Belgaum, 34. [4] Briggs' Ferishta, III. 89. [5] Briggs' Ferishta, III. 90-92.

Chapter VII. History. Bijápur Kings, 1489-1686. *Asad Khán, 1511-1549.*

concluded. In 1543 Bijápur attacked on three sides, by Burhán Nizám of Ahmadnagar, by Jamshid Kutab Sháh of Golkonda, and by Rám Ráya of Vijayanagar, was on the brink of ruin. Following Asad Khán's advice Ibráhim Sháh bought off Burhán Nizám and Rám Ráya and turned his whole strength against Golkonda. After taking some forts Asad Khán followed Kutab Sháh close to Golkonda, completely defeated him, and in a combat inflicted a wound which disfigured Kutab Sháh for life. Asad Khán returned victorious to Bijápur and was honoured by the king.[1] After this, probably in 1544-45, Burhán Nizám again attacked Bijápur. He was once more met by Asad Khán and a fifth time routed with heavy loss. In reward for this fresh success Ibráhim added several districts to Asad Khán's estate.[2] Soon after this Ibráhim Adil Sháh on slight suspicion put many of his nobles to death and made himself so hateful to others that a plot was formed to dethrone him and raise his brother Abdulla to the throne. The plot was discovered and Abdulla fled for safety to Goa. Ibráhim believed that Asad Khán was a party to this plot and he was forced to retire to Belgaum. With the aid of the Portuguese Nizám Sháh and Kutab Sháh, Abdulla proclaimed himself king and marched to Bijápur. Asad Khán was asked to join in the revolt but angrily declined. The sudden illness of Asad Khán destroyed the insurgents' chance of success. As Burhán Nizám was passing Belgaum on his way to Bijápur he heard that Asad was dangerously ill. Contrary to agreement Burhán stopped in the hope that on Asad's death he might be able to seize the fort of Belgaum. To prepare the way he sent a Bráhman spy to buy over Asad's men. Asad recovered, and, hearing what was going on, seized Burhán Nizám's spy and killed him, and put to death as many of the garrison as seemed to have been tampered with. This open breach with Burhán encouraged Ibráhim's supporters; the insurrection was quelled, and Abdulla was forced to retire to Goa where he remained till his death in 1554. In 1549 Asad Khán sent word to Ibráhim that he was dying and wished to see him before he died. Ibráhim started for Belgaum, but, before he arrived, Asad Khán had died at Mandoli three miles south-west of Belgaum. His tomb or *darga* in the Belgaum camp is still worshipped both by Musalmáns and Hindus. Asad's son Muhammad Kishwar Khán was made governor of Hukeri, Belgaum, and Ráybág, and the rest of Asad's estates and treasures went to the king.[3] According to Ferishta,[4] besides for his prowess as a soldier and his skill as a statesman, Asad Khán was famous as the patron and protector of all the learned and distinguished men in the Deccan. He lived at Belgaum in the greatest magnificence. He had 250 household servants, Georgians, Circassians, Hindus, and Abyssinians. He had sixty large and 150 small elephants, and, in his stables

[1] Briggs' Ferishta, III. 94. [2] Briggs' Ferishta, III. 95.
[3] Briggs' Ferishta, III. 100-101, 115. According to Portuguese historians a tenth of Asad Khán's riches valued at ten million ducats or £2,250,000 were used to bribe their government to give up Abdulla's cause, Briggs' Ferishta, III. 517.
[4] Briggs' Ferishta, III. 101-102.

Bijapur Kings, 1489-1686.

Asad Khán, 1511-1549.

besides those of mixed breed were 450 Arab horses. In his kitchens 100 fowls, thirty sheep, and 2700 pounds (100 Deccan *mans*) of rice were daily cooked. He set the fashion, which all men of rank followed, of wearing a gold waistband and a dagger. He attempted to manage elephants with a bit and bridle but the bit failed to control them in their fits of fury. Both Hindus and Musalmáns still worship him as the guardian of Belgaum. In the fine Sáfa mosque are still kept his sabre-proof quilted jacket, his Kuran, and his leaden-soled shoes, heavier than a man can lift, wearing which he used to leap on the platform at the south wall of the mosque.

After Asad Khán's death (1549) one Seif-ud-din Ein-ul-Mulk rose in Ibráhim's favour and was made commander-in-chief. In 1550 one Sher Khán built the town of Sháhápur, originally called Sháhpet as the *petta* or market of the fort of Belgaum.[1] In 1551 war again broke out between Ahmadnagar and Bijápur, and a brilliant victory was lost by the king's distrust of his commander Ein-ul-Mulk. Disgusted with the king Ein-ul-mulk retired to his estates and possessed himself of the country watered by the Mán in Sátára, and of Válva, Miraj, and other districts possibly parts of north Belgaum. Two fruitless attempts were made to dislodge Ein-ul-Mulk from his new possessions. In 1557 Ibráhim Adil Sháh died leaving sons, two of whom because of their leaning towards the Shia faith, were under watch, the eldest Ali at Miraj and the younger Tahamásp at Belgaum. When the king was on his death-bed Muhammad Kishwar Khán, Asad Khán's son, who possessed great wealth and influence, sided with the elder son Ali, and after Ibráhim's death released him from Miraj and placed him on the throne as Ali Adil Sháh (1557-1579). In 1558 Muhammad Kishvar Khán, who was made commander-in-chief, was sent as ambassador to Rám Ráya the regent of Vijayanagar (1542-1565) to enter into a league with him against Ahmadnagar. The embassy was successful and Rám Ráya was of great assistance to Bijápur. Though useful Rám Ráya proved a dangerous ally. He grew arrogant and wrested several districts from Bijápur probably parts of east Belgaum.[2] Enraged with his insolence Kishwar Khán negotiated a league against Rám Ráya to which the four Musalmán kings of Bijápur, Ahmadnagar, Golkonda, and Bidar became parties.

Overthrow of Vijayanagar, 1565.

In 1565 this league ended in the complete defeat of Rám Ráya at the battle (25th January) fought on the banks of the Krishna eighteen miles south of Tálikoti in the Muddebihál sub-division of Bijápur. Though the overthrow of Vijayanagar was complete, the jealousy of Bijápur and Ahmadnagar prevented either power from annexing any part of the conquered country. As much of it as had formerly belonged to Bijápur and had been lately usurped by Rám Ráya was recovered by Vitta Gauda Pátil of Avrádi on the Bhima. This Vitta Gauda is the ancestor of the Navalgund chief, now the *desái* of Sirsangi, about twelve miles north-east of Saundatti. Under Ibráhim Adil Sháh he commanded a body of horse and foot, and, in reward for his services, obtained the chief hereditary office of the

---

[1] Stokes' Belgaum, 45.

[2] Silcock's Bijápur, 27. An undated inscription of Sadáshiv Ráy the nominal ruler of Vijayanagar (1542-1573) has been found at Murgod about twenty-five miles east of Belgaum. Dr. Burgess' Archæological Lists, 46.

Chapter VII. History. Bijápur Kings, 1489-1686. *Their Conquests.*

division of Kokkatanur now in Athni. He distinguished himself at the battle of Tálikoti, where he supplied and commanded 1000 horse and 2000 foot. After the battle he took the fort of Torgal in East Belgaum, the sub-divisions of Terdal and Yádvád, the Parasgad villages of Sattigeri, Saundatti, Govankop, Yakkundi, Murgod, Asundi, and Huli, and the Bádámi village of Mutkavi. In 1566 Ali Adil Sháh rewarded Vitta Gauda by creating him Sar Desái of Torgal and conferred on him many rights and honours.[1]

In 1568 the natural dislike and suspicion of Ahmadnagar and Bijápur once more brought on a war. Kishwar Khán was presented with his father's standard the Angry Lion, and was sent to ravage Ahmadnagar, a service which cost him his life. In 1570 Ahmadnagar and Bijápur again joined to form a league. With the assistance of the Musalmáns of Kalikat they determined to attack all the Portuguese possessions and ruin their power. The heroic defence of Cheul against the Ahmadnagar army and of Goa against Bijápur ended in the total defeat of the allies.[2] Still the alliance had important effects. The feeling between Ahmadnagar and Bijápur grew more friendly, and in 1573 they agreed that Bijápur would not stand in the way of Ahmadnagar's conquest to the north and north-east and that Ahmadnagar would in no way hinder the spread of Bijápur power to the south. Ali Adil Sháh accordingly turned his attention to the country still held by Vijayanagar. In 1573, before reducing Dhárwár and the surrounding territory, Ali Adil Sháh marched on Turkul, that is Torgal. This in 1566 the king had himself granted to Vitta Gauda, or, as Ferishta calls him Venkatti Yesov Ráy, but Vitta had since refused to acknowledge Bijápur as his overlord. After a siege of seven months Vitta Gauda or Venkatti gave himself up and was put to death with torture.[3] Vitta's estates seem to have remained in his family. By the capture of Dhárwár and Bankápur in the same year, Belgaum and Kittur ceased to be frontier districts. The change reduced their military importance, but probably increased their safety and wealth.[4] In 1583 the English traveller Fitch found Belgaum, the first town between Goa and Bijápur, a good market for diamonds, rubies, sapphires and other precious stones.[5] From this time, for more than a century, the whole of the Bombay Karnátak remained under Bijápur.

In 1580 Ali Adil Sháh was assassinated and was succeeded by his nephew Ibráhim Adil Sháh (1580-1626) a minor. In 1582, taking advantage of the confusion which prevailed at Bijápur, the kings of Ahmadnagar, Golkonda, and Bidar besieged Bijápur, but the energy of Dilávar Khán, a Bijápur nobleman, forced the invaders to raise the siege. The Nizám Sháhi army returned to Ahmadnagar, on the way plundering Hukeri, Ráybág, and Miraj.[6] In 1593 prince Ismáil the brother of king Ibráhim II., who, since 1580, had been

---

[1] Stokes' Belgaum, 36.

[2] Briggs' Ferishta, III. 521, 523; Faria y Souza in Kerr's Voyages, VI. 423; Da Cunha's Cheul, 49, 54.

[3] Briggs' Ferishta, III. 135.

[4] Stokes' Belgaum, 37.

[5] Fitch in Harris' Voyages, I. 207.

[6] Briggs' Ferishta, III. 154, 443.

Chapter VII. History. Bijápur Kings, 1489-1686. Disorder, 1593.

kept a state prisoner at Belgaum, won the governor and garrison of Belgaum to his side, possessed himself of the fort, and broke into open revolt. Burhán Nizám of Ahmadnagar promised him help, and most of the Bijápur nobles openly or secretly sympathised with him. Ibráhim sent an army under Eliás Khán to quell the rebellion and besiege Belgaum where the prince still remained. During the siege Ein-ul-Mulk, a commander in Ibráhim's army, outwardly aiding the siege, secretly strengthened Ismáil's garrison by sending them grain and other necessaries and at last openly declared in Ismáil's favour. The siege was broken and Eliás Khán retired to Bijápur. Ein-ul-Mulk with an army of thirty thousand men marched to Belgaum and persuaded prince Ismáil to quit the fort and move towards Bijápur. Before they started a second army under a fresh general Hamed Khán came from Bijápur. Hamed Khán professed great respect for Ismáil and attachment to his cause. Tempted by the prospect of Hamed Khán's support Ein-ul-Mulk and prince Ismáil left Belgaum. When too far from the fort to seek safety in flight, Hamed Khán fell on them, slew Ein-ul-Mulk, and captured prince Ismáil who was shortly after put to death.[1] Of Bijápur rule in Belgaum during the rest of the sixteenth and the early part of the seventeenth century little information has been traced. From 1569 till 1615 Hukeri was held by a Bijápur officer, named Ranadulla Khán, who in 1616 was succeeded by his son Rustam Zamán. Afterwards Rustam Zamán was promoted to Miraj and Kolhápur, and Hukeri was given to one Abdul Kharid. 1629-30 was a rainless year, followed by famine and pestilence.[2]

War with the Moghals, 1631.

The spread of Moghal power southwards over Gujarát in 1584 and Khándesh in 1590, received a check after the fall of Ahmadnagar in 1600. The military and civil talents of Malik Ambar recovered most of the Ahmadnagar territories for his master Murtaza Nizám Sháh II. (1605-1631) and maintained his power till Malik Ambar's death in 1626. In 1631 the Moghal general Ásaf Khán laid siege to Bijápur. His provisions were cut off and he was forced to withdraw revenging himself by cruelly wasting the Bijápur country as far west as Miraj and Ráybág.[3] In 1635, after the submission of Daulatabad, the Emperor Sháh Jahán's (1626-1657) title to the Ahmadnagar country was disputed by the first of modern Maráthás, Sháhji, the father of the great Shiváji, who was supported by Bijápur. Sháh Jahán sent his general Khán Zamán against Sháhji who was driven from the north towards Miraj and Kolhápur. Khán Zamán, weary of fruitless pursuit, employed his forces in laying waste the country about Kolhápur, Miraj, and Ráybág. He took and destroyed the towns, carried off the people, and pressed forward every means of ruin till Bijápur made peace and left him to pursue Sháhji. This war ended in the final overthrow of the Ahmadnagar kingdom (1636), the establishment of Moghal power as far south as the Bhima, and the transfer of the rest of Ahmadnagar to Bijápur on payment of a tribute to the Delhi Emperor.[4] In 1643 Abdul Kharid, the last Musalmán chief of Hukeri who had been ousted by the

---

[1] Briggs' Ferishta, III. 176-182.
[2] Grant Duff's Maráthás, 46.
[3] Elliot and Dowson, VII. 30.
[4] Grant Duff's Maráthás, 52.

Chapter VII.
History.
Bijápur Kings, 1489-1686.
Marátha Raids, 1648-1680.

Marátha chief of Panhála died and an attempt to reinstate his son failed.[1] In 1648 Belgaum seems to have formed part of the service-estate or *jágir* of Muhammad bin Zabit Khán, originally an Abyssinian slave of the name of Rehán, then a leading officer in the Bijápur army.[2] In 1649 Linga Gauda the fourth descendant of Vitta Gauda of Torgal received some lands as a reward for distinguished service in the field. In 1656, seven years after Shiváji's revolt against Bijápur, Muhammad Sháh who succeeded Ibráhim Adil Sháh in 1626 died, leaving behind him Ali Adil Sháh II. (1656-1672) a youth of nineteen. In 1657 Aurangzeb, then viceroy of the Deccan, began an unprovoked war with Bijápur and marched against the young king. The Bijápur army was led by Muhammad Khán of Belgaum now general and prime minister. Owing to the treachery of Muhammad Khán, who was bought by Aurangzeb, the Moghal army arrived unopposed before Bijápur. The city was saved by the alarming illness of Sháh Jahán which took Aurangzeb suddenly to Delhi. A hasty peace was concluded and the Moghal army retired from Bijápur.[3] Muhammad Khán the traitor was asked to court under promise of protection. As he entered the city, he was dragged from his elephant and murdered,[4] and his estate bestowed on his son Khawás Khán.[5] The peace with the Moghals enabled Ali Adil Sháh to turn his arms against his rebel subject Shiváji the founder of the Marátha empire. In 1659 under Afzul Khán an army was sent against Shiváji. Afzul Khán made his way west as far as Mahábaleshvar, and there near Pratápgad was deceived and slain by Shiváji and his army destroyed. Shiváji followed up this success by seizing the fort of Panhála about ten miles north-west of Kolhápur, and with it the Kolhápur district including the Sankeshvar sub-division of Belgaum.[6] The Bijápur officer Rustam Zamán who held Miraj and Kolhápur, according to letters from English merchants at Rájápur and Kárwár, was believed to have been bribed by Shiváji and to have shared in the plunder of towns in his own estate or *jágir*.[7] When too late to save Kolhápur Rustam Zamán was ordered to march against Shiváji. With 3000 horse and a small body of infantry he advanced to Panhála; was defeated with great loss, and was driven across the Krishna followed by Shiváji who plundered the country as far as Bijápur, levied contributions, spread terror, and baffled pursuit.[8] In 1661 the Bijápur king took the field against Shiváji and regained Panhála. In spite of this loss Shiváji's power spread so rapidly that in 1662 Bijápur agreed to cede him the Konkan from Kalyán to Goa, and the Deccan from the north of Poona to the south of Miraj.[9] In 1666, in spite of this favourable settlement, Shiváji joined the Moghals in attacking Bijápur. In 1668 Ali Adil Sháh was so humbled that he concluded a peace with the Moghals and made an agreement with Shiváji under which the

---

[1] Moor's Narrative of Captain Little's Detachment, 14. [2] Stokes' Belgaum, 40.
[3] Grant Duff's Maráthás, 70-71; Elphinstone's History, 516.
[4] Silcock's Bijápur, 39; Grant Duff's Maráthás, 75.
[5] Grant Duff's Maráthás, 75. [6] Grant Duff's Maráthás, 79; Stokes' Belgaum, 41.
[7] Grant Duff's Maráthás, 80; Stokes' Belgaum, 41.
[8] Grant Duff's Maráthás, 80. [9] Grant Duff's Maráthás, 85.

Bijápur king engaged to pay £30,000 (Rs. 3,00,000) to prevent Shiváji levying the one-fourth or *chauth* of the Bijápur revenues.[1] From 1668 to 1686 Hukeri is said to have been held by Induráv Ghorpure.[2] In 1672 Ali Adil Sháh died leaving a son, Sultán Sikandar (1672-1686) a child of five years. Khawás Khán who in 1661, as second in command, had accompanied Ali Adil Sháh in his expedition in the Karnátak was made regent. Before his death Ali Adil Sháh suggested that the leading nobles should be put in charge of the different provinces of the kingdom, the Bombay Karnátak being assigned to Abdul Karim Khán the founder of the family of the Sávanur Nawábs. The regent set aside these arrangements fearing that the nobles when in charge of their provinces would treat his authority with little respect. Khawás Khán's decision caused much ill-feeling at Bijápur.[3] In 1673, taking advantage of the dissensions at Bijápur, Shiváji retook Panhála, and on his way to the sack of Hubli in Dhárwár plundered Belgaum.[4] From this time Shiváji seems to have been master of great part of Belgaum. In face of this fatal advance of Marátha power the Bijápur nobles set aside their private disputes. In 1673 Abdul Karim Khán was sent against the Maráthás and regained possession of the open country round Panhála. While he was busy in the west, a Marátha force appeared plundering near Bijápur. Abdul Karim was recalled to defend the capital, and, between Bijápur and Miraj, was attacked and forced to come to terms. In 1674 Abdul Karim Khán again marched to retake Panhála but was again defeated. In 1674, at his capital on Ráigad hill in Kolába, Shiváji assumed the titles and ensigns of royalty, and, in the same year, to strengthen his hold on the Belgaum country he is said to have built 360 strong places. Among these were the forts of Parasgad, Kathárigad, and Huli in the Parasgad sub-division. These and many other forts, each with a temple to Shiváji's patron goddess Bhaváni, were finished within eighteen months. To realize his claims on the surrounding country these forts were garrisoned, and, under grants from Bijápur, a fort cess or *gad-patti* was levied on the neighbouring villages.[5] In 1675 the regent Khawás Khán was assassinated because he had agreed to hold Bijápur as a province of the Moghal empire. The chief authority fell into the hands of Abdul Karim Khán, who defeated the Moghals in several actions and forced them to enter into terms honourable to Bijápur.[6] In 1679 on the death of the regent Abdul Karim Khán, the Moghals again laid siege to Bijápur. Abdul Karim Khán's successor applied for aid to Shiváji, though in the year before Shiváji had taken several of the Bijápur-Karnátak districts. Shiváji made a vigorous attack on the Moghal possessions in the Deccan. At this juncture his eldest son Sambháji, who was a prisoner at Panhála, revolted against his father and joined the Moghal army at Bijápur. Shiváji marched towards Bijápur, hovered around the besieging army, and by cutting off its supplies, forced Diláwar Khán the Moghal general to raise the siege. At the end of the rains Diláwar Khán attacked the open country and

[1] Grant Duff's Maráthás, 99. [2] Stokes' Belgaum, 42. [3] Grant Duff's Maráthás, 118. [4] Stokes' Belgaum, 42. [5] Stokes' Belgaum, 42. [6] Grant Duff's Maráthás, 120.

Chapter VII.
History.
Bijápur Kings, 1489-1686.
Máratha Power, 1680.

plundered Athni which then belonged to Shiváji. Athni or Hattani was an important centre of commerce which a few years before had large dealings with the English factory at Kárwár on the Kánara coast.[1] After the plunder of the town Diláwar Khán proposed to sell the Hindu inhabitants of Athni as slaves while Sambháji was anxious to keep them as subjects. Diláwar persisted in selling the people and Sambháji in disgust was reconciled to his father.[2] At the time of his death in 1680 Shiváji held the Belgaum country south to the Harankáshi a feeder of the Ghatprabha,[3] together with the forts of Párgad and Kálánandigad in Belgaum, Bhimgad in Khánápur, Vallabhgad, Mahipálgad, Pavitragad in Chikodi, and Murgod, Parasgad, Kathárigad, and Huli in Parasgad. Shiváji was succeeded by his son Sambháji. In 1681 Muhammad Akbar, the fourth son of the emperor Aurangzeb, rebelled against his father and sought Sambháji's protection. The village of Dodsay about twenty miles north of Belgaum was fixed for his residence, and, in compliment to his guest, Sambháji changed its name to Pádshápur or Páchhápur.[4] In 1683 the party in power at Bijápur attempted to recover the rich districts on the Krishna which had fallen into Shiváji's possession, and Miraj was retaken. This ill-judged aggression led to a final breach between the Maráthás and Bijápur, and prepared the way for the Moghal overthrow of the Adil Sháhi kingdom. In 1683 Aurangzeb left Delhi with a vast army intent on subduing the Deccan.[5] In 1684 he ordered his son Sultán Muázzim to march and retake the south-western districts which Shiváji had won from Bijápur.[6] Muázzim marched southwards and captured Gokák in 1685.[7] In 1686 Aurangzeb crippled Golkonda and turned his whole strength on Bijápur.

Fall of Bijapur, 1686.

After a gallant defence the city fell on the 15th of October 1686, and with the fall of Bijápur the Adil Sháhi dynasty came to an end. After the fall of Bijápur the Moghals drove the Maráthás out of Belgaum, except Hukeri now the Chikodi subdivision. The rest of the district practically formed part of the Moghal empire. A Bijápur noble Abdul Ráuf Khán, son of the late Abdul Karim Khán entered the Moghal service, and, with the title of Diláwar Khán Bahádur Diláwar Jang, was appointed *mansabdár* or governor of Bijápur country. Abdul Ráuf Khán was granted in *jágir* or estate, the twenty-two petty divisions or *máháls* subordinate to Banká-pur, Ázamnagar[8] or Mustafabad[9] that is Belgaum, and Torgal

---

[1] Orme's Historical Fragments, 86, 258; Ogilby's Atlas, V. 247; Hamilton's Description of Hindustán, II. 233; Moor's Narrative, 307.

[2] Orme's Historical Fragments, 86, 87.

[3] Grant Duff's Maráthás, 133.

[4] Grant Duff's Maráthás, 136.

[5] Grant Duff's Maráthás, 142.

[6] Grant Duff's Maráthás, 149.

[7] Orme's Historical Fragments, 144.

[8] According to Mr. Stokes (Belgaum, 45), after the fall of Bijápur, the fort of Belgaum remained for some years in possession of Aurangzeb's second son Ázam and from him was called Ázamnagar. This seems doubtful. According to Orme (Historical Fragments, 287) Belgaum was called Ázamnagar under the Bijápur kings. The province of Ázamnagar formed the western boundary of the district of Bankápur, and it contained within it the district of Gokák of which the town of Gokák was the head place.

[9] Belgaum was called Mustafabad in memory of its commandant or *kiládár* named Mustafa, who thoroughly repaired and strengthened the ramparts. Stokes' Belgaum, 45.

Abdul Ráuf Khán at first made Bankápur in Dhárwár his head-quarters. About the close of the seventeenth century he established himself at Sávanur and became the founder of the family of the present Nawábs of Sávanur. He was employed on various services and subdued the refractory landlords or *desáis* of the Bombay Karnátak. After they were reduced the *desáis* continued to administer the country paying a yearly tribute or *peshkash* to Abdul Ráuf Khán. Among these *desáis* the most important within Belgaum limits was Mudi Mallapa the Lingáyat *desái* of Kittur, who held Sampgaon and Bidi. The founders of this family were two brothers of the name of Hire or the elder Mulla, and Chik or the younger Mulla, who, towards the close of the sixteenth century, came into the district with the Bijápur army as moneylenders, and settled at Sampgaon. By distinguished services in the field the elder Mulla received the title of Shamsher Jang Bahádur and obtained a grant of the *sardeshmukhi* of the Hubli district. The fifth *desái* established himself at Kittur which was formerly sometimes called Gijaganahalli or Weaver-bird Town, and also became master of Sampgaon and Bidi. His son Mudi Mallapa was in power when Ráuf Khán made his settlement with the *desáis*. The other chief with whom Ráuf Khán made his settlement was the *desái* of Navalgund whose estates were continued to him. The parts of the district which for some years did not belong the Moghals was Hukeri in the west which was held by an independent *desái* the ancestor of the present Vontámurikar. During the disturbed times of Shiváji's plundering raids the Hukeri *desái* seems to have firmly established his power. He renounced all allegiance to Bijápur, assumed the independent title of *sansthánik* or estateholder, and by frequent encroachments gained a firm hold over his district. After the fall of Bijápur the Moghals allowed the Hukeri *desái* to remain undisturbed.[1] As the Moghals felt that there could be no security in Belgaum till the Maráthás were driven out of the neighbourhood, they continued to press them hard, till in 1690 Panhála was taken and placed under the charge of a Moghal officer.[2] In 1689 the power of the Maráthás was much reduced by the capture and execution of Sambháji, whose infant son Sháhu remained in Aurangzeb's power. In spite of the loss of their leader the managers of the Marátha state showed much energy and ability. Their forces swarmed all over the country, and their leaders exacted *chauth, sardeskmukhi*, and *ghásdána* from every district they entered.[3] In 1692 they retook Panhála and the fort of Torgal and defeated a Moghal officer stationed at Miraj.[4]

Condition, 1695.

Towards the close of the seventeenth century (1695) the Italian traveller Gemelli Careri passed through Goa, Kánara and Belgaum on his way to Galgalle about fifteen miles north of Kaládgi to see the Moghal camp. From Sámbráni in Kánara he arrived at Kakeri, a thinly peopled village about twenty-eight miles south-east of Belgaum. A march of twelve miles north brought him to Itgi, which, though made

[1] Stokes' Belgaum, 44.
[2] Grant Duff's Maráthás, 159, 163.
[3] Stokes' Belgaum, 45.
[4] Grant Duff's Maráthás, 166; Stokes' Belgaum 45.

Chapter VII.
History.
The Moghals, 1686-1723.
Condition, 1695.

up of cottages, had excellent land for tillage and sport, the stags and other game feeding tamely. A march of ten miles through a rich country took him to Tigdi, a small town defended by an earthen fort. From Tigdi he went to Vanur, and thence through a country full of green and delightful trees to Mamdápur, a city of mud houses enclosed with a low wall but with a good hill fort of lime and stone. From Mamdápur he went four miles to Betgire a walled town. A six-mile journey took him to Kalligudi, where, at a dear rate, he tasted ripe grapes like those of Europe. He then went to Yádvád, twenty-five miles east of Gokák, the largest city he had seen since he left Goa, but then visited with a plague. It had two enclosures. Within the first enclosure was an ill-built stone fort and a market, and within the second enlosure a garrisoned fort with mud and straw houses about it. All traders from the south bound for the Moghal camp at Galgalle halted at Yádvád. After visiting the Moghal camp he left Galgalle, passed through a country infested with robbers and enemies to Christianity, and returned to Yádvád, where he was disappointed in not finding any caravans or Christians on their way to Goa. On the 28th of March 1695, he started from Yádvád and arrived at the village of Kalligudi. From Kalligudi he marched to Mamdápur, ten miles south-east of Gokák, where he spent the night and passed the whole of the 29th in travelling. He spent the night under bushes in a field, in much dread of robbers, and next day made his way to Belgaum. Though with little but mud and thatched houses, Belgaum was a populous city on account of its trade. It had a large market and a good Musalmán fort built of stone and girt by a deep ditch full of water. In proportion to the size of the fort and the garrison the number of cannon was small. Next day (31st March) a Moor led him to Sháhápur a mile south, where he found a caravan of oxen ready to start for Bardes or Goa. The Kánarins or Goanese belonging to the caravan showed Careri much kindness, satisfying his three days' hunger with fowls and rice, but no bread, as the people were not in the habit of eating bread. He set out riding with the caravan and passed the night in a wood near the village of Jámboti near Khánápur belonging to a Say, that is *desái*, or prince of the same name, as the Moghals allowed some lords to possess these barren countries for a yearly tributo. After a few hours' riding, on the first of April, he passed by some cottages where were the officers of the custom house and guards of the roads who were worse than thieves. The night was spent on a mountain near some little huts of country people who had not a chicken or anything else Careri could eat. Travelling through such a country was difficult. There were no beasts of carriage; a man who had no horse of his own had to mount an ox. There were no provisions, rice, pulse, and meal being found only in great towns. There were no caravanserais or rest-houses on the road; at night a clear sky or else a tree was all a man's covering. There was no safety from daring thieves, and the country was disturbed by the raids of Marátha soldiers.[1]

[1] Churchill's Voyages, IV. 217-219; 249-250.

Chapter VII.
History.
Sátára, 1707-1730.

On Aurangzeb's death in 1707 prince Ázam, who aimed at the throne of Delhi, released Sháhu, the son of Sambháji, and on condition of stedfast allegiance promised him the territories which Aurangzeb had won from Bijápur. The release of Sháhu led to the establishment of two Marátha principalities under two of Shiváji's grandsons, Sátára under Sháhu and Kolhápur under Sambháji. In 1709 Sháhu's authority was much strengthened by an agreement with Daud Khán the Moghal viceroy of the Deccan, under which he and such Marátha chiefs as acknowledged Moghal authority were allowed one-fourth of the revenue of the Deccan, the right of collecting and paying their share being reserved by the viceroy.[1] In 1713 this treaty came to an end, and the Marátha armies again spread themselves over the Moghal territories collecting their tribute. In 1719 through the influence of the Sayeds who deposed the emperor Ferokshir (1713-1719), Sháhu received three imperial grants for the *chauth* or one-fourth and the *sardeshmukhi* or one-tenth of the revenues of the six Deccan provinces, among them Bijápur which included Belgaum. The third grant was for the *svaráj* or home rule of sixteen districts and forts. The only one of the sixteen districts included in the Maráthi *svaráj* or home rule which affected Belgaum was Panhála. Among the Belgaum forts which passed to Sháhu was Bhimgad in Khánápur and Phonda the centre of the Phonda Panch Maháls one of which was Khánápur.[2] Fatehsing Bhonsle, Rája of Akalkot, was appointed to collect the *chauth* and *sardeshmukhi* dues of the country in which Belgaum was included. But, owing to the power of Kolhápur and of the Sávanur Nawáb, for some years the Sátára government failed to enforce their rights over Belgaum.[3]

The Nizam, 1723.

In 1720 Chin Kilich Khán, Nizám-ul-Mulk, the Governor of Málwa, helped the emperor Muhammad Sháh (1719-1748) to get rid of the Sayeds. In 1723 he retired to the Deccan as viceroy and assumed independence. From that time the country south of the Narbada ceased to form part of the Moghal empire.[4] It was probably about this time that as viceroy of the Deccan Nizám-ul-Mulk quelled a disturbance in the Bijápur-Karnátak in which Belgaum was included, and appointed a new *subhedár* to that district. He is also said to have taken Athni and the fort of Belgaum.[5] After a short time Athni passed from the Nizám to Kolhápur.

Bájirão Peshwa, 1726.

In 1726 Peshwa Bájiráo (1720-1740), with a large army under Fatehsing Bhonsle, crossed the Krishna and marched as far south as Seringapatam, plundering the country through which they passed.[6] In 1730 after several repulses the Kolhápur chief yielded his claims to the chiefship of the Maráthás to Sháhu, and accepted Kolhápur as a distinct and independent state. Under the terms of a treaty then concluded, with a few exceptions the whole territory between the Krishna and the Varna on the north and the Tungbhadra on the

---

[1] Grant Duff's Maráthás, 188.
[2] Grant Duff's Maráthás, 200; Stokes' Belgaum, 47.
[3] Stokes' Belgaum, 47, 48.
[4] Grant Duff's Maráthás, 211.
[5] Stokes' Belgaum, 48.
[6] Grant Duff's Maráthás, 218.

Chapter VII. History. Sátára, 1726-1730.

south was assigned to Kolhápur, and Miraj Athni and Tásgaon on the north of the Krishna to Sátára.[1] In reward for the help given to Kolhápur, Jayappa the *desái* of Navalgund, the most distinguished member of the family and a man reputed to be wise and able, received among others the Parasgad villages of Hanchinál Saundatti and Sangráshikop. The object of his treaty was not so much to give over to the Kolhápur branch the sovereignty of the country ceded by the treaty, as to exclude the Kolhápur chief from all that lay to the north of the Krishna and from any share in the management of the rest of the Marátha territories. The object with which this treaty was concluded seems to have been gained as the Belgaum district seems at no time to have been in the possession of the Kolhápur chiefs, but, except the portions held by the Sávanur Nawáb and other petty chiefs, continued to be managed by Sháhu and the Peshwa.[2] The Nizám also divided the revenue with Sháhu and the Peshwa in such parts of the Bombay Karnátak as were not in the Marátha home rule or had not wholly been granted in private estates. About the same time (1730) Nág Sávant, the second son of Phond Sávant (1709-1737) of Sávantvádi, took the Hire and Chandgad districts above the Sahyádris, established a post at Chandgad about twenty-two miles west of Belgaum, and built the fort of Gandharvagad about four miles north-east of Chandgad.[3] Thus in 1730 Sháhu shared authority in the present district of Belgaum with the *desái* of Hukeri who was still independent in the west corner, with the Vádi chief in the south-west hills, and with the Sávanur Nawáb into whose hands, as his deputy, Nizám-ul-Mulk had passed the town and fort of Belgaum, and who held other parts of Southern, Eastern, and Central Belgaum. In 1734 Jayappa the *desái* of Navalgund built the fort of Saundatti.

The Sávanur Nawáb, 1746.

In 1736 the Deccan claims of Peshwa Bájiráv (1720-1740) were enhanced by the hereditary grant of the *sardeshpándegiri* or five per cent on the revenue of the six provinces.[4] The collection of the Maráthadues in the country between the Krishna and the Tungbhadra was yearly farmed to bankers. In 1746 Majid Khán, the Nawáb of Sávanur, who had long before thrown off dependence on the Moghals, resisted the authority of the Marátha farmer, named Bápu Náik Bárámatikar. In consequence of this a Marátha army under Peshwa Báláji's (1740-1761) cousin Chimnáji Bháu marched against the Sávanur Nawáb. The Nawáb was not strong enough to face the Maráthás and had to agree to a treaty under which he promised to yield thirty-six of his districts, among them Pádshápur, Kittur, Parasgad, Yádvád, Gokák, and Torgal. He was allowed to keep twenty-two districts together with the forts of Belgaum and Torgal which were his family possessions.[5] These possessions do not seem to have passed into the hands of the Maráthás. On Sháhu's death in 1749 Peshwa Báláji's scheme for usurping the sole authority offended his cousin Sadáshivráo Bháu. Sadáshiv left Poona in disgust and

---

[1] Grant Duff's Maráthás, 224.
[2] West's Kolhápur, 6; West's Southern Marátha Country, 22.
[3] Bombay Gazetteer, X. 441.
[4] Grant Duff's Maráthás, 235.
[5] Bom. Gov. Sel. CXII, 206.

Chapter VII.
History.
The Peshwás. 1746-1776.

was appointed Peshwa to the Kolhápur chief. About this time Kolhápur seems to have recovered the Chandgad district from Nág Sávant who had held it since 1730, and obtained the cession of the forts of Párgad, Kálánandigad, and Chandgad, together with a grant of land yielding £500 (Rs. 5000) a year.[1] Shortly after a settlement was effected between Peshwa Báláji and Sadáshivráo under which Sadáshivráo left Kolhápur and returned as prime minister to Poona. Towards the close of 1753 Peshwa Báláji made a land-quelling or *mulkgiri* expedition into the Karnátak to recover the arrears of the Marátha tribute. Beyond Marátha limits the distinction between revenue collecting and war disappeared. Whenever a village resisted, its officers were seized and forced to pay by threats and sometimes by torture. The garrisons of fortified places who made an unsuccessful resistance were put to the sword.[2] In February 1754, on the return of the army from Maisur the Maráthás took Gokák, which, though it had been ceded by the 1746 treaty, was still in the possession of the Sávanur Nawáb.[3] After taking Gokák the Marátha army marched west against a kinsman of the Vádi chief who still held the district of Hire. The *desái* of Hire was compelled to cede the Peshwa half of his land; the other half of forty-seven villages was continued to him, and was held by a descendant of his as late as 1840.[4] The neighbourhood of the Marátha army alarmed Iláchi Beg the Sávanur Nawáb's governor of Belgaum, and he wrote to Goa for help. But the Portuguese dread of the Marátha power, which had lately (1740) driven them out of almost all their possessions in the North Konkan was so strong that the Governor of Goa declined (15th May 1754) to help.[5] In 1755, in consequence of the refusal of Abdul Hakim Khán the Sávanur Nawáb to give up a Marátha deserter who had entered his service, the Marátha army under Peshwa Báláji, helped by the Nizám, marched against Sávanur, and so reduced the Nawáb that in 1756 he was forced to come to terms.

The Patvardhans.

This treaty deprived the Nawáb of eleven districts which are now in Dhárwár. As some compensation he was given part of the district of Parasgad. Probably about this time Belgaum fort passed to the Peshwa. The Peshwa seems not to have taken the lands of Belgaum under direct management, but to have left them for the most part to the *desáis* who were held responsible for the revenue.[6] In 1761, to check the power of Kolhápur and as a safeguard against the disorders which followed the death of Sambháji of Kolhápur, Báláji Peshwa gave the fort of Miraj and a military land grant or *saranjám* to Govind Haripant Patvardhan, one of his most active supporters. In 1763 Bálaji Peshwa reduced the Hukeri *desái* who since Shiváji's time had been independent, and, with other parts of the Karnátak, handed his district to the Kolhápur chief on condition of receiving a yearly present or *nazar* of £50,000 (Rs. 5,00,000).[7] In 1764 Govind Haripant Patvardhan of Miraj received as a military grant or *saranjám* to himself and his two nephews, Parshurám Rámchandra of Tásgaon and Nilkanthrái Trimbak of Kurundvád, lands yielding a yearly

---

[1] Grant Duff's Maráthás, 272. [2] Grant Duff's Maráthás, 281.
[3] Stokes' Belgaum, 49. [4] Stokes' Belgaum, 50. [5] Stokes' Belgaum, 50.
[6] Grant Duff's Maráthás, 287,289; Stokes' Belgaum, 51. [7] Stokes' Belgaum, 52.

Chapter VII.
History.
The Peshwás, 1746-1776.
The Patvardhans.

rental of £250,000 (Rs.25,00,000). Among the lands thus assigned, within Belgaum limits, were the villages in the Ainápur and Mánjre *karyáts* or divisions; eight detached villages or *phutgáms* of Hukeri, and the two *prants* or districts of Yádvád and Sháhápur near Belgaum. The yearly tribute of £14,000 (Rs. 1,40,000) paid by the Kittur *desái* also went to the support of the Patvardhan contingent. In 1769 Peshwa Mádhavráo (1761-1772), enraged by the continual inroads of Kolhápur marauders, deprived Kolhápur of Hukeri, and, in 1770, appointed a mámlatdár of his own, named Rámchandra Mahádev Paránjape, who, at the same time, held the fort of Manoli about twelve miles south of Chikodi in pledge for money advanced to Kolhápur. Late in the year the Kolhápur districts of Manoli and Chikodi were seized and given to the Patvardhans. This was the origin of the long and bitter enmity between Kolhápur and the Patvardhans, marked by a series of attacks and reprisals which continued as late as the early part of the nineteenth century.[1]

Haidar Ali, 1764.

Before these quarrels disturbed the peace of Belgaum a new power had risen in the south under Haidar Ali. This adventurer, about 1762, had deposed the Hindu king of Maisur and usurped authority. Taking advantage of the disastrous defeat of the Maráthás at the battle of Pánipat in 1761 (7th January) and their wars with the Nizám, Haidar Ali defeated the Sávanur Nawáb Abdul Hakim Khán, and in 1764 succeeded in stretching the northern limits of his kingdom across the Malprabha and Ghatprabha nearly to the banks of the Krishna.[2] In Belgaum his posts seem not to have passed the Malprabha as he held neither Gokák nor Belgaum.[3] These aggressions of Haidar's stirred the Maráthás to action and in the same year (1764) two armies, one under Gopálráo Patvardhan of Miraj and the second under Peshwa Mádhavráo (1761-1772) were sent to clear the Bombay Karnátak of Haidar's troops. The first army under Gopálráo Patvardhan was routed by Haidar's general Fazl-ul-la Khán; the second, under Peshwa Mádhavráo, succeeded in driving Haidar's troops out of the Bombay Karnátak, and in compelling (1765) Haidar to give up all claims on the Sávanur Nawáb and his country.[4] In 1772 Peshwa Mádhavráo died of consumption, which he believed was due to the curses heaped on him by the Kolhápur Ráni Jiji Bái, because in 1770 he had seized her two districts of Manoli and Chikodi. Shortly before Mádhavráo's death these two districts were restored to Kolhápur,[5] but the quarrels between Kolhápur and the Patvardhans did not cease. The death of Peshwa Mádhavráo in 1772, the murder of the young Peshwa Náráyanráo in 1773, the usurpation of authority by Rághoba or Raghunáthráo in 1773, and the opposition of the Poona ministers to Rághunatháro's claims to the headship of the Marátha state, were events of which the enemies of the Poona government, Kolhápur, Maisur, and Haidarabad were not slow to take advantage. The Kolhápur minister Yashvantráo Sindia, emboldened by an alliance with Haidar

---

[1] Stokes' Belgaum, 52, 53.
[2] Wilks' South of India, I. 461; Grant Duff's Maráthás, 330.
[3] Stokes' Belgaum, 52.
[4] Grant Duff's Maráthás, 331-332; Wilks' South of India, I. 462-466.
[5] Stokes' Belgaum, 54.

The Peshwás, 1746-1776.

Ali, made frequent raids on the Patvardhan territories; in September 1773 Haidar Ali sent his son Tipu with a strong detachment to recover the districts taken from him in 1765; and in 1774 Nizám Ali and his brother Salábatjang of Adoni entered the Marátha districts and levied contributions as far as Athni and Miraj.[1] In 1773 Konherráo Trimbak Patvardhan of Kurundvád marched into Kolhápur, destroyed many villages, and defeated the minister Yashvantráo at Bhoj twelve miles north-west of Chikodi. Towards the close of the year he again invaded the kingdom with greater success.[2] Vámanráo Patvardhan acted against Salábatjang and compelled him to retire. Against Haider Ali's son Tipu Peshwa Raghunáthráo marched in person. But before hostilities against Tipu were begun, the opposition of the Poona ministers to Raghunáth burst forth. This, and his want of money led Raghunáth to conclude a treaty by which Haidar Ali acknowledged Raghunáth as the sole head of the Marátha state and agreed to pay him and him only a yearly tribute of £60,000 (Rs. 6,00,000).[3]

Maisur, 1776-1790.

Shortly after the conclusion of the treaty of Surat with the Bombay Government, on the 6th of March 1775, Raghunáth proposed to Haidar that Haidar should take the whole of the Marátha territory up to the right bank of the Krishna holding himself ready to help Raghunáth with troops and money.[4] Under this agreement, in April 1776, Haidar marched northwards, and, before the rains, pushed his conquests as far as the territory of the Sávanur Nawáb. The Poona ministers sent a small force under Konherráo Trimbak Patvardhan to drive Haidar's garrisons from Sávanur. This expedition failed. In a battle near Dhárwár Konherráo was defeated and slain, and Pándurang Pant was taken prisoner by Haidar's general Muhammad Ali. In 1777 Parshurám Bháu of Tásgaon, now the leader of the Patvardhans, assembled a large army at Miraj, and, with the Nizám's troops, took the field against Haidar. He crossed the Krishna, but, as Ibráhim Beg the Nizám's general was bribed by Haidar, Parshurám was forced to recross the Krishna without risking an action.[5] By the end of 1778 the whole country south of the Malprabha in Belgaum and south of the Krishna in Bijápur passed into the hands of Haidar Ali. He found the country chiefly held by hereditary *desáis*, and for the present he agreed to receive their accustomed tribute or *peshkash*, on the condition of prompt payment as a free gift of a farther sum equal to their former payment.[6] The chief Belgaum *desáis* whom Haidar treated in this way were the *desáis* of Navalgund and Nargund, now in Dhárwár, and of Kittur. The Navalgund *desái* had to pay a present or *nazarána* of £42,500 (*Huns* 1,00,000). When the country was subject to them the Maráthás had assumed the management of all government or *khálsat* villages in the *desáis'* estates and continued to the *desáis* only the private or *inám* villages and their hereditary claims or *hakvartans* in government villages. Haidar restored the charge of all the villages to the *desáis*.[7]

---

1 Grant Duff's Maráthás, 363, 369; Stokes' Belgaum, 53.
2 Stokes' Belgaum, 54.
3 Wilks' South of India, II. 160; Grant Duff's Maráthás, 366.
4 Wilks' South of India, II. 173.
5 Grant Duff's Maráthás, 400.
6 Wilks' South of India, II. 187.
7 Stokes' Belgaum, 55.

Chapter VII.
History.
Maisur, 1776-1790.

The Poona ministers were too fully occupied with the war against Raghunáth and the English to allow them to make any serious attempt to dislodge Haidar. Haidar did not remain quiet. In 1777 he helped the Kolhápur minister Yashvantráo, a supporter of Raghunáth with money, and enabled the minister to drive off Rámchandra Hari a Poona officer who had been sent to retake Manoli and Chikodi which had been given to Kolhápur by Mádhavráo Peshwa (1761-1772) immediately before his death. On Rámchandra's defeat Mahádáji Sindia was sent against Kolhápur with a large army. As Haidar's promised force did not appear in time the Kolhápur minister was forced to come to terms. He agreed to pay £150,000 (Rs. 15 *lákhs*) for which Chikodi and Manoli were given as security, and to abstain from plundering the neighbouring districts and from harbouring rebels against the Peshwa.[1] After Mahádáji Sindia left in 1777 Parshurám Bháu of Tásgaon again began attacking Kolhápur and laid siege to Akkivát about fifteen miles north of Chikodi. Akkivát was gallantly defended by two brothers, but the death of both in an assault and want of provisions forced the garrison to surrender.[2] About the same time Khem Sávant II. (1755-1803) of Sávantvádi fomented a disturbance in Kolhápur with the result that the Kolhápur minister attached as much of the country as was held by Hire *desái*, a kinsman of the Sávantvádi chief, and took his fort of Gandharvagad. In 1778 the Kittur *desái* Irappa, backed by Haidar Ali overran and occupied Gokák. In 1779 to establish friendly relations with Abdul Hakim Khán, the Sávanur Nawáb, Haidar married his daughter to the Nawáb's son and his second son to the Nawáb's daughter. Not only were those of his own territories which were conquered during the late war (1776-1778) restored to the Nawáb, on payment of a tribute, but Parasgad including Sampgaon and Bidi, Gokák Pádshápur and Yádvád which had been taken from him by the Maráthás in 1756, were also given back to him. The Nawáb's authority over these districts was nominal. Parasgad with Sampgaon and Bidi, which since 1756 had belonged to the Kittur *desái*, another vassal of Haidar, were continued to the *desái* after a nominal transfer to the Nawáb. The Kittur *desái* also kept Gokák which he had occupied in 1778. Pádshápur, Yádvád and Belgaum never belonged to Haidar. They were held by the Maráthás throughout the whole of this time.[3] In 1779 Parshurám Bháu succeeded not only in reconquering Gokák for the Peshwa but in taking the Kittur *desái* prisoner. Gokák continued to belong to the Peshwa till 1783, when it was given in military grant or *saranjám* to the Patvardhans at a yearly revenue calculated at £9811 (Rs. 98,110).[4]

In 1779 the escape of Raghunáth from the banks of the Narbada and his reception by General Goddard at Surat induced the Poona ministers to form an alliance with Haidar and the Nizám. Both of these powers thought themselves aggrieved by the English and the object of the alliance was to drive the English out of India. To induce him to join this alliance, the Poona ministers agreed to acknowledge

---

[1] Grant Duff's Maráthás, 400; West's Kolhápur, 8. [2] Stokes' Belgaum, 58.
[3] Stokes' Belgaum, 56; Wilks' Mysore, II. 207; Bom. Gov. Sel. CXIII. 210.
[4] Stokes' Belgaum, 56-57.

Chapter VII.

History.

Maisur Power, 1776-1790.

Haidar's right to the Marátha territory south of the Krishna on payment of a yearly tribute of £110,000 (Rs. 11 *lákhs*).[1] Kolhápur was also induced to join by the cession of Manoli and Chikodi. This cession was only in name, as for twelve years, they remained undisturbed in the hands of Parshurám Bháu, to liquidate a contribution of £150,000 (Rs. 15 *lákhs*)[2] imposed on Kolhápur to meet the expense of the late wars. In 1781 Haidar's demands on the local estate-holders or *desáis* with whom he had negotiated in 1778 rose so high that Lingáppa the chief of Navalgund, after great disturbances, sought shelter in the Peshwa's territory. On the 17th of May 1782 the treaty of Sálbái brought to a close the war between the English and the Maráthás. While the treaty of Sálbái was being negotiated, Nána Phadnavis (1774-1800) the minister at Poona persuaded Haidar to restore the territory south of the Krishna, threatening, if his demand was not complied with, to join the English against Haidar. The rivalry between Nána Phadnavis and Mahádáji Sindia enabled Haidar to evade the Marátha demand. Haidar died in the latter part of 1782 (20th December) and was succeeded by his son Tipu (1782-1799). In 1782 Nána Phadnavis called on Tipu for arrears of tribute which he acknowledged to be due but evaded paying. Nána then formed an alliance with the Nizám to recover from Tipu the districts which both had lost through Haidar's encroachments. A hitch in the terms of the agreement enabled Tipu to strengthen his frontier by taking into his own hands the fortresses,[3] hitherto, under Haidar's arrangement with Raghunáth in 1774, held by their Marátha possessors.[4] In 1785 Tipu seized Nargund about thirty miles north-east of Dhárwár, Rámdurg, and Kittur, placing in Kittur a strong Maisur detachment. Tipu was not satisfied with the mere occupation of these forts; he forcibly circumcised many Hindus south of the Krishna and 2000 Bráhman disciples of Shankrácharya destroyed themselves to avoid the rite.[5] These outrages roused the energy of Nána Phadnavis who in 1786 formed an offensive alliance with the Nizám against Tipu. Their first efforts were directed to the recovery of the Marátha districts between the Krishna and the Tungbhadra. While the main army of the confederates advanced towards Bádámi in Bijápur and then on Dhárwár, Tukoji Holkar and Ganesh Pant Beheri were detached with 25,000 horse to attack a body of Tipu's troops under Burhán-ud-din near Kittur and to drive his garrisons from that district. Holkar's detachment succeeded in driving out Tipu's troops from every part of Kittur except the fort which was invested for more than a month, but with no result.[6] Though the balance of advantage in the war leaned to Tipu's side, fears of an English invasion led him in April 1787 to give Kittur and other places to the Maráthás. In the three years ending 1787, during which Kittur was under Tipu, his lieutenant Badr-ul-Zamán Khán took the management of the *desái's* estate or *jágir*

---

[1] Wilks' South of India, II. 208-210; Grant Duff's Maráthás, 441.
[2] Stokes' Belgaum, 57.
[3] Grant Duff's Maráthás, 465.
[4] Wilks' South of India, II. 536.
[5] Grant Duff's Maráthás, 446.
[6] Grant Duff's Maráthás, 468-69.

Chapter VII.
History.
Maisur Power, 1776-1790.

lands into his own hands, stripped him of all power, and set apart a sum for his support.[1] While the war between the Maráthás and Tipu kept the south in disorder the west was also disturbed. The chief of Nesari in Kolhápur joined the chief of Anur in a rebellion against his master the Kolhápur chief, and possessed himself of the fort of Vallabhgad about fifteen miles south-west of Chikodi, Gandharvagad about seventeen miles north-west of Belgaum, and Bhimgad about twenty-five miles south-west of Belgaum. In 1787 the Kolhápur army crushed the power of the rebels and took the three forts.[2] About the same time (1786) Parshurám Bháu took from the Torgal chief the fort of Manoli, about twenty-five miles south-east of Gokák, and added it to his possessions.

Third Maisur War, 1790-1792.

Tipu never intended to carry out the treaty of 1787. As soon as the Marátha army had recrossed the Krishna Kittur fort was again seized by the Maisur troops. On this occasion the *desái* Mallasarjya was taken prisoner, but he soon escaped and took refuge in the Marátha camp.[3] It was not till Tipu's attacks on Trávankor had broken the ties that bound the English to his alliance and set them free to join a confederacy against him, that the Poona government decided to punish Tipu's bad faith. In 1790 (1st June) a treaty was concluded between the English the Maráthás and the Nizám, whose object was to attack Maisur. Parshurám Bháu Patvardhan, who was appointed commander of the Marátha army, repaired to Tásgaon to make preparations. The English had promised to help Parshurám with two battalions and a suitable force of artillery. The English troops, consisting of the 8th and 11th battalions of native infantry, one company of European artillery, and two companies of gun lascars, with six field pieces, sailed from Bombay under Captain Little, disembarked at Sangameshvar in Ratnágiri on the 29th of May, ascended the Ámba pass by the 10th of June, and joined the Marátha army at Tásgaon in the latter part of June. July was spent in preparation. Besides by the English Parshurám Bháu was aided by a partisan officer named Dhondhu Pant Gokhale in command of 1000 horse. The confederate army crossed the Belgaum limits on the 19th of August and the English officers caught their first sight of the Krishna from the rising ground above Kágvád about twenty-three miles west of Athni. Thence they marched to the Krishna and encamped at Yedur, a favourite halting place with a magnificent grove of mangoes and tamarinds, about ten miles south of Kágvád. The Krishna was crossed in basket boats and the detachments were employed from the 10th to the 16th of August in getting over the guns and baggage. The army remained camped at Kaláli on the south bank of the Krishna till the 19th when they left the river, and, passing some miles west of Ráybág, in three marches reached the Ghatprabha opposite Gokák.[4] At Gokák a company of English officers went to see the falls whose thundering roar had been in their ears all the night. The town

---

[1] Stokes' Belgaum, 58. [2] Bom. Gov. Sel. VIII. 504.
[3] Grant Duff's Maráthás, 481; Stokes' Belgaum, 58.
[4] Moor's Narrative of Captain Little's Detachment, 2, 3.

Chapter VII.
History.
Third Maisur War, 1790-1792.
Condition, 1790.

of Gokák was remarkably neat and clean, then, as now, owing its prosperity to its weavers. The fort contained no artillery. On the 31st of August the British battalions started from Gokák and marched about twenty-five miles south-east to Manoli, camping for the night at Sidápur. On the 4th of September they crossed the Malprabha and entered Tipu's territory. They next marched to Saundatti going by way of Ugargol round Parasgad hill. From Saundatti they reached Gurl Hosur where they remained one day and then went on to Kallur within Dhárwár limits.[1] The Maráthás succeeded in driving out Tipu's garrisons from fortified villages and rapidly occupied the country. The people helped to expel Tipu's militia, or *sibandis*, and the militia, who were easily reconciled to a change of masters, enlisted with Parshurám Bháu, and aided him in collecting the outstanding revenue.[2] During this time the army was busy with the siege of Dhárwár which was gallantly defended by Tipu's general Badr-ul-Zamán. When the siege of Dhárwár had lasted from September to December with varying success and little progress, an additional English force was called in. A detachment under Colonel Frederick, composed of the 2nd Bombay regiment and the ninth battalion of native infantry sailed from Bombay on the 19th of November (1790), entered the Jaygad creek, reached the foot of the Ámba pass by the 14th of December, and, after passing through Sátára and Kolhápur, appeared on the 26th before Chikodi, a large and respectable town with an extensive market and a good manufactory of cloth chiefly for local use. The neighbourhood was famed for grapes of extraordinary size and flavour.[3] On the 27th of December the detachment marched about fifteen miles south to Hukeri, a poor town belonging to Parshurám Bháu, but with clear traces of former greatness. From Hukeri they marched ten miles south to Pádshápur, a pretty little village commanded by a decent fortification on a hill. From the number of water-courses the journey took eight hours. On the 28th of December they crossed the Márkándeya. On the 29th after leaving Pádshápur they passed through a thick forest called Manoli-Bári or the Manoli pass, ten miles of which was rugged and stony. The forest ran south for fifteen miles and lost itself in the hills to the south of Murgod. In some parts where the rivers took too great a sweep the forest was considered the boundary between the Maráthás and Maisur.[4] The detachment halted at Nesargi or Nesauri, a small village about fifteen miles south of Pádshápur. On the 30th of December they marched six miles to Imsal, a miserable village where sums of money were collected and distributed among the poor. On the 31st they marched eighteen miles south to Dodvád a pretty large place with a good-looking fortification lately repaired. After leaving Dodvád, Colonel Frederick joined the army at Dhárwár. After the fall of Dhárwár, on the 4th of April, the army moved south of the Tungbhadra as far as Seringapatam. Parshurám Bháu accompanied the English

---

[1] Stokes' Belgaum, 60.
[2] Grant Duff's Maráthás, 486.
[3] Moor's Narrative, 14.
[4] Moor's Narrative, 151.

Chapter VII.
History.
Third Maisur War, 1790-1792.
Condition, 1792.

army to Seringapatam, leaving the conquered country in the hands of Dhondu Pant Gokhale, who was authorized to collect money from the Kittur *desái* for Parshurám Bháu. In February 1792 the third Maisur war (1790-1792) was brought to a close. The victorious army moved northwards and again passed through Belgaum. On the 7th of May 1792 the army marched from Betigeri in Dhárwár to Dodvád, and from Dodvád to Murgod by a very good road. In point of soil the country round Murgod was as rich as the best garden mould. A little north of Murgod were some gardens with a well of excellent water. On the 9th of June they entered the Manoli forest, the rugged and stony ground wearying their cattle. They halted at Jamnahal a very poor village. For two miles north of Jamnahal the road was rugged and confined by trees. A march of fourteen miles brought them to Gokák where there was an extensive manufacture and sale of silk and cotton. On the 12th they crossed the Ghatprabha, and, after a march of three miles reached the village of Árbhávi near which was a beautiful mango grove enclosing a handsome building and a well ornamented with sculptures in the Kánarese style. After continuing their march for eight miles through a fairly good country they halted at Bhendvád about fifteen miles south-east of Chikodi. A nine miles' march through a stony barren tract brought them to Ráybág, a small village with no good houses, poorly inhabited, and with nothing to tempt settlers except some gardens to the north of the town. From Ráybág they marched north and crossed the Halhalla, or according to the Musalmáns the Dudhnála or Milk Stream, with the two villages of Birdi and Chinchani on the two banks. They found Chinchani a neat and populous village. From Chinchani they marched north and halted at Kudchi on the south bank of the Krishna. Kudchi had been a Musalmán town of some note, but Bráhman intrigues fomented by Parshurám Bháu had so distressed it that most of the Musalmáns had left. From Kudchi they crossed the Krishna to Ainápur. They found the Krishna the boundary line of the Marátha and Kánarese languages, and they also marked a difference in the style of houses on the two banks of the river. South of the Krishna the houses were flat-roofed and covered with mud or clay; north of the Krishna the roofs were pitched and thatched. Ainápur was a pretty large village with several neat buildings, both in the Hindu and Musalmán styles. They passed the villages of Katral, Tangri, and Shinál, and halted at Athni in a rich country reached by a very good road. The town belonged to Rástia who had spent much money in improving it. He had made several buildings, and, in 1785, planted an avenue of mango trees for about ten miles to the Krishna. The town was large, well-peopled, and thriving, trading with Surat in the north, Bombay in the west, and Ráichor in the east. The manufactures were silk and cotton cloth. From Athni they marched about seven miles east to Burchi a small village. Five miles farther east brought them to Aigali a good-looking village. From Aigali a fair road across an open country, apparently well peopled and capable of tillage, led them to Talsang

Chapter VII.

History.

Kolhápur Power, 1795 - 1799.

a respectable town. From Talsang they passed into Bijápur.[1]

As, under the treaty of Seringapatam, concluded in February 1792, the Marátha frontier was extended to the Tungbhadra, Parasgad and the Kittur *desái's* lands, which had been subject to Tipu, again became part of the Marátha country. These districts were assigned to Parshurám Bháu, who, in the late war had been forced to raise troops largely in excess of the number for which the Patvardhan's military grant or *saranjám* had been assigned. He placed a mámlatdár in Kittur and made it subordinate to Dhárwár, the *desái* receiving only an allowance for his support. On his return from Seringapatam, Parshurám Bháu found that by intrigues and by raising troops with the money obtained from the Kittur *desái*, Dhondu Pant Gokhle had grown so strong that he was forced to temporise with him. In 1793, just after his return, Parshurám turned his arms against Kolhápur and completely humbled the Kolhápur chief. About this time the district or *sarkár* of Ázamnagar or Belgaum, forming a part of the province or *subha* of Bijápur, contained fifteen subdivisions yielding a yearly revenue of £135,451 (Rs. 13,54,510).[2] The intrigues which followed the suicide of Mádhavráo Peshwa in 1795 and the accession of the last Peshwa Bájiráo (1795 - 1817) took Parashurám Bháu to Poona where he quarrelled with Nána Phadnavis. Parshurám Bháu remained at Poona till 1798. During his absence Nána incited the Kolhápur chief to attack Parshurám Bháu's districts. After the rains of 1796 the Kolhápur chief plundered some villages belonging to Parshurám Bháu and took the fort of Vallabhgad above Sankeshvar. He laid siege to Tásgaon, took and sacked it, burning Parshurám Bháu's palace to the ground. He also took possession of Chikodi and of Manoli after a siege of one month. The forts of Saundalgi about ten miles north-west, and of Birdi about sixteen miles north-east of Chikodi, were also captured by the Kolhápur troops with some loss owing to the obstinate resistance of the garrison who mined the chief towers and blew them into the air as the assailants entered. Towards the close of 1797 the Kolhápur army again entered Belgaum. Gokák was forced to pay a tribute of £12,000 (Rs. 1,20,000), the Kittur *desái* was mulcted in a large sum as tribute, and officers were left to manage the country and collect the revenue on behalf of Kolhápur.[3] Dhondhu Pant Gokhale, who through Bájiráo's friendship had been appointed the Peshwa's governor or *sar-subhedár* in the Bombay Karnátak, was the only officer of the Peshwa who opposed the Kolhápur troops. In 1798, he defeated unaided the Kolhápur army near Dhárwár, but instead of

[1] Moor's Narrative, 252 - 271 ; 300 - 308.

[2] The details are : Haveli yielding Rs. 2,78,350, Ájere Rs. 56,250, Kápsi Rs. 30,000, Mahpor Rs. 78,990, Gokák Rs. 11,250, Sháhápur Rs. 46,867, Mansari Rs. 15,000, Tole Rs. 37,500, Merkikhanápur Rs. 37,500, Mujali Rs. 50,193, Kanti Rs. 53,893, Sholápur Rs. 61,125, Sedelgaum Rs. 12,872, Tabevali Rs. 3,18,750, and Talari Rs. 1,75,975. Waring's Maráthás, 245. The Athni sub-division with a yearly revenue of Rs. 69,466 formed part of the district or *sirkár* of Bijápur Darubzefi.

[3] Bom. Gov. Sel. VIII. 506.

Chapter VII.
History.
Kolhápur Power, 1795-1799.

making a proper use of his victory he robbed the down-trodden chief of Navalgund of his two districts of Navalgund and Gadag in Dhárwár. The chief, the ancestor of the *desái* of Sirsangi in Belgaum, since 1756, had been deprived of his large estates by the Peshwa, who gave him some villages for his private support. In 1790 Parshurám Bháu promised to help him to recover his estates. The Peshwa's government, while refusing to release the lands of the estateholders until the expenses of the third Maisur war (1790-1792) had been reimbursed, granted ten more villages for the Navalgund chief's support, which are those still remaining with the family, except Belári which was given in exchange for Gurl Hosur. The chief was not satisfied with this small concession. He intended to go to Poona to negotiate the release of his whole estate, but the confusion which followed the death of Mádhavráo Peshwa (1774-1795) made him put off his visit. In 1798, while brooding over his misfortunes, he was deprived of Navalgund and Gadag by Dhondhu Pant Gokhale. The beaten Kolhápur army was reinforced and defeated Gokhale, and, with the object of binding the *desái* to his interest, the Kolhápur chief restored him the whole of his former estate.[1] In 1799 Nána Phadnavis was reconciled to Parshurám Bháu. Before beginning operations against Tipu in the fourth Maisur war (13th February-4th May 1799), Parshurám received orders from Poona to watch the Kolhápur chief, who was always friendly to Tipu, and to prevent him laying the country waste. Parshurám Bháu marched south and retook all the forts between the Ghatprabha and the Malprabha. In September he passed from Gokák and halted in great force at Chikodi. The Kolhápur army of 16,000 men, led by the chief in person, was camped on the low hills near Patankodi, a small village three miles east of Nipáni. In the battle which followed Parshurám Bháu was mortally wounded. He was taken prisoner, carried into the presence of the Kolhápur chief, and, though this is denied by all belonging to Kolhápur, was cut to pieces.[2] After the death of Parshurám Bháu his son Rámchandra, commonly called Appa Sáheb, fled to Poona for aid. His prayer was granted as both the Peshwa and Sindia were more than ever anxious to repress Kolhápur. A large body of Poona troops, with five battalions under Major Brownrigg from Sindia's disciplined levy, marched against Kolhápur,[3] while Dhondhu Pant Gokhale, the Peshwa's *sar-subhedár* or governor of the Bombay Karnátak, was also directed to march to Kolhápur. The Peshwa's army appeared before Kolhápur in November 1799 and the siege lasted till March 1800. The siege would have been disastrous to Kolhápur, but for the death of Nána Phadnavis on the 13th of March 1800. By Nána's death power passed to the party at Poona, who were hostile not to Kolhápur but to the Patvardhans. The Peshwa Bájiráo was the Patvardhans' bitterest enemy, and Sindia had long wished

[1] Stokes' Belgaum, 62-63.

[2] In 1790 Captain Moor described Parshurám Bháu as a man about fifty or fifty-five years of age with a stature rather under the common size. Though not very well looking he had something interesting and a great deal of good nature in his countenance. Narrative, 17.

[3] Bom. Gov. Sel. VIII. 507; Grant Duff's Maráthás, 547.

Chapter VII. History. Kolhápur Power, 1795-1799.

to possess himself of their extensive and rich estates. It was this treachery which prevented the capture of Kolhápur. Rámchandra Patvardhan, hearing of the arrangement between Bájiráo and Sindia retired from Kolhápur, and Sindia's five battalions were ordered to attack the Patvardhan estates. Sidojiráo Nimbalkar, commonly called Appa Sáheb *desái* of Nipáni, who, under Sindia's directions, had been engaged in a series of forays into the Miraj country, besieged the fort of Neráli between Sankeshvar and Hukeri. The siege was at first unsuccessful. On the arrival of Sindia's troops the garrison left the place, and Neráli was taken in the name of the Nipáni *desái*.[1] Sindia's battalions were shortly after recalled; but the Nipánikar at the head of a body of horse plundered and wasted the country from Miraj to Bijápur.[2] At this time Sindia forced the Peshwa to cede Manoli and Chikodi to Kolhápur and they were taken by Sindia's and the Nipáni *desai's* troops nominally on behalf of Kolhápur.

Colonel Wellesley, 1800.

On the 4th of May 1799 the fourth Maisur war was brought to an end by the capture of Seringapatam, the death of Tipu, and the destruction of Musalmán power in Maisur. Among other territory the English, who had borne the burden of the war, obtained Sunda in North Kánara on the western border of Dhárwár. On the fall of Seringapatam, Dhundhia Vágh, who under Haidar had risen to a high rank from a common soldier and who since 1794 had been imprisoned by Tipu for refusing to become a Musalmán, was set at liberty. On his release he began to plunder, and, finding pursuit too hot in the English territory, retired north into the Marátha country, and, at Dhárwár, gathered round him a desperate band. Before going to Kolhápur Dhondhu Pant attacked Dhundhia, and captured his family and all his effects. After this defeat in August or September 1799, Dhundhia entered the Kolhápur service. He soon after quarrelled with the Kolhápur chief and in November began to plunder the country, while Dhondhu Pant Gokhale and other Marátha chiefs were engaged in the siege of Kolhápur. He plundered several places near Kittur, took the title of the King of the Two Worlds, and was joined by the discontented of all classes, chiefly Musalmáns from Aurangabad and Haidarabad, and by almost the whole of Tipu's cavalry. By the 18th of June 1800 Dhundhia had gained possession of the whole country north of the Tungbhadra and threatened the territory lately acquired by the English. Colonel Wellesley, afterwards the Duke of Wellington, who was in Maisur, represented that it was impossible to settle the Marátha frontier so long as Dhundhia remained at large. The Poona government seemed gladly to take advantage of Colonel Wellesley's proposal to clear the Marátha country of Dhundhia and his men, and ordered Dhondhu Pant Gokhale and Appa Sáheb the son of Parshurám Bháu to co-operate with Colonel Wellesley. It was arranged that Dhondhu Pant Gokhale was not to cross the Malprabha till Colonel Wellesley had crossed the Varda. Dhondhu Pant did not keep to this arrangement, a mistake which

---

[1] Bom. Gov. Sel. VIII. 510. [2] Grant Duff's Maráthás, 551.

Chapter VII. History. Colonel Wellesley, 1800.

cost him his life. Colonel Wellesley crossed the Tungbhadra with a large army on the 26th of June 1800, and the Varda on the 7th of July. More than a week before Colonel Wellesley had crossed the Varda and while Dhundhia was camped at Hubli in Dhárwár, Dhondhu Pant, contrary to agreement, crossed the Malprabha, and entered the Kittur country nominally to act against Dhundhia, really with the object of making peace with him. He restored to Dhundhia his family and all the effects that had fallen into his hands in 1799. Dhundhia suspected Gokhale of double dealing and marched against him, and, to the south of Kittur, on the 30th of June, attacked the rear guard which was commanded by Gokhale, and put his force to flight. Dhondhu Pant was killed, and, in fulfilment of a vow made when he was defeated in 1799, Dhundhia dyed his moustaches in Gokhale's heart-blood.[1] Dhundhia remained in the Kittur country until Colonel Wellesley's arrival at Sávanur drew him in that direction. He did not dare to risk an engagement, and fled. Towards the end of July he lay at Saundatti with his main force. After clearing Dhárwár of Dhundhia's adherents, on the 29th of July, Colonel Wellesley, accompanied by Appa Sáheb the son of Parshurám Bháu and Bápu Gokhale the nephew of Dhondhu Pant, crossed the Bennihalla at Alagvádi, about fifteen miles south of Saundatti. When he heard that Colonel Wellesley had reached Alagvádi, Dhundhia at once broke from Saundatti. He sent one part of his army west to Dodvád, a second east, and a third with baggage north to Manoli. On the 30th of July Colonel Wellesley marched from Alagvádi to Ugargol east of Parasgad hill, and hearing that Dhundhia was opposite Manoli with his baggage, in the hope of surprising him, pressed on twenty-six miles to the Malprabha opposite Manoli. At three on the same afternoon Colonel Wellesley directed a cavalry onset on the enemy's camp. Lieutenant-Colonel Torin attacked their left with the 1st and 4th Regiments, and Colonel Stevenson and Colonel Peter their front and right with the 25th Dragoons and the 2nd Regiment of cavalry. Dhundhia's camp was strong with its rear to the Malprabha, covered by the fort of Manoli on the other side of it, and a deep stream along its front and left. The 2nd Regiment of cavalry was the only corps which forced its way into the camp, but every person in the camp was either killed or driven into the river. All the baggage, two elephants, and many camels horses and bullocks were taken. Numbers were drowned or shot in trying to cross the river, and many women and children were taken prisoners. Major Blaquiers with four troops of the 25th Dragoons pursued to the east a party which appear to have been outside of the camp, and drove them into the river. Six of Dhundhia's guns had been passed over the swollen stream before the attack. Half an hour after the camp was carried a party of the 25th Dragoons attempted to swim the river and seize a boat which was lying under the fort of Manoli. The force of the flood carried them below the spot where the boat lay. But two officers Lieutenant Fitchet and Jackson succeeded in stemming the current, brought

---

[1] Wellington's Supplementary Despatches, II. 51; Grant Duff's Maráthás, 551.

Chapter VII. History. Colonel Wellesley, 1800.

back the boat and with its aid the guns were soon taken, and to prevent them falling into the enemy's hands were destroyed.[1] About 5000 men were driven into the Malprabha and drowned. Among the rest one of the leaders, Bubber Jang, dressed in armour, rode his horse into the river and was drowned. During the action the Kolhápur fort of Manoli helped Dhundhia by firing on the English. After the action it was abandoned by the Kolhápur garrison, and, before Appa Sáheb Patvardhan's troops could get into it, was taken by the Páligár of Talur about eight miles north-west of Manoli.[2] His Marátha allies were of little use to Colonel Wellesley. None but Bálkrishna Bháu, Appa Saheb's agent, gave him any help. They would not obey his orders, and did so much harm plundering and wasting the country that Colonel Wellesley had to order them to camp at a distance.[3] After his defeat at Manoli Dhundhia made towards Kittur. From near Kittur he passed through a woody country round by the sources of the Malprabha. His want of boats forced him to make this march which proved so long and so trying that before it was over numbers of his troops had deserted him. He passed through Khánápur on the 4th of August, and on the 7th he arrived at Sháhápur about a mile south of Belgaum. Colonel Wellesley, starting from Saundatti on the 3rd of August, arrived at Kittur on the 5th. While he stayed at Kittur till the 10th preparing boats for the passage of the Malprabha, Colonel Stevenson, with Lieutenant Colonel Bowser's detachment and the 4th Regiment of Native Cavalry, lightly equipped, was detached on Dhundhia's track, with the object of cutting off part of his baggage. This detachment afterwards crossed the Malprabha before Colonel Wellesley, and for some time menaced Dhundhia's rear. Colonel Stevenson's detachment was ordered not to push the rebel force closely until the troops under Colonel Wellesley's personal command were forward enough to support their operations. Dhundhia, continuing his march east along the Ghatprabha, tried to pass the Ghatprabha west of Gokák, but, under Colonel Wellesley's orders, was prevented by the Chikodi *desái* named Nariti Sirjari. Colonel Stevenson's detachment continued its march along the Ghatprabha, while Colonel Wellesley, having passed the Malprabha, moved along its left bank. To prevent Dhundhia crossing the river with any large body of troops by the fords of the Malprabha east of Manoli and near Bádámi, Lieutenant Colonel Capper's brigade, with the Marátha cavalry, was detached by the road to the right of the Malprabha, and was ordered to occupy the passes most likely to be fordable. On the 22nd of August, Lieutenant Colonel Capper, marching through the valley of Parasgad, assaulted the fort of Huli and carried it by escalade. Though after the action of Manoli on the 30th of July, on condition that they committed no aggression, Colonel Wellesley had given this garrison a *kaul* or promise of safety from attack, they had plundered the baggage of the dragoons as it passed the fort on the march to

---

[1] Wellington's Supplementary Despatches, II. 81-84.
[2] Wellington's Supplementary Despatches, II. 86, 200.
[3] Wellington's Supplementary Despatches, II. 85.

Chapter VII.
History.
Colonel Wellesley, 1800.

Saundatti on the 1st of August. From Huli, Colonel Capper proceeded on the same day to Sungdal, another fort of great strength, about eight miles east of Huli, occupied by a petty chief in the interest of Dhundhia. As it was impossible to use ladders in storming this fort, the gateway was attacked and the outer gate carried. Inside of the outer gate the passage was too narrow for a gun carriage. The gun was taken off the carriage and borne to the inner gate under a heavy fire from the fort. This gallant enterprise was successfully accomplished by Sir John Sinclair and a detachment of the Coast and Bombay artillerymen, and the gate was speedily burst open. Hearing that the petty chief of Talur had guns, stores, and ammunition belonging to Dhundhia, Colonel Wellesley, on the 24th of August, despatched Lieutenant Colonel Montresor with a detachment to seize and destroy them. This service was satisfactorily performed. In Talur were found and destroyed one iron and four brass guns with excellent carriages, several tumbrils, a quantity of ammunition, and several Company's muskets with ammunition. The hill fort of Kathárigad was abandoned on Colonel Montresor's approach.[1] After evading pursuit through South Bijápur and the Nizám's country, on the 9th of September 1800, Dhundhia was killed at Kongal in the Nizám's territories. The parts of Belgaum wrested from Dhundhia were given to Appa Sáheb Patvardhan, from whom the Kolhápur chief had taken them between 1796 and 1799. During these wars the country suffered severely. Of eight bodies of troops manœuvring through it, Dhundhia's, the Chikodi *desái's*, Sindia's, the Kolhápur chief's, Bápu Gokhale's, Appa Sáheb's, and Colonel Wellesley's, all but Colonel Wellesley's lived on plunder.

Disorder, 1802.

Towards the end of 1801 war with Holkar called Sindia to the north, and Manoli and part of Chikodi came into the sole possession of the Nipáni *desái*, who held them on behalf of the Peshwa. In October 1802 Holkar drove the Peshwa Bájiráo from Poona and forced him to take refuge with the English. On the 31st of December 1802, under the treaty of Bassein, in return for cessions of territory the English undertook to restore the Peshwa to power in Poona and to guard his territories against attack. When, under the treaty of Bassein, the English undertook to keep order in the Peshwa's dominions, Belgaum was torn to pieces by the pretensions of seven independent authorities who held power in or near the borders of the district. Among these seven authorities were the Kolhápur chief who still held part of the district, which had been gained in his wars with the Patvardhans; Appa Sáheb Patvardhan who had as much of his estates restored to him by Colonel Wellesley as were wrested from Dhundhia Vágh: Sidojiráo Appa, *desái* of Nipáni, who maintained 300 horse and 400 foot; Sadáshiv Pandit who held the fort and country round Belgaum yielding a yearly revenue of £4000 (Rs. 40,000), and kept a force of 1000 horse and 2000 foot, supported by his estates in north Poona; Mallaserjya, *desái* of Kittur, who held

---

[1] Wellington's Supplementary Despatches, II. 156-57.

Chapter VII. History. Disorder, 1802.

the country round Kittur yielding a yearly revenue of £40,000 (Rs. 4,00,000), and kept a force of 1000 horse and 4000 foot, and was bound to pay the Peshwa a yearly tribute of £6000 to £7000 (Rs. 60,000-70,000). Among the servants of the Peshwa was Bápu Gokhale, who commanded a force of 2000 foot besides Pendháris, of whom he had at least 1000. He had also 1000 infantry with two or three guns. To pay these troops he held Gadag and Navalgund in Dhárwár, which yielded a yearly revenue of £50,000 (Rs. 5,00,000). He also made large sums from the plunder of the country near his districts. Amritráo, the adoptive brother of Bájiráo Peshwa, held Parasgad and Annágiri in Dhárwár, yielding a yearly revenue of £5000 (Rs. 50,000). Few of the actual estate holders had any legal hereditary right to their possessions which had generally been granted to their ancestors for military service. For years the Peshwa's government had been too weak to attempt to enforce the conditions of service on which the grants were originally made. The changes of fortune which befell the different estate-holders had been occasioned more by their disputes with each other, than by any exertion of authority on the part of the Poona government of which they were the nominal servants. The weakness of the Poona government, the troubles which shook the Marátha empire, and the example of others almost always led officers in command of troops and garrisons to make their authority permanent, and in some cases hereditary in their own family. The mode of paying them by orders on the revenues of the countries in which they were employed led to the complete establishment of their personal authority and the subversion of that of the Peshwa. It was also customary, as was done in the case of Parshurám Bháu, to assign the revenues of a district for a stated period to such estateholders as might have incurred an expense in the service of the Peshwa beyond the produce of their estates, and such temporary grants were often permanently annexed to their former possessions. The temporary allotment of a country to an estate-holder or the assignment of revenue to an officer of government for the payment of his troops usually ended in the independent establishment of the estate-holder or officer in the assigned country, or in a ruinous contest for the recovery of the state right. This system made every Marátha province a scene of petty warfare and enabled the subjects of the state to assume rights to which they had no other claim than usurpation and violence.[1]

General Wellesley's March, 1803.

According to the terms of the treaty of Bassein (31st December 1802) Major General Wellesley, who after Dhundhia's death had returned to Seringapatam, marched through the district on his way to Poona to reinstate Bájiráo as Peshwa. General Wellesley passed across Belgaum along the old road from Dhárwár by Sangoli, Nesargi, Nagar-Manoli, and Yedur. In their march through the Marátha territories the British troops were everywhere received as friends, and almost all the chiefs near their line of march joined their forces and accompanied the British army to

[1] Notes on the Transactions in the Marátha Empire (1804), 85.

Chapter VII.

History.

General Wellesley's March, 1803.

Poona. The friendliness of the estate-holders or *jágirdárs* and of the people was chiefly due to the fame which the British arms had won in General Wellesley's campaign against Dhundhia Vágh in 1800, and to the care and skill with which General Wellesley arranged for the supplies of his troops to the gain instead of to the loss of the people through whose country his route lay. This friendly feeling helped the English army without loss or distress to perform this long march in the trying month of April, in a season of severe famine.[1] Among the estate-holders who aided the British force, not from any loyal spirit to the Peshwa but from former knowledge of General Wellesley, were the *desái* of Nipáni who joined the British force at Nesargi with 300 horse and 100 infantry, and the *desái* of Kittur, who contributed 100 horse and 100 infantry to act with the British force. The Kittur *desái* also consented to give a small fort at Sangoli to serve as a post to keep up communications and guard the hospital and boats stationed there. The Kittur contingent, though furnished in a loyal spirit, was of little service. They had to receive constant advances to keep them from starving.[2] While the Nipáni *desái* was absent in Poona, the Kolhápur chief harassed his districts and persuaded the Talur *desái* Chandrappa to attack Manoli. Chandrappa besieged Manoli for some days and wasted the Nipáni country until General Wellesley sent Major General Campbell to guard Nipáni. Manoli was relieved, and as the Talur *desái* refused to come to terms and fled to Kolhápur, his fort at Talur was handed to the Nipáni *desái*.

Nipáni, 1804-1816.

In reward for his loyalty in joining the British army the Kittur *desái* escaped the intended loss of his estates, and in March 1804 the Nipáni *desái* received the title of *sarlashkar* and grants for lands in military service or *fauj saranjám* valued at £54,112 (Rs. 5,41,120) a year, besides the Manoli district and the petty division or *pargana* of Hukeri. The Kolhápur chief resisted the Nipáni claims to Manoli, and the two went to war. The war lasted six years (1804-1809). In 1808 the Nipáni *desái* completely defeated Kolhápur. In 1809, through the Peshwa's intercession, peace was concluded, by which, besides the disputed districts to be held on behalf of the Peshwa, the Nipáni *desái* received a Kolhápur princess in marriage.[3] In 1809 the Kittur *desái* Mallaserjya (1782-1816), who had been taken to Poona after the Peshwa's pilgrimage to Belári in 1805, entered into an agreement by which he promised to pay the Peshwa a yearly tribute of £17,500 (Rs. 1,75,000). In return for this agreement he received grants for his estates and the title of *pratáprão*. In commemoration of his title, near Nandgad town, the *desái* built a fort and called it Pratápgad.[4] In spite of his marriage with a daughter of the house, the Nipáni *desái* did not long remain at peace with Kolhápur. In 1811 he defeated the Kolhápur chief, marched on Kolhápur, and besieged it. The Honourable Mounstuart Elphinstone, who was Resident at Poona, interfered, and, on the 1st of October 1812, a treaty

---

[1] Notes on the Transactions in the Marátha Empire (1804), 11.
[2] Bom. Gov. Sel. CXIII. 196. [3] Bom. Gov. Sel. VIII. 512.
[4] Stokes' Belgaum, 71.

Chapter VII. History. Nipáni, 1804-1816.

was concluded by which the Kolhápur chief gave up all claim to Chikodi and Manoli. In 1813 the Nipáni *desái* was summoned by Bájiráo to Poona. He went but refused to comply with certain claims made by the Peshwa or to give up territory belonging to Kolhápur. The British authorities interposed, but Bájiráo artfully contrived to persuade the *desái* to trust to his lenience and to resist his demands. By this insidious conduct the *desái* was led to forfeit one-fourth of his estates to the Peshwa.[1] At the close of the rainy season of 1816 a detachment of the Poona subsidiary force was sent to enforce the forfeiture. The duty was not completed till the middle of December and then proved fruitless, for no sooner had the detachment returned to Poona, than the *desái* retook his lost possessions.[2]

The Peshwa's Overthrow, 1817.

The Peshwa's end was drawing near. His government of the Bombay Karnátak was hateful to the people. His revenue farmers ruined the small landholders who formed the bulk of the people. They and the traders were anxious to drive out the Marátha estateholders and their servants, because they ruined trade by arbitrary exactions, and often plundered traders of their whole property.[3] While they were hateful to the people the estateholders were not liked by the Peshwa, and they in turn hated their overlord. When the crisis came, the people volunteered, and, on behalf of the British, drove the Peshwa's officers out of the country. Most of the officers in charge of forts and districts stood by the Peshwa. Of the estateholders, a few, especially Appa Sáheb of Nipáni, served him but without will or spirit. The rest, among them the Patvardhans and the Kittur *desái*, were active in helping the English. In 1817, according to the terms of the treaty of Poona (13th June), the Peshwa, among other districts, ceded Dhárwár and Kushgal to the English. As, in the event of a rupture with the Peshwa, the early occupation of these lands was of great importance to the advance of an English army from the south Colonel Thomas Munro immediately took possession of Dhárwár fort. On the 5th of November the Peshwa's fate was sealed at the battle of Kirkee. After the battle, General Munro, in spite of the slender means at his disposal, succeeded in bringing the whole of Dhárwár and South Bijápur under the English.[4] On the 26th of February 1818 he reduced Bádámi and Bágalkot, and pressed up the right bank of the Ghatprabha to overrun the whole Marátha lands to the south of the Ghatprabha, and then be free to carry his arms north. The breakdown of some gun-carriages on the 26th delayed him, so that he did not reach Gokák till the 7th of March. On the 8th he crossed the Ghatprabha, and marching two days up the left bank recrossed to Ghodgeri, and, on the 11th, camped at the headquarter town of

---

[1] Grant Duff's Maráthás, 621. [2] Stokes' Belgaum, 72.
[3] Gleig's Life of Munro, I. 412.
[4] The troops under General Munro were three troops of the 22nd Light Dragoons, three artillerymen, eleven companies of native infantry, four companies of Maisur infantry, and four companies of Pioneers. His ordnance included one eight-inch mortar, one three and a half inch howitzer, two iron eighteen-pounders, two iron twelve-pounders, and four brass twelve-pounders. Stokes' Belgaum, 74.

Chapter VII.
History.
The Peshwa's Overthrow.
Siege of Belgaum, 1818.

Pádshápur which forthwith surrendered. Judging it unsafe to leave any fort in his rear in the enemy's hands, General Munro marched towards Belgaum which was then held on behalf of the Peshwa. He arrived before Belgaum on the 20th of March 1818 and took possession of the town or *petha* without delay, in order, before further operations, to gain cover as near to the fort as possible. The fort was found in perfect repair. It had a broad and deep wet ditch, was surrounded by an open space or esplanade six hundred yards broad, and was garrisoned by 1600 men. The Pioneers were set to work to prepare a battery of three twelve-pounders at a mosque opposite the north face of the fort. To favour their progress, a five and a half inch mortar and a six-pounder opened from the town. On the 21st the battery opened within eight hundred yards of the fort, and was answered by five guns which were nearly silenced in the course of the following day. On the night of the 22nd an enfilading or raking battery of two guns was completed in the town and swept the north face and the gateway. A gun opened on the enfilading battery from a small tower or cavalier within the works, and the fire of the twelve-pounder battery was returned from the curtain to the left of the gate. These efforts of the besieged were partly defeated on the 24th when the approach was begun and carried one hundred and forty yards. Next day the enemy fired nothing but gingals or wall muskets and the approach advanced 120 yards. On the 26th the garrison again showed artillery, and opened from the flag staff battery, which had been nearly destroyed by the previous fire of the twelve-pounders. They likewise produced a new gun on the right of the gate, but could not stop the approach which was carried forward 100 yards through very hard ground. On the 27th the mortar was moved from the enfilading to the twelve-pounder battery and threw shells all the night, while an advance of 100 yards more was made. This was prolonged 120 yards next day, the enemy's fire was reduced to two guns. On the 30th 120 yards more were added. On the 31st the magazine in the mosque belonging to the twelve-pounder battery blew up, and the garrison instantly sallied to take advantage of the confusion which they supposed the explosion must have caused. When within 100 yards, the battery guard under Lieutenant Walker of the 2nd Battalion of the 4th Regiment, and the artillery detail under Lieutenant Lewis, advanced to meet them, and, under a heavy fire of guns and small arms from the walls, drove them back into the fort. Colonel Newall, who saw this act of gallantry, praised with the two officers mentioned, the marked bravery of Lieutenant Macky, of His Majesty's 53rd Regiment, who, unable to join the detachment of his corps with Brigadier-General Pritzler, took his tour of general duty in Brigadier-General Munro's force. After the explosion, the repair of the twelve-pounder battery occupied the 1st of April during which an eight-inch mortar was opened, the five and a half inch mortar was taken back to the enfilading battery, and the approach was carried fifty yards further. The approach was now so well advanced that, within 550 yards of the wall, a breaching battery for two eighteen pounders was begun and finished on the 2nd. On the morning of the 3rd of April it opened on the left of the gateway with great effect.

Chapter VII. History. The Peshwa's Overthrow. *Siege of Belgaum, 1818.*

The garrison had still two guns able to fire on the side of the attack; and, as they considerably annoyed the breaching battery, to silence them two twelve-pounders were brought into battery 100 yards to the left. The enemy's guns were silenced on the 4th, when a large part of the outer wall to the left of the gate, and some of the inner wall, were brought down. Next day the destruction was still more rapid. All the batteries continued firing and shells were thrown all night long. Before daylight on the 6th a twelve-pounder was got within 150 yards of the gate and the firing was kept up with as great vigour as on the 5th. The twelve-pounder on the advanced battery opened on the 7th, but burst after firing fifteen rounds. The breach of the curtain was widened, but the garrison still kept up a smart fire. On the 8th the original twelve-pounder battery was abandoned, and two of its iron guns were brought into the battery near the gate. On the 9th they opened with excellent effect on the curtain to the right, where the enemy's gingals and matchlockmen had previously found good cover, and made a practicable breach in the outer wall. Seeing this breach the commandant sent out to propose terms, and, as the terms were not agreed to, on the morning of the 10th the batteries continued to fire till the commandant surrendered at discretion. On the same day (10th April) a detachment of British troops took possession of the outer gateway, and on the 11th, the Pioneers were employed in opening both entrances, as they were built up within and were strongly barricaded. On the 12th of April the garrison marched out. They acknowledged to have had twenty killed and fifty wounded during the siege; the British loss was twenty-three. The fall of this important fort, in spite of the want of ordinary means, was honourable to the energy and zeal of the besiegers. The exertions of the Artillery and the men of the 22nd Dragoons, serving in the batteries, were unremitting, and the labours of the Pioneers were equally meritorious in constructing, besides several batteries, an approach 750 yards long through extremely hard ground. General Munro took the field without any staff. He was even without an engineer, though this want was supplied by the judgment and energy of Colonel Newall, the second in command, who personally directed every operation. The ordnance found in the fort included thirty-six pieces, mostly of large calibre, and sixty gingals and small brass guns. The place was well supplied with stores. It was a matter of congratulation that the garrison surrendered without further opposition. The three eighteen-pounders were so run at the vent, that three fingers might be introduced into them, and they had consequently lost considerably in power. The walls of the fort were everywhere solid and massive, and being more than a mile and a half round, gave the garrison abundant room to avoid shells. After the capture of the fort the force had to halt at Belgaum till the 17th, to organize means for future operations and to put the results of the capture on a firm basis.[1] Leaving a company of the 2nd Battalion of the 9th Regiment in possession of the fort, General Munro returned towards the Ghatprabha, which, for the third time,

---

[1] Blacker's Marátha War, 292-94.

Chapter VII.
History.

he crossed on the 21st. Next day he reached Nagar-Manoli about twenty miles south of Chikodi, where he was joined by General Pritzler with the main body of the reserve. From Nagar-Manoli he marched to Sholápur, and took the fort of Sholápur on the 14th of May (1818).

The Nipáni Chief, 1818.

The fall of Belgaum completed the conquest of the Peshwa's territory south of the Krishna. Except the Nipáni *desái* none of the estateholders had resisted and no more fighting remained. The Kittur *desái* had given great help by furnishing materials during the siege of Belgaum. Even the *desái* of Nipáni, though he joined the Peshwa, never acted cordially against the British troops, and on the 7th of May, with the Peshwa's brother Chimnáji Appa, he gave himself up to Captain Davis of the Nizám's Reformed Horse.[1] As a punishment for his adherence to the Peshwa and for the slowness of his submission to the English, the Nipáni *desái* was deprived of Manoli and Chikodi, except the villages of Nipáni, Sirgat, and Belkur, which were made over to the Kolhápur chief in return for his hearty co-operation with the British. The Nipáni *desái* was greatly dissatisfied with this arrangement and was ready to join any combination against the English which he thought likely to be successful. He at first hesitated to give up the two districts and endeavoured to negotiate. General Munro, who was at Yedur on the 31st of May on his way back from Sholápur, marched towards Nipáni, intending to lay siege to the fort in case the *desái* delayed to give up the districts. This move and the dissatisfaction of his own people compelled the *desái* to yield as soon as the army arrived before Nipáni. His people's dislike to the Nipáni *desái* was the result of a long course of cruelty and ill-treatment. From the beginning of his career he had been in the practice of extracting money by throwing into prison every rich man in his own lands, and in any other villages over which he could exercise power. He used also to seize and keep in confinement any young women of the neighbourhood who were of unusual beauty. When General Munro came to Nipáni, many rich and well-to-do people had been in prison for ten or twelve years; and it was said that every year many died from cruel treatment. General Munro heard only of a few prisoners, and these he ordered to be released. After leaving the place he learned that about 300 were still in confinement. He wrote to the *desái* to release them, and some were set at liberty; but, as many were still kept in confinement, General Munro directed that some of the *desái's* villages on the south bank of the Krishna should not be restored until all were released. Strange stories are still current of the *desái's* cruelty. His palace at Nipáni is built on the edge of a deep lake. High up overhanging the water a narrow open stone ledge or balcony stands out from the palace wall. Along the outer edge of this balcony the *desái* was fond of arranging a row of young women. When they were ready he used to pass inside of the row of trembling girls, and suddenly thrusting out his hand hurl one off the ledge and watch her dying struggles in the deep water below. These acts of cruelty so enraged his people that when General Munro was near Nipáni the heads of

His Cruelty.

---

[1] Bombay Courier, 16th May 1818.

Chapter VII.

History.

The British, 1818-1884.

most of the *desái's* villages asked him to let them pass to the English. They wanted no help. All they asked was leave to drive out the *desái's* garrisons, and the promise that they would not be allowed to pass back under the *desái*.[1] In accordance with his arrangement with the people General Munro for two years held parts of Athni belonging to the Nipáni *desái*. In part of Parasgad which had lately been resumed by the Peshwa, when the people submitted to General Munro, they made a special stipulation that they were not to be again placed under the *desái*. As during the war most of the estateholders had sided with the English, in 1818, when the country came to be settled, they were continued in their estates. The Patvardhans held Gokák and parts of Athni, and had large possessions in Pádshápur. The Kittur *desái*, whose lands were raised to the position of an independent state or *svasthán*, held Sampgaon and the greater part of Bidi. The Khánápur district was resumed as he held it to pay for a body of troops which he was no longer required to keep. As Chikodi and Manoli were made over to Kolhápur, all that remained to the English as *khálsát* or state land was Khánápur, and parts of Pádshápur and Parasgad. On General Munro's recommendation, Mr. Chaplin, Collector of Belári, was appointed, under Mr. Elphinstone, Principal Collector of the Marátha Country south of the Krishna, and Political Agent with the Kolhápur chief and the Southern Marátha Jágirdárs. On the 1st of November 1819, when Mr. Elphinstone became Governor of Bombay, Mr. Chaplin succeeded him as Commissioner of the conquered country.

Kittur Rising, 1824.

Since it has come into the hands of the English the peace of the district has been more than once broken. Forfeitures caused by these disturbances and by the misrule of estateholders have led to a large accession to Government territory in the Bombay Karnátak. In 1822 Shivlinga Rudra the Kittur *desái*, who sheltered bands of robbers in his territory to the annoyance of his neighbours, was severely rebuked by Government. On the 12th of September 1824, a servant of the Kittur *desái* came to Mr. Thackeray, the principal Collector at Dhárwár, to bring word that his master was dying, and to deliver a letter purporting to be from his master announcing the adoption of a son. The letter was dated the 10th of July, but it was stated that the child had not been adopted till the day the letter was received. The Civil Surgeon was at once sent to Kittur. He found the *desái* dead, and from the appearance of the body judged that he had been dead several hours, probably before the messenger had left Kittur for Dhárwár. The circumstances connected with the alleged adoption seemed to Mr. Thackeray most suspicious. Though he knew that he could not adopt without leave, the *desái* had never applied for leave to adopt. When Mr. Thackeray had seen him a few months before, though he was very ill and had spoken freely of his affairs, he never expressed any wish to adopt. The signature to the letter was scarcely legible and the characters were different from the *desái's* usual handwriting, which was remarkably good and clear. Mr. Thackeray came to the conclusion that if the adoption had taken

[1] Gleig's Life of Munro, II. 269.

Chapter VII. History.

The British, 1818-1884.

Kittur Rising, 1824.

place it did not take place till the *desái* was either dead or senseless. In reporting these circumstances to Government, Mr. Thackeray pointed out that the *desái's* family included his wife, a girl of eleven, his stepmother, and the young widow of his brother who had died two years before. The remaining relations, like the child who was said to have been adopted, belonged to branches so remote that their descent from the common ancestor could not be traced. Mr. Thackeray reported that he had gone to Kittur to inquire into the alleged adoption, and to keep order until the decision of Government should be known. As, even if the estate did not lapse to Government there must be a long minority, he proposed to conduct the administration by means of two managers one on the part of Government and the other on the part of the *desái* family. On the receipt of Mr. Thackeray's report he was told to make known to the *desái's* family that the British Government did not recognise the adoption. Mr. Thackeray was desired to take charge of the state and to make an inquiry into the circumstances of the adoption. At the same time Government declared that if inquiry showed that the boy who was said to have been adopted was a descendant of the *desái* who held the country before Tipu's conquest, the boy would be allowed to succeed. On the other hand if it appeared that the claimant was neither a descendant of the ancient *desái* nor a near connection of the late *desái* by the female line, the adoption was to be disallowed. Mr. Thackeray's inquiries showed that the *desái* died on the night of the 11th instead of on the 12th of September; that he had made no adoption; and that after his death Konur Mullapa, his manager and other attendants invested the child with the insignia of *desái*. This was acknowledged by the parties concerned. They also confessed that they had put a pen in the dead man's hands, and so written his signature to the letter dated the 10th of July which was sent to Mr. Thackeray. Because of his share in these frauds, and also because he was concerned in the removal of treasure and jewels, Konur Mallappa, who had been appointed manager on the part of Government, was removed. In reporting these proceedings Mr. Thackeray wrote: 'All is quiet. I anticipate no disorder, and I expect to be able to manage the country without military assistance.' He afterwards submitted the result of his inquiries into the family pedigree, which showed that no descendant of the ancient *desái*, and no near connection of the late *desái* by the female line was alive. While these reports were under consideration Government were shocked by the news of a rising at Kittur which had resulted in the death of the Political Agent and other officers. On the 21st of October, Mr. Thackeray, finding that a number of the late *desái's* treasury guards were commanded by a thief, determined to place a guard of Government sepoys at each gateway. He also required the headmen to give a bond rendering themselves responsible for the safety of the treasury. The headmen refused without the orders of Chinavva, the late *desái's* stepmother, who had lately claimed the management of the state. Mr. Thackeray wished to call on the ladies to explain matters, but they refused to see him that day, promising to see him on the day after. On the 22nd they still refused to see him, and none of the leading men would accompany him to their house.

As Mr. Thackeray heard that the militia and messengers were coming in from the villages round he asked Captain Black, the commander of a troop of gunners or *golandáz*, who had accompanied him, to bring two guns into the fort and post them at the gateways. On the morning of the 23rd, when the artillery officer went to the fort to change guard, he found the outer gate locked, and the inner fort full of armed men, and was refused admittance. Mr. Thackeray sent several messages, and, as they were not attended to, he ordered up the two other guns, and declared that if the gate was not opened in twenty minutes he would blow it open. At the end of the twenty minutes, Captain Black, Captain Sewell, and Lieutenant Dighton, of the gunners or *golandáz* were preparing to blow open the gates when a sally was made by the garrison. The guns were seized and the officers and all with them were cut down. Mr. Thackeray rode up and tried to restore order but fell by a shot and his body was cut to pieces. The rest of the British detachment was attacked and cut up, and Messrs. Stevenson and Elliot, assistants to the Political Agent, who had hid themselves in a house, were made prisoners with some native officials and sepoys. Gursiddappa, the leader in these proceedings, and Chinavva the late *desái's* stepmother had stirred up the spirit that led to this murderous onslaught. When they found what had happened they were not a little alarmed and anxiously protected the European prisoners. As the portion of the Doab Field Force, which was stationed in Belgaum was too weak to act against so strong a fort as Kittur, which was said to be garrisoned by some 5000 desperate men, troops were rapidly collected from all quarters. A proclamation was issued offering a free pardon to all who would surrender before a fixed date, except Gursiddappa, and even Gursiddappa was promised his life, if he forthwith surrendered. The leading men and the troops in Kittur were warned that they should be held responsible for the safety of the prisoners. Meantime the people of Kittur addressed several letters to Government complaining of Mr. Thackeray's acts and demanding that the independence of the state should be respected. They also endeavoured to enlist on their side the Chief of Kolhápur. On the 30th of November Kittur fort was invested and Mr. Chaplin the Commissioner in the Deccan who had hurried to the spot called on the insurgents to surrender. They demanded more favourable terms before releasing the prisoners but were referred to the proclamation. On the morning of the 2nd of December the prisoners were released, but, as the fort was not surrendered, it was attacked on the third and an advanced fortified post was carried. On this post a battery was raised which next day effected a practical breach and the garrison surrendered at discretion. The troops engaged on this occasion were the 1st Bombay European Regiment and two companies of Her Majesty's 46th Foot, a battery of Horse and a company of Foot Artillery, the 4th and 8th Madras Light Cavalry, the 23rd Madras Native Infantry and the 3rd and 6th Regiments of Bombay Native Infantry, the whole under the command of Lieutenant-Colonel Deacon, C.B. The casualties were three killed and twenty-five wounded. Among the killed were Mr. Munro, the Sub-Collector of Sholápur, who had come to the scene of action after Mr. Thackeray's

Chapter VII.

History.

The British, 1818-1884.

Kittur Lapsed, 1824.

death and was mortally wounded in the attack on the advanced post. The Kittur territory thus lapsed to the British Government. It was partitioned into three sub-divisions, Kittur Sampgaon and Bidi, containing in all 286 villages and seventy-two hamlets. The revenue for the year immediately after the lapse (1825) amounted to £33,364 14*s.* (Rs. 3,33,647) which in three years increased by upwards of £2200 (Rs. 22,000). This revenue was exclusive of lands of the yearly value of £2004 (Rs. 20,040) which were held by servants of the late *desáis*, and other lands of the yearly value of £2092 12*s.* (Rs. 20,926) which were held by militia or *shetsandis.* Liberal provision was made for the ladies of the *desái's* family who were kept under watch in Bail-Hongal fort.[1]

Second Kittur Rising, 1829.

In 1827 Báva Sáheb the Kolhápur Chief, whose turbulence was a perpetual source of annoyance, was deprived of Chikodi and Manoli on the ground that he had shown a disregard for the friendship of the British Government and had repeatedly infringed the rights of the landholders of British villages. Besides land yielding a yearly revenue of £1000 (Rs. 10,000) the chief was compelled to cede Akkivát in Chikodi in consequence of the number of robberies committed by its inhabitants on land proprietors and others under British protection and because it was a general resort of robbers.[2] In 1829 a widespread rising took place at Kittur. This rising was headed by one Ráyappa a village watchman of Sangoli, a retainer of the Kittur *desái*, who had received a pardon for his share in the 1824 outbreak. Rendered desperate by the confiscation of his service land and exasperated by a quarrel with the clerk of his village, Ráyappa gathered many disaffected people round him, and, taking the boy who was alleged to have been adopted by the late *desái*, attempted to raise a revolt with the object of restoring Kittur independence. The *desáis* of Kittur had been very popular especially with the poorer classes of their people. Early in 1829, Ráyappa who had then about a hundred men, began by burning the *mámlatdár's* office at Bidi. Afterwards his followers increased to a thousand and they plundered and burned many other villages in Bidi, now Khánápur. They spent their days in the Balagunda and Handi Badagnáth hills in the south corner of the district and at night divided into plundering parties. Ráyappa once came to Kanabaragi about four miles north of Belgaum in the hope of seizing Belgaum fort by a rush at the time of changing guard, but he made no actual attempt to carry out this plan. Krishnaráo the mámlatdár of Sampgaon was told to arrest Ráyappa. He placed the treasure £5000 (Rs. 50,000) on the top of the mosque in Sampgaon, and, leaving a guard of peons, started for Bidi. According to the popular account it was against Krishnaráo that the revolt was raised, and it was by Krishnaráo's exertions that the revolt was quelled. It was hoped that the rising might be put down without military force. But when the Kittur militia refused to serve and the disorder continued to spread, the help of strong detachments became necessary. The regular troops were not well

---

[1] Bom. Gov. Sel. CXIII. 199-203; Sir T. Colebrook's Life of Mountstuart Elphinstone, II. 167-168. Welsh's Military Reminiscences, II. 298-299.

[2] Stokes' Belgaum, 82.

Second Kittur Rising, 1829.

suited for pursuing bands of robbers through close and difficult country. Krishnaráo, after scouring the forests in vain, came from Bidi to Mugutkhán Hubli sixteen miles south-east of Belgaum with a large body of militia and some horse. He learned that Ráyappa had avoided him, and had passed by a little known path through Kádaroli to Sampgaon where he had burned the mámlatdár's office and destroyed the records. Krishnaráo hurried forward and overtook Ráyappa's band at the little pond to the north of Sampgaon. He had ten horsemen with him, and succeeded in killing four of the rebels. The rest retired to Suttagatti near which they divided into two large bands, one of which returned with Ráyappa to Kittur hill by Sangoli, while the other plundered and burned Marikatti. Krishnaráo attacked the Marikatti band on Nesaragi hill, and dispersed it, killing ten or twenty and taking about a hundred prisoners. At this time it was deemed advisable to remove to Dhárwár Iravva, the late *desái's* widow who was living at Bail Hongal. This nearly excited another rising; a thousand men gathered at Anegol to resist her removal. On receiving a promise of pardon most of them submitted and the rest joined Ráyappa. Iravva died at Dhárwár in July; it was supposed by poison taken either by herself or administered to her. Soon after this the insurrection was quelled. Krishnaráo the mámlatdár, discovered that Lingana Gauda of Khudánpur, had wished his own son to be adopted on the death of the late *desái*, and resented the refusal with which his proposal was met. This man was chosen as a fit instrument to betray Ráyappa. Men were sent to join the rebels and suggest that they should call in Lingana, who would bring three hundred men. Ráyappa took the bait and wrote to Lingana Gauda to ask him to join. The mámlatdár sent Lingana Gauda with a body of men; and, as he was timid and weak, Yenkana Gauda of Neginahál who was bold and courageous, was sent with him to support him. They joined Ráyappa and continued with him for a fortnight plundering. One day, when Ráyappa had laid aside his arms and was bathing, Lakkappa, a watchman of Neginahál, rushed on him and clasped him round the body; another secured his weapons, and the rest overpowered him, bound him hand and foot on a stretcher, and carried him in triumph to Dhárwár. He was condemned to be hanged at Nandgad, the scene of his chief robbery. As he passed along the road to the gallows he pointed out a spot for his burial, stating that a great tree would spring from his body. He was buried in the spot he had chosen and a magnificent banian close to the road near Nandgad is shown as the tree which grew from Ráyappa's grave. Under the shade of this tree a temple has been built, to which people in want of children money or health come from great distances. Husbandmen, too, on their way to the Nandgad market stop to promise Ráyappa an offering if their grain sells well. Ráyappa's outbreak lasted about four months. His betrayers were rewarded with gifts of land; Lingana was presented with Kaloli near Kittur and Yenkana Gauda with a village in Dhárwár.

On the 17th of March 1830 under Regulation VII. of that year, the Government of Bombay brought under the regulations the

Chapter VII.
History.
The British, 1818-1884.

territories of the Bombay Karnátak which had been acquired either by conquest from the Peshwa or by treaty and agreement from other states. The territories were formed into the district of Dhárwár.

Nipáni, 1831.

In 1831 Appa Sáheb of Nipáni, whom age and a feeling of the power of Government had kept quiet if not well disposed, endeavoured to impose a child on Government as his heir.[1] It was discovered that one of his wives Táibái had been taken to a house in Nipáni, on the pretence that she was about to bear a child. A widow, who expected soon to be delivered, was also taken to the house; and when the child was born, he was placed in Táibái's arms, and said to be her offspring. The widow was murdered. Information of this intrigue and crime was given by the owner of the house in which it took place, and he soon after died with suspicious suddenness. His story was confirmed by the discovery of the widow's body. In consideration of the Nipáni chief's age and of his services to the British in 1800 and 1803, Government did not immediately confiscate his military grant or *saranjám* lands. They determined to punish the *desái* by declaring that his military estates were to lapse on his death, and that no son of his body or of his adoption should be recognized as heir to them.

Belgaum Collectorate, 1836.

On the 28th of April 1836 the Collectorate of Dhárwár was divided into two Collectorates a northern and a southern. On the recommendation of Mr. Dunlop who was then acting principal Collector of Dhárwár, the Belgaum Collectorate was made to consist of ten sub-divisions, Parasgad, Sampgaon, Pádshápur, Chikodi, Bágalkot, Indi, Muddebihál, Hungund, Bádámi, and Bidi. Mr. Ravenscroft the first Assistant Collector took charge of the Belgaum Collectorate on the 3rd of May 1836. Nearly two years passed before Government agreed to allow the civil headquarters to be fixed at Belgaum. Ankalgi, Gokák, Murgod, and Manoli were all proposed, and at one time Gokák was almost determined on. Mr. Dunlop, the Collector, in a series of letters, pointed out the disadvantages likely to arise from the headquarters being fixed at any other station than Belgaum, and at length persuaded Government to adopt his views. The order fixing Belgaum as the civil headquarters is dated the 9th of March 1838. The Collector was also Political Agent. A first assistant, with enlarged powers, was stationed permanently at Kaládgi. Soon after the formation of the Belgaum Collectorate the sub-divisions of Indi and Muddebihál were handed to the new Collectorate of Sholápur.

---

1 The Nipáni *desái* seems always to have been noted for his discontent and his cruelty. In 1819 Mr. Elphinstone represented him as turbulent and discontented by the loss of Chikodi and Manoli, but conscious of his own weakness. In 1822, from his indifference, Mr. Chaplin suspected him of secretly hoping to profit by the unsettled state of Kolhápur. In 1823 Mr. Elphinstone found him the only discontented estateholder in the Bombay Karnátak. He was cruel and furious in passion, harsh and unrelenting in the management of his estate, and deaf to the remonstrances of his people. In 1826 for neglect of duty he flogged two grooms so severely that one of them died on the spot and the life of the other was long despaired of. In spite of these faults, when meeting Europeans, he was frank and gentlemanlike, good-humoured and cordial. Bom. Gov. Sel. CXIII. 215. Welsh's Military Reminiscences, II. 283, 334.

The British, 1818-1884.

Chinchani Lapsed, 1836.

Government had decided to deny the privilege of adoption to certain estateholders, as it was considered desirable to reduce the area of alienated land as much as possible. One of the first estates which lapsed in consequence of this decision was the military estate of Chinchani. Govindráo the proprietor belonged to the Tásgaon branch of the Patvardhan family. He died on the 31st of December 1836 and his land passed to Government. It included the sub-divisions of Gokák and several separate villages. This addition to Belgaum was managed in the Political Department until 1839, when by Act VIII. it was brought under the Acts and Regulations. Unlike other Patvardhan lands, which were well managed and prosperous, when Gokák lapsed it was impoverished and was a famous resort of thieves. The Nipáni *desái* had for some time been in failing health. He was very infirm and subject to fits, under which, for a time, he used completely to lose his senses. On the 28th of June 1839 he died, having previously adopted Morárráo, son of his half-brother Raghunáthráo, as heir to his *deshkat* or civil estates which were estimated to be worth £1500 (Rs. 15,000) a year. The military or *saranjám* estate was resumed and divided among Belgaum, Dhárwár, and Sholápur. The chief parts which fell to Belgaum were the divisions of Athni and Honvád, and the flourishing town of Nipáni. These acquisitions were managed by the Political Agent, until, under Act VI. of 1842 they were brought under the Acts and Regulations. The year after the death of the Nipáni *desái* his six widows began to quarrel. The eldest had charge of the heir and the five others kept up continued complaints against her. She died in the end of 1840, and the management passed to the next eldest widow. Two of the remaining ladies induced Raghunáthráo, the late *desái's* half-brother, to seize his son whom the late *desái* had adopted, and with the aid of 300 Arabs to take possession of the fort and set the authorities at defiance. The military had to be called in before the fort submitted. It was attacked on the 20th of February 1841 and surrendered on the following day. The Arab ringleaders were punished with imprisonment; and all who had joined in the insurrection forfeited their pensions. The fort was dismantled at the expense of the *desái*, who had also to pay the cost of the expedition. On the 4th of May 1842, Gopálráo, the representative of a divided branch of the Miraj family of Patvardhans, died without an heir, and his estate lapsed to Government. In it were nine villages now in Belgaum, of which Ainápur on the Krishna is the largest. The estate was brought under the Acts and Regulations by Act III. of 1863.

Nipáni Lapsed, 1840.

Kolhápur Rising, 1844.

The years 1844 and 1845 are memorable for the serious risings in Kolhápur and Sávantvádi, which from their close neighbourhood caused uneasiness and disturbance within Belgaum limits. In 1843 great abuse and mismanagement in Kolhápur led Government to appoint Dáji Krishna Pandit as minister to improve the administration. His reforms aroused the alarm of the garrison or *gadakaris* of Sámángad about fifteen miles west of Hukeri and of Budhargad in Kolhápur, who shut the gates of their forts and defied Government. A force of 1200 men, with four mortars and two nine-

Chapter VII. History. The British, 1818-1884. *Kolhápur Rising, 1844.*

pounders, moved from Belgaum, and arrived before Sámángad on the 19th of September. The place was not taken until the 13th of October, after battering guns had been brought from Belgaum and a breach made. Meanwhile the insurrection spread and developed into a rising of the Kolhápur people against the British power. On the 10th of October the garrison of Budhargad plundered the division of Chikodi and robbed the mámlatdár's treasury. This insurrection was not got under till December, and meanwhile a similar outbreak had taken place in Sávantvádi. The Sávantvádi rising began with the garrison of Manohar about thirty-five miles north-west of Belgaum on the 10th of October. In a short time outrages became general, and the movement grew still more formidable when Phond Sávant, a man of note, joined the insurgents. In 1828 and 1832 Phond had headed outbreaks against the Sar Desái of Vádi. In 1838 he had been admitted to an amnesty and had since lived in the Vádi state, where he was treated with unusual generosity and kindness. In November 1844, with his eight sons, he openly espoused the cause of the rebels, and persuaded Anna Sáheb, the eldest son of the Sar Desái, a boy of sixteen, to escape from Vádi and lend the cause the support of his name. This insurrection and the Kolhápur disturbances covered the country round with confusion and alarm. There was an organized conspiracy to seize the forts of Dhárwár and Belgaum and excite a rebellion against the British throughout the Bombay Karnátak. To prevent insurgents crossing into Belgaum a large body of militia were raised and posted in various strong positions along the Sahyádris, and parties of regular troops were distributed at Bidi, Kittur, Hubli, Talevádi, Chikodi, and Patna. Notwithstanding these precautions Belgaum did not escape disturbance. On the night of the 30th of December two or three hundred rebels attacked and plundered the custom station at Párvád, and on the 2nd of January the Kumkumbi custom-house was plundered. Chandgad and Párgad were threatened, but a timely reinforcement of militia saved them. A large number of insurgents met below Talevádi, but fear of the garrison prevented an attack on the custom-house. In Bidi alone about 800 militia were employed. Bhimgad was occupied, and as, on the night of the 11th of January, Sávarda two or three miles west of Patna was attacked by a band of rebels, a party of regulars was sent from Belgaum to guard Patna. Alarm and danger continued until the forts of Manohar and Mansantosh in Sávantvádi had been taken and the rebels scattered. In February 1845 Colonel, afterwards Sir James, Outram drove one body of rebels from the forest below the Rám pass and most of the leaders, among them Phond Sávant and his sons, took refuge in Goa. The government of Goa declined to surrender them choosing to regard them as political refugees. By March 1845 the country near the Sahyádris was reported quiet.

Sávantvádi Rising, 1844.

While the Kolhápur rebellion was engaging the attention of Government, Shivlingáppa, the feigned adopted son of the Kittur *desái*, attempted to raise a revolt in Sampgaon and Bidi. A treasonable correspondence was discovered between him and the *desái* of Chachdi about twenty-five miles east of Belgaum. Sums of money were distributed through the districts, and many servants of the late *desái* promised aid. It was intended to ask help from the mercenary Arabs of the Nizám's territories, and applications were made to men in Kolhápur and Goa. The plot was discovered partly by the aid of the Vontamuri *desái*, Shivlingáppa's father-in-law. Sufficient legal evidence to secure conviction could not be obtained and the conspirators escaped punishment. Shivlingáppa spent the rest of his life dependent on the bounty of the Vontamuri chief. The adherents of the family still regard a son of his as the lawful *desái* of Kittúr.[1] On the 29th of April 1845 Vámanráo Patvardhan of Soni died leaving no heir. Soni was part of the Miraj military grants or *saranjám*, and became Vámanráo's when the estate was divided. It now lapsed to Government. Seven villages which were added to Belgaum were brought under the Acts and Regulations by Act III. of 1863. In 1848 Belgaum received a further addition by the lapse of the Tásgaon estate. Parshurám Bháu Patvardhan died on the 8th of June 1848. On his death-bed he addressed a letter to Government praying that his widow might be allowed an heir to his military lands or *saranjám*. His prayer was not granted as he had mismanaged his estate and done nothing entitling him to special consideration. His widow tried to impose a child on Government but the imposture was detected. These Tásgaon villages, which included the lands of Saudi on the Krishna and of Yádvád, were brought under the Acts and Regulations by Act III. of 1863. On the 1st of January 1862 the Tásgaon sub-division, which had previously been included in Belgaum, was handed to Sátára. On the 19th of October 1857 Trimbakráo Appa Patvardhan, who was either called the Shedbálkar or the Kágvádkar, died leaving no son. As Government had not allowed him to adopt an heir his estate lapsed. Fifty-six villages were placed under Belgaum and for two years were managed by an agent or *kárbhári*. A mámlatdár was afterwards appointed, till, in 1863 the villages were distributed over the Gokák, Belgaum, and Athni sub-divisions, and were brought under the Acts and Regulations by Act III. of that year.

Tásgaon Lapsed, 1848.

The Mutinies, 1857-58.

In 1850 Phond Sávant's younger sons had been allowed to return to Vádi and pardoned for the part they had taken in the 1845 rebellion. Phond and his elder sons, Nána, Bába, and Hanumant *desáis* were not included in the amnesty but remained under watch in Goa. On the night of the 2nd of February 1858, taking advantage of the difficulties which the Mutinies had brought on Government, the three brothers escaped from their guard and immediately began to stir disturbances all along the forest frontier from Sávantvádi to Kánara. On the 6th of February, one or two hundred men attacked the police post at Talevádi and attempted to fire the custom-house. On the 8th Varkund was attacked and the custom-house at Dudvál was burnt to the ground. A large body of military were called out and the Brigadier at Belgaum placed two companies

[1] Bom. Gov. Sel. CXIII. 204.

Chapter VII.
History.
The British, 1818-1884.
The Mutinies, 1857-58.

of the 28th Native Infantry with fifty Europeans at the disposal of the civil authorities. A special Commissioner was appointed to try offences against the State. The insurgents took a strong position on Darshanigudda hill on the Kánara border in the pass below Talevádi. This position was attacked by the field force on the 24th of February. It was hoped that the whole gang would be taken. But the force had left their encampment at Hemádgi at four in the afternoon of the 23rd instead of at night; their movements had been watched, and, when the top of the hill was reached, the enemy were gone. A company of the 28th Regiment of Native Infantry under Lieutenant now Major H. L. Nutt, and Lieutenant now Lieutenant-Colonel E. W. West had been sent round in advance to crown the hill under cover of the night. On their way they were fired into and a native officer was killed. At the close of 1858 peace was sufficiently restored to allow most of the regular troops to be withdrawn from Bidi. The Sávantvádi locals, the police, and the militia undertook to suppress the rising. Meanwhile villages had been plundered and several outrages and murders had taken place. Large rewards were offered for the apprehension of the leaders and measures were taken to prevent them passing into the open country. Before the end of the year the gang had been reduced to about twenty-five men who maintained themselves in the forests of Kánara and Bidi. They were led by three brothers named Rághoba or Rávba, Chintoba, and Shánta Phadnavis, while a Sidi called Bastian was a noted leader. Chintoba was killed in a combat fought on the 5th of July 1859 in the Hámod forests in Kánara. The rebel band was forty or fifty strong and was attacked by Lieutenants Giertzen and Drever with two *náiks* and twelve men. The rebels were dispersed with the loss of three men killed and several wounded. Eleven guns, eight swords, and all their ammunition were taken. The gang was finally broken on the night of the 5th of December 1859. News reached Lieutenants Giertzen and Drever that the rebels were hid somewhere in the hills near Diggi in the Dingorli forests in Kánara. They determined to surprise and capture them. Parties were posted so as to prevent their escape and Lieutenant Giertzen, with fourteen of the Belgaum police, taking the rebels' watch-fire as his guide, advanced cautiously through the forest creeping on guided by the fire across a difficult rocky slope covered with underwood. He came to within a couple of yards of the rebels before they took alarm. Lieutenant Giertzen killed Bablu, and two other men, Rávba and Shánta, who were sitting with Bablu over the fire, tried to escape but were seized by the hair and dragged out after a short struggle. This put an end to the rising.[1]

While these events were occurring in outlying parts of the district the town of Belgaum was in considerable danger. Mr. Seton Karr was at this time Collector and Magistrate at Belgaum, while General Lester, an old Artillery officer of sound judgment, commanded the Southern Division of the Army which had its head-

[1] Stokes' Belgaum, 92.

quarters at Belgaum. The Belgaum garrison had been drained of its European troops for the Persian war; and the Native Regiment which was quartered at Belgaum was the newly raised 29th. As at Kolhápur the officers of the 29th had full trust in the loyalty of their men and suspected no evil. General Lester's wise precautions probably prevented an outbreak. The fort was put in a state of defence, and its breaches repaired. His only Europeans were a battery of artillery and a depôt of Her Majesty's 64th, who had been withdrawn for service in Persia, including about thirty men fit for duty with upwards of 400 women and children. The artillery were quartered in the fort and the European and Eurasian inhabitants of the town were formed into a small volunteer corps and drilled daily. The Sáfa mosque was ordered to be closed for religious service lest its nearness to the arsenal might be a source of danger.[1] On the 10th of August 1857 the European reinforcements despatched from Bombay reached Belgaum by way of Goa. Like their brethren who came to the relief of Kolhápur they arrived in tatters, stripped of shoes almost of clothes by the rains and storms of July, but eager for work. This reinforcement enabled General Lester to seize a few of the civil and military conspirators against whom there was sufficient evidence for trial. One of these was a Musalmán *munshi*, a favourite with the officers whom he had taught. The *munshi* was found to be a disciple of the head of the Western India branch of the Wahábi sect who lived in Poona, and who was a prime instigator of the rebellion. Letters from this *munshi* to regiments at Kolhápur and other stations, full of treasonable matter, had been intercepted and furnished evidence against him. They showed how widespread was the conspiracy and how large an element in every station was ready to revolt if only they were satisfied that the movement would be general. This plot was discovered mainly through the zeal and intelligence of a police chief constable of Belgaum, a Christian convert named Mutu Kumár who afterwards received the grant of a village in acknowledgment of his services. The *munshi* was found guilty and executed, and with him an emissary from one of the chiefs who had been employed in corrupting the troops. Five men of the 29th were soon after convicted of mutiny and executed, and four were transported for life.[2] The danger passed over and no actual outbreak took place. Another important event connected with the Mutinies was the execution at Belgaum of the Bráhman chief of Nargund in Dhárwár. In 1858 the Nargund chief raised the standard of revolt against the British Government, and on the 29th of May surprised

---

[1] Stokes' Belgaum, 35, 94.

[2] LeGrand Jacob's Western India, 212-215. A letter from Belgaum written by a sepoy of the 29th Regiment, but purporting to be from several sepoys to their brethren of the 74th Bengal Native Infantry, was intercepted in Bombay. It was sent to Colonel Lester on the 13th of June 1857. After presenting their compliments the writer or writers went on: We are your children, do with us as it may seem best to you, in your salvation is our safety. We are all of one mind; on your intimation we shall come running. You are our father and mother. We have written a small letter, but from it comprehend much. You are the servants of Raghunáth and we your slaves. Write to us an answer as soon as you receive this. LeGrand Jacob's Western India, 215 note.

Chapter VII. History. The British, 1818-1884.

the Political Agent Mr. Manson at night when asleep in the village of Suriban about twelve miles north of Nargund, killed him, cut off his head, and fastened it over the gate of Nargund fort. A British force under Lieutenant-Colonel G. Malcolm marched towards Nargund, and, in the confusion which followed the capture of Nargund, the chief escaped, but was pursued and captured. He was taken to Belgaum, confined in the main guard of the fort, and was tried and sentenced to death. He was carried on a cart drawn by Mhárs through the town to Hay Stack Hill, on which the gallows were raised and was there executed.

Since 1858 the peace of the district has been unbroken. In 1864 (1st May) Kaládgi, now Bijápur, was formed into a separate Collectorate and took from Belgaum the three sub-divisions of Bádámi, Bágalkot, and Hungund.

CHAPTER VIII.

LAND ADMINISTRATION.[1]

Chapter VIII.
Land Administration.
Acquisition, 1818-1857.

THE city of Belgaum was taken by General Munro on the 15th of March 1818, and the fort of Belgaum on the 11th of April following. The fall of Belgaum completed the conquest of the Peshwa's territories south of the Krishna. The political charge of the whole tract was at first vested in Mr. Elphinstone. Afterwards Mr. Chaplin, the Collector of Belári, was placed in charge and styled the Principal Collector of the Marátha Country south of the Krishna, and Political Agent with the Rája of Kolhápur and the southern estate-holders or *jágirdárs*.[2] In 1821 the chief of Sángli ceded eight villages from the Sháhápur *pargana* instead of expenses on account of troops under articles of stipulation dated the 12th of December 1820. In September 1824 the *desái* of Kittur died without issue. The *desái's saranjám* or military estate villages therefore lapsed to Government. But, in consequence of a rising stirred up by the manager of the late *desái*, the estate was not taken possession of till the 5th of December 1824.[3] The country thus acquired was at first divided into three sub-divisions or *tálukás*, Kittur, Sampgaon, and Bidi, and afterwards into two Sampgaon and Bidi. The next acquisition of territory was that of Chikodi and Manoli in 1827. These were taken from the Rája of Kolhápur by a revised treaty dated the 23rd of October 1827, owing to his suspicious and turbulent conduct. This treaty was modified by the articles of agreement between the Rája of Kolhápur and the British Government, drawn up on the 15th of March

---

1 The chief reports from which materials have been taken for the Land Administration of Belgaum include the survey reports in Bom. Gov. Sel. LXXXI. XCIV. CXVIII. and Bom. Gov. Rev. Rec. 175 of 1855, 17 of 1856, 164 of 1856, 91A of 1861, 131A of 1880, and Bom. Gov. Rev. Comp. 1062 of 1881.

2 On the first of June 1818, the Peshwa signed articles of surrender by which he ceded to Government the *pargana* of Páchhápur; one village from *pargana* Yellur; twelve villages from *killa* Kalánidhigad; Hire Gandharvagad and the village at its foot; five villages from *pargana* Ajamnagar; four villages from *pargana* Vithal Vishrám; *taraf* Maneri; twenty-six villages from *tappa* Chandgad; *pargana* Khánápur; four villages from *taraf* Sakhali; one village from *pargana* Nargund; two villages from *pargana* Navalgund; *taraf* Ugargol; five villages from *taraf* Morab; three villages from *karyát* Bettigeri; *taraf* Yakkundi; four villages from *pargana* Govenkop; one village from *taraf* Konur; three villages from *karyát* Assundi; four villages from *karyát* Huli; the village of Saundatti; two villages from *pargana* Honvád; nine villages from *pargana* Athni; one village from *pargana* Gadi Kokatnur; one village from *pargana* Bidri; one village from *pargana* Gotc; two villages from *pargana* Terdál; and two villages from *piánt* Miraj.

3 Details are given in the History Chapter.

Chapter VIII.
Land Administration.
Acquisition, 1818-1857.

1829.[1] On the 31st of December 1836 Govindráv Chinchnikar of the Tásgaon branch of the Patvardhan family died without heirs and his *saranjám* or military estate lapsed to Government. It included the *pargana* of Gokák, some villages from the *parganás* of Yádvád, Terdál, Gadi Kokatnur, Athni, and Bidri, and two villages from the *pránt* of Ráybág. On the 12th of December 1837 two villages from the *pargana* of Terdál lapsed to Government on the death of Nilkanthráv Kurundvádkar of the younger branch of the Patvardhan family. On the 28th of June 1839 on the death of the *desái* of Nipáni his *saranjám* or military estate was resumed. It comprised the *pargana* of Athni with the town or *kasba* of Athni, six villages from *pargana* Gadi Kokatnur, twelve from Honvád, one from Jamkhandi, one from *karyát* Nesargi, and four other villages. This territory was at first managed by the Political Agent of Kolhápur and the Southern Marátha native states, but subsequently by Act VI. of 1842, it was made subject to the Acts and Regulations of Bombay. On the 4th of May 1842 Gopálráv Mirajkar, the chief of the fourth share of the Miraj estate, died without issue and his estate lapsed to Government. This consisted of one village from each of the *pránts* of Hukeri, Miraj, Ráybág, and three from that of Bijápur. In 1848 the district received a further addition by the lapse of the Tásgaon estate on the death without heirs of Parashurám Bháu Patvardhan on the 8th of June. His estate consisted of the two *parganás* of Saundi on the Krishna and of Yádvád now in Gokák. Subsequently in August 1848 Chintámanráv Krishna Vádikar died without heirs and this caused the lapse of two villages from *pránt* Miraj. In the following year, 1849, Ashte[2] from *pargana* Shábápur, Belgundi, Kangráli, and Nilgi were resumed from Raghunáthráv Jayvant Mantri of Islámpur. On the 19th of October 1857 Trimbakráv Appásáheb Patvardhan of Shedbál or Kágvád died without heirs and his estate lapsed to Government. This lapse brought an addition to the Belgaum district of *taraf* Mugalkhod, four villages from *pargana* Yádvád, one from *pargana* Kokatnur, and seven other villages. This area was managed by a *kárbhári* for about two years; the villages were then put under the charge of a mámlatdár, and, in 1863, they were distributed between the Gokák, Belgaum, and Athni sub-divisions, and brought under the Acts and Regulations by Act III. of 1863.

Changes, 1836-1864.

By Regulation VII. of 1830 the Marátha country acquired by conquest from the Peshwa and other native chiefs, was formed into a district called the Dhárwár Collectorate. In 1836 (April 28th) Government ordered that the principal collectorate of Dhárwár should be divided into two collectorates. In 1838 (March 9th) Belgaum was

---

[1] In 1829 the territory forming the Chikodi and Manoli *parganás* comprised the *karyáts* of Yelli-Manoli, Majati, Sadalgi, and Kabbur; three villages from *karyát* Adgal; twenty villages from *karyát* Sholápur; nine villages from *karyát* Sávgaon; eighteen villages from *karyát* Lát; seven villages from *karyát* Nez; thirteen villages from *karyát* Nesargi; three villages from *karyát* Ráybág; eleven villages from *pránt* Miraj; one village from *pránt* Kágal; *karyát* Sindogi; *taraf* Vatnál; *pargana* Murgod; *karyát* Sattigeri; and four other villages.

[2] It was subsequently granted in *inám* to Bápusáheb for his services in the 1857 Mutinies.

fixed as the civil head-quarters.[1] When it was formed into a separate district, Belgaum included ten sub-divisions, Páchhápur with eighty-six villages, Sampgaon with 106 villages, Bidi with 237 villages, Chikodi with 141 villages, Parasgad with ninety-six villages, Bágalkot with 123 villages, Bádámi with 133 villages, Hungund with 138 villages, Indi with 175 villages, and Muddebihál with 161 villages. The total number of villages was 1396 with about 681,338 people, and a yearly revenue of about £146,898 (Rs. 14,68,980). Some time after this new district of Belgaum was formed, the Indi and Muddebihál sub-divisions were transferred (1838-39) to the new district of Sholápur. The number of the Belgaum sub-divisions was increased by the formation of the two new sub-divisions of Athni and Gokák.[2] Between 1836 and 1864 the Belgaum district continued to receive constant additions by the lapse of *jágir* or alienated villages.[3] In 1864 the sub-divisions of Bágalkot, Hungund, and Bádámi were transferred from Belgaum to the new Collectorate of Kaládgi. In 1866 Páchhápur was named Belgaum and in 1881 Bidi was named Khánápur.

Chapter VIII.

Land Administration.

Changes, 1836-1864.

Staff, 1884.

District Officers.

The administration of the district in revenue matters is entrusted to an officer styled Collector, on a yearly pay of £2790 (Rs. 27,900). This officer, who is also the chief magistrate and executive head of the district, is assisted in his work of general supervision by a staff of four assistants of whom two are covenanted and two are uncovenanted servants of Government. The sanctioned yearly salaries of the covenanted assistants range from £840 to £1080 (Rs. 8400-10,800), those of the uncovenanted assistants or deputies are £360 (Rs. 3600) each. For fiscal and other administrative purposes the lands under the Collector's charge are distributed among seven sub-divisions. Of these five are generally entrusted to the covenanted assistants or assistant collectors, and two to one of the uncovenanted assistants, called the district deputy collector. The other uncovenanted assistant who is styled the head-quarter or *huzur* deputy collector is entrusted with the charge of the treasury. These officers are also magistrates, and those who hold revenue charges have, under the presidency of the Collector, the chief management of the different administrative bodies, local fund and municipal committees, within the limits of their revenue charges.

Sub-Divisional Officers.

Under the supervision of the Collector and his assistants the revenue charge of each fiscal sub-division is placed in the hands of an

[1] Ankalgi, Gokák, Murgod, and Manoli were proposed, and, had not the Collector Mr. Dunlop strongly advocated Belgaum, Gokák would probably have been chosen. A first assistant collector was stationed at Kaládgi.

[2] When Belgaum was first formed there were no petty divisions or *mahdls*. Some time after the petty divisions of Chandgad, Hukeri, and Murgod were formed.

[3] At the end of 1836 the lapse of the Chinchni *jágir* to Government added seventy-six villages to the Belgaum Collectorate. The next additions were the *parganás* of Athni and Honvád in 1839 on the death of the Nipáni *desái*, and six villages on the death in 1842 of one Gopálráv a representative of a divided branch of the Mirajkar family. In 1845, by the lapse of the Soni estate, the Collectorate received a further addition of seven villages. In 1848 the Tásgaon estate lapsed and the *parganás* of Saundi in the present (1884) Athni sub-division and of Yádvád in the present Gokák sub-division were added to the Collectorate. In 1857 the Kágvád *jágir* lapsed, and fifty-six of its villages were added to the Collectorate, and subsequently in 1863 distributed among the Belgaum, Gokák, and Athni sub-divisions.

Chapter VIII.

Land Administration.

Staff, 1884.

officer styled *mámlatdár*. These officers, who are also entrusted with magisterial powers, have yearly salaries varying from £180 to £300 (Rs. 1800-3000). Three of the fiscal sub-divisions, Chikodi Belgaum and Parasgad, contain subordinate divisions called *mahâls* placed under the charge of officers styled *mahálkaris*, who, except that they have no treasury to superintend, exercise the revenue and magisterial powers generally entrusted to a mámlatdár and have yearly salaries varying from £60 to £72 (Rs. 600-720).

Village Officers.

In revenue and police matters the charge of the 895 Government villages is entrusted to 987 headmen or *pátils*, of whom sixty-two are stipendiary and 925 are hereditary. Five of the stipendiary and eighty of the hereditary *pátils* perform revenue duties only. Five of the stipendiary and eighty of the hereditary *pátils* attend to matters of police only. Fifty-two stipendiary and 765 hereditary *pátils* are entrusted with both revenue and police charges. The *pátil's* yearly pay depends on the amount of revenue collected from his village. It varies from 6*s.* to £20 4*s.* (Rs. 3-202), the average receipts amounting to £3 3*s.* 6¼*d.* (Rs. 31 *as.* 12½). The above sums are paid to the *pátils* who are actually performing the duties of the office. The hereditary *pátils* also hold lands assigned as service emoluments which are called *vatan* lands. The heads of the families hold shares in the *vatan* property, and they and all the members of their families are styled *vatandárs*. The right of any member of the family to perform service is settled under Bombay Act III. of 1874. The *vatan* lands represent an annual grant of £2065 (Rs. 20,650). The whole yearly charge is £5201 (Rs. 52,010) of which £3136 (Rs. 31,360) are paid in cash. To keep the village accounts, draw up statistics, and help the headmen in performing their duties, fourteen stipendiary and 763 hereditary village accountants are entertained. Their yearly salaries, which are in proportion to the revenue collected by them, amount to £5103 (Rs. 51,030); they vary from 12*s.* to £21 14*s.* (Rs. 6-217) and average £6 11*s.* 4⅛*d.* (Rs. 65 10⅝ *as.*). Like the headmen the hereditary accountants or *kulkarnis* are *vatandárs* and their rights to service are settled under Bombay Act III. of 1874. No land is specially assigned to them for service; but certain *kulkarnis* hold land of the aggregate yearly value of £671 (Rs. 6710) which is subject to a quit-rent to meet the amount of remuneration due to the officiating *kulkarni*.

Village Servants.

Under the headmen and accountants are 5232 inferior village servants. Of these 2383 are liable for revenue and 2849 for police duties. Of those liable for revenue duties 1111 are Sanadis, 559 Mhárs, 321 Talvárs or watchmen, 175 Kolkárs or messengers, forty-two Tahsildárs, eighteen Náiks, one Vir, twenty-one Gastis or patrols, eighty-three Tarâls or porters, one Aparadha, three Mángs, two Dalvais, twenty Kolis, twelve Chaughulás, six Natikars, six Karbedis, and two Bárikis or crop-watchers. Of those liable for police duties 2737 are Sanadis, nineteen Gastis, eleven Tarâls, one Náik, one Kolkár, one Khot, and seventy-nine Gadkaris or fort-guards. Village servants are either Musalmáns, Native Christians, or Hindus belonging to the Marátha, Lingáyat, Jain, Dhangar, Berad, Upar, and Mhár castes. The total yearly grants for the support of this establishment amount to £9100 (Rs. 91,000) being £1 14*s.* 9⅜*d.*

(Rs.17 *as.* 6¼) to each man or a cost to each village of £10 3*s.* 4⅛*d.* (Rs.101 *as.* 10¾); of this charge £7882 (Rs.78,820) are met by grants of land and £1218 (Rs.12,180) are paid in cash. The yearly cost of the village establishment of the district may be thus summarised:

Chapter VIII.

Land Administration.

Staff, 1884.

Village Servants.

Belgaum Village Establishment, 1884.

	£	Rs.
Headmen	5201	52,010
Accountants ...	5774	57,740
Servants	9100	91,000
Total ...	20,075	2,00,750

This is equal to a charge of £22 8*s.* 7½*d.* (Rs. 224 *as.* 4⅝) a village or about sixteen per cent of the district land revenue.

Revenue Management, 1818-1850.

The state of the revenue administration in Belgaum from the accession of British rule in 1818 to the introduction of the survey settlement in 1850 differed in no way from that described in the Dhárwár Statistical Account.

Survey, 1849-1861.

The first thirty years' revenue survey settlement was introduced into 108 villages of Parasgad in 1849-50 and by 1860-61 the whole district was surveyed and settled. Compared with the tillage rental before the survey, the survey rental on the tillage area of the whole district showed a reduction of about fourteen per cent. The following statement gives the chief details of the settlements introduced in the Belgaum district by the revenue survey between 1849 and 1861:

Belgaum Survey Settlements, 1849-1861.

Survey Group.	Villages.	Settlement Year.	Survey. Before.	Survey. After.	Survey. Increase per cent.	Survey. Decrease per cent.
			Rs.	Rs.		
Parasgad	108	1849-50	69,786	70,814	1·5	...
Gokák	47	1849-50	30,384	23,764	...	21·6
Yádvád	10	1851-52	7669	6598	...	14·0
Athni	58	1851-52	62,654	47,334	...	24·4
Athni	21	1852-53	20,061	19,022	...	5·1
Sampgaon	106	1852-53	1,44,476	1,22,773	...	15·0
Páchhápur	9	1852-53	25,887	20,781	...	19·7
Chikodi	141	1853-54	1,38,780	99,621	...	28·2
Páchhápur	33	1853-54	16,834	12,580	...	25·5
Bidi	40	1853-54	39,782	37,725	...	5·1
Bidi	123	1855-56	19,302	18,129	...	6·0
Páchhápur	10	1855-56	2097	1833	...	12·6
Kágvád	49	1860-61	61,266	66,778	8·9	...
Total ...	750	...	6,38,928	5,47,692	...	14·2

Parasgad, 1849-50.

Parasgad, with 108 Government villages, was measured in 1847-48 and 1848-49; it was classed and the new rates were introduced in 1849-50.[1] The tract was irregular in shape, with an extreme length of forty-three miles and an extreme breadth of thirty miles. It was bounded on the south by Dhárwár and Navalgund; on the east by the estates or *jágirs* of Nargund, Rámdurg, and Torgal; on the north by Gokák; and on the west by Sampgaon. A low rugged sandstone range

[1] Capt. Wingate, Surv. Supt. 246 of 24th December 1849, Bom. Gov. Rev. Rec. 131A of 1880, 155-180.

Chapter VIII. Land Administration. Survey. *Parasgad, 1849-50.*

running north-west and south-east divided Parasgad into two nearly equal parts. To the south and west the hills were steep rising sharply out of a far-stretching rich black-soil plain. To the north and east the hills sloped into a rough stony upland with poor sandy soil. Further north, trap overlay the sandstone and the surface soil was shallow and poor. The river Malprabha, entering from the west and leaving some miles beyond Manoli to the east, divided the sub-division into two unequal parts. The climate, though nowhere moist enough for rice, was generally well suited to dry-crop tillage. The rainfall varied considerably in different parts. It was most abundant and certain in the west and grew gradually more uncertain towards the east, where, along the borders of Navalgund and Nargund, the crops were liable to fail from want of rain. The villages above and near the hills had the best supply of rain, while those of the Sattigeri group in the north-east had the worst. Parasgad contained 108 Government and twenty-five alienated villages. Of these, sixty-six Government and fifteen alienated villages formed the charge of the *mámlatdár* who was stationed at Saundatti, and the remaining forty-two Government and ten alienated villages were the charge of the *mahálkari* whose head-quarters were at Murgod. The Government villages contained 336,556 acres of which 46,480 were hills rivers and roads and the remaining 290,076 were arable. According to the survey census Saundatti contained 6265, Murgod 5649, and Manoli 5570 people. The largest villages Hosur, Ugargol, Huli, and Asundi, which were purely agricultural, each contained about 2000 persons. Eight to ten other villages had 1000 to 2000 and the rest less than 1000 people. The population was chiefly agricultural. The Parasgad husbandry was almost confined to dry-crop tillage, there was no rice and little garden land. The finest gardens were at Manoli on the north bank of the Malprabha where water was abundant within twenty feet of the surface. The gardens were watered from wells. Except in rare instances, the waters of the Malprabha were not used for irrigation. The chief garden crops were plantains, sugarcane, and vegetables. The leading dry-crops were red *jvári*, cotton, gram, and wheat. White *jvári* was also grown in a limited number of plain villages east of Parasgad where the rain was uncertain. About three parts were early crops and one part late. Among the early crops red *jvári* was by far the most important and covered at least one-half of the whole arable area. Of the late crops cotton was the most important. It was widely grown in the black soil plain to the south and west of the hills, and to a small extent in light soil. Manure and rotation of crops were valued. Manure was applied every two or three years to light soils. It was also used once in three to five years in the western black soils where rain was abundant. It was hardly ever used in the plain soil from Saundatti east where sheep were folded on the fields by the better class of tillers. In the black plain where numerous carts were freely used for field purposes, the husbandry on the whole was good. Above the hills the tillage was not so good because the country was too rough for carts, and manure had to be carried to the fields on bullocks. Carts from nearly every village easily reached the Belgaum-Kaládgi road which passed through the north of the sub-division. Owing to the badness of this route to Vengurla, little produce went by it except for the Belgaum market. Traders sent most of their cotton to Kumta and received their Bombay supplies from Rájápur. The traffic was carried on by means of pack bullocks. The manufacturing and trading towns were Saundatti, Murgod, and Manoli. About a thousand looms wove coarse cotton fabrics, some of which went to Kánara and the coast, and the rest were used locally. Murgod and Manoli were also noted for their dyed and printed stuffs the preparation of which supported upwards of two hundred families. All these towns sent cotton, wheat, and other raw produce to the coast, and brought English cloth and metal, and betelnut pepper and other articles of local use. Growers sold most of their surplus produce at Saundatti, Murgod, Manoli, Bailhongal, Gurl Hosur, and other markets. A few western landholders took their produce to Belgaum. The local markets were well placed for nearly all the villages except perhaps those of the Sattigeri group which had no important market near them. As a rule the same produce prices prevailed over the whole sub-division.

Of the twenty-five alienated villages, ten paid a quit-rent and fifteen were held rent-free. Of the 108 Government villages forty came under the English in 1817-18, fifty-six were taken from Kolhápur in 1827-28, seven lapsed on the death of Nilkanthráv Sinde between 1843 and 1848, and five were resumed after the Inám Commission's inquiry. The forty villages that came under British management in 1817-18 belonged to the Saundatti-Phutgaon and Yakkundi groups. Shortly after their acquisition they were surveyed and assessed by the late Mr. Thackeray. At the beginning of British rule the existing Marátha system of levying a very high standard assessment or *kamál*, nominally on a limited portion of the village lands and granting the rest rent-free or at low rates, led the first British officers to set an unduly high value on the land. From this cause the assessment of these forty villages was fixed greatly too high. The evil was aggravated by a fall in the price of field produce, so that it speedily became impossible to realize the full rates. Accordingly from time to time the revenue officers made arbitrary reductions until the original assessment existed only in name. In 1842-43 all acre rates above these figures were lowered to 6*s.* and 4*s.* (Rs. 3 and Rs. 2). Rates below 4*s.* (Rs. 2) remained as before. Since 1842-43 no further change had been introduced in these forty villages. No systematic inquiry had been made into the assessment of the remaining villages though in 1842 the land of the fifty-six Kolhápur villages was measured in acres. The lands of the twelve villages, which had lapsed or been resumed between 1843 and 1853, had not been measured. In ninety-six Parasgad villages, during the twenty-one years ending 1848-49, the tillage area fell from 88,957 acres in 1828-29 to 70,662 acres in 1848-49 or twenty per cent; and the remissions from £5141 to £163 (Rs. 51,410 - Rs. 1630) or 96·8 per cent. The revenue for collection rose during the same period from £7441 to £8446 (Rs. 74,410 - Rs. 84,460) or 13·5 per cent. The only two years of extensive failure of crops were 1832-33 and 1838-39. The details are:

Chapter VIII.
Land Administration.
Survey.
Parasgad, 1849-50.

Parasgad, 96 Villages: Land Revenue, 1828-1849.

Year.	Tillage. Area.	Tillage. Rental.	Remissions.	For Collection.	Year.	Tillage. Area.	Tillage. Rental.	Remissions.	For Collection.
	Acres.	Rs.	Rs.	Rs.		Acres.	Rs.	Rs.	Rs.
1828-29...	88,957	1,25,822	51,410	74,412	1840-41...	63,286	87,637	21,432	66,205
1829-30...	86,009	1,17,458	52,094	65,364	1841-42...	65,915	92,555	26,691	65,864
1830-31...	88,212	1,15,186	53,654	61,482	1842-43...	63,229	83,272	11,485	71,787
1831-32...	85,867	1,11,976	41,593	70,383	1843-44...	58,636	68,873	4144	64,729
1832-33...	71,741	82,992	50,102	32,890	1844-45...	58,786	67,897	8489	59,408
1833-34...	78,289	1,04,481	46,781	57,700	1845-46...	58,903	66,125	4999	61,126
1834-35...	75,528	1,16,128	38,845	77,283	1846-47...	62,769	70,320	2468	67,852
1835-36...	72,323	1,08,592	41,712	66,880	1847-48...	67,436	79,558	2932	76,626
1836-37...	72,808	1,08,622	37,412	71,210	1848-49...	70,662	86,097	1634	84,463
1837-38...	71,673	1,02,286	31,508	70,778					
1838-39...	60,999	74,541	31,513	43,028					
1839-40...	63,010	86,919	27,521	59,398	Average...	70,475	93,204	28,020	65,184

The old assessment was excessive and very unequal. Some groups were much more heavily rated than other groups and the rates varied greatly even in villages belonging to the same group. The most heavily assessed group was Saundatti-Phutgaon. The inequality and heaviness of the assessment had greatly prevented the spread of tillage. Between 1828-29 and 1845-46, in the eighteen Saundatti-Phutgaon villages, 16,797 acres or forty-nine per cent of the 1828-29 tillage area had fallen waste, and in the rest of the sub-division tillage had shrunk from eighteen to twenty-nine per cent. The following statement shows the effect on tillage of heavy, moderate, and light rates:

Parasgad Assessment, 1823-1846.

Villages.	Year.	Tillage. Area.	Tillage. Increase.	Tillage. Decrease.	Average Acre Assessment.	Average Acre Collections.	Probable Average New Acre Rate.
		Acres.	Per Cent.	Per Cent.	Rs. a. p.	Rs. a. p.	Rs. a. p.
Heavy.							
Háro-belvadi	1823-24 ...	3118	...	42	2 8 9	0 14 10	1 4 6
	1845-46 ...	1815			2 1 1	1 13 10	
Hosur	1833-34 ...	2618	...	32	...	1 10 2	1 2 6
	1845-46 ...	1780			...	1 12 9	
Saundatti	1823-24 ...	7689	...	59	2 12 0	1 13 5	1 2 6
	1844-45 ...	3115			2 12 7	1 8 9	
Hirekumi	1823-24 ...	1696	...	79	2 6 9	0 10 8	1 2 0
	1845-46 ...	363			2 3 1	1 12 4	
Huli	1823-24 ...	2376	...	41	2 1 10	0 12 5	1 0 6
	1847-48 ...	1423			1 11 5	1 11 5	
Hanchinál...	1823-24 ...	5188	...	63	2 9 2	0 12 0	1 0 0
	1845-46 ...	1916			2 1 11	1 11 5	
Markumbi...	1823-24 ..	614	...	...	2 2 7	2 2 7	1 5 0
	1845-46 ...	617			2 11 0	2 11 0	
Moderate.							
Inchal	1833-34 ...	1197	8	...	0 12 11	0 12 11	1 0 0
	1845-46 ...	1292			1 1 3	1 1 3	
Yekeri	1833-34 ...	100	28	...	0 12 5	0 12 5	0 10 0
	1845-46 ...	128			0 12 5	0 12 5	
Aladkatti	1833-34 ...	508	11	...	0 14 11	0 14 11	0 12 0
	1845-46 ...	562			1 0 7	1 0 7	
Rámápur	1834-35 ...	1301	...	5	0 12 7	0 12 7	0 12 0
	1845-46 ...	1242			0 12 3	0 12 3	
Light.							
Karikatti	1822-23 ...	393	84	...	0 9 8	0 4 5	0 11 0
	1847-48 ...	722			0 5 11	0 5 8	
Katmali	1833-34 ...	324	21	...	0 5 1	0 5 1	1 1 0
	1845-46 ...	392			0 7 6	0 7 6	
Chulki	1833-34 ...	1022	31	...	0 9 2	0 8 9	1 0 0
	1845-46 ...	1334			0 12 11	0 12 9	
Sattigeri	1833-34 ...	1427	47	...	0 6 11	0 6 11	...
	1845-46 ...	2102			0 5 6	0 5 6	

Chapter VIII. Land Administration. Survey. Parasgad, 1849-50.

Under the survey settlement the 108 Government villages were arranged in five classes, the first with sixteen, the second with twenty-seven, the third with thirty-three, and the fourth and the fifth each with sixteen villages. The sixteen first class villages, with a highest dry-crop acre rate of 3s. $1\frac{1}{8}$d. (Rs. $1\frac{9}{16}$), lay in the plain along the borders of Sampgaon and Dhárwár, and had a climate favourable for dry-crop tillage and a good market for surplus produce. The twenty-seven villages of the second class, with a highest dry-crop acre rate of 2s. 9d. (Rs. $1\frac{3}{8}$), lay in the plain to the north and east of the first class, with a less favoured climate and the same markets as the first class. The thirty-three villages of the third class, with a highest dry-crop acre rate of 2s. 6d. (Rs. $1\frac{1}{4}$) were partly in the plain to the east of the second class and partly along the hills from the south-east to the north-west as far as the borders of Gokák. Both in climate and in markets these villages were less fortunate than those of the second class. The sixteen villages of the fourth class, with a highest dry-crop acre rate of 2s. 3d. (Rs. $1\frac{1}{8}$), lay in the extreme east with still less favourable climate and prices. The sixteen villages of the fifth class, with a highest dry-crop acre rate of 2s. (Re. 1), lay near Sattigeri in the extreme north-east and were badly off both in climate and in markets. Well-watered garden lands amounted to about 350 acres of which 334 were held at an average acre rate of 6s. $3\frac{7}{8}$d. (Rs. 3 as. $2\frac{7}{12}$). The average acre rate paid by gardens in different villages varied from £1 3s. $9\frac{5}{8}$d. (Rs. 11 as. $14\frac{1}{4}$) in Manoli to $7\frac{5}{8}$d. ($5\frac{1}{12}$ as.) in Kurabgatti. The survey assessment fixed a highest garden acre rate of 10s. (Rs. 5), an average acre rate of 4s. 6d. (Rs. $2\frac{1}{4}$), and a whole garden assessment of about £80 (Rs. 800). The new rates raised tho rental from £6979 to £7081 (Rs. 69,790-Rs. 70,810) or about one per cent. The details are :

Parasgad Survey Settlement, 1849-50.

Class.	Villages.	Former 1841-1846 Tillage.		Survey. Tillage.		Survey. Waste.		Survey. Total.		Highest Dry-crop Acre Rate.
		Area.	Collections.	Area.	Rental.	Area.	Rental.	Area.	Rental.	
		Acres.	Rs.	Acres.	Rs.	Acres.	Rs.	Acres.	Rs.	Rs. a.
I	16	14,116	28,088	20,310	23,166	2883	3033	23,193	26,199	1 9
II	27	15,067	17,710	18,724	17,944	9021	7564	27,745	25,508	1 6
III	33	17,861	16,334	21,471	15,432	14,256	9578	35,727	25,010	1 4
IV	16	10,321	6772	11,266	7,569	6033	2922	17,299	10,491	1 2
V	16	15,095	5862	15,890	6,703	4317	1214	20,207	7917	1 0
Total ...	108	72,480	69,786	87,661	70,814	36,510	24,311	124,171	95,125	...

Gokák, 1849-50.

The measuring of Gokák was begun in 1847-48 and finished in 1848-49; the classing was begun in 1848-49 and completed early in 1849-50; and the survey settlement was introduced in 1849-50.[1] Gokák lay immediately north-west of Parasgad. On the west it was bounded by the Páchhápur and Chikodi sub-divisions; on the north by some detached Kolhápur villages and by the estates or *jágirs* of the Patvardhan family; and on the east by the Yádvád petty division or *mahál*. Except three outlying villages to the east,

---

[1] Capt. Wingate, Surv. Supt. 246 of 24th December 1849, Bom. Gov. Rev. Rec. 131A of 1880, 180-197.

Chapter VIII.
Land Administration.
Survey.
Gokák, 1849-50.

the tract was compact. It was enclosed on the south and west by a range of sand-stone hills, while to the north and east it was open and fairly level. The hills to the west though of no great height were extremely rugged, and were covered with a dense growth of low trees and brushwood. Near their north end, the Ghatprabha entered Gokák from the west, and, in passing the hills, formed the famous falls of Gokák, three miles to the west of Gokák town. Immediately to the north of the falls, trap overlaid the sandstone and covered the whole tract to the east and north. The climate was not so favourable as in Parasgad where it was generally well suited to dry-crop tillage. On and to the west of the hills the rainfall was ample, often too heavy for dry-crop tillage. But in the plain to the east of the hills it was so scanty and doubtful that according to a local saying a good monsoon came only once in twelve years. Besides the Yádvád petty division Gokák contained forty-seven Government and twenty-three alienated villages, forming the charge of the mámlatdár whose head-quarters were at Gokák. Of the alienated villages, twenty-two were subject to the payment of quit-rent and one was held free of assessment. The Government villages contained an area of 188,478 acres of which 54,099 came under hills roads and water-courses. The soil formed from the trap in the east and north of the hills was generally poor. That from the sandstone close to the hills was often little better than pure sand and required frequent manuring. It did not want much rain, and, with the help of manure, yielded fair crops. On the uplands, the trap soils were extremely poor, and, as the soil did not hold moisture, the crops were very apt to fail. In lower positions, chiefly along the banks of the Ghatprabha which ran nearly through the centre of the tract, the trap soil gradually deepened into fair black soil of which large tracts stretched along the river. On the whole the soil of Gokák was closely like that of north-east Parasgad. It was very inferior to the Dhárwár soil. The husbandry was extremely slovenly. Many fields were half or not at all tilled. This slovenly tillage was a sure sign of poverty. It might be attributable to an excessive or badly distributed assessment, a precarious climate, and a poor soil. In Captain Wingate's opinion it was chiefly due to an irregular and defective assessment. The people did not work well because their work was badly paid. In a few villages the fields were better tilled, and though they paid twice or three times as much as their neighbours, the people were much more prosperous. The leading dry-crops were red *jvári*, cotton, gram, and wheat. About three parts were early crops and one part late. At intervals of one to three years, manure was applied to all light soil, but seldom to black soil, and not at all when the fields were some way from the village sites. There was hardly any export of field produce owing to the large local demand at Gokák nearly half of whose 12,337 people lived by weaving, dyeing, and printing cotton fabrics. Of late years the price of cotton goods had fallen and the weavers were depressed. This fall in the price of cotton cloths was accompanied by a corresponding fall in the price of raw cotton. Captain Wingate (24th December 1849) believed that within the last thirty years money had grown three times dearer and therefore the people's

Chapter VIII. Land Administration. Survey. *Gokák, 1849-50.*

assessment represented three times as much produce as it had formerly represented. He feared that money was growing still scarcer. This at any rate the people believed. They said it did not matter whether their crops were good or were bad, in neither case could they turn them into money. The very low price of cotton was no doubt a chief cause of this evil state. Cotton was rising and things for the time were looking better. Still there was no reason to suppose the advance in cotton would last. To increase exports, Captain Wingate was satisfied, was the only way to bring in money. The inland districts were every year drained of considerable sums and little was spent locally. Unless their exports were helped, the burden of the land assessment must go on growing heavier. The gain from lowering assessments would not last. As money grew scarcer, the new rates would become as grievous as the old, and fresh reductions would be necessary. Without the help of good roads and an increase of exports, low assessments could ensure no lasting gain.

The only part of the tract for which Gokák was not the great market was a few of the most easterly villages which had the large markets of Mahálingpur and Rabkavi, two manufacturing towns in the Mudhol and Patvardhan territories, at a convenient distance. Near Gokák prices were a little higher, but they varied little in different parts of the tract. Throughout the sub-division cart-roads were greatly wanted. Owing to the wretched state of the roads, Gokák was not approached from the west by carts, and hardly from any other direction. Many other villages were as badly placed.

The Gokák sub-division lapsed to Government in 1836, on the death of Govindráv Patvardhan of Chinchni, a grandson of the well known Parashurám Bháu (1740-1799). At that time it had been fifty-six years in the hands of the Patvardhan family. For several years before the lapse the officer in charge was a *mámlatdár* named Bába Bhátkhande who managed the district on the usual native plan, but apparently with unusual liberality. Most of the land was let either at short rent or *ukti* rates or on leases or *kauls*, the revenue was collected in eight instalments from November to June, and when a landholder was unable to pay, his balance was allowed to stand over till the next year. Under English management the short rent or *ukti* rates became permanent and the leases or *kauls* were stopped. The revenue was taken in four instalments between December and March two for the early and two for the late harvest. These changes were unfavourable to the landholders. Under the Patvardhans there was a great variety of land measures, each village having its own standard. Soon after the villages came under British management, the district and village officers were ordered to keep all the land in *kurgis*, one *kurgi* being the area a two-bullock seed-drill can sow in a day. The work of making the change was left to the district and village officers and was done so roughly that the *kurgis* varied nearly as much as the old measures. The survey measurings showed that in tilled land the *kurgi* varied from one to thirty acres; the average *kurgi* in different villages varied from 3½ to 17½ acres; and the average *kurgi* for the whole sub-division was 6½ acres.

Chapter VIII.
Land Administration.
Survey.
Gokák, 1849-50.

With so uncertain a land measure the village clerks were able to conceal cultivation. In Hulkund the returns for the past year (1848) showed 307 *kurgis* as the area held for tillage and 345 (245 ?) or much more than one-half as the waste; measurements showed the tilled area to be 1614 acres and the waste 1032. In Talkatnal the village returns showed 377 *kurgis* cultivated and 215 waste; measurements showed 2183 acres under tillage and 468 acres waste that is the waste was one-fifth instead of three-fifths of the tillage. These and other instances showed that the old system failed to protect the interests of Government, and failed to supply trustworthy data by which a revenue officer could regulate or even understand the assessment. The under-estimate of tillage and the over-estimate of waste was probably old and was not necessarily fraudulent, as to under-estimate the tillage was a common device for lessening the pressure of a heavy assessment. During the thirteen years ending 1848-49 the tillage area had fallen from 55,873 acres in 1836-37 to 47,913 acres in 1848-49 or fourteen per cent; the remissions from £2644 to £58 (Rs. 26,440 - 580) or about ninety-eight per cent; and the revenue for collection had risen from £2368 to £2975 (Rs. 23,680 - Rs. 29,750) or 25·6 per cent. The details are:

Gokák, 47 Villages: Land Revenue, 1836-1849.

Year.	Tillage. Area.	Tillage. Rental.	Remissions.	For Collection.
	Acres.	Rs.	Rs.	Rs.
1836-37 ...	55,873	50,122	26,443	23,679
1837-38 ...	61,227	43,731	5625	38,106
1838-39 ...	60,318	42,758	19,098	23,655
1839-40 ...	58,510	41,373	6641	34,732
1840-41 ...	59,699	40,624	5139	35,485
1841-42 ...	54,791	37,948	5287	32,661
1842-43 ...	50,819	32,596	297	32,299
1843-44 ...	48,558	30,306	825	29,481
1844-45 ...	47,254	29,581	1436	28,145
1845-46 ...	47,645	29,210	2928	26,282
1846-47 ...	48,659	30,665	250	30,415
1847-48 ...	49,357	30,674	928	29,746
1848-49 ...	47,913	30,330	578	29,752
Average ...	53,125	36,147	5806	30,341

During the twenty-five years ending 1848-49 Gokák had declined from faulty assessment rather than from over-assessment. In some villages the average acre rate varied between 2¼*d.* (1½ *as.*) and 4⅞*d.* (3¼ *as.*), and in others between 2*s.* 9*d.* (Rs. 1⅜) and 5*s.* (Rs. 2½). Under the survey settlement for assessment purposes the villages were divided into six classes. The first class, with a highest dry-crop acre rate of 3*s.* 6*d.* (Rs. 1¾), contained three villages in the extreme west above the hills, with a favourable climate for dry-crop tillage, rain being usually abundant and droughts rare. The second class, with a highest dry-crop acre rate of 3*s.* (Rs. 1½), contained two villages, Dhupadhál above the hills but to the north of the first class and with a less favoured climate, and Gokák whose lands were below the hills where the rainfall was much less certain. These two villages were near each other and enjoyed the advantage of the Gokák market. The third class, with a highest dry-crop acre rate of 2*s.* 6*d.* (Rs. 1¼), comprised eight villages along and east of the western range of hills with a climate greatly inferior to that of the first class. The fourth class, with a highest dry-crop acre rate of 2*s.* 3*d.* (Rs. 1⅛), included eight villages in the plain, east and north of the third class, with an extremely uncertain rainfall. In the fifth class were fourteen villages, with a highest dry-crop acre rate of 2*s.* (Re. 1). They lay still further in the plain and had a still more uncertain climate. The sixth class, with a highest dry-crop acre rate of 1*s.* 9*d.* (14 *as.*), included twelve villages along or beyond the east of the sub-division very badly placed in respect to markets and climate. About twelve acres of poor rice land in two villages among the hills to the west, were assessed at dry-crop rates. About 1400 acres of dry-crop land in villages along the Ghatprabha, known as *madi* land, were subject to more or less frequent flooding during the monsoon freshes. These floodings were a gain especially in seasons of scanty rainfall. Some of the flooded lands were assessed at the dry-crop acre rate at an increase of a quarter and the rest at an increase of an eighth. Wheat, gram, and vegetables were grown in 400 acres of garden land. Only 266 acres were entered in the accounts as garden, the rest had been entered as dry-crop land. The assessment on the 266 acres tilled in 1848 was £82 6*s.* (Rs. 823) of which £41 6*s.* (Rs. 413) were on account of twenty-seven acres near Gokák. The highest acre rate adopted for the whole garden land at the new settlement was 10*s.* (Rs. 5) and the average acre rate was 4*s.* 6*d.* (Rs. 2¼). The effect of the new rates was a fall in the rental from £3033 to £2376 (Rs. 30,330 - Rs. 23,760) or 21·7 per cent. The details are:

Chapter VIII. Land Administration.

Survey.

Gokák, 1849-50.

Gokák Survey Settlement, 1849-50.

Class.	Villages.	Former 1839-1849. Tillage.		Survey. Tillage.		Survey. Waste.		Survey. Total.	
		Area.	Collections.	Area.	Rental.	Area.	Rental.	Area.	Rental.
		Acres.	Rs.	Acres.	Rs.	Acres.	Rs.	Acres.	Rs.
I ...	3	2806	5594	3052	3052	157	157	3209	3209
II ...	2	2443	2123	2288	1680	830	506	3118	2186
III ...	8	7384	4276	7562	4135	2323	1307	9885	5442
IV ...	8	8212	6403	7727	4669	5170	3231	12,897	7900
V ...	14	13,066	5267	12,107	5360	10,464	4414	22,571	9774
VI ...	12	17,153	6671	15,087	4868	6743	2001	21,830	6869
Total ...	47	51,064	30,334	47,823	23,764	25,687	11,616	73,510	35,380

Ten villages of Yádvád were measured in 1848 and 1849 and classed in 1851-52; the new rates were introduced on trial in 1851-52 and sanctioned for thirty years in 1855.[1] Yádvád, including the mahálkari's share of the Gokák sub-division, belonged to the estate of Parashurám Bháu of Tásgaon, which lapsed to the British on his death without heirs in 1848. These villages lay close to the north-east of the rest of Gokák and to the south of Athni from which it was separated by about twenty miles of estate land. Of the nineteen villages of the Yádvád group only ten were under Government management. To the remaining nine,

Yádvád, 1851-52.

[1] Capt. Anderson, Surv. Supt. Southern Marátha Country, 267 of 26th July 1853, Bom. Gov. Sel. LXXXI. 38-48.

Chapter VIII.
Land Administration.
Survey.
Yádvád, 1851-52.

which belonged to the estate of the Kanjalgi *desái*, the revision of assessment did not extend. The Government villages contained 37,846 acres of which 34,380 were arable and 3466 unarable. The population was 6494 or 110 to the square mile. The land included in this group differed little from Athni. The bulk of the soil was black, but much of it was poor, stony, and shallow, particularly in the northern trap villages. As in Athni the climate was very precarious, and the husbandry and condition of the people much on a par with what was found in the whole subdivision. The usual and chief dry-crops were wheat, *jvári*, and cotton. Two markets held within the limits of the group, a larger one at Yádvád and a smaller one at the alienated village of Kaujalgi, and several others at no great distance from the borders, secured a ready sale for local produce. The surplus grain was carried to the western markets, especially to Sankeshvar in Chikodi, where a return freight of Konkan produce was obtained. A small quantity of cotton was kept for local use and the rest went to the coast. The road lately made from Lokápur on the Kaládgi-Belgaum road, by Yádvád to Sankeshvar, greatly aided the local exports. Coarse cotton cloth weaving supported about a hundred, and mixed silk and cotton about twenty families. Most of the goods were sold at the Mudhol market. Parashurám Bháu, to whom these villages belonged, was very deeply involved in debt. For fourteen years before his death they had been mortgaged nominally to a wealthy banker named Náráyanráv Anant Válambe, but really to two clerks of this banker who were called *kamávisdárs* or managers and on whom civil and criminal jurisdiction over the district was conferred. The supreme authority still remained with Parashurám to whom the two clerks yearly forwarded accounts and sent remissions for sanction. After the chief's sanction was received, remissions were taken from the net revenue in his accounts; but these remissions went to the pockets of the managers not to the pockets of the landholders. To frighten landholders from throwing up their land, outstanding balances were purposely kept. The system was carried to such an extent that when the district lapsed to the English, the outstanding balances in the ten Government villages amounted to no less than £7803 (Rs. 78,030), the average gross revenue during the first three years of English rule being £841 (Rs. 8410) of which about one-tenth was remitted. Some years before the chief's death, with his consent, a Government clerk was appointed to supervise the revenue affairs of the group, against which the people loudly complained. This supervision lasted for three years and ceased shortly before the death of the chief. In 1848-49, when Parashurám Bháu died, the area under tillage was 15,756 acres and the gross assessment was £1034 (Rs. 10,340) of which £114 (Rs. 1140) were remitted and £920 (Rs. 9200) were collected. In 1849-50 the area under tillage was 11,637 acres and the gross assessment was £778 (Rs. 7780), of which £133 (Rs. 1330) were remitted and £645 (Rs. 6450) collected; and in 1850-51 the land under tillage was 11,258 acres and the gross assessment was £712 (Rs. 7120), of which £34 (Rs. 340) were remitted and £678 (Rs. 6780) were collected. For the survey settlement a highest dry-crop acre rate of 1*s.* 9*d.* (14 *as.*) was proposed. Of garden land there was only one

Government number of four acres assessed at 2*s*. 6*d*. (Rs. 1¼) the acre. The new rates caused a fall in the rental from £767 (Rs. 7670) to £659 (Rs. 6590) or fourteen per cent. The details are :

Chapter VIII. Land Administration. Survey. *Yádvád, 1851-52.*

Yádvád Survey Settlement, 1851-52.

Class.	Villages.	Former Tillage. Rental.	Survey. Tillage. Area.	Tillage. Rental.	Tillage. Acre rate.	Waste. Area.	Waste. Rental.	Total. Area.	Total. Rental.
		Rs.	Acres.	Rs.	As.	Acres.	Rs.	Acres.	Rs.
I.	10	7669	13,202	6593	8	5296	2431	18,498	9024

During the twelve years ending 1862-63 the tillage area rose from 13,202 to 21,380 acres or sixty-two per cent; and collections from £890 to £1273 (Rs. 8900 - Rs. 12,730) or forty-three per cent. During the same period remissions fell from £121 (Rs. 1210) to £2 (Rs. 20) or ninety-eight per cent. The details are :[1]

Yádvád Survey Results, 1851-1863.

Year.	Tillage. Area.	Tillage. Rental.	Remissions.	For Collection.	Waste. Area.	Waste. Rental.	Waste. Grazing Fees.	Quit-rent.	Collections.
	Acres.	Rs.	Rs.	Rs.	Acres.	Rs.	Rs.	Rs.	Rs.
1851-52 ...	13,202	6593	1206	5387	5296	...	563	2954	8904
1852-53 ...	15,886	7839	...	7839	7136	3295	...	1514	9353
1853-54 ...	16,851	8555	15	8540	4721	2061	349	1891	10,780
1854-55 ...	18,296	9218	15	9198	3223	1385	287	1914	11,399
1855-56 ...	19,167	9638	15	9623	2361	960	244	1915	11,782
1856-57 ...	20,773	10,273	15	10,258	612	247	80	2004	12,851
1857-58 ...	21,889	10,542	58	10,484	117	41	18	1927	12,429
1858-59 ...	21,128	10,429	15	10,414	391	162	45	1913	12,372
1859-60 ...	20,713	10,247	15	10,232	867	369	102	1919	12,253
1860-61 ...	21,184	10,441	15	10,426	614	258	78	1905	12,409
1861-62 ...	21,084	10,419	15	10,404	698	298	66	2154	12,624
1862-63 ...	21,380	10,550	15	10,535	464	193	45	2152	12,732

Athni, 1851-52.

Fifty-three Athni villages were measured between 1848-49 and 1851-52, and classed in 1850-51 and in 1851-52.[2] New rates were introduced on trial into the fifty-three villages in 1851-52 and were finally sanctioned by Government in 1855. With a population of 48,478 the fifty-three villages contained 524 square miles or 335,454 acres, of which 284,300 were arable and 51,154 unarable. These Athni villages had all belonged to various estates which had lapsed to Government. The chief lapse was the Nipáni *desái's* forty-two villages in 1839. The main body of the sub-division formed the most northern part of Belgaum. About a dozen villages also lay along the Krishna and bordered the western boundary of Bágalkot. To the west and north-west of the main body of Athni were several villages but none were included in the fifty-three. Of the fifty-three villages sixteen formed the charge of the Galgali mahálkari, and the remaining thirty-seven were under the mámlatdár at Athni, in whose charge were also the remaining twenty

1 Major Anderson, Surv. Supt. 53 of 6th February 1864, Bom. Gov. Sel. LXXXI. 46, 123.

2 Capt. Anderson, Surv. Supt. 267 of 26th July 1853, Bom. Gov. Sel. LXXXI. 22-38.

Chapter VIII.
Land Administration.
Survey.
Athni, 1851-52.

villages of the sub-division. Athni was generally rough and uneven with a surface of trap. In the west a broken chain of bare bushless flat-topped hills rose from the plain. The more level country was a series of long rises and hollows with, in many of the hollows, small running streams fringed with a few hundred paces of fair and often of good soil. Up the slopes of the rises the soil grew shallower and poorer, and the tops were rock sometimes in bare sheets of a hundred yards sometimes with an inch or two of soil hardly fit to grow grass. The black soil was of uncertain depth. Close to the Krishna it was always deep and rich, and the banks well wooded chiefly by *bábhul*. In the east, where the climate was specially bad, both the people and the tillage were miserably poor. The yearly Krishna floods so enriched the soil along its banks that it yielded excellent crops without manure and with almost no rain. About 200 families lived by weaving coarse cotton cloth and about 120 families by weaving blankets. Both the cotton and woollen fabrics were for local use. Athni was the chief market. It was attended by people from the neighbouring villages and by traders from the minor markets of Honvád, Telsang, and Ainápur. From Athni cotton and grain went to Miraj and salt and other articles came from the Konkan. The people of the villages to the south of Athni also attended the market held at the large town of Rabkavi in Sángli. The people of the mahálkari's group had the small market of Galgali, and, also, within a convenient distance, the large markets of the alienated towns of Mudhol and Jamkhandi. Thus the villages round Galgali and those about and especially to the west and south of Athni town, had an advantage over the north-eastern villages with respect to markets. The roads were in general fair, the prevailing even surface of the country offering no serious obstruction to traffic. From the fall of Bijápur in 1686 up to 1730 when it passed from Kolhápur to Sátára, Athni and the neighbouring parts were most unsettled, without security either of life or of property. Under Sátára, from about 1730 to 1749, much had been done to improve the country. Land was given on leases at a nominal rent, population and cultivation increased, and greater security prevailed. In 1750 Athni passed from Sátára to the Peshwa, under whom the district was made over to various estate holders. A fair degree of prosperity continued till about 1790. In 1792 a famine almost emptied the country of people. After the famine, troubled times and the farming system reduced the people to great poverty. For two years after the fall of the Peshwa the sub-division was under British management, and was then made over to Appa Desái of Nipáni. On his death in 1839 it lapsed to the British, by whom existing land measures and rates were continued. Under the native system, though the assessment on the better lands was generally very high, reductions were often made either under the name of *kkand-tota* or by adding a tract of poor land either rent-free or at a nominal assessment. A large balance was also allowed to remain outstanding from year to year, and reduced as much as possible in any specially good years. The proprietor used the threat of realizing outstandings to force the landholder to continue cultivating. The proprietor limited his demands

Chapter VIII. Land Administration. Survey. *Athni, 1851-52.*

solely by the capacity of the landholder. In some estates the people were ground to their last farthing, in others they enjoyed considerable ease. A minute knowledge of the means of every cultivator enabled the proprietor to raise a very large revenue without ruining any one; at the same time under their system any increase of capital or advance in condition was impossible. During the twelve years ending 1850-51 the tillage area fell from 121,930 to 92,369 and averaged 108,160 acres. It steadily fell till 1845-46 when it was 100,307 acres. During the next two years it rose, but it again began to fall speedily till it reached 92,369 acres in 1850-51. During the same period the amount for remissions fell from £854 (Rs. 8540) in 1839-40 to nothing in 1850-51, and averaged £555 (Rs. 5550). For the first three years the amount was very large. In 1842-43 it was £423 (Rs. 4230) and in 1843-44 it rose to £943 (Rs. 9430). It then fell rapidly till 1846-47 when it was £233 (Rs. 2330). Next year it more than doubled but disappeared in 1850-51. The amount for collection varied from £5257 (Rs. 52,570) in 1839-40 to £3451 (Rs. 34,510) in 1849-50 and averaged £4058 (Rs. 40,580). From 1839-40 to 1845-46 the amount fell from £5257 to £3798 (Rs. 52,570 - Rs. 37,980), it rose in 1846-47 to £4303 (Rs. 43,030), and again fell to £3451 (Rs. 34,510) in 1849-50. In 1850-51 it rose slightly to £3742 (Rs. 37,420). The details are:

Athni, 42 Villages: Land Revenue, 1839-1851.

Year.	Tillage.		Remissions.	For Collection.	Year.	Tillage.		Remissions.	For Collection.
	Area.	Rental.				Area.	Rental.		
	Acres.	Rs.	Rs.	Rs.		Acres.	Rs.	Rs.	Rs.
1839-40 ...	121,930	61,108	8535	52,578	1846-47 ...	111,098	45,357	2331	43,026
1840-41 ...	118,054	56,679	12,810	43,869	1847-48 ...	113,353	45,167	6227	39,940
1841-42 ...	116,145	54,161	12,219	41,942	1848-49 ...	105,582	40,162	2342	37,820
1842-43 ...	118,599	50,406	4226	46,180	1849-50 ...	97,463	36,015	1505	34,510
1843-44 ...	105,154	44,620	9433	35,187	1850-51 ...	92,369	37,419	...	37,419
1844-45 ...	102,862	42,395	5866	36,529					
1845-46 ...	100,307	40,030	2047	37,983	Average ...	108,160	46,127	5545	40,582

During the five years ending 1850-51 the tillage area in twenty-three villages immediately about Galgali and some to the west of the hilly tract, fell from 42,172 to 35,673 acres or fifteen per cent; remissions fell from £362 (Rs. 3620) to nothing; and collections from £2692 to £2440 (Rs. 26,920 - Rs. 24,400) or nine per cent. The details[1] are:

Athni, 23 Villages: Land Revenue.

Year.	Area.	Rental.	Remissions.	Collections.
	Acres.	Rs.	Rs.	Rs.
1846-47	42,172	30,536	3621	26,915
1847-48	40,281	27,731	4874	22,857
1848-49	37,379	24,130	2239	21,891
1849-50	35,146	21,925	380	21,545
1850-51	35,673	24,396	...	24,396
	38,130	25,744	2223	23,521

[1] Capt. Anderson, Surv. Supt. 318 of 8th Dec. 1855, Bom. Gov. Sel. XCIV. 10.

Chapter VIII.
Land Administration.
Survey.
Athni, 1851-52.

Under the survey settlement the fifty-three villages were divided into two classes, the first of twenty-three and the second of thirty. The first class of twenty-three villages, which were either close to Galgali or to the west of the hills, had a highest dry-crop acre rate of 1*s.* 9*d.* (14 *as.*). The second class of thirty villages, to the east of the hilly tract, with an inferior climate and poorer markets, had a highest dry-crop acre rate of 1*s.* 6*d.* (12 *as.*). Of 853 acres of garden land one-fourth was in Athni alone and nearly the whole of the rest was in the eastern villages. Sugarcane and plantains were grown in many gardens but rarely to any extent. Want of capital prevented the landholders growing superior crops. The bulk of the garden crops were vegetables, wheat, and other grains. The gardens were generally watered from dug wells and in many instances by *budkis* or water-lifts from stream pools. The old average acre rate on the whole garden land was 2*s.* 8*d.* (Re. 1 *as.* 5⅛); the new assessment gave a highest acre rate of 3*s.* 6*d.* (Rs. 1¾) and an average of 2*s.* 6⅜*d.* (Re. 1 *as.* 4¼). The effect of the survey rates was a fall in the rental from £6265 (Rs. 62,650) to £4733 (Rs. 47,330) or twenty-four per cent. The details[1] are:

Athni Survey Settlement, 1851-52.

Class.	Villages.	Former Tillage.	Survey.						
			Tillage.			Waste.		Total.	
		Rental.	Area.	Rental.	Acre rate.	Area.	Rental.	Area.	Rental.
		Rs.	Acres.	Rs.	As. p.	Acres.	Rs.	Acres.	Rs.
I. ...	23	26,799	38,464	19,448	8 1	25,192	10,637	63,656	30,085
II. ...	30	35,855	78,530	27,886	5 8	62,549	16,286	141,079	44,172
Total ...	53	62,654	116,994	47,334	6 6	87,741	26,923	204,735	74,257

In 1851-52 the year of settlement the area held for tillage was 116,994 acres and the gross survey assessment was £4733 (Rs. 47,330) of which £955 (Rs. 9550) were remitted. In 1852-53 the tillage area rose to 124,648 acres bearing, according to the revised rates, an assessment of £5442 (Rs. 54,420) the whole of which was realized. In the twenty-three villages placed in the first class the result of the survey settlement during the three years ending 1853-54 was a rise in the tillage area from 38,464 acres to 49,225 acres or twenty-eight per cent, and in the rental from £1945 (Rs. 19,450) to £2595 (Rs. 25,950) or thirty-three per cent. The details[2] are:

Athni, 23 Villages: Survey Results, 1851-54.

Year.	Tillage.		Waste.		Total.	
	Area	Rental.	Area.	Rental.	Area.	Rental.
	Acres.	Rs.	Acres.	Rs.	Acres.	Rs.
1851-52 ...	38,464	19,448	25,192	10,637	63,656	30,085
1852-53 ...	44,098	23,689	20,800	7126	64,898	30,815
1853-54 ...	49,225	25,945	13,986	4178	63,211	30,123

[1] Bom. Gov. Sel. LXXXI. 32, 33.
[2] Capt. Anderson, Surv. Supt. 318 of 8th Dec. 1855, Bom. Gov. Sel. XCIV. 11.

In the fifty-three villages of Athni, the result of the survey settlement during the ten years ending 1862-63 was a rise in tillage from 130,684 to 177,643 acres or thirty-six per cent, and in collections from £6721 to £8547 (Rs. 67,210 - Rs. 85,470) or twenty-seven per cent. During the same period remissions fell from £102 to £3 (Rs. 1020-30) or ninety-seven per cent. The details[1] are :

Chapter VIII. Land Administration. Survey. *Athni, 1851-52.*

Athni, 53 Villages : Survey Results, 1853-1863.

Year.	Tillage.		Remissions.	For Collection.	Waste.			Quit-Rent.	Collections.
	Area.	Rental.			Area.	Rental.	Grazing Fees.		
	Acres.	Rs.	Rs.	Rs.	Acres.	Rs.	Rs.	Rs.	Rs.
1853-54 ...	130,684	56,699	1019	55,680	73,146	17,442	2663	8863	67,206
1854-55 ...	139,021	59,243	970	58,273	66,548	15,411	3251	8899	70,423
1855-56 ...	143,979	61,073	1044	60,029	62,682	14,093	2879	8787	71,695
1856-57 ...	153,221	63,868	975	62,893	53,566	11,828	2789	8789	74,471
1857-58 ...	159,899	65,560	276	65,284	46,935	9656	2482	9073	76,289
1858-59 ...	164,629	66,398	267	66,131	42,336	8862	2457	9754	77,674
1859-60 ...	166,283	66,834	267	66,567	41,299	8691	2821	9797	79,185
1860-61 ...	169,792	67,587	257	67,330	38,237	8083	2786	10,854	80,958
1861-62 ...	174,277	68,522	139	68,383	34,357	7372	2688	13,012	84,083
1862-63 ...	177,643	69,691	33	69,658	31,222	6313	2673	13,136	85,467

1852-53.

The remaining twenty-one Athni villages were measured during 1849-50 and 1851-52, and classed in 1851-52.[2] The new rates were introduced in 1852-53 and sanctioned in 1857. These twenty-one villages formed the western part of the mámlatdár's division of Athni. They contained 66,592 acres, of which 42,322 were arable, with a population of 12,921 or 127 to the square mile. The villages of Athni and Tásgaon were much mixed. Athni was at first chiefly composed of part of the lapsed Nipáni estate to which, as they lapsed, other neighbouring villages were added, forming a very straggling and inconvenient sub-division. In 1848, on the lapse of the Tásgaon estate, the villages near Tásgaon and Athni were formed into a separate mámlatdár's charge, in which were included eight neighbouring villages of the Soni estate which lapsed in 1845. Except a block of twelve villages in the west the villages were scattered singly or in twos and threes throughout the estates of the Sángli, Miraj, and Shedbál Patvardhans. They were bounded on the east north and west by Sátára and its subordinate estates, and on the south-west, south, and south-east by the lands of Kolhápur and Jamkhandi. All the villages lay on the north or left bank of the Krishna. Almost all were to the east of a range of hills which ran nearly north and south some eight miles east of Tásgaon. The bulk of the country to the east of the hills was barren. The patches of superior soil were but a small proportion of the whole area and the rest was poor. The level plain of the Krishna was of deep alluvial soil which was continually renewed by the silt left by the yearly floods. The rainfall was scanty and

[1] Major Anderson, Surv. Supt. 53 of 6th February 1864, Bom. Gov. Sel. LXXXI. 122. Out of the quit-rents for 1858-59 and 1860-61, £66 16s. (Rs. 668) and £1 4s. (Rs. 12) were left outstanding.

[2] Captain Anderson, Surv. Supt. 318 of 8th Dec. 1855, Bom. Gov. Sel. XCIV. 3-20.

Chapter VIII.
Land Administration.
Survey.
Athni,
1852-53.

uncertain. The people were generally poor, and gave little care or labour to their fields. Manure was not used in dry-crop land. In most of the land *kharif* or early crops were grown. Grain was the chief produce. Cotton was grown in nearly every village but in no great quantity. Some parts of the alluvial Krishna lands were given to tobacco. Except a little cotton and blanket weaving there were no manufactures. Athni was the only market of any consequence. The import and export trade centred in the markets of Athni, Sángli, Tásgaon, and Miraj. Of the twenty-one villages ten had belonged to the Nipáni estate which lapsed in 1839-40, and the rest were acquired after 1839-40, either by lapse or by transfer. During the eight years ending 1851-52, in sixteen villages the tillage area varied from 20,660 to 24,218 and averaged 22,599 acres; remissions varied from £52 (Rs. 520) in 1847-48 to nothing in 1851-52 and averaged £19 (Rs. 190); and the amount for collection varied from £1396 (Rs. 13,960) in 1844-45 to £1634 (Rs. 16,340) in 1848-49 and averaged £1532 (Rs. 15,320). The details are:

Athni, 16 Villages : Land Revenue, 1844-1852.

Year.	Tillage.		Remissions.	For Collection.	Year.	Tillage.		Remissions.	For Collection.
	Area.	Rental.				Area.	Rental.		
	Acres.	Rs.	Rs.	Rs.		Acres.	Rs.	Rs.	Rs.
1844-45 ...	20,660	14,282	325	13,957	1849-50 ...	23,585	15,919	300	15,619
1845-46 ...	20,756	14,782	299	14,483	1850-51 ..	21,900	14,994	...	14,994
1846-47 ...	23,428	16,164	58	16,106	1851-52 ...	22,301	15,202	...	15,202
1847-48 ...	23,942	16,373	518	15,855					
1848-49 ...	24,218	16,354	16	16,338	Average...	22,599	15,509	190	15,319

For the survey settlement the villages were divided into six classes. In the first class, with a highest dry-crop acre rate of 4*s.* (Rs. 2), were two villages on the Krishna, having every advantage of climate and well placed as regards markets; in the second class, with a highest dry-crop acre rate of 3*s.* 6*d.* (Rs. 1¾), were three villages near but inland from the first class and with a poorer climate; in the third, fourth, and fifth classes, with highest dry-crop acre rates of 3*s.*, 2*s.* 6*d.*, and 2*s.* (Rs. 1½, Rs. 1¼, and Re. 1), were three villages between those of the first and sixth classes, the rate decreasing as the village was further east. In the sixth class, with a highest dry-crop acre rate of 1*s.* 9*d.* (14 *as.*), were thirteen villages similarly placed to the twenty-three Athni villages which had been settled in the previous year and assessed at the same rate. Garden tillage was found in nearly all the villages and chiefly in Chinchni, Nágaj, Dhauli, and Jambgi. The Government garden area of 893 acres was watered from wells by the leather bag or by water-courses led from some stream whose water was pounded by a temporary dam. The garden acre rate varied from 8*s.* 3*d.* (Rs. 4⅛) to 1*s.* (8 *as.*) and averaged 4*s.* 5½*d.* (Rs. 2 *as.* 3$\frac{8}{12}$). The crops included little sugarcane or other superior produce; they were chiefly wheat, turmeric, and vegetables. The effect of the new rates was a fall in the rental from £2006 (Rs. 20,060) to £1902 (Rs. 19,020) or five per cent. The details are:

Athni Survey Settlement, 1852-53.

Class.	Villages.	Former. Tillage Rental.	Survey. Tillage. Area.	Tillage. Rental.	Tillage. Acre Rate.	Waste. Area.	Waste. Rental.	Total. Area.	Total. Rental.
		Rs.	Acres.	Rs.	Rs. a. p.	Acres.	Rs.	Acres.	Rs.
I	2	7337	2868	4690	1 10 2	90	101	2958	4791
II	3	7574	9179	6411	0 11 2	1657	977	10,836	7388
III	1	462	832	378	0 7 3	72	12	904	390
IV	1	812	1034	542	0 8 5	1331	580	2365	1122
V	1	463	1589	464	0 4 8	154	33	1743	497
VI	13	3413	16,965	6537	0 6 2	7660	2268	24,625	8805
Total ...	21	20,061	32,467	19,022	0 8 10	10,964	3971	43,431	22,993

Chapter VIII.

Land Administration.

Survey.

Athni, 1852-53.

During the thirteen years ending 1864-65 the result of the new rates was a rise in the tillage area from 32,467 to 42,749 acres or thirty-two per cent; and in collections from £1711 (Rs. 17,110) to £2606 (Rs. 26,060) or fifty-two per cent. For the same period remissions fell from £410 to £9 (Rs. 4100-90) or ninety-eight per cent. The details[1] are:

Athni, 21 Villages: Survey Results, 1852-1865.

Year.	Tillage. Area.	Tillage. Rental.	Remissions.	For Collection.	Waste. Area.	Waste. Rental.	Waste. Grazing Fees.	Quit-Rents.	Collections.
	Acres.	Rs.	Rs.	Rs.	Acres.	Rs.	Rs.	Rs.	Rs.
1852-53 ...	32,467	19,022	4097	14,925	10,964	3971	1084	1098	17,107
1853-54 ...	31,047	19,262	80	19,182	11,275	3834	...	1067	20,249
1854-55 ...	32,923	20,018	80	19,933	9647	2728	...	1165	21,098
1855-56 ...	34,044	20,373	349	20,024	8686	2483	556	1093	21,673
1856-57 ...	34,901	20,645	328	20,317	7890	2276	539	1531	22,387
1857-58 ...	35,518	20,842	80	20,762	7273	2079	438	1612	22,812
1858-59 ...	37,326	21,561	80	21,481	6105	1716	407	2060	23,087
1859-60 ...	38,530	21,931	80	21,851	5487	1409	350	2232	24,433
1860-61 ...	40,571	22,330	80	22,250	2885	651	825	2687	25,762
1861-62 ...	42,804	22,843	80	22,763	874	239	900	2720	26,383
1862-63 ...	42,895	22,855	80	22,775	782	227	137	2707	25,619
1863-64 ...	43,162	22,937	80	22,857	533	147	262	2708	25,827
1864-65 ..	42,749	22,686	87	22,599	451	139	653	2807	26,059

Taking together the fifty-three villages settled in 1851-52 and the twenty-one villages settled in 1852-53, during the sixteen years ending 1854-55 the tillage area rose from 174,147 to 177,900 acres or two per cent, remissions fell from £1217 (Rs. 12,170) to £8 (Rs. 80) or ninety-nine per cent, and collections fell from £11,892 (Rs. 1,18,920) to £9568 (Rs. 95,680) or 19·5 per cent. The details[2] are:

[1] Bom. Gov. Sel. XCIV. 16, 126. In 1858-59, £47 (Rs. 470) were left outstanding.
[2] Bom. Gov. Sel. XCIV. 18.

Chapter VIII.

Land Administration.

Survey.

Athni, 1852-53.

Athni Tillage and Revenue, 1839-1855.

Year.	Tillage.		Remissions.	For Collection.	Collections.[1]	Grazing Fees.
	Area.	Rental.				
	Acres.	Rs.	Rs.	Rs.	Rs.	Rs.
1839-40 ...	174,147	1,07,612	12,167	95,445	1,18,922	1184
1840-41 ...	170,580	1,03,150	16,636	86,514	1,09,440	1435
1841-42 ...	167,708	1,00,449	15,951	84,498	1,06,804	1597
1842-43 ...	164,799	96,560	7691	88,869	1,06,776	1790
1843-44 ...	150,253	82,410	13,769	68,641	86,951	2705
1844-45 ...	148,756	79,075	9086	69,989	88,084	2559
1845-46 ..	147,351	79,998	4127	75,871	93,298	2936
1846-47 ...	163,772	90,251	5808	84,443	1,01,768	2471
1847-48 ...	164,228	87,501	8887	78,614	96,558	4014
1848-49 ...	154,259	78,763	4233	74,530	91,683	4578
1849-50 ..	143,946	71,429	2183	69,246	86,691	5252
1850-51 ...	138,212	74,985	...	74,985	93,160	4583
1851-52 ...	147,531	66,991	9554	57,437	73,875	4727
1852-53 ...	157,115	73,441	4097	69,344	85,200	5340
1853-54 ...	168,466	78,002	475	77,527	92,456	4473
1854-55 ...	177,900	81,012	80	80,932	95,680	4336

Sampgaon, 1852-53.

Sampgaon, with 106 Government villages, was measured in 1849-50 and 1850-51, and classed in 1850-51 and 1851-52.[2] The rates were introduced in 1852-53 and the settlement was sanctioned in 1857. It was a small compact tract, divided from west to east by the river Malprabha. Sampgaon was under the charge of a mámlatdár whose office was at the town of Sampgaon, with a mahálkari stationed at Belvadi. Besides 106 entire villages Government had a share in three villages which partly belonged to Government, the remaining share being in the hands of estate holders. Of the 106 Government villages fifty-nine formed the charge of the mámlatdár and forty-seven of the mahálkari. Sampgaon included much variety of soil and appearance. The west was generally more or less hilly, but the country sloped east and gradually merged into the great black or cotton soil plain to which the eastern half of the sub-division belonged. In the south-west many low ranges of quartz and iron-ore hills, about 150 feet high, ran north and south about a quarter or half a mile apart. The Malprabha ran slowly along a deep bed between high steep banks. Its valley which was almost solely of black soil was extremely rich. North of the Malprabha the trap range, which the Dhárwár-Belgaum road crossed near Bágevádi, stretched into the sub-division and then gradually sank into the plain. On the north and north-west, where the sand-stone hills of Gokák were prolonged into Sampgaon, the climate was exceedingly good owing to its westerly position and the nearness of the western hills. Both in the early and later rains, the rainfall was ample and certain. Some villages under the hills had almost too much moisture for the better crops. On the other hand, the eastern villages sometimes suffered from the failure of the early rains. Still, on the whole, no part of the Bombay Karnátak had a better climate than Sampgaon. Throughout the sub-division the fields were exceedingly well tilled, and the use of manure was general. The chief crops were *jvári*, wheat, and *bájri*. Cotton was grown only for local use, though both climate and soil were well

[1] Includes collections from alienated land. Bom. Gov. Sel. XCIV. 18.
[2] Capt. Anderson, Surv. Supt. 318 of 8th Dec. 1855, Bom. Gov. Sel. XCIV. 35-58.

suited for its growth. In the west sugarcane and considerable quantities of rice were grown. The people were generally in easy circumstances, though in a few villages the pressure of the old assessment had caused indebtedness. The villages were exceedingly well placed for markets. Within their limits were the large markets of Bailhongal, Sampgaon, Deshnur, Nesargi, Vanur, Belvadi, and Mugutkhán Hubli. Both the smaller markets of Kittur and of Bágevádi were just over the boundary, and the great market of Nandigad lay at no inconvenient distance from the south of the sub-division. The north had easy communication with Belgaum by the Kaládgi road through Nesargi. The made Dhárwár-Belgaum road skirted the west and placed both of these towns within easy reach. With Dhárwár there was little traffic, but Belgaum was a great centre of local trade. The whole, or nearly the whole, of the surplus produce of the villages north of the river found its way to Belgaum, being generally taken to market by the growers. The people had a natural turn for trade, and, when field work was slack, used their farm cattle in carrying produce. The villages north of the Malprabha had about 5000 cotton-weavers. Deshnur and Bailhongal had each about 200 looms, and Sampgaon, Mugutkhán Hubli, Marikatti, and other villages had a smaller number. Each weaver generally worked on his own account. A few had four or five looms worked by hired labour. The products were coarse cotton cloth, turbans, robes, and waistcloths. Some of the articles were sold in the neighbouring markets for local use and the rest were sent by Belgaum to the Konkan. Sampgaon formed part of the Kittur *desái's* estate which lapsed to Government in 1824. Under the *desái's* rule the rates of assessment were notoriously corrupted, the gross revenue of villages being exaggerated or diminished to suit the purpose of the moment. There was always inequality in the old rates. In 1825-26 the sub-division was surveyed, but the old rates were continued except in a few villages. During the twenty-six years ending 1851-52 the tillage area rose from 78,647 to 86,356 acres or 9·8 per cent; and the amount for collection from £12,664 to £14,303 (Rs. 1,26,640 - Rs. 1,43,030) or about thirteen per cent. During the same period remissions fell from £875 (Rs. 8750) to nothing. The details are:

Chapter VIII.

Land Administration.

Survey.

Sampgaon, 1852-53.

Sampgaon, 106 Villages: Land Revenue, 1826-1852.

Year.	Tillage.		Remissions.	For Collection.	Year.	Tillage.		Remissions.	For Collection.
	Area.	Rental.				Area.	Rental.		
	Acres.	Rs.	Rs.	Rs.		Acres.	Rs.	Rs.	Rs.
1826-27 ...	78,647	1,35,395	8754	1,26,641	1840-41 ...	80,237	1,26,979	1921	1,25,058
1827-28 ...	78,253	1,30,926	7959	1,22,967	1841-42 ...	79,573	1,25,567	9401	1,16,166
1828-29 ...	79,389	1,28,840	9260	1,10,580	1842-43 ...	80,166	1,26,858	1151	1,25,507
1829-30 ...	80,685	1,29,998	7430	1,22,568	1843-44 ...	77,845	1,22,376	831	1,21,545
1830-31 ...	79,887	1,29,805	19,202	1,10,603	1844-45 ...	75,666	1,17,188	1605	1,15,581
1831-32 ...	80,305	1,28,958	15,891	1,13,067	1845-46 ...	76,178	1,17,303	887	1,16,416
1832-33 ...	77,555	1,25,760	36,125	89,635	1846-47 ...	81,679	1,29,229	316	1,28,913
1833-34 ...	79,692	1,33,859	30,188	1,03,671	1847-48 ...	84,490	1,35,864	16	1,35,848
1834-35 ...	79,696	1,34,545	11,858	1,22,687	1848-49 ...	87,401	1,40,098	31	1,40,067
1835-36 ...	78,215	1,31,021	12,153	1,18,868	1849-50 ...	82,680	1,36,762	...	1,36,762
1836-37 ...	78,948	1,28,594	18,733	1,09,861	1850-51 ...	82,083	1,35,334	3	1,35,331
1837-38 ...	79,587	1,29,996	8394	1,21,602	1851-52 ...	86,356	1,43,301	...	1,43,031
1838-39 ...	78,012	1,28,379	21,322	1,07,057					
1839-40 ...	80,351	1,27,688	15,740	1,11,948	Average ..	80,137	1,30,006	9136	1,20,808

Chapter VIII.
Land Administration.
Survey.
Sampgaon, 1852-53.

Under the survey settlement the 109 villages were divided into eight classes, with highest dry-crop acre rates ranging from 4*s*. 6*d*. to 3*s*. (Rs. 2¼ - 1½). The settlement officer Captain Anderson enumerates these classes in the following order.[1] The first class, with a highest dry-crop acre rate of 3*s*. 6*d*. (Rs. 1¾), included seven villages in the east of Sampgaon, far from large markets and liable to a somewhat scanty rainfall; the second class, with a highest dry-crop acre rate of 4*s*. (Rs. 2), included thirty-five central villages with a certain rainfall sufficient for dry-crop tillage; the third class, with a highest dry-crop acre rate of 3*s*. 6*d*. (Rs. 1¾), included seven western rice villages well placed for markets but with a rainfall somewhat too heavy for the better dry-crop tillage; the fourth class,[2] with a highest dry-crop acre rate of 4*s*. 6*d*. (Rs. 2¼), included thirty-seven villages in the centre of Sampgaon north of the Malprabha and near large markets, with a certain rainfall sufficient for dry-crop tillage; the fifth class, with a highest dry-crop acre rate of 4*s*. (Rs. 2), included eleven villages to the east of the fourth class with a somewhat less certain rainfall; the sixth class, with a highest dry-crop acre rate of 3*s*. 6*d*. (Rs. 1¾), included seven villages in the north with a less certain rainfall than the fourth and fifth class villages; the seventh class, with a highest dry-crop acre rate of 4*s*. (Rs. 2), included four villages in the west of the fourth class, nearest to Belgaum; and the eighth class, with a highest dry-crop acre rate of 3*s*. (Rs. 1½), was the hill village of Gajminhál[3] in the extreme north, with a somewhat uncertain rainfall and inconvenient markets.

The Government and alienated rice lands, which occurred in fifty-eight villages of the second, third, fourth, and seventh classes, included a total area of 3974 acres. The average acre rate was 7*s*. 2¼*d*. (Rs. 3 *as*. 9½) and the highest 16*s*. (Rs. 8), except in the market town of Mugutkhán Hubli, on the Dhárwár-Belgaum road, where it was 18*s*. (Rs. 9). The *bágáyat* or garden lands, with an area of 1304 acres of which 421 were alienated, were found almost solely in the northern villages where water was near the surface and many streams flowed during the greater part of the year. About three-quarters of the whole of the garden lands were watered by *páts* or small canals led from neighbouring streams. The chief garden crops were sugarcane and vegetables. The 883 acres of Government garden land were assessed at £317 (Rs. 3170) or an average acre rate of 7*s*. 2⅛*d*. (Rs. 3 *as*. 9$\frac{5}{12}$). On well-watered land the acre rate varied from 9*s*. 6*d*. to 4*s*. (Rs. 4¾ - 2) and on channel watered land from 10*s*. to 2*s*. 6*d*. (Rs. 5 - 1¼). The old average acre rate was between 9*s*. and 10*s*. (Rs. 4½ and 5). The new rates caused a fall in the rental from £14,448 to £12,277 (Rs. 1,44,480 - Rs. 1,22,770) or fifteen per cent. The details are:

---

[1] Bom. Gov. Sel. XCIV. 49.
[2] It included the large market town of Bailhongal.
[3] Its inhabitants were Berads or Rámoshis who had the name of gaining a living by thieving. The former low rate of assessment tempted them to occupy more land than they could properly till, part of which was relinquished on the imposition of an increased rate. Bom. Gov. Sel. XCIV. 50.

Chapter VIII.

Land Administration.

Survey.

Sampgaon, 1852-53.

Sampgaon Survey Settlement, 1852-53.

Class.	Villages.	Former.	Survey.						
		Tillage	Tillage.			Waste.		Total.	
		Rental.	Area.	Rental.	Acre Rate.	Area.	Rental.	Area.	Rental.
		Rs.	Acres.	Rs.	Rs. a. p.	Acres.	Rs.	Acres.	Rs.
I	7	7178	5039	6066	1 3 3	773	405	5812	6471
II	35	32,677	24,624	30,935	1 4 1	8257	5297	32,881	36,232
III	7	3967	3872	4496	1 2 7	1194	672	5066	5168
IV	37	71,016	39,945	58,633	1 7 6	4800	4342	44,745	62,975
V	11	18,241	10,451	12,966	1 3 10	414	325	10,865	13,291
VI	7	7129	6903	6021	0 13 11	1674	682	8577	6703
VII	4	3755	2729	3052	1 1 11	263	282	2992	3334
VIII	1	523	1048	604	0 9 3	319	92	1367	696
Total ...	109	1,44,476	94,611	1,22,773	1 4 9	17,694	12,097	112,305	1,34,870

During the thirteen years ending 1864-65 the result of the survey settlement was a rise in tillage from 94,611 to 127,689 acres or thirty-five per cent; and in collections from £13,073 to £19,031 (Rs. 1,30,730 - Rs. 1,90,310) or 45·6 per cent. During the same period remissions fell from £1696 (Rs. 16,960) to nothing. The details[1] are :

Sampgaon, 106 Villages : Survey Results, 1852-1865.

Year.	Tillage.		Remissions.	For Collection.	Waste.			Quit-Rent.	Collections.
	Area.	Rental.			Area.	Rental.	Grazing Fees.		
	Acres.	Rs.	Rs.	Rs.	Acres.	Rs.	Rs.	Rs.	Rs.
1852-53 ...	94,611	1,23,153	16,955	1,06,198	17,694	...	3809	20,723	1,30,730
1853-54 ...	100,740	1,31,424	...	1,31,424	21,078	15,390	...	23,848	1,55,272
1854-55 ...	102,262	1,33,060	...	1,33,060	20,119	14,422	...	24,025	1,57,085
1855-56 ...	105,643	1,36,200	583	1,35,617	18,432	12,402	3043	23,515	1,62,175
1856-57 ...	110,846	1,40,575	764	1,39,811	13,729	8580	2851	23,520	1,66,182
1857-58 ...	114,787	1,43,324	332	1,42,992	10,316	6403	2360	23,757	1,69,109
1858-59 ...	117,498	1,45,106	16	1,45,090	7995	5038	2313	31,339	1,78,741
1859-60 ...	120,864	1,48,287	16	1,48,271	6946	4385	2404	29,745	1,80,420
1860-61 ...	122,331	1,49,977	39	1,49,938	5686	3379	1928	31,648	1,83,514
1861-62 ...	123,012	1,50,944	31	1,50,913	5669	3245	1958	34,091	1,86,962
1862-63 ...	123,994	1,51,893	16	1,51,877	5666	3211	1852	33,467	1,87,196
1863-64 ...	126,491	1,53,935	14	1,53,921	4117	2298	1558	33,034	1,88,513
1864-65 ...	127,689	1,55,031	...	1,55,031	3776	2081	1931	33,352	1,90,314

Páchhápur, 1852-53.

Nine Páchhápur villages were measured and classed in 1851-52 and 1852-53. The rates were introduced in 1852-53, and the settlement was sanctioned in 1857.[2] These villages lay round the town of Belgaum; their names were Belgaum, Khásbág, Hindalgi, Sindoli, Mannur, Kurchi, Kanbargi, Dhámni, and Muchandi. The climate was too wet for the better dry-crops. Sindoli and Muchandi in the east had a somewhat more moderate rainfall than Belgaum, while in Mannur in the west the fall was a little heavier and even less favourable for dry-crops than in Belgaum. The abundant rain and damp fostered luxuriant grass crops in soil which under other circumstances would yield little. The staple tillage was rice, for which both climate and soil were well suited. In the lower rice lands the under soil remained moist throughout the

[1] Bom. Gov. Sel. XCIV. 54, 128.

[2] Capt. Anderson, Surv. Supt. 318 of 8th Dec. 1855, Bom. Gov. Sel. XCIV. 58-69.

Chapter VIII.
Land Administration.
Survey.
Páchhápur, 1852-53.

year and grew considerable quantities of sugarcane. After the rice harvest, almost everywhere, enough moisture stayed in the soil to bring to perfection a second crop of wheat, gram, or more commonly field peas. The land was generally exceedingly well cultivated. The population of Belgaum and the included village of Khásbág amounted to about 30,000 including between 13,000 and 14,000 who lived in the camp. Kanbargi and Dhámni had each about 1500 and Kurchi and Muchandi upwards of 1000. Belgaum had between 400 and 500, and most of the other villages had ten to thirty weavers of coarse cotton cloth. The produce of the looms was for local use. Every Wednesday and Saturday a market was held in Belgaum, and in the Sángli town of Sháhápur close to Belgaum every Saturday. At these large markets the people found an excellent demand for their surplus rice, grass, and vegetables. Each market day about 1500 bullocks laden with salt, cloth, and grain, came from the plain districts to the Belgaum market. Almost all the imports were for local use. The people were on the whole in good circumstances, though many had become involved by holding to heavily assessed land in the hope of better times.

Only in the town of Belgaum with an average acre rate of £1 1*s.* 7½*d.* (Rs. $10\frac{13}{16}$) and the included village of Khásbág with an average acre rate of 18*s.* 4½*d.* (Rs. $9\frac{3}{16}$) was the average of the old assessment excessive. In the other villages the average assessment was by no means excessive though in individual cases it was unduly high. The rice acre rates ranged from $1\frac{1}{8}$*d.* to £4 (1¼ *as.*-Rs. 40); the dry-crop acre rate from 1½*d.* to 10*s.* (1 *a.*-Rs. 5); and the garden acre rates from 2*s.* to £1 6*s.* (Rs. 1-13). Of 3446 acres of Government rice land up to 1840-41 between 3100 and 3200 were regularly held for tillage. During the twenty-five years ending 1851-52 the whole tillage area rose from 7400 to 9020 acres or twenty-two per cent; and the revenue for collection from £2409 to £2535 (Rs. 24,090 - Rs. 25,350) or five per cent. During the same period the remissions fell from £204 (Rs. 2040) in 1827-28 to £4 (Rs. 40) in 1851-52 or ninety-eight per cent. The details are:

Páchhápur Land Revenue, 1827-1852.

Year.	Tillage.		Remissions.	For Collection.	Year.	Tillage.		Remissions.	For Collection.
	Area.	Rental.				Area.	Rental.		
	Acres.	Rs.	Rs.	Rs.		Acres.	Rs.	Rs.	Rs.
1827-28 ...	7400	26,124	2038	24,086	1841-42 ...	8066	28,394	143	28,251
1828-29 ...	7554	27,212	337	26,875	1842-43 ...	8429	26,898	221	26,677
1829-30 ...	7567	27,780	1719	26,061	1843-44 ...	7936	24,566	217	24,349
1830-31 ...	7451	36,161	3801	22,360	1844-45 ...	7831	23,272	243	23,029
1831-32 ...	7530	25,610	1113	24,497	1845-46 ...	7636	22,682	577	22,105
1832-33 ...	7064	26,589	6158	20,431	1846-47 ...	7920	23,939	476	23,463
1833-34 ...	7423	25,782	2306	23,476	1847-48 ...	8024	23,524	174	23,350
1834-35 ...	7439	27,545	1577	25,968	1848-49 ...	8574	24,706	251	24,455
1835-36 ...	7462	24,434	187	24,247	1849-50 ...	9026	26,388	278	26,110
1836-37 ..	7748	25,703	2728	22,975	1850-51 ...	8888	25,690	16	25,674
1837-38 ...	7946	27,958	328	27,630	1851-52 ...	9020	25,387	35	25,352
1838-39 ...	7975	28,269	6841	21,428					
1839-40 ...	8030	28,179	604	27,575					
1840-41 ...	8054	28,171	903	27,268	Average...	7920	26,039	1331	24,708

Under the survey settlement the nine villages were placed in two classes, the first containing Belgaum and the included village of

Survey.
Páchhápur, 1852-53.

Khásbág, for which a highest rice acre rate of £1 4*s.* (Rs. 12) and a highest dry-crop acre rate of 3*s.* 3*d.* (Rs. $1\frac{5}{8}$) were fixed because they had the advantage of nearness to a large market and of unlimited manure. These highest rates gave an average acre rate of 10*s.* $6\frac{1}{8}$*d.* (Rs. 5 *as.* $4\frac{1}{12}$) against the old average of 14*s.* $\frac{3}{4}$*d.* (Rs. 7 *ps.*6). For the remaining seven villages a highest rice acre rate of 18*s.* (Rs. 9) and a highest dry-crop acre rate of 2*s.* 9*d.* (Rs. $1\frac{3}{8}$) were fixed except in Mannur which had a highest dry-crop acre rate of 2*s.* 3*d.* (Rs. $1\frac{1}{8}$) as it lay further to the west and was less suited for dry-crop tillage. The garden or *bágáyat* lands were of no importance; of a total of 116 acres only fifty-six were unalienated. Except one acre watered by a channel, the whole was watered from wells by the water-bag. The acre rate fixed on this land varied from 11*s.* to 4*s.* 6*d.* (Rs. $5\frac{1}{2}$ - Rs. $2\frac{1}{4}$) and averaged 7*s.* $11\frac{1}{8}$*d.* (Rs. 3 *as.* $15\frac{5}{12}$). Vegetables were the chief produce, little was given to sugarcane or other superior crops. The new rates caused a fall in the rental from £2589 to £2078 (Rs. 25,890 - Rs. 20,780) or about twenty per cent. The details are :

Páchhápur Survey Settlement, 1852-53.

Class.	Villages.	Former Tillage Rental.	Survey. Tillage. Area.	Survey. Tillage. Rental.	Survey. Tillage. Acre Rate.	Survey. Waste. Area.	Survey. Waste. Rental.	Survey. Total. Area.	Survey. Total. Rental.
		Rs.	Acres.	Rs.	Rs. a. p.	Acres.	Rs.	Acres.	Rs.
I ...	2	13,425	2802	8895	3 2 10	2417	2956	5219	11,851
II ...	7	12,462	6576	11,886	1 12 11	1436	1175	8012	13,061
Total...	9	25,887	9378	20,781	2 3 6	3853	4131	13,231	24,912

The result of the survey settlement, during the thirteen years ending 1864-65, was a rise in the tillage area from 9378 to 12,518 acres or thirty-three per cent; and in collections from £3245 to £4278 (Rs. 32,450 - Rs. 42,780) or about thirty-two per cent. During the same period remissions fell from £248 (Rs. 2480) to £10 (Rs. 100) or ninety-six per cent. The details[1] are :

Páchhápur Survey Results, 1852-1865.

Year.	Tillage. Area.	Tillage. Rental.	Remissions.	For Collection.	Waste. Area.	Waste. Rental.	Waste. Grazing Fees.	Quit-Rent.	Collections.
	Acres.	Rs.	Rs.	Rs.	Acres.	Rs.	Rs.	Rs.	Rs.
1852-53 ...	9378	20,781	2481	18,300	3853	..	3690	10,464	32,454
1853-54 ...	10,027	23,275	104	23,171	3358	2124	...	10,050	33,221
1854-55 ...	9869	23,065	...	23,065	3343	2067	..	9660	32,725
1855-56 ...	10,282	23,275	249	23,026	2882	1881	3111	9839	35,976
1856-57 ...	10,832	24,056	206	23,850	2512	1690	2614	9759	36,223
1857-58 ...	10,831	23,776	146	23,630	2586	1669	2331	9720	35,681
1858-59 ...	11,023	23,943	146	23,797	2363	1560	5344	9899	39,040
1859-60 ...	11,227	24,157	146	24,011	2193	1431	5581	9856	39,448
1860-61 ...	11,429	24,156	146	24,010	1972	1349	6809	10,747	41,566
1861-62 ...	11,610	24,330	130	24,200	1817	1285	4302	11,501	40,008
1862-63 ...	11,686	24,404	130	24,274	1755	1246	6214	11,564	42,052
1863-64 ...	11,918	24,566	108	24,458	1563	1168	3441	11,596	39,495
1864-65 ...	12,518	25,532	104	25,428	1645	1201	5362	11,988	42,778

[1] Bom. Gov. Sel. XCIV. 65,129.

Chapter VIII.

Land Administration.

Survey.

Chikodi, 1853-54.

Chikodi, with 141 Government villages, was measured between 1849-50 and 1852-53 and classed during 1852 and 1853.[1] The revised rates were introduced in 1853-54 and the settlement was sanctioned in January 1858 for the usual period of thirty years. Chikodi adjoined no Belgaum sub-divisions except Gokák and the Ankalgi petty division of Páchhápur. On the north-east, north, and west Chikodi was bounded by estate or Kolhápur territory. A small group of Kolhápur villages lay in Chikodi and the Chikodi village of Bekeri was isolated in Kolhápur. Chikodi included 208 villages of which 141 were Government and sixty-seven were alienated. The Government villages covered 534 square miles with 117,768 people or 221 to the square mile. Of the 208 villages sixty-two Government and thirty-nine alienated formed the Chikodi mámlatdár's charge and seventy-nine Government and twenty-eight alienated villages were under the Hukeri mahálkari. Chikodi had two well marked natural divisions, the valley of the Ghatprabha and its feeder the Harankáshi in the south and the valley of the Krishna with its feeder the Dudhganga in the north. The two drainage areas were separated by a steep-sided trap tableland 300 to 400 feet above the two valleys. Except near the Harankáshi where was much black soil, the southern lands were impoverished by the ruins of sandstone rocks, and, to yield good crops, required constant manuring. The central tableland was the poor shallow trap upland which is known as *mál*. Especially close to the Krishna the north had much rich black soil. The position of the villages, in a tract from twenty-five miles from the Sahyádris in the west to about sixty miles in the east, caused much variety of climate in the different villages. Along the eastern frontier the south-west rains were uncertain and often scanty; in the centre and west as a rule they were certain and sufficient, and some of the western villages were too wet for the better dry-crop tillage. In the central tableland villages the rain was somewhat scantier and less certain than in neighbouring low land villages.

About nine-tenths of the population were agricultural. Most of the manufacturing population were cloth-weavers of whom there were 2034, over 500 in Yamkanmardi, about 250 in Chikodi, and the rest scattered in small numbers. Besides cloth-weavers about 800 earned a living by lacquering, by dyeing, and by weaving coarse blankets or *kámlis*. The products of the handlooms were waistcloths, turbans, and other ordinary articles of local use. Especially in the west Chikodi was well off for markets. In many small towns within and near the sub-division weekly markets were held. The chief of them were Yamkanmardi, Daddi, Sadalgi, and Ghodgiri. Nipáni and Sankeshvar, two alienated towns, and Chikodi were places of considerable trade, convenient stations between the interior and the coast, with which a made road from Nipáni over the Phonda pass gave easy communication. The centre and west of the sub-division were specially well off for roads. The Belgaum-Tásgaon road, which was then being carried on to Sátára, passed through it from

[1] Capt. Anderson, Surv. Supt, 180 of 12th May 1857, Bom. Gov. Sel. CXVIII, 1-16.

north to south by Daddi and Chikodi. This road again branched off at Gotur by Sankeshvar to Nipáni and Kolhápur. Another road joined Chikodi with Nipáni, another Hukeri with Chikodi, and another Gokák with Hukeri. Except in the wet west and south-west where *náchni vari* and other inferior grains were commoner, the chief grain crop was Indian millet or *jvári*. Wheat was sparingly grown in the east and in the Krishna valley villages. The use of manure was general. The husbandry was good, the fields were well tilled, and the landholders were well-to-do. As a border tract Chikodi suffered grievously during the eighteenth century troubles. In 1827 it passed from the Kolhápur chief to the British. In nine villages, at the time of the survey, traces of the old crop rate system remained. This survived in the case of 1344 acres of garden which had to pay a special and very heavy cess when sugar-cane was grown. During the twenty years ending 1852-53 tillage rose from 75,715 to 83,057 acres or 9·7 per cent; and during the twenty-six years ending 1852-53 the revenue for collection rose from £10,773 to £11,201 (Rs. 1,07,730 - Rs. 1,12,010) or four per cent. During the same period remissions fell from £568 (Rs. 5680) in 1827-28 to £148 (Rs. 1480) in 1852-53 or seventy-four per cent. The details are:

Chapter VIII.

Land Administration.

Survey.

Chikodi, 1853-54.

Chikodi, 136 Villages: Land Revenue, 1827-1853.

Year.	Tillage.		Remissions.	For Collection.	Year.	Tillage.		Remissions.	For Collection.
	Area.	Rental.				Area.	Rental.		
	Acres.	Rs.	Rs.	Rs.		Acres.	Rs.	Rs.	Rs.
1827-28 ...	...	1,13,406	5679	1,07,727	1842-43 ...	76,816	1,06,364	894	1,05,470
1828-29 ...	...	1,16,966	19,213	97,753	1843-44 ...	75,625	1,02,754	445	1,02,309
1829-30 ...	...	1,15,706	23,870	91,836	1844-45 ...	74,060	99,016	183	98,833
1830-31 ...	...	1,16,945	34,968	81,977	1845-46 ...	75,049	1,00,403	192	1,00,211
1831-32 ...	...	1,17,012	24,403	92,609	1846-47 ...	77,978	1,06,920	15	1,05,905
1832-33 ...	...	1,18,868	46,662	72,206	1847-48 ...	79,477	1,09,533	...	1,09,533
1833-34 ...	75,715	1,11,409	27,922	83,487	1848-49 ...	81,057	1,11,725	...	1,11,725
1834-35 ...	75,306	1,10,487	10,292	1,00,195	1849-50 ...	82,193	1,12,095	...	1,12,095
1835-36 ...	75,188	1,09,987	16,268	93,729	1850-51 ...	80,979	1,10,553	1219	1,09,334
1836-37 ...	74,862	1,08,846	45,492	63,354	1851-52 ...	82,482	1,13,114	1212	1,11,902
1837-38 ...	76,372	1,09,846	10,919	98,927	1852-53 ...	83,057	1,13,492	1481	1,12,011
1838-39 ...	75,568	1,05,648	44,847	60,801					
1839-40 ...	77,445	1,07,812	10,292	97,520					
1840-41 ...	77,064	1,08,351	3093	1,05,258	Average...	77,726	1,10,134	12,810	97,324
1841-42 ...	77,333	1,07,234	3501	1,03,733					

Under the survey settlement the 141 villages were arranged in seven classes; forty-one in the first; forty-four in the second; twenty-seven in the third; ten in the fourth; nine each in the fifth and sixth; and one in the seventh. The forty-one first class villages, with a highest dry-crop acre rate of 4*s.* (Rs. 2), were in the west and north-west of the sub-division and were most favoured both in climate and in markets; the forty-four second class villages, with a highest dry-crop acre rate of 3*s.* 6*d.* (Rs. 1¾), were partly in the extreme west where the rains were somewhat excessive and partly to the east of the first class villages where the rainfall was less certain; the twenty-seven villages of the third class, with a highest dry-crop acre rate of 3*s.* (Rs. 1½), were to the east of the eastern group of the second class, many of them on the poor central tableland and were not so well placed either for climate or for markets; the ten villages of the fourth class, with a highest dry-crop acre rate of 2*s.* 6*d.* (Rs. 1¼),

Chapter VIII.
Land Administration.
Survey.
Chikodi, 1853-54.

lay in the east where the rainfall was somewhat scanty; the nine villages of the fifth class, with a highest dry-crop acre rate of 2*s.* (Re. 1), lay in the extreme east where the rainfall was often scanty; the nine villages of the sixth class, with a highest dry-crop acre rate of 1*s.* 9*d.* (14 *as.*), lay in the south-west where the rainfall was too heavy for good dry-crop tillage; Bekeri the only village in the seventh class had a specially low highest dry-crop acre rate of 1*s.* 6*d.* (12 *as.*) because it lay by itself about eight miles beyond the east border of the sub-division where the rainfall was very uncertain. Of a total area of 2473 acres of rice land found in fifty-one villages, all but 640 were alienated. Nearly the whole of the rice land was in villages of the first second and sixth classes. In villages of the first and second classes a highest acre rate of 16*s.* (Rs. 8) was adopted and in villages of the sixth a highest acre rate of 14*s.* (Rs. 7). Garden or *bágáyat* cultivation covered 5622 acres of which 2685 were Government and 2937 alienated. Water could generally be found at no great depth, and there were also many streams whose waters were used either by lifts or *budkis* or with the help of a channel by throwing fair weather dams across them. At the time of the survey over 2000 acres were under sugarcane. The old garden rates were excessively high. In five villages the acre average was over £1 (Rs. 10) and the whole average was 10*s.* 7⅜*d.* (Rs. 5 *as.* $4\frac{1}{2}$) a rate which the neglected state of many of the gardens shewed to be excessive. Under the survey settlement the highest acre rate was 12*s.* (Rs. 6) and the average acre rate was 7*s.* 6*d.* (Rs. 3¾).

The effect of the new assessment was a fall in the rental from £13,878 to £9962 (Rs. 1,38,780 - Rs. 99,620) or twenty-eight per cent. The details are:

Chikodi Survey Settlement, 1853-54.

Class.	Villages.	Former.	Survey.						
		Tillage.	Tillage.			Waste.		Total.	
		Rental.	Area.	Rental.	Acre Rate.	Area.	Rental.	Area.	Rental.
		Rs.	Acres.	Rs.	Rs. a. p.	Acres.	Rs.	Acres.	Rs.
I ...	41	87,560	41,786	53,113	1 4 4	14,885	5663	56,671	58,776
II ...	44	27,793	24,682	22,043	0 14 3	6908	2695	31,590	24,738
III ...	27	13,044	18,040	12,558	0 11 2	9501	2865	27,541	15,423
IV ...	10	2513	4252	2769	0 10 5	2613	739	6865	3508
V ...	9	5833	16,852	7408	0 7 0	10,896	2282	27,748	9690
VI ...	9	1467	1881	1331	0 11 4	1210	356	3091	1687
VII ...	1	570	863	399	0 7 5	782	213	1645	612
Total ...	141	1,38,780	108,356	99,621	0 14 9	46,795	14,813	155,151	1,14,434

In 140 villages the result of the survey settlement, during the thirteen years ending 1865-66, was a rise in the tillage area from 107,344 to 170,719 acres or fifty-nine per cent; and in collections from £13,014 to £19,538 (Rs. 1,30,140 - Rs. 1,95,380) or fifty per cent. During the same period remissions fell from £1235 (Rs. 12,350) to £4 (Rs. 40) that is a reduction of 99·75 per cent. The details[1] are:

---

1 Bom. Gov. Sel. CXVIII. 84, 85.

Chapter VIII.

Land Administration

Survey.

Chikodi, 1853-54.

Chikodi, 140 Villages: Survey Results, 1853-1866.

Year.	Tillage.		Remissions.	For Collection.	Waste.			Quit Rent.	Collections.
	Area.	Rental.			Area.	Rental.	Grazing Fees.		
	Acres.	Rs.	Rs.	Rs.	Acres.	Rs.	Rs.	Rs.	Rs.
1853-54 ...	107,344	98,549	12,350	86,199	46,770	...	3128	40,808	1,30,135
1854-55 ...	116,514	1,04,847	...	1,04,847	43,320	13,208	...	37,420	1,42,267
1855-56 ...	118,694	1,05,819	585	1,05,234	41,315	12,366	2522	37,981	1,45,737
1856-57 ...	127,060	1,10,188	631	1,09,557	34,784	10,322	2418	37,253	1,49,228
1857-58 ...	131,761	1,11,680	42	1,11,638	31,591	9513	2348	38,471	1,52,457
1858-59 ...	136,417	1,14,512	57	1,14,455	28,791	8604	2407	38,529	1,55,391
1859-60 ...	144,982	1,20,417	36	1,20,381	24,142	7089	3007	38,530	1,61,918
1860-61 ...	150,824	1,23,886	36	1,23,850	21,017	6123	3021	48,211	1,75,082
1861-62 ...	154,791	1,25,752	36	1,25,716	17,902	5230	3082	50,305	1,79,103
1862-63 ...	158,498	1,26,921	36	1,26,885	14,616	4486	3439	51,084	1,81,408
1863-64 ..	166,339	1,29,141	44	1,29,097	6341	2314	2802	51,456	1,83,355
1864-65 ...	169,664	1,30,381	44	1,30,337	4940	1958	3995	58,075	1,92,407
1865-66 ...	170,719	1,31,236	44	1,31,192	4864	1930	3997	60,186	1,95,375

Páchhápur, 1853-54.

The thirty-three and a half Government villages, of which thirty-one and a half were in the Ankalgi petty division of Páchhápur, were measured in 1851 and 1852 and classed in 1853 and 1854.[1] The revised rates were introduced on trial in 1853-54, and sanctioned for thirty years in January 1858. Under the mahálkari were thirty-seven villages, of which five and a half were alienated. The remaining two villages were part of the charge of the Páchhápur mámlatdár. The half village was Banibági whose settlement was made by Government, and half the proceeds handed to the sharer. The Ankalgi group lay immediately to the south-east of Chikodi. The villages were either in the valley of the Márkándeya or on the sandstone hills which shut in the valley. Most of the valley villages had superior soil and raised excellent dry-crops, as the monsoon was almost always abundant. The rainfall was somewhat less certain near Gokák, and in the extreme west the rainfall was too heavy for good dry-crops. The thirty-three Government villages comprised an area of 62,877 acres and had a population of 16870 or 172 to the square mile. The comparatively low average population was due to the large proportion of hill land, more than half of the area being unarable. The people were generally fairly off, especially in the valley villages. All but 387, most of whom were Páchhápur weavers, lived by agriculture. All the villages were well placed for markets. Within the tract were the markets of Páchhápur and Ankalgi, and at no inconvenient distance were the large trade centres of Gokák and Belgaum. There were also several minor markets. Twenty of the thirty-three villages came into the hands of the British Government on the fall of the Peshwa, and the rest since then by lapse at different times. In the early years of English rule the land was surveyed and the measurements formed the basis of the revenue accounts since 1826-27. The old assessment continued in force. It was unequal, but, on the whole, was not excessive. In Ankalgi and Álur, the old average dry-crop acre rate exceeded 6*s*. (Rs. 3). In twenty villages of Páchhápur the tillage accounts for the eight

[1] Captain Anderson, Surv. Supt. 180 of 12th May 1857, Bom. Gov. Sel. CXVIII. 17-24.

Chapter VIII.

Land Administration.

Survey.

Páchhápur, 1853-54.

years ending 1826 were missing. During the twenty-seven years ending 1852-53, the tillage rose from 7097 to 8481 acres or nineteen per cent. The revenue for collection during the thirty-five years ending 1852-53 rose from £637 to £1244 (Rs. 6370 - Rs. 12,440) or ninety-five per cent, and remissions during the same period fell from £113 to £2 (Rs. 1130-20) or ninety-eight per cent. The details are:

Páchhápur, 20 Villages: Land Revenue, 1818-1853.

Year.	Tillage.		Remissions.	For Collection.	Year.	Tillage.		Remissions.	For Collection.
	Area.	Rental.				Area.	Rental.		
	Acres.	Rs.	Rs.	Rs.		Acres.	Rs.	Rs.	Rs.
1818-19 ...	...	7499	1130	6369	1837-38 ...	6221	9487	748	8739
1819-20 ...	...	7185	318	6867	1838-39 ...	6879	9716	784	8932
1820-21 ...	...	7888	381	7507	1839-40 ...	6666	10,002	1464	8538
1821-22 ...	...	8722	271	8451	1840-41 ...	6985	9689	192	9497
1822-23 ...	...	9161	458	8703	1841-42 ...	6992	9804	43	9761
1823-24 ...	...	9333	1324	8009	1842-43 ...	6960	9337	...	9337
1824-25 ...	...	9479	1324	8155	1843-44 ...	6976	9385	6	9379
1825-26 ...	...	9923	1066	8857	1844-45 ...	7019	9354	3	9351
1826-27 ...	7097	11,093	1085	10,008	1845-46 ...	7117	9556	17	9539
1827-28 ...	7061	11,140	701	10,439	1846-47 ...	7053	9647	27	9620
1828-29 ...	7164	11,275	1618	9657	1847-48 ..	7438	10,353	...	10,858
1829-30 ...	7412	11,609	1158	10,451	1848-49 ...	8307	12,054	...	12,054
1830-31 ...	7385	11,500	551	10,949	1849-50 ...	8280	11,800	...	11,800
1831-32 ...	7341	11,379	1830	9549	1850-51 ...	8406	12,000	...	12,000
1832-33 ...	6789	10,260	3733	6527	1851-52 ...	8620	12,669	...	12,669
1833-34 ...	6865	10,333	2338	7995	1852-53 ...	8481	12,465	24	12,441
1834-35 ...	6255	9670	792	8878					
1835-36 ...	5583	8891	915	7976					
1836-37 ...	5870	9212	2379	6833	Average ..	7134	10,082	762	9320

The thirty-three Government villages were divided into four classes, the first containing twenty-one villages, the second eight, and the third and fourth two each. The twenty-one first class villages, with a highest dry-crop acre rate of 4*s.* (Rs. 2), lay in the centre of the district and had a sufficient and certain but not excessive rainfall; the eight second class villages, with a highest dry crop acre rate of 3*s.* 6*d.* (Rs. 1¾), included some villages in the north-east of the petty division on the Gokák frontier where the monsoon was somewhat lighter than in the first class, and other villages in the west of the tract where the rainfall was somewhat excessive; the two third class villages, with a highest dry-crop acre rate of 3*s.* (Rs. 1½) were somewhat badly placed in the eastern hills; the two fourth class villages, with a highest dry-crop acre rate of 2*s.* 6*d.* (Rs. 1¼), lay in the extreme west of the tract where the rainfall was excessive and tillage was almost entirely confined to the poorer grains. Chandan Hosur included in the first class and Ashtagi in the second class were the villages of the mámlatdár's division. Of 304 acres of rice land 140 were alienated. Nearly the whole was in Ashtagi for which a highest acre rate of 18*s.* (Rs. 9) was adopted; in the remaining villages the rate was 16*s.* (Rs. 8). Over the whole rice land the rates gave an average of 7*s.* 9⅛*d.* (Rs. 3 *as.* 14$\frac{1}{12}$). Of 174 acres of garden land all but forty-four were alienated. The new garden rates on the forty-four acres gave an acre average of 6*s.* 10⅞*d.* (Rs. 3 *as.* 7¼). The effect of the new rates was a fall in the rental from £1683 to £1253 (Rs. 16,830 - Rs. 12,530) or 25·5 per cent. The details are:

Páchhápur Survey Settlement, 1853-54.

Class.	Villages.	Former.	Survey.						
		Tillage.	Tillage.			Waste.		Total.	
		Rental.	Area.	Rental.	Acre Rate.	Area.	Rental.	Area.	Rental.
		Rs.	Acres.	Rs.	Rs. a. p.	Acres.	Rs.	Acres.	Rs.
I ...	21	12,700	8377	9139	1 1 5	1246	761	9622	9900
II ...	8	3,647	2436	2712	1 1 10	1089	885	3525	3597
III ...	2	279	748	506	0 10 10	40	13	788	519
IV ...	2	208	522	173	0 5 4	232	71	754	244
Total ...	33	16,834	12,083	12,530	1 0 7	2606	1730	14,689	14,260

In these thirty-three villages the result of the survey settlement, during the thirteen years ending 1865-66, was a rise in the tillage area from 12,083 to 15,294 acres or 26·6 per cent, and in collections from £2181 to £2438 (Rs. 21,810 - Rs. 24,380) or 11·8 per cent. During the same period remissions fell from £179 (Rs. 1790) to nothing. The details[1] are:

Páchhápur, 33 Villages: Survey Results, 1853-1866.

Year.	Tillage.		Remissions.	For Collection.	Waste.			Quit Rent.	Collections.
	Area.	Rental.			Area.	Rental.	Grazing Fees.		
	Acres.	Rs.	Rs.	Rs.	Acres.	Rs.	Rs.	Rs.	Rs.
1853-54... ...	12,083	12,534	1787	10,747	2606	...	545	10,520	21,812
1854-55... ...	12,942	13,344	...	13,344	2155	1376	...	10,342	23,686
1855-56... ...	13,592	13,818	53	13,765	1106	622	273	6926	20,964
1856-57... ...	13,707	13,945	12	13,933	866	486	192	6918	21,073
1857-58... ...	14,312	14,391	3	14,388	711	895	193	6890	21,471
1858-59... ...	14,492	14,606	8	14,598	741	430	185	6867	21,650
1859-60... ...	14,385	14,493	...	14,493	817	464	873	6964	21,830
1860-61 ...	14,424	14,425	...	14,425	800	468	192	8102	22,779
1861-62... ...	14,440	14,509	8	14,501	741	416	184	8465	23,150
1862-63... ...	14,920	15,120	8	15,112	756	423	191	8106	23,409
1863-64... ...	15,176	15,281	8	15,273	516	286	44	8116	23,433
1864-65... ...	15,193	15,300	...	15,300	503	280	61	8514	23,875
1865-66... ...	15,294	15,360	...	15,360	418	236	151	8865	24,376

Bidi, 1853-54.

Forty villages of the Kittur petty division in Bidi were measured in 1850 and 1851, and classed in 1853-54.[2] The new rates were introduced on trial in 1853-54, and were sanctioned in January 1859. The portion of the Bidi sub-division included in the petty division of Kittur was about twelve miles long and five to six miles broad. It was bounded on the north-east by Sampgaon and on the south-east by Dhárwár. The villages were very irregular and stragglingly placed as regarded Kittur the mahálkari's head-quarters. Round Kittur itself the country was generally hilly. In the extreme south-west the villages were close to hills which were covered with low brushwood, and were connected with the great Kánara forest. In these villages the monsoon was much heavier than to the east,

[1] Bom. Gov. Sel. CXVIII. 80,81.
[2] Captain Anderson, Surv. Supt. 180 of 12th May 1857, Bom. Gov. Sel. CXVIII. 24-32.

Chapter VIII. Land Administration. Survey. *Bidi, 1853-54.*

and the dry-crop tillage was inferior. Along the east and in the Malprabha valley the country was more open. It had much superior black soil, and in spite of somewhat excessive rain, good *jvári* and other dry-crops were raised. The abundant rainfall and the waving character of the country were well suited for rice which was grown to a great extent and was the staple of the tract except in the east where dry-crops and rice were grown in about equal quantities. The mahálkari's division had an area of 54,157 acres or eighty-five square miles with a population of 31,108 or 366 to the square mile which the large area under rice made possible.[1] Of the whole population 1827 were weavers. Nearly half of them were in Kittur and the rest were scattered in greater or smaller numbers throughout the other villages. The people were well-to-do. The land-rent was on the whole moderate, and the high road from Dhárwár to Belgaum ran north-west and south-east directly through the villages of the *mahál,* giving ready communication with both those large markets, each of which was about fifteen miles from the nearest point. All the villages formerly formed part of the Kittur *desái's* estate which lapsed to the British in 1824. In Kittur as in Sampgaon, though great inequality prevailed, the general average was by no means excessive; it was kept down by the low assessment on land granted to be reclaimed from forest at low rates, and newly made rice lands which bore only dry-crop rates. In some western villages the whole assessment was fixed on the rice-land and a certain area of dry-land was attached to each rice-field. This plan was adopted in many Bombay Karnátak rice districts, and prevailed largely through the wilder parts of Bidi. During the twenty-seven years ending 1852-53 in the forty Bidi villages tillage rose from 19,627 to 25,012 acres or twenty-seven per cent; and the revenue for collection from £3475 to £3865 (Rs. 34,750-Rs. 38,650) or eleven per cent. During the same period remissions fell from £226 (Rs. 2260) to £3 (Rs. 30) or 98·7 per cent. The details are:

Kittur, 40 Villages: Land Revenue, 1826-1853.

Year.	Tillage.		Remissions.	For Collection.	Year.	Tillage.		Remissions.	For Collection.
	Area.	Rental.				Area.	Rental.		
	Acres.	Rs.	Rs.	Rs.		Acres.	Rs.	Rs.	Rs.
1826-27 ...	19,627	37,006	2258	34,748	1841-42 ...	22,664	37,219	1685	35,534
1827-28 ...	19,829	36,821	1453	35,368	1842-43 ...	22,702	37,300	632	36,668
1828-29 ...	19,876	36,493	567	35,926	1843-44 ...	22,255	37,698	272	37,426
1829-30 ...	19,683	36,053	2120	33,933	1844-45 ...	22,063	36,986	141	36,845
1830-31 ...	19,470	34,479	3784	30,695	1845-46 ...	20,615	32,870	72	32,798
1831-32 ...	19,309	33,863	2650	31,213	1846-47 ...	21,535	33,823	...	33,823
1832-33 ...	19,616	33,677	6991	26,686	1847-48 ...	23,360	37,088	...	37,088
1833-34 ...	19,502	34,416	5252	29,164	1848-49 ...	24,616	39,154	...	39,154
1834-35 ...	19,704	34,213	4350	29,863	1849-50 ...	25,064	39,518	67	39,451
1835-36 ...	19,799	33,559	3665	29,894	1850-51 ...	25,050	38,649	...	38,649
1836-37 ...	19,648	32,361	2787	29,574	1851-52 ...	24,497	38,176	...	38,176
1837-38 ...	20,624	33,103	1065	32,038	1852-53 ...	25,012	38,682	31	38,651
1838-39 ...	21,904	35,710	4375	31,335					
1839-40 ...	21,929	35,662	1588	34,074					
1840-41 ...	22,649	36,880	912	35,968	Average ...	21,578	35,978	1730	34,248

Under the survey settlement the forty villages were brought under three classes, the first of six, the second of twenty-seven, and

[1] Bom. Gov. Sel. CXVIII. 25.

Chapter VIII.
Land Administration.
Survey.
Bidi,
1853-54.

the third of seven villages. The six first class villages, with a highest dry-crop acre rate of 3*s.* 3*d.* (Rs. 1⅝), were Kittur, and five others in the east of Kittur and north of the Malprabha wherethe rains were heavy but not too heavy for dry-crop tillage; the twenty-seven second class villages, with a highest dry-crop acre rate of 2*s.* 9*d.* (Rs. 1⅜), were in the centre, to the west of the first class and with heavier rain less suited for dry-crop tillage; and the seven third class villages, with a highest dry-crop acre rate of 2*s.* 3*d.* (Rs. 1⅛), were in the south-west near the hills where the rain was too heavy for the better kinds of dry-crop grains. Of 13,741 acres of rice land 5263 acres were alienated. For all the villages a highest acre rate of 16*s.* (Rs. 8), the same as in Sampgaon, was fixed, and an average acre rate of 6*s.* 3*d.* (Rs. 3⅛). In eighteen acres of garden or *bágáyat* a highest acre rate of 9*s.* (Rs. 4½) was fixed and an average acre rate of 7*s.* 9*d.* (Rs. 3⅞). The effect of the new rates was a fall in the rental from £3978 to £3773 (Rs. 39,780-Rs. 37,730) or five per cent. The details are:

Kittur Survey Settlement, 1853-54.

Class.	Villages.	Former. Tillage. Rental.	Survey. Tillage. Area.	Tillage. Rental.	Tillage. Acre-rate.	Waste. Area.	Waste. Rental.	Total. Area.	Total. Rental.
		Rs.	Acres.	Rs.	Rs. a. p.	Acres.	Rs.	Acres.	Rs.
I ...	6	8626	5119	8299	1 9 11	1814	1602	6933	9901
II ...	27	20,267	13,436	19,770	1 7 7	4586	2878	18,022	22,648
III ...	7	10,889	7912	9656	1 3 6	2268	1035	10,180	10,691
Total ...	40	39,782	26,467	37,725	1 6 10	8668	5515	35,135	43,240

In the forty villages of Kittur, during the thirteen years ending 1865-66, the result of the survey settlement was a rise in the tillage area from 26,467 to 35,985 acres or thirty-six per cent; and in collections from £3707 to £5518 (Rs. 37,070-Rs. 55,180) or forty-nine per cent. During the same period remissions fell from £689 (Rs. 6890) to nothing. The details are[1]:

Kittur Survey Results, 1853-1866.

Year.	Tillage. Area.	Tillage. Rental.	Remissions.	For Collection.	Waste. Area.	Waste. Rental.	Waste. Grazing Fees.	Quit Rent.	Collections.
	Acres.	Rs.	Rs.	Rs.	Acres.	Rs.	Rs.	Rs.	Rs.
1853-54 ...	26,467	37,725	6892	30,833	8668	...	1960	4277	37,070
1854-55 ...	30,123	40,400	...	40,400	5232	3217	1251	4150	45,801
1855-56 ...	31,701	41,002	196	40,806	3700	2645	1135	4487	46,428
1856-57 ...	32,544	41,573	221	41,352	2923	2224	1043	4455	46,850
1857-58 ...	33,283	42,149	14	42,135	2374	1810	885	4699	47,719
1858-59 ...	33,391	42,580	11	42,569	2331	1775	1139	4759	48,467
1859-60 ...	33,937	43,120	11	43,109	1828	1328	1363	4768	49,240
1860-61 ..	34,388	43,676	11	43,665	1653	1186	1449	7128	52,242
1861-62 ...	35,212	44,941	11	44,930	1594	1072	1632	7141	53,703
1862-63 ...	35,549	45,203	11	45,192	1347	930	1672	7236	54,100
1863-64 ...	35,929	45,538	11	45,527	1094	803	1208	7099	53,834
1864-65 ...	35,953	45,587	8	45,579	1099	803	2063	7139	54,781
1865-66 ...	35,985	45,643	...	45,643	1099	803	2159	7374	55,176

[1] Bom. Gov. Sel. CXVIII. 82-83.

Chapter VIII.
Land Administration.
Survey.
Bidi, Páchhápur, 1854-55.

In 1855 the survey settlement was introduced into 125 villages of Bidi which were in the mámlatdár's charge, and into fifty-four villages of Páchhápur.[1] In this year in Bádámi seven quit-rent alienated villages, portions of detached alienated land in forty-three villages, and an allowance on account of abolished *deshmukhi* rights, were resumed. The revenue from all these amounted to more than £1200 (Rs. 12,000). Many other lands were resumed by the Inám Commission. During this year a good road was made from Bágalkot to Sirur and continued from Sirur to Amingad. Another from Amingad to Hungund and from Hungund to Ilkal opened communication between Belgaum and Bágalkot, and means of ready transit from Belgaum and Kaládgi were now available. A road from Roán to Budangad and a line from Kittur to Nandgad were also constructed during this year. These works cost £1865 (Rs. 18,650) of which £1000 (Rs. 10,000) were contributed by private persons.[2]

Bidi, 1855-56.

The Bidi sub-division, with 123 villages, was measured and classed in 1854-55.[3] The new rates introduced in 1855-56 were sanctioned on the 10th of May 1856. These villages included the whole of the western or Sahyádri portion of the sub-division. Rice was the staple crop as the rains were too heavy for the better dry-crops. The practice of *kumri* or wood-ash tillage prevailed largely in Bidi. To preserve the trees, the practice was stopped in 1854. The order stopping wood-ash tillage was disregarded and could not be enforced without considerable expense. As the profits of wood-ash tillage were very great, in 1856 Government arranged that in each of the forest villages certain lands should be assigned for wood-ash tillage and divided into twenty to thirty acre numbers assessed at 3*d*. (2 *as.*) an acre. It suited the landholders to take a number and till parts of it in rotation, for after two years' cropping all clearings required six to ten years' rest. The villages were small and most of the people were poor, though they were not so badly off as most forest tribes. The northern villages had the advantage of being within ten or fifteen miles of Belgaum. The average collections during the ten years ending 1854-55 in the 123 villages, of which twenty-seven came into the hands of Government in 1854-55, were £1548 (Rs. 15,480). The details are:

Bidi Revenue, 1845-1855.

Year.	Collections.	Year.	Collections.
	Rs.		Rs.
1845-46 ...	14,488	1850-51 ...	13,780
1846-47 ...	14 604	1851-52 ...	13,261
1847-48 ...	15,929	1852-53 ...	15,076
1848-49 ...	16,474	1853-54 ...	16,935
1849-50 ...	14,986	1854-55 ...	19,300

1 Bom. Gov. Rev. Rec. 17 of 1856, 243-245. Captain Anderson, Surv. Supt. 59 of th March 1855, Mr. Bell, Collector, 221 of 10th March 1855, and Gov. Res. 3978 of 27th April 1855, and 1825 of 3rd May 1855, Bom. Gov. Rev. Rec. 175 of 1855, 233-238, 250-255.

2 Mr. Seton Karr, Collector, 565 of 27th May 1856, Bom. Gov. Rev. Rec. 17 of 1856, 239-256.

3 Captain Anderson, Surv. Supt. 50 of 1st March 1856, Bom. Gov. Rev. Rec. 164 of 1856, 141-152.

Chapter VIII.

Land Administration.

Survey.

Bidi, 1855-56.

Under the survey settlement the 123 villages were divided into four classes with different rates of assessment. The first class included the villages nearest Belgaum with a sufficient rainfall for rice. As they approached the Sahyádris the remaining villages fell in a lower and lower class, the fourth class including those on the skirts of the hills. In the first class were thirteen with a highest dry-crop acre rate of 1*s.* 9*d.* (14 *as.*); in the second thirty-nine with a highest dry-crop acre rate of 1*s.* 6*d.* (12 *as.*); in the third fifty-four with a highest dry-crop acre rate of 1*s.* 3*d.* (10 *as.*); and in the fourth seventeen villages with a highest dry-crop acre rate of 1*s.* (8 *as.*). The survey settlement lowered the rental from £1930 to £1813 (Rs. 19,300 - Rs. 18,130) or six per cent. After the settlement all waste land of fair quality was promptly taken up. The details are:

Bidi Survey Settlement, 1855-56.

Class.	Villages.	Former. Collections 1854-55.	Survey. Tillage. Rental.	Survey. Waste. Rental.	Survey. Total. Rental.	Highest Acre Rate. Dry-crop.	Highest Acre Rate. Rice.
		Rs.	Rs.	Rs.	Rs.	Rs. a.	Rs. a.
I ...	13	4485	5784	2568	8352	0 14	7 0
II ...	39	6078	7199	2826	9625	0 12	6 0
III ...	54	6836	4604	3418	8022	0 10	4 8
IV ...	17	1903	542	1022	1564	0 8	4 0
Total ...	123	19,302	18,129	9384	27,463	...	...

In the 123 villages of Bidi, during the twenty-seven years ending 1881-82, the result of the survey settlement was a rise in the tillage area from 19,009 to 42,842 acres or 125 per cent; and in collections from £2047 to £3052 (Rs. 20,470 - Rs. 30,520) or forty-nine per cent. During the same period remissions fell from £345 (Rs. 3450) to nothing. The details are:

Bidi Survey Results, 1855-1882.

Year.	Tillage. Area.	Tillage. Rental.	Remissions.	For Collection.	Waste. Area.	Waste. Rental.	Waste. Grazing Fees.	Quit-Rent.	Collections.
	Acres.	Rs.	Rs.	Rs.	Acres.	Rs.	Rs.	Rs.	Rs.
1855-56 ...	19,009	17,195	3450	13,745	48,818	...	2555	4174	20,474
1856-57 ...	32,616	19,656	...	19,656	34,809	9233	3588	4426	27,665
1857-58 ...	34,918	20,430	...	20,430	36,159	9461	4649	4380	29,459
1858-59 ...	37,669	21,535	...	21,535	33,598	8578	1411	3672	26,618
1859-60 ...	45,892	22,908	...	22,908	29,831	7460	1275	3683	27,866
1860-61 ...	48,388	23,742	...	23,742	26,974	6761	1163	6613	31,518
1861-62 ...	50,167	24,470	...	24,470	31,553	9018	2072	7478	34,020
1862-63 ...	48,695	24,123	...	24,123	33,052	9680	1768	7626	33,517
1863-64 ...	48,989	24,431	7	24,424	33,084	9288	1578	7604	33,606
1864-65 ...	48,672	24,327	...	24,327	33,357	9415	2085	7598	34,010
1865-66 ...	46,964	23,859	...	23,859	35,298	10,042	1939	7651	33,449
1866-67 ...	45,938	23,620	32	23,588	36,377	10,348	1644	7606	32,838
1867-68 ...	44,740	23,232	133	23,099	38,351	10,870	1897	7590	32,586
1868-69 ...	41,991	22,137	40	22,097	41,178	12,015	1999	7578	31,674
1869-70 ...	41,449	21,832	...	21,832	48,122	14,461	1875	7611	31,318
1870-71 ...	41,842	21,827	...	21,827	48,552	14,688	2276	7598	31,696
1871-72 ...	41,829	22,139	3	22,136	47,770	14,855	1988	7560	31,684
1872-73 ...	42,545	22,268		22,268	47,369	14,242	1795	7582	31,645
1873-74 ...	43,125	22,446	...	22,446	43,909	13,468	1811	7576	31,833

Chapter VIII.
Land Administration.
Survey.
Bidi, 1855-56.

Bidi Survey Results—continued.

Year.	Tillage.		Remissions.	For Collection.	Waste.			Quit Rent.	Collections.
	Area.	Rental.			Area.	Rental.	Grazing Fees.		
	Acres.	Rs.		Rs.	Acres.	Rs.	Rs.	Rs.	Rs.
1874-75 ...	43,601	22,676	...	22,676	43,433	13,233	1672	7576	31,924
1875-76 ...	43,306	22,645	...	22,645	43,728	13,264	1606	7579	31,830
1876-77 ...	43,414	22,736	...	22,736	43,620	13,173	1403	7579	31,718
1877-78 ...	43,138	22,745	...	22,745	43,253	13,124	1011	7579	31,335
1878-79 ...	42,797	22,667	...	22,667	46,956	13,833	1041	7579	31,287
1879-80 ...	43,059	22,923	...	22,923	47,010	13,577	773	7579	31,275
1880-81 ...	42,983	22,913	...	22,913	35,810	10,513	780	7580	31,273
1881-82 ...	42,842	22,853	...	22,835	35,991	10,564	76	7595	30,523

Páchhápur, 1855-56.

In ten Páchhápur villages new rates were introduced in 1855-56 and sanctioned in May 1856.[1] Of these ten villages, all of which were attached to the fort of Párgad, seven lay above the Sahyádris and three on the slopes or at the foot of the Sahyádris. The survey settlement arranged the ten villages into two classes, a first class of five villages, with a highest dry-crop acre rate of 10½*d.* (7 *as.*) above the Sahyádris, and a second class of five villages, with a highest dry crop acre rate of 10½*d.* (7 *as.*) ; of these five villages of the second class, three were on the slopes or at the foot of the Sahyádris, and two were at a great distance from the Belgaum-Vengurla made road. The rates on rice land, 12*s.* (Rs. 6) in the first and 10*s.* (Rs. 5) in the second class, were a trifle higher than those proposed in Bidi for similar localities, and those on dry land were a little lower. The rice was grown solely for export and the dry crops for home use. The soil and climate of Páchhápur were slightly less favourable to dry crops than those of Bidi. The effect of the new rates was a fall in the rental from £210 to £183 (Rs. 2100 - Rs. 1830) or about thirteen per cent. The details are :

Páchhápur Survey Settlement, 1855-56.

Class.	Villages.	Former.	Survey.				
		Collections 1854-55.	Tillage Rental.	Waste Rental.	Total Rental.	Highest Acre Rate.	
						Rice.	Dry-Crop.
		Rs.	Rs.	Rs.	Rs.	Rs.	Rs. a.
I. ...	5	1158	1035	412	1447	6	0 7
II. ...	5	939	798	223	1021	5	0 7
Total...	10	2097	1833	635	2468	...	...

Kágvád, 1860-61.

In 1860-61 survey rates were introduced for twenty years into forty-nine Kágvád villages.[2] The Belgaum share of the Kágvád estate or *jágir* included two parts; twenty-seven plain villages beginning near Kágvád about ten miles south-east of Miraj and stretching south-east across the Krishna to below Yádvád the mahálkari's division of Gokák; and the Keni *karyát*, a compact

---

[1] Capt. Anderson, Surv. Supt. 50 of 1st March 1856, Bom. Gov. Rev. Rec. 164 of 1856, 152-154.

[2] Capt. Anderson, Surv. Supt. 114 of 23rd February 1861, Bom. Gov. Rev. Rec. 91 A. of 1861, 243-251.

group of twenty-two villages, whose centre was about fourteen miles north-west of Belgaum. The plain villages were scattered singly or in small groups of three or four, the two extreme villages being about sixty miles apart. The villages included almost every variation of climate from nearly the best to the worst in Belgaum. They were generally mixed with the Government villages of Chikodi, Athni, and Gokák. The chief produce of the plain villages was wheat and *jvári*. The Keni *karyát* division was a rice district and lay immediately to the south-west of the south-western villages of Chikodi. The fall of rain was somewhat too heavy for the better dry-crops, *rági* and *sáva* being the chief dry grains. Rice, sugar-cane, and hemp were the staple products of the division. The Kágvád estate lapsed in 1857-58 on the death of the chief without heirs. The old rates were moderate and were continued till 1860-61. Under the chief, most of the villages were mortgaged to bankers whose clerks took part in the management and besides the land-rent levied extra cesses. The people were not very prosperous. The rates were very unequal, and there was no certainty of tenure, as a higher bidder might at any time oust a holder. During the three years ending 1859-60 the collections rose from £5700 (Rs. 57,000) in 1857-58 to £6127 (Rs. 61,270) in 1859-60 or seven per cent and remissions fell from £370 (Rs. 3700) in 1857-58 to £79 (Rs. 790) in 1859-60 or 78·6 per cent. The details are :

Kágvád Land Revenue, 1857-1860.

Year.	Collections.	*Lávni Tota* or Permanent Reductions.	Remissions.
	Rs.	Rs.	Rs.
1857-58 ...	57,000	4062	3702
1858-59 ...	59,867	4314	905
1859-60 ...	61,266	3832	788

Under the survey settlement the plain villages were arranged in six classes, the first containing two, the second one, the third five, the fourth three, the fifth ten, and the sixth six villages. The highest dry crop acre rate fixed for the first class was 4*s.* (Rs. 2), for the second 3*s.* 6*d.* (Rs. 1¾), for the third 2*s.* 9*d.* (Rs. 1⅜), for the fourth 2*s.* 3*d.* (Rs. 1⅛), for the fifth 2*s.* (Re. 1), and for the sixth 1*s.* 9*d.* (14 *as.*). The Keni *karyát* villages were formed into a separate group with a highest dry-crop acre rate of 1*s.* 9*d.* (14 *as.*). In 1212 acres of Government garden land scattered through the plain villages in the first three classes the highest acre rate fixed was 10*s.* (Rs. 5) and the average 6*s.* (Rs. 3), and in the second three classes the highest was 8*s.* (Rs. 4) and the average 5*s.* (Rs. 2½). There was no garden land in Keni. In the Keni rice land the highest acre rate was 14*s.* (Rs. 7). The survey settlement raised the rental from £6127 to £6677 (Rs. 61,270 - Rs. 66,770) or 8·9 per cent. The details are:

Chapter VIII.

Land Administration.

SURVEY.

Kágvád, 1860-61.

Kágvád Survey Settlement, 1860-61.

CLASS.	Villages.	FORMER. Tillage Rental.	SURVEY. Tillage Rental.	Waste Rental.	Total.	Highest Dry-Crop Acre Rate.
		Rs.	Rs.	Rs.	Rs.	Rs. a. p.
I. ...	2	13,208	11,120	188	11,308	2 0 0
II. ...	1	6365	7556	150	7706	1 12 0
III. ...	5	12,839	12,645	330	12,975	1 6 0
IV. ...	3	3395	3629	130	3759	1 2 0
V. ...	10	8227	12,345	702	13,047	1 0 0
VI. ...	6	6624	7257	35	7292	0 14 0
Keni.						
I. ...	22	10,518	12,221	560	12,781	0 14 0
Total ...	49	61,266	66,773	2095	68,868	...

Revision Survey, 1880-1884.

The original survey was thus completed in 1861. In 1880 the thirty years' leases of the original survey began to fall in. The first group which came for revision was 109 villages of Parasgad in 1880. The details are:

Belgaum Revision Survey, 1880-1884.

GROUP.	Villages.	Year.	Rental. Former.	Revision.	Increase per cent.
			Rs.	Rs.	
Parasgad ...	109	1880-81	1,20,669	1,69,867	40·8
Gokák ...	70	1883-84	68,100	84,332	23·8

Parasgad, 1880.

In 109 Parasgad villages remeasurement was begun in 1877 and classing and dividing the land into survey numbers or fields, according to the revision rules adopted in Dhárwár, were completed in 1879.[1] In 1880, at the close of the thirty years lease, the revision of the original survey settlements was begun in 109 villages of which 108 had been settled in 1849-50 and one Kotur in 1864-65. One of the original 108 villages, Háro-Belvadi, was in Dhárwár; the rest still formed the Parasgad sub-division of Belgaum. The area of this tract amounted to 340,736 acres or 532 square miles, an increase of 0·3 per cent on the original survey. Parasgad lay in the south-east of Belgaum, with the town of Belgaum about twenty miles to the west and the town of Dhárwár about fifteen miles to the south. All along the southern frontier the sub-division marched with Dhárwár, and the south of it was an extension of the great Dhárwár black plain of *regad* or cotton soil. Through the middle of the subdivision a plateau or range of highly quartzose sandstone hills stretched nearly east and west, underlying the trap, which it separated from the primary formations of Dhárwár and Southern India. The soil south of the hills was black and of great depth; in the north and centre the soil was often sandy or a mixture of black and brown. As regards the dry-crop tillage the climate varied in different parts. In the western villages the rainfall was very good and certain; towards the east and north-

[1] Mr. Fletcher, Surv. Supt. 1A. of 20th March 1880; Col. Anderson, Surv. Comr. 300 of 3rd April 1880; Bom. Gov. Rev. Rec. 131A of 1880, 269-387.

east the supply was less certain and less well timed. During the eight years ending 1879-80 the rain returns varied at Saundatti from 15·77 inches in 1876-77 to 36·78 inches in 1877-78 and averaged 26·41 inches.[1] During the thirty years ending 1879-80 local produce prices had risen for Indian millet or *jvári* from 124 pounds the rupee in 1850-51 to 23 pounds in 1879-80 or an increase of 439 per cent; for millet or *bájri* from 124 to 24 pounds or an increase of 417 per cent; and for wheat from 124 to 11 pounds or an increase of 1027 per cent.[2]

Though not on any main stream of traffic, the Parasgad villages were furnished with local and trunk roads though most of them were merely fair weather tracks. After rain even the main Belgaum-Kaládgi road became impassable in places. A comparison of the average returns for the ten years ending 1859 and 1879 showed

---

[1] The details are: Saundatti, 1872, 22·57 inches; 1873, 17·96; 1874, 27·74; 1875, 36·40; 1876, 15·77; 1877, 36·78; 1878, 27·80; 1879, 26·27.

[2] The rupee prices in each year at Saundatti and Murgod were:

Parasgad Produce Rupee Prices, 1850-1880.

Year.	Saundatti.			Year.	Saundatti.		
	Jvári.	*Bájri.*	Wheat.		*Jvári.*	*Bájri.*	Wheat.
	Pounds.	Pounds.	Pounds.		Pounds.	Pounds.	Pounds.
1850-51 ...	124	124	124	1865-66 ...	32	30	28
1851-52 ...	120	116	120	1866-67 ...	40	44	36
1852-53 ...	116	108	116	1867-68 ...	44	48	32
1853-54 ...	116	108	116	1868-69 ...	58	56	40
1854-55 ...	96	100	96	1869-70 ...	56	60	44
1855-56 ...	72	72	64	1870-71 ...	60	60	48
1856-57 ...	106	84	120	1871-72 ...	60	56	52
1857-58 ...	116	88	120	1872-73 ...	72	78	32
1858-59 ...	104	80	112	1873-74 ...	52	32	20
1859-60 ...	80	60	80	1874-75 ...	60	52	56
1860-61 ...	76	56	76	1875-76 ...	42	46	28
1861-62 ...	72	44	68	1876-77 ...	42	45	34
1862-63 ...	76	60	76	1877-78 ...	18	18	11
1863-64 ..	76	60	76	1878-79 ...	24	23	11
1864-65 ...	13	16	16	1879-80 ...	23	24	11
				Average ..	68	61	62

Year.	Murgod.			Year.	Murgod.		
	Jvári.	*Bájri.*	Wheat		*Jvári.*	*Bájri.*	Wheat.
	Pounds.	Pounds.	Pounds.		Pounds.	Pounds.	Pounds.
1850-51 ...	128	132	118	1865-66 ...	32	32	24
1851-52 ...	128	120	114	1866-67 ...	40	48	32
1852-53 ...	124	116	110	1867-68 ...	44	52	28
1853-54 ...	124	118	110	1868-69 ...	64	60	36
1854-55 ...	104	104	90	1869-70 ...	66	64	38
1855-56 ...	80	76	60	1870-71 ...	70	62	42
1856-57 ...	104	88	114	1871-72 ...	72	64	46
1857-58 ...	110	92	112	1872-73 ...	76	84	28
1858-59 ...	112	84	110	1873-74 ...	48	36	18
1859-60 ...	90	62	76	1874-75 ...	64	54	52
1860-61 ...	82	58	72	1875-76 ...	26	50	24
1861-62 ...	84	52	66	1876-77 ...	46	48	30
1862-63 ...	78	62	70	1877-78 ...	14	14	10
1863-64 ...	76	62	72	1878-79 ...	24	24	10
1864-65 ...	12	18	14	1879-80 ...	24	24	13
				Average ...	71	65	58

Chapter VIII.
Land Administration.
Revision Survey.
Parasgad, 1880.

a spread from 122,932 to 162,373 acres in the tillage area and an increase in collections from £9703 to £12,003 (Rs. 97030-Rs. 1,20,030). The following statement gives a summary of the details[1] :

Parasgad Land Revenue, 1849-1879.

Year.	Occupied.	Unoccupied.	Collections.	Remissions.	Outstandings.
	Acres.	Acres.	Rs.	Rs.	Rs.
1849-1859 ...	122,932	30,750	97,030	735	3954
1859-1869 ...	165,737	8104	1,17,157	...	...
1869-1879 ...	162,373	6513	1,20,026	163	2081

During the thirty years ending 1879-80 the population returns showed a fall from 71,860 to 60,969 or fifteen per cent[2]; of farm cattle from 20,846 to 14,149 or thirty-two per cent; of cows, buffaloes and their young from 36,629 to 13,144 or sixty-four per cent; of sheep and goats from 36,406 to 16,780 or fifty-four per cent; and of horses and ponies from 647 to 404 or thirty-eight per cent. Houses showed an increase from 15,580 to 17,109 or ten per cent; carts from 560 to 2123 or 279 per cent; wells and water-lifts from 534 to 709 or thirty-three per cent; and ponds from fifty-eight to sixty-two or seven per cent. The tillage, on the whole, was careful. The crops were chiefly dry-crops. In the southern black soils cotton was abundantly grown every third year with wheat, *jvári*, safflower, and linseed. Of the red and sandy soils

---

1 The details are :

Parasgad, 108 Villages : Tillage and Revenue, 1849-1879.

Year.	Tillage.				Waste.			Quit Rent.	For Collection.	Outstandings.
	Area.	Rental.	Remissions.	For Collection.	Area.	Rental.	Grazing Fees.			
	Acres.	Rs.	Rs.	Rs.	Acres.	Rs.	Rs.	Rs.	Rs.	Rs.
1849-50 ...	89,422	71,339	6173	65,166	45,905	24,514	8417	33,800	1,02,383	10,669
1850-51 ...	94,421	76,059	...	76,059	48,561	24,725	8343	29,812	1,09,214	26,602
1851-52 ...	107,392	86,332	...	86,332	37,504	15,945	2453	29,748	1,18,533	2438
1852-53 ..	125,032	1,00,159	1102	99,057	35,244	14,020	1828	29,581	1,30,466	...
1853-54 ...	123,738	99,689	...	99,689	32,005	12,386	1816	34,284	1,35,789	10
1854-55 ...	130,717	1,05,199	47	1,05,152	26,984	8455	814	34,241	1,40,207	...
1855-56 ...	132,672	1,06,082	26	1,06,056	25,612	7666	806	34,572	1,41,434	...
1856-57 ...	139,278	1,09,592	...	1,09,592	20,729	5486	711	34,579	1,44,882	17
1857-58 ...	142,035	1,11,026	1	1,11,025	18,614	4455	641	34,429	1,46,095	...
1858-59 ...	144,611	1,12,171	...	1,12,171	16,345	8620	529	34,854	1,47,054	...
1859-60 ...	146,654	1,12,994	...	1,12,994	14,516	2913	537	34,858	1,48,384	...
1860-61 ...	149,283	1,14,858	...	1,14,358	13,044	2424	637	38,261	1,53,256	...
1861-62 ...	151,711	1,15,714	...	1,15,714	12,006	2221	757	41,332	1,57,803	...
1862-63 ...	153,469	1,16,428	...	1,16,428	10,949	1997	651	41,333	1,58,412	...
1863-64 ...	159,634	1,17,547	...	1,17,547	4887	880	578	41,660	1,59,786	...
1864-65 ...	160,921	1,18,832	...	1,18,832	4661	883	681	41,680	1,61,193	...
1865-66 ...	161,302	1,18,614	...	1,18,614	4848	861	648	45,019	1,64,281	...
1866-67 ...	161,653	1,18,846	...	1,18,846	4765	861	596	43,658	1,63,100	...
1867-68 ...	161,926	1,19,121	...	1,19,121	4866	878	393	43,475	1,62,969	...
1868-69 ...	160,814	1,19,120	...	1,19,120	6504	1264	449	43,541	1,63,110	...
1869-70 ...	160,793	1,19,328	...	1,19,328	6970	1381	827	43,910	1,64,065	...
1870-71 ...	161,460	1,19,787	...	1,19,787	6777	1310	635	43,627	1,64,039	...
1871-72 ...	161,663	1,19,990	...	1,19,990	6977	1350	550	43,150	1,63,690	...
1872-73 ...	161,918	1,20,070	...	1,20,070	6892	1382	708	43,505	1,64,283	...
1873-74 ...	162,542	1,20,403	...	1,20,403	6430	1238	372	43,477	1,64,252	...
1874-75 ...	162,899	1,20,379	...	1,20,379	6179	1189	540	43,772	1,64,691	...
1875-76 ...	163,046	1,20,465	...	1,20,465	6079	1158	461	44,356	1,65,282	...
1876-77 ...	163,222	1,20,503	1628	1,18,875	6186	1224	458	44,165	1,63,498	15,427
1877-78 ...	163,280	1,20,521	...	1,20,521	6111	1203	288	44,468	1,65,277	...
1878-79 ...	162,902	1,20,446	...	1,20,446	6538	1303	307	43,994	1,64,747	5386

2 The fall was supposed to be due to the famine and to the disease and emigration which accompanied it. Bom. Gov. Rev. Rec. 131A of 1880, 275.

Chapter VIII.

Land Administration.

Revision Survey.

Parasgad, *1880.*

grain, pulse, and oilseeds were the usual produce. As a rule these soils were devoted to early or *kharif* crops and as much manure as possible was given them. During the thirty years ending 1879-80 garden tillage nearly doubled, the perennial streams from the hills being used for irrigation. The chief garden crops were sugarcane, plantains, and vegetables. Plantains were chiefly grown in the finest well gardens of Manoli. Inchal and Markumbi had fine vegetable gardens watered by channels from hill streams. Most Malprabha villages had flourishing gardens watered by lifts from the river. The chief crops were *jvári* both the early or red and the late or white covering forty-two per cent, cotton covering fifteen, wheat nine, *bájri* five, and *tur* three per cent. Murgod was the most important local market and the centre of the local cotton trade. The growers sold their cotton to the dealers who sent it to Vengurla. In amount of weekly sales Manoli and Saundatti ranked next to Murgod and to their markets the produce of the local looms was brought for sale. Small weekly markets held at Assundi, Yakkundi, and Hirekop were of no importance. Of about 600 cotton and woollen looms most were in the towns of Murgod and Manoli, where were also a considerable number of dyers and calico printers. Of the population about 51 per cent were agricultural, 15 per cent part agricultural, and 34 per cent non-agricultural chiefly in Saundatti and Murgod. The people were better off and thriftier than the Deccan landholders. About one-third of the fields were sublet and two-thirds were tilled by the holders themselves.[1] The presence of a large trading population and latterly the pressure of the famine had caused a very great number of sales, leases, and mortgages. Between 1875 and 1878 the ordinary sale price of land ranged from twice to 133 times the yearly assessment. In leases the payment was always in a lump sum in advance; mortgages were uncommon. The mortgagee usually tilled the land instead of receiving interest on his capital, while the Government rent was paid sometimes by himself and sometimes by the owner of the land. In Parasgad the former survey was found to have classed the good soils too low and the poor soils too high. As in Dhárwár a system of partial reclassing was adopted enough to ascertain the former standard. All watered land was reclassed to ascertain changes in area and water supply. Under the revised assessment the villages were arranged in five classes. The first class contained eighteen villages lying along the south-western border, for which a highest dry-crop acre rate of 4*s.* 3*d.* (Rs. 2⅛) was fixed; the second, including the two towns of Saundatti and Murgod, comprised thirty villages in a line along the north-east of the first class and between them and the range of hills, with a highest dry-crop acre rate of 3*s.* 6*d.* (Rs. 1¾); the third class consisted of twenty-nine villages, including the

[1] The proportion of the land sublet, 33⅓ per cent, is large and is accounted for in part by the large proportion of alienated or *inám* land in the group, *inámdárs* as a class finding it more convenient to sublet their land. The non-agricultural population was also numerous in the group, and where such is the case the proportion of land sublet is almost always high. Mr. W. M. Fletcher, Surv. Supt. 1A of 20th March 1880. Bom. Gov. Rev. Rec. 131A of 1880, 277.

Chapter VIII.
Land Administration.
Revision Survey.
Parasgad, 1880.

town of Manoli, immediately to the north-east of the second class, with a highest dry-crop acre rate of 3*s.* (Rs. 1½); the fourth class of seventeen villages, to the north-east of the third class, with a highest dry-crop acre rate of 2*s.* 7½*d.* (Rs. 1$\frac{5}{16}$); and the fifth class of fifteen villages lying together in the northern corner of the sub-division, with a highest dry-crop acre rate of 2*s.* 3*d.* (Rs. 1⅛). The rice land amounted to about fifty-two acres of which twenty three were private and twenty-nine were Government land; the Government rice land was assessed at an average acre rate of 5*s.* 9½*d.* (Rs. 2 *as.* 14⅓). The garden land had increased from 505 acres in the 1849-50 survey to 972 acres at the revision or ninety-two per cent. Of the 972 acres, 559 were Government and had an average acre rate of 5*s.* 5⅞*d.* (Rs. 2 *as.* 11$\frac{11}{12}$). Land under wells which had been in existence at the former settlement was assessed within the highest dry crop acre rate, while land under new wells received no additional rate for irrigation. For wells that received water by soakage from Government reservoirs the usual addition up to double the dry-crop rate was made. The total bag-watered or *motasthal* area had risen from 389 acres to 732 acres and the *pátasthal* or channel-watered from 116 acres to 240. Of the channel-watered area 128 acres were Government and were assessed at a highest acre rate of 16*s.* (Rs. 8) giving an acre average of 11*s.* 4½*d.* (Rs. 5 *as.* 11). The new rates caused a rise in the rental from £12,067 to £16,987 (Rs. 1,20,670-Rs. 1,69,870) or 40·8 per cent The details are:

Parasgad Revision Settlement, 1880.

Class.	Villages.	Survey. Tillage.		Revision Survey. Tillage.		Waste.		Total.		Increase of Assessment per cent.	Highest Dry crop Acre Rates.
		Area.	Rental.	Area.	Rental.	Area.	Rental.	Area.	Rental.		
		Acres.	Rs.	Acres.	Rs.	Acres.	Rs.	Acres.	Rs.		Rs. a.
I. ...	18	33,818	36,585	34,094	55,097	50	74	34,144	55,171	50·6	2 2
II. ...	30	40,939	34,309	41,333	50,438	714	234	42,047	50,672	47·0	1 12
III. ...	29	38,466	26,497	38,986	35,140	1265	365	40,251	35,505	32·6	1 8
IV. ...	17	22,870	14,053	23,072	17,723	1130	310	24,202	18,033	26·1	1 5
V. ...	15	27,271	9226	28,002	11,469	1701	232	29,703	11,701	24·3	1 2
Total...	109	163,364	120,669	165,487	169,867	4860	1215	170,347	1,71,082	40·8	...

Gokák, 1883-84.

The seventy villages of Gokák were measured in 1880-81, and the revised settlement was introduced in 1883-84.[1] The villages formed an irregular compact group whose greatest length was from west to east, and whose breadth was greatest along the eastern border obliquely north-west and south-east. The sub-division was crossed from east to west by the sand-stone which divided the primary rock of the south from the Deccan trap. In the sand-stone tracts the soil was generally middling or poor; in the trap tracts there was the usual mixture of poor shallow soil in the uplands and of deep

---

[1] Bom. Gov. Rev. Comp. 1062 of 1881. Of these seventy villages 47 of the old Gokák sub-division had been settled in 1849-50; ten of the old Yádvád petty division had been settled in 1851-52; one lapsed village had been settled in 1854-55; and twelve of the old Kágvád estate had been settled in 1860-61 for twenty years.

Chapter VIII.
Land Administration.
Revision Survey.
Gokák, 1883-84.

black soil in the lowlands. To the south and west of the sub-division stretched a low rugged range of sand-stone hills thickly covered with low brushwood and cactus. The river Ghatprabha crossed the western border round the northern side of the hills, and found its way south-east for a few miles; it then leaped some 200 feet over the Gokák falls, turned north-east, and passed into the Mudhol state over the eastern border of the sub-division. The third of the sub-division which lay north of the Ghatprabha was chiefly an open tract of trap. South of the river, except in the east, sand-stone prevailed and the country was open and waving except a rugged and broken tract in the west of Gokák. In the extreme east and along the banks of the Ghatprabha and large streams, was much black soil. Elsewhere the land was sandy and poor. The climate varied greatly in different parts, the rainfall which in the west was generally good and certain, further east became more and more scanty. The country about Yádvád was in the belt of doubtful rainfall which was found everywhere in the Deccan at a certain distance from the Sahyádris. In this part of the belt the rainfall was untimely rather than scanty. During the eight years ending 1879-80 the rain returns varied at Gokák from 14·02 inches in 1876-77 to 31·25 inches in 1877-78 and averaged 21·52 inches.[1] During the thirty years ending 1878-79 local produce prices had risen for Indian millet or *jvári*, from 100 pounds in 1849-50 to 22 pounds in 1878-79 or an increase of 354 per cent; for millet or *bájri*, from 96 pounds to 23 pounds or an increase of 317 per cent; and for wheat, from 80 pounds to 10 pounds or 700 per cent.[2]

The sub-division was well supplied with roads. By Sankeshvar it had communication with the port of Vengurla by the Ámboli pass, and by Nipáni and the Phonda pass with the port of Devgad. There was easy communication with the great Belgaum-Poona road; with Belgaum, Kaládgi, and Nargund by minor made roads serviceable except during the heaviest rain. The whole country was now open to trade while at the former settlement the only crossing of the Sahyádris fit for carts was the old Rám pass.

The result of the rise in produce prices and the opening of roads had been in the forty-seven villages of the old Gokák sub-division,

[1] The details are: Gokák town, 1872, 20·73 inches; 1873, 15·77; 1874, 18·84; 1875, 24·74; 1876, 14·02; 1877, 31·25; 1878, 24·54; 1879, 22·26.

[2] The details are:

Gokák Produce Rupee Prices, 1849-1879.

Year.	*Jvári.*	*Bájri.*	Wheat.	Year.	*Jvári.*	*Bájri.*	Wheat.	Year.	*Jvári.*	*Bájri.*	Wheat.
	Lbs.	Lbs.	Lbs.		Lbs.	Lbs.	Lbs.		Lbs.	Lbs.	Lbs.
1849-50 ...	100	96	80	1859-60 ...	64	68	64	1869-70 ...	46	45	24
1850-51 ...	102	105	81	1860-61 ...	57	66	42	1870-71 ...	28	42	14
1851-52 ...	104	112	88	1861-62 ...	59	58	46	1871-72 ...	35	36	14
1852-53 ...	100	108	84	1862-63 ...	39	39	29	1872-73 ...	30	38	20
1853-54 ...	66	56	50	1863-64 ...	18	20	12	1873-74 ...	30	38	20
1854-55 ...	70	56	52	1864-65 ...	30	32	16	1874-75 ...	58	60	24
1855-56 ...	72	60	56	1865-66 ...	20	22	18	1875-76 ...	45	47	31
1856-57 ...	68	56	52	1866-67 ...	26	22	13	1876-77 ...	26	26	19
1857-58 ...	64	76	62	1867-68 ...	57	59	34	1877-78 ...	22	24	10
1858-59 ...	64	72	63	1868-69 ...	67	54	43	1878-79 ...	22	23	10

The average for *jvári* was fifty-three pounds; for *bájri* fifty-four pounds; and for wheat, thirty-nine pounds.

Chapter VIII.
Land Administration.
Revision Survey.
Gokák, 1883-84.

comparing the average of the ten years ending 1859 and the ten years ending 1879, a spread from 65,103 to 86,273 acres in the tillage area and an increase in collections from £3671 to £4610 (Rs. 36,710 - Rs. 46,100). The following statement summarises the details:[1]

Gokák, 47 Villages: Land Revenue, 1849-1880.

Year.	Tillage.	Waste.	Collections.	Remissions.	Outstandings.
	Acres.	Acres.	Rs.*	Rs.	Rs.
1849-1859 ..	65,103	17,683	36,714	479	1966
1859-1869 ...	83,690	2187	45,507	5	...
1869-1879 ...	86,273	1500	46,095	53	1795
1879-80	81,012	7281	44,322	...	...

During the thirty years ending 1879-80, in the fifty-eight villages settled between 1849 and 1854, the returns showed a fall, in population from 46,637 in 1849-50 to 42,462 in 1879-80 or about nine per cent[2]; in farm cattle from 11,524 to 10,143 or twelve per cent; in cows, buffaloes, and their young from 24,951 to 12,644 or forty-nine per cent; in sheep and goats from 24,839 to 14,345 or forty-two per cent; and in horses and ponies from 315 to 247 or 21·6 per cent. Houses showed a rise from 10,092 to 11,989 or 18·8 per cent; carts from 106 to 539 or 408 per cent; wells and water-lifts from 353 to 805 or 128 per cent; and ponds from twenty-three to twenty-four or four per cent.

---

[1] The details are : *Gokák Tillage and Revenue, 1849-1880.*

Year.	Tillage.				Waste.			Quit Rent.	For Collection.	Outstandings.
	Area.	Rental.	Remissions.	For Collection.	Area.	Rental.	Grazing Fees.			
	Acres.	Rs.	Rs.	Rs.	Acres.	Rs.	Rs.	Rs.	Rs.	Rs.
1849-50...	53,103	26,495	4051	22,444	23,122	12,475	1953	12,833	37,230	8273
1850-51...	53,895	29,773	...	29,778	30,524	14,041	1711	7915	39,399	10,332
1851-52...	55,578	31,273	5	31,268	29,045	12,909	1634	7813	40,715	1044
1852-53...	60,668	33,706	620	33,088	23,649	10,060	1448	7773	42,309	...
1853-54...	62,794	35,167	48	35,119	19,214	7666	1216	9133	45,468	13
1854-55...	67,629	38,017	4	38,013	14,697	5123	2070	9204	49,287	...
1855-56...	70,307	38,857	16	38,841	12,285	4454	1766	9130	49,737	...
1856-57...	74,425	40,517	39	40,478	9372	3531	1316	9077	50,871	...
1857-58...	76,128	41,220	7	41,213	7874	2952	1096	9097	51,406	...
1858-59...	77,008	41,393	4	41,389	7049	2827	1309	9080	51,778	...
1859-60...	78,062	41,822	12	41,810	6208	2553	1438	9047	52,295	...
1860-61...	79,982	42,555	4	42,551	4673	2012	1164	10,835	54,050	...
1861-62...	81,260	43,016	4	43,012	3898	1820	1184	10,589	54,785	...
1862-63...	82,554	43,783	10	43,773	3072	1291	1064	10,515	55,352	...
1863-64...	84,550	44,525	4	44,521	1012	472	1129	10,636	56,286	...
1864-65...	85,790	45,049	4	45,045	692	400	1506	11,426	57,977	...
1865-66...	86,102	45,222	4	45,218	445	288	1047	11,515	57,780	...
1866-67...	86,228	45,279	4	45,275	432	276	1869	12,270	59,414	...
1867-68...	86,309	45,409	4	45,405	573	296	1408	11,141	57,954	...
1868-69...	86,045	45,285	4	45,281	864	430	1373	12,092	58,746	...
1869-70...	85,910	45,221	4	45,217	1135	567	1297	11,134	57,648	...
1870-71...	86,614	45,615	4	45,611	944	460	1593	11,209	58,413	...
1871-72...	86,653	45,633	4	45,629	1022	509	1306	11,110	58,045	...
1872-73...	86,373	45,501	4	45,497	1378	671	1842	11,112	58,451	...
1873-74...	86,448	45,466	20	45,446	1377	604	98	11,111	56,655	...
1874-75 ..	86,478	45,453	4	45,449	1365	626	119	11,113	56,681	...
1875-76...	86,494	45,456	...	45,456	1367	632	120	11,111	56,687	...
1876-77...	86,250	45,403	493	44,910	1714	713	153	9536	54,599	15,092
1877-78 ..	86,221	45,398	...	45,398	1807	748	144	11,266	56,808	1661
1878-79...	85,285	45,236	...	45,236	2898	1195	431	11,463	57,130	1194
1879-80...	81,012	43,790	...	43,790	7281	2519	532	11,361	55,683	...

[2] Disease emigration and other causes connected with the 1876-77 famine contributed to this fall, Bom. Gov. Rev. Comp. 1062 of 1881.

The chief crops in the Gokák villages were: Indian millet both red and white covering 38·98 per cent, millet thirteen per cent, and cotton eleven per cent of the area under tillage. The villages were well supplied with roads. Weekly markets were held at Gokák where goods worth £900 (Rs. 9000) were sold, at Yádvád where goods worth £90 (Rs. 900) were sold, at Mamdápur, and at Ankalgi. The weaving of cotton and woollen cloth supported 614 looms 420 of which were in the town of Gokák. Most of the weavers were Lingáyats who also dyed cloth. The costly cotton fabrics of Gokák found a market in Kolhápur, Miraj, Bijápur, and other large towns. Of the population of 51,539 or 112 to the square mile about 48½ per cent were agricultural, 12½ part-agricultural, and 39 non-agricultural. The people were fairly off. Sales of land were rare and the terms varied greatly. Leases and mortgages were much commoner than sales. The garden lands received most attention and labour, and had the benefit both of manure and of change of crop. In the poorer dry-crop soils tillage was often careless. Only in the western villages where rainfall was certain, was much of the unwatered land manured. The chief garden crops were sugarcane, plantains, wheat, and vegetables. Under the former assessment too little difference had been made between the rates in good and in poor soil; the former classification was unduly low in good soils and too high in poor soils. A larger proportion than usual of the Gokák lands were remeasured and reclassed. Considering the improvement in roads and the rise in produce prices Colonel Anderson thought that some addition to the old rates might fairly be made. Under the revision settlement the villages were arranged in six classes. The first class of three villages in the extreme west above the hills, with a favourable climate for dry-crop tillage was assessed at a highest dry-crop acre rate of 4*s.* 3*d.* (Rs. 2⅛); the second class of two villages, Dhupdál and Gokák, both with a worse climate than the first class but with the advantage of a specially good market, were assessed at a highest dry-crop acre rate of 3*s.* 6*d.* (Rs. 1¾); the third class of ten villages, in a belt along the foot of the hills with a climate much like Gokák, was assessed at a highest dry-crop acre rate of 3*s.* (Rs. 1½); the fourth class of twelve villages, in a belt east of the third class and with a worse climate, was assessed at a highest dry-crop acre rate of 2*s.* 7½*d.* (Rs. 1$\frac{5}{16}$); the fifth class of twenty-three villages, still further east and with a still less favourable climate, was assessed at a highest dry crop acre rate of 2*s.* 4½*d.* (Rs. 1$\frac{3}{16}$); and the sixth class of twenty villages, still further in the plain with a risky rainfall, was assessed at a highest dry-crop acre rate of 2*s.* (Re. 1). Of seventy-six acres of rice land forty-seven were Government and twenty-nine private. An average acre rate of 3*s.* 3*d.* (Rs. 1⅝) was proposed. Of 3699 acres of garden lands 2082 were Government and were assessed at an average acre rate of 2*s.* ½*d.* (Re. 1 *ps.* 4). Land under wells which were in existence at the former settlement was assessed within the highest dry-crop acre rate and no addition owing to irrigation was made to the assessment of lands under new

Chapter VIII. Land Administration. Revision Survey. *Gokák, 1883-84.*

wells.[1] All wells whose water supply was enhanced by soaking from Government ponds had the usual additional assessment up to double the dry-crop rate. The total bag-watered area had risen from 2386 to 3680 acres and the channel-watered from two to nineteen acres. Of the channel-watered acres, sixteen were Government with an average acre rate of 6*s.* 11¼*d.* (Rs. 3 *as.* 7½). The effect of the new rates was a rise in the rental from £6810 to £8433 (Rs. 68,100 - Rs. 84,330) or 23·8 per cent. The details are :

Gokák Revision Settlement, 1883-84.

Class.	Villages.	Former. Tillage. Area.	Former. Tillage. Rental.	Survey. Tillage. Area.	Survey. Tillage. Rental.	Survey. Waste. Area.	Survey. Waste. Rental.	Survey. Total. Area.	Survey. Total. Rental.	Increase per cent.	Highest Dry-crop Acre Rate.
		Acres.	Rs.	Acres.	Rs.	Acres.	Rs.	Acres.	Rs.		Rs. a.
I.	3	4444	4564	4510	5959	173	49	4683	6008	30·6	2 2
II.	2	3067	2402	3211	2860	534	287	3745	3147	19·1	1 12
III.	10	16,772	8722	17,865	11,491	1073	310	18,938	11,801	31·7	1 8
IV.	12	18,253	9452	18,887	12,076	1821	643	20,708	12,719	27·8	1 5
V.	23	51,984	23,800	58,004	28,134	5102	1698	58,106	29,832	18·2	1 3
VI.	20	40,436	19,160	41,737	23,812	1551	492	43,288	24,304	24·3	1 0
Total ...	70	134,906	68,100	139,214	84,332	10,254	3479	149,468	87,811	23·8	...

Survey Results, 1849 - 1882.

The following statement[2] shows the chief changes in remissions, revenue for collection, and outstandings, since the introduction of the revenue survey. These details show that the Government demand has risen from £67,512 (Rs. 6,75,120) in 1849-50 to £86,780 (Rs. 8,67,800) in 1881-82, the revenue for collection from £65,518 to £82,190 (Rs. 6,55,180 - Rs. 8,21,900), and the remissions from £1995 to £4590 (Rs. 19,950 - Rs. 45,900). During the same period the outstandings have fallen from £2,152 to £23 (Rs. 21,520 - Rs. 230).

Belgaum Survey Settlement Results, 1849 - 1882.

Year.	Government. Occupied. Rental.	Government. Occupied. Remissions.	Government. Occupied. For Collection.	Government. Waste. Rental.	Government. Waste. Grazing Fees.	Alienated. Rental.	Alienated. Quit Rent.	Total. For Collection.	Outstandings.	Settled Villages.
Before Survey.	Rs.	Rs.	Rs.	Rs.	Rs.	Rs.	Rs.	Rs.	Rs.	Rs.
1844-45 ...	6,37,739	26,908	6,10,831	...	18,864	...	2,30,957	8,60,652	18,722	...
1848-49 ...	7,12,904	13,578	6,99,326	...	29,872	...	2,32,137	9,61,835	4796	...
Survey.										
1849-50 ...	6,75,123	19,945	6,55,178	...	29,664	...	2,25,112	9,09,954	21,524	154
1852-53 ...	6,95,238	32,841	6,62,397	..	25,742	...	2,04,217	8,92,356	4613	339
1855-56 ...	7,11,819	9155	7,02,164	...	23,061	...	1,83,221	9,08,446	2410	863
1858-59 ...	7,56,355	5228	7,50,132	...	20,700	...	1,92,672	9,63,504	2211	865
1863-64 ...	8,11,740	27	8,11,713	27,281	17,644	5,02,642	2,35,098	10,64,665	733	904
1868-69 ...	8,21,584	50	8,21,534	31,037	22,884	4,88,785	2,49,744	10,98,662	...	...
1873-74 ...	8,30,293	20	8,30,273	29,799	18,069	4,80,785	2,51,288	10,99,630	...	...
1874-75 ...	8,30,951	4	8,30,947	29,886	11,246	4,80,318	2,51,521	10,98,714	...	...
1875-76 ...	8,31,390	...	8,31,390	29,536	10,399	4,79,600	2,52,216	10,94,205	...	...
1876-77 ...	8,31,534	3900	8,27,634	29,733	10,645	4,80,098	2,50,166	10,88,445	...	...
1877-78 ...	8,31,462	1545	8,29,917	30,230	8968	4,79,622	2,51,957	10,90,842	86,428	...
1878-79 ...	8,30,310	...	8,30,810	35,341	8729	4,79,253	2,52,206	10,91,245	9859	...
1879-80 ...	8,23,489	202	8,23,287	43,399	8216	4,78,046	2,53,814	10,85,317	9944	...
Revision.									1351	...
1880-81 ...	8,67,940	...	8,67,940	42,867	12,160	5,08,376	2,52,185	11,32,285	790	107
1881-82 ...	8,67,801	45,902	8,21,899	43,851	11,024	5,07,903	2,56,339	10,89,262	232	...

[1] Gov. Res. 1028 of 25th Feb. 1874. [2] Supplied by the Survey Commissioner.

1864-65.

In 1864-65 twenty-two inches of rain fell. The monsoon set in favourably early in June and was heavy in July, partial in August and September, and short in October. The outturn of what had promised to be a specially fine early harvest was below the average. Locusts damaged the crops in Sampgaon and Parasgad. The supply of fodder was abundant. Except a few cases of cholera and bad fever in Bidi, public health was good.[1] The collections were £134,043 (Rs. 13,40,430), £23 (Rs. 230) were remitted, and £2 (Rs. 20) left outstanding. The rupee price of Indian millet or *jvári* was twenty-one pounds.

1865-66.

In 1865-66 twenty inches of rain fell. The season was not favourable and the crops were barely average.[2] Besides from scanty rain the crops in two sub-divisions suffered from locusts. There was some cholera but public health was generally good. Cattle were healthy, the mortality being slight. Collections fell from £134,043 to £127,073 (Rs. 13,40,430 - Rs. 12,70,730), £22 (Rs. 220) were remitted, and £6 (Rs. 60) left outstanding. The rupee price of Indian millet rose from twenty-one to eighteen pounds.

1866-67.

In 1866-67 twenty-seven inches of rain fell. The monsoon began favourably about the middle of June.[3] In the latter part of the month it held off for some time. But during July and the first fortnight of August the fall was general and beneficial. In the second fortnight of August and the first fortnight of September there was little rain, and, in the latter part of September, the fall was heavy in some places and scanty in others. In October the fall was again general and favourable to the early harvest and to the sowing of the late crops. In November no rain fell and the rice suffered but except on plain and gravelly soils, the late crops throve well. Cotton was healthy and promising. The season was about an average one, and public health was generally good. A few cases of cholera and fever occurred especially in Belgaum and Bidi. Collections rose from £127,073 to £128,730 (Rs. 12,70,730 - Rs. 12,87,300), £25 (Rs. 250) were remitted, and £17 (Rs. 170) left outstanding. The rupee price of Indian millet fell from eighteen to forty pounds.

1867-68.

In 1867-68 twenty-six inches of rain fell. After the first falls of rain in June which enabled the husbandmen to sow their early crops, July August and September passed with very little rain.[4] A heavy fall in October saved the early harvest and secured a more than average late harvest. Public health was generally good. The collections rose from £128,730 to £131,372 (Rs. 12,87,300 - Rs. 13,13,720), £53 (Rs. 530) were remitted, and £55 (Rs. 550) left outstanding. The rupee price of Indian millet fell from forty to forty-four pounds.

1868-69.

In 1868-69 twenty-nine inches of rain fell. At the beginning and up to the middle of the monsoon the fall of rain was general and sufficient. The latter rains were short and both the early and the late harvest suffered. Still the season was not unfavourable

---

[1] The Collector, 1508 of 22nd Dec. 1864.
[2] Bom. Gov. Rev. Rec. 75 of 1866, 50.
[3] Bom. Gov. Rev. Rec. 57 of 1867, 7.
[4] Bom. Gov. Rev. Rec. 59 of 1868, 318.

Chapter VIII.
Land Administration.
Season Reports.

and public health on the whole was good.[1] Collections fell from £131,372 to £127,090 (Rs. 13,13,720 - Rs. 12,70,900), £26 (Rs. 260) were remitted, and there were no outstandings. The rupee price of Indian millet remained stationary at forty-four pounds.

1869-70. In 1869-70 twenty-eight inches of rain fell. The monsoon began well.[2] Later on in September, in the first fortnight of October, and in November, the rainfall was scanty and the crops suffered. But a late fall turned a short into an unusually good harvest. Except much fever in Bidi public health was good. Cattle-disease prevailed slightly. The collections rose from £127,090 to £128,348 (Rs. 12,70,900 - Rs. 12,83,480), £22 (Rs. 220) were remitted, and there were no outstandings. The rupee price of Indian millet rose from forty-four to thirty-three pounds.

1870-71. In 1870-71 thirty-three inches of rain fell. The south-west rains began favourably but owing to the unseasonableness of the latter rains the early crops, especially the rice, suffered and the sowing of the late crops was kept back.[3] The early harvest was good and the late harvest was moderate. Cotton suffered from excess of moisture. Public health was good except slight fever in Bidi. The collections fell from £128,348 to £127,494 (Rs. 12,83,480 - Rs. 12,74,940), £27 (Rs. 270) were remitted, and nothing was left outstanding. The rupee price of Indian millet fell from thirty-three to forty-three pounds.

1871-72. In 1871-72 twenty-three inches of rain fell. Except in the east and north where the fall was short the rains began well. Rain was very scanty in July and Indian millet was withering in August when a fall saved it.[4] A general fall late in September secured the early harvest and helped the sowing of the late harvest. The early crops were below the average, but the late harvest was fair. The collections fell from £127,494 to £126,741 (Rs. 12,74,940 - Rs. 12,67,410), £22 (Rs. 220) were remitted, and £7 (Rs. 70) left outstanding. The rupee price of Indian millet rose from forty-three to twenty-six pounds.

1872-73. In 1872-73 twenty-five inches of rain fell. Except in Belgaum the rainfall was not seasonable for rice in Bidi, Sampgaon, and Chikodi. Cold winds in October and heavy rain in December when the crop was lying cut, damaged what would otherwise have been a good early harvest.[5] The December rain helped the late harvest, and cotton and wheat were good. Cholera was widespread but mild. The tillage area rose from 1,106,645 to 1,107,039 acres and the collections from £126,741 to £126,914 (Rs. 12,67,410 - Rs. 12,69,140), £22 (Rs. 220) were remitted, and £8 (Rs. 80) left outstanding. The rupee price of Indian millet fell from twenty-six to thirty-two pounds.

1873-74. In 1873-74 twenty-two inches of rain fell. In Bidi and Sampgaon the early crops suffered slightly from want of rain and in Sampgaon and Chikodi from locusts; in other sub-divisions the

[1] Bom. Gov. Rev. Rec. 65 of 1869, 253.
[2] The Rev. Comr. S. D. 74 of 7th January 1870.
[3] Bom. Gov. Rev. Rec. 95 of 1871, 83-84.
[4] Bom. Gov. Rev. Rec. 81 of 1872, 338.
[5] The Rev. Comr. 6369 of 31st December 1872.

early harvest was not below the average, and the late crops were good except in Gokák and Athni where they were damaged by scanty rain and dry winds.[1] The cotton was middling. Fever prevailed in Bidi and a few cases of dengue fever occurred in Sampgaon. Slight cattle-disease prevailed in Chikodi. The tillage area rose from 1,107,039 to 1,113,083 acres and the collections from £126,914 to £127,056, (Rs. 12,69,140 - Rs. 12,70,560); £87 (Rs. 870) were remitted, and £40 (Rs. 400) left outstanding. The rupee price of Indian millet fell from thirty-two to forty-four pounds.

1874-75.

In 1874-75, forty-one inches of rain fell. The early crops suffered from excessive rain and the late crops except cotton which was bad were fair.[2] Fever and ague prevailed in Sampgaon, Bidi, Gokák, and Athni, and cattle-disease appeared in Sampgaon, Bidi, Chikodi, and Athni. The tillage area rose from 1,113,083 to 1,114,780 acres, collections fell from £127,056 to £125,924 (Rs. 12,70,560 - Rs. 12,59,240), £22 (Rs. 220) were remitted, and £27 (Rs. 270) left outstanding. The rupee price of Indian millet fell from forty-four to forty-five pounds.

1875-76.

In 1875-76 thirty-five inches of rain fell. Except in Athni where scanty rain and two floods in July and September did much harm, the early crops were good.[3] In Sampgaon and Parasgad rats and locusts did some damage. There was a good rainfall in October and except in Athni the late harvest was good. Cholera was fatal in 2553 cases and fever in 9500. The tillage area fell from 1,114,780 to 1,114,584 acres and the collections from £125,924 to £125,770 (Rs. 12,59,240 - Rs. 12,57,700); £22 (Rs. 220) were remitted, and £27 (Rs. 270) left outstanding. The rupee price of Indian millet rose from forty-five to thirty-six pounds.

1876-77.

In 1876-77 twenty-one inches of rain fell. The June and July rainfall was good and the crops promised well.[4] Later on no rain fell, and except on river-banks and in a few watered lands the early crops almost entirely failed in Athni, Gokák, Parasgad, and part of Chikodi. Owing to the want of rain the late crops yielded a very small harvest. As there was no fodder, cattle had to be taken west to the Sahyádris. Cholera proved fatal in 3994 cases. The tillage area fell from 1,114,584 to 1,113,907 acres, and the collections from £125,770 to £114,178 (Rs. 12,57,700 - Rs. 11,41,780), £472 (Rs.4720) were remitted, and £11,823 (Rs. 1,18,230) left outstanding. The rupee price of Indian millet rose from thirty-six to twenty pounds.

1877-78.

In 1877-78 thirty-nine inches of rain fell. A good fall[5] in May and June was followed by a failure of rain in July and part of August. Rain in September saved the early crops and excessive moisture in October damaged them. On the whole the yield of the early harvest was above the average except in Gokák and part of Chikodi. The cold weather harvest was good. Cholera proved

---

[1] The Rev. Comr. S. D. 5026 of 29th December 1873.
[2] The Rev. Comr. S. D. 4718 of 29th December 1874.
[3] The Rev. Comr. S. D. 3876 of 31st December 1875.
[4] The Rev. Comr. S. D. 330 of 10th February 1877.
[5] The Rev. Comr. S. D. 138 of 19th January 1878.

Chapter VIII. Land Administration. Season Reports.

fatal in 7000 cases, and fever and ague were prevalent. The tillage area fell from 1,113,907 to 1,112,035 acres; the collections rose from £114,178 to £122,978 (Rs. 11,41,780 - Rs. 12,29,780); £22 (Rs. 220) were remitted, and £3680 (Rs. 36,800) left outstanding. The rupee price of Indian millet fell from twenty to twenty-four pounds.

1878-79. In 1878-79 forty-one inches of rain fell. Late rains in October damaged the early crops except rice and the late harvest suffered greatly from rats and locusts.[1] Cholera and fever prevailed. The tillage area fell from 1,112,035 to 1,104,981 acres, and the collections from £122,978 to £122,509 (Rs. 12,29,780 - Rs. 12,25,090), £22 (Rs. 220) were remitted, and £2375 (Rs. 23,750) left outstanding. The rupee price of Indian millet fell from twenty-four to twenty-five pounds.

1879-80. In 1879-80 thirty-seven inches of rain fell. The fall was seasonable, the harvest favourable, and public health good.[2] The tillage area fell from 1,104,981 to 1,078,798 acres; the collections rose from £122,509 to £123,172 (Rs. 12,25,090 - Rs. 12,31,720); £42 (Rs. 420) were remitted, and £250 (Rs. 2500) left outstanding. The rupee price of Indian millet fell from twenty-five to thirty-eight pounds.

1880-81. In 1880-81 twenty-eight inches of rain fell, but, except in Athni, the fall was below the average.[3] The early harvest which was suffering was saved by heavy rain in September and October and the late crops were sown favourably and yielded a good harvest. Locusts did some damage to sugarcane but the other crops were gathered before they appeared. Public health was good. The tillage area fell from 1,078,798 to 1,073,919; the collections rose from £123,172 to £128,581 (Rs. 12,31,720 - Rs. 12,85,810); £22 (Rs. 220) were remitted, and £107 (Rs. 1070) left outstanding. The rupee price of Indian millet fell from thirty-eight to fifty-six pounds.

1881-82. In 1881-82 thirty-two inches of rain fell. Except in Khánápur, Chandgad, Hukeri, Gokák, and Athni the fall was below the average, and was unseasonable for the early crops, especially for rice.[4] Over almost the whole district the cold weather harvest was good. Cholera proved fatal in 1402 cases. The tillage area fell from 1,073,919 to 1,072,820 acres and the collections from £128,581 to £124,117 (Rs. 12,85,810 - Rs. 12,41,170), £4841 (Rs. 48,410) were remitted, and £39 (Rs. 390) left outstanding. The rupee price of Indian millet rose from fifty-six to fifty-two pounds.

1882-83. In 1882-83 the rainfall was thirty-seven inches. On the whole the season was not favourable.[5] Locusts appeared in Chandgad and Khánápur at the end of the season but there were then no crops which the insects could damage. The season almost throughout the district was good for sugarcane. Cholera visited the Belgaum Gokák and Athni sub-divisions. Out of 579 attacks, 275 cases proved fatal. Fever was prevalent in the Khánápur sub-division and carried off 1300 people in 116 villages. The tillage area rose from 1,072,820 to 1,076,299 acres and the collections from £124,117

---

[1] Gov. Res. 4617 of 30th Aug. 1879. [2] Gov. Res. 4549 of 31st Aug. 1880.
[3] Gov. Res. 6538 of 2nd November 1881. [4] Gov. Res. 8390 of 30th Nov. 1882.
[5] The Collector, 3167 of 31st July 1883; the Rev. Comr. 2159 of 27th August 1883.

to £126,734 (Rs. 12,41,170 - Rs. 12,67,340); £2457 (Rs. 24,570) left outstanding. The rupee price of Indian millet rose from fifty-two to fifty pounds.

Chapter VIII.

Land Administration.

Revenue Statistics, 1864-1883.

The following statement shows the chief yearly statistics of rainfall, prices, tillage, and land revenue, collections, remissions, and balances during the nineteen years ending 1882-83:

Belgaum Tillage and Land Revenue, 1864-1883.

Year.	Rainfall.	Tillage.	Land Revenue.				Indian Millet Rupee Prices.
			Remitted.	For Collection.	Outstanding.	Collected.	
	In.	Acres.	Rs.	Rs.	Rs.	Rs.	Pounds.
1864-65...	22	...	227	13,40,447	21	13,40,426	21
1865-66...	20	...	218	12,70,783	57	12,70,726	18
1866-67...	27	...	251	12,87,467	165	12,87,302	40
1867-68...	26	...	527	13,14,263	547	13,13,716	44
1868-69...	29	...	264	12,70,903	...	12,70,903	44
1869-70...	28	...	218	12,83,475	...	12,83,475	33
1870-71...	33	...	272	12,74,940	...	12,74,940	43
1871-72...	23	1,106,645	221	12,67,479	72	12,67,407	26
1872-73...	25	1,107,039	218	12,69,222	82	12,69,140	32
1873-74...	22	1,113,063	873	12,70,966	403	12,70,563	44
1874-75...	41	1,114,780	218	12,59,510	267	12,59,243	45
1875-76...	35	1,114,684	218	12,57,969	268	12,57,701	36
1876-77...	21	1,113,907	4720	12,60,012	1,18,234	11,41,778	20
1877-78...	39	1,112,035	218	12,66,578	36,797	12,29,781	24
1878-79...	41	1,104,961	218	12,48,842	23,749	12,25,093	25
1879-80...	37	1,078,798	420	12,34,216	2497	12,31,719	38
1880-81...	28	1,073,919	218	12,86,880	1070	12,85,810	56
1881-82...	32	1,072,820	48,412	12,41,563	392	12,41,171	52
1882-83...	37	1,076,299	24,571	12,68,791	1455	12,67,336	50

Alienated Villages, 1884.

Of the 1133 Belgaum villages, 239 are entirely *inám* or private, of which three will lapse to Government on the death of the present holders.[1] Of the 239 village grants, forty-nine are political and military or *saranjám*; thirteen are *devasthán* or temple; seventy-four are personal; eighty-one are *vatani*, that is to hereditary village officers; three are granted to village servants useful to the community and nineteen to village servants useful to Government. Of the holders seventy are Hindus, twelve Musalmáns, and one is a Native Christian. Of the seventy Hindus, thirty-five are Bráhmans, twenty-three Maráthás, eight Lingáyats, three Kshatris, and one is a Gosávi. Some of these grantees or *inámdárs* live in their villages and some in neighbouring villages; five are minors and are under the guardianship of the district judge of Belgaum. Their estates are managed by a Government administrator and by their own agents. The rest are managed by the *inámdárs* themselves. They are entered in the name of one family, but, as a rule, are not kept in the hands of one family. In a few cases the revenues are divided among the sharers. The nineteen villages granted to village servants useful to Government were granted to the garrison of Bhimgad and Párgad hill-forts. They are entered in the Government accounts under the heading of *gadkaris*; their revenue is collected by the village officers and is kept in deposit till the time comes for paying the allowances. The estates which are held on political tenure and as grants to hereditary village officers or *vatan ináms* cannot be alienated, mortgaged, or sold.

---

[1] The Collector Mr. Jervoise, 1730 of 17th May 1884.

Chapter VIII.
Land Administration.
Alienated Villages, 1884.

Those which have been turned into private property under the summary settlement rules have generally passed from their original owners. There is no notable difference in the character of the tillage in alienated and in Government villages. The people of alienated villages are not generally so well off as in Government villages, as, in addition to the land tax, they have generally to pay a cess to the proprietor when a marriage, thread-girding or other ceremony takes place in their families. They get no remission or advances in times of scarcity and distress, and have no such certain hold of their lands as the holders of Government villages. They therefore do little to improve their fields. Except a few *kadim* or old and *jadid* or new holders of grants the husbandmen are mere tenants-at-will. In the Hire estate and in some private Khánápur and Chikodi villages payment is made in kind. In other cases the land dues are paid in cash as in Government villages. Except in the Sirsangi Deshgat in Parasgad where the survey settlement has been introduced, the rents are fixed at the proprietor's pleasure. The rates are generally higher or equal to, and seldom lower than the rates in the neighbouring Government villages. Village proprietors seldom take steps to improve their lands. In some cases tenants who have dug wells or otherwise improved the land have been allowed to hold at the old rent for four or five years.

In almost every private village lands are set apart for village grazing free of assessment. Tenants have no rights in the forest lands of the village, but they may cut without leave any unreserved trees on their numbers. When *inámdárs* apply to the Collector to recover revenue due from their tenants or underholders, assistance is given to them under the provisions of the land revenue code.

CHAPTER IX.

JUSTICE.

Chapter IX.

Justice.

1818-1882.

THE present district of Belgaum formed a part of the Southern Marátha Doab or between-stream land which was conquered from the Peshwa in 1817-18. The country formally came under British rule after General Munro's proclamation of the 11th February 1818. General Munro introduced civil administration into the newly conquered country, and under the title of Principal Collector and Political Agent exercised the functions of chief judicial, police, and revenue officer over the whole of it. The head-quarters of the district were at Dhárwár. The Southern Marátha Doab was divided into twenty-one sub-divisions, in each of which a mámlatdár aided by three or four group managers or *zilledárs* conducted the revenue, magisterial, and police administration. At the beginning of British rule petty civil claims and disputes were disposed of by the village officers; claims of more importance were entertained by the mámlatdárs and referred for final decision to *pancháyats* or juries. The highest class of cases were filed before the Principal Collector and were referred by him to juries for decision, subject to final trial on appeal before himself. About the year 1820 or 1821 a separate judicial officer called the *adálat peshkár* or court clerk was appointed to each subdivision, but he seems to have been little more than a clerk to the mámlatdár. His office was soon abolished and munsifs were appointed who gradually introduced the judicial system prescribed in the General Regulations. The Principal Collector was aided by a judicial assistant under the title of registrar. In 1830 by Regulation VII of the same year the Southern Marátha Doab was brought under the General Regulations of 1827 for the Bombay Presidency and was named the Dhárwár Zilla. In 1836 Belgaum was formed into a separate district for revenue purposes; but Belgaum remained under the jurisdiction of the District Judge of Dhárwár till 1869 when it was made a separate judicial district.

Civil Courts.

1870-1882.

In 1870 the number of courts was five, the number of suits settled was 3421, and the average duration was two months and twenty days. In 1875 the number of courts was the same as in 1870, the number of suits settled was 4733, and the average duration was three months and three days. In 1880 the number of courts was the same as in 1870, the number of suits settled was 3524, and the average duration was five months. At present (1883) the district is provided with a District Judge and four sub-judges. Of the four sub-judges the first class sub-judge of Belgaum besides special jurisdiction above £500 (Rs. 5000) over the whole district, including Bijápur has ordinary jurisdiction over the Belgaum and Khánápur subdivisions; the second class sub-judge of Chikodi has charge over the Chikodi and Gokák subdivisions; the second class sub-judge of Saundatti has charge over the Parasgad and Sampgaon subdivisions; and the sub-judge of Athni has charge over the Athni sub-division.

Chapter IX.
Justice.

The average distance of the Belgaum court from its furthest six villages is thirty-four miles; of the Chikodi court thirty-six miles; of the Saundatti court twenty-seven miles; and of the Athni court nineteen miles.

Civil Suits.
1870-1882.

During the thirteen years ending 1882 the average number of suits decided was 3851. During the first four years ending 1873, the totals show a gradual rise from 3421 in 1870 to 4723 in 1873. During the next three years the returns show alternate falls and rises. In 1877 the total fell from 3841 in 1876 to 3581 and again rose to 3841 in 1878. During the four years ending 1882 the totals fell continuously from 3841 in 1878 to 3243 in 1882. Of the total number of cases decided, fifty-nine per cent have on an average been given against the defendant in his absence, the lowest being forty-five in 1882 and the highest sixty-eight in 1874. Except in 1874, when there was an unusual rise to sixty-eight or nine per cent above the average, and in 1880 1881 and 1882 when there were unusual falls to fifty-three or six per cent, fifty-one or eight per cent, and forty-five or fourteen per cent below the average, the proportion of cases decided in the defendant's absence showed slight variations from the average, the rise or fall being one to four and at the most five per cent:

Belgaum Ex-parte Decrees, 1870-1882.

Year.	Suits.	Decided Ex-parte.	Percentage.	Year.	Suits.	Decided Ex-parte.	Percentage.
1870 ...	3421	1951	57	1878 ...	3841	2327	60
1871 ...	3740	2167	58	1879 ...	3638	2180	60
1872 ...	4100	2580	63	1880 ...	3524	1883	53
1873 ...	4723	3001	64	1881 ...	3387	1752	51
1874 ...	4295	2928	68	1882 ...	3243	1481	45
1875 ...	4733	2888	61				
1876 ...	3841	2407	63				
1877 ...	3581	2057	57	Total ...	50,067	29,602	59

Of contested cases during the thirteen years ending 1882 an average of 21·99 per cent have been decided for the defendant, the percentage varying from 26·45 in 1875 to 18·68 in 1872, and the number keeping always below 200 during this period, except in 1875 when it was 246. In 204 or 6·29 per cent of the suits decided in 1882 the decree was executed by putting the plaintiff in possession of the immovable property claimed. The number of this class of cases varied from 209 out of 3524 in 1880 to 126 out of 3638 in 1879. In 560 or 17·26 per cent of the 1882 decisions, decrees for money due were executed by the attachment or sale of property. Of these 470 or 14·49 per cent were executed by the sale of immovable property and ninety or 2·77 per cent by the sale of movable property. The number of attachments or sales of immovable property varied from 1835 in 1875 to 470 in 1882, and of movable property from 264 in 1875 to sixty-two in 1881. During the thirteen years ending 1882 the number of decrees executed by the arrest of debtors varied from 244 in 1873 to eight in 1877. During the three years ending 1872 the number varied from 152 in 1871 to 187 in 1872. In 1873 the number suddenly rose from 187 in 1872 to 244 in 1873; but in 1874 it suddenly fell to 120 and continued falling to eight in 1877. During the five years ending 1882 the number continuously rose from eight in 1877 to seventy-one in 1882. The following table shows that during the same thirteen years (1870-1882) the number of civil prisoners varied from 160 in 1878 to eight in 1881:

Chapter IX.

Justice.

Civil Suits.

1870-1882.

Belgaum Civil Prisoners, 1870-1882.

Year.	Prisoners	Days.	Release.				
			Satisfying the Decree.	Creditors' Request.	No subsistence Allowance.	Disclosure of Property.	Time-Expired
1870 ...	38	1237	4	9	20	3	2
1871 ..	29	1708	3	7	13	4	2
1872 ...	36	1552	3	13	18	1	1
1873 ...	75	2538	7	7	40	3	16
1874 ...	68	2266	8	7	22	7	24
1875 ...	87	2730	7	7	33	8	32
1876 ...	95	3129	5	6	13	5	66
1877 ...	123	3646	15	5	6	2	95
1878 ...	160	5502	17	11	13	...	119
1879 ...	23	698	1	9	11	...	2
1880 ...	13	394	...	3	9	...	1
1881 ...	8	390	...	...	7	...	1
1882 ...	20	716	1	7	8	...	4

The following statement shows in tabular form the working of the district civil courts during the thirteen years ending 1882:

Belgaum Civil Courts, 1870-1882.

Year.	Suits Disposed.	Average Value in £.	Uncontested.				
			Decreed Ex-parte.	Dismissed Ex-parte.	Decreed on Confession.	Otherwise Disposed of.	Total.
1870	3421	11·0	1951	19	219	443	2632
1871	3740	14·2	2167	31	203	564	2965
1872	4100	13·3	2580	22	252	518	3372
1873	4723	14·7	3001	27	176	631	3835
1874	4295	13·2	2928	25	187	502	3592
1875	4788	20·4	2888	88	183	694	3808
1876	3841	15·0	2407	83	102	508	3095
1877	3581	24·3	2057	72	151	412	2692
1878	3841	11·4	2327	103	151	550	3131
1879	3638	14·7	2180	126	148	472	2926
1880	3524	20·2	1883	166	167	567	2783
1881	3387	21·2	1752	164	161	535	2612
1882	3243	14·9	1481	153	206	603	2443

Years.	Contested.				Execution of Decrees.			
	For Plaintiff.	For Defendant.	Mixed.	Total	Arrest of Debtor.	Decree-holder put in Possession of Immovable Property.	Attachment or Sale of Property.	
							Immovable.	Movable.
1870 ...	542	189	58	789	170	171	1189	168
1871 ...	517	180	78	775	152	168	1039	141
1872 ...	511	136	81	728	187	151	1077	134
1873 ...	718	175	...	888	244	174	1492	182
1874 ...	557	146	...	703	120	181	1468	228
1875 ...	684	246	...	930	32	168	1835	264
1876 ...	589	157	...	746	82	156	1552	189
1877 ...	698	191	...	889	8	164	810	104
1878 ...	577	133	...	710	21	164	1387	185
1879 ...	556	156	...	712	25	126	1644	160
1880 ...	564	177	...	741	42	209	979	139
1881 ...	606	169	...	775	65	189	565	62
1882 ...	615	185	...	800	71	204	470	90

Chapter IX.
Justice.
Registration.

The Registration Department employs seven sub-registrars, all of them special or full-time officers. One of these sub-registrars is stationed at each sub-divisional head-quarters. In addition to supervision by the Collector as District Registrar, a special scrutiny, under the control of the Inspector General of Registration and Stamps, is carried on by the divisional inspector. According to the registration report for 1882-83 the gross registration receipts for that year amounted to £1046 (Rs. 10,460) and the charges to £787 (Rs. 7870) thus leaving a credit balance of £259 (Rs. 2590). Of 4948, the total number of registrations, 4796 related to immovable property, 132 to movable property, and twenty were wills. Of 4796 documents relating to immovable property 2247 were mortgage deeds, 1487 deeds of sale, 76 deeds of gift, 816 leases, and 170 miscellaneous deeds. Including £166,126 (Rs. 16,61,260) the value of immovable property transferred, the total value of the property affected by registration amounted to £169,590 (Rs. 16,95,900).

Magistracy.

At present (1882) twenty-four officers share the administration of criminal justice. Of these one is the District Magistrate, five are first class magistrates, seven second class and eleven third class. Of the first class magistrates two are covenanted European civilians, two are uncovenanted civil officers, also called deputy collectors, and one is the cantonment magistrate. The District Magistrate has a general supervision over the whole district. In 1881 the District Magistrate decided three original and six appeal cases and the five first class magistrates decided 2015 original cases. Three of the first class magistrates, invested with appellate powers, decided thirty-seven appeals against the decisions of the second and third class magistrates in their revenue charges and one had also divisional magistrate's powers. The *huzur* deputy collector has magisterial charge of the town of Belgaum and the cantonment magistrate of the cantonment. The remaining three first class magistrates divide the rest of the district between them according to their revenue charges. This gives them each an average area of 1552 square miles and about 261,355 people. Of magistrates of the second and third classes, there are eighteen, all of them natives of India. Of these seven are head *kárkuns* who aid the mámlatdárs and have no separate charges, and one is the special magistrate of the Here estate, who has charge of his own *inám* villages. The remaining ten *táluka* and *mahál* magistrates have an average charge of 465·6 square miles with about 84,035 people. In 1881 they decided in all 1498 original cases. Besides their magisterial duties these officers exercise powers as mámlatdárs, mahálkaris, and head *kárkuns* to mámlatdárs. 902 hereditary police *pátils* or village heads are entrusted with petty magisterial powers under section 14 of the Bombay Village Police Act VIII. of 1867. Of the whole number six hold commissions under section 15 of the Act.

Village Police, 1882.

The village police consists of the headman called the police *pátil* and one to twenty-eight *shetsandis* or militia, and, in the Chikodi Gokák and Athni sub-divisions, instead of militia village watchmen under the name of *gastis* or men of the rounds, *taráls* or Mhárs who attend upon travellers, *kolkars* or messengers, and *náiks* or village head servants who are by caste either Dhangars that is

Chapter IX.
Justice.
Village Police, 1882.

shepherds or Kolis that is fishermen who are paid either by land only or partly by land partly by cash. The number of militia or *shetsandis* at the different villages varies according to their size. No Mhár or *jáglya* watchmen do police duty. In the Belgaum and Khánápur sub-divisions a class of hereditary village police called *gadkari* or hill-fort men stand on an entirely different footing from the militia or *shetsandis*. They are the descendants of the hereditary garrisons of the three hill-forts of Pargad and Kálánandigad in the Belgaum subdivision and of Bhimgad in the Khánápur sub-division. They do duty in turn in some of the neighbouring villages and towns. The police headmen are under the direct orders of the District Magistrate but their nomination and dismissal rest with the Commissioner. The Belgaum district, with 1279 towns and villages and a population of 864,014, has 3556 police *shetsandis* or militia paid in land taxed at £6293 14*s*. (Rs. 62,937) and by £1210 (Rs. 12,100) in cash. The proportion of militia to population is one to 242·97. The *gadkaris* or hill-fort guards are paid £80 (Rs. 800) in land and £726 16*s*. (Rs. 7268) in cash, averaging £3 7*s*. (Rs. 33½) a year to each man. Their duties are chiefly confined to looking after the safety of their village, and aiding the district police in tracing crime and guarding and escorting criminals.

Crime.

The chief local obstacle to the discovery of crime and the conviction of offenders is the neighbourhood of the native states of Kolhápur and Sávantvádi, and the presence of *jágir* or estate villages within district limits. Perjury, forgery, criminal misappropriation, breach of trust, receiving stolen property, trespass, and adultery are the characteristic crimes of the higher classes. Field disputes are frequent and cause numerous agrarian offences, chiefly of the nature of assault, hurt, even murder, robbery, mischief, false complaint, and false evidence. The pressure of creditors through the medium of the civil courts, causes an occasional grievous hurt, robbery, or murder chiefly for revenge. The chief local criminal classes are Bedars who are mostly cattle-lifters, and the wandering tribes, Lamáns, Kaikádis, Vadars, and Beldárs who are more or less given to thieving and often join into gangs for highway and gang robberies.

Police, 1882.

In the year 1882 the total strength of the district or regular police force was 663. Of these, under the District Superintendent, one was a subordinate officer, 108 inferior subordinate officers, fourteen mounted and 539 foot constables. The cost of maintaining this force was for the Superintendent a total yearly salary of £767 6*s*. (Rs. 7673); for the subordinate officers, on yearly salaries of not less than £120 (Rs. 1200) and the inferior subordinate officers on yearly salaries of less than £120 (Rs. 1200), a total yearly cost of £2591 (Rs. 25,910); and for the foot and mounted constables a cost of £5015 8*s*. (Rs. 50,154). Besides their pay a total sum of £230 (Rs. 2300) was yearly allowed for the horse and travelling allowances of the Superintendent, £395 14*s*. (Rs. 3957) for the pay and travelling allowances of his establishment, £193 14*s*. (Rs. 1937) for the horse and travelling allowances of subordinate officers, and £668 8*s*. (Rs. 6684) a year for contingencies and petty charges. Thus the total yearly cost of maintaining the police force amounted to £9861

Chapter IX. Justice.

Police, 1882.

10*s.* (Rs. 98,615). On an area of 4656 square miles, and a population of 864,014, these figures give one constable for every seven square miles and 1303 people, and a cost of £2 2*s.* 4½*d.* (Rs. 21$\frac{3}{16}$) to the square mile, or 1¾*d.* (1⅛ *as.*) to each head of the population. Of the total strength of 663, exclusive of the Superintendent, eleven, one officer and ten men, were in 1882 employed as guards at district, central, or subsidiary jails; forty-six, six of them officers and forty men, were engaged as guards over treasuries and lock-ups, or as escorts to prisoners and treasure; 532 ninety-two of them officers and 440 men were stationed in towns, municipalities, and cantonments. Of the whole number, exclusive of the Superintendent, 334 were provided with fire-arms and forty-two with swords or with swords and batons and 286 were provided with batons only; 174, of whom sixty-five were officers and 109 men could read and write, and fifty-one men were under instruction. Except the Superintendent who was a European the members of the police force were natives of India. Of these thirty-seven officers and 223 men were Muhammadans, seven officers and six men Bráhmans, seven officers and twelve men Rajputs, four officers and thirty-one men Lingáyats, thirty-seven officers and 210 men Maráthás, one officer and one man Jains, thirteen officers and thirty men Hindus of other castes, one officer a Pársi, and two officers and one man Christians.

Offences, 1874-1882.

The returns for the nine years ending 1882 show a total of 161 murders, fifty-two culpable homicides, 245 cases of grievous hurt, 452 gang and other robberies, and 25,512 other offences. During these nine years the total number of offences gave a yearly average of 2936 or one offence for every 294 of the population. The number of murders varied from thirteen in 1881 to twenty-three in 1874 and averaged eighteen; culpable homicides varied from two in 1876 to thirteen in 1877 and averaged six; cases of grievous hurt varied from sixteen in 1878 to forty-three in 1875 and averaged twenty-seven; gang and other robberies varied from thirty-one in 1875 to sixty in 1878 and averaged fifty; and other offences varied from 2277 in 1874 to 3786 in 1877 and averaged 2835 or 96·56 per cent of the whole. Of the whole number of persons arrested the convictions varied from forty-seven per cent in 1874 to sixty-eight in 1877 and 1881 and averaged fifty-eight per cent. The percentage of the stolen property recovered varied from thirty-five in 1881 to seventy-nine in 1878. The details are:

Belgaum Crime and Police, 1874-1882.

Offences and Convictions.

Year.	Murders and Attempt to Murder.				Culpable Homicide.				Grievous Hurt.				Dacoities and Robberies.			
	Cases.	Arrests.	Convictions.	Percentage.	Cases.	Arrests.	Convictions.	Percentage	Cases.	Arrests.	Convictions.	Percentage.	Cases.	Arrests.	Conviction.	Percentage.
1874 ...	23	48	31	65	3	5	2	40	19	60	18	22	46	96	17	18
1875 ...	16	48	10	21	4	3	1	33	43	94	56	60	31	48	9	19
1876 ...	18	42	27	64	2	2	2	100	36	59	39	66	57	280	157	56
1877 ...	18	36	9	25	13	24	3	12	36	50	27	54	52	220	113	51
1878 ...	22	31	15	48	6	18	5	33	16	15	8	53	60	37	18	49
1879 ...	14	23	14	61	8	9	4	44	32	38	11	33	56	78	42	54
1880 ...	16	30	18	60	7	7	5	71	25	36	24	67	57	85	37	44
1881 ...	13	13	7	54	3	5	4	80	26	38	15	40	43	53	28	53
1882 ...	21	33	21	64	6	3	2	67	22	34	17	50	50	39	4	10
Total...	161	304	152	50	52	71	28	39	245	419	210	51	452	936	425	46

Offences, 1874-1882.

Belgaum Crime and Police, 1874-1882—continued.

Year.	Offences and Convictions—continued.										
	Other Offences.				Total.				Property.		
	Cases.	Arrests.	Convictions.	Percentage.	Cases.	Arrests.	Convictions.	Percentage.	Stolen.	Recovered.	Percentage.
1874 ...	2277	3766	1562	41	2368	3975	1625	47	6552	2633	40
1875 ...	2371	3610	1812	50	2465	3805	1888	51	3277	1511	46
1876 ...	2685	3920	2183	56	2798	4303	2408	56	3207	1218	38
1877 ...	3786	6376	4423	69	3905	6706	4575	68	6377	4519	71
1878 ...	2850	3430	2190	64	2954	3526	2236	66	5550	4292	79
1879 ...	2787	3535	2067	58	2887	3677	2138	58	5378	2574	48
1880 ...	3191	4160	2252	54	3298	4318	2336	54	3555	1337	38
1881 ...	2999	3233	2222	69	3084	3342	2276	68	2920	1015	35
1882 ...	2566	2557	1516	59	2665	2664	1560	59	2902	1240	43
Total...	25,512	34,587	20,227	58	26,422	36,314	21,042	58	39,718	20,339	51

Jails.

Besides the lock-up at each mámlatdár's office, there is a district jail at Belgaum and a subordinate jail at Athni. The number of convicts in the Belgaum jail on the 31st of December 1882 was forty-two, of whom thirty-two were males and ten females. During the year 1883, 499 convicts, of whom 433 were males and sixty-six females were admitted, and 465 of whom 396 were males and sixty-nine females were discharged. During the year the daily average of prisoners was sixty and at the close of the year the number of convicts was seventy-six, of whom sixty-nine were males and seven females. Of these 359 males and sixty-three females were sentenced for not more than one year; thirty-five males were for over one year and not more than two years; thirteen males and one female were for more than two years and not more than five years; six males and two females were for between five and ten years; and none were for over ten years. Eight male prisoners, one for life and seven for a term, were sentenced to transportation; and eight male prisoners were sentenced to death. The daily average number of sick was two. During the year four prisoners died two of bowel complaint and two after being admitted into hospital. The total cost of diet was £112 8*s* (Rs. 1124) or an average of £1 16*s*. 3*d*. (Rs. 18⅛) to each prisoner.

CHAPTER X.

FINANCE.

Chapter X.

Finance.

District Balance Sheet.

For account purposes the present district of Belgaum was formed in August 1864. The earliest available district balance-sheet is therefore that for 1865-66. Though since then a few account changes have been made, most of the items can be brought under the corresponding heads in the forms now in use. Exclusive of £54,266 (Rs. 5,42,660), the adjustment on account of alienated land, the total transactions entered in the district balance-sheet for 1881-82 amounted, under receipts to £295,745 (Rs. 29,57,450) against £229,568 (Rs. 22,95,680) in 1865-66, and under charges to £341,634 (Rs. 34,16,340) against £287,078 (Rs. 28,70,780). Leaving aside departmental miscellaneous receipts and payments in return for services rendered, such as post and telegraph receipts, the 1881-82 revenue under all heads, imperial, provincial local, and municipal came to £219,350 (Rs. 21,93,500), or on a population of 864,014, an individual share of 5*s.* (Rs. $2\frac{1}{2}$). The corresponding receipts in 1865-66 amounted to £208,528 (Rs. 20,85,280) which according to that year's approximate population of 838,750, gave an individual share of 4*s.* $11\frac{1}{2}$*d.* (Rs. $2\frac{3}{4}\frac{3}{8}$). During the period of nearly seventeen years between the dates of the two balance-sheets the following changes have taken place under the chief heads of receipts and charges.

Land Revenue.

Land Revenue receipts, which form 59·2 per cent of £219,350 (Rs. 21,93,500) the entire revenue of the district, have risen from £123,187 (Rs. 12,31,870) in 1865-66 to £129,948 (Rs. 12,99,480) in 1881-82. This increase is chiefly due to the revision of assessment, and lapses of alienated land. Land Revenue charges have risen from £10,761 (Rs. 1,07,610) in 1865-66 to £22,048 (Rs. 2,20,480) in 1881-82. The following statement shows the land revenue collected in each of the seventeen years ending the 31st of March 1882:

Belgaum Land Revenue, 1865-1882.

Year.	£	Year.	£	Year.	£	Year.	£
1865-66 ...	123,187	1870-71 ...	127,494	1874-75 ...	179,797	1878-79 ...	180,766
1866-67 ...	128,730	1871-72 ...	126,741	1875-76 ...	176,930	1879-80 ...	181,066
1867-68 ...	131,372	1872-73 ...	172,642	1876-77 ...	151,282	1880-81 ...	179,342
1868-69 ...	127,090	1873-74 ...	172,420	1877-78 ...	179,280	1881-82 ...	184,214
1869-70 ...	126,347						

The figures from 1872-73 to 1881-82 include the revenue of alienated lands amounting approximately to £50,000 (Rs. 5,00,000) which is adjusted every year by debit and credit.

Stamps.

Stamp receipts have risen from £10,635 (Rs. 1,06,350) in 1865-66

Chapter X.

Finance.

Excise.

to £12,126 (Rs. 1,21,260) in 1881-82, and charges have fallen from £384 (Rs. 3840) in 1865-66 to £383 (Rs. 3830) in 1881-82.

During the five years ending 1876-77 the average annual excise revenue of Belgaum amounted to £13,486 (Rs. 1,34,860). During the famine of 1876-77 the revenue fell to £8715 2*s.* (Rs. 87,151). It recovered in 1880-81, and by 1882-83 had risen to £21,419 (Rs. 2,14,190). The expenditure for the same year amounted to £592 (Rs. 5920) against £440 12*s.* (Rs. 4406) in 1881-82, before which no special establishment was employed for the collection and protection of the excise revenue. Until 1879-80, twelve shops, seven in the cantonment and five in the town of Belgaum, were licensed for the sale of imported foreign spirits on payment of a yearly fee of £5 (Rs. 50) each. Two of the Belgaum town shops were closed in 1880-81 but were re-opened in the next year. One additional shop was opened in the Kolhápur cantonment in 1881-82 and in Nipáni in 1882-83. Until 1879-80, the privilege of making and selling country liquor was sold at yearly auctions to each sub-division. The privilege included the right to draw and sell toddy that is fermented palm juice of wild date. Since 1879-80 the spirit contract has been separated from the toddy contract. In 1881-82, the central distillery system was introduced. A three years' contract was given to a capitalist on his guaranteeing a minimum yearly payment of £13,500 (Rs. 1,35,000) on account of still head duty leviable on liquor issued from the distillery at the rate of 5*s.* (Rs. 2½) the gallon of 25° under proof and of 3*s.* 4⅛*d.* (Re. 1 *as.* 10¾) the gallon of 50° under proof. The contractor is bound to sell liquor at prices not exceeding 9*s.* (Rs. 4½) the gallon for 25° under proof and of 6*s.* 6*d.* (Rs. 3¼) the gallon 50° under proof. In 1881-82, 18,212 gallons of 25° under proof and 53,515 gallons of 50° were issued for sale. The issues for 1882-83 were 29,675 gallons of 25° under proof and 44,700 gallons of 50° under proof. These figures include the liquor supplied to shops in villages belonging to native states which for excise purposes are joined to Belgaum with the consent of the chiefs who receive yearly compensation. Besides the minimum amount he guarantees on account of still head duty the contractor pays £40 (Rs. 400) a month as a contribution towards the cost of the excise establishment. Three stores or depôts, at Belgaum, Chikodi, and Gokák have been established for the distribution of liquor. The stores or depôts are maintained at the cost of the contractor. They have proved of great use and have increased the legitimate sale of liquor. It has been decided at the close of the present farm in July 1884 to raise the still head duty to 6*s.* (Rs. 3) a gallon of 25° uuder proof leaving the highest selling price the same as at present. It has also been determined to substitute liquor of 60° under proof for liquor of 50° under poof and to charge duty on 60° under proof liquor at 3*s.* 1½*d.* (Rs. $1\frac{9}{16}$) the gallon, the highest selling price being fixed at 5*s.* (Rs. 2½). The present contractor has built a distillery at Belgaum which has been bought by Government for £3450 (Rs. 34,500). There are 92 country spirit shops in Belgaum district proper, and 98 in the native state villages. The materials from which the country spirit is made are *moha* flowers and the bark of the *hewra* tree, both of which are produced locally.

Chapter X.
Finance.
Excise.

Toddy is drawn from date cocoa and wild-palm trees. It is not distilled, and is used in its unfermented or naturally fermented state for drinking and bread-making. In 1881-82 the exclusive right of drawing and selling toddy was sold for £3900 (Rs. 39,000) and the amount was recovered by twelve equal instalments. A tax on toddy yielding trees was sanctioned in June 1882 but was not introduced until August 1883. The rates levied are 6*s.* (Rs. 3) on a cocoa or brab palm tapped, and 2*s.* (Re. 1) on a date or other wild palm tapped. There are 78 toddy shops in the district proper and thirty-two in native state villages. The yearly toddy revenue now amounts to £6000 (Rs. 60,000). The farm for retailing *bháng* or hemp used as an intoxicating drink and *gánja* or hemp prepared for smoking yielded £256 8*s.* (Rs. 2564) in 1882-83 against £287 12*s.* (Rs. 2876). The drugs are produced locally and are also brought from Sátára and other districts. Thirty-nine shops are licensed for the sale of the drugs. Opium details are given under Customs.

Justice.

Law and Justice receipts have risen from £1259 (Rs. 12,590) in 1865-66 to £1323 (Rs. 13,230), and charges from £7980 (Rs. 79,800) in 1865-66 to £15,128 (Rs. 1,51,280) in 1881-82. The rise in expenditure is due to an increase in the number and pay of the officers and establishments.

Forest.

Forest receipts have risen from £3094 (Rs. 30,940) in 1865-66 to £12,979 (Rs. 1,29,790)) in 1881-82, and charges from £996 (Rs. 9960) to £6695 (Rs. 66,950). The increase in receipts is due to better prices, and to improved methods of working the myrobalan and firewood forests; the rise in charges is due to the increased strength of the forest staff.

Assessed Taxes.

The following table shows the amounts realized from the different assessed taxes levied between 1865-66 and 1881-82. The variety of rates and incidence prevents any satisfactory comparison of the results:

Belgaum Assessed Taxes, 1865-66 – 1881-82.

Year.	Amount	Year.	Amount	Year.	Amount	Year.	Amount
Income Tax.	£.	*Trade and Profession Tax.*	£.	*Income Tax.*	£.	*License Tax.*	£.
1865-66 ...	2102			1869-70 ...	10,140	1878-79 ...	9548
		1868-69 ...	2800	1870-71 ...	16,715	1879-80 ...	9491
License Tax.		1869	69	1871-72 ...	2000	1880-81 ...	4652
1867-68 ...	5327			1872-73 ...	2294	1881-82 ...	4284

Customs.

Customs receipts have fallen from £2473 (Rs. 24,730) in 1865-66 to £1081 (Rs. 10,810) in 1881-82, and charges from £310 (Rs. 3100) in 1865-66 to £47 (Rs. 470) in 1881-82. The receipts under this head consist of sale proceeds of opium and auction sales of the right to sell opium and of fines levied and forfeitures made under the Opium Act. Licenses for the retail sale of opium, of *madat* a preparation of opium and betel leaves, and of *chandol* or smoking opium are put to auction every year. Opium required for sale by the licenseholders has to be brought from the Collector's treasury, which is supplied from Bombay by purchase made on behalf of Government by the Commissioner of Opium. The license-holders buy about 765 pounds of opium a year.

Chapter X. Finance. Salt.

There are no local salt works. Salt is brought into the district on pack-bullocks from Goa and other parts of the Konkan below the Sahyádris. The making of earth salt was carried on in some of the native states round Belgaum till it was stopped under the orders of Government in 1877-78. The chiefs concerned receive a yearly compensation of £275 (Rs. 2750).

Political.

Political charges have fallen from £3070 (Rs. 30,700) in 1865-66 to £2816 (Rs. 28,160) in 1881-82. Political charges consist chiefly of the pay and allowances of the Political Agent Kolhápur and Southern Marátha Country and of his assistants, and the pay of their establishment and contingent charges.

Military.

Military charges have fallen from £150,971 (Rs. 15,09,710) in 1865-66 to £80,474 (Rs. 8,04,740) in 1881-82. This fall is due to the decrease in the number of troops stationed at Belgaum.

Registration.

Registration receipts have fallen from £1410 (Rs. 14,100) in 1865-66 to £928 (Rs. 9280) in 1881-82, and charges from £875 (Rs. 8750) in 1865-66 to £712 (Rs. 7120) in 1881-82.

Education.

Education receipts have fallen from £2643 (Rs. 26,430) in 1865-66 to £747 (Rs. 7470) and charges from £5910 (Rs. 59,100) in 1865-66 to £4713 (Rs. 47,130) in 1881-82.

Police.

Police receipts have risen from £73 (Rs. 730) in 1865-66 to £255 (Rs. 2560) in 1881-82 and charges have fallen from £14,025 (Rs. 1,40,250) in 1865-66 to £9494 (Rs. 94,940) in 1881-82.

Transfer.

Transfer receipts have risen from £29,267 (Rs. 2,92,670) in 1865-66 to £84,748 (Rs. 8,47,480) in 1881-82 and transfer expenditure from £21,658 (Rs. 2,16,580) to £132,804 (Rs. 13,28,040). The increase in receipts is chiefly due to receipts on account of Government savings bank deposits, pension fund receipts and remittances of cash from other treasuries, and receipts on account of local funds. The increased charges are due to the withdrawals of deposits from the savings bank and the payment of advances of loans and charges on account of local funds.

Balance Sheet. *1865-1882.*

In the following balance sheet for 1865-66 and 1881-82, the figures shown in black type on both sides are book adjustments. On the receipt side the items of £54,266 (Rs. 5,42,660) and £53,731 (Rs. 5,37,310) represent the additional revenue the district would yield, had none of its lands been alienated. On the debit side the items of £9648 (Rs. 96,480) and £2246 (Rs. 22,460) entered under land revenue represent the rental of lands granted to village headmen engaged on both revenue and police duties, to village clerks, and to village watchmen. The items of £38,216 (Rs. 3,82,160) for 1881-82 and £43,746 (Rs. 4,37,460) for 1865-66, under allowances and assignments, represent the rental of the lands granted to district hereditary officers and other non-service claimants. The items of £6402 (Rs. 64,020) and £7739 (Rs. 77,390), entered under police, represents the rental of the lands granted to *shetsandis* or militia and watchmen for doing police duties. On the other hand cash allowances are treated according to the nature of the allowances. Cash payments made to village headmen, except those solely engaged

Chapter X.
Finance.
Balance Sheet.
1866-1882.

on police duties, and to village watchmen are included in £22,048 (Rs. 2,20,480), the total of the land revenue charges:

Belgaum Balance Sheet, 1865-66 and 1881-82.

Receipts.

Head.	1865-66.	1881-82.
Land	a1,46,281	1,29,948
	53,731	54,266
Stamps	10,685	12,126
Excise	11,259	15,476
Justice	1259	1323
Forests	3094	12,979
Assessed Taxes	2130	4290
Miscellaneous	78	213
Interest	454	3496
Customs	2478	1081
Public Works	1153	6724
Military	14247	4962
Post	2854	14,758
Telegraph	313	1434
Registration	1410	928
Education	2643	747
Police	78	250
Medical	...	27
Jail	...	229
Total ...	2,00,301	2,11,017
Transfer Items.		
Deposits	19,647	15,236
Cash Remittances	1722	52,514
Pension Funds	...	1502
Local Funds	7898	15,496
Total ...	29,267	84,748
Grand Total ...	2,29,568	2,95,745
	53,731	54,266

Charges.

Head.	1865-66.	1881-82.
Land	10,761	22,048
	2346	9648
Stamps	884	383
Excise	...	229
Justice ... Civil	1183	7668
Justice ... Criminal ...	6797	7265
Forests	996	6695
Assessed Taxes	150	...
Adminstration...	...	242
Political	3070	2816
Allowances	15,862	3003
	43,746	38,216
Pensions	1206	2461
Minor Department	...	2100
Miscellaneous	70	1328
Customs	310	47
Public Works	42,768	43,501
Military	1,50,971	80,474
Post	3082	3863
Telegraph	2868	3254
Registration	875	712
Education	5010	4713
Police	14,025	9494
	7739	6402
Medical	1678	2247
Jail	...	4061
Printing...	16	14
Cemeteries	2087	17
Miscellaneous	1351	...
Total ...	2,65,420	2,08,880
Transfer Items.		
Deposits...	18,974	49,447
Cash Remittances	1097	64,611
Interest	5880	2195
Local Funds	1049	16,551
Total ...	31,658	1,32,804
Grand Total ...	2,87,078	3,41,684
	53,731	54,266

a This amount includes £23,044 of land revenue collected for the preceding year.

Revenue other than Imperial.

Local Funds.

Since 1863 district local funds have been collected to promote rural education, supply roads, wells, rest-houses, dispensaries, and other useful works. In 1881-82 the receipts amounted to £15,496 11*s.* (Rs. 1,54,965½) and the expenditure to £16,551 10*s.* (Rs. 1,65,515). The local fund revenue is drawn from three sources, a special cess of one-sixteenth in addition to the land tax, the proceeds of certain subordinate local funds, and certain miscellaneous items. In 1881-82 the special land cess, of which two-thirds are set apart as a road fund and the rest as a school fund, yielded a revenue of £10,101 16*s.* (Rs. 1,01,018). The subordinate funds, including a toll fund, yielded £2019 14*s.* (Rs. 20,197). Interest on Government securities invested on behalf of certain funds and Government and private contributions amounted to £2726 19*s.* (Rs. 27,269½); and miscellaneous receipts including certain items of land revenue amounted to £310 (Rs. 3100). This revenue is administered by district and sub-divisional com-

Chapter X.

Finance.

Local Funds.

mittees partly of official and partly of private members. The district committees consist of the Collector, the assistant and deputy collectors, the executive engineer, and education inspector as official, and the proprietor of an alienated village and six landholders as non-official members. The sub-divisional committees consist of an assistant collector, the mámlatdár, a public works officer, and the deputy education inspector as official, and the proprietor of an alienated village and three landholders as non-official members. The sub-divisional committees bring their requirements to the notice of the district committee who prepare the budget. For administrative purposes the district local funds are divided into two sections, one set apart for public works the other for instruction. The receipts and disbursements during the year 1881-82 were :

Belgaum Local Funds, 1881-82.

PUBLIC WORKS.					
Receipts.	£.	s.	**Charges.**	£.	s.
Balance on 1st April 1881 ...	5713	4			
Two-thirds of Land Cess ...	6734	12	Establishment	1276	0
Tolls	789	4	New Works	5010	10
Ferries	451	2	Repairs	3290	14
Cattle Pound	281	4	Medical Charges	503	19
Contributions	712	8	Miscellaneous	305	6
Miscellaneous	292	16	Balance 31st March 1882	4588	1
Total ...	14,974	10	Total ..	14,974	10
INSTRUCTION.					
Receipts.	£.	s.	**Charges.**	£.	s.
Balance on 1st April 1881 ...	2239	0	School Charges	4997	7
One-third of Land Cess	3367	4	Scholarships	120	16
School Fee Fund	834	14	School Houses, New...	536	0
Contributions Government ...	1638	3	Do. Repairs	387	12
Do. Private	268	8	Miscellaneous	123	6
Government Securities	118	0	Balance 31st March 1882	2309	4
Miscellaneous	18	16			
Total ...	8474	5	Total ...	8474	5

Since 1863 the following local fund works have been carried out at a cost of £66,289 (Rs. 6,62,890). To improve communication 570 miles of roads with thirty-six small bridges and drains have been made and repaired, and 123 miles of roadside planted with trees. To improve the water-supply fifty-five new wells, seventy-four ponds, and five water troughs have been made and repaired. To help village education, 21 new schools have been built and 130 old schools repaired, and for the comfort of travellers forty rest-houses and two bungalows have been built. Besides these works 104 village offices or *chávdis*, seventy-nine cattle pounds, and three dispensaries have been built and repaired.

Municipalities.

Belgaum has seven municipalities. Those at Belgaum, Athni, Gokák, Nipáni, and Yamkanmardi have been established under Act XXVI of 1850, and those at Saundatti and Yellama under

Chapter X.

Finance.

Municipalities.

Act VI of 1873. Each of these municipalities is administered by a body of commissioners with the Collector as president and the assistant or deputy collector in charge of the sub-division as vice president. At Yellamma's hill, near Saundatti, which is the scene of a large yearly fair, the municipality is temporary. In 1881-82 the total district municipal revenue amounted to £7743 (Rs. 77,430). Of this £3685 (Rs. 36,850) were recovered from octroi dues, £625 (Rs. 6250) from house tax, £669 (Rs. 6690) from toll and wheel taxes, £7 (Rs. 70) from assessed taxes, and £2757 (Rs. 27,570) from miscellaneous sources.

The following statement gives for each municipality, the receipts, charges, and incidence of taxation during the year ending the 31st of March 1882:

Belgaum Municipal Details, 1881-82.

Name.	Date.	People (1881).	Receipts. Octroi.	House Tax.	Tolls and Wheel Tax.	Assessed Taxes.	Miscellaneous.	Total.	Incidence.
			£.	£.	£.	£.	£.	£.	s. d.
Belgaum ...	1st Dec. 1851 ...	23,115	1850	24	263	3	1406	3546	3 1
Athni ..	1st Oct. 1853 ...	11,186	888	...	...	2	386	1276	2 3
Gokák ...	1st July 1853 ...	10,307	350	67	...	...	178	595	1 2
Nipáni ...	1st Sept. 1854. .	9777	505	331	...	1	254	1091	2 3
Saundatti ...	1st Jan. 1876 ...	7133	92	81	...	1	500	674	1 11
Yamkanmardi	21st April 1854.	4491	...	122	...	...	7	129	0 7
Yellamma ...	1st Oct. 1878 ...	...	...	...	406	...	26	432	
Total ...			3685	625	669	7	2757	7743	

Name.	Charges. Staff.	Safety.	Health.	Schools.	Works. Original	Works. Repairs	Miscellaneous.	Total.
Belgaum	457	125	1555	94	923	299	295	3748
Athni	185	53	385	92	293	111	125	1194
Gokák	93	8	458	5	94	5	26	689
Nipáni	118	10	150	57	1514	31	44	1924
Saundatti	54	5	115	...	14	7	18	213
Yamkanmardi ...	19	5	33	42	22	10	14	145
Yellama	41	8	40	...	370	137	9	605
Total ...	917	214	2736	290	3230	600	531	8518

CHAPTER XI.

INSTRUCTION.

Chapter XI.
Instruction.

Schools, 1883.

In 1882-83 there were 187 Government schools or an average of one school for every six inhabited villages, alienated as well as Government, with 16,380 names on the rolls and an average attendance of 10,470 pupils or 4·49 per cent of 232,869 the population between six and fourteen years of age. Besides Government schools there were fifteen other schools of which nine were maintained by missionaries, and six were private or indigenous schools.

Staff.

In 1882-83, under the Director of Public Instruction and the Education Inspector Southern Division, the schooling of the district was conducted by a local staff 530 strong, including a deputy educational inspector with a yearly salary of £180 (Rs. 1800) aided by an assistant deputy inspector drawing £90 (Rs. 900) a year, and schoolmasters and assistant masters with yearly salaries of £4 16*s.* to £420 (Rs. 48-4200).

Cost.

In 1882-83, excluding superintendence charges, the expenditure on these schools amounted to £9138 6*s.* (Rs. 91,383) of which £2716 2*s.* (Rs. 27,161) were debited to Government and £6422 8*s.* (Rs. 64,224) to local and other funds.

Instruction.

Of the 202 Government and aided schools, 156 taught Kánarese, forty-two Maráthi, and four Hindustáni. Of the 187 Government schools, one, the High School, taught English and Sanskrit to the Matriculation standard, one first grade anglo-vernacular school taught the first three standards only, eight were anglo-vernacular schools that is vernacular schools with an English class, and the rest, 168 boys and nine girls schools, were simple vernacular schools.

Schools.

The Government Belgaum High School was established under the title of the Sardárs' High School by subscriptions from the Sardárs of the Southern Marátha Country in 1850. After some time the sons of respectable merchants and others were admitted into the school and later on it was made public. Since 1872 it has become a purely Government institution. In the same year the school building, which originally belonged to the Sardárs of the Southern Marátha Country, was made over to Government. In 1882 a public subscription of £600 (Rs. 6000) was raised, which Government doubled, to build two new wings and add a play ground and gymnasium. The school is conducted by one head master and twelve assistant masters and has an average attendance of 155 boys. Boys of all castes who have passed the third Anglo-Vernacular standard are admitted and are taught from the fourth to the seventh or Matriculation standards.

Chapter XI.

Instruction.

Schools, 1883.

An agricultural class and a drawing class have also been attached to the school. The monthly fees varies from 3*s.* to 4*s.* (Rs. 1½-2), and the average yearly cost of each pupil is £9 16*s.* 8*d.* (Rs. 98⅓). The Sardárs of the Southern Marátha Country contributed to the school and sent to it their relations and nominees till 1880, when they gave their support to the Rájárám College in Kolhápur, and sent their children there. Besides Government schools, Belgaum had fifteen private schools at the end of 1882-83. Of the fifteen aided schools, of which six were maintained by the London Mission, one was a High School teaching up to the Matriculation standard, three were First Grade European and Eurasian schools, and the remaining six were vernacular schools. Of the six vernacular schools, five were for boys and one for girls. The London Mission High School at Belgaum, which was established in 1832 by the Reverend J. Taylor, teaches to the Matriculation standard. In 1882 the number on the rolls was 314, the average attendance 288, and the monthly fee 9*d.* to 2*s.* (Re. ⅜-1). The London Mission Maráthi boys school at Belgaum was opened in 1842 by the Reverend J. Taylor. In 1882 the number on the rolls was ninety-five, the average attendance sixty-eight, and the monthly fee 3*d.* (2 *as.*). The London Mission Kánarese boys school at Belgaum was opened in 1850 by the Reverend J. Taylor. In 1882 the number on the rolls was ninety-one and the average attendance seventy-one. The London Mission Kánarese boys school at Bail Hongal was opened in 1862. In 1882 the monthly fee was 3*d.* (2 *as.*), the number on the rolls seventy-two and the average attendance sixty-three. The St. Mary's Pensioners English and Eurasian school for boys and girls at Belgaum was established in 1854. In 1882 the number on the rolls was thirty-five, the average attendance thirty-three, and the monthly fee was 2*s.* (Re. 1). The Convent Boys English and Eurasian school at Belgaum was opened in 1868 by the Roman Catholic chaplain. In 1882 the number on the rolls was thirty-one, the average attendance 22·7, and the monthly fee was nothing to 2*s.* (Re. 1) in proportion to the boys' means. The Convent Girls English and Eurasian school at Belgaum was opened in 1868 by the Roman Catholic chaplain. In 1882 the number on the rolls was ten, the average attendance 9·5, and the monthly fees varied from nothing to 4*s.* (Rs. 2) in proportion to the girls' means. The Belgaum Police inspected school was opened in 1863. In 1882 the number on the rolls was fifty-three all constables, and the average attendance 5·8. No fee was charged. The Márutigalli Maráthi girls private aided school at Belgaum is a large and flourishing school. It was opened in 1856 by Mrs. Seton Carr and is supported partly by the Belgaum municipality which contributes £30 (Rs. 300) a year, and partly by the people's contributions. The school has a reserve fund of £150 (Rs. 1500). The monthly charges amount to £4 10*s.* (Rs. 45). In 1882 the number on the rolls was 101 and the average attendance forty-six. No fee was charged. The London Mission Kánarese girls' school at Belgaum was opened in 1875. In 1882 the number on the rolls was seventy-five and the average attendance thirty-five. No fee was charged. The private aided school at Sankeshvar was opened in 1882 by Mr. Sakhárám Náráyan. In 1882 the monthly fees varied from 6*d.* to 1*s.* (4-8

Schools, 1883.

as.) the number on the rolls was 155, and the average attendance 106. The private school at Karikatti in Parasgad was opened in 1865 by Mr. Gurubasáppa Gurushántáppa. In 1882 the number on the rolls was forty and the average attendance thirty. No fees were charged, but the people subscribe £6 (Rs. 60) a year. The private aided school at Shamnevádi in Chikodi was opened in 1877 by Mr. Vishnu Bálkrishna Joshi. In 1882 the number on the rolls was thirty-one, the average attendance twenty-three, and the monthly fees varied from 3*d.* to 6*d.* (2-4 *as.*). The private aided school at Kenjanur was opened in 1881 by Mr. Chanbasáppa Shivalingáppa. In 1882 the number on the rolls was twenty, the average attendance fifteen, and the monthly fees varied from 3*d.* to 1*s.* (2-8 *as.*). The private aided school at Hulkund in Gokák was opened in 1881 by Mr. Datto Shivrám. In 1882 the number on the rolls was twenty-two and the average attendance fifteen. No fee was charged, but the people subscribed £5 (Rs. 50).

Progress, 1830-1883.

The following details show the increased means for learning to read and write offered by Government to the people during the last fifty-three years. The first Government vernacular school was opened at Belgaum in 1830, and the second eight years after in the same town. Two years later, in 1840, a third vernacular school was opened at Gokák, and in 1850 the High School was established in the town of Belgaum. Thus in 1850 there were twelve Government schools in the district. In 1855-56 the number of schools in the district amounted to fourteen[1] one of them being a High School and the rest vernacular schools with 1498 names and an average attendance of 1320. After 1855-56, another vernacular school was opened at Athni in 1856. In 1865-66, the district contained 56 schools, one of them being a High School and tho rest, including the Training College, vernacular schools with 4380 names and an average attendance of 3612. In 1875-76 there were schools with 7823 names and an average attendance of 6120. Of these schools, including seven for girls, 129 were vernacular, six were anglo-vernacular, and one was a High School. In 1879-80 there were 164 schools with 9726 names and an average attendance of 6933. In 1882-83 the number of schools had risen to 189, the names to 16,380, and the average attendance to 10,470. A comparison with the returns for 1855-56 gives for 1882-83 an increase from 14 to 187 in the number of schools, and from 1498 to 16,380 in the number of pupils.

[1] The details are: *Belgaum Schools, 1830-1855.*

School.	Language.	Year.	School.	Language.	Year.
High School ...	......	1850	Bidi ...	Kanarese...	1838
Belgaum ...	Maráthi ...	1830	Bail Hongal ...	Do. ...	1838
Do. ...	Kanarese...	1838	Hukeri	Do. ...	1854
Sadalgi	Maráthi ...	1841	Khánápur ...	Maráthi ...	1843
Gokák	Kanarese...	1840	Jamboti	Do. ...	1849
Saundatti ...	Do. ...	1838	Chikodi	Do. ...	1855
Sampgaon ...	Do. ...	1838	Itgi	Kánarese...	1843

Chapter XI. Instruction.

Girls Schools.

Two Government girls schools were opened in 1867 in Athni and Belgaum. During the six years ending 1873-74 the number of girls schools had risen to seven with 267 names on the rolls and an average attendance of 181. In 1882-83 the number of girls schools was nine with 512 names on the rolls and an average attendance of 252.

Readers and Writers.

The 1881 census returns give, for the chief races of the district, the following proportion of persons able to read and write. Of 791,277, the total Hindu population, 10,322 (males 10,056, females 266) or 1·30 per cent below fifteen and 1939 (males 1922, females 17) or 0·24 per cent above fifteen were under instruction; 708 (males 659, females 49) or 0·08 per cent below fifteen and 21,866 (males 21,724, females 142) or 2·76 per cent above fifteen were instructed; 291,812 (males 145,687, females 146,125) or 36·87 per cent below fifteen and 464,630 (males 217,284, females 247,346) or 58·71 per cent above fifteen were illiterate. Of 66,351, the total Musalmán population, 870 (males 824, females 46) or 1·31 per cent below fifteen and 155 (males 154, female 1) or 0·23 per cent above fifteen were under instruction; 88 (males 77, females 11) or 0·13 per cent below fifteen and 1424 (males 1391, females 33) or 2·14 per cent above fifteen were instructed; 24,944 (males 12,630, females 12,314) or 37·59 per cent below fifteen and 38,870 (males 18,371, females 20,499) or 58·58 per cent above fifteen were illiterate. Of 6337 Christians, 158 (males 92, females 66) or 2·49 per cent below fifteen, and 75 (males 58, females 17) or 1·18 per cent above fifteen were under instruction; 32 (males 15, females 17) or 0·50 per cent below fifteen and 1137 (males 1022, females 115) or 17·94 per cent above fifteen were instructed; and 1764 (males 872 females 892) or 27·83 per cent below fifteen and 3171 (males 1602, females 1569) or 50·03 per cent above fifteen were illiterate:

Belgaum Education, 1881.

	Hindus.		Musalma'ns.		Christians.	
	Males.	Females.	Males.	Females.	Males.	Females.
Under Instruction.						
Below Fifteen ...	10,056	266	824	46	92	66
Above Fifteen ...	1922	17	154	1	58	17
Instructed.						
Below Fifteen ...	650	49	77	11	15	17
Above Fifteen ...	21,724	142	1891	33	1022	115
Illiterate.						
Below Fifteeen ...	145,687	146,125	12,630	12,814	872	892
Above Fifteen ...	217,284	247,346	18,371	20,499	1602	1569
Total ...	397,332	393,945	33,447	32,904	3661	2676

Pupils by Race.

Before 1855-56 no returns were prepared arranging the pupils according to race and religion. The following statement shows that of the two races of the district the Musalmáns have the larger proportion of their boys and girls under instruction:

Chapter XI.
Instruction.
Pupils by Race.

Pupils by Race, 1855-56 and 1882-83.

Race.	1855-56. Pupils.	1855-56. Percentage of Pupils.	1882-83. Pupils.	1882-83. Percentage of Pupils.	1882-83. School-going Population.	1882-83. Percentage on School-going Population.
Hindus ...	1442	96·26	14,466	88·79	214,510	6·74
Musalmáns ...	56	3·74	1827	11·21	18,359	9·95
Total ...	1498	100	16,293	100	232,869	6·99

Of 15,868, the whole number of boys in Government schools at the end of 1882-83, 2719 were Bráhmans, 5224 Lingáyats, 981 Jains, 439 Kshatris, 106 Prabhus, 472 traders, 1719 cultivators, 1225 craftsmen, 81 shopkeepers, 180 labourers, 211 low castes, 23 miscellaneous; 1807 Musalmáns; 78 Christians; and 3 Pársis. Of 512 the total number of girls on the rolls in 1882-83, 486 were Hindus, 20 were Musalmáns, and 6 were entered as Others.

Schools, 1855-1883.

The following tables, prepared from special returns furnished by the Education Department, show in detail the number of schools and pupils with the rates of fees and the cost to Government:

Belgaum School Return, 1855-56, 1865-66, and 1882-83.

Classes.	Schools.			Pupils. Hindus.			Pupils. Musalmáns.		
	1855-56.	1865-66.	1882-83.	1855-56.	1865-66.	1882-83.	1855-56.	1865-66.	1882-83.
Government.									
High School	1	1	1	...	140	145	...	2	...
Anglo-Vernacular ...	...	...	9	...	...	322	...	..	13
Vernacular	13	55	177	1442	4153	14,025	56	221	1794
Total ...	14	56	187	1442	4293	14,492	56	228	1807

Classes.	Pupils—continued. Pársis.			Pupils—continued. Total.			Average Daily Attendance.		
	1855-56.	1865-66.	1882-83.	1855-56.	1865-66.	1882-83.	1855-56.	1865-66.	1882-83.
Government.									
High School	...	17	7	...	159	152	...	136	143
Anglo-Vernacular ...	...	...	6	...	...	341	...	...	247
Vernacular	...	6	68	1498	4380	15,887	1320	3612	10,080
Total ...	...	23	81	1498	4539	16,380	1320	3748	10,470

Classes.	Fees.			Cost per Pupil.			Receipts. Government.		
	1855-56.	1865-66.	1882-83.	1855-56.	1865-66.	1882-83.	1855-56.	1865-66.	1882-83.
Government.				£. s. d.	£. s. d.	£. s. d.	£	£	£
High School ...	...	3s.	3s. to 4s.	...	8 9 0½	9 16 8	...	727	828
Anglo-Vernacular...	...	...	2s.	...	...	1 16 3	...	...	174
Vernacular	1½d.	1½d to 6d.	1½d. to 9d.	0 6 8¾	0 12 5½	0 12 3	306	1061	1511
Total ...	...	...	...	...	...	...	306	1788	2513

Chapter XI.
Instruction.

Schools, 1855-1883.

Belgaum School Return, 1855-56, 1865-66, and 1882-83—continued.

Classes.	Receipts—continued.								
	Local Cess.			Municipality.			Private.		
	1855-56.	1865-66.	1882-83.	1855-56.	1865-66.	1882-83.	1855-56.	1865-66.	1882-83.
Government.		£	£			£	£	£	£
High School	...	...	14	...	...	24	...	564	836
Anglo-Vernacular ...	...	...	...	...	...	63	...	...	68
Vernacular	...	208	3373	...	...	66	27	684	147
Total ...	...	208	3387	...	...	153	27	1248	1051

Classes.	Receipts—continued.						Expenditure.		
	Fees.			Total.			Inspection and Instruction		
	1855-56.	1865-66.	1882-83.	1855-56.	1865-66.	1882-83.	1855-56.	1865-66.	1882-83.
Government.									
High School	...	63	296	...	1354	1998	...	1153	1295
Anglo-Vernacular ...	...	...	143	...	...	448	...	...	448
Vernacular	109	312	992	442	2265	6089	442	1965	5073
Total ...	109	375	1431	442	3619	8535	442	3118	6816

Classes.	Expenditure—continued.								
	Buildings.			Scholarships.			Total.		
	1855-56.	1865-66.	1882-83.	1855-56.	1865-66.	1882-83.	1855-56.	1865-66.	1882-83.
Government.		£	£			£	£	£	£
High School	...	...	...	...	...	116	...	1153	1411
Anglo-Vernacular ...	...	...	...	...	...	...	...	...	448
Vernacular	...	282	1136	...	...	...	442	2247	6209
Total ...	...	282	1136	...	..	116	442	3400	8068

Classes.	Cost to											
	Government.			Local Cess.			Other Funds.			Total.		
	1855-56.	1865-66.	1882-83.	1855-56.	1865-66.	1882-83.	1855-56.	1865-66.	1882-83.	1855-56.	1865-66.	1882-83.
Government.	£	£	£		£	£	£	£	£	£	£	£
High School... ...	...	727	828	...	...	50	...	426	534	...	1153	1412
Anglo-Vernacular ...	...	...	174	...	...	...	...	...	274	...	...	448
Vernacular	305	107	1374	...	218	3851	136	968	984	441	1293	6209
Total ...	305	834	2376	...	218	3901	136	1394	1792	441	2446	8069

Town Schools, 1882-83.

A comparison of the present (1882-83) provision for teaching the district town and village population gives the following results. In the town of Belgaum, in 1882-83, eight schools under Government management had 1324 names on the rolls and an average attendance of 956·8. Of these schools, one was a High School, one a first grade anglo-vernacular school, and one a Hindustáni school. The average yearly cost[1] of each pupil in the High School was £9 16*s*. 8*d*.

[1] The cost for each pupil shewn in these statements is what the pupil costs the state not what the pupil pays in fees. The rates of fees are given in the School Return page 485.

Town Schools, 1882-83.

(Rs. $98\frac{1}{2}$) ; in the other schools it varied from 6*s.* 6*d.* to £3 12*s.* (Rs. $3\frac{1}{4}$ -36). Since 1864, 150, or a yearly average of 7·5 pupils have passed the yearly University entrance test examination from the Belgaum High School.[1] In addition to the Government schools, in 1882-83, nine private or aided schools in the town of Belgaum had 726 names on the rolls, an average attendance of 563·11, and an average yearly cost of each pupil varying from 10*s.* to £2 4*s.* (Rs. 5-22).[2] In 1882-83, the town of Gokák had five schools with 529 names on the rolls, an average attendance of 362, and an average yearly cost for each pupil varying from 7*s.* to 12*s.* (Rs. $3\frac{1}{2}$ - 6). In the town of Athni four schools had 375 names on the rolls, an average attendance of 267, and an average yearly cost for each pupil varying from 5*s.* $1\frac{1}{2}$*d.* to 14*s.* $10\frac{1}{2}$*d.* (Rs. $2\frac{9}{16}$ - $7\frac{7}{16}$). In the town of Chikodi three schools had 337 names on the rolls, an average attendance of 250, and an average yearly cost for each pupil varying from 6*s.* to 12*s.* (Rs. 3 - 6). In the town of Sampgaon two schools had 166 names on the rolls, an average attendance of 106, and an average yearly cost for each pupil varying from 12*s.* to 15*s.* 6*d.* (Rs. 6 - $7\frac{3}{4}$). In the town of Nipáni three schools had 418 names on the rolls, an average attendance of 292, and an average yearly cost for each pupil varying from 8*s.* 3*d.* to 10*s.* (Rs. $4\frac{1}{8}$ - 5). In the town of Sankeshvar one school had 183 names on the rolls, an average attendance of 126, and an average yearly cost for each pupil of 8*s.* $1\frac{1}{2}$*d.* (Rs. $4\frac{1}{16}$). In the town of Bail Hongal three schools had 316 names on the rolls, an average attendance of 197, and an average yearly cost for each pupil varying from 6*s.* 3*d.* to 6*s.* $4\frac{1}{2}$*d.* (Rs. $3\frac{1}{8}$ - $3\frac{3}{16}$). In the town of Kittur four schools had 611 names on the rolls, an average attendance of 442, and an average yearly cost for each pupil varying from 6*s.* $1\frac{1}{2}$*d.* to 11*s.* 9*d.* (Rs. $3\frac{1}{16}$ - $5\frac{7}{8}$). In the town of Nandgad three schools had 463 names on the rolls, an average attendance of 356, and an average yearly cost for each pupil varying from 7*s.* $7\frac{1}{2}$*d.* to 12*s.* $4\frac{1}{2}$*d.* (Rs. $3\frac{13}{16}$ - $6\frac{3}{16}$). In the town of Saundatti two schools had 268 names on the rolls, an average attendance of 172, and an average yearly cost for each pupil varyiug from 9*s.* $7\frac{1}{2}$*d.* to 13*s.* (Rs. $4\frac{13}{16}$ - $6\frac{1}{2}$). In the town of Murgod one school had 155 names on the rolls, an average attendance of 121, and an average yearly cost for each pupil of 8*s.* 3*d.* (Rs. $4\frac{1}{8}$). In the town of Sadalgi one school had 120 names on the rolls, an average attendance of 82, and an average yearly cost for each pupil of 6*s.* $7\frac{1}{2}$*d.* (Rs. $3\frac{5}{16}$). In the town of Manoli one school had 200 names on the rolls, an average attendance of 135, and an average yearly cost for each pupil of 7*s.* $1\frac{1}{2}$*d.* (Rs. $3\frac{9}{16}$). In the town of Hukeri one school had 180 names on the rolls, an average attendance of 119, and an average yearly cost

---

[1] The details are: 1864, two ; 1865, five ; 1866, three ; 1867, four ; 1868, five ; 1869, seven ; 1870, eight ; 1871, eight ; 1872, thirteen ; 1873, eleven ; 1874, eight ; 1875, seven ; 1876, three ; 1877, six ; 1878, two ; 1879, ten ; 1880, ten ; 1881, nineteen ; 1882, ten ; 1883, nine.

[2] Of these one was a high school, three first grade anglo-vernacular schools and one first grade anglo-vernacular school for girls and four vernacular schools. Since 1871, 46 pupils have passed the University entrance examination. The details are : 1871, none ; 1872, two ; 1873, one ; 1874, four ; 1875, five ; 1876, two ; 1877, one ; 1878, none ; 1879, none ; 1880, seven ; 1881, five ; 1882, four ; 1883, fifteen.

Chapter XI. Instruction.

for each pupil of 11*s.* (Rs. 5½). In the town of Yamkanmardi one school had 153 names on the rolls, an average attendance of 104, and an average yearly cost for each pupil of 7*s.* 6*d.* (Rs. 3¾). In the town of Kongnoli one school had 110 names on the rolls, an average attendance of 82, and an average yearly cost for each pupil of 7*s.* 6*d.* (Rs. 3¾).

Village Schools.

Exclusive of the forty-three schools in the seventeen towns of Belgaum, Gokák, Athni, Chikhodi, Sampgaon, Nipáni, Sankeshvar, Bail-Hongal, Kittur, Nandgad, Saundatti, Murgod, Sadalgi, Manoli, Hukeri, Yamkanmardi, and Kongnoli, the district of Belgaum was in 1882-83 provided with 135 schools, or an average of one school for every eight inhabited villages. The following statement shows the distribution of these schools by sub-divisions:

Belgaum Village Schools, 1882-83.

Sub-Division.	Villages.	Population.	Schools.	Sub-Division.	Villages.	Population.	Schools.
Belgaum ...	152	95,780	27	Parasgad ...	124	75,177	18
Sampgaon ...	122	102,108	26	Gokák ...	121	82,722	19
Khánápur ...	205	72,485	15	Athni ...	91	95,780	24
Chikodi ...	222	198,838	40				

Chámbhárs and Mhárs and the boys of other depressed classes are allowed to attend Government schools in a place set apart for them either in the veranda or in the school room. When the local feeling is strongly opposed to this arrangement, the Mhár lads are allowed to attend by night. In Belgaum town a Mhár class of twenty-five boys is taught by a Mhár teacher who was brought up in the Government vernacular school of Eksambi in Chikodi. The class is composed of nineteen boys and eight men and is taught from seven to nine in the evening.

Newspapers.

There are three local papers at Belgaum, the Belgaum Samáchár or Belgaum News published on Monday with an issue of 250 copies, the Karnátak Mitra or the Karnátak Friend published on Wednesday with an issue of 150 copies, and the Jnyán Bodhak or Adviser of Knowledge published on Sunday with an issue of 150 copies. These newspapers contain editorials on miscellaneous topics, private notices, local news, and extracts from other papers. Their circulation is confined to the central and southern divisions of the Bombay Presidency. The rates of yearly subscription vary from 4*s.* to 6*s.* 6*d.* (Rs. 2-3¼).

Libraries.

Belgaum has nine libraries. Except two at Belgaum these libraries are mere reading rooms, containing a few ordinary books and taking in papers only of local interest. In the fort of Belgaum is an excellent Station Library. The Belgaum Native General Library, which has a building of its own, is the oldest institution of the kind in the Belgaum district, having been established in 1848 by Mr. J. D. Inverarity then Collector. It is chiefly maintained on subscriptions raised at monthly rates varying from 6*d.* to 4*s.* (Rs. ¼-2). Its yearly income is about £25 (Rs. 250) which is raised from about eighty-five subscribers. Thirteen papers four English, three Anglo-vernacular, and six vernacular are taken. It also receives free of charge the Educational Record from the Educational

Chapter XI.

Instruction.

Libraries.

Department. Occasional excessive expenditure is met from the permanent fund of £50 (Rs. 500). The Belgaum municipality has lately presented the library with £10 (Rs. 100) to buy books. It has at present 1036 books, of which 622 are English, 284 Maráthi, thirty-four Sanskrit, thirty-one Kánarese, and sixty-five Gujaráti. Of 622 English books forty-four are books of reference, 136 are historical, 118 scientific, ninety-four classical, 151 novels, and seventy-nine miscellaneous. The library is much used both by Government officials and the more educated class of townsmen.

The following statement gives the details of native libraries and reading rooms:

Belgaum Native Libraries and Reading Rooms, 1882-83.

No.	Place.	Date.	Books.	Newspapers.			Members.	Monthly Fee.	Yearly Income.
				English.	Anglo-Vernacular.	Vernacular.			£
1	Belgaum	1848	1036	4	3	6	94	6*d.* to 2*s.*	25
2	Chikodi	1866	90	...	...	...	22	Ditto.	5
3	Nipáni	1875	8	...	3	4	...	Ditto.	5
4	Gokák	1865	62	...	...	2	19	Ditto.	8
5	Athni	1865	60	1	2	7	16	Ditto.	16
6	Sampgaon	1866	264	1	2	8	28	Ditto.	10
7	Khánápur	1868	35	1	2	3	35	Ditto.	5
8	Saundatti	1870	94	1	3	7	24	Ditto.	19

CHAPTER XII.

HEALTH.

Chapter XII.
Health.
Diseases.

ITS height of 1500 to 2000 feet above the sea and its short distance of twenty-five to seventy-five miles from the sea combine to make the climate of Belgaum cool, pleasant, and healthy. At the same time its dampness during the south-west rains (June-October) and the extreme dryness of the air at other times forms a sudden change which is trying to the weak, and is apt to cause liver disease, cold, neuralgia, and rheumatism.

Malarious fevers, though prevalent, are seldom severe or fatal, and people from other districts suffering from malarious fevers generally improve by a residence in Belgaum. Epidemics of measles and chicken-pox are not uncommon before and after the rains, but, as a rule, they are mild. Small-pox has always been mild. Dengue was introduced in 1872 from Aden and Poona, but it was confined to a few isolated cases, and never spread as an epidemic. Cholera is chiefly imported, although it occasionally rages as an epidemic in certain parts of the district. The sporadic cases are few, and are amenable to treatment. The 1877 famine was accompanied by a severe outbreak of cholera which proved fatal in a large number of cases. On the setting in of the rains this epidemic disappeared, and remittent fever took its place, passing into an intermittent fever of a severer type than had been known for years in Belgaum.

Hospitals, 1882.

In 1882, there was one civil hospital and five grant-in-aid dispensaries. The number of patients treated was 21,327, of whom 21,021 were outdoor and 306 indoor patients; the cost was £1909 (Rs. 19,090). The following details are taken from the 1882 reports:

Belgaum.

The Belgaum civil hospital probably dates from 1836 when Belgaum was chosen to be the district head-quarters. The prevailing diseases are malarious fevers, bronchitis, worms, and rheumatism. In 1882 cholera prevailed all over the district, and several times appeared in the city, but never in an epidemic form. Out of thirty-one cases seventeen proved fatal. 2384 outdoor and 258 indoor patients were treated at a cost of £1257 16*s*. (Rs. 12,578).

The Belgaum grant-in-aid dispensary was opened in 1859. The commonest diseases are malarious fevers, ophthalmia, bowel complaints, and worms. In 1882 7014 outdoor and five indoor patients were treated at a cost of £151 12*s*. (Rs. 1516).

Chapter XII.

Health.

Dispensaries.

The Gokák dispensary was opened in 1867. The prevailing diseases are malarious fevers, ophthalmia, worms, skin diseases, and ulcers. In 1882 cholera prevailed in May and June, 392 successful vaccinations were performed, and 2552 outdoor and fifteen indoor patients were treated at a cost of £144 (Rs. 1440).

Athni.

The Athni dispensary was opened in 1871. The prevailing diseases are ophthalmia, worms, skin diseases, malarious fevers, and rheumatism. In 1882 cholera prevailed in May and June, 433 successful vaccinations were performed, and 4952 outdoor and nineteen indoor patients were treated at a cost of £134 6*s.* (Rs. 1343).

Saundatti.

The Saundatti dispensary was established in 1875. The commonest diseases are malarious fevers, ophthalmia, chest affections, bowel complaints, and skin diseases. In 1882 no epidemic occurred, 195 children were successfully vaccinated, and 1972 outdoor patients were treated at a cost of £121 2*s.* (Rs. 1211).

Chikodi

The Chikodi dispensary was opened in 1882 in a hired bungalow, 136 children were successfuly vaccinated, and 2147 outpatients and nine inpatients were treated at a cost of £98 16*s.* (Rs. 988).

Infirm People.

According to the 1881 census 2199 persons (males 1268, females 931) or 0·25 per cent of the population were infirm. Of the total number 2052 (males 1171, females 881) were Hindus; 140 (males 90, females 50) Musalmáns; and 7 Christians all of whom were males. Of 2199 the total number of infirm persons, 151 (males 103, females 48) or 6·86 per cent were of unsound mind, 1186 (males 626, females 560) or 53·93 per cent were blind, 573 (males 330, females 243) or 26·05 per cent were deaf and dumb, and 289 (males 209, females 80) or 13·14 per cent were lepers. The details are :

Belgaum Infirm People, 1881.

	Hindus.		Musalmáns.		Christians.		Total.	
	Males.	Females.	Males.	Females.	Males.	Females.	Males.	Females.
Insane	101	46	2	2	...	...	103	48
Blind	583	537	41	23	2	...	626	560
Deaf-mute ...	297	221	28	22	5	...	330	243
Lepers	190	77	19	3	...	...	209	80
Tota. ...	1171	881	90	50	7	...	1268	931

Vaccination.

In 1883-84 under the supervision of the Deputy Sanitary Commissioner Southern Deccan Registration District the work of vaccination was carried on by twelve vaccinators with yearly salaries varying from £16 16*s.* (Rs. 168) to £28 16*s.* (Rs. 288). They were distributed over the rural parts of the district, one of them attending to the work of the Belgaum Town and Cantonment. Besides the vaccinators the medical officers of Belgaum Jail, Chikodi, Gokák, Saundatti, and Athni carried on vaccine operations. The total number of operations was 29,190 besides 1753 re-vaccinations compared with 10,341 primary vaccinations in 1869-70.

The following statement shows the sex, religion, and age of the persons primarily vaccinated :

Chapter XII.

Health.

Vaccination.

Belgaum Vaccination Details, 1869-70 and 1883-84.

Year.	Primary Vaccinations.									
	Sex.		Religion.					Age.		Total.
	Males.	Fe-males.	Hindus.	Musalmáns.	Pársis.	Christians.	Others.	Under one Year.	Above one Year.	
1869-70 ..	5695	4646	9145	877	...	76	243	3272	7069	10,341
1883-84 ...	14,782	14,418	25,086	2686	3	181	1244	10,991	18,209	29,200

In 1883-84 the total cost of these operations, exclusive of those performed in dispensaries, was £659 18*s.* (Rs. 6599) or about 5$\frac{3}{8}$*d.* (3$\frac{3}{4}$ *as.*) for each successful case. The charges included supervision and inspection £279 12*s.* (Rs. 2796), establishment £343 18*s.* (Rs. 3439), and contingencies £36 8*s.* (Rs. 364). Of these the supervising and inspecting charges were met from Government provincial funds, £349 12*s.* (Rs. 3496) were borne by the local funds of the different sub-divisions, and £30 14*s.* (Rs. 307) by the Belgaum Municipalty.

Cattle Disease.

Seven forms of cattle disease are known in the district. *Hirebeni* or green disease, *kundrog* a disease caused by insufficient food, *bairog* or tongue disease, *kálbeni* or hoof disease, *damirog* or *gundgi rog* chest diseases, and *nebin byáni* or *tuhaki byáni* and *mahárog* or the great disease thought to be an animal cholera. In *hirebeni* the neck of the animal swells, saliva flows from the mouth, and a swelling forms in the eye. The animal hangs its head and refuses to eat. Great thirst is followed after a day and a half by diarrhœa. The urine becomes tinged with red or mixed with blood, the animal loses strength, lies down, and after a day or two dies. The dung is fetid and contains small portions of the entrails. The people treat the disease with the juice of the *nim* tree Azadirachta indica. *Kundrog* is said to be caused by insufficient or bad water. It lasts about three days and is sometimes fatal. The attack generally begins with a trembling fit. In *bairog* the tongue becomes black and covered with ulcers. Saliva flows from the mouth and the animal can neither eat nor drink. The disease is often cured by rubbing the tongue with *nellikai* or Phyllanthus emblica. In the disease called *kálbeni* the hoofs became full of small worms. It can generally be cured by applying worm poisons for about two months. In the disease called *nebin byáni* or *tuhaki byáni* the attack is sudden like cholera among men. During the attack the cattle neither eat nor drink. They are dull and restless and frequently pass reddish urine. Death generally follows in four or five days. In the disease called *damirog* or *gundgirog* the breathing becomes hard and the eyes bloodshot. The lungs seem to become congested, breathing is difficult, and the animal dies in one to fifteen days. In *mahárog* the nostrils are parched, the mouth swells, and the dung is watery. The people consider this a form of animal cholera.

Births and Deaths.

The total number of deaths shown in the Sanitary Commissioner's yearly reports for the eighteen years ending 1883 is 420,965 or an average mortality of 23,387 that is, according to the 1881 census, of

Chapter XII. Health. Births and Deaths.

twenty-seven in every thousand people. Of the average number of deaths 10,980 or 47·94 per cent were returned as due to fevers, 1948 or 8·32 per cent to cholera, 587 or 2·51 per cent to small-pox, 2104 or 8·99 per cent to bowel complaints, and 7466 or 31·96 per cent to miscellaneous diseases. Deaths from violence or injuries averaged 300 or 1·28 per cent of the average mortality. During the thirteen years ending 1883 the number of births was returned at 313,055 or an average yearly birth-rate of 24,081, or, according to 1881 census, twenty-eight per thousand. An examination of the death returns shows that fever, which, during the eighteen years ending 1883 caused an average yearly mortality of 10,980 or 47·94 per cent, was below the average in the nine years ending 1874 and in 1882 and 1883, and in the seven years ending 1881 was above the average. The six years ending 1871 had less than 6000 deaths from fever, the lowest total being 4126 in 1870, two years 1872 and 1873 had between 6000 and 7000, and three years 1874 1882 and 1883 had between 8000 and 10,000, the lowest total being 8428 in 1874. Of the seven years above the average, three years 1875 1876 and 1881 had between 11,000 and 15,000, two years 1879 and 1880 had between 15,000 and 20,000, and two years 1877 and 1878 had between 20,000 and 26,000. Of the deaths from cholera, which amounted to 35,074 and averaged 1948, 8357 or 23·82 per cent happened in 1877, 7808 or 22·26 per cent in 1869, 5757 or 16·41 per cent in 1878, and 4950 or 14·11 per cent in 1876. The only other years which were over the average were 1875 with 2736 and 1866 with 1962. Of the nine years below the average, 1882 had 1334 deaths, 1872 had 617, 1883 had 479, three years 1868 1870 and 1881 had between 300 and 400, and three years 1867 1871 and 1873 had below fifty. The remaining three years 1874 1879 and 1880 were free from cholera. Of the deaths from small-pox which amounted to 10,574 and averaged 587, 1292 or 12·21 percent happened in 1871, 3133 or 29·62 per cent in 1872, and 1112 or 10·51 per cent in 1877. Besides these years, three years had a more than average mortality from small-pox, 1867 with 887, 1875 with 693, and 1876 with 796. Of the twelve years below the average, two years 1874 and 1883 had between 550 and 400, three years 1866 1869 and 1870 between 400 and 300, two years 1868 and 1873 between 300 and 200, 1878 had 105 deaths, 1882 had forty-seven, and the remaining three years 1879 1880 and 1881 had below ten. Of the deaths from bowel complaints, which amounted to 37,878 or 2104 a year, eight were above the average and ten were below the average. The smallest number of deaths from bowel complaints in any one of the eighteen years was 308 in 1867, and the largest was 5632 in 1877. Injuries, with a total mortality of 5405 and an average of 300, varied from 160 in 1869 to 529 in 1877. Other causes with a total mortality of 134,393 and an average mortality of 7466 varied from 3365 in 1867 to 29,347 in 1877.

During the thirteen years for which birth returns are available the yearly totals varied from a lowest of 11,773 in 1878 to a highest of 35,078 in 1883 and averaged 24,081 or according to the 1881 census, twenty-eight in every thousand people. The details are :

Chapter XII.

Health.

Births and Deaths.

Belgaum Births and Deaths, 1866-1883.[1]

Year.	Deaths.							Births.
	Cholera.	Small-pox.	Fevers.	Bowel Complaints.	Injuries.	Other Causes.	Total.	
1866	1962	852	5518	417	198	4750	13,197	...
1867	4	887	5850	308	168	3365	10,582	..
1868	363	220	5420	365	172	4126	10,666	...
1869	7808	320	5060	442	160	6395	20,185	...
1870	302	326	4126	490	187	5807	11,238	...
1871	40	1292	5808	1656	276	5395	14,467	16,747
1872	617	3138	6761	1921	316	7420	20,168	17,609
1873	16	299	6610	1439	313	7044	15,721	19,845
1874	...	537	8428	1953	322	8437	19,677	24,912
1875	2736	693	14,772	2858	322	8683	30,064	30,257
1876	4950	796	12,681	3054	281	9259	31,021	27,563
1877	8357	1112	25,267	5632	529	29,347	70,244	22,425
1878	5757	105	25,381	2540	463	9962	44,208	11,773
1879	...	6	18,922	1901	424	5421	26,674	19,170
1880	...	5	15,666	2545	339	4943	23,498	24,184
1881	349	4	11,874	3026	327	4552	20,132	31,015
1882	1334	47	9932	3412	337	4958	20,015	32,477
1883	479	440	9565	3919	271	4534	19,208	35,078
Total ...	35,074	10,574	197,641	37,878	5405	134,393	420,965	313,055
Average ...	1948	587	10,980	2104	300	7466	23,387	24,081

[1] The deaths returns are believed to be fairly correct and the birth returns to be incomplete.

CHAPTER XIII.

SUB-DIVISIONS.

Chapter XIII.
Sub-Divisions.
Athni.

Athni, in the north-east of the district, is bounded on the north and north-east by Jath, the Bijápur sub-division of Bijápur, and Jamkhandi, on the east and south-east by Jamkhandi, on the south by Gokák and the Sángli and Kolhápur states, on the west by Miraj, and on the north-west by the Tásgaon sub-division of Sátára and by Sángli. It contains sixty-five Government and seventeen private or *inám* villages with 786 square miles, a population of 105,961 or 134 to the square mile, and a yearly land revenue of £15,862 (Rs. 1,58,620).

Area.

Of the 786 square miles, 743 have been surveyed in detail. According to the revenue survey returns, 195 square miles are occupied by the lands of alienated villages. The rest contains 343,483 acres or 89·81 per cent of arable land, 11,255 acres or 2·94 per cent of unarable land, 1820 or 0·47 per cent of grass, and 25,862 acres or 6·76 per cent of village sites, roads, rivers, and streams. From the 343,483 acres of arable land 96,925 acres have to be taken on account of alienated lands in Government villages.

Aspect.

The west of Athni is broken by bare flat-topped hills which rise from the plain in a succession of clearly marked terraces. The leveller country is a series of long undulations with small streams of running water in the hollows, bordered by belts of good soil. On the rises the soil is poorer and thinner supporting only the scantiest vegetation, and in places bare rock stretches for hundreds of yards. Among these bare stretches of rock, are more or less extensive tracts of black soil of uncertain depth, the waving trap being in one place several feet and a few yards off only some inches below the surface. The level plain of the Krishna is of deep rich alluvial mould whose strength is continually renewed by fresh deposits of silt. Its banks are generally wooded with *bábhul* groves which also cover many of the islands in its bed. Except a few *nimb* and tamarind trees near the sites of some of the villages the rest of Athni is bare and desolate. Along the Krishna the village sites are close together. In other parts, particularly in the north-east, the villages are five or six miles from each other. The sub-division is divided by a range of hills, which, rising in Sátára, runs nearly north and south, and, entering the district some eight miles east of Tásgaon, as it draws near the river, breaks into low single hills. To the east the country is barren with an occasional patch of good soil. The rainfall is scanty and uncertain and failure of crops is common. Westward when the hills are passed, the

Chapter XIII.
Sub-Divisions.
ATHNI.

improvement is marked and rapid. Except in the west where they are enclosed by hedges most of the villages are surrounded by walls ten to twelve feet high, furnished with three or four gates. The south, crossed by the winding Krishna, is an open plain of fine black soil with many small rich villages.

Soil.

For three or four miles on each side of the Krishna, and in the south-west, south, and south-east the soil is black and fertile. Bordering the Don a strip of land about nine miles by six is a rich loamy soil particularly suited for *rabi* or late crops. Except in the valleys of the Krishna and Don, the soil is coarse and poor and is best suited for *kharif* or early crops. The only garden lands are patches watered from wells. In the black soil there is little watering even from wells.

Climate.

Athni has generally a dry and healthy climate, but in years of excessive rain the cold months are feverish. Especially towards the east the early rainfall is often uncertain and partial. At Athni during the ten years ending 1882 the rainfall varied from 7 inches in 1876 to 34 inches in 1878 and averaged 24 inches.

Water.

In the south-west, south,and south-east, the chief source of water is the Krishna, and in the west and north-west the Agarni, a feeder of the Krishna, which runs from the north to the south of the sub-division and falls into the Krishna. Besides these two rivers are many small streams, most of which dry during the hot months. When these streams dry the people dig holes or shallow wells in their beds. Away from rivers and streams the chief supply is from wells and ponds which sometimes dry or get fouled in the hot months, and the people have to fetch water long distances from rivers and streams or stream-bed wells.

Stock.

According to the 1882-83 returns the farm stock included 1404 two-bullock and 1935 four-bullock ploughs, sixteen riding and 2121 load carts, 28,931 bullocks, 16,832 cows, 10,871 she-buffaloes, 3595 he-buffaloes, 1338 horses, 57,676 sheep and goats, 755 asses, and twenty-six camels.

Crops, 1882.

In 1881-82 of 233,353 acres held for tillage, 36,119 acres or 15·47 per cent were fallow or under grass. Of the remaining 197,234 acres 9478 were twice cropped. Of the 206,712 acres under tillage, grain crops occupied 157,136 acres or 76·01 per cent, 118,945 of them under Indian millet, *jvári* (M.) or *jola* (K.), Sorghum vulgare; 23,766 under spiked millet, *bájri* (M.) or *saji* (K.), Penicillaria spicata; 13,610 under wheat, *ghau* (M.) or *godi* (K.), Triticum æstivum; 471 under maize, *makai* (M.) or *mekke jola* (K.), Zea mays; 188 under rice, *bhát* (M.) or *bhatta* (K.), Oryza sativa; 120 under Italian millet, *rála* (M.) *káng* (M.) or *navni* (K.), Panicum italicum; 35 under *náchni* (M.) or *rági* (K.), Eleusine corocana; and one under barley, *java* (M.) *godhi* (K.), Hordeum hexastychon. Pulses occupied 17,251 acres or 8·34 per cent, 10,844 of them under gram, *harbhara* (M.) or *kadli* (K.), Cicer arietinum; 2084 under cajan pea, *tur* (M.) or *togri* (K.), Cajanus indicus; 1956 under *kulthi* (M.) or *hurli* (K.), Dolichos biflorus; 828 under *mug* (M.) or *hesaru* (K.), Phaseolus mungo; 10 under peas, *vatáni* (M.) and (K.),

Chapter XIII. Sub-Divisions. Athni.

Pisum sativum; 3 under lentils, *masur* (K.), Ervum lens; and 1526 under other pulses. Oil-seeds occupied 5958 acres or 2·88 per cent, 449 of them under rape, *shiras* (M). and (K.), Brassica napus; 54 under linseed, *javas* (M.) or *agsi* (K.), Linum usitatissimum; 45 under gingelly seed, *til* (M.) or *yellu* (K.) Sesamum indicum; and 5410 under other oil-seeds. Fibres occupied 24,287 acres or 11·74 per cent, 24,259 of them under cotton, *kápus* (M.) or *hatti* (K.), Gossypium herbaceum; and 28 under Bombay hemp, *tág* (M.) or *sanabu* (K.), Crotalaria juncea. Miscellaneous crops occupied 2080 acres or 1·00 per cent, 585 under chillies, *mirchi* (M.) or *menasinakai*, (K.), Capsicum frutescens, 352 under sugarcane, *us* (M.) or *kabbu* (K.), Saccharum officinarum, 332 under tobacco, *tambáku* (M.) or *hágesoppu*, Nicotiana tabacum, and the remaining 811 under various vegetables and fruits.

People, 1881.

The 1881 population returns show that of 105,961 people 95,045 or 89·69 per cent were Hindus, 10,909 or 10·29 per cent Musalmáns and 7 Christians. The details of the Hindu castes are 5110 Bráhmans; 11,617 Jáins, traders; 4 Komtis, grain-dealers; 2 Gujars, shopkeepers; 13,328 Maráthás, 1219 Radis, 709 Hanbars, 432 Guravs, 362 Kunbis, 341 Rajputs, 291 Lonáris, 269 Lamáns, 184 Chhatris, and 46 Tiláris, husbandmen; 1054 Panchâls, metal-workers; 1047 Ghanigerus, oilmen; 588 Sális, weavers; 583 Badgis, carpenters; 536 Sonárs, goldsmiths; 461 Kumbhárs, potters; 262 Shimpis, tailors; 137 Jingars, saddlers; 115 Hatkárs, handloom-weavers; 78 Lohárs, and 44 Ghisádis, blacksmiths; 27 Uppárs, saltmakers; 17 Kásárs, coppersmiths; and 14 Otáris, smelters; 27,434 Lingáyats; 620 Nhávis, barbers; 258 Parits, washermen; 9333 Dhangars, cowherds; 30 Gavlis, milkmen; 3436 Kolis, and 110 Bhois, fishermen; 27 Kalávants, musicians; 1770 Biadarus, labourers; 329 Korvis, basket-makers; 257 Beldárs, quarrymen; 250 Ilgers, palm-juice sellers; 188 Desbávals, bakers; 105 Rámoshis, watch-men; 70 Buruds, bamboo-workers; 60 Golls, or Gopáls, beggars; 29 Vadars, diggers; 20 Kaikádis, labourers; 120 Dásarus, 55 Gosávis, 37 Gondhlis, 29 Davris, 18 Kelikelars, 7 Bháts, and 2 Pichátis, beggars; 6433 Mhárs and 2796 Mángs, village servants; 1749 Chámbárs, leather-workers; 350 Dhors, tanners; 231 Láds, mutton-sellers; and 15 Bhangis, scavengers.

Chikodi.

Chikodi, in the extreme north-west of the district, is bounded on the north by Kolhápur and Athni, on the east by Gokák, on the south by Belgaum Gokák and Shahápur, and on the west by Kolhápur and the Kolhápur states. It contains 158 Government and fifty-seven private or *inám* villages with 840 square miles, a population of 245,614 or 292 to the square mile, and a yearly land revenue of £26,144 (Rs. 2,61,440).

Of the 840 square miles 670 have been surveyed in detail. According to the revenue survey returns, 243 square miles are occupied by the lands of alienated villages. The rest contains 312,055 acres or 81·63 per cent of arable land, 10,538 acres or 2·75 per cent of unarable land, 962 acres or 0·25 per cent of grass, 23,153 acres or 6·05 per cent of forests, and 35,555 acres or 9·30 per cent of village sites, roads, rivers, and streams. From the 312,055 acres of arable

Chapter XIII. Sub-Divisions. CHIKODI.

land 117,397 acres have to be taken on account of alienated lands in Government villages.

Aspect.

North Chikhodi is an open well-tilled black soil plain dotted with many rich villages. Two or three miles to the south the sub-division is crossed from east to west by a range of barren hills, and in the south, near Dádi Páchápur and Masti Kariat, the level is broken by occasional rises and hollows, covered with a scanty growth of stunted teak and other less valuable trees. The extreme south near Katabeli and Biran Holi is a land of hills and forests with little tillage. Near the Harankáshi and Krishna rivers are wide stretches of black soil, while the waterparting between the Krishna and the Ghatprabha is a tableland of poor soil 300 to 400 feet above the plain. As the supply of rain is chiefly from the south-west the early harvest is the more important.

Soil.

The rich black soil of the north gradually passes west into red. In the south, the soil is gritty and poor. The sub-division is famous for its sugarcane and fruit and vegetable gardens.

Climate.

In the north the climate is pleasant and healthy, in the centre it is fair, in the south damp and unhealthy. Towards the east the rainfall is partial, but in the south near the hills it is abundant. At Chikodi during the ten years ending 1882 the rainfall varied from 11 inches in 1873 to 37 inches in 1877 and averaged 25 inches.

Water.

In the north the chief supply of water is from the Krishna which runs from west to east. In the north-west, west, and south-west, the Dudhganga and the Vedganga, and in the south the Harankáshi and the Ghatprabha are the chief sources of water-supply. Besides these rivers many streams feed the Krishna, but in the hot season most of them dry or stand in pools. Besides these natural sources of water many wells and ponds yield a good and healthy supply. At Hukeri four reservoirs are filled with sweet healthy water brought three miles from Manoli. Nipáni has a large reservoir and nine ponds in different parts of the town, but the supply is somewhat scanty.

Stock.

According to the 1882-83 returns the farm stock included 4102 two-bullock and 4569 four-bullock ploughs, 220 riding and 5382 load carts, 53,055 bullocks, 2800 cows, 29,758 she-buffaloes, 12,495 he-buffaloes, 2223 horses, 86,268 sheep and goats, 821 asses, and eleven camels.

Crops, 1882.

In 1881-82 of 179,867 acres held for tillage, 25,237 acres or 14·03 per cent were fallow or under grass. Of the remaining 154,630 acres 11,938 were twice cropped. Of the 166,568 acres under tillage, grain crops occupied 114,608 acres or 68·80 per cent 79,522 of them under Indian millet, *jvári* (M.) or *jola* (K.), Sorghum vulgare; 15,004 under spiked millet, *bájri* (M.) or *sáji* (K.), Penicillaria spicata; 7884 under Italian millet, *rala* (M.) *káng* (M.) or *navni* (K.), Panicum italicum; 4795 under *náchni* (M.) or *rági* (K.), Eleusine corocana; 2309 under rice, *bhát* (M.) or *bhatta* (K.), Oryza sativa; 1409 under wheat, *ghau* (M.) or *godi* (K.), Triticum æstivum; 843 under maize, *makai* (M.) or *mekke jola* (K.), Zea mays;

146 under chenna, *sáva* (M.) and (K.), Panicum miliare; 65 under *kodra* (M.) *harika* (K.), Paspalum scrobiculatum; 56 under barley, *java* (M.) *godhi* (K.), Hordeum hexastychon; and 2575 under other grains of which details are not given. Pulses occupied 19,271 acres or 11·57 per cent 10,027 of them under cajan pea, *tur* (M.) or *togri* (K.), Cajanus indicus; 4318 under *kulthi* (M.) or *hurli* (K.), Dolichos biflorus; 3781 under gram, *harbhara* (M.) or *kadli* (K.), Cicer arietinum; 335 under *mug* (M.) or *hesaru* (K.), Phaseolus mungo; 241 under *udid* (M.) or *uddu* (K.), Phaseolus radiatus; 167 under peas, *vatáni* (M.) and (K.), Pisum sativum; 12 under lentils, *masur* (K.), Ervum lens; and 390 under other pulses. Oil-seeds occupied 7482 acres or 4·49 per cent, 424 under rape, *shiras* (M.) and (K.), Brassica napus, 133 under gingelly seed, *til* (M.) or *yellu* (K.), Sesamum indicum; 19 under linseed, *javas* (M.) or *agsi* (K.), Linum usitatissimum, and 6906 under other oilseeds. Fibres occupied 9988 acres or 5·99 per cent, 9395 of them under cotton, *kápus* (M.) *hatti* (K.), Gossypium herbaceum; 531 under brown hemp, *san* (M.) *pundi* (K.), Hibiscus cannabinus; and 62 under Bombay hemp, *tág* (M.) *sanabu* (K.), Crotalaria juncea. Miscellaneous crops occupied 15,219 acres or 9·13 per cent, 8769 under tobacco, *tambáku* (M.) or *hagesoppu*, Nicotiana tabacum; 3247 under chillies, *mirchi* (M.) or *menasinakai* (K.), Capsicum frutescens; 2006 under sugarcane *us* (M.) or *kabbu* (K.), Saccharum officinarum; and the remaining 1197 under various vegetables and fruits.

People, 1881.

The 1881 population returns show that of 245,614 people 228,507 or 93·03 per cent were Hindus, 17,067 or 6·94 per cent Musalmáns, and 40 Christians. The details of the Hindu castes are: 9279 Bráhmans; 21 Káyasth Prabhus, writers; 22,000 Jains, traders and husbandmen; 77 Gujars, shopkeepers; 59 Komtis, grain-dealers; 51 Bhátiás, cotton-dealers; 24 Nárvekárs, moneylenders; 14 Bándekars, grain-parchers; 34,726 Maráthás, 8929 Kunbis, 5554 Hanbars, 2309 Tiláris, 1545 Chhatris, 730 Rajputs, 410 Guravs, 249 Lonáris, 93 Lamáns, 51 Radis, and 24 Mithgávdás, husbandmen; 2513 Pancháls, metal-workers; 2286 Sális, weavers; 1656 Hatkárs, hand-loom weavers; 1048 Badgis, carpenters; 995 Sonárs, goldsmiths; 758 Kumbhárs, potters; 613 Ghánigerus, oilmen; 550 Shimpis, tailors; 306 Lohárs, blacksmiths; 144 Jingars, saddlers; 124 Kásárs, coppersmiths; 55 Uppárs, salt-makers; 21 Ghisádis, blacksmiths; and 16 Otáris, brass-smelters; 76,366 Lingáyats; 876 Parits, washermen; 864 Nhávis, barbers; 12,192 Dhangars, cowherds; 235 Gavlis, milkmen; 4460 Kolis and 366 Bhois, fishermen; 27 Ghadsis, musicians; 6274 Biadarus, labourers; 1011 Korvis, basket-makers; 724 Kolátis, rope-dancers; 245 Beldárs, quarrymen; 155 Buruds, bamboo-workers; 155 Ilgers, palm-juice sellers; 140 Dombáris, tumblers; 59 Vadars, diggers; 41 Kaikádis, labourers; 37 Bhandáris, palm-tappers; 30 Golls or Gopáls, beggars; 24 Rámoshis, watchmen; 13 Rávals, weavers; 2 Kaláls, liquor-sellers; 194 Gosávis, 159 Gondhlis, 103 Pichátis, 83 Dásarus, 69 Kánphátes, 54 Davris, 13 Bháts, 8 Danding-Dásarus, 6 Kelikelars, 5 Vásudevs, and 4 Oshtams, beggars; 17,897 Mhárs and 4617 Mángs, village servants; 2636 Chámbhárs, leather-workers; 792 Dhors, tanners; 331 Láds, mutton-sellers; 7 Chalvádis, Lingáyat beadles; and 3 Bhangis, scavengers.

Chapter XIII.
Sub-Divisions.
GOKÁK.

Goka'k in the east is bounded on the north by Athni, on the north-east by Sángli and Jamkhandi, on the east by Mudhol, on the south-east by Sángli and Belgaum, on the south by Rámdurg Parasgad and Sampgaon, on the west by Gad Hinglaj and Chikodi, and on the north-west by Kolhápur. It contains eighty-five Government and thirty-five private or *inám* villages with an area of 670 square miles, a population of 93,029 or 138 to the square mile, and a yearly land revenue of £13,144 (Rs. 1,31,440).

Area.

Of the 670 square miles, all of which have been surveyed in detail, 162 square miles are occupied by the lands of alienated villages. The rest, according to the revenue survey returns, contains 240,819 acres or 73·96 per cent of arable land, 5541 acres or 1·70 per cent of unarable land, 75 or 0·02 of grass, 61,200 acres or 18·79 per cent of forests, and 17,968 acres or 5·51 per cent of village sites, roads, rivers, and streams. From the 240,819 acres of arable land 88,511 acres have to be taken on account of alienated lands in Government villages.

Aspect.

Gokák lies along the Ghatprabha river near the centre of the district. On the left bank of the river most of the country is a black soil plain. Eastwards also the land is open but the soil is poorer with a considerable mixture of red. The west and south-west are covered with ranges of low bare sand-stone hills.

Soil.

Among the western hills the soil is poor and largely mixed with nodules of sandstone. Here and there in this hilly tract are patches of fine sand where small crops of coarse grain are raised. The north and south have a mixture of red and black soil, and in the east near Yádvad the soil is rich black.

Climate.

Gokák has the worst climate in Belgaum, feverish during the cold months and oppressive during the hot months. In the western hills the rainfall is abundant; but towards the east it is partial. At Gokák, during the ten years ending 1882, the rainfall varied from 7 inches in 1876 to 33 inches in 1877 and averaged 21 inches.

Water.

Besides the Ghatprabha, which flows north-east through the sub-division, several of its feeders, small streams which dry during the hot months, cross Gokák on their way to the Ghatprabha. The water of the ponds and wells is scanty and unwholesome.

Stock.

According to the 1882-83 returns the farm stock included 6416 two-bullock and 1599 four-bullock ploughs, eleven riding and 1798 load carts, 26,467 bullocks, 17,493 cows, 10,411 she-buffaloes, 5341 he-buffaloes, 721 horses, 55,952 sheep and goats, 653 asses, and one camel.

Crops, 1882.

In 1881-82 of 140,453 acres held for tillage, 20,561 acres or 14·63 per cent were fallow or under grass. Of the remaining 119,892 acres 8777 were twice cropped. Of the 128,669 acres under tillage, grain crops occupied 93,949 acres or 73·01 per cent, 70,726 of them under Indian millet, *jvári* (M.) or *jola* (K.), Sorghum vulgare; 11,052 under spiked millet, *bájri* (M.) or *saji* (K.), Penicillaria spicata; 9123 under wheat, *ghau* (M.) or *godi* (K.), Triticum æstivum; 2176 under Italian millet, *rála* (M.) *káng* (M.) or *navni* (K.), Panicum italicum; 593 under maize, *makái* (M.) or *mekke jola* (K.), Zea mays; 190 under *náchni* (M.) or *rági* (K.), Eleusine corocana; 69 under rice, *bhát* (M.) or *bhatta* (K.), Oryza sativa; 6 under chenna, *sáva* (M.)

Chapter XIII. Sub-Divisions. Gokák.

and (K.), Panicum miliare; and 14 under other grains of which details are not given. Pulses occupied 12,242 acres or 9·51 per cent, 5156 of them under *kulthi* (M.) or *hurli* (K.), Dolichos biflorus; 3349 under gram, *harbhara* (M.) or *kadli* (K.), Cicer arietinum; 2839 under cajan pea, *tur* (M.) or *togri* (K.), Cajanus indicus; 61 under *mug* (M.) or *hesaru* (K.), Phaseolus mungo; one under peas, *vatáni* (M.) and (K.), Pisum sativum; and 836 under other pulses. Oilseeds occupied 7020 acres or 5·45 per cent, 223 of them under gingelly seed, *til* (M.) or *yellu* (K.), Sesamum indicum; 168 under linseed, *javas* (M.) or *agsi* (K.), Linum usitatissimum; and 6629 under other oilseeds. Fibres occupied 13,898 acres or 10·80 per cent, 13,785 of them under cotton, *kápus* (M.) *hatti* (K.), Gossypium herbaceum; 101 under Bombay hemp, *tág* (M.) *sanabu* (K.), Crotalaria juncea; 12 under brown hemp, *san* (M.) *pundi* (K.), Hibiscus cannabinus. Miscellaneous crops occupied 1560 acres or 1·21 per cent, 675 under chillies, *mirchi* (M.) or *menasinakai* (K.), Capsicum frutescens; 213 under sugarcane, *us* (M.) or *kabbu* (K.), Saccharum officinarum: 78 under tobacco, *tambáku* (M.) or *hagesoppu*, Nicotiana tabacum; and the remaining 594 under various vegetables and fruits.

People, 1881.

The 1881 population returns show that of 93,029 people 87,094 or 93·62 per cent were Hindus, 5909 or 6·35 per cent Musalmáns, 14 Christians, 11 Pársis, and one a Jew. The details of the Hindu castes are 2655 Bráhmans; 2100 Jains; 3 Gujars, traders; 4076 Chhatris, 3342 Maráthás, 2940 Radis, 1070 Hanbars, 213 Rajputs, 120 Lamáns, 69 Guravs, 26 Lonáris, husbandmen; 5925 Uppárs, salt-makers; 1377 Sális, weavers; 1126 Panchál, metal-workers; 482 Ghánigerus, oilmen; 393 Badgis, carpenters; 343 Patvegárs, dyers; 314 Shimpis, tailors; 308 Kumbhárs, potters; 235 Sonárs, goldsmiths; 158 Lohárs, blacksmiths; 43 Jingars, saddlers; 28,981 Lingáyats; 521 Nhávis, barbers; 134 Parits, washermen; 12,343 Dhangars, cowherds; 44 Gavlis, milkmen; 2401 Kolis and 107 Bhois, fishermen; 52 Devlis, temple servants; 7830 Biadarus, labourers; 530 Korvis, basket-makers; 199 Dombáris, tumblers; 196 Beldárs, quarrymen; 188 Ilgers, palm-juice sellers; 148 Korchars, hunters; 37 Golls or Gopáls, beggars; 15 Kaikádis, labourers; 14 Vadars, diggers; 12 Rámoshis, watchmen; 146 Dásars, 88 Gosávis, 37 Gondhlis, 35 Oshtams, 12 Bháts, and 2 Vásudevs, beggars; 3265 Mhárs, village servants; 1866 Mángs, village servants; 261 Chámbhárs, leather-workers; 245 Dhors, tanners; 61 Láds, mutton-sellers; and 6 Chalvádis, Lingáyat beadles.

Parasgad.

Parasgad in the south-east is bounded on the north by Gokák, on the east by Rámdurg and Torgal, on the south by Dhárwár, and on the west by Sampgaon. It contains 110 Government and twenty-three private or *inám* villages, with an area of 640 square miles, a population of 91,826 or 143 to the square mile, and a yearly land revenue of £18,744 (Rs. 1,87,440).

Area.

Of the 640 square miles, all of which have been surveyed in detail, 100 square miles are occupied by the lands of alienated villages. The rest, according to the revenue survey returns, contains 280,587 acres or 82·12 per cent of arable land, 1893 acres or 0·55 per cent

Chapter XIII.
Sub-Divisions.
PARASGAD.

of unarable land, 83 acres or 0·02 per cent of grass, and 59,080 acres or 17·29 per cent of village sites, roads, rivers, and streams. From the 280,587 acres of arable land 109,072 acres have to be taken on account of alienated lands in Government villages.

Aspect.

A low range of sand-stone hills lying north-west and south-east divides Parasgad into two nearly equal parts. South-west of the hills, whose southern face is steep and rugged, is a plain of fine black soil with many rich villages and hamlets which suffered severely in the 1876-77 famine. The north-east which is broken by low hills, is a high waving plateau the soil mostly poor and sandy, overgrown with bush and prickly pear. In the extreme north the sand-stone gives place to trap and the soil is generally shallow and much of it poor. The Malprabha enters the sub-division from the west, and, after a winding easterly course, turns north, and, forcing its way through a wild ravine some four miles from Saundatti, crosses the eastern border into Rámdurg.

Soil.

In parts of the north of the sub-division the soil is sandy and poor. In other parts it is generally black and of excellent quality. The most important crop of the southern half of the sub-division is cotton which is grown once in three years in turn with grain-crops.

Climate.

During the hot weather the climate is oppressive, but during the cold and rainy seasons it is pleasant. In some parts in the north and in the east the rainfall is scanty and uncertain; but in the south and west and in the immediate neighbourhood of the Sahyádris it is plentiful. At Saundatti, the head-quarters station of the sub-division, during the ten years ending 1882 the rainfall varied from 13 inches in 1873 to 41 inches in 1874 and averaged 23 inches.

Water.

The Malprabha, which runs north-east through the middle of the sub-division, and several of the Malprabha's local feeders are the chief water supply. Before the close of the hot season almost all the small streams dry and stagnate and the well and pond water is both scanty and unwholesome.

Stock.

According to the 1882-83 returns the farm stock included 5740 two-bullock and 1769 four-bullock ploughs, thirty-three riding and 3010 load carts, 25,683 bullocks, 13,623 cows, 9608 she-buffaloes, 3690 he-buffaloes, 808 horses, 51,007 sheep and goats, and 630 asses.

Crops, 1882.

In 1881-82 of 152,787 acres held for tillage, 12,535 acres or 8·20 per cent were fallow or under grass. Of the remaining 140,252 acres 13,732 were twice cropped. Of the 153,984 acres under tillage, grain crops occupied 106,941 acres or 69·45 per cent, 63,057 of them under Indian millet, *jvári* (M.) or *jola* (K.), Sorghum vulgare; 31,065 under wheat, *ghau* (M.) or *godi* (K.), Triticum æstivum, 6753 under Italian millet, *rála* (M.) *káng* (M.) or *navni* (K.), Panicum italicum; 6042 under spiked millet, *bájri* (M.) or *saji* (K.), Penicillaria spicata; 9 under rice, *bhát* (M.) or *bhatta* (K.), Oryza sativa; 9 under *kodra* (M.) or *harika* (K.), Paspalum scrobiculatum; 2 under maize, *makái* (M.) or *mekke jola* (K.), Zea mays; and 4 under other grains of which details are not given. Pulses occupied 12,013 acres or 7·80 per cent, 4221 of them under cajan pea, *tur* (M.) or *togri* (K.), Cajanus indicus; 3840 under *kulthi* (M.) or *hurli* (K.), Dolichos biflorus; 3411 under gram, *harbhara* (M.) or *kadli* (K.), Cicer arietinum; 181 under *mug* (M.) or *hesaru* (K.), Phaseolus mungo; and 360 under other pulses. Oilseeds occupied 7901 acres or 5·13 per cent, 1265 of them under linseed, *javas* (M.) or *agsi* (K.), Linum usitatissimum; 67 under gingelly seed, *til* (M.) or *yellu* (K.), Sesamum indicum; and 6569 under other oilseeds. Fibres occupied 26,671 acres or 17·32 per cent 26,608 of them under cotton, *kápus* (M.) or *hatti* (K.), Gossypium herbaceum; and 63 under Bombay hemp, *tág* (M.) *sanabu* (K.), Crotalaria juncea. Miscellaneous crops occupied 458 acres or 0·29 per cent, 88 under sugarcane, *us* (M.) or *kabbu* (K.), Saccharum officinarum; 87 under chillies, *mirchi* (M.) or *menasinakai* (K.), Capsicum frutescens; 2 under tobacco, *tambáku* (M.) or *hagesoppu*, Nicotiana tabacum; and the remaining 281 under various vegetables and fruits.

Chapter XIII. Sub-Divisions. PARASGAD.

The 1881 population returns show that of 91,826 people 85,442 or 93·04 per cent were Hindus and 6384 or 6·95 per cent Musalmáns. The details of the Hindu castes are: 2618 Bráhmans; 1023 Jains, 17 Komtis, and 7 Gujars, traders; 4038 Chhatris, 3321 Maráthás, 1943 Radis, 1066 Hanbars, 433 Lamáns, 411 Rajputs, and 99 Guravs, husbandmen; 2542 Uppars, salt-makers; 1771 Pancháls, metal workers; 1363 Ghánigerus, oilmen; 1177 Sális, weavers; 1155 Hatkárs, hand-loom weavers; 409 Kumbhárs, potters; 402 Shimpis, tailors; 203 Lohárs, blacksmiths; 211 Badgis, carpenters; 174 Sonárs, goldsmiths; 16 Kásárs, coppersmiths; 13 Jingars, saddlers; and 7 Otáris, smelters; 31,905 Lingáyats; 876 Nhávis, barbers; 350 Parits, washermen; 12,681 Dhangars, cowherds; 1939 Kolis and 105 Bhois, fishermen; 4 Kalávants, musicians; 6708 Biadarus, labourers; 472 Korvis, basket-makers; 248 Desháváls, bakers; 223 Beldárs, quarrymen; 208 Ilgers, palm-juice sellers; 147 Dombáris, tumblers; 95 Golls or Gopáls, beggars; 86 Buruds, bamboo-workers; 65 Rávals, weavers; 31 Vadars, diggers; 78 Dásarus, 77 Kelikelars, 67 Gosávis, 40 Oshtams, 36 Pingles, 22 Gondhlis, and 15 Bháts, beggars; 2687 Mángs and 1365 Mhárs, village servants; 262 Chámbhárs, leather workers; 136 Láds, mutton sellers; 68 Dhors, tanners; 27 Chalvádis, Lingáyat beadles.

People, 1881.

Sampgaon in the south-east is bounded on the north by Gokák, on the east by Parasgad, on the south by Dhárwár, and on the west by Belgaum and Khánápur. It contains 139 Government and one private or *inám* villages with an area of 424 square miles, a population of 119,843 or 282 to the square mile, and a yearly land revenue of £23,913 (Rs. 2,39,130).

SAMPGAON.

Of the 424 square miles, all have been surveyed in detail. According to the revenue survey returns, twenty-two square miles are occupied by the lands of alienated villages. The rest contains 217,179 acres or 86·70 per cent of arable land, 4223 acres or 1·67 per cent of unarable land, 1277 acres or 0·50 per cent of grass, 16,627 acres or 6·59 per cent of forests, and 12,927 acres or 5·12 per cent of village sites, roads, rivers, and streams. From

Area.

Chapter XIII. Sub-Divisions.

the 217,179 acres of arable land 52,998 acres have to be taken on account of alienated lands in Government villages.

SAMPGAON. *Aspect.*

Sampgaon has much variety of soil and surface. From the hilly west, the country gradually sinks eastwards into a great black cotton plain. In the south-west ranges of quartz and iron stone about 150 feet high and a quarter to half a mile apart run nearly north and south. Further south round Kittur though well peopled with many small villages and hamlets the land is generally hilly, and in the extreme south-west are timber-covered hills some of which have been set apart as Government forest land.

Soil.

The soil for the most part is black with a few red and stony patches in the south.

Climate.

Except during the hot east winds of March and April and an occasional cold blighting east wind in November and December, the climate is temperate. In December January and February the west and south, where the rainfall is heavy are feverish. At Sampgaon during the ten years ending 1882, the rainfall varied from 15 inches in 1872 and 1873 to 38 inches in 1874 and averaged 29 inches.

Water.

In the middle of the sub-division the chief source of water is the Malprabha which crosses the middle of the sub-division from west to east. Feeders of the Malprabha water the land on either bank but all except three dry or stand in pools during the hot weather. The well and pond water is healthy and sufficient.

Stock.

According to the 1882-83 returns the farm stock included 9271 two-bullock and 1561 four-bullock ploughs, ten riding and 5025 load carts, 25,345 bullocks, 16,399 cows, 17,492 she-buffaloes, 8576 he-buffaloes, 928 horses, 28,067 sheep and goats, and 456 asses.

Crops, 1882.

In 1881-82 of 158,320 acres held for tillage, 18,598 acres or 11·74 per cent were fallow or under grass. Of the remaining 139,722 acres 17,726 were twice cropped. Of the 157,448 acres under tillage, grain crops occupied 115,281 acres or 73·21 per cent 70,119 of them under Indian millet, *jvári* (M.) or *jola* (K.), Sorghum vulgare; 17,360 under Italian millet, *rála* (M.) *káng* (M.) or *navni* (K.), Panicum italicum; 14,310 under rice, *bhát* (M.) or *bhatta* (K.), Oryza sativa; 7811 under wheat, *ghau* (M.) or *godi* (K.), Triticum æstivum; 2595 under *náchni* (M.) or *rági* (K.), Eleusine corocana; 2266 under spiked millet *bájri* (M.) or *saji* (K.) ,Penicillaria spicata; 17 under chenna, *sáva* (M.) and (K.), Panicum miliare; 11 under maize, *makái* (M.) or *mekke jola* (K.), Zea mays; and 792 under other grains of which details are not given. Pulses occupied 18,637 acres or 11·83 per cent, 7331 of them under cajan pea, *tur* (M.) or *togri* (K.), Cajanus indicus; 4776 under *kulthi* (M.) or *hurli* (K.), Dolichos biflorus; 3177 under gram, *harbhara* (M.) or *kadli* (K.), Cicer arietinum; 976 under *mug* (M.) or *hesaru* (K.), Phaseolus mungo; 687 under peas, *vatáni* (M.)and (K.), Pisum sativum; 309 under *udid* (M.) or *uddu* (K.), Phaseolus radiatus; 37 under lentils, *masur* (K.), Ervum lens; and 1344 under other pulses. Oilseeds occupied 3504 acres or 2·22 per cent, 209 of them under rape, *shiras* (M.) and (K.),

Brassica napus; 198 under gingelly seed, *til* (M.) or *yellu* (K.), Sesamum indicum; one under linseed, *javas* (M.) or *agsi* (K.), Linum usitatissimum; and 3096 under other oilseeds. Fibres occupied 16,452 acres or 10·44 per cent, 15,949 of them under cotton, *kápus* (M.) or *hatti* (K.), Gossypium herbaceum; 500 under Bombay hemp, *tág* (M.) *sanabu* (K.), Crotalaria juncea; and 3 under brown hemp, *san* (M.) *pundi* (K.), Hibiscus cannabinus. Miscellaneous crops occupied 3574 acres or 2·27 per cent, 2368 of them under chillies, *mirchi* (M.) or *menasinakai* (K.), Capsicum frutescens; 604 under sugarcane, *us* (M.) or *kabbu* (K.), Saccharum officinarum; 133 under tobacco, *tambáku* (M.) or *hágesoppu*, (K.) Nicotiana tabacum; and the remaining 469 under various vegetables and fruits.

People, 1881.

The 1881 population returns show that of 119,843 people 109,713 or 91·54 per cent were Hindus, 10,027 or 8·36 per cent Musalmáns, and 103 Christians. The details of the Hindu castes are: 2031 Bráhmans; 3161 Jains, traders; 206 Nárvekars, moneylenders; 55 Bándekars, grain-parchers; 6 Gujars, shopkeepers; 6023 Maráthás, 3098 Chhatris, 1011 Hanbars, 461 Tiláris, 350 Guravs, 323 Rajputs, 136 Radis, 43 Kulmárus, and 13 Lamáns, husbandmen; 5056 Sális, weavers; 2347 Panchális, metal-workers; 931 Ghánigerus, oilmen; 727 Shimpis, tailors; 676 Kumbhárs, potters; 443 Sonárs, goldsmiths; 425 Badgis, carpenters; 326 Lohárs, blacksmiths; 50 Kásárs, coppersmiths; 17 Jingars, saddlers; and 15 Otáris, brass-smelters; 50,731 Lingáyats; 1062 Nhávis, barbers; 528 Parits, washermen; 10,170 Dhangars, cowherds; 2996 Kolis, 295 Bhois, and 12 Gábits, fishermen; 7435 Biadarus, labourers; 641 Korvis, basket-makers; 303 Buruds, bamboo-workers; 251 Beldárs, quarrymen; 232 Ilgers, palm-juice sellers; 172 Dombáris, tumblers; 147 Rávals, weavers; 51 Gopáls, beggars; 35 Vadars, diggers; 8 Rámoshis, watchmen; and 5 Kaláls, liquor-sellers; 141 Dásarus, 104 Gosávis, 41 Gondhlis, 14 Kelikelars, 10 Oshtams, 5 Bháts, and one Vásudev, beggars; 3207 Mángs and 2718 Mhárs, village servants; 249 Chámbhárs, leather-workers; 91 Láds, mutton-sellers; 64 Chalvádis, Lingáyát beadles; 64 Dhors, tanners.

BELGAUM.

Belgaum in the west is bounded on the north by Kolhápur and Chikodi, on the east by Gokák and Sampgaon, on the south by Khánápur and Sávantvádi, and on the west by Kolhápur and Sávantvádi. It contains 122 Government and eighty-one private or *inám* villages with an area of 663 square miles, a population of 128,477 or 193 to the square mile, and a yearly land revenue of £15,041 (Rs. 1,50,410).

Area.

Of the 663 square miles 486·5 have been surveyed in detail. According to the revenue survey returns, 279 square miles are occupied by the lands of alienated villages. The rest contains 158,983 acres or 64·73 per cent of arable land, 3471 acres or 1·41 per cent of unarable land, 2528 acres or 1·02 per cent of grass, 68,813 acres or 28·01 per cent of forests, and 11,803 acres or 4·80 per cent of village sites, roads, rivers, and streams. From the 158,983 acres of arable land 37,372 acres have to be taken on account of alienated lands in Government villages.

Chapter XIII.
Sub-Divisions.
BELGAUM.
Aspect.

In north-west Belgaum, the old Pádshápur sub-division, long sandstone ridges border and in many places cross the central plain. The villages are built on the banks of streams which rise in the hills, and except a few which fall into the Ghatprabha, flow north-east to the Márkandaya. Round Belgaum town are raised, rounded, bare plains of an ochry gravel in places almost as hard as stone. Along the brooks which run in the hollows between these uplands are large flats of rich black loam. Towards the south-east near Nágevádi, within the limits of the Malprabha valley, the land is plain and open. But to the west, where only the district stretches to the crest of the Sahyádris, the surface is covered first by swelling hills neither very high nor very steep, and with broad spaces fit for tillage at their bases. Further west near Chándgad the hills are steeper and more covered with brushwood, and the extreme west is a series of valleys running east and west between spurs from the Sahyádris. These western tracts are well watered draining north along Chandgad, Pátna, and Hira into the Ghatprabha at Mohanji.

Soil.

In the south and east the soil is a mixed red and black suitable for Indian millet and rice. In the west and north the soil is chiefly red with a few plots of black. The red soil is poor and after every crop requires a fallow. In the hilly west *kumri* or wood-ash tillage is allowed. The bushes are cut during the hot months and burnt to ashes before the rains set in. Only coarse grain is sown and the yield is poor.

Climate.

In the west close to the Sahyádris the climate is damp and unhealthy; and fever is common both during the rainy and the cold seasons. During the cold weather the east sometimes suffers from blighting east winds. Otherwise the climate of the east is pleasant, the heat of the hot weather being tempered by cool sea breezes, and the rainfall being moderate. At Belgaum, during the ten years ending 1882, the rainfall varied from 33 inches in 1880 to 71 inches in 1882 and averaged 50 inches.

Water.

Except in seasons of failure of rain the supply of water is abundant. The sub-division is crossed by many unfailing streams which flow either to join the Ghatprabha in Gokák or the Malprabha in Khánápur. Besides these streams many ponds and wells have a good and plentiful supply.

Stock.

According to the 1882-83 returns the farm stock included 11,781 two-bullock and 1226 four-bullock ploughs, 343 riding and 3585 load carts, 28,604 bullocks, 22,777 cows, 14,737 she-buffaloes, 10,238 he-buffaloes, 439 horses, 7368 sheep and goats, and forty-one asses.

Crops, 1882.

In 1881-82, of 113,313 acres held for tillage, 47,622 acres or 42·02 per cent were fallow or under grass. Of the remaining 65,691 acres 5564 were twice cropped. Of the 71,255 acres under tillage, grain crops occupied 58,101 or 81·54 per cent, 19,841 of them under rice *bhát* (M.) or *bhatta* (K.), Oryza sativa; 14,037 under Indian millet, *jvári* (M.) or *jola* (K.), Sorghum vulgare; 10,617 under *náchni* (M.) or *rági* (K.), Eleusine corocana; 6441 under chenna, *sáva* (M.) and (K.), Panicum miliare; 2944 under *kodra* (M.) or *harika*

Crops, 1882.

(K.), Paspalum scrobiculatum; 2143 under Italian millet, *rála* (M.) *káng* (M.) or *navni* (K.), Panicum italicum; 476 under wheat, *ghau* (M.) or *godi* (K.), Triticum æstivum; 53 under spiked millet, *bájri* (M.) or *saji* (K.), Penicillaria spicata; 33 under maize, *makái* (M.) or *mekke jola* (K.), Zea mays; and 1516 under other grains of which details are not given. Pulses occupied 7631 acres or 10·70 per cent, 3048 of them under Cajan pea, *tur* (M.) or *togri* (K.), Cajanus indicus; 1367 under peas, *vatáni* (M.) and (K.), Pisum sativum; 1233 under lentils, *masur* (K.), Ervum lens; 1003 under *kulthi* (M.) or *kurli* (K.), Dolichos biflorus; 417 under gram, *harbhara* (M.) or *kadli* (K.), Cicer arietinum; 14 under *udid* (M.) or *uddu* (K.), Phaseolus radiatus; and 549 under other pulses. Oilseeds occupied 2529 acres or 3·55 per cent, of which 2325 were under gingelly seed, *til* (M.) or *yellu* (K.), Sesamum indicum; 108 under mustard, *rái* (M.) *sásive* (K.), Sinapis racemosa; and 96 under other oilseeds. Fibres occupied 1628 acres or 2·28 per cent, 1405 of them under cotton *kápus* (M.) *hatti* (K.), Gossypium herbaceum; 195 under Bombay hemp, *tág* (M.) *sanabu* (K.), Crotalaria juncea; and 28 under brown hemp, *san* (M.) *pundi* (K.) Hibiscus cannabinus. Miscellaneous crops occupied 1366 acres or 1·91 per cent, of which 773 under chillies, *mirchi* (M.) or *menasinakai* (K.), Capsicum frutescens; 480 under sugarcane, *us* (M.) or *kabbu* (K.), Saccharum officinarum; and the remaining 113 under various vegetables and fruits.

People, 1881.

The 1881 population returns show that of 128,477 people 113,617 or 88·43 per cent were Hindus, 11,151 or 8·67 per cent Musalmáns, 3568 or 2·77 per cent Christians, 88 Jews, and 53 Pársis. The details of the Hindu castes are: 6031 Bráhmans, 269 Mudliars, 70 Káyasth Prabhus, and 43 Naidus, writers; 2778 Jains, traders; 729 Bándekars, grain-parchers; 711 Nárvekars and 77 Kalváris, money-lenders; 76 Komtis, grain-dealers; 36 Márwáris, usurers; 19 Bhátiás, traders; 7 Gujars, shopkeepers; 49,880 Maráthás, 4836 Kunbis, 2754 Tiláris, 2730 Hanbars, 687 Chhatris, 559 Rajputs, 43 Lonáris, 38 Guravs, 19 Kámáthis, 8 Lamáns, and 7 Radis, husbandmen; 1915 Sális, weavers; 1109 Pancháls, metal-workers; 1076 Shimpis, tailors; 886 Badgis, carpenters; 856 Ghánigerus, oilmen; 708 Sonárs, goldsmiths; 703 Kumbhárs, potters; 267 Lohárs, blacksmiths; 220 Patvegárs, dyers; 145 Jingars, saddlers; and 12 Ghisádis, blacksmiths; 13,209 Lingáyats; 645 Nhávis, barbers; 471 Parits, washermen; and 117 Madrásis, servants; 1640 Dhangars, cowherds and 115 Gavlis, milkmen; 609 Kolis and 186 Bhois, fishermen; 19 Kalávants, musicians; 8 Devlis, temple-servants; 5346 Biadarus, labourers; 622 Bhandáris, palm-tappers; 266 Beldárs, quarrymen; 242 Buruds, bamboo-workers; 195 Dombáris, tumblers; 175 Ilgers, palm-juice sellers; 145 Korchars, labourers and hunters; 60 Korvis, basket-makers; 58 Desháváls, bakers; 30 Kaláls, liquor-sellers; 22 Rávals, weavers; and 10 Vadars, diggers; 160 Gosávis, 45 Gondhlis, 14 Davris, 12 Bagdis, 10 Bháts, 8 Joshis, 6 Dásars, 4 Kelikelars, 3 Pingles, and 3 Vásudevs, beggars; 6707 Mhárs, and 979 Mángs, village-servants; 1007 Chámbhárs, leather-workers; 91 Bhangis, scavengers; 72 Dhors, tanners; and 2 Láds, mutton-sellers.

Chapter XIII.
Sub-Divisions.
KHÁNÁPUR.

Kha'na'pur in the south-west is bounded on the north by Belgaum, on the east by Sampgaon and Dhárwár, on the south by North Kánara, and on the west by Goa and Sávantvádi. It contains 215 Government and twenty-five private or *inám* villages with an area of 633 square miles, a population of 79,264 or 125 to the square mile, and a yearly land revenue of £11,308 (Rs. 1,13,080).

Area.

Of the 633 square miles, 626·7 have been surveyed in detail. According to the revenue survey returns, eighty-six square miles are occupied by the lands of alienated villages. The rest contains 159,669 acres or 45·57 per cent of arable land, 1796 acres or 0·51 per cent of unarable land, 1690 acres or 0·48 per cent of grass, 174,534 acres or 49·81 per cent of forests, and 12,664 acres or 3·61 per cent of village sites, roads, rivers, and streams. From the 159,669 acres of arable land 36,400 acres have to be taken on account of alienated lands in Government villages.

Aspect.

The Khánápur sub-division is varied and in parts beautiful. Especially in the south and south-west it is crowded with hills and dense forest, the people are few and unsettled, and, except in patches, tillage disappears. Towards Jámboti and in the north-west near Bailur in Belgaum, the hills are especially lofty, their bases far stretching, their outlines bold and clear cut, and their sides clothed with rich evergreen brushwood. In the centre, north-east, and east, along the Malprabha valley the country is an open well tilled black soil plain with many rich and populous villages.

Soil.

Except towards the east where there is poor black soil, the soil is red and stony, some parts so poor that after a crop it has to rest several years.

Climate.

The climate is temperate and healthy during the hot months, feverish in the cold season, and sickly during the south-west rains. At Khánápur during the ten years ending 1882 the rainfall varied from 46 inches in 1880 to 77 inches in 1878 and averaged 63 inches.

Water.

In the north the chief source of water is the Malprabha, which runs west to east, and, besides the Malprabha, many of its local feeders hold water till the middle of the hot weather. Except in some parts in the east the supply of well water though ample is bad.

Stock.

According to the 1882-83 returns the farm stock included 10,494 two-bullock and ten four-bullock ploughs, eight riding and 2618 load carts, 25,955 bullocks, 23,213, cows, 7869 she-buffaloes, 7712 he-buffaloes, 271 horses, 6271 sheep and goats, and 137 asses.

Crops, 1882.

In 1881-82 of 94,727 acres held for tillage, 36,143 acres or 38·15 per cent were fallow or under grass. Of the remaining 58,584 acres 2706 were twice cropped. Of the 61,290 acres under tillage, grain crops occupied 52,321 acres or 85·36 per cent, 28,048 of them under rice, *bhát* (M.) or *bhatta* (K.), Oryza sativa; 11,784 under *náchni* (M.) or *rági* (K.), Eleusine corocana; 6539 under Indian millet, *jvári* (M.) or *jola* (K.), Sorghum vulgare; 2806 under chenna, *sáva* (M.) and (K.), Panicum miliare; 1580 under Italian millet, *rála*

Chapter XIII. Sub-Divisions. KHÁNÁPUR. Crops, 1882.

(M.) *káng* (M.) or *navni* (K.), Panicum italicum; 1342 under *kodra* (M.) or *hárika* (K.), Paspalum scrobiculatum; 198 under spiked millet, *bájri* (M.) or *sáji* (K.), Penicillaria spicata; 19 under maize, *makái* (M.) or *mekke jola* (K.), Zea mays; and 5 under wheat, *ghau* (M.) or *godi* (K.) Triticum æstivum. Pulses occupied 5722 acres or 9·33 per cent, 2926 of them under *kulthi* (M.) or *hurli* (K.), Dolichos biflorus; 1147 under peas, *vatáni* (M.) (K.), Pisum sativum; 555 under gram, *harbhara* (M.) or *kadli* (K.), Cicer arietinum; 207 under cajan pea, *tur* (M.) or *togri* (K.), Cajanus indicus; 52 under lentils, *masur* (K.), Ervum lens; and 835 under other pulses. Oil-seeds occupied 2184 acres or 3·56 per cent 1677 of them under gingelly seed, *til* (M.) or *yellu* (K.), Sesamum indicum; and 507 under other oilseeds. Fibres occupied 64 acres or 0·10 per cent, 33 of them under Bombay hemp, *tág* (M.) *sanabu* (K.), Crotalaria juncea; 25 under brown hemp, *san* (M.) *pundi* (K.), Hibiscus cannabinus; and 6 under cotton, *kápus* (M.) *hatti* (K.), Gossypium herbaceum. Miscellaneous crops occupied 999 acres or 1·63 per cent, 433 of them under sugarcane, *us* (M.) or *kabbu* (K.), Saccharum officinarum; 232 under chillies, *mirchi* (M.) or *menasinakai* (K.), Capsicum frutescens; 84 under coffee, *káphi* (M.) or *bundu* (K.), Coffea arabica; and the remaining 250 under various vegetables and fruits.

People, 1881.

The 1881 population returns show that of 79,264 people 71,859 or 90·65 per cent were Hindus, 4815 or 6·07 per cent Musalmáns, and 2590 or 3·26 per cent Christians. The details of the Hindu castes are: 2692 Bráhmans; 2312 Jains; 1161 Nárvekars, moneylenders, 540 Bándekars, grain-parchers; 6 Márwáris, traders and merchants; 28,523 Kunbis, 8666 Maráthás, 2029 Hanbars, 662 Chhatris, 120 Rajputs, 40 Lamáns, and 32 Kulmárus, husbandmen; 940 Sonárs, goldsmiths; 857 Lohárs, blacksmiths; 694 Kumbhárs, potters; 541 Badgis, carpenters; 438 Shimpis, tailors; 436 Ghánigerus, oilmen; 359 Sális, weavers; 37 Jingars, saddlers; 25 Otáris, brass-smelters; 5 Kásárs, coppersmiths; 8944 Lingáyats; 491 Nhávis, barbers; 450 Parits, washermen; 1371 Dhangars, cowherds; and 125 Gavlis, milkmen; 345 Kolis and 88 Bhois, fishermen; 45 Devlis, temple servants; 1916 Biadarus, labourers; 644 Bhandáris, palm-tappers; 302 Korvis, basket-makers; 254 Beldars, quarrymen; 231 Buruds, bamboo-workers; 153 Dombáris, tumblers; 58 Golls or Gopáls, beggars; and 22 Vadars, diggers; 225 Gosávis, 20 Joshis, 18 Gondhlis, 8 Bháts and 4 Pingles, beggars; 3612 Mhárs and 805 Mángs, village-servants; 298 Chámbhárs, leather-workers; 189 Láds, mutton sellers; and 126 Dhors, tanners.

CHAPTER XIV.

PLACES.

Chapter XIV.

Places.

AINÁPUR.

Aina'pur, on the Athni-Kágvád road about thirteen miles south-west of Athni, is a large village with in 1872 a population of 4416 and in 1881 of 4357. The village has a post office and a Government Kánarese school. Outside of the village, to the south near a large pond is the tomb of a Musalmán saint called Pir Káji. In 1639 the French traveller Mandelslo notices it as Eynatour.[1] In 1791 Captain Moor, afterwards author of the Hindu Pantheon, who was then serving with the British detachment which was sent to help the Maráthás against Tipu, describes Ainápur as having a large Musalmán population with several good buildings both in the Hindu and Musalmán styles.[2] In 1842 Ainápur with eight other villages lapsed to the British Government on the death without heirs, of Gopálrav the representative of one branch of the Miraj Patvardhans.[3]

AKKIVAT.

Akkivat village, about twelve miles south-west of Chikodi, was besieged in 1777 by Parshurám Bháu of Tásgaon. Though gallantly defended by two brothers, their death in an assault and the pressure of famine forced its surrender to Parshurám.[4] In 1827 the Kolhápur Chief was compelled to hand Akkivat to the British Government as it was a den of robbers who caused ceaseless annoyance to the neighbouring British villages.[5]

Fort.

In 1842 a committee of inspection described Akkivat fort as a stone fort about 800 feet irregularly square and consisting of bastions and curtains with an unfinished ditch on the north-east and south-west. The defences consisted of twelve bastions of various sizes fit for ordnance and joined by curtains. They were built of uncemented stone work and averaged twenty to twenty-five feet high including parapets all partly out of repair. The fort ditch was most imperfect and only a few feet deep. There were two gateways in the north and in the east. The entrance to the north gateway was flanked by the main work but contained only one weak gate. The east gateway was a small narrow unfinished sallyport made

---

1 Harris' Voyages, II. 129.
2 Moor's Narrative of Captain Little's Detachment, 300-301.
3 Stokes' Historical Account of the Belgaum District, 88.
4 Stokes' Belgaum, 56.
5 Stokes' Belgaum, 82.

Chapter XIV. Places.

through the wall and easily blocked. The fort had a good water-supply but offered no protection against shells. It was well inhabited and on the sloping earthen mound or glacis on the north and east had a number of straggling houses.

Ánkalgi.

A'nkalgi, about fifteen miles south-west of Gokák, is a large village on the Márkandeya with a population in 1872 of 2315 and in 1881 of about 2000. Ánkalgi has a Kánarese school, a temple of Lakshmi, and a Lingáyat religious house or *math*. The income of the spiritual head or *svámi* of the house consists chiefly of gifts and offerings from the Lingáyats of the surrounding villages. The *svámi* spends his time in receiving those who come to visit him, and in visiting the chief neighbouring fairs and religious festivals. Ánkalgi was one of four places proposed for the headquarters of the collectorate before Belgaum was chosen on the 9th of March 1838.[2]

Arbhávi.

Arbha'vi is a small village on the Gokák-Ráybág road four miles north of Gokák, with in 1881 a population of 806. In 1791, under the name of Aarbyengh, Captain Moor described it as having a beautiful mango grove enclosing a handsome building and a well ornamented with sculptures in the Kánarese style.[3]

Athni.

Athni, 16° 40′ north latitude and 75° 7′ east longitude, about seventy miles north-east of Belgaum, is a municipal town the head-quarters of the Athni sub-division, with in 1881 a population of 11,186. Athni stands on waving ground about ten miles north of the Krishna, on the south bank of a small watercourse which is dry during the hot weather. The old town is ruined and the ditch filled. Two graceful and well built gates ornament the northern and southern entrances to the town. The 1872 census showed a population of 11,588 of whom 10,245 were Hindus and 1343 Musalmáns. The 1881 census showed 11,186, or a decrease of 402, of whom 9724 were Hindus and 1462 Musalmáns.

Trade.

Athni has a weekly market on Sunday and Monday and a considerable traffic is carried on in cattle. The town has about thirty traders chiefly Bhátiás, Bráhmans, Jains, Lingáyats and Márwár Vánis, with capitals varying from £2500 to £10,000 (Rs. 25,000-Rs. 1,00,000). Of the thirty traders nine are independent and the rest are agents of Bombay, Chiplun, Jamkhandi, and Miraj merchants. The chief imports are cocoanuts, dates, dry fish, gunny bags, rice, salt, and sugar from Bombay and Chiplun. The chief exports are clarified butter, cotton, and wheat. During the fair season the exports and imports from and to Athni find their way to Bombay in steamers and native craft by Chiplun and during the rains by rail from the Bársi Road station about ninety miles north of Áthni. The town is noted for its wheelwrights and for the making of saltpetre.

Management.

Besides the sub-divisional revenue and police offices Athni has a municipality, a sub-judge's court, a post office, a dispensary, a library, and six schools. The municipality was established in

---

1 Report dated Belgaum, 5th July 1842.
2 Stokes' Belgaum, 86. The three other places were Gokák, Manoli, and Murgod.
3 Moor's Narrative, 266.

Chapter XIV. Places. ATHNI. *Management.*

1853. In 1882-83 it had an income of £1253 (Rs. 12,530), chiefly raised from octroi, and an expenditure of £1404 (Rs. 14,040) chiefly incurred in sanitation and on roads and other public works. The water supply is from two reservoirs and fifteen public and ninety-six private wells. Of the reservoirs which are not far to the south of the town one is used for drinking and the other for watering cattle. The drinking reservoir was begun by the municipality in 1865 and finished in 1871 at a cost of £1156 (Rs. 11,560). It supplies drinking water for six months and also acts as a feeder to wells in the town. Of the fifteen public wells six are fit for drinking and nine are brackish. Of the ninety-six private wells, eight are used for drinking. Of the whole number of 111 wells, both public and private, forty-six have steps and sixty-five have no steps. Of the fifteen public wells two, the Modhal and the Kumbhár, are important. The Modhal is thirty feet in diameter and at all seasons of the year contains twenty feet of water. This well was built by the municipality in 1874-75 at a cost of £365 (Rs. 3650). It is used solely for watering cattle. The Kumbhár well, which is used for drinking, contains sweet water and has been recently repaired by the municipality at a cost of £428 (Rs. 4280). The municipal market which was built at a cost of about £727 (Rs. 7270) contains sixty stalls which are let by the year to petty dealers in grain, vegetables, fruit, and cloth. The market days are Sunday and Monday. Besides the market stalls the town has 275 shops where grain and other articles are sold. The dispensary which was opened in 1871 in 1882-83 treated nineteen in-patients and 4952 out-patients at a cost of £134 6*s*. (Rs. 1343). A public garden surrounds the dispensary. The library was built by private enterprise in 1865 at a cost of £150 (Rs. 1500). It is maintained from a yearly subscription of £16 (Rs. 160) and a municipal contribution of £6 (Rs. 60). Of the six schools three are Government and three local. Of the three Government schools two are for boys and one for girls. Of the two boys' schools one is an Anglo-vernacular school to which the municipality makes a yearly grant of £36 (Rs. 360). Athni has the remains of a mud fort, and, within the fort, two mansions or *vádás*, one of which served as the office of the mámlatdár and the other still serves as the residence of a Sardeshpánde. In one enclosure are two temples of Siddheshvar and Amriteshvar and a mosque.

History.

The earliest mention of Athni which has been traced is by the French traveller Mandelslo in 1639 who notices Atteny city as one of the chief markets between Bijápur and Goa.[1] About 1670 the English geographer Ogilby notices Attany as a great trading town two days from Bijápur.[2] In 1675 the English traveller Fryer notices Hattany as a mart town in Bijápur.[3] In 1679 Huttaney was a considerable mart taken from Shiváji by the Moghal general Dilávar Khán who sacked it. Dilávar Khán wished to sell the people as slaves. Sambháji, the son of Shiváji, who some time before had rebelled against his father and joined Dilávar Khán, opposed the suggestion, and, as Dilávar Khán

[1] Harris' Voyages, II. 129. [2] Atlas, V. 247. [3] East India and Persia, 175.

Chapter XIV. Places. Athni. History.

paid no attention to his remonstrances, Sambháji in anger left his camp and became reconciled to his father. At this time the English factory at Kárwár had large dealings with Athni which ceased during the disturbances which filled the latter part of the century.[1] About 1720 Athni was taken by Nizám-ul-Mulk the Deccan viceroy.[2] He soon after made it over to his ally the Kolhápur chief, who, in 1730, handed it to Sháhu of Sátára.[3] In 1774 Basálat Jang the governor of Bijápur is mentioned as levying contributions as far as Athni and Miraj.[4] In 1788 Rennell calls its Atoni or Huttany an English factory in the heart of Viziapur.[5] In 1792 Captain Moor calls it Atni a large town well peopled and thriving. It was a place of much trade importing merchandise from Surat, Bombay, Ráichur, and Náráyanpeth in the Nizám's country. The staple export was grain and there were manufactures of silk and cotton robes and piece goods. The town was enclosed by a wall and ditch of no great strength and the stone fort was not worth speaking of. On the north and east the town was entered by fairly well built gates. The chief building was a rest-house about a mile to the east of the town in a grove of trees. It was square and when finished would have room for 500 travellers. There were two handsome and beautifully built gates on the south and the west. They had been built by Rástia to whom the town belonged and were each said to have cost more than £1200 (Rs. 12,000). In the centre of the enclosure was a religious building apparently ancient. It was a Hindu temple with a Musalmán dome. An avenue of mango trees which were planted by Rástia in 1785 led south from the town nine or ten miles to the Krishna.[6] Athni lapsed to the British Government on the death without heirs of the Nipáni chief in 1839.[7]

Bágevádi.

Ba'geva'di, a large village about ten miles south-east of Belgaum, with in 1881 a population of 4534, has a school and a weekly market held on Tuesday. In 1827 Captain Clunes mentions Bagivaree on the Belgaum-Dhárwár road as a post-runner's station with 400 houses, twelve shops, a watercourse, and wells.[8] About a mile east of Bágevádi is Chik or Little Bágevádi where a copper-plate of the seventh Devgiri Yádav king Krishna (1247-1260) was found in the possession of a weaver. The plate is in three sheets and bears on its seal a figure of the monkey god Hanumán. It is dated the full-moon of *Áshádh* or June-July 1249 (S. 1171). It records, at the command of king Kanhara, a gift of land in thirty-two shares in the village of Santheya Bágevádi in the Hubli[9] sub-division of the district of Kuhundi[10] to sixty-six Bráhmans attached to a shrine

---

[1] Orme's Historical Fragments, 121, 193; Hamilton's Description of Hindustán, II. 233; Stokes' Belgaum, 43. [2] Stokes' Belgaum, 48.
[3] Grant Duff's Maráthás, 224; Stokes' Belgaum, 48.
[4] Grant Duff's Maráthás, 369; Stokes' Belgaum, 53.
[5] Memoir of a Map of Hindustán, 174.
[6] Narrative, 301-307. [7] Stokes' Belgaum, 87. [8] Itinerary, 71.
[9] As the inscription notices that Bágevádi village was included in the Hubli Twelve, this Hubli must be the modern Mugutkhán Hubli five miles south-east of Bágevádi, not the great Dhárwár Hubli.
[10] The Kuhundi or Kundi district of three thousand villages, a division of the

Chapter XIV.
Places.
Bágevádi.

of Mádhavdev. The granter is Krishna's minister Mallisaitti living at Mudugal, apparently the place of that name in the Nizám's country on the Bijápur frontier about 130 miles east of Belgaum. The grant is described as having been afterwards ratified by Mallisaitti's son Chaundisaitti who gave this copper-plate in token of confirmation. The copper-plate gives an interesting list of the names of the sixty-six Bráhman donees, several of which are the same as names used at the present day. With each name is given its surname and the name of the family stock or *gotra*, and, in several cases, the names of the fathers of the grantees. Of the thirty-two shares, six Bráhmans get whole shares, forty-two half shares, seventeen quarter shares, and one gets three-quarters of a share.[1]

Bail Hongal.

Bail Hongal, about six miles east of Sampgaon, is an old town with in 1872 a population of 9001 and in 1881 of 7806. The town stands on rising ground, in the middle of a large plain or *bail* to the east of a large pond. The town is noted for its breed of bullocks and for its coarse cotton waistcloths and robes. Its position on the borders of the Sampgaon and Parasgad subdivisions gives importance to its weekly market which is held on Friday.

Trade.

Bail Hongal is an important trade centre with about thirty independent traders chiefly Lingáyats, Jains, and Bráhmans with capitals varying from £500 to £10,000 (Rs. 5000 - Rs. 1,00,000). The chief imports are silk and cotton yarn, women's robes and bodicecloths, men's waistcloths and headscarves, and betelnuts molasses and indigo. Silk and cotton yarn are bought in Bombay through agents and brought by steamers and native craft to Vengurla and from Vengurla to Bail Hongal in carts. Women's robes are brought for local use from Gadag in Dhárwár and bodicecloths from Guledgudd in Bijápur and from Hubli in Dhárwár. Betelnuts and molasses are brought from Yellápur in Kánara both for local use and for transport to Sholápur and Bijápur. Indigo waistcloths and headscarves are brought from Madras for local use. Of exports cotton is the chief. It is bought on market days from husbandmen and petty dealers, and also from surrounding villages by local traders and by the agents of Belgaum and Vengurla merchants. It is then sent to Vengurla.

The town has a post office and a branch of the London Church Missionary Society with a Mission house and a chapel. The chief object of interest is an old Hindu temple to the north of the town outside the walls. Though at present used as a Ling shrine and dedicated to Basaveshvar it appears to have originally been a Jain temple. A yearly fair is held in *Kártik* or October-November when about 12,000 people attend. The temple has two inscribed stone tablets of the twelfth century, both belonging to the Ratta chiefs (875-1250) of Saundatti and Belgaum. The first tablet, on

---

Kuntala province, included the greater part of the Belgaum district and the native states to the north of it and the southern parts of the Bijápur district. Fleet's Kánarese Dynasties, 20 note 1.

[1] Fleet's Kánarese Dynasties, 73; Journal Bombay Branch Royal Asiatic Society, IX. 246-249.

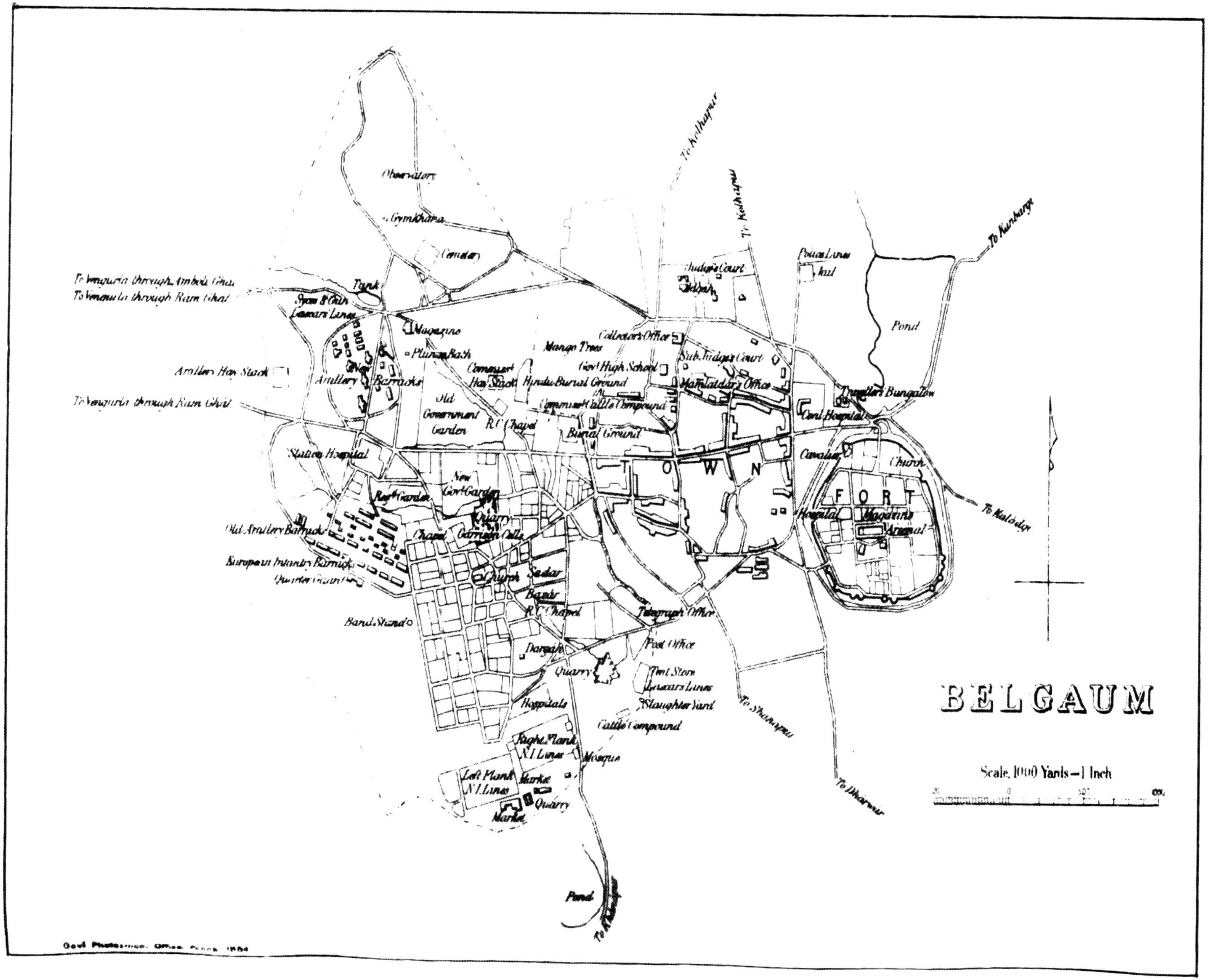
BELGAUM
Scale, 1000 Yards = 1 Inch
FORT
TOWN
Church
Magazine
Arsenal
Hospital
Cavalier
Civil Hospital
Traveller's Bungalow
Pond
Police Lines
Jail
Judge's Court
Collector's Office
Sub Judge's Court
Govt High School
Mamlatdar's Office
Hindu Burial Ground
Burial Ground
Mango Trees
Observatory
Gymkhana
Cemetery
Tank
Magazine
Plunge Bath
Commissariat Hay Stack
Artillery Hay Stack
Artillery
Barracks
Old Government Garden
R.C. Chapel
Station Hospital
New Govt Garden
Quarry
Chapel
Garrison Cells
Church
Sadar Bazar
Old Artillery Barracks
European Infantry Barracks
Quarter Guard
Band Stand
Dargah
Telegraph Office
Post Office
Tent Store
Lascars Lines
Slaughter Yard
Cattle Compound
Hospitals
Right Flank N.I. Lines
Left Flank N.I. Lines
Mosque
Market
To Kolhapur
To Kalhapur
To Kanbarge
To Kaladgi
To Shahapur
To Dharwar
To Vengurla through Amboli Ghat
To Vengurla through Ram Ghat
To Vengurla through Ram Ghat
Govt Photozinco Office Poona 1884

Chapter XIV.
Places.
BAIL HONGAL.
Inscriptions.

the right front of the temple, has an inscription of seventy-three lines in Old Kánarese characters and language, but the letters are so worn that neither the sense of the inscription nor its date can be made out. The emblems at the top of this tablet are a *ling* and a priest in the middle, with the sun to the right, and a cow and calf with the moon beyond them to the left. The second tablet, now set upright on the left front of the temple, lay in the hedge surrounding the town. It is in Old Kánarese characters and language and has fifty-one lines of about thirty-nine letters each. The inscription is dated 1164 in the reign of the Ratta chief Kártavirya (1143-1164). It mentions a Jain *basti* and probably records the building of this very temple and grants made to it. The emblems at the top of this tablet are in the middle a seated figure of Jinendra, on its right a standing figure full front, with the moon above it; and on its left a cow and calf with the sun above them.[1]

BELAVDI.

Belavdi, about twelve miles south-east of Sampgaon, with in 1872 a population of 3284 and in 1881 of 3160, has an old temple of Virbhadra said to have been built by Jakhanácharya. The temple has a fragment of an inscription dated 1070 in the reign of the Western Chálukya king Someshvar I. (1068-1077). A yearly fair attended by about 1500 people is held in *Chaitra* or March-April. A weekly market is held on Tuesdays.

BELGAUM.

Belgaum, 15° 52′ north latitude and 74° 42′ east longitude, about forty-five miles north-west of Dhárwár, seventy miles from the coast, 110 miles south-west of Bijápur, and about 200 miles south of Poona is the head-quarters of the Belgaum district and sub-division, and is the chief military station in the Karnátak. The 1881 census showed that Belgaum is the seventeenth city in the Bombay Presidency with a town site of 289 acres and a population of about 23,000 or seventy-nine to the square acre.[2] Belgaum stands from 2100 to 2260 feet above the sea from which in a straight line it is about fifty miles distant. The town stands on one of the laterite hills which form the eastern slope of the water-shed of the Márkandeya river, which flows from south-west to north-east three miles north of Belgaum, and of its feeder the Belári which flows about two miles south of Belgaum.[3] The Belári and its small western feeders drain nearly the whole station as well as the low-lying ground to the south-east which is almost wholly under rice or sugarcane. Excluding the Native Infantry Lines in the south-west, Belgaum may roughly be compared to an isosceles triangle with the fort at its apex; the British Artillery and Infantry Lines along its base about $1\frac{1}{4}$ miles

---

[1] Indian Antiquary, IV. 115; Fleet's Kánarese Dynasties, 82.

[2] The exact number is 23,115, excluding 9582 the population of Belgaum Cantonment.

[3] The water-parting of the Belári watercourse is crossed by the Kolhápur road near a bungalow long occupied by Mr. Grey, a former Collector of Belgaum, and hence known as the Collector's bungalow, in the north at a considerable height above the station. On the same line further east is the old double-domed mosque erected in 1561 by Kishwar Khán, the son of the celebrated Asad Khán. (See above p. 371 and below p. 527). The mosque has been turned into the hospital and guard-room of the jail. Near the jail are the Police Lines from which the ground slopes rapidly forming the western boundary of the water-shed of the Turakmatti or One Tree Hill.

Chapter XIV.
Places.
BELGAUM.
Aspect.

long; and in the centre the Town, the Cantonment, the Commissariat Cattle Lines, and the Officers' and Pensioners' bungalows. The two sides of the triangle are each about 2¼ miles. They include an area of 289 acres, and contain besides the troops a population of about 23,000. Within station limits only the native town in the centre and the cantonment to its west are thickly peopled. The rest of the station is mostly open plain set apart for parade grounds, or occupied by gardens, mango groves, haystacks, and quarries.

The country round Belgaum is hilly, and grows more rugged towards the crest of the Sahyádris which lie about twenty-five miles to the west. Among the hills wind the rich valleys of many feeders of the Krishna which broaden eastwards till they merge into the Krishna plain. From Mahálakshmi hill to the west of the station, Belgaum seems surrounded by low hills. Yellurgad hill, whose height of about 800 feet above the station makes it the chief local landmark, lies about nine miles to the south; Belgundi hill is about six miles to the south-west; Vaijnáth hill, with its well-known Shaiv temple which gives its name to the hill, is about twelve miles to the west; Kákti hill which forms a continuation of the Sutgatti range is about five miles to the north; and the Kanbargi range is about four miles to the north-east. To the east the hills are lost in the high land which rises above the rice fields close to the station. Except the Kákti hill all these hills and spurs belong to the Sahyádri range with typical flat trap tops and level grassy terraces with a few solitary trees. Close to the station are rice fields and grass lands belonging to Belgaum and the surrounding villages. A quarter to half a mile to the south are the Sángli town of Sháhpur and the villages of Hassur and Hassoti, reached either by the Dhárwár, Kapleshvar, or Khánápur roads. Much of the country round is well suited for the manœuvres of infantry, and close to the barracks in the west are fine stretches of plain. But the ground is not suited to cavalry or artillery exercise, as, where it is not rocky, it is full of deep dangerous cracks. Three miles east of the fort, to the north of the road leading to Kanbargi village, is the artillery range, while the British Infantry range is about half a mile to the west of the barracks, and the Native Infantry lines are about a mile further west. Except to the west and south-west, the station contains a large number of fine trees, which, with occasional groves, make the whole town and its surroundings seem richly wooded. The only building which rises above the trees is the Camp Protestant Church of St. Mary's.

Geology.

The raised ground on which the station stands is of laterite and trap. The laterite, or iron clay, which forms a thick layer over the trap, is a porous clayey rock which allows water to pass rapidly through it. Chemically it is composed of peroxide of iron, alumina, lime, magnesia, and silica, and contains twenty-five to thirty-five per cent of metallic iron. The twisted tubes or pores of the laterite are often filled with clay which is readily washed out. Under ground this rock is so soft that it can be easily dug out with a spade, but on exposure to the air it rapidly hardens to stone. It is largely used for building and most Belgaum houses have been built from quarries within the town and cantonment limits. Some wells are cut through forty-five to seventy-five feet of laterite to the underlying trap; in other places the trap comes to within fifteen feet of the surface. The great Deccan trap series ends a little to the south and east of Belgaum. The thickness of the trap near Belgaum has been estimated at 2000 to 2500 feet. Trap is used for building and crumbled trap or *murum* as road metal.

Soil.

The soil of Belgaum is crumbled laterite two or three feet deep, and black soil which is a mixture of ruined trap and vegetable matter. The crumbled laterite is more or less barren, is heavy and sticky when wet, and during the dry season rises in fine brick-red dust.[1] The black soil is very rich yielding alternate crops of rice, beans, pulse, and sugarcane. In the centre of the town is a large patch of black soil in places at least fifteen feet deep believed to be partly artificial.[2]

Water.

The Belgaum water-supply is entirely drawn from wells cut in the laterite subsoil which are deeper in the north and west than in the south and east. As the water soaks through this porous iron rock it is freed from impurities. Except during the rains, when in some of the dirtiest quarters of the town the surface washings and other impurities have found their way into the wells, cholera in Belgaum is seldom due to bad water. Except in the south-east where the water is brackish and generally fails at the end of the dry season, the Belgaum wells afford a plentiful supply throughout the year.[3]

Ponds.

Belgaum has five reservoirs, the fort or *killyáche tale*, the two Kapleshvars, the Argan, and the Jakirhonda. The fort reservoir, which is the largest, lies north of the fort between the Jail hill on the west and the Kanbargi road on the east. It has an area of about sixty acres and is fed partly by springs and partly by the drainage of the Turakmatti and Jail hills. An embankment along the Kanbargi road to the east of the lake is said to have been built by the Musalmáns. Its water is used for watering the roads and is carried by sluices to fields along the valley to the north of the Kaládgi road. It dries during the hot weather when crops are raised in its bed. On the Nárali Purnima or cocoanut full-moon in August the regimental sepoys go in procession to the lake, worship it instead of the sea, and throw cocoanuts into it. The Musalmáns also drown the Muharram biers on *tábuts* in this lake. The two Kapleshvar reservoirs, which are joined by sluices, lie near the south end of the town on either side of the Sháhpur road. The water is used for the neighbouring fields and for watering the roads. During the hot weather the neighbouring poor drink the water of the left hand pond. The Argan pond on the Vengurla road near the Station Hospital is a small unbuilt pond. The water though muddy lasts throughout the year and is used for watering cattle. The Jakirhonda reservoir on the Khánápur road to the east of the Native Infantry Lines fills the south-east corner of a lake which is called Nágar Kere or the Cobra pond in an eleventh century Jain inscrip-

---

[1] Surgeon-Major C. T. Peters, M.B.
[2] Sanitary Commissioner's Report for 1868, Sec. VII. 121.
[3] In the neighbouring town of Sháhpur the water is brackish and unpalatable.

Chapter XIV.
Places.
Belgaum.

tion in the fort.[1] The ruined dam of the old lake still shows. The soil within its limits is so full of water that a hole one or two feet deep yields an abundant supply which is often used by blanket-makers and dyers. The new pond is dammed by an earthen embankment built in 1877-78 as a famine work and is provided with a sluice for watering the neighbouring fields. The fort ditch also holds water at the end of the rains which is used for the neighbouring fields.

Nágjhari Springs.

The Nágjhari or Cobra springs, whose water is held to be the best in Belgaum, lie to the south of the cantonment at the upper end of the old Nágar Kere lake. The springs are in two groups one close to the Khánápur road and the other a little to the west, about 600 feet to the left of the Native Infantry Lines. Both groups are surrounded by fields and approached by foot-paths. Near them, especially near the western group are magnificently wooded old gardens which the Belgaum and Sháhpur people often use for garden dinners or *van-bhojans* and *churmurchatnis* in which fried rice or *churmurás* and a condiment or *chatni* of parched gram are eaten with other sweetmeats. Each group of springs consists of two square ponds surrounded by stone walls above which small openings are left to allow the water to escape. The ponds were formerly stocked with large tame fish but of late the fish have disappeared. The water is considered light and digestive and the place is holy with some ascetics' huts and shrines. In 1878-79 the Belgaum municipality paid Government £128 (Rs. 1285) to survey a scheme for bringing water by an open canal from Tudye village about ten miles south-west of the town. The survey was favourable and the scheme is under consideration.

Streams.

Besides the wells, ponds, and springs noted above a few streams or *nálás* in and around the station of Belgaum flow during the rainy season. The Bogárve rises in the hill to the west of the British Infantry Barracks, and, passing between the barracks and the station hospital, separates the town from the camp and joins the Belári behind the post office and the Ordnance Lines. The Belári, which is larger than the Bogárve and which forms the south boundary of the lands of Belgaum, takes its rise among the hills to the south of the British Infantry Barracks, is fed by the drainage of the hills to the south-west of the camp and the upper Nágjhari springs, flows close to the rear of the Native Infantry Lines, and, skirting the south-west and south-east boundaries of the camp, receives the waters of the Bogárve, and the united stream flows south-east through the rice fields between the town and the fort on the north and Sháhpur on the south. From this, keeping north, it receives the waters of the Belgaum stream, which rises from the pond formed below the lower Nágjhari group, and, changing its course to the north-east falls into the Márkandeya river near the village of Honga. Except a little of the raised ground to the west of the New Artillery Barracks, which is drained by a small stream running north-west across the Vengurla road into the Márkandeya river, these streams drain the whole station of Belgaum.

---

[1] Stokes' Belgaum, 18.

Climate.

The circular belt of hills round Belgaum condenses the clouds and helps to increase the rainfall. The mean yearly rainfall[1] recorded in the ten years ending 1867 was 52 inches; in the five years ending 1875, 49·7 inches; in the famine year of 1876, 39·95 inches; and in the six years ending 1882, 47·47 inches. The fall becomes less when the surrounding belt of hills is crossed, whether north towards Kolhápur, north-east towards Bijápur, or south-east towards Dhárwár. By concentrating the rainfall the hills cause luxuriant vegetation and render the climate more equable than that of most other places in Western India. At the same time, they make a heavy mist overhang the camp between sunset and sunrise, accompanied by slight malarious fever throughout the year, especially in November December and January. Its height above the sea and the freshness of its sea breeze make the climate of Belgaum pleasant and on the whole healthy. Still the great change from the dry east winds of the fair months to the damp of the monsoon is trying especially to new-comers and to the weakly.

Divisions.

For administrative purposes Belgaum is divided into civil and cantonment limits. The civil limits include the town and the line of bungalows to its north; the cantonment limits include the camp to the west of the town and the fort to the east, with the open space or esplanade all round the fort. The town of Belgaum is bounded on the north by the high ground on the Vengurla road occupied by the Judge's Court and the residences of civil officers, on the east by the fort, on the south by a belt of fields with the town of Sháhpur beyond, and on the west by the camp. Within these limits the town, which is almost circular in shape, contains an area of about 300 acres, with a population of 23,115, and a municipal revenue of £3710 (Rs. 37,100). The site on which the town stands has not been surveyed but the ground appears to fall rapidly to the south-east. Its natural drainage is carried off by the Bogárve and by a smaller stream which meets it, while on the south-east a water-course running alongside of the Dhárwár road drains the south-east of the town. These two water-courses discharge during the rains into the Belári on the south, and are dry during the fair season. Formerly the town was disfigured by many plots of low open ground, apparently quarries, where water used to gather during the rainy season. These have now been filled by town sweepings and are used as building sites. In the south-west a few rice and sugar-cane fields are included within town limits, but these open spaces also are every year being taken for houses. The town is shaded and hid by lines and groves of well grown mangoes, tamarinds, banians, bamboos, *umbars*, and *pimpals*.

For municipal purposes, the town is divided into four wards. These are subdivided into fifty-four sections called *vádás* or *gallis* generally named after the principal residents. The boundaries of the different sections are uncertain. Kapleshvarváda, named after the Kapleshvar temple, is in the extreme south of the town. The population chiefly consists of Kunbis and Shimpis, and has much increased during the

[1] Details are given above, p. 43.

Chapter XIV.
Places.
BELGAUM.
Divisions.

past few years.[1] One Bráhman house the Bhátes are the oldest residents of the place. The section has several small shops where among other things good snuff is prepared and sold; and a few pounders or *láts* for making *pohes* from parched rice. The rest-houses or *dharmshálás* of the Kapleshvar temple are used for performing the ten days' funeral ceremonies, and the Gosávi's hut beyond the pond is often the resort of parties from Belgaum and Sháhpur who come to drink sugarcane juice during the hot season. The Bhádurgiváda to the west of Kapleshvarváda, named after the *bhádurgi* plant which grew there in abundance, is chiefly occupied by bricklayers and masons. The number of houses has been steadily increasing. Tángdiváda, to the east of Bhádurgiváda, called after a former resident named Tángdi, is occupied by Kunbi cultivators. Pátilváda to the north of Tángdiváda is occupied by houses of the pátil family of Belgaum, the chief pátil's house having generally on the front wall a coloured drawing of a tiger hunted by a horseman. This is an old street and the number of houses has for many years remained the same. The most southerly road between the fort and the camp passes through this street, by the side of which are some sweetmeat shops. At its western end near the camp are a few shoemakers' houses, and the Dhed's well believed by Mr. Stokes to be the oldest masonry in the town. Kángliváda, to the north of Pátilváda, is called after one of its chief residents; Mujávarváda, to the north of the Kángliváda, is called after the Mujávars or sweepers of Asad Khán's mosque who lived in it; Sheriváda to the north of Mujávarváda is named after one of its residents; Mathváda, to the east of Sheriváda, contains a Lingáyat *math*; Kulkarniváda to the north-west of Mathváda is an old street and contains the houses of the Belgaum Kulkarnis who are Deshasth Bráhmans. It has many houses of Jain cultivators and in the west has a temple of Rámling. Anantshayanváda to the north of Kulkarniváda has in the centre a temple of Anantshayan or Vishnu sleeping on his serpent bed, and is inhabited chiefly by Deshasth Bráhmans with a few Jain and Kunbi houses. At its eastern end is a small temple of Máruti called Nava or New Máruti, the old Máruti being the one in Máruti Galli. Basvannaváda, to the north of Anantshayanváda, has a temple, in the middle of the road, of Basvanna or Shiv's Bull, where a cultivator's fair is held on the first day of *Chaitra* that is March-April. New bullocks are yoked to the large field carts, and about thirty carts are furiously driven three times round the temple. *Ambil* or gruel is handed to the assembled Mhárs. Next day a bonfire is lighted in front of the temple and the ceremonies of walking over the fire and rubbing with ashes are performed. This street contains the houses of Deshasth Bráhmans, Jains, Kunbis, and a few carpenters and smiths, and has been much improved of late years. Behind Basvanna's temple is a Jain Basti or religious house, with, in front of it, a large round stone pillar with a small image of

[1] The names of most of these sections or *vádás*, are given in the census papers of 1820 and are still shewn in the books of the Belgaum village accountant. These papers show that, except in the north-west and south-west within the last fifty years, the town limits have not much spread but that many new houses have been added.

Párasnáth in a niche at the end. In the temple is a seated image of finely polished black stone about two feet high said to have been brought from the Jain temples in the fort.[1] At its feet are two images of white marble of half its size and several small brass images of different Jain saints. Bráhmanical Hindus object to go into the temple, as the image is naked. At the eastern end is the temple of Dyámava or Lakshmi, from which this part is sometimes called Lakshmi or Mahálakshmiváda. The goddess first lived in the fort and was moved by the Musalmáns to a place on the esplanade where there is still a small temple of the goddess and where the twelve-yearly fair in honour of Dyámava is held. The image of the goddess whose ministrant is a Badgi or carpenter is made of wood, painted red, has ten hands, and rides on a lion. Deshpándeváda, to the north of Basvanna or Mahálakshmiváda which of late has been much improved, is inhabited by Deshasth Bráhmans some of whom have the surname of Deshpánde. In the centre is Bhadbhade's mansion a two-storeyed house generally used by Jágirdárs or landed proprietors when they visit Belgaum. Hanmant or Márutigalli, to the north of Deshpándeváda, contains the temple of Máruti, a two-storeyed building surrounded by rest-houses and shrines. The temple has lately been repaired and out-houses built, and some images which had long lain neglected in the fort have been placed in this temple. The only old part of the building of Máruti's temple is a shrine of Chandramauleshvar. The front hall was built by subscription raised among the people of Belgaum. This Máruti is supposed to be the guardian deity of the town, and many Hindus visit the temple every day. The street is chiefly occupied by Deshasth Bráhmans mostly Government officers. The other inhabitants are the Kunbi ministrants of Máruti's temple and a few Sonárs and Shimpis. The street is at present flourishing. Áditvár or Ravivár peth, called after a market formerly held on Sunday to the east of Márutigalli, has much improved of late years and is improving. It is occupied by wholesale grain and salt merchants chiefly Shenvi Bráhmans and Lingáyats, who have a religious house. Ganpatigalli to the north-west of Áditvárpeth takes its name from a temple of Ganpati, and is chiefly occupied by rich Telis or oilmen who also drive bullock carriages or *sárvats* for hire. Near the north end of the street are a few shops of Musalmán tin workers. Kodolkarváda to the west of Ganpatigalli is named after a rich Kunbi named Kodolkar, and, besides by a few Kunbi and Bráhman houses, is chiefly occupied by weavers who make coarse white cloth and women's robes. It has two Sutár's and Lohár's yards where carts are made. Burudgalli to the north of Kodolkarváda is solely occupied by Buruds or basket-makers and is shaded by clumps of bamboos. Bápatgalli to the north-west of Burudgalli is named after its original Bráhman landowner Bápat. The ground which the street occupies was under cultivation, and,

---

1 In the temple is a large bell which is said to have been made about ten years ago from an old bell which, according to the writing on it, was 150 years old. It was probably a Portuguese bell brought about 1740 from some of the Portuguese churches in the Konkan.

Chapter XIV.
Places.
BELGAUM.
Divisions.

except the owner's dwelling, all the houses have been built by Kunbis within the last fifty years. The street has an old mosque built in Musalmán times (1350-1750). Bogárvegalli to the west of Kodolkarváda, reaching to the western border of the town leading to the camp, takes its name either from the houses or the caste of Bogárs or coppersmiths who used to live in it. Many new houses have lately been built, and the place has a few Bráhman and Kunbi houses and is the head-quarters of Belgaum prostitutes. The street has two pony stands and two cart stands or *addás* where ponies and carts can be had on hire. At the western end is a Gosávi monastery with several old tombs in the yard. Opposite its eastern end is a public well called *Bára Gadgadyáchi Vihir* or the Twelve-Pulley Well. Kelkarváda or Kelkarbág to the north of Bogárvegalli was formerly the garden of a Konkanasth Bráhman named Kelkar. The garden had many cocoa palms and strings of pack bullocks from the Konkan used to rest under them. Almost all the houses have been recently built and the ward is occupied chiefly by Bráhmans and a few Kunbis. The water of this place is excellent and the public well formerly belonging to the Kelkars, supplies numbers of people throughout the year. Kelkarbág also includes a street which leads north from the western end of Márutigalli towards the Khade bázár, has the Sungathankar's three-storeyed palace at its northern end and is occupied by wealthy Bráhmans, Government officers, and two great bankers. Gondhliváda to the north of Kelkarbág formerly contained a few Gondhlis' houses. Many new houses have since been built and the street is occupied mostly by Shenvi Bráhmans. The other main streets are Samádevtigalli called from a temple of the goddess Samádevti and chiefly occupied by Shenvi Bráhmans; Nárvekargalli called from its residents who are chiefly Nárvekars or Vaishyas; Shirágshettigalli to the north called after an old merchant named Shirág; Chámbhárváda to the north-east almost wholly occupied by shoemakers; Káktivesváda, on the road leading to Kákti village chiefly occupied by Dhangars, Kunbis, and Musalmáns; Kangráliváda to the west called after the headman of Kangráli who owned it; Khadakváda to the south called from a layer of surface rock; Bhadkali to the south called from a former resident; Chavátváda to the east; Shettiváda to the north, the former residence of the Shetti or leading banker of Belgaum with a well known Máruti's temple the oldest in Belgaum; Kotválváda to the east called after an old police station; Bágvánváda to the north chiefly occupied by Bágváns or fruit and vegetable sellers; Chandáváda to the north called after a woman ramed Chandábái; Khade bázár, formerly called Budhvár and Shanvár bázár, because markets were held here on Wednesdays and Saturdays, takes it new name from a road leading from the camp to the fort. It is chiefly inhabited by Márwáris and Káchis and dealers in cloth from Bombay. Kákarváda to the east chiefly inhabited by Kákars or Pendháris; Dhorgalli to the south-west inhabited by Dhor tanners and formerly inhabited by Madras Mhárs when Madras troops occupied Belgaum; Baghadleváda called from a landholder named Baghadle who lived here; Kámátváda chiefly inhabited by cultivators; Vadváda called from a banian tree; Kasábváda the butchers' quarter; Hajámváda the barbers' quarter;

Bhendi bázár formerly the site of a vegetable market, and now occupied by shops of various trades; Bhoiváda the fishermen's quarter; Pángulváda called after an old resident named Pángul; Bhátkandiváda the rice-sellers' quarter; Máliváda the gardeners' quarter; Mensiváda called from a number of its inhabitants whose surname is Mensi; Rámnandváda called from a landholder of that name who formerly held it; and Arlikatti Deshpándeváda called after the Deshpándes of Arlikatti who owned the ground.

Population.

The earliest record of Belgaum population is in 1820, when it had 7652 people lodged in 1309 houses. One-third of these were Maráthás, one-sixth Musalmáns mostly connected with religious establishments, one-sixth Lingáyats, one-eighth Jains, one-ninth Bráhmans chiefly Deshasths and Karhádás, and the rest artisans of various sorts.[1] The choice of Belgaum as the head-quarters of the Collectorate and as the chief military station in the Karnátak brought a large accession to the population, chiefly Márwári traders, Madrási Mhár and Pendhári camp followers, and upper class Hindus in Government service. In 1852 the population of Belgaum including the village of Khásbág and probably Sháhpur amounted to about 30,000 including between 13,000 to 14,000 who lived in the camp. In 1866 the town population numbered 16,514 increasing to 19,371 and to 24,366 in the next two years.[2] In 1870 the opening of the Ámboli pass and the direct communication with the port of Vengurla in Ratnágiri brought a further increase to the trade and population of the town. The 1872 census showed a population of 26,947, of whom 19,384 were Hindus, 5517 Musalmáns, 1757 Christians, and 289 Others. The 1881 census gave for the city a population of 23,115 and for the cantonment of 9582, that is a total population of 32,697. Of these 22,939 were Hindus, 7136 Musalmáns, 2481 Christians, 53 Pársis, and 88 Jews. This on 1725 square acres gives an average density of about nineteen to the square acre.

Houses.

Belgaum does not appear to have been a large town either under the Musalmáns (1350-1750) or under the Maráthás (1750-1818). In 1820 two years after its capture it had 1309 houses lodging about 7700 persons, and of these a good many must have been added in 1818 when about 300 houses in the fort were pulled down. In 1820 the houses which were thinly scattered are described as better than in most parts of India, those of the upper class being uniform, substantial, and roomy, and those of the lower classes respectable cottages.[3]

In 1872 Belgaum had 4388 houses, 827 of which were of the better, and 3561 of the poorer sort. These lodged 26,947 persons or an average of 6·14 persons to each house. Of late the town has spread towards the north-west and south-west and many houses have been built chiefly by husbandmen who hold land near the town. In 1881 the number of houses was increased to 7713. All the houses are tiled.

---

[1] Local Records. [2] Mr. C. W. Richardson.

[3] Hamilton's East India Gazetteer, I. 165. The house of the Peshwa's mámlatdár Vyankáji Yashvant Mánjrekar near the Samádevati temple still shows signs of openings for guns. Near it are a few Musalmán tombs supposed to be of Arab sepoys, who from time to time died in the mámlatdár's service.

Chapter XIV. Places. BELGAUM. *Houses.*

By far the greater number of houses consist of a ground floor: very few buildings have an upper storey. The better class of houses have a raised plinth sometimes of cut stone, but usually of blocks of laterite of which also the walls are built. A few of the houses are *chausopi* that is with open yards surrounded by verandas. The poorer houses are built of mud mixed with cut hay, or of plastered sun-dried bricks between wooden supports. The floors of the poorer class of houses are in many cases on or below the level of the ground. The houses as a rule face the street in an unbroken line. The rear line is extremely irregular as the houses vary in depth from twenty or thirty to seventy feet. The central rooms of the very deep houses are extremely dark and ill-aired, the only air coming from the front and back doors and through the tiles which seldom fit tightly and are often moved by monkeys who wander at large over the house-tops. All houses have a back court yard in which usually stand a *tulsi* pillar and a well. Within a few feet of the well formerly was a pit privy, but these have lately been replaced by open privies. In most yards vegetables and plantains are grown and cowdung cakes dried. The waste water instead of being carried away is generally left to soak into the yard.

Roads.

In 1848 the leading men of Belgaum formed a committee and in four months by voluntary subscriptions repaired all the roads and lanes of the town, extending to a length of between nine and ten miles.[1] In reward for their public spirit Government granted the people of Belgaum a sum of £600 (Rs. 6000) to improve the town. Still much remained to be done in widening the old roads and in making new roads until the municipality was established in 1852. In 1853-54, £59 (Rs. 590) and during the next four years £40 to £50 (Rs. 400-500) were spent. In 1864-65 £242 (Rs. 2420) were spent, and, from 1865 to 1880, £253 (Rs. 2530) have been yearly spent on roads. There are at present fifty-seven sections of roads known by the names of the streets through which they pass. Most of these sections have been metalled within the last eight or ten years, and a few of crumbled trap or *murum* are being gradually metalled. Every day all the municipal roads are cleaned by Mhár sweepers. The sweepings consisting of grass rubbish dry leaves and decayed bones are gathered in dust-bins in different parts of the town, removed in carts, and thrown into a pit to the south of the town. The sweepings were at first used to fill old quarry holes and the low lying spaces in and near the town. When rotten and decayed the sweepings are sold as manure. The leading streets are lighted with kerosine lamps, of which seventy-one are kept alight at a yearly cost of £155 (Rs. 1554). During the dry weather nine carts water the roads at a yearly cost of £65 (Rs. 650). The town is surrounded by a hedge chiefly of *kárvi* or milk bush with openings for the roads. These openings are called gates or *veses*, and some of them are said to have formerly been provided with gateways and gates which were closed at night. The chief gates are the Pátil, the Bogár, and the Gondhaliváda in the west; the Kangráli and Kákti

---

[1] The example thus set down was followed in several towns and villages of the district. Thornton's Gazetteer, 66.

Gates.

in the north; the Fort in the east; and the Dhárwár and Kapleshvar in the south. The Pátil and Bogár gates have traces of old gateways. The Kákti gate had a built gateway under the banian tree to the west of the high school where dead bodies are rested on their way to the burning ground. The Bogárve was the largest gate, as the term is still applied to any unusually broad passage. The other gates have been opened as the town limits extended. Near the Kotvál chávdi in Sherkhánváda are traces of a gate which must have led to the fort. At each of the present gates is a police post a small pretty building and a municipal toll bar. Besides the gates several small openings lead out of the town, where tollmen are stationed.

Communications.

The surrounding hills make Belgaum difficult of access. On the west the barrier of the Sahyádris is pierced only in two or three places. About ten miles to the north a line of rugged hills runs west and east, and, except by the bridges on the Poona road, the Márkandeya and the Ghatprabha, which run in the same direction, can be crossed only during the dry season. About fifteen miles to the south the river Malprabha runs west and east. Four hill forts are visible from Belgaum Yellurgad nine miles to the south commanding the country between the Khánápur and the Dhárwár roads; Mahipálgad on the Vaijnáth hills eight miles north-west of Belgaum under which the new Vengurla road passes; Kálánandigad twenty-two miles west of Belgaum on a hill near the Rám pass road about 200 feet higher than the country round; and Kákti fort four miles north of Belgaum on a line of hills running parallel to the Poona road.

Railway.

When (1889) the West Deccan railway is finished Belgaum will have a second class station 242 miles from Poona. The exact position of the Belgaum station has not been fixed; the site will depend chiefly on military considerations. Till the railway is finished the only available port is Vengurla in Ratnágiri seventy-eight miles to the west, which is little better than an open roadstead. Steamers have always to lie a long distance off-shore and during the monsoon the port is closed. Kárwár about ninety miles to the south-west is except Bombay the best harbour on the west coast. Marmagaon about fifteen miles south of Goa will be the terminus of the south branch of the Southern Marátha Railway.

Trade.

Belgaum has about 250 traders chiefly Bráhmans, Lingáyats, Nárvekars, Maráthás, Gujarát and Márwár Vánis, Pársis, and Musalmáns with capitals varying from £500 to £20,000 (Rs. 5000 to Rs. 2,00,000). Some have capital of their own and others trade on borrowed funds. Almost all are independent traders. The chief imports are timber, ironware, glass and other European articles, metal vessels, salt, and cocoanuts. Timber is bought at the Government stores in Kánara and sold at Belgaum to private persons and contractors. Ironware, glassware, and other European articles are brought from Bombay by Vengurla in the fair season and by Poona during the rains; they are sold to petty dealers and to consumers. Brass and copper vessels are brought from Poona and Sángli for local use; salt and cocoanuts are brought from Goa and Vengurla both for local use and to be sent inland. The chief

Chapter XIV. Places. BELGAUM. *Trade.*

exports are of grain, rice, wheat, gram, millet, and pulse; and of cloth waistcloths and women's robes. Grain is bought by grain merchants at Belgaum from petty corn dealers and growers and sent to Goa and Vengurla. The waistcloths and robes are brought by cloth merchants from local weavers and are either sold to Konkan merchants or sent to Dhárwár and Bijápur. The chief industry is cotton weaving with a yearly outturn valued at about £11,500 (Rs. 1,15,000). The making of carpets and copper vessels and spinning and dyeing raw silk are the only other industries. Oil-pressing is a very thriving calling in Belgaum and several of the well-off Telis let bullock carriages called *dhamnis* or *sárvats* on hire. Belgaum has seven tanneries to the south of the cantonment near the distillery; six dyers in indigo, and twenty-two in safflower or *kusumba*. There are two lime kilns and two small tile kilns to the south of the town.

Markets.

The municipal vegetable market in the heart of the town was built by the municipality in 1866 at a cost of about £760 (Rs. 7600). The market has fifty-two stalls which yield a yearly rent of about £120 (Rs. 1200). The stalls are arranged in the form of a square enclosing an open space which is occupied by cloth merchants on the Saturday weekly market. All round on the outside of the market is an open space which is occupied by squatters who come daily with vegetables and on Saturday by people from the neighbouring villages who come with small quantities of grain. Beyond it is a further open space where cartmen are allowed to stand with their grain and wood carts. At the Saturday weekly market all kinds of grain, country cloth, groceries, firewood, grass, earthen vessels, and vegetables are brought from the villages within a radius of twenty miles from Belgaum and exposed for sale. A cattle and timber market is also held on Saturday in an empty plot of ground to the east of the town and fort where milch buffaloes and cows, he-buffaloes and bullocks, ponies, timber, rafters, and bamboos are sold. The other municipal markets are the mutton market and slaughter-house built in 1872 at a cost of £416 (Rs. 4160) and yielding a yearly income of £70 (Rs. 700); a fish market built in 1872 at a cost of £102 10*s.* (Rs. 1025) and yielding a yearly revenue of £4 (Rs. 40); a beef market built in 1873 at a cost of £124 14*s.* (Rs. 1247) and yielding £15 (Rs. 150); a second slaughter-house yielding £18 (Rs. 180); and a cart stand built in 1875 at a cost of £347 (Rs. 3470) and yielding £40 (Rs. 400). Besides the special market room provided by the municipality, both sides of the Khade Bázár road are occupied by shops of Nárvekars, Bohorás, and Márwáris where groceries, woollen and silk cloths, English piece-goods, and oilman's stores are sold. The Bhendi Bázár has a few cloth merchants' shops where handloom waistcloths, turbans, and women's robes are sold. In the same street ready-made native clothing iron and brassware and confectionery are sold at a few shops. All the wholesale grain and salt merchants live and have their shops in the Áditvár Peth.

Management.

Belgaum is throughout the year the seat of a Judge, cantonment magistrate, chaplain, and civil surgeon, and during the rains of the Collector, the assistant and deputy collectors, superintending and executive engineers, deputy sanitary commissioner, divisional forest officer, police superintendent, assistant superintendents revenue survey, and the educational and deputy educational inspectors. It is also the head-quarters of the chief revenue and police offices of the Belgaum sub-division, and is provided with a municipality, a civil hospital and dispensary, jail, post and telegraph offices, travellers' bungalow, eighteen schools, temples and mosques, and prayer places.

Municipality.

The municipality was established in 1851 and was raised to a city municipality on 1st April 1883. In 1851 the municipal revenue, chiefly from a house-tax, was £40 (Rs. 408), which increased in 1859 to £218 (Rs. 2185). In 1864-65 octroi took the place of the house-tax, and the revenue increased to £724 (Rs. 7240), further increasing to £1395 (Rs. 13,950) in 1869-70, £1601 (Rs. 16,010) in 1877-78, and £2848 (Rs. 28,480) in 1880. In 1882-83 the income of the municipality chiefly raised from octroi (Rs. 19,157), a conservancy cess (Rs. 8357), market fees (Rs. 2624), and a wheel-tax (Rs. 2527) was £3710 (Rs. 37,102); and the expenditure, chiefly incurred in public health (Rs. 14,282), conservancy (Rs. 9038), and road repairs (Rs. 5496) was £3931 (Rs. 39,310). The municipality has made a factory for turning nightsoil into poudrette. At first people refused to use the poudrette. But a trial showed its value as a manure and it is now in demand.

Jail.

The jail, on a ridge about a quarter of a mile north of the town, is built round the *dargha* or tomb built by Kishvar Khán the son of Asad Khán in 1561.[1] Part of the tomb has been turned into a guardroom and hospital.[2] The jail building was originally a factory or industrial school for Thags. In 1866 it was made into a sub-jail with accommodation for about 108 prisoners. It is now classed as a temporary jail for prisoners sentenced to less than two years' imprisonment. Additional sheds have also been built. The prisoners are made to work in the jail garden and in a stone quarry close by; they are also hired to work for the municipality, who pay their wages. The travellers' bungalow at Belgaum is on the Poona-Harihar mail road. It has three rooms and was built in 1841 at a cost of £252 (Rs. 2520); the yearly charge of maintenance is £13 4*s*. (Rs. 132). Of the eighteen schools eight are Government, four are mission, one is a girls' school, and five are private schools. Of the Government schools one is a high school, one a first grade Anglo-vernacular school, two are Kánarese, two Maráthi, one Hindustáni, and one a night school. Of the mission schools, one is a high school, one a Maráthi school, one a Kánarese school, and one is for girls.

The six chief temples are Dyámava's, Kapleshvar's, Máruti's, Shiv's, Vishnu's, and Vithoba's. All are modern and have no historical or architectural interest.

Fair.

In honour of Dyámava a large fair is held in Belgaum once every twelve years. A large car about fifty feet high is built and

---

[1] Kishvar Khán was buried at Bijápur not in this tomb.

[2] In five places the *dargha* bears marks of shot directed from Belgaum fort at General Munro's first battery in 1818.

Chapter XIV. Places. BELGAUM. *Fair.*

a figure of the goddess is set on the car and drawn in procession through the thoroughfares of the town. At the 1872 fair the car was so heavy that, though pulled by some 200 men three days were required to drag it through the town. When the car reached the green between the town and the fort of Belgaum twelve buffaloes and hundreds of goats were offered as sacrifices. The head of the buffalo which was borne in procession before the car, was carried round the town, and buried, and over it a small hut was built. During the twelve days on which Dyámava remains in a temporary shed on the green no corn-mills are allowed to grind.[1]

There are two mosques one near the jail, the other near the new police lines. Both show signs of repair and rebuilding. According to a local story a British officer began to pull them down for their stones, but fell sick and did not recover till he had put both buildings in repair.

Cantonment.

The[2] cantonment lies to the west and south-west on somewhat higher ground than the town and is separated from it for about 600 yards by the Bogárve stream and the Kolhápur road. Twenty-four pillars mark the camp boundaries which include an area of 1524 acres and contain a population of 9852. The chief divisions are the Sadar Bázár forming part of the eastern boundary, the most thickly peopled part of the camp, the Officers' and Pensioners' Lines within 600 yards west and 300 yards north of the Sadar Bázár, and the Regimental Lines at the western and southern ends. There are also the Tent Lascars' Lines near the post office. The surface of the camp is waving with a general slope from north-west to south-east. Except a small piece of ground at the north-west the drainage of the camp is towards the Bogárve and Belári water-courses, which meeting at the south-east corner behind the post office run through the rice fields between Belgaum and Sháhpur, and pass to the south-east of the fort. Besides single large trees in the enclosures of the Officers' and Pensioners' houses, and in the Native Infantry Lines, the camp has large *khirni* groves round Asad Khán's tomb and mango groves behind the post office in the south-east and near the north-eastern boundary.

Gardens.

Besides small gardens mostly attached to Officers' and Pensioners' houses, and several strips of garden in the old British Infantry barracks and in the Artillery Lines, the camp has three gardens, the old station garden, the new station garden, and the Soldiers' garden. The two station gardens, with an area of about fifty-nine acres, occupy two pieces of ground behind the station hospital and the Artillery Lines. The gardens are managed by the Cantonment Magistrate with a small paid establishment for the benefit of soldiers and residents in the cantonment. Both gardens have wells worked with leather bags or *mốts*. The new gardens have many flower beds, a band-stand, and seats. For the Soldiers' garden a plot about seven acres has been set apart between the lines of the British regiment and

[1] Details are given in the Dhárwár Statistical Account.
[2] The Cantonment account owes much to additions and corrections by Lieutenant-Colonel T. Trueman, Cantonment Magistrate of Belgaum.

the station hospital. Potatoes, peas, and other vegetables are grown. A small garden of about 1½ acres near the right flank Native Infantry lines is let to a Pársi merchant.

Besides the European and Native regimental barracks, there are sixty-two officers' and forty pensioners' bungalows, and 1032 native houses in the Sadar Bázár. For the British Infantry troops there are twelve small single storeyed barracks built during the five years ending 1841. One of these barracks is used as a theatre, four as married men's quarters accommodating 100 families, and the rest accommodate thirty-two non-commissioned officers and 304 men. Two large single storeyed barracks were built in 1866 to accommodate eight native cavalry officers and eighty-two men. Seven double storeyed barracks were built in 1874-75 to accommodate three single and seven married native cavalry officers and 260 men. During the five years ending 1841 three field battery barracks were built of which one is used for stores. The double storeyed barracks are fine buildings of black basalt and were built at an average cost of £8800 (Rs. 88,000). Except one block which cost £15,560 (Rs. 1,55,600) and holds forty-four men each holds thirty-six men. Subsidiary accommodation includes quarters for seven staff sergeants, quarter-guards with prisoner's rooms and ten cells, canteen and coffee-shop in one block, workshops, gymnasium and drill shed, library, and recreation room, two school rooms for adults and children, sergeant's mess, quartermaster's stores and office, orderly room, court-martial room and pay office, temperance hall which is the old artillery canteen, two plunge-baths, two ball-courts, one skittle-alley and one bowling-alley. The gun-shed in the old artillery barracks is used as a public works workshop, and the old artillery stables are empty. The new artillery barracks, on the highest ground in the cantonment to the north of the infantry barracks, were built in 1874. Three of these accommodate seven native cavalry officers and 131 men, and one eighteen married men, and the stables attached accommodate 110 horses. These barracks have also all the subsidiary buildings complete for a battery of field artillery. They are well built and on the best site in the cantonment. In addition to the usual buildings necessary for a battery there is a hot-air bath for horses, a ball-court, skittle-alley, and a plunge-bath.

The Native Infantry Lines in the extreme south of the camp contain complete hut accommodation for two native regiments. They are well built and neatly laid out, but the right flank lines are too close to a pond on the right side, and of late years the regiments occupying them have suffered from fever and bowel diseases. The right flank lines were built in 1869 by the men of the regiment and last repaired in 1880. The left flank lines were built in 1866 by the men of the regiment and were last repaired in 1881. Each flank has two wings of barracks separated from each other by a wide road, where the men gather at muster time. Each wing has eight lines containing two barracks. Each barrack contains ten rooms for the men and one for the native officers on each side. The men's rooms are about ten feet long and six feet broad, and

Chapter XIV. Places. BELGAUM. *Cantonment.*

are divided into two compartments. The outer compartment which is smaller is used for bathing, while the inner serves both as a cooking and sleeping room. These rooms are occupied by single as well as by family men. The waste water is carried by means of small gutters and used for watering plantain, jack, and mango trees planted in each row of buildings. The sweet basil plant with its mud stand is often seen in front of the rooms occupied by Hindu sepoys. The lines have all necessary subsidiary buildings including a hospital. A few old huts to the south belonging to the old lines are used as shops in the regimental bázárs. One or two small temples dedicated to Mahádev or Máruti are outside of the lines.

Each infantry regiment has its own rented mess-house, and the officers of the battery rent one of the bungalows as a mess. The tent lascars' lines at the south-east end of the camp are mud huts with thatched roofs. The Commissariat Lines lie about half a mile to the east of the artillery barracks. Of the 130 bungalows in the officers' lines and in the pensioners' lines, five are first class bungalows with a monthly rent of £6 (Rs. 60) or more, thirteen second class houses with a monthly rent of £5 to £6 (Rs. 50 - 60), thirteen third class with rents of £3 10*s.* to £5 (Rs. 35 - 50), and fifty-nine fourth class houses with rents of £2 to £3 10*s.* (Rs. 20 - 35). The forty bungalows in the Pensioners' Lines, with monthly rents of £3 10*s.* to 10*s.* are inhabited by civil officials as nearly all the pensioners have died or left the place. Except one or two which are two-storeyed most of the bungalows are one-storeyed buildings, large, airy, built mostly of laterite, and tile-roofed. Besides the veranda which in many cases surrounds the building, the bungalows contain a hall with side rooms and one or two back rooms. The servants' quarters are by themselves in the enclosure. Most of the houses are owned by Márwáris and Sávkárs of Belgaum and Sháhpur.

Of the houses in the Sadar Bázár the better class have a good plinth two or three feet high and are built of cut stone with laterite walls or entirely of laterite. The walls of the poorer houses are built of mud and bricks sometimes with very small entrances. Most of the houses are one-storeyed and all are tiled, but they are badly aired dark and unwholesome. The camp water-supply is obtained from ninety-four wells, seventy-two of which in the Sadar Bázár and in the officers' and pensioners' houses are private, and twenty-two public wells for the use of troops. The best water is from a well near the quarry near St. Mary's Church, which is chiefly used by the British officers and troops. Besides the native regimental bázárs, the chief markets are beef mutton and vegetable markets in the Sadar Bázár. Of the 120 shops in the Sadar Bázár, forty sell firewood, twenty-six sell fish, twenty-three are Europe shops, twelve sell vegetables, eight earthen vessels, seven fruit, and four sell oil.

Roads.

Four roads, Bogárve's road, Samádevati road, Post Office road, and the Vengurla road join the cantonment with the town. The cantonment roads are in good order and clean and are provided with side drains.

Troops.

The troops stationed at Belgaum in 1882-83 were a Field Battery of Artillery of 162 men and 110 horses; seven companies of a British Regiment, 770 men including one company stationed in the fort; two regiments of Native Infantry (old strength) 1424 rank and file. The establishment of a field column carriage consists of 28 draught bullocks, 56 pack bullocks, 82 mules, 24 draught bullocks attached to the battery, 55 litter-bearers, and 25 carts. The present establishment includes 38 draught bullocks, 75 pack bullocks, 24 draught bullocks attached to the battery, 55 litter-bearers, and 25 carts. Accommodation for these is provided in the Commissariat Cattle lines called Modikhána near the eastern extremity of the camp, between the old cemetery and the old Government garden.

Staff.

The station staff comprises the Brigadier General commanding, Deputy Assistant Adjutant General, Deputy Assistant Adjutant General for Musketry, Cantonment Magistrate, Executive Engineer, Executive Commissariat Officer, Camp Chaplain, Fort Chaplain, Roman Catholic Chaplain, Staff Surgeon, and Barrack Master. Almost all of these officers live in the cantonment.

The Commissariat Lines lie about half a mile to the east of the Artillery barracks, while the godowns are inside the fort near the west entrance. The slaughter-house is on the south side of a grove of trees opposite the staff lines. It includes a meat shed and hanging shed, both nearly new and with the latest improvements, three cattle sheds, and a sheep shed.

St. Mary's Church.

St. Mary's Church is a handsome building in the Lombardo-Gothic style with entrance porches on the west and south and aisles connected with a lofty nave by flying buttresses between which are eight clerestory windows. The church is adorned by the use of different coloured stones and by a rich stained glass window, which was given by subscription in 1870. The chancel is approached by six steps of Kolhápur marble. The church was begun in 1864 at the same time as the Kirkee church both from designs by the Reverend F. Gell, and was consecrated in 1869 by Bishop Douglas. It holds 700 persons and cost £11,580 (Rs. 1,15,800). In 1875 the compound was enclosed with a fence and railing and laid out as a garden. In front of the west porch, almost at the meeting of the four chief cantonment roads, stands a lofty memorial cross raised by the officers and men of the 64th Regiment to comrades who fell in the 1857 Mutinies and in Persia.[1] Near the garrison cells is a chapel belonging to the London Mission Society where Presbyterians usually worship.

Roman Catholic Chapels.

There are three Roman Catholic chapels, St. Mary's of Mount Carmel near the Native Infantry Lines, St. Anthony's in the Sadar Bázár, and a third near the Commissariat Cattle Lines. St. Mary's Chapel was built in 1823 by subscriptions among the Roman Catholic community of Belgaum and the European troops, was enlarged in 1833 and in 1851, and improved in 1884. It is a tiled building about forty feet long and twenty-five feet broad with laterite

---

[1] The Rev. C. Walford, M.A., Chaplain of Belgaum.

Chapter XIV. Places. BELGAUM. *Roman Catholic Chapels.*

walls and 400 to 450 seats. Round the church is a large enclosure in which is a school building and several tombs. Till 1856 when it was transferred to the Bombay Catholic Bishopric the church was under the Archbishop of Goa and the priest was a Carmelite. The congregation numbers 700 to 800 persons including European and Eurasian Roman Catholic soldiers and officers and Madrási Christians. Two morning and evening services are held. The duties of the Jesuit priest are to hold daily divine service, two masses and an evening service on Sundays, to go to the military hospitals, teach the catechism in the Regimental schools and two English and two Tamil schools connected with the chapel. The large bungalow to the south-east, now rented, belongs to the chapel and till 1881 was occupied by nuns who were withdrawn in that year. St. Anthony's Chapel in the Sadar Bázár is chiefly intended for the evening prayers of the Madrási Christians. It is in charge of the priest in St. Mary's chapel. The chapel near the commissariat cattle lines for Goanese Catholics is under the jurisdiction of the Archbishop of Goa.

Asad Khán's Dargha.

The only Hindu temples are small buildings in the camp near the native infantry lines and the Nágzari springs. There are two Musalmán shrines, one in the *khirni* grove behind the Roman Catholic chapel to Asad Khán the Bijápur general who held Belgaum fort from 1511 to 1549, and the other to Murád Alli Sháh a *fakir*. Asad Khán, who died at Mandoli three miles south-west of Belgaum and was buried here, is held in high honour by all Belgaum Musalmáns. He was remarkable for his judgment talents and learning, and for his physical strength and prowess as a swordsman. For nearly forty years he was the patron and protector of all the noble and distinguished men in the Deccan. He lived universally respected and esteemed and maintained a splendour and magnificence suited to his high station.[1] Asad Khán is supposed to have died at the age of 150 and it is said, but with little truth, that as long as his memory is honoured Belgaum will be free from cholera. In the Muharram, all the biers or *panjás* are brought and pay their respects at Asad Khán's tomb. About thirty royal umbrellas hang round the shrine and about two dozen ostrich eggs near the front of the building are presents offered by Asad Khán's devotees. Almost all classes of natives and especially the sepoys pay their devotion at Asad Khán's shrine, where incense flowers and cocoanuts of the value of about £1 (Rs. 10) are offered every Thursday and dancing girls pay their respects by dancing before the shrine every Thursday night. To the original building a front was added by a Bráhman mámlatdár of Belgaum.

Hospitals.

The station hospital to which all British soldiers are sent is between the British Infantry and the Royal Artillery Lines. It contains beds for ninety-four men and fifteen women and has quarters for the apothecary, assistant apothecary, matron, and apprentices. The Native Infantry Regiments have each their hospitals. There are three infection huts one near the Royal

---

1 Stokes' Belgaum, 33-34. Details are given in the History Chapter.

Artillery Lines and two near the right flank Native Infantry Lines. Two positions for cholera camps were chosen in 1869 one on the Khánápur road about six miles south of Belgaum near the village of Machha, the other near Yermale village about eight miles to the south-west. Two more sites have been chosen further south in the direction of Khánápur, but it has not been found necessary as yet to use any of the four camps. Lock hospital rules are in force within a radius of five miles from Belgaum. The station has a first class lock hospital with a building bought and remodelled by Government at a cost of £485 (Rs. 4850). The staff consists of a surgeon, hospital assistant, and a matron. The number of prostitutes on the rolls in 1882-83 was 145 chiefly Madras Mhárs and Maráthás.

Cantonment Fund.

The cantonment is managed by a committee from a fund which in 1882-83 yielded an income of £1664 (Rs. 16,640). The fund is administered under rules laid down by Act III of 1867. The cantonment committee consists of the Brigadier General, the District Magistrate, Deputy Sanitary Commissioner, Executive Engineer, and two members nominated by the Commander-in-chief, with the Cantonment Magistrate as its Secretary. The committee is responsible for the proper administration of the fund. The executive duties of the committee are performed by the Cantonment Magistrate who has a staff under him.

Magazine.

The station has no proper regimental magazine, the reserve and spare ammunition of the British and Native Infantry regiments being kept in the old ordnance store in the fort. Near the Royal Artillery barracks is the main magazine; but it is of faulty build and is used for keeping powder and blank cartridges for the Royal Artillery.[1] The garrison cells lie between the church and the cantonment garden and have accommodation for fifteen prisoners. The post and telegraph offices are close to the Staff Lines. The telegraph office is of the third class.

Observatory.

Belgaum is one of the five military stations in the Presidency where in 1851 meteorological observatories were established.[2] The observatory is in the enclosure of the station hospital and is in charge of the senior medical officer of the hospital and under the administration of the medical department. The system of observations comprises two sets of daily observations one taken at nine in the morning and the other at six in the evening. Four complete sets of twenty-four hourly observations for four days in every month are also recorded. At each observation the instruments and phenomena noted include the barometer, dry and wet bulb thermometers, the direction of wind, the cloudiness, and the rainfall. Twice a day are recorded the maximum and the minimum thermometers in the shade, and once a day the maximum thermometer exposed to the sun's rays during the day and the minimum thermometer laid

---

[1] The magazine is a large high building with two rooms divided by pillars of open arches like the aisles of a church divided from a nave.

[2] The five stations are Belgaum, Poona, Deesa, Karáchi, and Bombay-Colába. Chambers' Bombay Meteorology, 125, 129.

Chapter XIV.
Places.
BELGAUM.
Observatory.

on grass open to the sky at night. The observations are registered on printed forms which are filled and regularly forwarded by the head of the medical department to the Reporter of the Colába Observatory in Bombay to have the calculations examined and results compiled. Once a year the registers and compilations are sent by the Reporter to Government to be forwarded to Her Majesty's Secretary of State for India.

The observatory possesses tables of corrections for index errors of the various thermometers and of the barometer which corrections are regularly applied to the observations. In the beginning of the system the observers at the station were European soldiers who were drafted from their regiments for the duty, and, before entering on this duty, were put through a course of practical training at the Colába Observatory. The self-registering thermometers are placed in a wooden revolving stand at a distance of 18½ feet from the nearest building and four feet from the ground. They are fully exposed to the air and protected from the sun's rays, but it is impossible to prevent rain from getting at them during the revolving storms which occur at the beginning of the south-west monsoon at the close of May. The readings of the thermometer are supposed to be too high as the construction of the stand is not adapted to a tropical sun. The barometer and dry and wet bulb thermometers are in a shed in the north-east veranda of the hospital guard-house. The shed is thirteen feet by six and is made of wooden bars two inches apart. It has a flagged floor and a post in the middle rising from the floor to the roof. The barometer is suspended in the room and the dry and wet bulb thermometers on it, the thermometer being four feet seven inches from the floor, the dry bulb two feet seven inches, the wet bulb being three feet one inch from the wall. A new tower has been erected near the Gymkhána.

Fort.

The fort of Belgaum, one of the six works kept as Government forts in the Bombay Presidency,[1] is about three quarters of a mile to the east of the town and about 1½ miles from the camp and on a somewhat lower level. It is commanded by rising ground about 1000 yards to the north. Except where the town almost abuts on the fort and is about 150 yards from its west or weakest face, the ground close to the fort is an esplanade 600 yards broad with a slight outward rise. Rice and sugarcane fields lie to the south and east. The fort is about 1000 yards long and 800 yards broad. It is an irregular oval of 2900 yards perimeter, with the outer work of the main gate attached to it in the form of the mouth of a jar. It occupies an area of about 100 acres, and owes its principal strength to the width of its steep wet ditch and the height of its stone walls.

The ditch, at present forty to fifty feet deep and about seventy-two feet wide, is nowhere dry, and, except during the hot weather, is in most places filled with water, especially towards the

[1] Govt. of India, Mily. Dept. 1027 dated 17th July 1879. Belgaum is a station of secondary importance and not a strategical point for a first class fortress. It has not to defend an arsenal but to protect an arsenal depôt. It has no Government buildings of much importance. It has been kept to maintain a hold on the neighbouring districts.

east and south where as the ground is low about fifteen feet are stored at the end of the rainy season. The water is unwholesome and in places is covered with scum. In the hot season when large quantities of water are drawn to the neighbouring fields, the ditch is dry and becomes a grazing ground for cattle. Except that the greater portion of its facing or revetment has given way, the ditch is in good repair. The average height of the walls which are backed by substantial earthworks, and are accessible from all parts, is thirty-four feet. The fort is well covered by the glacis or earth slope especially where it is most subject to attack from its nearness to the town of Belgaum. The wall contains a large number of the carved stones which are found on Jain and other temples, including some richly relieved figures of Ganpati and Vishnu built in without design as the blocks fitted.[1] The scarp wall which had failed in places was repaired in 1883. The fort has six bastions, one cavalier or outwork, and two gateways.

Inscriptions.

In three places stones with Persian and Arabic inscriptions record the dates of the building or re-building of the fort or part of the fort.

On the north-east wall in a recess in the parapet is a six-line inscription in the Persian character which runs:

> 'Ya'qub 'Ali Kha'n who is a joy to the heart, and by whose benevolence the world is prosperous, built the wall of the citadel strengthening it with a strong foundation like the wall of Alexander.'

The date-verse gives the date (A. D. 1530 H. 937.) Another inscription in the south-east of the fort relates to the re-building of that portion of the wall. The inscription runs:

> 'Oh Opener! The fort having been destroyed by the rains, it was again made strong and firm. It was entirely renewed in the time of 'Abdul Husain, the powerful. A reckoning according to the date of the Hijrah was written down: know it to be the year 1043 (that is A.D.1632). Written by 'Abdul 'Aziz'.[2]

Gates.

The fort is entered by two gates the main gate in the north and the new gate in the west. The main gate which was built in 1631 by one Bándeh Ali crosses the ditch by a massive masonry causeway flanked by high and thick walls. This gate is covered by a very large outwork which would require a strong garrison to hold it. The outer as well as the inner gateways are furnished with heavy folding gates which are kept in good order. A third gateway between these two was pulled down by the British and there are traces of a fourth folding gate a little to the south of the inner gateway. In a small well built and painted niche in the wall

---

[1] Besides the figures of Ganpati and Vishnu are rows of sharp cut lotus flowers, a warrior brandishing his sword, slim dancing women, and musicians. Hero-stones or *virgals* raised in honour of the dead are also built into the walls. These stones are divided into three panels or compartments, the lowest panel representing the fight in which the warrior was slain, the central panel showing two damsels bearing him to heaven, and the uppermost showing him in heaven adoring the *ling*. On one slab, on the bastion under the flag staff battery, the central compartment instead of the usual damsels has a gigantic hand and arm pointing upwards; the body of the deceased warrior follows its direction with arms raised towards the sky. This is a *sati* stone showing how the sacrificed wife guides her husband to heaven. Stokes' Belgaum, 25.

[2] Dr. Burgess' First Archæological Report, 5.

Chapter XIV.
Places.
BELGAUM.
Fort.

just inside the main gate on the right side is a black stone image of the goddess Durga vulgarly called Durgadi, the guardian deity of Hindu forts. It was probably placed there in Marátha times (1750-1818). The hereditary worshipper is a Jain, who, in the shape of presents of cocoanuts and copper coins, enjoys an income of about 2*s*. (Re. 1) a week from the Hindus of the town. Many men flock to the place on Fridays and Tuesdays. On each side of the road leading through the gate are large stalls, covered from above by a stone terrace supported by pillars and arches taken chiefly from Jain temples. At the end of the left hand stall are two carved pillars placed upside down. The road with the Engineer's stores and workshops and the Station Library on the right and the old main guard rooms and the church on the left leads to an old arched gateway, the remains of the *Nagárkhána* in front of Asad Khán's *mahál* or palace which stood in front of the Safa Masjid. The western gateway is simply a well built arched opening in the rampart made for public convenience. The ditch is here simply filled in so as to carry the roadway across a solid causeway. Besides these two gateways several underground passages are said to lead out of the fort, especially one to Yellurgad about nine miles to the south.[1] One of these openings was found when part of the wall in the south-east was being re-built.

Except in the south-east where the ground is low and is sometimes flooded during the rains the interior of the fort is level. It is adorned with beautiful trees. When the British took possession of the fort, besides the garrison and the commandant Lakshmanbhat Thákur, who lived in a large mansion of which the present Station Library forms a part, the fort contained 200 to 300 people and ten Bráhman, ten Lingáyat and ten Jain families chiefly Government officers. Of these only one family, the Khares, now live in the town of Belgaum. These were ordered to leave the fort with their property in seven days, and no Hindu or Musalmán was allowed to live in the fort. British officers were given sites for building bungalows most of which at present by sale or gift have again become the property of Hindu and Musalmán townsmen. About thirty-five bungalows are occupied by European officers, clergymen, and pensioners. The bungalows are large airy one-storeyed buildings with walls and tiled roofs, in the centre of large hedged enclosures with bright flowers and finely grown trees. Most of the gardens have a well and behind, or to one side, are the servants' quarters, stables, and other out-houses. The fort also contains a magazine, an ordnance store, a commissariat store, and barracks for one strong company of British infantry. The value of the Government buildings in the fort is estimated at £27,500 (Rs. 2,75,000).

Besides barracks for the use of a detachment of the European regiment stationed in the camp, the fort has small single storeyed barracks built in 1860 with room for four officers and eighty-five men and one double storeyed barrack accommodating seven

[1] An opening is shown at Yellurgad which is said to communicate with the Belgaum fort.

Chapter XIV. Places. BELGAUM.

married men.[1] The subsidiary accommodation includes a quarter guard with prisoners' rooms and cells, canteen and coffee shops, school room, plunge bath, and skittle and bowling alleys. The fort has an excellent supply of water from forty-eight wells six of them public and forty-two private. The wells are stone built and are generally worked by bags drawn by bullocks. The best water is said to come from a well inside the arsenal which is not available for public use. From the well outside the arsenal and close to the Safa mosque water is drawn for the use of the troops and the European residents of the fort.[2]

Roads.

The fort is connected with the town and cantonment by two roads leading out of two gates. The road from the main or north gate after crossing the esplanade meets the Khade Bázár road at the east end of the town, and the road through the new or west gate meets the Dhárwár road and passes either through or outside the town by the Post Office into the Cantonment. The Kaládgi road runs south-east passing the fort on the north and north-east, while the Vengurla road runs west from the main gate, meeting the Kolhápur road near the Huzur Kacheri. Inside the fort a well made road, with several branches leading to the bungalows and the barracks, passes along the fort wall and below the earth works which support the wall. The conservancy arrangements in the fort are under the Cantonment Magistrate. A plot of land by the side of an old Musalmán burying-ground to the north-west of the pond below the Jail hill seems at one time to have been set apart as a graveyard. It contains a tomb about five feet high dated 1821 and several inscribed stones whose letters have been effaced by weather. For long Europeans who have died in the fort have used the camp burying ground.

The fort contains a church, an arsenal, a commissariat yard, public works stores and offices, an ordnance office, and a station library. The chief objects of interest are Asad Khán's Safa mosque and three old Jain temples.

Church.

The fort church, called Christ Church, is a small building 112 feet long with a pleasing interior. It was built in 1833 at a cost of £1135 (Rs. 11,350) and contains several monuments and memorial windows. Its apse was designed by General Merriman R. E. to commemorate the services of Mr. C. J. Manson, C.S. Political Agent

---

[1] This barrack is one of the three old Jain temples in the fort.

[2] In 1868 an analysis of the water of this well gave :

Chloride of Sodium	5·57	grains to the gallon.
Sulphate of Soda	2·27	,, ,,
Carbonate of Soda	1·61	,, ,,
Nitrate of Lime	·46	,, ,,
Carbonate of Lime	6·23	,, ,,
Silica	2·80	,, ,,
Carbonate of Magnesia	3·21	,, ,,
Oxydisable Organic Matter	·42	,, ,,
Total ...	22·57	,, ,,

Total solids by evaporation 21·98; Clark's degree of hardness 10°·33. The water was destitute of colour, odour, and taste, deposited hardly any sediment, and contained traces of nitrous acid. Surgeon-Major C. T. Peters, M.B.

Chapter XIV.
Places.
Belgaum.
Ordnance Depôt.

Southern Marátha Country who was murdered by the Bráhman chief of Nargund in 1858.[1] The church font is of a very handsome design in black marble.[2] A third class ordnance store was kept in the fort till the end of March 1881. A few stores are left in charge of a park sergeant, under the orders of the Officer Commanding the Royal Artillery. It is a compact block of buildings surrounding an oblong plot of ground whose outer measurements are 200 yards by seventy with a large open space in the centre 180 yards by fifty. It contains two large store rooms one 184 feet by 24 and the other 114 by 24; workshops, two guard-rooms, staff sergeants' quarters, armoury, magazine, and woodyard. As there are no proper regimental magazines the reserve and spare ammunition both of the British and of the native regiments are kept in the old ordnance store. A small magazine at the back of the old store is not used. The commissariat store rooms are close inside the west entrance of the fort, while the lines lie about half a mile to the east of the artillery barracks in the cantonment. The executive engineer's office and the public works stores and workshops are inside the north entrance to the fort. The Station Library is in a house behind the public works stores and offices which form part of the old commandant's mansion. In the south-west corner of the front wall of the Library a Persian inscription in six lines, dated A.D. 1648, records that in the time of Khán Muhammad, a Bijápur officer of note in whose estate or *jághir* Belgaum probably lay, the fort wall was finished by Muhammad bin Zabit Khán.[3]

Safa Mosque.

Close to the south of the arsenal between the north and the west gates is Asad Khán's fine mosque called the Masjid-i-Safa or the Pure Mosque. The front measures 81′ 5″ in length and the mosque is 58′ 7″ deep. Over the mosque door, in very illegible Persian, is the following inscription:

> 'In the time of Adil Aya'm son of Adil Kha'n, a man of high rank, who bore the palm of excellence from all the world, of good counsel, the aim of merit, the defender of the faith who utterly uprooted the unbelievers from the country of the Deccan, Asad Kha'n, the best of all upright men, built this house of God, by good fortune, and with much labour. By the grace of God he called it the Pure Mosque. The lustre of the religion of the Prophet grew greater.'

The mosque formed part of a group of buildings all the rest of which have been pulled down. Asad Khán's palace or *mahál*, is

---

[1] The inscription on Manson's tablet runs:

> 'This tablet was erected by Government in recognition of the able and devoted public services of Charles James Manson of the Bombay Civil Service who, when Acting Political Agent, Southern Mara'tha Country, was barbarously murdered by a band of rebels in the night of the 29th May, 1858, at the village of Suraban. The Apse and Memorial window at the east end of the Church were erected by his Friends in affectionate remembrance of his public worth.'

Of six other tablets one is to Lieutenant W. P. Shakespeare, A. P. Campbell, and Ensign W. Caldwell who fell in the Kolhápur and Sávantvádi insurrection in 1844.

[2] The Rev. C. Walford, M.A., Chaplain of Belgaum.

[3] Stokes' Belgaum, 40; Dr. Burgess' First Archæological Report, 5.

said to have been to the south of the mosque. Opposite the palace were his kitchens, and to the right looking from the front of the mosque stood the *Divánkhána* or hall of audience. The road to this group of buildings led under an arch on the site of the present arsenal which was so high that an elephant with his rider could pass beneath it. The present arch which faces the main gate of the fort was straight opposite the arch which has been removed. That arch was the place where the *naubat* or large kettledrum was beaten at stated hours and for salutes.[1] In the mosque are preserved Asad Khán's quilted jacket which was sabre-proof;[2] his Kurán, and a pair of shoes, too heavy for an ordinary man to lift, with soles of lead and uppers of iron, which were used by Asad Khán in gymnastic exercises. On the south wall of the mosque is a very solid and heavy round platform (6′ 5″ long 5′ 1″ broad and 3′ 10″ high) on which Asad Khán is said to have often sprung dressed in full armour and wearing his lead-soled shoes. Another of his feats of strength, according to local story, was to lift the great iron stool before the mosque by the edge of the fountain. His sword was kept in the mosque till it was stolen by a soldier a year before the mutiny. In 1857 when the mutiny broke out the authorities in Belgaum, on account of its nearness to the arsenal, ordered the mosque to be closed. Since then it has not been used for service. In 1882 the closed doors of the mosque opened of themselves. The people said it was Asad Khán and became much excited. The doors were closed, and, as Asad Khán made no further sign, the excitement passed off. A British soldier is believed to have climbed into the mosque after a tame rabbit and opened the door from the inside. The fort has another mosque beyond and to the east of the Naubat Khána, a plain neat building with no inscription and with one large and three small tombs.

Jain Temples, 1200.

Of[3] the three old Jain temples one is just outside the commissariat enclosure, another is inside the enclosure, and a third is at a short distance from it. The shrine of the old laterite temple outside of the enclosure is entirely gone. It was probably pulled down when the road was made behind it. The shrine door has been blocked and the temple hall is used as a tent store. The remains of the temple include a porch the whole width (42′) of the building, with a screen wall in front and a hall or *mandap*, thirty-two feet square, raised on sixteen pillars and sixteen pilasters. The porch is fourteen and a half feet high in the middle and faces south. The screen wall is carved with figures almost all playing on musical instruments or dancing. Below the figures are diamond-shaped ornaments cleverly designed and all different. The hall door is of delicately carved porphyry smeared with paint and clay. Over the centre is a kneeling figure and above the cornice are two other figures and two lions. The four central hall pillars stand on a platform raised

[1] Stokes' Belgaum, 23-25. The late Mr. E. B. Eastwick (Murray's Bombay Hand-Book, 235) gives a different translation of the inscription from that given in the text from Stokes' Belgaum, 23.

[2] The jacket is said to have been prepared with one single thread.

[3] Dr. Burgess' First Archæological Report, 1-5.

Chapter XIV.
Places.
BELGAUM.
Jain Temples, 1200.

about three and a half inches above the floor. The aisles are separated from the central area by a latticed or perforated stone screen joining the other pillars four on each side. Of this screen only one piece between the front wall and the first pillar of the right hand row remains. All along the side walls is a narrow plinth and opposite the middle the plinth passes well forward as if for an image seat. Above, about five and a half feet from the ground, is a stone shelf eighteen inches wide and six feet long. The stone beams over the columns are very massive and the beams which cross the centre aisle have an opening over them nearly equal to their own depth, to allow the beams of the side aisles to overlap the bearings both in the central and in the outer aisle. Except cobras on the capitals and four dancing satyrs on the blocked shrine door, there are no representations of living creatures inside. The shafts of the pillars are each a single stone, and some of the slabs in the walls measure six feet by four and in some instances even more. The foundations of the whole building have sunk in some places and made the walls crack.

The large temple inside of the commissariat enclosure consists of an open hall or *mandap* (24′ × 18′) with three porches and surmounted by a carefully carved dome, an inner temple or *shála* (20′ × 18′), a small antechamber (7′ × 7′), and a shrine (8′ × 8′). The hall is surrounded by a low screen wall from which rise the pillars supporting the roof. Above the level of the screen the pillars are round with square bases. They are of the black Belgaum porphyry which takes a high polish and is strongly magnetic. A cobra head forms the ornaments on the ends of all the brackets. In each of the eight architraves which support the dome are carved five small cells or *mandirs*, each containing a sitting Jina, and, between the cells, are four attendants or supporters, standing figures each under a small canopy. Over the brackets, which project inwards, have been carved slabs. Two on the north-east are gone; on one that remains on the north is a figure on horse-back with a high cap, a canopy or umbrella over his head, and a woman behind him. The next is similar but the animal's head is gone. The third animal is a fancy alligator or *makara* a large-headed gaping and short-legged dragon similarly mounted. The fourth slab on the south-west has a man with a shield mounted on the shoulder of a larger man who carries a badly broken woman on his left shoulder. The animal on the south-east slab is too broken to be made out. The animal on the last slab appears to have been a ram. In the centre of the dome is a beautiful pendentive boldly designed and well executed but damaged at one point. The pendentive hangs from a circle about eight feet in diameter and its point is about thirteen feet from the raised circular flag stone which is four inches above the floor. The dome springs at a height of eleven feet from the floor. The door leading from the hall to the inner temple has been very gracefully carved though two clumsy ashlar pillars lately put in to strengthen the building greatly interfere with the view. On the centre of the lintel is a sitting Jina and above the cornice are four sitting men. On the neat side pillar colonettes are five bands with human groups in some of which the figures though little more than an inch high are

Jain Temples, 1200.

in strong relief. Inside the bands of human figures is a band of rampant lions, their necks adorned with high frills. Outside of the colonettes is a band of holy swans, another of lions, and a third of human figures mostly on bended knees. The pillars of the inner temple or *shála* are square and massive, relieved by having all the chief fronts, the triangles on the base and neck, carved with flowers. The roof of the area between the four central columns is carved and with cut corners. The central stone is gone. In the front wall of this chamber, which is three and a half feet thick, are two small recesses closed by sliding stones one foot nine inches high. A richly carved door leads to the small antechamber in front of the shrine. On the under side of the door cornice is carved a dancing figure between two musicians. Above is a damaged figure which appears to have had eight arms. On each side of this door is a niche in the wall neatly carved in which were probably figures of Jain divinities or of the temple builders. The antechamber is plain with carved roof, its corners cut off by four carved stones. The corners of the square thus formed are cut off by four other stones and the central square is filled by a stone carved with a lotus. The door leading to the shrine is neatly carved and is in good preservation. The outer line of sculptures is a series of small grinning lions each supporting a second lion. Over the centre is a Jina with two fans and on the extreme top are four lions. The shrine contains no image but the throne on which the object of worship sat remains. The back of the seat which is now black with smoke, is carved to represent the usual cushion behind Jain images. Over the cushion on each side of the position for the head a plant rises with many circular or wheel-shaped flowers. At the ends of the cushion small colonettes support the back rail of the throne and a lion over a man. Above is an elephant with riders. At each side of the shrine is a deep niche in the wall. In the spire above the shrine is a small square chamber such as is common in Jain temples for a second image.

The third Jain temple, at a short distance from the Commissariat enclosure, has been turned into quarters for married soldiers, with such additions from the outside that it is impossible to recognize it as a temple. Besides these three, there seem to have been other temples in the fort as many of the gate posts to houses both inside the fort and outside are pillars from old Jain temples. Two finely carved slabs were unearthed in a garden in the camp in 1874.

Inscriptions.

Early in the present century two Ratta inscription tablets are said to have been removed from one of the fort temples to the museum of the Bombay Branch of the Royal Asiatic Society. The inscriptions were in the Old Kánarese language and very inaccurate copies of them have been preserved in a book belonging to the library of the London Mission Society's establishment at Belgaum. One of the inscriptions begins with the mention of king Sena II. born in the Ráshtrakuta or Ratta race. The genealogy is then continued to the brothers Kártavirya IV. and Mallikárjun who ruled together from about 1199 to 1218. Mention is then made of a certain king Bicha and of his sons. The inscription then proceeds to record grants made in 1205 (*Shak* 1127 the *Raktákshi*

Chapter XIV.
Places.
Belgaum.
Inscriptions.

samvatsar) when the sun was beginning to turn north, on the second day of the bright fortnight of *Pausha* or December - January while the great chieftain Kártaviryadev and his younger brother the heir apparent Mallikárjundev were exercising imperial sovereignty at their capital of Venugrám, to the high priest Shubhchandra-bhattárkdev for the purposes of the Jain temple of the Rattas which had been built by king Bicha. The lands granted were at the village of Mambarváni in the Korvalli subdivision of the Kundi Three thousand. The second inscription, the historical part of which is to the same purport, records grants of lands at Belgaum (Venugrám) on the same day to the same person and for the same purpose.[1]

Fort.

In 1823 a committee of inspection described Belgaum fort as in a wide plain surrounded at a distance of five or six miles by ranges of hills, the hills to the south being wooded and forming part of the Sahyádris and the hills to the north stretching towards Pádsháhpur. The fort was irregularly round and enclosed by a deep wet ditch holding water for the greater part of the year. The ramparts were of stone and sufficiently high and strong to give Belgaum fort a place among the first class forts of the Bombay Karnátak. The fort was well covered by a sloping earthen mound or glacis especially in the west where its nearness to the town made it most subject to attack. The interior was level and stretched about 1000 yards long by 800 broad. The only good buildings were the commandant's house, two stone temples used as magazines, and a large house in which commissariat stores were kept. The fort was well suited for a military store.[2] Except the works at the gateway which had been breached and the masonry of the parapets which had fallen in places the fortifications were in good repair. In 1826 Colonel Welsh, the commandant of the Doab Field Force, described the fort as an irregular stone fortification egg-like in form. It was about a mile and a half in circumference with very high ramparts and only one gateway. The curtains were disproportionately long and the bastions consequently small and insufficient. The ditch was very wide and deep but not being repaired its sides were beginning to decay and many breaches were forming from heavy rains washing away the earth and the stones falling from their own weight. As communication with the town and the cantonment was stopped during the rains, Colonel Welsh made a causeway over the ditch on the western face where a large breach had prepared materials. The general staff of the Doab Field Force lived in the fort and had built their own houses. The houses were surrounded by excellent gardens and the inside of the fort was so beautifully wooded that it was more like a large garden than a military station. It was without exception the pleasantest and healthiest Indian station Colonel Welsh had ever

---

[1] Journal Bombay Branch Royal Asiatic Society, X. 184.

[2] In 1825 Lieutenant A. Lawe, Superintending Engineer of Forts recommended Belgaum fort as eminently suited for a military depôt chiefly on account of its strength and convenience. The buildings in the fort he valued at £12,000 (Rs. 1,20,000) and there was room for many more. The fort could hold a large garrison and required a large force to invest it. The ditch was very broad and deep, the rampart of cut blue stone was in good repair, and broad enough to admit of heavy artillery on all parts.

Chapter XIV.

Places.

BELGAUM.

Fort.

known.[1] In 1828 the fort is described as standing in a plain, a work of great strength and extent. The ramparts were faced with stone flanked by massive round bastions and protected by an admirable wet ditch cut out of the rock, with an earth slope or glacis and an advanced work in front of the chief gateway. Two old temples and some ruined native houses were found in its large interior.[2] In 1872 a committee was formed to report on the condition and requirements of the defence and armament of Belgaum fort. The committee reported that the fort was irregularly round, its interior being 800 to 850 yards in diameter. It was surrounded by a deep and broad ditch dry in the hot weather but holding water for the greater part of the year. The defences, within the ditch, consisted of an earthen rampart retained by a massive stone and lime escarp wall. The rampart was twelve to eighteen feet high above the general level of the interior and varied in breadth but was everywhere solid enough to resist heavy smoothbore guns. The counterscarp was ruinous, the wall in many places having fallen into the ditch. On the south and west from eight to fifteen feet of the scarp wall was high enough above the glacis or sloping earthen mound to be exposed to direct fire from without. The ramparts had no traverses. On the north-west side of the fort was a cavalier battery capable of mounting eight heavy guns with bastion outwork, and round the ramparts were eight towers with stone parapets, each capable of holding one or two heavy guns. The fort had two entrances the old Marátha gateway with a strong outwork in front to cover it and a new gateway cut directly through the rampart and crossing the ditch by an earthen bank. The fort had an arsenal and a powder magazine and an ample water-supply from wells. Immediately round the fort were low cultivated fields. But about 1000 yards off, on the north-west opposite the cavalier and bastion, high ground commanded the interior of the fort.[3]

History.

Belgaum is an old town. It is called Venugrám or the Bamboo Village in inscriptions of the twelfth and thirteenth centuries.[4] Old Belgaum is believed to have stood a little to the south-east of the modern town, and the embankment of the mud fort of old Belgaum is still shown a short distance from the second milestone on the Dhárwár road. The fort is said to have been built by a Jain king. Round the fort was a moat and the remains of a high turret at one corner are still seen. On the south was a well, whose stones are

---

[1] Military Reminiscences, II. 249-252. Colonel Welsh gives a sketch of the fort with forty-three references, a side view of the fort, and a sketch of his own bungalow.

[2] Hamilton's Gazetteer, I. 165.

[3] Report No. 217 Miscellaneous dated Belgaum 14th November 1872.

[4] Indian Antiquary, IV. 139; Journal B. B. Roy. As. Soc. IX. 296. Besides in inscriptions, the old name is preserved in the writing at the end of copies of the Vedas written by Belgaum Bráhmans which is always: 'Written at Venugrám.' Stokes' Belgaum, 18. *Venu* or *Velu* is a common Sanskrit term for bamboos and until lately Belgaum was thickly surrounded by clumps of bamboo. Within living memory the different parts of the city were separated by thick bamboo hedges and robberies in broad daylight by men hid in the bamboo thickets were not uncommon. A MS. account of Belgaum fort written about 1820 describes the *petta* or town of Belgaum as hidden and guarded by a high impassable bamboo hedge.

Chapter XIV. Places. BELGAUM. History.

said to have been taken to build the present fort. The pond belonging to old Belgaum was called Nágarkere or the Cobra pond, and within a mile of Belgaum the Khánápur road passes over the ruined dam of this pond.[1] The earliest known mention of Belgaum is as Velugrám in a Goa Kádamba inscription dated 1160 found at Golihalli a mile south of Bidi. Belgaum was then the chief town of a district known as the Belgaum Seventy and was governed, along with the Palasige or Halsi Twelve thousand and the Konkan Nine hundred, by the sixth Goa Kádamba chief Shivchitt or Permádi. Within the next fifty years Belgaum had passed to the Rattas of Saundatti and Belgaum (850-1250). Two inscriptions in Belgaum fort dated 1205 both mention Venugrám. One mentions Venugrám as the Ratta capital and the other records that lands in Venugrám were assigned for the maintenance of one of the fort temples.[2] An inscription dated 1208 and found at Hannikeri, about six miles north-west of Sampgaon, has the first mention that the Ratta capital was moved from Sugandhvarti or Saundatti to Venugrám or Belgaum, and that, in addition to the Kundi Three thousand, the Rattas held the Belgaum Seventy which they had conquered from the Goa Kádambas.[3] About 1250 Belgaum passed from the Rattas to the Devgiri Yádavs (1150-1310). In 1375, according to Ferishta, the fortress of Belgaum was included in Vijaynagar territory.[4] During the three following years Mujáhid Sháh Bahmani (1375-1378) unsuccessfully turned his arms against the forts from Goa to Belgaum and Bankápur.[5] In 1472 under orders from Virupáksha of Vijayanagar, Vikram Ráy Rája of Belgaum, helped by the Hindu chief of Bankápur in Dhárwár, tried to retake Goa. Muhammad Sháh Bahmani put himself at the head of a large army and marched against Belgaum, which is described as a fortress of great strength, surrounded by a deep wet ditch, and near it a pass whose only approach was fortified by redoubts.[6] According to Ferishta Vikrama Ráy, who commanded the fort, at first asked terms which were refused. He then defended himself with great vigour and prevented Khwája Máhmud Gawán the Bahmani general from filling with wood and earth the wet ditch in which lay the chief strength of the fort. The besiegers then began to form trenches and dig mines, apparently at this time a new feature in Deccan warfare. Three mines were sprung and made practicable breaches in the fort wall. The breaches were at once stormed, and, in spite of a gallant defence and the loss of two thousand of the besiegers, Muhammad Sháh succeeded in gaining the ramparts. The citadel had yet to be carried, but Vikram Ráy despairing of success, disguised himself and was admitted to the Bahmani king's presence as a messenger from the Belgaum chief. In the king's presence he discovered himself saying that he had come with his family to kiss the foot of the throne. Muhammad admiring his courage received him into his order of nobles. The new territories were added to the estates of Khwája

1 Stokes' Belgaum, 19.
2 Jour. B. B. R. A. Soc. X. 185; Dr. Burgess' First Archæological Report, 2.
3 See below Hannikeri. 4 Briggs' Ferishta, II. 313; Scott's Deccan, I. 27.
5 Grant Duff's Maráthás, 26. 6 Briggs' Ferishta, II. 337-338.

Máhmud Gawán who had distinguished himself during the siege.[1] In a distribution of the Bahmani territory made in 1478 by the Bahmani minister Khwája Gawán the country from Junnar to Sátára and the forts of Goa and Belgaum were placed under the governorship of Fakr-ul-Mulk.[2] In 1481 the Vijaynagar king Narsingh attempted to recover Goa. The attack was repelled by Muhammad Sháh Bahmani II. (1463-1518) who is mentioned as visiting Belgaum and examining the city and fortifications.[3] About 1488 Bahádur Giláni, the Bahmani governor of the Konkan broke into rebellion and seized Belgaum and Goa.[4] In 1493 Bahádur Giláni was killed by an arrow and his estate including Belgaum was conferred on Ein-ul-Mulk Giláni.[5] In 1498 the Bahmani territories were divided and the estate of Belgaum and the neighbouring districts were assigned to Bijápur.[6] In March 1510 when the news of Dalboquerque's capture of Goa reached Belgaum, the Hindus rose, drove out the Bijápur garrison and resumed their former allegiance to the Vijaynagar kings.[7] In 1511 Belgaum was taken from Ein-ul-Mulk Giláni, and, together with the title of Asad Khán, was granted to Khosru Turk, a Persian of the province of Lár and a Shia by religion, in reward for delivering the young king Ismáil Adil Sháh (1511-1534) from the treachery of his guardian Kamál Khán Dakhani.[8] Asad Khán held Belgaum for thirty-eight years (1511-1549) during which he was the mainstay of Bijápur power. His is the greatest name Belgaum history can boast. He is the hero of the Belgaum Musalmáns and is now a saint whose power, so long as he is pleased by worship, keeps the cholera spirit from ruining his beloved Belgaum.[9] In 1519 Asad Khán completed the building of the Safa Mosque in Belgaum fort,[10] and, in 1530, the wall of Belgaum fort was finished by one Yakub Ali Khán.[11] About 1535 Yusuf Khán of Kittur accused Asad Khán of meditating the surrender of Belgaum fort to Burhán Nizám of Ahmadnagar, who, like Asad Khán, was a Shia. Under Yusuf's advice the king summoned Asad Khán to Bijápur, but Asad Khán pleaded sickness and remained at Belgaum. After fruitless attempts to poison him, lands near Belgaum were given to Yusuf, that, when the chance offered, he might seize the minister. Once near Belgaum while Asad was riding alone some distance ahead of his guard, Yusuf Khán attacked him with a troop of horse. Asad Khán, who was a man of giant strength and a famous swordsman, single-handed attacked and put Yusuf Khán and his troops to flight, and, with the help of his guard, made Yusuf's men prisoners. King Ibráhim professed much anger at Yusuf's conduct, confined him, and asked Asad Khán to do with him what he pleased. Asad Khán blamed his own ill-luck and set Yusuf's men free with presents.[12] Taking advantage of this quarrel between Ibráhim and Asad Khán

[1] Briggs' Ferishta, II. 330; Stokes' Belgaum, 14.
[2] Briggs' Ferishta, II. 502-503; Scott's Deccan, I. 168-169; Grant Duff's Maráthás, 29.
[3] Briggs' Ferishta, II. 516-517.
[4] Briggs' Ferishta II. 539-543.
[5] Briggs' Ferishta, II. 543.
[6] Stokes' Belgaum, 23.
[7] Commentaries of Dalboquerque, III. 37.
[8] Briggs' Ferishta, III. 45.
[9] Stokes' Belgaum, 33-34.
[10] Mosque Inscription see above p. 538.
[11] Wall Inscription see above p. 535.
[12] Briggs' Ferishta, III. 89.

Chapter XIV.
Places.
Belgaum.
History.

Burhán Nizám of Ahmadnagar and Amir Barid of Bidar spread reports that Asad Khán had promised to give them Belgaum. In 1542 the Ahmadnagar king attacked the Bijápur territory and moved south towards Belgaum. About 1545 the Bijápur king Ibráhim Adil Sháh discovered a plot to dethrone him and place his brother Abdulla on the throne. Abdulla fled to Goa and as Asad Khán was suspected of being a party to the plot he was forced to retire to Belgaum. With the aid of the Portuguese, of Burhán Nizám Sháh of Ahmadnagar, and of Kutubsháh of Golkonda, Abdulla proclaimed himself king and marched to Bijápur. As Burhán Nizám was passing Belgaum on his way to Bijápur he heard that Asad was dangerously ill. In the hope that on Asad's death he might be able to seize the fort of Belgaum Burhán stopped at Belgaum. To prepare the way Burhán sent a Bráhman spy to buy over Asad's men. Asad recovered and hearing what was going on, seized Burhán Nizam's spy and killed him, and put to death as many of the garrison as seemed to have been tampered with. In 1549 Asad Khán sent word to Ibráhim that he was dying and wished to see him before he died. Ibráhim started for Belgaum, but, before he arrived, Asad Khán had died at Mandoli three miles south-west of Belgaum. His tomb or *dargha* in the Belgaum camp is still worshipped both by Musalmáns and Hindus. Asad's son Muhammad Kishwar Khán was made governor of Hukeri, Belgaum, and Ráybág, and the rest of Asad's estates and treasures went to the king. According to Ferishta,[1] besides for his prowess as a soldier and his skill as a statesman, Asad Khán was famous as the patron and protector of all the learned men in the Deccan. He lived at Belgaum in the greatest magnificence. He had 250 household servants, Georgians, Circassians, Hindus, and Abyssinians. He had sixty large and 150 small elephants, and, in his stables, besides those of mixed breed, were 450 Arab horses. In his kitchens 100 fowls, thirty sheep, and 2700 pounds (100 Deccan *mans*) of rice were daily cooked. He set the fashion, which all men of rank followed, of wearing a gold waistband and a dagger. He attempted to manage elephants with a bit and bridle, but the bit failed to control them in their fits of fury. In 1550 one Sher Khán built the town of Sháhpur, originally called Sháhpet as the *petta* or market of the Fort of Belgaum.[2] In 1557 Ibráhim Adil Sháh died leaving his younger son Tahamásp, who had Shia leanings, under watch at Belgaum. In 1583 the English traveller Fitch found Belgaum the first town between Goa and Bijápur, a good market for diamonds rubies sapphires and other precious stones.[3] In 1593 prince Ismáil the brother of king Ibráhim II., who, since 1580, had been kept a state prisoner at Belgaum, won the governor and garrison of Belgaum to his side, possessed himself of the fort, and broke into revolt. Burhán Nizám of Ahmadnagar promised him help, and most of the Bijápur nobles openly or secretly sympathised with him. Ibráhim sent an army under Eliás Khán to quell the rebellion

---

1 Briggs' Ferishta, III. 101-102.
2 Stokes' Belgaum, 45. Sháhpur now belongs to the Sángli chief.
3 Fitch in Harris' Voyages, I. 207.

and besiege Belgaum where the prince still remained. During the siege Ein-ul-Mulk, a commander in Ibráhim's army, outwardly aiding the siege, secretly strengthened Ismáil's garrison by sending them grain and other necessaries and at last openly declared in Ismáil's favour. The siege was broken and Eliás Khán retired to Bijápur. Ein-ul-Mulk with an army of thirty thousand men marched to Belgaum and persuaded prince Ismáil to quit the fort and move towards Bijápur. Before they started a second army under a fresh general Hamed Khán came from Bijápur. Hamed Khán professed great respect for Ismáil and attachment to his cause. Tempted by the prospect of Hamed Khán's support Ein-ul-Mulk and prince Ismáil left Belgaum. When too far from the fort to seek safety in flight, Hamed Khán fell on them, slew Ein-ul-Mulk, and captured prince Ismáil who was shortly after put to death.[1] In 1631 the main gate of Belgaum fort was built by a Bijápur officer named Bándeh Ali.[2] In 1640 excessive rain ruined the south-east corner of the Belgaum fort wall and it was rebuilt by one Abdul Husain Amin.[3] In 1648 Belgaum seems to have formed part of the estate or *jághir* of Khán Muhammad a leading officer in the Bijápur army in whose time the fort wall was finished by one Muhamad bin Zabit Khán.[4] In 1673, taking advantage of dissensions at Bijápur, Shiváji retook Panhála fort in Kolhápur, and on his way to the sack of Hubli, plundered Belgaum.[5] About 1680 the English geographer Ogilby mentions Bellegam-Chapour or Belgaum-Sháhpur as one of four very eminent castles in the Cuncan or Konkan.[6] On the 30th of March 1695 the Italian traveller Gemelli Careri, on his way from the Moghal camp at Galgale about fifteen miles north of Kaládgi, to Goa, came to Belgaum. Though with little but mud and thatched houses, Belgaum was a populous city and a place of much trade. It had a large market and a good Musalmán fort built of stone and girt by a deep ditch full of water. In proportion to the size of the fort and the garrison the number of cannon was small.[7] In 1730 the town and fort of Belgaum were held by the Sávanur Nawáb who had received them from Nizám-ul-Mulk. In 1746 the Sávanur Nawáb, feeling himself unable to face the Maráthás, agreed to a treaty by which he was allowed to keep twenty-two districts together with the forts of Belgaum and Torgal which were his family possessions.[8] In 1754, a Marátha army returning from Maisur attacked Iláchi Beg the Sávanur Nawáb's governor of Belgaum,[9] and apparently soon after the fort passed to the Peshwa. In a Marátha revenue statement prepared about 1789 Ázamnagar or Balegaon appears as the head of a district or *sarkár* with fifteen sub-divisions or *parganás* yielding a yearly revenue of £135,451 (Rs. 13,54,516).[10] In 1802 the fort and

---

[1] Briggs' Ferishta, III. 176-182. [2] Stokes' Belgaum, 39. See above p. 535.
[3] Stokes' Belgaum, 40. Wall Inscription see above p. 535.
[4] Library Inscription see above p. 538. [5] Stokes' Belgaum, 42.
[6] Atlas, V. 250. [7] Churchill's Voyages, IV. 217-219.
[8] Bom. Gov. Sel. CXII. 208. [9] Stokes' Belgaum, 50.
[10] Waring's Maráthás, 245. According to Mr. Stokes (Belgaum, 45), after the fall of Bijápur, the fort of Belgaum remained for some years in possession of Aurangzeb's second son Ázam and from him was called Ázamnagar. This seems doubtful. According to Orme (Historical Fragments, 286-287) Belgaum was called Ázamnagar

Chapter XIV.
Places.
BELGAUM.
History.

country round Belgaum, with a yearly revenue of £4000 (Rs. 40,000), were held by Sadáshiv Pandit who kept a force of 1000 horse and 2000 foot supported by estates in north Poona. In the Third Marátha War General Munro arrived before Belgaum on the 20th of March and took possession of the town or *petta* without delay, in order, before further operations, to gain cover as near to the fort as possible. The fort was found in perfect repair. It had a broad and deep wet ditch, was surrounded by an open space or esplanade six hundred yards broad, and was garrisoned by 1600 men. The Pioneers were set to work to prepare a battery of three twelve-pounders at a mosque opposite the north face of the fort. To favour their progress, a five and a half inch mortar and a six-pounder opened from the town. On the 21st the battery opened within eight hundred yards of the fort, and was answered by five guns which were nearly silenced in the course of the following day. On the night of the 22nd an enfilading or raking battery of two guns was completed in the town and swept the north face and gateway. A gun opened on the enfilading battery from a small tower or cavalier within the works and the fire of the twelve-pounder battery was returned from the curtain to the left of the gate. These efforts of the besieged were partly defeated on the 24th when the approach was begun and carried one hundred and fifty yards. Next day the enemy fired nothing but wall muskets and the approach advanced 120 yards. On the 26th the garrison again showed artillery, and opened from the flagstaff battery, which had been nearly destroyed by the previous fire of the twelve-pounders. They likewise produced a new gun on the right of the gate, but could not stop the approach which was carried forward 100 yards through very hard ground. On the 27th the mortar was moved from the enfilading to the twelve-pounder battery and threw shells all the night, while an advance of a hundred yards more was made. This was prolonged 120 yards next day, the enemy's fire was reduced to two guns, and on the thirtieth 120 yards more were added. On the 31st the magazine in the mosque, belonging to the twelve-pounder battery, blew up, and the garrison instantly sallied to take advantage of the confusion which they supposed the explosion must have caused. When the sallying party were within 100 yards of them the battery guard, under Lieutenant Walker of the 2nd battalion of the 4th Regiment, and the artillery detail under Lieutenant Lewis, advanced to meet them, and, under a heavy fire of guns and small-arms from the walls, drove them back into the fort. Colonel Newall, who saw this act of gallantry, praised, with the two officers mentioned, the marked bravery of Lieutenant Macky of His Majesty's 53rd Regiment, who, unable to join the detachment of his corps with Brigadier-General Pritzler, took his tour of

---

under the Bijápur kings. The province of Ázamnagar formed the western boundary of the district of Bankápur, and it contained within it the district of Gokák of which the town of Gokák was the head place. Belgaum was called Mustafabad in memory of one of its commandants or *kiladárs* named Mustafa, who thoroughly repaired and strengthened the ramparts.

general duty in Brigadier-General Munro's force. After the explosion, the repair of the twelve-pounder battery occupied the 1st of April during which an eight-inch mortar was opened, the five and a half inch mortar was taken back to the enfilading battery, and the approach was carried fifty yards further. The approach was now so well advanced that within 550 yards of the wall a breaching battery for two eighteen-pounders was begun and finished on the 2nd. On the morning of the 3rd of April the breaching battery opened on the left of the gateway with great effect. The garrison had still two guns able to fire on the side of the attack; and as they considerably annoyed the breaching battery, to silence them two twelve-pounders were brought into battery 100 yards to the left. The enemy's guns were silenced on the 4th, when a large part of the outer wall to the left of the gate and some of the inner wall were brought down. Next day the destruction was still more rapid. All the batteries continued firing and shells were thrown all night long. Before daylight on the 6th a twelve-pounder was got within 150 yards of the gate and the firing was kept up with as great vigour as on the 5th. The twelve-pounder on the advanced battery opened on the 7th, but burst after firing fifteen rounds. The breach of the curtain was widened, the garrison still keeping up a smart fire. On the 8th the original twelve-pounder battery was abandoned and two of its iron guns were brought into the battery near the gate. On the 9th they opened with excellent effect on the curtain to the right, where the enemy's ginjal[1] and matchlock men had previously found good cover, and made a practicable breach in the outer wall. Seeing this breach the commandant sent out to propose terms. As the terms were not agreed to, on the morning of the 10th, the batteries continued to fire till the commandant surrendered at discretion. On the same day (10th April) a detachment of British troops took possession of the outer gateway, and, on the eleventh the Pioneers were employed in opening both entrances, as they were built up within and were strongly barricaded. On the 12th of April the garrison marched out. They acknowledged to have had twenty killed and fifty wounded during the siege; the British loss was twenty-three. In spite of the want of ordinary means this important fort fell before the energy and zeal of the besiegers. The exertions of the Artillery and the men of the 22nd Dragoons, serving in the batteries, were unremitting, and the labours of the Pioneers were equally meritorious in constructing, besides several batteries, an approach 750 yards long through extremely hard ground. General Munro took the field without any staff. He was even without an engineer, though this want was supplied by the judgment and energy of Colonel Newall the second in command, who personally directed every operation. The ordnance found in the fort included thirty-six pieces, mostly of large calibre, and sixty wall muskets and small brass guns. The place was well supplied with stores. It was a matter of congratulation that the garrison

[1] Lieutenant Lake (Sieges of the Madras Army, 70) describes ginjals as long matchlocks of various calibres, used as wall pieces. They are commonly fixed like swivels and carry iron balls not more than a pound in weight. In the field they are sometimes carried on the backs of camels.

Chapter XIV. Places. BELGAUM. *History.*

surrendered without further opposition. The three eighteen-pounders were so run at the vent, that three fingers might be introduced into them, and they had consequently lost considerably in power. The walls of the fort were everywhere solid and massive, and being more than a mile and a half round, gave the garrison abundant room to avoid shells. After the capture of the fort the force had to halt at Belgaum till the 17th, to organize means for future operations and to put the results of the capture on a firm basis.[1]

In an account of Belgaum fort written about 1820 Belgaum is described as consisting of the fort and *petta*. The country rose gradually above the fort in almost every direction. The town was to the west of the fort separated by a large esplanade and concealed and protected by a high and impenetrable bamboo hedge. A number of large trees grew in the neighbourhood.[2] In 1821 Belgaum had 1309 houses and 7652 people. The houses were better than in most parts of India those of the upper class being uniform substantial and roomy and those of the lower classes respectable cottages.[3] In 1826 Colonel Welsh, in charge of the Doab Field Force with its head-quarters at Belgaum, described the town as extensive populous and wealthy. Its skirts were barely out of the reach of cannon from the western face of the fort and the cantonment was about the same distance on the other side.[4] In 1828 Belgaum town and fort were visited on a tour of inspection by Sir John Malcolm then Governor of Bombay.[5] About this time Belgaum is described as an old town most of its merchants and bankers residing at Sháhpur. The town stood high and within the influence of the sea breeze. It was famous for its healthy climate, fresh strengthening air, and excellent water.[6] On the 9th of March 1838 Belgaum was chosen as the civil head-quarters of the district, though A'nkalgi Gokák Manoli and Murgod were all proposed and Gokák was at one time almost determined on. In 1848 the people of Belgaum raised subscriptions and repaired the town roads and lanes, and during the years before 1862 much was done to improve the town.[7] During the 1857 mutinies Belgaum was in considerable danger. The fort was put in a state of defence and its breaches repaired. A battery of artillery was quartered in the fort and the European and Eurasian inhabitants of the town were formed into a small volunteer corps and drilled daily. The Safa mosque was ordered to be closed as its nearness to the arsenal was a source of danger. On the 10th of August 1857 reinforcements arrived from Bombay, of which Belgaum was badly in want chiefly on account of the drain caused by the Persian War. A Wahábi Munshi who was the ringleader of the conspiracy was tried with five men of the disaffected regiment. All six were found guilty and executed and four more were transported for life. The danger was overcome chiefly through the tact of General Lester in military command of Belgaum and no actual outbreak occurred. In 1858 the mutinous Bráhman chief of Nargund, who had murdered Mr. Manson, the Political Agent of Dhárwár, was brought for trial

---

[1] Blacker's Marátha War, 292-294.
[2] MS. Account of Forts (1820-1827).
[3] Hamilton's Gazetteer, I. 165.
[4] Military Reminiscences, II. 250.
[5] Military Reminiscences, II. 339.
[6] Hamilton's Gazetteer, I. 165.
[7] Thornton's Gazetteer, 86.

to Belgaum. He was confined in the main guard of the fort, tried, and sentenced to death. He was carried on a cart drawn by Mhárs through the town of Haystack Hill where the gallows were erected and was there hanged.[1]

BELVANKI HILL.

Belvanki or Old Panhala Hill about 1000 feet above the plain, lies near Belvanki village about six miles north-west of Athni. Its rugged sides are partly covered with low thorn bushes. A narrow and difficult footpath leads up the hill to a cave dedicated to the god Siddheshvar. The hill-top belongs to the chief of Sángli and is tilled with wheat and gram by Lingáyats and Maráthás.

BHIMGAD FORT.

Bhimgad Fort, in the village lands of Tanáli, is built on a detached spur of the Sahyádris about sixteen miles south-west of Khánápur. The spur has steep sides and a flat top which is reached by a flight of rock-cut steps. The fort is 1380 feet long from north to south and 825 broad from east to west; the whole inside of the fort is overgrown with brushwood. The fort has one gateway and the walls are still in good order. The water-supply is from a spring. Tigers, wolves, bears, bison, and *sámbhar* occasionally visit the hill. In 1827 a committee of inspection described Bhimgad fort as situated in a bay or basin formed by the Sahyádris immediately north of the Khele pass. Bhimgad occupied the summit of an extraordinary rock with sides about 300 feet in perpendicular height. Except on the south where a pathway broad enough to admit of two or three men abreast led to the summit, the fort was inaccessible. The defences were almost entirely natural, requiring little artificial help. The gateway was formed by a small thatched building connected on each side with a slight wall of defence very weak and assailable even without scaling ladders. The gateway commanded the footpath and the approach in some degree, but an invading force would find cover almost everywhere from the fire of the garrison. The *petta* or lower fort was about 400 feet below the upper and was inaccessible on every side except by a footpath leading eastward where a neck of hills formed an easy communication with the principal range. On this, the east side, the defences of the lower fort were trifling and could be easily surmounted with short scaling ladders. On the other sides, the south and the west, there was a fearful descent of 400 feet into the valley below, partly hill and partly rock. The water-supply, consisting of a small spring to the west and a reservoir to the north, was scanty and entirely failed during the two hottest months of the year. The surrounding hills rose about 700 feet above the level of Bhimgad and lay within range of shot and shell. In the upper fort were two guns an eight and a three pounder and one wall musket. None of the gateways in the lower fort had any powder or shot. The committee found that the fort could not be effectually destroyed as the masonry at the top of the footpath could be rebuilt in a short time. When the fort was examined it was guarded by an irregular force of 175 men.

History.

Bhimgad was one of the forts which Shiváji held at the time of his death in 1680.[2] In 1719 it was given to Sháhu with the sixteen

[1] Sir LeGrand Jacob's Western India, 226. [2] Grant Duff's Maráthás, 133.

Chapter XIV.
Places.
BHIMGAD FORT.

districts included in his own rule or *svaráj*.[1] About 1787, with Vallabhgad and Gandharvgad, Bhimgad was forcibly taken from Kolhápur by the Nesargi chief, but shortly afterwards the chief and his confederates were put down, their army was dispersed, and the forts retaken. In 1820 Marshall notices Bhimgad as built on a lofty rock nearly steep on two sides and of most rugged and steep ascent on others. It was surrounded by a double line of hills and was reached by a series of rude ascents and broken descents, almost every step being from rock to rock.[2] In 1844 Bhimgad fort among other places was occupied as a guard against bodies of insurgents who threatened the Belgaum district.

BHOJ.

Bhoj village, about thirteen miles north-west of Chikodi, with in 1881 a population of 4150, has a copperplate grant dated 1208 (S. 1130 *vibhava samvatsar*) of Kártavirya IV. and Mallikárjun (1200-1218) brothers and joint rulers belonging to the Ratta dynasty of Saundatti and Belgaum (875-1250).[3] In 1773 Bhoj was the scene of the defeat by Yesáji Shinde the Kolhápur minister of Konherráv Trimbak Patvardhan of Kurundvád who was marauding into the heart of the Kolhápur country and had destroyed many villages.

BIDI.

Bidi, twelve miles south-east of Khánápur, with a population in 1872 of 1911 and in 1881 of 2086 was the head-quarters of the Bidi subdivision till 1868-69 when they were transferred to Khánápur. The local trade is confined to rice, cocoanuts, oil, salt, and plantains. There is a Portuguese mission with a chapel and two schools one for Kánarese and the other for Musalmán boys. The only object of interest is a pond with stone steps to the east of the village. About 1690 Bidi with Sampgaon was held by the *desái* of Kittur.[4] In 1779 Bidi was given to the Sávanur Nawáb by Haidar Ali, but, after a nominal transfer, it was continued to the Kittur *desái*. In 1829 the Sángoli Ráyappa outbreak began with the burning of the mámlatdár's office at Bidi. In 1844 a party of 800 troops was stationed at Bidi to guard against the insurgents who threatened the district.

BIJGARNIGUDD.

Bijgarnigudd Hill, about 1500 feet above the plain, lies about six miles south-west of Bidi and eight south-west of Khánápur. It is an isolated hill with on its flat brushwood-covered top (300′ × 285′) the remains of a fort called Hanmantgad or Máchigad. An easy ascent of 750 steps leads to the fort which has two gateways and a ruined wall with two bastions. In one of the gateways is an image of Máruti or Hanumán from which the fort takes one of its names. The water-supply is from a rock-cut cistern.

CHANDGAD.

Chandgad, the head-quarters of the Chandgad petty division, with in 1872 a population of 2211 and in 1881 of 2574, lies twenty-two miles west of Belgaum. Besides the revenue and police offices of the petty division, Chandgad has a post office, a vernacular school, and a temple of Ravalnáth (100′ × 38′) with a Persian inscription. The god is believed to keep off cholera. Chandgad has a ruined mud fortlet or *ghadi*. In 1827 the *ghadi* was described as

---

[1] Stokes' Belgaum, 47.
[2] Statistical Reports, 87.
[3] Fleet's Kánarese Dynasties, 83.
[4] Stokes' Belgaum, 44.

CHANDGAD.

a place of no strength useful only to protect the persons and property of the inhabitants during incursions of predatory horse. There were forty irregulars and one small gun in the fort. In 1724 Nág Sávant, a son of the great Phond Sávant of Sávantvádi, overran and reduced the Chandgad petty division and established a post or *thána* at Chandgad.[1] In 1750 Chandgad fort with Párgad and Kálánandigad and land valued at £500 (Rs. 5000) a year were granted by the Kolhápur chief to Sadáshivráv Bháu the Peshwa's cousin, who, dissatisfied with his treatment at Poona, had made overtures to Kolhápur and got himself appointed Peshwa of Kolhápur.[2] In 1820 Chandgad had 277 houses and 1088 people.[3] In 1844 Chandgad and Párgad were threatened by insurgents but a timely reinforcement of irregulars saved the forts from attack.[4]

CHIKODI.

Chikodi, 16° 25′ north latitude and 74° 38′ east longitude, about forty miles north of Belgaum is a large town the head-quarters of the Chikodi sub-division, with in 1872 a population of 6184 and in 1881 of 5699. The town lies among a group of hills about ten miles south of the Krishna. It is a place of considerable trade with the inland country and with Rájápur on the Ratnágiri coast with which it is connected by a made road passing through Nipáni, Kolhápur territory, and the Phonda pass. Of imports rice is brought from Ajre village in Kolhápur about twenty-seven miles to the south-west by Musalmán dealers. It is also carted from Belgaum and Dhundshi in Dhárwár by Chikodi Lingáyats who visit these places to sell tobacco and chillies. Wheat is imported from Bágalkot and Guledgudd in South Bijápur in exchange for molasses, and cocoanuts, curry-stuff, dates, spices, and salt from Rájápur in Ratnágiri. Many kinds of cloth are brought from Bombay by Márwár Vánis who have opened shops in the town. Of exports cotton, hemp, molasses, and tobacco go to Rájápur, sugar to Poona, betel leaves[5] chillies and tobacco to Belgaum and Dhundshi, and molasses to Bágalkot and Guledgudd in South Bijápur. The chief industries are the weaving of ordinary women's robes headkerchiefs and the lower kind of blankets and waistcloths, and there is a little work in brass and copper. Superior hand-woven cloth is also imported from Bijápur. A few Chikodi goldsmiths have a local name for their skill in setting diamonds. The busy months of brisk trade are February March and April. A weekly market is held throughout the year on Thursdays when gram, millet, rice, wheat, and salt are sold by Jains, Lingáyats, and Maráthás. Besides the revenue and police offices of the Chikodi sub-division the town has a post office, a subordinate judge's court, and a small mud fort. Of five schools three are government and two private. Of the three government schools two, an anglo-vernacular and a primary school are for boys, and one a vernacular school is for girls. Between the fort and the

[1] Stokes' Belgaum, 49.
[2] Stokes' Belgaum, 50. Sadáshivráv soon after resigned his appointment under Kolhápur and returned as prime minister to Poona.
[3] Marshall's Statistical Reports, 70. [4] Stokes' Belgaum, 89.
[5] Betel leaves worth about £700 are grown in six or seven betel leaf gardens in the town of Chikodi and sent to Belgaum.

Chapter XIV.
Places.
CHIKODI.

town is a water-course called *kund* two feet deep and as many broad, the water of which is believed to cure fever. A municipality was established at Chikodi but abolished as the income was less than the expenditure. About 1680 the English geographer Ogilby notices Secoery as a village of some note on the road from Goa to Bijápur. Seven *kos* from it was Ráybág and five *kos* distant was a *pagod* from which the city of Mirsie (Miraj) with its castle and towers could be plainly seen.[1] In 1720 Captain Moor described Chikodi as a large and respectable town with an extensive market pleasingly situated on a rivulet. The town had a good manufacture of cloth chiefly for the dress and convenience of the country people and a good Thursday market. The neighbourhood of the town was famous for grapes of extraordinary size and flavour.[2] In 1827 Captain Clunes notices Cheekorie as a town belonging to Kolhápur with 600 houses seven shops and wells.[3]

DEGÁMVE.

Dega'mve village, three miles south-west of Kittur has a small but elaborately sculptured temple of the god Kamal Náráyan and the goddess Mahálakshmi built by Kamaládevi the wife of the sixth Goa Kádamba chief Permádi (1147-1175). In the temple are four inscriptions one on a pillar, and twô to the right and the fourth to the left of the central shrine. Inscriptions one and three are much defaced but curiously enough are repeated in inscriptions two and four in Devnágari and Kánarese character and each supplies the deficiencies of the other. Two of the inscriptions are dated 4275 of the Kali age or A.D. 1175 in the twenty-eighth year of king Permádi.[4]

DESHNUR.

Deshnur, about ten miles north of Sampgaon, had in 1872 a population of 2566 and in 1881 of 602. The village has a Government Kánarese school and a few families who make the coloured wooden toys usually known as Gokák toys.

Hill.

Deshnur Hill, about 1300 feet above the plain, is about half a mile north of the village. It contains quarries of white stone, and has a flat top cultivated with gram and millet, chiefly by Bedars Lingáyats and Maráthás. Tigers, leopards, wild hog, jackals, and deer are occasionally found on the hill.

DODVÁD.

Dodva'd, about thirteen miles south-west of Saundatti, is a large village in the Sángli state. In 1790 Captain Moor described Dodvád as a pretty large place with good looking newly repaired fortifications.[5]

DONGARGAON HILL.

Dongargaon Hill is nine miles south-west of Khánápur. It is a sloping well-wooded hill with a flat uncultivated top on which is a religious house of the Kánpháta saint Matsyendranáth with a shed in which some Kánpháta monks live throughout the year. The water-supply is from a spring. The hill is sometimes visited by tigers, leopards, wolves, and *sámbhar*.

GANDHARVGAD FORT.

Gandharvgad Fort, about 400 feet above the plain, lies in a spur of the Sahyádris about twenty-one miles west of Belgaum.

---

[1] Atlas, V. 248. [2] Moor's Narrative, 14. [3] Itinerary, 34.
[4] Fleet's Dynasties, 92; Jour. B. B. R. A. Soc. IX. 262, 266, 289, 299, 310.
[5] Moor's Narrative, 15.

Gandharvgad Fort.

The hill on which the fort is built has bare sides with an easy ascent on one side and a difficult ascent on the other side. Of the fortifications which occupied a space about 1000 feet square the greater part are gone and only walls appear lining the ravines. In 1827 a committee of inspection described Gandharvgad as a hill fort of little strength, composed of a mud fort about twelve feet high set on a projecting neck of hill about 400 feet above the plain. The hill was scarped on the west and south but could be easily climbed from the north, where it was connected with the range of hills to the east, and was protected by a low wall and a thicket which formed a very indifferent defence. The water-supply was from a well and a small pond which dried in the hot weather. The fort was garrisoned by twenty-four irregulars. Gandharvgad was built about 1724 by Nág Sávant the second son of the great Phond Sávant of Sávantvádi.[1] In 1778 the Kolhápur chief captured Gandharvgad, but in 1793 it was restored to Sávantvádi through Sindia's influence.[2] About 1787 the chief of Nesargi rose against his master the chief of Kolhápur and took Gandharvgad among other forts; but soon after, the chief and his confederates were put down, their army was dispersed, and the forts retaken.[3]

Ganimardi Hill.

Ganimardi Hill, about 600 feet above the plain, is in the village lands of Hirenandihalli about ten miles south of Sampgaon. In its brushwood covered slopes are some black stone quarries. Neither its flat top nor its sides are cultivated. Jackals and wolves infest the hill and it is occasionally visited by bears.

Gokák.

Goka'k, 16° 10′ north latitude and 74° 53′ east longitude, about thirty miles north-east of Belgaum, with in 1881 a population of 10,205, is a municipal town, the head-quarters of the Gokák sub-division, famous for its paper and wood industries. The town lies in the lowland between the south bank of the Ghatprabha and the low range of hills which prevent the river from running southwards. It is walled and has a ditch on the south and west. To the east it is commanded by a hill with a ruined fort. The 1872 census showed a population of 12,612 of whom 10,506 were Hindus and 2079 Musalmáns. Of 10,307 the total 1881 population 8799 were Hindus and 1508 Musalmáns. Except a few, which are thatched or tiled, most of the houses have mud-roofs. Gokák is famous for its paper and wooden toy making. It was once noted for its cotton and silk weaving, dyeing, and copper and brass work, but these industries have declined. Of paper makers there are about ten families who make a coarse paper used for envelopes and packing purposes known as Gokák paper. Toy making employs about ten families of Chatris. The materials are the soft light wood of the *sávar* or Bombax malabaricum, and a clay which, when dry, becomes extremely light. The wood comes from the Belgaum sub-division and the earth is found near Gokák town. The toys are chiefly fruit, vegetable, and animal figures, very exact copies of nature. They are sold at the shops of the makers or exported by purchasers at 1½*d.* to £3 (1 *a.* to Rs. 30) each. The toy-makers find

---

[1] Stokes' Belgaum, 50. [2] Stokes' Belgaum, 56. [3] Stokes' Belgaum, 59.

Chapter XIV. Places. Gokák.

steady employment, a family's monthly earnings varying from £1 to £1 10*s*. (Rs. 10-15).[1] Besides the revenue and police offices of the Gokák sub-division, the town has a municipality, a post office, and a subordinate judge's court. The municipality which was established in 1853 had in 1882-83 an income of £662 (Rs. 6620) chiefly raised from an octroi and house tax; and an expenditure of £929 (Rs. 9290) chiefly spent on sanitation and road repairs. Most of the water used in the town comes from the Ghatprabha. There are no ponds but twenty-six wells without steps and nine with steps. The well water is brackish, and is not used for drinking. Gokák has a bad name as one of the chief local cholera centres and about seventy per cent of the municipal revenue is spent on sanitation.[2] The dispensary was established in 1867. In 1882 it treated fifteen in-patients and 2552 out-patients at a cost of £144 (Rs. 1440).

The only objects of interest in the town are two mosques and a *ganjikhána*, and a Jain temple.

Fort.

Gokák fort also known as Panchamigudd lies on an isolated peak behind and to the west of Gokák town. The ascent for about 900 feet is by a footpath and the rest of the way by steps. The fortified top is about a quarter of a mile long from north to south and about half a mile broad from east to west. The fort has one gateway, three temples, a cave, and a reservoir. It is said to have been built by one of the Adilsháhi kings of Bijápur (1489-1687).

Falls.

The[3] Gokák or Cow Falls[4] are in north latitude 16° 11′ and east longitude 74° 50′ about 3½ miles north-west of Gokák town about two miles south-east of the irrigation bungalow at Dhupdal and two miles east of Konnur on the right bank of the river. The proposed Gokák Road station on the Western Deccan Railway will be about five miles north-west of the falls and three miles north of Dhupdal.

The Ghatprabha rises south of the Amboli pass on the edge of the Sahyádris and flows across the high land near the Sahyádris in a series of flat steppes with slight falls throughout the trap formation and steep falls through gorges where it meets sandstone or quartzite rocks. After a winding course of about eighty-five miles, during which it receives the waters of two large feeders the Támraparni and Harankáshi, the Ghatprabha takes a mighty leap of 170 feet over a sandstone cliff in the picturesque gorge of Gokák. Except close to the river the country above the falls is barren and commonplace. On the left bank bare trap hills rise from black soil plains and on the right bank lies a woody plain broken by bushy sandstone hills. Below the falls, past the town of Gokák, the country for miles is a black soil plain sprinkled with *bábhul*.

In singular and taking contrast to their dull surroundings are the falls whose bold cliffs and raging torrents lead to a still pool and a deep winding gorge with rocky sides fringed with the bright green *karanj* and the pale feathery bamboo. The falls are horse-shoe-shaped with at the crest a greatest flood breadth of 580 feet. Above

[1] Details given above pp. 350-351. [2] Municipal Report for 1881-82 p. 73.
[3] Contributed by Mr. R. B. Joyner, C. E.
[4] Perhaps from *go* cow and *kakku* an old Kánarese word for a waterfall.

Chapter XIV.

Places.

GOKÁK.

Falls.

the fall the river is a rapid with a slope of 43′ in 2000′, the steepest part being close above the crest of the falls. Except in its width and the colour of its water the general features of the fall, its height, shape, and the rapid above, are much like those of Niagara. As above the falls the Ghatprabha has a drainage area of over a thousand miles, much of it with a very heavy rainfall, the volume of water in the July floods is probably greater than that of most of the world-famed waterfalls. In the great flood of the 15th of July 1882, the highest since 1822 which is said to have been a few feet higher, the greatest depth on the crest was twenty feet and the discharge at the falls was 135,700 cubic feet or 3800 tons a second.[1] With the close of the rainy season the quantity of water rapidly declines. In November the average discharge is about 700 cubic feet a second, in December 250 cubic feet, and in January an average of 170 cubic feet or 4¾ tons.

During the rains the thick reddish brown water sweeps far over the brink of the cliff and falls with a dull roar which can be heard for miles. The broken water and heavy brown spray shoot almost to the top of the fall and hide most of it from below or in front. The fine spray often rises several hundred feet over the crest of the rocks and, blown by the wind, falls in heavy showers. During the rains almost a finer sight than the falls is to stand on the water level near the crest of the fall, and looking up the steep rapid, to let the monster waves fill the view to the sky line, raging in wild tumult, and, against the mighty rocks, dashing in lofty columns of spray with a roar which deadens the deep bass of the falls. The falls are in greatest beauty between October and December. The water is clear, the rockets and spray dazzle like snow, or, when the sun is low, gleam in brilliant bows, and the pool is a lovely green warmed by a brownish tint caught from the rich reddish hue of the high wall-like cliffs that rise a hundred feet above the crest of the fall. According to the quantity of water they form two or three separate falls. One of the falls is unbroken throughout its descent and its greater speed contrasts pleasingly with the neighbouring fall which is partly broken about half-way down. From the cliffs in places through clefts in the rock, gush jets of water each keeping down to the pool a fresh green ribbon of water plants. Flocks of blue rock pigeons circle in mid-air almost like butterflies, the face of the rocks is alive with little brown red-faced monkeys, and great fish lie basking near the surface of the pool. On either side of the pool are huge masses of rock fallen from the crest of the cliff and washed to one side by the mighty force of the water. The pool has a greatest breadth of about 600 feet and a greatest depth of forty-three feet below fair weather and of sixty-five feet below high flood level.

---

[1] That is the river in flood represents a mass of water 200 times the ordinary flow of the Thames falling from a height equal to the top of the tower of the Bombay High Court. In twenty-one seconds the discharge would form a volume of water equal to the mass of the Bombay Secretariat and in one minute would flood three and a half square miles one inch deep. Taking, as determined by Captain Newbold in 1844, one-fiftieth of the bulk of the water as clay in suspension, the sediment of the river in full flood would in seventeen minutes form a mass as large as the Secretariat building.

Chapter XIV.
Places.
Gokák.
Falls.

The bed seems to be a smooth unbroken layer of hard quartzite with a cross dip of seven degrees about the same as the dip in the layers exposed in the scarp above.[1]

The best views of the falls are obtained by going down a fissure called The Crack on the right bank of the river. As this fissure is a joint in layers of rock at about right angles to the dip of the bed, the sides overhang about 7° from the perpendicular. The entrance is about 200 feet from, and in front of, a small hut on the foot road to Gokák 700 to 800 feet from the large temple of Maháling-eshvar in Konnur village. In passing down the crack there is a drop of five or six feet, then a crawl through a small hole down about 150 feet of a rough steep underground passage, and then along the length of the fissure, which, but for a canopy of leaves and creepers, is open to the sky.[2] The narrow vent ends at the foot of the perpendicular scarp. The footpath then passes down steep broken rocks covered by a bamboo thicket, and then over flood-blackened boulders held together to the water's edge by the roots of old Pongamia glabra or *karanj* and Terminalia tomentosa or *matti* trees. The views on this pathway are of marvellous beauty. When the water is low enough, it is possible to enter a cave called the Cave of the Winds about ten feet up the cliff facing the falls. From the foot of the falls the cliff over which part of the flood water dashes is seen to overhang its base by about 150 feet. Other good views may be had from the top of the cliff on the left bank, but the height of the bank somewhat dwarfs the fall.

The geology of the neighbourhood is interesting. About two miles above the falls the great Deccan trap area ends and beautiful quartzite sandstone begins. The sandstone is here very thin and just below the falls gives place to gneiss. If soundings did not show the same slope in the bottom of the pool as in the beds above, the falls would seem to have eaten through the sandstone into the gneiss. The trap outflows might seem to have been the original cause of the Gokák falls by forcing the drainage over the Gokák range instead of letting it flow to the north and east. But Mr. Foote[3] thinks that the sandstone scarp must have existed in something like its present shape before the pouring out of many, if not of all, the Deccan trap flows as he found a remnant of a trap flow lapping the base of the scarp. Below the falls at the end of the gorge the river flows between two curious conical hills. The left hill, with a small temple on the top, is called Shringagudd or the Demons' Hill, and the right hill, at the foot of which lies Gokák town, is called Malik Sáhebgudd or Malik Sáheb's hill from the tomb of a Musalmán

---

[1] Of a moonlight view of the falls in December 1822 Mr. Elphinstone wrote: 'When I reached the top of the fall the softened beauty of the rocks and woods, the stillness of the basin and the deep solitude, only broken by the voice of the waters, inspired me with feelings of elevation and delight. The cascade itself appeared in all imaginable grandeur. The upper parts were indistinctly seen and the bottom scarce at all. All other objects lay in complete repose, and the cascade alone full of sound and motion, entirely occupied the mind. One felt as if in the presence of a superior being, and filled with a reverential and almost superstitious awe.' Colebrooke's Elphinstone, II. 141, 145.

[2] Captain Newbold unsuccessfully excavated the base of the fissure in the hope of finding organic remains.

[3] Geological Survey of India, Memoirs XII, Part I. 90.

saint of that name which crowns it. Malik Sáheb's hill rises 590 feet above the Gokák plain and like Shringa's hill is of gneissic schist with a capping of quartzite conglomerate sandstone on which are perched the remains of a fort and some ruined buildings. This capping of hard rock by saving the soft schists below from weathering has probably made the hill. At the head of the rapid which is rather more than 2000 feet long is a pool about 1½ miles long. This pool, which in parts is over thirty feet deep, has its dry weather water surface forty-three feet above the crest of the falls. At the beginning of the rapid the river widens to 1250 feet because it meets the crest of an anticlinal axis of the sandstone beds. The quartzite layers of rock here slope towards the falls at an average rate of one foot in forty, but as they near the falls, the slope becomes much steeper with a sharp dip of 7° across the flow of the river. As might be expected, the upper of these curved layers is much weakened in jointing with the peculiar result that the river rushing down the slope with mighty force has torn up and overturned or carried away the loose jointed layers at the top, and the cross slope of the layers has intensified this effect so that, except when in flood, the river flows in channels which it has torn till it reached the more solid layers of unjointed rock below. Huge blocks of rock are tilted up a little and the enormous pressure of the water drives stones underneath the rocks which act as wedges and keep up the blocks. Another flood comes with another lift at the rock and a larger wedge and so the huge rock is slowly tilted till the force of the water or even its own weight upsets it. This rock-tilting may be seen in different stages all along the rapid. The open-jointed top layer varies in thickness from six inches or one foot to three or four feet. Occasionally the surface of a layer is a conglomerate of beautiful white and pinky quartz and rounded and angular pebbles, and in places beautiful ripple marks are well shown on the surface of the sandstone. Captain Newbold noted that the direction of the ripple marks was usually about S. 25° W. longitudinally indicating the E.S.E. and W.N.W. direction of the current which caused them. He noticed that the ripple marks on the sandstones of Kadapa and Karnul had a generally similar direction. The upheaval and the destruction of the upper layers of rock are much helped by the multitude of pot-holes which have been drilled into the rock by the churning of stones to which the great velocity of the water rushing over uneven surfaces has given a circular motion. These pot-holes are very numerous and vary in breadth from six or nine inches to seven or eight feet. The holes generally get larger as they go down for three or four feet when the water seems to have less swirl and the holes are not often more than about six feet deep. Sometimes the unequal hardness of the rock causes holes of very eccentric shape and often two or more neighbouring holes have joined to form fairies' palaces with vaulted roofs. The cross dip of the layers causing the blocks of stone to tilt across the direction of the stream has probably increased the number of pot-holes by forming barriers and consequently increasing the swirl. The destruction of the rapid appears to go on comparatively quickly and the fall must once have been much higher. The eating back must proceed now

Chapter XIV.
Places.
Gokák.
Falls.

very slowly as the greatest force of the water has reached the hard and compact layers of rock. Near the foot of the cliff a layer of soft shaly sandstone has weathered out to a great depth in parts and this in time must help to bring down some of the hard layers above.[1]

This weathering of the softer layer has formed a ledge by which visitors with cool heads and not easily cowed spirits can pass behind the falling water. This ledge is reached by climbing down the left bank of the river a little more than a quarter of a mile below the fall. About eighty feet above the river bed the path leads back to the foot of the falls close to the foot of the scarp and above the heap of enormous boulders by the side of the pool. The ledge is at first of some breadth and some height above the water but in one place it is only ten feet or less above the water according to the season. Towards the right bank, with the lie of the rock, the ledge gradually rises and as on this side there is neither a path to the top of the cliff nor to the edge of the pool, the return has to be made back along the left bank. Boots and socks and as much clothing as possible should be taken off; there should be little or no wind, and there should never be enough water to make the waves wash over the low part of the ledge. The pathway caused by the wearing of the soft rock is at first high enough or projecting enough to stand upright on and sometimes it runs many feet into the rock. At other places it is very narrow and sometimes low. Luckily the slope is inwards to the rock or the passage would not be possible as it is wet and covered with a green slime as slippery as soap. Most of the journey must be done crawling, sometimes even sitting or lying. The awful din, the frightful upward blasts of icy wind, the deluges of water, the seething roaring waves below, the blinding spray, the darkness, and the knowledge that a slip is sure and sudden death combine to make the passage a terrifying ordeal. When little water passes over the fall, the danger is slight, but in floods, when the ledge is partly below the level of the pool, the journey is impossible.

The lowest dip in the lip of the falls, over which water flows even in the hot weather, is almost exactly 170 feet above the summer level of the pool below and 1941 feet above mean sea level. The greatest height of the cliff over which flood water is sometimes hurled is about 200 feet. The side cliffs of the pool rise about 100 feet over the lip of the falls. In early cold weather mornings the column of spray can be seen rising 200 feet or 300 feet above the fall.

The people hold the fall in great awe. They say that much of the wearing and cutting of the rock is the work of the Pándav brothers. The large Lingáyat temple of Mahálingeshvar on the right bank is held in high honour, and, at certain times, numbers come from the

---

[1] Of this shaly band Captain Newbold wrote : 'The lower portions of the sandstone are interstratified with layers of shale whose softness aids the undermining. These shales are of a purplish brown and yellowish brown with minute spangles of mica disseminated and between the lamina contain incrustations of common alum (sulphate of alumina). The alum is earthy and impure and sometimes has a mammilated surface resembling the alum incrustations in the ferruginous shales cresting the copper mountain near Belári. It is found in considerable quantities in the small cave at the foot of the falls.' Journal Bengal Asiatic Society, XIV. 272.

Chapter XIV.

Places.

GOKÁK.

Temples.

country round to worship and bathe in the pot-holes and enjoy a half religious picnic. Some of the lower orders hold the falls in great dread. Awful demons live in a temple at the bottom of the pool, whose waters abound in enormous and fierce crocodiles.

The river banks on each side of the fall have long been a chosen site for temples. The earliest buildings have probably disappeared. Even of those from the ninth to the thirteenth centuries, only fragments are left on the steep slope of the north bank of the river, overgrown by prickly pear and other thorn bushes. On the south or right bank of the river, reached by a flight of fifteen steps, is the large temple of Mahálingeshvar (70′ × 42′). It is a plain structure with eight porches, each of which has three pillars, with a row of single pairs inside. The temple is built of large stones, and the ceilings are flat. Four pillars in the centre of the hall or *mandap* are 8′ 9″ high exclusive of the brackets, and have square bases, octagonal mouldings, then a square plain block, round neck and capital, and a square abacus. The pillars of the porches have round smooth shafts. The brackets of the capitals have the cobra ornament. On each side of the door leading into the antechamber is a perforated panel. On the door posts door-keepers with four hands hold the trident or *trishul* and the drum or *damru*. Two smaller door-keepers bear the mace and fruit and on the walls behind them is Kártiksvámi on the right and perhaps Brahma with a mace in his right hand on the left. The shrine door is plain and the back of the hall or *mandap* has been repaired since the temple was built. The outside of the roof is much injured. In the east porch is a long inscription in Old Kánarese characters, but so besmeared with paint that parts of it cannot be read. The date, which appears to be about 1153, is effaced, but the inscription belongs to the seventh Ratta chief Kártavirya III. (1143-1164). Another inscription in one of the temples is dated 1087 (*Shak* 1009 *Prabhava samvatsara*) and belongs to the fifth Ratta chief Kannakaira II. (1082-1096).

On the east opposite the shrine is another temple with four square old looking columns inside and four perfectly plain shafts in front. Behind the second pair of columns at the entrance to an open fronted antechamber to the shrine are two pillars of the usual broken square form. The door to the shrine is somewhat elaborately carved with two male and two female figures below on the posts. On the step are two conch shells forming the bud of a flower as in Vaishnav temples and in Jain temples of Neminúth the twenty-second *tirthankar*. The shrine contains a *ling*. Behind the door are large holes for a massive bar and the walls are of great thickness. On the east side is a shelf and below it is the water conduit. The pillars are all single blocks and the temple appears much older than that now in use. Behind this temple is a small shrine facing east with antechamber and porch about six feet high inside. The shrine door is tastefully carved and has a Ganpati on the lintel. It has square pillars. The outside walls have fallen away. South of this and facing north is another apparently very old shrine. It has four pillars in the floor and a veranda with pilasters and two columns in antis. The temple is on the model of a Buddhist cave, and though the walls

Chapter XIV.
Places.
GOKÁK.
Temples.

have been rebuilt in more modern times, it appears to be a fragment of one of the earliest Gokák temples. The pattern of the temple door is peculiarly like the cave pattern. To the west of this very old temple is a neat little temple, ruined in front. It is perhaps the most modern of the group and has four columns inside the hall, of the same style as the Mahálingeshvar temple but more elegant. The screen has four square columns and two pilasters. The antechamber has two small pillars in front. The shrine door is very neat but without animal figures. The floors of the shrine and antechamber have been recently dug in search of treasure. To the west of the Mahálingeshvar temple are the remains of another smaller temple. On the opposite or north side of the river are five or six ruined temples. From the crest of the rock 132 rock cut-steps lead to the river bed before it flows over the fall. At the bottom of the steps is a little temple to Basav of which only the shrine and the entrance remain. Over the porch or antechamber to the shrine is a carved slab, in the centre of which is Káli with a crooked sword, heavy ear-rings, a heavy chain over the brow instead of the usual skull necklace. In her hands she holds a shield a human head and a mace or sceptre. At her left foot is a figure on a dog and at her right foot one beating a drum. The next compartment near the shrine has a dancing four-armed Devi with smaller figures on each side. In the corner compartment to the right is Ganpati. On the compartment to the right a woman with a strap across her bosom, seizes a smaller woman by the hair; below is a dog and a sheep. In the front compartments are three dancing women, one with a strap across her breasts; and with these are other smaller figures in the same compartments. On the east side compartment is a figure of the Varáh or boar incarnation of Vishnu with large breasts and a small figure on an animal; and in the last or corner compartment is a dancing Devi with four arms, straps, and small figures below. On the lintel is Shiv or Vishnu with Párvati or Lakshmi seated on his knee. Loose slabs lie about, representing the same pair, and a three-faced Brahma. Higher up the hill are fragments of four other temples in the same style but entirely ruined. Beside them is a much larger temple, surrounded by prickly pear and partially filled with earth, and almost unbearably infested by bats. The pillars are square like the pillars of the older temple on the north side, but the torus of the capital is circular. It has been a triple temple facing south and directly opposite the larger temple on the other side with the falls in a line between. Further east is a smaller temple, not over six feet high, with four plain columns in the hall and pilasters with two columns in antis in front. The antechamber and shrine are small and the walls are thin, being formed of large slabs set on edge. No sculptures are left to show the sect to which the temple belonged. West of these is a fragment of another, about five feet high, plain, with two square pillars.

Márkandeya Gorge.

The Márkandeya rises in a spur of the Sahyádris about forty miles west of Belgaum, and after a course of sixty or seventy miles meets the Ghatprabha just below the Gokák gorge, immediately above the town of Gokák. About a mile above the meeting the Márkandeya leaves the range of sandstone hills by a rocky chasm whose breadth at over 100 feet above the stream is only 420 feet. For six or seven

Chapter XIV.

Places.

GOKÁK.

Márkandeya Gorge.

miles above this rocky chasm the river runs through a remarkably picturesque gorge. The entrance of the gorge is about two miles from Gokák camp. From the entrance a footway leads over the rocks at the base of the cliffs on the right bank of the river a few miles up the gorge to much frequented temples of Malappa and Nirvanappa. The way to these shrines leads through one of the most beautiful spots in the Deccan. The Márkandeya tumbles and rushes over and through gray gneiss rocks. Above on either side from 300 to 450 feet above the river, their bases often starting from the water's edge, tower bright red sandstone cliffs contrasting beautifully with the steep green wooded slopes below. The river is in places overshadowed by trees. In others it spreads over golden sands, or falls in miniature cascades through gray and ruddy boulders. Still glassy pools reflect the bright green-leaved *karanj* and the white-stemmed *matti* with the red rocks high above.[1] But for stray wild-date palms the scenery would be much like parts of North Wales.

History.

The earliest mention of Gokák is probably as Gokáge in an inscription of 1047 which mentions Akkádevi the aunt of the Western Chálukya king Someshvar I. (1042-1068) as laying siege to the fort of Gokáge.[2] In 1685 Gokák is mentioned as a town of note and the head-quarters of a district or *sarkár* that surrendered to the Moghals.[3] In 1719 Gokák was among the territory included in Shάhu's own rule or *svaráj.*[4] Some time between 1719 and 1754 Gokák fell to the Sávanur Nawábs who built the mosque and Ganji-khána which overhang the river. In February 1754 Gokák was taken by the Peshwa.[5] In 1778 Gokák was occupied by Irappa the Kittur *desái*, but in 1779 it was reconquered for the Peshwa by Parshurám Bháu Patvardhan who took the *desái* prisoner. The Gokák sub-division then continued to belong to the Peshwa till 1783 when it was given in military grant or *saranjám* to the Patvardhans at an estimated yearly revenue of £9811 (Rs. 98,110). In a Marátha revenue statement prepared about 1789 Gokák appears under the Azimnagar or Balegaon *sarkár* as the head-quarters of a *pargana* or sub-division with a yearly revenue of £1125 (Rs. 11,250).[6] In 1790 Captain Moor described Gokák as a town of considerable extent and trading importance pleasantly situated on the eastern acclivity of a hill. . On the north the town was watered by the Ghatprabha which had deep water immediately opposite to the town but could be well forded about a quarter of a mile to the east. The town was enclosed by a wall and ditch on the east and south, and to the west it was commanded by a hill with a ruined fort. The river bank had another fortification which with the town gave a pleasant view from the opposite side but was not of much strength. The town had a large cotton and silk weaving industry.[7] Major Price, whose Memoirs of the Early Life and Services of a Field Officer were published by Major Moor in 1839, visited Gokák

---

[1] *Karanj* is Pongamia glabra; *matti* Terminalia tomentosa.
[2] Fleet's Kánarese Dynasties, 45.
[3] Orme's Historical Fragments, 144; Stokes' Belgaum, 43.
[4] Stokes' Belgaum, 47.
[5] Stokes' Belgaum, 49.
[6] Waring's History of the Maráthás, 245.
[7] Moor's Narrative, 260-261.

Chapter XIV.
Places.
GOKÁK.
History.

in 1790, and describes it as, next to Miraj and perhaps Tásgaon, by far the most considerable town he had seen in the country. The walls and dwelling-houses were built of sun-dried clay with more than ordinary neatness and regularity. Next to Bilgi in North Kánara Gokák was the neatest and most cleanly town Major Price had seen. It had a large manufacture of women's robes, turbans, and shoulderclotlis or *dupettás.* The fort to which the town formed a *petta* was of some size and lay along the south bank of the Ghatprabha. Round the fort were vestiges of a useless ditch. A castle, if it deserved the name, lay on a conical-looking hill west of the town.[1] In 1797 the Kolhápur chief forced Gokák to pay him a tribute of £12,000 (Rs. 1,20,000). In the Third Marátha War Munro reached Gokák on the 7th of March 1818 and crossing the Ghatprabha advanced to Páchhápur.[2] In 1836 on the death without heirs of Govindráv Patvardhan of Tásgaon Gokák town and sub-division lapsed to the British Government.[3] During the two years ending 1838, when the question of the civil head-quarters of the Belgaum district was under discussion, Gokák was one of five towns proposed and at one time was all but chosen.[4] In 1850 Sir George Wingate estimated the value of the yearly exports of Gokák cotton fabrics at £10,500 (Rs. 1,05,000). In the 1876-77 famine the weaving and dyeing suffered severely and large numbers of the weavers either left or died. In 1881 Gokák town is mentioned as owing its importance to the manufacture of cotton cloth for which it had 420 looms. Women's robes and waistcloths varying in price from 2*s.* 6*d.* to £2 (Rs. 1¼-20) were made and exported, the richer kinds to Bijápur Kolhápur and Miraj, and the inferior sorts below the Sahyádris by the Phonda pass where they were much used by the poorer classes of the coast population.[5]

GOLIHALLI.

Golihalli, about one mile south of Bidi, has temples of Kalmeshvar, Rámling, and Siddhaling. Near the Kalmeshvar temple is an inscription which appears to record a grant made by one of the Kádambas as an underlord of the Western Chálukya king Someshvar III. or Bhulokmalla (1126-1139).[6] Just outside the village is another inscription on a stone in front of a small temple of Basava. At the top of the stone are emblems. In the centre is a shrine with a *ling* in its case or *shálunkha* and a worshipper. To the left is a figure of Basav with the sun above it, and to the right a cow and a calf with a crooked knife above them and above the knife the moon. The inscription is dated in the fourteenth seventeenth and twenty-sixth years of the Goa Kádamba chief Permádi (1147-1175), who is described as governing the Konkan Nine-hundred, the Palasige or Halsi Twelve-thousand, and the Velugrám or Belgaum Seventy, and as ruling happily at his capital of Gove or Goa.

---

1 Stokes' Belgaum, 59; Memoirs, 211-212. 2 Stokes' Belgaum, 74.
3 Stokes' Belgaum, 87. The Gokák sub-division was a noted resort of thieves and plunderers. Ditto. 4 Stokes' Belgaum, 86.
5 Survey Superintendent's Letter 47 of 1881 and Survey Commissioner's Letter 273 of 1881.
6 Journal Bombay Branch Royal Asiatic Society, IX. 263; Fleet's Kánarese Dynasties, 52.

It records the grant of land and cash endowments to a temple of Hemmeshvar in the district of Kirusampgádi.[1]

Chapter XIV. Places. GUDALGI.

Gudalgi village, nine miles north of Athni, is noted for two Lingáyat spirit-scaring gods, Kádsidh and Pádsidh. The person possessed with a spirit is brought before the gods on three no-moon nights one after another. Every time he is brought the possessed person cries out bitterly as though beaten and says 'I will go, I will go.' The spirit is believed to leave the patient on the third no-moon visit.

HALSI.

Halsi, or **Halasige,** in the Bidi sub-division about ten miles south-east of Khánápur, with in 1881 a population of 2500, is an old town, the chief capital of the Early Kadambas (A.D. 500) and a minor capital of the Goa Kádambas (980-1250). The town has no manufactures and no trade except in rice and plantains. Halsi has three large temples two, Varáhnarsimh's and Suvarneshvar's in the town and the third Rámeshvar's on a hill about two miles to the west. Varáhnarsimh's is an old Vaishnav temple (90' × 54') ascribed to Jakhanácharya. Suvarneshvar's is a good sized building out of repair. Someshvar's is a small temple on the hill with a sacred pool. The temple is held in great local veneration and a Soma sacrifice was performed here as late as about 1870. The sacrifice lasted about ten days and was attended by about 2000 persons. A yearly fair is held at the temple on the full-moon of *A'shvin* or September-October when about 2000 people assemble. On the full-moon of *Kártik* or November, the palanquin of Varáhnarsimh is carried to the temple of Rámeshvar attended by about 500 persons. In the temple of Varáhnarsimh, on a stone tablet about ten feet high by three feet broad, is an inscription. For a third from the top the tablet is covered with a large sculpture representing Narsimh, Lakshmi, and other figures. The inscription covers an equal portion in the middle and the rest of the stone is blank. The writing extends over sixty lines in two parts recording two different gifts in different years. The first part of thirty-six lines bears date Thursday the new moon of *Áshádh* or June-July in the year 4270 of the Kali age (A.D. 1169). It records the gift, by the sixth Goa Kádamba king Permádi or Shivchitt (1147-1175), of Sindvalli village in the Kálgiri subdivision of the Palsi or Halsi district,[2] for the performance in the rites of the holy Narsimh whose shrine had been established of the pure city of Palsi or Halsi by Matayogi who had practised

Inscriptions.

[1] The details of the grant are: In the fourteenth year, some rice land, a flower garden near the king's betel plantation, two houses, a monastery, a house where jars are made, a *mána* or four *shers* of oil for every oil mill to be devoted to the god's lamp, and a further quantity of oil from all the oil mills in the village. The donor of this grant is the king's *dandnáyak* or head of the police. The grant made in the seventeenth year is lost but the donors are given as the merchants of one village and the people of nine villages, thirty-six travelling merchants, some head merchants, some basketmakers and cultivators. The twenty-sixth year grant records the gift of a toll at the rate of twenty for every loaded cart. The donors are the merchants of the four towns which constitute the district of Kirusampgádi. Journal Bombay Branch Royal Asiatic Society, IX. 300-403. Dr. Burgess (Lists, 43) notes another Kádamba grant at Golihalli dated Kaliyuga 4283 or A.D. 1181.

[2] Journal Bombay Branch Royal Asiatic Society, IX. 262, 278-284. For the interchange of *p* and *h* in Kánarese see Rice's Mysore, I. 395. The Kálgiri mentioned in this inscription, which has not been identified, may be Ptolemy's (A.D. 150) Kalligeris which seems to have belonged to this part of the country.

Chapter XIV.
Places.
Halsi.
Inscriptions.

contemplation by faith, knowledge, and action.[1] The latter part of twenty-four lines is dated Thursday the twelfth of the bright half of *Mágh* or January-February in the year 4272 (A.D. 1171) of the Kali age.[2] It records the gift by Vishnuchitt (1147-1173) the younger brother of, and joint ruler with, Shivchitt of thirteen fields in Bhálak village in the Kálgeri subdivision in the Palsi or Halsi district, for the proper performance of the worship of the god Narsimh.[3] About 1860 in a small mound close to a small well called Chakratirth, on the Nandgad road about three miles north of Halsi six copper-plates were found. The copper-plates which vary from three to five sheets in one set, and, in size, from 8⅞″ to 5¼″ long by 2⅝″ to 1⅜″ broad, are all in the Sanskrit language and in the Western India Buddhist Cave-alphabet characters[4] not yet developed into the Old Kánarese character. All record grants of an old dynasty of Kadamba kings whose capitals were at Banavási and Halsi and who were Jains by faith. The exact date of these early Kadamba kings cannot be fixed as the plates contain no reference to any known era. From the type of the alphabet, and the allusions which they contain to contemporary events, the plates may be assigned to about the fifth century after Christ. Almost all the plates begin and end with a Jain salutation. Except one which records a gift of land to a private person, all record gifts of land or villages in furtherance of the Jain religion. Five of the plates mention Paláshika or Halsi, and one records the building of a Jain temple at Halsi. Four plates record grants of land and three record grants of villages. Besides these seven an eighth copper-plate in four massive sheets was found at Halsi. It belongs to the Goa Kádambas, and has, on its seal, the representation of a Narsimh with the words Shri-Vira-Jayakeshi Malavarmári. The plate records that on Thursday the twelfth of the bright half of *Chaitra* in the year 4288 of the Kali age (A.D. 1186), an image of Varáhdev was made to be set in front of Narsimh in the centre of the village of Paláshika, and that a village was granted to it by the seventh Goa Kádamba king Jaykeshi III. (1175-1188).[5]

Copper-Plates.

---

[1] The initial date of the Kali age is the spring equinox of B.C. 3102. Indian Antiquary, V. 152.

[2] The original has 4270 by a mistake of the engraver who merely copied the year of the first part, notwithstanding that he put the right cycle year two years later than the cycle year of the first part.

[3] At the end of the inscription is the following curious record : Among the shares of the twelve Bráhmans one share was acquired by Narsimh. All the ornaments of Narsimh purchased with five hundred gold *nishkas* were deposited in the house of the Vaishnav Padmanábh, and were stolen by him. When the time for putting on the ornaments arrived, king Jaykeshidev (father of the brothers Shivchitt and Vishnuchitt) found out the theft, took away the Vaishnav's three shares in the village of Sampat and gave the three shares worth five hundred *nishkas* to Narsimh. At the time of the consecration of Narsimh two fields were given by a banker living in the city of Panas (Halsi ?). A Vaishnav named Dugjan gave a flower garden outside the village and one Vrishabh of Chintogirivâli gave a flower garden inside the village. King Shivchitt gave a plantation of betel palms inside the village. Some respectable merchants also gave a contribution. The wise man Shankarárya had this written on the stone having seen it on a copper plate.' Journal Bombay Branch Royal Asiatic Society, IX. 280-281, 284-286.

[4] Compare Bombay Gazetteer, XVI. 607-610; Archæological Survey of Western India IV. Plates XLIV.-LX.

[5] Journal Bombay Branch Royal Asiatic Society, 230, 241-246; Fleet's Kánarese Dynasties, 93.

Chapter XIV. Places.

HALSI. *History.*

Halsi, called Paláshika Palashika Palshi and Halasige in inscriptions, is an old town and was one of the capitals of a dynasty of Kadamba kings in the fifth century. A Jain temple at Halsi was built by one of these kings and pious countrymen and citizens were ordained by the king to worship Jinendra. During the eleventh twelfth and thirteenth centuries, Halsi was a minor capital of a dynasty of Kádambas whose chief city was Goa (980-1250). During their rule the still existing temple of Narsimh was built about 1170 and a small temple of Varáh afterwards added about 1185.[1]

HANNIKERI.

Hannikeri village, about four miles north-west of Sampgaon, with in 1872 a population of 1608 and in 1881 of 499, has an old plain Jain temple of Brahmadev. The village has an inscription of the Ratta kings of Saundatti and Belgaum (875-1250) on a stone tablet bearing date 1208. The inscription is of the sixteenth Ratta chief Lakshmidev I. and speaks of him as a descendant of the Ráshtrakuta king Krishna II (875-901). This is the first inscription which mentions that the capital of the Rattas was moved from Sugandhvati or Saundatti to Venugrám or Belgaum and that in addition to the Kundi Three-thousand they also possessed the Venugrám Seventy.[2]

HIREKUMBHI HILL.

Hirekumbhi Hill, about 325 feet above the plain, lies about eight miles east of Saundatti. It is a steep flat-topped hill covered with brushwood and prickly pear, and climbed by a footpath. On the top are two small mosques and a hut with a resident Musalmán family in charge of the mosques. Wild hog and panthers occasionally visit the hill.

HILTALMARDI HILL.

Hittalmardi Hill, near Kulavli village, stands eighteen miles south-east of Sampgaon, on a brushwood covered slope. A pass in the hill, chiefly used for grain carts leads to Kittur and Alnávar. The top is tilled with millet and rice by Hindus and Musalmáns who live in temporary huts during the rainy season.

HUKERI.

Hukeri, in 16° 13′ north latitude and 74° 40′ east longitude, about fifteen miles south of Chikodi, is the head-quarters of the Hukeri petty division, with in 1872 a population of 5365 and in 1881 of 5523. The town stands on the east bank of a large water-course which flows into the Hirankeshi a feeder of the Ghatprabha. Hukeri has the offices of the petty divisional officer or *mahálkari*, of the chief constable, a post office, and two schools one anglo-vernacular and the other private. A municipality was established in 1854 but abolished in 1864 as the income did not pay the expenses. A weekly market is held on Mondays, when chillies gram and molasses come from the neighbouring villages and rice is brought from Ajre in Kolhápur, about twenty-five miles to the west, by Bágbán Musalmáns. From Hukeri molasses and hemp go to Rájápur in Ratnágiri and chillies to Belgaum. The only manufactures are coarse sackcloth robes for women and cheap blankets. Trade is briskest during February March and April. Besides several tombs

---

[1] See above p. 565. [2] Fleet's Kánarese Dynasties, 82.

Chapter XIV.
Places.
HUKERI.

and ruined water channels the only objects of interest in the town are two mosques called the Gajbara Sáheb's and the Chini *ghumat* now used as lodging houses by European officers visiting the town. Gajbara Sáheb's mosque on rising ground to the east of Hukeri near the Gokák road was built about 1498 by Keta Gauda a *desái* of Nandi village about five miles north of Chikodi. The Chini *ghumat,* which is the only building in the district on which painted tiles are used as an ornament, and the Kadam Rasul mosque near it were built by Rustam Zamán (1616-1667) a Bijápur officer. In his time also was built another mosque beside the road near the great dome and the small tomb and well close by. An inscription on the well is a passage from the Kurán.[1] A yearly fair or *uras* in honour of the two *ghumats* is held for two days in February. From two to three thousand people come and a little trafficking is done in sweetmeats and ironware.

History.

The earliest known mention of Hukeri is in 1327 when Hukeri and Ráybág appear as the two Belgaum towns where, on his conquest of the Karnátak, the emperor Muhammad Tughlik (1325-1351) stationed officers.[2] In 1347 the name of the *Amir* of Hukeri occurs in the list of the new nobility or *Amir Jadidas* whom the emperor summoned to Daulatabad and who revolted.[3] About 1500 Hukeri and its neighbourhood were in charge of Fateh Bahádur a captain of one thousand horse.[4] In 1502 Yusuf Adil Sháh jealous of his growing power took the Bijápur command from Ein-ul-mulk Giláni and reduced his possessions to the districts of Hukeri and Belgaum. During his rule, which lasted for the forty-three years ending 1546, Ein-ul-mulk Giláni built the Hukeri fort and palace aqueducts and cisterns and the largest of the Hukeri tombs.[5] In 1542 Ein-ul-mulk joined Burhán Nizám of Ahmadnagar against Bijápur, but rejoined Bijápur service on Burhán's defeat and was rewarded by Ibráhim Sháh with the estate of Kittur.[6] Ein-ul-mulk was succeeded in the Hukeri command by his brother Fateh Mulk (1547-1568) in whose time a third tomb to the east was built.[7] The successors of Fateh Mulk in the Bijápur command were two Bijápur officers Randulla Khán in 1569 and his son Rustam Zamán in 1616. Rustam built the Chini *ghumat* and the Kadam Rasul mosque near it, planted a garden around, and built a well. On Rustam's promotion to Miraj, Hukeri with Kolhápur was given to one Abdul Kharid. Kharid was dethroned by the Rája of Panhála, died in 1643, and an attempt to secure the succession for a surviving son failed.[8] From 1668 to 1686 Hukeri is said to have been held by Induráv Ghárpure.[9] During the disturbed times of Shiváji's plundering raids (1664-1680) the Hukeri *desái* seems to have fairly established his

---

[1] Stokes' Belgaum, 22-23, 39. [2] Stokes' Belgaum, 11.
[3] Briggs' Ferishta, I. 437. [4] Stokes' Belgaum, 23.
[5] The small tomb to the left of the largest tomb was built in 1515 by Ein's brother Seif Khán. [6] Briggs' Ferishta, III. 90-92.
[7] Stokes' Belgaum, 23. No monuments are now to be found in the tombs. They may have been destroyed or the three bodies may have been taken for burial to Bijápur.
[8] Moor's Narrative, 14-15. [9] Stokes' Belgaum, 42.

Chapter XIV.

Places.

Hukeri.

power. He renounced allegiance to Bijápur, assumed the independent title of estateholder or *samsthánik*, and by frequent encroachments gained a firm hold over his district. On the Moghal destruction of Bijápur in 1687 Hukeri was the only part of Belgaum that remained to the Maráthás, and it continued to be held by an independent *desái* the ancestor of the present Vontámurikar. In 1763 Mádhavráo the fourth Peshwa (1761-1772) reduced the Hukeri *desái*, and, with other parts of the Karnátak, handed his district to the Kolhápur chief on condition of receiving a yearly present or *nazar* of £50,000 (Rs. 5,00,000).[1] In 1769 Mádhavráo Peshwa, enraged by the continual inroads of Kolhápur marauders, deprived Kolhápur of Hukeri and in 1770 appointed a mámlatdár of his own.[2] In 1791 Captain Moor found Hukeri a poor town with a poor Musalmán population. It belonged to Parshurám Bháu and bore clear traces of former greatness. Captain Moor notes its tombs, three of them of superior workmanship, and several wells and cisterns.[3] In 1804 Hukeri with the Chikodi and Manoli sub-divisions were given by the Peshwa to the Nipáni *desái* in reward for help rendered to General Wellesley.[4] In 1827 Captain Clunes notices Hukeri on the Poona- Belgaum road belonging to Kolhápur, with 300 houses, twenty shops, and an aqueduct.

Huli.

Huli, about five miles east of Saundatti, with in 1872 a population of 2118 and in 1881 of 1299, is an old place with temples and inscriptions. The chief object of interest in the village is a handsome but ruined temple of Panchlingdev originally a Jain *basti*. The temple is in three parts a large outer many-cornered hall or *mandap* (51′ × 45′) with three porches and twenty-two pillars, four of the pillars in a central group, twelve round these, and two at each of the porches. The outer hall leads to an inner hall (41′ 9″ × 25′) with a triple shrine at the back and one at each side. The Jina figures, corresponding to the figures of Ganpati over the shrine doors of a Shaivite temple, have been hewn off all the lintels except that over the entrance to the shrine at the south end which has the finest door. The temple faces east and has on two of its outer hall pillars Kánarese inscriptions probably written when the temple came to be used by Lingáyats. Except in some compartments with carved lotuses the roofs are plain. The temple probably belongs to about A.D. 1100. At the foot of the hill to the north of the village is a group of temples in ruins, probably of about the same age. One of these, built of hard compact bluish stone, has a hall about forty-three feet from north to south. The four central pillars, except the snake on the bracket, are similar to those at Belgaum.[5] The short pillars on the screen are of different forms, some six-sided some eight-sided and some round. The door of the shrine is of porphyry richly carved, and, on the lintel is Shri or Lakshmi with elephants pouring water over her. Standing against the ruins of an old temple close by, is a large inscription, in good preservation. All round are fragments of buildings with pillars of the

[1] Stokes' Belgaum, 52. [2] Stokes' Belgaum, 52. [3] Moor's Narrative, 14-15. [4] Stokes' Belgaum, 70. [5] See above Belgaum, pp. 539-540.

Chapter XIV.
Places.
Huli.
Temples.

plainest and roughest style, slabs of granite and porphyry carved stones, and fragments of inscriptions. Below this ruined temple is a pond to the north of which is a temple with an inscription in the west wall with a figure of Vishnu resting on his cobra. Over the shrine door is Lakshmi with elephants. On the west side of the pond are several shrines. The most southerly is the antechamber and shrine of a temple with a standing figure on the lintel of the door. The next has a highly carved door with the usual figure on the lintel. To the north of this is another shrine with six pillars of the hall still left, with figures carved in high relief round their bases.[1] These figures are now defaced. The antechamber has had two small pillars in front one still standing and there are traces of a screen between the middle pair. Except a lotus carved in the roof of the hall the roofs are flat. Two niches, which probably held inscriptions, are empty. This temple bears clear marks of wilful destruction. To the west of these, overgrown with prickly pear, is an old shrine with a small open hall. The door from the outer hall to the inner and larger hall is richly carved with a wonderful variety of twined cobras. North-west from this is a modern shrine with a remarkable snake figure. Carved slabs lie about or are built into the surrounding walls, some in slaty stone with very spirited Vaishnav carvings. East-south-east from the pond, on a mound, is another temple with a round hall. The outside is plain and the door of the shrine has lines of dancers and Nága figures. Inside there is a Lingáyat inscription, a curious Nága figure, and a Ganpati probably brought from some other temple. Of three inscriptions at Huli two belong to the reigns of the Western Chálukya kings Vikramáditya V. (1018-1042) and Someshvar II. (1068-1075) and one to the Kalachuri Bijjala (1156-1167).[2]

Fort.

In 1842 Huli fort is described as an oblong stone fort (150′ × 100′) on the south edge of a small range of hills north of and overlooking the town and about 200 feet above the plain. Its defences consisted of circular stone bastions at the angles connected by curtains varying in height from twenty-two to thirty-three feet and containing a rampart ten feet broad and a ruined parapet four feet high. It had no ditch. The chief gate to the fort was blocked with stones and the only entrance was by a small ruined door in a very small sallyport on the south face covered by a stone outwork. The water-supply was ample but there were no houses and no protection from shells. The fort was strong enough to resist infantry but was powerless against shells and by knocking off its parapets it might easily be taken by escalade.[3] At present (1884) except the north wall which has fallen down its stone walls are in good order. The interior is overgrown with prickly pear and brushwood and the only buildings are a gateway, a pond, a well, and two powder magazines.

History.

On the fall of Vijaynagar after the battle of Tálikot (1565), with various other places in Belgaum, Huli fell to the Navalgund

---

[1] These figures have (1881) solid iron rings round their necks.
[2] Fleet's Kánarese Dynasties, 43, 48, 59.
[3] Inspection Committee's Report of 5th July 1842.

Chapter XIV. Places. Huli. History.

chief Vitta Gauda.[1] In 1674 Huli fort is said to have been built by Shiváji and it was one of many which are recorded to have been held by him at the time of his death.[2] While in pursuit of Dhundia Vágh, General Wellesley gave the garrison of Huli on the 30th of July 1800 a *kaul* or promise of safety on condition that they committed no aggression. On the 1st of August they plundered the baggage of the British Dragoons as it passed the fort on the march to Saundatti and on the 22nd Lieutenant Colonel-Capper attacked the fort and carried it by escalade.[3]

Hunur Hill.

Hunur, also called **Pavitra** or **Paijhar Hill,** about 270 feet above the plain lies near Hunur village about twenty miles south of Chikodi. A difficult ascent without any rock-cut steps leads to the open unfortified top (150′ × 125′). The hill has a nearly round fort standing by itself, its sides consisting partly of rock and partly built with stones and earth. The fort has no gateways and no buildings and is mostly ruined, portions of the walls remaining here and there. The hill is infested with wolves and jackals. Pavitragad is mentioned as one of the ten Belgaum forts held by Shiváji at the time of his death in 1680.[4] In 1853 Paijhargad or Pavitragad is described as situated on the highest point of a long wavy isolated hill running nearly east and west. The only good approach to the fort was on the south by a very rugged and stony path which led from Hunur under the south wall to the east gateway. The north side was very steep, the west spur very easy and the hill all round not hard to climb. Hunur and Masti villages lay to the south and south-west of the fort. A path partly good and partly stony and narrow, led from Sutgatti on the Belgaum-Kolhápur road; and there were two other roads to the fort from Hatargi five miles to the west and Hukeri six miles to the north. The fort about 300 feet above the plain was fashioned out of a large knoll or mound about the middle of the hill.[5] The surface of the mound was originally surrounded by large masses of rocks of irregular shape and size. In making the fort the top of the mound was levelled, walls of large square stones raised on the rocks, and the intervals filled in. Including both natural and artificial formations[6] the walls from base to top varied in height from twenty-five to fifty feet. The fort had one entrance on the east where about twelve stone steps led, through an opening in the wall between two towers or bastions to the left, to a small wooden gateway. The opening in the wall was broad enough to allow of four persons passing abreast through it. The bastions afforded little or no protection to the defences, as they were solid and without parapets or loopholes for firing. The interior of the

---

[1] According to the Local Chronicle of Torgal, Ali Adil Sháh (1557-1579) the fourth Bijápur king, on a promise of safety enticed a man named Nágráj from the sallyport of Huli and treacherously took him captive. The date of the event is given in the Chronicle as Shak 1478 (A.D. 1556). Indian Antiquary, VII. 34.

[2] Stokes' Belgaum, 42; Orme's Historical Fragments, 86, 87.

[3] Supplementary Despatches, II. 124.

[4] Grant Duff's Maráthás, 133.

[5] A cultivated plain surrounded the hill. The hill sides were covered with loose stones and low brushwood.

[6] The artificial formation varied from twenty-five to fifty feet.

Chapter XIV.
Places.
HUNUR HILL.

fort was a small level space following the irregular rock formation and only two furlongs round. It was surrounded by the remains of a low parapet wall two to three feet high with, at irregular distances, the remains of fourteen small round bastions. Save two small rooms near the gate for the sentry and a small recess in the north parapet said to have been the magazine, the fort had no buildings. At the south-west corner was a high solid tower seventeen feet high and twenty-five feet round at the top. The tower was fast going to decay and had probably been climbed by a ladder as it bore no traces of steps. The water-supply was from two wells but both were dried up. The larger well (38′ × 30′ × 65′) had remains of steps but was choked with a part of its inner wall which was struck by lightning about 1800. The smaller well (21′ × 17′) was thirteen feet deep. In 1853 the fort was empty and almost entirely in ruins. During the Kolhápur insurrection in 1844 the people of Hunur village sought safety in it and after the insurrection it was dismantled. The fort was said to have been built by a Kolhápur king about 1550 and always contained a small garrison to whom the fort and ground were granted as *inám*.

JÁMBOTI.

Ja'mboti, on the road leading by Kunkumbi and the Chorle pass into Portuguese territory is a small town eighteen miles south-west of Belgaum, with in 1881 a population of 634. The town consists of two parts, the *kasba* the residence of a *desái* now almost deserted and the *peth* or market place a mile distant. In 1820,[1] when it was visited by Dr. Marshall, Jámboti was ruled by a Marátha *sardesái* named Venkatráv who formerly gained his income from plunder. Though dangerous to his neighbours Venkatráv treated his own people well. Compared with the neighbouring towns Jámboti was notably neat and comfortable. Nor did the *desái* show any signs of the robber. He kept the pomp of a Hindu chief, had his own civil and criminal courts, drew a large income from the revenues of several villages, and was surrounded by a number of Bráhmans. As he failed to show any satisfactory claim to the lands he held Government deprived him of most of his villages including Jámboti and turned him into a pensioner, with a yearly allowance for three generations of £500 (Rs. 5000) and the revenues of two villages. The present (1883) *desái* who receives a pension of £63 (Rs. 630), was a minor at his father's death. In 1870 he was placed under the guardianship of Mr. A. E. Grey, then Collector of Belgaum, who managed the estate, paid off the family debts, and saved a large sum for his ward. On coming of age the *desái*, who had been given a fair Maráthi education in the Sávantvádi chief's house to whom he is closely related, fell into dissipated habits, wasted the savings, and ran into debt. Many of the people of Jámboti have left their homes and the town or *kasba* is half ruined. In the suburb or *peth* are still some fairly prosperous Lingáyat and Nárvekar Vánis, and a market is held every Tuesday where the people from the villages round make weekly purchases.

The Jámboti forest lands abound in game, tigers being occasion-

[1] Statistical Reports, 106.

ally found. Nánásáheb, the father of the present *desái* was a great sportsman and every year generally killed several tigers. In 1695 the Italian traveller Gemelli Careri going from Belgaum to Goa passed the night in a wood near what he calls the village of Jámboti. The village belonged to a *say* that is *desái* as the Moghals allowed some lords to possess these barren countries for a yearly tribute.[1]

JOGI HILL.

Jogi Hill, about 875 feet above the plain, lies about a mile south-west of Chikodi. It has no cultivation either on its sides or on its flat unfortified top. It is infested with wolves and jackals.

JUGAL.

Jugal, about fifteen miles north-east of Chikodi, is a large village on the Krishna with in 1872 a population of 2367 and in 1881 of 2281. The village has an old tomb of a Musalmán saint named Masabati. In memory of the saint a yearly fair is held in the seventh Musalmán month Rajab and is attended by 2000 to 3000 people. The village has a Kánarese school.

JULPEN HILL.

Julpen Hill, about 730 feet above the plain, stands near Hirekodi village from miles from Chikodi. It is a flat bare hill with a flat top on which millets of both sorts are grown by Lingáyats and Holerus. The hill is infested with wolves and jackals.

KÁBUR.

Ka'bur, about twelve miles south-west of Chikodi, is a large garden village, with in 1872 a population of 2722 and in 1881 of 2443. The village lies on a channel which waters about fifty gardens within the limits of the village. The produce is sugarcane, vegetables, and, except rice, all varieties of grain. The village has an old ruined temple of Ishvardev (128′ × 48′) with an inscription which has not been made out. Outside the village are two ruined tombs or *ghumats* believed to belong to Moghal times. The Poona-Londa or Belgaum branch of the West Deccan railway will have a second class station called Chikodi Road near Kábur forty-four miles north-east of Belgaum station.

KÁDROLI.

Ka'droli village on the Malprabha about six miles south of Sampgaon, with in 1881 a population of about 1600, has in the bed of the river a temple of Shankarling of about the tenth century. The temple, of which except three shrines and an antechamber nothing remains intact, is built of large black stones. The central shrine is about eight feet and each of the side shrines five feet six inches square. The roofs and capitals of columns have been washed away by the river. Except a few letters on one of the columns and on an old loose image of Ganpati the temple has no inscription. In the veranda of a modern temple in the village is an inscribed stone tablet (1′ 8″ broad and 6′ high) which originally stood in front of the Shankarling temple but was moved into the village for safety. At the top of the slab are a *ling* with a priest in the middle, the bull *Nandi* with the sun above it to the left, and a cow and calf with the moon above them to the right. The inscription is in Old Kánarese letters excellently preserved. The language is Sanskrit but the idiom and inflexions

---

[1] Churchill's Voyages, IV. 249-250.

are Old Kánarese. The inscription records a yearly cash grant for decorating the image of the god Shankardev with clothes and ornaments on Sunday the full-moon of *Paush* or December-January *Shak* 997 (1075) during the reign of the Western Chálukya king Someshvar II. (1068-1075). A large fragment of an inscribed stone lies uncared for in the village.[1]

KÁGVÁD.

Ka'gva'd is a large village about twenty-two miles west of Athni, with in 1872 a population of 4098 and in 1881 of 3407. Kágvád has a little trade in cotton, a post office, and a Kánarese school. The village has temples of Brahmanáth and Satvái. The image of Brahmanáth usually called Kaggodaráya, from which the village takes its name, is generally placed in an underground cell near which is an inscribed stone tablet. Satvái or Mother Sixth, considered by the lower classes as the destroyer and by the upper classes as the guardian of infants, is worshipped by women of all castes during the three months after a child is born. A yearly fair attended by about one thousand people is held in honour of Satvái in *Mágh* or February-March. In 1827 Captain Clunes calls the village Kagwaur, and notices that it belonged to the Patvardhans and had 384 houses, twenty shops, and twenty-five wells.[2]

KÁLÁNANDIGAD.

Ka'la'nandigad, on the Rám pass road about twenty miles west of Belgaum, is a ruined fort, on the highest point of one of the Sahyádri spurs. The fort is built on a peaked hill with partly wooded sides. The only ascent is on the north by a steep footpath about a mile and a half long. The fort is 1350 feet broad from east to west by 825 feet long from north to south, and has two gateways and ruins of walls cresting the ravines. An old temple and a small ruined building probably a storehouse are the only other remains. In 1827 a committee of inspection described Kálánandigad as a triangular fort on the top of a hill twenty miles west of Belgaum about 700 feet above the plain with a gentle ascent. On two sides it was formed by the perpendicular scarp of the rock which varied from forty to seventy feet in height, and, on the third side, it was defended from the adjoining hill[3] by a masonry wall only sixteen feet high in most places and in one place twelve. The water-supply was from a deep rock-cut well about six feet in diameter. Of ordnance there were two eight-pounders badly mounted, a three-pound tumbril without shot, and about 100 pounds of powder. The garrison consisted of 140 irregulars. In 1842 another committee of inspection described the fort as 900 feet above the level of the plain and as occupying the entire crest of one part of a hill.[4] This part was triangular in shape, the north side or base being about 1000 feet long, the south-east and south-west sides being about 600 feet each, and the entire breadth of the fort from north to south being about 300 feet. The works on the north and south-east sides were upon a natural scarp varying in height from thirty-eight to fifty feet. These works were very low

---

[1] Fleet's Kánarese Dynasties, 48; Bom. Arch. Rep. I. 9-10. [2] Itinerary, 33.
[3] This adjoining hill commanded the fort within 500 yards.
[4] A spur of the hill on nearly the same level stretches to the south-west rising about 900 feet distant to as great a height as the fort.

KÁLÁNANDIGAD.

with gun-holed parapets. The south-west front rose from the slope of the hill, the works in this part consisting of curtains and bastions about twenty feet high including very strong parapets five feet high. Except near the west angle, where the broken wall was badly built with loose stones, these works were well built of stone. About twenty feet from the foot of the works was a small ditch. Of two gates one on the north front was small and ruined, the other on the south-west front had two doors in bad order. The ascent to the north gate was steep and well flanked by the fort, the approach to the other gate was from the south-west and the works round its two doors were in good order. The committee observed that on two sides the fort might be considered impregnable, while, for an attack on the south-west front from the adjoining hill, ordnance especially mortars would be necessary.

KALHOLE.

Kalhole on a feeder of the Ghatprabha, about seven miles north-east of Gokák, with in 1872 a population of 2192 and in 1881 of 1648, has an old Jain temple or *basti* with an inscription. A fair is held at the temple in December when about 1500 people come. The inscription belongs to the Ratta chiefs and brothers Kártavirya IV. and Mallikárjun (1199-1218) whose capital is said to have been at Belgaum. It bears date Saturday the second of the bright half of *Paush* or December-January at the time of the beginning of the sun's course to the north in *Shak* 1127 (1205), and records the building of a Jain temple of the sixteenth *tirthankar* Shántináth at Kalpole[1] in the Kundi Three thousand and the grant of a field and certain cash dues to the temple priest.[2]

KANMADI.

Kanmadi village, with in 1872 a population of 2802 and in 1881 of 2426, lies about twenty-four miles north-east of Athni. The village has temples of Haridev and Mallikárjun and an old shrine of Daridevi in whose honour a yearly fair is held in *Chaitra* or March-April attended by five or six thousand people. The village contains a Government Kánarese school.

KHÁNÁPUR.

Kha'na'pur, 15° 37′ north latitude and 74° 34′ east longtitude, on the Malprabha about sixteen miles south of Belgaum is the head-quarters of the Khánápur sub-division, with in 1872 a population of 3516 and in 1881 of 4016. Besides the revenue and police offices of the Khánápur sub-division, the town has a school, a post office, a rest-house, and a Portuguese mission with a chapel. The town has a small trade in rice and plantains. Khánápur will be one of the stations on the Belgaum-Londa branch of the Poona-Belgaum railway. About 1720 Khánápur was a large entrepot or *utar peth* for Goa merchants with drugs, China goods, metals, and spices. They were met here by Hubli Nargund and Navalgund merchants with cloth cotton and saltpetre. This trade was destroyed about 1810 by the Kittur *desái* who removed it to Nandgad seven miles south-east of Khánápur.[3] In 1827 Khánápur with the neighbouring village of Thadkod had 453 houses, nine shops, a temple, and wells.[4]

---

[1] For the Kánarese interchange of *p* and *h* see above p. 565.
[2] Jour. Bo. Br. Roy. As. Soc. X. 220; Pali Sanskrit and Old Kánarese Inscriptions, 95; Fleet's Kánarese Dynasties, 83.
[3] Marshall's Statistical Reports, 97.
[4] Clunes' Itinerary, 72.

Chapter XIV.
Places.
KHAROSHI.

Kharoshi, on the Chikodi-Hukeri road about four miles south of Chikodi, is a large village, with in 1881 a population of 2024. The village has a temple of Ghanti Basvanna, a moderate sized building not in good order. A yearly fair in honour of the god is held on the last Monday of *Shrávan* or July-August when about 500 Lingáyats assemble.

KIRAVLE.

Kiravle also called Gorakhnáth hill lies about eight miles west of Khánápur. A sloping brushwood covered ascent leads to a flat uncultivated top with a monastery of the Kánpháta or slit-ear saint Gorakhnáth occupied by a few Kánpháta Gosávis. The water-supply is from a spring on the hill.

KITTUR.

Kittur, 15° 35′ north latitude and 74° 51′ east longitude, about fourteen miles south of Sampgaon, is an old town and till 1867 was the head-quaters of a petty division. In 1857 Kittur had a population of 7500; in 1872 of 7166 of whom 5545 were Hindus 1579 Musalmáns and forty-two Christians; and in 1881 of 6300. Markets are held twice a week on Mondays and Thursdays. About 1000 persons attend and cattle cloth cotton and grain are sold. Weaving and glass bangle-making are the chief industries. Kittur has a school a post office and a small temple with an old inscribed stone. The temple is dedicated to Basav and is not very old.

Inscription.

The inscribed stone in the temple belongs to the twelfth century and records a grant by the Kádambas of Goa. The emblems at the top of the stone are, in the middle a *ling* on a pedestal; to the left a figure of Basav with the sun above it; and to the right a worshipper with the moon above him and beyond him a cow and a calf and over them a crooked knife. The inscription, which is in thirty-nine lines in the Kánarese character, is unfinished, as the last words have no meaning, as it breaks off without the usual signs of ending, and as much blank space remains after the last line. It begins with salutations to Shiv, to Ganpati, and to Sarasvati, and, after a long list of complimentary attributes of the eighth Goa Kádamba chief Jaykeshi III. (1175-1188), records that in the Kaliyug year 4289 that is A.D. 1188 on Sunday the eighth of the bright half of *Áshádh* or June-July, two priests came to settle a dispute before the prime minister Ishvarárya Dandnáyak. The two priests were Shivshakti the *Ácharya* of Shri Kalleshvar of Attibávi well in Kittur and Kalyánshakti the *ácharya* of the original god of that place. Shivshakti maintained that a plot of ground in Kittur belonged to Kalleshvar, and Kalyánshakti asserted that the plot belonged to the original place god. The two parties entered into an agreement in the presence of the prime minister. Shivshakti said: 'Whereas this plot of ground, Álakolanakeyi, belonged of old to Kalleshvardev (but) Devráshi, the father of Kalyánshakti, unauthorizedly brought it under cultivation in the Chande State (?), and had a grant written in his own favour, I am now prepared to undergo the red-hot ploughshare ordeal in support of my statement that it has belonged from of old to Kalleshvardev.' Kalyánshakti, under oath with the holy symbols on his head, replied: 'If the Chande State (?) gave this plot of ground, Álakolanakeyi, to my father Devráshi and to myself on behalf of the original place god, it has not been unauthorisedly brought under cultivation.' When the parties had stated their case, the minister said 'Go both of you before the assemblage of the

Trial by Ordeal. 1188.

KITTUR.
Trial by Ordeal, 1188.

bankers of Degámve village which has been granted for ever to Bráhmans.'[1] The parties agreed to this, and, on Sunday the dark seventh of *Áshádh* or June-July, in the same year (1188), in front of the temple of Mallikárjun of Degámve, Shivshakti underwent the red-hot ploughshare ordeal, and made oath that the piece of land, Álakolanakeyi, belonged from of old to the god Kalleshvar of Attibávi; while Kalyánshakti taking the sacred symbols on his head, declared that it was the property of the original place god. Next day, Monday, the eighth of the same dark fortnight, the Degámve bankers, meeting in the assembly hall and examining Shivshakti's hand decided that he had won his cause, that Kalyánshakti had lost it, and that the plot of ground called A'lakolanakeyi belonged to the god Kalleshvar of Attibávi, and they gave a certificate of success to Shivshakti. The inscription then goes on to state that one Sántana Náyaka built the temple of Kalleshvar of Attibávi and bought and granted the wet crop land called Álakolana and also some untilled land for incense, offerings, and lights for the god and for repairs. Some other cash gifts are also mentioned by gardeners reapers and cultivators. Among other gifts were a *visa*[2] for every animal load and an *aravisa* for every man load.[3]

Fort.

The chief interest of Kittur is its fort. In 1825 Lieutenant Lawe, the superintending engineer of forts, described Kittur as a weak and ruined fort consisting of a lower fort and a citadel. The lower fort, which was uneven rocky and full of large pits, occupied one-sixth of the space of Belgaum fort. Nearly half of this space was taken up with the remains of the wet ditch and rampart of an older fortification. The upper fort or citadel, with a deep quarry in its centre had one-tenth the area of Belgaum fort, and was too small to accommodate even a single building. The fortifications consisted of a mud rampart seven feet thick, faced with loose stone for about one-third of its height. The scarp had in many places fallen and the counterscarp was very low. The parapet which was not more than three feet high was entirely built of mud. With reference to a proposal to abandon Belgaum and fix the military cantonment at Kittur Lieutenant Lawe found entirely in favour of Belgaum. Kittur fort was ruined, low, and exposed, its yearly repairs would amount to about £500 (Rs. 5000), and in the first instance about £80,000 (Rs.8,00,000) would be wanted to make the fort secure. Nor had Kittur any good buildings, not even the needful space for barracks for 700 men.[4] Three years later (1828) Colonel Welsh, who was in charge of the Karnátak Field Force, formed a very different opinion of Kittur. To his mind the ruined works of Kittur fort were extraordinarily strong. The upper battery was a strong citadel nowhere commanded though conspicuous for many miles in every

[1] Degámve village is three miles south-west of Kittur. It has an old and elaborately carved temple. See above p. 554.

[2] A *visa* is either five *sers* or one-sixteenth of something which is not specified. Mr. J. F. Fleet, C. S., C.I.E.

[3] Jour. B. B. R. A. Soc. IX. 307-309.

[4] Only two buildings in the lower fort were capable of being turned into an arsenal and a hospital for about seven companies of native troops. The other houses and huts were poor and dirty.

Chapter XIV. Places. KITTUR. *Fort.*

direction and surrounded by highly cultivated country, ill adapted for carrying on approaches. Though the outer wall was destroyed, he engaged with one regiment to defend the citadel against any enemy without mortars and shells.[1] In 1862 Kittur fort is noticed as ruined and of no natural strength though water and supplies were easily available.

A line of stones marks (1882) the site of the gateway where Mr. Thackeray fell in the 1824 insurrection.[2] Near it is a ditch about sixteen feet deep, partly filled with grass and bushes. About eighty yards beyond is a second ditch and remains of the fort walls and part of a solidly built stone gateway. To the east is a modern temple and about 150 yards further east are the ruins of the fort palace. The fort stretches some way beyond the palace ruins and at this point is defended by a ditch.[3] About a hundred yards beyond the fort is the site of the palace of the *desái's* wives. Beyond this to the south is a curious building, a temple built by an oilman during the time of the last Kittur *desái.* About twenty feet from the ground a gallery passes along the centre of the building and throws forward two wings towards the road. The gallery has a number of figures, the Kittur *desái* in the middle, his two wives on his left, and his minister on his right. At the end of each group is the statue of an English officer in knee breeches and a round hat.[4]

History.

The earliest known mention of Kittur is by its present name in an inscription of about the close of the twelfth century. It had a well, apparently a large step-well or cistern called Attibávi and a temple of Kalleshvar enjoying a grant of land. The land grant was disputed and by order of the minister of Jaykeshi III. (1175-1188), the ruling Goa Kádamba chief, the parties were referrd to a fire ordeal before the merchants of Degámve village, three miles west of Kittur, and, as the red-hot ploughshare did not burn the hand of the man who stood for Kalleshvar, the case was decided in that god's favour.[5] In 1534 Kittur formed the estate of Yusuf Khán a Turkish nobleman and an adherent of the great Asad Khán of Belgaum. In the same year Yusuf blinded and deposed Mallu Adil Sháh the king of Bijápur. About the close of the seventeenth century the most important of the Karnátak *desáis* was Medi Mallápa the Lingáyat *desái* of Kittur who held Sampgaon and Bidi. The founders of this family were two brothers of the name of Hire or the elder Mulla, and Chik or the younger Mulla, who, towards the close of the sixteenth century, came into the district with the Bijápur army as moneylenders, and settled at Sampgaon. By distinguished services in the field the elder Mulla received the title of Shamsher Jang Bahádur and obtained a grant of the *sardeshmukhi* of the Hubli district. The fifth *desái* established himself at Kittur which was formerly sometimes called Gijaganahalli or Weaver-bird

---

[1] Welsh's Military Reminiscences, II. 299. [2] See below p. 580.

[3] Although so completely ruined the place bears all the traces of great strength; and its utter demolition is chiefly due to the townspeople moving away its stones and building materials for new houses. Mr. E. B. Eastwick in Murray's Bombay Handbook, 238. [4] Murray's Bombay Handbook, 238. [5] See above p. 577.

Chapter XIV.
Places.
Kittur.
History.

Town, and also became master of Sampgaon and Bidi. His son Mudi Mallapa was in power when Ráuf Khán Nawáb of Sávanur made his settlement with the *desáis*. In 1746 the Nawáb of Savanur had to cede Kittur along with some other districts to the Maráthás.[1] In 1778 Haidar Ali who had conquered the whole country south of the Malprabha in Belgaum and south of the Krishna in Bijápur agreed to receive from the Kittur *desái* his usual tribute or *peshkash*, on the condition of prompt payment, as a free gift, of a farther sum equal to his former payment.[2] In this year the Kittur *desái* occupied Gokák in addition to Parasgad, Sampgaon, and Bidi which he had held since 1756. In 1779 Parshurám Bháu obtained Gokák and took the Kittur *desái* prisoner.[3] In 1785 Tipu seized Kittur and Nargund and Rámdurg in Dhárwár and placed a strong Maisur detachment in Kittur. The Maráthás formed an offensive alliance with the Nizám against Tipu and while the main army of the confederates advanced towards Bádámi in Bijápur and then on Dhárwár, Tukoji Holkar and Ganesh Pant Behere were detached with 25,000 horse to attack a body of Tipu's troops under Burhán-ud-din near Kittur and to drive his garrisons from that district. Holkar's detachment succeeded in driving out Tipu's troops from every part of Kittur except the fort which was invested for more than a month, but with no result.[4] Though the balance of advantage in the war leaned to Tipu, in April 1787 fears of an English invasion led him to give Kittur and other places to the Maráthás. In the three years ending 1787, during which Kittur was under Tipu, his lieutenant Badr-ul-Zamán Khán took the management of the *desái's* estate or *jághir* lands into his own hands, stripped him of all power, and set apart a sum for his support.[5] Under the treaty of Seringapatam, concluded in February 1792, the Marátha frontier was extended to the Tungbhadra and Parasgad, and the Kittur *desái's* lands, which had been subject to Tipu, again became part of the Marátha country. These districts were assigned to Parshurám Bháu, who, in the late war had been forced to raise troops largely in excess of the number for which the Patvardhan's military grant or *sarinjám* had been assigned. He placed a mámlatdár in Kittur and made it subordinate to Dhárwár, the *desái* receiving an allowance for his support. In the latter part of June 1800 Dhundia Vágh, the great Marátha freebooter, came into the Kittur country. On 30th June he surprised the Marátha general Dhondo Pant Gokhale near Kittur, attacked his rear guard, and put his whole force to flight. Gokhale was killed, and, in fulfilment of a vow made when he was defeated in 1791, Dhundia dyed his moustaches in Gokhale's heart's blood. Dhundia remained in the Kittur country until General Wellesley's arrival in Dhárwár drove him in that direction. On the 30th of July 1800 a part of Dhundia's army was destroyed at Manoli twenty-five miles north-east of Kittur, and he retired precipitate in the direction of Kittur, whence he effected his escape through the neighbouring forests and by passing round along the

---

[1] Bom. Gov. Sel. XII. 208. [2] Wilks' South of India, II. 187.
[3] Stokes' Belgaum, 56. [4] Grant Duff's Maráthás, 468-69. [5] Stokes' Belgaum, 58.

Chapter XIV. Places. Kittur. History.

source of the Malprabha. General Wellesley in his pursuit came to Kittur on the 5th of August and was kept for six days making boats for crossing the Malprabha.[1] In 1802 Mallasarjya the *desái* of Kittur (1782-1816) held the country round Kittur, yielding a yearly revenue of £40,000 (Rs. 4,00,000) and kept a force of 1000 horse and 4000 foot, and was bound to pay the Peshwa a yearly tribute of £6000 to £7000 (Rs. 60,000-70,000). In the same year as General Wellesley was going from Seringapatam to Poona to reinstate Bájiráv Peshwa, several of the Belgaum estateholders aided the British force and among them the *desái* of Kittur contributed 100 horse and 100 foot to act with the British. The Kittur *desái* also consented to give a small fort at Sángoli to serve as a post to keep open communications and guard the hospital and boats stationed there. The Kittur contingent, though furnished in a loyal spirit, was of little service. They had to receive constant advances to keep them from starving.[2] In reward for his loyalty in joining the army which was going to reinstate the Peshwa, the Kittur *desái* was continued in the enjoyment of his estates. In 1809 the Kittur *desái*, who had been taken to Poona after the Peshwa's pilgrimage to Belári in 1805, entered into an agreement by which he promised to pay the Peshwa a yearly tribute of £17,500 (Rs. 1,75,000). In return for this agreement he received grants for his estates and the title of Pratápráo. In honour of his title the *desái* built a fort near Nandgad town and called it Pratápgad.[3]

In 1817 and 1818, when affairs came to a crisis between the English and Bájiráv Peshwa the Kittur *desái* was one of the few Belgaum estateholders who actively aided the English. During the siege of Belgaum (21st March-12th April, 1818) he gave great help by furnishing materials.[4] In September 1824, on the death of the Kittur *desái*, an attempt was made to set up an adopted son. Mr. Thackeray the principal Collector at Dhárwár reported the circumstances to Government and on the receipt of his report Government refused to recognize the adoption. Mr. Thackeray was desired to take charge of the state and to make an inquiry into the circumstances of the adoption. While Government were considering Mr. Thackeray's reports news arrived of a rising at Kittur on the 23rd of October which had resulted in the death of Mr. Thackeray and the imprisonment of his two assistants Mr. Stevenson and Mr., now Sir Walter, Elliot. Troops were collected and a proclamation was issued offering a free pardon to those who would surrender before a fixed date. On the 30th of November Kittur fort was invested and the insurgents were called on to surrender. They demanded more favourable terms before releasing the prisoners but were referred to the proclamation. On the morning of the 2nd of December the prisoners were released, but, as the fort was not surrendered, it was attacked on the third and an advanced fortified post was carried. On this post a battery was raised which next day effected a practical breach and the garrison surrendered at discretion. The

---

[1] Wellington's Supplementary Despatches, II. 158. Eleven of General Wellesley's Despatches (524-535) are dated Kittur 7th-11th August 1800. Ditto, 91-105.
[2] Bom. Gov. Sel. VIII. 512.
[3] Stokes' Belgaum, 71.
[4] Bombay Courier, 16th May 1818.

casualties were three killed and twenty-five wounded. Among the killed was Mr. Munro, the sub-collector of Sholápur and nephew of Sir Thomas Munro.[1] The Kittur state thus lapsed to Government.

In 1828 Colonel Welsh, then commanding the Doab Field Force, describes Kittur as formerly a flourishing town and beautiful fort in a most fertile spot. It was a heap of ruins but still worth seeing as the ruins showed that it once was a place of great strength. Two-thirds of the palace was ruined but what remained served to show its former splendour. The chief porch was 100 feet long by thirty feet wide supported on beautiful teak pillars. The roof was very fine of massive carved teak and the other parts of the building above and below had long narrow rooms all neatly finished. Beautiful granite slabs were lying about, one line of them ten feet by seven all perfectly smooth.[2]

In 1829 another widespread rising took place at Kittur. This rising was headed by one Ráyappa a village watchman of Sángoli village twelve miles north of Kittur, a retainer of the Kittur *desái* who had received a pardon for his share in the 1824 outbreak. Rendered desperate by the confiscation of his service land and exasperated by a quarrel with the clerk of his village, Ráyappa gathered many disaffected people round him, and, taking the boy who was alleged to have been adopted by the late *desái*, attempted to raise a revolt with the object of restoring the independence of Kittur. Ráyappa began by burning the mámlatdár's office at Bidi, and, after troubling the Khánápur and Sampgaon sub-divisions for four months, was eventually betrayed and hanged at Nandgad. His betrayers were rewarded with lands.[3]

KONGNOLI.

Kongnoli, on the Belgaum-Kolhápur road about twenty-two miles north-west of Chikodi, is a trading town of some importance with in 1872 a population of 5143 and in 1881 of 5061. The town lies in the extreme north-west corner of the district on the south bank of the Dudhganga a feeder of the Krishna. Kongnoli has a travellers' bungalow, a rest-house, a post office, and two Government schools, one anglo-vernacular and the other for girls. The town has a large trade sending rice to Belgaum and various places in Kolhápur and importing cloth, date, salt, spices, and sugar through the Ratnágiri ports of Rájápur and Vengurla. A weekly market is held on Thursdays when cotton, yarn, grain, molasses, and tobacco and from 2000 to 3000 cattle form the chief articles of trade. The weaving of women's robes, waistcloths, and inferior blankets are the only industries. Before the 1876-77 famine paper was made at Kongnoli, but during the famine many of the paper-makers left and the industry has died.

---

[1] Details are given above pp. 401-404; Bombay Gazette, 3rd November, 8th December, 15th December and 22nd December 1824. The booty captured was estimated to amount to £160,000 (Rs. 16,00,000) in cash, £40,000 (Rs. 4,00,000) in jewels, besides many horses, one thousand camels, and several elephants. Among the ordnance and military stores captured were thirty-six brass and iron guns, fifty-six matchlocks, twenty-five swords, and a great quantity of powder and stone and iron shot.

[2] Military Reminiscences, II. 297-299. Colonel Welsh gives a sketch of Kittur fort.

[3] Details are given above pp. 404-405.

Chapter XIV. Places.

In 1827 Colonel Welsh described Kongnoli fort as extensive but poor with a good faussebraye or mound and a good ditch.[1] In 1862 the fort was described as ruinous with no well but ample supplies.[2]

KOKATNUR.

Kokatnur is a small village twelve miles south-east of Athni, with in 1872 a population of 2744 and in 1881 a population of 2250. The village has a Government school, and workers in iron who make nutcrackers bridles and bits. About a mile east of the village, on the Pápnáshini river, is a temple of Yellamma in honour of whom a yearly fair is held in December when about 4000 people come. In 1565 the Kokatnur *pargana* was given in grant or *jághir* to the ancestor of the present *desái* of Sirsangi for his services under Ibráhim Adilsháh in the campaign which led to the battle of Tálikot and the destruction of Vijaynagar in 1564.[3]

KONNUR.

Konnur, the Kondanuru of inscriptions, is a large village on t Ghatprabha, about five miles north-west of Gokák, with in 1872 a population of 4008 and in 1881 of 3437. Near the Gokák falls on the Ghatprabha, within the limits of Konnur village, are several ruined temples of about the eleventh century.[4]

Cell-Tombs.

To[5] the south of the village, close at the foot of the sandstone hills, are a number of the slab-walled and slab-roofed cell-tombs or *kistvaens* which have been found near Haidarabad in the Deccan and in other parts of Southern India,[6] and which have a special interest from their likeness to the old stone chambers in England of which the best known are Wayland Smith's cave and Kit's Coty House.[7] Many of these cell-tombs, for there seems no doubt that they are tombs, are scattered over the plain. The most interesting feature is a group of fifty more or less perfect rooms. All the stone slabs used as walls and roofs are of the neighbouring quartzite sandstone. They show no signs of tooling, but seem to have been roughly broken into shape. The cell or *kistvaen* is usually formed of six slabs of flat unhewn stone. Two upright slabs, four to six feet long and four to six feet high, are set north and south parallel to each other and four or five feet apart. Across the north end almost always between, not overlapping the ends of the east and west slabs, is set a third upright slab of the same height as the side slabs. The front or south face of the room instead of a single slab has two smaller slabs placed so as to leave an opening between them generally about two feet wide. On these five upright side or wall slabs is laid as a roof a large level eight inch thick slab which almost overlaps the walls and completes the cell. In almost every case from the opening in the south face a small passage is carried at

---

[1] Military Reminiscences, II. 282. [2] Government List of Civil Forts, 1862.
[3] Stokes' Belgaum, 36. [4] See above Gokák p. 561.
[5] Contributed by Mr. R. B. Joyner, C. E.
[6] Compare Fergusson's Rude Stone Monuments, 467-476; Forbes Leslie's Ancient Races of Scotland, 187; Transactions Bombay Literary Society, III. 342-348.
[7] Wayland Smith's Cave is in Berkshire; Kit's Coty House is in Kent. Fergusson's Rude Stone Monuments, 116, 122. Similar *kistvaens* or cell-tombs have been found in Southern India. They were formerly called dolmens. But as *dolmen* means table-stone it is more correctly applied to the level stones poised on uprights which apparently are not ruined cell-tombs but are of uncertain use either altars for sacrifice or judgment seats.

I.

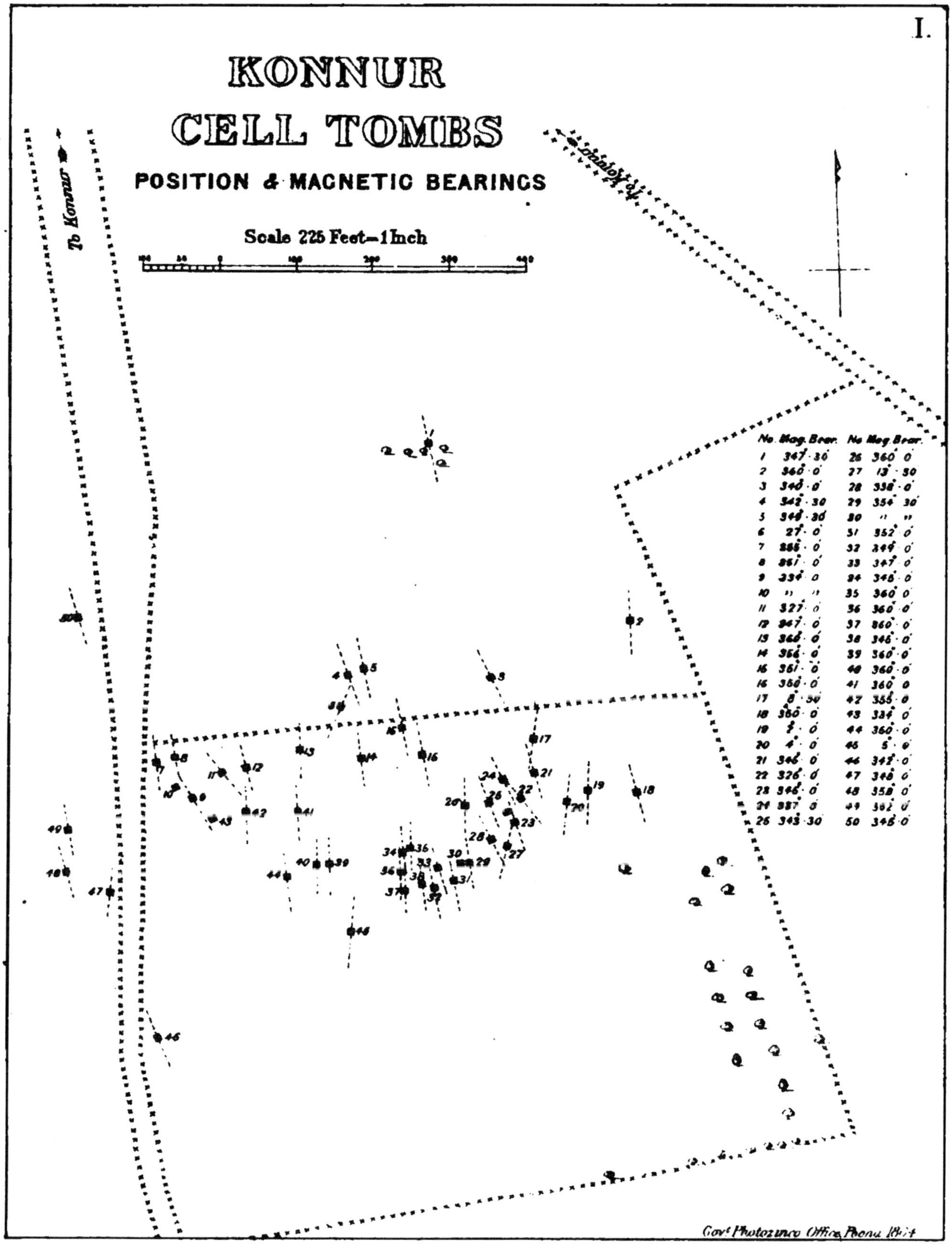

No.	Mag. Bear.	No.	Mag. Bear.
1	347°·30′	26	360° 0′
2	360°·0′	27	13°·30
3	340°·0′	28	338°·0′
4	342°·30	29	354° 30′
5	349°·30′	30	" "
6	27°·0′	31	352°·0′
7	355°·0′	32	349°·0′
8	351°·0′	33	347°·0′
9	334°·0	34	348°·0′
10	" "	35	360° 0′
11	327°·0′	36	360°·0′
12	347°·0′	37	360°·0′
13	360°·0′	38	346°·0′
14	356°·0′	39	360°·0′
15	361°·0′	40	360°·0′
16	360°·0′	41	360° 0
17	8°·30′	42	355°·0
18	360°·0′	43	334° 0′
19	2°·0′	44	360°·0′
20	4°·0′	45	5°·0′
21	346°·0′	46	342°·0′
22	326°·0′	47	348° 0′
23	346°·0′	48	358° 0′
24	337° 0′	49	362° 0′
25	343°·30	50	348°·0′

PLAN OF CELL-TOMB Nº I.

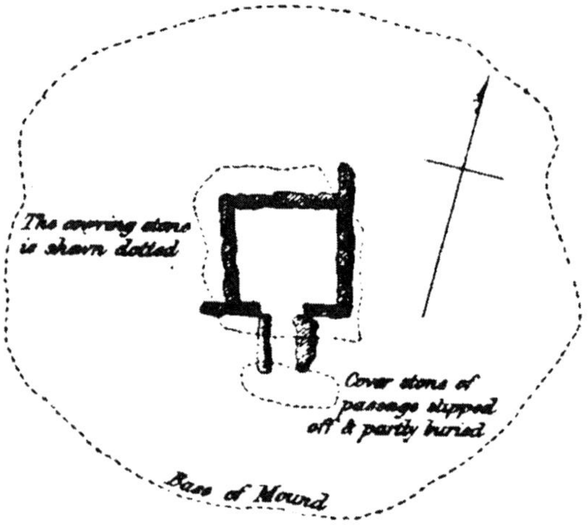

PLAN & SECTION OF CELL-TOMB Nº 46 SHEWING POSITIONS OF ARTICLES FOUND.

Scale, 1 inch — 12 feet.

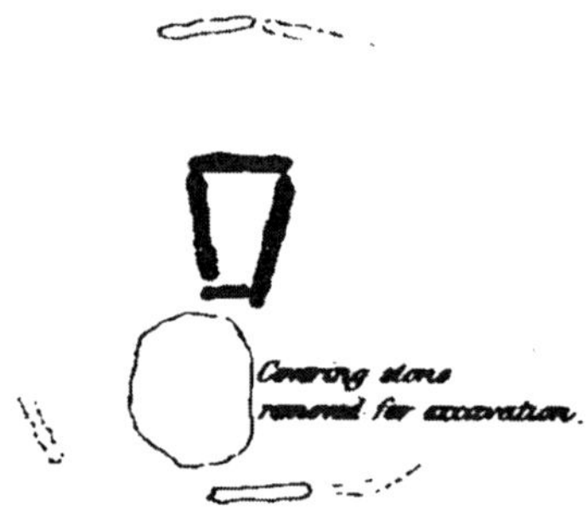

A. A. A. Positions of bits of earthenware bowls.
B. — do — part of tooth & small bits of bone.
C. — do — small bits of bone.

SKETCHES OF PIECES OF EARTHENWARE BOWLS.

Scale, ½ full size.

PLAN & SECTION OF CELL-TOMB Nº 13 SHEWING CURB & REMAINS OF MOUND.

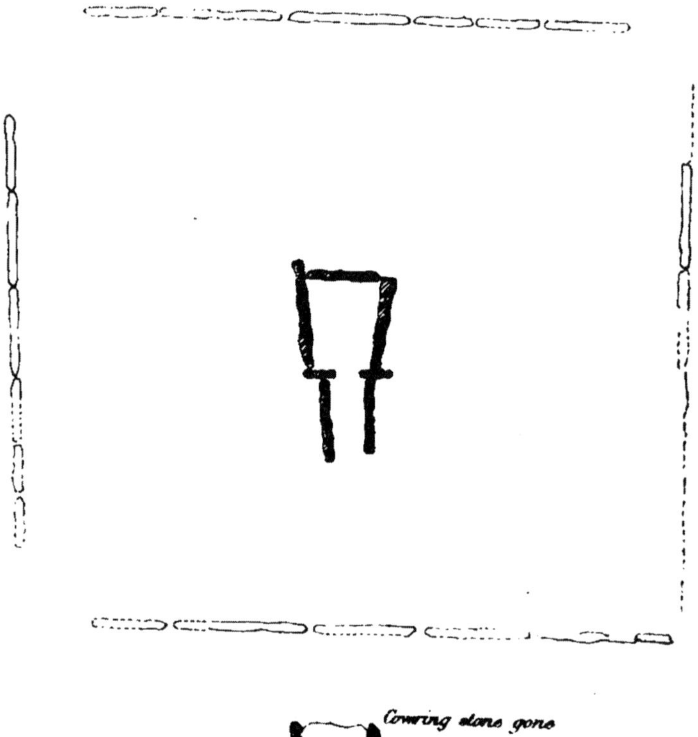

Scale, 1 inch — 12 feet.

KONNUR CELL TOMBS

Govt. Photozinco Office, Poona, 1884.

Chapter XIV.

Places.

KONNUR.

Cell-Tombs.

right angles to the chamber by laying down two stone slabs three to five feet long, about two feet high, and one foot to eighteen inches apart, and on these two slabs laying a third to form a roofed passage. In the chief group of fifty only seven have their large covering stones and of the seven only five have passages more or less complete. Over each cell-tomb a cairn of small stones and earth seems originally to have been piled probably forming a semispherical or domed mound about eight feet high. In almost every case remains of these mounds or covers are seen. Many of the chambers are ruined and of some only a few stones are left, the large slabs having probably been taken for building. Some of the better preserved chambers were surrounded by a square rough-hewn stone kerb which in some instances is in fair order. In one measured instance the kerbed space, formed by stones four to five feet long by six inches thick, measured thirty-four feet by thirty-three. This kerb was probably a plinth on which the covering mound rested which in some cases seems to have been carefully built of rough stone boulders set in mud.[1] An examination of the magnetic bearing of the axes of these chambers showed that of forty-eight chambers in the main group the axes of ten pointed due north, of thirty-two pointed west of north, in one case as much as 34° west, but most were much nearer north than west. The remaining six pointed east of north one as much as 27° east and the rest only a few degrees east. This variation in direction is probably due either to carelessness or to the fact that the north was taken from the east as fixed by the sun rising on days when the sun rose either north or south of east.

The people call them Pándavs' houses and say the Pándavs built them as sun shades.[2] The complete or almost complete weathering away of the mounds of earth and stones which originally covered these burial-rooms shows that they must be of great age. As *konne* is the Kánarese for a room and *uru* is a village, it seems probable that the village takes its name from its cell-tombs or burial rooms and that Konnur means the Room-village.[3] To find what were the inner arrangements of these cell-tombs number forty-six of the main group was opened. It had clearly never been touched. There were marked remains of the encasing or covering mound, the top stone or roof was unmoved, and the inside of the cell was filled or nearly filled. In some respects this cell was different from most

---

[1] It may be suggested that the object of this stone fence, of the circle of stones round other old burial heaps (Compare Bombay Gazetteer, XIV. 414-416), and of the Buddhist rail was to ward evil influences from the dead. The early guardian form of the idea seems to live in the circle of stones each the home of a *shipái* or watchman which surround the central stone in which lives Vetál the early or primitive Deccan and Konkan Shiv. (Compare Bombay Gazetteer, Poona Statistical Account).

[2] With the name Pándav houses may be compared the Malabár name Pándu kulis for the burial chambers described by Mr. Babington. Transactions Bombay Literary Society, III. 342-348.

[3] The form Kondanuru which (Journal Bom. Br. Roy. As. Soc. X. 180, 294) appears as the name of the village in twelfth century inscriptions, may perhaps mean room or cave village.

Chapter XIV. Places. KONNUR. *Cell-Tombs.*

of the other cells. It was by itself, was somewhat smaller and differently shaped from the others, and, unlike any of the others, had no southern passage. The roof or top-stone was removed by bars and wedges. When it was taken off the inside was found to be packed with small boulders and hard brown earth. As the stones at the top were much too large to have been put in through any crevice after the roof was on, the tomb had clearly never been opened. All the earth and stones taken out of the cell were carefully sifted. About eighteen inches from the roof were found the greater part of a large human double tooth with some small bits of bone. The cell was three feet eight inches to three feet ten inches deep and a few inches from the floor were some more small pieces of bone. At three feet three inches, three feet eight inches, and three feet ten inches from the roof were pieces of common baked earthenware. The material was the same as the present village pottery. The shape of the bowls was peculiar apparently a flat hemisphere. A piece of what seemed to be burnt slag from a potter's kiln was also found. The position of the tooth seemed to show that the body was buried sitting and facing the south. After being set there the body seems to have been packed with earth and stones a pressure which probably broke the clay jars. Nothing in this tomb threw any light on the use of the southern passages in the other tombs.[1]

KUDCHI.

Kudchi, about twenty miles south-west of Athni and three miles south-west of Ainápur, is a large village with in 1872 a population of 2932 and in 1881 of 5343. Kudchi has a post office and two schools one a Government Kánarese school and the other a private Hindustáni school. There is a local manufacture of carpets. When the West Deccan Railway is finished (1889) Kudchi will have a station 179 miles south-east of Poona and sixty-three miles north-east of Belgaum. On an island in the Krishna about a mile east of the town, in a *bábhul* and tamarind grove, is a black stone tomb of Shaikh Muhammad Sirájjenadi Pirdadi a Musalmán saint and missionary. Among the numerous converts he made was a princess of Balkh named Masapli. She accompanied her preceptor to India and died here after a life of charity and benevolence. The saint died at Kulburga and was buried there, but in his honour a tomb was built near the tomb of the princess. Yearly fairs are held at the tombs. Ferishta notices Kunchi in Ráybág, probably Kudchi ten miles north-east of Ráybág, as being the first *jághir* town of Hassan Gango (1347-1358) the founder[2] of the Bahmani dynasty granted to him by Muhammed Tughlik (1325-1351). In 1791 Captain Moor notices Kudchi on the Krishna as a Musalmán town of some note, but Bráhman intrigues fomented by Parashurám Bháu had so distressed it that most of the Musalmáns had left.[3]

---

[1] Taken with the circular hole in one of the side slabs in the cell-tombs described by Captain Meadows Taylor (Journal London Ethnological Society, New Series, I. 164) near Haidarabad and with other early burial practices, it seems probable that the southern passage was for the soul to go out and in by.

[2] Briggs' Ferishta, II. 285.

[3] Moor's Narrative, 301.

Kumbha'rdi Hill lies seventeen miles south-east of Khánápur. A sloping wooded ascent leads to a flat uncultivated top with a monastery of the Kánphata saint Handi Bhadangnáth. Near the monastery are three cattle sheds occupied throughout the year by a few Kánphata Gosávis.

KUNKUMBI.

Kunkumbi village, about nineteen miles north-west of Khánápur, with in 1881 a population of 635, has temples of Kunkumbeshvar and Máhulidevi. Máhulidevi's shrine (97' × 54') though modern is regarded as holy as it stands at the source of the Malprabha. The local belief is that every twelve years, when Jupiter enters Sagittarius, the Ganges comes to visit the Malprabha at its source and remains there for a year. At this time devotees from various parts of the district and from Goa come and purify themselves by bathing in the river.

MAHIPÁLGAD FORT.

Mahipa'lgad Fort stands on the highest point of a range of hills about ten miles west of Belgaum. The fort hill is fairly wooded and the fortifications are built in a corner of a considerable plateau. An easy ascent of about 300 feet leads to the fort which is about 1400 feet long from east to west and 600 feet broad from north to south. The fort has one gateway and walls of brick and rubble on three sides.[1] Of twenty acres the whole area of the fort, ten are occupied with houses and enclosures and the rest are overgrown with grass. There is a large well in the fort. In 1827 a committee of inspection described Mahipálgad as an extensive hill fort situated about the middle of a range of hills. It was built of stones with round towers on the angles and sides. The wall was low and in many places, especially on the west face, was open to escalade. The top was covered with brushwood. The fort belonged to Chintámanráv the Sángli chief. At his death in 1680 Shiváji is said to have held Mahipálgad along with nine other Belgaum forts.[2]

MALLAYAN.

Mallayan, or Adi Hill, about 630 feet above the plain, lies near Adi village about twelve miles north-west of Chikodi. It is a flat hill with a flat barren top. The hill sides are partly tilled with millet by Jain and Marátha husbandmen. The water-supply is from a spring and a small pond on the hill.

MALPRABHA.

Malprabha. See SOGAL.

MANGSULI.

Mangsuli, a village belonging to the Athni *desáis,* with in 1872 a population of 3072 and in 1881 of 3160, lies sixteen miles west of Athni. The village has a temple of Mallaya or Mártand in honour of whom a yearly fair is held in *Chaitra* or April when 7000 to 8000 people come and large numbers of cattle and ponies are sold. The village has a Government Kánarese school.

MANOLI.

Manoli, about six miles north of Saundatti, is a large town on the Malprabha, with in 1872 a population of 6232 and in 1881 of

---

[1] On one side the wall only lines the crest of a ravine.

[2] Shiváji's Bakhar. The nine other Belgaum forts were Párgad and Kálánandigad in Belgaum, Bhimgad in Khánápur, Pavitragad and Vallabhgad in Chikodi, and Huli Kátharigad Murgod and Parasgad in Parasgad.

Chapter XIV.
Places.
MANOLI.
Fort.

4621. Manoli has an important dyeing industry. The only objects of interest are a ruined fort and old temples with inscriptions. The fort is a sandstone work standing on a peninsula round which the river winds. The walls are still fairly preserved. In 1820 Manoli fort was described by Mr. Grant a sub-engineer as a small work with stone-faced ramparts and surrounded by a ditch. Between the rampart and the ditch was a space about nine feet at the end of which was a weak stone wall forming an imperfect covering mound or faussebraye which as seen from the opposite side added greatly to the apparent depth of the ditch. The wall was very substantial on the south or river face where it had a footpath and parapet. The works were further secured on this side by a strong and high abutment wall and parapet in advance of the counterscarp and washed by the river. The ditch on this face was very deep and generally held water. Of late (1820) the west face had been greatly strengthened by a hidden way and glacis carefully built, and, at the time Mr. Grant wrote, great exertions were being made to continue the same round the north and west works. The entrance to the fort was on the west through two ill guarded gateways. The buildings in the town or *petta* were irregularly placed close to the north and west works. The soil in the neighbourhood was poor but afforded much wood for fuel. The fort had a large boat capable of carrying an eighteen-pounder. In 1842 the fort was described by an inspection committee as about 500 feet square with the Malprabha flowing close on the south-east. The defences of the fort consisted of four large strong round angular bastions and one in the middle of the north face all capable of holding ordnance. The bastions were unconnected by curtains. The height of the works, which were well built of stone and in good order, was generally about thirty-four feet. The ramparts were narrow and only fit for musketry while the parapets were low and not in good order. At the foot of and all round the works was a narrow space or berm about fifteen feet broad at the edge of which was a well-built raised mound or faussebraye of stone work in good order about eighteen feet above the bottom of the ditch and five or six feet broad. The ditch was dry and from twenty to twenty-six feet broad with a descent at the counterscarp of fourteen to fifteen feet. The sloping mass of earth or glacis was imperfect. On the west north and east the ditch and the narrow space or berm were filled with impenetrable prickly pear. The entrance was on the west front with two gates. The first gate leading out of the fort was very strong; the second which was close and at right angles to the first was of no strength. The gates were covered by the same works as the other parts of the fort as they took a curve to shelter the entrance. There was another entrance in the south front by a small passage leading through the rampart into the ditch and so by a doorway out to the river made through the counterscarp and the sloping mass of earth or glacis. Both the passages were very small and probably made for bringing water from the river into the fort. Both the passages could be easily filled. At the south-east angle and inside of the fort within a few feet of the ramparts was a small citadel or *ghadi* enclosing a space about 100 feet square and opened to the east. It had four high stone

Chapter XIV.

Places.

MANOLI.

bastions all in good order. The gates were so placed as not to be seen on entering the fort. The fort contained the ruins of a large number of houses and was uninhabited. The water-supply was not plentiful and the fort afforded no protection against shells. The committee were of opinion that from the good order of the works the fort was strong and if well-garrisoned was capable of making a good defence. Heavy ordnance would, they thought, be necessary for its capture.

Temples.

Inside the fort are the remains of some temples, the chief of which are to Hanumán and Udachava. The roof of the vestibule of Hanumán's temple is carved in compartments or panels with a net-work of snakes. At either end are curiously carved stones about a foot square on which are represented triple-bodied dolphins. The Udachava temple has an inscription dated 1252 of the seventh Devgiri Yádav king Kanhara or Krishna (1247-1260). To the west of the town in an enclosure surrounded by a high wall, are the temples of Panchling Dev. They consist of eight temples two very small and two larger than the rest. One of these two is a triple temple, Jain in style. Except the spire it is well preserved. The roofs have now become flat and a clumsy lion is placed over the front or north face. On the lintel of the doorway of one of the others is Lakshmi with her elephants. The other large temple facing the rest is regarded as the chief of the group. It has a dark inner hall or *mandap* and an open outer hall with several carved stones and a large inscription on a stone tablet. The inscription is dated 1223 and belongs to the fifth Devgiri Yádav king Singhan II. (1209-1247). These Panchling temples are built of coarse-grained stone and are in no way remarkable for carving. From the snake head on the bracket and the general style, apart from the inscriptions, the temples appear to belong to the end of the twelfth century or perhaps a little earlier.

Dyeing.

Dyeing is practised by nine or ten families of the Bangar caste. They dye cotton and yarn red green yellow and dark blue. The white yarn is first dipped in water mixed with oil and the ashes of the prickly pear. Six dippings are necessary to perfect the colour, but more than two or three dippings are seldom given. The yarn thus dipped is made into bundles called *has*. The bundles are soaked for a night in a kettle containing water which has been mixed with the powder of *suranja* the roots of a plant growing in Sholápur, in the proportion of a *sher* of *suranja* to each *has*. Next morning the *has* of yarn is dipped in the river which gives to the water a piquant flavour which is much liked by drinkers. The yarn is then laid in the sun spread on smooth specially prepared stones and is dried five to ten days. This part of the process is very pleasing to the people of Manoli. The air is filled with a soft soothing perfume.[1]

History.

The earliest mention of Manoli is as Munipur or Munivalli in a stone inscription of the seventh Devgiri Yádav king Krishna.[2]

---

[1] According to some accounts this sweet dye was formerly used in Saundatti and gave the town its name *Sugandhvarti* or the fragrant.

[2] Bombay Archæological Survey, Second Report, 233.

Chapter XIV. Places. MANOLI. *History.*

In 1786 Parshurám Bháu took Manoli fort from the Torgal chief and added it to his possessions.[1] In his pursuit of Dhundia General Wellesley, on the 30th of June 1800, hearing Dhundhia was opposite Manoli with his baggage, in the hope of surprising him, pressed on twenty-six miles to the Malprabha opposite Manoli. At three on the same afternoon General Wellesley directed a cavalry onset on the enemy's camp. Lieutenant-Colonel Torin attacked their left with the 1st and 4th Regiments, and Colonel Stevenson and Colonel Peter their front and right with the 25th Dragoons and the 2nd Regiment of cavalry. Dhundhia's camp was strong with its rear to the Malprabha, covered by the fort of Manoli on the other side of it, and a deep stream along its front and left. The 2nd Regiment of cavalry was the only corps which forced its way into the camp, but every person in the camp was either killed or driven into the river. All the baggage, two elephants, and many camels horses and bullocks were taken. Numbers were drowned or shot in trying to cross the river, and many women and children were taken prisoners. Major Blaquiers with four troops of the 25th Dragoons pursued to the east a party which appeared to have been outside of the camp, and drove them into the river. Six of Dhundhia's guns had been passed over the swollen stream before the attack. Half an hour after the camp was carried a party of the 25th Dragoons attempted to swim the river and seize a boat which was lying under the fort of Manoli. The force of the flood carried them below the spot where the boat lay. But two officers, Lieutenant Fitchet and Jackson, succeeded in stemming the current, brought back the boat, and, with its aid the guns were soon taken, and to prevent them falling into the enemy's hands were destroyed. About 5000 men were driven into the Malprabha and drowned. Among the rest one of the leaders, Bubber Jang, dressed in armour, rode his horse into the river and was drowned.[2]

MANOLI.

Manoli, better known as Nagar Manoli to distinguish it from the old town of Manoli in Parasgad, is a large village twelve miles south of Chikodi with in 1881 a population of 2546. In 1770 the fourth Peshwa Mádhavráv (1761-1772) appointed a mámlatdár of Hukeri who held the fort of Manoli in pledge for money advanced to Kolhápur.[3] Late in the same year the Manoli and Chikodi districts were given by the Peshwa to the Patvardhans and this was the origin of the long and bitter enmity between Kolhápur and the Patvardhans marked by a series of attacks and reprisals which continued as late as the early years of the nineteenth century.[4] In 1796 the Kolhápur chief took possession of Manoli and Chikodi after a siege of one month. In his pursuit of Dhundia while General Wellesley was fighting with Dhundia's troops at the Saundatti Manoli, the Kolhápur garrison of Nagar Manoli helped Dhundhia by firing on the English. After the action it was abandoned by the Kolhápur garrison, and, before Appa Sáheb Patvardhan's troops could get into it, was taken by the Páligár of Talur about eight miles north-west of Manoli. Towards

---

1 See above p. 388.
2 Wellington's Supplementary Despatches, II. 81-84.
3 Stokes' Belgaum, 53.
4 Stokes' Belgaum, 53.

MANOLI.

the end of 1801 Manoli and part of Chikodi came into the sole possession of the Nipáni *desái* who held them on behalf of the Peshwa. In 1802-3, while the Nipáni *desái* was absent in Poona with General Wellesley's force, the Kolhápur chief harassed his districts and persuaded the Talur *desái* Chandrappa to attack Manoli. Chandrappa besieged Manoli for some days and wasted the Nipáni country until General Wellesley sent Major-General Campbell to guard Nipáni. Manoli was relieved, and as the Talur *desái* refused to come to terms and fled to Kolhápur, his fort at Talur was handed to the Nipáni *desái.* For his loyalty in helping to reinstate the Peshwa the Nipáni chief was granted the Manoli district and the Hukeri petty division. The Kolhápur chief resisted the Nipáni claims to Manoli and the two went to a war which lasted for six years (1809-1814). In 1812 Mr. Elphinstone concluded a treaty by which the Kolhápur chief gave up all claim to Chikodi and Manoli.[1] In the third Marátha War General Munro came to Manoli on the 22nd of April 1818 and was there joined by General Pritzler with the main body of the reserve. As the Nipáni *desái* joined the Peshwa he was deprived of the Manoli and Chikodi districts and they were made over to the Kolhápur chief in return for his hearty co-operation with the British. In 1827 Bába Sáheb the Kolhápur chief, whose turbulence was a perpetual source of annoyance, was deprived of Manoli and Chikodi on the ground that he had shown a total disregard for the friendship of the British Government and had repeatedly infringed the rights of the landholders of British villages. In the same year Captain Clunes calls Nagarmanowlee, a Kolhápur village on the Poona-Belgaum road with ninety-six houses and one shop.[2]

MUGUTKHÁN HUBLI.

Mugutkha'n Hubli is a large village on the Dhárwár road about eighteen miles south-east of Belgaum with in 1872 a population of 4234 and in 1881 of 4196. The village has a travellers' bungalow and a small tent-making industry. The village is called Mugutkhán Hubli after a Bijápur officer named Mugutkhán whose tomb is in the village.[3] Its old name Hubli appears in a Devgiri Yádav copperplate, dated 1249, where a Devgiri Yádav minister reigning at Mudgal in the Nizám's territories grants lands in Bágevádi village in the Hubbali district in the Kuhundi country.[4]

MURGOD.

Murgod about fifteen miles north-west of Saundatti is the head-quarters of a petty division with in 1872 a population of 7181 and in 1881 of 4895. The town is a flourishing cotton and grain mart, and, besides the revenue and police offices of the petty division, has a post office and a Kánarese school. The village has a temple of Mallikárjun and a yearly fair is held on the first of the bright half of *Márgshirsh* or November-December in honour of Chitambareshvar. The fair lasts six days and is attended by three to four hundred people. A little to the north of the town are some gardens with sweet water.

---

[1] Stokes' Belgaum, 71. [2] Itinerary, 33. [3] Ráo Bahádur Tirmalrao Venkatesh.
[4] Journal Bom. Br. Roy. As. Soc, IX, 249. For Bágevádi Kuhundi and Mudgal see above pp. 513-514.

Chapter XIV. Places. MURGOD.

In 1565, after the battle of Tálikot, Murgod with several other Parasgad villages was taken by Vitta Gauda, the ancestor of the present *desái* of Sirsingi.[1] At his death in 1680 Shiváji is said to have held the fort of Murgod.[2] In 1792 Captain Moor described Murgod as in a country whose soil was as rich as the best garden mould. A little to the north of Murgod were some gardens with a well of excellent water.[3] About 1836 Murgod was one of the four places proposed for the head-quarters of the collectorate before Belgaum was chosen on the 9th of March 1838.[4]

NÁGARHÁL HILL.

Na'garha'l Hill, about 850 feet above the plain, lies near Julpen hill about four miles north of Chikodi. It has a flat top on which millet is raised by Lingáyats and Holerus. The water-supply is from two springs.

NÁGARPACHAMI HILL.

Na'garpachami Hill, about 390 feet above the plain, lies about a quarter of a mile from Chikodi. It is a flat hill with a roundish uncultivated top. The hill is not inhabited and has no springs or passes. It is infested with jackals.

NANDGAD.

Nandgad,[5] on the Belgaum-Haliyál road about seven miles south-east of Khánápur, is a town of some importance, with in 1872 a population of 5748 and in 1881 of 7912. The town has a post office, a weekly market on Wednesdays, and three schools, two Maráthi and Kánarese for boys and one for girls. Nandgad is an important trade centre and has about thirty traders chiefly Shenvi Bráhmans with capitals varying from £500 to £3000 (Rs. 5000 - 30,000). The chief imports are betelnuts, cocoanuts and cocoanut oil, dates, oil, and salt. These articles are brought either in carts or on pack-bullocks from Native Christian traders of Goa and are sold to local traders. None of these imported articles are passed inland or sent to Dhárwár by Nandgad traders. But from the agents of Goa traders at Nandgad most of these articles are bought in exchange for wheat and other grain by the agents of Gadag Hubli and Navalgund traders in Dhárwár. The town has no direct export trade. Not far from the town is a ruined fort called Pratápgad which was built by Malla Sarya Desái of Kittur in 1809 to commemorate the grant to him of the title of Pratápráv by Peshwa Bájiráv (1796 - 1818).[6] The Desái is said to have encouraged merchants to settle here by drawing them from Khánápur. The whole manufacturing population of Khánápur was taken by persuasion and force and nine years' exemption from taxes was granted to new settlers.[7] Ráyappa the leader of the second or 1829 Kittur rising was condemned to be hanged at Nandgad, as the scene of his chief robbery. As he passed along the road to the gallows he pointed out a spot for his burial, stating that a great tree would spring from his body. He was buried in the spot he had chosen, and a magnificent banian, close to the road near Nandgad, is shown as the tree which grew from Ráyappa's grave. Under the shade of this tree a temple

---

[1] Stokes' Belgaum, 36. [2] Shiváji's Bakhar. [3] Moor's Narrative, 302.
[4] Stokes' Belgaum, 86. The other three places were Ánkalgi Gokák and Manoli.
[5] The town is generally called Peth Nandgad.
[6] Stokes' Belgaum, 71. [7] Marshall's Statistical Reports, 97.

has been built, to which people in want of children money or health come from great distances. Husbandmen, too, on their way to the Nandgad market stop to promise Ráyappa an offering if their grain sells well.[1]

NAUL TIRTH.

Naul Tirth. See SOGAL.

NESARGI.

Nesargi, on the Belgaum-Kaládgi road about seven miles north of Sampgaon, with in 1881 a population of 2102, has a travellers' bungalow and a fine old ruined temple of Basav. The town has a weekly market on Monday, and weaving and bangle-making industries. A fair is held at the Basaveshvar temple once in twelve years. The temple has an inscription dated 1219 of the Ratta chieftain Kártavirya IV. (1199-1218). The inscription records the building of three *ling* temples by Bacheyanáyak a local officer in charge of the Nesargi group of six villages. The inscription also mentions various grants of land tithes and duties made over for the maintenance of these temples at the command of Kártavirya.[2] In 1791 Captain Moor calls Nesargi the little village of Nesauri where Captain Little's detachment halted fifteen miles from Pádsháhpur.[3] In his pursuit of Dhundia Vágh in 1800 General Wellesley was joined at Nesargi by the *desái* of Nipáni with 300 horse and 100 infantry.[4]

NIPÁNI.

Nipa'ni, 16° 23′ north latitude and 74° 26′ east longitude, on the Belgaum-Kolhápur road about forty miles north of Belgaum and thirteen miles west of Chikodi, is a large municipal town with in 1872 a population of 9371 and in 1881 of 9777. Besides the municipality Nipáni has a travellers' bungalow, a rest-house, a post office, four schools, a library, and a dismantled fort. The 1872 census showed a population of 9371 of whom 8167 were Hindus 1198 Musalmáns and six Christians. Of 9777 the 1881 population 8735 were Hindus, 1039 Musalmáns, and three Christians. The town has a large trade and a crowded weekly market on Thursdays.

Trade.

It has about 100 traders Lingáyats, Jains, Shimpis, Márwár and Gujarát Vánis, and Bráhmans with capitals varying from £500 to £2500 (Rs. 5000-25,000). Of imports rice comes from Belgaum and Kolhápur; betelnuts, cardamoms, and pepper from Havig traders at Sirsi in Kánara; cattle from the neighbouring villages on the Krishna; cocoanuts and dates salt spices sugar and coppersheets from Bhátiás, Gujarát and Márwár Vánis, and Musalmáns of Vengurla and Rájápur; and cloth brass vessels catechu nutmeg almonds and cloves from Bombay and Poona traders. Of exports large quantities of molasses and some tobacco, chillies, hemp, and cotton go to Rájápur in Ratnágiri. On the market day two to three thousand cattle are offered for sale and people from the neighbouring villages come in large numbers to buy and sell. Waistcloths, women's robes, and cheap blankets are made in the town. The municipality was established in 1854 and in 1882-83 had an income of £1052 (Rs. 10,526) and an expenditure of £1726 (Rs. 17,265). The chief sources of income were octroi and taxes on houses and animals, and the chief items of expenditure were water works and

---

[1] Stokes' Belgaum, 85.
[2] Jour. Bom. Br. Roy. As. Soc. 250-259.
[3] Moor's Narrative, 301.
[4] Bom. Gov. Sel. VIII. 512.

Chapter XIV.
Places.
NIPÁNI.

conservancy. The late *desái* of Nipáni built a reservoir at Shirguppi about two miles west of Nipáni and brought the water from it into the town by pipes. This reservoir is still in working order and the municipality have supplemented it by building a pond in the middle of the town. A water-course running to the east of the town is used for washing and for watering cattle. Further to improve the water-supply of the town a new pond with an earthen embankment has been made near Shirguppi and a masonry reservoir (100′ × 100′ × 8′) near Nipáni. It is proposed to connect this pond by pipes with the *desái's* pond and to distribute water over the town by pipes. Nearly £2700 (Rs. 27,000) have been spent on the works which are not yet finished, and are unsatisfactory as the new pond has turned out leaky. The municipality owns real property valued at £11,660 (Rs. 1,16,600). The town has four Government and two private schools. Of the four Government schools three, anglo-vernacular vernacular and night, schools are for boys and one for girls. The fort, which was dismantled in 1843, was described in 1827 as an eight-cornered building well built of mud, the interior of the wall said to be of stone. Round the fort was a deep wet ditch about twenty feet broad, and a narrow space or berm at the foot of the walls about twenty-five feet broad. The narrow space or berm was enclosed by the revetment of the ditch, and was pierced by loopholes which formed a second line of defence. Since 1822 an extensive line of rampart had been building round the town embracing the fort. The work was of stone and had a considerable ditch before it. In 1827 only the south side was finished, and, looking to the cost, it was not thought possible for the *desái* ever to complete it. If it was ever completed the committee considered that it would prove a most formidable defence though so small as not to contain a garrison of more than four or five hundred men. The gate of the fort was well sheltered from surprise, and near it was a bridge over the ditch on beams of wood. On the west there was a small gate but without any means of crossing the ditch. It was probably intended to have a drawbridge here.[1] Though dismantled the fort (1882) remains strongly built of stone with a wet ditch and a handsome gateway. Close to the gateway is a palace built about 1800 by Siddojiráv Nimbálkar. The interior of the palace has nothing remarkable. The pillars in the court are of teak and neatly carved. About 300 yards south-west of the fort is the travellers' bungalow to the left of the Kolhápur road.[2]

History.

Nipáni is a town of recent growth. No copper-plates or inscribed stones have been found in Nipáni and the earliest known mention is in 1800 when its *desái* Siddojiráv Nimbálkar, commonly called Áppa Sáheb was engaged, under Sindia's directions, in a series of forays into the Miraj country and in the siege of Nerali fort between Sankeshvar and Hukeri. In the same year the Nipáni *desái's* and Sindia's troops took over, nominally on behalf of Kolhápur, the districts of Chikodi and Manoli which the Peshwa was obliged by Sindia to cede. In 1801 war with Holkar called Sindia to the north and the Nipáni

---

[1] MS. Report. [2] Murray's Handbook of Bombay (2nd Ed.), 258-259.

desái got possession of Manoli and part of Chikodi. In 1802 Siddojiráv Nimbálkar with 300 horse and 400 foot was one of the seven Karnátak chiefs whose rival claims were ruining the Belgaum district. In 1802-3 the Nipáni chief with 300 horse and 100 infantry accompanied General Wellesley in his march from Seringapatam to Poona to reinstate Bájiráv as Peshwa. While the Nipáni *desái* was absent in Poona the Kolhápur chief harassed his districts and persuaded Chandrappa the *desái* of Talur about fifty miles south-east of Nipáni to attack Manoli. Chandrappa besieged Manoli for some days and wasted the Nipáni country until General Wellesley sent Major-General Campbell to guard Nipáni. Manoli was relieved, and, as the Talur *desái* refused to come to terms and fled to Kolhápur, his fort at Talur was handed to the Nipáni *desái*.[1] In reward for his loyalty in joining the cause of the Peshwa, General Wellesley gave the Nipáni chief a certificate of merit.[2] From the Peshwa the *desái* received the title of Sarlashkar and grants of lands in military service or *fauj saranjám* valued at £54,112 (Rs. 5,41,120) a year besides the Manoli district and the petty division or *pargana* of Hukeri. The Kolhápur chief resisted the Nipáni claims to Manoli, and the two went to war. The war lasted six years (1804-1809). In 1808 the Nipáni *desái* completely defeated Kolhápur. In 1809, through the Peshwa's intercession, peace was concluded, by which, besides the disputed districts to be held on behalf of the Peshwa, the Nipáni *desái* received a Kolhápur princess in marriage.[3] In spite of his marriage with a daughter of the house, the Nipáni *desái* did not long remain at peace with Kolhápur. In 1811 he defeated the Kolhápur chief, marched on Kolhápur, and besieged it. The Honourable Mountstuart Elphinstone, who was Resident at Poona, interfered, and, on the 1st of October 1812, a treaty was concluded by which the Kolhápur chief gave up all claim to Chikodi and Manoli. In 1813 the Nipáni *desái* was summoned by Bájiráv to Poona. He went but refused to comply with certain claims made by the Peshwa or to give up territory belonging to Kolhápur. The British authorities interposed, but Bájiráv artfully contrived to persuade the *desái* to trust to his lenience and to resist his demands. By this insidious conduct the *desái* was led to forfeit one-fourth of his

---

[1] Stokes' Belgaum, 70.

[2] This certificate, which the *desái* family has preserved, runs (Murray's Handbook, 258-259): 'Siddoji Ráo Nimbálkar joined me with the body of Marátha troops under his command, in the month of March 1803 when I was on my march to Poona with the British troops to restore the Peshwa to the exercise of the powers of H. H.'s Government. This service having been effected by the arrival of H. H. at Poona Siddoji Rao Nimbalkar accompanied the British army on its march from Poona in the month of June following to oppose the confederacy then forming by the Northern Marátha chiefs against the British Government and their allies, Rao Pandit Pradhan and the Nizam. He served during the war which ensued in a manner satisfactory to me. His troops were engaged with the enemy repeatedly and always conducted themselves well, and Siddoji Rao Nimbalkar distinguished himself, and them in a late action against a formidable band of freebooters who had assembled upon the frontiers of the Peshwa's territories and cut off the supplies of the city of Poona. I have given him this paper in testimony of my approbation of his conduct and that of his troops. I request that all British officers and others to whom this paper may at any time be shown, will consider Siddoji Ráo Nimbálkar as the friend of the British Government.

(Signed) ARTHUR WELLESLEY,
Major-General.

Poona, March 6th, 1804.'

[3] Bom. Gov. Sel. CXIII. 196.

Chapter XIV. Places. NIPÁNI. *History.*

estates to the Peshwa.[1] At the close of the rainy season of 1816 a detachment of the Poona subsidiary force was sent to enforce the forfeiture. The duty was not completed till the middle of December and then proved fruitless, for no sooner had the detachment returned to Poona, than the *desái* retook his lost possessions.[2] In the third Marátha war, except the Nipáni *desái*, none of the estate-holders resisted, and even the *desái* of Nipáni, though he joined the Peshwa, never acted cordially against the British troops, and on the 7th of May, with the Peshwa's brother Chimnáji Appa, he gave himself up to Captain Davis of the Nizám's Reformed Horse.[3] As a punishment for his adherence to the Peshwa and for the slowness of his submission to the English, the Nipáni *desái* was deprived of Manoli and Chikodi, except the villages of Nipáni, Sirgat, and Belkur, which were made over to the Kolhápur chief in return for his hearty co-operation with the British. The Nipáni *desái* was greatly dissatisfied with this arrangement and was ready to join any combination against the English which he thought likely to be successful. He at first hesitated to give up the two districts and endeavoured to negotiate. General Munro, who was at Yedur on the Krishna on the 31st of May on his way back from Sholápur, marched towards Nipáni, intending to lay siege to the fort in case the *desái* delayed to give up the districts. This move and the dissatisfaction of his own people compelled the *desái* to yield as soon as the army arrived before Nipáni. His people's dislike to the Nipáni *desái* was the result of a long course of cruelty and ill-treatment. From the beginning of his career he had been in the practice of extracting money by throwing into prison every rich man in his own lands, and in any other villages over which he could exercise power. He used also to seize and keep in confinement any young women of the neighbourhood who were of unusual beauty. When General Munro came to Nipáni, many rich and well-to-do people had been in prison for ten or twelve years; and it was said that every year many died from cruel treatment. General Munro heard only of a few prisoners, and these he ordered to be released. After leaving the place he learned that about 300 were still in confinement. He wrote to the *desái* to release them, and some were set at liberty; but, as many were still kept in confinement, General Munro directed that some of the *desái's* villages on the south bank of the Krishna should not be restored until all were released. Strange stories are still current of the *desái's* cruelty. His palace at Nipáni is built on the edge of a deep lake. High up overhanging the water a narrow open stone ledge or balcony stands out from the palace wall. Along the outer edge of this balcony the *desái* was fond of arranging a row of young women. When they were ready he used to pass inside of the row of trembling girls, and suddenly thrusting out his hand hurl one off the ledge and watch her dying struggles in the deep water below. These acts of cruelty so

---

[1] Grant Duff's Maráthás, 621. [2] Stokes' Belgaum, 72.
[3] Bombay Courier, 16th May 1818.

enraged his people that when General Munro was near Nipáni the heads of most of the *desái's* villages asked him to let them pass to the English. They wanted no help. All they asked was leave to drive out the *desái's* garrisons, and the promise that they would not be allowed to pass back under the *desái*. In accordance with his arrangement with the people General Munro for two years held parts of Athni belonging to the Nipáni *desái*. In parts of Parasgad which had been lately resumed by the Peshwa, when the people submitted to General Munro, they made a special stipulation that they were not to be again placed under the *desái*.

In 1819 Mr. Elphinstone represented the Nipáni chief as turbulent and discontented by the loss of Chikodi and Manoli but conscious of his own weakness. In 1822, from his indifference, Mr. Chaplin suspected him of secretly hoping to profit by the unsettled state of Kolhápur. In 1823 Mr. Elphinstone found him the only discontented landholder in the Karnátak. He was cruel and furious in passion, harsh and unrelenting in the management of his estate, and deaf to the remonstrances of his people. In spite of these faults, with Europeans he was frank and gentlemanlike, good humoured, and cordial. In 1827 Colonel Welsh the commandant of the Doab Field Force describes him as a very affable though poor prince and a distinguished soldier. He lived in a respectable palace within a doubled walled citadel with a wet ditch all round. His little fortress was a perfect model and he had begun a large fort of which this was to be the citadel.[1] After spending a large sum he abandoned the project but the work of some of the completed bastions was very solid. A half-finished palace also stood near the further extremity of the projected fortifications with a fine stone wall and a large reservoir near it. He had also built some waterworks which supplied water to the town and the fort by aqueducts leading from springs in a range of hills three miles west.[2] In 1828 Colonel Welsh calls Appa Desái his favourite of all the Marátha chiefs, indeed of all the native princes he had ever known. He had a frank and dignified manner and was said to be a favourite of Sir John Malcolm.[3]

In 1831 the chief, whom age and a feeling of the power of Government had kept quiet if not well disposed, endeavoured to impose a child on Government as his heir. It was discovered that one of his wives Táibái had been taken to a house in Nipáni, on the pretence that she was about to bear a child. A widow, who expected soon to be delivered, was also taken to the house; and when the child was born he was placed in Táibái's arms, and said to be her offspring. The widow was murdered. Information of this intrigue and crime was given by the owner of the house in which it took place, and he soon after died with suspicious suddenness. His story was confirmed by the discovery of the widow's body. In consideration of the Nipáni chief's age and of his services rendered to the British army in 1800 and 1803, Government did not immediately confiscate his

---

[1] Colonel Welsh (Military Reminiscences, II. 285) gives a sketch of the Nipáni citadel.

[2] Military Reminiscences, II. 283-288. [3] Military Reminiscences, II. 333-335.

Chapter XIV.
Places.
NIPÁNI.
History.

military grant or *saranjám* lands. They determined to punish the *desái* by declaring that his military estates were to lapse on his death, and that no son of his body or of his adoption should be recognized as heir to them.[1] On the 28th of June 1839 the chief died, having previously adopted Morárráo, son of his half-brother Raghunáthráo, as heir to his *deshkat* or civil estates which were estimated to be worth £1500 (Rs. 15,000) a year. The military or *saranjám* estate was resumed and divided among Belgaum, Dhárwár, and Sholápur. The chief parts which fell to Belgaum were the divisions of Athni and Honvád, and the flourishing town of Nipáni. These acquisitions were managed by the Political Agent until, under Act VI. of 1842, they were brought under the Acts and Regulations. The year after the death of the Nipáni *desái* his six widows began to quarrel. The eldest had charge of the heir and the five others kept up continued complaints against her. She died in the end of 1840, and the management passed to the next eldest widow. Two of the remaining ladies induced Raghunáthráo, the late *desái's* half-brother, to seize his son whom the late *desái* had adopted, and with the aid of 300 Arabs to take possession of the fort, and set the authorities at defiance. The military had to be called in before the fort submitted. It was attacked on the 20th of February 1841 and surrendered on the following day. The Arab ringleaders were punished with imprisonment; and all who had joined in the insurrection forfeited their pensions. The fort was dismantled at the expense of the *desái,* who had also to pay the cost of the expedition. The present (1884) *desái* is a minor educated at the Rájkumár College in Káthiáwár and his estate is managed by his mother.

NIRVÁNEPAN HILL.

Nirva'nepan Hill, about 700 feet above the plain, lies about a mile from Chikodi. It is a flat bare hill infested by wolves and jackals.

PARASGAD FORT.

Parasgad Fort lies in the village lands of Saundatti about a mile to the south. The fort stands on the south-west edge of a range of hills immediately overlooking the blacksoil plain below. The top, which measures about 1500 feet from north to south by about 1000 feet from east to west, is irregular and a good deal covered with prickly pear and brushwood with a sprinkling of banians and tamarinds. The sides are of rock and almost perpendicular. The ascent which is about 325 feet from foot to top is long irregular and difficult. The walls are built of stone and are ruined in places. Most of the sixty bastions are out of repair. The only buildings are a ruined cistern holding no water and a small temple of Máruti just enough to hold two persons. There is a hollow in the rock with a spring esteemed sacred by the people and an underground cave which has not been explored. In 1842 a committee of inspection described the fort as about three miles south-west of Saundatti on the south-west corner of a wide piece of table-land about 400 feet above the plain. The fort was irregularly

---

[1] Bom. Gov. Sel. CXIII. 216-219.

Parasgad Fort.

four-sided (550 × 500 yards) with its longest side on the tableland. Inside the fort was a small square ruined *gadhi*. The defences consisted of ramparts and bastions. The ramparts were narrow and in good order. The bastions were of stone built at irregular intervals and joined by stone curtains. On the east part of the north front the bastions were hardly more than fifteen feet high including parapets which in places were very high. The bastions were capable of holding ordnance. These defences, being on the edge of precipices on the south-west and a large part of the north face, were impregnable. The western face was the strongest, the rocks being very high and forming a perfect natural scarp. The south face was not so rugged and as a ravine ran in front of a part of the north face the works there were doubled. The fort had two entrances one on the south-west front by a steep path leading to a gateway in some work at the foot of the natural rocky scarp. From this work a flight of stone steps in a cleft of the rock led into the upper fort by a small doorway which could be easily blocked. The other entrance was in the east front from the tableland. The water-supply consisted of a pond in a ravine which ran dry early in the hot weather, and a fine spring in the lower works at the foot of the hill in a small cavern in the rocks. The fort was uninhabited and had the ruins of many houses. Parasgad is said to have been built by Shivάji in 1674,[1] and it is mentioned in a list of ten Belgaum forts which Shivάji held at the time of his death. In 1746 the Sávanur Nawáb was forced to give up the Parasgad district to the Maráthás, but it was restored to him in 1756.[2] In 1802 the districts of Parasgad and Annigeri in Dhárwár with a revenue of £5000 (Rs. 50,000) were held by Amritráv the adopted son of Raghunáthráv Peshwa.[3]

Párgad Fort.

Pa'rgad Fort, on the Belgaum-Sávantvádi frontier about thirty-five miles west of Belgaum, is built on a peaked hill in the Sahyádris about 2000 feet above sea level. The hill sides are wooded, except in places where they have been laid bare by brushwood clearing or *kumri*. The ascent to the fort is steep by rock-cut steps. The fort which is about forty acres in area is mostly out of repair. Part of the walls, which only line the crests of ravines, and one gateway are fallen. The water-supply is from six reservoirs four of which are in repair. A temple of Bhaváni and two broken pieces of cannon are the only other remains in the fort. In 1827 a committee of inspection described Párgad as an extensive hill fort in the Sahyádris 1900 feet high, about thirty-one miles from Belgaum and two miles north of the Rám pass. It was formed by the basaltic band of rock which crowns so many of the Sahyádri hills. The perpendicular scarp varied from forty to 100 feet and was inaccessible in every part except at the gateway where the masonry was only fourteen feet high. The fort was overlooked and commanded on several sides especially on the north where a hill approached as near as 1200 feet. The water-supply was from

---

[1] Stokes' Belgaum, 42. [2] Bom. Gov. Sel. CXII. 208. [3] See above p. 395.

Chapter XIV. Places. Pа́rgad Fort.

numerous wells supplied by springs. A reservoir in the fort also held water till February. A stone-built temple, the commandant's house, an eight-pounder, and three *Jamburás* were the only other remains in the fort. The garrison consisted of 360 irregulars. A second committee of inspection in 1842 described the fort as about forty-five miles west of Belgaum on a spur of the Sahyádris about 1200 feet above the plain. The spur contained two distinct heights the most northern of which formed the fort. The hill was triangular in shape, its eastern side forming the base being about 2400 feet, its south-west front about 1800, and north-west front about 1650 feet, and the entire breadth of the hill from east to west was about 1200 yards. The crest of the hill with a natural scarp all round of thirty to sixty feet formed, without any help from art, a strong and almost impregnable position; for though in many places the scarp had a slight slope it was nowhere sufficiently sloped to admit of an assault. The works crowning the crest of the scarp were strong stone walls twelve to twenty feet high, and, according to the form of the hill, flanked in various places with bastions fit for ordnance. At the north angle round which the road led to the gate the rock was particularly high bold and rugged and was crowned by a double line of works of masonry completely commanding the road to the gate which was placed in the north-west front about 600 feet from the western angle of the hill. The only entrance to the fort was up a flight of steps about fifty yards long on the top of which was a small gate facing south-west and much exposed. The passage up the steps was steep and well flanked by the works. The south-east end of the fort was the weakest point forming a sharp acute angle without any defences. The fort was inhabited, but water was scarce and had to be brought by the people from a village outside the slope of the hill to the north-west not far from the gate. The committee observed that even without defences the hill would be regarded as a very strong position; but formed into a fort, with the defences as they then (1842) existed, it should be deemed a fort of great strength requiring ordnance for its capture. Párgad appears among the ten Belgaum forts held by Shiváji at the time of his death in 1680. In 1749 Párgad fort was ceded to Sadáshivráv the cousin of the third Peshwa Báláji.[1] In 1844 Párgad and Chandgad were threatened by insurgents, but a timely reinforcement of irregulars saved them.[2]

Rámtirth.

Ra'mtirth, a small village within Jamkhandi limits about fifteen miles north-east of Athni, is in great local repute for its holiness. The village is on a water-course called the *pápnáshini* or sin-destroyer, and, near the village, is a hill called A'nandparvat or the Mount of Joy, with a cave containing an image of the goddess Ánandnáyaki or Our Lady of Joy. To the east of the cave is a fine old temple of Rámeshvar with well carved pillars.[3] A large yearly

[1] Grant Duff's Maráthás, 272. [2] Stokes' Belgaum, 89.

[3] The temple is said to have originally been dedicated to Venkateshvar and to have been called Rámeshvar after Rám paid it a visit. Venkateshvar is said to have directed Rám to go to Ceylon when Rám was searching for Sita; and, to please the god, on his return from Ceylon, after killing Rávan and winning back Sita, Rám is said

Chapter XIV.

Places.

Sadalgi.

fair is held in honour of the god on *Maháshivrátri* the thirteenth of the dark half of *Mágh* (February-March).

Sadalgi, about two miles north of the Vedganga branch of the Krishna and ten miles north of Chikodi, is a large village, with in

---

to have stopped here and called the temple after his own name. Ceremonies in honour of forefathers, as well as certain birth and marriage rites, are performed at this stream. The following suggestions are offered regarding the reason of the holiness of this and of other Indian springs; the reason why so many of the holiest springs are called Rámtirths or Rám pools; the reason why the water of holy springs and streams is believed to cleanse from sin; and the reason why the waters of holy springs and streams is of special avail in ancestral funeral rites. The feeling of the holiness of water and the value of water in religious rites seems based on the nearly universal early belief that pain and disease are caused by evil spirits, the ghosts of the dead. Things which relieved pain and cured disease were held to be spirit-scarers and therefore became holy. Water, the quencher of thirst, for the pains of thirst like the pangs of hunger were at first supposed to be the work of an evil spirit, the scarer of the swoon-spirit the healer of diseases and of wounds, holds one of the highest places among spirit-scarers. Hence the use of water in holy water, in lustration and purifying rites, and in baptism. Springs whose waters were found specially healing were deemed specially spirit-scaring, and so became peculiarly holy. The reason why so many specially healing and sacred springs are, like this Athni spring, called Rámtirth or Rám's pool, is apparently not so much that Rám went to them as that their healing or spirit-scaring power is enough to cure even Rám's complaint. Rám's was a most serious complaint. In killing Rávan he killed a Bráhman (Muir's Sanskrit Texts, IV. 413-415) and Rávan's spirit haunted him, a terrible disease as no spirit is so hard to shake off as the Brahmarákshas or Bráhman spirit. Rám wandered till he found a spring whose spirit-scaring power was so great that it drove from him the haunting spirit of Rávan. Hence springs wells and rivers, the spirit-scaring power of whose waters can drive away even a haunting Bráhman spirit, become Rámtirths or pools in which Rám bathed and was cured. Why do the waters of holy wells cleanse from sin? The reason seems to be that the idea of sin is a branch of the early belief that spirit possession is the cause of disease. That sin was originally a form of spirit possession appears from the fact that the early sins are acts which expose the sinner to spirit attacks. Omissions or misdoings of the ritual, whose object is to keep off spirits, are sins because they expose the omitter or misdoer to spirit attacks. So among Jains, Buddhists, and Lingáyats, and, to a less extent, among Bráhmanic Hindus, the sin of sins, or as a Jain would say the one sin, is to take life. The taking of life is the great sin, because by taking life a spirit is made homeless and in wrath seizes the sinner who ruined its home. So in this Athni stream, as in other holy streams, the healing water which scares the haunting spirits becomes the *pápnáshini* or sin-destroyer. The reason why this Athni Rámtirth, like other Rámtirths and other holy springs and streams, is used in ancestral funeral rites apparently is, that, of the two great classes of disease-causing spirits, the house-spirit or *gharchebhut* and the outside-spirit or *báhirchebhut*, in early times the house-spirit was most feared because he was always at hand, and, in most cases, had grounds for being angry. In the practice of mourners bathing in a spirit-scaring stream, as in other details, the chief object of early funeral rites seems to have been to drive the spirit of the dreaded dead from the house and out of any relation whom it had begun to haunt. When the present later and kindlier funeral ideas, whose theory is that the object of funeral rites is to help the loved dead to heaven, took the place of the earlier dead-scaring ideas, the old practice of getting rid of a haunting spirit by the chief mourner bathing in a healing or spirit-scaring stream was continued under the priestly adaptation that the bathing of mourners in sacred pools helps the loved dead on their way to heaven. Similarly, the practice of throwing the bones and ashes of the dead into water seems to have lasted from early times because priestly ingenuity was able to adapt the old practice to new and higher ideas. As water scares spirits, spirits cannot cross water. The spirit, or at least one and the strongest of the spirits, of the dreaded dead, which remains in the bones and ashes, if the bones and ashes in which it lives are thrown into water cannot come back: still less can it come back if the ashes or bones are thrown into a spirit-destroying pool. This seems the basis of the present Hindu practice of throwing the bones and the ashes of the dead into water, or better into the sea, or still better into a holy stream or spring. The present higher and kindlier ideas of the dead have been reconciled to the old spirit-scaring practice by the priestly explanation, that by the way of holy water the spirit of the loved dead passes easily to heaven.

Chapter XIV. Places.

SADALGI. *Sugar-making.*

1872 a population of 6383 and in 1881 of 7240. A weekly market is held on Tuesdays when grain chiefly is sold. Coarse waistcloths blankets and women's robes are woven, but the chief industry in the town and neighbourhood is sugar-making. Sugarcane juice is mixed with milk-bush ashes which contain potash and boiled till it turns into liquid molasses. The liquid molasses is then stored in an earthen pot and from this pot it is thrown into a large cloth-lined bamboo basket placed on logs of wood about five inches from the floor. The basket is covered about an inch thick with a layer of the *havasi* waterweed and carefully closed with planks or mats. About a foot from the basket a pit about three feet deep and about six feet round is dug and plastered to receive the treacle as it drops from the basket. Some time, usually a week, is allowed for the liquid to crystallize at the end of which the crystallized part is removed. The basket is again covered as before and allowed to stand another week for further crystallization. The process is repeated until the whole crystallizable part of the liquid is collected. The crystallized sugar is then spread upon a cloth and finely powdered. The treacle is removed from the pit as it fills and is stored in large pots, to be used in making country liquor.

SAMPGAON.

Sampgaon, 15° 36′ north latitude and 74° 50′ east longitude, about eighteen miles south-east of Belgaum, is the head-quarters of a sub-division, with in 1872 a population of 3678 and in 1881 of 3629. Besides the sub-divisional revenue and police offices Sampgaon has a post office, a library, two schools one of them for girls, and an old mosque. A weekly market is held on Sundays when cattle, cloth, cotton, and grain are sold. The village has also a few looms. A fair in honour of Basava and Dyámava, attended by about 5000 people, is held once in ten or twelve years. The old mosque though small and low-roofed is a beautiful building well proportioned and pleasing. Over the prayer niche or *mehráb* three verses from the Kurán are inscribed.[1] The earliest mention of Sampgaon is in 1683 when Aurangzeb's son Prince Muhammad Muazzam is mentioned as besieging the fort of Sampgaon and taking it after a gallant attack of two days.[2] Towards the end of the seventeenth century the founder of the Kittur Desái family, who came into the district with the Bijápur army, settled at Sampgaon.[3] Sampgaon lapsed to Government after the Kittur outbreak of 1824. In the Sángoli Ráyappa outbreak of 1829 the Sampgaon mámlatdár's office was burnt and the records were destroyed.[4]

SANKESHVAR.

Sankeshvar, more correctly Shankheshvar or the Conch-god, about eight miles north-west of Hukeri, is one of the richest villages in the Chikodi sub-division, with in 1872 a population of 8905 and in 1881 of 8106. The village has a large traffic with fifty traders, who export cotton to Chiplun and Vengurla and import dry cocoanuts, dates, spices, and curry-stuff.[5] The only industry is the weaving of waistcloths, women's robes, and blankets. A weekly

---

1 The three verses are Surah LXI. 13, XII. 64, and VI. 161. Professor H. Blochmann in Ind. Ant. IV. 6.
2 Kháfi Khán in Elliot and Dowson, VII. 314.
3 See above p. 377.
4 Stokes' Belgaum, 83.
5 See above p. 313.

Chapter XIV.
Places.
SANKESHVAR.

market is held on Fridays when grain, copper, ironware, vegetables, cotton, yarn, blankets, waistcloths, and women's robes are bought and sold. The village has a post office, three schools two of them private, an old temple, and a monastery. The temple of Shankarling, which is said to have been built by Jakhanácharya, is eighty-two feet long and forty-eight feet broad. It has three inscriptions one of them of the seventeenth Ratta chieftain Kártavirya IV. (1199-1218) and bearing dates 1199 and 1202 (*S.* 1121 and 1124). A yearly fair in honour of the god lasting for three days is held on *Maháshivrátri* the thirteenth of the dark half of *Mágh* or February-March, and is attended by two to three thousand people. The monastery or *math* of the Sankeshvar Svámi is a large building about two acres in circumference. The chief gate faces north, and, by the south gate, flows a rivulet called the Kashmal Hiranikeshi. A sacrifice chamber or *yajnamantap* with room for 1000 persons is built on the bank of the rivulet. The present *svámi* is the twelfth in succession and was chosen by the late *svámi* as his favourite disciple. The devotees of the *svámi* are Bráhmans, Rajputs, Maráthás, Shimpis, Pánchals, and Gábits, and his jurisdiction extends from the Malprabha to the Himálayas (?) and from the Nizám's territories to the Konkan coast. Besides tribute from disciples and re-admission fines paid by excommunicated followers, the monastery enjoys a yearly revenue of about £3000 (Rs. 30,000) from thirty *inám* villages.[1] As this large income hardly suffices to maintain the monastery, and feed every year 10,000 Bráhmans in the holy month of *Shrávan* or July-August, the *svámi* is generally on tour levying contributions from his followers. According to the local account Shankaráchárya (about A.D. 800), the great apostle of the Smárt or Vedánt sect of Shaivism, had four disciples one of whom Vishvarupáchárya was stationed at the great Shringeri monastery in West Maisur. Shankarbhárati or Devgosávi a successor of Vishvarupáchárya left Shringeri about 1570 on a pilgrimage to Benares.[2] From Benares he desired to visit the Himálayan cave of Govindbhágvat-pujya-pádáchárya the teacher of the great Shankaráchárya. He left his followers at the cave entrance, and told them that if he did not return by a certain day they were to choose one of their number as their spiritual head or *guru* and to return to Shringeri. As the day passed with no sign of Shankarbhárati, his followers started for Maisur and chose one of their number to be teacher or *guru*. They came to Kudálgi at the holy meeting of the Tung and Bhadra, about thirty miles south of Harihar, and stopped there for a few days when Shankarbhárati returned and joined them. He meant to go to Shringeri but the head at Shringeri did not allow him to enter as he had brought with him a second head whose election during the lifetime of the first was contrary to the custom of the monastery. The people of Shringeri

[1] Fifteen of these villages are in Kolhápur, five in Belgaum, three in the Nizám's territory, two each in the Patvardhan estate, Sátára, and Sávantvádi, and one in Bijápur.

[2] Neither Vishvarupáchárya nor Shankarbhárati appears in the list of the Shringeri Gurus published by Mr. Rice (Mysore and Coorg, I. 380). The list has a Shankaránand Bhárati who was consecrated in 1428 and died in 1454.

Chapter XIV. Places. SANKESHVAR.

sided with the head of the monastery and Shankarbhárati was not allowed to enter the town. He started a monastery at Kudálgi and established his new head in it putting him in possession of several villages he had acquired in the Nizám's territories. Shankarbhárati again started for Benares and on his way visited the temple of the goddess Haridradevi in Vallabhgad fort two miles north of Sankeshvar. The goddess is said to have desired the *svámi* to go and worship Shankarling at Sankeshvar. The *svámi* began to worship the god after his daily bath in a sacred pool called Shuklatirth in the Kashmal Hiranikeshi rivulet and continued his worship. Randulkhán (1569-1615), an officer of Hajrat Ibráhim Yedal a minister of the Bijápur king was so pleased with the *svámi's* devotion that he granted him some villages which enabled the *svámi* to open two more monasteries at Kolhápur and at Sankeshvar. The third *svámi* after Shankarbhárati acquired some further villages from a Kolhápur chief about 1670 and additions to the *inám* continued till 1838. The number of villages at present enjoyed as *inám* by the monastery is thirty yielding a yearly revenue of £3000 (Rs. 30,000).[1]

The earliest known mention of Sankeshvar is in 1488 when Bahádur Giláni, the Bahmani governor of the Konkan, broke into rebellion, took Belgaum and Goa, and established his head-quarters at Sankeshvar. Máhmud II., the fourteenth Bahmani king (1482-1518), came to punish the rebel, and from Jamkhandi passed to Sankeshvar whose fortifications were unfinished and which submitted to him in three days. In 1659 Sankeshvar fell to Shiváji as part of the Kolhápur district.[2] In February 1834, when the late Dr. J. Wilson was at Sankeshvar on a missionary tour, he saw the yearly fair which was attended by about 10,000 people and the great car of the god forty-five feet high was dragged a few yards. Among the commodities for sale, copper-ware, especially household images, was most in demand.[3]

SAPTASÁGAR.

Saptasa'gar, on the south or right bank of the Krishna about twelve miles south-west of Athni, is a small village of great local holiness, with in 1881 a population of 1655. It is the local belief that at this village the water of the seven Puránik seas or *ságars* brought by the seven great seers was mixed with the water of the Krishna. This is said to have given the village its name and bathing here in the Krishna is regarded as very purifying.[4] The village has a Government Kánarese school.

SAUNDATTI.

Saundatti, 15° 46′ north latitude and 75° 11′ east longitude, about forty miles south-east of Belgaum, is a municipal town, the head-quarters of the Parasgad subdivision, with in 1881 a population of 7133. The 1872 census showed a population of 8180 of whom 7298 were Hindus and 882 Musalmáns. The 1881 census showed

---

[1] Ráv Bahádur Gurshidapa Virbasapa. [2] Stokes' Belgaum, 41.
[3] Oriental Christian Spectator, V. 143.
[4] The village is also called Sarpságar from a story that the Puránik king Janmejaya performed here a serpent or *sarp* sacrifice for the absolution of his ancestors. The sacrifice is said to have been performed on the bank of the Krishna and a little digging still discovers ashes.

7133 or a fall of 1047 probably due to the 1876-77 famine. Of the 1881 total, 6443 were Hindus and 690 Musalmáns. Besides the revenue and police offices of the Parasgad sub-division Saundatti has a municipality, dispensary, sub-judge's court, post office, a collector's bungalow, two schools four old temples and a ruined fort. The municipality, which was established in 1876, had in 1882-83 an income of £269 (Rs. 2690) and an expenditure of £505 (Rs. 5050). The income is chiefly derived from octroi, a house tax, and a grant-in-aid from provincial or local funds, and the chief items of expenditure are public health and works. The water-supply of the town is poor, consisting of two wells with steps and seventy-three wells without steps. Of the step wells one gives good drinking water and the other is used for watering cattle. Of the drawing wells only eleven contain wholesome water fit for drinking. During the year 1882-83 the municipality spent about £200 (Rs. 2000) in building a stone and cement well called the Hanamgiri well with four pulleys for drawing water. The dispensary was established in 1875. In 1882 it treated 1972 out-patients at a cost of £121 2*s*. (Rs. 1211). Of the two schools one is an anglo-vernacular school for boys and the other a Kánarese girls' school. A weekly market is held on Wednesdays when cloth, cotton, oil, salt, and spices are sold. About fourteen families live by weaving. The town has four old temples of Ankusheshvar, Purandareshvar, and Shankarlingdev, and a Jain temple all plain, ruinous, and in no way remarkable.

Inscriptions.

Saundatti has six inscribed tablets with inscriptions of Ratta chiefs varying in date from 875 to 1229. The first inscription is on a stone slab built into the wall to the left of the Jain temple. The emblems at the top of the stone are a seated figure of Jinendra in the middle, on its right a crooked knife with a cow and a calf beyond it, and on its left the sun with the moon above it. The inscription is in fifty-three lines of large and slanting Old Kánarese characters and records distinct grants made by three Ratta chiefs of Saundatti and Belgaum. It mentions two Jain temples built in Saundatti, called Sugandhvarti in the inscription, by Prithvirám the first, and Sena I. the seventh, Ratta chiefs; and gives a rather confused list of six or seven grants of land made by some of the Ratta chiefs and one in 1097 by the great Western Chálukya king Vikramáditya VI. Three of the grants are made to Jain temples and four to the preceptors of the donors and two of them are dated 875 and 1097. The inscription gives the Ráshtrakuta king Krishna (875-911) as the overlord of Prithvirám, and mentions near Sugandhvarti the river Malhári apparently the Malprabha. The second inscription is on a stone slab built into the right wall of the same Jain temple. The emblems at the top of the stone are in the middle a seated Jina with two half figures, a Yaksha and Yakshini above fanning him with brushes of peacock's feathers, to the right a cow and calf with the sun above them, and to the left a seated figure with the moon above it. The inscription is in fifty-one lines in the Old Kánarese character and is dated 981. It records, after much praise of the Kandur Jain sect and its preceptors, a grant of 150 *mattars* of land by the fourth Ratta chief Shánta to a Jain

Chapter XIV. Places. SAUNDATTI. *Inscriptions.*

temple that he had built at Saundatti and an equal grant to the same temple by his wife Nijikabbe or Nijiyabbe. In the beginning the inscription records the grant of a measured portion that had been set apart for the temple of the Ratta Jina. The grant is said to have been made with the consent of certain husbandmen, and a further gift is recorded of one *mána*[1] of oil on each oil-mill for the lamp of the god at the festival of Dipávali.[2] The third inscription dated 1048 is on a broken tablet in the temple of Ankusheshvar.[3] The fourth inscription is an Old Kánarese inscription on a stone slab built into the wall in the interior of the temple of Ankusheshvar. The floor of the temple is below the level of the ground, the door is the only means of lighting the interior and the inscription is so placed that the light admitted by the door does not fall upon it. The inscription is much injured. It is in two parts. The first part gives the genealogy of the Ratta chief Anka as the subordinate of the Western Chálukya king Trailokyamalladev (1042-1068) and records a grant made by him at his capital of Sugandhvarti in 1049. The second part records a grant made by the princess Bhágaldevi and her husband the eleventh Ratta chief Kártavirya II. (1088-1096) in 1088. The fifth inscription is on a stone, now in the mámlatdár's office, which was dug out of the courtyard in front of the same Jain temple. The stone is a fragment on which thirty-three lines are preserved. The emblems at the top of the stone are in the middle a seated Jinendra, on its right a seated figure with the sun above it, and on its left a cow and calf with the moon above them. The inscription gives the genealogy of the ninth Ratta chief Kártavirya II. who is mentioned as subordinate to the Western Chálukya king Someshvar II. (1077-1084).[4] Inscription six is on a stone tablet which used to stand in one of the chief streets of Saundatti but is now kept in the mámlatdár's office. The emblems at the top of the stone are a *ling* in the middle, to the right of the *ling* an officiating priest with beyond him a seated figure and above them the sun, and to the left a cow with beyond it a crooked knife and above them the moon. The inscription is in Old Kánarese in ninety-three lines of small and very finely engraved characters, an exceptionally good specimen of inscription sculpture. The inscription begins with the mention of the eleventh Ratta chief Lakshman or Lakshmidev I. of the Ráshtrakuta race, the supreme lord of the Kundi district in the Kuntal country, and carries the Ratta genealogy to the last Ratta chief Lakshmidev II. The circle of villages known as the Sugandhvarti Twelve was administered by Munichandradev the royal spiritual preceptor of the Ratta chiefs assisted by three counsellors, one of whom was a local chief named Mallikárjun. In giving the genealogy of Mallikárjun the inscription mentions two local families, the chiefs of Banihatti near Jamkhandi, and the chiefs of Kolár the modern Korti Kolhár on the Krishna about thirty miles south of Bijápur. Mallikárjun of Banihatti married Gauri the heir apparent of the Kolár chiefship. Their son Keshiráj

[1] A *mána* is an oil measure equal to 2 lbs. (4 *shers*). Mr. J. F. Fleet, C.S., C.I.E.
[2] Jour. B. B. R A. S. X. 171-172, 208-212. [3] Dr. Burgess' Antiquarian Lists, 46.
[4] Jour. Bom. Br. Roy. As. Society, X. 213.

Chapter XIV.
Places.
SAUNDATTI.
Inscriptions.

combined the two chiefships, Mallikárjun, as is mentioned above, serving as one of the Saundatti counsellors. The inscription goes on to record how Keshiráj, having three times visited and vowed strict vows at the *ling* shrine of the god Mallikárjun at Shrishail in Telingana, brought back with him a *ling* made out of the rock of the sacred hill, and set it up in a temple of Mallikárjundev or Mallináthdev which he built in the name of his father near the Nágarkere pond outside the city of Saundatti. The inscription notices the appointment of a high priest of the temple, and records various grants of lands and tithes made to the temple in 1229-30 (*Shak* 1151 *Sarvadhári samvatsar*) by order of the spiritual preceptor Munichandradev while the great chieftain king Lakshmidev was ruling at his capital of Venugrám or Belgaum.[1]

Fort.

The fort is to the west of the town on a small isolated hillock. The top of the hillock is irregular and occupied by the interior of the fort. The sides are rocky and covered with a dense growth of prickly pear. Up to the chief gateway on the east the ascent is not very steep and a roadway has been made; but inside the gateway the ascent is rather steep up some twenty-five or thirty steps. The walls with a greatest height of sixty feet are strongly built of large hewn stones and have eight bastions. The fort, which is about 325 feet from north to south and 450 feet from east to west, has a chief gateway on the east and two posterns or sallyports on the north and south. On the higher part of the fort is a modern temple of Hanumán and just below it on the south is a stand apparently meant for a beacon fire. Inside the fort is a masonry pond and a building which has been adapted as a collector's bungalow. On a clear day Yellurgad fort near Belgaum thirty-eight miles to the west of Saundatti can be seen from the ramparts and even signals can be interchanged. In 1827 a committee of inspection described the fort as a tolerably regular nine-sided polygon on a small hill very easy of ascent. The rampart was well revetted and varied in height from twelve to thirty feet and had corner towers for flank defences. There was something like a raised mound or faussebraye in front of part of the wall about six feet high and faced with loopholes but much out of repair. The ditch with a depth of about nine feet was very imperfect and irregular. Within the fort was a small square work with corner towers. It had no ditch and was much out of repair. The water-supply was from a large well of excellent water. A second committee of inspection in 1842 described it as a very compact and well built little fort on a small rising ground about 600 feet west of the town. The fort was eight-sided, about 300 feet in diameter, and surrounded by a ditch. The defences consisted of eight circular stone built bastions varying from forty to seventy-five feet in height and capable of holding ordnance. The bastions on each side of the gate were extremely well built. The curtains joining the bastions were about 120 feet long, well built of stone and varying in height from twenty-four to sixty feet. The ramparts were narrow parapets of stone, loopholed, and in good order: except the north-east face,

---

[1] A photograph of the stone is given in Plate XXVII. of Mr. Hope's Series (1866) for the Architectural Committee of Western India.

Chapter XIV.
Places.
SAUNDATTI.
Fort.

where it was imperfect, a narrow space or berm from fifteen to forty-five feet wide went round the foot of the works. At the edge of the berm, twenty feet above the ditch, was a raised mound or fausse-braye a good deal injured but in excellent order on the west front. The ditch was twenty-five feet deep but not regular and forty feet broad. On the west face the ditch was partly cut out of the rock forming a good natural escarp and counterscarp; where there was no rock the ditch was faced or revetted with stone. The earth slope or glacis was formed by the natural slope of the hill which was rather steep on the north. The entrance to the fort was on the east front, the road to it being well commanded and flanked from the fort. Of its two gates the inner was large and strong. It was covered by a semicircular work with ramparts parapets and loopholes. The outer gate passing through this work on the left hand was strong and was commanded from the bastions. There was a third ruined gateway. Inside the fort was a square work well built of stone and enclosing a temple. It was a work built for defence with two bastions on the west front and ramparts which formed the roof of a corridor supported inside on stone pillars all round. The parapets were small of stone work and loopholed. The entrance to this inner work was up a flight of steps through a simple well commanded door. The water supply was abundant from a small pond which never failed, and another on the north outside the works. This pond was surrounded by a high wall entered from the fort by a small door which could easily be blocked by the garrison. The committee remarked that it was a very compact and well built little fort but too small for a large garrison. It was exceedingly well suited for an office or *kacheri* as it had a good house which formerly belonged to the *desái*.

History.

Saundatti, called Sugandhavarti Savandhavatti and Savadhavatti, or the Fragrant City, in inscriptions varying from the ninth to the thirteenth century, was the head-quarters of a petty division of twelve villages under the Kundi district called the Sugandhavarti Twelve, and, until about 1210 when Belgaum took its place, was a capital of the Ratta chiefs of Saundatti and Belgaum (850-1250). Inscriptions found in Saundatti show that two Jain temples were built in Saundatti by two Ratta chiefs in 876 and 981, and about 1230 a Shaivite temple of Mallikárjun by Keshiráj a local chief of Kolhár in Bijápur in memory of his father Mallikárjun who served as a councillor to the Saundatti governor of the Ratta kings who had then transferred their capital to Belgaum. The temple was built on the bank of a large pond called Nágarkere outside the city. Keshiráj is also described as having built the pond and planted a grove round it. The list of tithes presented to the god by three guilds and others of the town show that Saundatti was then a rich place with considerable trade.[1]

---

[1] The tithes granted are one hundred betel leaves on each beast-load of betel leaves and fifty leaves on each head-load; a spoonful on each grain sold in each rice shop; two betelnuts on each shop; one spoonful of green ginger molasses and turmeric from each grocer's shop; a handful of cotton from each cotton-dealer; a ladleful of oil from each oil-mill; a clay pot from every potter's kiln; two bundles on every cart-load of vegetables, and four bundles on each beast-load. Jour. B. B. R. A. Soc. X. 283-284.

In 1730 Saundatti, with other Dhárwár villages, was granted to the Navalgund *desái* by the Sávanur Nawáb;[1] and in 1734 the *desái* built the fort of Saundatti.[2] In the campaign against the freebooter Dhundia General Wellesley was at Saundatti from the 1st to the 3rd of August 1800.[3]

SAVDI.

Savdi, on the Krishna about ten miles south-east of Athni, is a large village with in 1872 a population of 2979 and in 1881 of 2634. About a mile south of the village, on the north bank of the Krishna, in a shady mango and tamarind grove, is the tomb of a Musalmán saint where a yearly fair is held in *Chaitra* or March-April. The village has a Government school.

SENDUR HILL.

Sendur, or **Ra'suba'i Hill,** about 670 feet above the plain lies about five miles south-west of Nipáni. It is a round hill partly covered with trees and brushwood and ending in a conical peak. A pass across the hill which is seldom used for traffic leads to Ajre village in Kolhápur. On the hill is a spring and a temple dedicated to the goddess Rásubái. Rice, wheat, and Indian millet are grown on the hill sides by Lingáyats and Maráthás who live in two villages on the hill containing a population of about 2500. The hill is not used as a health resort, but people from the neighbouring villages sometimes go to it for its spring and temple. Wolves and jackals infest the hill.

SHAMSHERGAD FORT.

Shamshergad Fort is on a hill about 1800 feet above the plain in the lands of Nandgad village about seven miles south of Khánápur. The hill is isolated, and has rocky partly wooded sides and a flat top. An easy ascent by a footpath leads to the fortified top. The fort (1980′ × 900′) has walls of stone and earth, one gateway, and one sallyport. The interior of the fort is full of brushwood and has a well without water.

SHEDBAL.

Shedbal, about twenty miles west of Athni, is a large village with in 1872 a population of 3833 and in 1881 of 3065 chiefly Jains. When (1889) the West Deccan Railway is finished Shedbal will have a third class station 169 miles south-east of Poona and seventy-three miles north-east of Belgaum. The village is chiefly remarkable for an old temple of Basav with a Siláhára inscription dated 1156 (*S.* 1078). The temple has three images in a row in the temple and a *ling*. A large lamp-pillar stands in front of the temple so placed that when lamps are lit on it, the light falls only on the *ling* and the middle Basav image and not on the two side images. A yearly fair is held in honour of Basav on *Maháshivrátri* in February-March, attended by about 2000 people. The village has a Kánarese school.

SHURPÁLI.

Shurpa'li, or **Marnur,** on the Krishna, about twenty miles south-east of Athni, is a large village with in 1872 a population of 2124 and in 1881 of 1448. The village is regarded as the Benares of the neighbourhood and a banian tree on the Krishna not far from

---

[1] Stokes' Belgaum, 62. [2] Stokes' Belgaum, 62.

[3] Nine of General Wellesley's Despatches, Nos. 514 to 522, are dated Soondooty 1st to 3rd August 1800. Supplementary Despatches, II. 83-90.

Chapter XIV. Places.

the village is said to have grown from a tear shed by Parshurám. Under the tree is a temple of Narsimh in honour of whom a yearly fair attended by about 1000 Bráhmans and lasting for two days is held in *Vaishákh* or May-June. The Bráhmans who attend the fair are fed on the second day by twenty-three Bráhmans of the village who hold it in *inám* from a Musalmán chief. There is a Kánarese school.

SOGAL.

Sogal village, about twelve miles north-west of Saundatti, lies at the foot of a quartzite scarp below a picturesque waterfall on the Malprabha. The stream rises in the valley above Sogal and runs south-west through a dip in a ridge of quartzite rock. Close to Sogal it takes a clear leap over a semicircular cliff fifty to sixty feet high. Above the chief fall is a pretty spot with two smaller falls, an old temple and a grove.[1]

Malprabha Gorge or Naul Tirth.

Nine miles south-east of Sogal is the Naul Tirth or Peacock's Pool, a beautiful gorge through which the Malprabha enters the Kaládgi basin. The local story of the name is that a peacock hardpressed by pursuers and too weary to fly over the chain of hills which rise to the north of the gorge, rested on a large rock, and called piteously. The river heard its cry, clove the hills, and the peacock escaped. Ever since the waters have kept to the new passage. The gorge forms a true Mexican canon or river chasm, with cliffs so close to the river bed that without climbing them it is almost impossible to pass from end to end of the gorge.[2] In the upper or south-western half the cliffs are about 300 feet high, and the river bed is hardly fifty feet wide. Even in moderate floods the water fills its narrow bed from wall to wall, and during heavy floods, it rises thirty to fifty feet in the gorge, in its rush bearing along stones and rocks whose furious swirl has worn great holes in the rock which, as at Gokák, are sacred bathing places. In its lower or north half the gorge widens and the walls lose height till the quartzite beds sink into a flat which stretches far to the north-east. Near the top of the lower or north half of the gorge, a remarkable detached rock stands below the left bank on a steep slope above the present water level. This rock has kept its place while the upper and lower parts of the beds to which it belonged have slid into the torrent and been swept away. There is nothing to show that the river water ever reached this rock. If the water reached the rock it must have been ponded into a lake stretching miles behind the head of the gorge and of such a lake no trace is left. In the bed of the river, within water reach the hard quartzites are so highly polished that at times walking is dangerous. In most places the polished surface is covered with a thin film of dark grayish black in contrast to the beautiful pale red and pink of the unstained quartz. At the narrowest part of the gorge the fairweather flow is only twenty feet wide, 127 feet above the bed the width from cliff to cliff is only 264 feet, and at 200 feet the width is only 500 feet. At[3] the mouth of the gorge at sixty feet above the fair weather water level, the width

---

[1] Foote in Geological Memoirs, XII. Part I. 98-101. [2] Mr. R. B. Joyner, C.E.
[3] Measurements taken by Mr. R. B. Joyner, C.E.

is about 200 feet, and at the foot of the steep sides the width of the river is seventy feet. At this spot is a pool whose depth varies from thirty-six feet in the dry weather to seventy-four feet in the great flood of July 1882 when the river rose thirty-eight feet.

SOMESHVAR HILL.

Someshvar Hill, about 350 feet above the plain, lies about thirteen miles north-west of Saundatti. It is a steep hill covered with poor trees and has a flat uncultivated top. A footpath leads from Sogal three miles to the south to Murgod three miles to the west, but it is not used for traffic. A large spring and a temple of Someshvar with a yearly fair on *Mahâshivrâtri* in February-March are the only objects of interest on the hill.

SUTGATTI.

Sutgatti, fourteen miles north of Belgaum and the first stage on the Poona road, has a travellers' bungalow and two very large Indian fig trees. The first near the travellers' bungalow has a stem forming a wall of timber extending forty feet. The tree rises to a great height and the branches spread out 100 feet round the trunk. The other tree is a mile from the bungalow, and though not very high covers a larger surface of ground.[1]

TALVÁRKOP.

Talvárkop, an uninhabited village on the Malprabha about twelve miles north-east of Khánápur, has a small but old temple of Shankarling in the river-bed said to have been built by Jakhanáchárya. The neighbourhood of the temple is called Bilva Kshetra or the Bel Holy Bathingplace, and people come here every Monday for a purifying bath.

TANGDI.

Tangdi village, six miles east of Athni, has an exorcist who cures snake-bites. According to the exorcist, after a snake-bite the patient should take the name of the saint Adigudi Imám Sáheb, and closing his eyes tie a thread round his neck. He should then be taken to the exorcist who repeats some charms and drives out of the patient the spirit of the serpent.[2]

TÁVANDI.

Távandi a small village of 441 people on the Belgaum-Kolhápur road about fifteen miles south-west of Chikodi, has on a neighbouring hill a small temple of Bharmapa said to be a Jain god. A yearly fair attended by about 1000 persons chiefly Jains is held in honour of the god in *Kártik* or October-November.

VAKKUND.

Vakkund village, twelve miles south-east of Sampgaon with in 1881 a population of 428, has a fine old Jakhanáchárya temple still in good repair. The beautiful perforated stone work of this temple and the remains of other temples are objects of great interest. The village still has some clever workers in stone.

VALLABHGAD FORT.

Vallabhgad, or Hargápur, about fifteen miles south-west of Chikodi, is an isolated hill about 300 feet above the plain. The top has a nearly round fort (275′ × 200′) with, in places, a natural wall of rock and in others artificially built walls of stone and earth. The wall has given way in many places and the fort is much out of repair. It has two ruined gateways, four springs, and a well. The north

[1] Murray's Bombay Handbook, 236.
[2] The art of curing snake-bite, according to the exorcist, could be learnt only by those who without fear or harm can vomit five times and re-eat as many times what they have vomited.

Chapter XIV.
Places.
Vallabhgad Fort.

side of the hill is cultivated with millet by poor Maráthás and Lingáyats and on the east and west slopes is a village with three hamlets and a population of 1200 chiefly Lingáyats, Maráthás, and Musalmáns. Jackals infest the hill. In 1842 a committee of inspection described Vallabhgad as a small fort about 300 feet above the plain. The fort was triangular with two sides each about 650 feet long and a third or south side of about 400 feet. The fort was built on a natural scarp varying in height from twenty to thirty feet except on the south front where the gate was placed. The defences consisted of stone walls with parapets varying in height externally from twenty-four to thirty feet but of very little height within, the ground being on nearly the same level with the parapets. The entrance was on the south front by two gateways. There was only one gate which was placed between the two gateways and was of fair strength. The water-supply from a deep spring was very scanty. Two small cavaliers in bad order were the only remains of artillery. On the east and west slopes of the hill close to the works were small villages. Vallabhgad was among the ten Belgaum forts which Shiváji held at the time of his death in 1680.[1] In 1786 the Nesargi chief rebelled against his overlord of Kolhápur and deprived him of Vallabhgad, Gandharvgad, and Bhimgad, but in 1787 he was put down, his army was dispersed, and the forts retaken by Kolhápur.[2] In 1796 while Parshurám Bháu was at Poona his old enemy the Kolhápur chief took the fort of Vallabhgad.[3]

Yamkanmardi.

Yamkanmardi, about twenty miles south of Chikodi and about eight miles south-west of Hukeri, is a municipal town with in 1872 a population of 5296 and in 1881 of 4491. The town is said to have been founded about 1780 by Virpan Ambáji a Kolhápur mámlatdár. It has about 300 looms making waistcloths, women's robes, and blankets. A weekly market is held on Tuesdays, when dry cocoanuts, dates, gram, wheat, and cloth are chiefly sold. The municipality was established in 1854. In 1882-83 it had an income of £150 (Rs. 1505) and an expenditure of £109 (Rs. 1090). The income was chiefly raised from a house tax, and the chief items of expenditure were conservancy and road repairs. Besides the municipality the town has a post office, a Kánarese school, and a ruined fort.

Fort.

In 1827 a number of Kolhápur freebooters took refuge in the fort and Colonel Welsh of the Doab Field Force with a company of H. M.'s 41st Regiment, a company of the Bombay European Regiment, a troop of Horse Artillery, two squadrons of Native Cavalry, and two hundred men from each of the native corps under the command of Major Henry proceeded to the spot. The town was large and contained many excellent houses. The fort or *ghadi* was a very strong place with six bastions two of them very large. One of these two bastions commanded the rest of the works, and was capable of containing a garrison of about 200 men, who could drive any enemy out of any part of the

---

[1] Shiváji's Bakhar. [2] Stokes' Belgaum, 59. [3] Stokes' Belgaum, 61.

interior. Round the fort was a deep and dry ditch through which a passage with two gateways led into the fort. Inside was the house of the commandant and a pond of good water. After some deliberation and a show of resistance the garrison came out with their arms.[1]

YÁDVÁD.

Ya'dva'd, twenty-five miles east of Gokák, is the second town in the Gokák sub-division. In 1695 the Italian traveller Gemelli Careri stopped at what he calls Edour on his way from Goa to the Moghal camp at Galgale about fifteen miles north of Kaládgi. He found it the largest city he had seen since he left Goa, but then visited with a plague. It had two enclosures. Within the first enclosure was an ill-built stone fort and a market, and within the second enclosure a garrisoned fort with mud and straw houses about it. All traders from the south bound for the Moghal camp at Galgale halted at Yádvád. Returning to Goa Careri stopped at Yádvád and was disappointed not to find any ox caravans or Christians on their way to Goa.[2] In 1746 Majid Khán the Savanur Nawáb, unable to face a Marátha army, had to give up Yádvád among other districts.[3] In 1764 the Yádvád *pránt* formed part of a military grant or *saranjám* from the Peshwa to the Miraj Patvardhans. In a revenue statement of about 1790, prepared from Marátha records, Yádwari appears as the head of a *pargana* in the Torgal *sarkár* yielding a revenue of £4600 (Rs. 46,000).[4] Yádvád lapsed to Government on the death without heirs of Parshurám Bháu of Tásgaon in 1849.[5] In 1853 Yádvád had a cotton and mixed silk and cotton industry supporting about 400 people.[6] As it contained a large number of the artisan and labouring classes Yádvád suffered much during the famine of 1876-78.[7]

YEDUR.

Yedur, or Edur, about twelve miles north-east of Chikodi is a large village on the Krishna, with in 1872 a population of 2592 and in 1881 of 2192. The village has a modern temple of Virbhadra (145'×145') on an old foundation. About 1830 additions were made to the building, and a rest-house was attached by one Annáji Narsinh Deshpánde of Páchhápur. Two inscriptions in the temple, dated *Shak* 1752 (A.D. 1830) and *Shak* 1758 (A.D. 1836), probably record these additions. The revenue of the village, which has been granted for the maintenance of the temple, is managed by the grantees who live in the village. A yearly fair in honour of the god is held on *Mahâshivratri* in February-March and lasts for a month. People, chiefly Bráhmans and Lingáyats, come from as far as Poona and Belári, and sweetmeats, iron and copperware, waistcloths, handkerchiefs, and women's robes are sold to the value of about £5000 (Rs. 50,000). Its situation on the Krishna, with a famous temple and a magnificent grove of mangoes and tamarinds, make Yedur a favourite halting place. In

---

1 Welsh's Military Reminiscences, 263-267. Colonel Welsh gives a general view and a ground plan of Yamkanmardi fort.

2 Churchill's Voyages, IV. 219, 249.

3 Bom. Gov. Sel. CXII. 208.

4 Waring's Maráthás, 243.

5 Survey Superintendent's Letter, 267 of 1853.

6 Survey Superintendent's Letter, 267 of 1853.

7 Survey Superintendent's Letter, 47 of 1881.

Chapter XIV. Places.

1754 Peshwa Báláji Bájiráv halted at Yedur with his army on its way to the Karnátak.[1] In 1790 the British detachment under Captain Little, sent with Parshurám Bháu to oppose Tipu Sultán, encamped at Yedur on the 9th August and crossed the Krishna in bamboo baskets covered with buffalo hides.[2] In his march from Seringapatam to Poona to reinstate Bájiráv, General Wellesley halted for two days at Yedur, or as he calls it Eroor.[3] On the 31st of May 1818 General Munro camped at Yedur on his march to Nipáni.[4]

Yellamma's Hill.

Yellamma's Hill, about five miles south-east of Saundatti and about a mile north of Ugargol village, takes its name from a shrine of the goddess Yellamma which is held in great veneration throughout the Bombay Karnátak, and is visited yearly by about one hundred thousand pilgrims. The shrine is built in the bed of the Sarasvati a small stream which runs north from the hill into the Malprabha. The temple stands in the middle of a courtyard surrounded by arcades of pointed arches. In the west gate are some pillars like those in the Jain temple in Belgaum fort, and, on the base of one, is a short Kánarese inscription covered with whitewash. The inscription is dated 1514 (*Shak* 1436, *Bháva samvatsar*), and records the finishing of an upper storey over the stone *mantapa* of the west door which Bommappa Náyak of Bági or Ráybág (the Náyaka) of the great king the brave Shri Krishna (1508-1529) caused to be built at the feet of the goddess Jattaka-Mahammáye.[5] Though locally said to be about 2000 years old, in its present form the temple, excluding perhaps the sanctuary, appears to have been built within the seventeenth or eighteenth century, and its predecessor does not appear to be older than the thirteenth century. To the north is a small shrine of Ganpati with two rough pillars on one of which is a Kánarese inscription of about eleven lines. In honour of the goddess fairs are held on the full-moon of *Chaitra* or April-May and on the full-moon of *Márgshirsh* or November-December. The *Chaitra* fair is small attended by from 15,000 to 30,000 pilgrims; but on the *Márgshirsh* fair from 30,000 to 70,000 people assemble from all parts of Belgaum, as well as from Dhárwar, Bijápur, Sátára, Belári, Miraj, Sángli, and Tásgaon. From 1000 to 2000 traders drive a profitable trade in cocoanuts, plantains, sweetmeats, copper and brass vessels, cloth, silk thread, wild ox tails, beads, turmeric, and redpowder or *kunku.* The priests who officiate at the temple and stay on the hill are Lingáyats of forty families divided into eight divisions or *bans.* The turn of each family to officiate comes every fourth day. Except $\frac{3}{8}d.$ ($\frac{1}{4}$ *a.*) a head levied from every pilgrim for the temple use, no fixed fees are paid by pilgrims. Almost every pilgrim gives, in addition to the fee, clothes, cocoanuts, cash, and ornaments. Of these the money

Temple.

Fairs.

---

[1] Stokes' Belgaum, 50.
[2] Memoirs of the Early Life and Services of a Field Officer, 206-207.
[3] Gurwood's Despatches of Wellington (1799-1818), I. 123. [4] Stokes' Belgaum, 78.
[5] Jour. B. B. R. A. S. XII. 343-344. *Mantapa* is an open hall or temporary shed built on festive occasions, or an open temple or halting place for images when carried in procession. A *náyaka* is a military officer with administrative functions. Mr. J. F. Fleet, C. S., C.I.E.

YELLAMMA'S HILL.

contributions, which are estimated to bring in about £1000 (Rs. 10,000) belong to the priests. The clothes and ornaments are presented to the goddess and become temple property, the clothes being sometimes sold for the benefit of the temple or burnt if they are kept long enough to rot. Some of the cash offerings are called *mudupu* or vowed money. This is set apart for feasts and charitable works belonging to the temple and amounts to about £250 (Rs. 2500) a year. Nothing is known of the origin of the shrine. Yellamma is said to be the same as Renuka the mother of Parshurám. The old story is told of Renuka's sudden love for a heavenly minstrel, her husband ordering Parshurám to kill his mother for her unchaste desires, Parshurám killing her, and, when desired to ask a boon in reward for his obedience, requesting that his mother might be restored to life. It is said that even after she was restored to life her husband's curse smote her with leprosy, but after long devotion to two seers she was cured. In honour of her cure she is said to have built this temple as this hill was her original abode from which she used to go and bring water from the Malprahári or Malprabha river.

In the early years of British rule the practice of farming the temple revenue from pilgrims and other sources was continued. In 1834 the farm of Yellamma's temple was sold for £570 (Rs. 5700). The three great fair days were (1834) the full-moons of April May and June. Each person coming to the fair paid $\frac{3}{8}$*d.* ($\frac{1}{4}$ *a.*), men and women who came stark naked under a vow usually for children or for the cure of skin diseases or to offer prayers paid 1$\frac{7}{8}$*d.* (1$\frac{1}{4}$ *a.*) each,[1] and carts coming up the hill paid 2*s.* (Re. 1). Numerous other offerings were made to the goddess, in the shape of clarified butter, clothes, cocoanuts, and ornaments, and the hook-swinging or *shedi* ceremony, at a cost of £1 16*s.* (Rs. 18) to be paid as indulgence to the temple farmer, was a great source of income. The ceremony consisted of swinging round with two hooks fastened through the skin of the back. In 1834 it was performed by 175 persons.[2]

Municipality.

A temporary municipality[3] was established on the hill on the 1st of October 1878 to improve communications, build rest-houses, and carry out sanitary arrangements. In 1882-83 the municipal

---

[1] Naked processions have ceased since 1855 and at present (1884) persons under vows to go naked before the goddess apply sandal paste or tie *nim* branches from the shoulder to the knee. People do not go naked before the goddess but walk several times round the temple clad in *nim* leaves and then appear before the goddess in a robe or waistcloth. Barren women offer to the goddess lampstands, silver cradles with golden figures of children, burn camphor on the temple spire, or light a thousand lamps round the temple.

[2] At the April full-moon of 1834, 15,000 people were present at the fair of whom forty-four swung. One of the victims was an old woman of eighty hardly able to stand. It was generally believed that her skin would give way, but she went through her trial well, and expressed a wish to die after the swinging was over. The usual practice was to squeeze lime-juice into the wound and place a leaf on the wound as a plaster. Extract paras 35, 40, 41, and 42 of Mr. S. A. N. Shaw's MS. Report, Chechree, 10th March 1835.

[3] The municipality is within the boundaries of Ugargol village. Its limits are confined to the hills round the temple and to the approaches to them, and do not include the village site of Ugargol.

income, chiefly derived from farmed tolls on pilgrims and visitors during the fair days, was £471 (Rs. 4714), and the expediture, which was chiefly incurred in making three new roads and in keeping old roads in repair, was £500 (Rs. 5000). The municipality owns three rest-houses, six wells, and two pools.

YELLURGAD FORT.

Yellurgad is a ruined fort at the extreme west end of a high trap ridge about seven miles south-east of Belgaum. The fort is a trigonometrical survey station 3365 feet above sea level and 797 feet above the sill of the chief gate of Belgaum fort. Yellurgad was described in 1827 as a small square hill fort consisting of a stone rampart with round towers on each side, and commanding a good view of the hill slope and of the country round. It was too high for escalade, but was defenceless as its northern walls had fallen. An underground passage in the fort was said to communicate with Belgaum fort. The committee were of opinion that its works were too weak to admit of defence, but, as it might prove a hiding place for thieves, it ought to be destroyed.

APPENDIX.

The following is a list[1] of plants and seeds which were used as articles of food by the poorer classes during the famine of 1876-77 in the different sub-divisions of the Belgaum district:

CLASS I.—Seeds.

1. Seeds of the Bambusa arundinacea and other species, *veluche tándul* (M.); 2. Indigofera glandulosa, *godi bármond* (K.), *gahun bármond* or *gavácha malmandi* (M.); 3. Indigofera linifolia, *malmandi* or *javalai malmandi* (K.), *javáricha malmandi* or *barbora* (M.); 4. Jasminum latifolium, *kusari* (M.); 5. Amaranthus frumentaceus, *ádvi rájgira* (K.); 6. Tamarindus indica, *chinch* (M.); 7. Acacia arabica, *bábhul* (M.); 8. Sophora tomentosa, *káshi bábhul* (M.); and 9. Erythrina indica, *pángára* (M.).

CLASS II.—Herbs and Rinds.

10. Husks of the Penicillaria spicata, *sejji* (K.) or *bájri* (M.); and 11. the rind of the ripe fruit of the Musa paradisiaca and other species, *kelyáchi sál* (M.).

CLASS III.—Fruits.

12. The unripe fruit and blossom of the Musa paradisiaca and other varieties, *keliche phul áni phal* (M.); 13. Coccinia indica (unripe fruit), *tondli* (M.); 14. Randia uliginosa (unripe fruit), *pendhare* (M.); 15. Opuntia dillenii (ripe fruit), *nivdung* (M.); 16. Ficus indica (unripe fruit), *vad* (M.); 17. Ficus tjiela, *pimpri* (M.); and 18. Ficus glomerata, *umbar* (M.).

CLASS IV.—Sprouts.

19. The young sprouts of the Bambusa, *veluche komb* (M.); and 20. sprouts of the Caryota urens, *surmádáche komb* (M.).

CLASS V.—Leaves of Stalks and Herbs.

21. The herb Lactuca gorœana, *pátri bháji* (M.); 22. The herb Lactuca(?), *háli bháji* (M.); 23. Leaves of the Moringa pterygosperma, *shevgyáchi bháji* (M.); 24. The herb Portulaca quadrifida, *chirgoli* (M.); 25. The herb Amaranthus frumentaceus, *ádvi* (wild) *rájgira* (K.); 26. The herb Amaranthus polygamus, *chavli* (M.); 27. Leaves of the Morus indica, *shetut* (M.), *chichuk* (K.); 28. Leaves of the Cassia (?), *guradi* (or hill) *hanavri* (K.); 29. Leaves of the Cassia sophora, *yemmi* (or buffalo) *hanavri* (K.); 30. Leaves of the Cassia auriculata, *tarota hanavri* (K.), *tarvad* (M.); 31. Leaves of the Cassia tora, *tarota* (M.); 32. Leaves of the Sophora tomentosa, *káshi bábhul* (M.); 33. Leaves of the Tamarindus indicus, *chinch* (M.); 34. Tribulus terrestris, *gokhru* or *saráta* (M.); 35. Ficus glomerata, *umbar* (M.); 36. Ficus tjiela, *pimpri* (M); 37. Santalum album, *chandan* (M.); 38. A creeper not identified, *jiti* (M.); 39. A creeper not identified, *mustik* (M.); 40. A creeper not identified, *malli* (M.); 41. Achyranthes aspera, *aghάda* (M.); 42. Not identified, *yelvat* (M.); 43. Not identified, *savdadu* (M.); 44. Indigofera glandulosa, *malmandi* (M.); 45. Cocculus villosus, *dágdi* (M.); 46. Anethum (?), *ránshepu* (M.); 47. Not identified, *chonchi* (M.); 48. Zizyphus rugosa, *churnu* or *turan* (M.); 49. Cyanotes axilloris (?), *ichka* (M.);

[1] Contributed by Surgeon-Major C. T. Peters.

Appendix.

50. The plant Tonidium suffruticosum, *ratan purush* (M.); 51. Poinciana elata(?), *saphet sankeshvari* (M.); 52. Not identified, *supari* or *vassu* (K.); 53. Leaves of the Celastrus paniculatus, *kanguni* (M.); 54. Leucas linifolia, *tumba* (M.); 55. Not identified, *murchand* (M.); and 56. Dæmia extensa, *kurtigia* (M.).

CLASS VI.—Pith.

57. The pith of the Plantain Musa paradisiaca and other varieties, *kelicha gábha* (M.); 58. The pith of the wild plantain Musa textilis, *chavaicha gábha* (M.); 59. The pith of the Caryota urens, *surmádácha magaj* (M.).

CLASS VII.—Roots and Tubers.

60. Colocasia, and Caladium and Arum (certain varieties) tuber, *alu* (M.); 61. Dioscorea bulbifera tuber, *kadu káranda* (M.); 62. Musa textilis, *chavaicha gadda* (M.); 63. Polygonum (?), *sogali mula* (M.); and 64. Not identified, *phirsi mula* (M.).

The following notes will help to form an idea as to the nutritive value or otherwise of these substances. It is to be regretted that some of the specimens were received in a semi-putrid state and others without their fruits or blossoms and could not be identified. Others such as the rhizomes, tubers, and seeds had to be grown before some of them could be identified, while some although they had been successfully grown, the writer of this article having had to leave Belgaum, the plants had to be left behind before they blossomed.

CLASS I.—Eaten in all Seasons.

The seeds *veluche tándul* and the sprouts *veluche komb* of the Bambusa arundinacea and B. spinosa. The seeds of the wild bamboo according to Buchanan are gathered for food in Maisur and the South Konkan. In Belgaum it is not an unusual thing to see the thorny varieties of the bamboo producing seeds, which exactly resemble oats in size and appearance and are called the bamboo rice. The tender shoots are used in making curries and pickles. The seeds of the JASMINUM LATIFOLIUM, *kusarichi phale*, are pounded into flour and made into cakes. The fruits ripen in May and June when they are eagerly sought after, being wholesome. The seeds of the AMARANTHUS FRUMENTACEUS, *rájgira*, are generally used for making bread or cakes especially during fasts. The tops, stalks, and leaves of several wild varieties of the AMARANTHUS are generally used as spinage; those of the A. POLYGONOIDES being especially considered a delicacy and ordered for invalids.

AMARANTHUS POLYGAMUS *chavli*, A. OLERACEUS *tándulja*, and A. FRISTIS *máth*, are cultivated and considered to be very wholesome as pot-herbs.

MUSA PARADISIACA AND OTHER VARIETIES, *kel*.

The unripe fruit, the blossom and the pith (*kelichágábha*) are usually eaten cooked as vegetable curry. Professor Johnstone considers the plantain fruit to approach most nearly the potato in composition and nutritive value.

COCCINIA INDICA, *tondli*.

This creeper is common in hedges during the rains, the fruit is cooked as a vegetable, the ripe fruit of the cultivated variety is eaten raw.

RANDIA ULIGINOSA, *pendhare*.

The fruit is ovoid about a couple of inches long and of a yellow colour; the unripe fruit is used in curries.

OPUNTIA DILLENII, *nivdung*.

The fruit when ripe is generally eaten by children, it has a faint sweetish taste.

CARYOTA URENS, *surmád* or *bherle mád*.

The fruit of the tree yields a kind of coarse sago. In the Konkan people generally pound the pith and make gruel of it. During the famine this was made into flour with which they made cakes, either alone or mixed with the flour of the *rági* Eleusine corocana.

LACTUCA GORŒANA, *pátri*.

This herb appears to be the same as that described by Dalzell and Gibson as the Microrhynches sarmentosus. There appear to be two varieties.

one stemless, the leaves appear as if attached directly to the root. The other has long stalks and corresponds with Roxburgh's Prenanthes acaulis and P. racemosa. The latter is common in Zanzibar where, according to Sir John Kirk, K.C.M. G., it is used by the natives as a pot-herb. It is known among them as the wild salad plant. It finds a place in the African flora as Lactuca goroeana which name has been adopted here. The two varieties mentioned here are found growing at all seasons about houses, roadsides, pasture lands, and old damp walls; taste slightly bitter and are used as vegetables and considered to be a stomachic and very similar in effect to that of the dandelion.

MORINGA PTERYGOSPERMA, *shevga*.

The leaves, blossoms, and pods are eaten cooked as curries, but they are considered heating and when taken in excessive quantities cause purging.

PORTULACA QUADRIFIDA, *chirgoli*.

A succulent plant, the whole herb is used as a pot-herb. P. oleracea and P. meridiana are also used as pot herbs; according to Roxburgh the P. quadrifida is supposed by the natives to produce stupefaction.

DIOSCOREA BULBIFERA, *kadu karánda*.

The tuber is eaten by the poorer classes after it has been roasted and then steeped in cold water to take away the bitter taste. (Graham's Catalogue p. 219).

CALADIUM, COLOCASIA, AND ARUMS, *alu*.

Several varieties of the Caladium, Colocasia, and Arum are cultivated for the tubers which are used as curries, and sometimes they are eaten boiled like potatoes, and taken with salt after the skin has been removed. A little limejuice is added to the wild varieties in order to remove the acrid taste that they may possess.

CLASS II.—Eaten in times of Famine.

INDIGOFERA GLANDULOSA, *godi* or *gahun bármand* or *gavácha malmandi*; I. LINIFOLIA, *javálai malmand* or *javoricha malmandi*.

The seeds of the I. glandulosa are black elongated about a line in length and dotted over with numerous pits on the surface and those of the I. linifolia have a white roundish husk which when removed leaves a fine seed resembling poppy seeds, having a smooth surface; found in the cold weather. These grains are made into flour for making bread like the cereals.

ANETHUM (?), *Ránshepu*.

This plant exactly resembles the Anethum graveolens, *shepu*, in structure and fragrance which is cultivated as a spinaceous vegetable. It is perhaps a wild variety of the Anethum.

TAMARINDUS INDICA, *chinch*.

The seeds are generally eaten roasted by children in ordinary years, and are pounded and boiled in water for sizing country blankets; in times of scarcity and famine, like the mango seeds, they are eaten (Roxburgh). Tamarind leaves are slightly acid and are sometimes eaten in curries.

ACACIA ARABICA, *bábhul*.

The seeds and pods of the *bábhul* are used in the hot season as food for sheep and goats when grass is scarce. If properly shelled and cooked *bábhul* seeds would afford a wholesome and nutritious food.

SOPHORA TOMENTOSA, *káshi bábhul*.

The pods sent resembled the pods of this plant, if so they are not generally used as food, and according to Rumphius the seeds which are very bitter are considered a specific in cholera. The seeds of some of the Acacia, however, as the Acacia leucophlœa, are eaten ground and mixed with flour and the pods used as vegetable. The leaves as well as the seeds were used as articles of food.

ERYTHRINA INDICA, *pángára*.

The seeds of the Indian coral tree are not known in ordinary seasons

Appendix.

to have been used as an article of diet; when boiled they are believed to resemble beans.

PENICILLARIA SPICATA, *sejji* or *bájri*.

The husks were evidently used with a view to add to the bulk of the flour prepared from other articles.

MUSA PARADISIACA, *kel.*

The rind of the ripe plantain was used even by the upper classes, cooked as curry.

FICUS INDICA, *vad*; FICUS TJIELA, *pimpri*; FICUS GLOMERATA, *umbar*.

The fruits of these plants were used in their green state, or simply boiled and taken with salt and gave rise in many cases to fatal diarrhœa. If cooked properly they might have been wholesome, as they are generally eaten by birds. The leaves of the *pimpri* and *umbar* are stated to have been also used as food.

MORUS INDICA, *shetut pála* (M.), *chichuk* (K.).

The leaves are a favourite food of the silk-worm which feeds greedily on the tender leaves. It is considered to be wholesome as a vegetable by the natives. They also use it as a remedy for *achra* a sort of venous tumour forming under the tongue.

SANTALUM ALBUM, *chandana*, *shrigandha*.

The leaves of the sandalwood are generally given to goats which are very fond of the tender tops. They are considered to be wholesome as an article of food.

CASSIA AURICULATA, *tarvad*; CASSIA TORA, *tarota*; CASSIA SOPHORA, *kasunde* (M.), *yemmina novri* (K.); CASSIA (?), *gurdna novri* (K.).

The word *gurd* in Kánarese means wild and *yemmi* a buffalo, indicating that the plant is eaten by buffaloes. *Yemmina novri* is said to be wholesome and used as *chatni* or relish. The Cassia auriculata is sometimes used as vegetable. *Shegunshi*, Cassia (?), is said to be a bushy plant growing on hill sides throughout the year. The leaves are said to be wholesome when cooked as spinage. They are also used as a cure for rheumatism and supposed to be heating.

ZIZYPHUS RUGOSA, *toran* or *churan*.

The fruit is eaten, the leaves are mucilaginous and may be wholesome. The wild silk or *tasar* worm feeds on the leaves of this plant and that of the Z. jujuba or *bor* tree.

POINCIANA ELATA, *saphet sankeshvari*.

The plant is probably the P. elata which is the only one of the Poincianas bearing white flowers. The leaves are said to be wholesome.

MUSA TEXTILIS, *chavai* or *ránkel*.

The pith and root of this plant would have similar properties to those of the plantain, and as the root stock contains a large quantity of starch it would be useful as an article of food.

POLYGONUM (?), *sogalichi muli*.

This plant grows by the river sides. Roxburgh says some of the Polygonums are eaten by cattle greedily.

The undermentioned plants are well known for their medicinal properties, and with a few exceptions would not be considered as wholesome articles of food:

TRIBULUS TERRESTRIS, *saráta* or *gokhru*; ACHYRANTHES ASPERA, *ágháda*; COCCULUS VILLOSUS, *dágadi*.

The leaves of the *dágadi* are made into curry and given to patients who are under a course of the roots (Roxburgh).

IONIDIUM SUFFRUTICOSUM, *ratan purush*.

The leaves and tender stalks are mucilaginous.

CELASTRUS PANICULATUS, *kanguni*; LEUCAS LINIFOLIA, *tumba*; DŒMIA EXTENSA, *kurtigia*.

Besides those already mentioned the following plants could not be identified: *Jiti* a creeper, *mustik* a creeper, *malli* a creeper, *yelvati*, *saudadu*, *chonchi* vegetable, and *ichka* plant. *Ichka* is perhaps the Cyanotis axillaris which Dr. Gray mentions in his Sholápur List. *Murchandi*, *supari* or *vassu* leaves, and *phirsi* a root.

INDEX.

E.

F.

G.

H.